D1071293

ANTHROPOLOGICAL STUDIES
IN THE EASTERN HIGHLANDS OF NEW GUINEA

James B. Watson, *Editor*

Volume I. The Languages of the Eastern Family of the East New Guinea
Highland Stock

*Anthropological Studies
in the Eastern Highlands of New Guinea*
James B. Watson, *Editor*

VOLUMES PUBLISHED:

I. The Languages of the Eastern Family of the East New Guinea Highland Stock, edited by Howard McKaughan
II. Physical Anthropology of the Eastern Highlands of New Guinea, by R. A. Littlewood

The Languages of the Eastern Family of the East New Guinea Highland Stock

Edited by HOWARD McKAUGHAN

UNIVERSITY OF WASHINGTON PRESS

SEATTLE AND LONDON

This book is published with the assistance of a grant from the National Science Foundation.

Library of Congress Cataloging in Publication Data
Main entry under title:

The Languages of the eastern family of the east
    New Guinea highland stock.

    (Anthropological studies in the eastern highlands
of New Guinea, v. 1)
    Reports of research by the New Guinea Micro-
evolution Project.
    Bibliography: p.
    1.   Papuan languages.   2.   Kainantu region—
Languages.   I.   McKaughan, Howard, 1922-   ed.
II.   Title.   III.   Series.
PL6601.A35   499'.12   72–13131
ISBN 0–295–95132–X

Foreword

This is the first volume of a monograph series, 'Anthropological Studies in the Eastern Highlands of New Guinea,' which will report the results of the New Guinea Micro-evolution Project, an interdisciplinary research project. Nine volumes in all are planned. The present volume of studies in language will be followed by studies in physical anthropology, human geography, archaeology, and ethnography. Each volume, in addition to developing technical, descriptive, and analytical matters peculiar to its own topic, is intended to throw light on a set of problems common to the series.

The central theoretical problem of the Micro-evolution Project is change, specifically the diversification of several related peoples of the Eastern Highlands of Australian New Guinea. Four of these are the 'study peoples,' the principal research concern of the project. On linguistic grounds, the study peoples have putatively all sprung from a single source, that is, from a single original people. Through time, in response to various factors not initially known but in some cases discoverable, they have diversified. Each study people is unmistakably, though in varying degrees, related to its congeners, as is evident in numerous more or less profound similarities. But each people is now also distinct from its congeners in identifiable, sometimes marked, and conceivably significant ways.

The term 'micro-evolution' of the project title refers to the details of differentiation or specialization of the study peoples and to the causes or meaning of their specialization, insofar as cause or meaning can be recognized. Micro-evolution here implies a central question of roughly this form: In what ways have these peoples specialized or diversified since their putative common past? In response to what factors? To what extent have they been distinctly shaped, in other words, and what selective processes have shaped them? A logical corollary is the question: To what degree and in what ways have the study peoples remained alike, either through continuity or through parallel development?

The four study peoples are today known respectively as Gadsup, Tairora, Auyana, and Awa. Their territories, though each touches at least one of the others, are fairly discrete. Each people speaks a different language and manifests different physical and genetic characteristics. Each follows a way of life distinct in some respects from those of the others. A main purpose of the project has been to assess in detail the character and distinctness of each study people, broadly speaking, in language, race, and culture. In addition, the investigators have endeavored to assess the habitat of each of the study peoples, recognizing, where possible, environmental factors in their specialization. Through archaeology, some control of the temporal dimension has also been sought.

A more extended statement of the research purposes and methods of the Micro-evolution Project, as well as of the personnel of the research group, will be found in a paper published in the *Journal of the Polynesian Society* (Watson 1963). Considerable detail concerning individual projects, collective research design, and preliminary findings is also contained in grant applications, nineteen research memoranda (including reports of two research conferences), and several published papers. The monographs of Anthropological Studies in the Eastern Highlands of New Guinea are intended, however, to stand as the principal publications of the Micro-evolution Project. Insofar as possible, they will provide full details of their respective topics without requiring immediate reference to material published elsewhere. Indeed, the principal collaborators in the project have agreed to present their major findings and conclusions in the monographs of this series rather than in occasional, scattered publications.

The topical monographs are conceived and written to stand on their own in still another sense. The present volume, for example, is a purely linguistic assessment of the Eastern Family of the East New Guinea Highland Stock (Wurm 1962a). The languages of the study peoples (and other closely related languages) are described and compared. The degree and character of their relationship are gauged in light of their differentiation. The light that language can shed upon differentiation will thus be seen. Whatever the eventual micro-evolutionary conclusions about the study peoples, however, the present volume can be judged solely on linguistic grounds. Its significance, in other words, is not limited to questions of micro-evolution. With the publication of this volume, in any event, the Eastern or Kainantu group will surely rank as one of the best known families of language in New Guinea.

A theoretical synthesis is projected as the final volume of the series. Each preceding volume will therefore reflect the micro-evolutionary concern of the project only as far as possible within the terms of its special topic. Given the language data alone, it would not be possible to consider, or to give adequate reasons for, all aspects of the specialization of the study peoples. The linguist could not decide, for example, if the study peoples were more or less differentiated with respect to language than with respect to genetic or other specialization. Nor, if he knew the answer to that, would he be able to evaluate its significance. He would not be able to tell if the several study peoples show the same order of relative distance in other respects that they display in language. Conceivably, each monograph might recapitulate the micro-evolutionary theorizing of its predecessors in a sort of cumulative commentary running throughout the series, but with such a scheme the repetition and successive revisions of theory would surely become burdensome. A final reason for the deliberate focus of the topical volumes is that some readers may be interested primarily in language, for example, or in population genetics, with but a marginal concern—or perhaps none—for the archaeology or the cultural and psychological character of the speakers of the given languages. A linguistic reader will, in fact, find the contents of the present volume developed so as to enhance their value to him as a linguist, whatever his meta-linguistic concerns may be. The best answers to the central questions of the project, on the other hand, will arise from a synthesis, in the final volume, of all of the findings of the several topical researchers.

A comprehensive historical treatment of the Micro-evolution Project must also await the final volume of the monograph series. Indeed, the history of the project is still being written. The analysis of data and the writing of monographs continue in several phases of the project—in one case further field work is being undertaken. A brief sketch of the project's early history may nevertheless be appropriate here. A surprising number of individuals have been involved from the initial stages of planning to the present. Beginning in the mid-1950's with a committee of from six to eight members, anthropologists of six West Coast universities (the Universities of British Columbia, Washington, Oregon, the University of California at Berkeley, Stanford, and the University of California at Los Angeles), rather large-scale objectives and broad research aims in New Guinea were considered. The present plan emerged about 1958 as a proposal for a more specific attack on a single area of that vast island by a series of researchers of different specialties sharing the particular theoretical concerns outlined above. Accordingly, the present writer was sent to New Guinea in 1959, with the support of a small grant from the National Science Foundation, to produce a planning and feasibility report and to scout a suitable location for the coordinated study.

In 1961, with further support from the National Science Foundation, Dr. Howard McKaughan, now professor of linguistics at the University of

Hawaii, went to the Kainantu subdistrict of Australian New Guinea as one of the first three field researchers for the Micro-evolution Project. He spent a year there, working in each of several locations within the several language areas of the Kainantu or Eastern Family. In much of this work he had the cooperation of the Summer Institute of Linguistics, New Guinea Branch, and in particular of the various contributors to this volume, nearly all of them his collaborators in the field. I should like here to add my appreciation to his for the close working relationship and field comradeship that all the researchers of the Micro-evolution Project have had with the Summer Institute of Linguistics, whose New Guinea base, Ukarumpa, is located within the boundaries of the study area and has also served most of us as a base when we were not at the immediate site of research.

It is doubly fitting that the first volume to appear in Anthropological Studies in the Eastern Highlands of New Guinea should deal with language. Not only were linguistic studies, as noted, carried out as part of the initial field work, but there has been no more intensively collaborative phase of this generally collaborative research project: Professor McKaughan counts some seventeen coauthors in this volume.

There is a further reason to believe it will prove useful to the monograph series to have the linguistics volume appear first. Language, more than anything else, has been used as tag or identifier for the historical units of study with which the research group has been concerned. Without attempting to recognize more profound reasons, it is fair to say that we have found no better "trace element" than speech. This is not to argue that languages are invariably less pervious than breeding pools or culture spheres; but differences of speech are immediately obvious and irreducible, in contrast to different sets of genes or differences of custom. One recognizes the speech of another at once as being his own or alien. The audible reality of dialect and language difference is clear for the study peoples themselves, that is, even while they are oblivious to genes and tend to overlook all but relatively gross differences of custom. The study area is one in which local varieties of speech are not merely numerous in fact but are quite well known and widely remarked.

Languages have seemed strategic to the micro-evolutionary conception in two other ways. First, with the methods of lexicostatistics and phono-statistics the study languages initially held some promise of providing acceptable measures of distance among the study peoples—whether or not of actual time depth in years. Such measures are presented in the pages that follow. Second, with the methods of linguistic reconstruction it would be possible to go far in establishing the character of the *Ursprache* of the study peoples, either for a particular semantic domain like *Urverwandt-schaftsterminologie,* or more generally. The latter possibilities are by no means fully realized as yet in the Micro-evolution Project, for linguistic reconstruction is a very painstaking business. The point is simply that the possibilities exist and, along with what has so far been achieved, contribute to making the languages of the study peoples a basic element in the research scheme.

The publication of this series of monographs is being made possible by a grant from the National Science Foundation, whose continued support of this project is gratefully acknowledged.

JAMES B. WATSON

Seattle

Preface

This volume is one of a series on Anthropological Studies in the Eastern Highlands of New Guinea. The plan for this part of the series has been to bring together in one place all linguistic studies on the languages of the Eastern Family of the East New Guinea Highland Stock which have been written since I went to New Guinea in 1961. Other parts of the series will be concerned with cultural, physical, archaeological, ecological, and demographic phenomena of these peoples.

The research reported here has been carried out by myself and by the following members of the Summer Institute of Linguistics.

Darlene Bee received her doctorate in linguistics from Indiana University (1967), and has also studied at the University of Washington and the University of Hawaii. She initiated her field work under the Summer Institute of Linguistics with the Usarufa in 1958 and has taught linguistics under SIL in summer sessions in Australian, American, and New Zealand schools. In the last case, she has served as principal of the school.

Chester and Marjorie Frantz started their linguistic field work under SIL with the Gadsup in 1958. Both were educated in the United States, he at Gordon College (B.A.) and Fuller Seminary (B.D.). The Frantzes received their linguistic training through SIL summer sessions at the University of Oklahoma.

Kathleen Barker Glasgow studied at Moody Bible Institute in Chicago and later did her B.A. in home economics. She studied linguistics with SIL and began her field work with Darleen Bee in the Usarufa in 1958. She and her husband are now working under SIL with the Burera in Australia.

Jean Goddard received her B.A. from Gordon College in 1954. Her linguistic training was at SIL summer sessions at the University of North

Dakota. She started her field work under SIL with the Agarabi in 1960.

Alan Healey obtained a B.S. degree from Melbourne University and his Ph.D. in linguistics from the Australian National University (1965). His field work under SIL began in 1958 and has been primarily with the Telefol, one of the languages of the West Sepik District in New Guinea. He has taught linguistic courses for SIL in its various schools in Australia.

Joyce Hotz received her undergraduate education at Northwestern College, Minneapolis (B.A. 1969). Her graduate training in linguistics was through SIL at the Universities of North Dakota and Oklahoma. She started her field work in New Guinea with the Waffa in 1961 and has taught basic linguistics for SIL at the Queensland University, Brisbane.

Harland Kerr studied agricultural science (Ph.D. 1955) and anthropology at the University of Sydney, and linguistics at the University of Hawaii. His field work has been with the SIL primarily in Wiru (since 1958), a language of the Southern Highlands District of New Guinea. He is director of the Australian branch of SIL schools, the Wycliffe School of Linguistics, giving courses during summer sessions at the Queensland University, Brisbane. Dr. Kerr's writings include articles on Philippine languages.

Richard and Aretta Loving were educated in the United States, he in agricultural economics and she in education and nursing. The Lovings studied linguistics under SIL at the Universities of Oklahoma and North Dakota. They have taught basic linguistics at the SIL sessions at the Queensland University, Brisbane. The Lovings started their field work with the Awa in 1959.

Lorna Luff took her B.A. at the University of Sydney and studied linguistics under SIL at its Australian school. She started her field work with the Agarabi in 1957.

Doreen Marks studied at the Melbourne Bible Institute and took a nursing program in Adelaide. She studied linguistics in Melbourne under SIL. Doreen initiated her linguistic field work with the Auyana in Kosena in the Kainantu subdistrict in 1958.

Desmond and Jennifer Oatridge both attended the Melbourne Bible Institute. Desmond held a trade apprenticeship for six years, part of the time in the New Hebrides. Jennifer studied nursing and midwifery at St. Helen's in Brisbane and National Women's in Adelaide. The Oatridges took linguistics work in Melbourne under the auspices of SIL, and have served as teaching staff for courses offered at Queensland University. They started their linguistic field work with the Binumarien under SIL in 1959.

Mary Stringer was educated at Adelaide Teacher's College and the Adelaide Bible Institute. She studied linguistics at the SIL schools in Melbourne and Oklahoma and was assigned by SIL to the Waffa in 1961. She has taught basic linguistic courses at the Australian SIL schools, most recently at Queensland University in Brisbane.

Alex and Lois Vincent studied in Australia and the United States, respectively. Alex started work under SIL with the Tairora in 1956, and Lois joined him in 1958, after working with Doreen Marks in the Auyana at Kosena. Alex studied linguistics with SIL in Australia and Lois did her basic work at the SIL sessions at the Universities of Oklahoma and North Dakota. Both have served on the SIL teaching staff in Australia and at the University of Oklahoma.

Howard McKaughan, editor of the volume, studied at the University of California at Los Angeles, and Dallas Theological Seminary, and received his Ph.D. in linguistics at Cornell. He served with the Summer Institute of Linguistics in various capacities from 1946 to 1962, teaching courses in schools in the United States and Australia, and directing field work in the Philippines. His field work has been with the Chatinos of Mexico and the Maranao of the Philippines as well as with the New Guinea languages described in this volume. In 1961 he joined the faculty of the University of Washington, and in 1963 he moved to the University of Hawaii, where he is professor of linguistics and the associate dean of the Graduate Division. Besides the research reported here, he has published several monographs and articles of interest to Philippine linguists.

My research was supported for 1961 and 1962 by the National Science Foundation through the New Guinea Micro-evolution Project, which was headed by Professor James B. Watson of the University of Washington. In 1963 I moved to the University of Hawaii, and as a member of the staff of the Department of Linguistics and the Pacific and Asian Linguistics Institute, I continued my writing as I had time. In addition to the support from the National Science Foundation and that of the departments mentioned, I received a grant from the East-West Center for Cultural Interchange of the University of Hawaii in their Senior Scholar Program of the Institute for Advanced Projects. This grant to support part time research was in 1966-67. I wish to express appreciation to these agencies for their support.

The assistance of the New Guinea Branch of the Summer Institute of Linguistics is also gratefully acknowledged. The objectives of this organization include research of the lesser known languages of the world in order to prepare literary materials, translated documents of educational and cultural interest, technical linguistic descriptions of all kinds, and translations of the Scriptures. The research results here would have been impossible for a single linguist in the time allotted to the project. I am sure I speak for the research team of the Micro-evolution Project when I express appreciation for this organization's assistance.

The accompanying map of New Guinea indicates the study area where the peoples live whose languages are described here. The specific Eastern Highlands areas with relative locations, names, and principal sites where

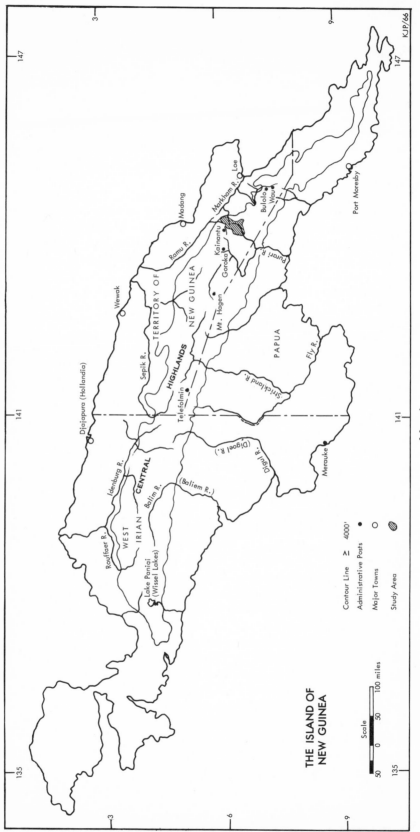

THE ISLAND OF
NEW GUINEA

Scale

50   0   50   100 miles

Contour Line ≥ 4000'

• Administrative Posts

○ Major Towns

▨ Study Area

Map 1

KJP/66

the researchers of the Micro-evolution Project carried out their investigations are indicated on the second map. The linguistic materials do not always come from the particular villages where anthropologists of the team stayed later (that is, after I had done my field work). However, the linguistic materials are representative of the languages and should be comparable with the results obtained from the ethnographic, geographic, and physical studies.

This volume is divided into five parts, the first four presenting descriptive studies of the subfamilies of the Eastern Highland Family, and the fifth giving the linguistic relations obtaining between the languages. A number of the articles presented here have been published elsewhere. Specific references are indicated in the footnotes, and are marked by an asterisk in References Cited.

Grateful acknowledgment is hereby made to the following for permission to republish.

American Anthropologist, published by the American Anthropological Association.

Linguistic Circle of Canberra Publications, the Australian National University.

Oceania Linguistics Monographs, published by the University of Sydney.

Oceanic Linguistics, published by the University of Hawaii.

Papers on Seven Languages of Papua–New Guinea, published by the Linguistic Society of New Zealand.

Summer Institute of Linguistics Publications on Linguistics and Related Fields, a series of the Summer Institute of Linguistics of the University of Oklahoma.

The descriptive studies in the first four parts of this volume are in general based on a taxonomic framework. This is partially because of the orientation of the authors, and partially because descriptions of aspects of individual languages based upon incomplete knowledge of those languages is, in my opinion, more cogently presented in this framework. A transformational-generative approach requires a more thorough understanding of the language in order to prepare rules powerful enough to generate acceptable sentences without generating those that are not acceptable. We must wait until we know more about these languages, it seems to me, before we can formulate such rules. Perhaps the descriptions here with the texts to expand them will allow for a certain amount of transformation-generative rule writing. At any rate, we have not held up the material in order to write such rules.

Part V brings together what is known of a comparative nature. Studying closely related languages, and also closely related dialects within those languages, is fraught with problems. Words often look alike, but seem to represent inconsistencies in their sound changes. When we discover a regular sound change, we are elated, there being so much that we do not yet

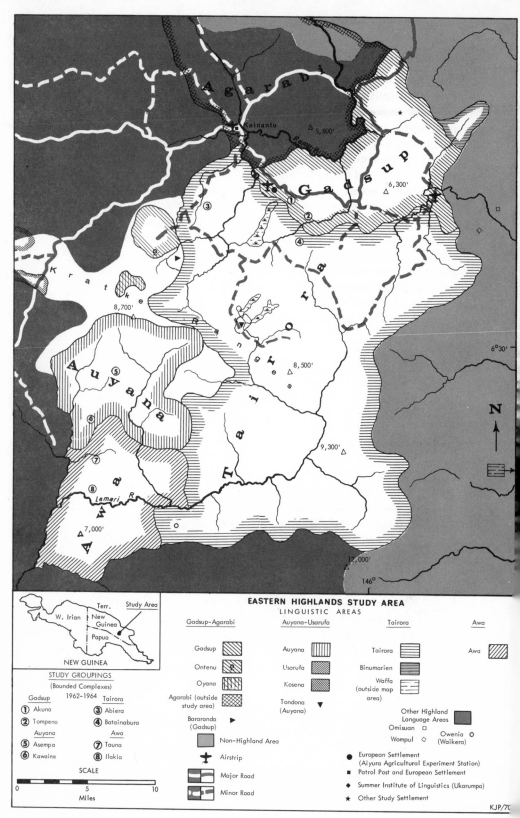

EASTERN HIGHLANDS STUDY AREA

LINGUISTIC AREAS

Gadsup-Agarabi	Auyana-Usarufa	Tairora	Awa
Gadsup	Auyana	Tairora	Awa
Ontenu	Usarufa	Binumarien	
Oyana	Kosena	Waffa (outside map area)	
Agarabi (outside study area)	Tondona (Auyana)		
Bararanda (Gadsup)		Other Highland Language Areas	
		Omisuan □ Owenia ○ (Waikera)	
		Wompul ◇	

Non-Highland Area

✚ Airstrip

Major Road

Minor Road

● European Settlement (Aiyura Agricultural Experiment Station)
■ Patrol Post and European Settlement
◆ Summer Institute of Linguistics (Ukarumpa)
★ Other Study Settlement

NEW GUINEA

W. Irian — Terr. New Guinea — Study Area — Papua

STUDY GROUPINGS
(Bounded Complexes)

Gadsup	1962-1964	Tairora
① Akuna		③ Abiera
② Tompena		④ Batainabura
Auyana		Awa
⑤ Asempa		⑦ Tauna
⑥ Kawaina		⑧ Ilakia

SCALE

0 — 5 — 10

Miles

N

6°30'

146°

KJP/7C

Map 2

understand about similarities and differences in these languages. Dr. Bee's work on comparative and historical problems in these languages is important, pointing to the direction of results possible which may someday reach the proportions of the better known fields such as the North American Indian languages. Dr. Kerr gives us details on the kinship system. Closed linguistic systems such as this seem to preserve forms for a longer period of time and are fruitful in this area for comparative work.

A substantial amount of text material has been included in this volume since it is my belief that published texts are invaluable for interested linguists. I am sure that these studies can be extended through the texts, and in some cases, can be corrected. I can only wish that time would have permitted an analysis of the texts, and that a further check could have been made with the recorded tapes. However, a halt must come at some point.

I am sure that I express the hope of the other authors represented here when I urge continued interest in and support for research on the languages and peoples of this area of the world.

HOWARD MCKAUGHAN

Just before going to press we received word that Dr. Darlene Bee had tragically died on April 7, 1972, in a plane crash in New Guinea. She had just completed a summer as principal of the Summer Institute of Linguistics courses in New Zealand, and was returning to the Usarufa for further field work. It is fitting that special recognition be given her here for her most significant contributions to this work and to linguistics in general. She wrote four major chapters here and co-authored two others. She also assisted in editing several other chapters, contributing to this volume more than any other one individual of her institute colleagues.

Dr. Bee's work is pioneering both in its descriptive nature and in the steps taken forward in historical and comparative linguistics for New Guinea. At her death, she was working on a new textbook to teach general linguistics, a text she called *Neo-Tagmemics*. She was also perfecting her translation of the Gospel of John in Usarufa (the manuscript with her latest corrections found in the plane wreckage), and was looking forward to further translation and linguistic work with her beloved friends, the Usarufa. They, we, and a host of other friends mourn her passing. I am sure that I speak for the other contributors, and for her colleagues in the Micro-evolution Project and the Summer Institute of Linguistics, when we express here our respect for Darlene, and by these lines pay fond tribute to her memory.

H.M.

Contents

xix

PART TWO: AUYANA-USARUFA

PART THREE: GADSUP-AGARABI

PART FOUR: TAIRORA-BINUMARIEN-WAFFA

Illustrations

PART ONE: *Awa*

I. Introduction

HOWARD McKAUGHAN

Awa is spoken by an estimated twelve hundred to fifteen hundred speakers located both north and south of the Lamari River in the southeastern corner of the Eastern Highlands District. It belongs to the Kainantu group of languages which includes Tairora, Gadsup, Auyana, and Awa as the major representatives. These in turn form the Eastern Family of the East New Guinea Highland Stock.

The following descriptions of Awa are written in a taxonomic framework. Units, both phonological and grammatical, are identified, their variations indicated, and their relationships to each other described. The phonological description concerns segmental and prosodic features, but does not deal with units larger than the syllable. The grammatical descriptions identify units on the morpheme, word, phrase, clause, and sentence levels.

The Awa sound system is fairly easy for the Westerner to duplicate. Syllables are simple, the major patterns being a single vowel nucleus (V) with preceding and/or following single consonants (C). Thus we have the following: CV, CVC, V, and VC. There are twelve consonants and seven vowels. The consonants are about the same as those found in other languages of the area. A unique feature in Awa is the seven vowel system in a group of languages that have six. Where the other related languages have two front (*i, e*), two central (*a, aa*) and two back (*u, o*), Awa has three front, one central, and three back. The low front and the low back vowels make Awa sound quite different from the other languages. We have symbolized these two vowels by the digraphs *eh* and *ah* respectively.

Tone in New Guinea languages has now been attested in many cases. Awa has a four-tone system—high, falling, rising, and low. Though these tones are easily contrasted in lexical environments, the functional load is not seemingly as high as for the more commonly known tone languages. The range of phonetic variation within each tone is wide, varying according to preceding tones. High tones step gradually up in a sequence, and low tones step gradually down. Low tone has the highest frequency of occurrence, while the falling and rising tones together account for less than 10 percent of the total distribution. Tone perturbation obscures the basic lexical tone when items occur in phrases or sentences. The relations between tones and their relation to bases and affixes are described in Chapter III.

Most Awa sentences are composed of a verb nucleus with its various closely related elements, and substantives with their satellites. The satellites of both verbs and nouns are often enclitics. That is, the satellite elements are phonologically dependent on the nucleus preceding, but have greater freedom of occurrence than do affixes.

Many of the satellite elements occur with both nouns and verbs. For the most part, those elements that mark internal or listlike relations (modify in some way the base) are limited to a specific class, while those that mark linear or syntactic relations are not so limited. Though noun bases may occur with more than thirty different suffixes or enclitics, the noun base may optionally occur alone and often does. The satellite elements thus optionally make explicit relations that can be indicated, at least in many cases, by other syntactic devices such as order, juxtaposition, or intonation.

The Awa sentence is typical of New Guinea Highland languages in that very frequently the sentence is composed of more than one clause. In such sentences verbal affixes indicate the relation between clauses by markers in the dependent clause to anticipate the subject to follow in an independent clause, and also in certain instances to relate a contrary to fact clause or an obligation to their respective clause partners.

Besides the interclause relation markers, verbs in Awa contain morphemes, or fusions of morphemes to mark subject-tense (4 tenses), aspect (7), and mode (6), and may also with some stems indicate the direct and indirect objects. Awa stands in this instance between Tairora on the one hand whose verbs mark these categories by fusions of morphemes, and Gadsup on the other, whose verbs contain affixes that can be separated out as individual units. Awa in some instances uses fusions, and in others uses individual morphemes. At any rate, the system is complicated by morphophonemic rules, multiplicity of morphemes in a close-knit phrase or sequence, and tonal perturbation. These complications are described in the papers to follow.

A number of the papers published here have been published in scattered journals elsewhere, as indicated in the footnotes. The editor has worked closely with the Lovings on the Awa papers, co-authoring a number of them. Some of the papers published elsewhere have different orthographies.

These, whenever possible without changing the information, have been altered for the sake of consistency both between papers on Awa and with the papers on other languages. Texts were collected by the editor with assistance from R. Loving on translation.

II. The Dialects of Awa

RICHARD LOVING

Among Awa villages there is a direct relationship between dialect difference and the distance between villages. This phenomenon is not peculiar to Awa, but has been reported elsewhere.[1] What is unique about the Awa dialect pattern is that of the eight different villages each has certain dialectal differences.[2] On a straight cognate comparison no village has more than 98 percent similarity with any other village. Awa speakers not only easily recognize but also point out to the investigator specific differences in pronunciation between village dialects with even the highest percentage of shared cognates. On the other hand, there appears to be mutual intelligibility between even the most divergent dialects, and speakers in any one Awa village will name the other seven villages as those which are *mota ehweh* 'one talk'. The percentage of shared cognates between word lists collected from individuals representing the different villages varies from 71 percent to 98 percent. Diversity between pairs of dialects thus ranges from 2 percent to 29 percent noncognates. This suggests a recognition of major dialect groupings rather than an analysis in terms of eight coordinate dialects. This paper posits four dialects for Awa.

The word list used for the comparison of these dialects consisted of one hundred items, including object words, pronouns, and verbal constructions. Seventy-five of the one hundred items were taken from Swadesh's 100-word

---

[1] This was noted by Diebler and Trefry in 1960 in their survey of the Chimbu subdistrict in the Eastern Highlands and suggested specifically for Awa by McKaughan (see Chap. XXXV).

[2] The word village here is used to include clusters of two or more hamlets as much as a half hour's walk from one another. All the villages except Yona and Amoraba consist of hamlets.

list.[3] The remaining items consisted primarily of verbal constructions and sequences elicited to establish shared grammatical features. These served to ascertain the existence of any dialectal differences involving the categories of number, person, tense, aspect, and mode. It was found when comparing these items that though there were differences (often predictable) between the morphemes signaling these various categories, the categories themselves were remarkably consistent throughout all the dialects of Awa. Word-list items were considered cognates when 50 percent or more of the phonemes of compared items were the same. Thus grammatical features are not reflected in the cognate percentages given here. Nevertheless, a comparison of these grammatical features did reveal that in the dialects of Awa the variation between grammatical categories is much less than the variation between lexical items.

TABLE 1
CHART OF COGNATE PERCENTAGES

Dialects	Villages	T.S.C.*	Agam	Mo	Am	Tain	Yo	Taw	Il
Tauna	Tauna	550	71	76	75	76	81	84	87
Ilakia	Ilakia	560	75	78	80	78	80	83	
Northeastern {	Tawaina	575	76	79	80	81	92		
	Yona	583	80	84	84	82			
Southern {	Tainoraba	600	90	95	98				
	Amoraba	608	94	97					
	Mobuta	604	95						
	Agamusi	581							

*Total Shared Cognates with each of the other villages.

▱   Shared cognates between villages south of the Lamari River.

▱   Shared cognates between villages north of the Lamari River.

▢   Shared cognates between villages across the Lamari River.

The chart of cognate percentages indicates the dialects, villages, total shared cognates (T.S.C.), and the percentages of cognates between villages. The villages are listed vertically in geographical order beginning with Tauna in the northwest, proceeding eastward, and then south of the Lamari River to Tainoraba and listing east to west and then finally south to Agamusi. The horizontal listing begins with Agamusi and continues back in order to Ilakia. Listing the Awa villages in this manner makes it possible to observe (A)

[3] Swadesh (1955a). The materials on which these comparisons are based were collected by the author during August, 1964, from speakers whose parents (as well as themselves) were born and raised in the village represented.

the relationship between geographical and dialectal distance between the villages, and (B) a grouping of the percentage of shared cognates between villages north, south, and across the Lamari River. The villages of Tauna, Yona, and Amoraba each have less than 100 but more than 60 speakers, Mobuta has approximately 175 speakers, and the remaining villages each have between 200 and 250 speakers.

The four dialects of Awa will be called Tauna, Ilakia, Northeastern, and Southern. Each of these except the Southern dialect is located north of the Lamari River in the Kainantu subdistrict. The hamlets of Tauna, located in the northwest corner of the Awa area, comprise the most divergent dialect of the language. In the word list used for the comparison, Tauna has 87 percent shared cognates with Ilakia, which is the closest village both geographically and dialectally. McKaughan using basically the Swadesh 100-word list supplemented by a list of 100 additional items indicates for the two dialects 92.6 percent probable cognates in his first list and 71 percent in his second list. One might suspect that borrowed words from the nearby villages of the Auyana language might account for some of the differences between Tauna and Ilakia since phonetically these two dialects sound quite similar to this investigator. Although there is presently no Auyana word list available with which to compare the Tauna data, there are indications that borrowings from Auyana actually account for very few of the divergences of Tauna as compared to other Awa dialects. Among nouns, which comprise over half of the word list, only one ends in -*ma,* the Auyana classifier which occurs with nonverbal forms. And in this case the word *idama* 'bark' is still a cognate with the Ilakia word *itawa.* McKaughan's investigations also lend support to this position. He writes, 'No Awa dialect seems to be especially close to any of the Auyana dialects. ... We can only conclude that there has been no particular long-standing influence between, for example, Tauna and Kawaina [dialect of Auyana], the present closest neighbors across this language boundary' (see Chap. XXXV, Sec. 3.5.3.).

The hamlets of Ilakia located near the center of the northern part of the Awa area comprise the second most divergent of the Awa dialects. With each of the four villages in the Southern dialect Ilakia has at least two more shared cognates than does Tauna. With the two villages comprising the Northeastern dialect, however, Ilakia has exactly one less shared cognate than does Tauna. Since the percentage of shared cognates in the latter case runs between 80 percent and 84 percent a difference of only one cognate has little significance. Therefore one can say that the Tauna and Ilakia dialects, though distinct themselves, differ to almost the same degree when compared to the Northeastern dialect. Furthermore the difference between the Ilakia and Southern dialects is less than between the Tauna and Southern dialects.

The Northeastern dialect consists of the hamlets of Tawaina and the village of Yona. These two villages have 92 percent shared cognates. It is interesting to note that Tawaina has more shared cognates with Tauna and Ilakia than with the Southern dialect while Yona has more shared cognates with the Southern dialect than with Tauna or Ilakia.

The Southern dialect is located south of the Lamari and north of the Aziana rivers in the Wananara subdistrict and consists of the villages of Tainoraba, Amoraba, Mobuta, and Agamusi. More than half of the Awa speakers (over 700 out of approximately 1,200) live in this area. Within the Southern dialect, speakers in the village of Agamusi are the most divergent.

Adding up the total number of shared cognates for each village gives a good over-all linguistic picture of the Southern dialect. Tainoraba has a total of 283, Amoraba 289, Mobuta 287, and Agamusi 279. Thus we see that Amoraba has the most shared cognates with the other villages having a dialect total of 2 more shared cognates than Mobuta, 6 more than Tainoraba, and 19 more than Agamusi. This same relationship between villages in the Southern dialect remains when comparing the total number of shared cognates for each of the eight villages in the language. Amoraba has a language total of 4 more cognates than Mobuta, 8 more than Tainoraba, 27 more than Agamusi, 25 more than Yona, 37 more than Tawaina, 51 more than Ilakia, and 62 more than Tauna.

The linguistic center of the Awa language is thus probably south of the Lamari River in the Southern dialect. The village of Amoraba emerges as linguistically and geographically the most central village in both the Southern dialect and, perhaps, in the entire Awa language area.

III. Awa Phonemes, Tonemes, and Tonally Differentiated Allomorphs

RICHARD LOVING

1. INTRODUCTION

Tonally differentiated allomorphs in noun phrases as well as the tonomes and segmental phonemes of Awa will be described in this paper.[1]

An interesting feature of Awa noun phrases is that most noun suffixes do not have basic tonemes but derive their tonemes depending on: (A) the suffix stem class of which they are a part; (B) the toneme of the preceding syllable; (C) whether or not the preceding toneme has been perturbed; (D) the class of the stem on which they occur.

In the first few days of language study, minimal toneme pairs of object words in isolation indicated the presence of phonemic tone levels.

A unique feature of segmental phonemes in Awa is the occurrence of /eh/ as a seventh vowel phoneme in an area of five and six vowel languages.

2. SEGMENTAL PHONEMES

The segmental phonemes of Awa include nine consonants: *p, t, s, k, q, m, n, w, y;* and seven vowels: *i, u, e, o, eh, a, ah.*[2]

---

[1] The material for this paper was gathered over a one and a half year residence at the village of Mobuta under the auspices of the Summer Institute of Linguistics. The author is indebted to Eunice Pike, Dorothy James, and Alan Pence for editorial help in preparation of this paper. The paper was first published as pp. 23-32 in *Papers in New Guinea Linguistics, No. 5,* Linguistic Circle of Canberra Publications (Series A: Occasional Papers, No. 7) (Australian National University, 1966), and is used here in its present form by permission.

[2] [My data indicate that there are 12 consonants rather than the 9 cited by Loving, adding *b, d,* and *g.* In Sec. 2.2 Loving analyzes the voiced stops as variants of the voiceless. His interpretation seems to be based upon the fact that voiced phones never appear in initial position. He interprets voiceless stops occurring between vowels as a sequence of glottal stop and one of the stop phonemes. He then makes the voiced

2.1. *Consonantal Contrast*

The stops and affricate /p, t, s, k, q/ contrast as in: *ipisehq*[3] 'He cries', *itiă* 'raw', *ísiq* 'He plucks', *kíkíq* 'It is crowded', *iqisá* bird name. The nasals /m, n/ contrast as in *níeq* 'They gave me', *míehq* 'He is there.' The semivocoids /w, y/ contrast as in: *ehyehyéhtiq* 'drought', *ehwĕh* 'talk'.

2.2. *Consonantal Variation*

A voiced variant of the stops /p, t, k/ occurs intervocalic following front vowels as in [ibiȼæʔ] 'He cries', [idigiʔ] 'He stands', [kîgíʔ] 'It is crowded.'[4] A voiced flap variant of the stop /t/ and a voiced fricative variant of the stops /p, k/ occur intervocalic following central and back vowels as in [ɔře] 'woman', [ubɐe] 'sand', [ogɔ̃] 'alive'. A voiced affricate variant of the affricate /s/ occurs following /n/ as in [wɔndžɔ̃] 'ghost'. A velar variant of the nasal /n/ occurs preceding the stop /k/ as in [awɔŋkɔ̃] 'tree' [my data have *awɔŋgɔ* H. M.].

A voiced alveopalatal grooved fricative occurs as an allophone of /y/ pre-

variety between vowels a variant of the phoneme rather than a phoneme in its own right.]

[I find in my data, however, that the voiceless and voiced stops contrast following the nasals. Phonemes /p/ and /b/ following the bilabial nasal occur as in the following examples: *tampehra* 'banana', *kampi kampi* 'point', *arampehri* 'work'; *anahmbi* 'banana', *ahmbahra* 'bean', *ahmbiuq* 'belly', *kamborah* 'cassowary'. The voiceless and voiced aleveolar stops contrast following the aleveolar nasal as in the following examples: *ambanta* 'skirt or garment (lap-lap)', *tontonah* 'gray hair', *pentoruq* 'old or dry banana leaf', *tauntau* 'quick'; *kandi* 'arrow', *ahnde* 'many', *kahndigara* 'greater'. The velar stops contrast after the velar nasal which is an allophone of the alveolar nasal: *pankeqme* 'stand', *monke* 'blue', *anonka* 'body', *sosunkura* 'pupil (eye)'; *mengamehnga* 'animal', *mangara* 'blue', *tawehngi* 'ant', *ongi* 'garden'. This sequence also occurs in the reverse order in *tiriyehgnah* 'lime'. These contrasts added to the intervocalic occurrence of voiced obstruents in contrast to the voiceless stops do not permit, in my view, the interpretation given by Loving.]

[A few comments about the phonetic characteristics of the segmental phonemes of Awa are also in order at this point. Between vowels, the voiced bilabial and velar obstruents are stops following front vowels and fricatives elsewhere. The aleveolar voiced obstruent is flapped. The affricate phoneme (*s*) is aleveolar to alveopalatal and is voiced following a nasal as Loving indicates. Loving covers the variants of the nasal phoneme and also the semivowels adequately. The vowels are high, front and back; mid, front and back; and low, front and back, the phoneme /ah/ being a back rounded vocoid as are the other two back vowels (here and elsewhere the digraph is used as is *eh* for [æ]). The central phoneme indicated as /a/ varies from the mid position [ə] to the low central position [a]. As Loving indicates in Section 2.4, the front back and central vowels are short in initial and medial positions, but long in final positions. The phoneme /a/ is the low variant when long, but tends toward the mid position in initial and medial occurrence. H.M.]

[3] Except where examples of tonemes are given, low toneme throughout this paper will be unwritten.

[4] [In the original article, Loving presented the medial voiceless stops as sequences of glottal plus stop. Thus initial voiceless stops and medial voiced stops and fricatives were treated by him as allophones. I prefer to present the material as outlined in footnote 2, above. I have therefore omitted Loving's 'phonemic' transcriptions, leaving only the phonetic entry as in the original article. H.M.]

ceding the vowel /i/ and less frequently fluctuates with [y] in other environments as in: [əži] tree name, [əɓuži] woman's name, [əžu] ~ [əyu] 'seed', [ožôʔmedôʔ] ~ [oyôʔmedôʔ] 'They pulled up.'

2.3. Vocalic Contrast

The seven vowels contrast as in: *píti* 'heart', *putuputu* 'thunder', *petaté* 'banana', *pontŏ* 'harp', *pehtahqkotah* 'naked', *pátéqta* 'plate', and *pahtahni* 'person'.[5]

2.4. Vocalic Variants

Word initial /um/ is actualized etically as a portmanteau phone, [m·], as in [m·oʔ] /umoq/ 'rat'.

The vowels /i, u, a/ occur as short vowels initially and medially. Word final, either in isolation or at the end of a phonological phrase, these vowels occur with length as in: [idobîbĭ·] 'noise', [puřuɓuřu·] 'thunder', [kəɓəra·] 'bird'.

2.5. Distribution of Segmental Phonemes in Relation to the Syllable and Word

A syllable consists of a single vowel nucleus plus an optional onset and an optional coda; that is, the patterns CV, CVC, V, VC occur. All consonants except glottal stop occur syllable initial. Only nasals and glottal stop occur syllable final. Any vowel may fill the slot of any syllable type. Only one toneme occurs with any one syllable.

Within a phonological word, any consonant may occur intervocalic. All but /y, q/ occur word initial. Only /q/ occurs word final. Across syllable boundaries the following consonant clusters occur: /mp/, /nt/, /ns/, /nk/, /qm/, /qn/, /qp/, /qt/, /qk/ [the last three sequences not found in my data H.M.]. These clusters occur only word medial, never initial or final.

The seven vowels each occur word initial, medial, and final, and also preceding and following each of the consonants.

The vowels /o, eh, a, ah/ have not been observed preceding either /eh/ or /ah/ within words. All other combinations of vowels are possible in sequences of two. In sequences of three, the following combinations have been observed: /iahu/ *ániahú* 'mother and daughter', /iahe/ *ahpíahe* 'tomorrow', /iahu/ *iwiáhiaq* 'He is thinking', /iaho/ *iwiáho* 'think', /iehi/ *ahpièhî* 'grass ashes', /iai/ *katiaiq* 'slippery', /iueh/ *íúéh* 'our mouth', /uehi/ *nuehĭ* 'my chin', /eoe/ *koweoe* 'Go and bring!', /oia/ *ahpitoia* 'disintegrated', /ehia/

---

[5] [Note: Whenever Loving uses *t* between vowels, it represents the flapped voiced alveolar obstruent which I symbolize as /d/. A sequence of *qt* equates with my voiceless stop *t*. Parallels to this are the same for *p = b, qp = p; k = g* and *qk = k*. It is not possible in Loving's transcription, nor from his description, to know if the obstruents are voiced or voiceless before nasals. I have *pondo* for 'harp'. H.M.]

ehîa 'silent', /aio/ *aiô* 'toe joint', /aoi/ *paoiq* 'He married', /aie/ *aie* 'foot!', /aea/ *maeawě* 'animal fat', /ahoe/ *iwiáhoe* 'Think!' In sequences of four the following combination occurs: /iahoe/ *iwiáheo* 'Think!'

Any syllable type may occur word initial, medial, or final. A sequence of V syllables within a word occurs in contrast with a sequence of VCV syllables in which the C is /w/ or /y/ as in: *aiaq* 'stem', *ayǎ* 'intestines', *atàhûe* 'why', *áhwánah* 'different'.

3. TONEMES

Awa tonemes include high, falling, rising, and low.

3.1. Tonemic Contrast

In one-syllable words there is contrast between these tonemes as in: *náh* 'breast', *nâh* 'taro', *pǎh* 'fish', *nàh* 'house'.

In two-syllable words ten of the possible sixteen toneme combinations occur as in: *táti* 'dew', *tápǎh* beetle name, *áhtè* 'afraid', *nâhpô* 'Is it a taro?', *nâhmǐq* 'It is a taro', *âhqmè* frog name, *àhqkí* 'yam', *màhgô* man's name, *àhtě* 'ear', *àhtè* 'woman'. Of the sixteen possible patterns, note that four of the six which do not occur are those in which the initial toneme is rising. The two remaining patterns, high-falling and falling-high, occur on the last two syllables of three-syllable words as in: *wènáwêh* 'his sister's husband', *áwêhwá* 'sister's husband'.

In three-syllable words all tonemes contrast word final as in: *kàmpòtá* 'cassowary', *àyàhtǎ* 'hair', *òtìtâ* 'taboo', *kapata* 'bird'. All tonemes except rising contrast word medial as in: *kàpáhtè* bird name, *kàpâhtà* 'bamboo', *àyàhpà* 'belly'. All tonemes except rising contrast word initial as in: *tónànà* 'bark belt', *môqkàkè* 'someday', *nònàhwè* 'fog'. Of the sixty-four possible combinations of these tonemes on three-syllable words, twenty-three have been found to occur. See examples above and the following: *òyétá* 'egg', *áwìǎh* 'his tibia', *nònáwěhq* 'ditch', *pòpâhkíq* 'whistle', *nánúêh* 'my sister's husband', *wènáwêh* 'his sister's husband', *áwêhwáh* 'sister's husband', *èhîǎ* 'silent', *àhkàhmpǔ* 'deaf', *wáhnèpâh* 'casuarina', *téhqtàté* 'two', *téhqtúkàh* 'trap', *átúó* 'his lips'.

3.2. Tonemic Variants

High toneme has a range of phonetic variants as follows. Utterance final high occurs as a phonetic upglide from high, while nonfinal highs in a series step gradually up from a high mid pitch to the final upglide. Elsewhere high toneme occurs as phonetic high pitch.

Examples: *ikahtahse* /íkáhtáhsé/ oppossum name; *tehtate* /téhtàté/ 'two'; *otita* /ótìtà/ 'taboo'; *kahqtoqpe* /kàhqtóqpè/ 'potato'.

Falling toneme has a range of phonetic variants as follows. Following high toneme it glides from high to mid. Between high and low, or utterance final following high, it glides from high to low. Utterance final following other than high it glides from mid to low. Utterance medial following tonemes other than high its pitch is level mid.

Examples: *awehwa* /áwêhwá/ 'sister's husband'; *nanuweh* /nánúwêh/ 'my sister's husband'; *kapahta* /kàpâhtà/ 'bamboo'; *ahkahmpu* /àhkâhmpû/ 'deaf'; *ayahqno* /àyàhqnô/ 'head'.

Rising toneme occurs as a glide from low to low mid as in: *apiah* /àpìǎh/ 'nose'; *o* /ǒ/ 'new'.

Low toneme has a range of phonetic variants as follows. Utterance final low occurs as a phonetic downglide from low. The final low in a series of lows preceding high toneme is low in pitch, while nonfinal lows in a series step gradually down from a low mid pitch to the final low in the series. Elsewhere low toneme occurs as phonetic low pitch.

Examples: *tahmemiah* /tàhmèmìàh/ opossum name; *ahte* /àhtè/ 'woman'; *tunsotetiq* /tùnsòtètíq/ 'afternoon'; *kahqtoqpe* /kàhqtóqpè/ 'potato'.

3.3. Tonemic Distribution

All of the tonemes occur with each of the vowels word final. High, falling, and low tonemes occur with each of the seven vowels word medial. High and low tonemes occur with each of the vowels word initial. Falling toneme occurs with /o/ and /ah/ word initial. It is expected that a larger corpus of data will reveal the occurrence of falling toneme with more of the vowels word initial. Not more than two falling tonemes have been observed in sequence. Rising toneme occurs only word final.

Low toneme is the most frequent in occurrence. The next most frequent is high toneme. Rising toneme is the least frequent. In ten pages of Awa folktale text the percentage of occurrences were as follows: low 68 percent, high 22.8 percent, falling 5.4 percent, and rising 3.8 percent. The percentage of rising tonemes would be higher in a listing of lexical items since word-final rising tonemes are perturbed to low tonemes phrase medially in text.

4. TONALLY DIFFERENTIATED ALLOMORPHS IN NOUN PHRASES

Two types of tonemic perturbation occur throughout the language:

A. A word-final rising toneme becomes low whenever followed by another word in the same phonological phrase as in: *pĕh* 'just' plus *póétáhq* 'pig' becomes *pĕh póétáhq* 'just a pig'; *pĕh* 'just' plus *nâh* 'taro' becomes *pĕh nâh* 'just taro'.

B. A word-initial low toneme becomes a falling toneme whenever preceded in the same phonological phrase by a word whose final toneme is rising as in: *pĕh* 'just' plus *tàhnú* 'flea' becomes *pèh tàhnú* 'just a flea'; *pĕh* 'just' plus *kàpàtà* 'bird' becomes *pèh kàpàtà* 'just a bird'.

Within verb phrases the tonemes of a verb stem are perturbed not only by certain modifiers which preceded them, but also by the suffixes with which they occur. Within noun phrases, however, noun stems are never perturbed by their suffixes, most of which have no basic tonemes.[6] These stems may only be perturbed by words which occur in satellite positions in noun phrases.[7]

4.1. Tonally Differentiated Allomorphs of Noun Stems and of Noninitial Modifiers in Noun Phrases

In addition to the general perturbation just described, unperturbed satellite words in noun phrases are grouped into three classes depending on how they perturb the word which contiguously follows. Noun stems in their phonological relationships with suffixes fall into the first two of these classes.

Class I satellite words cause following one-syllable words to perturb to rising toneme and cause multisyllable words to perturb to low for the first toneme and to high for all subsequent tonemes as in: *kàwèq* 'good' plus *nàh* 'house' becomes *kàwèq nǎh* 'good house'; *ànòqtàh* 'big' plus *kàpàtà* 'bird' becomes *ànòqtàh kàpátá* 'big bird'.

All satellite words whose final toneme is low or falling occur in Class I. In addition to those words, the following satellite words whose final toneme is rising, and satellite words whose final toneme is high occur in Class I: *wìèhq* 'yellow', *wàhqtŏ* 'short', *ŏ* 'new', *sèhìyŏ* 'foolish', *àùqmǎ* 'poor hunting', *ànǎh* 'selfish', *tàhùqtáhúq* 'red', *sùànsúá* 'fast', *èyòyó* 'light', *ìwìáh* 'thinking', *wítéh* 'laughing'.

Class II satellite words cause following words to perturb to all high tonemes as in: *pàpùsǎ* 'black' plus *wéh* 'man' becomes *pàpùsà wéh* 'black man'; *kàpàntéh* 'sick' plus *kàpàtà* 'bird' becomes *kàpàntéh kápátá* 'sick bird'.

Nouns or pronouns plus the suffix *-tahnsa*[8] 'similar', and nouns plus the suffix *-te* 'from' occur in Class II, as in: *tóqpìàtàhnsǎ* 'like an earthworm' plus *wèh* 'man' becomes *tóqpìàtàhnsà wéh*[9] 'earthwormlike man'; *kàìnèn-túpèqtě* 'from Kainantu' plus *màhpì* 'boy' becomes *kàìnèntúpèqtè máhpí* 'the boy from Kainantu'.

The following satellite words occur in Class II: *àhpĕhq* 'no good', *pàpùsǎ* 'black', *sòpùyǎ* 'thin', *tàpòítìǎ* 'dark', *tàmùnsìǎ* 'close by', *ítàkátìqtàhq* 'many',

---

[6] Certain grammatical noun phrases which always have pause are not treated, since pause always interrupts the phonological phrase.

[7] Words which occur in satellite positions in noun phrases will hereafter be referred to in this paper simply as satellite words.

[8] The tone of these suffixes depends on the stem-final toneme which precedes them, and therefore the tonemes are not written when the suffix is listed in isolation.

[9] This perturbation takes precedence over that described in the second paragraph of Section 4.

ítìă 'raw', *kàpàntéh* 'sick', *tàkàhtíéh* 'looking', *títí* 'cooking', *sùkéh* 'sleeping', *íteh* 'understanding', *àqpí* 'chopping', *kèqkí* 'burning'.

Class III satellite words do *not* cause tonemes in following words to be perturbed as in: *ítè* 'not' plus *nàh* 'house' becomes *ítè nàh* 'not a house'; *ítè* 'not' plus *kàpàtà* 'bird' becomes *ítè kàpàtà* 'not a bird'.

This class includes the clitic *ítè* 'not', the modifiers *mòqkě* 'all', *pěh* 'just', and all possessives. The possessives are made up of noun or pronoun plus -*ne* possessive marker as in: *wěně* 'his' plus *póétáhq* 'pig' becomes *wènè póétáhq* 'his pig'; *póétáhqné* 'the pig's' plus *àhqkí* 'yam' becomes *póétáhqné áhqkí* 'the pig's yam'.

Notice that the general perturbation described in the first paragraph of Section 4 still occurs even though the satellite word is in Class III as in: *wěně* 'his' plus *kàpàtà* 'bird' becomes *wènè kàpàtà* 'his bird'; *něně* 'my' plus *nàh* 'house' becomes *něnè nàh* 'my house'.

Perturbed satellite words in turn cause all following satellite and head words in a noun phrase to be perturbed to all high tonemes as in: *ítòqkě* (Class I) 'no good' plus *sèhìŏ* (Class I) 'foolish' plus *pàtòsă* (Class II) 'blind' plus *wèhùqkè* 'people' becomes *ítòqkè sèhíó pátósá wéhúqké* 'bad, foolish, deaf people'; *àwàhtì* (Class I) 'sick' plus *pàtòsă* (Class II) 'blind' plus *àhtàtì* 'girl' becomes *àhwàtì pàtósá áhtátí* 'sick, deaf girl'.

4.2. Tonally Differentiated Allomorphs of Noun Suffixes

Noun suffixes are divided into those with a basic toneme and those without a basic toneme. Those without a basic toneme are further divided into suffix classes set up on the basis of the particular pattern with which they derive tonemes when occurring with noun stems.

4.2.1. *Noun suffixes which have basic tonemes.* The tonemes of these suffixes remain unchanged. These suffixes include -*è* augmentative, -*tàpà* 'large', -*tàpîtă*, -*tàpîtàmô*, -*tàpîtàqpómò* dubitative, as in: *tàhnú* 'flea' plus -*è* augmentative becomes *tàhnúè* 'a flea'; *nàh* 'house' plus -*tàpà* 'large' becomes *nàhtàpà* 'big house'; *ànòtâh* 'big' plus *nàhtàpà* 'big house' becomes *ànòtâh nàhtàpà* 'great big house'.

The suffix -*tàníáhq* 'very long' remains unchanged when following unperturbed noun stems as in: *nàkà* 'vine' plus -*tàníáhq* 'very long' becomes *nàkàtàníáhq* 'a very long vine'. Following perturbed noun stems, however, this suffix has a sequence of high tonemes as in: *ànòtâh* 'big' plus *nàhkàtàníáhq* 'very long vine' becomes *ànòtâh nàkátáníáhq* 'a big long vine'.

4.2.2. *Noun suffixes without basic tonemes which follow unperturbed noun stems.* Factors influencing the tonemes which these suffixes have are: (A) the toneme of the preceding syllable; (B) whether or not the preceding toneme has been perturbed; (C) the phonological class of the stem on which the suffix occurs.

Suffixes without basic tonemes are divided into suffix classes as follows:

Suffix Class I is made up of those one-syllable suffixes which have a high toneme when following a stem-final high or rising[10] toneme, and have a rising toneme when following a stem-final low or falling toneme. The suffixes in this class are: *-miq* predicative, *-me* identificational, *-teh* conjunctive plural.

Examples: *póétáhq* 'pig' plus *-me* identificational becomes *póétáhqmé* 'the pig'; *ànôwǎ* 'mother' plus *-teh* conjunctive plural becomes *ànôwàtéh* 'his mother and others'; *àhtè* 'woman' plus *-miq* predicative becomes *àhtèmǐq* 'It is a woman'; *àyàhtâ* 'hair' plus *-me* identificational becomes *àyàhtâmě* 'the hair'.

Suffix Class II is made up of those one-syllable suffixes which have a falling toneme when following a stem-final low, falling, or rising toneme, and have a low toneme when following a stem-final high toneme. The suffixes in this class are: *-po* question marker, and *-seq* personal dual.

Examples: *àhtè* 'woman' plus *-po* question marker becomes *àhtèpò* 'Is it a woman?'; *ànôwǎ* 'mother' plus *-seq* personal dual becomes *ànôwàsêq* 'and his mother'; *nâh* 'taro' plus *-po* question marker becomes *nâhpò* 'Is it a taro?'; *póétáhq* 'pig' plus *-po* question marker becomes *póétáhqpò* 'Is it a pig?'

Suffix Class III is made up of those one-syllable suffixes whose toneme is determined by the class of the preceding noun stem as well as its stem-final toneme. The suffixes are: *-pa* 'to, at' (animate); *-ne* possessive marker; *-ka* actor marker; *-taq* 'at, on'; *-sahq* purposive collective. They have: (A) rising toneme when following all Class I noun stems whose stem-final toneme is low, falling, or rising; (B) low toneme when following all Class I noun stems whose stem-final toneme is high; (C) high toneme when following all Class II noun stems.

Examples: *nâh* 'taro' plus *-sahq* purposive collective becomes *nâhsǎhq* 'taro collecting'; *àhtè* 'woman' plus *-ne* possessive marker becomes *àhtènè* 'the woman's'; *ápòkèh* (Class I) 'tree top' plus *-ka* actor marker becomes *ápòkèhkǎ* 'The tree top did it'; *tàhnú* (Class I) 'flea' plus *-ka* actor marker becomes *tàhnúkà* 'The flea did it'; *òyétá* (Class II) 'egg' plus *-taq* 'at, on' becomes *òyétátáq* 'on the egg'; *pǎh* (Class II) 'fish' plus *-sahq* purposive collective becomes *pàhsǎhq* 'fish collecting'.

Suffix Class IV is made up of those two-syllable suffixes whose toneme is determined by the class of the preceding noun stem as well as its stem-final toneme. The suffixes are: *-sape* causational, referential; *-tate* dual; *-tato* trial; *-mati* plural; *-kaqta* 'elongated'; *kaqkaq* conjunctive; *-taqte* instrumental; *-piqpeq* 'in'; *-tapa* 'over, across'.

They have: (A) low-high tonemes when following all Class I noun stems whose stem final toneme is low or falling; (B) low-rising tonemes when

---

[10] For ease of description we are giving basic tonemes of the stems.

following all Class I noun stems whose stem-final toneme is high; (C) falling-rising tonemes when following all Class I noun stems whose stem-final toneme is rising; (D) high-high tonemes when following all Class II noun stems.

Examples: *kàpàtà* 'bird' plus *-tato* trial becomes *kàpàtàtàtó* 'three birds'; *nâh* 'taro' plus *-mati* plural becomes *nàhmàtí* 'many taros'; *tàhnú* (Class I) 'flea' plus *-tate* 'two' becomes *tahnutatĕ* 'two fleas'; *ápòkĕh* (Class I) 'tree top' plus *-kaqkaq* conjunctive becomes *ápòkèhkâqkăq* 'and a tree top'; *òyétá* (Class II) 'egg' plus *-tate* 'two' becomes *òyétátáté* 'two eggs'; *păh* (Class II) 'fish' plus *-mati* plural becomes *pàhmátí* 'many fish'.

Suffix Class V consists of one suffix *-tahnsa* 'similar' and has: (A) low-high tonemes when following all nouns whose stem-final toneme is low or falling; (B) low-rising tonemes when following all nouns whose stem-final toneme is high; (C) falling-rising tonemes when following all nouns whose stem-final toneme is rising.

Examples: *nàh* 'house' plus *-tahnsa* 'similar' becomes *nàhtàhnsá* 'like a house'; *tàhnú* 'flea' plus *-tahnsa* 'similar' becomes *tàhnútàhnsă* 'like a flea'; *păh* 'fish' plus *-tahnsa* 'similar' becomes *pàhtàhnsă* 'like a fish'.

Suffix Class VI consists of two suffixes which have: (A) low-falling tonemes when following all nouns whose stem-final toneme is low or falling; (B) high-low tonemes when following all nouns whose stem-final toneme is high or rising. The suffixes in this class are: *-pomo* dubitative; *-poqpoq* dubitative conjunctive.

Examples: *nâh* 'taro' plus *-pomo* dubitative becomes *nâhpòmô* 'A taro?'; *nàh* 'house' plus *-poqpoq* dubitative conjunctive becomes *nàhpòqpôq* 'And a house?'; *tàhnú* 'flea' plus *-pomo* dubitative becomes *tàhnúpómò* 'A flea?'; *păh* 'fish' plus *-poqpoq* dubitative conjunctive becomes *pàhpóqpòq* 'And a fish?'

4.2.3. *Noun suffixes without basic tonemes which follow perturbed noun stems.* Following perturbed noun stems, suffixes in suffix Classes II, V, and VI have the same tonemes which they have when following unperturbed stem-final high tonemes as in: *àwàhtè* 'sick' plus *àhtàtí* 'girl' plus *-po* question marker becomes *àwàhtè àhtătípŏ* 'Is it a sick girl?'; *kàwèq* 'good' plus *àhtàpâh* 'yam' plus *-tahnsa* 'similar' becomes *kàwèq àhtápáhtàhnsă* 'like a good yam'; *pàtòsà* 'blind' plus *àhtè* 'woman' plus *-pomo* dubitative becomes *pàtòsà áhtépómò* 'A blind woman?'

Following perturbed noun stems, suffixes in suffix Classes I, III, and IV have all high tonemes as in: *àwàhtè* 'sick' plus *àhtàtì* 'girl' plus *-ne* possessive marker becomes *àwàhtè àhtátíné* 'the sick girl's'; *pàtòsă* 'blind' plus *ahte* 'woman' plus *-tate* dual becomes *pàtòsà áhtétáté* 'two blind women'.

IV. A Preliminary Survey
of Awa Noun Suffixes

RICHARD and ARETTA LOVING

1. INTRODUCTION

Awa nouns may be defined as those word bases which may occur with suffixes to indicate number and size.[1] Other suffixes which occur with nouns may or may not occur with other parts of speech, but analysis is not yet complete enough for details. This paper does not purport to be a complete analysis of Awa nouns. As the title indicates, it is only a preliminary survey of the suffixes which may occur with nouns, indicating their structural categories, their morphophonemic variants, and their distribution as related to the word base. Prefixes (indicating obligatory possession and used in general with body parts and kinship terms) are covered in Chapter V. Person names seem to act more like pronouns than nouns, and are also left to a later discussion of that phase of the language.[2] It is felt, however, that sufficient information is at hand to give a preliminary picture of the structure indicated by noun suffixes.

[1] This paper was originally published as pp. 28-43 in *Studies in New Guinea Linguistics*, Oceania Linguistic Monographs No. 6 (Sydney: University of Sydney, 1962). It is reissued here in this format by permission.

The material for this paper was gathered by the authors during 1960-61 under the auspices of the Summer Institute of Linguistics. The main informant was Iera, a monolingual young man approximately nineteen years old from the village of Mobuta. The paper was first drafted in early 1961 for an SIL workshop, and included in a series of mimeographed papers designated as '1961 Workshop Papers of the Summer Institute of Linguistics, New Guinea Branch, Ukarumpa, Territory of New Guinea.' We are indebted to colleagues of SIL, New Guinea, for help with this draft. In late 1961 the paper was completely revised and rewritten under the guidance and editorship of Howard McKaughan.

[2] Person names are distinguished from other nouns in that they occur with the vocative suffix *(-o): paetao* 'Peta!'

19

2. STRUCTURAL CATEGORIES MARKED BY NOUN SUFFIXES

Those suffixes in Awa which indicate listlike relations, that is, class membership, are said to mark 'internal relations'. Such suffixes include those which mark size, number, place, and so on. Pittman prefers to describe such under morphology.[3] In contrast to this, certain other noun suffixes in Awa show a relation between the noun and other word bases in the sentence. These indicate 'sequence' relations, and are syntactic in nature. Such suffixes mark the subject, instrument, or location, and so forth, of an action; or they mark possession, similarity, or conjunction, and so forth, between nouns. A complete description of Awa grammar would treat the latter suffixes at the same time all sequence relations involving nouns were described. It seems important here, though not describing all sequence relations involving nouns, to distinguish between those noun suffixes that mark internal relations, and those that mark external relations.

2.1. Internal Relations

2.1.1. Size. Three suffixes affixed to Awa nouns indicate the size of the noun base involved: *(-daba)*[4] indicates that the base is 'large', *(-kadaN)*[5] indicates that the base, a small object, is 'elongated', and *(-daniyahq)* indicates that the base, a larger object, is 'very long'. Examples: *poedahdaba* 'large pig', *pakada* 'stick used for handling sweet potato in fire', *nahgadaniyahq* 'long vine'.

2.1.2. Number. Awa nouns may occur with dual, trial, or plural suffixes, *(-tade)*, *(-tado)*, and *(-madiN)* respectively. Thus *iyaN* 'dog' may be inflected to indicate that two dogs are in view, *iyatade;* or to indicate that three dogs are involved, *iyatado;* or that more than three are indicated, *iyamadi.*

2.1.3. Place. The fact that the noun base is a location or a place is indi-

---

[3] Pittman (1959) suggests that the morphology of a language may be defined as 'the set of structural signals which relates its word roots (and/or their expansions) to one another in substitutions.' He further suggests that the syntax of a language is 'the set of structural signals which relates its word roots (and/or their expansions) to one another in sequence.'

[4] Awa phonemes include consonants /p, t, k, q, b, d, g, s, m, n, y, and w/. In general voiced plosives are stops following front vowels, fricative or the alveolar flap elsewhere; /n/ is velar before velar phonemes, alveolar elsewhere; /y/ is a retroflexed grooved fricative before /i/, the nonsyllabic semivowel elsewhere. Vowels include /i, e, eh/, high mid and low front vowels; /u, o, ah/, high mid and low back vowels; and /a/, the low central vowel. Tone has not been indicated in the paper since it carries no grammatical functional load, and since its analysis is not yet settled.

[5] Awa forms enclosed in parentheses are citation forms and indicate that the suffix has various allomorphs. Such citation forms are considered primary. Final *N* on both suffixes and words is a morphophoneme, retained as a phoneme only when /s/, /k/, or a vowel follows it (see Sec. 3). Suffixes are listed with the final *N* when enclosed in parentheses, but not in the examples since these are given in their phonemic shape. Words are also listed with final *N* only if in citation form.

cated by the suffix *(-peq)*. Thus *naho,* an allomorph of *nahN* 'house', plus *-peq* becomes literally 'house-place' and may be translated by 'at', 'to', or 'in the house'; or *nahopeq* may refer specifically to the small house where women go to bear children. Village names optionally occur with *(-peq)*: *mobutapeq* 'Mobuta'.

2.1.4. *Predicative.* The existence of the noun base is expressed by the suffix *(-mideN)*: *iyamide* 'It is a dog.'

2.1.5. *Emphasis.* The suffix *(-de)* emphasizes the noun base. This may be the slight emphasis of mere repetition. In answer to the question 'What did you say?' the answer may be a repetition of the noun plus the emphatic marker followed by 'I said': *poedahde uge* 'A pig, I said.' Additional emphasis may be given by laying extra stress on the suffix: *poedahde* (with the *-de* receiving strong stress) 'A pig!' This suffix may occur twice with the same base; in such cases, it emphasizes the suffix immediately preceding it. Example: *poedahq* 'pig' plus *(-madiN)* plural plus *(-de)* emphasis plus *(-po)* question marker plus *(-de)* emphasis, yields *poedahmadineboe* 'Is it many pigs?!' Here the allomorph of the emphasis marker, *-e,* augments the plural, 'many pigs', and then emphasizes the question.

2.1.6. *Endearing term.* The suffix *(-moneN)* indicates endearment and occurs with kinship terms when possessed by first persons: *nanibaqmone* 'my dear younger brother' (male speaking); *itedibaqmone* 'our dear younger brother' (male speaking).

2.1.7. *Kinship indicator.* The suffix *(-kawa)*[6] optionally occurs with certain nouns to indicate that such are kinship terms: *wenabakawa* 'his younger brother'. This affix does not occur when such terms are possessed by first person.

2.2. *External Relations*

2.2.1. Certain suffixes mark a sequence relationship between noun and verb. These suffixes indicate that the noun is the subject, instrument, location, causation, or purpose of the action.

A. *Subject.* The suffix *(-kaN)* indicates that the noun is the subject of the action expressed by the verb: *poedahka nehde* 'The pig is eating.'

B. *Instrument.* The instrument by which the action of the verb is accomplished is shown by the suffix *(-tateN)*: *sogitaten amuduwedede*[7] 'With a knife he cut.'[8]

C. *Location.* Certain suffixes indicate that the noun is related to the verb as the location of the action. Included in this category are affixes to indicate

---

[6] When *(-kawa)* occurs, the resulting combination must be classified with pronouns and person nouns. This suffix may be related to *(-moneN)*.

[7] Though the word boundary follows final /n/, syllable division precedes it.

[8] Translation equivalents are sometimes given in the order of Awa to assist the reader.

(a) direction toward or location at *(-taq)*, (b) direction toward or location at for personal nouns *(paN)*,[9] (c) direction from *(teN)*, (d) location within *(-piq)*, (e) location on top *(-so)*, (f) location over, across *(-tabaN)*. Examples follow:

mahditaq mado	'On the bed set (it).'
adeniyopa pokuno	'To your brother go.'
sotapeten koweo	'From the garden bring (it).'
unapipeq usado	'In the bag stuff (it).'
nahnsadapeq miehde	'On top of the house he is.'
wanitaba pokide	'Across the water he went.'

D. *Causation.* The noun may be related to the verb in such manner as to explain the reason for the action of the verb. This is done by the suffix *(-sabe)*. Examples:

sunkikidesabe bokide	'Because of darkness he went.'
wenabasabe ibisehde	'For his younger brother he is crying.'
poerahsabe ahdeide	'Of the pig he is afraid.'
poedahsabe nide	'A pig I want.'

E. *Purposive.* The noun may be related to verbs of 'coming' or 'going' to express the purpose of the action. The suffix *(-sahq)* indicates this relation, and also marks the noun as collective; that is, indicates that a collection or grouping of items is in view: *namusahq madape pokide* (for grass down hill went) 'He went downhill for grass', or 'He went downhill to collect grass.'

2.2.2. Certain suffixes mark a sequence relationship between two or more nouns. These include possession, conjunction, similarity, and identification.

A. *Possession.* Noun bases may possess something or someone and this is indicated by the suffix *-ne: iyane nah* 'the dog's house'. That which is possessed need not always be actualized in the same sentence. The boy's knife may be requested by saying *mahbine wenio* (boy plus possessive, give me) 'Give me the boy's.'

B. *Conjunction.* There are three morphemes marking conjunction in Awa: *(-seq)*, *-deh,* and *(-kakaq)*. A connection between a personal noun (a noun designating a person either expressing who or what he is, such as boy, girl, man, etc.) and another personal noun (or pronoun) is indicated by *(-seq)* suffixed to both nouns (or noun and pronoun) in the sequence: *naniyoseq naniweseq* 'my brother and my husband'.

---

[9] *(-taq)* may sometimes occur with personal nouns with a probable difference in meaning from *(-paN)*, though that difference has not yet been precisely located: *anowataq* or *anowaba* 'at mother'.

When a personal noun is connected to two or more additional personal nouns (or pronouns), the suffix *-reh* is used, again suffixed to each word in the sequence. The suffix in this instance either pluralizes the nouns in question or indicates conjunction: *nanodeh nanibodeh naniyodeh* 'my mother, my father, and my brothers' (female speaking).

To avoid ambiguity in number an Awa speaker may pluralize the nouns in such a sequence by the suffix *(-madiN)*. In this instance, *(-seq)* would occur as the conjunction marker: *mahbigonseq ahdadigonseq animaigonseq* (where *-gon* is an allomorph of the plural morpheme) 'the teenage boys, girls, and little boys'.

Both *-deh* and *(-seq)* may occur (though infrequently) with the same base: *nanodehdeq*[10] *miahwe* 'My mothers (and another, or and others) are here.' In this case *-deh* indicates plural, and *(-seq)* a connection between the noun and some other noun or nouns not actualized, but understood in the context.

The third conjunction marker, *(-kakaq)*, indicates a connection between a nonpersonal noun and one or more other nonpersonal nouns. Nouns considered a part of the sequence may not appear actualized, being understood only by context. The conjunction marker occurs with each noun actualized. Examples: *umokakaq* 'a rat also', *umokakaq nahgakakaq* 'a rat and a rope', *umokakaq nahgakakaq namukakaq* 'a rat, a rope, and grass'.

If in a sequence of two nouns, *(-kakaq)* occurs only on the second, the morpheme indicates that the affixed noun modifies the preceding base by amplifying it. In such cases, the noun base may be personal or nonpersonal. Thus the word 'wife' or 'woman' plus 'child' (a personal noun) suffixed with *(-kakaq)* relates the information that the woman in question is the one having a child. The word for 'girl' plus the word for 'hat' (nonpersonal) affixed with *(-kakaq)* points out the girl having or with a hat: *ahde aninkakaq* 'a woman having a child'; *ahdadi ayahukakaq* 'a girl with a hat'.

It is possible that even when amplification is indicated, the noun modified will appear only in context. Such instances are ambiguous: that is, *(-kakaq)* may indicate either conjunction or amplification; *ayahukakaq* 'with a hat' or 'a hat also'.

C. *Similarity.* Likeness or similarity to something may be expressed by the suffix *(-tahnsaN)*. The word for snake, *padikigiah*, with *-tahnsa* suffixed to it compares it with something else. The object to which the suffixed base is compared, if expressed, precedes the suffixed base. It may, however, be indicated in the context only: *ah padikigiahtahnsa* 'The path is like a snake'; *padikigiahtahnsa* '(It is) like a snake.'

D. *Identification.* The suffix *(-meN)* points out or refers to a before-mentioned noun which may or may not be actualized in the context: *poedahme pokide* 'The pig (the one in view or under discussion) went.'

---

[10] *-deq* is an allomorph of *(-seq)*.

2.2.3. Six morphemes in Awa express some question or doubt. Rather than relating the noun to another word base, these seem to be 'sentence relators'. We class these as external relation markers since they seem to act somewhat like a questioning intonation in English. These suffixes are also grouped together because of their phonemic similarity. Recurring partials are immediately obvious, but it has not yet been possible to assign separate meaning to the individual parts. Each morpheme as indicated below contrasts with the others. However, a relationship in meaning is again apparent even to the point of it being difficult for the analysts to distinguish by translation between them.

A. The suffix (-*po*) marks a question: *iyapo* 'Is it a dog?' or 'A dog?'

B. The suffix (-*popoq*) indicates a doubt or question as to whether one of two or more things may be that in view. This suffix may occur in reply to a question indicated by (-*po*). If more than one base appears in question, (-*popoq*) occurs with each. Examples: *poedahpopoq* 'a pig maybe (or something else maybe)'; *poedahpopoq umopopoq* 'a pig or a rat maybe'.

C. The suffix (-*pomo*) often alternates with (-*po*) to mark a question. The suffix (-*pomo*) seems to carry more emphasis. This emphasis is often augmented by an intonational emphasis on each word. (-*pomo*) may also occur in answer to a question as does (-*popoq*). In answer to the question: *iyapo* 'Is it a dog?', the response may be, *iyapopoq* 'A dog maybe (or something else)', or it may be *iyapomo* 'A dog? (You don't seem to know, and I'm sure I don't either).'

D. and E. Two suffixes, (-*dabidamo*) and (-*dabidapomo*), express doubt, but we have not yet been able to distinguish them semantically. The former is more frequent in occurrence. Both seem to indicate a more serious doubt or lack of knowledge than either (-*popoq*) or (-*pomo*). The question *poedahpo* or *poedahpomo* 'Is it a pig?' may receive any of four different answers: (a) *poedahpopoq* 'A pig or something else.' (b) *poedahpomo* 'A pig? (I'm sure I don't know).' (c) *poedahdabidamo,* and (d) *poedahdabidapomo.* The last two seem to express serious doubt: 'A pig perhaps (but unlikely so—I just don't know, and I don't think anyone knows).'

F. The suffix (-*dabido*) occurs only infrequently. It may be a questioning of the veracity of a statement. The question *poedahdabido* 'A pig?' may thus receive the emphatic affirmative answer: *poedahde* 'A pig!'

3. MORPHOPHONEMICS

3.1. *Noun and Suffix Classes*

Nouns and their suffixes may be divided into three classes. Class I forms end with a glottal stop, Class II with an alveolar nasal, and Class III with a vowel: *poedahq* 'a pig', *wahN* 'possum', *paseh* 'fish'; (-*kakaq*) conjunctive, (-*kadaN*) 'elongated', (-*ka*) subject.

The final glottal stop of Class I forms is retained only when a following form begins with a vowel, or a nasal, or if the form is said in isolation (before silence):

poedahq + (*-madiN*) > *poedahqmadi*	'pigs'
poedahq + (*-tade*) > *poedahtade*	'two pigs'
poedahq + *kowedo* > *poedah kowedo*	'Bring a pig.'
poedahq + *awo* > *poedahq awo*	'Give him pork.'
poedahq + *nahno* > *poedahq nahno*	'Eat pork.'
ida + (*-kakaq*) + (*-po*) > *idaakapo*	'and firewood'
ida + (*-kakaq*) + (*-mideN*) > *idaakaqmide*	'It is also firewood.'

A final nasal of Class II forms is retained only preceding /s/, /k/, and vowels. Citation forms are given with *N* since the nasal is not actualized as a phoneme when given without a following form. Examples:

aniN = *ani*	'child'
aniN + (*-tade*) > *anitade*	'two children'
aniN + (*-po*) > *anipo*	'Is it a child?'
aniN + (*-sabe*) > *aninsabe*	'because of a child'
aniN + (*-ka*) + *nehde* > *aninka nehde*	'The child is eating.'
aniN + *awanie* > *anin awanie*	'I will give it to the child.'
aniN + *sewedo* > *anin sewedo*	'Come get the child.'
poedahq + (*-madiN*) + (*-ka*) + *nahwe* > *poedahqmadinka nahwe*	'The pigs are eating.'
poedahq + (*-madiN*) + (*-po*) > *poedahqmadipo*	'Pigs?'

3.2. Suffix Allomorphs

Most Awa suffix allomorphs are described here by citing a primary allomorph, and then indicating any morphophonemic changes that take place in other allomorphs of that morpheme.

A. Most suffixes with initial /d/ in the primary form have allomorphs without the /d/. These include the following: (*-de*)[11] emphatic, (*-daba*) 'large', (*-dabidamo*) and (*-dabidapomo*) dubitative, (*-dabido*) veracity questioner, (*-daniyahq*) 'very long'. The primary allomorph of these morphemes occurs with Class I forms (remembering that glottal stop is in turn lost). The allomorph without initial /d/ occurs with Classes II and III:

poedahq + (*-de*) > *poedahde*	'A pig!'
wahN + (*-de*) > *wahne*	'A possum!'
kogo + (*-de*) > *kogoe*	'A fly!'

[11] The suffix *-deh* conjunctive personal plural appears only in the one form.

B. Another group of suffix allomorphs may be described by citing a primary allomorph that occurs with Class I and II forms. The allomorphs occurring with Class III forms then may be described as follows:

a. Initial voiceless stops and the sibilant of primary allomorphs of this group (or words) become voiced when occurring with Class III forms. Examples:

mahbi + (*-ka*) + *awide* > *mahbiga awide*	'The teenage boy gave it.'
mahbi + (*-po*) > *mahbibo*	'A teenage boy?'
mahbi + (*-tade*) > *mahbidade*	'two teenage boys'
poedahq + (*-sabe*) + (*-tahnsaN*) > *poedahsabedahnsa*	'because of something like a pig'
mahbi + *kowedo* > *mahbi gowedo*	'Bring the teenage boy.'
poedahq + (*-tado*) + *kowedo* > *poedahtado gowedo*	'Go bring the three pigs.'
mahbi + (*-sabe*) > *mahbiyabe*	'referring to teenage boy'
mahbi + *sewedo* > *mahbi yewedo*	'Take the teenage boy.'

b. Initial /m/ of the primary allomorphs listed below (or words) becomes /w/ when occurring with Class III forms:

ida + (*-madiN*) > *idawadi*	'firewood' (plural)
ida + *menio* > *ida wenio*	'Hand me the firewood.'

The following is a list of the primary allomorphs described above.[12]

(*-ka*)	subjective	(*-tahnsaN*)	'like, similar'
(*-kadaN*)	'elongated'	(*-teN*)	'from'
(*-paN*)	personal 'to, at'	(*-sabe*)	causational
(*-piq*)	'within'	(*-sahq/-sabatahq*)	purposive collective
(*-po*)	question marker	(*-so*)	'top'
(*-popoq*)	'maybe, or'	(*-meN*)	identificational
(*-pomo*)	emphatic question	(*-mideN*)	predicative
(*-taq*)	'to, at'	(*-moneN*)	endearing term
(*-tade/-te*)/		(*-tateN*)	instrumental
(*-natade/-nate*) dual			
(*-tado/-natado*)	trial		

C. Certain suffixes have allomorphs which do not follow the above description when following Class III forms. These are as follows: *-seq ~ -deq* personal dual conjunctive; *-kakaq ~ -akaq* conjunctive; *-kawa ~ -wa* kinship indicator; *-peq ~ -ipeq*[13] place marker. The first of the above allo-

---

[12] Suffix (*-piq*) is cited as a Class I form arbitrarily (see Sec. 4.2.1). *-sahq* and *-sabatahq* occur in free fluctuation. (*-tade/-te*) occur in free fluctuation; following (*-daba*) 'large' any one of the four dual forms may occur. *-tado* and *-natado* occur in free fluctuation following (*-daba*).

[13] An allomorph *-beq* has been noted the following six times in the language: (A)

morphs is the primary allomorph occurring with Class I and Class II. The second allomorph listed occurs with Class III forms: *keweseq keweninseq* 'a widow and a widower'; *wehdeq* 'and a married man'.

D. The plural suffix (*-madiN*)[14] has a number of allomorphs: *so ∼-mahq ∼-ba ∼-sonso ∼-do ∼-go ∼-madi*.

-so occurs with the following nouns of Class I: *keweq* plus *-so* becomes *keweso* 'widows'; *nanwehq* plus *-so* becomes *nanwehso* 'my husbands'; *nanibaq* plus *-so* becomes *nanibaso* 'my young brothers' (male speaking). In the last example, the alternant *-madi* may also occur: *nanibaqmadi* 'my young brothers'. Allomorph *-so* also occurs with the following nouns of Class II: *ibainiN* plus *-so* becomes *ibaininso* 'brides'; *keweniN* plus *-so* becomes *keweninso* 'widowers'; *menahweN* plus *-so* becomes *menahwenso* 'grooms'.

-mahq occurs with one noun of Class I: *naniyoqmahq* 'my brothers' (female speaking); and three nouns of Class II: *nanahnimahq* 'my sons', *nanidahmahq* 'my sons-in-law' (female speaking), *naniyahumahq* 'my daughters'.

-do occurs with one noun (Class III): *ahdedo* 'wives'.

-go occurs with the following (Class III): *ahdadigo* 'girls', *mahbigo* 'teenage boys', *animaigo* 'little boys'.

-ba occurs with the suffix (*-daba*) 'large': *poedahdababa* 'large pigs'.

-sonso occurs with the suffix (*-daniyahq*) 'very long': *nahgadaniyahsonso* 'very long vines'.

-madi has the widest distribution and occurs with nouns of Classes I and II not listed above. Another allomorph related to *-madi* has the shape *-wadi/-adi* when occurring with all nouns of Class III not listed above: *poedahqmadi* 'pigs', *animadi* 'children', *idawadi/idaadi* 'firewood' (plural).

4. Distribution of Suffixes

4.1. *Relative Order*

The following illustrates the relative order of the suffixes.

1		2	
(*-daba*)	'large'	(*-tada*)	dual
(*-kadaN*)	'elongated'	(*-tado*)	trial
(*-daniyahq*)	'very long'	(*-madiN*)	plural
(*-kawa*)	kinship indicator	(*-sahq*)	purposive collective
(*-so*)	'on top'	*-deh*	conjunctive plural

with three bound stems, *mah-* 'this way', *se-* 'that way', and *mi-* 'that before-mentioned way'; and (B) with three village names: *kahinehntu, kahimidahi,* and *ponah*. Of the latter, Kainantu is introduced, Kaimirai is a Fore village, and Pona is an Awa village.

14 (*-madiN*) is a Class II morpheme as indicated by final *N*. Allomorphs in this section are given without final *N* since all examples occur before silence. When these allomorphs occur before /s/, /k/, or a vowel, the final nasal is retained: *mahgigonseq* 'and a teenager'.

3		9	
(*-tateN*)	instrumental	(*-teN*)	'from'
(*-paN*)	personal 'to, at'		
(*-seq*)	personal dual	**10**	
(*-moneN*)	endearment	(*-sabe*)	causational

4		11	
(*-ka*)	subjective	(*-tehnsaN*)	'like'
-ne	possessive		

5		12	
(*kakaq*)	conjunction	(*-po*)	question
		(*-pomo*)	emphatic question
6		(*-popoq*)	'maybe, or'
(*-taq*)	'to, at'	(*-dabidamo*)	serious doubt
(*-tabaN*)	'over, across'	(*-dabidapomo*)	serious doubt
		(*-dabido*)	veracity
7		(*-mideN*)	predicative
(*-piq*)	'in, inside'	(*-meN*)	identificational

8		13	
(*-peq*)	'place'	(*-de*)	emphasis

4.2. *Limitations*

Although we have listed thirteen orders, rarely do more than four or five suffixes occur with one base at the same time. Usually only two or three suffixes so occur.

4.2.1. *Mutually obligatory suffixes.* Suffix (*-so*) 'on top' is always followed by (*-taq*) 'to, at' and (*-peq*) 'place' taking the form (*-sodapeq*) 'at a place on top', 'on top'. Note that this combination is mutally exclusive with the size suffixes. If an Awa wishes to indicate something big or long, he uses a free form when *-sodapeq* occurs: *anotah nahnsodapeq kehde* (big house-on-top-it is) 'It is on top of the big house.'

The suffix (*-piq*) 'in, inside' is always followed by (*-peq*) 'place'. Primarily this combination occurs with nouns that have an inside such as bamboo or a container: *kabadapipeq* 'inside the bamboo'.

The suffix (*-teN*) 'from' is always preceded by either (*-taq*) 'to, at', (*-peq*) 'place', or (*-paN*) 'to, at' (personal): *sotapete* or *sotate* 'from the garden', *unapipete* 'from within the bag', *naniyopate* 'from my brother' (female speaking).

4.2.2. *Mutually exclusive suffixes.* Any suffix occurring in the same order is of course mutually exclusive with any other suffix listed in that order.

Note that size morphemes occur in Order 1, number morphemes (though some are structurally portmanteau) occur in Order 2, and that morphemes dealing with question or doubt occur in Order 12.

Suffixes to indicate purpose, instrument, subject, and causation are mutually exclusive. Only one of these four may occur with any one noun base at one time.

The following examples illustrate the relative orders and some of the limitations mentioned above.[15]

poedah^{1}-daba-bo^{12}	'Is it a big pig?'
mahbi-gon^{2}-se^{3}-ne^{4}	'teenagers' and (others' things)'
poedahq-ne^{4}-akaq^{5}	'pig's and (other's)'
so-madin^{2}-kaka^{5}-ta^{6}-peq^{8}	'at the gardens and (some other places)'
unah-pi^{7}-peq^{8}	'inside a netbag'
iyan-sabe^{10}-rahnsa^{11}-pe^{12}-e^{13}	'Because of being like a dog?!'
so-ta^{6}-pe^{8}-ten^{9}-sabe^{10}-bo^{12}-e^{13}	'Because of being from the garden?!'

5. Special Features

5.1. *Suffixes Not Related to the Word Base to Which They Are Attached*

A suffix may be attached to a word base and yet not be grammatically related to that particular base.[16] The word to which it is grammatically related is unexpressed, being understood from context only. This causes the suffix to appear out of its usual order. Examples thus far located indicate that such an affix occurs last. Examples follow.

A. *Plural. poedahq-madi-ne-adin koweo* (pig-plural-possessive-plural bring) 'Bring the pigs' (things).' Here the first suffix pluralizes 'pig', the second marks a possessive relation between 'pig' and some other noun understood in the context. The third suffix pluralizes that noun understood in the context.

B. *Subject. poedahq-madi-ne-ga wegide* 'The pigs' (food) fell.' The first suffix pluralizes the base, the second marks possession, and the third relates a noun understood in context to the verb as its subject. In instances where the grammatical relation is between the base affixed and another noun or verb, possession and subject are mutually exclusive. Here subject marker occurs after possessive indicator and cannot be related to the base to which it is attached.

C. *Instrument. mahbi-ne-datan amuduo* 'Cut it with the boy's (knife).' The first suffix (Order 4) marks possession, and the second (usually Order 3) marks an instrumental relation between a noun understood in context and the verb.

---

[15] Hyphens within an Awa form indicate morpheme boundaries; numbers above the suffix indicate relative order.

[16] These examples give excellent support to a paper by Pittman (1954).

D. *Location within. poedahq-me-pi-peq miehde* 'The pig is within (the garden).' The first suffix, *(-meN)* identificational, is an Order 12 suffix. Suffixes *(-piq)* 'within' and *(-peq)* 'place' are Orders 7 and 8, respectively. Here the combination *-pipeq* marks the location mentioned by a noun understood by context only. The grammatical relation is between that understood noun and the verb.

5.2. *Suffixes Whose Order Is Not Always Fixed*

Certain suffixes have occasionally been observed to shift position.

A. *Conjunctive (-kakaq).* The suffix *(-kakaq)* usually occurs as an Order 5 affix. However, note the following examples.

> poedah-kȧka-sȧbe nide   'I want a pig also.'
> poedah-sabe-akaq nide   'I want a pig also.'

The reverse order above seems to have no effect on meaning, and either utterance is acceptable. In the following example, *(-kakaq)* again occurs out of its usual order. In this case, informants have not accepted the usual order: *naho-pe-ten-kaka koweo* 'Bring from the house also.'

B. *Locational (-taq) and place marker (-peq).* Usually these suffixes combine with *(-taq)* preceding *(-peq)*: *poedah-ta-pe sodiq abiado* (pig-to-at-place salt sprinkle) 'Sprinkle salt on the pork.' The reverse sequence has been noted with a corresponding change of meaning: *poedah-pe-ta sodiq abiado* 'Sprinkle salt all over (or throughout) the pork.' The conjunctive *(-kakaq)* may follow this reverse sequence: *poedah-pe-ta-kaka sodiq abiado* 'Sprinkle salt all over the pork also.'

V. Possessive Prefixes Occurring with Inalienable Awa Nouns

HOWARD McKAUGHAN and ARETTA LOVING

---

1. INTRODUCTION

Awa nouns are either alienable or inalienable. The inalienable nouns occur obligatorily with prefixes to indicate possession. The citation form for these nouns occurs with prefix *a-* which is nonspecific third person singular: *a-bobiyah* 'someone's back'.[1] Possession is indicated for alienable nouns by the suffix *-ne*: *iya-ne nah* 'the dog's house', *se-ne nah* (they-possessive house) 'their house'. Some of the inalienable body parts may occur with possession indicated by a prefix, or by a combination of the suffix *-ne* with the noun or pronoun preceding the item and prefix *a-*. For example, one can say *si-uta* 'their eyes' or *se-ne a-uta* (they-possessive possessive-prefix-eye) 'their eyes'.

General semantic categories for inalienable nouns are body parts and kinship terms. However, these semantic categories are not sufficiently well-defined to use as the only basis for classification. For example, the following body parts are alienable and do not occur with the prefixes: *nah* 'breast', *nahnaoq* 'nipple', *pidi* 'heart', *pe* 'penis', and *tehtakaweh* 'front teeth'. All kinship terms, identifiable by the suffix *-wa ~ -kawa* marking the class, are inalienable. Because of the similarity in required allomorphs of the pronoun prefixes, we have also included the following with the kinship terms even though they do not occur with *-wa ~ -kawa*: *-wahpeq* 'village', *-wahdah* 'relatives' or 'the in-group', *-wa* 'spirit', and *-wiq* 'name'.

The possessive prefixes mark six categories in the pronominal series: first, second, and third person singular; a nonspecific third person singular; and third person and nonthird person plural. Except for the nonspecific

[1] Hyphens are used to separate morphemes for the convenience of the reader.

third person singular, free personal pronouns also mark these categories. The first, second, and third person singular free pronouns are *ne, te,* and *we,* respectively. The third person plural free pronoun is *se,* and the non-third person plural is *ite.* The similarity between the free pronouns and the prefixes used with inalienable nouns will be immediately apparent.

Certain general morphophonemic rules are applicable to all combinations of prefixes and bases. (A) Consonant-final allomorphs when occurring with bases that begin with *w* add *u* between the prefix and the base: *nan-* plus *wadena* becomes *nanuwadena* 'my father-in-law'. (B) The final *a* of allomorphs is lost preceding bases beginning with vowels and becomes *i* preceding bases that begin with *y*: *a-* plus *-edo* becomes *edo* 'someone's brother-in-law'; *adena-* plus *yoq* becomes *adeniyoq* 'your younger brother'. (C) Two like vowels reduce to one: *si-* plus *iyobeq* becomes *siyobeq* 'their toes'.

2. PREFIXES WITH SINGLE ALLOMORPHS

Prefixes to indicate possession by the second person singular and third person singular both specific and nonspecific occur with only one allomorph each for all inalienable nouns. The second singular is *adena-,* the third singular specific is *wena-,* and the nonspecific third singular is *a-.* Examples follow: *adena-* plus *-ahde* becomes *adenahde* 'your ear'; *adena-* plus *-yoq* becomes *adeniyoq* 'your younger brother'; *wena-* plus *-yau* becomes *weniyau* 'his daughter'; *wena-nuo* 'his neck', *a-bowa* 'someone's father', and *a-nahno* 'someone's sister'.[2]

3. PREFIXES WITH MULTIPLE ALLOMORPHS

Prefixes to indicate first person singular and the plural forms for nonthird person and third person have a number of allomorphs. Allmorphic variation is dependent partially on morphological conditioning and partially on phonological conditioning.

3.1. *With Body Parts*

In general for inalienable body parts first person singular is marked by the prefix *ni-,* the plural nonthird person is marked by *i-,* and the third person plural is marked *si-.* An allomorph *n-* occurs in free variation with *ni-* ('I') with bases that begin with *ah,* or with *w* (resulting in *nu-* by morphophoneme Rule B). An allomorph *iu-* may occur freely fluctuating with *i-* ('our' or 'your plural') with bases beginning with *w.* The prefix *si-* does not have alternants with body parts. Examples follow: *ni-ahqmo ~ n-ahqmo*

---

[2] Suffix *-wa ~ -kawa* is optional in some cases, obligatory in others, and always absent in other cases. Rules for these occurrences have not yet been fully worked out. We only include the suffix in these examples when obligatory. The suffix is always excluded when the possessive prefix is first person singular or nonthird person plural. Allomorph *-wa* follows stem final vowels and *-kawa* follows stem final consonants.

'my cheek', *ni-weh ～ nu-weh* 'my mouth', *ni-uta* 'my eye', *ni-i > ni* 'my foot', *i-wehhi ～ iu-wehhi* 'our/your chins', *i-ahqmo* 'our/your cheeks', *i-tu* 'our/your livers,' *i-ko* 'our/your shoulders', *si-ahte* 'their ears', *si-nuo* 'their necks', *si-iyopeq > siyopeq* 'their toes'.

3.2. With Kinship Terms

The kinship terms that concern us here are listed below. Groups II and III may be phonologically defined in that they begin with *n* and *w* respectively. Other kinship terms no doubt will fall into one of the three groups designated.

Group I

1. *-baq*	'younger brother of male'
2. *-bo*	'father'
3. *-dahN³*	'son-in-law'
4. *-do ～ -edo*	'brother-in-law'
5. *-duwana*	'husband's brother's wife'
6. *-obane*	'wife's sister's husband'
7. *-yauN ～ -ayauN*	'daughter'
8. *-yoq ～ -ayoq*	'brother of female'

Group II (bases with initial *n*)

1. *-nah*	'grandchild'
2. *-nahbu*	'grandfather'
3. *-nahbuq*	'daughter-in-law'
4. *-nahno*	'sister of male' or 'older sister of female'
5. *-no*	'mother'
6. *-noibo*	'parents'
7. *-nahda ～ dahda*	'grandmother'
8. *-nahniN ～ ahniN*	'son'
9. *-nahtahna ～ -ahtahna*	'mother-in-law'
10. *-nonanah ～ -onanah*	'younger sister of female'

Group III (bases with initial *w*)

1. *-weh*	'older brother-in-law of female' or 'younger sister-in-law of male'
2. *-wehq*	'husband'
3. *-wehia*	'sister-in-law of female'
4. *-wadena*	'father-in-law' or 'elder brother-in-law of married female'

³ The morphophoneme *N* is actualized as the nasal phoneme only preceding *s*, *k*, and vowels. A final glottal stop in the base is retained only before vowels, a nasal, or silence.

5. *-wah*   'older brother of male'
6. *-wahpeq*   'village'
7. *-wahdah*   'relative' or 'the in-group'
8. *-wa*   'spirit'
9. *-wiq ~ -kiq*   'name'

3.2.1. *First person singular.* With Group I, first person singular is indicated by the allomorph *nani-*.[4] Items 3 and 6 may also occur with a shortened form *ni-*. With Group II, *nani-* is shortened to *nai-* with allomorphs beginning with the nasal except for item 9. An allomorph *na-* may also occur with items 1, 2, 4, and 5. Items 8, 9, and 10 may appear with allomorph *nen-* with the second of the two allomorphs of the base. Note that with item 9, *nen-* is the only allomorph used to mark the first person singular.

With Group III, which all begin with *w*, the *nani-* base allomorph becomes *nanu-* with all forms except 8 and 9. Forms 8 and 9 take *neni-* which may be shortened to *ni-* for these forms or to *nenu-* with number 8.

3.2.2. *Nonthird person plural.* Nonthird person plural with kin terms is marked basically by *itedi-*. This form is shortened to *itei-* for Group II, and becomes *iteiu-* for Group III. In certain cases these forms have additional alternants. The form *ited-* may occur with the second allomorph of items 8, 9, and 10 of Group II. Besides *iteiu-*, the base form *itedi-* may occur with items 8 and 9 of Group III. The prefix may also become *iteyu-* with these items or even *ited-* with item 8 or *itei-* with item 9.

3.2.3. *Third person plural.* The third person plural possessive pronoun with kinship terms is marked by the prefix *si-* in all cases except item 8 of Group II and items 6 and 7 of Group III. A longer form, *sensi-* may also occur with all items in Group I; items of Group II except 8, 9, and 10; and with items 8 and 9 of Group III. The allomorph *sensu-* may appear with all items of Group III except 9. This allomorph in turn may be shortened to *su-* for items of Group III except for numbers 8 and 9. Items 8, 9, and 10 of Group II take allomorphs *s-*, *sen-*, or *sens-* (or even *si-*) with the second listed allomorphs of these bases.

4. SUMMARY

Pronominal prefixes with Awa inalienable nouns which have multiple allomorphs are shown in Table 2. Forms occur with all nouns listed unless otherwise noted. It may be that free alternants are sometimes traceable to individual speakers or to sociolinguistic groups. The variation, as indicated, is wide but not always agreed upon by all speakers.

---

[4] Reference is always to occurrence with the first of two allomorphs of the base unless otherwise noted.

TABLE 2
PRONOMINAL PREFIX VARIANTS

	With Body Parts	With Kinship Terms		
		Group I	Group II	Group III
First singular	*ni-* *n-* (_/ah, w)	*nani-* *ni-* (3, 6)	*nai-* *na-* (1, 2, 4, 5) *nen-* (_/2nd allomorph of 8, 9, 10)	*nanu-* (except 8, 9) *neni-*, *ni-* (8, 9) *nenu-* (8)
Nonthird plural	*i-* *iu-* (_/w)	*itedi-*	*itei-* *ited-* (8, 9, 10)	*iteiu-* *itedi-*, *iteyu-* (8, 9) *ited-* (8) *itei-* (9)
Third plural	*si-*	*si-* *sensi-*	*si-* (except 8) *sensi-* (except 8, 9, 10) *s-*, *sen-*, *sens-* (_/2nd allomorph of 8, 9, 10)	*si-* (except 6, 7) *sensi-* (8, 9) *sensu-* (except 9) *su-* (except 8, 9)

VI. Awa Verbs, I: The Internal Structure of Independent Verbs

RICHARD LOVING and HOWARD McKAUGHAN

1. INTRODUCTION

Verbs in Awa[1] are central to the clause. When inflected, they may stand alone manifesting the clause with its obligatory grammatical relations of subject and predicate. No other part of speech may occur as the predicate of a clause, nor indicate these two relations. When occurring as predicate, a verb must contain morphemes to indicate subject and tense. Morphemes to indicate an object and the categories of aspect and mode may also occur with verb bases.

The present paper deals only with the internal structure of independent verbs. It is meant as a preliminary survey to set the direction of research rather than as a definitive statement. Research is not yet complete.[2] Further investigation may modify present results, and will most certainly add to them. However, sufficient data are at hand to give a good picture of the complications encountered in the verb structure of a New Guinea language.

The independent verb has the following characteristics: (A) It contrasts with dependent verbs in that it may not contain morphemes to anticipate following clauses, nor may it occur subordinate to other verbs. (B) The independent verb must always contain morphemes to indicate the subject of the clause, and the tense of the verb base. (C) This verb occurs as the

[1] For classification of New Guinea Highland languages, see Wurm (1960, 1961 a,b,c, and 1962a,b,c,d).

[2] Loving is responsible for preliminary analysis, while McKaughan has been responsible for the theoretical framework and presentation. The paper was first published as pp. 31-44 in *Verb Studies in Five New Guinea Languages,* Summer Institute of Linguistics Publications in Linguistics and Related Fields No. 10, 1964, and is reissued here in its present format with permission.

predicate of independent clauses; that is, those clauses which may occur as a sentence, independent of other constructions. (D) Its general internal structure includes, besides the stem, a direct or indirect object (obligatory with some stems, optional with others), certain optional aspectlike morphemes, obligatory tense-subject affixes, and optional modelike affixes, generally in the order given here.

2. MORPHOPHONEMICS

The following is a summary of some of the general morphophonemic facts. Variation in individual morphemes will be mentioned when the particular morpheme is discussed. Additional research will be necessary before we can give a complete study of the morphophonemic variation within the verb structure.

2.1. *Verb Stems*

We define a verb stem as a nuclear morpheme or morphemes which potentially occurs with markers to indicate a subject referent (and sometimes an object referent) as well as other grammatical categories such as tense, aspect, and mode.

2.1.1. Verb stems fall into two major classes. Affixes are morphophonemically different for each class. In general, Class I includes stems whose last vowel is /a/, and Class II those stems whose last vowel is /i/, /u/, /e/, /eh/, or /ah/.[3] Certain stems do not follow this phonological classification and must therefore be listed. The last vowel of some stems may be followed by a consonant (usually alveolar nasal or glottal stop). For purposes of description, we set up as basic, or as a point of reference, consonant-final forms or vowel-final forms in cases where a final consonant may not occur. Morphophonemic statements are therefore related to the basic forms. The following are a few examples of the two classes. Class I: *pehbeq-* 'to turn', *pugeq-* 'to untie', *súq-* 'to throw away', *suga-* 'to sleep', *taga-* 'to look, see it', *táhtoq-* 'to hold'; Class II: *idad-* 'to say', *kekí* 'to burn', *kogahn-* 'to sew', *paban-* and *suehq-* both meaning 'to split', *pagun-* 'to shove' *s-* 'to come', *subíq-* 'to hit', *sáhnsáh-* 'to count', *úq-* 'to plant', *wídé-* 'to laugh'.

2.1.2. All verb stems with initial /m/, /s/, or voiceless stops (/p/ /t/ /k/) when following morphemes basically ending with a vowel, have alternants beginning with /w/, /y/, or a voiced obstruent (/b/ /d/ /g/), respectively: *mewe + mado > mewe wado* 'Take and put it!'; *suga- + suga + iq > sugàyugàiq* 'He kept sleeping', *anìmâi + pokiq > anìmai bokiq* 'The boy went', *taga + taga + iq > tagadagaiq* 'He kept looking.'

2.1.3. Verb stems which may occur with final glottal stop have

---

[3] See footnote 4, Chap. IV, for a statement of the phonemes of Awa, used as a basis for the transcription here. In addition, we have marked tones here as high (´), low (no mark), rising (`), and falling (^).

allomorphs (A) with the glottal stop, (B) without the glottal, and (C) with final /d/.

A. Stem alternants with final glottal occur preceding suffixes with initial nasal: *tahtoq-* + *madehq* > *tahtoqmadehq* 'He touched it', *mugiq-* + *-nintehq* > *mugiqnintehq* 'He vomited on me.' Alternants with final glottal stop also occur preceding suffixes with initial vowels which mark an indirect object referent: *tahtoq-* + *-(a)t-ehq* > *táhtoqatéhq* 'He held it (for him).'

B. Stem alternants without final glottal occur preceding consonants other than nasals: *tahtoq-* + *tahtodiq* > *tahtotahtodiq*[4] 'He repeatedly hit it.' Stems from Class II have alternants without the final glottal preceding vowels other than those initial to morphemes marking the possessed direct object: *túq-* + *-íq* > *túíq* 'He came downhill', *mugiq-* + *-ewehq* > *mugiewéhq* 'He vomited a lot.'

C. Stems from Class I which have final /q/ in the basic form have alternants with final /d/ preceding vowels other than those of the indirect object morphemes: *tahtoq-* + *ehq* > *táhtodéhq* 'He held it', *pugeq-* + *ana* > *pugedanâ* 'He will untie it.'

2.1.4. Stems which have a basic final alveolar nasal have alternants without the final nasal preceding the past tense marker, the first and second person plural indirect object morpheme, and morphemes with an initial nasal: *paban-* + *(daiq~-taiq* > *pabatàiq* 'He has chopped it', *paban-* + *-(i)tehq* > *pabaitéhq* 'He chopped it for us', *pagun-* + *-madehq* > *pagumadéhq* 'He pushed.'

2.1.5. Stems of both classes listed with final vowels appear sometimes with and sometimes without that final phoneme. The distribution of these alternants has not yet been completely defined. The following general observations are made as an indication of the type of distribution found.

A. Stems having final /a/ have alternants without that vowel preceding suffixes beginning with vowels other than /i/: *taga-* + *-ehq* > *tagehq* 'He looked', *suga-* + *-ana* > *sugana* 'He will sleep!'

B. Stems with final /eh/ and /ah/ usually retain these vowels: *sahnsah-* + *-iq* > *sáhnsáhíq* 'He counts', *wideh-* + *-ewehq* > *widéhewéhq* 'He laughed.'

C. Stems having final /i/ have alternants without that vowel preceding suffixes with initial /i/: *keki-* + *-iq* > *kekíq* 'He burns', *api-* + *-ina* > *apinâ* 'He will cut.'

2.2. Verb Affixes

Throughout the paper we give paradigms to illustrate the allomorphic variations that occur in general with Class I and Class II stems. In most cases, specific alternants must be described for each morpheme. Some-

---

[4] When following stems that have a final /q/ basically, the voiceless stops remain.

times verb stems which act as Class I stems with some affixes seem to cross lines and act as Class II stems with other morphemes. We do not attempt a classification and subclassification of stems at this time.

One general comment can be made here regarding lateral morphemes sometimes occurring with initial /d/. Such affixes appear with initial /s/ following stems which occur with final /q/, or if the affix is initial in the word: *pugeq-* + *-duwehq* > *pugesúwéhq* 'He finished untying it', *síyúq* (from *-diy* + *-uq*) 'I gave them', but *keki-* + *-duwehq* > *kekidúwéhq* 'He finished burning it.' In one instance, that of the past tense morpheme, the alternant has initial /t/: *paban-* + *-q* > *pabatàiq* 'He chopped it.'

We now turn to a discussion of the various morphemes found in the Awa independent verb.

3. TENSE-SUBJECT COMPOUNDS AND PORTMANTEAUS

Awa independent verbs, as we have indicated, must include the subject of the clause. This subject may or may not be more explicitly defined by a noun (see Chap. IV), or its phrase, or a free pronoun: *wehgà póédáhq tagehq* (man pig saw-he) 'The man saw the pig', *we tàgehq* (he saw-it) 'He saw it', *tagehq* (he-saw-it). Awa independent verbs must also contain a morpheme to indicate the time of the action: tense and subject morphemes are obligatory.

The following tenses occur: near past, indicating an action that has recently taken place, or is still in process: *tagoq* 'I saw it' (today); past, indicating an action which has taken place previous to the day a person is speaking, but within easy memory: *tagadàuq* 'I saw it' (yesterday or before); far past, indicating an action that has taken place at some time in the remote past: *tagawaq* 'I saw it a long time ago'; and future, indicating an action that has not taken place: *tagani* 'I will see it.'

Awa subjects indicated in the verb are first, second, or third persons, in singular, dual, or plural number. At some place in the system (see *Certituative,* Sec. 6.1.3.), all nine contrasts occur. Not all paradigms illustrate the same contrasts.

A characteristic of Awa verb structure is the close-knit phonological relation between tense and subject morphemes. Recurring partials occur for each, but the distribution of allomorphs is so interdependent that contrastive forms are found in the combinations rather than entirely in the individual morphemes. In some cases the phonological fusion of morphemes has progressed to the degree that partials are difficult to define and describe as such. In the latter case we refer to the fusion as a portmanteau, but if individual morphemes can be identified, we refer to the combination as a compound (K. Pike 1967: 545).

3.1. Near Past Tense-Subject Compounds

3.1.1. The following matrix illustrates compound morphemes which indicate the various person subjects with the near past tense.[5] We use *tag-*, an alternant of *taga-* 'to see', a Class I stem.

	1st	2nd	3rd
Sing	*tag(oq)*	*tag(áhnaq)*	*tag(ehq)*
Dual	*tag(óyaq)*	*tag(éhyaq)*	
Pl	*tag(ónaq)*	*tag(ahq)*	

Contrast for all three persons is found only in the singular, and for the three numbers in first persons as opposed to nonfirst persons. In this set, we identify the tense morpheme as *-o ~ -a ~ -eh,* the first allomorph occurring before first person morphemes, the second before the second person singular and nonfirst person dual morphemes. In turn, we note that *-yaq* indicates dual number for all persons, *-naq* the first and the third singular, and the nonfirst plural subjects. Further examples follow: *tahtod(oq)* 'I held it', *pehbed(ahnâq)* 'You turned it', *me(éhq)* 'He took it.'

However, we observe that the sequences of morphemes *-oq, -ehq,* and *-ahq* contrast, as do *-oyaq* and *ehyaq,* as well as *-onaq* and *-ahnaq.* We recognize, for example, the combination *-onaq* as 'near past we' but *-ahnaq* as 'near past you': *meonâq* 'We took it', *meahnâq* 'You took it.' The meaning carried by the suffixes thus is overtly indicated by the combination of the morphemes. We readily identify the partials, but the combined form is needed to recognize the meaning of the two in sequence.

3.1.2. Class II verb stems occur with alternants of the same compounds. We illustrate with the stem *wideh-* 'to laugh'.

	1st	2nd	3rd
Sing	*widéh(uq)*	*widéh(ónaq)*	*widéh(iq)*
Dual	*widéh(úyaq)*	*widéh(óyaq)*	
Pl	*widéh(únaq)*	*widéh(oq)*	

With Class II stems, the near past tense alternants are *-u ~ -o ~ -i,* the first alternant occurring before first person markers, the last before third person singular, and the second before the others. Further examples fol-

---

[5] We use the term 'matrix' instead of 'paradigm' since we wish to indicate the way contrastive features of person and number intersect, forming a cell whose occupant is thus illustrated relative to the occupants of other cells. We are indebted to K. Pike (1962b) for this suggestion. The matrix is arranged in this particular format in order to highlight tense morphemes in a column. The usual paradigmatic listing does not do this.

low: *kekí(úq)* 'I burned it', *mugi(onâq)* 'You vomited', *iwiáh(iq)* 'He thought.'

3.1.3. The morphemes indicating person of subjects have alternants in various environments which help to separate first singular, third singular, and second-third plural subject morphemes. A matrix of principal alternants follows:

	1st	2nd	3rd
Sing	*-ga ~ -q*	*-na ~ -naq*	*-de ~ -q*
Dual	*-ya ~ -yaq*	*-ya ~ -yaq*	*-ya ~ -yaq*
Pl	*-na ~ -naq*	*-wa ~ -q*	*-wa ~ -q*

Note the lack of contrast for different persons in the dual, the lack of contrast between second and third persons except in the singular, and the fact that first person plural and second person singular are marked by the same (or homophonous) morpheme(s). The distribution of person allomorphs follows. Alternants with the final glottal stop occur in final position, that is, when not followed by another morpheme: see above matrices. Alternants occur having only the initial consonant of the first form listed in the matrix when preceding the interrogative or augmentative morphemes: *kekio(n)ô* 'Did you burn it today?', *pokù(g)e* 'I went!' Vowel final allomorphs occur elsewhere:[6] *tageh(da)pómo* 'He might have seen it', *tageh-(ya)pómo* 'You two might have seen it.'

3.2. Past Tense-Subject Compounds

Compounds marking the past tense and various persons of subject can be indicated by the following matrix.

	1st	2nd	3rd
Sing	*tag(àdauq)*[7]	*taq(adonâq)*	*tag(adàiq)*
Dual	*tag(adàuyâq)*		*tag(adoyâq)*
Pl	*tag(adàunâq)*		*tag(adôq)*
Sing	*wídéh(udàuq)*	*wídéh(udonâq)*	*wídéh(udàiq)*
Dual	*wídéh(udàuyâq)*		*wídéh(udoyâq)*
Pl	*wídéh(udàunâq)*		*wídéh(udôq)*

The variants of the past tense morpheme are thus *-adau ~ -ado ~ -adai* with Class I stems, and *-udau ~ -udo ~ -udai* with Class II stems. With

---

[6] Person allomorphs appear as ø in some places with dependent verbs. Such instances are described in the following chapter.

[7] Note the form *keki-a-t-adauq* (hyphens used to indicate morpheme divisions) where the past tense-subject compound has initial /a/. We therefore, by analogy, suggest that the stem *taga-* 'to look' has an allomorph *tag-*, the /a/ belonging to the compound suffix rather than to the stem.

both sets of allomorphs, the first occurs with first person morphemes, the third with third singular, and the second with other person markers. Further modifications to this general statement are (A) that alternants without the initial vowel (-dau ~ -do ~ -dai) occur following most Class II stems with final /i/:[8] keki(dai)q 'He has burned it'; and (B) alternants with initial /t/ (-tau ~ -to ~ -tai) occur following stems of either class (or suffixes) which may have final /n/ or /q/: paban- + -adai + -q > paba(tài)q 'He has split it', tahtoq- + -adau + -yaq > tahto(tau)yaq 'We two held it.' Further examples of the past tense-subject compounds follow: pok(udonaq) 'You have gone', keki(dàiq) 'He has burned it', sug(adôq) 'They have slept.'

3.3. Far Past Tense-Subject Compounds

The following matrix illustrates the far past tense-subject compounds, and the distribution of the various allomorphs.

	1st	2nd	3rd
Sing	tag(ahwaq)	tag(onaq)	tag(óq)
Dual	tag(ahwayâq)		
Pl	tag(ahwanâq)		
		tag(oyaq)	
		tag(oq)[9]	
Sing	wídéh(owaq)	wídéh (unaq)	wídéh(úq)
Dual	wídéh(owayâq)		
Pl	wídéh(owanâq)		
		wídéh(uyaq)	
		wídéh(uq)	

The far past tense morpheme then is -ahwa ~ -o[10] with Class I stems, and -owa ~ -u with Class II stems, the first with first person morphemes, and the second with the other person morphemes. Further examples follow: keki(ówaq) 'I burned it a long time ago', pehbed(ahwánaq) 'We turned it a long time ago.'

3.4. Future Tense-Subject Portmanteaus

The following matrix illustrates the fusion of future tense and various subject morphemes. Though some phonemes occur in these fusions which also occur in the compounds just discussed, note that the relative order of such is reversed, and that a description assigning all phonemes in the sequences to some morpheme would unduly complicate the description.

[8] Alternants without the initial vowel have also been observed with a few Class II stems with final /a/: sansa(dai)q 'He counted.'

[9] Note that tagoq 'They saw it long ago', and tagoq 'I saw it today' (as well as other verb forms in these cells) are homophonous. Homophonous forms may be distinguished in Awa by the use of the free pronouns. These include né 'I', ade 'you', we 'he', ite 'we, we two, you two, and you all', and se 'they': se tagoq 'They looked a long time ago', né tagoq 'I looked today', we tagoq 'He saw it long ago.'

[10] The distribution of the alternants distinguished by tone has not yet been determined.

	1st	2nd/3rd
Sing	*tag(anì)*	*tag(ankèh)*
Dual	*tag(ayèh)*	*tag(agèh)*
Pl	*tag(anèh)*	

	1st	2nd/3rd
Sing	*wídéh(ini)*	*wídéh(inkeh)*
Dual	*wídéh(oyeh)*	*wídéh(igeh)*
Pl	*wídéh(oneh)*	

Second and third person forms contrast only for singular and plural. Perhaps for this reason, speakers sometimes use what seem to be dependent medial verb forms in third person independent constructions. These forms are as follows:

	3rd (Class I)	3rd (Class II)
Sing	*tag(anâ)*	*wídéh(inâ)*
Dual	*tag(ayèheda)*	*wídéh(oyèheda)*
Pl	*tag(anèheda)*	*wídéh(onèheda)*

Future pormanteaus also occur to indicate first person, exclusive of hearer, subjects. These forms are as follows:

	1st exclusive (Class I)	1st exclusive (Class II)
Dual	*tag(ayèheta)*	*wídéh(oyèheta)*
Pl	*tag(anèheq)*	*wídéh(onèheq)*

Sequences *-eta, -eq,* and *-eda* (third person) occur with dependent verbs as morphemes, but here these morphemes have lost their meaning, so we consider them a part of the portmanteau.[11]

In many of the future portmanteaus we note the recurring partial /eh/, perhaps characteristic of this tense. Further, in the dual forms, we note the phoneme /y/. Again the phoneme /n/ occurs with forms indicating 'we' and 'you', but this phoneme also occurs in all singular forms, and also with the 'they' forms. We cannot directly equate a future tense morpheme with the phoneme /eh/, nor person morphemes with those identified so far. We conclude that there is a fusion of morphemes to indicate future tense with various subjects and call the fusions portmanteaus.

The following observations are pertinent to the distribution of the portmanteaus. Following Class I stems, portmanteaus have initial /a/; following Class II stems, they have initial /i/ with singular forms and an initial /o/ in other subject-future forms.

---

[11] See Chap. VII, Sec. 2.1.2, for these morphemes.

The following illustrate further the future portmanteaus: *keki(oyèh)* 'We two will burn it', *sug(anèheda)* 'They will sleep', *pok(onèheq)* 'We but not you will go', *tag(agèh)* 'You two or more will see it', 'They will see it', 'They two will see it.'

3.5. Summary

The verb structure with (T)ense-(Su)bject complexes may be represented in summary by the following diagram. Commas are to be read as 'or,' and lines may be followed from left to right and up or down.

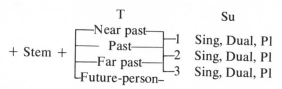

4. Nonsubject Person Morphemes

Besides the subject, Awa independent verbs may contain a nonsubject referent morpheme. With some verbs it is obligatory. The nonsubject referents may be related to the action as the indirect object, or as a possessed direct object, that is, something possessed by the subject.

4.1. Possessed Direct Object Morphemes

All verb stems which semantically may take an object (transitive stems), and which do not obligatorily occur with such, optionally contain a possessed direct object. The following morphemes indicate an indefinite object and the person to whom that object belongs.

-nuw	'that which is mine'	*-yuw*	'that which is ours or yours'
-auw	'that which is yours or his'	*-duw*[12]	'that which is theirs'

In most verbs, these morphemes occur directly following the stem: *keki-(nuw)éhq* 'He burned that which is mine' or 'He burned mine.' This sentence may be expanded: *wegà néne sòn keki(nuw)éhq* (he my garden burn-(mine) he-near-past) 'He burned my garden.'

Two verb stems, *-ahb-* 'to please, like', and *-ahdi-* 'to displease, not like',

---

[12] One could assign person to the first consonant, and direct possessed object, or indefinite object to *-uw*. Similarities occur with the indirect objects (Sec. 4.2), but we prefer to treat these sequences as one morpheme, saving descriptive complications when treating the indirect objects. The status of *w* following /u/ and *y* following /i/ is not clear. Since vowel sequences with other than high vowel initials may be interrupted by /w/ or /y/, we suspect that some contrasts may occur such as /iya/ and /ia/, or /uwa/ and /uah/. However, such have not been clearly located. We have written *w* and *y* in this paper where clearly heard.

require a possessed direct object morpheme, and in these cases that morpheme is a *prefix*. An allomorph *suw-* instead of *-duw* 'theirs,' occurs with these stems (Sec. 2.2). Examples follow: *(nuw)ahbehq* 'He/it pleases me', *(auw)ahdíehq* 'It displeases him/you', *(suw)ahdíehq* 'It displeases them.'

The verbs 'to hit' and 'to give' must occur either with a possessed object, or an indirect object morpheme described in the next section, though the two morphemes may not occur with the same stem at the same time. The following illustrates: *subiq-* 'to hit': *wegà néne póedáhq subiq(núw)-éhq* (he my pig hit-(mine)-he-near-past) 'He hit my pig', *subiq(nuw)éhq* 'He hit what is mine.'

The verb 'to give' is indicated in Awa by the absence of any verb stem, leaving only the combination of affixes. The affix complex requires both the subject, and either a possessed direct object indicator, or an indirect object morpheme. Note the following: *wegà néne póedáhq (núw)éhq* (he my pig (mine)-he-near-past) 'He gave my pig', *wegà sene póedáhq (súw)éhq* 'He gave their pig', *(aúw)éhq* 'He gave what is yours/his.' The combination of affixes with the indirect object to indicate 'to give' follows in the next section.

4.2. Indirect Object Morphemes

4.2.1. Obligatory indirect object morphemes. We have noted that the verbs 'to hit' and 'to give' require either the possessed direct object morphemes, or the indirect object indicators. The set of morphemes indicating indirect object contrast with the possessed direct object morphemes since they are expanded in the clause by different constructions; compare the examples in the previous section with the following: *wegàh néne póedáhq món aní (aw)íde* (he my pig another child (to-him)-near-past-I-augmentative) 'He gave my pig to another person!' In this latter instance, the indirect object marker *(-aw)* refers to the individual indicated by *món aní*, the indirect object, whereas *-nuw* in a similar sentence in the last section referred to the 'pig', the direct object. The indirect object morphemes used initially in a sequence of affixes to indicate the verb 'to give' follow: *-niy* 'me'; *-aw* 'you, him'; *-iy* 'us, you all'; *-siy* 'them'.

Allomorphs of these markers occurring with *subiq-* 'to hit' are *n-* 'me', *ø-* 'you, him, them', and *iy-* 'us, you all'. These alternants replace the first phoneme of the stem except in the case of *ø-*: *nubíq* 'He hit me', *subíq* 'He hit him, you, them', *iyubíq* 'He hit us, you all.'

Some verb stems always occur with an indirect object morpheme. The stem *-adab-* 'to call' requires these affixes preceding the stem, while *te-* 'to call' requires indirect object suffixes. The first has a zero alternant for 'you, him': *(niy)áhdabiq* 'He called me', *(ø)áhdabiq* 'He called him, you', *(síy)áhdabiq* 'He called them.' With *te-* 'to tell it', and with other verb stems when it applies, allomorphs without the final /y/ occur preceding consonants or the vowel /i/: *te(níy)éq*[13] 'They told it to me', *te-* + *-niy* + *-iq* > *teníq* (by reduction of like vowels) 'He told it to me', *te(aw)íq* 'He told it to him.'

The following stems are usually idiomatic, and occur only with the near past third person singular subject compound. The indirect object prefix is obligatory with these stems. All known stems are *-er-* 'to hurt, pain', *-ahdedak-* 'to recall, remember', *-witag-* 'to forget', *-dupib-* 'to hunger', *-yahbankid-* 'to be full', and *-waqnahw-*[14] 'to rest'. A zero alternant of the morpheme 'you, him' occurs with the first two verbs listed. The other verb stems occur with the alternant *-a* for this person. Since these are prefixes, *siy-* occurs instead of *-diy* 'them'. Examples follow: *(ø)édiq* 'It hurts you, him', *(níy)édiq* 'It hurts me', *(a)bitagiq* 'It was forgotten by him, he forgot', *(iy)ahdekakéhq* 'It is remembered by us, we remember it.'

4.2.2. *Optional indirect object morphemes.* Indirect object morphemes are optional with verbs not discussed in the previous section; but in such cases, must be followed by the benefactive morpheme *-t*. With the benefactive, the indirect object markers indicate the person to whom, for whom, upon whom, or instead of whom the action is performed. A direct object is always implied, and may or may not be manifested by a noun or free pronoun. But the direct object cannot be indicated in the verb when the benefactive morpheme is present. The indirect object markers occur with the following forms preceding the benefactive indicator: *-n* ~ *-in* ~ *-nin* 'me'; *-a* 'you, him'; *-i* 'us, you all'; *-di* 'them'. Examples follow: *taga(nín)t-éhq* 'He saw it (for me)', *tag(a)t-éhq*[15] 'He saw it (for you, him)', *wehgà ábotàhne póedáhq tag(a)t-éhq* (man Abota's pig saw-(for him)-he) 'The man saw Abota's pig for him.'

4.3. *Summary*

Verb structure with the possessed (D)irect (O)bject or (I)ndirect (O)bject morphemes may be summarized as follows: (T)ense-(S)ubject subnumerals with S indicate different (S)tems.

$$(1) \quad +S_1 \pm \begin{bmatrix} DO \\ IO \end{bmatrix} + \text{T-Su}$$

$$(2) \quad +DO + S_2 + \text{T-Su}$$

[13] Allomorphs of various morphemes occur with initial /e/ instead of the /o/ indicated in matrices illustrating occurrences with Class II stems (cf. Sec. 3.1.2). The stems *s-* 'to come' and *idad-* 'to say' are other examples.

[14] The compound allomorph *-aq* occurs with this stem: *awaqnahwag* 'It is resting to him, he rests.' Some of the morphemes making up the verb stems above follow: *-ahdedak-* 'to recall' from perhaps *ahde* 'ear' and *da* 'on'; *-dupib-* 'to hunger' from *adu* 'insides'; *-yahbankid-* 'to be full' from *ayahba* 'stomach' and *kiq* 'full'. Some nouns have obligatory possessive prefixes (body parts usually) which are similar to the indirect object prefixes obligatory to some verb stems.

[15] See 2.1.5.A for *tag-* as the stem alternant here.

$$\begin{aligned}
&(3) \quad +S_3 + \begin{bmatrix} DO \\ IO \end{bmatrix} + \text{T-Su} \\
&(4) \quad +IO +S_4 + \text{T-Su} \\
&(5) \quad +S_5 + IO + B + \text{T-Su}
\end{aligned}$$

5. ASPECTLIKE MORPHEMES

Awa independent verbs optionally include in their internal structure aspect-like morphemes. These affixes are grouped together (A) because of their semantic similarity—dealing with kind of action or time span, and (B) because they occur preceding tense-subject complexes.

Morphemes included in this section mark punctiliar, completive, benefactive, continuative, habituative, repetitive, and inceptive actions. The first three are mutually exclusive; the continuative may occur with the first three, and with the repetitive, but not with most habituative forms. The habituative and the repetitive may occur with the punctiliar completive and the benefactive as well as the continuative.

5.1. *Punctiliar*

A punctiliar morpheme indicates that the action of the verb occurs at a point in time, momentarily, or that the action is to be viewed in its entirety: *tag(ad)èhq* 'He saw it, he glimpsed it, he caught a glimpse of it.' The punctiliar morpheme includes *-ma ～ -mad ～ -a ～ -ad*. Alternants with initial /m/ follow /q/, the first preceding past tense or reduplicated stem, and the second elsewhere: *uq-(ma)tàiq* 'He has planted it', *táhtoq(mad)èhq* 'He held, touched it.' Alternants with initial vowel follow morphemes with finals other than /q/, the first preceding past tense, the second elsewhere: *anti(a)tàiq* 'He has poured it', *keki(ad)èhq* 'He has burned it.'

5.2. *Completive*

A completive morpheme indicates that the action has been finished: *taga-(dúw)èhq* 'He finished looking.' Allomorphs include *-du ～ -duw ～ -aduw:* the first precedes consonants, the second precedes vowels, and the third follows reduplicated stems. Examples follow: *keki(du)tàiq* 'He has finished burning it', *keki(dúw)èhq* 'He finished burning it a bit ago', *kekigeki(adúw)-èhq*[16] 'He burned it over and over.'

5.3. *Benefactive*

The benefactive morpheme *-t* must be preceded by an indirect object marker. The benefactive indicates that the subject acts on behalf of, instead of, onto, or to another party: *kekidi(t)èhq* 'He burned it for them', *néne*

---

[16] Unless otherwise noted, morpheme alternants following Class I stems also follow other suffixes.

póédáh wegà kabadanín(t)éhq (my pig he search-me-(for)-he-did) 'He looked for my pig for me.'

5.4. *Continuative*

The morpheme *-ew* indicates that an action continues over a limited period of time. This morpheme may either follow the other aspectlike morphemes or occur without them, preceding the tense-subject markers. Examples of the continuative follow: *tag(éw)anìe* 'I will watch', *u(ew)-adàiq* (plant-(continuative)-past-he) 'He has been planting it', *p(éw)éhq* 'He continually shot.'

5.5. *Habituative*

Habituative and repetitive concepts are generally indicated by some form of reduplication—usually of the verb stem. The habituative indicates an action that always takes place—a matter of habit. The repetitive stresses the fact that the action takes place over and over.

The habituative is usually indicated by the complete reduplication of the stem: *(tagadaga)iq* 'He always looks.' The reduplicated stem may be followed by *-aduqadud,* perhaps a reduplicated form of the completive morpheme. No additional meaning seems to be indicated: *tagadaga(aduqa-dûd)iq* 'He always looks.' Note that allomorphs of tense-subject complexes which follow Class II verb stems also follow forms indicating the habituative regardless of the class of the verb stem. Some stems may occur with *-aduqadud* with or without stem reduplication, though the former is more common: *(wídéh-wídé)(aduqadud)iq, wídé(aduqadud)iq* 'He always laughed.'

Stems which may only occur with the third person singular subject are marked for the habituative by the suffix *-weguw ~ -waguw ~ -aguwaguw.* The first two of these occur with stems having /g/ in the final syllable, the choice of vowel depending on the vowel preceding /g/—/e/ following /e/, /a/ following other vowels: *megu(weguw)iq* 'It is always falling', *taqnobà-gu(waguw)iq* 'It is always lost', *todáhgu(waguw)iq* 'It is always burnt.' Other stems of this group occur with the third allomorph: *adupibì(agu-waguw)iq* 'He is always hungry', *níyéd(aguwaguw)iq* 'It is always hurting me.'

Habituative forms may occur with punctiliar and completive morphemes. In such cases, the punctiliar and completive morphemes are repeated with the stem reduplication: *(subiq-ma)(subiq-mad)iq* 'He is always hitting', *(taga-du)-(taga-dud)iq*[17] 'He is always looking, finishes, and looks again.'

---

[17] The completive morpheme has an alternant *-dud* before vowels, probably from *-duq* acting as do Class I stems with final /q/.

5.6. *Repetitive*

The repetitive contrasts with the habituative in that (A) repetitive forms act as do Class I stems, but habituative forms always act as do Class II stems with reference to suffix allomorphs, and (B) punctiliar and completive morphemes occur following the repetitive reduplicated form[18] but these morphemes may be repeated with hatituative forms. Note the following examples: *(pugepuged-ad)éhq* 'He unties it over and over', *pugeq(ma)-pugeq(mad)éhq* 'He always unties it', *(kekigeki-adúw)éhq* 'He finished burning it over and over', *(tagadaga-dúw)éhq* 'He is looking repeatedly.'

The continuative morpheme may not occur with *-aduqadud* of the habituative. However *-ew* does occur with *-waguw* (and other allomorphs) with the effect that the action becomes a continued repetitive: *todáhgu(waguw-ew)éhq* 'It is continually, repeatedly burned.'

Punctiliar or completive morphemes may also occur with the continuative and repetitive forms. The resultant meanings express continual repetition either of completed acts, or individual acts. When the continuative morpheme occurs with the repetitive and either a punctiliar or a completive morpheme, the latter may optionally be repeated with the reduplication: *(pugepuged-àd-ew)éhq* or *(pugeq-ma)(pugeq-mad-éw)éhq* 'He continued to untie and untie and untie', *(pugepugey-adùw-ew)éhq* or *(pugesu)(puge-sud-éw)éhq* 'He continually finished untying.'

5.7. *Inceptive*

The sequence of a future portmanteau and one of the tense compounds indicates an action which is about to take place. We discuss this sequence as an aspect because it occurs in the same relative position as do other aspects, and because of the parallel in meaning. Future portmanteaus preceding tense compounds have *-ana* with 'I' and *-anie* with 'you' forms. Other forms are the same as the first person exclusive, and the third person portmanteaus described in Section 3.4. Tense compounds following the future have the same initial vowels as occur with Class II stems. The following illustrate: *tag(anà-uq)* 'I am about to see it', *tag(anìe-unaq)* 'You were about to see it a long time ago', *tag(anà-udàiq)* 'He was about to see it'; *wídéh(oyèhetauyaq)* 'We two are about to laugh', *wídéh(onèhe-udoq)*[19] 'You all were [past] about to laugh', *wídéh(onèheda-uq)* 'They were about to laugh a long time ago.'

5.8. *Summary*

The relative distribution of aspectlike morphemes can be summarized as follows, following the lines as indicated:

---

[18] When the continuative occurs with the repetitive, it is possible to have a repetition of the punctiliar or completive morphemes.

[19] The final /q/ of the portmanteau does not occur in this environment.

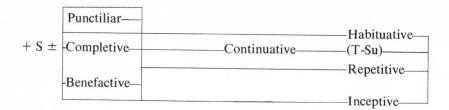

6. MODELIKE MORPHEMES

We have grouped the remaining affixes under this section, calling them modelike since they express the manner in which the action is conceived by the subject, and since they follow the tense-subject complexes. The modes are imperative, avolitional, certituative, dubitative, interrogative, and augmentative. The first three of these modes are marked by fusions which include tense-subject-mode morphemes. The rest of the mode markers occur as separate morphemes.

6.1. *Compounds Including Mode Morphemes*

The imperative and avolitional mode indicators occur in compounds including the near past tense and various subject markers, while the certituative mode indicator occurs with future tense-subject portmanteaus. Tense morphemes seem to have lost their particular time difference, overshadowed by the mode.

6.1.1. *Imperative.* Compounds including the imperative indicate that the subject must perform the action designated in the stem: *tagáhno* 'You look at it.' The imperative compound has not been observed following punctiliar, completive, or continuative aspects, though it may occur following the others. The following matrix illustrates these compounds. Forms appear only with second person subjects.

	Class I stems	Class II stems
Sing	*tag(áhno)*	*wídéh(úno)*
Dual	*tag(ahtao)*	*wídéh(otao)*
Pl	*tag(ahdo)*	*wídéh(odo)*

In these compounds we may assign tense to the first vowel *(-ah ~ -u ~ -o)*, imperative mode to the last vowel *(-o)*, and the second person with the various numbers to the remainder *(-n, -ta,* and *-d)*. Note that the first vowels are similar, but not the same in distribution, to vowels indicating the near past tense discussed in 3.1. Person-number indicators except for *-n* as second person singular are not paralleled elsewhere. Further, certain stems, which must be listed from the two classes, occur with *-o* in the singular instead of *-ahno* or *-uno: póbi(o)* (Class I) 'Blow it', *tid(o)* (Class II) 'Cook it.' This circumstance would necessitate describing zero alternants of the tense and person indicators in this instance. We prefer, then, to treat the sequence as a fusion, partials recognizable, but interdependent in the compound.

The compounds, then, occur with initial vowel /ah/ following Class I Stems, and initial /u/ with singular forms, or /o/ with dual and plural forms following Class II stems. This statement is modified by the listing of certain stems occurring with -o for the entire compound marking imperative second singular.[20]

6.1.2. *Avolitional.* Certain compounds include a negative imperative mode, or the avolitional as we term it. These compounds indicate warnings by the speaker against the performing of the action expressed in the verb stem: *tagehyehò* 'We two shouldn't look at it', 'It isn't good that he look.' The following matrix illustrates the compounds.

	1st	2nd	3rd
Sing	*tag(ehnehò)*		*tag(èhnehò)*
Dual	*tag(ehyehò)*	*tag(ehò)*	
Pl	*tag(ehnehò)*		
Sing	*wídéh(onèhò)*	*wídéh(inehò)*	*wídéh(inehò)*
Dual	*wídéh(oyehò)*	*wídéh(iyehò)*	
Pl	*wídéh(onehò)*		

In these compounds we suggest the general possibility of final /o/ being imperative, the preceding /eh/ being the negative aspect of the mode, the consonants /n/ and /y/ being person-number indicators, and the first vowel being tense. Again variants of the morphemes in the specific distributions would necessitate complicated description. Note that the mode indicators are the least variable, but that the tense vowel is the most, changing from /ah/ to /eh/ of the imperative after Class I stems before the avolitional; and from /u/ or /i/ after Class II stems to /o/ of the imperative throughout with the first person indicators, and /i/ elsewhere before the avolitional.

We further call attention to the fact that with compounds including avolitional, contrasts between singular and plural first persons are neutralized with Class I stems, that second and third person as well as dual and plural contrasts are all neutralized, and that due to phonological conditioning, even the first and second person contrast in the singular is neutralized with Class I stems.

6.1.3. *Certituative.* Compounds which include the certituative mode also include the future-subject portmanteaus. These compounds, besides marking the subject, indicate that the action is certain to take place: *taganàuq*

[20] Additional stems occurring with the -o alternant for the singular imperative are *tahtoq-* 'to hold', *agi-* 'to broil', *sabiq-* 'to pick', *sahnsah* 'to count', *keki* 'to burn', *api* 'to cut'.

'I will certainly look at it.' Note the following:

	1st	2nd	3rd
Sing	*tag(anà-uq)*	*tag(anìe-wóq)*	*tag(anà-wiq)*
Dual	*tag(ayèheta-uq)*	*tag(ahèheta-woq)*	*tag(ayèheda-woq)*
Pl	*tag(anèheq-múq)*	*tag(anèheq-múq)*	*tag(anèheda-woq)*

Compounds with Class II stems have initial /i/ with singular subjects and initial /o/ with other subjects.

Note that the pattern of allomorphic variations for the certituative morpheme (*-uq* ～ *-muq* ～ *-moq* ～ *-woq* ～ *-wiq*) is not a familiar pattern: allomorphs with /u/ found with first persons, with /i/ following third singular, and those with /o/ elsewhere (cf. allomorphs with Class II stems in Sec. 3.1). In addition alternants with initial /m/ occur with first and second plural compounds, initial vowel with first singular and dual, and initial /w/ elsewhere.

The future-subject portmanteaus occurring with the certituative morphemes are the same as those occurring to mark the inceptive (Sec. 5.7).

6.2. Individual Mode Morphemes

Morphemes to mark dubitative, interrogative, and augmentative occur as individual morphemes, not parts of compounds. These morphemes may also occur with other parts of speech.[21] Various morphemes occur with verbs to indicate doubt or question. We describe the morphemes expressing doubt under dubitative and interrogative sections, and the morpheme indicating emphasis under augmentative.

6.2.1. *Dubitative.* The morphemes *-pomo* and *-popoq* express doubt. The exact difference in meaning has not yet been determined. It is possible that the first directs attention to a question, whereas the second expresses a statement of doubt: *tagehda(pómo)* 'He saw it? Maybe', *tagehda(pópoq)* 'Maybe he saw it.' The morpheme *-mo* seems to freely replace *-pomo,* with the same meaning: *tagehda(mo)* 'He might have seen it, possibly.'

Dubitative morphemes follow tense-subject compounds: *tagadoyâ-(pómo)* 'You two may have seen it?' *tagahwanâ(pópoq)* 'We may or may not have seen it a long time ago.'

Dubitative morphemes with the future tense-subject portmanteaus occur following a sequence of a future tense-subject portmanteau, plus the interrogative morpheme, plus a subject morpheme. In the following matrix *-popoq* could replace *-pomo.*

---

[21] See Chapter IV, Section 2.2.3, where six morphemes expressing some question or doubt are described, occurring with nouns.

	1st
Sing	*tag(anà-bu-ga-pómo)*
Dual	*tag(ayèheta-bu-ya-pómo)*
Pl	*tag(anèheda-bu-na-pómo)*

	2nd	3rd
Sing	*tag(anìe-bo-ya-pómo)*	*tag(anà-bi-da-pómo)*
Dual	*tag(ayèheta-bo-ya-pómo)*	*tag(ayèheda-bo-ya-pómo)*
Pl		*tag(anèheda-bo-wa-pómo)*

The future portmanteaus occurring first in the sequence are the same as those used in the certitutative mode compounds, except that *-aneheda* occurs with first and second plural forms rather than *-aneheq* (see Sec. 6.1.3). The dubitative morpheme occurs last, and is directly preceded by the regular subject morphemes, though redundant (see Sec. 3.1.3). The interrogative morpheme, following the future portmanteaus, with its alternants here of *bu ~ -bi ~ -bo* (see Sec. 2.1.2), seems to redundantly emphasize the doubt. Note the familiar pattern of alternation: *-bu* with first persons, *-bi* with the third person singular, and *-bo* with the other persons.

Third person future portmanteaus may precede the dubitative: *taganà-(bomo)* 'Will he perhaps see it?' In such instances, *-bo* may replace *-bomo: taganà(bo)* 'Will he perhaps see it?'

6.2.2. *Interrogative.* The interrogative mode is signaled by *-po* which has various alternants. Alternant *-o* follows the tense-subject compounds. Except with forms including 'you all, they', *-o* replaces the vowel of the subject morpheme in the near past and past compounds, as well as the vowel of 'you' and 'you two' forms of the far past compounds: *widéhoyô* 'Did you two just laugh?', *tagonô* 'Did you see it a long time ago?' With 'you all' and 'they' forms, this alternant replaces the entire subject marker: *tagah(ô)* 'Did they just see it?', *tagad(ô)* 'Did they see it?', *tago(ô)* 'Did they see it a long time ago?', *tagò(ô)* 'Did he see it a long time ago?' This alternant of the interrogative morpheme follows 'we two' and 'we' forms of the far past compound: *tagahwaya(o)* 'Did we two see it?', *tagahwana(o)* 'Did we see it?'

The alternant *-o* may replace *-pomo* in the matrix given in the last section. When so occurring, the *-o* replaces the final vowel of all person markers, and replaces the entire person marker in the 'you all, they' form: *taganabidô* 'He might see it?' *taganehedaboô* 'They, you all might see it.' Such forms seem to be abbreviations for those listed in the matrix.

The interrogative has further alternants occurring directly after the future portmanteaus. These are *-nkono ~ -nkoyo ~ -bo*. The first of these occurs with portmanteaus including 'I' and 'we'; the second with 'we two'; and the third with the other persons: *taganì(noknô)* 'Will I see it?', *tagayèh(nkoyô)* 'Will we two see it? The future-subject portmanteaus including second person occurring with the interrogative are *-ani* (singular), *-ayeh* (dual), and *-aneh* (plural).[22] *tanganìbô* 'Will you see it?,' *tagayehbô* 'Will you two see it?', *taganèhbô* 'Will you all see it?' The forms *tagankèhbô* and *tagagèhbô* are only used to refer to third person subjects freely alternating with the other third person forms (see Sec. 3.4).

The alternant *-bo* also follows mode morphemes, and in such cases questions whether or not the statement was made: *tagáhnô* 'You look!', *tagahno(bô)* 'You look!? (is that what you said?).' This alternant may also follow the emphatic marker used with tense-subject complexes with the same meaning: *tagehde(bô)* 'He saw it!? (is that what you said?).'

6.2.3. *Augmentative.* The suffix *-e* adds emphasis to the verb complex. With tense-subject compounds the augmentative replaces the vowel of the subject morpheme: *tagehd(e)* 'He just now saw it!', *tagadàid(e)* 'He saw it!', *tagahwày(e)* 'We two saw it a long time ago!' It replaces the entire subject morpheme in the case of the first and third singulars of the far past: *tagahwa(e)* 'I saw it long ago!', *tagó(we)* 'He saw it long ago!' Note in the last example that with the third singular far past forms, the augmentative occurs as *-we*.

The augmentative may follow the future-subject portmanteaus: *tagankèh(e)* 'You, he just saw it!', *taganhèh(e)* 'We saw it!'

The augmentative may also occur following mode markers. In these cases, the *-e* emphasizes that the statement it occurs with, in fact, has been made: *tagáhno(e)* 'Look at it! (that's just what I said!).'

Following the certituative mode compound, the augmentative requires the person subject markers preceding it: *taganìewóq* + *-naq* + *-e* > *taganìewóne* 'You certainly will see it!' With 'you all' and 'they' forms the augmentative is added directly to the certituative form without the person subject: *taganèheqmó(e)* 'You all certainly will see it!', *taganèhedawò(e)* 'They certainly will see it!'

The augmentative may occur with tense-subject complexes, followed by *-bo* to question the occurrence of the statement (not its fact), and then *-bo* in turn may be followed by a second *-e* to augment the force of *-bo*: *tag-ahw-(e)-bô-e*) 'They saw it!? (is that exactly what was said!?).'

6.3. *Summary of Modelike Morphemes*

Modelike morphemes may be graphed as follows for their relative distribution:

---

[22] These forms may be from the first person portmanteaus, or from other portmanteaus with certain modifications. The phoneme sequences of /eta/ and /eda/ may be morphemes. See Sec. 3.4.

```
        ┌T-Su-Imperative ──┬─┤
        │
        ├T-Su-Avolitional ─┼─┤              ┌─┤          ┌─┤
+ S +  ─┤                  ├Augmentative┴─Interrogative┴Augmentative
        ├T-Su-Certituative─┼─┤
        │
        └T-Su-Dubitative ──┴─┤
```

7. SUMMARY OF INDEPENDENT VERB STRUCTURE

We have indicated specific distributions as we have discussed the various morpheme sequences and complexes. In general, the direct or indirect object morphemes occur contiguous to the stem (preceding or following depending on the stem). Aspect morphemes may follow the object morphemes, or the stem. The obligatory tense-subject complexes may follow the stem, the object morphemes or the aspect morphemes. Mode morphemes follow the tense-subject complex, occurring with objects and/or aspects optionally. A summary diagram representing in general the internal structure of the Awa independent verb follows:

$$
+ S_1 \pm \begin{bmatrix} DO \\ \\ IO \end{bmatrix} \pm \text{Aspect} + \begin{bmatrix} T\text{-}Su^{23} \\ \\ T\text{-}Su\text{-}mode \end{bmatrix} \pm \text{Mode}
$$

[23] Dubitative mode, being mutually exclusive with mode compounds, follows only tense-subject compounds, not mode compounds.

VII. Awa Verbs, II: The Internal Structure of Dependent Verbs

ARETTA LOVING and HOWARD McKAUGHAN

1. INTRODUCTION

This paper continues the description of Awa verbs begun in the preceding chapter, and is concerned with the dependent verb.[1] The Awa dependent verb has the following characteristics. (A) It occurs as the predicate of dependent clauses—that is, clauses whose occurrence is either limited to the occurrence of at least one other clause in the same larger construction, or whose occurrence depends on context outside of the sentence in the form of either a question, or an understood continuation of the discourse: *pokiniéna ménsámehnsá táhdudáhduiq* 'In order to go, he is tying up his things'; or to the question, 'Why is he tying his things?', one may respond, *pokiniéna* 'In order to go he (is doing it).' (B) The dependent verb contains certain morphemes in its internal structure which do not occur with independent verbs: for example, markers to anticipate either the subject of a following clause, or the clause itself. (C) The dependent verb contains morphemes and complexes which vary morphophonemically in certain ways not found in independent verbs. The distinctive markers and their variants found in dependent verbs form the basis for this part of the description of Awa verbs.

We distinguish two types of dependent verbs in Awa: (A) those which occur in a dependent clause which must be *followed* by one or more clauses, or which appear without other clauses in the same sentence, and (B) those

[1] Aretta Loving is responsible for early analysis of this part of the description of Awa verbs. As in the preceding chapter, McKaughan is responsible for the theoretical framework and presentation. The paper first appeared as pp. 1-30 in *Verb Studies in Five New Guinea Languages,* Summer Institute of Linguistics Publications in Linguistics and Related Fields No. 10, 1964, and is reissued here by permission.

which occur in a dependent clause which must be *preceded* by one or more clauses. We call the first a dependent medial verb, and the second a dependent final verb.

2. DEPENDENT MEDIAL VERBS

Dependent medial verbs are characterized by markers to anticipate the subject of a following clause, or by markers which anticipate a second clause.

2.1. *Anticipatory Subject Markers in Dependent Medial Verbs*

Most Awa medial verbs indicate both the subject of the clause in which they occur, and the subject of a following clause.[2] The first subject is marked by morphemes which appear as part of compounds or portmanteaus including tense. These complexes and their relative distribution have been described in the preceding chapter. We refer to morphemes indicating a subject to follow as (A)nticipatory (S)ubject (M)arkers.

Anticipatory subject markers indicate the person and number of the subject to follow. The markers are:

> *-na* ~ *-ena* anticipating 'I' or 'he'
> *-ah* ~ *-ø* ~ *-e* anticipating 'you'
> *-ta* ~ *-eta* anticipating 'we two' or 'you two'
> *-q* ~ *-eq* anticipating 'we' or 'you all'
> *-da* ~ *-eda* anticipating 'they two' or 'they'

Allomorphs with initial /e/ follow future portmanteaus, or compounds involving future portmanteaus, and avolitional compounds. Allomorph *-ah* occurs following morphemes with final /a/, replacing that phoneme. Other allomorphs listed occur elsewhere. Note the following examples: *tagogo(na) bòkiq* 'When I looked, he went', *tagog(ah) bokónaq* 'When I looked, you went', *tagoga(ta) bokóyaq* 'When I looked, you two went', *tagoga(q)* 'When I looked you all ...', *tagoga(da)* 'When I looked, they ...', *tagayeh(éta)* 'We two will look, and we two ...'.[3]

The internal structure of a medial dependent verb with anticipatory subject markers may be represented as follows:

$$+ \ S_1 \ \pm \begin{bmatrix} DO \\ IO \end{bmatrix} \pm \ \text{Aspect} \ + \begin{bmatrix} \text{T-Su} \\ \text{T-Su-M} \end{bmatrix} + \ \text{ASM} \ \pm \ \text{Mode}$$

---

[2] S. A. Wurm (1961a) has given a general résumé of the fact that different sets of morphemes occur 'with verbs in utterance-final and non-utterance final positions' in Central New Guinea languages. These sets of morphemes may indicate a subject to follow, or show various types of relationship between the actions referred to by the related clauses.

[3] The subject of the second clause is redundantly marked in the independent verb, described in the preceding chapter.

We now turn to a discussion of the ASM's with the various tense and mode complexes.

2.1.1. *ASM's following tense-subject compounds.* Anticipatory subject markers with tense compounds always signal a *different* subject in the following clause from that of the dependent clause. Preceding ASM's, the first person singular morpheme of the far past tense-subject compound occurs as a *-ø* alternant: *tag-ahwa-(ø)-na* 'When I saw it long ago, he . . .'. Also preceding ASM's the third singular far past compound is *-owa; tag(ówa)na* 'When he saw it long ago, I . . .'. Other than these differences, all tense-subject compounds (and all aspect morphemes preceding such) occur as described in Chapter VI preceding the anticipatory subject markers. The following examples illustrate the internal structure of medial verbs with ASM's following tense-subject compounds.

> *tag-oga-na* 'When I saw it, he . . .'
> *tag-adàuyá-da* 'When we two had seen it, they . . .'
> *tagahwana-ta* 'When we saw it long ago, you two . . .'
> *tag-ad-óg-ah* 'When I glimpsed it, you . . .'
> *taga-du-tàuya-na* 'When we two had finished seeing it, he . . .'
> *tag-a-t-ahwána-na* 'When we saw it for him long ago, he . . .'

2.1.2. *ASM's following future-subject portmanteaus.* Future-subject portmanteaus occurring in dependent medial verbs differ somewhat from the forms included in independent verbs. The portmanteaus with medial verbs exhibit number contrasts, while person contrasts are carried either by free pronouns or by the form of the ASM. ASM's may follow the future portmanteaus to anticipate the same or different subject as the dependent clause, under the following conditions.

When indicating the *same* subject, the ASM's follow portmanteaus marking singular (*-ani*), dual (*-ayeh*), and plural (*-aneh*). The future singular when indicating first or third persons has an alternant *-a,* varying freely with *-ani.* Note that these forms are the same as portmanteaus in independent verbs marking first persons. The ASM's following these portmanteaus occur with initial /e/ except when following /a/. The number of forms possible with these combinations is limited to the following since same subjects are depicted.

tag-ani-éna 'I will see it, I . . .', or 'He will see it, he . . .'
tag-a-na (same meaning)
tag-anì-e 'You will see it, you . . .'
tag-ayèh-eta 'We two will see it, we two . . .', or 'You two will see, you two . . .'
tag-ayèh-eda 'They two will see it, they two . . .'
tag-anèh-éq 'We will see it, we . . .', 'You all will see it, you all . . .'
tag-anèh-eda 'They will see it, they . . .'

The anticipatory subject markers indicate different subjects when following the future portmanteaus -*ankehe* future singular, and -*agehe* future plural. Note that these morphemes are alternants of the independent portmanteaus, having an additional /e/.[4] Person differences may be clarified by the use of free pronouns.[5] In the following example, note the possible ambiguities: *tag-ankehe-éna* 'I will see, he . . .', 'He will see, I . . .', 'You will see, he . . .', 'You will see, I . . .'.

2.1.3. ASM's *following tense-subject mode compounds*[6]

A. Conditional compounds occur with dependent verbs, but may not occur with independent verbs. This mode indicates a condition whose fulfillment is necessary to another action: *nene podiah me(ehna)na* 'If you take my arrow, I . . .'. The conditional compound includes tense, subject, and conditional mode. The following matrix illustrates the situation.

	1st	2nd	3rd
Sing	*tag(ahna)-*	*tag(ehna)-*	*tag(ahna)-*
Dual	*tag(ehya)-*		
		tag(ehdra)-	
Pl	*tag(ahna)-*		
Sing	*wídéh(ona)-*	*wídéh(ina)-*	*wídéh(ina)-*
Dual	*wídéh(oya)-*		
		wídéh(ida)-	
Pl	*wídéh(ona)-*		

Note that certain contrasts in person and number found elsewhere are here lost. Compounds with Class II verbs have initial /o/ with first persons, initial /i/ elsewhere, the same initials observed with avolitional compounds. Conditional compounds with Class I words have /ah/ and /eh/, but the pattern is different from any we have observed thus far: /ah/ with 'I', 'he', and 'we' forms; /eh/ with 'we two', and 'you', and 'you all, they' forms (dual or plural). We suggest again that the first vowel indicates tense (near past), the consonant the person-number subject, and the final vowel the mode. However, the partials act together in the compound for total meaning.

Anticipatory subject markers following the conditional compounds indicate a different subject from that of the dependent clause. The following illustrate: *me(éhya-na)* 'If we two take it, he . . .', *pok(ida-q)* 'If they go, we . . .', *kek(iná-ta)* 'If you burn it, we two . . .'.

---

[4] The /e/ may be an obligatory occurrence of the augmentative morpheme. Compare Sec. 2.1.3.C.

[5] See Chap. VI, footnote 9.

[6] ASM's have not been observed following the imperative mode compounds.

B. Avolitional compounds occurring in dependent medial verbs differ somewhat from those occurring in independent verbs paralleling differences observed for the future portmanteaus.

Following avolitional compounds, the ASM's may signal the same or a different subject in the related clauses.

When indicating the same subject, the ASM's follow -ehneho (avolitional singular or plural), or -ehyeho (avolitional dual) with Class I stems, and the same compounds with initial /o/ with Class II stems. Examples follow: *tag(ehneho-éna)* 'He should not look, so he . . .', *wídéh(oyeho-éda)* 'They two might laugh, so they two . . .', *me(éhneho-é)* 'You shouldn't take it, so you . . .', *pok(oneho-éq)* 'We ought not to go, so we . . .'.

Anticipatory markers indicate a different subject is to follow when they occur with the avolitional compounds which parallel those occurring in the independent verbs. Examples follow: *'tag(ehneho-éna)* 'I might see it, so he . . .', *wídéh(inedho-é)* 'It isn't good that he laugh, so you . . .', *me(ého-éq)* 'They shouldn't take it, so we . . .', *pok(òyeho-éda)* 'We two might go, so they . . .'.

C. Following certituative compounds, the ASM's indicate a different subject from that of the dependent clause. Certituative compounds with medial verbs require the augmentative morpheme preceding the ASM. This in turn requires a subject morpheme except in the 'you all' and 'they' forms. In order to compare the dependent forms with the independent, we give the matrix with forms of the verb 'to go'. The internal structure illustrated is stem plus future portmanteau plus certituative plus person-subject plus augmentative plus anticipatory subject.

	1st	2nd
Sing	. . . .[7]	*pok-inìe-wo-n-e-éna*
Dual	*pok-oyèheta-u-y-e-éna*	*pok-oyèheta-wo-y-e-éna*
Pl	*pok-onèheq-mú-n-e-éna*	*pok-onèheq-mo-e-éna*

	3rd
Sing	*pokina-wi-d-e-éna*
Dual	*pok-oyèheda-wo-y-e-éna*
Pl	*pok-onèheda-wo-e-éna*

The second person column of this matrix could be translated: 'You certainly will go, he . . .', 'You two certainly will go, he . . .', 'You all certainly will go he . . .'.

2.1.4. *Preceding individual mode morphemes.* Anticipatory subject

---

[7] We have been unable to elicit the certituative first person singular form followed by a different subject. Informants insist that *pokinàugeéna* 'I intend to go, so I . . .' must be followed by an independent verb with the same subject.

markers precede the individual mode morphemes.[8] Medial dependent verbs contain a mode morpheme not found in the independent verbs. We refer to this mode as contrary to fact since it marks an action which is alleged to be different from the actual facts: *méoganadaidí pokìdino* 'If I had taken it (but I didn't), he would have gone.' This mode is indicated by *-taidi(n)* ~ *-daidi(n)*, the first occurring with morphemes with final /q/, replacing that phoneme, the second elsewhere. Final /n/ is actualized before a following vowel, /k/, or /s/. Interrogative and augmentative mode markers occur with dependent forms only when those forms do not have other clauses in the same sentence: *tagogana-bô* 'When I saw it, (did) he?' or 'When he saw it, (did) he? (Is that what you said?)'; *tagogana-è* 'When he saw it, he did it!'

The following illustrate the ASM preceding contrary to fact and dubitative morphemes: *tagoga(na-daidí)* 'If I had seen it, he . . .', *tagoga(na-bopoq)* 'Maybe I saw it, and he . . .'.

2.2. (A)nticipatory (C)lause (M)arkers in Dependent Medial Verbs

Dependent medial verbs in Awa may contain morphemes to indicate that a clause will follow (or occurs in the context). These morphemes do not give information as to the following subject. Three such anticipatory clause markers have been located in our research thus far. Each of them is mutually exclusive with the ASM's.[9] Preceding these ACM's, subject morphemes indicating 'I', 'he', or 'you all, they' have *-ø* alternants. The ACM's parallel each other in that an allomorph of each occurs following the phoneme sequence /na/,[10] with other allomorphs elsewhere.

2.2.1. *General anticipatory clause marker.* The ACM with the widest distribution is *-boq* ~ *-daq* ~ *-taq*. This morpheme indicates that the verb in which it occurs is dependent, that is, its action is dependent in some way on that expressed in a related independent clause. The relation between clauses seems to be the same whether an ASM or this general ACM[11] occurs with the dependent verb.

Allomorphs of the general anticipatory clause marker include *-boq* following future portmanteaus and avolitional compounds, *-daq* and *-taq* elsewhere; *-daq* follows the phoneme sequence /na/, *-taq* elsewhere.

Future portmanteaus preceding the general anticipatory clause marker are the same as those occurring with independent verbs: *me(ankèh-boq)*

---

[8] The augmentative morpheme is obligatory in certain complexes such as medial certitutives. In such cases, the augmentative precedes the ASM, but may also follow it: *pokinàwideénae* 'He intended to go, so I (did it)!'

[9] The morpheme *-sabe* has been observed following ASM's, but in nonpredicate functions.

[10] The phoneme sequence /na/ is a morpheme ('I' or 'you') in some instances and may be the historic reason why the sequence, whether a morpheme or not, conditions the following allomorph.

[11] Further research is needed related to interclausal syntactic and semantic relations. We trust this will clarify the use of the general ACM.

'He will take it, so . . .', *kek(iní-boq)* 'I will burn, so . . .', *pok(igèh-boq)* 'They will go, so. . .'. Avolitional compounds have alternants preceding this general morpheme which may be derived from the compounds occurring with independent verbs; that is, these forms occur in the medial verbs with *-boq* without the final /o/: *me(éh-boq)* 'They ought not to take it, so . . .', *pok-(onèh-boq)* 'I shouldn't go, so . . .'.

Following tense compounds, the person markers indicating 'I', 'he', or 'you all, they' preceding -daq ~ -*taq* occur as -ø alternants: *tag-o-ø-taq* 'When I saw it then . . .', *tagehtàq* 'When he looked, then . . .', *tagahtàq* 'When they saw it, then . . .'; but note *tagáh(na-daq)* 'When you saw it then . . .'.

Forms with allomorph *-boq* may not be followed by mode markers. Otherwise there seem to be no limitations: *mieh(ta-pópoq)* 'Maybe when he was here . . .', *mieh(tád-e)*[12] 'When he was here!', *mieh (tá-po)* 'When he was here?'

2.2.2. *Time anticipatory clause marker.* The morpheme *-gake* ~ *-kake* may be included in dependent verbs to mark a specific time when the dependent action occurred. This morpheme has only been observed with past, far past, and conditional compounds. The first of the two allomorphs occurs following the phoneme sequence /na/, the second elsewhere. Subject morphemes indicating 'I', 'he', or 'you all, they' preceding *-gake* ~ *-kake* occur as -ø alternants. The following illustrate: *pok-udàu(kake)* 'When I left, then . . .', *tag-ona(gake)* 'At the time you saw it . . .', *me-ahna(gake)* 'If and when I take it, then . . .'.

Mode morphemes may follow the time anticipatory clause marker: *pokudàikake(bopoq) ménsámehnsá tabanagadide* 'Maybe when (at the time) he went, the things disappeared.'

2.2.3. *Cause anticipatory clause marker.* The morpheme *-yabe* ~ *-sabe* ~ *-nsabe* has a wide usage in Awa.[13] More research is necessary before we can give its full distribution and meaning. Dependent medial verbs may contain this morpheme to indicate that the action in the dependent clause is the cause or reason for the action in the independent clause related to it: *meónsábé bokiq* 'Because I took it, he went.' Allomorph *-yabe* occurs following the phoneme sequence /na/, *-sabe* after morphemes with final /q/ replacing that phoneme (but not after any of the person morphemes in tense or mode compounds), and *-nsabe* elsewhere. The following illustrate: *tageh(nsábé)*[14] 'Because he saw it . . .', *wídéhudàuna(yabé)* 'Because we laughed . . .', *pokona(yabé)* 'Since I might go . . .', *meótá(sábé)* (with *-taq*)

---

[12] An allomorph *-tad* occurs preceding vowels as does a *d* final allomorph of certain Class I stems. See Chap. VI, Sec. 2.1.3.C.

[13] See Chap. IV, Sec. 2.2.1.D, for *-sabe* with nouns.

[14] As with other ACM's, person morphemes indicating 'I', 'he', and 'you all, they' with tense compounds occur with -ø alternants preceding *-yabe* and its alternants.

'Because I took it, then . . .'.
2.2.4. The internal structure of the dependent medial verb with anticipatory clause markers may be summarized as follows:

$$+ S_1 \pm \begin{bmatrix} DO \\ IO \end{bmatrix} \pm \text{Aspect} + \begin{bmatrix} \text{T-Su} \\ \text{T-Su-mode} \end{bmatrix} + \text{ACM} + \text{Mode}_2$$

3. DEPENDENT FINAL VERBS

We define a dependent final verb in Awa as one which occurs in a clause which must be preceded by another clause, and one which contains one of the morphemes to be described in the following sections. Two types occur: verbs containing a morpheme marking the partner of a dependent medial contrary to fact clause, and verbs containing a compound marking an obligation which must be preceded by a dependent medial conditional clause. In such instances we have an interdependency between two clauses. The medial dependent verbs have been described in previous sections. We turn then to the final dependent verb.

3.1. *Dependent Final Verb with Contrary to Fact Mode Morpheme*

A contrary to face mode in a dependent final verb is marked by *-idino: méotátaodí poku(idino)* 'If I had taken it, I (would have) gone.' Morpheme *-idino* is preceded by *-ø* alternants of person morphemes in compounds indicating 'I', 'he', or 'you all, they'. All other forms must occur with *-e*[15] directly preceding *-idino,* replacing the vowel of the person morpheme: *pok-ú-y-eidino* ' . . . , we two would have gone.' The only mode marker observed following *-idino* is the interrogative *-bo,* questioning whether or not the statement was made: *pokùidinobo* ' . . . , would have gone (did you say?)'. Further illustrations of the internal structure of final dependent verbs with *-idino: tageh(idino)* ' . . . , he would have looked' (near past), *tagah-wayéidino* ' . . ., we two would have seen it' (far past), *tagadonéidino* ' . . . , you would have seen it' (past).

3.2. *Dependent Final Verb with Imperative Mode Compounds*

A final clause which contains a verb with imperative mode compounds must be preceded by a clause containing a verb with the conditional mode compound: *mahtaq miahnana bok(ono)* 'If he is here, I must go.' The compounds comprise the imperative compounds occurring with independent verbs, and also compounds marking the other persons which do not occur with independent verbs. The following matrix illustrates.

---

[15] Probably the augmentative with its meaning neutralized.

	1st	2nd	3rd
Sing	*tag(ahno)*	*tag(áhno)*	
Dual	*tag(ehyo)*	*tag(ahtao)*	
Pl	*tag(ahno)*	*tag(ahdo)*	
Sing	*wídéh(ono)*	*wídéh(úno)*	*wídéh(ino)*
Dual	*wídéh(oyo)*	*wídéh(otao)*	
Pl	*wídéh(ono)*	*wídéh(odo)*	

With Class I verb stems, there is no contrast between second and third person forms. With Class II stems, all three persons contrast in singular forms. The initial vowel (probably the tense morpheme) has the following alternants: with Class I stems, initial /eh/ occurs with 'we two' forms, /ah/ with all other forms; with Class II stems, initial /u/ occurs with 'you', initial /i/ with 'he', and initial /o/ elsewhere. Further examples follow: *me(áhtao)* '. . . , they two must take it', *pok(òdo)* '. . ., they must go.'

3.3. *Summary*

The final dependent verb may be summarized as follows:

$$+ \; S_1 \; \pm \; \begin{bmatrix} DO \\ IO \end{bmatrix} \; \pm \; Aspect \; + \; T\text{-}Su \; + \; \begin{bmatrix} \text{Contrary to fact final} \\ \text{Imperative compound} \end{bmatrix}$$

VIII. An Outline of Awa
Grammatical Structures

RICHARD LOVING

1. INTRODUCTION

Four levels of Awa grammatical structure, the clause, sentence, phrase, and word, are described in this paper.[1] Previous papers have described the noun suffixes, noun prefixes, independent verb affixes, and dependent verb affixes. This paper is intended to complete the grammar outline of the Awa language describing the four grammatical levels mentioned, including their interrelationships.

2. CLAUSE STRUCTURES

Awa clauses are grammatical units with one and only one predicate tagmeme, manifested by verbs and verb phrases, and filling slots on the sentence, clause, and phrase levels. Awa clauses are either transitive, intransitive, stative, or quotative; and either independent, dependent, or included. Though included clauses as defined in this paper are in some sense dependent because they never occur in isolation, they are formally different from both independent and dependent clauses and thus treated as a distinct clause type.

2.1. *Independent, Dependent, and Included Clause Distinctions*

On the basis of their internal structure and their distribution in a larger grammatical unit, that is, the sentence, Awa clauses are either independent or dependent.

[1] The material for this paper was gathered during a two-year residence in the village of Mobuta under the auspices of the Summer Institute of Linguistics. Assistance from SIL colleagues at the University of Oklahoma is gratefully acknowledged as is also editorial assistance from Howard McKaughan.

2.1.1. An independent clause occurs either last in a sequence of two or more clauses or alone as the filler of an independent sentence slot. The predicate tagmeme in an independent clause is manifested by a verb construction with suffixes indicating the person and number of the subject. Such constructions also optionally occur with overt mode suffixes.

2.1.2. A dependent clause occurs preceding one or more clauses in an independent sentence. The predicate tagmeme of a dependent clause is manifested by a verb construction with one or more of the following dependent markers: (A) anticipatory subject markers,[2] (B) simultaneous or sequential markers,[3] and (C) conditional, contrary to fact, focus, or dependent imperative mode markers. Motion verbs occurring without person, number, and tense markers also manifest the predicate tagmeme of dependent clauses.

2.1.3. Included clauses occur as manifestations of a nonpredicate tagmeme, that is, as the fillers of the modifier slot in head-modifier phrases and as the fillers of the axis slot in axis-relator phrases. The predicate tagmeme in an included clause is manifested by a verb construction with suffixes indicating the person and number of the subject. Such constructions, however, occur only in the conditional and the declarative modes and never occur with unfused mode morphemes.

2.1.4. Independent and dependent clauses thus differ from included clauses in the following respects: (A) different external distribution, that is, occurrence in tagmemes on different levels and (B) different potentialities for verbal suffixation. Independent and dependent clauses differ from each other in the following respects: (A) different external distribution within the sentence and (B) different verbal suffix requirements.

2.2. Transitive, Intransitive, Stative, and Quotative Clause Distinctions

Awa clauses are also transitive, intransitive, stative, or quotative on the basis of the occurrence in them of different classes of verb stems and different optional and/or obligatory tagmemes.

2.2.1. In transitive clauses the obligatory predicate tagmeme is manifested by a verb construction, the nucleus being a transitive verb stem. Transitive clauses occur with the following optional clause level peripheral tagmemes:

[2] Anticipatory subject markers indicate the person and number of the subject of the following clause. The subject of the independent clause is marked by another series of affixes.

[3] Simultaneous and sequential markers indicate whether the action of the following clause is simultaneous with or sequential to the action in the first clause. When occurring with these markers, verb stems are not inflected with suffixes indicating the person, number, and tense of the clause in which they occur. Since there is never a change of subject in clauses following a verb construction containing simultaneous or sequential markers, the subject of the following clause is also the subject of the first clause. All sequential and most simultaneous verb constructions occur with anticipatory subject markers which indicate the number but not the person of the subject of the following clause.

subject, indirect object, object, referent, time, location, and instrument.

2.2.2. In intransitive clauses the obligatory predicate tagmeme is manifested by a verb construction, the nucleus being an intransitive verb stem. These stems are never associated with direct or indirect objects. Intransitive clauses occur with the following optional clause level peripheral tagmemes: subject, referent, time, location, and purpose.

2.2.3. In stative clauses the obligatory predicate tagmeme is manifested by a verb construction, the nucleus in this case being a stative verb stem. The stative verb stems indicate existence in reference to something or someone. This class includes the three stems *k-* 'is' (inanimate); *m-* 'is' (animate); and *up-* 'becomes, changes into.' Stative clauses occur with the following optional clause level peripheral tagmemes: referent, time, location, subject, and complement. The complement tagmeme occurs only with stative clauses.

2.2.4. In quotative clauses the obligatory predicate tagmeme is manifested by the quotative verb signaled by the absence of any overt verb stem leaving only the person, number, and tense marker. The quotation, obligatory in quotative clauses, is manifested by either sentences, clauses, phrases, or words. Quotative clauses have not been observed to occur with optional clause level peripheral tagmemes.

2.2.5. Transitive, intransitive, stative, and quotative clauses contrast (A) by a different class of verb stems manifesting the nucleus of the predicate tagmeme in each case and (B) by different optional clause level tagmemes. In addition transitive clauses differ from each of the other three clause types by verbal affixation, and quotative clauses differ from each of the other three types by the occurrence of a second obligatory tagmeme.

2.3. *Peripheral Tagmemes in Clauses*

Optional (peripheral) tagmemes in Awa clauses are the same regardless of their distribution within various clause types. Relators in these tagmemes are either obligatory, optional, or always absent.

2.3.1. The object, indirect object, and complement peripheral tagmemes never occur with relators. An object (O) tagmeme functions as the goal of the predicate (P) of a transitive verb. An indirect object (IO) tagmeme functions as the recipient of the goal of the action of a transitive verb. Both of these peripheral tagmemes occur in transitive clauses and are manifested by nouns, noun phrases, or pronouns.

Examples: *naino* (IO) *poedahq ayahqno* (O) *awuke* (P) (my-mother pig head I-gave-her) 'I gave my mother a pig's head.' *pehe ehweh* (O) *ne* (IO) *teniq* (P) (lying talk me he-told-me) 'He told lying talk to me.'

A complement (C) tagmeme functions as part of the comment in stative clauses, usually in apposition to other nouns, or noun phrases.

Examples: *mahbi* (S) *omenahwe* (C) *ukina* (P) (young-man groom he-will-become) 'The young man will become a groom.' *ide ahnte* (C) *kehde* (P) (not much there-is) 'There isn't much.'

2.3.2. The subject and time peripheral tagmemes occur with optional relators in transitive, intransitive, and stative clauses.

The subject (S) tagmeme functions as either the performer of an action or as the subject of a stative verb. It is manifested by nouns, noun phrases, pronouns, or actor axis-relator phrases.

Examples: *weh* (S) *pokiq* (P) (man he-went) 'The man went.' *meg-in-ka* (S) *pitegide* (P) (drop-it-actor it-broke) 'Dropping broke it.'

The time (T) tagmeme indicates either a point in time or a unit of time and is manifested by either temporals or temporal axis-relator phrases.

Examples: *ahbiah* (T) *pokinie* (P) (tomorrow I-am-going) 'Tomorrow I am going.' *tag-eh-taq* (T) *pokiq* (P) (see-he-temporal he-went) 'When he saw it, he went.'

2.3.3. The referent, location, instrument, and purpose tagmemes occur with obligatory relators and are manifested by axis-relator phrases. The referent and location tagmemes occur with transitive, intransitive, and stative clauses; the instrument tagmeme occurs only with transitive clauses; and the purpose tagmeme occurs only with intransitive clauses.

The referent (R) tagmeme usually occurs clause initially and is manifested by referential, causal, or reason axis-relator phrases: *ian-sabe* (R) *kabaduge* (P) (dog-referential I-search) 'I'm looking for the dog.' *poedah-puwa-na*[4] (R) *nehte* (P) (pig-causal-and-he he-ate) 'Because he's a pig he ate it.' *tag-ani-boq* (R) *ko weo* (P) (see-I-will-reason go you-bring-it!) 'So I can see it, go and bring it!'

The location (L) tagmeme indicates the location or direction of an action, person, thing, or event and is manifested by either locatives or location axis-relator phrases. The various location tagmeme markers will be covered in greater detail under the discussion of phrase level structures: *anehe* (L) *siq* (P) (behind he-comes) 'He is coming behind.' *unah-bipeq* (L) *tagahno* (P) (string-bag-inside-of you-look!) 'Look inside the string bag.' *tag-eh-dapeq* (L) *kabaduge* (P) (see-he-place I-searched) 'I searched at the place where he saw it.'

The instrument (I) tagmeme indicates the means by which an action is executed and is manifested by instrument axis-relator phrases: *aah-tate* (I) *nubiq* (P) (club-instrumental he-hit-me) 'He hit me with a club.'

The purpose (Pu) tagmeme indicates the purpose for the action expressed by the intransitive verb stem and is manifested by purposive axis-

---

[4] The cause marker *puwa-* is unique in that it obligatorily occurs with anticipatory subject markers even when following nouns, noun phrases, and pronouns. In most of the constructions in which the marker *-na* occurs in this paper it anticipates either 'he', 'she', 'it', or 'I'. Only the most appropriate translation as indicated by the context will be given.

relator phrases. No difference in meaning has been noted between the purpose relators -*sahq* and -*sabatahq*: *wene anin-sahq* (Pu) *siq* (P) (his child-purposive he-came) 'He came for his child.' *wi-sabatahq* (Pu) *pokiq* (P) (urine-purposive he-went) 'He went to urinate.'

2.3.4. Rarely three and usually no more than two optional tagmemes have been noted to occur in a clause in Awa text materials. Tagmemes which are manifested by axis-relator phrases occur initially in a clause and the instrument and purposive tagmemes tend to occur immediately preceding the predicate tagmeme. The remaining tagmemes are quite flexible in order of occurrence, although the subject, time, and location tagmemes usually precede the indirect object and object tagmemes. Even so, relators or the context must often be relied upon to identify peripheral tagmemes in clauses.

2.4. *Focus in Clauses*

Clause level tagmemes in Awa may be put into focus, that is, become the focus of attention in the clause, by the addition to the tagmeme of the focus enclitic -*we* phonologically alternating with -*me*. The focus enclitic may occur with the predicate tagmeme or with any of the peripheral tagmemes except the purpose tagmeme. There are no other restrictions on its distribution within a clause. The tagmeme which occurs with the focus enclitic (f) is also set off from what follows by definite features of intonation and pause. The gloss of the focused items in the following examples of tagmemes in focus is in italics: *ne-ga-we* (Sf) *tagoq* (P) (I-actor-focus I-see) '*I* see it.' *ki tag-o-me* (Pf) *ide miehde* (P) (moving-uphill see-I-focus negative he-is) '*I went uphill to look* and he wasn't there.' The focus mode enclitic never occurs with more than one clause level tagmeme in any one clause. However, several focus enclitics may occur within the single clause level tagmeme. Although the items in a list are usually connected by conjunctions, they may occur with focus enclitics instead: *ahki-me ahnko-we topah-me* (Of) *meo* (P) (yams-focus taro-focus sweet-potato-focus you-take!) 'Take the *yams, taro, and sweet potato!*' *ade-we ne-we* (Sf) *aiq tagahdioye* (P) (you-focus I-focus completely we-two-know) '*You and I* really understand.'

2.5. *Summary and Examples of Clause Types*

There are twelve clause types based on the kind of predicate (transitive, intransitive, stative, or quotative) and the clause structure (independent, dependent, or included). These clauses may be charted as follows.

	Transitive	Intransitive	Stative	Quotative
Independent	Ind-Trans	Ind-Int	Ind-St	Ind-Quo
Dependent	Dep-Trans	Dep-Int	Dep-St	Dep-Quo
Included	Inc-Trans	Inc-Int	Inc-St	Inc-Quo

The peripheral tagmemes permitted in each clause type are dependent upon the verb class (transitive, intransitive, etc.) and have been stated in Section 2.3. The minimal form of the clause is a single predicate and the observed maximal form is a predicate and three peripheral tagmemes. The following are examples of each clause type.

A. *Independent-transitive clause.* *keki-nu-ehq* (P) (burn-mine-he) 'He burned mine.' *wega* (S) *nene so* (O) *kekinuehq* (P) (he my garden he-burned-mine) 'He burned over my garden.' *wehegah* (T) *madapeq* (L) *kekinuehq* (P) (noon downhill he-burned-mine) 'At noon he burned mine down there.'

B. *Independent-intransitive clause.* *pok-iq* (P) (go-he) 'He went.' *metaq* (T) *sehekahpeq* (L) *pokiq* (P) (a-little-while-ago forest-place he-went) 'A little while ago he went to the forest.' *wehbuwana* (R) *idasabadahq* (Pu) *pokiq* (P) (because-he's-a-man to-get-firewood he-went) 'Because he's a man, he went in order to get firewood.'

C. *Independent-stative clause.* *k-ehd-e* (P) (inanimate-is-it-augmentative) 'There are.' *we* (S) *unahpipeq* (L) *ahnte* (C) *kehde* (P) (he inside-the-string-bag many nuts there-are) 'He has plenty of nuts inside the string bag.' *wepuwana* (R) *amahnaga* (T) *ahnte* (C) *kehde* (P) (because-it's-he now many there-are) 'Because it's he, he now has plenty.'

D. *Independent-quotative clause.* *pokuno* (Q) *iq* (P) (you-go! he (said)) 'He said, "You go!" ' The augmentative mode marker -*e* optionally follows the quotative verb and obligatorily follows all quotations which end in nouns, noun phrases, or declarative mode verb constructions: *poedahd-e* (Q) *id-e* (P) (pig-augmentative he-(said)-augmentative) ' "A pig," he said.' *nene nahtapeq tagahno unahpipeq kehde* (Q) *ide* (P) (my at-the-house you-look! inside-the-string-bag there-are he-said) ' "Look inside my house! It's inside the string bag," he said.'

E. *Dependent-transitive clause.* *keki-nu-ehda-na* (P) (burn-mine-he-and I) 'He burned mine, and I . . .'. *nene so* (O) *wega* (S) *kekinuehtana* (P) (my garden he he-burned-mine-and-I) 'He burned off my garden, and I . . .'.

F. *Dependent-intransitive clause.* *pok-ida-na* (P) (go-he-and-I) 'He went, and I . . .'. *metaq* (T) *idasabadahq* (Pu) *pokidana* (P) (a-little-while-ago to-get-firewood he-went-and-I) 'A little while ago he went to get firewood, and I . . .'.

G. *Dependent-stative clause.* *k-ehda-na* (P) (inanimate-is-it-and-I) 'There are, and I . . .'. *we* (S) *unahpipeq* (L) *ahnte* (C) *kehdana* (P) (he in-the-string-bag many there-are-and-I) 'He has plenty in his string bag, and I . . .'.

H. *Dependent-quotative clause.* *pokuno* (Q) *ida-na* (P) (you-go! he-(said)-and-I) ' "You go!" he said, and I . . .'. *nene nahtapeq kehde; ko tagahno; pehedah ko weo* (Q) *ida-na* (P) (my at-the-house there-are; go you-look!

quickly go you-bring! he-(said)-and I) ' "It's inside the house. Go and look! Quickly go bring it!" he said, and I . . .'.

I. *Included-transitive clause.* The morphemes or words between solidi in each of the following examples are not part of the included clauses but are rather either relators or fillers of the head tagmeme in modifier-head noun phrases: *kek-i-/taq/* (P) (burn-he-/temporal/) 'when he burned'; *we* (S) *nene sotapeq* (L) *keki/taq/* (P) (he my garden-place /when/-he-burned) 'when he burned off my garden'; *wehekah* (T) *nene sotapeq* (L) *keki* (P) */ani/* (noon my garden-place he-burned /one/) 'the one who burned off my garden at noon'.

J. *Included-intransitive clause.* *pok-i/dapeq/* (P) (go-he-/general-place-marker/) 'where he went'; *we* (S) *metaq* (T) *poki/dapeq/* (L) (he a-little-while-ago /where/-he-went) 'where he went a little while ago'; *idasabadahq* (Pu) *poki /ani/* (to-get-firewood he-went /one/) 'the one who went to get firewood'.

K. *Included-stative clause.* *k-ehn-/sabel/* (R) (inanimate-is-it-/referential/) 'concerning there being'; *ahnte sehgadu* (C) *keh /madakotaq/* (L) (many mud-holes is /ground at/) 'the ground where there are many mud holes'; *ide kaweq madako keh-dabete* (L) (not good ground is-/from/) 'from where the poor ground is'.

L. *Included-quotative clause, pokuno* (Q) *i-/taq/* (you-go! he-(said)-/temporal/) 'when he said, "You go!" '; *menio* (Q) *in/sabel/* (R) (you-give-me! he-(said)-/referential/) 'concerning his saying, "You give it to me!" '; *ehsa miahno* (Q) *i /ani/* (quiet you-be! he-(said) /one/) 'the one who said, "You be quiet!" '.

TABLE 3

SUMMARY OF CLAUSE STRUCTURE

Clause	⌈V trans⌉		⌈IO⌉		⌈DO⌉		⌈Instrument⌉
	V intrans	± Subject ±	ø	±	ø	± Ref ± Time ± Loc ±	Purposive
	⌊V stative⌋		⌊ø⌋		⌊ø⌋		⌊Complement⌋
	V quot	+	quotation				

3. SENTENCE STRUCTURES

Awa sentences are the minimal units which can occur as complete utterances. These range in length from a single word to a complex sequence of many clauses. An independent clause occurring alone in a response situation is a dependent sentence. Thus, at some points in grammatical analysis, clause and sentence structures coincide. However, sentences differ from clauses in their manner of expansion and also in that sentences may: (A) be less than a clause, that is, contain no predicate tagmeme, and (B) be more than a clause, that is, contain more than one predicate tagmeme.

3.1. Basic Sentence Types

On the basis of their relationship to the linguistic or nonlinguistic context Awa sentences are either independent or dependent, and on the basis of internal structure they are either clause or nonclause sentences. The four major sentence types intersect in a two-dimensional matrix which has as its axis independent versus dependent and clause versus nonclause sentence types. Numbers refer to sections of this chapter in which the various sentence types are described.

		Clause	Nonclause
Independent	3.2	3.2.1	3.2.2
Dependent	3.3	3.3.1	3.3.2

3.2. Independent Sentences

Sentences which are not dependent on the linguistic or nonlinguistic context and can therefore occur alone as complete utterances without ambiguity are independent sentences. These are further divided on the basis of their internal structure into clause and nonclause sentences.

3.2.1. Independent sentences with clause constituents comprise the vast majority of sentences analyzed in Awa text materials. Determined by the occurrence and/or type of dependent clause constituents, independent sentences are either simple, compound, or complex. Included clauses may occur in each of these three sentence types.

3.2.1.1. Simple independent sentences contain only one independent clause, which in turn optionally has included clauses manifesting peripheral tagmemes. The minimal form of this sentence type is one independent clause and the maximal form is one independent (Ind) and two included (Inc) clauses: *pokiq* (Ind) 'He went.' *abiahnsai* (Inc) *ani tagehtaq* (Inc) *pokiq* (Ind) (he-frowns one when-he-saw he-went) 'When he saw the angry one he left.'

3.2.1.2. Compound independent sentences contain an obligatory dependent final clause which includes either (A) dependent imperative or (B) contrary to fact mode markers. The minimal form of this sentence type is two dependent clauses and the maximal form is one included (Inc) and two dependent (Dep) clauses.

A. A dependent imperative sentence contains a dependent imperative final clause preceded by a dependent clause containing a fused conditional mode person number marker: *pokinana* (Dep) *mahtaq miahno* (Dep) (if-he-goes-I here I-must-be) 'If he goes, I must stay here.' *abiahnsai* (Inc) *ani sinana* (Dep) *pokono* (Dep) (he-frowns one if-he-comes-I I-must-go!) 'If the angry one comes, I must go!'

B. A contrary to fact independent sentence contains a dependent final clause with *-idino* result contrary to fact marker. The condition contrary to fact marker *-dahidi* immediately precedes this final clause and is itself preceded by a dependent clause: *meehnanadahidi* (Dep) *teawuidino* (Dep) (if-he-had-taken-it-(but he didn't)-I I-would-have-told-you) 'If he had taken it, I would have told you.' *pukina* (Inc) *poedahq sinanadahidi* (Dep) *tagoidino* (Dep) (he-will-die pig if-he-had-come-(but he didn't)-I I-would-have-seen) 'If the dying pig had come, I would have seen it.'

3.2.1.3. Complex independent sentences contain a sentence-final independent clause preceded by one or more dependent clauses. Both dependent and independent clauses optionally occur with included clauses filling slots in peripheral tagmemes. The minimal form for this sentence type is one dependent and one independent clause. The maximal form is one independent (Ind), with multiple dependent (Dep) and included (Inc) clauses.

Examples: *tagehdana* (Dep) *pokuq* (Ind) (he-saw-me-and-I I-went) 'He saw me and I left.' *taqnobagi* (Inc) *kokode tagena* (Dep) *padabehdana* (Dep) *monaninka tagehnsabe* (Inc) *sahtate subiqmadena* (Dep) *ayo sosuehdana* (Dep) *wene ahde tiwe* (Dep) *naduehde* (Ind) (it-is-lost chicken seeing-I (with an arrow)-missed-and-he someone-else concerning-his-seeing with-a-club killing-it feathers he-pulled-out-and-she his wife cooking she-ate) 'After seeing the chicken that had been lost, I missed it (with an arrow), and someone else saw it, killed it with a club, pulled out its feathers, and his wife cooked and ate it.'

3.2.2. Independent sentences with nonclause constituents are interrogative, interrogative word, exclamatory, and vocative.

A. Interrogative nonclause sentences consist of a word or phrase with the interrogative mode marker *-po: poedah-po* (pig-interrogative) 'A pig?' *meta-po* (a-while-ago-interrogative) 'A while ago?'

B. Interrogative word nonclause sentences consist of an interrogative word occurring optionally with the following markers: (a) the referential or actor relator and (b) the interrogative mode marker. When it occurs, the interrogative mode marker is sentence final. Examples: *aneq-sabe-po* (what-referential-interrogative) 'Why?' *aneq-sabe* (what-referential) 'Why?' *ane-po* (what-interrogative) 'What is it?'

C. Exclamatory sentences consist of exclamatory words: *ehneh* 'Oh!' *uwoibo* 'Whew!' *oyaq* 'Well!'

D. Vocative sentences consist of words or phrases obligatorily occurring with the vocative suffix *-o: akahmpu anin-o* (deaf one-vocative) 'Oh, deaf one!' *kehdani-o* (Karen-vocative) 'Oh, Karen!'

3.3. *Dependent Sentences*

Sentences which are dependent on the linguistic or nonlinguistic context and cannot therefore occur alone as complete utterances without ambiguity are dependent sentences. They are further divided on the basis of their internal structure into clause and nonclause sentences. All dependent sentences with clause constituents occur only as responses in a linguistic or nonlinguistic context.

3.3.1. Response clause sentences consist of (A) axis-relator phrases with their axis slot filled by included clauses, (B) dependent clauses with anticipatory subject markers, or (C) either (A) or (B) with the contrary to fact condition and/or focus mode marker.

3.3.1.1. Any peripheral clause tagmeme which is manifested by an axis-relator phrase with its axis slot filled by an included clause and which is dependent on a preceding interrogative or understood clause may manifest a response clause dependent sentence. Specifically, these axis-relator phrase response sentence types are: referential, causative, reason, temporal, locative, and actor. In the examples which follow the material within parentheses is a free English translation of a question which could easily have precipitated the response being illustrated.

A. *Referential response.* (Why is she sad?) *wene ani ide wahdo poginsabe* (her child not short concerning-his-going) 'Concerning her child going a long distance away.'

B. *Causative response.* (Why is she beating him?) *ahbabaq ani miehpuwana* (bad child because-he-is) 'Because he is a bad child.'

C. *Reason response.* (Why should I bring it?) *taganiboq* 'So I can see it.'

D. *Temporal response.* (When did you see him?) *pokitaq* 'When he went.'

E. *Locative response.* (Where did you lose it?) *pokotapeq* 'The place where I went.'

F. *Actor response.* (What broke it?) *meginka* 'Dropping did.'

3.3.1.2. Any dependent clause with anticipatory subject markers which is dependent on a preceding interrogative or understood clause may manifest a response clause dependent sentence. Specifically, these dependent clause response sentence types are sequential, declarative, conditional, avolitional, and certituative.

A. *Sequential response.* (Are you coming?) *nena* 'After eating.' *tagena* 'After looking.'

B. *Declarative response.* (When will you bring it?) *taganiena* 'After I see it.' *siniena* 'After I come.'

C. *Conditional response.* (When are you coming?) *padabaginana* 'When it's finished.' *padahinana* 'When the sun shines.'

D. *Avolitional response.* (Why is he leaving?) *tagehnehoena* 'Since he shouldn't look.' *subinehoena* 'Since it's not good that he be killed.'

E. *Certituative response.* (When will he get them?) *pokinawideena* 'After he certainly goes.' *taganawideena* 'After he certainly sees them.'

3.3.1.3. The temporal, sequential, and conditional response dependent sentences optionally occur with a condition contrary to fact mode marker and/or a focus mode marker. When both markers occur, the focus mode marker is sentence final. The following examples illustrate the occurrence of these mode markers with a temporal response sentence: *tagotatahiti* 'If I had seen it (but I didn't).' *tagotaqme* 'While I was watching.' *tagotatahidime* 'If I had seen it (but I didn't).'

3.3.2. Dependent sentences with nonclause constituents consist of words or phrases in either a response or clarifying afterthought context.[5]

3.3.2.1. Response nonclause sentences contain relators, mode markers, both, or neither.

3.3.2.1.1. Response nonclause sentences containing relators are: referential, causative, temporal, locative, actor, instrumental, and purposive.

. A. *Referential nonclause.* (Why are you fixing that?) *poedahqsabe* 'Concerning the pig.' *waninsabe* 'Concerning the water.'

B. *Causative nonclause.* (Why can't the bird get out of the spider's web?) *pagegepuwana* 'Because it's so strong.' *peh kadipuwana* 'Because he's so very small.'

C. *Locative nonclause.* (Where did he come from?) *sehekahpete* 'From the forest.' *nahtapete* 'From the house.'

D. *Temporal nonclause.* (When are you going?) *motaq* 'In a little while.' *amahnaga* 'Right now.'

E. *Actor nonclause.* (What messed that up?) *poedahka* 'The pig did.' *adene aninka* 'Your child did.'

F. *Instrument nonclause.* (How did you cut yourself?) *sogitate* 'With a knife.' *kabahdatate* 'With bamboo.'

G. *Purposive nonclause.* (Why did he go?) *idasabadahq* 'To get firewood.' *wisabadahq* 'To urinate.'

3.3.2.1.2. Response nonclause sentences containing mode markers are dubitative, rhetorical, augmentative, and certituative.

A. *Dubitative response.* (What's that moving over there?) *kabadapomo* 'A bird, maybe.' *poedahpomo* 'A pig, maybe.'

B. *Rhetorical response.* (What's that moving over there?) *kabadamino* 'A bird, isn't it?" *poedahqmino* 'A pig, isn't it?'

C. *Augmentative response.* (What's that moving over there?) *kabadane* 'A bird.' *poedahde* 'A pig.'

D. *Certituative response.* (What's that moving over there?) *kabadamide* 'Most certainly a bird.' *poedahqmide* 'Most certainly a pig.'

3.3.2.1.3. The dubitative and rhetorical mode markers may also occur with any of the response nonclause sentences containing relators. Examples of these will be given with the purposive relator: (Why did he go?) *idasabadah-*

---

[5] Awa text material also contains fragmentary nonclause sentences which result from the speaker either being interrupted or changing his mind about what to say and therefore breaking off an utterance before it would normally have been completed. However, since such fragments do not represent accepted sentence structure, they will not be included in this description.

pomo 'To get firewood, maybe.' *idasabadahqmino* 'To get firewood, didn't he?'

3.3.2.1.4. Response nonclause sentences which contain neither relators nor mode markers are content information response, and yes or no response. A. *Content information response.* (Who's there?) *ne* 'Me.' *adenaboe* 'Your father.' B. *Yes or no response.* (Have you seen it?) *kowe* 'Yes.' *idagaumo* 'No.' 3.3.2.2. A clarifying afterthought nonclause sentences is always dependent on the sentence or sentences which precede it. Quite often an Awa speaker will add an afterthought which clarifies a point in the preceding linguistic context. (He grabbed the baby chicken and ran away.) *ianka* 'The dog did.' *mi kadiq ani* 'That little child.' (After I hit him he ran away crying.) *nene nokah* 'My brother-in-law.' *maqinsega* 'What's-his-name did.'

TABLE 4
SUMMARY OF SENTENCE TYPES

	Clause	Nonclause
Independent	Simple Compound Complex	Interrogative Exclamatory Vocative
Dependent	Axis-relator ASM marked Contrary to fact	Axis-relator Modal Yes-No

4. PHRASE STRUCTURES

Awa phrases consist of either a word plus an enclitic or two or more words, and fill slots on the phrase, clause, and sentence level. Verb phrases manifest clause level predicate tagmemes and thus may also be clauses and sometimes sentences as well. Phrases occurring in isolation are always sentences. However, phrases differ from clauses and sentences in their manner of expansion and also in that the majority of phrases neither contain verbs nor occur alone. Awa phrases include the following five types: axis-relator, modifier-head, coordinate, double-centered, and appositional.

4.1. *Axis-Relator Phrases*

An axis slot filled by a word, modifier-head phrase, or included clause, and a relator slot filled by a focus, actor, or peripheral tagmeme relator enclitic constitutes an axis-relator phrase. In clauses the referent, location, instrument, and purpose tagmemes are obligatorily manifested and the subject and time tagmemes are optionally manifested by axis-relator phrases.

4.1.1. Referential axis-relator phrases consist of an axis slot filled by an included clause, modified noun phrase, noun, or pronoun and a relator slot filled by the referential enclitic *-abe,* following vowels, alternating with *-sabe,* following consonants.[6] A referential axis-relator phrase obligatorily manifests either the referent tagmeme in clauses or referential response clause and nonclause sentences: *pokin-sabe* (he-went-referential) 'concerning his going'; *anotah poedahq-sabe* (big pig-referential) 'regarding the big pig'; *wen-sabe* (him-referential) 'concerning him'.

4.1.2. Causal axis-relator phrases consist of an axis slot filled by an included clause, modified noun phrase, noun, or pronoun and a relator slot filled by the causal enclitic *-puwa-.* A causal axis-relator phrase obligatorily manifests either the referent tagmeme in clauses or causal response clause and nonclause sentences: *poki-puwa-na* (included clause) (he-went-causal-he) 'because he went'; *anotah poedah-puwa-na* (modified noun phrase) (big pig-causal-he) 'because it's a big pig'; *we-puwa-na* (pronoun) (him-causal-he) 'because it's he'.

4.1.3. Reason axis-relator phrases consist of an axis slot filled by an included clause and a relator slot filled by the reason enclitic *-boq.* A reason axis-relator phrase obligatorily manifests either the referent tagmeme in clauses or reason response clause sentences. The included clause filling the axis slot always contains either future tense or avolitional mode markers: *pokini-boq* (I-will-go-reason) 'so I can go'; *pokoneh-boq* (I-should-not-go-reason) 'since I shouldn't go'; *meehneh-boq* (he-shouldn't-take-it-reason) 'since he shouldn't take it'.

4.1.4. Location axis-relator phrases consist of an axis slot filled by an included clause, modifier-head phrase, noun, pronoun, or locations, and a relator slot filled by one of the following locative enclitics: *-peq* 'place'; *-taq* 'on, at'; *-pete* 'from'; *-pi* 'at' (specific); *-pa* 'with, at' (animate); *-so* 'on top of'; *-pipeq* 'within'; *taba* 'over, across'; and *-tabeq* general place marker occurring with included clauses. A location axis-relator phrase obligatorily manifests the location tagmeme in clauses, location response clause and nonclause sentences, and the locative modifier slot in modifier-head noun phrases.

Examples: *sehekah-pete* (forest-from) 'from the forest'; *poki-dapeq* (he-went-place) 'the place where he went'; *anowa-ba* (mother-with) 'with his mother'.

4.1.5. Instrument axis-relator phrases consist of an axis slot filled by a noun or modifier-head noun phrase and a relator slot filled by the instrumental enclitic *-tate.* An instrument relator axis phrase obligatorily manifests the instrument tagmeme in clauses and instrument response nonclause sentences: *sah-tate* (club-instrument) 'with a club'; *sogi-tate* (knife-instrument) 'with a knife'.

---

[6] The markers *-sabe, -boq, -taq,* and *-kake* were handled by Aretta Loving and Howard McKaughan in the initial analysis of Awa dependent verbs as anticipatory clause markers (see Chap. VII, Sec. 2.2).

4.1.6. Purposive axis-relator phrases consist of an axis slot filled by a noun or modifier-head phrase and a relator slot filled by the purposive enclitic -*sahq* freely alternating with -*sabatahq*. A purposive axis-relator phrase obligatorily manifests the purpose tagmeme in clauses and purpose response nonclause sentences: *ahnte ahkin-sahq* (many yams-purposive) 'to get a lot of yams'; *wi-sabatahq* (urine-purposive) 'to urinate'.

4.1.7. Actor axis-relator phrases consist of an axis slot filled by an included clause, modifier-head phrase, noun, or pronoun, and a relator slot filled by the actor enclitic -*ka*. An actor axis-relator phrase manifests the subject tagmeme in clauses and actor response clause and nonclause sentences: *megin-ka* (it-dropped-actor) 'Dropping did'; *anotah poedah-ka* (big pig-actor) 'The big pig did'; *we-ga* (he-actor) 'He did.'

4.1.8. Temporal axis-relator phrases consist of an axis slot filled by an included clause or by a bound temporal stem and a relator slot filled by the temporal enclitics -*taq* general temporal or -*gake* specific temporal. A temporal axis-relator phrase manifests the time tagmeme in clauses and temporal response clause and nonclause sentences: *tago-taq* (I-saw-temporal) 'when I saw it'; *me-taq* (while-ago-temporal) 'a little while ago'; *sina-gake* (he-will-come-specific temporal) 'when he will come'.

4.1.9. Focus axis-relator phrases consist of an axis slot filled by an axis-relator phrase, modifier-head phrase, noun, pronoun, or predicate tagmeme, and a relator slot filled by the focus mode enclitic -*we* phonologically alternating with -*me*. A focus axis-relator phrase may manifest any clause level tagmeme except the purpose tagmeme; *poedahka-we* (pig-actor-focus) 'The pig did'; *ade-we* (you-focus) 'you'; *tago-me* (I-looked-focus) 'I looked.'

4.2. Modifier-Head Phrases

One or more preceding modifier tagmemes and a head tagmeme constitute a modifier-head phrase. Occasionally as many as three modifiers occur preceding a head tagmeme but usually no more than two. Modifier tagmemes are manifested by either a modifier word or by a modified modifier phrase. Modifier-head phrases are divided into three subtypes determined by whether the head tagmeme is manifested by a noun, verb, or modifier.

4.2.1. Modified noun phrases manifest the axis tagmeme in axis-relator phrases, and the subject, object, complement, indirect object, and quotation tagmemes in clauses. Modifiers may be grouped dependent upon their occurrence related to the head. Although no more than three orders occur in a given modified noun phrase, orders of modifiers are fixed relevant both to the base and to each other. One may say 'a black female pig', but not 'a female black pig'. In the following paragraphs, the modifiers are grouped by orders counting out from the head, but the stated order only means that relative to preceding orders, the higher number occurs farthest from the base. At no time are there twelve possible orders in a given phrase.

4.2.1.1. First-order modifiers are the specifier, locative, and type modifiers. A. The specifier is an included clause occurring as a modifier (see Sec. 2.1.3). When occurring as a specifier, included clauses are in the declarative or conditional mode: *metaq poki* (M) *ani* (H) (awhile-ago he-went one) 'the one who went awhile ago'; *sina* (M) *ahdadi* (H) (she-is-coming girl) 'the girl who is coming'.

B. Locative modifiers consist of a locative axis-relator phrase in which the relator slot is filled only by the locative suffix *-pete* 'from': *sehekahq-pete ka* (forest-from animal) 'an animal from the forest'; *ide-pete ani* (up-over-there-from one) 'the one from up over there'.

C. Type modifiers are *awehq* 'wild' and *mahq* 'here': *awehq poedahq* (wild pig) 'a wild pig'; *mahq ka* (here animal) 'a tame pig'.

4.2.1.2. Second-order modifiers are the genders *awehq* 'male' and *anehe* 'female': *anehe poedahq* (female pig) 'a female pig'; *anehe mahq ka* (female here animal) 'a tame female pig'.

4.2.1.3. Third-order modifiers consist of color words: *pabusa poedahq* (black pig) 'a black pig'; *ega anehe poedahq* (roan female pig) 'a female roan pig'.

4.2.1.4. Fourth-order modifiers are size words: *kadiq* 'small,' *akahtaq* 'medium', and *anotah* 'large'. Size may be redundantly indicated by suffixation of the head element when these size modifiers occur in a phrase: *kadiq poedahq* (small pig) 'a small pig'; *anotah poedahq-aba* (large pig-big) 'a great big pig'; *kadiq ega poedahq* (small roan pig) 'a small roan pig'. Occasionally size modifiers occur with the head tagmeme understood: *kadiq menio* (small you-give me!) 'Give me a small one!"

4.2.1.5. Fifth-order quality modifiers indicate something about the condition of the manifesting element of the head tagmeme: *idoke poedahq* (worthless pig) 'a no-good pig'; *kaweq kadiq poedahq* (good small pig) 'a good small pig'.

4.2.1.6. Sixth-order modifiers are the conjunctive and attributivized modifiers.

A. The conjunctive modifier consists of a noun or modifier-head noun phrase with the conjunctive suffix *-kakaq* meaning 'with' or 'has' in this context: *atah-kakaq poedahq* (offspring-with pig) 'pig with an offspring'; *naon-kakaq idoke poedahq* (sore-with worthless pig) 'worthless pig with a sore'.

B. An attributivized modifier consists of a verb stem with the attributivizer *-a:* *tid-a ahki* (cook-attributive yam) 'cooked yam'; *tida kaweq poedahq* (cooked good pig) 'tasty cooked pork'. Occasionally these attributive modifiers occur with the head tagmeme understood: *tida menio* (cooked you give me!) 'Give me a cooked one!"

4.2.1.7. Seventh-order similative modifiers consist of a noun or modifier-head noun phrase with the similative suffix *-dahnsa: kokode-dahnsa kabada* (chicken-like bird) 'a bird the size of a chicken'; *ebahdahnsa tida ahki* (like-a-stone cooked yam) 'hard as a rock cooked yam'.

4.2.1.8. Eighth-order quantity modifiers indicate something about the quantity of the manifesting element of the head tagmeme: *mobediah kabada* (five bird) 'five birds'; *ahnte kokodedahnsa kabada* (many like-a-chicken bird) 'many birds the size of chickens'. Occasionally these quantity modifiers occur with the head tagmeme understood: *ahnte menio* (many you-give-me!) 'Give me many of them!'

4.2.1.9. Ninth-order modifiers are the possessive and demonstrative modifiers.

A. Possessive modifiers indicate the possessor of the manifesting element of the head tagmeme and consist of a noun, modifier-head noun phrase, or pronoun with the possessive suffix *-ne: poedahq-ne topah* (pig-possessive food) 'pig's food'; *wene ahnte poedahq* (he-possessive many pig) 'his many pigs'.

B. Demonstrative modifiers indicate the distance and/or elevation of the manifesting element of the head tagmeme from the speaker: *inse poedahq* (that-down-over-there pig) 'that pig down over there'; *mi ahnte poedahq* (that many pig) 'those many pigs'.

4.2.1.10. The negative modifier *ide* 'not' modifies only the immediately following element. Thus, although it occurs in tenth order, the negative modifier only modifies the noun when it contiguously precedes it:[7] *ide poedahq* (negative pig) 'not a pig'; *ide ia* (negative dog) 'not a dog'.

4.2.1.11. The limiter modifier *peh* 'just, only' modifies only the immediately following element. Thus, although it occurs in eleventh order, the limiter modifier only modifies the head noun when it contiguously precedes it: *peh poedahq* (just pig) 'just a pig'; *peh ia* (just dog) 'just a dog'.

4.2.2. Modified verb phrases manifest the predicate tagmeme in clauses. The four modifiers in verb phrases are described in their order of occurrence preceding the head tagmeme.

4.2.2.1. First-order intensive modifiers include two items already described under modified noun phrases. However, when the size modifier *anotah* 'large' and the quantity modifier *ahnte* 'many' occur preceding verbs they take on an intensive meaning instead of size and quantity meanings: *anotah niediq* (very it-hurts-me) 'It hurts me very much.' *ahnte pehedahniq* (very he-runs) 'He runs very fast.'

4.2.2.2. Second-order similative modifiers consist of a noun, pronoun, modifier-head noun phrase, or actor axis-relator phrase with the similative suffix *-tahnsa: kambodanka-tahnsa pehedahniq* (cassowary-does-like he-runs) 'He runs like a cassowary does.' *adetahnsa anotah pehedahniq* (like-you very he-runs) 'Like you he runs very fast.'

---

[7] Note that here the negative and limiter are considered as modifiers of noun heads. When they modify modifiers, they are part of modifier-modified phrases (see Sec. 4.2.3).

4.2.2.3. The negative *ide* 'not' modifies only the immediately following element. Thus, although it occurs in third order, the negative modifier only modifies the verb head when it contiguously precedes it: *ide pokiq* (negative he went) 'He didn't go.' *ide teniq* (negative he tells me) 'He hasn't told me.'

4.2.2.4. The limiter modifier *peh* 'only, just' modifies only the immediately following element. Thus, although it occurs in fourth order, the limiter modifier only modifies the verb head when it contiguously precedes it: *peh tagoq* (just I-see) 'I just looked.' *peh ahnte pehedahniq* (just very he-runs) 'He just really runs.'

4.2.3. Modified modifier phrases manifest the modifier tagmeme in both modified noun and modified verb phrases. The three modifiers in modifier phrases are described in their order of occurrence preceding the head tagmeme.

4.2.3.1. The first-order intensive modifier functions as described under Section 4.2.2.1 when preceding condition modifier heads: *anotah kaweq* (very good) 'very good'; *ahnte kaweq* (very good) 'very good'.

4.2.3.2. The second-order negative modifier functions as described under Section 4.2.2.3 when preceding any modifier head: *ide kaweq* (negative good) 'not good'; *ide wahto* (negative short) 'long'.

4.2.3.3. The third-order limiter modifier functions as described under Section 4.2.2.4 when preceding any modifier head: *peh pabusa* (just black) 'just black'; *peh tida* (just cooked) 'just cooked'.

4.3. *Coordinate Phrases*

Two or more head tagmemes with a coordinate relationship between them indicated by conjunctive suffixes following each head tagmeme constitute coordinate phrases. These phrases consist of pronouns, nouns, or noun phrases with conjunctive suffixes and manifest the subject, object, indirect object, referent, and location tagmemes in clauses. They also fill the possessive modifier slot in phrases. Coordinate phrases are either personal or nonpersonal depending on the head tagmemes and the conjunctive suffixes with which they occur.

4.3.1. Personal coordinate phrases are used whenever more than one person is indicated in a coordinate phrase.

4.3.1.1. When a maximum of two singular personal nouns or pronouns are connected, the suffix *-deq,* following vowels, alternating with *-seq,* following consonants, occurs with each of the two head tagmemes: *we-deq ne-deq* (he-and I-and) 'he and I'; *ade-deq ne-de-ka* (you-and I-and-actor) 'You and I did.' Note that the actor marker need only occur once following the final conjunctive marker to apply to both head tagmemes. This is also true of each of the other markers which occur following conjunctive suffixes. Personal and nonpersonal conjunctives never occur together in the same coordinate phrase. Only one of the head tagmemes need be a personal noun or pronoun for the personal conjunctive to occur with both head tagmemes: *we-deq wene ian-seq* (he-and his dog-and) 'he and his dog'.

4.3.1.2. When more than two personal nouns or pronouns occur in a coordinate phrase, the suffix *-deh* (plural personal conjunctive) occurs with each of the head tagmemes: *naino-deh nanibo-deh naniyo-deh* (my-mother-and-my-father-and my-brother-and) 'my mother, father, and brother'. Whenever a plural pronoun is connected to only one other pronoun or noun, the plural personal conjunctive occurs with each of the head tagmemes: *ite-deh we-deh* (we-and he-and) 'we and he'.

4.3.2. Nonpersonal coordinate phrases are used whenever two or more nonpersonal items are to be connected in a coordinate phrase. The nonpersonal conjunctive is *-agaq,* following vowels, alternating with *-kakaq,* following consonants. Examples: *ahkin-kakaq tobadu-akaq sah-kakaq* (yam-and tuber-and sugar-cane-and) 'yams, tubers, and sugar cane'; *kokode-agaq poedah-kakaq* (chicken-and pig-and) 'chicken and pig'.

4.4. Double-centered Phrases

A verbal auxiliary preceding a main verb constitutes a double-centered verb phrase. These phrases manifest the predicate tagmeme in clauses: *ki tagehq* (going-up he-saw) 'He went up and looked.' *ko weo* (going-level you-bring!) 'Go and bring it!'

Occasionally a peripheral clause level tagmeme occurs between the verbal auxiliary and the main verb: *ki toya subidaide* (going-uphill drum he-beat) 'Going uphill he beat the drum.'

4.5. Appositional Phrases

Words or phrases which have the same referent stand in an appositional relationship and constitute an appositional phrase: *mi kadiq ani nene nokah* (that little child my brother-in-law) 'that little child, my brother-in-law'; *we mi kadiq ani* (he that little child) 'he, that little child'.

The constituents of appositional phrases are usually contiguous as illustrated. They may, however, be separated by the predicate tagmeme when the speaker amplifies some preceding peripheral clause tagmeme after having formally completed the clause: *we* (O) *subiq* (P) *nanibaq* (O) (him he-beat-him my-younger-brother) 'He beat him, my younger brother.' *we* (S) *subiq* (P) *nanibaka* (S) (he he-beat-him my-younger-brother-did) 'He beat him, my younger brother did.'

Appositional phrases and clarifying afterthoughts have the same characteristic intonation. These may or may not be identical depending on whether an already present tagmeme is enlarged upon by the clarifying afterthought. Examples in which they are the same have already been illustrated. In the following example the clarifying afterthought is *not* an appositional phrase because it introduces a tagmeme not previously present in the clause: *we* (O) *subiq* (P) *nanibaka* (S) (him he-beat-him my-younger-brother-did) 'He beat him, my younger brother did.'

4.6. *Summary of Phrases*

The following outlines the phrases described for the readers' convenience.

A. *Axis-relator:* referential, causal, reason, locative, instrumental, purposive, actor, temporal, and focus.

B. *Modifier-head:* modified NP, modified VP, and modified modifier.

C. *Coordinate:* personal and nonpersonal.

D. *Double-centered.*

E. *Appositional.*

5. WORD STRUCTURES

Awa words are grammatical units consisting of a single morpheme or a stem with derivational or inflectional affixes and filling slots on the phrase, clause, and sentence level. On the word level, only verbs and nouns have any complexity of internal structure, and these have been described in previous chapters. Therefore membership in word classes as outlined here is based primarily on distribution in various slots rather than differences in internal structure.

5.1. *Verbs*

Awa verbs are words which occur as the head of modifier-head verb phrases and as head of clause level predicate tagmemes. Verbs are either inflected or uninflected.

5.1.1. Inflected verbs occur as the head of most dependent and of all independent and included clause level predicate tagmemes. Except when occurring with simultaneous and sequential markers, inflected verbs obligatorily contain markers indicating the person and number of the subject of the verb. Inflected verbs are either simple, complex, or optionally complex.

5.1.1.1. Simple inflected verbs never occur with nonsubject person morphemes. They manifest the predicate tagmeme in intransitive, stative, and quotative clauses. Examples: *pok-iq* (go-he) 'He went.' *k-ehq* (inanimate-is-it) 'There are.'

5.1.1.2. Complex inflected verbs occur with either a direct or indirect object morpheme and manifest the predicate tagmeme in transitive clauses: *nu-b-iq* (me-hit-he) 'He hit me.' *te-aw-iq* (tell-him-he) 'He told it to him.'

5.1.1.3. Optionally complex inflected verbs occur with an optional clause level object or indirect object tagmeme in transitive clauses. Although these verbs never occur with obligatory nonsubject person morphemes, they do optionally occur with (A) possessed direct object morphemes and (B) indirect object morphemes which obligatorily precede the benefactive morpheme -*t*.

Examples: *keki-nu-ehq* (burn-mine-he) 'He burned mine.' *keki-nin-t-ehq* (burn-me-benefactive-he) 'He burned it for me.'

5.1.2. Uninflected verbs occur as the head of dependent clause level tagmemes and are either verbal auxiliaries or motion verbs.

5.1.2.1. Verbal auxiliaries occur in the first part of double-centered verb phrases. This class consists of the following members: *ko* 'going level'; *ki* 'moving uphill'; *tu* 'moving downhill'; *se* 'coming level'; *madu* 'carrying downhill'; and *mo* 'carrying uphill or level'.

5.1.2.2. Motion verbs manifest the predicate tagmeme only in intransitive clauses and indicate the direction, elevation, or speed of the subject of the clause. This class consists of the following members: *tunse* 'moving downhill'; *pehedah* 'moving quickly, running'; *kide* 'moving uphill'; *kude* or *pokue* 'moving away from'; and *sude* 'moving toward'.

5.2. Nouns

Awa nouns are words which optionally occur with suffixes indicating number or size. Nouns manifest the subject, indirect object, complement, object, and quotation tagmemes in clauses, occur as the head tagmeme in modifier-head noun phrases, occur obligatorily suffixed as the modifier tagmeme in similative and possessive noun phrases, and fill the axis slot of axis-relator phrases. Nouns are either: (1) never owned, (2) inalienable, or (3) alienable.

5.2.1. Never-owned nouns include personal names, place names, and the names of certain objects and phenomena.

5.2.1.1. Personal names are not only never owned, but are never modified except by the negative modifier. They may, however, with the appropriate suffixes manifest the modifier tagmeme in possessive and similative noun phrases. When manifesting the locative tagmeme, personal names occur only with the enclitic *ba* 'at, with' (animate): *odetah-ba* (Aretta-with) 'with Aretta'.

Personal names occurring with the vocative suffix *-o* manifest vocative sentences: *odetah-o* (Aretta-vocative) 'Oh, Aretta!'

5.2.1.2. Place names like personal names are neither possessed nor modified except by the negative modifier. Unlike personal names, however, place names occur with neither the vocative suffix nor the possessive suffix. They may occur unsuffixed as modifiers: *mobutah weh* (Mobuta man) 'a man from Mobuta'.

Place names usually occur with locative markers—though never with *-ba* 'at, with' (animate)—manifesting the location tagmeme in clauses: *mobutah-pete* (Mobuta-from) 'from Mobuta'.

5.2.1.3. The names of certain objects and phenomena are nonpossessed. These may occur as the head tagmeme in modifier-head noun phrases. Unlike personal names and place names, however, they never occur in the modifier slot in phrases: *tehdeh* 'light'; *ibo* 'rain'; *io* 'moon'.

5.2.2. Inalienable nouns occur with prefixes indicating one of six categories of possession. These categories include first, second, third, and nonspecified third person singular; third person plural; and nonthird person plural. Inalienable nouns include kin terms, most body parts, and several other miscellaneous nouns.

5.2.2.1. Only kin terms may occur with the kin indicator -*kawa* alternating with -*wa: si-bowa* (their-father) 'their father'; *wena-wehkawa* (her-husband) 'her husband'.

5.2.2.2. Most body parts are inalienable: *i-du* (our-insides) 'our insides'; *aden-ahsa* (your-jawbone) 'your jawbone'.

5.2.2.3. Miscellaneous nouns consist of the following members: -*wi* 'name', -*wa* 'spirit', -*wahpeq* 'village', and -*wahdah* 'relatives'. Examples: *itei-wiq* (our-name) 'our name'; *nanu-wahpeq* (my-village) 'my village'.

5.2.3. A few nouns may occur with the possessive prefixes indicated above or in a possessive noun phrase.

5.2.3.1. Nouns which optionally occur with possive prefixes are *ani* 'child', *ehweh* 'talk', and *ahde* 'wife': *nen-ani* (my-child) 'my child'; *wen-ehweh* (his-talk) 'his talk'.

5.2.3.2. Most nouns in Awa are alienable and occur without possessive prefixes but are optionally possessed in a possessive noun phrase: *ia* 'dog'; *wene ia* 'his dog'.

5.3. *Pronouns*

Awa pronouns are words which may either substitute for nouns or occur in apposition to nouns or noun phrases in an appositional phrase. Pronouns manifest the subject, indirect object, complement, object, and quotation tagmemes in clauses and with the appropriate suffixes they occur as the modifier in similative and possessive noun phrases. Subject to semantic limitations, most of the suffixes which occur with nouns also occur with pronouns. Pronouns, however, never occur as the head of head-modifier noun phrases. Pronouns are either personal or demonstrative.

5.3.1. Personal pronouns are either simple or intensive. In both sets there is a distinction between first, second, and third person singular, and between third and nonthird plural.

5.3.1.1. Simple personal pronouns are the only words which may occur with the suffixes -*tiahdiah* 'alone, by one's self' and -*pataq* 'only, alone'. The five pronouns are listed below.

	1st	2nd	3rd
Sing	*ne*	*ade*	*we*
Pl		*ite*	*se*

5.3.1.2. Intensive personal pronouns never occur with the two suffixes listed in Section 5.3.1.1. Intensive personal pronouns have more force and emphasis than do simple personal pronouns. They are formed by reduplication of all or some of the phonemes of the simple personal pronouns. This is illustrated by a comparison of the simple personal pronouns with the intensive personal pronouns below.

	1st	2nd	3rd
Sing	*nene*	*adede*	*wewe*
Pl		*iteite*		*seye*

5.3.2. Demonstrative pronouns always occur with the pronominalizer *-na* and indicate information concerning the distance and elevation of the referent relative to the speaker. Demonstrative pronouns are either simple or intensive.

5.3.2.1. Simple demonstrative pronouns consist of the five following words: *mina* 'that'; *mahna* 'this'; *insena* 'that down over there'; *idena* 'that up over there'; and *isena* 'that level over there'.

5.3.2.2. Intensive demonstrative pronouns are formed by a reduplication of the demonstrative pronoun stem (but not the pronominalizer) and consist of the following three words: *inseisena* 'that way down over there'; *ideidena* 'that way up over there'; and *iseisena* 'that level way over there'.

5.4. *Minor Word Classes*

Modifiers, temporals, interrogatives, exclamatory words, hesitation words, response words, and locatives constitute minor word classes in Awa.

5.4.1. Modifiers are a class of words which manifest the modifying tagmemes in noun, verb, and modifier modifier-head phrases. Modifiers are either restricted or unrestricted. Restricted modifiers occur only in noun modifier-head phrases. These modifiers occur not only with noun phrases but also with verbs and modifiers manifesting the head tagmeme in modifier-head phrases. These include the intensives (*anotah, ahnte*), the negative (*ide*), and the limiter (*peh*).

5.4.2. Temporals manifest the time tagmeme in clauses: *ahdina* 'the day after tomorrow'; *mętaq* 'a little while ago'.

5.4.3. Interrogatives occur with or without the interrogative marker *-bo* as fillers of independent sentences which have nonclause constituents, and without the interrogative marker as fillers of peripheral clause level slots in sentences which have clause constituents: *atahi* 'how'; *aneq* 'what'.

5.4.4. Exclamatory words occur as fillers of independent nonclause exclamatory sentences: *ehneh* 'Oh!'; *uwoibo* 'Whew!'

5.4.5. Hesitation words occur in appositional phrases: *maq* 'er'; *aaa* 'uh'.

5.4.6. Response words occur as nonclause response sentences. Any word may occur in this slot and the following words occur only there and as fillers of the quotation tagmeme in clauses: *kowe* 'Yes'; *ee* 'Yes'; *idekaumo*

'No'; *aqa* 'No'; *atahinabomo* 'Who knows?'; *anetanibo* or *anetaninkahnaq* 'Forget it!'

5.4.7. Locatives manifest the location tagmeme in clauses: *anehe* 'behind'; *awenah* 'beneath'.

IX. Awa Texts

Compiled by HOWARD McKAUGHAN

---

1. INTRODUCTION

The following texts were collected in the villages of Mobuta and Ilakia in 1962. The first twelve are from the former and the rest from the latter. An informant first put the stories into a tape recorder with the freedom of no interruption. The stories were then transcribed from the tape, an Awa dictating phrase by phrase what was on the recorder. Dick Loving of the Summer Institute of Linguistics did much of the word-for-word translation in the rough draft, there being for Mobuta a very nearly monolingual situation.

These texts are unanalyzed. Word division and even sentence breaks are tentative. A semicolon marks a break between clauses, with a clause or clauses to follow. However, not all such medial sentence breaks are so indicated, and a period may at times appear instead of a semicolon. The reader-analyst will need to compare the material with the descriptions given in the preceding chapters. Most of the descriptive materials were written after the texts were collected.

The orthographic representation follows that used in the descriptive studies for the most part. But the transcription is only semiphonemic. Tone is not indicated. Capital letters introduce Awa sentences indicating the beginning of the intonation contour and a period at the end closes the contour, at least in most cases. The low front vowel is represented by the digraph *eh,* and the low back vowel by *ah,* there being no glottal aspirate in Awa. Some confusion may exist in the recording of *a* for *ah* and sometimes even for *eh* due to varying placement of these vowels by different speakers (and perhaps to the recorder's ear). Certain morphophonemic shifts occur, not always accurately recorded: /p>b/, /t>r/, /k>g/, /m>w/, /s>y/, and /q>r/. For conditions, see the descriptive materials.

The value of these texts rests primarily in their usefulness as data for further analysis. Further analysis will result in correcting various aspects of the texts such as the indication of word division by spaces. The texts are not consistent in this respect now. Analysis of levels larger than the word and sentence will also be of interest to many. If opportunity is afforded, the addition of prosodic features and some correction of other phonological matters would greatly improve the texts.

In their current form, however, they should prove of value to students who may be assigned either to apply the descriptive materials to them for practice in identifying recurring partials, or to try their hand at analysis of raw data. It should be noted in this respect that paragraph divisions in the free translations are arbitrary. The numbering of every five sentences in the free translation will assist the reader to keep his place.

The translation under the Awa sentences gives the general semantic equivalent for each word. Hyphens between English words indicate that more than one English word is necessary to convey the meaning of one Awa word (or stretch of speech written between spaces!). Since the translation was done at an early stage of the study, it is not always exact. This will present a challenge to the student, making it necessary to apply the principle that form is primary.

The texts have been chosen for their content as well as to exemplify the linguistic properties of the language. The Awa often deal with the spirit world, tell many 'Two Brother' stories, and have, or at least tell about, adventures with death in various forms. I leave further comments about their customs and beliefs to the ethnographers.

2. The Bat and the Python

1. Manika manika mahbe rarega mahbirarega abahronae irareruwera
     First-people/supernatural-people young-men two sing-sing the-talk hap-
uwara.
pened.

2. Marutapeq maru abahruwara.
     Marutape down-hill sing-dance.

3. Ahrari rarega setaq kiyeriqrayatauye irareruwera tobaran sume unahpi
     Girl two there-up want-the-two talk-they bean-seed string-bag put-in
usabe usabe usabe usabe.
put-in . . .

4. Kahwerarera uwara setagarioyara.
     Good happen they-looked-two.

5. Abaruwe abaruwe abaruwe abaruwe abaruwe abaruwe abaruwe.
     Dance-and-play-drum continually.

6. *Kuyara mena tuwekuwana.*
   Went-toward-two them down-went.
7. *Tuwekuwana ahnansaipeq pokuyeiq anansaipeq pokuyansabe.*
   Down-went on-edge-place went place went-two-because.
8. *Ahrari rarerehq tehtare ahrarirare pokuwe.*
   Girl two-and two girls-two went.
9. *Kiesinainkaqmera.*
   Up-hill-they-followed.
10. *(Mi)tate mo tauyansubuyehra murutatuorute mo rauyan subuyehra.*
    From-there again drum-beat-two Marutatora again drum beat-two.
11 *Mena ahrarirarewe kurarera kiesinaenkaqmera.*
    Those girls-two cross-over up-hill-behind-came.
12. *Singehnkaqmera pokwe bokwe bokwe bokwe bokwe bokwe bokwe.*
    Followed them went and went and went.
13. *(Marutapete—aaa) tahbehnabete ki rauya suwiyame.*
    (Marutape—I mean—) Tabanabe-from up drum beat-two.
14. *Kuwehbete seiratiyoyeiq.*
    Kuwabe-from they-followed-them.
15. *Kuwabete seiraqtiyoyana.*
    Kuwabe the-two-followed-them.
16. *Mahbirure pokwe bokwe.*
    Young-men-two went went.
17. *Tahbiyapete ki rauya subuyame.*
    Tabaiya-from up they went-up.
18. *Tahbanabete kiratiyoyeiq.*
    Tabanabe-from girls-followed.
19. *Saurepete ki rauya suwiyame.*
    Chauripe-from up they followed.
20. *Tahbiyapete kiratiyoyeiq.*
    Tabiyape-from they-followed.
21. *Wegiyabarapete ki rauya suwiyaime.*
    Wegiyabara-from up they followed.
22. *Saurapete kiratiyoyeiq.*
    Chauripe-from they-followed-them.
23. *Wegiyabarapete seratiyoyame.*
    Wegiyabara-from they-followed.
24. *Mobutapete tauya subuyeiq.*
    Mobuta-from they beat-it.
25. *Mobutapete tiyoyame.*
    Mobuta-from they-followed-them.
26. *Naniyapete ko rauya suwiyansabe.*
    Naniyape-from level drum beat-they-two.
27. *Aqau sewe kotao irarena sewe kotao irarena.*

No go back they-said go back they-said.
28. *(Mi)taq mo poriah airiuyanabe.*
There again arrows bundled.
29. *Aqau itewe itensabe insabe ite inehngaroye iraruyeiq.*
No we we-want-you want we follow-will two-said.
30. *Iraruyansabe nabokwe bokwe.*
They-said-this those-went went.
31. *Kuwipipete maru tauyan subuyame.*
Kuwipipe-from down drum they-went-beating.
32. *Naniyapete koyatiyeiq.*
Naniyape-from they-followed.
33. *Naniyapete kuwipipete tuwi ira tiyoyame.*
Naniyape-from Kuwipipe they went following.
34. *Ayaonsatate ko rauya subuyeiq.*
Ayaonsa-from down drum beating.
35. *Ayaonsatate ko iratiyoyame.*
Ayaonsa down they-followed.
36. *Momoratate ki rauya subuyeiq.*
Momorata-from there drum beating.
37. *Mumuratate ki ratiyoyame.*
Momorata-from they followed.
38. *Orenahmiyatate ki tauya subuyeiq.*
Orenamiyata-from down drum beating.
39. *Ki rauya subuyana tahpah tahpahn akeqme orenahsabitabera.*
Down drum beat flying-fox [bat] flying-fox couple Orena-tree-went-
down-in.
40. *Orenah awahipeq tupekwiyenawe.*
Orena base went-out-of-sight.
41. *Aganian akeqme pokuwe.*
Python couple went-on.
42. *Wanin ayahrapeq anotawa wani tuwana.*
Water edge big water went-down.
43. *Mi wantitaq mo sarewe mena uwana mena uwana.*
That water-on again bridge that happen that happen.
44. *Minaga awehkawaga mahtaq suno mahtaq suno uwana.*
That husband here you-come here you-come he-said.
45. *Aqau are ogesaonao enasabe uge aqau irarunsabe.*
No you gate/stile no-good I-say no she-said.
46. *Aqa suno mahbesuno uwana.*
No come here-come he-said.
47. *Aqau are ogesaonao enayabe uge irarunsabe.*
No you stile no-good I-said she-said.
48. *Pehpehera suno unsabe pehpeheransure.*

Quickly come he-said quickly-she-came.

49. *Isebeq keagurabera ebeq pokuwana anahkawa anae keaguwe pokwe*
    Over-it they-went first went-he wife behind second went went went.
pokwe pokwe bokwe.

50. *Anowansabe poriahwe mewena suwe.*
    Mother-reference arrows brought came.

51. *Nahopeq indoirarunsabe.*
    House-in put-them-down.

52. *Tunse anowawe tunse tutagowana.*
    Down mother down to-see-them.

53. *Ahre miyonsabe ehweh onaneq mire aite meyano iraruwana.*
    Wife was-there-because talk cross it-is there-from bring-her he-said.

54. *Aqa ne nega iwiyahuwe ire meogeq we wega nensabe.*
    No I I thought not took she she me-reference.

55. *Iwiyahwe kienirahreq mipeq indounsabe.*
    Though go-up-hill together there-stay.

56. *Mena mewe mipeq atena uwana.*
    That carry there put-down happen.

57. *Miyowana kiyamiyonsabe.*
    Being-there pregnant-she.

58. *Kiyamiyonsabe tagariyowana animaqme.*
    Pregnant looked-he child-bore.

59. *Mo aneq ani mon aneqani maqmaronsabe.*
    Again what child another what-child bore.

60. *Mipi awena awehkawawe pokewonsabe.*
    There gave her-husband-them left.

61. *Anowa korenime wega kiyutaq pehrah kire gire gire gire pokwe pokwe*
    Mother old-one she came-up walking go-up up up went went went.
pokwe pokwe gire.

62. *Giragowana ayahungawa miyonsabe.*
    Go-up-see daughter where-she-was.

63. *Mengarir animari maqme mitasa arena andayapipeq marena pokuwana.*
    Those children bore there put-she container-inside put left.

64. *Andayapipeq marena pokewonsabe.*
    Container-inside put left.

65. *Anowa korenime kire (ki) andayan (ki) paiyahsiruwowana mipete*
    Old woman went-up (up) container (up) threw-down there-from many
yigeritaq animari (miq), tehnsuwiq aguwahrena.
children (?), coals leaped-and-land.

66. *Tehnsuwi aguwahrena uwana.*
    Coals leap-into happen.

67. *Mena anowawe sureseragome.*
    That mother-her came-look.

68. *Tehnsuwiriya gonsabe.*
    Coals had-them.
69. *Ai abowawe ire wahn ehwehi.*
    Yipes father not small talk.
70. *Waukene animire irarena sewe(we) mipeq marena uwana.*
    Man's child said carried there put happen.
71. *Anowansabe ehwehin anine animire ehweh inehbo.*
    Mother talk person's child talk no-good.
72. *Pokuno aruwena.*
    You-go she-said.
73. *Eqmaq auwowana.*
    Like-this given-her.
74. *Pokwe bokwe bokwe bokwe bokwe bokwe bokwe bokwe bokwe bokwe*
    She left and went and went and went.
    bokwe.
75. *Mahna ahwun sahqme wahtotaq mo nehniye inehboq.*
    This gave sugar-cane short-distance again I-eat no-good.
76. *Arene nahme koragahrabe wahtotaq mo nahno iraruwanawe.*
    Your house go-see short-distance again you-eat told-her.
77. *Aqau aruwena wahtotaq mo nowana.*
    No she-said short-distance again eat.
78. *Abowawe anehen gure gure gure.*
    Father followed came came.
79. *Koragome mipi miyonsabe, mo subi suqmaqme.*
    Saw-he there she-was, then hit hit-she.
80. *Nawe parabaruwena.*
    Ate-her finished.
81. *Ayaqno mewena ayahongawa miyopi meyarowana.*
    Head he-took her-daughter where-was carried-put.
82. *Ayahongawaga wiyaena gabara tiwe tehnonahpi gisugopi wiyaena*
    Daughter taro-shoots bamboo cooked coals where-sleep taro-shoots
    gahbara tiwe.
    bamboo cook.
83. *Mibe suwowana kuriqmaq aowana kareyaruwena.*
    There threw-it leaped-up gave shouted.
84. *Nahnabaq keahngekuwehnaq mena ayahungauwa.*
    House-big pulled-out-grass that daughter.
85. *Wenahrega menahme maruwe kekiyarena pokwe bokwe bokwe bokwe*
    His-wife that-house down set-fire went went went . . .
    bokwe bokwe.
86. *Koragome anowan subisan ahnaregonsabe.*
    See mother killed signs-of-action.
87. *Anowa subiseh anahnaragonsabe ayahnsame ayaqnome.*

Mother kills signs bones head.

88. *Unahpipeq usawena pokwe bokwe bokwe.*
     String-bag-in put went went.

89. *Poqnah suwapeq ayaqno mipimaru marena wewe mipi tumiyare.*
     Potna village head there-put down she there down-was.

90. *Iraerareruq erurowe, parabagire.*
     Was-told-us always, finished.

1. There were two young men who were Manikas [supernatural people] and they were going to a singsing [festival]. They went down to Marutape for their singsing. There were two girls who wanted the two young men, and they were talking about it and they kept putting beans in their net bag. Now this is what happened. 5. The two girls watched and the boys danced and played the drum and sang and kept on doing that. The two of them followed the boys. They went on down and came to the edge of that place. The two went to the edge of the village. The girls went there. They followed them uphill. 10. From there the boys went along beating their drums—going from Marutatora they went along still beating their drums. Those two girls crossed over and followed them. They followed them and kept on following them. From Marutape—I mean from Tabanabe—they went along beating the drums. Then from Kuwabe the girls followed them. 15. From Kuwabe they followed the boys. The two young men kept on going. From Tabaiya they went on up beating the drums. The girls followed them from Tabanabe. Then from Chauripe they followed along as the boys beat their drums. 20. From Tabiyape the girls followed them. From Wegiyabara they followed along. From Chauripe they followed them. From Wegiyabara they followed them. From Mobuta they [the boys] went along beating their drums. 25. From Mobuta the girls followed them. From Naniyape they went along beating the drums. 'No, go back,' they said, 'go back home,' they said. There they stopped and bundled up some arrows. 'No, we want you, we want you so we will follow you,' the girls said. 30. When they said this, the boys went on. From Kuwipipe they went on down beating their drums. Then from Naniyape the girls followed them. From Naniyape, from Kuwipipe they went on down following them. 35. From Ayaonsata they followed them along. From Momorata they went up beating their drums. From Momorata they went along following them. Then from Orenamiyata they went down beating their drums.

As they were beating their drums, the flying fox, that flying fox couple [one of the girls and the bat who was in the form of a boy] went down into the ground at the Orena tree. 40. At the Orena tree trunk those two went out of sight. The python couple went on. They came down to the edge of a river, a big river. The python made himself into a bridge over that water. That husband of hers told her, 'You come on over here, come on over here across me.' 'No,' she said, 'you are no good as a bridge. I say, that it is not good,' she said. He said, 'Don't talk like that, come on over'; this is the way it happened. 45. 'No, you aren't any good as a bridge as I said,' she said. 'You come over here quickly,' he said, and she went over. They crossed over the river; he went first,

and his wife followed behind, and they continued to travel.
50. With reference to her mother, she brought some arrows and came. Now he went down to see his mother and to see the arrows. Because his wife was there, the mother talked crossly at him. 'Where did you bring her from?' she said. He said, 'It is really not I that thought that way, I did not take her, she is the one that wanted me.' 55. 'So we came up here together, and she stayed with me. She is the one that came and settled here with me.'

While she was there she became pregnant. She got pregnant, and she bore children. Now what sort of children were they? What sort of children were they that she bore? 60. Now her husband left them in her charge and went out.

Her old mother came walking up to visit her coming along little by little. She went up to see her daughter. Now those small children which she had, she put inside of a container and left. 65. After she put them inside the container and had gone, her old mother came along and took off the top of the container and all the children (snakes) leaped out and landed in the coals of the fire. They leaped out and landed in the coals. Then the mother [of the children] came and saw what happened. They were in the coals of the fire. 'Yipes,' she said, 'their father will not talk just a little bit.' 70. 'Those are that person's children,' she said and carried them and put them back in the container. Now the wife of that one said to the mother, 'These were this person's children and it is not good that you stay and that he talk to you. You'd better go,' she said. This is the way it was and the way she talked to her. So the old mother left and went far away. 75. The wife gave her some sugar cane and told her that it would not be good to eat the sugar cane near their place.

'You go to your home, and after a while you eat this,' she told her. But in a short distance the old mother ate the sugar cane. The father of the children followed her coming along. He saw her where she was and heard her because she was hitting the sugar cane [to break it so she could eat it]. 80. The python ate her. When he finished eating, he took her head and carried it and put it where the daughter was. Now the daughter put some taro shoots in a bamboo on the coals near where the python slept. She cooked taro shoots in a bamboo. Then she threw it down into him and scalded him, and he yelled in pain. She then pulled some grass from the roof of the house. 85. His wife then went down and set fire to the house and then she left, going and going. She looked and found the traces where the python had killed her mother. She put her mother's bones and her head inside a string bag and left that place. Then she put the head there at Potna [part of Ilakia], and that is where she stayed. This is what they have always told us. 90. The story is finished.

3. ADDENDUM TO PYTHON STORY

Another storyteller from Mobuta told the python story. This portion gives additional information.

1. Kobekuyana mipipeq peh suwansuwa suwansuwa ki giyamiyoweiq.
   Out-of-sight there just quickly quickly up became-pregnant.
2. Kiyamiyonsabe awehkawawa kiyamiyarena wahme pawena meyawa

Being-pregnant husband she-pregnant possum shot brought-gave
meyawan uwana naruq naruruweiq.
brought-gave do ate ate.

   3. *Naruqnaruruwana aigaratape we naruwena, ayahqnopeq awa, ayahq-*
        Ate-ate feet she eat, head give, head he eat (feet) head husband eat,
   nope we naruwena (aigaratapeq) ayahqnopeq awehkawa naruwena, aigara-
   lower-part wife eat, raw he-eat-eat.
   tapeq anahkawa nawa, iriya naruqnarureuweiq.

   4. *Ire rira ire rira naruq.*
        Not cooked not cooked eat.

   5. *Narurunsabe ire gahwerone tiwe nahnaneqme tiwene gahwerone, ire*
        Eat-reference not good cook thing cook good, not good, dog-like per-
   gahwerone, iyatahnsa waukeo unweiq anahkawaga.
   son said wife.

   6. *Iyatahnsa waukeunsabe ine aganiyeme minarahnsa tagariyoge are wau-*
        Dog-like person-reference I python that-like know-I you person not
   kenime ire tagariyame teyauweiq.
   know he-told-her.

   7. *Anahkawasabe, teyauwana ite waukewe ite waukewe tirane gahwere*
        Wife-reference, said we person we person cook good raw not good
   iriyane ire gahwe mugiyorahinae awehkawansabe teyauweiq.
   vomit husband she-said.

   8. *Teyauwana kiamena aganiya maqmarena wehe maqmarena parikigiyah*
        Telling pregnant python bore adder bore small-snake bore small-black-
   maqmarena rahtaba maqmarena, (maq——) min garikaironga mingarikai-
   snake bore, (bo——) those small-animals those-small-animals bore-reference
   ronga maqmarenaronsabe mena anowan gorenime kire gire gire gire gire.
   that mother old-one came came came.

   9. *Kiragome tahpahn akeq pokuyarabeq ahnara ragome ire ayaungawane*
        Come-see bat couple went track look-for not daughter track, look-for
   ahna, ragonsabe ayaungawane ahnara iregonsabe, pokwe.
   daughter track not-have, go.

   10. *Ebahpipeq kiragome minanimari ahwiruwe wenanimari mipi nahmari*
        Rocky-place look those-children embrace her-children there breasts feed
   nariyena mipi miyonsabe.
   there they-are.

   11. *Wae nainahno e irarena, anowaga ayaungawansabe ibisoweiq.*
        Oh my-mother yes she said, her-mother daughter-reference cry.

   12. *Ibisonsabe aiq mire mahbeq miyahno ena, wene mahripeq (miq)*
        Cry oh be here you-go do, her bed (here) be-here do her bed put.
   miyahno ena wene mahripeq atena.

   13. *Mahripeq atena, anowansabe animari sawiwe mewahtao aruwena*
        Bed put-her, mother children held [to shoulder] be-here said hold

sawiwe mewahtao aruwena, pokwe we topahnsahq pokunsabe, awehkawawe
stay-here said, went she sweet-potato-for went, her-husband possum went.
wahnsah pokwe.

14. *Awehkawa wahnsah pokwe uwana, (no————) anowa ngorenime*
    Her-husband possum went do, (moth————) her-mother old-one (an-
(awau soiriq) ahnden soiri karunsabe soiri runsabe awahu koreninso
other wind) plenty wind blew wind blew another old-woman was-there
miyopi iraparewe miyowana mipi tumiyaniye aruwena, wene (animari)
fire-built was-there there I-go-stay say, her (children) (chil————) daughter
(ani————) ayaungawane animarime maeqme runse irabi tumiyowana,
children carry go-down fire down-be-there, fire down-be-there that old-
irabi tumiyowana mena mengorenime (a—) aganiyen garirani maqmaron
woman (a—) python small-child born child just quickly bag-from slipped-
aninga peh suwansuwa unahpipeten giyebeguwe, giraipeq tabiguweiq.
out, fire-place was-burned.

15. *Iraipeq tabiguwana mon animarime ogamiyowana mon ani tabikunsabe*
    Fire-place burned other children alive other child burned not good is,
ire gahweruge ena, mon garir animari kabehwe awenahpeq marenawe.
other small children out-of-sight underneath put.

16. *(Moq) mo ogamiyo waukerumarine aboboraq usaroweiq.*
    (Other) other alive persons on-top put-she.

17. *Usarena ayaungawansabe mon ani tabikirana maroge iraruweiq.*
    Put daughter other child burned put said.

18. *Wae abowa ire wahn abiyahnsahnsi waukweni animire ire gahwerone*
    Wow its-father not little angry person children not good said not good
irareruwena ire gahwerone irareruwena, pokwe pokwe arene nahtepe
tell-her, go go your house go talk tell-her.
pokingae ehweh teyawena.

19. *Topahme agewe unahpipe usatena, mahmahnaga wahtotaq mari sahqme*
    Sweet-potato cooked bag put, now short down cane down eat not-good.
maru naniye inehboq.

20. *Arene nahme wahtotaq maru nahno iraruwe.*
    Your house short down eat said.

21. *Eqmaqwowana bokwe bokwe bokwe, bokwe bokwe bokwe bokwe*
    Left go go go, go go, kept going.
bokwe bokwe bokwe uwana, bokwe bokwe bokwe.

22. *Poqnabete senhpeq tahnsunah suwahpesabe kibeku gibeku.*
    Poqnabe up-hill that Tansuna village up-over go-out-of-sight.

23. *Minsawehraq sahqsahq mari noweiq.*
    That-village hit-with-stick-cane down ate.

24. *Maru nowana (awehkawawe) abowawe mo mahrawe kobaiq-maqme,*
    Down ate (husband) father other like-this came-around, look-for follow
tagowana pokiyanah ahnara kagu, no mahrawe kobaiq-maqme tagowana

track where, more like-this around-go look-for follow-tracks where do do.
pokiyanahnara kagu uwe uwe uwe uwe uwe uwe.

25. *Tuwana ruwana ruwana ruwana, mo mahrawe tubaiqmaqme tagome.*
    Go-down go-down, again like-this circle look-for.

26. *Anaipete tasahn soron sororena, pake bake bakeunsabe mibe miyahre*
    Behind-from beat cane cane-beat, tap tap tap there she-is said, quickly
    aruwena, pehpehera (ayahqnopinse) (maq) ahnuwopi ahnuwopi sebahq
    (strike-with-head) (what) her-neck her-neck struck she-there, aii do jumped.
    miyowana, wae ena gurinahnuweiq.

27. *Gurinahnuwana subiqmaqme.*
    Jumped kill-her.

28. *Ahrahnawan goreni subiqme.*
    Grandmother old killed.

29. *Nawe nawe nawe nawe nawe nawe nawe nawe, parabarena peh mora*
    Eat eat eat, finished just only head carry, head teeth grip go go go.
    ayahqno mewena, ayahqno awehbi pahqmena bokwe bokwe bokwe bokwe.

30. *Ayaungawansabe aren anome mahrawe subiqme.*
    Daughter your mother like-this killed.

31. *Naruwoge irarena, ayahqno mo (aneq) anahkawame mo reaunsabe, ire*
    Ate said, head again (what) wife more gave, not good thought, she
    gahwerone iwiyahruwena, we suwansuwa)wiyaenahgabaq) ebah pare
    quickly (Wiya-bamboo) stone heat put Wiya-bamboo cook make-good,
    arena wiyaenahgabara tiwe gahwerarena, awehkawa tahno tehn ahpi
    her-husband edge-fire edge-fire path sleep, *(kis)* bamboo there opening
    giyugonsabe, (kis) kabahra mibeq eraperaruwowana kuribena, iyahnabo
    explode, that python man *(piq)* burned-him.
    aganiye weh (piq) tabitiyonsabe.

32. *Mo ebahn koyokeqmaqme aboboraq akariyarena, nah maruwe keki-*
    Other stone take-some-fire on-top cover-him, house down set-fire, run run
    yarena, peherah peherah peherah peh- anahkawa peherah peherah tunse
    run wife run run go-down go-down go-down.
    runse runse runse.

33. *Tutagoma anowa subisa ahnara tutagoma, naino mahpisubiqme.*
    Look her-mother killed sign down-look, my-mother here-killed.

34. *Nahne irareruwena, tuwe ibisaruwena ibisaruwena, tunse poqnabeq*
    Ate she-said, down cried cried, go-down Poqnabe brought mother old
    tumena anowan gorenine (unah—) unahpi usawe ayahqnome unahpi
    (bag) bag-in put head bag-in put.
    usawe.

35. *Enduwan awaipe awahngan awaipe mari arena, are nainowe airi*
    Entuwa-tree base tree base down put, you my-mother bundle Kananda
    kanandah mahkana miyehnanawe.
    here will-be.

36. *Ine tehweh miyahno irareruwena, aganiyen ahrari miyahno irareruwena,*
     I Tewe I-am she said, python girl I-am said, her-mother bones there
anowane ayahnsa mipi matiyehranawe.
put-and-stay.
37. *Irahkiyah suwahpete turuturuqne awahwaga ayahnsa unahpeq usabe*
     Ilakia village Tultul older-brother bones bag reference put-there-stay.
matiyehre.
38. *Miran ehweh iraruq irarurunaq.*
     That talk is-said said.
39. *Parabagi.*
     Finished.

1. When they [the couples] went on out of sight, the girl very quickly got
pregnant. When she got pregnant over there, her husband went out hunting
possum and brought it in and gave it to her over and over. She would eat and
eat it. When she ate it, she would eat the lower part and he would have the head.
He would eat the top half; that is, the husband would eat the head and he would
give his wife the bottom half. He would always eat his part raw. He did not cook
it. 5. Now with reference to his eating it raw, his wife would say, 'You do not
do well, you should cook that, it is for cooking and you do not do well. You are
like a dog,' she said. He would respond, 'As for being like a dog or a person, I am
a python, and I know how to be like one, but you are a person and you do not
know.' But his wife would reply, 'We are people; we are people, and cooking is
the right way to eat it; raw is not good; one will vomit it out,' she told her
husband.

After she told him this, she being pregnant bore a python, an adder, a small
snake, and she even bore a little black snake. With reference to those small
animals which she bore, we must tell about that old mother of hers who kept on
coming and came up there. She came up to find her [daughter] and was looking
for her tracks where the bat couple had gone, but as she looked for her
daughter's tracks, she noticed that they were not the tracks of her daughter.
10. So she came on and looked at the cave where her daughter was embracing
those children, since the children were there feeding at her breast. 'Oh, it is my
mother.' 'Yes,' she said, and her mother cried for her daughter. She cried and
said, 'It's enough, you go in here first. You go in first,' and she put her on her bed
there.

Now after she had put her on her bed, that is, her mother, she held the
children, and her daughter said, 'You stay here holding the children.' And the
daughter went out for sweet potato. Her husband had gone to hunt possum.
When her husband had gone for the possum, her old mother, because the wind
blew hard, that old woman built a fire and was there; and she said, 'I'll go down
there'; and her children, I mean her daughter's children, were the ones she
carried and went down to be by the fire. When she was there by that fire, one of
the pythons, one of the small children which her daughter bore, quickly slipped
out of the string bag, and was burnt to death in the fire. 15. After he was
burned in the fire, the live ones were there and the old lady said regarding the

burned one, 'I did not do well.' So she put the burned one out of sight underneath the other small children. She put the other ones that were alive on top.

After she had done that she told her daughter where she put the dead one.
'Yipes, its father will be plenty angry; it is a person; you have not done well,'
she told her. 'You have not done well at all,' she told her; 'You better get going
to your own house,' she told her. So she put sweet potatoes cooked on the coals
in her bag, and said, 'Now it is not good that you eat the sugar cane close to
this place.' 20. 'You eat this a short distance away from the house,' she said.

She left and went and went and went. From Poqnabe uphill with reference to
Tansuna she went out of sight and disappeared. Now near the village she
pounded the sugar cane with a stick and was eating it there. As she ate it down
there, her husband, I mean the children's father, went around like this [motion-
ing in a circle], and was looking for her tracks. Again like this in a circling
way he kept looking for her tracks and kept looking for them. 25. He went
down and down and circled and looked for her. And over behind there she was
beating the sugar cane [against something]. He heard the tap tap tap, and
could tell where she was. Quickly he struck (with his head) at her in the neck.
'Aiii,' she cried and jumped. As she jumped, he killed her. He killed that old
grandmother and then ate her. He ate her, and when he was finished, he took
only the head back. He gripped the head in his teeth and he went on back.

30. He told her daughter, 'I killed and ate your mother like this.' And he gave
her head to his wife. 'You did not do well,' she thought. She quickly heated a
stone and put it there in a Wiya bamboo preparing it well. When her husband
was sleeping there at the edge of the fire, she put the open end of the bamboo
toward him and then it exploded. It burned that python-man. She took another
stone from the fire and covered him with that. Then she went down and set fire
to the house. Then she ran off, that wife, and went on down.

She looked and looked and found the signs where her mother was killed. 'He
killed my mother here and ate her,' she said, and then down there she cried
and cried, and went and brought the head to Poqnabe, and put it in a string
bag. 35. She then put it there at the base of the Entuwa—at the base of a tree.
'You are my mother in this bundle, and will be Kananda [the daughter's name]
and there it will be. I am Tewe [her mother's name],' she said. 'I am a python-
girl,' she said. So she put her mother's bones there. The Tultul's older brother
from Ilakia put the bones in a bag, and they are still there. This is a story from
long ago. It is now finished.

4. OLDER BROTHER STEALS WIFE OF YOUNGER

1. *Awahwaga abakawan giweq mena wah tagorogeq.*
   Older-brother younger-brother up-took with possum look-at.
2. *Wah tagarogeq ireta kiragano irarunsabe awahngapeq gire gire gire*
   Possum look-at beyond went-up to-look-said tree-place went-up up up
abogaipeq giwiyowana.
tree-top climb.

3. *Abogaipeq giwiyowana ahtapo irarunsabe irerebeq senahpeq kiragano*
   Tree-top climb road-where he-said on-beyond on-top go-up-look said.
irarunsabe.
4. *Senapeq kira gano irarunsabe.*
   On-top go-up look he-said.
5. *Awahngatapeq kire kire uwana.*
   Tree-place went-up went-up happen.
6. *Mo mitate ahtapo uwana, irerebeq kira gano irarunsabe.*
   More there-from path where-is-it, beyond go-up look he-said.
7. *Irerebe ki uwana nahga kirasuqmaqme.*
   Beyond up happen vine cut-off.
8. *Abakawa saberapeq awowana awena.*
   Younger-brother in-the-air left go-away.
9. *Wene ahre abakawane ahre awahwaga meyowe ire.*
   His wife younger-brother wife older-brother took it-is-said.
10. *Meyowana abakawa mo subi suwena.*
    He-took-her younger-brother again beat him.
11. *Awahwaga meyoweq.*
    Older-brother took.
12. *Parabagiq.*
    It is finished.

1. The older brother took his younger brother with him to look for possums. When they were looking for possums, the older brother told the younger to go on farther, so he went on up. He climbed up a tree and said, 'Where is [the possum's] path?' And the older brother told him to go on up some more and look. 'Go on up and look,' he said. 5. He went and went up the tree. Again from there he asked where [the possum] was, and he told him to go on up farther and look. He went on up farther, and he [the older brother] cut off the vine [that the younger brother used in climbing]. He left his younger brother suspended there in the air. Then the older brother took his younger brother's wife it is said. 10. He took her and killed his younger brother. The older brother took her. The story is finished.

5. Two Boys Get Married

1. *Tehrehwe tehrehwe anowane awahmbora tote tiyowana.*
   First first mother large intestines in-sight-came.
2. *Nehnowone senaga moronenaq nahnonsabe.*
   My-mother that cut-off eat.
3. *Niyurate samire arawe kamoro ehwininekonounsabe.*
   My-skin it-is how cut give.
4. *Kamoruniyo uwana.*
   You-cut-give-me happen.

5. *Niyurate saneuwe pokuwe.*
   My-skin part left.
6. *Monanson suwapeq pokuwe.*
   Another village went.
7. *Pokunsabe wen ani animehrewe toqme sehpiwe sehpiwe sehpiwe.*
   Went her child boy-two blade-grass break break break.
sehpiwe sehpiwe.
8. *Toqme sehpiwe sehpiwe toqme sehpiwe.*
   Blade break break blade break.
9. *Ayah tabanininera naenone nahtaq nahtaq nahtaq nahtaq nahtarena.*
   Hand bundle my-mother breast breast breast.
10. *Toparuwoyana kowe kuwarena sene awahndame paruq.*
    Grass-shoot-two go turn-back their testicles shoot.
11. *Naenone nahtaq nahtaq nahtarena mobaruwowana kowe kuwarena*
    My-mother breast breast breast-say again-shoot go turn-back his testicles
wene awahnda me barurunsabe.
there shoot.
12. *Mora koukuwana naenone nahtarena paruwowana peherah anowane*
    One went my-mother breast-on he-shoot go his-mother breast landed
nahtaq kensoq miyowe ire.
there say.
13. *Kensoq miyonsabe nenaningae iyarena arutabo iruwe ire.*
    Landed there my-child-it-is she-said sorry she-said say.
14. *Arutabo iruwana wen animararewe senemensamehnsa mewera pokuwe*
    Lonesome they-are her children-two their-things took went and went
bokwe bokwe bokwe bokwe.
and went.
15. *Iyah nahtuwo koragoyana (nahberiq) nahberiyonsebe.*
    Iya [bird] house-broken down-went-look-two (house) house-build.
16. *Nah beriyonsabe (mi)pe sugoye ire.*
    House build there slept say.
17. *Mowaukwewe wen animari nahpi sahrena pokuwe.*
    Another-person his children house-in plenty went.
18. *Koragome nahn konsebe soqme koragome animairare.*
    Went-look house has search went-look boy-two.
19. *Mipeq miyoyansabe mewe mahbe sitena meriq mena nahopeq merowe*
    There stay carry here came carry there house put say.
ire.
20. *Nahopeq merena anahkawansabe kerame unahme peh mirawe mahbe*
    House put his-wife band string-bag just like-this here put-down.
sahunounsabe.
21. *Mirawe auwana mahbiruwe mahpeq marena.*
    Like-this gave this-way outside did.

22. Mo sen anite aiten anitebo iraruwana.
Another he child-two where anyway said.
23. Pehipete mewe mahbiraroge irareruwena uwana.
Just-place carry young-men-made said happen.
24. Aiqmire awahnga ariranae iraarena sonsoq.
Go-we tree cut-top-out said make-garden.
25. Sonsoq marena mo siwiqmi uwara.
Garden make another came along.
26. Awahngatapeq kiegiye uwe wayao ariqmarera.
Tree climb-up do Wayao cut-top-did.
27. Mahbi nahngege orugege arugegena awahngame ayauwe ire.
Young-men singing *Orugege Arugegena* tree topping say.
28. Awahngame ayauwanawe ahraregaume awaipete tagariyowe ire.
Tree top girls-are base saw-them say.
29. Tagariyowara awahngame ayauwana ne sese gariq mahbi geraniye.
Saw tree top I those small young-men I-want.
30. Ne mahn gariq mahbi geraniye iraruwe ire.
I this small young-man I-want said say.
31. Iraruwana mon gariq ahrariga naenahnoreh mowe suwe ayoakaq
Said other small girl my-sister dear Suwi-bird feathers small young-man
kariq mahbiwe keraniye.
I-want.
32. Nega keraniye iraruwe ire.
I I-want said say.
33. Iraruwana anahnowahga nega geraniye ume arega irarenoera ehweh
Said her-sister I want do you tell-them talk do talk do say.
uwe ehweh uye ire.
34. Ehweh uyana anahnowaga mahbigauga maro towai kiwewe awaebi
Talk two sister young-men put cassowary bone set-base pierce say.
pearowe ire.
35. Awaebi pearowana tunserunse maru patorarirowe ire.
Base pierce come-down down pierced say.
36. Marupatorariwowana menawe ire pabuqmena kureyotaq menahwe
Down-pierced that not dirty G-string groom came say.
suwe ire.
37. Parabagire.
Finished.

1. Once in the early days, a certain mother's large intestines had come out. 'Mother, cut that off, so we can eat it.' 'But it is my skin, how can I cut if off, and give it to you?' 'You cut it and give it,' her children said. 5. 'It is my skin, and a part of me,' she said, and went away. She went away to another village. When she went away, her two sons broke off blades of grass and kept breaking off more.

They continued to break off spears of grass, and when they had a big bundle of them [so they could hold them with two hands], they had it in mind to shoot the blade at their mother's breast. 10. The two of them would shoot the spears of grass at her, and the spears would go and then turn back and hit the boys in the testicles. They would say, 'At my mother's breasts, at my mother's breasts,' and shoot some more; but the blades would turn back and hit them in their own testicles. The boys wanted a blade of grass to hit her on the breast, and so they continued to shoot and one did land on her breast, they say. When it landed there, she said, 'It is my children for sure doing that,' and she was very sorry, they say.

When her children became lonesome, they took up their belongings and left and went and went and went. 15. They went and looked for a broken down Iya [bird] nest, and fixed it up. They fixed up a house and slept there, it is said. Now another person came along to where the two boys were in that house. As he looked, he searched in the house and found the two boys. They were there, and he took and brought them to his place and put them down in his house.

20. When they were settled in his house, he told his wife, 'You put here arm and leg bands, and string bags.' He acted on them outside in this way [so the boys were not seen]. His wife asked him, 'Where do these two young people come from anyway?' 'Oh, they just came, and they are now our young men,' he told her. 'Let us go and top some of the trees,' he said, 'and make a garden.'

25. While they made the garden some others came. They [the two boys] climbed up to the top of the tree and cut out the top of the Wayao tree. While the young men were up there they were singing 'Orugege Arugegena,' they say. When they were cutting out tops of the trees, some girls saw them from the base of the tree. While they were looking at them as they were chopping in the tree, one of them said, 'I want those young fellows.' 30. 'I want this small person,' she said. When she said this, the other young girl said, 'My dear sister, I want the one that has the Chuwi bird feathers. I want him,' she said. The two said this, and her sister replied, 'Yes, I want him. You talk to them about it.'

The two argued about it, they say. As the two argued, they set cassowary bones at the base of the tree to wound them. 35. When they came down, it pierced them, they say. At the time that they were wounded, they were so young that their G-strings were not even dirty yet. Then those fellows came to be married young men, they say. The story is finished.

6. Two Brothers Separate

1. Mo waukwega awahwareh abakawarehga.
   Other man older younger.
2. Abakawaga wahnsahq bokuwana.
   Younger possum-get hunt.
3. Wahnsah pokuwana arupibiunsabe, wahnsah pokuwana arupibiunsabe.
   Possum went hungry, possum went got-hungry.
4. Awahwane sopipete awahwane sopipete anotah nirupibere ena.
   Older garden older garden big hungry is.

5. *Awahwa poerahq subiniyena, irasabetahq pahoyabetahq kabiyansa-*
   Older pig I-kill, fire-wood-get greens cane-shoots are, sweet-potato are,
   batahq ena, topahnsahq ena, irabarena ahbiyah sanoniniye poerahq subi
   build-fire tomorrow mumu-make pig kill do.
   sumaqme.
6. *Sanoniniye irarena topahnsabe irayabe kabarebonsabe.*
   Mumu-make-I build-fire sweet-potato wood look-for.
7. *Abakawawe saekapeq pokuwe.*
   Younger forest went.
8. *Wahnsabatahrewowana arupibiunsabe sahqatewe awahwane sotate*
   Possum-hunt hungry-get sugar-cane older garden cane take-eat.
   sahqtewe nonsabe.
9. *Awahwawe penguana kire sotapeq kiragowana, sahq atewe nonsabe*
   Older evening went-up garden looked, sugar-cane took ate sugar-cane
   sahq atewen niyatagiyena.
   took saw.
10. *Tagiyena nene sota sahq mensega atewe nehramo.*
    Saw my garden cane who took ate-it.
11. *Sahqnesega atewe nerapomo unwana ena, ehweh ena anotah ehweh unsabe.*
    Sugar-cane who took-ate anyway did, talk do big talk happen.
12. *Abakawaga asume ire suwogeq ire ranahreipeq suwogeq aborahq*
    Younger pulp not throw-away not thicket throw in-sight pulp put.
    asume maroge.
13. *Anonsahqme naruwoge iraruwe ire.*
    Big-cane ate said say.
14. *Aneq niye atewe nahno.*
    Why take you eat.
15. *Aneniye atewe nahno.*
    I take eat.
16. *Ine mokakeyabe sahqme matiyoge nirupibinakake nana.*
    I someday sugar-cane give hungry eat.
17. *Anesabe iragwe nahno ena, anota ehwehwe abiyahnsansasunsabe.*
    Why uncooked eat did, big talk older-brother-frown.
18. *Awahwaga anota abiyahnsasunsabe.*
    Older big frown.
19. *Abakawawe pokwe bokwe bokwe bokwe bokwe uwana.*
    Younger went and went and went.
20. *Sahunsuwahpeq sebeq, mobuta (maq⸺) manikanga sahunsuwahpeq*
    Chaun other-side-water, Mobuta (Ma⸺) Manika Chaun-village went.
    pokunsabe.
21. *Awahwawe poerahqme takatare subiq marena tatare poerahq subiq*
    Older pig two killed down-put two pig killed put.
    marena.

22. *Nanibaq ehig miyaro subiqme nabiniboq.*
    My-brother where is kill give-eat.
23. *Aiqmiyaro uwanawe.*
    Where is-he?
24. *Arega anotah ehweh abiyahnsa anindahnayabe, ne pokuge.*
    You big talk frown put-on-me, I left.
25. *Poerahq arebataq nahno irareruwana, pokuwe pokwe pokwe bokwe*
    Pig you eat said, went and went and went.
    bokwe bokwe bokwe bokwe bokwe.
26. *Tunse tunse tunse tunse tunse tunse tunse.*
    He-went-down and down and down.
27. *Tunse awahronah suwahpete tumiyowana sensebeq awahronah suwah-*
    He-went-down Awalarosa village other-side over Awalarosa village
    peq mahberiyopeq mire marapeqnsebeq agahkahmahtahbah suwahpeq
    this-side it-is down-hill Agakamataba village there he-was.
    mipipeq miyowana.
28. *Awahwawe ibisawena abakawansabe nirutaboi ire irarena.*
    Older cried younger sorry said say.
29. *Ibisawena tunse poerahqme mewe kabahrapipe tiwe mewena.*
    Cried went-down pig carried bamboo-in cooked carried.
30. *Abakawa nawina abakawa marunawiniyena kabahrapipe tiwe mewena.*
    Younger give-him younger down-give bamboo-in cooked carried.
31. *Pokwe bokwe bokwe bokwe bokwe bokwe bokwe bokwe, bokwe bokwe*
    Went and went and went (older—younger) my-older-one sugar-cane
    (awahwagawe—abakawagawe) nenuwabiyao sahrurahnsabepoq pehriyah-
    just-there my-older-brother sugar-cane just-there he sang did.
    sabeyabe nenuwahbiyaho sahrurahsabepo pehriyahsabeyabe ena igongo
    uwana.
32. *Awahwaga poerahqme mahtaq subiniyena.*
    Older pig here kill-I.
33. *Subiniyena uraugatake pokuraona.*
    Kill-I-it look-at left.
34. *Poerahqme mahna (nawe) mewe nabiyoqmena tugegiweyo giweyo*
    Pig this (?) carry brought brought-down came came happen.
    giweyo uwana.
35. *Marako abiqme mo sinorapete tumeyo kiweyo kiweyo kiweyo uwana.*
    Ground name other Chinorape come-down come-up come come did.
36. *Kake mozino kake mozino kake mozino usabe.*
    [Fore] 'You eat it.'
37. *Are monahno are nahno are mo nahno irarunsabe.*
    You eat you eat you again eat he-told-him.
38. *Saho kambare suwansuwa irahne.*
    Fore not quickly understand.

39. Sahon ehwehme suansua irahne nanibaq pehmora wehika tehtare
Fore talk quickly understand my-younger just-one day two day you-
wehika miyahneyabe urahwe.
here be.
40. Sahone ehwehme ibora suansuwa irahneq irareruwana.
Fore talk today quickly understand tell-him.
41. Poerahqme we awahwa ire niya.
Pig his older not give.
42. Awahwa ire niya peh poerahq maru kuwemaqme.
Older not give just pig down split-off.
43. Kabahra kuwaqmaqme suwowana awaka wah miyowana.
Bamboo split-off throw-away meat possum was-there.
44. Auga poerahq miyowana.
Skin pig there.
45. Ahnde karekaironga mengamehnga kabara wah ebahnga kireq poerahq
Plenty animals animals birds possums ground-hogs wild-cat pig plenty
ahnde miyowana tira.
there cooked.
46. Poerahka ahnde mi mengamehnga ukuwana miyonsabe.
Pig plenty of animals be there.
47. Nondapiyahnga kabahranga awahu gabahra (taru) ogowana, ogowana
Greens bamboo unused bamboo (?) new, new greens more new.
nondapiahga mo ogowana.
48. Tiyahqme tiyahsahqme maru uqmarowana biyahno gowana.
Tiya-greens Tiyacha-greens down-hill stick-in ground greens.
49. Biyahgowana mena ibisabe ibisabe ibisabe ibisabe abakawa nirutaboi
Cane that cry and cry and cry younger lonesome there cry cry.
ire ena ibisabe ibisabe ibisabe.
50. Mipimarena ibisabi mipimarena tuwe kuwarena poerahq maru guwasuq-
Put-down cry put-down down-hill came pig down broke-up throw-away.
maqme suwowana.
51. (Po—) ogamiyonsabe poerahq maringa ogamiyonsabewe mipeq
(Er—) alive pig they alive-become there do-nothing say.
kierubaguwe ire.
52. Ehweh tainobin abo teniq karamoga.
Talk Tainobi father say Karamo.
53. Parabagi.
Finished.

1. Once there were two young men, an older and a younger brother. The younger brother went out to hunt possums. As he was hunting possums, he got hungry. At his older brother's garden he got very hungry. 5. Now his older brother had said, 'I'll kill a pig and get firewood and some greens and cane shoots

and sweet potato, build a fire, and tomorrow I'll make a mumu [oven-pit in the ground], and I'll kill a pig. I'll make a mumu so I'll build a fire and get sweet potatoes and wood.'

The younger brother had gone to the forest. When he was hunting for possums, he got hungry, and he took some sugar cane from his older brother's garden. He took the sugar cane and ate it up. His older brother went up there in the evening and looked at his garden; he saw that some sugar cane had been taken and eaten. 10. When he saw it, he said, 'Who took and ate it? Who took the sugar cane and ate it anyway?' he shouted out. His younger brother had not thrown away the pulp of the sugar cane into the thicket, but had left it in sight. He had eaten a lot of sugar cane, they say. His brother said, 'Why did you take it and eat it?' 15. 'Why did you take it and eat it? Sometime I'll want that sugar cane. Sometime I'll be hungry and want to eat it. Why did you eat it?' The older brother shouted, and was very angry. He was very very angry. The younger brother went and went and went.

20. He went to the village of Chaun on the other side of the river where the early Mobuta people lived. Now the older brother killed two pigs and he put them down there. 'Where is my younger brother,' he said. 'I want to give him these pigs to eat that I have killed. Where is he?' The younger brother said, 'You yelled at me and got mad at me, so I left.' 25. 'Well you just eat this pig,' he told him. But he went and went and went. He went down down down.

He went down to the village of Awalarosa on the other side there at Awalarosa; it is on this side down hill from Agakamataba, that is where he stayed. The older brother cried for the younger brother and was lonesome for him, it is said. He cried and he went down and carried the pig cooked in the bamboo. 30. He wanted to give this to his younger brother so he went down to give it to him carrying it cooked in bamboo. He went a long way and that older brother—I mean the younger brother—sang as he went, 'Oh my older brother, oh the sugar cane, oh my older brother the sugar cane,' etc. His older brother had said, 'I will kill a pig here. I'll kill it and then he will see it,' and he left.

He carried this pig along and brought it and came down with it. 35. He came down to the place where it is named Chinorape and called out, 'Come out and get it, come out and get it.' He even used Fore talk and said, 'You eat it. You go ahead and eat it,' he told him. The Fore is hard to understand but he quickly learned it. 'Fore talk is quickly understood, my brother, you be there only one or two days.' 40. 'Fore talk can be understood in a day,' he told him. His older brother didn't give him the pig; the older brother didn't give it, he just brought it down and split off some bamboo.

He split off the bamboo and threw it and some possum meat was there. Pig skin was there. 45. Plenty of animals, birds, possums, ground hogs, wild cats, pigs, plenty of animals were there to be cooked, pigs and plenty of those animals were there. Greens and bamboos and unused bamboo and other things came up, more and more new vegetables came into being [because he threw these pieces of the bamboo around]. Tiya greens and Tiyacha greens were stuck in the ground and sugar cane came up. After the cane came up, he cried and cried because he was lonesome for his younger brother. 50. He put these things down there, and he cried, and when he cried, all of these things came up and he carried and put them down there, broke the bamboo up and threw it down, and then all of these kinds of animals came alive; the pig came alive and these other things. This is what Tainobi's father told me—Karamo is the one. The story is finished.

7. TWO BROTHERS AND AN OLD WOMAN

1. Manika abarahrega wahnsarewoyana.
   Manika brothers possum-to-get.

2. Pehngunsabe pehnguwe ibokakaq ibonkakaruwe pehngunsube aiq
   Darkness dark rain-and rain-and-is darkness where stay-two-shall.
miyayankoyoera.

3. Awahnga awaipeq ababagorapipeq sewiyoyana.
   Tree-base old dead-one-place they-were-two.

4. Anabo gorenime sure seragome wene nahopeq miyoyansabe.
   That old-woman came came-look her house were-two.

5. Minawe itene ababagora mire eta.
   That our old-dead-tree it-is-two said.

6. Mipinsemiyayo mirarena se ehweh uwarawe itenowah paipeq mire eta.
   There-they-stay two-said their talk happen our-mother without-cause that
is-said.

7. Awahnga ahpeq mire eta sewiyowe iraruyansabe.
   Tree shade two said they-two said-two.

8. E, aruwena mewe nahopeq sitena.
   Yes, she-said carry house they-were.

9. Topahme nabiqnabiq aritena.
   Food prepared gave-two.

10. Mipimewato aruwena pimewato aruwena.
   There-be-two she-said there-be said.

11. Pokuwarena kaqabaqme sugeritena pokuwe.
   She-left under-bark-cape slept-two she-went.

12. Ayahnobeq insameq wene ayahnobeq insameq kaweruwena sure.
   Finger sharpen she fingers sharpen made-them-good came.

13. Seniobauq, maniobauq ayahnobe banturena, mahripeqme wene
   Chenobau, Maniobau finger hit-down, bed her fingers there strike.
ayahnobeq meya sabiyome.

14. Ebahmari abawari bibiq mipeq akariarera, pokuyana, mitaqme
   Rocks dead-wood place there covered, went, there finger clubbed
ayahnobeq sawewena ayahnobe sawewena.
fingers clubbed.

15. Qmqmm ena wene ayahnobe irayabe ayahnkaran kosoyowe ire.
   Oh-oh said she fingers fire hand pull-back said.

16. Koyowena kabehweragome mipeq ebahmari abawari konsabe.
   Pull-back lift-up-look there rocks dead-wood was.

17. *Airagoyan aniteyabe miraugwamo aruwena.*
Where-go two-children anyway she-said.

18. *Mina ruwekuwe ahnarah araqmena kure koragome.*
Those were-gone tracks tracking went go-look-for.

19. *Ahtapeq pokuyansabe kegaqmena kegaqmena paerah kure koragome.*
Path went chased chased ran went go-look desired-to-catch happen.
tatoraniyena uwena.

20. *Sundsabe seneiyame parikiwera, tahtorahrauwena kunsabe.*
Come their-dog rope-around-neck, try-catch came.

21. *Awaibi seneiya mere sariya tera.*
Tree-base their-dog is tied up.

22. *Mahtaq sinawe.*
Here she-came.

23. *Mobe pawiye inehbo awah ubukuwo irarena mere awaipeq mere*
Body bite no-good crotch bite they-said went base that-one tied there went.
sari atera pokuwe.

24. *Wayaotaba pehpeherah pokuwe.*
Wayao-big fast-walk went.

25. *Awahwawe ebeq pokuwanawe abakawawe anowan goreninga iyanobo*
Older-brother first went younger-brother mother old that-one old gave.
koreninga awu.

26. *Topahmarime awahwawe sahbe kabehwe sahbe kabehwe kopipeq*
Sweet-potato older sugar-cane put sugar-cane put away threw.
suwowanawe.

27. *Abakawawe naruqnaruqrewowe ire.*
Younger had-eaten they-say.

28. *Naruqnaruqunsebe naniyo naniyo unsabe are na wena nire arena*
As-two-eating give-eat give-eat happen you ate I want your I want he-
wena nire iraruwanawe, naniyo naniyounsabe uwana.
said, give-eat give-eat happen.

29. *Abakawawe ahnde ire gariq nonsabe.*
Younger plenty not good ate.

30. *Mitate ire gariq newon powana, awahwa anonata ebeq paera.*
There-from not good eat pounce-on, older big first travel.

31. *Awahngatapeq wayaon aberapeq paerah pokuwanawe.*
Tree Wayao top travel go.

32. *Abakawawe kigambaruq mena awaeipeq, kigambaruq mena awaeperena.*
Younger go-up-slide that base, up-slide-back that base-said.

33. *Abakawaweme subiniena sume.*
Younger kill-want came.

34. *Wene iyanga ponsabe peh awahipeq akahpi paepi.*
His dog it just crotch middle bit.

35. *Awaipeq tambehreh iyah ruweukuwe ire.*

Base Tambara banana hid they-say.

36. *Abakawawe tuweukuwanawe, sene iyame awaipeq wayaun awae*
Younger down-hid, their dog base Wayao base hidden.
ukuweire.

37. *Kuwanawe awahwawe wayaune wahte kabehrehwena abogaipeq peh*
Stay older Wayao skirt lift-up top just up-there stay they-say.
kieruba akuwe ire.

1. Two Manika brothers went out to hunt possums. Because it got dark and started to rain, the two said, 'Where shall we stay because of the darkness and rain?' The two of them were at the base of an old dead tree. An old woman came and she looked and the two were at her house. 5. 'That is our old dead tree,' the two said. 'Our mother, we are just here with nothing in mind,' they said. The tree is a shelter is what they indicated. That's why they were there. 'Oh, yes,' she said, and took them into the house.

She gave the two of them sweet potato that had been prepared for eating. 10. 'You two just be there,' she said. Then she left, and the two slept under a bark cloth, and she went. She sharpened her finger nails, she sharpened her finger nails, making them very sharp, and then came. 'Chenobau, Maniobau,' she said, and struck downward with her fingers. She stabbed into the bed with her fingers. They had put rocks and dead wood there and covered them over and left when she was stabbing there with her fingers.

15. 'Oh, oh,' she said as her fingers burned like fire, and she pulled back her hand, it is said. She pulled back [the covers] and lifted them up to look and there were rocks and dead wood there. 'Where have those two gone anyway?' she said. The two had gone out of sight so she went tracking them and looking for them. She chased and chased along the path, running and looking for them and wanted to catch them.

20. When she came, their dog was there with rope around his neck. She tried to catch them as she came. Their dog was tied at the base of the tree. When she came, they said, 'Don't just bite her body, bite her in the crotch'; that is what they told the one tied there, and they left. They went quickly to the big Wayao tree. 25. The older brother went first, but the old lady had given that to the younger brother.

The older brother had thrown the sweet potatoes out of sight into the sugar cane pulp. The younger brother had eaten and eaten, they say. In connection with his eating so much he said, 'Give me what is yours, I want it,' he said to him. 'Give it to me to eat, give it to me;' and he kept saying it. 30. But it was not good to eat of those things, for that person would pounce on him.

The older brother traveled a long way ahead. He went up to the top of the Wayao tree. The younger brother would try to go up and slide back, he'd go up a way and slide back to the base of the tree. Now she wanted to kill that younger brother when she came. His dog bit her just in the middle of the crotch. 35. At the base of the Tambara banana tree he hid, they say. The younger brother hid down there and their dog was there at the base of the Wayao tree. The younger one stayed there and the older lifted up the skirt of the Wayao tree and was up there in the top of it just staying there quietly doing nothing.

8. CONTACT WITH THE SPIRIT WORLD

1. *Wehroga teninsabe.*
   Wairo told-me.
2. *Mo mowaukwe wahnsabatahq.*
   Another another-man possum-hunt.
3. *Wahnsabatahq saekahpeq pokuwana saekahpeq pokuwena anotahn*
   Possum-hunt forest he-went forest he-went big rain.
   ibonsabe.
4. *Sahbonan kakaruwe.*
   Mist-in was.
5. *Ahnden ibonsunsabe saekahpe ibosubunsabe.*
   Plenty rain-came-down forest rained.
6. *Sure sure sure sure.*
   Came came came.
7. *Anomarako awai tanahgogopeq isena (tabigaq) naniyahpete saberi-*
   Large-area base Tanagogo there-side (?) Naniyape-from other-side
   yopeq ungumari tagaraga ona ungum sopiq marakoe mitare teawini.
   pines see-always where pine garden around there is I-talk.
8. *Tabigarabeq a—tanahgogopeq niwe tagirana mo marakon awiruq.*
   Tabigara er—Tanagogo, I forgot another ground name.
9. *Tanahgogopeq ungun awaipeq ibonsunsabe ungun awaipeq miyowana;*
   Tanagogo pine base rain-comes pine base was-there;
10. *Mo wahnsaga mo wahnsaga ire, awahngane nene nahne.*
    Other spirit other spirit not, tree my house.
11. *Nene nah mire anesabe mipeq miahnana ahnde soeri iro.*
    My house it-is why there you-are plenty wind blow.
12. *Ahnde soeririro ena se wenega iyahnabonensabe wene yahnebninsabe*
    Plenty wind-blow do there he friend his friend came.
    maho.
13. *Maho uwana ne iwiyahu awahnga awaipere iwiyahena miyoge.*
    Come happen I think tree base thought be.
14. *Mo waukega mahbete ogamiyo waukega iraruwana, wahnsagawe ire*
    Other person from-here living person said, spirit not tree base my house.
    awahngan awai nene nahne.
15. *Nene nahne iraruweiq.*
    My house he-said.
16. *Iraruwana abakawaga (aq—) mo wene yahnaboninga pukiya waukega*
    He-said younger-brother (er—) other his friend dead person my-house
    nenahopeq kibiangabo miyahnoena;
    stay-you you-go first;

17. Wene nahopeq miyo mowatoweiq.
  His house there stayed.

18. Mowatowana we we mipeq miyonsabe weniyahnabo ahqapena
  Stayed his his there were-there two-friend not-that spirit his-friend
wahnsaga weniyahnabo wahnsaga kiraqmaqme topahme nawena;
spirit up-went sweet-potato gave-eat;

19. Mo waukwega nahopeq sinahweq.
  Again person house came.

20. Wene boriyah mehpete boriyah nahopeq mo pahnahwe.
  His arrows door arrows house more shoot.

21. Ire soriwiyo ire meyo pehragahno.
  Not pull-out not take just-look.

22. Pehweraganana we yahnaboni we wene kiweyahno iraq.
  Just-look his friend he he can-take he-said.

23. Ogamiyo waukeyabe teyauweiq.
  Alive person he-told-him.

24. Ogamiyo waukega teyauwana ire irasa ogamiyo waukega ire irasa peh
  Alive person said not heed alive person not heed just he he thought
we wega iwiyahwe kawe poriahko meyoweiq.
good arrow take.

25. Poriyahgo meyowana, nemetaq teyaume anere ehweh teyango.
  Arrow take, I-just told what talk I-tell-you.

26. Mo waukene poriyahwe meanaboq peh robaroba miyahno.
  Other person arrows no-good just inactive be-there.

27. Tutuwe miyahno teyaume anere ehweh tayaugo uwana;
  Sit-down be-there I-told-you what talk I-told-you happen;

28. Ahnde wahnsane nahopeq ira bareyarowana ahnde nku aunuwe.
  Plenty spirits house fire build plenty smoke [Fore word].

29. Marako ipekakaq aununsabe arerega poriyah aebo meyahnana, aunire
  Ground go-on smoking you arrow stole took, smoking smoking is spirit
aunire ena wahnsagawe ehweh ire iraruweiq.
talk say said.

30. Wene iyahneboninka ehweh ire anesabe meyahnouwana ne metate
  His friend talk say why take-them I just told-you.
awenawe.

31. Mo waukega poriah mehpehtate mo banabe.
  Another man arrow door-way more shoot.

32. Baruwanawe ire soriwiyo ire meyo irarugeq.
  Shoot not pull-out not take I-told-you.

33. Nesebe meyahno iraruwana;
  Why you-take he-said;

34. Ne nirutaboirinsabe meyogeq poriyahyabe nirutaboirinsabe meyogeq
  I wanted-to take arrow wanted I-took I arrows want took he-said.

ne poriyahyabe ninsabe meyogeq iraruweiq.

35. *Iraruwana ire gawerone suwo.*
    He-said not good throw-them.

36. *Suwehnana yahnabo waukega meyahnowena suwowana poriyahwe*
    Threw that person took throw arrows wild-cat person arrows happen,
    kireq waukwena poriyah uwana, kireq waukena poriyah uwana suwowana;
    wild-cat person arrow happen threw;

37. *Kireq waukena wene boriyah mewena;*
    Wild-cat person his arrow took-went;

38. *Wene wahriq monkeq pagnahipeq mehpehtetahnsa mahrataq mo*
    His bed other room door-way-from here-on other shot;
    baruwowana;

39. *Serabete meyowana mewe tuparuwowana mewena wene wahripeq*
    There-on from-take carry throw-with-hand carry his bed stayed.
    kobiyoweiq.

40. *Wene wahripeq kowena uwana ne iwiyahome wahnsaga ehweh nera.*
    His bed stay happen I think spirit talk is.

41. *Wahnsaga ehweh (ne) nawe.*
    Spirit talk (I?) is.

42. *Newiyah mo waukega kahnga igoarehre.*
    I-think other person trap set.

43. *Wene ire ire wahne ahtaq mire waukwenine ahtarirana kahnga*
    He not not possum path on person path-on trap set.
    igoarehreq.

44. *Mokake mokake mokake nahgaqehya tag(u)we kambehrekinaraq*
    Someday other-time other-time vine get-old will-rot go-off like-this
    parawe mahrewe sahta suwo suraq suwo.
    club throw break throw.

45. *Sura suweinana mora nahga kahnaraq pariyahno anotahn gatarate*
    Break come-loose one vine have go-off big log set that log soft be.
    igoareh min gatawe mareq mareruwe.

46. *Kaweraginarahq motaq pariyahno.*
    Good-make little-while go-off.

47. *Mo wahnsa teyawena, mo wahnsaga miraoro miraruwana kireqme*
    Other spirit he-told, other spirit you-did-it do-it wild-cat not talk not
    ire ehwehme ire irasa pehsuwansuwa pehpaerah pokuarena;
    heed quick run went;

48. *Pahq waukwega igoarowana;*
    Just person set-trap;

49. *Kahngap igowarowana ahniporeh ki ehwehnseunsabe kireqme poku-*
    Trap set soon wild-cat talk wild-cat went other person trap sprung.
    warena mo waukwene kahngapiko pehriyonsabe.

50. Ne ehweh mena kopipete tagariyarauga arega gahngan igowa-
My talk that hidden I-saw you trap set-it I-saw.
taunana tagaraume.
51. Wene so wene so ahnahnsahraq weneso ahnahnsahraq igowa-
His garden his garden edge his-garden edge set he went-off did left.
tahune we pariyeni ena pokire.
52. Mekewewe keqme bokuno wahnsagawe ogamiyo waukwe teyaunsabe.
Go-out get go spirit alive person told-him.
53. Kayarena wahnsaga nahopeq kayarena pokwe.
Stay spirit house stay leave.
54. Kigeqmena kahngapite kigeqmena tunserunse.
Get-out noose-trap get-out down-came.
55. Mo mobuta waukweyabe mobuta manikansabe aqau, ne mirawe
Other Mobuta person Mobuta Manika no, I like-that spirit house stay
wahnsane nahpipeq kayarena suge.
sleep.
56. Suge mahngireqme nene gahngapi (su) pariyasabe.
Sleep this-wild-cat my trap (?) go-off.
57. Mewena suwe ire ahrerome ire nahwo peh weh arerego tiwe nahno
Bring came not woman not give just man you cook eat man cook eat
wehga tiwe nahrounsabe ahnebora tirewonsabe wahnsane nahopeq
soon before-cook spirit house person died tell-me.
kauwaukwenime putiyowe ire teniq.
58. Parabagiq.
Finished.

1. Wairo told me this story. There was a certain man who went hunting for possums. As he hunted, he went into the forest, and a big rain came. He was in the mist or fog. 5. Plenty of rain came down, and it poured there in the forest. He came on and on. There at a large area in Tanagogo, there on the other side of Naniyape where the pines can be always seen, where the pine forest is, that is, the ground I'm talking about—Tabigara—er, I mean Tanagogo—I forgot, it is another place. At Tanagogo he stayed at the base of a pine tree while it rained.

A certain spirit said, 'That's not a tree, that's my house. This is my house, why are you staying here? You have made the wind blow hard.' The wind was blowing hard, and he said this to his friend, 'You come on in.' When he told him to come in, the other one said, 'I was at the base of the tree.' The other person from here was a real person. The spirit indicated that it was not a tree trunk, but 'It is my house,' he said. 15. 'It is my house,' he said. When he said this, his younger brother, that is, the friend of the dead one, said, 'You can stay in my house, you go on in first.'

The two went in the house, and sat down there. He setttled him and they were there, and his friend—no not that way—the spirit went up and gave his friend sweet potato to eat. Another person came into the house. 20. His arrows were there at the door, and he wanted to shoot those arrows that were in the house. 'Don't pull them out of there, do not take them, leave them alone,' he said. 'Leave them alone, just his friend can take them,' he said. This is what he said to the real person. The real person did not pay any attention when he told him this, he just thought he would take the good arrows. 25. He took the arrows and the other said, 'What did I tell you a bit ago, what talk was it that I told you? Those arrows belong to that other person. It is not good that you take them. Just be there doing nothing. Sit down, and just be there, I told you. That is what I just told you to do,' he said.

A number of spirits built a fire in the house, and there was a lot of smoke there. There was smoke all around the ground and that is 'because you have stolen the arrows, that's why it is smoking and smoking.' This is what the ghost was telling him. 30. His friend said, 'Why did you take them? I just told you not to. Another man wants to shoot the arrows from the doorway too.' When he shot them, he said, 'Don't pull them out, don't take them away, I told you. Why did you take them?' he said. 'It is because I wanted to take them, because I wanted the arrows. That's why I took them. I wanted the arrows and took them,' he said. 35. When he said this, the other said, 'It is not good what you have done, throw them to me.' He threw them, and that person took them.

He took the arrows which belonged to that wild-cat person. He threw the arrows to the wild-cat person. The spirit person took his arrows and left. He took them to his bed and the other fellow was in his room like from here to the doorway. He took them from there and threw them at him, and he stayed on his bed.

40. He stayed on his bed. He thought, 'I think,' referring to what the ghost said, 'it is the spirit talking. I think that other person is setting a trap. It is not on a possum's trail, but it is on the path of people that he set the trap. Someday the vine [with which the trap is set] will get old and will rot and the trap will go off and, like this, the club will hit and crush someone.' 45. 'It will break and come loose and it will have only one vine so it will spring; I will set it on a big log and that log will get soft.' He fixed it up right so it would go off in a short while. He told all this to another spirit. The other spirit said, 'You do it,' so they did it; but the wild cat did not get in on this talk, and did not pay attention, but running quickly, he went along. That real person set the trap. After he set the trap, and pretty soon with reference to what was said before, the wild cat went, and that other person's trap went off. 50. 'Here is my talk, I know that it was hidden, and I saw that you set the trap.'

On the edge of his garden—on the edge—he set it and it went off, and he [the spirit] left. 'You go, go get it out,' the spirit said to the live person. He was just staying there and the spirit was staying in the house and he left. He pulled it out of the noose, got it out of the trap, and went on down the hill. 55. That other Mobuta person, a Mobuta Manika, said: 'No! I stayed and slept at that spirit's house like that. I slept and this wild cat was in my trap when it went off.' He brought it and came and said: 'Do not give it to the women, just to the men; you do that—cook it and eat it—men—cook it and eat it.' Pretty soon, before they cooked it, that person who had stayed in the spirit's house died. That is what has been told me. The story is ended.

9. WHY THE POSSUM HAS PART OF HIS TOE MISSING

1. Irahkiyah waukwega irahkiyah waukwega miyowana wene (soq———)
Ilakia person Ilakia person was-there his (gard———) his garden from-
wene sotate awanga nara, wisu, wisuwara ebahnganga noweiq.
tree fruit, Wichu-tree, Wichu-tree-fruit ground-hog ate.
2. Ebahnganga nonsabe nene sotate ebahnganga nehre iwiyahnuwena;
Ground-hog eating my garden-from ground-hog eats thought;
3. Inokahpeq pokwe kowahnah nuweiq.
At-night went watch do.
4. Inokahpeq pokwe kowahnah nuwe, peh wena metiriniye ena wah mireq
Night went watch do, just he carry-and-cooked I-will possum is carry-
meririniyena bokwe kowahnahnuwena;
and-cook went set-watch;
5. Kowahnahnuwana ebahngawe wahnsa ebahnga sure sure.
Watching ground-hog spirit ground-hog came came.
6. Kahq meogahq (merawena) abaqmena, wen anime inahonahni abaq-
Cape new-cape (put-on) covered, her child baby covered carry-on-back;
mena sehwiwena;
7. Sehwiwena sure sure.
Carry-on-back came came.
8. Irahkiyah waukwewe (soq———) wahnahnuriyowana;
Ilakia person (gard———) was-watching;
9. Wene (roq) wene awahngataq wahnahnuriyowana sure sure sure sure
He (er) he tree watching came came came, came came.
sure, sure sure.
10. Tagahriyowana mena surarena awahngatape suweiq.
Look-for that-one coming tree arrived.
11. Awahngatape sunsabe aiq putaq wahne iwiyahena;
Tree arrived indeed true possum he-thought;
12. Putaq wahne iwiyahena;
True possum he-thought;
13. Tagahriyome waukweni waukweni suweiq.
Look-for person person arrived.
14. Waukweni tautauq ahre.
Person red woman.
15. Tautauq ahre sunsabe ine wahne iwiyahuganawe ahre iwiyahruwena;
Red woman came I possum thought woman think;
16. Sunga—menaq—awahnga—serame sewewe unahpipeq usena;
Came—that-one—tree—fruit-picked picked bag-in put;
17. Usaruwena gahwerue putome naruwena ire gahwe pu——— irega———
Put-in good ripe ate not good rip——— not-go——— not ripe carry bag
ire putome mewe unahpeq usaruq.
put-in.

18. *Kahweruwe putome we naruwena ire putome mewe unahpeq usaru-*
    Good ripe she ate not ripe carry bag put-in.
ruweiq.
19. *Unahpeq usaru aruwena unsabe isena wahtaireme poirina;*
    Bag put-in did because that-there possum I- shoot;
20. *Ahre kahwe ahre miyahne ena;*
    Woman good woman is-there be;
21. *Iqmari mipinsuwena, peh ayahnga (noq) ahrene ayahtaq tahtaroweiq.*
    Bow put-aside, just hand (*noq*) woman hand held.
22. *Tahtarowana uwo uwo uwo ena;*
    Held *uwo uwo uwo* did;
23. *Peh (neq) ahnden ahre uweiq.*
    Just (*neq*) afraid woman said.
24. *Wensabe ahnden ahreunsabe, maho maho inen gahweq ahre tagoge ena;*
    She-refer afraid said, come come I good woman see said;
25. *Pehetaq tahtotiyoweiq.*
    Just hold-her.
26. *Tahtotiyowana abehqnaner ukume peh rahtotiyoweiq.*
    Holding worthless became just held-on.
27. *(Abe———) abehqnane awahngatahnsa nukume awahnga peh rah-*
    (Wor———) worthless-thing tree-like became tree just hold.
totiyoweiq.
28. *Ebahn ukume peh ebah tahtotiyoweiq.*
    Stone became just stone he-held.
29. *Mo moqmarin ukume peh rahtotiyoweiq.*
    Other rat became just held-on.
30. *Wahn uku peh rahtotiyoweiq, (aneq) abehqnane katahnsa kamari*
    Possum became just held-on, (what) worthless animal-like animal-
miyoq ukume peh rahtotiyoweiq.
plural is became just hung-on.
31. *Toirahnsan ukuwe peh rahtotiyoweiq.*
    Lizard became just hung-on.
32. *(Maqaneka—) abarahnsa marako uku peh rahtotiyoweiq.*
    (What-that—) decaying-like ground became just hung-on.
33. *Ne kahwe ahre nene niyurahnga ai tahgogeq.*
    I good woman my eyes indeed saw.
34. *Ire sorahsuwanauge ire sabiruwana uge ena;*
    Not let-go-intend-I not release I said;
35. *Ire auwanauge peh rahtotiyanauge iwiyah ena;*
    Not let-go just hold-I thought do;
36. *Peh rahtotiyowana mirau mirau mirau.*
    Just hold did did did.
37. *Iyarerena wahnsa ukuwana peh rahtotiyoweiq.*

Doing spirit became just hold-on.
38. *Peh rahtotawena unsabe mahn anime aneriroaruwena;*
    Just hold refer this child what-doing;
39. *Awehkawa—awehkawawe peh aqau ena peh rahtotiyoweiq.*
    Husband—husband just no said just hold-on.
40. *Ire ire sabiauwanauge ire suwanauge ena, peh rahtotiyowana iyahnabo*
    Not not release-I not release said, just hold-on that woman thought do
    ahre iwiyah iyarerena iwiyahwe.
    thought.
41. *Tagaraga ena iwiyahu niwiyahun iwiyahu.*
    I-know said thought thought thought.
42. *Irakau nunsabe mena pahq waukweni miyoweiq.*
    Not-release refer that spirit person was.
43. *Pahq waukweni miyoweiq.*
    Spirit person was-there.
44. *Pahq waukweni miyonsabe ine rahq mirenena erahq irengainae merahq*
    Spirit person was-there I that do that be-like that be-like-me said;
    mirengainae mirarena;
45. *Awehkawa iwiyah wiyahuweiq.*
    Husband thought thought.
46. *Awehkawa iwiyah wiyah uwana;*
    Husband thought thought did;
47. *Maeqmena sure sure sure sure.*
    Take-her came came came.
48. *Wene nahopeq meyatena, wene nahopeq meyatena irawe parewe parewe*
    His house take-her, his house take fire build build build.
    parewe parewe.
49. *Mipi atoweiq.*
    There put-her.
50. *Atowana(maq) mahpete mahpetengega ropah nawaqmaqme.*
    Put-her outside outside-people sweet-potato gave.
51. *Irauwana waukweni nura miyowiq.*
    Said person it-is there.
52. *Miyonsabe peh gahwe ahre mewena meyaroge iwiyahruwena;*
    Is-there just good woman brought put thought;
53. *(Abowa) awehkawa mipi mena wen aninseq men aninseq wen ani*
    (Father) husband there that her child-and that child-and her child put
    auwena uwana nahtaq mewena;
    do house brought;
54. *(Topahngo——) topahnsahq pokuno uwe.*
    (Sweet-potat——) sweet-potato go-for do.
55. *Anahkawa eqmaq auwena, anahkawa eqmaq auwena bokwe uwana;*
    Wife left return, wife left return go did;

56. *Anahkawa bokwe bokwe topahn goubuqme ubuqme topahme sahqme*
   Wife went went sweet-potato go-dig dig sweet-potato cane banana bring
   perahrewe koireuwena sure sure.
   came came.

57. *Ahnan sahrapete seiratiyome ahnan sahrapete iratiyowana wen aninga*
   Edge village came-listen edge village heard her child big cry.
   anotahn ibisoweiq.

58. *Anotahn ibisonsabe aiq peh garitaq ibisahno peh garitaq ibisahno.*
   Big cry-refer yipes just little cry just little cry.

59. *Topahnura nahn aningapoq peh awahnga nahna aninone are nano peh*
   Sweet-potato eat child just tree eat child you mother just tree eat-eat
   awahnga narunarurin anine awahngan sera nahn anine.
   child tree fruit eat child.

60. *Animone ropah nahno, (a—) topah nahn aningapoq.*
   Child-dear sweet-potato eat, (er—) sweet-potato eat person.

61. *Peh garitaq ibisahno, peh garitaq ibisahno iraruweiq.*
   Just little cry, just little cry said.

62. *Abowahga;*
   Father;

63. *Abowahga wen aninsabe iraruwana anowawe peh ahran sahrapete*
   Father her child-refer said mother just edge village listen yes here I-
   kiratiyopona e mahna giyuge mahna giyugana mire iraruweiq.
   come here I-come up said.

64. *(A—) irarunsabe ine nega ire iwiyahuwe aretaq ire surauge.*
   (Er—) said I I not think you not come.

65. *Nena sotaq miyarauga.*
   My garden was.

66. *Arega nemen sewanitaone nemen, sewanitaone irarena;*
   You me took me, came-took said;

67. *Anahkawawe abiyahnsa suweiq.*
   Wife frown came.

68. *Awehkawansabe nen aninsabe irareno.*
   Husband-refer my child-refer you-talked.

69. *Nena aninsabe irarenara ine nirutaboinire ena;*
   My child-refer you-talked I sorry she-said;

70. *Anahkawa ibisoq—abiyahnsan suweiq.*
   Wife cry—cross came.

71. *Abiyahnsan suwana mena inokahpeqme (abowa) awehkawame tiwe*
   Cross came that night (father) husband cooked ate;
   nauwana;

72. *Wene nahopeq pokewonsabe we we pokwe topahme kabahratumewena*
   His house went she she go sweet-potato bamboo-bring go bamboo-bring
   pokwe kabahratumewena topahme moriwe unahpipe suq (araq) arahqme

sweet-potato again-cook bag put (what) left-overs (raw things—cook—
(iriya maqaneq—agewe—maq) unahpipeq usaruq.
what) bag put.

73. *Agewe unahpesuq urewo newo newo.*
   Cooked bag put do do.

74. *Perarewe kai uwe unahpe usaru ruwe ewo newo newo.*
   Bananas scrape do bag put do and do.

75. *Aiq suq nokahnabu inokahpetahnsan ukunsabe, mena unahme sokah*
   Enough when sleep night-like became, that bag possessions do her-
   ena wenanime unahpe usabe togena;
   child bag refer hang-from-head;

76. *Towena pokwe pokwe bokwe bokwe bokwe bokwe bokwe bokwe.*
   Hang-things-head left go and go.

77. *Pokuwana tutagome (a——) wene nahpipeq mahripipeq ire sugoyansabe,*
   Go down-look (er——) her house bed not sleep, their-father her-husband
   sibowawe awehkawa pokwe bokwe.
   went went.

78. *Kiragome ahnansahrape kobekunsabe pehipehirah we motaq se motaq*
   Went-up-look edge-village out-of-sight quickly he soon they soon he soon
   we motaq semotaq uwo uwo uwo.
   follow do do do.

79. *Uwe uwe uwe ebahnabana anotahn ebah kiyonsa siyatawena, anowange*
   Do do do rock large rock door come-open, mother house inside went,
   nahopeq ke agena, ayotahpero ayotahpero mirahmboq mahrahmboewahne.
   Ayotape Ayotape this-way that-way [not Awa].

80. *Onda awahngengaho awahngengaho giyuwana, onsa pehirah.*
   Door open-it open-it call, door went-quickly.

81. *Siruwowana arokirahnsan onsa siruwowana anowa nahopeq ke agena;*
   Opened lock-like door opened mother house go inside;

82. *Wen ani ahnibora koyawiwe mahbeq maraniboume.*
   Her child close pulled here put-him.

83. *Abowaga mahotaoena;*
   Father come-you-two;

84. *Wene wen anine aigara korahtotawena uwana, anowaga sabiruwana*
   Her her child foot grabbed did, mother pulled father pulled, mother
   abowaga sabiruwana, anowaga sabiruwana abowaga sabiruwana, anowaga
   pulled father pulled, mother pulled father pulled, do do.
   sabiruwana abowaga sabiruwana, unga unga.

85. *Wen anine—wen anine aigara kirakuweiq.*
   Her child—her child foot pulled-off.

86. *Wen anine aigarame kirakuwara aiga—kirakuwana peh aigara mewena*
   Her child foot pulled-off foot—pull-off just foot took toe toe went-down;
   aisobeq aiyobeq mewena;

87. Tunse (mira-iraq-iraq-) mirawe ebahpipeq pokinsabe mirawe peh
Go-down (like that) that stone-in she-went like-that just foot pull-off;
aigara sehpirugana;
88. Sehpirugana sehpirugana aigara kirakuwe.
Pull-off pull-off foot pull.
89. Niyahpi maransabe tuge.
My-hand hold-refer come-down.
90. Tuiraruweiq.
Come-down-tell.
91. Tuwirarena wena wen ahrensabe peh mo arutaboi tuwe ire.
Come-down-say he him wife just more sorrow come say.
92. Irahkiyah manikanga irauwe ire.
Ilakia Manika told said.
93. Teniyeq.
Told-me.

1. There was once an Ilakia person who had a garden. A ground hog would eat the fruit from the trees—the Wichu fruit. 'A ground hog is eating from my garden,' he thought. So at night he went out in order to guard the garden. 'I'll just get that possum and cook him,' he said, so he went out to set a watch. 5. When he was watching, a ground hog, that is, a ground hog's spirit, approached. She [the ground hog] had on a new cape. Her child—a baby—was covered, and she was carrying it on her back. As she carried the baby on her back, she came and came. The Ilakia person was watching. He was watching at the tree and that one came closer and closer.

10. He was watching with anticipation, and that one arrived at the tree. With reference to the one arriving, he said, 'Oh, it is surely a possum. It is truly a possum,' he thought. As he waited a person arrived. It was a white woman. 15. Now with reference to that white woman, he said, 'I thought you would be a possum, but now I think it is a woman.' The thing that came to that place picked the fruit and put it in her string bag. As she did this, she ate the ripe fruit and the not-good, that is, the green fruit, she took and put into the bag. The ripe fruit she ate, and the green fruit she put in her bag. 'If that one putting things into her bag were a possum, I would shoot it.' 20. 'But it is a woman, a good woman there,' he said, and he put his bow and arrows aside. With just his hand he hung on to the woman's hand. While he was holding her she cried out, '*Uwo, uwo, uwo.*' She was very frightened. Now with reference to this one that was so frightened, he said, 'Come, come, I see that you are a good woman.' 25. He just held on to her.

While he was holding on to her, she became a worthless thing, but he just held on to her. She became a treelike thing, but he still held on to the stick. She became a stone, but he held the stone. Then she changed to a rat, but he just held on to her. 30. She became a possum, but he held on. She became all sorts of worthless things, but he hung on. She became a lizard and a whatever you may call it—decayed ground, but he still hung on. 'I saw a good woman with my eyes! I do not intend to let her go, I will not release her,' he said. 35.

'I do not intend to let her go, I'll just hold on,' he thought. He kept hanging on. While he did this, she became a spirit, but he held on. Regarding this one he was holding to, he said, 'What is this person doing?' The husband just said, 'No,' and held on. 40. 'I do not intend to release her, I do not intend to let her go.' As he held on, he thought, 'It is a woman who is doing this. I will always know this,' he thought and thought. Now with reference to his not letting her go he saw that this person was a spirit. She was a spirit-person. With reference to that spirit, he said, 'Why don't you just be like me, be like me,' he said. 45. This is the way that husband thought about it. The husband thought this way, and taking her he came and came. He took her to his house, and in taking her to his house, they built a fire. He settled her down there.

50. When he settled her there, some folks from the outside gave her sweet potato. They said, 'There is a person living there.' Now with reference to that person there the man thought, 'I have brought and put here a very good woman.' Now this husband stayed there with her child—he and the child which he had brought to the house were there. 'You go for sweet potatoes,' he told her. 55. She left, intending to come back; she went and went. That wife went, and she went to bring sweet potatoes, sugar cane, and bananas and then came back.

At the edge of the village, she came and listened. When she was at the edge of the village, she heard that her child was crying very loud. Now with reference to that loud crying, the man was saying 'You cry just a little; don't cry, don't cry. Here, are you a sweet potato eating child? Or do you just eat the fruit of trees? Your mother is just a fruit eating person; she just eats from the trees.' 60. 'My dear child, eat these sweet potatoes. Aren't you a sweet potato eating person? Just cry only a little. Just cry a little,' he said, that is, the father said.

As the father said this to her child, the mother was just at the edge of the village listening, and she said, 'Yes, here, I'm coming, I'm coming.' With reference to her he said, 'I didn't think about it, and I didn't go where you were.' 65. 'I was in my garden,' she said. 'You came and forced me to come here with you; you forced me to come here,' she said. His wife, in coming, was very angry at him. She said to her husband, 'You talked angrily at my child, you talked mean to my child, and I am very sorry for him.'

70. His wife was very cross as she came. Because she was cross, that night she cooked for her husband and he ate. When he had gone to his house, she left, taking sweet potatoes in a bamboo. She brought down the bamboo and the cooked sweet potato, putting it into the string bag, perhaps raw, I mean probably cooked, well, she put it in this string bag and left. She put the cooked things into the string bag and she kept on doing it. She scraped the bananas, and put them in the bag. 75. When he was asleep at night, she became like the night and hung these things from her head in the bag, and put her child there too and left. When she hung them from her head, she just left, going away very far.

Now he went down to look into her house and she was not asleep there in her bed. Their father, her husband, followed her. He went up to look but she had disappeared at the edge of the village—he then, that is, she or they, went after her. He kept following her, and she came to a large rock where there was a rock door and her mother was inside. She wanted to go inside there and called out, '*Ayotape Ayotape*,' this way and that way [not Awa]. 80. 'Open the door, open it,' she called. She went to the door and when it was opened, when the locklike door was opened by the mother, she went in the house. She pulled her child close to her and said, 'I'll put him here.'

Now the father called out, 'Come here you two.' He grabbed the child's foot. The father pulled and the father pulled and they kept tugging at the child's foot. . . . He pulled off that child's foot. He pulled off her child's foot, that is he pulled it off; he just took the foot—I mean the toe; he took just the toe off. Then he went down and she went into that cave there while he had just pulled the foot, having pulled it off. With reference to the fact that he held on to her hand, 'I came down here,' he told them. When he said this with reference to his wife he just had a lot more sorrow they say. The Ilakia Manika told this story, they say. That is what has been told to me.

10. ORIGIN OF LICE

1. Mo mo wehga nahn awiq onsopete, onsopete pokwe.
Other other man house name Onsope, Onsope-from left.

2. Sau sabatahq pokeniyena sau sabatahq pokeniyena pokwe.
Larva go-get go-will larva go-get go left.

3. Bokwe, orahbipeq kibekunka, orahbipeq kibekunka pokunga tunserunse.
Leave, Orabipe pass-by, Orabipe pass-by go-by go-down.

4. Agaurah suwahpeq iseberiyopeq agaurah suwahpeq inseberiyopete tunse.
Agaura village over-beyond Agaura village over-beyond came.

5. Kambarene nahtuwoipeq, kambare waukene nahtuwoipe uwana, mon
Stranger house-old, strange person house-broken is, other child larva
anine sauq awahngame uwana.
tree is.

6. Tainoraba waukwe ababarena we ababarena bokwe.
Tainoraba person wrong he wrong leave.

7. Agaurah suwahpeq seberiyopete waukene awahngan uwana aibo aibo
Agaura village over-beyond person tree was stole stole larva (er—*Koba
kobawe (ah—koban sauq sau mehweh) sauqme sauqme tuwe ruwe ruwe*
larva Fore talk) larva larva chop-out chop chop chop.
ruwe.

8. Mitaq marena.
There put.

9. Mahnaq arensebo arensebo nene awahngataqme arensebo uwana.
This you-who you-who my tree-on who did.

10. Abanganage abangange iraruwana.
Who-is who he-said.

11. Ine ehwehme ireyame ine ireyame peh inugo inugo iraruweiq.
My talk not my not just who who he-said.

12. Inugo iraruwana arewensebo arewensebo iraruwana.
Who he-said who-is-it who he-said.

13. Ine ehwehme ireiya arensebo uweiq.

My talk not who he-said.

14. *Arensebo unsabe (aq) irarena awahngane nene awahnga mire.*
   Who because (er) he-said tree-my my tree is.

15. *Are ahnde aibo iregawerone aibo iregawerone irareruwena.*
   You plenty stole not-good stole not-good said.

16. *Sure sure (seq) wahtotate wahtotate seragome we aibo sauq tunsabe*
   Come come (?) short short level-look he stole larva down-come larva
   sauq sabatahq tunsabe.
   get came.

17. *Ire arene awahnga mire, pokupokuwena (ko) iyahnabo awahnga*
   Not your tree is, went-went (and) that tree cut-off with head hit say.
   suwera tate ayahqnome subisuwowe ire.

18. *Ayahqnome subisuqmaqme mipi marena uwana.*
   Head-on hit there put do.

19. *Iyahnabo mi waukwewe tainoraba waukewe wen subiniyenaume wen*
   That that person Tainoraba person him hit he on-level-first hit he first
   onotahpeq subimaqme we ebeq subiqme subiqme.
   hit hit.

20. *Mipi marowana sahtate subiqme pokatate subiqme.*
   There did club hit ax hit.

21. *Maisarowe ire.*
   Buried say.

22. *Maisarowana marawe marun subuwana marun subuwana.*
   Buried like-this down hit down hit.

23. *Toringa irebeq karirapeq osorehnaneq karirapeq mibe kowe ire.*
   Blood over-there nettle hot nettle there they say.

24. *Konsabe korahq mo waukega korahq taganaho ena.*
   Where blood other person blood not-good-see is.

25. *Korahqmari kaweruwe kaweruwe kaweruwe marako ipeq suwana.*
   Blood good good good ground there threw.

26. *Me waukwenime we irarate akariwe awahngan airate awahnga anahrate*
   That person he wood cover tree bark tree leaves cover cover good say.
   akariwe akariwe kaweraruwowe ire.

27. *Kaweraruwana uwana, korahka bokwe bokwe bokwe, peh korahtate*
   Good did, blood went went went, just blood blood went went went no!
   korahka bokwe bokwe bokwe bokwe aqau nsebe pokwe.
   went.

28. *Yehbo maho uwe anahkawa giwaerowe ire.*
   Let's-go come do wife up-went say.

29. *Anahkawansabe giwaero uwana.*
   Wife up-went happen.

30. *Nanuwehqme ire mahran animire ire nanuwehqtahnsa mone.*
   My-husband not this child not my-husband-like dear.

31. *Are nsabono uwana.*
    You anyway happen.
32. *Ine aiq arena wehre ine arena wehq muge maho uwe ire.*
    I sure your husband I your husband I-say come do say.
33. *Ine arenawehq muge mahounsabe.*
    I your-husband I-say come.
34. *Ine tagariyoge nanuwehqme monanine are.*
    I know my-husband another you.
35. *Nanuwehqne auranabiyahme mone arene auranabiyahme mone iraruwe*
    My-husband face-other dear your face-other dear say say.
    ire.
36. *Irarunsabe are pehinone ine putaq arene wehre uwe ire wahnsaga*
    Say you lie I truly your husband say say spirit spirit said.
    wahnsaga irarunsabe.
37. *Anahkawawe sokame tuwe maqme.*
    Wife things down carried.
38. *Pokuweyehbo miyahno uwe gimaeqmena (po-tunse) (a——) pokwe*
    Go-let's go do go-along (leave-go-down) (er——) went went (we——)
    bokwe (bo——) kire gire gire gire gire gire gire.
    go-up go-up.
39. *Orahpipeq kibe kuwarena, (na—tainorab—) amorahbah miyahtate*
    Orapipe up hidden-came, (na—tainorab—) Amoraba there other-side
    seberiyopeq min sehwehraba sehraba pokwe bokwe orahpipeq kibe kuwah-
    that ridge-big ridge went went Orapipe over came.
    rena.
40. *Mina runse runse runse runse runse runse mina runse runse runse we*
    Went down down down kept going down he bury ground down put put-
    maisaro marakoraq maru marena marunatena anahkawame marunatena.
    down wife put-down.
41. *Marunatena mena awehkawawe mo wahnsayabe maho nen ahre subo*
    Put-down that husband other spirits come my wife kill we come do.
    nehbo maho uwe.
42. *Mairaniyena pokena mo wahnsahri mairaniyena pokena, (maq aneq—).*
    Take-her go other spirit take go, (now what—).
43. *Mahbete irawe wena kariya, wena kariya ira bariyehnehbo.*
    Here wood his cover, his cover wood burn-not.
44. *Mahna monira isena monira sena monira mahna monira sena monira*
    This wood that wood that wood this wood that wood plenty put-down.
    ahnde paqmaroge.
45. *Ahnde paqmaroge isesen irawe ire bariyo aqau aqau aqau bariyehnae*
    Plenty I-put-down wood fire not burn no no no burn burn.
    bariyehnaewe.
46. *Kiyape nehweh tahmbuewe.*

Kiap talk taboo.
47. *Tahmbe irareruqmaqme.*
Taboo said.
48. *Paqmaroge aqau reyawena uwana.*
I-put-down no do-it did.
49. *Anahkawawe mahni ira pariyo.*
Wife this wood burn.
50. *Pariyowana pariyowana parapaquwana.*
Burn burn burn.
51. *Mo sen ira pariyowana (prabag——) mina barabaguq.*
More there wood burn (fini——) that finished.
52. *Mo isenira pariyowana mina parabaguwana mo isenira pariyowana*
Other wood burn that finish other wood burn finish other wood burn
parabaguwana mo isenira pariyowana parabaguwana.
finish.
53. *Mitare mimora mahmore ise mora se mora itaretare barabarena.*
Those two that-one this other there other two-by-two burn.
54. *Irawe ahnde ira bagira parabarena.*
Wood plenty wood stack burn.
55. *Awehkawa maesiya awehkawa maesiyan ira parewe barewe barewe*
Husband bury husband bury wood burn burn burn burn on-top burn finish.
barewe aboborahte parewena pareruq.
56. *Pareruruwe uwe uwe uwe uwe uwe uwe uwe.*
Burn keep doing.
57. *Pariyowana pariyowana pehrah maro turonsabe.*
Burned burned just-few down came.
58. *Anotah irari konsabe awenahpete pehgari ira mewe parianiye ena.*
Big wood have underneath small wood took burn did.
59. *Awenahpeq marawe kabeh uwana.*
Underneath that uncover do.
60. *Kabehwe kabehwe kabehwe marawe tahtorowana waukenitate titirun-*
Uncover uncover uncover like-this hold person cold.
sabe.
61. *Anepomo irarena.*
What said.
62. *Kaneq otate marawe kaneq irageqmaqme.*
Bamboo section like bamboo light.
63. *Tagowana mipi waukweni (miyo) konsabe.*
Look there person (is) had.
64. *Anepomo irareruwena mena anotah kaneke suqmaqme o onge sumaqme.*
What exclaims that big bamboo poke it burn poke.
65. *Aurepi marawe tagowana awehkawa awehkawa miyonsabe.*
Eyes this look husband husband there.

66. *Wei ine ire iwiyahuge nanuwehqme pukiya, waukwega wahnsaga*
    Aiii I not think my-man dead, person spirit me come tell she look.
    inensabe maho iranawe we tagangaiena.
67. *We tagangaiena maho iranawe tuge iraruwena.*
    She look come tell came said.
68. *Irawe (tiraq) totarasa mewe.*
    Fire (?) coals took.
69. *Arahqnahn uwe obe kiwena ayahpi tatare mewena bokwe bokwe bokwe*
    Bundle go shoulder carry hand-two carry went went went.
    bokwe bokwe bokwe.
70. *Gire gire gire gire gire gire gire gire gire, gire, kiragowana mena mah-*
    Climb climb climb, climb, go-look that here over-went that husband
    beq kibekunsabe mena awehkawawe ahnde wahnsahri meriq mena sure sure.
    plenty spirits brought that come come.
71. *Seragomewe miyo mahripe ire miyonsabe.*
    Level-look there bed not stay.
72. *Aipopo pokire aruwena.*
    Where go said.
73. *Peherahn giragome.*
    Quickly go-up-look.
74. *Ahnahnsahrapeq pokunsabe, peherahn gire gire gire kiragowena mah-*
    Edge-village she-go, quickly he-climb climb go-look there-like-this look.
    ratatetahnsa tagome.
75. *Nahniyahpetetahnsa ira ira taratasate marawe tautaurunsabe ira iraga*
    Naniyape-from-like fire fire glowing there like-this-red fire fire fire
    iraga tehronsabe, sesena bokire iwiyah aruwena.
    burning, over-there went thought said.
76. *Pehpeherah naniyahpete kiyapene nahtatetahnsa tutagome.*
    Quickly Naniyape-from Kiap house-like-from look.
77. *Iyenirapetahnsa kobekunsabe iyenirapetetahnsa tutagome.*
    Iyenirape-like disappear Iyenirape-like look.
78. *Sesena irahkiyah suwapete wani anotah oibete wanitahnsa tunsabe.*
    Over-there Ilakia-from village water big Oibe-from water-like go-down.
79. *(M)itate tutagome.*
    From-there saw-her.
80. *Irahkiyah suwapetahnsa kiyunsabe.*
    Ilakia village-like go-up.
81. *Mirawe ire wahto uwe ire wahto uwe ire wahto uwe ire wahtonuwe.*
    Like-that not short do not short do not short do not short.
82. *Gire gire gire gire senahpeq amoraba miyahtate senahpeq mipi orah-*
    Climb climb climb up-hill Amoraba there from-up there Orapipe-from
    pipete tutagome.
    down-look.

83. *Poerahkautate marako awiq poerahkautate tu irobina nunsabe maruteh-*
    Pig-place ground name pig-place from flame there-down lit that go-up
ronasabe mina giyogeq mena runse.
that go-down.
84. *Poerahkaupete seragome.*
    Pig-place look.
85. *Panaroten se irobina unsabe merehraruwonsabe sesenagire ena.*
    Panaro that flame do carry-burning over-there do.
86. *Mo wahnsahri mita sitena.*
    Other spirit there put.
87. *Wega pehpehera peherah peherah, tahtoraniyenawe tahtoraniye iwiyah*
    He run run run, grab-I hold-I think do.
ena.
88. *Pehpeherah suwena, we ahrewe ephpeherah pokwe bokwe bokwe.*
    Run come, his wife run go go go.
89. *Wene nahopeq ire runsiya.*
    Her house not come-down.
90. *Ayokawane nahopeq ire wene nahopeq awehkawane nahopeq ire*
    Brother house not her house husband house not go-down.
runsiyame.
91. *Ayokawane nahopeq tunse.*
    Brother house come.
92. *Wei naniyoq mone namiyoqmone wahnsaga (m)ire irana pokuge*
    Oh my-brother dear my-brother-dear spirit is happen went said.
mirarena.
93. *Marawe ayahra kabehrawena ire wahton ayahra kabehwe.*
    Like-this hair lift-up not short hair left-up.
94. *Mahpipeq tutu uwe miyoweiq.*
    Here-in sat down stay.
95. *Ahngomepipeq wene awiqme ahngomepipeq tutuwe miyowana.*
    Base-head his name base-head sat-down stay.
96. *Wahnsawen gire.*
    Spirit came-up.
97. *Itensabe (niyahtehreq) itensabe ire niyahtehreq itensabe ire niyahtehre*
    You-two (afraid) you-two not afraid you not afraid me men's house me
ine wehne nahnga ine sabinaho ena.
hit-no do.
98. *Negawe itensabe niyahtehrana mo (itogeopo) wehne nahnga inen*
    I you afraid other (?) men's house me hit-no do.
subinaho ena.
99. *Ahre uge wahnsaga iraruweiq.*
    Afraid said spirit said.

100. Wahnsaga irarunsabe mena anahnowawe ahngomepipeq mipeq miyo-
        Spirit said that sister base-head there stay.
weiq.
101. Miyowana aipowe giruweguwana mira ena miraena.
        Stay where go-up go do like-that.
102. Mirawe wahnsa wahnsaga mirawe ine mahonsabe tuwerorabe au-
        Like-that spirit spirit like-that me come go-down no-catch.
ranubowe.
103. Miran ehweh ayokawa tiyauweiq.
        That talk brother told.
104. Ayokawa tiyauwana minaga ayokawane (maq aneq) ayahqnopipeq
        Brother told that brother (what what) base-head that plenty children
mena ahnde animari maqmaroweiq.
bore.
105. Oyerame nune oyera maqmarowe irarebona (maq) wakarareh (a—
        Eggs lice egg bore told (er) Wakara (er—what) Ubeyana—Ubeyana-
maqinse) ubeyanah—ubeyahnahreh—wene abowa wena abowareh anon-
and—his father his father Anontabu father.
tabune abowa.
106. Minge minge (ne nahq) ayahqnopeqme ahnde nu miyanawire we
        People people (?) head-place plenty lice desire-there his Manika that
manikanga mirawe iwiyah ipuwana wene ayahqnope ahnde nu miyahnahwe.
thought do his head plenty lice there.
107. Manikanga wene anahrowaga mipipeq miyehrane.
        Manika his sister there stay.
108. Miyehrana ahnde nu miyaniyanawire ire irehwehuno arene ayahq-
        Settle plenty lice desire not complain you head plenty lice-are talk not
nopeq ahnde numiyehre ehweh ire iraruno.
say.
109. Wene wene manikangawe anahnowaga ayahqnopeq miyowe.
        His his Manika sister head there.
110. Mirangebona ahnde nu miyanae wene wateiqipeqme wene ayahq-
        People-these plenty lice be his grass-skirt his head plenty lice settle.
nopeqme ahnde nu miyaniyanae.
111. Mira nehweh mirareruq eruroq.
        That talk always told.
112. Parabagi.
        Finish.

    1. A certain man left his place, a place named Onsope. 'I'll go hunt larva
[a big worm],' he said, and left. He passed by Orapipe, and went along, going
on down. He came down to Agaura and to a place over beyond Agaura. At
that place there were some foreigners' old broken-down houses. 5. A stranger's
old house was there. Another man's larva, that is, another person's tree where

the larva was, was there. At Agaura, at the place over beyond, he stole that man's tree, that is, he stole the larva from it (er—*Koba* is the Fore for larva), chopping it out from the tree. He put it down over there.

'Who is it, who is it that did this to my tree?' [the owner said]. 10. 'Who did it, who did it?' he kept saying. 'I'm not shouting about it, I'm just saying "Who did it?" ' he said; 'Who is it?' he said and he told him [in Awa] who did it. 'I'm not hollering about anything,' he said, 'just asking who did it.' This was all in reference to the fact that it was his own tree. 15. 'You stole plenty, you are not doing well, you stole and you are not doing well,' he told him. It was only a very short distance that he came to steal the larva. 'But it is not your tree,' he said, so he went and he cut a piece off of the tree, and he hit him over the head with it, they say. He hit him on the head with that thing that he had put there. That person who did this was a Tainoraba fellow. He [Tainoraba fellow] hit him [Awa fellow] as he was going along and kept hitting him. 20. That is where he did it, he hit him with a club, and he hit him with a big instrument, and then buried him.

He buried that one where he had struck him down. Now the blood got up on the nettles (the stinging kind), they say. With reference to that blood the killer said, 'It is not good that anyone should see it.' 25. So he fixed the place where the blood was, by throwing dirt over it. He covered the body with wood and with bark and leaves; he covered it over and made it good they say. When it had been made good, the blood got up and went away. Just that blood went and went. You don't say?

Well it [the blood-spirit] did go down, and it said to the man's wife, 'Let's go.' 30. Now his wife as she was going along thought to herself, 'This person is not my husband, it is not my dear husband. Who are you anyway?' she asked. 'I am indeed your husband; I say that I am your husband, so come on,' he said. 'I am your husband come along.' She said, 'I know my husband, and you are another person.' 35. 'My husband's face is one and your face is another,' she told him. But in answer to this, the spirit said, 'You are lying; in truth I am your husband.' This is what the spirit told her. The wife took down her possessions. 'Let's go, you go on,' he said, and went along; that is, they went up and kept on going.

They went up and over and came to Orapipe. It is the other side over the ridge from Amoraba that they went, and then they went over and came to Orapipe. 40. That one went down and down. He kept on going, and at the place where he had buried that one he stopped and had his wife stay there. When he had her stop there, he said to the other spirits, 'Come on, kill my wife; let's come and do this,' he said. 'We'll take her and go,' said the other ghosts, 'we'll just take her, and we'll go.'

There was the great pile of wood there where he buried the man, and with reference to this wood the spirit told her, 'There's plenty of wood here, I have put plenty of wood.' 45. 'I put down lots of wood, but don't you burn it.' In Kiap talk he said it is taboo, it is taboo he told her. 'I put it there, but don't you burn it,' he told her. But his wife burned some of the wood. 50. Then she burned and burned it. She burned that wood and finished part of it. She burned some more wood and finished it, and kept burning some more and finishing it. She would

take a piece here and a piece there and burn the pieces two by two. She burned
plenty of that wood which was stacked up there where her husband was buried.
55. And she kept on burning it. She burned and burned and burned it. She burned
it till she came down to only a few pieces left. Then most of the wood was
finished. She took some more and said, 'I'll burn this too.' She uncovered it underneath like this.

60. She uncovered and uncovered it, and she saw that there was a cold body
there. 'What is this anyway?' she said She took a section of bamboo and lit it.
She looked and there was a body there. 'What is this?' she exclaimed. She poked
the burning bamboo down in order to see. 65. She looked closely like this, and
saw her husband. 'Yipes, I didn't think my husband was dead! That person is a
spirit who told me to come.' and she looked at the body. She looked and thought,
'He told me to come here, and I came.' She took some coals of fire. Then she took
her bundle on her shoulder and took it [the fire] in her hands and left. She went
and went and went.

70. She climbed and climbed and then he came to look where she had been
but she had gone out of sight. Now that husband brought plenty of spirits and
came over there. He looked there, but she was not in her bed. 'Where has she
gone?' he said. Quickly he went up and looked. She had gone to the edge of
the village. He went and went up quickly to look. He went and looked and was
looking from a place like this. 75. Over at a place like Naniyape he saw the
fire glowing red like this, the fire was burning. 'She has gone over there,' he
thought and he quickly went over there. He quickly went over from Naniyape,
the Kiap's house, and from a place like that he looked. At a place like Iyenerape
she disappeared, from a place like Iyenirape he looked for her. 80. Over there
at Ilakia at the big river, from Oibe, the place near the river, he went down.
From there he saw her. So he went to a place like Ilakia. It was like that that
they went on and on a very long way.

They went and went up, going up at Amoraba she would be there. And there
from Orapipe he would look down at her. From Pig-place (that is the name of
the place) he would see the flame of her coals she was carrying and follow
her. He looked from Pig-place. 85. From Panaro she carried the flaming coals
and went on. He had the other ghost stay there and he ran and ran after her.
'I will hold her, I will grab her,' he thought. But his wife ran on and on.

She did not come to her own house. 90. She went to her brother's house, she
did not go to her husband's house. She went into her brother's house. 'Oh my
dear brother, my dear brother [she cried] the spirit did so and so, and I ran.'
Then she lifted up her brother's hair like this. There under his hair she sat down
in the hollow at the back of his head. 95. At that hollow place at the back of
his head she sat down and was there.

The spirit came up. 'I'm not afraid of you two, I'm not afraid,' he said. 'But
it is not good that the men's house hit me,' he said. 'I am really afraid of you.
It is not good that the men's house hit me.' 100. When the spirit said that, that
sister was there at the back of his head. She was there and that is where she went
up and stayed they say. 'That is the way it happened to me, the spirit kept telling
me to come and I went, but when I ran away he didn't catch me.' This is what
she told her brother, so after she told her brother these things she settled there

at the hollow place at the back of his head and bore plenty of children there.

105. They tell me that there were plenty of eggs of the lice there; Wakara and (I can't think of his name—er—uh) Ubeyana; it was his father and Anontabu's father that told me. Those people desired to be there on his head in the form of lice. That is the way the Manika did it, and so his head had plenty of lice in it. The Manika, his sister, was there at the back of his head. Now when there are plenty of lice all the time in your head, don't complain, don't complain if there are plenty of lice on your head. The Manika, that sister, is there on your head.

110. These people will be there as plenty of lice in your bark skirt or on the head—plenty of lice will always be there. That is the talk which has always been told to us. This story is finished.

11. 'HOME LIFE'

1. *Mo mahbiga mo mahbiga ahreyabe uwana, ahreyabe arena uwana;*
   Another young-man another young-man girl happen, girl have happened;

2. *Anahkawawe anahkawawe ahreriyabe uwana, ahreyabe uwana, pokuwe.*
   Wife wife girl happened, girl happened, left.

3. *Awehkuwa mahbiwe awahreuwana iragobaqmena;*
   Husband young-man sick wood-went-for-bring;

4. *Mewena mewena ira wahtaq atoge.*
   Bring bring fire wood here-on-put.

5. *Irawahtaq atoge irarunsabe tumewena mo bareruq.*
   Fire-wood here-on-put he-said down-bring more burn.

6. *Mon kungah ira kobaq mena meawena mahtaq atoge iraruwena, aweh-*
   More go-for fire bring carry girl here put-down he-said, husband he sick,
   kawa we awahreuwana, awahreu waukenunsabe tumewena mo bahreruq.
   sick-was person down-brought more burned.

7. *Mira uwana ire gaweq anahgomari nawe nawe ire gaweragu waukenin*
   There happened fire good possums ate ate not good-was person hap-
   uwana;
   pened;

8. *Mira iraunsabe (mi)na anahkawawe pokuwarena pokuwarena mo mon*
   That said that wife went went more more go-get bring bring gave
   gobaq mena meya uwana bareruwonsabe pokuwe.
   burned-get-and she-went.

9. *Bahnahriahriahri ahnahri ahri.*
   Always-and always.

10. *Ira baq mena meyawa meyawanuge irareruwena, aiq tubarubahguwe*
    Wood for bring give give it-is-said, never working he-was-there;
    miyowana;

11. *Mo wena wahrah waukega anesabe ire gawragono arewe.*
    Others his people person why not well you.

12. *Arewe anesabe ire gaweragono anahgo ire garitaq nahnagapopoq ire*

You why not well possum not few eaten-probably not well.
gaweqragoneunsabe.
13. *Aiyaitonsabe mipinsuwena;*
Laziness that-throw-out;
14. *Aiyaitonsabe ipinsuwe na mina pokuwe.*
Laziness that-throw-out and that-one left.
15. *Aiyaitonsabe pokuwe uwana pokwe bokwe tanahwe mon ahtaq mere*
Laziness he-left happened went went ashes again road carry settled an-
antugiqmaq mon ahtaq mere antugiqmaq mon ahtaq mere antugiqmaruwe
other road carry settled another road carry settled do do.
uwe uwe.
16. *Pokwe bokwe bokwe pokwe bokwe bokwe bokwe.*
Went went went and kept going.
17. *Bokwe bokwe bokwe me mahbiwe pokuwe tahme miyahtaq kobari-*
Went went went that young-man went Tame that-tree rope-for-hanging,
kiriowana, anahkawan ahrariwe me poerahq erowaga subena;
wife girl that pig his-brother-in-law killed;
18. *Erowaga poerah subuwana, poerah subuwana minaga pokuwarena,*
Brother-in-law pig killed, pig killed that-one left, that again gave again
mena mo nauwana mon auwana ne mahbibona ire nanae.
gave I young-man not eat.
19. *Mahbibona ire nanae.*
Young-man not I-eat.
20. *Taraqmoga nawehro ne mahbibona ire nanae irarunsabe.*
Taramo's husband I young-man not I-will-eat he-said.
21. *Poerahqme nahno mahna nahno irarunsabe.*
Pig-is eat-you this eat they-said.
22. *Iraruwana ire ire naniyenauge.*
Said no no eat-I-want.
23. *Ire naniye nauge irareruwena uwana;*
Not eat-I want he-said happen;
24. *Poerahqme nahno uwana nahno uwana;*
Pig-is eat happen eat happen;
25. *Ire ironsabe mipi suena;*
Not pay-attention here throw-away;
26. *Taba tunsoqmena mo auwana abiahpe te inuninununsabe.*
Taba down-carry more gave-him nose-place from get-well.
27. *Mibeq mina nangae arena poerahqme ayaqnowana;*
There that ate give pig-is not-eat;
28. *Me mahbiwe pokwe bokwe bokwe, tahmemiyahta kobarikiriowana;*
This young-man went and went, Tame-tree hang-self;
29. *Mahna anahkawa ahrari kure gure gure.*
That wife girl went went went.

30. Koragowana tahmemiahtaq parikiriyonsebe.
   Went-look Tame-tree hanged-self.
31. We we pokuwarena moweh kuwena, iyahnabonime parikiguweuwara
   She she left other-man went, that-one hanged-himself got-brought that
kowewera me maisarowire.
bury.
32. Parabagiq.
   Finished.

1. There was another man who was married to a certain girl. He went to the girl that was his wife. The husband, this young man, got sick and the wife went and brought wood for him. She brought and brought firewood and put it down for him. 5. She would put it down where he told her and bring it and he would burn it. She would go for more and bring wood in to him and he would say, 'Put it down here.' This husband of hers was sick.

With regard to this sick fellow, she would go out and bring in wood and he would burn it up. He was not well and he would eat and eat possums and not be well: and so it went. It is said that his wife would continually go out and bring in more wood and give it to him, and he would burn it up and she would go out. This is always the way it went. 10. She would bring in the wood and give it to him and he would just be there doing nothing. Others of his friends would say, 'Why aren't you well? Why aren't you well? You are not well because you have eaten so many possums. You should get rid of that fashion of laziness.' He got rid of that fashion and left.

15. Because of his laziness he left and went and went. He carried ashes and sprinkled them on one road and put them down on another road and carried on and kept doing this. He went and went a long long way. He went, that particular young man finally went, and hanged himself by a vine on a Tame tree; as for the wife, her brother-in-law had killed a pig.

Her brother-in-law killed a pig before that one had left. He gave him some of it and gave him some more but that one said, 'I am a young man, I will not eat it, I am a young man so I'll not eat it.' 20. It was Taramo's husband saying, 'I am a young man and I'll not eat it,' it is said. 'But it is a pig, eat it, eat this,' they said. They told him this, but he said, 'I don't want to eat it, I don't want to eat it.' 'But it is a pig, eat it,' they said. 25. But he would not pay any attention to them and threw it down. And they got Taba insects for him, and gave him these, and he got well, But the pig that they gave him to eat, he refused.

That young man left, and hanged himself in a Tame tree. His young wife went and went. 30. She went looking and found he had hanged himself from the Tame tree. She then left and went to another man. As for the one who had hanged himself, others went and got him, and brought and buried him. The story is finished.

12. THE FOUNDING OF MOBUTA

1. Tehreh mobutareq tainorabareqne nahtuwo.

First Mobuta-and Tainoraba-and house-old.

2. *Nahtuwo sene marakowe morabi marako (tainoraba) tahmahbupeq*
House-old their ground two-own ground (Tainoraba) Tamabupe ground
marako awiqme marako awiqme.
name ground name.

3. *Manikanga maro marako abiqme tahmahbupeq mora nahtuwo tainor-*
Old-people were ground name Tamabupe one house-broken Tainoraba
aba waukereq mobutah waukweneqne mora nahtuwo uwana.
person Mobuta person-and one house-old was.

4. *Mobutahpe sewiyahna waukene poerahka sure sure.*
Mobuta future person pig came came.

5. *Pehipehinehweh mire sure surewe.*
Lie is come come.

6. *Motaq mire.*
Soon be.

7. *Ma aite ieniq.*
Er—where from—.

8. *Wahniansopete wahniyansopete tahgowana.*
Waniyansope Waniyansope from-saw.

9. *Mo waukega mo mo waukewega runse.*
Other person other other person came-down.

10. *(Tabanogopeq) awiraipete tunserunse.*
(Tabangope) Awiraipe-from came-down.

11. *Tabangopeq tunse.*
Tabangope came-down.

12. *Mahbeq seraqmobagu seraqmobagu unsabe.*
Here nothing-in-sight nothing happen.

13. *Wahnsa waukwega e mobutapeq wauke miya uwanabomo miyawa-*
Spirit person yes Mobuta person here knows here-are said.
pomo iraruwena.

14. *Miyapopoq metaganiye iwiyahruwenawe.*
Where I-see thought.

15. *Poerahka sure sure sure sure.*
Pig came and came.

16. *Mahpin seragowena wauke ire miyonsabe peh marako konsabe.*
Here came-see person not were just ground had.

17. *Pehipi marako konsabe.*
Just ground was.

18. *Ne tagaragaume sawarepete tagaragaume.*
I look ridge look.

19. *Wauke sure tabangope setaqnobagoseraqno bagonsebe seragoge aneq-*
Person came Tabangope went-out-of-sight disappear go why person not
sabe wauke ire miyahpomo uwana iwiyah ena.
here did think.

20. *Poerahka gurime, gurime, nahopeq gurimeq mahna mahma marakobi*
Pig rooted, rooted, house root here this ground here-root, more there
kurimaq moisebe isena nahtuwoipeq turuturuqne nahngeh guri maruwe.
Natuwope-at Tultul house rooted did.
21. *Gurime gawerarena uwana wene—wene poerahka gurime gurime*
Rooted make-good did he—he pig rooted rooted made-good.
gawerarena.
22. *Kiyamiyonganga kiyaninimena (wena) mena maqme, mahpin guriq*
Pregnant animal (he) this bore, here rooted bore bore good went went
maqme maqme gawerarena pokwe bokwe bokwe.
went.
23. *Abowaba topahnsabe taganegenaguwana, taganiyenagena uwana, wene*
Father sweet-potato looked-for, looked-for happen, her pig child one
poerahqme ani masusa (miq) miyonsabe.
there (?) put.
24. *Aiq maqmerarpomo iwiyah aruwena miyowana.*
Where bear thought is there.
25. *Tanahbiyoqme aboboraq (taq) poerahqme aboborapeq tanahbiyoqme,*
Ashes-sprinkle back-on (?) pig back sprinkle-ashes, sprinkle look-for
biyoqme kaberawowana sure sure.
came came.
26. *Tanah mo mitaq mere mere aq tanah mo mitaq mere aq uwe uwe uwe*
Ashes again there put put it ashes again on put they went along.
uwe uwe.
27. *Mahpin sewiyowana poerahq ebeq sewiyowana, abowawe aipomo ena*
Here they-were pig they were-at, father where it foot track track track
aigara araqme araqme araqme araqme araqme araqme.
track—.
28. *Araqmena sure sure.*
Tracks came came.
29. *Iyanirapete giragome mibeq mahbeq kibekunsabe sure sure kiyapene*
Iyanirape-from came-up look here up-come come come Kiap house
nahtate nahniyahpete tagome.
Naniyape-from look.
30. *Ahtaq ubehntapeq sebekonsabe mina sure.*
Path Ubentape there-come there come.
31. *Aiyahnsuwenorate wehrongore topahtaten seragome.*
Ayansuwenora-from Wero-old sweet-potato level-looked.
32. *Mahtaq sebe konsabe aigara araqmena.*
Here there is foot tracks.
33. *(Anabino) irawensabeq wainarorate giragome mahtaq kiragonsabe*
(Anabino) Irawensabe stream-place-up look here went-look Anabinota
anabinotapeq (tupo marakoraq) kibe kunsabe mine sure senagome ahre-
(ball ground) went-up come there come look wife woman house is place

rone inahopeq nah geh mipipeq marumaqme.
bore.

34. *Poerahqarahqmari maqme kawerarena mipi miyonsabe.*
Pig-place there good there were.

35. *Nene poerahqme mahbeq miyarapomo ena runse.*
My pig here they-are it came.

36. *Wene poerahq ahre arasa miyonsabe.*
His pig ear cut-off stay.

37. *Mipi maru topah maru nawena.*
There down sweet-potato down ate.

38. *Ahahkawansabe aqau itene poerahqme ire wahtotaq mati ehre ire*
Wife no our pig not short bore there not Amoraba, not Owibete ground
ahmorapeq, ire owibete marapeq mahnsepipeq mati ehre.
over-there bore them.

39. *Itene poerahq ire wahtotaq mati ehre ire wahto ire wahto mati ire*
Our pig not short-distance bore there not short not short bore not short
wahto ire wahto matiyehre.
not short bore-there.

40. *Pokuweyabo mahwe ewowana.*
Go-we come said.

41. *Mo amoraba waukwega amorapeq miyah mi waukega pokuwe.*
Other Amoraba person at-Amoraba was that person went.

42. *Saikahpete ebahnga gibawena ebahnga gibawena.*
Forest ground-hog up-shot ground-hog shot.

43. *Ano ano anongame ire nawasa peh aya peh aya no uwana.*
Big big big-was not give-eat just intestines just intestines gave did.

44. *Wa gitabehre aneq nanieno gitabehre uwana.*
Oh bitter what you-gave bitter was.

45. *Anongame ire nabinauge peh aya nahno peh aya nahno ena.*
Big not give-eat just guts eat just guts eat you.

46. *Mabuta wauke naunsabe ire gawerone ano naniyo ayame gitabehre.*
Mobuta person gave not good big give guts bitter.

47. *Gitapehre ire gawerone anonga naniyo unsabe.*
Bitter not good big-one give eat.

48. *Anongame ire arena aya nahnoena ayanaunsabe.*
Big-one not yours guts eat-you guts-gave.

49. *We abiyahnsanuwena.*
He found.

50. *Nene poerahq ire wahto maqme, miyehrabe pokiniye iwiyahena sure*
My pig not distance bore, where-bore go-I thought come come.
sure.

51. *Wene mensamehnsa mewena sure sureuwana.*
His possessions carried came came.

52. *Tainorahbah waukweninga tainorapeq miyo waukeninga aipo kono*
    Tainoraba person Tainoraba there person where go happen.
uwana.
53. *Ine nene poerahq miyehnsabe koraganauge, wauwane wensabe.*
    I my pig where look-for-want, return he.
54. *Pehipehin ehweh teyawena pehipehin ehweh teyawena (pokw-) sure*
    Lie talk told lie talk told when—came came came came came.
sure sure sure sure sure sure.
55. *Seragowana (mi)pi miyonsabe, aipo uwe se aborisabe aborisabe abori-*
    Level-look this where, where is come clear-ground clear-ground clear-
sabe nahme aborisabe (?) kawerarena (me) na.
ground house clear (?) good that.
56. *Mo waukwe tahmaro waukwe ko weriq mena meyarena.*
    More person few person go get brought here.
57. *Weni iyahnabo weni iyahnabo koweriqmena meyarena mahtape we*
    His friend his friend get-bring here place he be-here, always here stay said.
miyanae, ahriahri mahtaq miyawiyahonae arena.
58. *Tainorahbah waukweyabe ine kaweq marako ragonsabe pokuge teya-*
    Tainoraba person I good ground saw I-go told did.
wena uwana.
59. *Tainorahbah waukwewe ne mahpi miyanowe ninebataq miyana.*
    Tainoraba person I here will-stay only will-stay.
60. *Ire gawe inaugwe senahpeq tainorahpeq pokinaugwe irarena.*
    Not good I-want up-hill Tainoraba go-I said.
61. *We we sokawena pokwe bokwe.*
    He he possessions go go.
62. *Senahpeq tainorahpeq kiwiyowanawe.*
    Went-up Tainoraba up-settle.
63. *Mobutah waukewe sure, mahpinsewiyowana mo amoraba waukewe*
    Mobuta person came, here-settle other Amoraba person went up-hill
pokwe senahpeq amorapeq miyowana.
Amoraba settle.
64. *Wene naho naho manikanga maro nahtuwobime ire miyasa.*
    He old old Manika down house-broken not is-there.
65. *(Pokwe pokwe) mobutah wauke mahbepokuwana, amorabah wauke*
    (Go go) Mobuta person here-came, Amoraba person up-hill went,
senahpe pokuwana, tainorahbah waukwe isebeq tahpe pokuwana.
Tainoraba person level there went.
66. *Mahpime poerahka kureme gawerarena uwana.*
    Here pig root good happen.
67. *Miyawiya uwe uwe uwe uwana, mo tabankopeqme wauke waukerahn-*
    Stay stay there continually, again Tabankope person person-like spirit
sanuwe wahnsaga waukerahnsa nuwe serabanagu serabanagu unsabe wena-

person-like was-there disappear disappear is his-name Tabankope *disap-*
wiq tabankopere serabankopere arena uwana.
peared they say.

68. Na mahpime miyawe miyawe miyawe wiyame uwana.
Now here stay and be long time.

69. Wene poerahqmarime phe suwansuwa mora bopoqnahra suwansuwa
He pigs just quickly one moon quickly big quickly big-animals were.
anota suwansuwa anotangmari miyonsabe.

70. Suwansuwa ano nurare poerah suwansuwa ano nurare ena.
Quickly big grew pig quickly big grew did.

71. Mo mina mo nurowanamo matawena uwana.
Again there others grew others bore happen.

72. (M)inan suwansuwa ano nukuwana mo matawena uwana, mina
That quickly big grew others bore did, that quickly big grew killed ate
suwansuwa ano nukuwena subiqme nowana mah marakoraqme ahnde
here ground plenty people stay.
waukwe miyosabe.

73. Tainorapeq ahnde wauke miyonsabe, amorapeq pehreh tehtare wauke
Tainorape plenty people were, Amoraba just two people stay, two peo-
miyoyeiq, tehtehre waukwe miyoyansabe peh.
ple live just.

74. Tainorabare mobutahre mon serah ire garita waukwe miyanehbo.
Tainoraba-and Mobuta-and both alike not few people stay.

75. Amorahbah wauke pehrehtare wauke miyahno mira niwiyah arena,
Amoraba person just-two person live that thinking here, here ground
mah marakopime mobutapeq (ma) akahta amahnaga wene poerahka ire
Mobuta (?) half now his pig not Manika put-down.
manikanga atasa.

76. Ire manikanga mah marakora miyahno ire iyamire, manikangawe
Not Manika this ground be-there not tell-them, Manika Tainoraba vil-
tainorahbah suwahpeq marapeq miyahno arena uwanawe.
lage down-hill you-be set-them happen.

77. Wene poerahka wensabe mahowe maqme (su—) marakowe maqme
His pig him come bring (came) ground bring came.
suwana.

78. Mah marakopi poerahka miyehre (a—) waukeninse poerahse anonu-
Here ground pig settle (er—) people pigs grew.
ranae.

79. Poerahqme ire peh garitaq anonuranae anotah anonuranae irarewe
Pig not just few grew-big grew-big grew say is-said.
irariq.

80. Parabagiq.
Finished.

1. At first Mobuta and Tainoraba houses were broken down. The place where these two peoples owned ground together was called Tamabupe—that's the name of the area. The old people (Manika) were there and the area was named Tamabupe, and there was one broken-down house belonging to the Tainoraba and Mobuta people. The future Mobuta person's pig came and came [over here where we are]. 5. That's not true that he came and came. Pretty soon that will come in this story (er—from where—). From Winiyansope he saw it. Another person came down. 10. He came down from a Awiraipe. He came down to Tabangope. Here there was nothing in sight. A spirit-person said, 'Yes, but who knows where any Mobuta people are,' it is said. 'I will see if there are any,' he thought. 15. Now a certain pig came and came. She came over here to look and there were no people here, only the land, just the land. 'I will look and look, I will look from the ridge [she said]. A man came and went out of sight at Tabangope, so I'll look. 'Why is no one here?' she thought.

20. The pig rooted and rooted there. She rooted at the women's houses, here at this place, and she rooted over there at Natuwo's at the Tultul's house. She rooted and made it good for herself, that is, the pig rooted and made it good. Now the pig got pregnant and bore little ones. Here where she had rooted she bore and had made it good and had gone there. She looked for her owner (father) for sweet potatoes looking and looking for food. When she went to look, she left her piglets where she had been. 'Where did she bear those pigs?' he [her owner] wondered.

25. He sprinkled ashes on her back (the back of the pig is where he sprinkled the ashes), he sprinkled them on her back and came looking. He put, and kept putting ashes on her as he went along and kept doing this. They got near this place, the pig was going first. Her owner said, 'Where are they? Here are her footprints here and here.' Her tracks came on and on. From Iyanirape he came and looked, and came on up here and looked from the Kiap's house. 30. From Naniyape he came on the path to Ubenatape where there were tracks. He looked at old Wero's sweet potato garden, and there were tracks there too. At Trawensabe, at the stream, he went up and looked, he looked here and at Anabinota (the soccer field), he went up and came along here, he came and looked at the women's houses there where the house is, and found where she bore them. The piglets were born there, and she had made it good for them there.

35. 'My pig, are they really here?' he said. He cut the ears of his pig [the Awa always mark a tame pig by cutting the ear]. There he gave them sweet potato to eat. Now with reference to his wife, he explained to her, 'Our pig bore her young a long way over there, not at Amoraba or at the low ground, but she bore her young way down over there. Our pig bore her young a long, long way away.' 40. 'Let's go there,' her husband told her.

Another fellow at Amoraba was at Amoraba when that one left. He shot a ground hog up there in the forest. It was very big. Now he did not give him [the Mobuta person] any of it to eat. He just gave him the intestines. 'Wow, what you gave me was bitter,' he said. 45. 'That animal is big, but I'll not give you any of the good meat, you eat just the guts, just the guts are for you.' Now the Mobuta person said, 'With reference to what you gave me, it was awful. It was bitter and not good.' 'It was a big animal and it was not yours,' the other responded; 'You just eat the guts,' and he gave him that part.

He [Mobuta person] was angry at him. 50. 'My pig bore piglets a long way away. I'll go there where the little pigs are.' He carried off his possessions, and came on this way. A Tainoraba person was at Tainoraba and he asked the man where he was going. 'Oh, I want to look to see where my pig is; I'll return,' he said. But that was a lie that he told him, it was a lie and he went, that is, he came and came.

55. Now he looked around there to see where he would clear the area. He worked and worked clearing the area and making a place for a house. That person went and got a few more people, and brought them over. He went and got his friends, and brought them and said, 'Let's be here, we will settle down here always,' he said. He told the Tainoraba person, 'I will go to a good ground which I have seen.'

The Tainoraba person said, 'I'll just stay here alone.' 60. 'It's not good just me alone, but I'll go uphill to Tainoraba,' he said. So he took his possessions and went there. Up at Tainoraba he settled down. The Mobuta person came and came and settled down here. Another one, an Amoraba person, went and he was over there at Amoraba. The old broken-down house [of the old, old people] is no longer there [where the people lived before they moved to make the three villages]. 65. The Mobuta person came here, the Amoraba one went up the hill, and the Tainoraba person went over there on the level ground. Here the pig rooted around and made it good.

These people continued to stay on here. That other Tabankope person who is spiritlike, that is, a spirit who is like a person—the one who disappeared, his name was Tabankope—he disappeared they say. They have been here a long long time. The pigs grew up very quickly, in only a month they got big. 70. They grew very quickly, and the pigs got big fast. Other pigs grew, and they bore others. Those in turn grew up, and they killed them and ate them here on this ground where there were plenty of people settled. There were plenty of people also at Tainoraba, at Amoraba only a few, just two people stayed there, just two people. Tainoraba and Mobuta were alike in that a lot of people were in those places. At Amoraba there were just two people—'You two be there,' it was thought. 75. This ground at Mobuta is where that one's pig, not a Manika but the pig, settled in there half long ago. It was not a Manika, he did not tell them, 'You be here.' The Manika told the Tainoraba village, 'You be there downhill.' But here it was a pig that indicated where this ground should be. The people settled on this land, and the people and pigs increased a lot. The pigs were not just small ones, they grew very large, it is said. This story is finished.

13. THE KILLING OF ECHEGA

 1. *Minehweh esaya subito.*
    This-talk Echega killed.
 2. *Subito mapite mahbigaho pokurera, imbaruwa suwapeq poiraq kibi-*
    Killed from-here young-men went, Wananara village boy want-to-get-

yanaera.
go-up.
3. *Poiraq kibiyanaera kirorabete aikibera.*
   Boy want-go-get-go get-work-from finish-up.
4. *Tunsaqmaqme tutauraebeq.*
   Down-came came-down-from.
5. *Amorabahga subonaera arutauwara.*
   Amoraba will-kill give-it.
6. *Subonaera arutauwara inokapeq surarera nahniyahpeq segaiareraurau-*
   Kill give at-night came Nania came-and-slept-it-was-said.
wara.
7. *Sinowa sibowasabe aqao.*
   Their-mother their-father no.
8. *Amorabahga aura nubirana senauge uraunsabe.*
   Amoraba fellow skin hit return-because.
9. *Ahbiyepeqme kowara rirebera kure.*
   Next-morning bow-string renew went.
10. *Koirarenara kogotionana irakauninaraqme senae aruera mahpite*
    Level-going-to-go-and talk-and argue fight shouldn't from-here young-
wehwe.
men.
11. *Nahbiomi yegarahwe bokuwarera.*
    Young-men plenty went-over.
12. *Topanabiq nabiqebera agaupeqte wauke eqmaq awatauwana amora-*
    Sweet-potato for-eating Agaupe man sent gave Amoraba up-went-to-give-
peqme kireriyewarainsabe.
notice.
13. *Pokuwarere kogotionaeq munera kurome.*
    Went-they to-argue want went.
14. *Kogotionaeq munera gurominawe ire momaq aneriya nahopeqme peh*
    Argue want went not another I-forgot house-place just place-from.
mahbete.
15. *Senona tapeq mobarabaraoara.*
    First on-level shot-and-miss.
16. *Senono tapeq senono tapeq mobarabaraoara.*
    First on-level first on-level shot-and-miss.
17. *Senon tapeq mo barabaraonsabe aipoaruwera mina ebaeruwera.*
    First level again shot-and-miss finished there fight.
18. *Kowekuwe momahbeq mahbesewewanehbouraumemaq.*
    Came-back here this-place-they-stay-no-good.
19. *Mo anetaq seweq kuraunga ongio egawiyabo.*
    Again why they going garden destroy.
20. *Koragarowe senowa sibowehga (eqma suwa taowehra gorauminaga*

Went-to-look their-mothers their-fathers (?) came-back house (?).
erahtaq kowe) kuwerera nahpipeq (kewanae bouraume).
21. *Seabiqmiruena esegiyame nonsuwepea kuwana urehbena.*
    Skirmish Echega ditch/rut went fought.
22. *Urerana marebeh uwena tuwewarairana.*
    Fight down-hill did pulling-the-bow.
23. *Tondibe turuturuq koregaq esegiyame paraerara kowewera suraq-*
    Tondibe Tultul old-man Echega shot come-back come-back.
maqme.
24. *Mapime arauwerapo.*
    Here how-long.
25. *Mobutapeqme apataroraq kigairairana.*
    Mobuta-is three-on stay-over-night.
26. *Awaropeq tatareraq tunkairairana.*
    Awalarosa two down-hill-stay-and-sleep.
27. *Awaropeqte tuwekuwe mahpi tahtareraq kigairairana.*
    From-Awalarosa down-hill-back this-place two stayed.
28. *Mapite abepete morawe pokuwe.*
    Here from six went.
29. *Purotapeq tuwe kaiarena kire mokendi kirauwana.*
    Purosa down-hill stayed up-hill-went Okapa stayed.
30. *Sotaga poriah soriatairana.*
    Doctor arrow pulled-out.
31. *Petairabeqme pukurairana.*
    Darkness he-died.
32. *Tunse okandibetenatapeq tunse.*
    Come-down-from Okapa come-down.
33. *Kobarubeq tuwekaiarena.*
    Kobaru down-stay.
34. *Mina runse mataq tutaowana.*
    That come-down here come-down.
35. *Mata tunse mata tatareraq tumiarau.*
    Here down-came here two down-came.
36. *Moraraq maru matawera.*
    Together down carry-him.
37. *Ahbiapeqme maru maisatawe.*
    In-the-morning down buried.
38. *Iraruraun ehweh ira taunaeq.*
    It-was-said talk it was-told.

1. This talk is about the killing of Echega. When he was killed, the young men went from here, going up to Wananara to get work as servants. They wanted to go up there to get such work, and completed their negotiations

[trying to get the work]. Then they came on down from there.

5. A fellow from Amoraba threatened to kill one of them. Because of that threat of killing, they came on at night, coming along, they slept at Nania. Now with respect to their mothers and fathers, they had said not to fight. That Amoraba fellow was going to fight them, that's why they intended to go back again [to Amoraba]. So the next morning they renewed their bow strings and started out. 10. They were going to go over there and talk and argue that there shouldn't be a fight to kill a man from here. A lot of young men went over to argue. They took sweet potato to eat, and sent an Agaupe man over to give notice to Amoraba of their intentions. They really went over there to argue. They wanted to argue, so they went, not for some other . . . I forgot, uh . . . in the house.

15. At first then they [the Amoraba men] shot at them and missed. They short first and missed. They shot first and missed again. When they did this, they finished off fighting. Then they came back. It was not good to stay there. Also why, when they went, did they destroy their gardens? 20. Their mothers and fathers had told them to go watch their own gardens, but they went over there and skirmished.

As they skirmished, Echega fought from a ditch. He was fighting—just pulling out the bow [being in a shooting position] Tondebe, the old Tultul [from Amoraba] shot Echega, then he [Echega] came back here. How long did they stay over? 25. They stayed over in Mobuta three days [after the fight]. Then they went down and stayed at Awalarosa two days. Six people went from here. At Purosa they went and stayed, then went on up and stayed at Okapa.

30. The doctor pulled out the arrow. But he died in the darkness. They came down, then, coming down from Okapa. They then stayed at Kobaru. Then they came on down here. 35. They came here, coming here in two days. They came together carrying him along. In the morning they buried him. This is what was told to us.

14. PYTHON STORY: ILAKIA

1. Nen awehpite irareyebe irariye woin ehwehpite (mowau—) (poqna-
My talk-from talking talk-I this talk-on (?) (Poqnabe—Poqnabe—)
beq—poqnabeq—) poqnabeteq mahbi tehtare mahbi (tehtare—) mahbi
Poqnabe-from young-man two young-man (two—) young-men two (er—)
tehtarega (a—) mo abahrugo mo abahruyeiq.
another dance other dance-two-did.

2. Tehtare mahbi rarega mo abah ruyehneh aipo ahrariwi tehtare ahrari
Two young-men two more dance two-did where girl two girl two we
tehtarega ite nakaeq nirupebei.
good I-desire.

3. Mahbi ine irupebe mahbiga ahbahrone iraruweiq.
Young-men them pleased young-men danced said.

4. Ita takuwena (a—) namon ahrasiga mo mahbitabe uwana (moq—)
So saying (er—) other girl other young-men did (other—) those girls

mon arahsiga mo mahbi teteuweiq.
those young-men want-take.

5. *Uwana aqau ne mahna waukweni mire inebo(q) (a—neq——) aganie*
   Happen no I this person it-is not-good (er—I——) python being py-
   nena wehya (anene) mina arerena aganie (irah——) aganie nena nepo-
   thon (what-do) this say python (no——) python become I-go-up person
   kinapoq waukweni mire tenirahno auguena mina aganie maraipeq pokuwe.
   it-is come-with-me-you said that python downhill went.

6. *Maraipeq bokuwe iraru maraqne bokuwanawi tahpah tahpah mahqma-*
   Down-hill went said ground went bat bat that-young-man like-that left.
   biwi aipo bokuweiq.

7. *Okahena mena arasirega (a—) naunah meoyapi totumari pehrame*
   Possessions those two-girls (er—) bag took beans pack bag put-in left
   unahn tabera bokwe maqmena ahnanupe teoyeiq.
   beside path were.

8. *Teyoyara abah rewena kuwerowana kuwerowana pokuweiq.*
   Come-two dance at-dawn morning left.

9. *Tenenaupeq tenaupeq pokuyena aipo kerimaqme.*
   Their-house their-house went-two like-that were-married.

10. *Gire gire gire gire ire takigarera mina tahpahngawi marawe mo buwah*
    Go-up go-up go-up up up-there-went that bat like-that flew and flew-
    mbuwah mbwahnuweiq.
    away.

11. *Mo buwah mbuwah nuwena iyebeq taweharutapeq pokuweiq.*
    So flew flew did up-there mountain-sky left.

12. *Pokuwana inaq inaq arati tahpahn keronaq arati kiwekuo kiwekuo.*
    Gone this this girl bat married girl you-go-back go-back.

13. *Kiwekuanawi aganien keronaq (mahbipeqnike) ahrayibeqneq kero-*
    Go-back python marry (young-man-it-was) girl-it-was married.
    weiq.

14. *Maraqnai poku boku boku boku.*
    Along-ground go go go go.

15. *Bokwe bokwe auyahpeq auyahpeqte mahbigaena pokuarena pinkiyo-*
    Go go Auyana Auyana-from young-men went went-and-stayed (er—)
    wana (a—) aipo nemahrainaugwe ayuwena mina ne mahnaneq mahnugeq
    enough I-am-like-this he-said that I this-thing this-one he-said python
    aruwenan aganie keukuweiq.
    changed.

16. *Neq waukweninka kekuwennaina (a—) neneiq maraqnawe parirawe*
    He person he-changed (er—) I-like ground uncoil go ledge his house
    parirawe onikiahpi wene nahopeq onikiahpi auyahpeq onikiahpipeq mipeke
    ledge Auyana ledge-place there coiled-up.
    keboqnaguweiq.

17. Keboqnaguwana aipo mo pareruqme miyowana mipi mo sekatena aipo
Coil-up enough then build-fire be-there there then put-her like-that he
we(w)i pokuwarena, motahq motahq taikahpipeq motahq kiyuwena kiraq-
went, hunt hunt forest-in hunt up-go cut brought-down brought-down gave.
nena murunka murunka nuweiq.
18. Ayahnta ayahnta murunka murunka nuwana, natuq naturuweiq.
Bone bone brought brought gave, ate ate.
19. Tiyaqmaqme ekupi tiya naruq; naruwana naruq; naruwana ina aipo
Cook fire-in cook eat; eat-and eat; eat that like-that he-went food down-
bebokuwarena topah tuwinaena topah tuwinaena pe pokuwarena pe moki
give food give again left again again shoot uncooked ate this-way come
pehwena isiya nasuwena mabeq kiraqmena maru tupesuwena pentuwekuweiq.
down throw-down go-back-bush.
20. Uwana uwana uwana irauwana—(pe—namoq—) amukikiruwana
Do do do like-this-do—(again—more—) get-full that-place slept.
iterapi tuntugoeiq.
21. Tanonkebi tanonkebi tuntugena aipo mena topah nabikatowana
Near-fire near-fire after-sleep like-that this food gave-husband left.
pokuweiq.
22. Peraikahpipeq taikahpe pokuwe pe pe mokibehwena tagenamoq
Went-bush forest went again again shoot-went looking again-went got-
penamuru amutakiwe kaweruena pemina kiraqnena eberaipeq tahq
full good again-this cut-up one-side part bring-give.
marunkauweiq.
23. Murunkauwana nasuwena tagena moq pe mipi tuntuge nena mo
Bring-give went look other again here sleep-there again more food take-
topah tomenena pen tugekuweiq.
eat again go-sleep.
24. —Topah tuwahnowena mobarewe nagatoana inatumewe nabiqnena
—Food get-from-garden cook gave-cooked that-down-take eat-finish
menaqmoq ibeq mari tuperuruweiq.
again there down throw-away.
25. Uwana uwana aipo mina itaq marena pemera iniena uwana puweq.
Do do enough that there put again do-like-before do did.
26. Awahninga mukarini miyoweiq.
Wife got-pregnant she-was.
27. —Amuq—muq—— a—kia kia miyoweiq; amukikiquweiq; mukarini
—Stomach—stom——er—big big she-was; get-pregnant; get-pregnant
mukarini miyowana aire atuqmaqme (ina) mukarinimiyahneq.
pregnant she-was did said (er) pregnant-she-was.
28. Topahn tunowe mobarewe naniteyaho asuwena pe motahrina pokuweiq.
Food down-bring cook you-put-away said again hunt-possum left.
29. Pokuwaqmaqme kibehwena (ina) pe mina ibehq ki wanene ayuwena

Left up-shoot (er) again that up-there up ate said head cut-off down-
pehqno kiraqmena murungauweiq.
bring-give.

30. *Murungaundabe paitareuwe miraune ayuwena namoq pentuwe kuntabe*
     Down-bring-give wait she-said did then again-bring came-with that her-
inaq anowa koreni inaq unahmpi agiqmamaqme togatoweiq.
mother old that bag-in took-off put-on-head.

31. *Togatowana iteta mataoatuena we topah ndahrina anowa pokuweiq.*
     Putting-on-head there put-did she food get-cook mother left.

32. *Topah ndarina anowa pokundabe mena ibitondabe ibitondabe marawe*
     Food cooked mother went that cry cry like-that side-on here-on put-them.
tahwatoq marataq iraroweiq.

33. *Irarena mahpeq tumena mahpeq tumena kuwam pokuwana irepete-*
     Put outside she-was outside she-was out went outside-from-up-were adder
(mi)naq wahya pweguwa maqme pweguwaq maqme tahpi tahpipe tabiku-
fell-out there fell-out there coals coals burned-up.
weiq.

34. *Tahpipe tabikuwana mahpeq tumena irarowana mahpete uwo uwo*
     Coals burned-up outside was heard-it outside-from moan moan went look
untabe kiragome tahpin tabitoweiq.
coals burned.

35. *Tehtare tabitoweiq.*
     Two burned.

36. *Tehtareundabe kiwaq maqme—tanahga tanahgaq amboupeq tutaroweiq.*
     Two-because lift-up there—ashes-with ashes bottom put-in.

37. *Tutarena augiangamari augiangamari abobonaq abobonaq tutaroweiq.*
     Put-in alive alive on-top on-top fill-it.

38. *Tutarowana aipo anowawi ahpete kire kire kire kire.*
     Fill enough mother path-from came-up came came came.

39. *Kiragowana aqau wen anoba kirowana we menanimari tugahndabe*
     Came-look no her mother ask she those-children sleeping there I-
ibeq mearogeuweiq.
put-said.

40. *Anebepeq meyarogeuweiq.*
     Where I-put-them-said.

41. *Meyarogeundabe ehreraq irarogeundabe ayuwena moparebare uwe*
     I-put on-hook did did cook did good food cook good food cook fix-good
kaerarena topah mbarewe kaerarena topah mbarewe kaerarenaina marawe
like-that bag-in look-in—.
unahpipeq tagaweina—.

42. *Uwanaina nahnkawenaq nahnkaqenaq aipo mena unah kiagiqmaqme.*
     Happen breast-give nurse-good that-way that bag take-off.

43. *Marawe nahngawena marawe puewe tagomi puewe togomi tanahawahrin*

Like-that breast-give like-that take-out look take-out look ashes had.
koweiq.

44. *Tanahwahrin kontabe kontabe mahnawi abete tanah abiyamowena*
Ashes-were hang hang these from-where ashes where-ask like-that
marawe nahn kawiniena nah nah marauwena iye nontabe (ahq) wena
breast give breast breast like-this-gave not eat (oh) those all those-things
tomi menkamahrinka marawe tomi nah marawe kiwanowanawi.
like-that all breast like-that they-ate.

45. *Tatarega iye noweiq.*
Two not ate.

46. *Iye nontabe abeq kenabiyamoena marawe pehikahnuwe tagomi*
Not eat where they-are like-that search look there there burned were.
mipipeq mipipeq tabiqme koweiq.

47. *Tabiqme koantabe mahkarani aneneah aneneah nanabo ayuena*
Burned be-there that-small-child what what did-do said out-of-sight
pehipeqaupeq marena ireinae tahnda narumi puewe taga irawe taga
put not-do like I-told-you take-out look like-that look do-like I-said no
inaetahnda narumi aqawe wetonana aipoge kebehrankwe tabikoyo uweiq.
take-out only they-jump-out burned happen.

48. *Ayuwena ina (we——) wenanonkorenemi ahbeq katanaboena abowaga*
Said this (she——) her-mother-old where put-them father beat-no-
tubinaena topahmi barewe barawe barwew (a——) unahpi tuturutu
good food cooked cooked cooked (er——) bag-in put-put fill-up.
agatoweiq.

49. *Tuturutu agatowena (inamoq iyebeten ehwehtaq kowasuwogeiq)*
Put-put filled-up (uh-er what-sort talk-this belong-another) put-put
tuturutu agatowena ina mahngauq nangauqna tuturutu agatowana aipo
fill-up this get-ready all-night put-put fill-up then left.
pokuweiq.

50. *Kauqne bokwe bokwe bokwe bokwe kowekwe bokwe bokwe bokwe*
Afternoon went went went went went.
bokwe.

51. *Bokwe bokwe tahqni tahqni moraga moraga(w)ena mahtaba nenahbo*
Went went sugar-cane cane one one-given here no-good-you-eat go go go
bokwe bokwe bokwe bokwe bokwe toqmatapeq muru nahouweiq.
go Toqmata down go-said.

52. *Arene nahmi intekare aruwe toqmatapeq indetaq marunaho uweiq.*
Your house there-is be Toqmata there go-down-eat said.

53. *Marunaho uwana mena mena aipo iyeta tumena mena marawe*
Go-down-eat do carry take then up-there came take like-that came-
maruntubi tubiruwe.
down-hit hit.

54. *(Mahq——) mahrena arena marundahtah tuaroq tuaroq mahrara*

(There———) like-that do go-down tap tap on-this down-went.
muruweiq.

55. *Mahrawe tubi tubi tubi tubiruwena mahtena kobaiq meraga (maq)*
    Like-that hit hit hit hit here-coming went-around like-this (that) went-
ebete marawe we mara kowetagu ebete bokwe bokwe bokwe.
looked front he front circled went-looked front went went went.

56. *Mo aiyahbanahpetaq bokwe bokwe kobaiq; meraga ebetaq bokwe bokwe*
    Again Ayabana-on went went circled; around front went went went.
bokwe.

57. *Kobaiq meragawena tun tun tun tu mitate teromi aiq marawe mara*
    Circled around come come come from-there listen oh like-this like-
tuweiq.
this came.

58. *Baki baki baki uweiq.*
    Hit hit hit did.

59. *Untabe (ina) paitareuwe tere rere rere rere rere.*
    Happen (uh) waited came came came came came.

60. *Mahbete marawe (mi)naitaq, matate (aq) agno ita teungiyoweiq.*
    Here-from like-that almost, here (uh) her-head there bite-off-did.

61. *(O) giaqme mahna ahnabo waukweni ano kaukweni nawe nawe nawe*
    (Oh) sever this that-one person that person ate ate ate ate.
nawe.

62. *Naintatuwena nawe anaintatuwena manaq aqnomi baqmena pokuneiq.*
    Eaten eat eat-finish that her-head take-mouth leave.

63. *Ompimah marawe pahqmena pahqmena bokwe bokwe bokwe bokwe*
    Mouth-in this-way hold hold go go go go go.
bokwe.

64. *Aipo ayaungantabe arenano mari tubiqnena kiyugeena mina manaq*
    Then daughter your-mother down killed-I-her came-back-I this here her-
ayahqno mipeq mo kirutaireiq.
head there again dropped-it.

65. *Arubi mahpi mahwi taroweiq.*
    Lap here here hold-it.

66. *Mahwi rarowana e iraone irare paitare ayuwena miyowana miyowana*
    When-it hold you-did did wait said was-there was-there went again get-
pokwe pe motahrina raikahpeq bokuweiq.
possum forest left.

67. *Bokuntabe (a——) abehnti ranami tirena, abehnti rananami tiwarera*
    Go (er——) leaf-in bamboo cooked, leaf-in bamboo cook stone there
oniki mipipeq ekupipeq igowaroweiq.
fire-in put-in.

68. *(Igo——) mahpipeq mahraroweiq.*

(Uh—) this-place did-this-way.

69. *Ekutopopeq ikowarowana aipo ina motahkiewewena aipo (naq) naeq*
Fire-inside put-it then this again-went-look-possum then (oh) eat them
maqme amukiki rawena aqnontera mope pahqmena mibeq muruntuwena
stomach full its-head again took-mouth here went-down there-like near-
iterawe tahnogebi tun tungoweiq.
fire go sleep.

70. *Tugondabe menaq abehndi ranami marawe ampaho piyarowana apaho*
Sleep that-one greens bamboo like-that bottom put-in bottom put-in
peyarowana mipete kuripena aneq anepeq kuribowana mipi kurinahnumi.
this explode skin skin explode at-this jumped [with pain].

71. *Menaq oniki meyuwena itaq marawe parahboraq aboboraq marawe*
That stone took there like-this put-on top-on like-that put-on put-on left.
parahparena parahparena pokuweiq.

72. *Bokwe bokwe bokwe bokwe (menanunde menaq—) mena aqnonsara*
Go go go go (that-way that—) that head bag put-in went went went went.
unahpi tutawena bokwe bokwe bokwe bokwe bokwe.

73. *(A—wa) anowa koreni (maru) tubiqnondabe toriqmari teragena*
(Uh—) her-mother old-one (down) killed blood saw blood saw this cry
toriqmari teragena mina tebitawena tebitawena tunte tunte tunte.
cry went-down went went.

74. *Poqnabeq mahpi itenaq awahngana awehibi tehawehibi minteh awehebi*
Poqnabe here here tree [Mobuta dialect] base tree-base this tree-base
itepintu tumiyoweiq.
over-there under-it-is.

75. *Entowan awehebin tumiyoweiq.*
Entowa base under-it-is.

76. *Tumiyowana aipo ina waukwenintabe atehganaho asuwena muru*
Down-is enough there person Ategano said put-down tie-it tie-it vine tie-it.
ehtehuwe ehtehuwe nagatane ehtehuwe.

77. *Ehtehumen aqnonsara mipi marena marena waukwenintabe atehganao*
Tie-it her-head here put-it put person Ategano said Makanao said put-
arena makanaho arena itaroweiq.
there.

78. *Waukwenitabe itatarena aipoina.*
Person put-down finished.

79. *Mipinkehrare inawi poriyah mah(na) mote kawi naninka mina(w)i*
This-place-has that-give arrow this who gave person that here that head
matehq mina aqnomi eborariga matehq mina aqnomi.
Ebora is-here that her-head.

80. *(A—) aiparabagoiq.*
(Er—) finished.

1. This is the story that I am going to tell you. There were two young men from Poqnabe who were continually dancing. As these two were dancing, suddenly two girls came upon them and said, 'We are pleased and want these two.' These young men pleased them and the young men continued to dance, it is said. Having said that, these girls wanted to be with those young men.

5. This is the way it happened, but one of them said, 'No, I am not a person, I am a python, a python (what is it),' and he kept saying, 'I am a python, don't you understand? Since I am not a person but a python, why do you come up with me,' he said, and that python went on down the hill. As he went down the hill, it is said he went along the ground, but a bat, that is, a young man who was a bat, went along like this. The two girls gathered their possessions and the two took their net bags and put in some food; they put it in there and went along on the side of the path and stayed there. When they came there, the young men were dancing and it was morning so they left. The two went to their house like that and they got married.

10. He went up and up, that is, the bat flew away like that. He flew and flew up there into the mountains—into the sky and left. After he left, the girl that was with the bat is the one that he told, 'Go back, go back.' After she returned, the python, that is, the young fellow, and the other girl got married. They went and went and went along the ground.

15. That one from Auyana went and went, that is, the young man went along and stayed in a certain place. 'Enough,' he said, 'I am like this, I am really like this,' he said, and changed himself into a python. He would change himself into a person and then he would uncoil and be on the ground and be on an overhanging ledge at his house; he would be there on the ledge at Auyana, and he would coil up there. When he had coiled up there she would build a fire and they settled down there; that is where he settled her, and then he would go hunt for possum in the forest; he would go up to hunt for possum, cut it up, and then bring it down and this is the way they lived. He would bring bones and give her the bones and he would eat and eat. She would cook things on the fire and eat and eat them, and he would go get food, come down and give her the food, and then go again to hunt possums, but would eat them uncooked; this is the way he would do after coming, and he would throw down [the cooked food] and then go back to the forest.

20. This is the way he continued to do this—he would get full and then he would go to sleep near the fire, sleeping near the fire where she gave her husband plenty of food, and then he would leave. He went out to the forest and went again and again to hunt possum; he would get full, getting these food things, cut them up and bring part of it back for his wife. Having brought it, she would look at it and then he would sleep there again, as he took the food and ate it and then go out again. She would get sweet potato from the garden and cook it and give the cooked food to him; but he threw it down, having eaten the other food, he would throw it away. 25. He did and did this, doing just as he did before.

26. Now his wife got pregnant. She got really pregnant and was big with child, it is said. Her husband would bring food and she would cook it and set it to one side and he would go out and hunt again for possum. He went up and shot it and ate most of it up there, but he cut off the head and would bring it

and give it to her. 30. She would ask him to wait when he brought and gave it to her, but he kept doing it and doing it.

One time when he came, her old mother came. So she took the string bag off the hook and put it on her head. She took the string bag and she put sweet potatoes in it and the mother [of the children] left. When she went to get food, the children cried with reference to their mother leaving and she [the old mother] took them down. After she took them down, she went outside and was there outside when one of the adders fell out of the bag into the coals and was burned up. When he was burned up in the fire, she was outside and heard it. Hearing the moans from outside, she went to look and saw that he was burned up in the fire. 35. Two were burned up.

She lifted up the two and put them in [the bag] and filled it with ashes. Then she put in the live ones. The live ones she put in on top and filled it. After she put them in, then the mother came up the path and kept coming up. After she came up and looked, she asked her mother about them and her mother with reference to those children said, 'No, they are sleeping where I put them.' 40. 'They are there where I put them,' she said. So after she had said, 'I put them there on the hook,' she [her daughter] cooked and made ready, and cooked sweet potato; she fixed everything up well and made sweet potato, and then looked there inside the bag—it so happened that she wanted to nurse them, that is, to give them her breast, so she took the bag off the hook. So, like that she started to nurse them, and took them out and looked; she looked and there were ashes there. The ashes were there in the bag hanging there and she thought, 'Where did these ashes come from?' It was like that that she was going to nurse them, offering her breast, but not all of them were there to eat. Not all those persons were there eating at her breast. 45. Two of them were not eating. With reference to their not eating she thought, 'Where are they anyway; what has happened?' and she looked there, and there were the ones that were burned. With reference to those burned ones she said, 'What happened to the small children, what did you do?' she said. 'They were put out of sight, you did not do as I told you. You took them out, and you looked at them. I told you not to take them out, but they jumped out and were burned.' She talked this way to her old mother; 'Where shall I put them? Their father will beat us!' so she cooked and cooked sweet potato and she filled up the bag with it.

When she had filled it up—(uh-er what sort of talk is this, it belongs to another), after filling it up, she kept getting ready all night long and kept filling it up; then she left. 50. She went and went and went all afternoon. She went and went and she [her daughter] had given her some sugar cane; 'Here, it is not good that you should eat it now,' she told her, and she went and went and she went near Toqmata. 'You go down there to Toqmata to eat it,' she told her. 'Up there at your house at Toqmata, you go there, and eat,' she said. She went down carrying it and then she came on up and she kept going up and down and on the way she hit and hit it [the sugar cane in order to soften it].

Now she was doing like that as she went down, tap tap tap went the sugar cane as she went down. 55. It was like that as she hit and hit and hit it, then he [the python] came along looking for her, and he would go and circle around to the front like this [making a circling motion with the hand], and he would look in front and go and go. Over at Ayabana he went and circled around in front there, and went and went. When he circled, he came on and got in front and listened like this and like this he came. She came on hitting and hitting [the sugar cane]. So what happened is that he waited as she came and came.

60. Now she came around around like that and got near and he bit off her head. This one severed that one's head, and he ate up that person. When he had eaten her, he just ate and ate and finished it, and then he took her head in his mouth and left there. He held her head in his mouth this way and went and went and went. With reference to that daughter he said, 'I killed your mother down there, and I came back here and this is her head here,' and he dropped it there. 65. She held it here in her lap. As she held it she said to herself, 'You did that, you just wait!' and they were just there, and he went again, going out to hunt possum in the bush.

When he went, she cooked some greens in a bamboo. She had these greens in the bamboo, and she put a stone inside there with it. So at this place there there's what she did. She put it there with the bottom in the fire; he had gone out looking for possum, and was eating there and had become full, and again took its head in his mouth; he came back and was there near the fire and went to sleep. 70. While he was sleeping, the bottom of the bamboo with the greens in it was placed there in the fire. She had put the bottom there in the fire, and it exploded against his skin; when it exploded, he jumped as a result with pain. She took that stone like this and put it there on top of him. She put it on top of him and when she did that she went away.

She went and went and went and she put her [mother's] head in a bag and left there and went and went. She went down where her mother had been killed and she saw her blood there; there was plenty of blood and she saw it, and she cried and cried and then went and went from there. Here at Poqnabe at this tree here, this tree stump, in fact that tree stump over there, under it is where it is. 75. It is at the Entowa trunk underneath it.

When it was down there, in reference to that person she said, 'It is Ategano,' and then tied and tied it up with a vine and it is tied there. She tied it, having put her head in there, and said with reference to that person, 'Ategano or Makanao,' and she put it there. She, with reference to that person, put it there and this is finished.

It is where that person gave you those arrows. That is where the head is here at Ebora. That's where the head is. 80. Uh—it is finished.

15. HOW TO ESCAPE FROM THE SPIRITS

1. *Pehtauwara pehtauwara mopi meoyana (meoya—meoyan—) meoyana-*
   Sun-out sun-out there two-were-there (were—were-there—) when-
   tabe (ogaiq—ogaiq—) ogaitu ogaiq awewera.
   there (arrow—arrow—) pronged-arrow pronged-arrow they-made.
2. *Agantu tuawewera, mo gaeruwe mo gaeruwe.*
   Bamboo-arrow made, more made-good more made-good.
3. *Gawe eyoyantate pokuwarera, (aq—) pata rupa(w)era koyaq tuba(w)-*

Good did-it went, (er——) Pata-fish went-down-shoot Koya-fish went-down-
etaq.
shoot.
4. *Monayabo miyahutahu aruqmaqme.*
   More-eat you-two-go said.
5. *Ite ruwah ahrobetaq ite ruwah ahrobeta (a——) pata tubaweta.*
   Our ground river-on our ground river-on a (er——) Pata-fish down-shoot.
6. *Monayabo miyaho aruqmaqme.*
   More-eat you-two-go said.
7. *Ogaiqmari arau(w)era pokwe bokwe bokwe.*
   Bamboo-arrows took went went went.
8. *Bokuwarera ubianahnomarin gebaqme.*
   Went-two bamboos-for-irrigation pull-out.
9. *Arehuwera omi omi ibianahnomarin gebaqme.*
   Bundle bamboo bamboo irrigation-bamboos pull-out.
10. *Arehuwera tunte meni bariahga tunte unte unte unte.*
    Bundle-up down-went those brothers went-down went went.
11. *Gairapi muru mahri ruwe.*
    Sleeping-place-in down bed made.
12. *Iroya(i)peq awiqmiq awiqmi iroyapeq muru mahri ruwe.*
    Iroya-place name name Iroya down bed made.
13. *Gaerarera mina bariyahga mahri ruwe.*
    Made-did-good those brothers bed made.
14. *Gaerarerauyana aibenguntabe aibenguntabe ina omitaq mahtaq ruwe*
    Made-good-they-two darkness-came darkness that bamboo-on that-on
uwe uwe uwe uwe.
did did did did.
15. *Urumarenaboq abakantabe are mipi pehreradho (ayuwena——) are*
    Set-down younger-brother you here light-it (said——) you younger-brother
abakantabe mipi pehreraho ayuwena, (aq) awahwawi pokuwarena oq
here light-it said, (er) older-brother went bamboo took bamboo bundle
mena qon ara kewewena mena on ara kewewena aipo mo taqmaq.
took that bamboo bundle took then other put-down.
16. *Mo taqmaruwena uwena uwena uwena, uwena uwena; mahntebeq*
    Other put-down did did did, did did; over-there down put-it did.
muru mahrena uwara.
17. *(Aq——) ibeq tirahq tirah tubiyu we iniboq—(awahwa) abaka aipo*
    (Uh——) there strangle strangle kill he that—(older-brother) younger-
tenahpeq o maqmena pokuweiq.
brother then up-hill bamboo put-it he-went.
18. *O o tanahnarobeq maqmena (aq) tanahnarobeq maqmena pokuwana,*
    Bamboo bamboo up-stream put-it (uh) up-stream put-it went, (younger-
(abakae) awawawi nape rarobeq maqmena pokuwanami.

brother) older-brother down stream put-them he-went.

19. *Aipo abaka itaq, miyaho ayuwena awahwabeq (ne) tirah tibiyuweiq.*
Then younger-brother here, you-stay said older-brother (?) strangle killed.

20. *Tirahq tirahq mahpi marawe tirah tubiyuweiq.*
Strangle strangle here like-that strangle killed.

21. *Napeq o maqmena tuwegowana tirahq tirah tubiyuwana a——.*
Down-there bamboo put where-gone strangle strangle kill, uh——.

22. *(Maqme maru marera gibarewe ki ropah ki bariyoyeu topah topahn*
([Another speaker] Put down put-it went-up up sweet-potato up build-
gibarewe barewe. Barewe nabiqme kaweruwaera aipo——.)
fire sweet-potato sweet-potato cook cook. Cook ate fix-good then——.)

23. *Auagiayaera auagiayaera aipo mena bariaga mena abariaga maqmera*
Two-look-for two-look-for then those brothers those brothers put down
muru marera gire.
put came.

24. *Me mahripin giwera topahn gibarewe nera, abiqme.*
This bed-in came-up sweet-potato cooked ate, ate.

25. *Mera tagaro(y)ena tagaro(y)ena, aipo aikauqme inokahpeq ukun-*
Were-there looked looked, then night-came [Ilakia] night-came
tabe aipo are nanibaqmi tanahpeq (aiq) auagiyahu ayuena, tanahpeq
[Mobuta] being then you my-younger-brother up-stream (oh) two-look-
agiaho ayuenawi.
for he-said, up-stream search he-said.

26. *Awahwe napeq arobeq napeq arobeq tapata auwaigioweu awagewe*
Older-brother down stream down stream for-fish he-look look look.
agawe.

27. *Ageweruwana pawe itaqmaq pawe itaqmaruwe uwe.*
Did shoot put shoot put-did did.

28. *Tuwara ibeq menaq awawabiqne (aq——) tirahq tubiyuweiq.*
Went-down there that older-brother (er——) strangle kill.

29. *Tirahq mahpi marawe tirah tubiyuwana, (iyau——) (aq patawi——)*
Strangle here like-that strangle kill, *(Iyau——)* (er fish——) just came.
peh giuweiq.

30. *Minaq awahwawi tirahq tubi(e)yowana, peh giuwanawi.*
That older-brother strangle kill, just came.

31. *(A——) tanahpeq abakagabeqne papatawi paratanuwe.*
(Er——) up-stream younger-brother fish shot-and-shot.

32. *Koyaqmari patari pawe kaeraena, tuwana unahngakaq tuwanawi.*
Koya-fish-plural fish shot good-did, came-down bag came-down.

33. *Inaq awahwawi tirahq tubiqmarowana, puwana peh giuweiq.*
That older-brother strangle killed, refer-to just came.

34. *Peh gire gire, aipo menaq mahripi kiwena, kiwena abaka nonotahngi*

Just came came, then that bed-in stay, stay younger-brother first-up-went
wena auqmaroweiq.
he looked.

35. *Kewena auqmarowana, auqmarowana, aipo auqmaro.*
Stay looked, looked, then look.

36. *Auqmaron tarena tugena tagarowana, mena awahwa giuweiq.*
Look said came-down looked, that older-brother came.

37. *Tirahq tubiqmarowana, tirah tubiqmarowana, gire gire gire.*
Strangle kill, strangle kill, come come come.

38. *Genawe are ine napetaq auwagebah abakagawi nenuwaho are eraho-*
Came you I down search-for younger-brother my-older-brother you
nouweiq.
you what-doing-said.

39. *Inewi patawi peh tanahpeq mibeh ongahbonaena peh ratanayogeiq.*
I fish just up-stream that bamboo-finished just kill-them.

40. *Unahngaraq mipi mina muru maroge.*
Bag-in there that down put.

41. *Are erahonouwanawe, aqau ina aren awahwi (aq——) iya kaun iyana*
You what-do-said, nothing that you older-brother (er——) not have none
peh menaq omi peh auwage tagoge iraruweiq.
just that bamboo just look-I look I-said.

42. *Iraruwanana, iraruntabe inahte inegapeqne meh payopeqne.*
Said-it, said-reference stalling I-there there just-being.

43. *Ahbiyah tuweki natawi ketinayabo mitare ayuera, menaq abariga*
Morning comes daylight cook-eat stay-we said, those brothers slept.
pingauyeiq.

44. *Pinduwe tugoyana, tagena aipo mina kirahq tubiqmaro naninga (aq——)*
There they-two-slept, look then that strangle killed person (er——)
(aweraq) non tumiyoraho uweiq.
(aweraq) water go-bring-it said.

45. *Wani wani tumiyorahountabe pokuwarena, (aq——) tutagomi.*
Water water get-for-me went, (er——) went-down-look.

46. *Minaq wani tuwena tutagomi.*
That water went-down went-down-look.

47. *Awahwa weni yawa mipi miyoweiq.*
Older-brother his spirit there was-there.

48. *Wahnta wahnta pimiyowana, tutagena ipete (aq——) tuwekuweiq.*
Spirit spirit there-was, went-look from-there (er——) came-back.

49. *Menaq nonana ipeq murun tuwena, tuwekuwarena inan, gire.*
That water-container there down threw, came-back that-one, came.

50. *Aqau mahqehpipeqmi wahnta miyahwana, niwantuontabe murun*
No over-there spirit was-there, afraid-I-because down throw-I said, then
tuwoge ayuwena, aipo (naq) nonana marun tuwena, kiyuwana awahwega

(naq) container down threw, came-up older-brother (er) there let's-
(e) inahre tugayae ayuena, tugoweiq.
sleep said, slept.

51. *Wena awahngu tutagena uwana, tugontabitiq.*
   His spirit went-down-look did, he-slept.

52. *Tuwekagena, tagarowana aipo wahq aqmaqme tugena, tagarowana*
   Look-at, look-at then cloak cover sleep, look like-that club like-that
mahrawe tatabe marawe tatabe tubinageena, tatabe nugeena, wahq min
club I-will-hit, club-with will-I-do, cloak that poke-holes poke-holes
tarotabe tarotabe tarotabe.
poke-holes.

53. *Kairatena tepite tagarowe(inu) (murun tao) awe pehtutahpeq.*
   Did-good from-there watch (down do) there just-where-slept.

54. *Tuwena tutugahpeq tumena tahgaromi.*
   Came from-sleeping-place came he-look.

55. *Marawe abaka tubina abaka arahtiya tubiqmiyana, mahrawe tahntane*
   Like-that younger-brother hit younger-brother dead kill, like-that club-
mahrawe tararaqmaq, marawe tararaqmaruweiq.
thing like-that aim-at, like-that make-ready.

56. *Uwana tararaqma tararaqma ruwana tagena aipo awera garowana,*
   Did aim aim did look then was watching, aim aim reference wait did-it then.
tararaqma tararaqma untabe paitare uwaq maqme.

57. *Tugangiwetu tagarowana, menaq awahwa (tuwe), (tuge) guntabe aiq*
   When-asleep look, that older-brother (?), (?) sleep oh like-that I will-
marawe ine tubinio nabo mara enie ewena, aipo kiambokuwe.
hit like this I will-do, then get-up.

58. *Aba parahpanahpawe—(wahtenga)—wahtane abobonah kabonatena,*
   Wood cover-over—(cloak)—cloak-with on-top cover-over, wood spread-
aba tanena abobonah mo se kabonarena, (mi)naga kire eku ne okeq
out on-top other it cover-over, that-one came fire from pull get, that fire
mena, menaq eku nahenaq.
light-on-end.

59. *Oke mena tontane marawe marawe punini punini punini nuwena,*
   Pull get burning like-that like-that wave wave wave do, went went went.
gire gire gire.

60. *Motaq kiuwana ipete kiragomi.*
   Soon went-up from-there went-look.

61. *Menaq wahraru aiqmah miyehreena tago marawe marawe we aurapi*
   That cloak-under where is-he look like-that like-that he eye- in want-to-
peraranieena, marawe tatabiomi onikiraq ayahnobeq bahnkuweiq.
pierce, like-that club-pierce stone-on fingers split.

62. *Mahna ayahnobeq pahngiyuntabe naq ai waukweni ahbepo ayuena,*
   This finger split what oh person where said, there-from follow went-up,

(m)itate kaqmena kiuwana, kaqmena kiuwana, iraun tane mahrawe
follow went-up, fire-wood went like-that wave-to-light, fire take left.
punininuwena, iraun keq miyoweiq.

63. *Eku keqmiyontane motaqte obinimbininaruq.*
    Fire took-went from-here got-it-to-burn.

64. *Motate obinimbininaruruwena, (kaq) kaqmena kaqmena kaqmena,*
    There make-burn-do, (kaq) follow follow follow, my watchman
    nene wahntaq kaumpehrayuwena, itate kaqmena kaqmena kaqmena.
    exclamation-said, from-there follow follow follow.

65. *Kiuwana motate mo turatuq.*
    Went from-there more make-burn.

66. *Motate mo turaturuwana, kaqmena kiunkiun kiu.*
    From-there again make-burn, follow go-up go-up.

67. *Aipo tanaerapeq itenaq nah kobipeq sene nah kobi wai nahopeq*
    Then at-Tanaero that house used-to-be that house none men's house
    kibekuwe.
    went-in.

68. *Wah kia suwena mahrarupeq kerugeguroao.*
    Cloak cover over bed went-sleep.

69. *Kerugeguwana, ontarate ontarate uwo teq are waukwenitabe nahre*
    Went-inside-sleep, door-way-from door-way-from oh dung you person
    enauqnuga.
    I not-afraid.

70. *Peh mah senaq tuwitabe nahrena, mo kawoge.*
    Just this thing-there center/top-pole afraid, other throw-out-I.

71. *Se are sen anino arenene arene (wahnahtaq) (kaumparuwo) iraruweiq.*
    Dung you dung person you your (?) (?) he-said.

72. *Irarasuwena, mitate kiwe kuweiq.*
    When-said, from-there came came-away.

73. *Aipinisiq.*
    Finished.

1. When the sun was out, when the sun was shining, two people were there; they were there, and with reference to their being there they were making pronged arrows—arrows are what they were making. They were making bamboo arrows, and they kept making one and then the other, making them good. After they had finished making them good they left, and they went on down to catch Pata fish and Koya fish. Wanting some to eat, one of them said, 'You two go on first.' 5. There on our river on our river, (er) they went down to catch fish. Wanting more to eat one of them said, 'You two go on.' So they took up the bamboo for irrigating and went and went and went.

Two of them went along with the bamboos for irrigating, pulling them out. They stacked them up and pulled out these old irrigation pipes. 10. They stacked them and those brothers went on down and kept going down like that. They came down and made beds at a sleeping place. The name of the place was Iroya, its name was Iroya, and that's where they made those beds down there; those two brothers fixed it up well and made those beds. When the two had fixed the place up, darkness came so they got those bamboos over there and put them down there.

15. They set them down and with reference to the younger brother, he (the older one) said, 'You stay here and light it.' When he told the younger brother to stay there and light it, then the older brother went on and he took some of the irrigation bamboos; taking a bundle he went and then put some more down. He put more down and kept doing that and doing that; he put them down over there.

Then when he was there, someone strangled and killed him (the older brother)—the younger brother then had left and taken bamboo and put it up there. He put the bamboo upstream; he put it upstream and went there (the younger brother); the older brother went down the stream to put the bamboo and left. He had told the younger brother to stay there but the older brother was strangled and killed. 20. He was strangled and strangled like that, strangled and killed. It was down there where he put the bamboo, where he had gone that he was strangled and killed—[Another speaker inserts the following: One of them had put it down and gone up and they had really built a fire up there and cooked sweet potato; cooking it well they cooked and ate it and fixed it up well then]—the two looked for him [the older brother]; they looked for him and then those brothers, those brothers put the things down and at the place where they made the beds they came and cooked and ate the sweet potato, finishing their eating. 25. They were there and they kept looking and waiting for the older brother; then as it became night [Ilakia word] it became night [using the Mobuta word], one of them said, 'You, my younger brother, go on upstream; oh, you look for him there,' he said; 'Search up stream,' he said.

The older brother had gone down the stream, going downstream for fish, and so one of them looked and looked for him down there. He would go along fishing [shooting at the fish], putting it down and shooting and kept doing this. He went down there, that older brother, and there he was strangled and killed. Just like that he was strangled and killed, and then, oh! there he was, fishing, and he just came [his spirit] without fish. 30. That older brother who was strangled and killed just came on back. (Er) the younger brother went upstream and was fishing up there. He shot and shot fish in his bag and came back. But the older brother who was strangled and killed, well, that one just came on back [his spirit]. He just came and came, then he stayed there in that bed and he stayed there, but the younger brother was there first and he went and looked there.

35. When he stayed and looked, he kept looking and then he looked some more [suspecting something]. He looked at his head and then he came and he kept looking, and his older brother had come on back. The one who was strangled and killed, that one that was strangled and killed, came and came. When he came the younger brother said, 'I searched for you, my older brother; what have you been doing? I have just been upstream fishing, and I finished the bamboo there and just killed some fish.' 40. 'I put it in the bag and came on

down.' When he asked him, 'What have you been doing?' that older brother said, 'Just nothing; er, I didn't get any, I just put the bamboo down and was just looking,' he said. He said that, and with reference to what he said, he was stalling and said, 'I was just down there.'

It was getting toward morning and they cooked and ate and, 'Let's stay here,' he said; so those brothers slept there. While they were sleeping there, he looked there, and that one that had been strangled, that person said, 'Go get some water for me.' 45. With reference to that water that he wanted, the other went, and he went down still looking [with suspicion]. So he went down for the water and he kept looking. The older brother's spirit was staying there. His spirit, yes, his spirit was there, and he [the younger one] was looking from there and (er) he came back. But the water container he threw down, and he came back to that place. 50. He said, 'Nothing doing! There was a spirit over there, and it frightened me so I threw it down,' he said; then when he threw the container down, he came on back and his older brother said, 'Let's go to sleep'; so they slept.

Now he, when he went down and looked at his spirit, he went [pretended] to sleep. Now he watched and he watched, and then he covered himself over with his cloak and slept; but he kept watching like that and he [the older brother] thought, 'I'll just hit him with the club, I'll just do that,' but the other one had poked holes in his cloak; he poked holes in his cloak to watch him. He fixed it up good and was watching him from under there and was just down there where they slept. So when he came from the sleeping place he was there watching. 55. It was like that that he was going to hit the younger brother; he was going to just kill that younger brother just like that with that club; he made ready to hit him; it was like that that he aimed it at him. When he was aiming it at him and kept aiming it, the other one was there watching him, he was watching him as he aimed it at him and he waited and waited.

Then as he [the younger brother] watched that older brother went to sleep while he was there thinking, 'I'll hit him, I'll do it like that, I'll hit him'; then the other one got up. He covered over some wood with his cloak—he put his cloak over on top of some wood that he spread out and covered it over, and then went over to the fire and took out a brand and lit one end of it. He pulled it out and got it burning, waving it back and forth and then he left and went and went.

60. Soon the other got up and went over to look there. Remember that one had been there under the cloak and he was looking like that with his eye while his brother wanted to stab him and stab him with the club, but he stabbed down on the stones and split his fingers. With reference to splitting his fingers as he stabbed he said, 'What, where is that fellow?' So from there he went up and he followed and followed him, and like that the fire was going on the bamboo and he [the younger brother] was waving it back and forth to make the fire go as he took it and left. He took this fire and left from there, got it burning and as it was burning he left so the other followed and followed and followed him and swore furiously. From there he kept on following him. 65. So he went on up, and from there the other made the bamboo burn. When he made it burn, then the other followed and followed him.

So then there at Tanaero where those houses used to be but there are no houses there anymore, he [the younger one] went into the men's house. He took his cloak and covered himself, going in there to the place where his bed was. He went inside and slept, and then that other one [the spirit] from the doorway said, 'Teq, you people, I'm not afraid of you!' 70. 'I'm just afraid of that thing there which is the center or top pole. As to that other one, I'll just throw him out.' So he swore and swore and swore at that fellow. But after he said that, he left and went away from there. It is finished.

16. FOOLING THE SPIRITS

1. *Mementahn aranontabe mementahn aranontabe wahnahnuwe tamaru-*
   Mementa fruit Mementa fruit looking draw-back-bow.
   toq.

2. *Tamurutowanu tamarutoweiq.*
   Draw-back draw-back.

3. *Maniraninka maniraninka mementahn aranontabe tamurutowana mok-*
   Old-people old-people Mementa-tree fruit draw-back possum-maybe
   arahq minoena naminoena tamurutowana (aq) ibete kitarena wahga wahga
   thought eat-it-thought draw-back (er) there-from he-went-up man man
   ibeten gire gire.
   from-there came came.

4. *(Minaq—) mementahn ara kotiqna te tiqna uwo—.*
   (That—) Mementa fruit went-get-eat here went-get-eat do—.

5. *Kiuwana kiragome waukweni tamurutontabe waukweni tamurutontabe*
   Went-up look person draw-back person draw-back-you that worthless
   minatabe abehqna miyeate tamururahno nuwehgaiyo giuwana ahqwe nu-
   not-good not-good-you-pull-back my-one-talk came no my-one-talk here
   wehgayo mahbeq(i)ne mokawah motabewah moka nareatena tamaturoge
   possum-maybe possum-maybe possum eat pull-back-I what-said no that
   iraruntabe aqa ina waukwenine totariyana waukwene totariyana ine nene
   possum garden-is person garden that my garden that here here-I-come
   totariyana anaboni mahbeq mehkiuge iraruweiq.
   he-said.

6. *Iraruwana ina aqa ne nuwehgaiwah ina peh motabewah tamurutoga*
   Talked that no my friend that just possum-maybe pull-back you-talk.
   irarene.

7. *(Aq—) areahbete nani tamurutahno iraruntabe e ina ine arena wehgai*
   (Er—) you-where-from son you-draw-back said yes that I your friend
   mayoge matamurotogeq.
   I-am this pull-back.

8. *Paepeqme arene motabe tamurutogahwi.*
   Just-be-there you possum I-pull-back.

9. *Waukweni gione irarasuwena uwana;*
   Person came said happen;

10. *Anenunu anenunuena tauku oniki ukuerah merawe (m)irau (mi)-*
   What I-do tree-become stone become like-that like-that did (er—) other
ntarena (aq—)mo iyepite mazutaugwe tagaraho uweiq.
there I-get-out you-watch said.

11. *Mo iyepite mayutaugwe.*
   Other over-there-from get-out.

12. *Tagaraho ayuena (aq—) indeindetate mina tehweraq kiatagweine.*
   You-watch said (er—) down-from-there that tree-on climb-up.

13. *Ahmperaweraq ahmperawera kiatagwarena ai(n)gu iyepite magu-*
   Ampe-tree-up Ampe-tree-up-in he-climbed possum up get-him-out.
tangwe.

14. *Tagaraho ayuwena aipo (aq) arahtaq miyah nouwana mayoge untabe*
   You-watch said then (er) where-is are-you said I-here oh down down
ahqah napeq nape indeta tumiyaho.
farther be-down-there.

15. *Napeq mahndetaq tumiyahountabe moq oita tumena aipo mahtaq*
   Down here-farther you-be again there down-be then here shall-I-be said
menugo uwana aqa mo indeindeta tumiyahountabe mo mo utuwe kiqme.
no again on-down you-be again again on-farther go.

16. *Tetaq tuwekiqme.*
   Farther go-down.

17. *Tumiyowana moq mataq menugouwana aqa intebeq napeq tumiyaho*
   Down-went again here shall-I-be no on-farther down be-there said.
uweiq.

18. *Napeq tumiyahouwana mo airabiyo irarasuwena mahtaq mehyoq.*
   Down be-there-was then good said here I'll-be.

19. *Mehyotaq menugo uwana aqa mo indeindetaq tumiyahountabe mo*
   I-be here said no again on-farther you-go again on-farther.
indeidetaq.

20. *Tumiyowana mo aqa ina oriahpo indeindetapo indeindeta tumiyaho-*
   Was-there again no that short-way on-farther on-farther you-be down
untabe napeq tuwekiq.
down-more.

21. *Tuwekiruwe indeindeta tumiyowana ibete ina teh(w)ebete tabuku*
   Down-more down-on be-was there-from that up-from climb climb take-
tabubun gibagimaqme mah ntebiq tararaqmeena mahntepipeq tuperuwo-
be there way-over throw long-way threw-it.
(we)u.

22. *Tuperuwowana aipo (aq) mena aninga menaq wahntaga mipetaq*
   Threw-it then (er) that person that spirit there pounce.
mahtaiq.

23. *Mahtairewena ayah muru tegaranuweiq.*
   Pounce-there hand down stick-strike.

24. *Tabubutaq tabubutaq ayah muru tegara nawena aeseq mahnahne naq*
   Dead-branch dead-branch hand down stick went-in oh-dung this wha
mayuwana nabugo.
what-throw-away did.

25. *Irarayuwena uwana mena teh awebeten giwasuwo nanimi peherah more*
   Said did that tree top-from throw-down person quickly down slide-dowr
kokuba(w)ena peherah pokuweiq.
quickly left.

26. *Pokuwana mena aninga mena tabubutaq ayah mahrawe maq mahro*
   Left that person that dead-branch hand that-way what like-this dowr
muruma ahyataq mahtategara muruawena tabubutaq ahya muruntegarar
hand-on this-stick down-like-that dead-limb hand down-stick did;
awena;

27. *Aheteq irarasuwena mitate kiragomi.*
   Oh-dung he-said from-there came-look.

28. *Mena ta(w)ebete more suwena pokuntabe kaqmena kaqmena giuwana*
   That-one tree-from one threw gone follow follow went follow came
kaqmena kiuwana kaqmena giuwana kaqmena kiuwana;
follow came follow came;

29. *Minaga peh ese inten anino itare itareuena tuntun tuntu.*
   That-one just stay-there who person be-there be-there went went.

30. *Aipoq tetaq mahtahtuobi mahtahtuobitena wainahopeq tuwa aguwana*
   Enough tree-at here-place here-where-came man-house went inside went
tuwa aguwana seq indeinden anino.
inside who down-there person.

31. *Pehetare ugahwe ahqa(w)e indeinde pokone ayuwena;*
   Wait I-said-he no way-down he-went said;

32. *Giberah ontarate abonorahq kiuwana (iyeq—) iyenanino arentabeuq*
   Coming door-from center-place came (not—) not-person you-because
—nahrehrehnauqnuga.
—afraid-I-you.

33. *Moq mahyena tuwitabe peh tuwiga nahtehntabe mo suwoge.*
   Again that-one top-post just center-pole afraid again throw-away.

34. *Teq irawo irarasuwena itate maraweq marawe mo ayahbaqno agatena;*
   Dung do said throw-from like-this like-this again hand-noise [snapped
finger] said;

35. *Mo ayahbaqno agatena pokuweiq.*
   Again snap-finger did left.

36. *Patena.*
   The-end.

1. Now with reference to the Mementa fruit, that one watching drew back
his bow at the Mementa fruit. He drew it back and that's exactly what he did.

It was one of our old forefathers that drew back his bow, ready to shoot into the Mementa fruit because he thought that it was a possum who was eating the fruit; that is why he drew back prepared to shoot; he went up from there, that man, that man came up from there. It went and ate the Mementa fruit, and that's what it continued to do.

5. When he went up there, he saw a person, and with reference to his drawing the bow back to shoot that person, with reference to his drawing it back, the other said: 'It is not good that you do that; it is not good that you pull the bow back; you are my friend'; so when he came up, he told him: 'No, you are my friend here,' but he thought that maybe he was a possum, and he thought he would eat the possum, and he said, 'That's why I pulled back the bow'; and with reference to the one that told him, 'No,' he said, 'It is a person's garden, a man's garden, in fact my garden; that is why I came here,' he said.

After they talked, that one said, 'No you are my friend, it was just at a possum that I was going to shoot.' 'Where are you from, you who drew back your bow?' And with reference to what he said he answered, 'Yes, I am your friend, I am this one who pulled back the bow. You just be there; I thought you were a possum, and I made ready to shoot.' 'You are a person, you come on,' he said. 10. 'Now what can I do, I shall become a tree or a stone,' he thought, and it was like that that he acted; 'It was something else that I got out, so you watch,' he said [the one a person, the second a spirit]. 'It was over there that I got it [a possum] out. You watch there,' he said, and he told him [the spirit] to climb on up that tree over there. He went up the Ampe tree, it was up the Ampe tree that he went saying, 'I'll get out the possum from there. You watch,' he said, then he called out, 'Where are you'; with reference to his saying that he was there, he shouted, 'Oh, go on down farther, you be down there.'

15. With reference to his telling him, 'You be down there farther,' he again went on down there farther, and said, 'Shall I be here?' He replied, 'No, go on down and be farther, and go on farther down.' So he went on down farther. When he went down farther again, he said, 'Shall I be here?' 'No, go on farther down, and be there,' he said. So he went on down farther and he said, 'That's good, I'll be here.' He asked again, 'Shall I be here?' and the response was again, 'No, you go on down farther on.' 20. He was there again and he asked if it should be a short way, but in reference to his saying, 'Go on farther,' he told him to go even farther.

So he went on down more and more, and he was up there having climbed and climbed, and then he took it [a stick] and threw it way over there a long way; he threw it down. When he threw it, that person, that is, the spirit person, pounced on it. He pounced on it and struck down on the stick [which he had thrown down] with his hand. On that dead branch, that sharp stick, he struck his hand down and cried, '*Aheteq,* what is this, what did you throw down?'

25. After he said this, the one at the tree top who threw that thing down quickly slid down the tree, and then quickly left. When he left, that person there did this way with his hand on that sharp stick; he struck down on it, he struck his hand down like that on that dead stick. '*Aheteq,*' he said, and he came and looked from there, but the one that had been up the tree and thrown it down had left, so he [the spirit] followed and followed him coming on up

and following him. That one called, 'You stay there; who is it there? Be there,'
and he went and went. 30. So at this tree here where there used to be houses,
he went inside the men's house, and when he went inside, he asked 'Who is
down there? Wait, I said,' but he didn't wait, he kept on going. So when he
came, he was there at the door near the central open place, and he came, but
he said: 'I'm not afraid of a person, I am not afraid of you.' But that one
said, 'I am just afraid of the center post,' and he shouted; 'I'll throw him away.
Dung!' and that is what he kept saying and doing, and from there he did like
this, he made a noise with his hand [snapped his fingers]. 35. Again snapping
his fingers he left. That is the end.

17. ORIGIN OF REEDS FOR ARROWS

1. Mahbiga ainga gibawena, ainga gibawena, muru ahraritabe muru murun
Young-fellow possum hunt, possum hunt, down girl down down he-gave.
kauweiq.

2. Muruawiq, maroweiq; ahraritabe muruawiq, maroweiq.
Down-gave, put; girl down-gave, put.

3. Mahbiga ainga gibawena, muruawiq.
Young-man possum shoot, gave-it.

4. Maroena, (a—aipo ina—) muru ainga gibawena, mu(ru)nga mu(ru)nga
Put-it, (er—enough that—) down possum shoot, do do ate, ate, cook
neqeuwana, nayuwena, tinaru tinaru ayuwena uwana, (aq—) ongigiuweiq.
cook ate did, (er—) went-make-garden.

5. Ongi ongigiuwana, anamaeuku(w)e anamaeukuwe menaq mahbiga
Taro make-garden, child-became child-became that young-man boy-
anamaeukue anaqmaqme awahpipeq kiwaena, awahpipeq makimena, (m—)
became child-what edge came, edge here-came (uh—) wife wife plant.
awahningantabe awahninga uqmaro.

6. Nanitabe (aq—) pebi mani garai mani pebi mani garai mani pebi mani
Child (er—) bug give-me bug give-me bug give bug give bug give bug
garai mani uweiq.
give he said.

7. Pebi mani pebi mani garai mani pebi mani igiarena, aipo tate (aq)
Pebi give pebi give garai give pebi give came-said, enough there-from (er)
pembunahn suwe, pembunah tuwe uwe uwe uwe uwe.
flute play, flute play play play play.

8. (Aq) mahbi nuwo ayori more tahrawe.
(Er) young-man bird feathers again tied-put.

9. Mahbitanta nuwe kaeruwena, mahbi tuweukuwe.
Young-man-like was fix-up, young-man became.

10. Pempunah tawe uwe uwe pokuweiq.
Flute play play play left.

11. Pokuwarena, tungerenamo mena awaninga moq ongigiuwana, tagena mo

Left, down-stay that wife again taro-garden-fix, look again that bird
menaq nuwo ayoari mahta tahra ayomari (aq) moyeakatuwe.
feathers here tie feathers (er) pull-off-throw.
12. *Awahpipeq marena, ana maeukuwaq maqme menaq anamae ukuamaqme.*
Edge put, boy become what that boy became.
13. *Pebi manin garai mani pebi manin garai mani uweiq.*
But give-me bug give-me bug give bug give he-said.
14. *Giuwana tagena aipo mina moq anenga (m)irarea mirarea ronamo*
Came look then that again what-animal like-this like-this talks she-said
ayuena uwana, mena pebiwari ibe tuperu tuperu uwana, we mahna mahbi
did, that bugs there threw-it threw-it did, he that young-man my-husband-
nanuwehkarahnta irareneq.
like she-said.
15. *We mahna anenabi ayuena, kuwe anai ngaqme.*
He this what-you-eat she-said, she-came behind follow.
16. *Ina tunte aupe tumena, aupe tumena, awapipe tumena, tagarowana,*
That went-down out-of-sight went-down, out-of-sight went, edge came-
menaq unahmari (aq) nuwo ayori tuwe tahrawe.
down, she-watched, that bags (er) bird feather came-down put-on.
17. *Mahbitantan awena, mahbitantan awena, pokuntabe ae (aq) aboantabe*
Young-man-like was, young-man-like was, went oh (er) her-father her-
aboantabe ahqau are moq pehwe muru ngatarona, oganeka maqine onki
father no you possum shot down gave-me, new-young-man what garden
upipeq kiwaena, (anamae—) ukuwe anamae ukuwe.
place-where he-came, (boy—) became boy became.
18. *Kiwaena, inentabe (aq) pebi mani garai mani pebi mani garai mani*
Came-was-there, me-reference (er) bug give bug give bug give bug give
giarena, aipo mena mahbi tuweukuwe.
came-said, then that young-man down-became.
19. *Menari tahruwena pokoyana, poku pokuyana, tagatagaruge iraruweiq.*
Those tied-on went, went left, I-look she-said.
20. *Aboantabe iraruntabe aipo ongiqme omi pehqmena, mo webeq marou-*
Her-father she-said enough bamboo-for-lighting bamboo took, other
wana, totoruwana, webeq moarowana, totoruwana, webeq moarowana,
shelf put-on, dry-it, shelf put-on, dry-it, shelf put-it, dry, then (er—)
totoruwana, aipo (aq—) nahopeqtah ge(ag)uwe.
house-in collected.
21. *Wehwi nahopeqtah geaguwe.*
Men house-in collected.
22. *Ga(w)eruguana, penguwana, penguwana nahopeqtah giwe gaeuwana,*
Collected, get-night, night house-in collect collected, slept, then father that
tugowana, aipo abowaga menaq ongi wewena, webete naq ongi wewena,
bamboo he-brought, shelf-from then bamboo brought, (er—) lit-it fire-in

(aq—) turaqmaqme ekupi turaqmaqme.
lit-it.

23. *Marawe keqmena nogena, keqmena nogena uwana, aqau ne mahna*
     Like-that follow walk, follow walk did, no I this young-brother I this her
ahyokaeq ne mahna wen aboe uwana, mon atapipeq koturaqme.
father did, again fire-edge came-look.

24. *Irauwana aipo pehqnahbitem tuwe.*
     Like-this-did then room-in came.

25. *Pehqnahbin tehpi muru geroweiq.*
     Room-in edge down came-look.

26. *Mon gerowana, aqau ine mahpiqmi ahyokamiyoge, ahyokamiyoge,*
     Again came-look, no I here his-younger-brother-I-am, younger-brother-I,
are maebera tagariyountabe mo mahtate turaqmena, mo tiyotahpeq
you there-at look again here-from lit-it, again room again look, no I this
moge rowana, aqao ne mahna wene ahrahboq wen ahrahbo are mobenaq
his in-law his in-law you over-there look he-said.
tagario iraruweiq.

27. *Iraruntabe moq mena keqmena, mopi koturabuwana, aqahu ne mahna*
     Said again that lit-it, again went-into-another, no I this (er—) his
(aq—) wen ahrah miyoge iraruweiq.
in-law I-here he-said.

28. *Iraruntabe moq keqmena, mon tehpi mo turaguwana, mo aqaho ayoka*
     Said again lit, other fire-place again went-look, other no her-brother
miyoge iraruweiq.
I-here he-said.

29. *Untabe moq keqmena, mon atehpi muru ngerowana, moq aqaho ne*
     Happen again lit, other fire-place down light, again no I this-one I her-
mahna we ne ahyoka miyoge iraruweiq.
brother I-am he-said.

30. *Iraruntabe menaq ogeqmena, mona tehpi muru ngerowana, mo aqau*
     Said that bamboo-light, other room down light, again no I this (er) her-
ne mahna (aq) abowa miyoge iraruweiq.
father I-am he-said.

31. *Iraruntabe moq ina moq ongeqmena, mopi murun turatuwomeyahq.*
     Said again that again bamboo-lit, other-in down lit-it.

32. *Wenaq mipeq awehka mipeq miyoweiq.*
     He here husband here is

33. *Miyontabe are ine abowa mehyo nanine aniniyahwi.*
     Being-there you I her-father I-here I alive.

34. *(Aq-) kiraraq irararone, umoq peh tiwenara, tina tinaho omi*
     (Er—) that-talk you-say, possum just shot-and-brought, cook eat talk
anentabe giwe awitoqmaq awitoqnaq tono.
why go-up talk-that-way talk-that-way do.

35. *Irarasuwena, minaq ontane itaq muru aritoweiq.*
    He-said, that bamboo-with that down burned-him.
36. *Muru ariqme otoqme aunawe muru ariqme ariqme ariqme ariqme.*
    Down burned bamboo-with his-skin down burned burned burned burned.
37. *Muru ariqme, otoqme gaeragauwana, ipete kiambokuwarena, (aq)* down
    Down burned, burned he-fix-him, from-there get-up-leave (er) down
    muru kiambokuwe p(eh)erah p(eh)erah tuntarena, kawahupipeq tupekuwe,
    get-up-leave run run went-down, water-place jump-in, down washed.
    muru wehriruweiq.
38. *Wehriniruwe wehriq—wehriruwe wehriq wehriruwe.*
    Washed washed—washed washed washed.
39. *Kaerawena, aipo inaga tuwekuwemena, nahpeq ki(w)ena, tagarowara*
    Fix-up, then that-one came-back, house came-there, look his relatives go
    wena wahrah poku bokuaguwana, (aq) ayahra mintoqme.
    left, (er) hair curled/braided.
40. *Ayahra mintoqme.*
    Hair fixed.
41. *Gaerarena (aq-) pahowin tahrare.*
    Fix-good (er—) feather-head-dress tie-on.
42. *(Tahq)iwe gaerarena, (aq—) nuwo ayowineq iwe.*
    Did fix-good, (er—) bird feathers made.
43. *Aupeq marena, (aq) tagarowaga, wehke poku pokuwana, aipo tubi-*
    Out-of-sight put, (er) I-look, people went left, then feather [long]
    yahna tubiyahnagi utuwe.
    feather made-it.
44. *Kaerarena, (a—) nuwo ahyowi moyepewe arena, nuwo ahyo moyepe*
    Fix-good, (uh—) bird feather at-head put, bird feather at-head put, then
    arena, aipo (aq) mentantami wehke boku.
    (er) things people went.
45. *Boku ahpeq ahpeq boku.*
    Went path path went.
46. *Bokuakuwana, wehikah wehikah ahpeq boku boku, aguwana itate*
    Went, noon noon path went went, do there shield that cassowary-feather
    tamengapi mentu biahna uruwaromi kiaqme.
    fastened-it-on took-it.
47. *Peyarena, aipo menari ane raneruwe.*
    Put-on, then something skin put-on.
48. *Gaeruraena, ayahrantoqme.*
    Make-good, fix-hair.
49. *Gaeruraena, aipo mena itate pokuweiq.*
    Fix-good, then that-one there-from left.
50. *Mina tubiyahna anahpite me tamenga mahnane tamenga mehwiq*
    That feather leaf that shield these shield edge thing-like-that that-thing-in

marahna(na)neq   (m)inanepi   tubiyahna   pewena,   mitate   pokuweiq;
feather stick-on, from-there left; danced.
abahrawe.

51. Abahruwena, pokuwana, awehninkaga aqaho(aq—) unah merenae
Danced, left, his-wife no (er—) bag want-I-get grass-skirt want-get
wahte merenae wahq merenae.
cloak want-take.

52. Itare itaq miyaho, itaq miyahoena, kaqmena giu kaqmenan ngiu aqao
Wait there you-be, there you-be, follow go follow go no I this at-me-he-
ine mahna niwehguwo(w)ana, aren aboga aren aboga niwehguyana, pokuge.
angry, your father your father me-angry-at, go-I.

53. Ayuwena, motaq moye abahraruq.
He-said, over there he-dance.

54. Motaq moye abahraruruena, pokuwana, pokuwana bokuwana kaqmena
Again there danced, went, went went follow she-came, no be-there,
giena, aqao itare, kiera nibo.
I-want marry.

55. Itare itare itare kiera nibo itaq miyaho iyenaq ogahnero itaq miyaho
Wait wait wait I-want marry there be-you you-there new-young-man
uwana, iyenaq ogahnero kaqmena, kiuge itare itare kiera niboq itare
there be said, you-there new-young-man follow, go-up-I wait wait I-want
itareuwana, itate moye abahraga motaq moye abahraga nuwe nauwe.
marry wait wait-she-said, wait there dance other place dance do do.

56. Nauwena uwena uwena, kiuwana, itare itare.
Did did did, went-up, wait wait.

57. Unah mewenae wahq mewenae wahte mewenae.
Bag I-want-get cloak I-want-get grass-skirt want-get.

58. Iraruwana, kaqmena kaqmena kaqmena kiuwana, motaq moye
She-said, follow follow follow she-went, again there dance.
abahraruq.

59. Motaq moye abahraruq uwe uwe uwe uwe.
Again there dance do do do do.

60. (Aq) kirarena, (aq) tahraq menaneq.
(Er) went-up-he, (er) tree-on that-what?

61. Tahk(u)wahraq tahkwahra kiataguarena, (aq) mayebaq abogehbeq
Takwa-tree Takwa-tree he-climb-up, (er) up-there on-top on-top that
abogehbeq men tamenga itapeq nomiq tariwarena, (aq—) itate abogarapeq
shield that-place there put-down (er—) there-from up-on-top moss/reed
nanah nukuweiq.
he-became.

62. Kieukuwana, uwoena, mahntenaq awehibin kinuwen yuwe nu nu nu nu.
He-became-up-there, oh-she-said, there at-base she-went-around did did
did did did.

63. *Irarena, mipi minaq teh geukuwaqme.*
   Did-it, there this reed/tree she-became.
64. *Awehibi awehibi mipi kemari kuweiq.*
   Base base there those-things became-she.
65. *Awehninkawi.*
   His-wife-it-was.

1. There was a young man who used to go hunting for possum; he would go hunting for possum and would give it down there to a certain girl. He gave it to her, put it there, and gave it to that certain girl, putting it there. This young man, after shooting possum, would give it to her. When he put it there, then he would go again and shoot possum and keep doing this, and they would eat and eat it, cooking it and cooking it and keep eating it, and then she went out in order to make a taro garden.

5. When she went to make a taro garden, he would become a small child, that young man would become a small child and keep becoming a small child, and he would come and be there at the edge of the garden with reference to where his wife [to be] was planting. Now he would say continually to her, 'Give me a bug, give me a certain bug,' and he would keep saying [singing] this. He would continue to say and say, 'Give me a bug, give me a bug,' and then he would take out his small flute and keep playing and playing it. That young man tied on bird feathers on his head. This young man would fix himself up very nicely, becoming a good looking young man. 10. He would play his flute, keep doing this, and then leave.

After he left, she would go down and stay over night and then that wife [to be] again would go out to fix a taro garden and that young fellow would see her again, and he would pull off his feather decorations and put them down over there at the edge of the garden, and then he would become a small boy, he would become a very small boy. Then he would say to her again, 'Give me a bug, give me a bug,' [singing it]. After he came like this and she saw him, then that one said to herself, 'What sort of person is this that he talks like this?' and she threw those bugs over there; but said to herself, 'That one is very much like the young man who is to be my husband.' 15. 'I wonder what this is that he wants to eat?' she said, and she came along behind him and followed him. He went on down out of sight, and as he went out of sight, she came down to the edge and watched him and he came down and put on his feathers and his net bag. Then he was like a young man again; he became like a young man and with reference to the fact that she went down there, she said, 'Oh,' and then with reference to her father— it wasn't so good, for she thought, 'You went down there to shoot possums and give them to me,' [and she told her father] 'that young fellow came along to the garden where I was working, and he became a young lad, he became a young boy. He came and was there and he kept singing, "Give me a bug, give me that bug," then he would go away and become a young man again. He would tie on his feathers and leave and then when he left I spied on him,' she said.

20. Now when she told her father this, then he took some bamboos for torches and put them on a shelf, and dried them, putting them on the shelf to dry, and then after putting them there and drying them, then the men collected

together in the men's house. When they were collected there in the men's house and it had gotten dark and it was dark there in the house and the men were there, he fixed it up well; they slept and then that father brought the bamboos, he brought the bamboos from the shelf and he lit them in the fire, lighting them well. Then he would do like this; he would walk along and follow a certain one, and then that one would respond, 'No, I am the younger brother, I am this particular one, not the one you want,' and then again he would go to the edge of the fire and look. He would do like this again and then go into one of the small rooms. 25. He would go into the small room from the edge of the fire and go and look. When he went and looked, the one in the room would say, 'No, I'm just here, and I'm her younger brother, I am her younger brother, you go look over there'; and then he would go look over there with his torch; and in another room he would look and the one there would say, 'No, I am just her brother in-law aren't I? I am her in-law, you look over there,' that one said. He would do what that one said again and he would light his bamboo and again go look at another one; and this one too would say, 'No I am just here, I am her in-law.' Then again as a result he would light another bamboo, go from the fire place, and look and another one would say, 'No, I'm not the one, I'm her brother.' He again with reference to that would light another one, go from the fire place, make a light down there, and then that other one said, 'No, I'm not the one, I'm her brother.' 30. Then again he did it the same way, going into another small room and lighting it, and that one again said, 'No, I'm this one, I'm really her father,' he said. And again the same thing happened over again; he lit it to look for him.

Then he found that her husband was here in one of them. With reference to where that one was, her father said, 'You are the one!' and the young man answered, 'Yes, I am here, I am alive right here.' 'What is that talk that you kept saying that you were going to go and shoot and bring possum for cooking and eating? Why did you talk that way, making that kind of talk?' 35. When he said that, he burned him with that bamboo. He rammed down with the bamboo and burned and burned his skin and kept burning him. He burned him that way and really fixed him and after he had done that, the young man got up and left, and he ran and ran and went down to a pond of water and jumped in, and down there he washed himself. He washed and washed and washed and washed and washed.

When he was really fixed up, then that one came back from down there and came into the house and he looked for his relatives, but they had left, so he fixed his hair up. 40. He fixed his hair up, he really fixed himself up and put on his head feathers. They had gone on out of sight, and when he looked, the people had left, and then he just fixed up the long feathers and made them pretty. He finished, put on his head dress, put on those bird feathers on his head, and then went along where the people had gone.

45. He went along that path and kept going. When he had gone along, it got to be noon and he just kept going, and then fastened cassowary feathers on the shield, and took it along. So after he put those on, then he put some skin on the shield and made it very nice. He made himself up and again fixed his hair. When he had finished; he went on from there. 50. So he put those feathers and leaves on the shield, he put a fringe on the edge of the shield like that by

sticking feathers and things on it, and from there he went along and then he started to dance.

He danced and went, and then his wife said, 'Don't go, I want to get my net bag and my grass skirt and my cloak and bring them along. You just be there, you just be there and wait!' she said; and then followed him. She followed him and as he went he said, 'No, I'm going to do this because your father was very angry at me; your father got very angry at me and I'm leaving.' When he said that, again he danced over at that other place. He danced there again and went and went, and she followed him and said, 'No, don't go, you just stay because I want to marry you.' 55. 'Just wait, wait I want to marry you, you be there, you just be that new young man,' she said; 'You be that new young man,' and she followed him saying, 'I'm going up, so you wait; I want to marry you, wait, wait,' she kept saying; but he would dance again there and be there at another place and he would go and dance and he kept doing that. He kept doing and doing that, and he went up from there and she said, 'Wait, wait. I want to get my net bag and cloak and I want to get my grass skirt.' When she said that, she followed and followed him and as she went again, he danced over there. He would dance over there and he kept doing and doing that.

60. Finally he went on up a tree that was there. He climbed up the Takwa tree and he was up there, way up on top. He put down his shield there at that place, and he went up there, up on top and he became a certain kind of moss (or reed). When he became that up there, she said, 'Oh!' and was there at the base of the tree, and she went around and around and around it. When she did that, she became there this other kind of reed. There at the base, at the base she became that sort of thing. 65. That was his wife.

18. A 'SINGSING' ABOUT HANGING

1. Awehninga abahruwana, (aq—) anahgo ainka anahgome pehyahouwana,
    Wife singsing, (er—) possum possum possum he-went-shoot, went-
pehyahouwana, mahbigaena mahbigaenawi ahreawiq.
shoot, young-man young-man wife-give.
    2. Marena, (iye—iye no-) iye nonaneq.
    Put-it, (not—not—) not he-can-eat.
    3. Iye nonaneq, anahgo naumaqmaqme anahpeu taguw(e)u anahbetaguq
    Not he-can-eat, possum he-ate-and-ate weak-became no-account weak-
anahbetaguweiq.
became weak-became.
    4. Anahbetaguwana, aipo ina mipi meqeuwana, abahro naerauntabe
    Became-no-good, then that there always-was, dance go-because refer-that
nauntabewe anahbeutagena, marawe nahopete tagaroweiq.
no-good-he-was, like-this house-from look.
    5. Marawe oyarate inderan oyarate tagaroweiq.
    Like-this door-way-from that-way door-way-from look.
    6. Tagarowana, awehninga aratiga keokahuena, itebeq mo abahriniena,

Look, wife girl dress-up, there again make-dance, this her-brother
mehq ayokaga iyakahpewe tubiyahna utuwe.
feather-stick-in feather put-it-on.

7. *Irakauwana, aqnopi maqmena, abahruwena, pokuntabe are ibeq mo*
Make-and give, head-on put, make-singsing, go you there again singsing
abahrewe tegabaruwo ayumena, (aq—) mena awehkawi aqnopeq tanahqme
you-can-come-look said (er—) that husband head-on ashes-sprinkle fix,
gaeruwena, tanahqme gaeruwena, mina porah rahwebete tebe kuwe aqmena;
ashes-put work-good, that pig path-from here came sprinkle;

8. *Anduwena anduwena anduwena anduwena;*
Put-on put-on put-on put-on;

9. *Aipo tehra tahmemetaq mayoyapi mayonabi (aq) tahmemeta tebari-*
Then tree-in Tameme-tree-in this-ground this-ground (er) Tameme-tree
kirena.
he-went-hang-himself.

10. *Tebarikirena, ina ina tanah ahnduwena, mo tearena, teh ebeteru-*
Hang-self, that that ashes sprinkle, again put-on, tree up-in-saw, here
gahnana, ibeq parikiontabe ibeq parikiwe.
hanging here hang.

11. *Torantahra nurowana, aipo mo abahrena, mina awehninga tererere*
Swing he-was, then more dance, that wife came came call-out;
tere taweuwana;

12. *Iya kauntabe aiqme abono (aq) aiqme abono irareuwana, ira kanuntabe*
Not was-there where you-are (er) where you-are say, not be-there
tere mena tanah.
came that-one ashes.

13. *Mena okahyomari mote akaturuena, mena tanahrate (aq) ayahntawe*
Those decorations from-there took-off, those ashes-with (er) tracks
ayahntawe ayahntawe teragome.
tracking tracking look.

14. *Awehibi moye antuwarena, (aq) iyetaq tahmemetaq tebarikirowana,*
Base there sprinkle-he, (er) up-on Tameme-in hanged-self, Tameme-
tahmemtaq kongo, tahmemetaq kongo, iraruweiq.
tree-on sing, Tameme-on sing, she said.

1. A certain wife would always go to singsings [dances] and he went out for
possums, going out to hunt and shoot possums; that is, her young man—her
young man would hunt and give the possums to his wife. When he put it there,
it was not good for him to eat it. He was not supposed to eat it, but he ate and
ate and ate the possum, and he became weak, and got to be of no account because he got very weak. After he had become very weak, then he would always
be there, and with reference to the dances, when he was no good, he would stay
there at the house and watch. 5. He would be in the door way like this, looking
from the door way.

When he looked, his wife, that girl, would dress up and she would go over again to a singsing; her brothers would put on cockatu feathers, sticking them on and twisting them into it [their hair]. They made those things and gave them to her, and she put them on her head, and she would go to the singsing, but as she would go, he would say, 'You are there again at a singsing,' and he would just look. So he decided, that husband, to sprinkle ashes on his head and when he fixed up, he worked the ashes in well, and then he took a path of the pigs and from here he came along and sprinkled and sprinkled and sprinkled the ashes. Then he, here in the Tameme tree, here at this particular area, right there in the Tameme tree, he hanged himself. 10. He just went and hanged himself, but those ashes he had sprinkled along the way and put them right there up to the tree so that she could see where he had gone, and there with reference to that hanging, he just was there and hanged himself. He was up there swinging, but she had gone to more dances, so that wife came and called out for him, but he was not there and she kept saying, 'Where are you, where are you?' but he was not there so she followed the trail of the ashes. She took off those decorations that she had on, and then she followed the tracks of the ashes, tracking and tracking and looking for him. Right up to the base of the tree he had scattered the ashes, and then he was up there where he had hanged himself in the Tameme tree. He was there in the Tameme tree, and what she said was a sort of singsing, saying *"Tamemeta kongo, Tamemeta kongo."*

PART TWO: *Auyana-Usarufa*

X. Introduction

HOWARD McKAUGHAN

The bulk of the descriptive studies of the Auyana-Usarufa has been done be Darlene L. Bee of the Summer Institute of Linguistics. References and acknowledgment appear in the first footnote of each chapter. Her studies are of the Usarufa, spoken by some 1,000 persons. Data are from the village of Kaagu (Orona). The Auyana, a name covering the dialect spoken in the villages of Kosena, Arora, and Asempa among others and the dialect spoken in the village of Kawaina, is summarized by McKaughan and Marks. The collection of texts is also from the Auyana. The map of the Eastern Highlands Study Area shows the Auyana, north of the Awa (see Map 2). Villages of Asempa (5) and Kawaina (6) are located as is the area for Kosena and Usarufa.

Dr. Bee prefers that Usarufa be called a language rather than a dialect. Her studies do indicate a substantial difference between the two, and though Usarufa is more closely related to Auyana than to any of the other study languages (Awa, Gadsup, and Tairora), it may be as well to regard the Auyana-Usarufa as a subfamily rather than dialects of the same language. Criteria for establishing language versus dialect are yet to be formalized to the satisfaction of all. In this case, the differences between Usarufa and Auyana are more substantial grammatically, perhaps, than the differences between the various Awa dialects. The people insist on a difference, and though in this respect native reaction is dangerous, we will stick to the two names, Auyana and Usarufa. However, there is not this kind of difference between Kosena and Auyana, the language spoken in the village of Kosena being little different from that in Arora from where the Kosena people migrated within remembered history.

McKaughan and Marks summarize the Auyana phonology in the following chapter, so nothing more need be said here. The consonant and vowel system of Auyana is compared to the other languages in Chapter XXXV. The notes on the Auyana grammar in McKaughan and Marks are augmented substantially by the treatment by Bee on Usarufa. The phonological studies of Usarufa are of special interest in that they highlight (A) tone, a newly discovered feature of New Guinea languages; and (B) distinctive features, an approach not used by the other writers, new in its application to New Guinea languages. Bee's article in Part V (Chap. XXXVI) on comparative problems is also of interest along this line since she comments on the distinctive features in the other languages of the study group.

The original publishers of Chapters XII and XIII are indicated in the footnotes. The only difference between the original publications and those given here is the use of an orthography that is consistent with the other descriptions where it does not alter the information given.

The texts will afford an opportunity for further analysis and description of Auyana, and also give the reader-analyst an opportunity to compare Auyana and Usarufa.

XI. Notes on Auyana Phonology and Morphology

HOWARD McKAUGHAN and DOREEN MARKS

1. INTRODUCTION

Auyana is spoken by some 4,500 people living in the Kainantu subdistrict of the Eastern Highlands of New Guinea. This study is of the dialect spoken by about 350 people living in the village of Kosena.[1] These people moved from the Arora village within remembered history, and their dialect is representative of Central Auyana.

These notes, though incomplete and sketchy, will give the reader a basis for comparison with the Usarufa materials. The differences are matters of detail. However, it should be noted that the Usarufa say that the Auyana spoken in Kosena is not intelligible to them. Before conclusions can be drawn from the statement, however, further investigation needs to be made of what is meant by 'unintelligible.' The Usarufa descriptive materials in other chapters of this monograph give the descriptive details for the Auyana language group as opposed to the Awa, Gadsup, and Tairora. The final part of this monograph gives the comparative relations between the languages of the family including Auyana and Usarufa.

2. PHONOLOGY

2.1. *Phonemes (segmental)*

2.1.1. *Consonants.* Voiceless and voiced stops occur at bilabial, alveolar, and velar positions, and also the labiovelar position. The bilabial and alveolar stops contrast following the nasals: *aampaq* 'on the path', *aamba* 'path';

---

[1] The materials upon which these notes are based were gathered by Doreen Marks under the auspices of the Summer Institute of Linguistics. Data papers on the phonology and the noun morphology were written by Miss Marks and were used by McKaughan as a basis for this paper.

TABLE 5
PHONETIC SEGMENTS

		Consonants			
	Bilabial	Alveolar	Velar	Labialized	Glottal
Stops					
Voiceless	*p*	*t*	*k*	*kw*	*q*
Voiced	*b*	*d*	*g*	*gw*	
Fricatives					
Voiceless	[ɸ]*	*s*			
Voiced	[β]		[ǥ]	[ǥw]	
Lateral		[l] ~ [tl]			
Vibrant		[r]			
Nasals	*m*	*n*	[ŋ]		

	Semivowels
w	*y*

		Vowels	
	Front	Central	Back
High	*i*		*u*
Mid	*e*	*a*†	*o*
Low		*aa*	

* Symbols enclosed in square brackets are allophonic.
† The phonetic quality is usually symbolized by [ə] in this case and [a] for the low central vowel. The symbols here are chosen for practical purposes. Symbols /q/, /kw/, and /gw/ are also so chosen.

sindaampaq 'my alimentary track', *siyaamba* 'my arm'; *ontama* 'door', *undama* 'wind'. However, the velar phonemes do not contrast in this way. The voiceless varieties occur in initial position and following the nasal (which in turn is velar in position): *kesibako* 'my younger brother', *kwikomba* 'arm band', *kankamba* 'rubbish', *tunkwi* 'darkness'. The velars contrast in intervocalic positions: *anaabukoma* 'her husband's mother, her son's wife', *anaabugoma* 'her mother's father', *awaikoma* 'her husband', *amaaigoma* her sister-in-law'; *aukwaiqa* 'bird arrow head', *auqwaima* 'message'. Voiced stops have stop versus fricative allophones. The bilabial fricative fluctuates between voiced and voiceless varieties. The alveolar obstruent is a stop before a homorganic nasal, a lateral following /i/, and a flapped vibrant (sometimes fluctuates with *tl*), elsewhere. Examples: [ayaanaɸbiq] 'his finger nail', *oqomba* 'another', *tindauma* 'yesterday', [marama] 'ground', [silaumba] 'my knee'. Consonant phonemes are thus /p, b, t, d, k, g, kw, gw, q, s, m, n, w, y/.

2.1.2. *Vowels.* There are six vowels in Auyana as charted, using double vowel /aa/ to represent the low central vowel, and /a/ for the mid central vowel. Note the following examples: *iyamba* 'dog', *iyaamba* 'bush turkey', *anama* 'bamboo', *aanoma* 'later', *andama* 'string', *aamba* 'path', *unaane* 'It is a bag', *mayaamba* 'taro', *ema* 'you', *oyama* 'door'. Bee in chapter XIII describes five vowels for Usarufa, finding the central varieties to be in complementary distribution by interpreting the lower quality as a sequence of two and long with the higher being short and single. Her material resembles the Auyana since we use *a* and *aa* also. The other languages in the family also have at least six vowels, with Awa having a seventh.

3. NOUN MORPHOPHONEMICS

Phonemes are modified in various ways when morphemes are juxtaposed. This is the case with all types of words. However, we indicate some of the changes occurring in word structure when nouns are involved, leaving the verb morphophonemics for later analysis. A rather complete treatment is given by Bee in Chapter XIV. Indications are that the morphophonemics for Auyana are more consistent through both nouns and verbs whereas Usarufa rules change between noun and verb and close-knit noun phrases.

Nouns in Auyana are those word bases which may occur with the nominative suffix *-maN*.[2] Both nouns and their affixes may be divided into three classes: Class I terminates with /q/; Class II with a nasal; and Class III with a vowel. The nasal of Class II is not actualized unless an affix or another word base follows the item in question. A noun complex (word base plus affixes or a closely knit noun phrase consisting of a descriptive plus head noun) usually requires the nominative suffix whether said in isolation or as a part of a sentence. Examples of the three classes follow:

	Class I		Class II		Class III	
kaeq	'two'	*aaedaaN*	'old'	*moda*	'one'
kaweq	'good'	*eiyaiN*	'four'	*aki*	'short'
taaq	'sugarcane'	*ontaN*	'stone'	*padoi*	'arrow'
naaoq	'village'	*naaN*	'house'	*kisaa*	'sweet potato'
maankadaq	'knife'	*iyaN*	'dog'	*numa*	'bird'
abaq	'your brother'	*amosaN*	'your throat'	*ano*	'your mother'
(-paq)	'to, at'	*(-piN)*	'from'	*(-nei)*	instrument
(-kwadaq)	'together with'	*(-maN)*	nominative	*(-e)*	predicative

Combinations of morphemes result in the following morphophonemic changes.

3.1. *Class I*

Class I stems or affixes exhibit the following. (A) Final glottal stop is dropped preceding morphemes with initial voiceless stop: *kaeq* + *-qa* >

---

[2] Almost all affixes given have allomorphic variants. The *N* is a morphophoneme indicating a nasal which is actualized as bilabial or alveolar depending on phonological environment.

kaeqa (two + allomorph of nominative suffix) 'two'; *kaeq* + *padoi* >
kae padoima 'two arrows'; *kaeq* + *tomeyoq* > *kae tamayoqa* 'two sticks';
maiq +*-kabaN* > *maikabamba* (pit beside) 'beside the pit'. (B) Final
glottal stop becomes /d/ preceding initial vowel; *kaeq* + *iyampoi* > *kaed
iyampoima* 'two boys'; *oq* + *-e* > *ode* (star it-is) 'It is a star.' (C) Glottal
stop is retained before nasals, and sometimes in isolation: *kaeq* + *maankadaq* > *kaeq maankada* 'two knives'. Usually, however, the form is cited
with the nominative suffix: *kaeq* or *kaeqa* 'two', *kaeq maankadaqa* 'two
knives'.

3.2. *Class II*

Class II stems or affixes exhibit the following changes. (A) The final
nasal is lost before silence, becomes /m/ before bilabials, /n/ elsewhere:
iyaN +*maN* > *iyamba* 'dog', *aidaaN* + *padoi* + *-maN* > *aidaam padoima*
'old arrow', *oqoN* + *paasa* + *-maN* > *oqom paasama* 'another comb',
iyaN +*-toN* + *maN* > *iyantomba* 'lots of dogs', *aidaaN* + *tamayoq* + *-qa*
> *aidaan tamayoqa* 'old stick', *kuN* + *-e* > *kune* 'It is an axe', *eiyaiN* +
ontoN + *-maN* > *eiyain ontomba* 'four stones'. The nominative suffix has
a final nasal, but when forms with this suffix are cited in isolation, the final
nasal is lost: *poima* 'pig', *iyamba* 'dog', *noyaaqa* 'fish'. (B) Class II stems
or affixes cause a following initial nasal to become a voiced stop having the
same point of articulation as the original nasal: *eiyaiN* + *maankadaq* >
eiyaim baankadaqa 'four knives', *ontaN* + *maN* > *ontamba* 'stone',
oqoN + *noN* + *-maN* > *oqon domba* 'another river', *kuN* + *-ne* >*kunde*
'with an axe'.

3.3. *Class III*

Class III stems or affixes cause the following changes. An initial /p/ of a
following suffix (or word) becomes /b/ and an initial /k/ or /kw/ becomes
/g/ or /gw/: *ana* + *piN* + *-maN* > *anabimba* 'in the bamboo', *kigau* +
-paq + *-maN* > *kigaubaqa*[3] 'to the garden', *moda* + *kwaasi* + *-maN* >
moda gwaasima 'one person'.

The nominative suffix, which acts as a classifier, occurs final in the noun
complex. Thus before a verb the nominative suffix, being Class II, causes
the morphophonemic changes cited above. The nominative suffix occurs
only with the head noun in a close-knit noun phrase. This suffix has the
following allomorphs: (*-ma* ~ *-N*) ~*-qa,* the alternants in parentheses being
free following Class III items. The last alternant, *-qa,* occurs with Class I
stems. Following the description above, Class II items cause the nasal of
the suffix to become /b/. Hence we have such examples as *taaqa* 'sugar cane',
kobadamba 'beans', and *kisaama* 'sweet potato' from the three classes. The

---

[3] The suffix *qa* is an allomorph of *maN*.

alternant designated *-N* has the same morphophonemic characteristics as described for the final nasal of Class II items.

4. NOUN AFFIXES

Auyana nouns may occur with prefixes to indicate pronominal possessives, and with suffixes to indicate categories such as possession, similarity, conjunction, accompaniment, instrument, purpose, acquisition, locative, predicative, interrogative, and vocative.

4.1. *Person Prefixes*

Possessive prefixes occur with certain inalienable nouns including with others body parts and kinship terms. There are three prefixes indicating this personal possession:

s- ∼ su- ∼ si-   first person singular, dual, and plural
ø- ∼ a-   second and third person singular
t- ∼ tu- ∼ ti-   second and third dual, and plural

The distribution of allomorphs is phonologically defined. Thus: (A) *s-* and *t-* occur preceding /o/, /u/, /aa/, /i/; and *ø-* preceding /o/ and /aa/. Examples: *s-oiqa* 'my mouth', *s-udamba* 'my eye', *s-aaqa* 'my ear', *s-iqa* 'my nose', *ke s-idoma* 'my brother-in-law', *ke s-isaabugoma* 'my great grandparent', *ke s-aaninko* 'my son', *ke s-isaamba* 'my son-in-law'; *t-oiqa* 'their mouths', *t-udamba* 'their eyes', *t-aaqa* 'their ears', *t-iqa* 'their noses', *ø-oiqa* 'your/ his/her mouth', *ø-aaqa* 'your/his/her ear', *ø-aaninko* 'your/his/her son'. (B) *su-* and *tu-* occur preceding /w/: *su-wetamba* 'my leg', *tu-wetamba* 'their legs'. (C) *si-*, *ti-*, and *a-* occur elsewhere: *si-samaima* 'my foot', *si-dumba* 'my liver', *si-mosamba* 'my throat', *ke si-noma* 'my mother'; *ti-samaima* 'their feet', *ti-dumba* 'their livers', *ti-mosamba* 'their throats', *ti-nowama* 'their mother'; *a-udamba* 'your/his eye', *a-mosamba* 'your/his throat', *a-iqa* 'your/his nose', *a-nowama* 'his mother', *a-idowama* 'his brother-in-law', *a-isaankoma* 'his son-in-law', *a-isaabugoma* 'his great grandparent'.

Free forms of the pronouns may be used to avoid ambiguity. The first person singular of these forms is preferred before kinship terms as in the examples cited above. The free forms distinguish between the various persons and singular, dual, trial, and plural numbers.

	Sing	Dual	Trial	Pl
1st	*kema*	*kedaima*	*kesaama*	*kesaama*
2nd	*ema*	*kenadaima*	*kenadauma*	*kenadawaqa*
3rd	*kwema*	*mindadaima*	*mindadauma*	*mindadawaqa*

4.2. *Suffixes*

Suffixes may be grouped into those that indicate morphological relations, and those that mark syntactic relations. The former include dual, plural, limiter, augmentative, and state of being; the latter include suffixes to mark relations between nouns, or between nouns and verbs, and suffixes which indicate that the affixed base is an utterance.

4.2.1. Suffixes marking morphological relations

A. *Dual.* *-dai~kai: kwaasi-dai* 'two people', *iyampoi-dai* 'two boys', *si-yaan-kai-ma* (my-hand-dual-nominative) 'ten'.

B. *Plural.* *-yoN~-toN* (the first with Class III, the second with Classes I and II): *iyampoi-yom-ba* 'boys', *inaamadu-yom-ba* 'girls', *poi-yom-ba* 'pigs', *kwaasi-yom-ba* 'men', *kwaan-tom-ba* 'opposums', *iyan-tom-ba* 'dogs', *noyaa-tom-ba* 'fish', *mai-tom-ba* 'pits'.

C. *Limiter.* *-yaa: inaamadu-yaa unaamba kweum* (girl-only bag making) 'Only we girls make bags.'

D. *Augmentative.* *ye ~ -te: kwaasai-ye sininimba* (talk-augmentative talk-woman) 'a talkative woman', *oisan-ten malan kwaasi* (goods-augmentative put person) 'a man who keeps gathering riches'.

E. *Stative.* *-koN* (indicates that the base to which it is attached is viewed as in a state of being): *kwaasi-ko* 'a man' or 'state of being a man' or even 'an action characteristic of a man', *taai-go* 'tree, being a tree', *kadan-ko* 'white man', *aba-ko* 'his younger brother'.

4.2.2. Suffixes marking syntactic relations between nouns

A. *Possession.* *-a* singular, *-ti* plural: *ke sibon-a tomba* 'my father's food', *mora iyampoikon-a tomba* 'a boy's food', *kaed iyampoi-ti tomba* 'two boys' food'.

B. *Accompaniment*

a. *-kwadaq* indicates that the base to which it is attached accompanies some other one or thing (active): *kisaa-kwada tusin akayo* (sweet-potato-with squash cook) 'Cook the sweet potato along with the squash', *poi-kwada kwassin kweti* (pig-with man come-he) 'The pig is coming along with the man.'

b. *-te ~-ye* or *-se ~-e* indicate that the base to which the morpheme is attached is accompanied by another (passive): *poi-yen/poi-sen kwaasin kweti* 'The man is coming accompanied by a pig.' *-te* occurs with Classes II and III, *-e* following stative *-koN*, and *-ye/-se* elsewhere.

C. *Similarity.* *-daaN ~ -kaaN: idaankabayaan-kaam-ban aamba* (snake-like road) 'a path like a snake', *anda-daam-ba* 'vinelike'.

4.2.3. Suffixes marking syntactic relations between nouns and verbs

A. *Referent* (also indicates a question). *-yabaya~-tabaya* (the latter with Classes I and II): *taa-tabaya kwankai* (sugar-cane-for wants) 'Does he want sugar cane?'

B. *Instrument.* *-nei: nointantaaq-nei tubuqmai* (what-thing-with hit) 'What did he use to hit?'

C. *Purpose.* *-yaaq* ~ *-taaq* (the latter with Classes I and II): *kwaasai-yaaq-an kudai* (language-for talk) 'He went to talk', *kun-taaq-a naaum-paqan konaum* (axe-for house-in I-go) 'I will go into the house for an axe.'

D. *Locative*

a. *-paq* ~ *-baq* 'place at, to, on': *kigau-baq-a* 'to the garden', *mada-baq-a* 'on the ground'.

b. *-piN* ~ *-biN* 'in, on': *kigau-bim-ba* 'in the garden', *unaam-pim-ba* 'in the bag'.

c. *-keN* 'from': *kigauba-kem-ba* 'from the place of the garden', *anabin-kem-ba* 'from inside the bamboo'.

d. *-daq* ~ *-kaq* 'around, near, at': *kigau-daq-a* 'around the garden', *nan-kaq-a* 'on the house'.

e. *-dabaN* ~ *-kabaN* 'beside, along': *kudi-dabam-ba* 'beside the fence', *aan-kabam-ba* 'along the path'.

f. *-a* or *-aq* interrogative with *-piN* and *-keN: kigaubin-a* 'Is it in the garden?', *kigauba-ken-aq* 'Is it from the garden?'

4.2.4. *Suffixes marking predicative expressions*

A. *-we* ~ *-e* occurs final in an utterance and predicates the base to which it is attached: *kigau-we* 'It is a garden', *non-e* 'It is water.'

B. *-waqi* ~ *-aqi* occurs final and marks an interrogative: *kigau-waqi* 'Is it a garden?', *non-aqi* 'Is it water?'

C. *-o* occurs with personal names indicating that the person is being called: *konka-o* 'Oh, Konka!', *aqina-o* 'Oh, Aqina!'

5. VERB MORPHOLOGY

5.1. *General*

The verb complex in Auyana has both prefixes and suffixes. A substantially complete analysis and description which parallels the Auyana is given by Bee (see Chap. XIV) for the Usarufa. Analysis for the Auyana is not complete at this time. The categories marked by verbal affixation in Auyana include at least the following: tense-aspect, voice, person, mode, and certain affixes to indicate relationships between clauses and to anticipate the person subjects of a following clause.

Tense-aspect forms include present, future, past, far past, customary, and perfect. Voices include stative, completive, and benefactive. Persons include the subject of the verb, and, for a closed set of verbs, an obligatory object (prefixes of the same form used to mark person possessors with inalienable nouns). Number for persons include singular, dual, and plural, and persons are first, second, and third. However, not all possible contrasts are marked in all instances. Often the same morpheme is used for second and third persons plural and one for second and third person dual. In some instances the singular and plural for first person is the same morpheme. Rules for co-occurrence of classes of verb stems with the sets of morphemes to indicate person subject become complicated (see Chap. XIV). Modes include indicative, imperative, prohibitive, and interrogative.

The relative order of the affixes to the verb stem is in general as follows:

Verb Stem + Voice + Tense-Aspect + Person-Subject + Mode

Object person markers precede the particular verb stems that require them (e.g., to call, to show, to see, to give, etc.).

The morphophonemics resulting from combinations of affixes is complicated. Again, Bee has worked out most of the basic rules for the Usarufa (see Chap. XIV. Sec. 9). No attempt will be made here to demonstrate such modifications for Auyana.

5.2. Verb Affixes

Some of the Auyana verb affixes are as follows:

A. *Tense-aspect*. *kwe-* present continuative (a unique prefix), *-ya* (with dual persons) or *-na* future, *-ka ~ -da* past, *-ya ~ ma* perfect.

B. *Voice*. *-koN* stative, *-suwa* completive, *ta ~ -ga* comprehensive complexive (e.g., 'Split all the wood, not just part of it').

C. *Person-subject*. *-um* first singular and plural, *-ø ~ -a* second singular and second and third plural, *-i* third singular, *-u* first dual, *-ai* second and third dual.

D. *Mode*. *-e* indicative, *-o* imperative, *-bo* prohibitive, *-no* interrogative.

Some examples of verb forms with person affixes and two of the tenses follow.

kumo- 'to go, come down'

	Present	Past
1st sing/pl	*kum-um*	*kun-ka-um*
2nd sing/pl, 3rd pl	*kumo-ø*	*kun-ka-ø*
3rd sing	*kum-i*	*kun-ka-i*
1st dual	*kum-u*	*kun-ka-u*
2nd/3rd dual	*kumo-i*	*kun-ka-ai*

Other examples of verb forms:

kwe-isa-i (present-continuative-here-he) 'He hears.'
u-ma-sua-um (make-perfect-completive-I) 'I have made'
ati-yuwa-na-um-no (pour-completive-future-1st-singular-interrogative) 'Will I pour it all out?"
aqa a-ma-ka-a-no (already to-him-give-past-2nd-singular-interrogative) 'Have you already given it to her?'
u-ma-su-ka-um (make-perfect-completive-past-I) 'I had made.'
u-ma-sua-na-um (make-perfect-completive-future-I) 'I will have made.'
kwai-go-na-um (sleep-stative-future-I) 'I will be in the state of sleeping.'
naa-o (eat-vocative) 'You eat.'

na-sin-ka-i (eat-for-me-benefactive-he) 'He eats for me/us.'
na-sin-ka-da-i (eat-for-me-benefactive-past-he) 'He ate for me/us.'
na-i-bo (eat-he-prohibitive) 'He shouldn't eat!'

There are numerous suffixes with final verbs. Many of the suffixes that occur with nouns also occur with verbs. We look forward to continued analysis.

XII. Usarufa Tone and Segmental Phonemes

DARLENE BEE and KATHLEEN BARKER GLASGOW

1. INTRODUCTION

1.1. *General*

Both S. Wurm (1962a) and A. Capell (1949) have pointed out the significant occurrence of tone in New Guinea languages. It is the purpose of this paper to describe more fully the occurrence of tone in one of the languages of the East New Guinea Highland Stock.[1] After describing the phonemic status of tone in Usarufa, its distribution and perturbation, the authors will include a description of Usarufa segmental phonemes.

1.2. *Definitions*

The *syllable* is defined as a unit of tone placement. Each syllable therefore has only one mora of length, a feature of the toneme; and a single vowel as its peak. The two syllable patterns, vowel (V) and consonant-vowel (CV), are the basis for interpretation of consonant versus vowel and of contoid clusters. Vowel clusters constitute syllable clusters.

The *morphological word* is defined as the smallest meaningful unit which may be uttered in isolation. It is thus morphologically rather than phonologically determined.

[1] This paper was originally published as pp. 111-27 in *Studies in New Guinea Linguistics,* Oceania Linguistics Monographs No. 6 (Sydney: University of Sydney, (1962), and is reprinted here, in slightly revised form, by permission. The authors gathered the material for this paper over a period of eighteen months' residence in the village of Mairapaqa of the Orono district. The area occupied by Usarufa speakers lies about thirty miles south and west of Kainantu in the Eastern Highlands District of New Guinea. Although a great percentage of the adult population speaking Usarufa are bi- or even multilingual, few understand or speak Neo-Melanesian. Therefore, the material used in this paper was gathered monolingually.

The *phonological phrase* may contain one or more words and is a unit having one stress, whose placement is determined by the nucleus of falling and/or high tones as described in Section 3.1.

1.3. *Symbolization*

A single *a* will be used in both phonetic and phonemic transcription to represent the mid-central vocoid ə. Glottal stop will be represented in both cases by *q* and preglottalized consonants by apostrophe plus consonant: *'p, 't, 'k, 'm,* etc. Length will be indicated by a colon following the segment: *m;, n;, a;,* etc. High tone will be represented by an acute accent (´); over the vowel, falling tone by a caret (ˆ) over the vowel, and low tone will be unmarked. Phonetic mid tone will be marked only in the section describing the phonetic qualities of high and low tones—in which case a macron (¯) over the vowel will be used. In phonetic transcription only, stress will be marked by double quotation marks (") preceding the stressed syllable. In phonemic transcription stress being subphonemic will be unmarked.

TABLE 6

SEGMENTAL PHONEMES

	Consonants			
	Bilabial	Alveolar	Velar	Glottal
Stops	*'p*	*'t t*	*'k*	*q*
Fricatives and flap	*b*	*r*	*g*	
Liquids	*w*	*y*		
	'w	*'y*		
Nasals	*m*	*n*		
	m:	*n:*		
	'm	*'n*		
		Vowels		
	Front	Central	Back	
High	*i*		*u*	
Low	*e*	*a*	*o*	

2. INTERPRETATION OF PHONEMES

2.1. *Consonant versus Vowel*

Nonsyllabic vocoids [y] and [w] are interpreted as consonants which occur only in consonant position of CV syllables and which are phonetically distinct from [i] and [u] by being nonsyllabic and having slight friction. Syllabic vocoids [i] and [u] are interpreted as vowels occurring only in vowel positions of V and CV syllables. For example:

[a"wé]	/awe-/	'Wait.'	(V-CV)
["aue]	/aue/	'It is flesh.'	(V-V-V)

["wíyiye]	/wíyiye/	'It is boiling.'	(CV-CV-CV)
["úiye]	/úiye/	'He is coming up.'	(V-V-CV)
["kéyune]	/ˈkéyune/	'I am coming.'	(CV-CV-CV)
["kéune]	/ˈkéune/	'I am doing.'	(CV-V-CV)

2.2. Complex Unit versus Sequence

Suspect vocoid clusters and contrastive long vocoids are interpreted as sequences of diverse or like vowels for the following reasons.

A. Nonsuspect vocoid clusters are common. For example:

| ["kéone] | /ˈkéone/ | 'You are doing. |
| [wae"m:á] | /waem:á/ | a type of tree |

B. Diverse tones may occur on suspect and nonsuspect vocoid clusters. For example:

["kéone]	/ˈkéone/	'You are doing.'
["áitauqa]	/áitauqa/	'foot'
[a"úram:a]	/aúram:a/	'eye'

C. Long vocoids occur with diverse tones and contrast with short vocoids. For example:

[a"ːma]	/aáma/	'breath'
[a:"má]	/aamá/	'sound'
[a"má]	/amá/	'to stick a post in the ground'
[o"ːtam:a]	/oótam:a/	'cargo'
["óʈam:a]	/óʈam:a/	'stone'

Suspect contoid clusters (preglottalized contoids and long nasals) are interpreted as single complex phonemes, 'p, 't, 'k, 'm, 'n, 'y, 'w, m:, and n:, because there are no nonsuspect consonant clusters on which to base a CCV syllable pattern and there are no nonsuspect CVC syllable patterns. By setting up either a CCV or both a VC and a CVC syllable pattern these segments could be interpreted as sequences of two diverse or like consonants. This would reduce the consonant phonemes from eighteen to ten and give the following consonant clusters: *qp, qk, qt, qw, qm, qn, mm,* and *nn.* This solution is adopted for orthographic purposes but is rejected for the phonemic analysis.

3. DESCRIPTION OF TONE

3.1. Conditioning of Stress

As in many of the languages of the Eastern New Guinea Highlands Stock, tone in Usarufa is closely linked with stress. In some of the Highland languages tone sequences are conditioned by stress while in others stress is conditioned by tone sequences. The latter is true in Usarufa. The three phonemic tones, high, falling, and low, condition stress as follows: stress occurs on the first high-tone syllable of a sequence of all high-tone syllables or of such a sequence following low-tone syllables; on the last high- or fall-ing-tone syllable preceding low tone; and on the last low-tone syllable in a sequence of all low tones. For example:

["má:mím:á]	/máámím:á/	a type of tree
[ma"yáímá]	/mayáímá/	'work'
[ílá"qóne]	/íráqóne/	'It is good.'
[a"nêma]	/anêma/	a type of bird
[ku'kabu"wo]	/'ku'kabuwo/	'Scrape it!'

3.2. *Phonetic Quality*

Phonetically high tone has a mid quality on final syllables following a se-quence of all low tones. Elsewhere its quality is high. Low tone has a mid quality on syllables preceding a high-low sequence. Elsewhere its quality is low. Falling tone has the quality of a high-low sequence but with only one mora of length instead of two.

The following contrastive sets provide evidence for the establishment of three tonemes and illustrate the conditioning of stress and of the phonetic qualities of the high and low tonemes.

["á:ma]	/áama/	'hunger'
[ā":má]	/aámá/	'breath'
[a:"mā]	/aamá/	'sound'
["púmá]	/'púmá/	'knife'
["póma]	/'póma/	'pig'
["pûma]	/'pûma/	a fern used as a trespass warning
[á"gúm:a]	/ágúm:a/	'lump'
["ábuma]	/ábuma/	'ripe'
[a"bûm:a]	/abûm:a/	'shoulder'
["ómá]	/ómá/	'wild cane'
[o"mā]	/omá/	'ditch'
["ôma]	/ôma/	'lid'
["wáíma]	/wáíma/	'tree kangaroo'
[wa"íma]	/waíma/	'house rat'
[wai"mā]	/waimá/	'needle'
["úniqa]	/úniqa/	type of sugar cane
[ú"nîqa]	/únîqa/	'cut worm'
[iya"mā]	/iyamá/	'water fall, spring'
[i"yámá]	/iyámá/	'feces'
[kā"búma]	/'kabúma/	'bowstring'
[kabu"mā]	/'kabumá/	type of tree

| ["káweqa] | /ˈkáweqa/ | 'glue' |
| [ka"wéqá] | /ˈkawéqá/ | 'cooked food' |

3.3. Distribution of Tonemes

The distribution of high, low, and falling tones is limited in that not more than one series of falling and/or high tones may occur on a morphological word. This same feature is manifested over two or more words in a phonological phrase. The distribution of falling tone is further limited in that it does not occur word or phrase finally,[2] and therefore always preceeds low tone. With these limitations all possible tone patterns occur on two-, three-, and four-syllable words. All patterns except five have been found on five-syllable words, and all but eleven patterns have been found on six-syllable words. Words of more than six syllables have not been charted. In Table 7, patterns expected but not yet observed are in parentheses.

3.4. Tone Perturbation

Two types of tone perturbation are present in Usarufa—*internal* and *external*. By *internal* we mean that perturbation which takes place within a word base when affixes are added; by *external* we mean that perturbation which takes place when two or more words come together to form a phonological phrase. Perturbation between phrases has not been observed.

For purposes of describing tone changes two word classes are distinguished in Usarufa, *nouns* and *verbs*. Each class manifests a different type of tone perturbation. *Verbs* manifest *internal* perturbation while *nouns* manifest *external*. The tone changes which occur in *noun phrases* will be dealt with here. The tone changes which occur within the *verb* are much more complicated and will be dealt with in a separate paper.

Within *noun phrases* there are two types of perturbation which occur; the perturbation of *descriptive noun phrases* and the perturbation of *possessive noun phrases*. In both types the perturbation is progressive, that is, that which precedes perturbs that which follows. Single modifiers and the first in a series of two or more always retain their basic tone pattern. Succeeding modifiers are perturbed in the same manner as nouns in descriptive phrases.

In *descriptive noun phrases* all the tones of the noun perturb to agree with the tone of the nominal suffix dropped from the modifier, binding modifier,

---

[2] Questions, emphatic predicated nouns, and proper name calling forms have a falling tone on the word final suffix with corresponding stress. This use of the falling tone is interpreted as intonation because it is fixed, unlike the tone of other suffixes; and because it creates a new tone pattern of more than one series of high tones, and, therefore, more than one stress. E.g.: [na:"nó"nô:] /naanóno?/ 'Are you going to eat it?'; ["keye"nô:] /ˈkéyeno?/ 'Are you coming?'; [a"páa":"nô] /aˈpááno!/ 'Daddy!'; ["tá:"rô:] /ˈtáaro!/ 'Am I ever hungry!'

TABLE 7
CHART OF TONE PATTERNS

Tone Sequence	Two-syllable	Three-syllable	Four-syllable	Five-syllable	Six-syllable
High	´ ´	´ ´ ´	´ ´ ´ ´	´ ´ ´ ´ ´	´ ´ ´ ´ ´ ´
High-low	´ `	´ ´ `   ´ ` `	´ ´ ´ `   ´ ´ ` `   ´ ` ` `	(´ ´ ´ ´ `)   ´ ´ ´ ` `   ´ ´ ` ` ` ´ ` ` ` `	´ ´ ´ ´ ´ `   (´ ´ ´ ´ ` `)   ´ ´ ´ ` ` ` ´ ´ ` ` ` ` ´ ` ` ` ` `
High-falling-low		´ ˆ `	´ ´ ˆ `   ´ ˆ ` `	´ ´ ´ ˆ `   (´ ´ ˆ ` `)   ´ ˆ ` ` `	(´ ´ ´ ´ ˆ `)   (´ ´ ´ ˆ ` `)   ´ ´ ˆ ` ` `
Falling-low	ˆ `	ˆ ` `	ˆ ` ` `	(ˆ ` ` ` `)	ˆ ` ` ` ` `
Low	` `	` ` `	` ` ` `	(` ` ` ` `)	(` ` ` ` ` `)
Low-high	` ´	` ` ´ ` ´ ´	` ` ` ´   ` ` ´ ´   ` ´ ´ ´	` ` ` ` ´ ` ` ` ´ ´   ` ` ´ ´ ´   ` ´ ´ ´ ´	` ` ` ` ` ´   ` ` ` ` ´ ´   ` ` ` ´ ´ ´ ` ` ´ ´ ´ ´ ` ´ ´ ´ ´ ´
Low-high-low		` ´ `	` ´ ` `   ` ´ ´ `   ` ` ´ `	` ´ ` ` ` ` ´ ´ ` `   ` ´ ´ ´ `   ` ` ´ ` `   ` ` ´ ´ ` ` ` ` ´ `	` ´ ` ` ` `   ` ´ ´ ` ` `   ` ´ ´ ´ ` ` ` ´ ´ ´ ´ ` ` ` ´ ` ` `   ` ` ´ ´ ` `   ` ` ´ ´ ´ ` ` ` ` ´ ` `   ` ` ` ´ ´ `   (` ` ` ` ´ ´ `) (` ` ` ` ` ´ `)
Low-falling-low	` ˆ `	` ` ` ˆ ` ` ˆ ` ` `	` ` ` ` ˆ `   ` ` ` ˆ ` ` ` ˆ ` ` ` `	(` ` ` ` ` ˆ `) (` ` ` ` ˆ ` `) (` ` ` ˆ ` ` `) ` ˆ ` ` ` ` `
Low-high-falling-low		` ´ ˆ `	(` ´ ´ ˆ `) ` ` ´ ´ ˆ `   ` ` ` ´ ˆ `	` ´ ´ ˆ ` `   (` ´ ´ ´ ˆ `)   ` ` ´ ´ ´ ˆ ` (` ` ` ´ ´ ˆ `) ` ` ` ` ´ ˆ `

and noun together in a phonological phrase. In the following examples the nominal suffixes of the modifiers are underlined.

	naam:á 'house'	'póma 'pig'	waayú'kama 'persor
wayám:a 'white'	wayán nám:á	wayá 'pómá	wayá 'káyú'kámá
netuqa 'many'	netuq nám:a	netu 'pómá	netuq wáyú'kámá
'páá'yamma 'little'	'páá'yan nam a	'páá'ya boma	'páá'ya wayu'kámá
taíma 'bad'	taí nam:a	taí boma	taí wayu'kama

Some compound words only perturb in the first member. For example, watá-ama 'speech'. Note -ama never perturbes to high, but watá- may perturb to either wátá- or wata- according to the rule. For example:

a'núm:á	'weak'	a'nú 'kátáama	'weak speech'
numamá	'bird'	numa wátáama	'bird speech'
íráqóm:a	'good'	íráqó 'kataama	'good speech'

In *possessive noun phrases*[3] either the initial possessor or the following noun may be emphasized. An *emphasized noun* is unperturbed, and therefore often consists of two phonological phrases. An *emphasized possessor* perturbs the tone of the noun to all low with the following exceptions: (1) possessors which drop a high-tone nominal suffix or therefore carry a high-tone possessive suffix do not perturb high-low sequence nouns to low tone; (2) possessors with stems of all low tone and not carrying a possessive suffix do not perturb nouns to low, as this would produce an all low sequence not observed in nouns or noun phrases. In the examples in Table 8 the tone perturbations which do not occur are numbered according to the exception(s) they follow.

4. DESCRIPTION OF SEGMENTAL PHONEMES

4.1. *Phonetic Quality and Evidence for Phonemic Status*

4.1.1. *Consonants.* Voiceless aspirated[4] stops occur in the bilabial /'p/, alveodental /'t/, and velar /'k/ positions. These stops occur phrase initially as plain stops and intervocalically as preglottalized stops.

Voiced fricatives occur in the bilabial /b/, and velar /g/ positions contrasting intervocalically with the voiceless aspirated stops /'p/ and /'k/. For example:

[e" 'píwámá]	/e'píwámá/	'that man over there'
[e"bíwámá]	/ebíwámá/	'that man up there'

---

[3] Possession is indicated either by possessive suffix on the modifier which always takes the tone of the dropped nominal suffix; or obligatory possessive prefix on such words as body parts, breath, name, offspring, and relationship terms; or both. E.g.: pogoni kamááma 'pig's sweet potato', pó áyaqa 'pig intestines', pógoni ayaqa 'pig's intestines'.

[4] Light aspiration occurs on voiceless stops, but is noncontrastive, occurring usually before high vowels, occasionally in fluctuation with nonaspirated stops before low front and back vowels, and not before the central vowel.

TABLE 8

TONE PERTURBATION OF NOUN IN POSSESSIVE PHRASE*

(Tone of emphasized noun in left subcolumn; tone with emphasized possessor in right subcolumn)

	múmá 'vomit'	*áyaqa* 'intestine'	*á'nóm:a* 'head'	*aítauqa* 'foot'
iyám:á 'dog'		(1)		
iyá'kóní 'the dog's'		(1)		
'póma 'pig'				
'pógoni 'the pig's'				
wáábímá 'water creature'		(1)		
wáábígoni 'the water creature's'		(1)		
numamá 'bird'		(1) (2)	(2)	(2)
numagóní 'the bird's		(1)		
'ko'kórima 'chicken'				
'ko'kórigoni 'the chicken's'				

* In spaces where neither possessive suffix nor prefix is present, a descriptive rather than possessive noun phrase is indicated and the tone is not pertinent to this chart. An all high-tone sequence does not occur on nouns that have obligatory possessive prefixes.

[pu" 'púmá]	/pu'púmá/	'game'
[ţu"búmá]	/'tubúmá/	a type of bird
[waa"kómá]	/waa'kómá	'the possum'
[waa"gómá]	/waagómá/	'the man'
[a'ki" 'kímá]	/a'ki'kíma/	'chicken hawk'
[a"gí'kímá]	/agí'kímá/	'a fright'

/r/ is a voiced alveolar flap occurring intervocalically following /i/ and in high-tone syllables following /a/ and preceding /i/, /e/ and /a/ as a lateral flap [1]; elsewhere it occurs as the flap [r]. For example:

[ţilu"m:á]	/'tirum:á/	'my liver'
[aru"m:á]	/arum:á/	'his liver'
[a"líburiqa]	/aríburiqa/	a type of sweet potato
[a"lá:tiyo]	/aráátiyo/	'Show him!'
[a:ra"má]	/aaramá/	'woman'
["óriqa]	/óriqa/	'very'

/t/ a voiceless alveolar contoid occurring only intervocalically may with some speakers fluctuate between a stop [t] and a grooved fricative [s]. This occurs mainly with borrowed words or with words which are cognate with languages having [s] as a phoneme. For example:

[ke"tí/ke"sí]	/'ketí/	'my' (cognate with Auyana
[mititima/misisima]	/mititima/	'European woman' (from
		Neo-Melanesian)

The alveolar phonemes /'t/, /t/, and /r/ contrast intervocalically as follows:

[ke"tááma]	/ketááma/	'we'
[ke" 'ţááma]	/ke'tááma/	'us'
["pí'ţoqa]	/'pí'toqa/	a type of sweet potato
["pítoqa]	/'pítoqa/	'a headdress'
[pi'ţu"m:á]	/'pi'tum:á/	'orange-brown dye'
[ţiru"m:á]	/'tirum:á/	'my liver'
[ma:"túma]	/maatúma/	'coconut'
[a"rúmá]	/arúmá/	'valley'

Voiceless glottal stop /q/ occurs intervocalically contrasting with its own absence. For example:

| [ko"qá] | /'koqá/ | 'a root vegetable' |
| [ko"áma] | /'koáma/ | 'a type of bird' |

Voiced nasals occur in the bilabial /m/ and alveolar /n/ positions; lengthened /m:/ and /n:/; and preglottalized /'m/ and /'n/. For example:

[a:"má]	/aamá/	'sound'
[a:"m:á]	/aam:á/	'path'
[a:'"me]	/aa'me/	'to carry in mouth'

["yómá]   /yóm:á/   a type of tree
["yóm:á]   /yóm:á/   'garden'
[yo" 'má]   /yo'má/   'to feel'

["ánama]   /ánama/   'leaf'
[á"n:áma]   /á"n:áma/   'vine'
[a" 'náma]   /a'náma/   'wall'

[a"nóm:a]   /anóm:a/   'big'
[a" 'nóm:a]   /a'nóm:a/   'head'

[ke"ná'kámá]   /'kaná'kámá/   'you two (subject)'
[ke"n:á'kámá]   /'ken:á'kámá/   'you two (object)'

Voiced nonsyllabic vocoids occur with slight bilabial /w/ and alveolar ' y/ friction, and preglottalized in each position /'w/ and /'y/. For example:

["pá:'yam:a]   /'páá'yam:a/   'small'
[pa"yá:m:a]   /'payáám:a/   'pandanus tree'
[a"'yúguma]   /a'yúguma/   'nothing'
[a"yúmá]   /ayúmá/   'stack'
[ṭe'wa"ríma]   /'te'waríma/   a proper name
["éwa:o'tama]   /ewaao'tama/   a type of yam

/w/ contrasts with /b/ as follows:

[a:"bá:ma]   /aabáama/   'sound of rain'
[a"wá:ma]   /awááma/   a type of tree
[aba"úmá]   /abaúmá/   'sun'
[a"wáuma]   /awáuma/   'navel'

4.1.2. *Vowels.* Voiced front vocoids occur unrounded in high /i/ and mid /e/ positions with open and close allophones. The open allophones [ι] and [ε] occur as follows:

[ι] occurs in fluctuation with [i] phrase medially in unstressed syllables before /n/, and in stressed syllables before /n/ when preceded by /i/ or /y/; and in fluctuation with [e] phrase finally following alveolar phonemes. For example:

[mi"nínímá/mι"nínímá]   /minínímá/   'that'
[ṭi"íniye/ti"ίniye]   /'tiíniye/   'He will say.'
["yíniye/"yίniye]   /yíniye/   'He will come.'
[ka:ya" ré/ka:ya"rί]   /'kaararé/   'two'

[ε] occurs in fluctuation with [e] phrase initially and medially before /n/, /'p/, /'t/, /'k/ and /q/ in stressed syllables; and in fluctuation with [a] phrase medially after /y/ or /r/ before /m or /m:/. For example:

["énaima/έnaima]   /énaima/   'yesterday'
["mé'poma/"mέ'poma]   /mé'poma/   'yellow beans'
["péṭóriqa/"pέtórîqa]   /'pé'tórîqa/   'brimmed hat'

[a:"qáá'kiye/a:"qáɛ'kiye]	/aaqáé'kiye/	'It's getting dark.'
["kéqo'keqa/"kɛqo'keqa]	/'kéqo'keqa/	'every kind'
[wa"yám:á/wa"yɛm:á]	/wayám:á/	'white'
[ila"má/ilɛ"má]	/iramá/	'fire'

The phonemes /i/ and /e/ contrast as follows:

[i"má]	/imá/	'how'
[e"má]	/emá/	'you'
[wai"má]	/waimá/	'needle'
[wae"m:á]	/waem:á/	a type of tree

The voiced central unrounded vocoid /a/ includes a low open [a] and a mid open [ə] allophone. The low allophone occurs only contiguous to itself in the morphological word; the mid allophone occurs elsewhere. For example:

["yá:m:ɔ]	/yáám:á/	'machete'
[yə"m:ɔ]	/yam:á/	'taro'
[kəna:"mɔ]	/kanaamá/	'time'
[kənə"mɔ]	/kanamá/	'ashes'

Voiced back vocoids occur rounded contrasting in high /u/ and mid /o/ positions. For example:

["ómá]	/ómá/	'wild cane'
["úmá]	/úmá/	'salt'
["kéone]	/'kéone/	'You are doing.'
["kéune]	/'kéune/	'I am doing.'

4.2. Distribution of the Phonemes

4.2.1. *General.* Syllable patterns are V and CV. The morphological word contains from two to thirteen syllables, and is the basis for the description of the distribution of the phonemes. For example:

/o.é/	'It is wild cane.'
/a.má/	'to stick a post in the ground'
/'pó.ma/	'pig'
/'ku.yu.bu.í.'ká.ra.u.na.ta.a.na.bi.yo/	'Were we supposed to sweep for him?'

All syllable combinations may occur with the following limitations of V syllable. Initially only three V syllables may occur contiguously. For example: /a.á.i.qa/ 'fight'.

Medially only two V syllables may occur contiguously following a CV syllable making a cluster of three vowels. For example:/'ko.a.ó.na.a.o/ 'Go look!'

Finally, only three V syllables may occur contiguously following a CV syllable making a cluster of three vowels. For example: /'ko.a.ó.na.a.o/ older sibling', /á.bá.ra.wa.a.o.e/ 'He is your twin, likeness.'

4.2.2. *Specific*. Consonants occuring initially are stops /'p/, /'t/ and /'k/; simple nasals /m/ and /n/; and simple liquids /w/ and /y/. For example:

/'p/	/'póma/	'pig'	/m/	/maan:áma/	'that'
/'t/	/'tawemá/	'bucket'	/n/	/naam:á/	'house'
/'k/	/'komá/	'pouting'	/w/	/waamá/	'man'
			/y/	/yaamá/	'tree'

In the consonant position of a word-final CV syllable all consonants may occur except stops /'p/, /'t/, and /'k/; and fricative /b/, /g/, /'w/, and /y/; and complex alveolar nasals /n:/ and /'n/. For example:

/t/	/'ketí/	'my'
/q/	/aaqá/	'rain'
/r/	/aaré/	'It's rain.'
/w/	/uwo/	'Do!'
/y/	/iyé/	'He comes.'
/m/	/aamá/	'sound'
/m:/	/aam:á/	'path'
/'m/	/áá'me/	'to carry in mouth'
/n/	/aané/	'It is a path.'

Elsewhere medially all consonants occur. For example:

/'p/	/'kaa'paqá/	'horizontally'
/'k/	/á'kaqa/	'final'
/'t/	/a'tóbaqa/	'on the corner, end'
/t/	/atéema/	'delicious'
/q/	/'káqom:a/	'another'
/b/	/aabáyaama/	'tomorrow'
/g/	/agayaao/	'Cook!'
/r/	/áráam:a/	'mushroom'
/w/	/awaiqá/	'male'
/'w/	/ware'wárêm:a/	a type of mushroom
/y/	/iyám:á/	'dog'
/'y/	/páá'yam:a/	'small'
/m/	/umoiyám:a/	'bad cough'
/m:/	/nam:áqá/	'neighborly visit'

/'m/	/'ka'mááqa/	'wilderness'
/n/	/ánama/	'leaf'
/n:/	/'kon:óqa/	'cucumber'
/'n/	/a'nóm:á/	'head'

All vowels occur initially and medially. For example:

/i/	/ima/	'bow'	/a'ki'kímá/	'hawk'
/e/	/emá/	'you'	/áá'pe'paaqa/	'grass'
/a/	/am:á/	'grate'	/iyám:á/	'dog'
/o/	/omá/	'ditch'	/'kon:óqa/	'cucumber'
/u/	/úma/	'salt'	/'pu'púma/	'game'

All vowels except /u/ occur finally. For example:

/i/	/wení/	'his'
/e/	/aané/	'It is a path.'
/a/	/wemá/	'he'
/o/	/wemo/	'Him!'

All vowel sequences may occur except *ie, iu, uo,* and *uu* which have not been observed. Cowel clusters of two occurring initially are *ei; ai, aa, ao, au; oi, oe, oa, oo; ui, ue.* For example:

/ei/	/eím:á/	'large cricket'	/oi/	/oímá/	type of bird
/ai/	/aítauqa/	'foot'	/oe/	/oé/	'It is wild cane.'
/aa/	/aáma/	'breath'	/oa/	/oámá/	type of grass
/ao/	/aónaao/	'Look!'	/oo/	/oótam:a/	'cargo'
/au/	/aúram:a/	'eye	/ui/	/uíye/	'He comes up.'
			/ue/	/úé/	'It is salt.'

Vowel clusters of two occurring medially are *ia, io; ei, eo, eu; ai, ae, aa, ao, au; oi, oe, oa, ou; ui, ua.* For example:

/ia/	/'kubián:ábáqa/	'quickly'
/io/	/'tio'taama/	'shirt' (from Neo-Melanesian)
/ei/	/'kéiye/	'He is coming.'
/eo/	/'kéone/	'You are doing.'
/eu/	/'kéune/	'I am doing.'
/ai/	/waíma/	'house rat'
/ae/	/waem:á/	type of tree
/aa/	/'kamááma/	'sweet potato'
/ao/	/náoma/	'sore'
/au/	/naumá/	'yarn'
/oi/	/'kóiqa/	'lizard'

/oa/	/ˈkoáma/	type of bird
/ou/	/ˈkóuraiye/	'He went away.'
/ui/	/ˈpúiye/	'He is dying.'
/ua/	/ˈpúábíyó/	'Is it a knife?'

Vowel clusters of two occurring finally are: *ee, eo; ae, aa; oe, oo; ue.* For example:

/ee/	/ˈkétee/	'They are talking.'
/eo/	/ˈkéteo/	'Are they talking?'
/ae/	/waé/	'It's a man.'
/aa/	/ˈkenamáa/	'just me'
/oe/	/ˈpóe/	'It's a pig.'
/oo/	/nanóo/	'Will they eat?'
/ue/	/ˈpúé/	'It's a knife.'

XIII. Usarufa Distinctive Features and Phonemes

DARLENE BEE

1. Introduction

1.1. *General*

Usarufa reflects many of the features which are common to the languages classified by Wurm (1962a) as the East New Guinea Highland · Stock.[1] It is therefore hoped that a presentation of some of the aspects of Usarufa phonemics and morphophonemics will give insight into problems of analysis faced by those studying other languages in the stock. The specific contribution which this paper hopes to make is in the area of distinctive features analysis which has heretofore been lacking in the descriptive statements of New Guinea languages.

Problems of interpretation and analysis are discussed in three of the articles in *Studies in New Guinea Linguistics*. [2] The problems are basically the same in all three articles: (A) interpretation of contoid and vocoid clusters and (B) the decision as to which if any of a series of phonetic variants to unite as single phonemes when a given variant is in identical complementary distribution with more than one other phonetically similar variant. Rosemary Young (1962) suggests several interpretational possibilities and selects the one most suitable for her purposes of comparison. R. and R. Nicholson (1962) go more deeply into the problems involved

---

[1] This paper was originally submitted as a Master's Thesis at Indiana University, Bloomington, and is based on materials collected under the auspices of the Summer Institute of Linguistics. It was later published as pp. 39-68 in *Papers in New Guinea Linguistics, No. 4,* Linguistic Circle of Canberra Publications (Series A: Occasional Papers, No. 6) (Australian National University, 1965).

[2] Oceania Linguistic Monographs No. 6, *Studies in New Guinea Linguistics* by members of the Summer Institute of Linguistics, New Guinea Branch, published by University of Sydney, Australia, 1962.

and show the implications of two different interpretations of the Fore system. Bee and Glasgow (see Chap. XII) rely heavily on pattern pressure and phonetic similarity for their conclusions. None of these analyses consider distinctive features and therefore miss some of the clues that such an approach might offer. This paper attempts to present the Usarufa material from a distinctive feature point of view and to show how such an approach does offer analytical clues and yet leave some areas open to nonunique solutions.

The Usarufa speaking area is located in a pocket surrounded by Kamano, Kanite, Fore, and a small segment of Auyana speakers. All of these languages except the Auyana have been classified by Wurm as members of language families distinct from Usarufa. Nevertheless most adult Usarufa speakers speak at least one of the three more distantly related languages and many speak all three. Contrariwise very few Fore, Kamano, or Kanite speakers are able to speak Usarufa. Also of note is the fact that except for the residents of the village of Ilafo, on whose ground a small group of Auyana speakers have settled, few Usarufa speakers admit to speaking or understanding Auyana, which is so closely related that the two may be dialects of one language. The problems of multilingualism will not be discussed here but there may be reflections of such multilingualism in the phonological systems of the speakers involved. Realizing this to be true it is nevertheless more convenient for purposes of this paper to present the Usarufa system as though the speakers were monolingual. It may be possible to use this material as a spring board for investigation of language contact. The influences of the growing knowledge and use of Neo-Melanesian (Pidgin English) will also have to be taken into such consideration.

1.2. *Definitions*

The following terms will be defined with reference to the Usarufa system.

Stress group: a phonological unit with one primary stress whose placement is determened by the distribution of pitch features within the unit. A stress group may consist of two or more morphemes within a single word or it may consist of one or more words. Morphemes and words are defined by morphological criteria which will not be discussed here. The stress group has been chosen as the unit of primary distribution for phoneme classes because it presents the least amount of interpretational ambiguity.

Consonants: those phonemes which are consonantal plus, vocalic minus, and which occur stress group initially and medially.

Vowels: those phonemes which are vocalic plus, consonantal minus, and which occur stress group initially, medially, and finally.

Liquid: that phoneme which is both consonantal and vocalic plus and which occurs only stress group medially.

Glide: that phoneme which is both consonantal and vocalic minus and which occurs stress group medially and finally. The distributional-distinctive feature basis for the distinctions between phoneme classes in Usarufa may be summarized in chart form as in Table 9.

TABLE 9
DISTINCTIVE FEATURES DISTRIBUTION IN STRESS GROUP

	Consonantal	Vocalic	Initial	Medial	Final
Consonants	+	−	+	+	−
Vowels	−	+	+	+	+
Liquid	+	+	−	+	−
Glide	−	−	−	+	+

2. PHONEMES

2.1. *Phonetic Inventory*

Defined in terms of position within the stress group the following vocalic phones occur, as summarized in Table 10.

TABLE 10
USARUFA VOCALIC PHONES

Stress Group Initial		Stress Group Medial		Stress Group Final	
[i]	[u]	[i]	[u]	[i]	[u]
		[ɩ]		[ɩ]	
[e]	[o]	[e]	[o]	[e]	[o]
[ɛ] [ə]		[ɛ] [ə]		[ə]	
[a]		[a]		[a]	
		[r]	[ɪ]		

Initially [ɛ] fluctuates with [e] when occurring with high pitch and preceding either an acute and/or checked consonant or the glide [ʔ]:
[ɛ́nəìmə̀/ɛ́nəìmə̀] 'yesterday'
[ɛ́ʔkurə̀iye/ɛ́ʔkùrə̀iyè] 'It is dark.'

Medially contiguous to acute phones [i] fluctuates with [ɩ]:
[mìnínímə́/mìnínímə́] 'that woman'
[tìíniyè/tìɩnìyè] 'He will say it.!
[yíniyè/yínɩyè] 'He will come.'

[e] and [ɛ] fluctuate under the same conditions as stress group initially:
[pétórî́ʔə́/pɛtórî́ʔə̀] 'brimmed hat'
[kè̀ʔò̀ʔkè̀ʔə̀/kɛ́ʔò̀ʔkè̀ʔə̀] 'every kind'

[ə] fluctuates with [ɛ] preceding unchecked nasal phones when following[1] or [y]:

[wə̀yə̀m:ə́/w̃ə̀yə̀m:ə́] 'white'
[ìlə̀mə́/ìlɛ̀mə́] 'fire'
and [l] occurs only following [i] and following [ə] if preceding acute vowel
phones or [a]:
   [tìlùm:ɔ́] 'my liver'
   [ə̀líɓùrì?ə̀]   a variety of sweet potato
   [ə̀láátìyò] 'Show him!'
   Finally [e] fluctuates with [ɪ] following acute phones and [r]:
   [kàày ̣ə́ré/kàày ̣ə̀rɪ̀] 'two'
   [nə̀núnè/nə̀núnɪ̀] 'I will eat.'
   [kóìyè/kóìyɪ́] 'He goes.'
[a] in all positions occurs only contiguous to [a]:
   [nààm:ɔ́] 'house'
   [áárə̀rəm:ə̀] 'his ear'
Nonvocalic phones occur within the stress group as demonstrated in Table 11.

TABLE 11
USARUFA NONVOCALIC PHONES

Stress Group Initial	Stress Group Medial				Stress Group Final
[p] [t̪] [k]	[ˀp]	[ˀ t]	[ˀk] [ˀ]		[ˀ]
[m] [n]	[ɓ]	[t]	[ɡ]		
[w] [y]	[m]	[n]			
	[m:]	[n:]			
	[ˀm]	[ˀn]			
	[wˡ]	[y]			
	[ˀwˡ]	[ˀy]			

2.2. *Interpretation*

The interpretation of sequences of nonvocalic phones within the stress
group presents the first major problem of analysis. The interpretation which
is chosen will affect the phoneme and distinctive feature inventories, the
description of syllable structure, and the statement of morphophonemic
change. The extent and nature of the effect must be considered when
making the decision as to which interpretation most adequately handles
the data.

Several possibilities of interpretation of sequences of nonvocalic phones
might be considered:

A. *Interpret the sequences of glottal plus consonant as clusters of two
diverse phonemes.* This interpretation simplifies (i.e., numerically) both
the phoneme and distinctive features inventories. The description of syllable
structure with this interpretation remains relatively simple. However a prob-

lem of determining syllable boundaries is introduced which also reflects into morpheme segmentation.

B. *Interpret sequences of glottal plus consonant as single complex phonemes.* This interpretation increases the number of phonemes and the number of distinctive features needed to define them. However, the increase is balanced by an exceedingly simple statement of syllable structure with no problem as to borders. Also, some aspects of morphophonemic change are more easily stated with this interpretation.

C. *Interpret long nasals as a cluster of two like phonemes.* With this interpretation consonant clusters would occur which with other interpretations are nonexistent and which would be restricted to like nasal phonemes. Syllable structure is more complex with this interpretation of problems of segmentation arise which tend to make this interpretation unappealing.

D. *Interpret long nasals as single complex phonemes.* This interpretation presents roughly the same advantages and disadvantages as interpretatio B.

E. *Interpret length as a prosodic feature occurring with nasal phonemes.* This interpretation reduces the phoneme inventory by two and does not introduce the complications of interpretation (C) into the description of syllable structure.

Weighing the advantages and disadvantages of each interpretation and combination of interpretations two solutions have been selected for discussion in this paper. The choice has not been because the two chosen are obviously greatly superior to all other possible combinations of interpretation but because they seem to have about equal simplicity rating and they most adequately satisfy certain intuitive feelings which have been acquired in the course of learning Usarufa as a medium of communication and in preliminary testing of native reaction through literacy experimentation.[3] The two solutions will be referred to as Solution I and II as follows:

Solution I (cluster solution). Adopting interpretations (A) and (E) interpret sequences of glottal plus consonant as clusters of two diverse phonemes and length as a prosodic feature of nasal phonemes.

Solution II (unit solution). Adopting interpretations (B) and (D) inter-

---

[3] The author resided in the Usarufa speaking village of Kaagu (Orona) for a period of approximately twenty-four months at various intervals between September 1958 to May 1962. During the period of residency in the village of Kaagu virtually all transactions and communications with the members of the village were carried on in Usarufa. Most of the data for phonemic analysis were gained monolingually, and Neo-Melanesian was used only to a limited extent for investigation and cross-checking of grammatical categories. Native reactions to many phonemic conclusions were checked informally with neighbors and friends in the village situation. A more formal check of native reaction to phonemic analysis as reflected in the orthography based on that analysis was carried out in the summer of 1961 in a pilot literacy class of five adult males of the village. The results, although by no means conclusive, tend to lend support to a unit solution. However, it will be worthwhile to attempt a similar literacy experiment based on the cluster solution.

pret sequences of glottal plus consonant and long nasal phones as single complex phonemes.

The decision as to which of the two solutions is to be preferred will be left to the objective evaluation of the reader.

2.3. *Inventory of Phonemes*

An articulatory description of phonemes and charts showing environmental contrasts by use of permutable sets appear in the appendixes to this chapter.

On the basis of complementary distribution which is described in Section 2.1 five vowel phonemes, /i/, /e/, /a/, /o/, and /u/, and one liquid /r/ may be established. The assignment of [ɩ] and [ɛ] which occur in fluctuation with [i] or [e] and [e] or [ə], respectively, to phonemes /i/ and /e/, respectively, has been made on the basis of the limiting factors involved. The phones which are least limited as to environmental factors for fluctuation have been united. The decision as to which phones to unite into single phonemes could have been avoided by use of the concept of neutralization of contrast in the environments involved.

The analysis of nonvocalic phones with Solution I gives a simple complementation statement for seven consonant phonemes, /p/, /t/, /k/, /m/, /n/, /w/, /y/, and a single glide phoneme, /ʔ/.

The analysis of nonvocalic phones in Solution II is not so immediately obvious. The difficulty arises from the fact that initial stop phones, [p], [t̪], and [k] are in complementary distribution with both medial [ɓ], [t] [ɡ] and medial [ʔp], [ʔt̪], [ʔk]. Which medial set, if either, should be united with the initial set? In a previous analysis it was decided that the initial set and the preglottalized or checked medial set were phonetically more similar and should therefore be united as allophones of single phonemes. However, an analysis of the distinctive features of the Usarufa System reveals that both the voicing and the friction which were used to determine the degree of phonetic similarity are nondistinctive to the system. This, therefore, leads to a reversal of the previous analysis and would analyze initial [p], [t̪], [k] and medial [ʔp], [ʔt̪], [ʔk] as separate phonemes, /p/, /t/, /k/, and /ʔp/, /ʔt/, /ʔk/, with [ɓ], [t], and [ɡ] as allophones of the former. It would, of course, be possible to avoid the problem entirely by again using the notion of neutralization of contrast.[4] In either case sixteen consonant phonemes result. This doubles the number of oral consonants and triples the nasal consonants. However, it may be noted that the total number of consonants is still

---

[4] For use in the establishment of a practical orthography this alternative has been selected. Thus only the medial sets are in contrast, the initial set representing a neutralization of that contrast. *b, t, g* would be the orthographic representation of the nonchecked medial set and *p, ʔt, k* the representation of the unchecked set. The initial set would be represented by *p, t,* and *k.*

relatively low. The nonvocalic phonemes in the two solutions may be compared as follows:

Solution I				Solution II			
p	*t*	*k*	*ʔ*	*p*	*t*	*k*	*ʔ*
				ʔp	*ʔt*	*ʔk*	
m	*n*			*m*	*n*		
				ʔm	*ʔn*		
				m:	*n:*		
w	*y*			*w*	*y*		
				ʔw	*ʔy*		

3. DISTINCTIVE FEATURES

3.1. *Inherent Features*

Six inherent features are needed to define the fourteen phonemes of Solution I and eight to define the twenty-three of Solution II. The fundamental source features, *consonantal/nonconsonantal* and *vocalic/nonvocalic* divide the phonemes into four classes: consonant, vowel, liquid, and glide. The *grave/acute* tonal opposition may be considered the primary resonating feature which divides both consonants and vowels into two oppositional classes. The *compact/diffuse* feature which affects only vowels and plain consonants may be considered a secondary resonating feature. The supplementary resonator *nasal/oral* divides consonants into two classes and a secondary tonal feature *sharp-flat/plain* occurs with the oral consonants.

In addition to the foregoing features Solution II introduces a tertiary tonal feature, *tense/lax* with nasal consonants and a secondary consonantal source feature of *checked/nonchecked* with all consonants.

The *sharp-flat* composite opposing *plain* is to be interpreted as follows: grave phonemes participate in the opposition *flat/plain* and acute phonemes in the opposition *sharp/plain*.

Table 12 shows the distinctive feature components of each phoneme. Symbols are to be interpreted as follows: plus (+) indicates that the feature listed is a component of the phoneme in question; minus (−) indicates that the feature opposed to the one listed is a component of the phoneme in question. A blank space indicates that the feature listed is irrelevant to the phoneme in question, that is, nowhere is that feature the only feature to distinguish that phoneme from some other phoneme. In three cases phonemes which might have been marked ø have been marked otherwise. These are: the marking of /t/ and /ʔt/ as compact minus; the marking of /k/ and /ʔk/ as grave plus; and the marking of /a/ as compact plus.

A close examination of the distinctive features presented in Table 12 and of the definitional distinctives which are shown in Table 13 will reveal that

TABLE 12
DISTINCTIVE FEATURES

Pho-neme	Conson-antal	Vocalic	Com-pact	Grave	Nasal	Sharp-flat	Check*	Tense
i	−	+	−	−				
u	−	+	−	+				
e	−	+	+	−				
o	−	+	+	+				
a	−	+	+	±				
ʔ	−	−						
r	+	+						
p	+	−	−	+	−	−	−	
t	+	−	−	−	−	−	−	
k	+	−	+	+	−	−	−	
w	+	−		+	−	+	−	
y	+	−		−	−	+	−	
m	+	−		+	+	−	−	−
n	+	−		−	+		−	−
m:	+	−		+	+		−	+
n:	+	−		−	+		−	+
ʔ*m*	+	−		+	+	+	+	−
ʔ*n*	+	−		−	+	+	+	−
ʔ*p*	+	−	−	+	−	−	+	
ʔ*t*	+	−	−	−	−	−	+	
ʔ*k*	+	−	+	+	−	−	+	
ʔ*w*	+	−		+	−	+	+	
ʔ*y*	+	−		−	−	+	+	

*Solution II only.

nowhere is compact (3) the only feature which distinguishes /t/, /ʔt/, or /a/ from any other phoneme nor is grave (4) the only feature to distinguish /k/ or /ʔk/ from any one other phoneme. Therefore these features would be expected to be left blank for these particular phonemes. However, since either the compact or the grave feature is needed to distinguish /t/ from /k/ and /ʔt/ from /ʔk/, and since the choice is more or less arbitrary, both have been marked as components of both phonemes. In the case of /a/ compact has been marked plus because of the ± marking of the grave feature. This may raise some theoretical problems and two alternate statements of the distinctive feature components of /a/ may be given:

A. /a/ may be considered compact (+), and grave (+), in which case /e/ and /o/ would be marked compact (±) and /i/ and /u/ compact (−).

In terms of the allophonic variants of the phonemes involved it seems unrealistic to consider /a/, the phonetic value of which is usually [ə], as more compact than /e/ which sometimes has the phonetic value of [ɛ].

B. The sharp-flat/plain opposition may be extended to the vowels as a flat/plain opposition. The vowels would then be defined as follows:

	Consonantal	Vocalic	Compact	Grave	Flat
i	−	+	−	−	−
u	−	+	−	+	+
e	−	+	+	−	−
o	−	+	+	+	+
a	−	+	+	+	−

This solution would eliminate the necessity for any complex middle term but does not as accurately reflect the phonetic facts since rounding is often hardly noticeable with the Usarufa /o/ and /u/.

The solution chosen, therefore, seems to best represent the phonetic actualizations of the phoneme and also gives a more elegant description of the system as a whole. The ± is to be read: in opposition to /e/, /a/ is grave (+), in opposition to /o/ it is grave (−).

Table 13, Definitional Distinctives, shows the feature or features whereby each phoneme is distinct from each other phoneme and is to be read as follows:

/p/ is distinguished from /t/ by feature number 4, that is, grave/acute;

TABLE 13
DEFINITIONAL DISTINCTIVES

```
 p
 4   t
 3   C   k
 5   D   5   m
 D   5   D   4   n
 6   F   6   5   D   w
 F   6   F   D   5   4   y
 2   2   2   2   2   2   2   r
 1   1   1   1   1   1   1   B   ʔ
B4   B  BC  B4   B  B4   B   1   2   i
 B  B4  B3   B  B4   B  B4   1   2   4   u
BC  B3  B4  B4   B  B4   B   1   2   3   C   e
B3  BC   B   B  B4   B  B4   1   2   C   3   4   o
BC  BC  B4  B4  B4  B4  B4   1   2   C   C   4   4   a
 7  47  37  57  D7  67  F7   2   1  B4   B  BC  B3  BC  ʔp
47   7  C7  D7  57  F7  67   2   1   B  B4  B3  BC  BC   4  ʔt
37  C7   7  57  D7  67  F7   2   1  BC  B3  B4   B  B4   3   C  ʔk
57  D7  57   7  47  57  D7   2   1  B4   B  B4   B  B4   5   D   5  ʔm
D7  57  D7  47   7   D  57   2   1   B  B4   B  B4  B4   D   5   D   4  ʔn
67  F7  67  57  D7   7  47   2   1  B4   B  B4   B  B4   6   F   6   5   D  ʔw
F7  67  F7  D7  57  47   7   2   1  B4   B  B4  B4   F   6   F   D   5   4  ʔy
 5   D   5   8  48   5   D   2   1  B4   B  B4   B  B4  57  D7  57  87  47  57  D7  m:
 D   5   D  48   8   D   5   2   1   B  B4   B  B4  B4  D7  57  D7  47  87  D7  57   4  n:
```

Code: 1—consonantal/nonconsonantal; 2—vocalic/nonvocalic; 3—compact/diffuse; 4—grave/acute; 5—nasal/oral; 6—sharp-flat/plain; 7—checked/unchecked; 8—tense/lax; B—1 and 2; C—3 and 4; D—4 and 5; F—4 and 6.

from /k/ by feature 3, compact/diffuse; from /m/ by feature 5, nasal/oral; from /n/ by combination D, that is, features 4 and 5, grave/acute and nasal/oral; and so on.

Table 14 summarizes the information of Table 13 and compares the relative functional load of each feature with reference to the number of pairs of phonemes it helps to define and the number of pairs in which it is the only feature which distinguishes the two phonemes in question.

TABLE 14
FUNCTIONAL LOAD OF FEATURES

Feature	As Only Feature		As Redundant Feature	
	Solution I	Solution II	Solution I	Solution II
1: Consonantal	12	21	48	102
2: Vocalic	12	21	48	102
3: Compact	3	4	16	30
4: Grave	7	11	41	118
5: Nasal	5	15	10	60
6: Sharp-Flat	3	6	6	24
7: Checked	. . .	7	. . .	49
8: Tense	. . .	2	. . .	4

Total pairs defined: 91 and 253 (Solutions I and II).

Pairs uniquely defined: 42 and 86.

When more than one feature distinguishes between two phonemes both are here called redundant.

A diagrammatic display of the phonemes in terms of the interrelation of distinctive features shows the functional load of each feature from another angle. On the diagrams which follow, each distinctive feature opposition (consonantal/nonconsonantal and vocalic/nonvocalic are combined for diagramming purposes into a consonantal/vocalic opposition) is represented by a line which intersects with other distinctive feature lines according to the distributional relationship of one feature to another. Phonemes are represented by dots within the areas defined by the intersecting distinctive feature lines. These dots are connected by lines to form geometric figures which illustrate the systematic arrangement within the system.

The composite diagrams show the entire phonemic system as defined by Solutions I and II, respectively. The individual diagrams are abstractions from the composite for Solution I and show the relationship of each phoneme participating in a given opposition to each other phoneme participating in that opposition.

Some may find these diagrams little more than geometric doodlings and see little meaning in them. Others, it is hoped, may see the systematic relationships between phonemes and distinctive features more clearly than other methods of presentation allow.

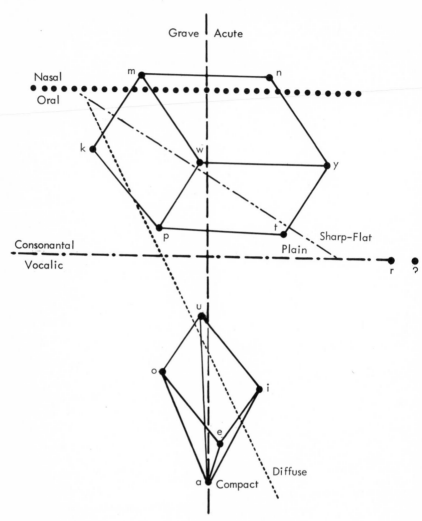

Figure 1. Composite diagram for Solution I

3.2. *Prosodic Features*

Both solutions require three degrees of pitch or three contrastive tones. Each syllable peak contains one of the three pitch features, high (´), low (unmarked), and falling (ˆ). Stress may be considered a component of the

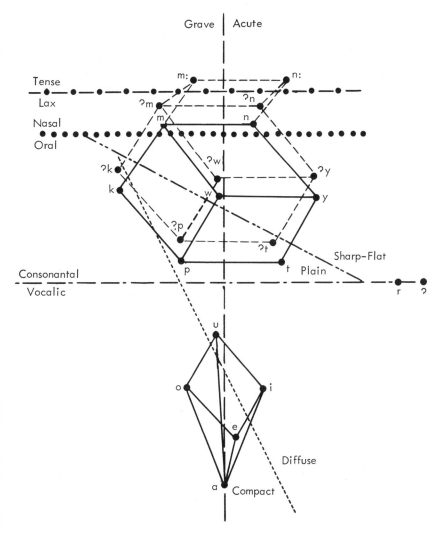

Figure 2. Composite diagram for Solution II

pitch feature being conditioned by tone placement.[5] Each stress group contains no more than one series of syllables with high and/or falling pitch. Therefore a sequence high-low-high is not possible within the system.

[5] A more definitive statement of the tone and stress features appears in Chapter XII.

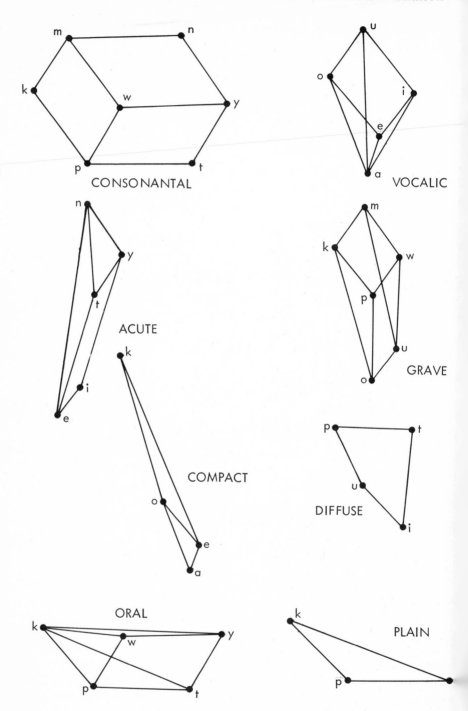

Figure 3. Oppositional subclasses

Phonemic pitch contrasts may be seen in the following sets of three syllable words:

high-high-low	*ápúm:a*	'lump'
high-low-low	*ápuma*	' ripe'
high-falling-low	*ápûm:a*	'shoulder'
high-high-low	*wáíma*	'tree kangaroo'
low-high-low	*waíma*	'house rat'
low-low-high	*waimá*	'needle'
low-low-high	*iyamá*	'water fall'
low-high-high	*iyámá*	'feces'
high-low-low	*úni²a*	a variety of sugar cane
high-falling-low	*únî²a*	'cut worm'
high-low-low	*káwe²a*	'glue'
low-high-high	*kawé²á*	'cooked food'
high-high-high	*káúmá*	'door step'
low-low-high	*kaum:á*	a type of tree
high-low-low	*páum:a*	'section'
low-high-low	*kapúma*	'bow string'
low-low-high	*kapumá*	type of tree
high-high-low	*kóáma*	type of bird
high-falling-low	*póâm:a*	type of bird (different from above)
high-low-low	*táoma*	'frog'

With Solution I a prosodic feature of length is added whose distribution is limited to stress group medial nasal phonemes. The most common occurrence of this length is in the second and final syllables of words. Contrasts may be seen in Section 7.

A noncontrastive lengthening of the vowel of a high pitch penultimate syllable or of a low pitch penultimate syllable preceding a high pitch final syllable is to be distinguished from the feature of length which occurs contrastively with nasal phonemes.

4. DISTRIBUTION OF PHONEMES

Although it is not the purpose of this paper to give a definite statement of the higher level units of Usarufa phonology, it is nevertheless appropriate to make some statement of the distribution of phonemes within such higher units. Reference has already been made to the distribution of phonemes within the stress group, but no mention has been made of the distribution of the phoneme within the syllable which is between the phoneme and the stress group in hierarchical classification. Therefore a few words will be devoted to a consideration of syllable structure and the distribution of phoneme classes within it.

The syllable structure of Solution I may be described in one of two ways:

A. Syllables consist of either an onset plus a peak or of a peak without an onset. The onset may consist of a single nonvowel phoneme or of a glide plus a consonant phoneme. The syllable peak consists of a single vowel phoneme.

B. Syllables consist of: an onset plus a peak; a peak and a coda; an onset, a peak, and a coda; or a peak with neither onset nor coda. All nonvowel phonemes may occur as syllable onsets, syllable peaks are single vowel phonemes, and the syllable coda is always a glide.

Whichever description is chosen, and the choice may depend on further acoustic examination of the data, the distribution of phoneme classes within the syllable is subject to the following restrictions: consonants may be preceded only by those phonemes which are consonantal minus and must be followed by at least one vowel; a liquid must occur intervocalically; a glide must be preceded by a vowel and may be followed by either a consonant or a vowel; and up to four vowels may occur in sequence.

The syllable structure as defined by Solution II is as follows: a syllable consists of either an onset plus a peak or a peak without an onset; single vowel phonemes occur as syllable peaks; and all other phoneme classes occur as onsets. The distribution of phoneme classes within the syllable is subject to the following restrictions: all nonvowel phonemes except unchecked consonants occur only intervocalically; unchecked consonants occur only preceding a vowel and may optionally be preceded by only a vowel phoneme; and up to four vowels may occur in sequence.

5. MORPHOPHONEMICS

The statement of morphophonemic processes which is given here is that which applies equally to all word and morpheme classes. Other types of morphophonemic change take place within and/or between specific word or morpheme classes but are more appropriately discussed in a morphological rather than a phonological context. Also not included in this discussion is a statement of the morphophonemics of tone or pitch which can only be discussed with reference to specific word classes. A discussion of the morphophonemics of the tone of nominals appears in Chapter XII.

The statement of morphophonemic change will be presented first as viewed from Solution I and then in terms of Solution II. Illustrative examples in Section 5.3 apply to both solutions.

5.1. *Solution I*

A cluster solution makes possible the statement of morphophonemic change in terms of phonological classification. All morphemes are classified as to whether they end with a glide (Q), a vowel (V), or a nasal (N). In combination within a word or stress group the (V) class remains unchanged;

in the (N) class before obstruents (N) is manifested as /ʔ/, before nasals as length of the nasal, and as /n/ before vowels; in the (Q) class (Q) is manifested as /ʔ/ except within the same word before vowels in which case it is manifested as /r/. Following morphemes of the (N) class /w/ and /y/ are replaced by /k/ and /t/ respectively. Following morphemes of the (Q) class within a word /m/ drops out. A formulization of the foregoing morphophonemic processes is:

$$
\begin{array}{lll}
V + p > Vp & N + p > ʔp & Q + p > ʔp \\
V + t > Vp & N + t > ʔt & Q + t > ʔt \\
V + k > Vk & N + k > ʔk & Q + k > ʔk \\
V + m > Vm & N + m > m: & Q + m > ʔm/ʔ \\
V + n > Vn & N + n > n: & Q + n > ʔn \\
V + w > Vw & N + w > ʔk & Q + w > ʔw \\
V + y > Vy & N + y > ʔt & Q + y > ʔy \\
V + V > VV & N + V > NV & Q + V > rV/ʔV
\end{array}
$$

5.2. Solution II

With a unit solution morphophonemic change is best stated in terms of morphological classification. All morphemes are classified into one or another of three classes on the basis of the types of morphophonemic changes which take place when morphemes come together within the same word or stress group. The basic form of a given morpheme is that form which occurs in isolation and/or following within the same word or stress group Class I morphemes. Morpheme initial obstruents are replaced by checked obstruents; initial nasals by tense nasal; initial /w/ and /y/ by /ʔk/ and /ʔt/, respectively, and initial vowels are preceded by /n/ when following Class II morphemes within the same word or stress group. Following Class III morphemes initial consonants are replaced by their checked counterpart with the exception that within the same word /m/ is replaced by /ʔ/; initial vowels are preceded within the same word by /r/ and between words within the same stress group by /ʔ/.

This may be tabulated as follows:

Basic or form occurring following Class I	Form occurring following Class II	Form occurring following Class III
p	ʔp	ʔp
t	ʔt	ʔt
k	ʔk	ʔk
m	m:	ʔm/ʔ
n	n:	ʔn
w	ʔk	ʔw
y	ʔt	ʔy
V	nV	rV/ʔV

5.3. *Illustration*

All examples are written phonemically.

5.3.1. *Nominals.* Citation forms occur with nominal suffix {-ma}.

Nouns

waamá	'man'
waam:á	'possum'
wáá^ɂa	'noise'
yóm:á	'garden'
yóma	'mud'

Descriptives

môrama	'one'
anóm:a	'big'
kaayaɂá	'two'

Descriptive + Noun

môrawama	'one man'
anóɂkama	'a big man'
kaayaɂwámá	'two men'
anóɂtoma	'a lot of mud'
kaayaɂyóm:á	'two gardens'

Noun + {-e} indicative

waaé	'It is a man.'
waané	'It is a possum.'
wááre	'It is a noise.'
yóné	'It is a garden.'
yóe	'It is mud.'

Noun + {-ko} stative + {-e} indicative

waakóé	'It is the man.'
waaɂkóé	'It is the possum.'
wááɂkóé	'It is noise.'
yóɂkóé	'It is the garden.'
yókoe	'It is the mud.'

Noun + {-pa} + {-e} indicative location

yóɂpáré	'It is in the garden.'
yopáré	'It is in the mud.'

5.3.2. *Verb.* Stem: *na-* 'to eat'; affixes: {ke-} present continuous; {-u}

first person singular subject; [ø₁] second person singular subject; [ø₂] third person plural subject; {-e} indicative; {-po} certituative.

kénaune	'I am eating.'
kénaane	'You are eating.'
kénaae	'They are eating.'
kénauˀpo	'I definitely am eating.'
kénaaˀpo	'You definitely are eating.'
kénaapo	'They definitely are eating.'

6. APPENDIX I: ARTICULATORY DESCRIPTION OF PHONEMES AND THEIR ALLOPHONES

/p/   A bilabial obstruent.

     [p]   A voiceless lightly aspirated bilabial stop which occurs stress group initially (with Solution I: medially following glottal stop).

     [ƀ]   A voiced bilabial fricative which occurs intervocalically, stress group medially.

/t/   Alveolar obstruent.

     [ṱ]   A voiceless lightly aspirated alveodental stop which occurs stress group initially (with Solution I: and medially following glottal stop).

     [s]   A voiceless grooved fricative which occurs only in fluctuation with /t/ in limited number of words (mainly in those words which are borrowed or which are cognate with words in languages which have an /s/ phoneme).

     [t]   A voiceless lightly aspirated alveolar stop which occurs only intervocalically stress group medially.

/k/   A velar obstruent.

     [k]   A voiceless lightly aspirated velar stop which occurs stress group initially (with Solution I: and medially following glottal stop).

     [g]   A voiced velar fricative which occurs intervocalically stress group medially.

/m/   A voiced bilabial nasal which occurs in all consonantal positions within the stress group.

/n/   A voiced alveolar nasal which occurs in all consonantal positions within the stress group.

/w/   A voiced high back nonsyllabic vocoid with slight bilabial friction which occurs in all consonantal positions within the stress group.

/y/   A voiced high front nonsyllabic vocoid with slight palatal friction which occurs in all consonantal positions within the stress group.

/r/   A voiced alveolar flap which occurs only stress group medially
           between vowels.
    [r]   An alveolar flapped vibrant which occurs intervocalically except
           following /i/ and between /a/ and /i/; /a/ and /e/; and /a/ and /a/.
    [l]   An alveolar lateral flap which occurs following /i/ and between
           /a/ and /i/; /a/ and /e/; and /a/ and /a/.

/ʔ/   A voiceless glottal stop which occurs stress group finally, inter-
           vocalically stress group medially (for Solution I: and before con-
           sonants stress group medially).

The following consonants are with Solution II only:

/ʔp/   A voiceless preglottalized bilabial stop which occurs intervocalic-
           ally stress group medially.

/ʔt/   A voiceless preglottalized alveodental stop which occurs inter-
           vocalically stress group medially.

/ʔk/   A voiceless preglottalized velar stop which occurs intervocalically
           stress group medially.

/ʔm/   A voiced preglottalized bilabial nasal which occurs intervocalic-
           ally stress group medially.

/ʔn/   A voiced preglottalized alveolar nasal which occurs intervocalic-
           ally stress group medially.

/ʔw/   A voiced preglottalized high back nonwyllabic vocoid with slight
           bilabial friction which occurs intervocalically stress group medi-
           ally.

/ʔy/   A voiced preglottalized high front nonsyllabic vocoid with slight
           palatal friction which occurs intervocalically stress group medially.

/m:/   A long voiced bilabial nasal which occurs intervocalically stress
           group medially.

/n:/   A long voiced alveolar nasal which occurs intervocalically stress
           group medially.

/i/   A voiced high front vocoid which occurs in all vocalic positions
           within the stress group.
    [i]   A voiced close high front vocoid.
    [ɩ]   A voiced open high front vocoid which occurs in fluctuation
           with [i] stress group medially contiguous to acute phones, and
           with [e] stress group finally following acute phones and [r].

/e/   A voiced mid front vocoid which occurs in all vocalic positions
           within the stress group.
    [e]   A voiced close mid front vocoid.

[ɛ] A voiced open mid front vocoid which occurs in fluctuation with [e] stress group initially and medially when occurring with high pitch and preceding either an acute and/or checked consonant or the glide /ɪ/ and with [ə] stress group medially preceding unchecked nasals when following /r/ or /y/.

/a/   A voiced central vocoid.

[ə] A voiced mid central vocoid which occurs in all vocalic positions within the stress group.

[a] A voiced low central vocoid which occurs only contiguous to another /a/.

/u/   A voiced high back vocoid which occurs in all vocalic positions within the stress group.

/o/   A voiced mid back vocoid which occurs in all vocalic positions within the stress group.

7. APPENDIX II: ENVIRONMENTAL CONTRASTS

7.1. *Initial Consonants and Medial Vowels*

píma	'a proper name'	*pé'ma*	'pour'
tí'a	'my pain'	*tero*	'Say it!'
kíma	'key'	*kemá*	'I'
wíma	'ginger root'	*nere*	'I eat.'
yíye	'He comes.'	*wemá*	'he'
		yemá	'they'
póma	'pig'	*púmá*	'knife'
tôma	'saw'	*túma*	'my body'
komá	'indifference'	*kúm:a*	'axe'
nom:á	'water'	*múmá*	'vomit'
yómá	'garden'	*nûm:a*	'lice'
		yúma	'bottom string of bag'
páá'a	'found'	*ká'ma*	'cut'
táá'a	'my ear'	*ma'má*	'put'
káá'a	'dew'	*wá'ma*	'chase'
máá'a	'ground'	*ya'má*	'test'
wáá'a	'noise'		
yaa'á	'sugar cane'		

7.2. *Medial Consonants: Obstruents*

ápûm:a	'shoulder'	*opó'a*	'a green'
ká'pû'a	'preparation'	*ó'poma*	'faded'
atú'a	'dead leaves'	*tótowaai'a*	an insect

aʔtuma	'a trap'	*oʔtóma*	'jews-harp'
ákúm:a	'lump'	*pókoma*	'the pig'
áʔkûʔa	'a smell'	*toʔkôm:a*	'blue'

7.3. Medial Consonants: Nasals

kemá	'I'	*amamá*	'digit'
kem:á	'me'	*yam:á*	'taro'
péʔma	'down'	*kaʔmam:á*	'chuck holes'
enám:a	a grass	*áname*	'leaf'
en:ákómá	'your character'	*án:áma*	'vine'
keʔnáám:á	'still'	*aʔnáma*	'wall'

XIV. Usarufa: A Descriptive Grammar

DARLENE BEE

The Usarufa area forms a small peninsula into the center of the eastern border of the East-Central Language Family so that except for the small Auyana-Kosena border it is geographically isolated from the rest of the Eastern Family.[1] Most of the Usarufa speak at least one, and many speak two or more, of the geographically neighboring languages. Of these Fore, Kanite, Keiagana, and Kamano-Kafe are more commonly known than Auyana-Kosena.[2] Thus the linguistic pressures that are currently operative come almost exclusively from the East-Central Language Family.

McKaughan, in Chapter XXXV, classifies Usarufa as a dialect of Auyana-Kosena and Wurm and Laycock (1961) suggest a similar classification.

[1] The research for the grammatical description presented here was carried out under the auspices of the Summer Institute of Linguistics. The grammar was originally written and presented to the faculty of the Graduate School of Indiana University in partial fulfillment of the requirements for the degree of Doctor of Philosophy.

Joseph Grimes, Kenneth L. Pike, Robert Longacre, and Benjamin Elson laid the foundation for understanding the theory and technique of grammatical analysis, linguistic theory in general and tagmemic theory in particular. Kathleen Barker Glasgow, also of the Summer Institute of Linguistics, assisted in the initial research and turned over all of her Usarufa materials. Fred W. Householder, Thomas A. Sebeok, C. F. Voegelin, Albert Valdman, and Carlton Hodge of Indiana University served on the research committee which directed the final writing and taught me much about linguistic theory, history, and application.

Financial assistance which made both the research and study program possible came from a National Defense Act Title IV Language Fellowship, a Student Interchange Grant from the East-West Center in Honolulu, a Staff Scholarship from the Summer Institute of Linguistics, and the Memorial Presbyterian and Brentwood Bible Churches of St. Louis, Missouri.

[2] In using hyphenated names for Auyana-Kosena and Kamano-Kafe I am following the preferences of D. Marks for the former and D. Drew and A. Payne for the latter. The three linguists have been working in the respective languages for several years and are producing translated materials in each.

Both present evidence which, given their interpretation, justifies their classification. However, their evidence does not point to a clear-cut choice but rather shows that the situation is a borderline case. Their decision, being largely academic, was made in favor of the dialect classification. However, practical considerations suggest that their evidence can be just as reasonably interpreted in favor of the language classification. Evidence from lexicostatistic studies based on application of the comparative method, from grammatical comparison and evaluation of degree of intelligibility based on observation over a period of ten years, suggests that this latter interpretation is preferable. I therefore choose the definition of the Eastern Family which recognizes four branches:

Northern branch—Agarabi, Gadsup, and Oyana
Western branch—Usarufa and Auyana-Kosena
Southwestern branch—Awa
Southern branch—Tairora, Binumarien-Kambaira, and Waffa.[3]

The grammatical description of Usarufa here presented is based on data collected during the period September, 1958, to May, 1962. Written in 1965, it has been revised on the basis of additional data collected during the period of 1965 to 1968. However, there has been no substantial change in the analysis.

The results rather than the processes of analysis are given so that the structural units making up the framework of Usarufa grammar and the rules by which they combine are brought into focus. It is hoped that the central core of patterns and rules given here will enable the non-Usarufa speaker to generate an infinite number of grammatically correct Usarufa utterances and that it will give him a functional introduction into the language.

The grammar progresses from lower to higher level units so that the beginning sections are more removed from actual utterances than are the later ones. It may be more satisfying for the reader who prefers to start with the sentence to begin with Sections 6 through 8. In any event it will be helpful to refer to Section 9 on morphophonemics periodically while reading the other sections.

Tagmemic theory as developed by Kenneth L. Pike and his associates of the Summer Institute of Linguistics has provided the theoretical orientation from which the analysis presented here has been made. However, the description given represents a departure from current models of tagmemic theory and formulization. The reasons for this departure are both theoretical and practical. The practical motivation for departing from standard

---

[3] I have chosen to label the branches geographically for reasons of convenience. Waffa was omitted from previous classifications but research by M. Stringer and J. Hotz shows that it is a member of the Southern Branch. According to Des Oatridge Kambaira is closely related to Binumarien.

tagmemic format can be summarized in the words of Joseph Grimes (1964):

... it is worthwhile to write a description from a single point of view but once or twice in the development of a particular linguistic theory: at the point where it is necessary to demonstrate that a language can be described using that theory. Once the demonstration is made, the theory goes into the linguist's tool box. From then on, any linguist who is not at the moment trying to prove that his own theory works ought to feel obligated to his readers to choose the right tool for each part of his job rather than try to drive a nail with a saw blade. He should, in other words, search for ways of treating data that render each kind of linguistic phenomenon clearest.

The introduction of rewrite rules and the extensive use of matrix displays is an attempt to relate interrelated levels of analysis. The reader should not be misled into thinking that because the description does not look like a tagmemic description it is therefore not one. To the extent of recognizing the primacy of both pattern and process, the importance of both form and meaning, the distinction between etic and emic, and the universality of tri-modal structuring, this is a tagmemic analysis. However, I have departed significantly from the interpretation of tagmemics that is taught at the Summer Institute of Linguistics' summer sessions and as represented by current tagmemic literature. It is not the purpose of this paper to go into the rationale behind the interpretational model I am following but the following interpretational concepts have influenced the form of the grammar here presented.

(1) Language in tagmemics is viewed as a highly complex unit of human behavior and as such is in Pike's terms viewed as being tri-modally structured. The three modes each represent a separate but interlocking hierarchy of increasingly more complex units. These modes are characterized as the *manifestation mode,* the structuring of the physical characteristics of a unit with its actual and potential range of variation; the *feature mode,* the structuring of the contrastive and identificational components of a unit with their semantic significances; the *distribution mode,* the structuring of the relational components of a unit as seen in the correlation of functional slot and a class of filler items.

(2) Since each mode of the behavioral unit called *language* is represented by a hierarchy of units each of which is also tri-modally structured, it is possible to fragment each modal hierarchy into three subhierarchies which in turn could be further fragmented into subhierarchies. In a total description of any given language such fragmentation soon becomes so unwieldy that the forest of detail blurs the individual trees of structure. In order to maintain a reasonable balance so that it is possible to distinguish the modes of a unit within a given hierarchy from the corresponding modes of a unit in another hierarchy and to determine the proportional relationship of each to the unit *language,* I propose to choose a focal mode for each

hierarchy based on the modal relationship of that hierarchy to the unit *language*. The nonfocal modes of the units of the hierarchy will be downgraded in descriptive emphasis.[4]

(3) The phonological hierarchy is representative of the manifestation mode of *language*. The focal mode of the hierarchy is therefore the manifestation mode of the phonological units of the language (physical manifestations and variations).

The lexical (semantic) hierarchy is representative of the feature mode of *language* and its focal mode is therefore the feature mode of the lexical units of the language (their formal and semantic profiles).

The syntactic hierarchy is representative of the distribution mode of *language* and its focal mode is the distribution mode of the syntactic units of the language (their relational significance).

(4) The threshold unit of each hierarchy is regarded not as a minimal component of the hierarchy but as a convenient starting point for descriptive analysis and is viewed as the level just below the awareness level of the native speaker. The syllable is probably the unit of the phonological hierarchy of which the native speaker is most immediately aware. The threshold unit of the phonological hierarchy is therefore defined as the unit just below the syllable, the phoneme. The word is the lexical unit of which the speaker is most immediately aware, and the level just below the word is chosen as the threshold of the lexical hierarchy with the morpheme regarded as the threshold unit. The clause (or simple one predicate sentence) seems to be the syntactic unit closest to the speaker's level of awareness and the level just below the clause is recognized as the threshold level of the syntactic hierarchy. The tagmeme is identified as the threshold unit of the syntactic hierarchy.[5]

(5) We are now ready to distinguish between the tagmeme and the tagmemic principle. The tagmeme as the threshold unit of the syntactic hierarchy is a relational unit representing the primary distributional matrix for the syntagmatic organization of linguistic structure. For those familiar

---

[4] This specifically rejects Crawford's proposed phonotagmemic hierarchy and also suggestions by others for a separate semantic hierarchy. The basis for this rejection is that it distorts the structural proportion of each hierarchy in its modal relationship to the unit *Language*. Multiplication of hierarchies is viewed as inappropriate rather than invalid.

[5] I am here in basic agreement with Pike's rather than Longacre's designation of minimal (threshold) units for each hierarchy. It should be pointed out, however, that I am suggesting a progression from level to level that is different from either of theirs. Tagmemes are here regarded as building directly into clauses. Word and phrase structure are viewed as lexical and not syntactic. So-called overlap between morphology and syntax is treated as part of systemic interaction between hierarchies in much the same way as morphophonemics is viewed here as interaction between the phonological and lexical hierarchies. These relationships are probably best described as processes.

with Longacre's work my use of the term roughly corresponds to his clause-level tagmeme. For those familiar with classical languages it is similar to but broader than the concept of case. The tagmemic principle is to be distinguished from the tagmeme. It is the principle of slot-class correlation by which the distribution mode of the units of each hierarchy is reflected. It is the system of hierarchical structuring which identifies the separate modes of the unit language and may be called the *grammar* of that language.

(6) The relationship of the units of one hierarchy to those of another hierarchy is mutually conditioning. For example, a lexical unit may be modified in its structural profile by its occurrence as manifesting a particular tagmeme and a particular lexical manifestation may restrict the occurrence of some one or more tagmemes. The interrelationship between hierarchies is expected to be greatest across the boundaries of shared modal characteristics. The borders of lexicon (feature mode) and syntax (distribution mode) may therefore be expected to be most blurred at the juncture of the distribution mode of lexical units and the feature mode of syntactic units.

The foregoing interpretation of the implications of Pike's tri-modal structuring of human behavior directly influenced the choice of format used to describe the grammatical structure of three levels of lexical and syntactic units in the Usarufa elements: morpheme, word, phrase and tagmeme, clause, and sentence.

I. INTRODUCTION

1.1. *Phonology and Orthography*

Usarufa phonemes divide into four classes defined as follows:

Vowels, i, e, o, u, and *a,* are those phonemes which are vocalic plus, consonantal minus, and occur stress group initially, medially, and finally.

Consonants, p, t, k, m, n, w, and *y,* are those phonemes which are consonantal plus, vocalic minus, and occur stress group initially and medially. Stress group medially *p* and *k* are usually lightly voiced with friction.

Liquid, r, is that phoneme which is both consonantal and vocalic plus and occurs only stress group medially.

Glide, ʔ, is that phoneme which is both consonantal and vocalic minus and occurs stress group medially and finally.

Complex phonemic units include preglottalized consonantal phonemes, *ʔp, ʔt, ʔk, ʔm, ʔn, ʔw, ʔy,* and long nasal units, *m:* and *n:.* These units occur only stress group medially.

Tone is distinctive with high, low, and falling contrasts. For greater detail of both tone and segmental phonemes see Chapters XII and XIII.

Examples throughout the text are written in the practical orthography used in publishing materials for Usarufa readers. This is done to simplify comparison between descriptive material and the growing body of Usarufa

literature. Rules for converting the phonemic orthography to the practical
orthography are given in Section 9. The following gives the main points
of those rules: glottal stop ʔ is represented by *q* and preglottalized consonantal units are represented as sequences of glottal plus consonant, for
example, *qy*. Exception to the representation of preglottalized consonants
as a sequence is made in the case of *qk* and *qp* which are represented as
k and *p,* respectively. The phonemes /k/ and /p/ are represented medially
as *g* and *b,* respectively. Lengthened nasals are represented by sequences
of two like nasals *mm* and *nn.* Low tone is unmarked, high tone is marked
by an acute accent (´), and falling tone by a circumflex (ˆ).

1.2. *Morphophonemics*

Detailed morphophonemic rules are given in Section 9. However, a summary of the most salient features will help the reader follow the examples
throughout the text more easily. Where there are morphophonemic changes
in the text illustrations that are not covered by this brief summary the reader
is reminded again to turn to Section 9.

Every morpheme is classified as belonging to one of three morphophonemic
classes, the vowel class (V), the nasal class (N), or the glottal class (Q).
The phonological shape of every morpheme is determined by the morphophonemic class of the morpheme immediately preceding it in the same stress
group (both within the word and across word boundaries). Every nominal
stem further belongs to one of two tone classes, symbolized 1 or 2, and
every verb stem to one of three tone classes. The tone class of a stem determines the type of tone sandhi which will occur in constructions of which
that particular stem is a constituent.

A characteristic of noun tone Class 1 is that the syllable nuclei of any morpheme or cluster of morphemes following a Class 1 stem will occur with the
low toneme while the syllable nuclei of any morpheme or cluster of morphemes following a Class 2 nominal stem will occur with the high toneme.
The morphotonemics of verb constructions is much more complex but the
defining characteristics of the three verb tone classes are: Class 1 stems occur with a low tone on the aorist tense morpheme *-ra*; Class 2 stems occur
with a high tone on the aorist tense morpheme; and Class 3 stems maintain
a relatively constant stem tone pattern throughout all constructions while
the other two tone classes vary the stem tone pattern according to construction type within which it occurs.

Characteristics of the vowel (V) class are that *p* and *k* change orthographically and phonetically to *b* and *g* following a V morpheme but all
phonemes remain phonemically unchanged. Characteristics of the nasal
(N) class are that *w* and *y* become *k* (i.e., /qk/) and *qt,* respectively, following N class morphemes; nasal phonemes are lengthened; stops are preglottalized; vowels are preceded by *n* and *r* becomes *k* (i.e., /qk/). Characteristics of the glottal (Q) class are that consonants are preglottalized ex

cept that within a word the sequence Q + *m* becomes *q*; vowels are preceded by *r* following a morpheme of the Q class except within a phrase and before *i*, and *r* becomes *k* (i.e., /qk/).

The effect of these morphophonemic and morphotonemic changes will be illustrated first with noun sufixation, then with descriptive phrases, and finally with verbal constructions.

(1) *Noun suffixations.* See Table 15.

TABLE 15
NOUN SUFFIXATIONS

Noun		Nominal (+ *ma*)	Indicative (+ *e*)	Stative + indicative (+ *koV* + *ma*)
*móra*V1	'one'	*mórama*	*mórae*	*móragoma*
*waa*V2	'man'	*waamá*	*waaé*	*waagómá*
*anó*N1	'big'	*anómma*	*anóne*	*anókoma*
*waa*N2	'possum'	*waammá*	*waané*	*waakomá*
*wááá*Q1	'noise'	*wááqa*	*wááre*	*wáákoma*
*kaaya*Q2	'two'	*kaayaqá*	*kaayaré*	*kaayakómá*

(2) *Descriptive phrases: móra-wama* 'one man', *anó-kama* 'big man', *kaayaq-wámá* 'two men'.

(3) *Verbal constructions.* See Table 16.

TABLE 16
VERBAL CONSTRUCTIONS

	Imperative *o*			Aorist *ra*
	1st *øN*	2nd sing *øV*	2nd-3rd pl *øQ*	3rd sing *iV* Indicative *e*
*na*V2b	*naano*	*naao*	*naaro*	*naráiye*
*δme*N1	*ámeno*	*ámiyo*	*ámero*	*ámikaiye*

The three person suffixes shown are zero morphemes belonging to three different morphophonemic classes. Also note that the reduction of *aa* to *a* in the descriptive phrase construction and the expansion of *a* to *aa* in the verbal construction are extra systemic defined outside the present context. For details see Section 9.

2. STEM FORMATION

All Usarufa morphemes may be regarded as bound either at the word level or at the phrase level. Three types of morphemes, however, may be recognized: *stems, affixes,* and *particles.* Stems are those morphemes or morpheme sequences which may occur with mood marking suffixes to form a single grammatically well-formed word level unit. Affixes must occur with at least one stem morpheme and particles function as both stems and affixes.

On the basis of occurrence or nonoccurrence with the negative particle iV1 and the person-subject suffixes, stems are divided into two major classes: *verbal* and *nominal*. *Verbal stems* are those stems which may occur with the negative particle-prefix and usually require a person-subject suffix. *Nominal stems* do not occur with either the negative particle or the person-subject suffixes.

Verbal stems may be classified as transitive versus intransitive and as stative versus nonstative on the basis of affix potential and tagmemic distribution. Nominal stems may be classified as noun, pronoun, or locative and further classified according to distributional restrictions and potential within higher level lexical or syntactic constructions. These subclasses are relevant at various levels of construction and will be indicated throughout the text as they apply.

The following series of rewrite rules specifies the levels of subclassification which will be used throughout the grammar.[6]

stem $\rightarrow$ {verbal (vs); nominal (nom.s)}

vs $\rightarrow$ $\left\{ \begin{array}{l} \{\text{transitive (vs}_{tr}); \text{ intransitive (vs}_{intr})\} \\ \{\text{stative (vs}_{st}); \text{ nonstative (vs}_{non\text{-}st})\} \end{array} \right\}$

nom.s $\rightarrow$ {noun (ns); pronoun (pro); locative (loc)}

ns $\rightarrow$ {quantifiable (ns$_q$); nonquantifiable (ns$_{nq}$)}

   ns$_{nq} \rightarrow$ {numeral (nd$_{nb}$); personal name (ns$_{pn}$)}

   ns$_q \rightarrow$ {common (ns$_c$); descriptive (ns$_d$); temporal (ns$_t$)}

   ns$_c \rightarrow$ $\left\{ \begin{array}{l} \{\text{animate (ns}_{ani}); \text{ inanimate (ns}_{inani})\} \\ \{\text{delta-one (}\delta\text{ns}_1); \text{ delta-two (}\delta\text{ns}_2)\} \end{array} \right\}$

pro $\rightarrow$ {personal (pro$_p$); location (pro$_{loc}$); interrogative (pro$_{int}$)}

pro$_p \rightarrow$ $\left\{ \begin{array}{l} \{\text{simple (pro}_{mx}); \text{ complex (pro}_{cx})\} \\ \{\text{exclusive (pro}_{ex}); \text{ reflexive (pro}_{rx})\} \\ \{\text{object (pro}_{obj}); \text{ nonobject (pro}_{non\text{-}obj})\} \end{array} \right\}$

   pro$_{mx} \rightarrow$ {singular (pro$_{p.sg}$); nonsingular (pro$_{p.non\text{-}sg}$)}

   pro$_{cx} \rightarrow$ {dual (pro$_{p.d.}$); plural (pro$_{p.pl}$)}

      pro$_{p.d.} \rightarrow$ {focus (pro$_{foc}$); nonfocus (pro$_{non\text{-}foc}$)}

pro$_{loc} \rightarrow$ {ani (pro$_{ani}$); inani (pro$_{inani}$); neutral (pro$_{neut}$)}

   {pro$_{ani}$; pro$_{inani}$} $\rightarrow$ {singular; dual; plural}

      dual pro$_{ani} \rightarrow$ {focus; nonfocus}

   pro$_{neut} \rightarrow$ {singular; plural}

LOC $\leftarrow$ {place name (loc$_{pn}$); directional (loc$_d$); positional (loc$_p$)}

---

[6] For the following abbreviations, and others used throughout this chapter, see Sec. 10.

Stems may also be classified as either simple or complx. Simple stems are monomorphemic roots. Complex stems are polymorphemic forms whose constituent elements are inseparable and which function in word or phrase level constructions as single units. These polymorphemic forms may consist of two or more stems; one or more simple stems plus specified obligatory affixes; or may be a combination of these with stem formative suffixes.

The following discussion will deal with types of noun, pronoun, locative, and verb stem complexities specifying the relevant subclassifications of each.

2.1. *Noun Stems*

On the basis of distribution within the phrase and of potential occurrence with number suffixes, noun stems are divided into quantifiable and nonquantifiable. Quantifiable nouns are further subdivided into common nouns, animate or inanimate; descriptives; and temporals. Nonquantifiable nouns are subdivided into numerals and personal names. Table 17 gives examples of each subclass with one example from each of the three morphophonemic classes. No example has been found of a numeral of the nasal (N) class, and personal names seem to be only of the vowel (V) class.

TABLE 17
Noun Stem Subclasses

	V	N	Q
Quantifiable Common			
Animate	*waa*V2 'man'	*waa*N2 'possum'	*kói*Q1 'lizard'
Inanimate	*yaa*V2 'tree'	*yáá*N2 'machete'	*yaa*Q2 'sugar cane'
Descriptive	*áté*V1 'delicious'	*anó*N1 'big'	*ikaa*Q2 'bitter'
Temporal	*êtaba*V1 'later'	*aabáyaa*N1 'tomorrow'	*íbê*Q1 'now'
Nonquantifiable			
Numeral	*móra*V1 'one'		*kaaya*Q2 'two'
Personal name	*Yáanu*V1		

Noun stem complexities may be divided into three major types: (1) stem plus stem constructions; (2) person prefix plus stem composite; (3) stem plus derivational affixation.

2.1.1. *Stem plus stem constructions.* New or unique concepts are often expressed by use of nominal compounds in which a common noun is preceded by either a nominal or a verbal stem or sequence. Sequences of noun stems on the basis of semantic and morphophonemic differences are divided into two types symbolized, ns-ns$_1$ and ns-ns$_2$.

2.1.1.1. The ns-ns$_1$ type of stem complex exhibits a unique morphotonemic structure whereby the tone class of the complex is determined by the second member of the compound and the tone of the first member is modified if the combined tones of the two stems conflict with the phonological limitations on permitted tone sequences. (There is one and only one nucleus of high tones within a single word and/or descriptive phrase.) This type of morphotonemic change occurs only in this particular constructional type. To illustrate the change in tone classification which occurs let x stand for the first member of the construction and y for the second. Numbers 1 and 2 represent the tone class of the stem with which it occurs. The change occurs as follows:

$$x1; x2 + y1 \rightarrow xy1$$
$$x1; x2 + y2 \rightarrow xy2$$

In other words the tone class of x is neutralized in the xy complex and the tone class of xy is the same as the tone class of y.

The semantic relationships between x and y in the ns-ns$_1$ stem construction include: (1) x is the possessor of y, or y is part of x; (2) x is the purpose for which y is used; (3) x is the material of which y is made; (4) x and y are coordinate parts of the whole represented by xy.

The following samples illustrate these semantic relationships and demonstrate the morphotonemic processes involved.

(1) *Possessor-possessed or whole part.* anabeyúN2 'the bottom of a bamboo tube used as a container' (*ana*V2 + *abeyú*N2 'bamboo' + 'bottom of a container'); *noniya*V2 'wave, waterfall' (*no*N2 + *iya*V2 'water + 'waterfall'); *póáwayaa*N1 'a pendant of pig tusks' (*po*V1 + *a-δwayaa*N1 'pig' + 'its-teeth'); *iyánáwayaa*N1 'a decoration made from dog's teeth' (*iyá*N2 + *a-δwayaa*N1 'dog' + 'its-teeth'); *iyánáráa*Q1 'puppy' (*iyá*N2 + *áráa*Q1 'dog' + 'offspring').

(2) *Purpose-object.* iráámáN1 'bark for firewood' (*iráa*N1 + *aáma*N1 'coals' + 'bark'); *iraaqta*V2 'fire blowing stick' (*iráa*N1 + *yaa*V2 'coals' + 'tree, wood'); *naamárû*Q1 'village' (*naa*N2 + *márû*Q1 'house' + 'ground, land').

(3) *Material-substance.* powaiV2 'a needle made from the bone of a pig' (*pó*V1 + *wai*V2 'pig' + 'needle'); *waakai*V2 'a needle made from the bone of a possum' (*waa*N2 + *wai*V2 'possum' + 'needle').

(4). *Part-part.* arawaaV2 'people' (*ara*V2 + *waa*V2 'woman' + 'man'); *unáákáqtò*V1 'clothes' (*unáá*N2 + *wáqtò*V1 'string bag' + 'skirt').

2.1.1.2. The ns-ns$_2$ construction differs from the ns-ns$_1$ in terms of morphotonemic process and semantic proportion. The morphotonemic process is the same as that which occurs in nominal suffixation and in descriptive phrases. The tone of the second stem is modified according to the tone class of the first stem and the tone class of the stem complex is the same as the tone class of the first rather than second stem. The process may be represented as follows:

$$x1 + y1/y2 \rightarrow xy1$$
$$x2 + y1/y2 \rightarrow xy2$$

Because of the phonological similarity between type ns-ns₂ stem complexes and descriptive phrases it is sometimes difficult to decide in a given instance whether a form is in fact a compound word or a phrase. Section 5 on phrase structure gives the formal basis for their separation. The semantic relationships reflected by ns-ns₂ constructions are as follows: (1) *x* modifies or limits *y*; (2) *x* and *y* are coordinate representatives of the whole represented by *xy*. Examples of ns-ns₂ stem complexes follow.

(1) *Modifier-modified. únó*N2 'ocean' (*ú*V2 + *no*N2 'salt' + 'water'); *únópíkááré*V2 'boat' (*únó*N2 + *pi*N + *kaáre*V1 'ocean' + 'in' + 'car'); *ayárekaare*V1 'trailer' (*ayáre*N1 + *kaáre*V1 'rear' + 'car'); *iyámáí*Q2 'toilet' *yi-δyá*N2 + *mai*Q2 'their-dung' + 'hole'); *abíqtátá*N2 'chair' *a-δbí*N2 + *yátâ*V1 'his-buttocks' + 'stick, board').

(2) *Representative part–representative part. waíwaa*N1 'wild animals' (*waí*V1 + *waa*N2 'rat' + 'possum'); or *póiya*N1 'domestic animals' (*pó*V1 + *iyá*N2 'pig' + 'dog'); *aíyayaa*N1 'twenty' (*a-δítau*Q1 + *a-δyáá*N2 'his-foot + 'his-hand').

2.1.1.3. Verb-noun compounds (vb-ns_c) are formed according to the following formula: vs + α-3rd + ns_c. The verb stem plus an alpha third person suffix combines with a common noun stem to form a compound in which the verb indicates a specific purpose to which the object represented by the noun is to be put, thus extending the semantic range of the noun itself. The following examples illustrate the construction and indicate the type of concepts which tend to be expressed by this type of construction. Most examples of this construction type denote a fairly recently introduced item. As the item becomes more fixed in the culture the tendency is to borrow a single term from the source culture: *waíyááré*V2 'bed' (*wae*Q2Rb + α-*i*V + *yaare*V2 'to sleep' + 3rd person + 'table'); *kúberaiuna*N1 'shirt' (*kubera*N3R + α-*i*V + *unáá*N2 'to put on' + 3rd person + 'string bag'); *wáínáúpá*Q2 'bedroom' (*wae*Q2Rb + α-*i*V + *naa*N2 + *u* + *pa*Q 'to sleep' + 3rd person + 'house' + 'inside' + loc).

2.1.2. *Person prefix plus stem composite.* A restricted number of noun stems occur with person prefixes. These prefixes occur only with those stems with which they are obligatory and change for person according to the delta series of person markers (see Sec. 3.4).[7] These noun stems are referred to as delta-nouns (δns) and are divided into two semantic categories.[8] Delta-noun type 1 (δns₁) includes kinship terms and kin-oriented categories, inalienable possessions shared by others. Delta-noun type 2 (δns₂) includes body parts and bodily processes or functions, inalienable possessions not shared by others. The relationship between the delta prefix and the noun stem is possessor-possessed. Delta stems enter into two types of stem con-

TABLE 18
CONSANGUINEAL KIN TERMS

Generation	Male				Female			
2nd removed	δnaabuV2* grandfather/grandchild				δraaraV2* grandmother/grandchild			
1st removed	δboV2 father/uncle	δnaoV2* maternal uncle/niece/-nephew			δnoV1 mother/aunt	δmaamuV2* paternal aunt/niece/-nephew		
	δaaniN1 son/nephew				δyaamuN1 daughter/niece			
Ego's	δwaaV2 older brother/cousin	δmanaaQ1 sister of male		δyobiV1 brother of female	δnaanoV2 older sister/cousin			
	δbaQ1 younger brother/cousin				δúN1 younger sister/cousin			
	δunanaaV1 parallel cousin δnogaaV1 cross cousin							

* Sex of either ego or relative is indicated depending upon which is elder.

[7] The treatment of delta person prefixes as a type of stem complex rather than as inflection affixes simplifies the over-all description of word and phrase structure and reflects more adequately the structural proportion involved.

[8] Words such as, *ábomma* 'tree trunk', *ánnáma* 'vine', *annomá* 'sap', *ánama* 'leaf', *arammá* 'fruit', etc., upon comparison with cognates in closely related languages seem to indicate that the third person delta prefix (*a*) has been petrified in the Usarufa forms. A common semantic category can be abstracted from these forms which can be related to the delta-two stems. Further historical-comparative studies promise to be interesting.

structions. The first type is a fusion of pronoun object stem and delta prefix which results in the resolution of ambiguities between second and third person designations. The second type of construction is a fusion of personal name and delta-one nouns. The details of these two construction types will be given in Section 2.1.2.1 following a brief discussion of the terms making up the two delta stem classes.

2.1.2.1. *Delta-one nouns.* Usarufa kinship and kin-oriented terms as indicated by delta stems are divided into three categories; consanguineal, affineal, and neutral. The consanguineal kin include sixteen terms with five distinctive semantic components: sex of relative, generation of relative, sex of ego, age of relative, and sex of intervening relative.[9]

Table 18 gives the consanguineal kin stems with an English gloss. The chart is arranged to show the interaction of semantic components.

Affineal kin include five terms which are distinguished in terms of generation, sex of relative or ego, and sex of intervening kin. These are represented in Table 19.

TABLE 19
AFFINEAL KIN TERMS

Generation	Male	Female
Neutral	δitaaN1 in-law	
Ego's	δiroV2 sibling-in-law	
	δwánéV2 wife's sister's husband	δmaaiV2 sister-in-law of woman
1st removed		δnaabúQ1* daughter-in-law or parent-in-law of woman

* Sex designate refers to either ego or relative depending upon which is the elder.

Kin-oriented terms are for nonconsanguineal and nonaffinal relationship for which there are kinlike social responsibilities. These terms include three categories of humans and two terms which do not refer to persons. The terms not referring to persons are those for language and homeland. The defining features of the three terms referring to humans are sex of referent and generation, for which there is either a positive or neutral designation.

[9] A component is considered distinctive if it is the only component which distinguishes between some two terms.

TABLE 20
KIN-ORIENTED TERMS

Generation	Human		Nonhuman
	Neutral	Female	
Neutral	ծraamaaV2 namesake		ծaaV1 language
Ego's	ծbarawaV1 twin/age-mate	ծmuqtoaaV1 age-mate of female	ծmaaQ1 homeland

2.1.2.2. *Delta-two nouns.* Body parts and bodily processes or states are indicated by delta-two stems except for *nae*V2 'blood'; *nááN*1 'breast, milk'; *agare*V2 'saliva'; and *mú*V2 'vomit'. Bodily processes or states included in the delta-two category follow:

ծaaV2	'voice'	ծmaN2	'shadow'	ծyáV2	'feces'
ծáaV1	'hunger'	ծmuQ2	'pleasure'	ծyaN1	'entrails'
ծaáV1	'breath'	ծqnuV2	'tears'	ծúyánáN2	'thoughts'
ծaáQ1	'ear, mind'	ծwiV2	'urine'	ծgayeV2	'shame'
ծiQ1	'pain'	ծwîQ1	'name'	ծweV2	'arrival'

The following is a selective sample of body parts:

ծaáraraN1	'ear'	ծóyauQ1	'mouth'
ծbíN2	'buttocks'	ծqnóN2	'head'
ծbûN1	'shoulder'	ծruN2	'liver'
ծiQ2	'nose'	ծrûQ1	'thigh'
ծítauQ1	'foot, leg'	ծuV1	'body, flesh'
ծiqtaN1	'chest'	ծúraN1	'eye'
ծmáábîV1	'tongue'	ծúwáayaaN1	'forehead'
ծmaaboN1	'heart, lung'	ծwayaaN1	'teeth'
ծnuwaraN1	'neck'	ծyaQ1	'intestines'
ծmûQ1	'belly, seed'	ծyááN1	'hand, arm'
ծóîQ1	'face'		

2.1.2.3. *Delta stem constructions.* Delta singular person prefixes may be fused with the object pronoun stem to resolve ambiguities in the second and third persons. This construction is the usual form of delta-one stems found in conversational discourse. It is used as a rare stylistic variant of the delta-two stems except for *ծwi*Q1 'name' and *ծoi*Q1 'face' where it commonly occurs as the more natural form. A possible explanation for this exception may be that both name and face may in special circumstances be shared by others in the same way as kin terms, that is, one shares one's name with one's namesake and one's face with close relatives to whom one bears a physical likeness. Table 21 illustrates this construction by comparing the fused and nonfused forms on the term for father. The structural formulas underlying the forms in the two matrices follow.

TABLE 21
TERMS FOR FATHER

	Nonfused			Fused	
Person	Singular	Nonsingular	Person	Singular	Nonsingular
1st	*tibomá*		1st	*keqtibomá*	
2nd		*tibomá*	2nd	*enaboámá*	*kenaboámá*
3rd	*aboámá*	*yiboama*	3rd	*wenoboámá*	*yenaboámá*

(1) Nonfused: δns + *ma*

{*ti₁; ti₂; a; yi*} + δ*bo*V2 + *ma*

{my; your; your/his; their} + father + nominal

(2) Fused: Pro_obj + δns + *ma*

{*ke*N1; *e*N1; *ke*N1; *we*N1; *ye*N1} + {*tibo; abo*} + *ma*

{me; you; you; him; them} + {my-father; his/your-father} + nominal

Personal names may be compounded with delta-one terms as follows: ns_pn + poss + δns₁. This formulization may be used in place of a given name to avoid name taboos. Married men are referred to by the name of their eldest child plus the morpheme meaning father (δ*bo*V2), that is, 'x's father'. This becomes a substitute for his given name which is used only by strangers. Other kin terms may occur in the δns₁ position, but the resulting construction tends to be limited in usage to referring to individuals having a particular name taboo relationship and is not used as a general substitute for the individual's name. There are a few instances where the formula 'x's mother' substitutes for the individual's given name, but this is not the general rule. Examples are: (1) *iqyarénabo* 'Iqyaré's father, Awááqo'; (2) *toqorínano* 'Toqori's mother, Taaqyaa'.

{Iqyaré; Toqorí} + *na* + *a*- {δ*bo*V2; δ*no*V1}

{Iqyaré; Toqorí} + poss + his/her {father; mother}

2.1.3. *Stem plus derivational affixation.* Two similar types of constructions may be regarded as primarily derivational. These are (1) nominal formative derivations and (2) stative derivations.

2.1.3.1. *Nominal formative derivations.* A small class of morphemes occurs as nominalizing enclitics. These may occur with word, phrase, and clause level constructions to transform the whole of the higher level construction to a single stem function unit. These nominal formatives always occur with at least one stem and indicate the following semantic categories:

inanimate, animate, personal or neutral animate, and female or neutral personal animate. Table 22 shows formatives that have been isolated.

TABLE 22
NOMINAL FORMATIVES

Animate			Inanimate
Human or personal		Neutral	
Female	Neutral		
*ini*N	*na*Q *wa*V *na*N *kano*Q	*wa*N	*yaqtaa*Q *ya*N

These formatives unite with nominal and verbal stems as follows:

{{ns + (*raa*N); pro$_{obj}$ + *raa*N}; {loc; [(n) + vn-*i*]}} + nf.

A noun stem may occur before a nominal formative either with or without the resemblance suffix (*raa*N). An object pronoun stem may occur before a nominal formative only if that stem is followed by the resemblance suffix. A single locative or a verb/verb phrase–third-person complex may also occur with the nominal formatives. Examples of each constructional type with representative formatives follow.

Verb and verb phrase plus noun formative [(n) + vb-*i*] + nf. (1) *naí-yáqtááQ2* 'something edible' (*na*V2b + α-*i*V + *yaqtaa*Q 'eat' + 3rd person + 'thing'). (2) *aayúkain-iniN1* 'a divorcee' (*aayuwa*N1Rb + *ra* + α-*i*N + *ini*N 'to get rid of' + aorist + 3rd person + 'female'). (3) *mááqaayoqi-yaqtaaQ1* 'binoculars' ([*mááQ1* + *aayo*Q2 + *o*V2b + α-*i*V] + *yaqtaa*Q 'outside' + 'a gaze' + 'do' + 3rd person + 'thing').

Pronoun plus resemblance and nominal formative: pro$_{obj}$ + *raa*N + nf. (1) *kekáá-káV2* 'a person like me' (*ke*N2 + *raa*N + *wa*V 'me' + resemblance + 'man'). (2) *nóikaa-kaaV1* 'what kind of a person' (*nói* + *raa*N + *wa*V 'what + resemblance + 'man').

Noun stem plus nominal formative: ns + (*raa*N) + nf. (1) *kawáániniN2* 'midwife' (*kawáá*N2 + *ini*N 'watching' + 'female'); (2) *aúbâganoQ1* 'native teacher' (*aúbâ*V + *kano*Q 'writing' + 'one'); (3) *inaQ2* 'policeman' (*i*V2 + *na*Q 'bow' + 'person'); (4) *áwáabiqwaN1* 'an insect that bites or stings (*áwáabi*Q1 + *wa*N 'fighting' + 'creature'); (5) *memewaV2* 'beggar' (*mem*V2 + *wa*V 'begging' + 'man'); (6) *iyákáá-kamma* 'a doglike creature' (*iyá*N2 + *raa*N + *wa*N 'dog' + 'like' + 'creature'); (7) *anóniboaqnaN1* 'giant' (*anó*N1 + *iboa*Q2 + *na*N 'big' + 'initiated' + 'being').

Locative plus nominal formative: loc + nf. (1) *wiyokaka*N1 'caterpillar' (*wíyô*N1 + *ra*N + *wa*N 'heaven' + 'at' + 'creature'); (2) *ámêrikapa-kenna*Q1 'an American' (*ámêrika* + *pa*Q + *ke*N + *na*Q 'America' + 'place' + 'from' + 'person'); (3) *wíyôpakenna* Q1 'angel or spirit being' (*wíyô*N1 + *pa*Q + *ke*N + *na*Q 'heaven' + 'place' + 'from' + 'person').

2.1.3.2. *Stative derivations.* Three types of constructions with the stative suffix (*ko*V) reflex derivational transformations: (1) noun subclass transformations; (2) resemblance stems; and (3) verbal transformations. In each case the derived stem may be classified as animate or inanimate nouns. The stative derivational formulization is

$$\{\{ns_d; ns_{nb}\}; \{ns; pro_{obj}\} + raaN; [(n) + vb\text{-}iV]\} + koV.$$

Descriptive and numeral subclasses may occur with the stative suffix to indicate 'the one with the characteristics of . . .'. Nominal and pronoun object stems with the resemblance suffix and the stative suffix indicate 'the one like . . .'. Verbs or verb phrases with the stative suffix occurring after the alpha third person suffix *i*V are transformed into abstract inanimate nouns.

$\{ns_d; ns_{nb}\}$ + *ko*V: (1) *mórago*V 'a person' (*móra*V1 + *ko*V 'one' + stative); (2) *kaayakó*V 'two persons' (*kaaya*Q2 + *ko*V 'two' + st); (3) *anóko*V 'the big one' (*anó*N1 + *ko*V 'big' + st); (4) *pááqyako*V 'the small one' (*pááqya*N1 + *ko*V 'small' + st).

$\{ns; pro_{obj}\}$ + *raa*N + *ko*V: (1) *wekáákó*V 'the one like him' (*we*N2 + *raa*N + *ko*V 'him' + resemblance + st); (2) *póraako*V 'the pig like one' (*pó*V1 + *raa*N + *ko*V 'pig' + resemblance + st).

$\{[(n) + vb\text{-}iV]\}$ + *ko*V: (1) *ítáígó*V 'hearing, believing' (*ɩta*Vla + α-*i*V + *ko*V 'hear' + 3rd person + st). (2) *aubama agatáígo*V 'writing' ([<*aúba*V1 + *ma*> + < *agaya*QR2 + *ra* + α-*i*V + *ko*V>] [<design + nom> + <cook + aorist + 3rd person + st>]).

2.2. *Pronoun Stems* (pro.s)

Pronoun stems are divided into three major types: *personal, locational,* and *interrogative.* Personal pronouns further divide into three binary sets: simple versus complex, exclusive versus reflexive, and object versus nonobject. Locational pronouns divide into three categories: animate, inanimate, and neutral. Except for five monomorphemic stems, all pronoun stems are polymorphemic and semantically complex.

2.2.1. *Personal pronouns* (pro$_p$). Thirty-seven complex personal pronoun stems are derived from a kernel matrix of five monomorphemic roots. Three persons, first, second, and third, and singular versus nonsingular number are distinguished by the simple stems.

2.2.1.1. *Simple versus complex stems.* From the kernel matrix four free pronouns may be formed by combination with mood suffixes. *kemá* 'I'; *emá* 'you'; *wemá* 'he'; and *yemá* 'they'. Nonsingular stems distinguishing

TABLE 23
KERNEL PRONOUN MATRIX

	Singular	Nonsingular
1st	keV2$_1$	
2nd	eV2	keV2$_2$*
3rd	weV2	yeV2

*This stem is not usually used in isolation except as part of complex stem forms; however, in the context of a sentence it may be so used. First person keV2 and second person nonsingular keV2$_2$ have been analyzed as separate stems. The subscripts indicate this homophony. Differences in the constructions in which they occur and clues from comparative-historical studies support the analysis chosen.

dual and plural are derived from the kernel matrix by combination with number or active accompaniment suffixes. Dual stems may indicate either that both persons are equally involved, or that the focus of the action or attention is on one of the two persons. The former will be called *nonfocus* and the latter will be referred to as *singular-focus*. This phenomenon of focus occurs with plural pronouns but as a phrase rather than a stem construction (see Sec. 5.3.3). Singular stems combine with the active accompaniment suffix, $karaQ$, to form the singular-focus dual forms, and nonsingular stems occur with number suffixes to form the plural and nonfocus dual stems.

The following formal description portrays the structure of dual and plural pronoun stems. A matrix of the actual stem forms is given in Table 24.

dual and plural $= \text{pro}_p + \{\text{num}; \text{accom}_{act}\}$

$\text{pro}_p + \text{accom}_{act} \rightarrow \text{pro}_{p\text{-sg}} + \text{accom}_{act}$

$\text{pro}_p + \text{num} \rightarrow \text{pro}_{p\text{-n.sg}} + \text{num}$

$$\text{pro}_{p\text{-n.sg}} + \text{num} \rightarrow \text{pro}_{p\text{-n.sg}} + \begin{Bmatrix} \{nakaV; rarataV\} \\ \{taaV; rawaQ\} \end{Bmatrix}$$

$$\text{pro}_{p\text{-n.sg}} + \{nakaV; rarataV\} \rightarrow \begin{Bmatrix} ke\text{V2}_1 + rarataV \\ ke\text{V2}_2 + nakaV \\ ye\text{V2} + \{rarata; naka\} \end{Bmatrix}$$

$$\text{pro}_{p\text{-n.sg}} + \{taa\text{V2}; rawaQ\} \rightarrow \begin{Bmatrix} ke\text{V2}_1 + taa\text{V}_2 \\ \{ke\text{V2}_2; ye\text{V2}\} + rawaQ \end{Bmatrix}$$

TABLE 24
PRONOUN STEM FORMS

	Dual		Plural
	Nonfocus	Singular Focus	
1st	*kerátá*V2 'we two'	*kegáráQ2* 'we two but especially I'	*ketáá*V2 'we'
2nd	*kenaka*V2 'you two'	*egáráQ2* 'you two but especially you (sing)'	*keráwá*Q2 'you'
3rd	*yenáká*V2* *yerátá*V2 'they two'	*wegáráQ2* 'they two but especially he'	*yeráwá*Q2 'they'

* Both constructions are acceptable and have the same semantic significance. The *ye*V2 + *naka*V construction is much more commonly used. The dual morphemes *rarata*V and *naka*V are nominal and pronominal, respectively (see Section 3.1.5). The latter occurs only with pronoun stems as part of complex stem formation while the former occurs with noun, locative stems as an inflectional suffix and with pronoun stems as part of the complex stem formations.

2.2.1.2. Exclusive and reflexive stems. The stems of the kernel pronoun matrix combine with the morpheme *namáa* to form an exclusive-reflexive morpheme *ri*Q and indicate only person, not number. Only the singular stems of the kernel pronoun matrix occur in the reflexive construction. Exclusive pronoun stems indicate an exclusion of all but the specified person or persons and combine with number suffixes to indicate both person and number. Either the nonsingular or the singular second person stem may be used for dual or plural second person exclusive. The nonsingular tends to be the preferred form even though this results in an ambiguity with first person which can only be resolved by context.

The exclusive and reflexive pronoun stem rules and matrices follow.

$$\text{pro}_{rx} = \text{pro}_p + namáaV^{10} + \text{reflexive}$$
$$\text{pro}_p + namáaV + \text{reflexive} \rightarrow \text{pro}_p + namaá + riQ$$
$$\text{pro}_p + namaá + riQ \rightarrow \text{pro}_{p\text{-}sg} + namaáV + riQ$$

Reflexive pronouns are: *kenamaari*Q1 first person, *enamaari*Q1 second person, *wenamaari*Q1 third person.

$$\text{pro}_{ex} = \text{pro}_p + namáaV + (\text{nb})$$
$$\text{pro}_p + namáaV + (\text{nb}) \rightarrow \text{pro}_p + namáaV + (\{rarataV; taa\})$$
$$\text{pro}_p + namáaV + (\{rarataV; taa\}) \rightarrow \{keV; eV; weV\} + namáaV + (\{rarataV; taaV\})$$

[10] The meaning of *namáa* cannot be specified at the present stage of analysis. It occurs both in the exclusive and reflexive constructions.

TABLE 25
EXCLUSIVE PRONOUN MATRIX

	Singular	Dual	Plural
1st	*kenamáa*V1 'only I; I alone'	*kenamáarata*V1	*kenamáataa*
2nd	*enamáa*V1 'only you; you alone'	*kenamáarata*V1 *enamaarata*V1	*kenamáataa* *enamáataa*
3rd	*wenamáa*V1 'only he; he alone'	*wenamarata*V1	*wenamáataa*

2.2.1.3. *Object stems.* The stems of the pronoun kernel matrix cited in Table 23 all belong to the vowel (V) morphophonemic class. The morphophonemic classes do not usually have any syntactic significance. However, in the case of these pronoun stems the morphophonemic class reflects the syntactic distinction between object and nonobject. The object pronoun stems are formed by transforming the stems of the kernel matrix from the vowel (V) to the nasal class (N) and, omitting the focus form, working through the rules for dual and plural stem formation.

$$\text{pro}_{obj} = \text{pro}_{p.non-obj} + V \to N + (nb)$$

The following comparisons of nonobject and object forms will illustrate the significance of the class changing transformation.

pro_{obj} + nom	pro_{obj} + nom
kemá 'I'	*kemmá* 'me'
ketáámá 'we'	*keqtáámá* 'us'
keV2 + (*taa*) + *ma*	keN2 + (*taa*) + *ma*
I + (plural) + nom	me + (plural) + nom

The following morphophonemic rules apply:

$V + m \to m$	$N + m \to mm$
$V + t \to t$	$N + t \to qt$

2.2.2. *Locational pronoun stems* (pro.s_{loc}). There are three categories of locational pronoun stems: *animate, inanimate,* and *neutral.* The last two are traditionally known as demonstratives. This label could be applied to all three categories but the labels chosen seem to more adequately describe the Usarufa construction. The locational pronouns are in complementary distribution with the third person personal pronouns and locate the third person referent with regard to his position in space relative to the speaker.

Animate and inanimate forms distinguish singular, dual, and plural;

neutral forms are either singular or nonsingular; and dual animate forms may be either focus or nonfocus. Locational-directional stems combine with nominal formatives, number siffix, and a stem forming suffix $naV1$ which may be followed by either a number or active accompaniment suffix. The specific details of combination follow: loc_d + {nf + (nb); nb; $naV1$ + ({nb; accom$_{act}$})}.

Stems formed with $naV1$ follow the ns-ns$_1$ pattern or morphotonemic change while all other stems follow the ns-ns$_2$ pattern, as described in Sections 2.1.1.1 and 2.1.1.2, respectively.

The locational-directional stems which occur in these constructions are as follows: *ebí*N2 'up there', *ení*N2 'near', *maa*N2 'here', *mema*N2 'down there', *mera*N2 'medium far', *meya*N2 'very far', *mi*N2 'there'.

For animate pronoun stems the foregoing directional stems undergo the following class changing transformation: $loc_dN2 \rightarrow loc_dV2$.

Noun formatives which occur with these locative stems are waV neutral animate and $yaqtaaQ$ inanimate. The number suffixes which occur are $nakaV$ and $rarataV$ dual, yuV collective, and $rawaQ$ plural.

Table 26 gives the specific co-occurrences or morphemes as they combine to form specific semantic composites.

TABLE 26
LOCATIVE PRONOUN CONSTRUCTION

		Animate	Inanimate		Neutral
Singular		$loc_dV + waV$	$loc_d + yaqtaaQ$		$loc_d + naV1$
Dual	Focus	$loc_dV + naV1 + karaQ$	$loc_d + naV1 + rarataV$	Non-singular	$loc_d \pm naV1 + rawaQ$
	Nonfocus	$loc_dV + nakaV$			
Plural		$loc_dV + yuV$	$loc_d + yaqtaaQ + + rawaQ$		

Examples of locative pronouns follow.[11]

Animate

maawámá	'he (this-being)'
maanákámá	'they two'
maanágaraqa	'they two (focus)'
maayúmá	'they here'

[11] The locative-directional stem used in the examples given is *maa*N2 'here'. In each translation the location specification and the categories animate, inanimate, and neutral are to be understood.

Inanimate

maaqtátááqá	'it (this-thing)'
maannáratama	'these two'
maaqtátáákáwáqá	'these

Neutral

maannáma	'this'
maannárawaqa	'these'

2.2.3. *Interrogative stems* (pro_{int}). Two interrogative morphemes combine with nominal affixes and nominal formatives to form interrogative stems. These morphemes occur only in larger constructions either on the stem level, as will be described here, or on the word and phrase level, as will be described in Sections 4.2.1 and 5.3.4. The two stems are *náa*V1 'which'; *nói*N1 'what'. They occur in the following stem constructions: (1) pro_{int} + loc + *a*Q (interrogative stem plus locative); (2) pro_{int} + nf + *a*Q (interrogative stem plus nominal formative); (3) pro_{int} + ref + *a*Q (interrogative stem plus referent); (4) pro_{int} + *ra* + *a*Q (interrogative stem plus *ra*).

2.2.3.1. *Locative interrogative stem* ($\text{pro}_{\text{int-loc}}$). The locative interrogative stems consist of the *náa*V1 stem and locative suffixes plus an interrogative suffix (*a*Q). These stems may substitute for any locative stem: *náa*V1 + loc + *a*Q. (1) *náabara*Q 'where (what place)' (*náa*V1 + *pa*Q 'which' + 'place' + interrogative); (2) *náakara*Q 'where (what position or direction)' (*náa*V1 + *ka*Q + *a*Q 'which' + loc + interrogative).

2.2.3.2. *Nominal interrogative stems* ($\text{pro}_{\text{int-n}}$). There are two nominal interrogative constructions. Inanimate and animate nominal formatives occur respectively with *nói*N1 and *náa*V1 to form interrogative noun substitutes: *nói* + (nf_{inani}) + interrogative and *náa* + nf_{ani} + *a*Q. (1) *nóina*Q 'what' (*nói*N + *a*Q 'what' + interrogative); (2) *nói-qtaqtaa*Q 'what' (*nói*N1 + *yaqtaa*Q + *a*Q 'what' + 'thing' + interrogative); (3) *náawa*Q 'who' (*náa*V1 + *wa*V + *a*Q 'which' + 'creature').

2.2.3.3. *Referent interrogative stem* ($\text{pro}_{\text{int-ref}}$). A single referent interrogative formed with the *nói*N1 stem and the referent suffix (*yaba*V) covers the semantic area of 'why' or 'for what reason' and 'what about' or 'concerning what'. The referent suffix may be abbreviated as *ya*.

$\left\{\begin{array}{l} \textit{nóiqtaba}Q \\ \textit{nóiqta}Q \end{array}\right\}$ 'why, what about'

*nói*N1 + *yaba*V + *a*Q   what + referent + interrogative

2.2.3.4. *Purpose interrogative stem* ($\text{pro}_{\text{int-ra}}$). The semantic area covered by this construction is very difficult to define. It seems in general to include manner or means of action and may usually be translated by 'how': (1) *naaraQ* 'why' (*naa* + *ra* + *aQ* 'which' + *ra* + interrogative); (2) *noraQ* 'what, how many' (*noi*N + *ra* + *a*Q 'what' + *ra* + interrogative).

2.3. *Locative Stems* (loc.s)

Locative stems are those stems which have their primary manifestation in the form: nominal stem plus locative suffix. They are of two semantic types: those which relate to location in space and those which relate to location in time. The former includes place names (loc_{pn}), directionals (loc_d), and positionals (loc_p); the latter may be general or specific.

2.3.1. *Location in space* (loc_{sp}). Stems relating to location in space occur in the following forms: (1) loc_{pm} + *pa*Q (place names); (2) loc_d + *ka*Q (directionals); (3) loc_p + *pa*Q (positionals).

2.3.1.1. *Place names.* The names of all villages, hamlets, gardens, and so on, consist of the proper name plus the place marking suffix (*pa*Q). The following are names of places which play a key role in Usarufa culture.

*Aayurabá*Q2 'Ogura' (*Aayura*V2 + *pa*Q) (Usarufa Village)

*Aayurapá*Q2 'Aiyura' (*Aayura*N2 + *pa*Q) (Government Agricultural Station)

*Iraabóbá*Q2 'Ilafo' (*Iraabó*V2 + *pa*Q) (Usarufa village)

*Kaagúbá*Q2 'Orona' (*Kaagú*V2 + *pa*Q) (Usarufa village)

*Kainaaqtúpá*Q2 'Kainantu' (*Kainaaqtú*N2 + *pa*Q) (subdistrict office)

*Kemaáyúpá*Q2 'Kemiyu' (*Kemaáyú*N2 + *pa*Q) (the medical-aid post)

*Moíbeba*Q1 'Moife' (*Moíbe*V1 + *pa*Q) (Usarufa village)

*Moképa*Q1 'Okapa' (*Moké*N1 + *pa*Q) (patrol post for the Kainantu subdistrict)

*Náápítípá*Q1 'The Coast', from the Neo-Melanesian *nambis* 'coast' (*Naapiti*N1 + *pa*Q)

2.3.1.2. *Directional* (loc_d). Directional stems usually indicate distance as well as direction and are formed from directional locative stems and the locational suffix (*ka*Q). Examples of directional stems:

*aáka*Q1 'by the fire'

*aakaká*Q2 'in the sunshine'

*abáká*Q2 'over, out of the way'

*abaroká*Q2 'in the open'

*memaká*Q2 'down there'

*mepiká*Q2 'to the side'

*meraká*Q2 'medium far'

*meyaká*Q2 'very far'

*ebíká*Q2 'up there'

*epíká*Q2 'there (near)'

*kêraka*Q1 'there (medium near)'

*maaká*Q2 'here'

*miká*Q2 'there'

*néka*Q1 'at a distance'

*pááká*Q2 'shallow'

*waaqóká*Q1 'very near'

2.3.1.3. *Positionals* (loc$_p$). Positional stems occur with the place suffix (*pa*Q) and indicate either specific position or position relative to something else. Examples of positional stems:

*áapa*Q1 'in the shade'	*áúkáapa*Q1 'in the middle, center'
*áitaba*Q1 'on a hillside'	*áwàba*Q1 'on the edge'
*ámepa*Q1 'on a hillside'	*ayáábá*Q2 'top end of the garden'
*aménáápá*Q2 'underneath (higher than speaker)'	*kaapa*Q2 'horizontal'
*ámènaapa*Q1 'underneath (lower than speaker)'	*kokupa*Q2 'vertical'
*ámûbayaaba*Q1 'on top'	*máápa*Q1 'outside'
*ámúraapa*Q1 'on top'	*naawátûpa*Q1 'just outside the house'
*áúpá*Q2 'hidden, on the inside'	*paába*Q1 'aside'

2.3.2. *Location in time* (loc$_t$). Stems indicating location in time are formed from temporal noun stems (ns$_t$) in combination with the location and place suffixes (*ka*Q and *pa*Q, respectively). Stems of the form ns$_t$ + *pa*Q tend to indicate a more specific though indefinite time than the stems of the form ns$_t$ + *ka*Q, which tend to be more general. Examples of time location stems:

ns$_t$ + *pa*Q	ns$_t$ + *ka*Q
*áupa*Q1 'the rainy season'	*áka*Q1 'last, finally'
*ayukába*Q1 'day before yesterday'	*anaaéka*Q1 'later'
*wágáábá*Q1 'at noon, before'	*énaika*Q1 'evening'

2.4. *Verb Stems* (vs)

Verb stems are either transitive (vs$_{tr}$) or intransitive (vs$_{intr}$) on the basis of lexicosyntactic interaction. Transitive verb stems occur in constructions which have an optional object tagmeme. These verb stems may be interpreted as having either definite or indefinite objects as part of their semantic make-up. A sentence such as *íkenaiye,* may be translated either 'He is not eating (he is not feeling well and unable to eat),' with an indefinite elliptical object, or 'He is not eating his food (he doesn't like it),' with a definite elliptical object. In such a case the context of situation would determine which interpretation should be given. The criterion then for determining whether a verb is transitive or not is whether in any of its occurrences it may occur with an overt object tagmeme. In the case of the above example, 'to eat' (*na*V2b) is classed as transitive on the basis of such constructions as, *kamááma íkenaiye* 'He doesn't eat sweet potato.' Intransitive verb stems never occur in constructions with an object tagmeme.

On the basis of co-occurrence potential with verbal affixes there is a distinction between those verb stems which may occur with the stative suffix (*ko*V), those which never occur with *ko*V, and those verb stems which only occur in the stative form.[12] Although the criteria for dividing verb stems into three categories cut across the transitive and intransitive classification there is some interaction. The transitive or intransitive status of a verb stem affects the co-occurrence potential of a stative verb with person suffixes. Transitive stative verbs occur with only third person subject suffixes whereas intransitive stative verbs may occur with first, second, or third persons.

Verb stem complexity is not as extensive as other types of stem complexity and is of such a nature that it could be treated as inflectional. Three types of verbal complexities will, however, be treated as complex stem formations. These are (1) delta person prefix plus verb stem (δ + vs); (2) verb stem plus the verb 'to put' (vs$_{tr}$ + *mara*); (3) verb stem plus the verb 'to sleep' (vs$_{intr}$ + *wae*).

2.4.1. *Delta verb stems* (δvs). A few verb stems occur with an obligatory person prefix in much the same set of person prefixes is used for both the noun and verb stems. The prefixes occur only with those stems with which they are obligatory. The semantic relationship between prefix and verb stem is the relationship of object (direct or indirect) to action. The following are the only delta verb stems which have thus far been found.

δ*aaya*V3	'to call'	δ*ra*V3	'to sting, burn'
δ*bugaya*Q3	'to poke'	δ*raate*V3	'to show'
δ*ikamo*N1Rb	'to hit'	δ*ukara*N2Rb	'to bite as food'
δ*me*N1a	'to give'	δ*upuyo*N2Ra	'to bite as animal'
δ*ona*V3	'to see, look'	δ*wauto*V3	'to awaken'
δ*ka*V2	'to put for someone, to like'	δ*yora*	'to hold for someone'

2.4.2. *Transitive verb plus the verb 'to put'* (vs-*mara*). The verb 'to put' (*mará*N2Ra) compounded with another verb stem adds a completive or inclusive aspect to the action. It differs from the completive and perfect suffixes in the scope of the action. In the latter the focus is on the completion of a single action, whereas in the construction with *mara* the focus is on the completion of other attending actions as well as the single action. The translations of the following forms are free but will illustrate the semantic significance of the vs-*mara* compounds as compared to forms with the completive and perfect suffixes: (1) *agátuwaiye* 'He is finishing the cooking of it' (*agaya*Q2Ra + *tuwa*N + α-*i*V + *e* 'to cook' + completive + 3rd person + indicative). (2) *agamaráiye* 'He is doing everything that needs to be done for the preparation and serving of a meal'

---

[12] This third distinction may be due to insufficient data.

(*agaya*Q2Ra + *mara*N2Ra + ∞ -*i*V + *e* 'to cook' + 'to put' + 3rd person + indicative). (3) *agayemáiye* 'He has prepared the food already hence it is now prepared.' (*agaya*Q2Ra + *ma* + α-*i*V + *e* 'to cook' + perfect + 3rd person + indicative).

2.4.3. *Intransitive verb stem plus verb 'to sleep'* (vs-*wae*). The verb 'to sleep' or 'to lie down' (*wae*Q2Rb) adds to an intransitive stem an aspect of duration. Usually verbs of motion are involved, and a stay of some extended period of time, at least a night, is implied.

Selected examples: (1) *kukae* Q2Ra 'to go down somewhere and spend a night or more' (*kumo*N2Ra + *wae*Q2Rb 'to go down' + 'to sleep'). (2) *ukae*Q2Ra 'to go up somewhere and spend a night or more' (*uyo*Q2Ra + *wae*Q2Rb 'to go up' + 'to sleep'). (3) *yawae*Q2Ra 'to come and spend a night or more' (*ye*V2a + *wae* Q2Rb 'to come' + 'to sleep').

2.4.4. *Reduced verb stems* (rvs). In a number of verbal constructions verb stems of the *R* class are reduced by the loss of their final syllable: {vs-vcv; vs-vv} R → vs-v.

Selected examples: (1) *agatáiye* 'He cooked it' (*agaya*Q2Ra + *ra* + α-*i*V + *e* 'cook' + past + 3rd person + indicative). (2) *watáiye* 'He slept' (*wae*Q2Rb + *ra* + α-*i*V + *e* 'sleep' + past + 3rd person + indicative).

3. AFFIX INVENTORY

Affixes will be presented under six categories, (1) nominal and pronominal, (2) locational, (3) tense-aspect and voice, (4) person, (5) mood, and (6) directional. Some affixes, particularly the mood suffixes, may be considered primarily syntactic markers. However, most are complexes of semantic components which can best be handled as part of the lexical section of the grammar. In order to show the systematic arrangement of semantic components most clearly, chart and/or matrix displays have been chosen. The distribution of these affixes including ordering and co-occurrence restrictions will be dealt with in Section 4, 'Word Structure'.

3.1. *Nominal and Pronominal Affixes*

Included in this category are those affixes which occur only with noun or pronoun stems and those affixes which mark nominal constructions. Specifically included are affixes of accompaniment, instrument, reference, possession, number, and resemblance.

3.1.1. *Accompaniment* (accom). Two suffixes fall into this category: *kara*Q active accompaniment (accompanied by), *te*V passive accompaniment (accompanying). The stems with which these suffixes occur are marked as either the active or passive subjects of accompaniment. In the form *x* + *kara*Q, *x* is marked as the active subject of accompaniment and does the accompanying. In contrast, the form *x* + *te*V indicates *x* as the passive subject of accompaniment, being the one who is accompanied. Both forms may be translated by 'with *x*', but the English ambiguity is not present in the Usarufa. The following sentences will illustrate both Usarufa constructions: *ketibogárá kéune* 'I come accompanied by my father', *ketiboté kéune* 'I come accompanying my father.' The analysis is:

$$< ketiboV2 + \{karaQ; teV\} > + < kéV + yeV2a + \alpha\text{-}uN + e >$$
$$\text{my-father} + \text{accom} + \text{pres. con} + \text{come} + \text{1st person} + \text{indic}$$

3.1.2. *Instrument* (inst). A single suffix occurs in this category indicating the instrument by which an action is performed: *napoV* 'with' (instrument).

3.1.3. *Referent* (ref). Included in this category is a semantic area similar to the Indo-European dative, including 'concerning', 'the reason for', indirect object, and benefactive. This entire area of meaning is represented by a single referent suffix: *yabaV* 'concerning, for,' etc.

3.1.4. *Possessives* (poss). Possessive suffixes indicate singular or plural possessor and distinguish between real or absolute possession and relative possession.

TABLE 27
POSSESSIVE SUFFIXES

	Singular	Plural
Relative	*ni*	*ti*
Absolute	*na*V	*mina*V

3.1.5. *Number* (nb). Number suffixes fall into two categories, those which occur with all nominal stem types and those which occur only with pronoun stems as part of complex stem formations.[13] The distinctions made by number suffixes are between collective and dual or plural. Singular forms are unmarked but it should be noted that a stem without number suffixes need not be interpreted as singular; it is merely noncommittal as to the number category involved.

TABLE 28
NUMBER MATRIX

	Dual	Plural	Collective
Nominal	*rarata*V *ra*V	*taa*V *rawa*Q	*yu*V
Pronominal	*naka*V		

3.1.6. *Resemblance*. The resemblance suffix *raa*N may occur as described in Section 2.1.3. on stem formation or it may occur in word, phrase, and

---

[13] Verb person-subject suffixes may historically be derived from nominal number suffixes. The third person dual or plural of the beta series is *ta*V; the form *tarata*V may occur for the dual and the first and second person dual forms in the same series is *taa*V.

clause constructions as will be described in the sections dealing with these higher levels.

3.2. *Locational Affixes* (loc)

Locational suffixes mark general or specific location in time or space or movement away from a specified location. Suffixes occur as shown in Table 29.

TABLE 29
LOCATIONAL SUFFIXES

Location in Time or Space		Movement Away
General	Specific	
*pa*Q place *ka*Q location	*noba*Q 'inside' *pi*N 'in, on' *ra*Q 'at'	*ke*N 'from'

3.3. *Tense-Aspect and Voice Affixes* (ts; vc)

The Usarufa tense-aspect category is primarily one of aspect rather than time although a time component is involved. In order to clarify the categories involved a brief definition of terms as used to define the Usarufa morphemes will be given.

3.3.1. *Tense-aspect*

Aorist: a tense-aspect indicating that an action either has taken place in some past time or that it must take place prior to some other action.

Recent past: a tense-aspect indicating an action which has taken place on the preceding day.

Remote past: a tense-aspect indicating an action which has taken place at least two days ago.

Customary: a tense-aspect indicating a past action which used to occur regularly as part of tradition or habit.

Frequentive: a tense-aspect indicating a past action which is or was repeated frequently.

Perfect: a tense-aspect indicating a past action whose results are still in evidence.

Present continuous: a tense-aspect indicating a nonpast action which is presently in progress or which is at the present a habitual action.

Future: a tense-aspect indicating an action which has not yet taken place or an action which the speaker either has not observed or is not certain as to the reality of its occurrence.

3.3.2. *Voice*

Stative: an action or substantive viewed as a state of being. Note the following examples: *puyo* + *ko*V (die + stative) 'to be dead', *no* + *ko*V (water + st) 'the state of being water or an action characteristic of water', *waa* + *ko*V (man + st) 'the state of being a man or an action characteristic of mankind', *akate* + *ko*V (break + st) 'the state of being broken'.

Completive: The subject of an action viewed as performing and completing it.[14]

Benefactive: An action performed in behalf of, on account of, instead of, or for the benefit of someone else.

The matrix in Table 30 gives the tense-aspect and voice morphemes as they reflect various semantic oppositions. The tense-aspect morphemes show contrast in the oppositions of past to nonpast and of time oriented to aspect oriented tense-aspects. The benefactive suffix is dimorphemic, consisting of the delta person prefix and the benefactive morpheme *ka*. The remote past is made up of the sequence aorist *ra* plus remote past *ro;* after morphophonemic rules have been applied, this results in the form *rero*.

TABLE 30
TENSE-ASPECT, VOICE MATRIX

Tense-Aspect					Voice	
Time			Aspect			
Past	*ra* *ta* *ra+ro*	(aorist) (recent) (remote)	*wao* *qo* *ma*	(customary) (frequentive) (perfect)	*ko*V *tuwa*NR *δka*V	(stative) (completive) (benefactive)
Non-past	*ké*V (present continuous) *no* (future)					

3.4. *Person Affixes* (per)

There are four series or sets of person markers. These have been set up on the basis of differences in the nature and number of person distinctions made, the semantic significance of the structural types with which each occurs, and the differences in the phonetic shapes of the forms in each series. The alpha (α), beta (β), and gamma (γ) series function as person-subject suffixes occurring with verb stems. The delta (δ) series occurs in complex stem constructions as obligatory prefixes described in Section 2.

---

[14] The classification of the completive morpheme with the voice suffixes rather than with the tense-aspect suffixes may cause some questioning. The basis for so doing was the fact that the morpheme in question is in complementary distribution with the voice suffixes and its occurrence is in the same structural slot with reference to the verb stem and other verb affixes as is the voice category.

The differences in person designations in the four series can best be seen in summary as presented in Table 31. Plus indicates that the person-number category or categories represented by a given cell is designated by a form in the person series. It may be noted that the alpha, beta, and gamma series make seven person-number distinctions while the delta series makes only four. The configurations of person-number distinctions shown in Table 31 represent the kernel matrices of each series. Subseries of each show different configurations of components as will be indicated in the following sections.

TABLE 31
SUMMARY OF PERSON-NUMBER MATRICES

Person	Alpha Series			Beta Series			Gamma Series			Delta Series	
	Sing	Pl	Dual	Sing	Pl	Dual	Sing	Pl	Dual	Sing	Pl
1st	+	+	+	+	+		+		+	+	
2nd	+			+	+	+	+		+		+
3rd	+	+	+	+		+	+	+	+	+	+

Before going into the details of each series it should be noted that the subclassifications which postulate subseries within the alpha and beta series are not as securely based as the division between the four series. The person-number configurations are complex and sometimes seem quite erratic. One feels that both homophony and neutralization of contrast are functioning. However, it is not always clear where the line should be drawn between the two. In order to facilitate the description of both verb and clause and sentence constructions in which person suffixes play a crucial role, the present analysis utilizes both neutralization and homophony. The subseries classifications may upon further analysis prove either inadequate or unnecessary but for the present they serve as a means to demonstrate the complexity of semantic component configuration and to simplify the statement of syntactic structure. If they should prove to be of no further value they will have been sufficiently useful to justify their inclusion here.

3.4.1. *Delta series (δ).* As has been indicated the delta series occurs as obligatory prefixes in the δns and δvs stem types. The functional relationship between prefix and stem is determined by the stem type. The relationship of prefix to noun stem is that of possessor-possessed, and of prefix to verb stem is that of object-action. The relationship in the benefactive suffix is the same as that of prefix to verb stem.

The four morphemes of the delta series distinguish between singular and nonsingular in second and third persons and between first person and non-first person in the nonsingular. It should be noted that the second person nonsingular form is homophonous with the first person form. These have been treated as homophonous on the basis of co-occurrence restrictions on the word, phrase, and clause levels. The forms of the delta series are shown in Table 32.

TABLE 32
DELTA MATRIX

	Sing	Non-sing
1st	ti_2	
2nd	a	ti_2
3rd		yi

3.4.2. *Alpha series (α).* The alpha or independent series of person markers has the widest occurrence and the greatest diversity of person-number configurations and phonetic shapes. Seven subtypes may be described as derived from a single kernel matrix of person forms. Each subtype is partially like and partially unlike other alpha types. Because of their obvious similarities of form they have been grouped as a single series of types. However, there are significant differences in the person distinctions made, syntactic relationships marked, and partial dissimilarities in the phonetic shapes of some of the forms which cannot be accounted for by the over-all morphonemic structure of the system. One significant syntactic difference in the distribution of alpha subseries is that subseries one through four occur in both sentence-final and sentence-nonfinal clause types while subseries five through seven occur only in nonfinal clauses. The differences in person distinctions made by the alpha subseries are shown in distinctions made by the alpha subseries are shown in Table 33. The actual phonetic

TABLE 33
SUMMARY OF ALPHA MATRICES

Person	Final						Nonfinal					
	α_1	α_2	α_4	α_3			α_5			α_6	α_7	
	Sing	Pl	Dual	Sing	Pl	Dual	Sing	Pl	Dual		Sing	Pl
1st	+	+	+	+	+		+	+		+	+	
2nd	+	+		+	+		+	+		+	+	+
3rd	+			+			+			+	+	

shapes of the alpha forms may be seen from the subseries matrices which follow the rules for generating each subseries.

3.4.2.1. *Alpha kernel matrix* (α_1). The alpha subseries one is taken as the kernel matrix from which each submatrix is generated. In the forms which appear in the cells of the alpha kernel matrix there are some obvious recurring partials which can be identified with specific semantic components. For example, *u* can be identified as first person and *y* as dual. This segmentation, however, proves of little value either with reference to the other components included in the matrix or elsewhere in the grammar. Although it may prove to be of historical and comparative significance, the forms are analyzed in terms of their synchronic significance as single morphemes with the note that further segmentation is possible. The person designations of the alpha kernel matrix or subseries one are, first, second, and third singular; first and second-third dual; and first and second-third plural.

TABLE 34
ALPHA KERNEL MATRIX (α_1)

	First	Second	Third
Singular	*úN*	*øN*	*iV*
Dual	*úyV*	*yV*	
Plural	*únataV*	*øV*	

3.4.2.2. *Rules for generating alpha subseries matrices*

3.4.2.2.1. *Subseries two* (α_2). By addition of *a* V/N to the forms in the α_1 matrix the forms in the cells of the α_2 matrix may be generated by application of the following rules.

$$\alpha_1 + a\ \{V;N\} \to \alpha_2$$
$$\{iV; øV\} + a\{V;N\} \to \{iV: øV\} + \{V;N\}$$
$$únataV + a\ \{V;N\} \to únataaV$$
$$xV + (a)\ \{V;N\} \to x(a)\,N$$
$$xN + (a)\ \{V;N\} \to x(a)V$$

(*x* is any α_1 form)

TABLE 35
ALPHA SUBSERIES TWO MATRIX (α_2)

	First	Second	Third
Singular	*únaV*	*naV*	*iN*
Dual	*úyaN*	*yaN*	
Plural	*únataaV*	*øN*	

3.4.2.2.2. *Subseries three* (α_3). The forms in the α_2 matrix may be rewritten in the cells of the α_3 matrix as follows:

$$\alpha_2 \to \alpha_3$$
$$\text{lsg : ld : lpl} \to \text{lsg-pl : ld}^{15}$$
$$\acute{u}nataa\text{V} \to \acute{u}na\text{V}$$
$$i\text{N} \quad \to ina\text{N}$$

TABLE 36
ALPHA SUBSERIES THREE MATRIX (α_3)

	First	Second	Third
Singular		*na*V	*ina*N
Plural	*úna*V	øN	
Dual	*úya*N	*ya*N	

3.4.2.2.3. *Subseries four* (α_4). The forms in the α_2 matrix may be rewritten in the cells of the α_4 matrix as follows:

$$\alpha_2 \to \alpha_4$$
$$x \{\text{V}; \text{N}\} \to x \ (x \text{ is any } \alpha_2 \text{ form})$$
$$\acute{u}nataa \to \acute{u}nana$$
$$i \quad \to ita$$
$$\emptyset \quad \to wa$$

TABLE 37
ALPHA SUBSERIES FOUR MATRIX (α_4)

	First	Second	Third
Singular	*úna*	*na*	*ita*
Dual	*úya*	*ya*	
Plural	*únana*	*wa*	

3.4.2.2.4. *Subseries five* (α_5). The α_3 forms may be rewritten in the cells of the α_5 matrix as follows:

$$\alpha_3 \to \alpha_5$$
$$\text{2-3d : 2-3pl} \to \text{2-3d,pl}$$
$$x \{\text{V}; \text{N}\} \to x \ (x \text{ is any } \alpha_3 \text{ form})$$
$$\{na, ya\} \to \{ena, iya\}$$
$$\{\acute{u}na, \acute{u}ya\} \to \{na, ya\}$$
$$\emptyset \to iya$$

---

[15] Rewrite the opposition of first person singular to first dual and first plural to the opposition of first person singular-plural to first dual.

TABLE 38
ALPHA SUBSERIES FIVE MATRIX (α_5)

	First	Second	Third
Singular		ena	ina
	na		
Plural		iya	
Dual	ya		

3.4.2.2.5. *Subseries six* (α_6). The α_6 matrix may be derived from the α_2 matrix by neutralization of the number contrasts and the forms from the α_2 matrix rewritten in the cells of the α_6 matrix as follows:

$$\alpha_2 \to \alpha_6$$
$$\text{sg} : \text{d} : \text{pl} \to \text{sg-pl}$$
$$x \{V; N\} \to x \ (x \text{ is any } \alpha_2 \text{ form})$$

TABLE 39
ALPHA SUB-SERIES SIX MATRIX (α_6)

First	Second	Third
úna	na	i

3.4.2.2.6. *Subseries seven* (α_7). The α_7 matrix may be derived from the α_6 matrix by reintroduction of a singular and plural contrast in the second person and the α_6 forms rewritten in the α_7 matrix as follows:

$$\alpha_6 \to \alpha_7$$
$$\text{sg-pl} \to \text{1sg-pl} : \text{3sg-pl} : \text{2sg} : \text{2pl}$$
$$i \to imma$$
$$\text{2pl} \to ma$$

TABLE 40
ALPHA SUBSERIES SEVEN MATRIX (α_7)

	First	Second	Third
Singular		na	
	una		imma
Plural		ma	

3.4.2.3 *Alpha composite matrix*. The matrix in Table 41 summarizes the forms of the alpha series relating the subseries to one another for comparision and quick reference.

TABLE 41
ALPHA COMPOSITE MATRIX (α)

Subseries	Singular			Dual		Plural	
	1st	2nd	3rd	1st	2nd-3rd	1st	2nd-3rd
α_1	*u*N	*ø*N	*i*V	*uy*V	*y*V	*unata*V	*ø*V
α_2	*una*V	*na*V	*i*N	*uya*N	*ya*N	*unataa*V	*ø*N
α_3	*una*V	*na*V	*ina*N	*uya*N	*ya*N	*una*V	*ø*N
α_4	*una*	*na*	*ita*	*uya*	*ya*	*unana*	*wa*
α_5	*na*	*ena*	*ina*	*ya*	*iya*	*na*	*iya*
α_6	*una*	*na*	*i*				
α_7	*una*	*na*	*imma*				*ma* (2nd)

3.4.3. *Beta series* (β). The beta or subjunctive person suffixes occur as person-subject markers of subjunctive constructions and as anticipatory subject markers in multiple clause sentences. The beta subseries are derived from a single kernel matrix of forms.

3.4.3.1. *Beta kernel matrix* (ß). The beta subseries one (ß$_1$) constitutes the beta kernel matrix. The person distinctions made are as follows: first, second, and third persons singular; first and second persons plural; first-second person dual; and third person dual-plural.

TABLE 42
BETA KERNEL MATRIX (ß$_1$)

	First	Second	Third
Singular	*ø*Q	*ø*V	*na*V
Dual		*ka*V	*ta*V
Plural	*taa*V	*ø*Q	

3.4.3.2. *Rules for generating beta subseries*

3.4.3.2.1. *Subseries two* (ß$_2$). The contrasts between first person singular and first-second dual, and between first person plural and third dual-plural, are neutralized by the following rules for rewriting ß$_1$ forms in the ß$_2$ matrix. The person-number configuration which results is unique.

$$\beta_1 \to \beta_2$$
$$\text{ø}Q_{1sg} \to ka\text{V}$$
$$taa\text{V} \to ta\text{V}$$

TABLE 43
BETA SUBSERIES TWO MATRIX (ß₂)

	Third	First	Second
Singular	*na*V		ø V
Dual		*ka*V	
	*ta*V		
Plural			ø Q

3.4.3.2.2. *Subseries three* (β_3). The β_3 matrix may be derived from the β_1 matrix and the β_1 forms rewritten in the cells of the β_3 matrix as follows:

$$\beta_{|1} \rightarrow \beta_3$$
$$1 : 2 : 3 \;\; \rightarrow 2 : 3$$
$$taV \rightarrow yaQ$$
$$naV \rightarrow naQ$$

TABLE 44
BETA SUB-SERIES THREE MATRIX (ß₃)

	Second	Third
Singular	ø V	*na*Q
Dual	*ka*V	
		*ya*Q
Plural	ø Q	

3.4.3.3. *Beta composite matrix*. The matrix in Table 45 summarizes the beta subseries.

TABLE 45
BETA COMPOSITE MATRIX (ß)

Subseries	Singular			Nonsingular			
	1st	2nd	3rd	1st-2nd dual	3rd dual-pl	1st pl	2nd pl
ß₁	ø Q	ø V	*na*V	*ka*V	*ta*V	*taa*V	ø Q
ß₂	*ka*V	ø V	*na*V	*ka*V	*ta*V	*ta*V	ø Q
ß₃		ø V	*na*Q	*ka*V(2d)	*ya*Q		ø Q

3.4.4. *Gamma series* (Υ). The gamma or imperative series has a single set of person forms which occur in imperative constructions. These forms bear resemblance to both alpha and beta forms, but differences in the semantic composition of the forms and the relationship of forms of the series to one another is significant. The forms Υ-*ka*V and ß-*ka*V both indicate second person dual subjects. However, the beta form cannot be called a second person dual morpheme in the same sense as the gamma form is since it is in opposition only to third person dual while the gamma form is opposed to both first and third persons dual. Differences in types of morphophonemic processes which the two forms participate in also suggest that two different but homophonous morphemes are involved. The gamma series makes the following person designations: first person singular-plural; second and third persons singular; first, second, and third persons dual; and second-third person plural.

TABLE 46
GAMMA MATRIX (γ)

	First	Second	Third
Singular	øN	øV	iN
Plural		øQ	
Dual	iV	kaV	taiV

3.5. *Mood Affixes* (md)

Two prefixes may be classed as mood affixes. The are *i*V negative and *paa*V 'only, just'.

Mood suffixes mark syntactic constructions and are complex semantic units. Morphemically mood suffixes may be either simple or complex. Moods indicated follow.

Designatory: indicating that a particular nominal construction or the subject of a particular action is pointed out for special attention or emphasis.

Indicative: indicating that an action is viewed as a simple statement of fact or that a nominal construction is in a state of existence.

Assertative: indicating the confirmation or strong affirmation of an action or event.

Interrogative: indicating a question or query.

Imperative: indicating a command or necessity or with nominal constructions emphasizing the fact of a state of existence and with personal names functioning as a vocative.

Causal: indicating that an action or given nominal is the determining factor in or cause of some other action, event, circumstance, or quality.

Nominal: indicating a substantive construction.

Prohibitive: indicating an action is forbidden as potentially harmful to the subject.

Indicative, designatory, assertative, and interrogative moods combine with additional components to form four categories of moods: *declarative,* which declares the fact of an action without reference either to the relationship of the subject to the action or of the action to any other action; *abilitative*, which indicates the ability or aptitude of the subject for performing a particular action or existing in a particular state; *conjunctive*, which indicates that the action specified is one of more than one action; *substantive*, which indicates existence, or state. The interesecting of these components is represented in Table 47 by the affixes which occur in the cells of the matrix.

TABLE 47
MOOD MATRIX

	Declarative	Abilitative	Conjunctive	Substantive
Designatory	. . .	*miye*	. . .	$mo + \alpha_1 + e_1$ *mo*
Indicative	e_1	e_2	$na + e_2$	e_1
Assertative	*po*	*mibo*	$na + mibo$	. . .
Imperative	o_2	. . .	. . .	o_2
Interrogative	o_1 $abo + \alpha_1 + o_1$	*abiyo*	. . .	a *abiyo*
Prohibitive	*bo*	. . .	. . .	. . .
Causal	$poa + ß_1$	. . .	. . .	. . .
Nominal	. . .	. . .	. . .	*ma*

The morphemically complex forms which appear in Table 47 have been handled as constructions on the preword level and are treated as single units on higher levels of structure. The analysis of these affixes follows : (1) *miye* abl desig (*mo* + α-*i*V + *e* desig + 3rd person + indic); (2) *mibo* abl assert (*mo* + α-*i*V + *po* desig + 3rd person + assert); (3) *abiyo* abl inter (aV + *po* + α-*i*V + o_1 nom inter + assert + 3rd person + inter); (4) *abo* + α_1 + o_1 inter (aV + *po* + α_1 + o_1 nom inter + assert + person + inter); (5) naV + *e* conj indic (conj + indic); (6) naV + *mibo* conj assert (naV + *mo* + α-*i*V + *po* conj + desig + person + assert); (7) *poa* + $ß_1$ (causal + person).

3.6. *Directional Affixes*

Two types of relationships between directional morphemes and the action signaled by the verb stem are to be distinguished. The first is simultaneity of the movement indicated by the directional morpheme and the action of the verb stem, and the second is a sequential relationship between the two. The former is marked by directional prefixes and the latter by reduced verb stems functioning as prefixes. The morphemes which indicate these relationships are shown in Table 48.

TABLE 48

DIRECTIONAL AFFIXES

Direction of movement	Simultaneity	Sequential
toward; to come	*ma*	*ya* (from *ye*V2a)
away; to go away	*mo*	*ko* (from *koo*V3)
up; to go or come up	*mu*	*u* (from *uyo*Q2Ra)
down; to go or come down	*maru*	*ku* (from *kumo*N2Ra)

Selected examples: (1) *momaraao* 'Put it away or aside' (*mo* + *mara*N2Ra + γ -ϕV + o_2 'away' + 'put' + 2nd person + imper); (2) *komaraao* 'Go put it away' (*ko* + *mara*N2Ra + γ -ϕV + o_2 'go away' + 'put' + 2nd person + imper); (3) *mamayaao* 'Bring it' (*ma* + *maya*Q2Rb + γ -ϕV + o_2 'toward' + 'get' + 2nd person + imper); (4) *yamayaao* 'Come and get it' (*ya* + *maya*Q2Rb + γ -ϕV + o_2 'come' + 'get' + 2nd person + imper).

4. WORD STRUCTURE

Stems may occur either without affixes in phrase level constructions or with one or more inflectional affixes in word level constructions. In the first instance the stem plus its attending affixes is a word. A word then may be described as a stem in some higher level construction. A word is distinctive in being a single stress group whose constituent morphemes are inseparable and which may occur with only one mood suffix.

Corresponding to the two major stem types there are two major types of words, *nominal* and *verbal*. The differences between the two types of constructions are marked by different potentials of occurrence with inflectional affixes. Where a given class of affixes may occur with both types there are co-occurrence restrictions with particular members of the class. Mood suffixes in particular differ in their potential of occurrence with nominal and verbal word constructions. Limitations on the occurrence of mood affixes will be specified in Section 4.4. The mood affixes which may occur with nominal stems are given in Table 49 and examples of each with various nominal stems are as follows.

TABLE 49

NOMINAL MOOD MATRIX (md$_n$)

	Declarative	Abilitative
Indicative	e_1	
Interrogative	*a*	*abiyo*
Nominal	*ma*	
Designatory	*mo*	*miye* *mo* + α_1 + e_1
Imperative (vocative)	o_2	
Causal	*poa* + β_1	

(1) pro.s + md (*ke*V2 + md): *kemá* 'I' (nom); *keá* 'Me?' (nom inter); *kemó* 'I am the one' (desig); *keé* 'It is I' (indic); *keábíyó* 'What about me?' (abl inter); *kemíyé* 'I mean me!' (abl desig).

(2) ns + md: *yaaqá* 'sugar cane' (*yaa*Q2 + *ma* 'sugar cane' + nom); *anóne* 'It is big' (*ano*N1 + *e* 'big' + indic); *inaarúá* 'Is it a girl?' (*inaaru*V2 + *a* 'girl' + ' nom inter); *ímiye* 'not, it is not, no' (*i*V1 + ¯*miye neg* + abl desig); *waamó* 'a man (not someone else)' (*waa*V2 + *mo* 'man' + desig); *Turúaao* 'Luluai!' (*Turúaa*V1 + o_2 Luluai + imper); *ibèrabiyo* 'Now?' (*ibe*Q1 + *abiyo* 'now' + abl inter); *inaarúmúné* 'I am a girl' (*inaaru*V2 + *mo* + $\alpha_1 u$N + e_1 'girl' + desig + I + indic); *anópoana* 'because it is big' (*ano*N1 + *poa* $_1$-*na* 'big' + causal + 3rd person).

(3) loc + md: *maakáqá* 'here (*maaka*Q2 + *ma* 'here' + nom); *ebíkárá* 'Up there?' (*ebika*Q1 + *a* 'up there' + nom inter); *Moképare* 'It is (at) Okapa' (*Mokepa*Q1 + *e* 'Okapa' + indic); *wagáábarabiyo* 'Do you mean earlier?' (*wagaaba*Q1 + *abiyo* 'before' + abl inter); *anurápóána* 'because it's on a mountain' (*anu*V2 + *ra*Q + *poa* + *na* 'mountain' + 'at' + causal + 3rd person).

Four major construction types will now be considered, (1) substantives, (2) pronouns, (3) locatives, and (4) verbs. Based on these four word-construction types eight word classes may be defined. These will be specified according to the construction type from which they are derived.

4.1. *Substantives*

Noun stems enter into constructions with nominal affixes to form five word classes, *noun* (n), *descriptives* (d), *numerals* (nb), *temporals* (t), and *proper names* (pn). Each word class may be considered a subclass of substantives with co-occurrence restrictions affecting the substantive suffix potential (sf.p) definitively. The differences in suffix potential for each class may be regarded as a special and obligatory reading of the substantive formula governed by the subclass of noun stem which occurs. Optional readings of the suffix potential for each word class are then without restrictions. Rules will be given to eliminate nonoccurring readings of the substantive suffix potential.

Table 50 summarizes the co-occurrence restrictions of suffix categories and word classes as specified by the structural rules and formulas which follow.

$$\text{sb} = \text{ns} + (\text{sf.p})$$

$$\text{sf.p} = (\left\{ \begin{array}{l} \{\text{st} + \text{poss}_{\text{rel-sg}}; \{\text{poss}_{\text{ab}}; \text{instr}\} + (\text{ref}) + (\text{md})\} \\ (\text{st}) + (\text{nb})_{\text{mx}} + (\{\text{poss}_{\text{rel-pl}}; (\text{accom}) + (\text{nb})_{\text{mx}} + (\text{ref}) + (\text{md})\}) \end{array} \right\}$$

4.1.1. *Rewrite rules.* The following rewrite rules applied to the above formulas specify limitations on the reading potential of suffix-potential formula and help define word classes.

TABLE 50
SUBSTANTIVE CO-OCCURRENCE POTENTIAL*

Word Class	Affix					
	Numeral	Possessive	Instrument	Stative	Accompaniment	
					Active	Passive
Noun						
Animate	+	+	−	+	+	+
Inanimate	+	+	+	+	+	−
Descriptive	+	+	+	−	+	−
Temporal	+	+	−	+	+	−
Numeral	−	+	+	−	+	−
Personal name	−	+	−	−	+	+

Plus indicates co-occurrence potential and minus indicates nonpotential.

* It should be noted that noun stems plus locative suffixes are not regarded as substantive constructions but as locatives.

$$ns \rightarrow \{ns_q; ns_{nq}\}$$
$$(1)\ ns_q + \lfloor(nb)\ \rfloor \rightarrow ns_q\ minus\ (nb)$$
$$accom \rightarrow \{accom_{act}; accom_{pass}\}$$
$$ns_q \rightarrow \{ns_{nb}; ns_{pn}\}$$
$$ns_{nq} \rightarrow \{ns_c; ns_d; ns_t\}$$
$$ns_c \rightarrow \{ns_{ani}; ns_{inani}\}$$

$$(2)\ \begin{Bmatrix} ns_{ani} \\ ns_d \\ ns_t \\ ns_{pn} \end{Bmatrix} + (\{accom_{act}; accom_{pass}\}) \rightarrow \begin{Bmatrix} ns_{ani} \\ ns_d \\ ns_t \\ ns_{pn} \end{Bmatrix} + (accom_{act})$$

$$(3)\ \begin{Bmatrix} ns_{ani} \\ ns_t \\ ns_{pn} \end{Bmatrix} + (instr) \rightarrow \begin{Bmatrix} ns_{ani} \\ ns_t \\ ns_{pn} \end{Bmatrix} minus\ (instr)$$
$$ns_{ani} \rightarrow \{ns_{ani}; ns_1\}$$

$$(4)\ \begin{Bmatrix} \delta ns_1 \\ ns_{pn} \end{Bmatrix} + (st + poss_{rel\text{-}sg}) \rightarrow \begin{Bmatrix} \delta ns_1 \\ ns_{pn} \end{Bmatrix} + (poss_{rel\text{-}sg})$$
$$\delta ns_1 \rightarrow \{ns_1 V; \delta ns_1 N: \delta ns_1 Q\}$$

$$(5)\ \delta ns_1 \{N; Q\} + (st) \rightarrow \begin{Bmatrix} \delta ns_1 \{N; Q\} + st \\ \delta ns_1 \{N; Q\} + (st) \end{Bmatrix} {}^{16}$$
$$\delta ns_1 V \rightarrow \{\delta ns_1 V; *\delta ns_1 V\}$$

[16] The occurrence of the stative suffix with delta-one stems of the N and Q class is not the usual type of optional relationship. Normally the stative suffix does occur but sociolinguistic factors such as intimacy of informality may change the seeming obligatory relationship to an optional one.

(6) $*\delta ns_1 V + (st) \rightarrow \{*\delta ns_1 V \text{ minus (st)}; *\delta ns_1 + (st)\}$[17]

(7) $\left\{ \begin{array}{l} \delta ns_1 V; \\ ns_{\{pn; \, d; \, nb\}} \end{array} \right\} + (st) \rightarrow \left\{ \begin{array}{l} \delta ns_1 \\ ns_{\{pn; \, d; \, nb\}} \end{array} \right\}$ minus (st)[18]

Distribution of word classes with the foregoing rewrite rules is summarized in Table 51.

TABLE 51
DISTRIBUTION OF REWRITE RULES

Word Class	Rule Number						
	1	2	3	4	5	6	7
Noun							
Animate	−	+	−	−	−	−	−
Inanimate	−	−	+	−	−	−	−
Delta-one	−	−	+	+	+	+	+
Descriptive	−	+	−	−	−	−	+
Temporal	−	+	+	−	−	−	−
Number	+	+	−	−	−	−	+
Personal name	+	−	+	+	−	−	+

4.1.2. *Definition of classes*. The five substantive word classes may be defined as follows:

Noun = ns_c + (sf.p + Rules $\{2; 3; 3\text{-}7\}$)
  Animate nouns = ns_{ani} + (sf.p + Rule 2)
  Inanimate nouns = ns_{inani} + (sf.p + Rule 3)
  Delta-one nouns = ns_1 + (sf.p + Rules 3-7)
Descriptive = ns_d + (sf.p + Rules 2, 7)
Temporal = ns_t + ($\{$sf.p + Rules 2, 3; loc$\}$)
Numeral + ns_{nb} + (sf.p + Rules 1, 2, 7)
Personal name = ns_{pn} + (sf.p + Rules 1, 3, 4, 7)

4.1.3. *Selected samples of substantive constructions*

4.1.3.1. *Noun*

(1) *waamá* 'man'
  *waa*V2 + *ma*
  man + nom

(2) *waagótáátábámá* 'about man'
  *waa*V2 + *ko*V + *taa*N + *yaba*V + *ma*
  man + st + pl + ref + nom

(3) *waagóní* 'the man's'
  *waa*V2 + *ko*V + *ni*
  man + st + poss$_{rel-sg}$

(4) *iyápóti* 'the children's'
  *iyápó*V1 + *ti*
  child + poss$_{rel-pl}$

[17] Reciprocal terms in the delta-one class may optionally occur with the stative suffix but usually do not.

[18] $\{ns_d; ns_{nb}\}$ + (st) → ns_c as described under the section describing stem constructions.

(5) *iyápógórátágáráqá* 'with the two children'
   *iyápó*V1 + *ko*V + *rarata*V + *kara*Q + *ma*
   child + st + dual + accom + nom

4.1.3.2. Descriptive

(1) *anómma* 'big'
   *anó*N1 + *ma*
   big + nom

(2) *anóqtabama* 'about bigness'
   *anó*N1 + *yaba*V + *ma*
   big + ref + nom

4.1.3.3. Number

(1) *kaayaqá* 'two'
   *kaaya*Q2 + *ma*
   two + nom

(2) *kaayakáráqá* 'with two'
   *kaaya*Q2 + *kara*Q + *ma*
   two + accom + nom

4.1.3.4. Temporal

(1) *aabáyaama* 'morning'
   *aabáyaa*V1 + *ma*
   morning + nom

(2) *nokáátabama* 'concerning night'
   *nokáá*N1 + *yaba*V + *ma*
   night + ref + nom

   (3) *aabáyaanapine* 'Good morning! (lit: it's in the morning) '
      *aabayaa*V + *na* + *pi*N + *e*
      morning + *na* + in + indic

4.1.3.5. Personal names.

The following examples illustrate two types of possessive and accompaniment constructions.

(1) *binae* 'It is Bee's'
   bi + *na* + *e*
   Bee + poss$_{ab}$ + indic

(2) *pasááqyani* 'Pasaaqya's'
   pasááqya + *ni*
   Pasaaqya + poss$_{rel\text{-}sg}$

(3) *tipínagara* 'with Timpina'
   tipína + *kara*Q
   Tipina + accom$_{act}$

(4) *naanúte* 'with Naanu'
   naanú + *te*V
   Naanu + accom$_{pas}$

TABLE 52
PRONOUN CO-OCCURRENCE POTENTIAL

Pronoun Subclass	Possessive	Accompaniment			Referent	Mood
		Instrument	Active	Passive		
Exclusive	−	−	+	+	−	+
Reflexive	−	−	−	−	+	+
Interrogative	+	+	+	+	+	+
Personal	+	−	+	+	+	+
Locational	+	+	+	+	+	+

4.2. *Pronouns* (pr)

The occurrence potential of pronoun stems with suffix categories is summarized in Table 52. The formulas for pronoun construction are as follows:

$$\text{pro.s} + (\{\text{poss}_{rel}; (\{\text{inst}; \text{accom}; \text{poss}_{ab}\}) + (\text{ref}) + (\text{md})\})$$

$$\text{pro.s} \rightarrow \left\{ \begin{array}{l} \text{pro}_{p\text{-ex}}; \text{pro}_{ref}; \text{pro}_{int} \\ \text{pro}_p; \text{pro}_{loc} \end{array} \right\}$$

Selection of pronoun stem subclass conditions the reading of the above formula and gives four primary reading potentials.

(1) $\text{pro}_{p\text{-ex}} + (\text{accom}) + (\text{md})$

(2) $\text{pro}_{p\text{-ref}} + (\text{ref})(\text{md})$

(3) $\text{pro}_p + \left\{ \begin{array}{l} \text{poss}_{rel} \\ (\{\text{accom}; \text{poss}_{ab}\}) + (\text{ref}) + (\text{md}) \end{array} \right\})$

(4) $\begin{array}{l} \text{pro int} \\ \text{pro}_{loc} \end{array} + (\left\{ \begin{array}{l} \text{poss}_{rel} \\ (\{\text{inst}; \text{accom}; \text{poss}_{ab}\}) + (\text{ref}) (\text{md}) \end{array} \right\})$

Readings numbers (3) and (4) must be further refined to define limits of subcatetory co-occurrence potential. This will be done by a set of rewrite rules.

4.2.1. *Rewrite rules.* $\{\text{pro}_p; \text{pro}_{loc}\} \rightarrow \{\text{pro}_{obj}; \text{pro}_{n.\,obj}\}$

(1) $\text{pro.s} + \left\{ \begin{array}{l} \text{poss}_{rel} \\ \\ \text{poss}_{ab} \end{array} \right\} \rightarrow \text{pro}_{n.obj} + \left\{ \begin{array}{l} \text{poss}_{rel} \\ \\ \text{poss}_{ab} \end{array} \right\}$

$\text{accom} \rightarrow \{\text{accom}_{pass}; \text{accom}_{act}\}$

(2) $\text{pro.s} + \text{accom} \rightarrow \left\{ \begin{array}{l} \text{pro}_{obj} + \text{accom}_{pass} \\ \\ \text{pro}_{n.obj} + \text{accom}_{act} \end{array} \right\}$

$\text{pro}_{n.obj} \rightarrow \{\text{pro}_{d.foc;\ sg}; \text{pro}_{d;\ p}\}$

(3) $\text{pro}_{n.obj} + \text{accom}_{act} \rightarrow \text{pro}_{d;\ p} + \text{accom}_{act}$

$\text{pro}_{d.foc;\ sg} \rightarrow \left\{ \begin{array}{l} \text{pro}_{p.sg} \\ \\ \text{pro}_{d.foc;\ loc.sg} \end{array} \right\}$

(4) $\text{pro}_{d.foc.sg} + \left\{ \begin{array}{l} \text{poss}_{rel} \\ \\ \text{poss}_{ab} \end{array} \right\} \left\{ \begin{array}{l} \text{pro}_{sg} + \left\{ \begin{array}{l} \text{poss}_{rel} \\ \text{poss}_{ab} \end{array} \right\} \\ \left\{ \begin{array}{l} \text{pro}_{d.foc} \\ \text{pro}_{loc.sg} \end{array} \right\} + \left\{ \begin{array}{l} \text{poss}_{rel} \\ \text{poss}_{rel} + \text{poss}_{ab} \end{array} \right\} \end{array} \right\}$

$\{\text{pro}_{loc}; \text{pro}_{int}\} \rightarrow \{\text{pro}_{ani}; \text{pro}_{inani}\}$ [19]

[19] This reclassification intersects with other reclassifying rules and applies to all locative pronouns whether subclassified by previous rules or not.

$$(5) \ \text{pro}_{obj} + \text{accom}_{pass} \rightarrow \left\{ \begin{array}{l} \text{pro}_{obj} \\ \text{pro}_{ani} \end{array} \right\} + \text{accom}_{pass}$$

$$(6) \ \text{pro.s} + \text{instr} \rightarrow \text{pro}_{inani} + \text{instr}$$

4.2.2. *Examples of pronoun constructions.* (1) *kenamáa* 'I alone' (pro$_{p\text{-}ex}$); (2) *kenamáari* 'myself' (pro$_{p\text{-}rx}$); (3) *náakararabiyo* 'Where is it?' (pro$_{int}$ + md) (*naakara*Q1 + *abiyo* 'where' + interrogative); (4) *keqtááqtábáma* 'about us' (pro$_{p.obj}$ + ref + md) (*keqtaa*N2 + *yaba*V + *ma* 'us' + ref + nom); (5) *kenákátí* 'our two' (*kenaka* V2 + *ti* 'us two' + poss); (6) *epíwánímínáé* 'It is his (he near)' (*epiwa*V2 + *ni* + *mina* + *e* 'he near' + poss$_{rel}$ + poss$_{ab}$ + indic).

4.3. *Locative* (loc)

A locative is marked by one or more locative suffixes. The locative nucleus (loc$_{nu}$) consists of either a locative stem, or a noun, pronoun, or verb plus a location in time or space suffix (see Sec. 3.2). To the locative nucleus may be added movement-away-from, number, referent, or mood suffixes. The rules from suffix combination are as follows:

$$\text{loc} = \text{loc}_{nu} + (\text{from}) + (\text{nb}) + (\text{ref}) + (\text{md})$$

$$\text{loc}_{nu} \rightarrow \left\{ \begin{array}{l} \text{loc.s} \\ \{\text{ns; pro; vb}\} + \text{loc} \end{array} \right\}$$

$$\text{vb} \rightarrow \text{vb}_{nu} + (\text{ts}) + \text{person}$$

$$\text{ns} \rightarrow \text{ns} + (\text{st}) + (\text{nb})$$

Selected examples: (1) *yópáké* 'from the garden' (*yo*N2 + *pa*Q + *ka*V 'garden' + 'place' + 'from'); (2) *kekáqá* 'to me' (*ke*N2 + *ka*Q + *ma* 'me' + loc + nom); (3) *naráunabaqa* 'where I ate' (*na*V2b + *ra* + *una*V + *pa*Q + *ma* 'to eat' + aorist + 'I' + loc + nom); (4) *yaayúqnóbaqtáámá* 'to the woods' (*yaayu*Q2 + *noba*Q + *taa*V + *ma* 'woods' + 'inside' + pl + nom); (5) *naaûpaqtabama* 'concerning the house' (*naa*N2 + *u* + *pa*Q + *taba*V + *ma* 'house' + 'inside' + 'place' + ref + nom).

4.4. *Verb* (vb)

There are three categories of verbs paralleling the three types of person suffixes. However, each type conforms to the following basic verb formula:

$$\text{vb} = (\text{neg}) + (\text{dir}) + (\text{ts})_{mx} + \text{vs} + (\text{vc}) + (\text{ts}_{mx} + \text{per} + (\{\text{ref; md}\})$$

A portion of this formula remains unchanged throughout a number of verbal constructions and will be referred to as a verb nucleus (v$_{nu}$).

$$v_{nu} = (\text{neg}) + (\text{dir}) + \text{vs} + (\left\{ \begin{array}{l} \textit{tuwa} \\ (\delta ka) + (ko) \end{array} \right\})$$

The potential for co-occurrences of particular tense, person, and mood suffixes characterizes the differences in the three verb categories. Each series of person suffixes has a different set of co-occurrence restrictions. These will be specified in the following sections.

4.4.1. *Alpha co-occurrence restrictions.* The alpha verb (α-vb) has the widest range of co-occurrence potential. The rules for the occurrence of alpha person suffixes in verb constructions are specified in the following formula, which indicates the actual morphemes or morpheme categories that may occur as manifestations of the structural slots in the basic verb formula.

$$\alpha\text{-vb} = \left\{ (keV)_{mx} + vb_{nu} + \left(\begin{cases} (\{ts; \ ra \ + \ ro; \ ta\})_{mx} \\ (ra)_{mx} + (no) \end{cases} \right) \right. $$

$$\left. + \alpha + \left(\begin{cases} assert; \ conj; \\ abl; \\ poa \ + \ \beta; \\ e_1; o_1; po \end{cases} \right); vb_{nu} \ + \alpha_3 \ + \ bo \right\}$$

The distribution of subseries of alpha person suffixes with mood suffixes is as follows:

$$\alpha_1 + e_1; o_1; po$$
$$\alpha_2 + md_{abl}$$
$$\alpha_3 + \{bo; \ poa \ + \beta\}$$
$$\alpha_4 + md_{conj}$$

The alpha person series may occur with all tense morphemes and with the indicative, interrogative, assertative, abilitative, conjunctive, causal, and prohibitive mood suffixes. These mood suffixes may occur with any of the tense morphemes except the prohibitive mood. The future tense suffix (*no*) may co-occur with either the past or present continuous suffixes but all other tense-aspect suffixes are mutually exclusive with one another. Alpha subseries number one occurs with indicative, interrogative, and assertative moods; subseries number three with prohibitive and causal moods; and subseries number four with the conjunctive moods. The tense and voice potential of the alpha verb shall be referred to as the alpha nucleus (α-vb$_{nu}$).

4.4.2 *Beta co-occurrence restrictions.* Beta person suffixes occur only with present continuous, past aorist, and future tense-aspect affixes and with indicative, interrogative, abilitative designatory, abilitative interrogative, and abilitative assertative moods. Beta subseries number three suffixes may occur with the imperative mood when also occurring with either voice or aorist suffixes or with both. The beta nucleus (β-vb$_{nu}$) is the tense and voice potential of the beta verb as defined by the following formula:

$$\beta\text{-vb} = \left\{ \begin{array}{l} (keV)_{mx} + vb_{nu} + (ra)_{mx} + (no) + \beta + \\ \qquad (\{ \begin{array}{l} \{e_1; \ abiyo; \ mibo; \ miye\} \\ abo \ + \alpha_1 \ + o_1 \end{array} \}) \\ (neg \ + (dir) \ + vs \ + ra \ + \beta_3 \ + o_2 \\ (neg) \ + (dir) \ + vs \ + vc \ + (ra) \ + \beta_3 \ + \}_2 \end{array} \right\}$$

4.4.3. *Gamma co-occurrence restrictions.* Gamma suffixes are the most restricted in their distribution, occurring only with one mood, the imperative, and with no tense affixes. The formula specifying the structure of the gamma verb is γ-vb $= v_{nu} + \gamma + o_2$.

4.4.4. *Co-occurrence of alpha and beta person suffixes.* In addition to the alpha and beta co-occurrence which relate to the structure of mood affixes already described there are two types of constructions in which the two series co-occur within the same word. These may be summarized and compared by the following formulas:

(1) β-vb$_{nu} + \beta_1 + mo + \alpha_1 + md$
(2) α-vb$_{nu} + \alpha + \beta$

The second of these formulas, which is related primarily to sentence structure, and the details of the specific subseries which occur will be specified in Section 8 on sentence structure. Type one might well have been included in the description of mood affixes for the semantic significance fits into the mood categories indicating sufficiency of action and the structuring can be described as a combination of mood affixes. The designatory suffix (*mo*) followed by the alpha-one person suffixes which agree in number and person with the beta person suffix preceding occurs with indicative, interrogative, and assertative mood suffixes. Since two variables are involved (both person and mood) and since the construction is restricted to beta verbs, it has been included in this description of word structure. The following example illustrates this construction: *nemamiye* 'He eats enough' (*na*V2b + β-*na*V + *mo* + α-*i*V + *e* 'to eat' + 3rd person + desig + 3rd person + indic).

A synopsis of other verb constructions follows in the next section. Person and mood variations are given in the present tense for the verb, *na*V2b 'to eat'. Tense-aspect and voice contrasts for the verb 'to eat' are given in the third person singular. These are followed by diagnostic sets for several verbs of various morphophonemic types. The English translations merely attempt to give an idea of the differences in the semantic significances of the various forms and are by no means a statement of the full semantic significance of any of the forms.

4.4.5. *Sample verb constructions*

4.4.5.1. *Present tense indicative, interrogative, and assertative moods*

$$na\text{V2b} + \alpha_1 + \{e_1; o_1; po\} \text{ 'to eat'}$$

First person singular (α-*u*N)   Second person singular (α-$\emptyset$N)
náune 'I eat.'   *náane* 'You eat.'
náuno 'Do I eat?'   *náano* 'Do you eat?'
náupo 'I certainly eat.'   *náapo* 'You certainly eat.'

Third person singular (α-iV)
naiyé 'He eats.'
naiyó 'Does he eat?'
náibo 'He certainly eats.'

First person dual (α-uyV)
náuye 'We two eat.'
náuyo 'Do we two eat?'
náubo 'We two certainly eat.'

Second-third person dual (α-yV)
náaye 'You/they two eat.'
náauo 'Do you/they two eat?'
náabo 'You/they two certainly eat.'

First person plural (α-$unata$V)
náunatae 'We (pl) eat.'
náunatao 'Do we (pl) eat?'
náunataibo 'We (pl) cer-
    tainly eat.'
náunataibo 'We (pl) certainly
    eat.'

Second-third person plural (α-$\emptyset$V)
nááé 'You (pl) or they eat.'
nááó 'Do you (pl) or they eat?'
náábo 'You (pl) or they certainly eat.'

4.4.5.2. *Present tense abilitative moods*
naV2 $+\alpha_2$ $+e_2$; *abiyo; mibo; miye*}

First person singular (α-unaV)
náunae 'I can eat.'
náunabiyo 'Can I eat?'
náunaibo 'I certainly can eat.'
náunamiye 'I am he who can eat.'

Second person singular (α-naV)
náanae 'You can eat.'
náanabiyo 'Can you eat?'
náanaibo 'You certainly can eat.'
náanamiye 'You are he who can eat.'

Third person singular (α-iN)
náine 'He can eat.'
náinabiyo 'Can he eat?'
náimibo 'He certainly can eat.'
náimiye 'He is the one who can eat.'

First person dual (α-uyaN)
náuyane 'We two can eat.'
náuyanabiyo 'Can we two eat?'
náuyamibo 'We two certainly can eat.'

náuyamiye 'We two are they who can
    eat.'

Second-third person dual (α-yaN)
náayane 'You/they two can eat.'
náayanabiyo 'Can you/they two eat?'
náayamibo 'You/they two certainly
    can eat.'
náayamiye 'You/they two are they
    who can eat.'

First person plural (α-$unataa$V)
náunataae 'We can eat.'
náunataabiyo 'Can we eat?'
náunataamibo 'We certainly can eat.'
náunataamiye 'We are the ones who
    can eat.'

Second-third person plural (α-$\emptyset$N)
náane 'You (pl) or they can eat.'
náanabiyo 'Can you/they eat?'
náámibo 'You/they certainly can eat.'
náámiye 'You/they are the ones who
    can eat.'

4.4.5.3. *Present tense prohibitive and causal moods*

$$naV2b + \alpha_3 + \{bo; poa + \beta\}$$

First person singular-plural
(α-*una*V; $\beta\emptyset$Q; β-*ta*V)
náunabo 'I/we shouldn't eat.'
náunaboaqa 'Because I eat.'
náunaboata 'Because we eat.'

Second person singular
(α-*na*V: β-$\emptyset$Q)
náanabo 'You shouldn't eat.'
náanaboaqa 'Because you eat.'

Third person singular
(α-*ina*N; β-*na*V)
náinabo 'He shouldn't eat.'
náipoana 'Because he eats.'

First person dual
(α-*uya*N; β-*ka*V)
náuyabo 'We two shouldn't eat.'
náuyapoaka 'Because we two eat.'

Second-third person dual
(α-*ya*N; β-*ka*V; β-*ta*V)
náayabo 'You/they two shouldn't eat.'
náayapoaka 'Because you two eat.'
náayapoata 'Because they two eat.'

Second-third person plural
(α-$\emptyset$N; β-$\emptyset$Q; β-*ta*V)
náábo 'You (pl) or they shouldn't eat.'
náápoaqa 'Because you (pl) eat.'
náápoata 'Because they eat.'

4.4.5.4. *Present tense conjunctive moods*

$$naV2b + \alpha_4 + na + e; mibo$$

First person singular (α-*una*)
náunanae 'I eat and . . .'
náunaqibo 'I certainly eat and . . .'

Second person singular (α-*na*)
náananae 'You eat and . . .'
náanaqibo 'You certainly eat and. . .'

Third person singular (α-*ita*)
náitanae 'He eats and . . .'
náitaqibo 'He certainly eats and . . .'

First person dual (α-*uya*)
náuyanae 'We two eat and . . .'
náuyanaibo 'We two certainly eat and . . .'

Second-third person dual (α-*ya*)
náayanae 'You/they two eat and . . .'
náayanaibo 'You/they two certainly eat and . . .'

First person plural (α-*unana*)
náunanatae 'We eat and . . .'
náunanataibo 'We certainly eat and . . .'

Second-third person plural (α*wa*)
nááwanae 'You (pl) or they eat and . . .'
nááwanaibo 'You/they certainly eat and . . .'

4.4.5.5. *Present tense subjunctive moods*

$$naV2b + \beta + \{e_1; abo + \alpha_1 + o_1; abiyo; mibo; miye\}$$

First person singular (β-$\emptyset$Q; α-*u*N)
nére 'I may eat.'
nérabuno 'May I eat?'
néqiyo 'May I be able to eat?'

Second person singular (β-$\emptyset$V; α-$\emptyset$N)
née 'You may eat.'
néabono 'May you eat?'
néabiyo 'May you be able to eat?'

néqibo 'I certainly may be able to eat.'

néqiye 'I may be the one who is able to eat.'

néibo 'You certainly may be able to eat.'

némiye 'You may be the one who is is able to eat.'

Third person singular (β-*naV*; α-*iV*)

nénae 'He may eat.'

nénabiyo 'May he eat?'

nenabiyo 'May he be able to eat?'

nénaibo 'He certainly may be able to eat.'

nenamiye 'He may be the one who is able to eat.'

First-second person dual
(β-*kaV*; α-*uyV*; α-*yV*)

nékae 'We/you two may eat.'

nékabuyo 'May we two eat?'

nékaboyo 'May you two eat?'

nékabiyo 'May we/you two be able to eat?'

nékaibo 'We/you two certainly may be able to eat.'

nékamiye 'We/you two may be the ones who are able to eat.'

Third person dual-plural
(β-*taV*; α-*yV*; α-*$\emptyset$V*)

nétae 'They may eat.'

nétaboyo 'May they two eat?'

nétaboo 'May they eat?'

nétabiyo 'May they be able to eat?'

nétaibo 'They certainly may be able to eat.'

nétamiye 'They may be the ones who are able to eat.'

First person plural
(β-*taaV*; α-*unataV*)

nétaae 'We may eat.'

nétaabuno 'May we eat?'

nétaabiyo 'May we be able to eat?'

nétaaibo 'We certainly may be able to eat.'

nétaamiye 'We may be the ones who are able to eat.'

Second person plural
(β-*$\emptyset$Q*; α-*$\emptyset$V*)

nére 'You (pl) may eat.'

néraboo 'May you eat?'

nérabiyo 'May you be able to eat?'

néqibo 'You certainly may be able to eat.'

néqiye 'You may be the ones who are able to eat.'

4.4.5.6. *Imperative mood*

$$naV2b + \gamma + o_2$$

First person singular-plural (γ-*$\emptyset$V*): *naano* 'I or we must eat.'

Second person singular (γ-*$\emptyset$V*): *naao* 'You must eat.'

Third person singular (γ-*$\emptyset$N*): *naino* 'He must eat.'

First person dual (γ-*iV*): *naiyo* 'We two must eat.'

Second person dual (γ-*kaV*): *naakao* 'You two must eat.'

Third person dual (γ-*taiV*): *naataiyo* 'They two must eat.'

Second-third person plural (γ-*$\emptyset$Q*): *naaro* 'You (pl) or they must eat.'

$$naV2b + ra \neq \beta_3 + o_2 \text{ (subjunctive-past)}$$

Second person singular (β-*$\emptyset$V*): *náreo* 'You must first eat.'

Third person singular (β-*naQ*): *nárenaro* 'He must first eat.'

Second person dual (*ß-ka*V): *nárekao* 'You two must first eat.'
Third person dual-plural (*ß-ya*Q): *náreyaro* 'They must first eat.'
Second person plural (*ß-ø*Q): *nárero* 'You must first eat.'

4.4.5.7. *Indicative mood, third person, tense and voice contrasts*

$$(kéV) + naV2b + (\begin{Bmatrix} tuwa\text{NR} \\ \delta ka\text{V} \end{Bmatrix}) + (\begin{Bmatrix} ma;\ wao;\ qo \\ ta:\ ra + ro; \\ (ra) + (no) \end{Bmatrix}) + 3\text{rd per} + o_1$$

Present continuous: *kénaiye* 'He is eating.' (*ké*V + vb)
Completive (present): *nátuwaiye* 'He finishes eating.' (vb + *tuwa*NR)
Completive (aorist): *nátukaiye* 'He finished eating.' (vb + *tuwa*NR + *ra*)
Benefactive (first person): *natíkáiye* 'He eats in my honor.' (vb + *ti-δka*)
Aorist (independent): *naráiye* 'He ate.' (vb + *ra*)
Aorist (subjunctive): *narénae* 'He first eats.' (vb + *ra* + ß)
Future (independent): *nániye* 'He will eat.' (vb + *no*)
Future (subjunctive): *nanénae* 'He wants to eat.' (vb + *no* + *ß*)
Customary: *néwaiye* 'He used to eat.' (vb + *wao*)
Frequentive: *néqiye* 'He ate often.' (vb + *qo*)
Perfect: *némáiye* 'He has eaten.' (vb + *ma*)
Recent past: *nétaiye* 'He ate yesterday.' (vb + *ta*)
Remote past: *narériye* 'He ate day before yesterday.' (vb + *ra* + *ro*)

4.4.5.8. *Diagnostic sets illustrating morphophonemic classes and change.*
The following sets include examples of each morphophonemic class (V, N, and Q), of reduced stem types (R), differences of final stem vowels (*a*, *e*, and *o*), and differences in tone types. The forms given are those which indicate the various morphophonemic types of subclasses.

V-class

(1) *a*V2a (vs$_{tr}$) 'to shoot at a target'
    aaó 'Shoot it!' (Second person singular imperative)
    aakao 'You two shoot it!' (Second person dual imperative)
    aiyé 'He shoots it.' (Present tense indicative)
    aráiye 'He shot it.' (Aorist indicative)
    ániye 'He will shoot it.' (Future indicative)

(2) *agata*V1a (vs$_{tr}$) 'to turn as a page or leaf'
    agataó 'Turn it!' (Second person singular imperative)
    agátáakao 'You two turn it!' (Second person dual imperative)
    agátáiye 'He is turning it.' (Present tense indicative)
    agátaraiye 'He turned it.' (Aorist indicative)
    agatániye 'He will turn it.' (Future indicative)

(3) *koo*V3 (vs$_{intr}$) 'to go away'
    kóaao 'Go away!' (Second person singular imperative)

kóokao 'You two go away!' (Second person dual imperative)
kóiye 'He goes away.' (Present tense indicative)
kóuraiye 'He went away.' (Aorist indicative)
kóiniye 'He will go away.' (Future indicative)

(4)　*ítaV1b* (vs_tr) 'to hear, understand, know, listen'
itaao 'Listen!' (Second person singular imperative)
ítáakao 'You two listen!' (Second person dual imperative)
ítaiye 'He hears.' (Present tense indicative)
ítaraiye 'He heard.' (Aorist indicative)
itániye 'He will hear.' (Future indicative)

(5)　*teV2a* (vs_tr) 'to say, talk'
tiyó 'Talk!' (Second person singular imperative)
tekao 'You two talk!' (Second person dual imperative)
tiyé 'He is talking.' (Present tense indicative)
tiráiye 'He said.' (Aorist indicative)
tíniye 'He will say.' (Future indicative)

N-class

(1)　*ɔ́meN1a* (vs_tr) 'to give'
amiyó 'Give it to him.' (Second person singular imperative)
ámèkao 'You two give it to him!' (Second person dual imperative)
ámiye 'He gives it to him.' (Present tense indicative)
ámikaiye 'He gave it to him.' (Aorist indicative)
amíniye 'He will give it to him.' (Future indicative)

(2)　*ataeN2Ra* (vs_tr) 'to chop'
ataiyó 'Chop it!' (Second person singular imperative)
atáekao 'You two chop it!' (Second person dual imperative)
atáiye 'He chops it.' (Present tense indicative)
atákáiye 'He chopped it.' (Aorist indicative)
ataíniye 'He will chop it.' (Future indicative)

(3)　*kumoN2Ra* (vs_intr) 'to go or come down'
kúmowó 'Go down!' (Second person singular imperative)
kúmokao 'You two go down.' (Second person dual imperative)
kúmiye 'He goes down.' (Present tense indicative)
kukáiye 'He went down.' (Aorist indicative)
kumíniye 'He will go down.' (Future indicative)

(4)　*peraN1Rb* (vs_tr) 'to pour over, paint'
peraao 'Paint it!' (Second person singular imperative)
péráakao 'You two paint it!' (Second person dual imperative)
péráiye 'He paints it.' (Present tense indicative)
pékaiye 'He painted it.' (Aorist indicative)
perániye 'He will paint it.' (Future indicative)

(5)　*puraN2Ra* (vs_tr) 'to peel with fingers, to shell'
puraaó 'Peel it!' (Second person singular imperative)

púráakao 'You two peel it!' (Second person dual imperative)
púráiye 'He peels it.' (Present tense indicative)
púkáiye 'He peeled it.' (Aorist indicative)
purániye 'He will peel it.' (Future indicative)
(6) *puyóN2Ra* (vs$_{intr}$; stative) 'to die'
puyuwó 'Die!' (Second person singular imperative)
púyôkao 'You two die!' (Second person dual imperative)
púiye 'He dies.' (Present tense indicative)
pukáiye 'He died.' (Aorist indicative)
puíniye 'He will die.' (Future indicative)
pukiyé 'He is dead.' (Present stative indicative)
pukuráiye 'He is dead.' (Aorist stative indicative)
pukíniye 'He will be dead.' (Future stative indicative)

Q-class

(1) *agáyaQ2Ra* (vs$_{tr}$) 'to cook, write'
agayaaó 'Cook it!' (Second person singular imperative)
agáyaakao 'You two cook it!' (Second person dual imperative)
agáyaiye 'He cooks it.' (Present tense indicative)
agatáiye 'He cooked it.' (Aorist indicative)
agayániye 'He will cook it.' (Future indicative)
(2) *káráQ3b* (vs$_{tr}$) 'to cut'
karaao 'Cut it!' (Second person singular imperative)
káráakao 'You two cut it!' (Second person dual imperative)
káráiye 'He cuts it.' (Present tense indicative)
kárataiye 'He cut it.' (Aorist indicative)
káraniye 'He will cut it.' (Future indicative)
(3) *kaúgóQ2Ra* (vs$_{tr}$; stative) 'to cook in the ashes or ground'
kauguwó 'Cook it!' (Second person singular imperative)
kaúgôkao 'You two cook it!' (Second person dual imperative)
kaúgíye 'He cooks it.' (Present tense indicative)
kautáiye 'He cooked it.' (Aorist indicative)
kaugíniye 'He will cook it.' (Future indicative)
kaugiyé 'It is cooked.' (Present stative indicative)
kauguráiye 'It is cooked.' (Aorist stative indicative)
kaugíniye 'It will be cooked.' (Future stative indicative)
(4) *kautoQ1Rb* (vs$_{tr}$; stative) 'to burn, char'
kautuwo 'Burn it!' (Second person singular imperative)
káútôkao 'You two burn it!' (Second person dual imperative)
káútíye 'He burns it.' (Present tense indicative)
káútaiye 'He burned it.' (Aorist indicative)
kautíniye 'He will burn it.' (Future indicative)
káúgiye 'It is burned.' (Present stative indicative)
káúguraiye 'It is burned.' (Aorist stative indicative)

    káúginiye 'It will be burned.' (Future stative indicative)

(5) *uyo*Q2Ra (vs$_{intr}$) 'to go or come up'

    uyuwo 'Go up!' (Second person singular imperative)

    úyôkao 'You two go up!' (Second person dual imperative)

    úiye 'He goes up.' (Present tense indicative)

    utáiye 'He went up.' (Aorist indicative)

    uíniye 'He will go up.' (Future indicative)

(6) *wae*Q2Rb (vs$_{intr}$; stative) 'to lie down, sleep'

    waiyo 'Lie down!' (Second person singular imperative)

    watáiye 'He lay down.' (Aorist indicative)

    waguráiye 'He is asleep.' (Aorist stative indicative)

5. PHRASE STRUCTURE

Words have the following three characteristics: (1) they contain a single stress group, (2) their constituent elements are inseparable, and (3) they contain a single closing suffix. On the basis of the word characteristics which they share, phrases are divided into three types. *descriptive, syntactic,* and *idiomatic*. The matrix in Table 53 specifies the features of each.

TABLE 53
PHRASE DEFINITION

	Constituent elements inseparable	Single stress group	Single closing suffix
Word	+	+	+
Descriptive phrase	−	+	+
Syntactic phrase	−	−	−
Idiomatic phrase	+	$+/-$	$+/-$

The plus-minus marking in the idiomatic phrase row of Table 53 indicates that there may be one or more stress groups or closing suffixes. This contrasts with the plus markings of the descriptive phrase row which indicate that only one stress group and closing suffix may occur and the minus markings of the syntactic phrase row which indicate that more than a single stress group and closing suffix always occurs.

5.1. *Descriptive Phrase* (DscP; $[x + y]_1$)

The descriptive phrase shares two features with the word, differing only in that its constituent elements are separable by expansion. The words of a descriptive phrase form a single stress group, and only the final word of the Phrase occurs with inflectional suffixes. The morphotonemic pattern of change is the same for the noninitial words of a descriptive phrase as for inflectional affixes (see Sec. 9.2.3.1).

The descriptive phrase structure is expressed by the following formula:

$$\text{DscP} = \begin{cases} \{\text{ns; loc; pro; vb} + \text{i}\} + \text{n} \\ \{\text{ns; pro}\} + \{\text{loc; t; DscP}\} \end{cases}$$

ns → (ns$_{nb}$) + (ns$_d$) + (ns$_d$) + ({ns$_t$; ns$_c$})
pro → {pro$_{int}$; pro$_{loc}$}

It will be noted that the noun stem in the basic formula may be rewritten as a sequence of noun stem types and that only interrogative and locative pronouns occur. Usually sequences of noun stem types are limited to three, but the full range is structurally possible. The following examples will illustrate the different types of fillers of the final position in the formula; this position may be considered the head of this construction type.

5.1.1. *Noun phrase* (NP$_1$) {ns; loc; pro} + n

(1) ns$_{nb}$ + n (number stem plus noun)
móra-namma 'one house'
[< *mórâ*V1 > + < *naa*N2 + *ma*>]$_1$
one + house + nom

(2) ns$_{nb}$ + ns$_d$ + ns$_d$ + n (number stem, two descriptive stems plus noun)
móra-ano-karogaro-namma 'A big red house'
[< *mórâ*V1 > + < *anó*N1 > + < *karogaro*N2 > + < *naa*N2 + *ma*>]$_1$
one + big + red + house + nom

(3) ns$_t$ + n (temporal stem plus noun)
nokáán-aawaqa 'food for at night (night food)'
[< *nokááN*1 > + < *aáwa*Q1 + *ma*>]$_1$
night + food + nom

(4) ns$_c$ + n (common noun stem plus noun)
ira-nómmá 'hot water (fire water)'
[< *ira*V2 > + < *nó*N1 + *ma*>]$_1$
fire + water + nom

(5) loc + n (locative plus noun)
yopake-kaayukae (a from-the-garden man) 'He is a man from the garden'
[< *yó*N2 + *pa*Q + *keN*> + < *waayúká*V1 + *e*>]$_1$
garden + place + from + man + indic

(6) pro$_{loc}$ + n (locative pronoun plus noun)
min-ááwáqá 'that food'
[< *mi*N2 > + < *aawa*Q1 + *ma*>]$_1$
that + food + nom

(7) pro$_{int}$ + n (interrogative pronoun plus noun)
náa-waayukama 'which man'
[< *náa*V1 > + < *waayuka*V1 + *ma* >]$_1$
which + man + nom

(8) nom$_{raa}$ + n (resemblance nominal plus noun)
ekáán-íyápómá 'children like you'
[< *e*V2 + *raa*N > + < *iyapo*V1 + *ma* >]
you + like + child + nom

5.1.2. *Locative phrase* (locP$_1$) {ns; pro} + loc

(1) pro$_{int}$ + loc (interrogative pronoun plus locative)
náa-yopake 'from which garden'
[< *náa*V1 > + < *yo*N2 + *pa*Q + *ke* >]$_1$
which + garden + place + from

(2) ns$_d$ + loc (descriptive stem plus locative)
átê-aapaqa 'in the delicious shade'
[< *átê*V1 > + < *áapa*Q1 + *ma* >]$_1$
delicious + in the shade + nom

5.1.3. *Temporal phrase* (TemP$_1$) {ns; pro} + t

(1) ns$_d$ + t (descriptive stem plus temporal)
anó-kanaama 'a long time'
[< *anó*N1 > + < *kanaa*V2 + *ma* >]$_1$
big + time + nom

(2) pro$_{int}$ + t (interrogative pronoun plus temporal)
nói-kanaama 'when (what time)'
*noi*N1 + *kanaa*V2 + *ma*$_1$
what + time + nom

(3) pro$_{loc}$ + t (locative pronoun plus temporal)
maa-kánáámá 'now (this time)'
[< *maa*N2 > + < *kanaa*V2 + *ma* >]$_1$
this + time + nom

5.1.4. *Embedded descriptive phrases* {ns; pro} + DscP

(1) *anó-yopake-kaayukae* (a big-from-the-garden-man) 'He is a big man
from the garden'
[< *anó*N1 > + [*yópáké kááyúkáé*]$_1$]$_1$
big + [< *yó*N2 + *pa*Q + *keN* > + < *waayúká*V1 + *e* >]$_1$
garden + place + from + man + indic

(2) *náa-paaqya-poma* 'which little pig'
[< *náa*V1 > + [*pááqya-poma*]$_1$]$_1$
which + [< *pááqya*N1 > + < *pó*V1 + *ma* >]$_1$
little + pig + nom

5.1.5. *Verb plus noun*

naí-númámá 'edible bird'
*na*V2b + *i*V + < *numa*V2 + *ma* >
eat + 3rd person + bird + nom

5.2. *Syntactic Phrase* (SynP [*x* + *y*]₂)

The constituent elements of a syntactic phrase are separate by expansion but they neither form a single stress group nor occur with only one set of inflectional affixes. The nonpermutability of its constituent elements distinguish it as a single unit. Two types of syntactic phrases occur, *possessive* and *co-ordinate*.

5.2.1. *Possessive phrase* (SynP$_{poss}$). A possessive phrase consists of a possessive and either a noun, locative, temporal, or a descriptive phrase. The possessive element of the phrase may be either a possessive personal name, a possessive pronoun, or a possessive noun or noun phrase. This may be expressed in terms of the following formula and set or rewrite rules.

$$\text{SynP}_{poss} = \text{poss} + \{\text{n; loc; t; DscP}\}$$
$$\text{poss} \rightarrow \{\text{pn}_{poss}; \text{pro}_{poss}; (x) + \text{n}_{poss}\}$$
$$x \rightarrow \{\text{ns; loc; pro; poss}\}$$
$$\text{ns} \rightarrow (\text{ns}_{nb}) + (\text{ns}_d) + (\text{ns}_d) + (\{\text{ns}_t; \text{ns}_c\})$$
$$\text{pro} \rightarrow \{\text{pro}_{int}; \text{pro}_{loc}\}$$

Selected examples:

(1) *ketí iyámmá* 'my dog'
    [< *ke*V2 + *ni*> + < *iya*N2 + *ma*>]₂
    I + poss$_{sg}$ + dog + nom

(2) *waagóní yópáqá* 'the man's garden'
    [< *waa*V2 + *ko*V + *ni*> + < *yó*N2 + *pa*Q + *ma*>]₂
    man + st + poss$_{sg}$ + garden + place + nom

(3) *ení wagááma* 'your day'
    [< *e*V2 + *ni*> + < *wagáá*V1 + *ma*>]₂
    you + poss + midday + nom

(4) *pasááqyani áúgen-unaamma* 'Pasaaqya's new string bag'
    [< *pasááqya* + *ni*> + [< *áúge*N1> + < *unaa*N1 + *ma*>]₁]₂
    Pasaaqya + poss$_{sg}$ + new + string bag + nom

(5) *aaragóní anóani iyákómá* 'the woman's mother's dog'
    [[< *aara*V2 +*ko*V +*ni*> +< *a-ðno* +*ni*>]₂ +< *iya*N2 +*ko*V +*ma*>]₂
    woman + st + poss$_{sg}$ + her mother + poss$_{sg}$ + dog + st + nom

(6) *anón-inarugoni unáámma* 'the big girl's string bag'
    [[< *anó*N1> + < *inaru*V2 + *ko*V + *ni*>]₁ + < *unáá*N2 + *ma*>]₂
    big + girl + st + poss$_{sg}$ + string bag + nom

5.2.2. *Co-ordinate phrases* (SynP$_{co}$). A co-ordinate phrase is a sequence of parallel nominal constructions such that x_1 (where *x* is any given nominal construction and subscript one is a given manifestation of that construction) may be followed in the same syntactic phrase by $x_2{}^n$ (where x is the same or parallel construction and subscript two is a second and different manifestation, superscript n indicates that he same construction may be successively repeated with different manifestations without structural limitation). A parallel construction is one in which the suffix configuration remains the same but the stem class and/or the lateral expansion is different. If both x_1 and $x_2{}^n$ are manifested by personal names the particle *uyaa* may be used following each item in the phrase.

The co-ordinate phrase formula: $\text{SynP}_{co} = x_1 + x_{2n}$ may be rewritten to show the sequences which may occur.

$$x_1 + x_2{}^n \rightarrow \left\{ \begin{array}{l} \{\text{sb; pro}\}_1 + \{\ \{\text{sb; pro}\}_2{}^n; \text{loc}_1 + \text{loc}_2{}^n\} \\ \{\text{pn}_1; \text{pn}_1 + uyaa\} + \{\text{pn}_2; \text{pn}_2 + uyaa\}^n \end{array} \right\}$$

Selected examples:

(1) *aaramá, waamá, iyápóma* 'women, men, and children'
$[< aaraV2 + ma> + < waaV2 + ma> + < iyápóV1 + ma>]_2$
woman + nom + man + nom + child + nom

(2) *kamáágara, aríkokokara* 'with sweet potatoes and green beans'
$[< kamááV1 + karaQ> + < aríkokoQ1 + karaQ>]_2$
sweet potato + accom + green beans + accom

(3) *waaqém úyáá, titiqmó úyáá, toqááó úyáá* 'Waaqeme, Titiqmo, and Toqaao'
$[< waaqémá + uyaa> + < titíqmó + uyaa> + < toqááo + uyaa>$
Waaqema + conj + Titiqmo + conj + Toqaao + conj

(4) *yópáké, naaôpake, yaayúqnóbáké* 'from the garden, the house, and forest'
$[< yóN2 + paQ + ke> + < naaN2 + ô + paQ + ke> + < yaayúQ2 + nobaQ + ke>]_2$
garden + place + from + house + o + place + from + woods + in + from

5.3. *Idiomatic Phrases* (IdP; $[x + y]_3$)

The constituent elements of an idiomatic phrase are inseparable, may form one or more stress groups, and may contain more than one set of inflectional suffixes. When an idiomatic phrase forms a single stress group and contains only one set of inflectional suffixes the line between word and phrase is difficult to draw. In such a case a combination of intuition and economy has been used to divide the two. The major types of idiomatic phrases which occur are *quantifiable substantive, numeral, pronoun, interrogative,* and *verb.* The following sections will present each type giving examples to illustrate different constructions.

5.3.1. *Quantifiable substantive phrases* (IdP$_{sb}$). The head word of the substantive phrase is either a noun, temporal, or descriptive occurring phrase finally. Four structural types occur as follows: (1) noun stem plus noun or noun phrase; (2) verb or verb phrase plus noun; (3) verb phrase plus nominal formative; (4) reduplicated quantifiable noun stems. The examples which follow will illustrate each type.

5.3.1.1. *Noun stem plus noun or noun phrase* (ns + {n;NP})

(1) *aa-wááyúkámá* 'interpreter (a sound or speech man)'
   [< *a-δaa*V2> + < *waayuka*V1 + *ma*>]₃
   his-voice + man + nom

(2) *áai-kataa-wataama* 'talk about customs'
   [*áai*N1> + < *wataa*V2> + < *wataa*V2 + *ma*>]₃]₃
   base of tree, custom + talk + talk + nom

5.3.1.2. *Verb or verb phrase plus noun* ({vb; VP} + n)

(1) *aa-ítarai-karamma* 'judge (a smart white man)' ('to have understood his voice, that is, to be smart')
   [[< *a-δaa*V2> + < *íta*V1b + *ra*1 + *i*N>]₃ + < *kara*N2 + *ma*>]₃
   his-voice + hear + aorist + 3rd person + white man + nom

(2) *aaq-itaraí-kárámma* 'judge (a white man who interprets)' ('His ears have heard, that is, he interprets.')
   [[< *a-δaa*Q1> + < *íta*V1b + *ra*2 + *i*N>]₃ + < *kara*N2 + *ma*>]₃
   his-ear + hear + aorist + 3rd person + white man + nom

(3) *ikátuwai-iyapoma* 'a child who dies shortly after birth.'
   [< *apδikamo*N1Rb + *tuwa*N + *i*V> + < *iyapo*V1 + *ma*>]₃
   him-hit + completive + 3rd person + child + nom

(4) *koaóna-yaaóna-waayukama* 'craftsman' ('Look carefully.')
   [[< *ko* + *a-δóna*V3> + < *ya* + *a-δóna*V3>]₃ + < *waayuka*V2 + *ma*>]₃
   go + it-see + come + it-see + man + nom

(5) *iyápóma-íma-akáí-wímmá* 'that which is aborted'
   [[< *iyápó*V1 + *ma*> + < *í*V1 + *ma*> + < *a-δka* + *i*V>]₃ +
   < *wí*N1 + *ma*>]₃
   child + nom + neg + nom + him-put for + 3rd person + ginger + nom

5.3.1.3. *Verb phrase plus noun formative* (VP + nf)

(1) *amam-íwainaqa* 'an unfortunate person' ('He doesn't have a shadow.')
   [[< *a-δma*N2> + < *í*V + *wa*V + *i*V]₃ + *na*Q + *ma*>]₃
   his-shadow + neg + to be + 3rd person + person + nom

(2) *maramá-airáínáqá* 'a surveyor' ('one who sorts the ground.')
   [[< *mara*V2 + *ma*> + < *aira*N1Rb + *i*V]₃ + *na*Q + *ma*>]₃
   ground + nom + so sort + 3rd person + person + nom

(3) *áá-wairaináqá* 'interpreter' ('one whose ears turn')
   [[< *a-δáá*Q1> + < *waira*N2R + *i*V]₃ + *na*Q + *ma*>]₃
   his-ear + turn + 3rd person + person + nom

(4) *iyápóma-íma-akáíyáqtááqa* 'abortive'
   [[< *iyápó*V1 + *ma*> + < *í*V1 + *ma*> + *a-δka* + *i*V]₃ + *yaqtaa*Q + *ma*>]₃
   child + nom + neg + nom + him-put for + 3rd person + thing + nom

5.3.1.4. *Reduplicated quantifiable noun stems* (sb$_{q.r}$). A class of quanti-

fiable noun stems (nouns, temporals and descriptives) occurs reduplicated with the first vowel of the stem changing to *aa* (v₁ → *aa*). The following are examples of these stems: *aati aatima* 'all the time', *aaga naaga* 'to catch breath', *negi naagima* 'crazy', *turi taarima* 'messy', *koyu kaayu* 'angry', *kaipu kaapu* 'squirming', *wataa wataama* 'discussion, talk', *yobo naabo* 'clumsy'.

Onomatopoetic phrases are characteristically reduplicated sequences. The following suggest the range or types of onomatopoetic expressions which occur; significantly absent is the category of animal sounds which often find expression in onomatopoetic form. The Usarufa regard such sounds merely as noise.

tágaq-naagaqa	the sound of scratching
táu-tauma	the sound of chewing
tabuq-tabaaqá	the sound of the shooting of many bows
naróq-náróqa	the sound of a stomach gurgling
karû-karuqa	the sound of crunchy food
parô-paraaqa	the sound of crackling flames
pakí-bakima	the sound of footsteps
paké-bakema	the sound of knocking
tága-tagama	the sound of paper rattling
kamu-gamááma	the sound of a burp

5.3.2. *Numerals* (IdP_{nb}). All but three of the Usarufa numerals are complex stem, word, or phrase constructions. The latter is the more common and will be described here. The numeral system may be described as consisting of twenty number distinctions, these being the twenty digits which are the sum of a man's fingers and toes. Any number beyond twenty may be indicated by increasing the number of men each adding twenty or that part of twenty which may be needed. Forty-one, for example, would be two men and one. The Usarufa's lack of interest in being specific about numbers beyond ten is reflected in the complexity of the numeral system.

The numeral system includes only three basic numerals: one (*móràV1*), two (*kaayaQ2*), and three (*kaomoV2*). All other numeral distinctions are combinations of these with morphemes meaning hands, feet, and man used as units of five. The combination two plus two adds a forth distinction which is used in the combination of the units of five to give the final required distinction. This construction is:

> *kaayaqté kaayaqté*Q2 'four'
> [< *kaaya*Q2 + *te*Q> + < *kaaya*Q2 + *te*Q>]₃
> two + *te*Q + two + *te*Q

Units of five have the following structure:
> nb + {n; loc}
> nb → {*móràV1* 'one'}
>   {*mákaV* 'both'}

n → ⎧ *tiyáákama* 'my two hands'⎫
    ⎨ *títauqa* 'my foot'   ⎬
    ⎩ *waayúkámá* 'man'   ⎭

loc → *tiyáápaqa* 'at my hand'

Thus the numbers five, ten, fifteen, and twenty are:

móra tiyaapaqa 'five (at my one hand)'
$[< mórâV1 > \; + < ti\text{-}\delta yááN1 \; + paQ \; + ma >]_3$
one + my-hand + place + nom

máka tiyaakama 'ten (both my hands)'
$[< máN1 + raV > \; + < ti\text{-}\delta yááN1 \; + raV \; + ma >]_3$
all + dual + my-hand + dual + nom

móra titauqa 'fifteen (my one foot)'
$[< mórâV1 > \; + < ti\text{-}\delta ítauQ1 \; + ma >]_3$
one + my-foot + nom

môra waayukama 'twenty'
$[< mórâV1 > \; + < waayúkáV1 \; + ma >]_3$
one + man + nom

The numbers six through nine, eleven through fourteen, and sixteen through nineteen are complex combinations of the foregoing as follows:

(1) *Six through nine*

    abapake mórama 'six'
    kaayaqá 'seven'
    kaomomá 'eight'
    kaayaqté kaayaqtéqá 'nine'

$[< aba \; + paQ \; + ke > \; + < \{1, 2, 3, \text{ or } 4\} >]_3$
sum + place + from
('from the sum (my hand, i.e., five), one, two,' etc.)

(2) *Eleven through fourteen*

tiyááka naekamá títaupake môrama 'eleven'
    kaayaqá 'twelve'
    kaomomá 'thirteen'
    kaayaqté kaayaqteqá 'fourteen'

$[< ti\text{-}\delta yááN1 \; + raV > \; + < naeN \; + raV \; + ma > \; + < ti\text{-}ítauQ1 \; +paQ \; +$
$keN > \; + nb]_3$
my-hand + dual + *nae* + dual + nom + my-foot + place + from + nb
('my hands completed, from my foot one, two,' etc.)

(3) *Sixteen through nineteen*

tiyááka naekamá môra títauqa abapaké morama 'sixteen'
                kaayaqá 'seventeen'
                kaomomá 'eighteen'
                kaayaqté kaayaqteqa 'nineteen'

$[<$ *ti- δyááN*1 + *ra*V$>$ + $<$*nae*N + *ra*V$>$ + $[<$ *môrâ*V1$>$ +
$<$ *ti-δítau*Q1$>$]₁ + $<$*aba* + *pa*Q + *ke*N$>$ + nb]₃
my-hand + dual + *nae* + dual + one + my-foot + sum + place +
from + nb

('my two hands completed, one foot and from that sum, one, two,' etc.)

Another construction can be used for twenty which utilizes both the hands and feet:

    tiyáámma títauq yáutama 'twenty' ('a circle of my hands and feet')

    $[<$ *ti-δyáá*N1 + *ma*$>$ + $<$ *ti-δítau*Q1$>$ + $<$ *yáuta*V1 + *ma*$>$]

    my-hand + my foot + circle + nom

5.3.3. *Pronoun phrases* (IdP$_{pro}$). Pronoun phrases are used to indicate singular and plural focus of plural personal pronouns. The structure is as follows:

    $<$ pro.s$_p$ + $<$*maqte*N1 + (*pa*Q) + (md)$>$]₃

    personal pronoun stem + all + place + mood

Singular focus: pro.s$_p$ → pro.s$_{p-sg}$.

Plural focus: pro.s$_p$ → pro.s$_{p-1pl}$; pro.s$_{p-3n.sg}$.

The resulting phrase nuclei are shown in Table 54.

TABLE 54
PRONOUN FOCUS PHRASE NUCLEI

	Singular focus	Plural focus
1st	*ké máqte*N1	*ketáá máqte*N1
2nd	*é máqte*N1	
3rd	*wé máqte*N1	*yé máqte*N1

The formula for plural focus phrases must be rewritten for a possessive construction as follows:

$[<$ pro.s$_p>$ + $<$ *máqte*N1 + (*pa*Q) + (md)$>$]₃ + poss$_{pl}$ → $<$ pro.s$_p$ +poss$_{pl}>$

The resulting forms contrast with singular possessive pronoun forms in second and third persons.

    ení 'your (sing)'   *etí* 'your (pl) but primarily your (sing)'
    wení 'his'   *wetí* 'their but primarily his'

When the place suffix (*pa*Q) occurs it seems to add the implication of 'all, everywhere'. The following examples will illustrate the semantic significances of various focus phrase constructions.

(1) *we-maqtemma* 'they all but primarily he'

    $[<$ *we*V2$>$ + $<$ *maqte*N1 + *ma*$>$]₃

    he + all + nom

(2) *we-máqtepaqa* 'they everywhere but primarily he'
$[< weV2> + < maqteN1 + paQ + ma>]_3$
 he + all + place + nom

(3) *ye-máqtemma* 'they all but primarily they' (a selected few)
$[< yeV2> + < máqteN1 + ma>]_3$
 they + all + nom

5.3.4. *Interrogative phrases*. Three interrogative phrases fall into the category of idiomatic phrase types, the constituent words being inseparable. Their structure follows.

$[< \text{pro}_{int} + ra> + oV2 + \{ma; \alpha_4 + \beta_1\}$
$[< \text{pro}_{int} + ra> + < umá + (md)>]_3$

 (1) *nora umá* 'how much, how many'
 (2) *náara umá* 'how, in what manner'
 (3) *nòra itaná* 'why' (third person subject)

nòra umábiyo 'How many are there?'
$[< nói + ra> + < umá + abiyo>]_3$
 what + for + do_{past} + abl inter

5.3.5. *Verb phrases* (VP). On the basis of separability, suffix potential, and stress group patterning all verb phrases are idiomatic phrases. However, on the basis of co-occurrence potential of constituent words and relative degree of productivity they may be divided into the idiom type and the inflectional type. The idiom type has a restricted co-occurrence potential of constituent words and a limited degree of productivity. The inflectional type is highly productive and the co-occurrence potential of constituent words is relatively unlimited within the range of class potential. There are three categories of the idiom type verb phrase: (1) delta phrases, (2) impersonal phrases, and (3) verbal idioms. The inflectional type falls into two categories: (1) adverbial phrases and (2) constructions with the verb 'to do'.

This rather rough categorization and classification merely provides the framework for a much more detailed study of verb phrases than is possible within the scope of this present grammar. The semantic significances of various verb phrase types have barely been touched and need further study. In the following sections the structural formulas for each phrase type are given along with sufficient examples to illustrate the range of categories which occur.

5.3.5.1. *Delta phrases* (VP$_\delta$). Typical of many New Guinea Highland languages Usarufa expresses states of being by verb phrases with either a body part term (δns$_2$) and a verb, or a noun and a verb with an object prefix (δvs). In both cases the person of the delta prefix agrees with the subject tagmeme of the clause or sentence in which it occurs. This tagmeme may be either overt or elliptical. The person-subject suffix of the verb is either third person agreeing with the noun of the phrase or it agrees in person with the delta prefix. The difference in the person-subject suffix agreement marks the two types of delta phrases. The structure of the two types is expressed in the following formulas. The numbered arrow heads indicate the type of agreement which occurs. The optional subject tagmeme is indicated by (S).[20]

$$\overset{\underset{\longrightarrow}{1}}{} \quad \overset{\underset{\longleftrightarrow}{1\ 2}}{} \qquad\qquad\qquad\qquad\qquad\qquad \overset{\underset{\longleftarrow}{2}}{}$$
(1) (S) |[< δns + (nom)> + (ns$_{\text{d-ad}}$) + < vb$_{\text{nu}}$ + (ts) + 3rd person + md>]$_3$

$$\overset{\underset{\longrightarrow}{1}}{} \quad \overset{\underset{\longrightarrow}{2}}{} \qquad\qquad\qquad\qquad \overset{\underset{\longleftarrow}{1}}{} \qquad\qquad \overset{\underset{\longleftarrow}{2}}{}$$
(S)[(< ns + nom>) + (ns$_{\text{d-ad}}$) + < δvb$_{\text{nu}}$ + (ts) + 3rd person + md>]$_3$

$$\overset{\underset{\longrightarrow}{1}}{} \quad \overset{\underset{\longleftrightarrow}{1}}{} \qquad\qquad\qquad\qquad\qquad\qquad\qquad \overset{\underset{\longleftarrow}{1}}{}$$
(2) (S) [< δns + (nom)> + (ns$_{\text{d-ad}}$) + < vb$_{\text{nu}}$ + (ts) + 3rd person + md>]$_3$

The difference in functional relationships marked by the two delta phrase types is that of a subject-action relationship between noun and verb in type one and an object-action relationship between the two in type two. The following examples illustrate each type.

Delta noun stems, third person-subject suffix (VP$_{\delta\text{-1ns}}$):

(1) *táa kéyaiye* 'I am hungry.' ('My hunger is dancing.')
    [< *ti-δáa*V1 > + < *ké*V + *ya*V2*b* + α-*i*V + *e*>]$_3$
    my-hunger + pres. con + dance + 3rd person + indic

(2) *táá kégaiye* 'I am afraid.' ('My ear is burning.')
    [< *ti-δáá*Q1 > + < *ké*V + *ka*V2a + α-*i*V + *e*>]$_3$
    my-ear + pres. con + burn + 3rd person + indic

(3) *tááqa kéitaiye* 'I believe.' ('My ear hears.')
    [< *ti-δáá*Q1 + *ma*> + < *ké*V + *íta*V1*b* + α-*i*V + *e*>]$_3$
    my-ear + nom + pres. con + hear + 3rd person + indic

(4) *táákaq wáiye* 'I remember.' ('It is at my ear.')
    [< *ti-δáá*Q1 + *raQ* + *ma*> + < *wa* + α-*i*V + *e*>]$_3$
    my-ear + at + nom + be + 3rd person + indic

(5) *tíbo kégaiye* 'I am tired.' (My shoulder is burning.')
    [< *ti-δbo*> + < *ké*V + *ka*V2a + α-*i*V + *e*>]$_3$
    my-shoulder + pres. con + burn + 3rd person + indic

(6) *tíqa kéiye* 'I am in pain.' ('My pain is doing.')
    [< *ti-δi*Q1 + *ma*> + < *ké*V + *o*V2*b* + α-*i*V + *e*>]$_3$
    my-pain + nom + pres. con + do + 3rd person + indic

(7) *títauqa pukiyé* 'My foot is asleep.' ('My foot is dead.')

---

[20] The nature of the optional descriptive-adverbial stem (ns$_{\text{d-ad}}$) in the formulas will be explained in Sec. 5.3.5.4 on adverbial phrases.

$[<\textit{ti-δitau}Q1 + \textit{ma}> + <\textit{puyó}N2Ra + \textit{ko} + α\textit{-i}V + e>]_3$
my-foot + nom + die + st + 3rd person + indic
(8) *títauqa áaga áaga kétiye* 'I am longing for someone.' ('My foot is gossiping.')

$[<\textit{ti-δitau}Q1 + \textit{ma}> + [\textit{aaga aaga}]_3 + <\textit{ké}V + \textit{te}V2a + α\textit{-i}V + e>]_3$
my-foot + nom + gossip + pres. con + say + 3rd person + indic
(9) *timaímmá kéyaiye* 'I am yawning.' ('My chin is dancing.')

$[<\textit{ti-δmaai}N2 + \textit{ma} + <\textit{ké}V + \textit{ya}V2b + α\textit{-i}V + e>]_3$
my-chin + nom + pres. con + dance + 3rd person + indic
(10) *tímùqa kéyaiye* 'I am full.' ('My stomach is dancing.')

$[<\textit{ti-δmû}Q1 + \textit{ma}> + <\textit{ké}V + \textit{ya}V2b + α\textit{-i}V + e>]_3$
my-stomach + nom + pres. con + dance + 3rd person + indic
(11) *tirummá kéitaiye* 'I believe.' ('My liver hears.')

$[<\textit{ti-δru}N2 + \textit{ma} + <\textit{ké}V + \textit{íta}V1b + α\textit{-i}V + e>]_3$
my-liver + nom + pres. con + hear + 3rd person + indic
(12) *tirummá kéiye* 'I am sad.' ('My liver is doing.')

$[<\textit{ti-δru}N2 + \textit{ma}> + <\textit{ke}V + \textit{o}V2b + α\textit{-i}V + e>]_3$
my-liver + nom + pres. con + do + 3rd person + indic
(13) *túgáíbáá kéiye* 'I am sleepy.' ('My sleepiness is doing.')

$[<\textit{ti-δúgáíbáá} + <\textit{ké}V + \textit{o}V2b + α\textit{-i}V + e>]_3$
my-sleepiness + pres. con + do + 3rd person + indic
(14) *tíyamma táiq-kéiye* 'I am angry.' ('My viscera are bad.')

$[<\textit{ti-δya}N1 + \textit{ma}> + <\textit{tái}Q1 + \textit{ma}> + <\textit{ké}V + \textit{o}V2b + α\textit{-i}V + e>]_3$
my-viscera + nom + spoiled + nom + pres. con + 3rd person + indic
(15) *tíyamma tágaguraiye* 'I trust, I am enlightened.' ('My viscera shine.')

$[<\textit{ti-δya}N1 + \textit{ma}> + <\textit{tága}V3 + \textit{ko} + \textit{ra} + α\textit{i}V + e>]_3$
my-viscera + nom + shine + st + aorist + 3rd person + indic

Delta verb stem, third person-subject suffix ($VP_{δ\text{-}lvs}$):
$$δvb_{nu} \rightarrow \{δvb_{nu}; vb + δka\}$$

(1) *ketikaiye* 'I like it.' ('It is for me.')
$<\textit{ké}V + \textit{ti-δka} + α\textit{-i}V + e>$
pres. con + me-for + 3rd person + indic
(2) *karímá kétikaiye* 'I am sick.' ('Sickness is for me.')
$[<\textit{karí}V2 + \textit{ma}> + <\textit{ké}V + \textit{ti-δka} + α\textit{-i}V + e>]_3$
sickness + nom + pres. con + me-for + 3rd person + indic
(3) *karímá étikaiye* 'I am getting well.' ('Sickness is darkening for me.')
$[<\textit{karí}V2 + \textit{ma}> + <\textit{ena}N2R + \textit{ti-δ-ka} + α\textit{-i}V + e>]_3$
sickness + nom + darken + me-for + 3rd person + indic
(4) *matíkaraiye* 'I was born.' ('She put for me.')
$<\textit{mara} + \textit{ti-δka} + \textit{ra} + α\textit{-i}V + e>$
Put + me-for + aorist + 3rd person + indic

(5) *yabááqnámá tikákaiye* 'I fell down.' ('The earth hit me.')
[< *yabááqná*V1 + *ma*> + < *ti-δikamo*N1Rb + *ra* + α-*i*V + *e*>]₃
earth + nom + me-hit + past + 3rd person + indic

(6) *taíyamma kétikaiye* 'I am sick.' ('Sickness is for me.')
[< *taíya*N1 + *ma*> + < *ké*V + *ti-δka* + α-*i*V + *e*>]₃
sickness + nom + pres. con + me-for + 3rd person + indic

Delta noun stem—delta prefix and person-subject suffix agree (VP$_{δ\text{-}2}$):

(1) *taáma kémaraune* 'I am breathing'. ('I am placing my breath.')
[< *ti-δaá*V1 + *ma*> + < *ké*V + *mara* N2Ra + α-*u*N + *e*>]₃
my-breath + nom + pres. con + put + I + indic

(2) *táákaq kémaraune* 'I am going to remember it.' ('I am placing it at my ear.')
[< *ti-δáá*Q1 + *ra*Q + *ma*> + < *ké*V + *maráN*2Ra + α-*u*N + *e*>]₃
my-ear + at + nom + pres. con + put + I + indic

(3) *timuqá kémaraune* 'I am pleased.' ('I have placed my pleasure.')
[< *ti-δmu*Q2 + *ma*> + < *ké*V + *maráN*2Ra + α-*u*N + *e*>]₃
my-pleasure + nom + pres. con + put + I + indic

(4) *tírûqa kéuyune* 'I am hurrying.' ('I have caused my thigh to go up.')
[< *ti-δrû*Q1 + *ma*> + < *ké*V + *uyo*Q2Ra + α-*u*N + *e*>]₃
my-thigh + nom + pres. con + go-up + I + indic

(5) *túwáayakaq kémaraune* 'I am learning it' ('I am placing it at my forehead.')
[< *ti-δuwááyá*N1 + *ra*Q + *ma*> + < *ké*V + *maráN*2Ra + α-*u*N + *e*>]₃
my-forehead + at + nom + pres. con + put + I + indic

(6) *túyánámmá kémaraune* 'I am thinking.' ('I am placing my thoughts.')
[< *ti-δúyáná*N2 + *ma*> + < *ké*V + *maráN*2Ra + α-*u*N + *e*>]₃
my-thoughts + nom + pres. con + put + I + indic

(7) *tíyapi kéitaune* 'I believe.' ('I have heard in my intestines.')
[< *ti-δya*Q1 + *pi* + < *ké*V + *íta*V1b + α-*u*N + *e*>]₃
my-intestines + in + pres. con + hear + I + indic

5.3.5.2. *Impersonal phrases* (VP$_{impl}$). The impersonal phrase is similar to the delta phrase type one in that the person-subject suffix is always third person agreeing with the noun of the phrase and the relationship between noun and verb is that of subject-action. However, delta noun stems do not occur and there is a significant difference in external distribution in that an overt subject tagmeme never occurs in the same clause as an impersonal phrase. The structural formula and illustrative examples follow:

[< ns + nom> + (ns$_{d.ad}$) + < vb$_{nu}$ + 3rd per + md>]₃

(1) *aammá kégaiye* 'The way is clear.' ('The path is burning.')
[< *aa*N2 + *ma*> + < *ké*V + *ka*V2b + α-*i*V + *e*>]₃
path + nom + pres. con + burn + 3rd person + indic

(2) *aaq ékiye* 'It is getting dark.' ('Weather is darkening.')
   [$<aa$Q2 $+ ma> + <ena$N2R $+ ko + \alpha\text{-}i$V $+ e>$]$_3$
   weather $+$ nom $+$ darken $+$ st $+$ 3rd person $+$ indic
(3) *aaqá kégaiye* 'It is a sunny day.' ('Weather is burning.')
   [$<aa$Q2 $+ ma> + <ké$V $+ ka$V2b $+ \alpha\text{-}i$V $+ e>$]$_3$
   weather $+$ nom $+$ pres. con $+$ burn $+$ 3rd person $+$ indic
(4) *aaqá kéiye* 'It is raining.' ('Weather is coming.')
   [$<aa$Q2 $+ ma> + <ké$V $+ ye$V2a $+ \alpha\text{-}i$V $+ e>$]$_3$
   weather $+$ nom $+$ pres. con $+$ come $+$ 3rd person $+$ indic
(5) *aaqá ikákiye* 'It has stopped raining.' ('Weather has been hit.')
   [$<aa$Q2 $+ ma> + <\delta ikamo$N1Rb $+ ko + \alpha\text{-}i$V $+ e>$]$_3$
   weather $+$ nom $+$ it-hit $+$ st $+$ 3rd person $+$ indic

5.3.5.3. *Verbal idioms* (VP$_{id}$). There are four types of verbal idioms as follows:
(1) Noun with nominal suffix plus verb: [$<$ns $+$ nom$> +$ vb]$_3$
(2) Noun stem plus verb: [$<$ns$> +$ vb]$_3$
(3) Reduplicated noun plus verb: [{[ns^r]$_3$; ns$_r$} $+$ vb]$_3$
(4) Verb stem with nominal suffix plus verb: [$<$vs $+$ nom$> +$ vb]$_3$

In each of the above constructions only a few verbs are potential fillers of the verb slot. The following examples give the more common ones which account for about two-thirds of the verbal idioms.

(1) *Noun with nominal suffix plus verb*

$x + o$V2b 'to do'

komá 'a pout' $+ o$V2b $=$ 'to be angry, to pout'
wááqa 'noise' $+ o$V2b $=$ 'to shout, to bark,' etc.
maabumá 'young man' $+ o$V2b $=$ 'to initiate a boy'
agayemá 'shame' $+ o$V2b $=$ 'to be bashful'

$x + te$V2b 'to say'

umoimá 'a cough' $+ te$V2b $=$ 'to cough'
áúqa 'inside' $+ te$V2b $=$ 'to hum'
awimá 'urine' $+ te$V2b $=$ 'to urinate'

$x + yorá$N2Rb 'to move'

anumá 'mountain' $+ yorá$N2Rb $=$ 'to move a stubborn child'
kámanama 'a rough leaf' $+ yorá$N2Rb $=$ 'to sand'

$x + mayá$Q2Ra 'to get, to take'

meyámmá 'purchase' $+ mayá$Q2Ra $=$ 'to buy'
moyámmá 'theft' $+ mayá$Q2Ra $=$ 'to steal'

$x + yo$V2a 'to be'

karagíqá 'sorrow' $+ ye$V2a $=$ 'to bemoan'

x + *pera*N1Rb 'to pour over'
nommá 'water' + *pera*N1Rb = 'to bathe'
ayammá 'color' + *pera*N1Rb = 'to paint'
naammá 'house' + *pera*N1Rb = 'to attend school'

$x + y$

ibiqá 'a cry' + *yara*N2b 'to weep' = 'to cry'
akuqá 'odor' + *íta*V1b 'to hear' = 'to smell'

(2) *Noun stem plus verb*

x + *o*V2B 'to do'

ákubitaa 'fragrance' + *o*V2b = 'to sniff, smell'
wíráá 'a laugh, smile' + *o*V2b = 'to laugh, be happy'
abáá 'lost' + *o*V2b = 'to search'
aayoq 'a gaze' + *o*V2b = 'to admire'

x + *ka*V2a 'to burn'

ópo 'dullness' + *ka*V2a = 'to fade'
áwáarara 'brilliance' + *ka*V2a = 'to shine'

x + *ya*V2b 'to dance' x + *wo*V2b 'to go'

áábê 'play' + *ya*V2b = 'to play'
imaamú 'rage' + *ya*V2b + 'to be beside oneself with anger'
arabé 'flight' + *wo*V2b = 'to fly'

(3) *Reduplicated noun plus verb*

ns$_r$ + *o*V2b 'to do'

aqteqte + *o*V2b = 'to shiver'
tete + *o*V2b = 'to wash, to scrub, to cut wood finely'
apibi + *o*V2b = 'to shake something'

ns$_r$ + *te*V2b 'to say'

této + *te*V2b = 'to be crackly dry'
kíki + *te*V2b = 'to be firmly planted'
títi + *te*V2b = 'to fit tightly together'
míqmiq + *te*Vb = 'to suck'
abububu + *te*V2b = 'to stutter'
ameme + *te*V2b = 'to mimic'

ns^r + *o*V2b 'to do'

amóqna moqna 'a kiss' + *o*V2b = 'to kiss'
kamu gamáá 'a burp' + *o*V2b = 'to burp'
turi táári 'messy' + *o*V2b = 'to be messy'
nagí naagi 'crazy' + *o*V2b = 'to be crazy'

$_{ns}$r + *te*V2b 'to say'

níkiq nikiq 'hiccough' + *te*V2b = 'to have the hiccoughs'

áagaa ágaa 'gossip' + *te*V2b = 'an itching foot indicating someone is thinking of you'
waku waku + *te*V2b = 'to hurry someone'

(4) *Verb stem with nominal suffix plus verb*
itama ónaao 'Ask him!'
$[<\textit{íta}V1b + \textit{ma}> + <a\text{-}\textit{δóna}V3 + \gamma\text{-}\textit{ø}V + o_2>]_3$
hear, listen + nom + him + see + 2nd person + imper

náma ónaao 'Taste it!'
$[<\textit{na}V2b + \textit{ma}> + <a\textit{ónaao}>]_3$
eat + nom + see

máqma ónaao 'Try it!'
$[<\textit{mayá}Q2Rb + \textit{ma}> + <a\textit{ónaao}>]_3$
take + nom + see

yoqma ónaao 'Feel it!'[21]

yaqma ónaao 'Test it!'[22]

timá miyo 'Tell him!'
$[<\textit{te}V2b + \textit{ma}> + <a\text{-}\textit{δme} + \delta\text{-}\textit{ø}V + o_2>]_3$
say + nom + him + give + 2nd person + imper

5.3.5.4. *Adverbial phrases* (VP_{ad}). A subclass of descriptive stems
($ns_{d.ad}$) occur immediately preceding a phrase final verb to indicate the
manner in which the action of the verb is performed. These include:

*arupú*V1	'straight'
*arútâma*V1	'well, straight, strong'
*iráqó*N1	'good'
*kabé kabé*V2	'quickly'
*kanaará*Q2	'well, right'
⎰ *mirá*N2 ⎱ ⎱ *miráuma*V ⎰	'thus'
*netuqyáá*N2	'plenty'
*ôri*Q1	'very'
*tái*Q1	'bad, spoiled'

Adverbial phrases may occur imbedded in other phrase types such as in
the fifth example of the following. In almost all constructions it is possible to
rewrite verb as verb or adverbial phrase—

$$vb \rightarrow \{vb; VP_{ad}\}$$

—whereas other verb phrase types have some restrictions on their external
distribution which require more specific rewrite rules.

[21] The nature of the optional descriptive-adverbial stem ($ns_{d\text{-}ad}$) in the formulas
will be explained in Sec. 5.3.5.4 on adverbial phrases.
[22] It is not clear what the meaning of the verb stem is in this case.

The examples which follow illustrate various of the adverbial descriptive stems.

(1) *ôri kénaiye* 'He eats very much.'
$[oriQ1 + <keV + naV2b + \alpha\text{-}iV + e>]_3$
very + pres. con + eat + 3rd person + indic

(2) *arútâma tiyo* 'Say it clearly!'
$[arutamaV1 + <teV2b + \gamma\text{-}\emptyset V + o>]_3$
straight + say + 2nd person + imper

(3) *miráum agayaao* 'Cook like this!'
$[miraumaV1 + <agayaQ2Ra + \gamma\text{-}\emptyset V + o>]_3$
thus + cook + 2nd person + imper

(4) *kabé kabé iyo* 'Come quickly!'
$[[kabe\ kabeV2]_3 + <yeV2a + \gamma\text{-}\emptyset V + o>]_3$
quickly + come + 2nd person + imper

(5) *táá ôri kégaiye* 'I am very afraid.'
$[<ti\text{-}\delta\acute{a}\acute{a}Q1> + [<ôri> + <keV + kaV2a + \alpha\text{-}iV + e>]_3]_3$
my-ear + very + pres. con + 3rd person + indic

5.3.5.5. Constructions with the verb 'to do' (VP$_{do}$). The verb 'to do', oV2b, is an auxiliary verb which occurs only in verbal phrases and equational clauses. In many of its functions it is like the English verb 'to be'. As a verbal auxiliary it may be used to form tense, voice, or mood contrasts instead of the usual suffixation. In this case the appropriate suffixes occur on the verb 'to do' and the main verb precedes it without suffixation. In equational clauses and descriptive or state of being phrases it functions as a copula.

Five categories of phrases with this verb will be considered.

(1) State of being phrases: ns$_d$ + oV2b$_{vb}$

(2) Desiderative phrases: $[<\beta\text{-}vb_{nu} + no + \beta> (\text{-}\beta) + o\text{V2b}_{vb\text{-}nu} + \alpha_1 + md>]$

(3) Abilitative phrases: $[<\beta\text{-}vb_{nu} + no + \beta> (\text{-}\beta) + <o\text{V2b}_{vb\text{-}nu} + \alpha_2 + abl>]_3$

(4) Continued action phrases: $[<vs + iQ>^n + o\text{V2b}_{vb}]_3$

(5) Repeated action phrases: $[vs^r + o\text{V2b}_{vb}]_3$

(1) *State of being phrases.* A descriptive stem plus the verb oV2b 'to do', expresses attribution: ns$_d$ + oV2b 'to do'.

> *pé* 'skinny' + oV2b = 'to be emaciated'
> *kó* 'pout' + oV2b = 'to be displeased'
> *kato* 'obedient' + oV2b = 'to be obedient'
> *kaúbi* 'disobedient' + oV2b = 'to be disobedient'
> *oyáá* 'light' + oV2b = 'to be easy, light'
> *kokó* 'warm' + oV2b = 'to be warm, dry'
> *táiq* 'bad + oV2b = 'to be big'

anó 'big' + *o*V2b = 'to be big'
pááq 'found' + *o*V2b = 'to be found'

(2) *Desiderative phrases*. Desire may be expressed by use of the future subjunctive with regular inflectional suffixation. However, an alternative and more common desiderative construction is the use of the beta verb nucleus with the future tense suffix in the form appropriate to the person-subject plus the verb 'to do' in any tense but with alpha-one person suffixes and moods. The following compares the two types of constructions.

nanaare (future subjunctive *na*V2b + *no* + *β-ø*Q + *e*)
nanaa onune (desiderative phrase)
$[<na$V2b + *no* + *β-ø*Q − *β-ø*Q + $<$ *o*V2b + *no* + *a-u*N + $e>]_3$
'I want to eat'.

(3) *Abilitative phrases*. A phrase construction similar to that of the desiderative phrase can be used to express capability of the subject to perform an action. The same subjunctive stem construction is used but abilitative moods are used with the verb 'to do'.

nané íne 'He is able to eat'.
$[<na$V2b + *no* + *β-na* − *β-na* + $<o$ + *i*N + $e>]_3$
to eat + fut + 3rd person + 3rd person + do + 3rd person + abl

(4) *Continued action phrases*. An action which is continued over a period of time may be expressed by use of the verb stem and the morpheme *i*Q plus any form of the verb 'to do' which will express the appropriate person, tense, voice, and mood distinctions.

(1) *náiq náiq onúne* 'I am going to eat and eat.'
$[<na$V2b + *i*Q$>^r$ + $<o$V2b + *no* + *α-u*N + $e>]_3$
to eat + *i*Q + do + fut + 1st person + indic

(2) *náiq-náiq-náiq uráiye* 'He ate and ate and ate.'
$[<na$V2b + *i*Q$>^{r-3}$ + $<o$V2b + *ra* + *α-i*V + $e>]_3$
eat + *i*Q + do + aorist + 3rd person + indic

(5 *Repeated action phrases*. An action which is made up of the repetition of some one action may be expressed by the reduplication of the verb stem without affixation plus the verb 'to do'.

úbó-ubo kéiye 'He is digging'.
$[ubo$N2Rb^r + $<ké$V + *o*V2b + *α-i*V + $e>]$
to plant + pres. con + do + 3rd person + indic

6. TAGMEME INVENTORY

A tagmeme will here be defined as that correlation of functional slot and manifesting class by which lexical units combine in syntactic constructions. This is a more restricted definition of the tagmeme than that used by leading tagmemicists (see Elson and Pickett, 1962:3, 57; Longacre, 1964:15; Pike, 1967: chap. xi). It yields tagmemes which are much like Longacre's clause level tagmemes and avoids the use of the term as a level oriented concept.

The tagmemes of Usarufa are either *nuclear* or *peripheral* depending upon whether or not they are restricted in occurrence or manifesting class by clause or sentence construction types. The following sections will give an inventory of the tagmemes which occur indicating manifesting classes and grammatical function.

6.1. *Nuclear Tagmemes*

Nuclear tagmemes are those tagmemes which are either restricted in their potential for occurrence to specific clause or sentence types or whose manifesting class is restricted by the type of clause or sentence in which they occur. These are the tagmemes which are significant in determining differences in clause and sentence construction types. There are four such tagmemes in Usarufa, *subject, object, complement,* and *predicate*.

Subject, object, and complement tagmemes are manifested by substantives, pronouns, or locatives which may be optionally expanded to higher level units as follows: {S; O; C} : {sb; loc; pro}

Optional rewrite rules:

> sb → {sb; SbP; Cl_{sb}}
>   SbP → {NP; NbP; TemP}
> Cl_{sb} → $(X)^n$ + P:vb + nf (where X^n is any tagmeme or tagmeme
>   sequence)
> loc → {loc; LocP; Cl_{loc}}
> Cl_{loc} → $(X)^n$ + P:vb + loc
> pro → {pro; ProP}

Obligatory rewrite rules for word units as they manifest either subject, object, or complement tagmemes will be given under the section which deals with each tagmeme. These obligatory rules apply both to the original statement of manifestation potential and to the head words of each of the complex units resulting from the above optional rewrite rules.

6.1.1. *Subject tagmeme* (S). The grammatical functions or semantic significances of the Usarufa subject tagmeme include both performer of an action and topic of an equation. The manifesting classes of the subject tagmeme are substantives, locatives, and pronouns. Restrictions on lexical form of each class may be stated in terms of the rewriting of the lexical formulas already given. In summary these rewrite rules specify the following: A subject tagmeme may be manifested by a substantive, a locative, or a pronoun. Only nonobject pronouns manifest subject tagmemes. Three subject allotagmas occur—equational subject, transitive subject, and intransitive subject. The equational subject is manifested by substantives, locatives, or nonobject pronouns while transitive and intransitive subjects are manifested only by substantives and pronouns. Relative-possessive suffixes do not occur with substantives or pronouns manifesting subject tagmemes. Nonobject pronouns manifesting transitive or intransitive subject tagmemes may be pronoun stems or stems plus mood suffix. Substantives manifesting transitive or intransitive subjects are noun stems with either conjunctive or mood suffixes and optional stative and number suffixes as may be grammatically possible in accordance with co-occurrence restrictions on stems and suffixes. Personal names only optionally require a mood or conjunctive suffix and temporal stems do not manifest transitive subjects.

The following is the formal statement of subject manifestation potential.

$$S: \{sb; loc; pro\}$$
$$pro \rightarrow pro_{n.obj}$$
$$S \rightarrow \{S_{eq}; S_{tr}; S_{intr}\}$$
$$\{S_{eq}; S_{tr}; S_{intr}\} : \{sb; loc; pro_{n.obj}\} \rightarrow$$

(1) $S_{eq}: \{sb; loc; pro_{n.obj}\}$

$$pro_{n.obj} \rightarrow pro.s_{n.obj} + (\left\{ \begin{matrix} poss_{ab} \\ accom \end{matrix} \right\}) + (ref) + (md)$$

$$sb \rightarrow ns + (\left\{ \begin{matrix} \{loc; poss_{ab}; inst\} \\ (st) + (nb) + (\{ref; accom\}) \end{matrix} \right\}) + (md)$$

(2) $S_{tr; intr}: sb; pro_{n.obj}$

$$pro_{n.obj} \rightarrow pro.s_{n.obj} + (md)$$
$$sb \rightarrow ns + (st) + (nb) + (md)$$
$$ns \rightarrow sb_q; sb_{nq}$$
$$sb_q; sb_{nq}\} + (st) + (nb) + (md) \rightarrow$$

    (1) $sb_q + (st) + (nb) + (md)$

    (2) $sb_{nq} + (st) + (md)$

      $sb_{nq} \rightarrow ns_{nb}; ns_{pn}$

$$\{ns_{nb}; ns_{pn}\} + (st) + (md) \rightarrow$$

    (1) $ns_{nb} + (st) + (md)$

    (2) $ns_{pn} + (st) + (md)$

$$S_{tr}: sb_q + (st) + (nb) + (md)$$
$$sb_q \rightarrow \{ns_c; ns_d\}$$
$$S_{intr}: sb_q + (st) + (nb) + (md)$$
$$sb_q \rightarrow \{ns_c; ns_d; ns_t\}$$

6.1.2. *Complement tagmeme* (C). The complement tagmeme occurs only in equational clauses and includes the functional categories of comment, citation, and complementation. Complement tagmemes may be manifested by substantives, locatives, and pronouns. The manifesting class must occur with a nominal mood suffix and relative-possessive suffixes do not occur with stems manifesting the complement tagmeme.

$$C: \{sb; loc; pro\}$$

$$pro \rightarrow pro.s + (\{accom; poss_{ab}\}) + (ref) + md_{nom}$$

$$sb \rightarrow ns + (\begin{Bmatrix} \{loc; poss_{ab}; inst\} \\ (st) + (nb) + (\{ref; accom\}) \end{Bmatrix}) + md_{nom}$$

$$loc \rightarrow \begin{Bmatrix} \{ns_c; vb\} + loc \\ loc.s \end{Bmatrix} + (\text{‘from’}) + (nb) + (\begin{Bmatrix} ref \\ accom \end{Bmatrix}) + md_{nom}$$

6.1.3. *Object tagmeme* (O). The object tagmeme functions as the goal of the action of a transitive verb. Its distribution is limited to transitive clauses and its occurrence is optional. Substantives, locatives, and pronouns may manifest object tagmemes. Instrument, referent, passive accompaniment, and relative-possessive suffixes do not occur with words manifesting the object tagmeme.

$$O: \{sb; loc; pro\}$$

$$pro \rightarrow pro.s_{obj} + (\{accom_{act}; poss_{ab}\}) + md$$

$$sb \rightarrow ns + (\begin{Bmatrix} \{loc; poss_{ab}\} \\ (st) + (nb) + accom_{act}) \end{Bmatrix}) + md$$

6.1.4. *Predicate tagmeme* (P). The predicate tagmeme is the central or nuclear tagmeme of all syntactic constructions. Differences of clause and sentence type are marked by changes in the manifesting class of the predicate tagmeme. The predicate tagmeme is the only obligatory tagmeme which occurs in all clause types and it is optional only in an equational clause which has a complement tagmeme. The predicate tagmeme includes functions of other tagmemes such as subject, object, referent, complement, and time and functions which are unique to it such as expression of action or occurrence and manner of action.

The predicate tagmeme of an equational clause may be manifested by the verbs *waV* or *maV* inanimate and animate verbs ‘to be’, and *oV2b* ‘to do’; by stative verbs; descriptive or state of being verb phrases; and by any substantive, locative, or pronoun construction with a verbal mood suffix. Transitive and intransitive predicate tagmemes are manifested by verbs and verb phrases. Greater detail as to the nature of these predicate slot fillers will be given in the next two sections which deal with clause and sentence structure.

The predicate tagmemes of each of the three major clause types are manifested as follows:

$$P_{eq}: \{vb; VP; sb; loc; pro\}$$

$$vb \rightarrow \{\{waV; maV\}; oV2b; vb_{st}\}$$

$$\{sb; loc; pro\} \rightarrow \{sb; loc; pro\} + md_{vb}$$

P_{tr}: {vb_{tr}; VP_{tr}}
P_{intr}: {vb_{intr}; VP_{intr}}

6.2. *Peripheral Tagmemes*

Those tagmemes which may occur without change in any clause type are classed as peripheral tagmemes. These include: location, time, accompaniment, referent-reason, instrument, and topic. The manifesting classes of these tagmemes are generally much more restricted than those of the nuclear tagmemes.

6.2.1. *Location tagmeme* (L). The location tagmeme indicates spatially the location or direction of an event, action, place, person, or thing. Locatives are the only manifestation of the location tagmeme on the word level with locative phrases and clauses being higher level manifestations.

The formal statement of the location tagmeme manifestations is: L:loc.

Optional rewrite rules:

loc → {loc; LocP; Cl_{loc}}

Cl_{loc} $(X)^n$ + P:vb + loc (where X^n is any appropriate tagmeme or tagmeme sequence)

Obligatory rewrite rules:

$$loc \rightarrow \begin{Bmatrix} \{ns_c; vb\} + loc \\ loc.s \end{Bmatrix} + (\text{'from'}) + (nb) + (md)$$

loc.s→ {$loc.s_p$; $loc.s_d$}

6.2.2. *Time* (T). The time tagmeme indicates either a unit of time or the location in time of some event or action. Temporals or locatives of time may occur as manifestations of time tagmemes with temporal phrases and clauses being higher level manifestations.

Time manifestations: T:{loc;t}

Optional rewrite rules:

t→ {t; TemP; Cl_{tem}}

Cl_{tem} → $(X)^n$ + P:vb + α_2 + ({*tao*Q2; *kanaa*V2})

Obligatory rewrite rules: loc→ $loc.s_t$ + ('from') + (nb) + (md)

6.2.3. *Accompaniment* (Acc). The accompaniment tagmeme indicates participation in an action by someone or thing other than the subject or object. It is manifested by either a substantive or pronoun with an accompaniment suffix: Acc: {sb; pro}

Optional rewrite rules:

sb → {sb; NP; NbP}

pro → {pro; ProP}

Obligatory rewrite rules:

sb → ns + (st) + (nb) + accom + (md)

ns → {ns_c; ns_d; ns_{nb}; ns_{pn}}

pro → pro.s + accom + (md)

6.2.4. *Referent-reason* (R). The referent-reason tagmeme functions as indirect object, benefactive, and reason for an action. Any word class plus the referent suffix may manifest this tagmeme and only those co-occurrence restrictions which govern the occurrence of the referent suffix are operative. Phrase units and clauses may manifest the referent-reason tagmeme as specified by the optional rewrite rules in the following statement of referent-reason manifestations: R: {sb; loc; pro; vb}

Optional rewrite rules:

$$sb \rightarrow \{sb; SbP\}$$
$$loc \rightarrow \{loc; LocP\}$$
$$vb \rightarrow \{vb; VP; Cl_{ref}\}$$
$$Cl_{ref} \rightarrow (X)^n + P{:}vb + ref$$
$$pro \rightarrow \{pro; ProP\}$$

Obligatory rewrite rules:

$$sb \rightarrow ns + (st) + (nb) + ref + (md)$$
$$loc \rightarrow \{loc.s; \{ns_c; vb\} + loc\} + (\text{'from'}) + ref + (md)$$
$$pro \rightarrow pro.s + (\{inst; accom; poss_{ab}\}) + ref (md)$$
$$vb \rightarrow vb_{nu} + (ts) + per + ref + (md)$$

6.2.5. *Instrument tagmeme* (I). The instrument tagmeme expresses the inamimate means by which an action is accomplished. It is manifested by an inanimate noun or pronoun occurring with the instrument suffix or by a noun or pronoun phrase whose head word occurs with the instrument suffix. The class of noun stems which may occur is limited to inaminate common nouns. Pronoun stems are limited to inanimate or neutral locative pronoun stems and the interrogative stem, *noi*N1 'what': I:{n; NP; pro; ProP}

$$n \rightarrow ns_{c.inani} + inst + (md)$$

$$pro \rightarrow \left\{ \begin{array}{l} pro.s_{loc.\ inani;\ neut} \\ pro.s_{inter\text{-}noiN1} \end{array} \right\} + inst + (md)$$

6.2.6. *Topic tagmeme* (Tp). The topic tagmeme might be better treated as a hyper-tagmeme. It differs from other tagmemes in that its manifesting class is a tagmeme rather than a lexical unit. Any nonpredicate tagmeme may occur as manifesting the topic tagmeme in which case it is brought into the focus of attention as being the topic of a given clause, sentence, paragraph, or discourse. The topic tagmeme occurs either clause initially or finally and is set apart from the rest of the clause by features of pause and intonation.

The manifesting class of the topic tagmeme may be expressed as follows:

$$Tp: X_{n.P}$$
$$X_{n\text{-}P} \rightarrow \{S; I; Acc; O; C; L; T; R\}$$

The following excerpt from an Usarufa folk tale will illustrate the use of the topic tagmeme. In the first sentence the topic tagmeme is manifested by the subject tagmeme which in turn is manifested by a descriptive phrase. In the second sentence the topic tagmeme is manifested by the object tagmeme which is manifested by a descriptive phrase.

T:S:NP   +   S:NP   +   P:VP   +   O:n   +   P:vb
[*móra-anon-uqmagoma*], *anón uqmagoma yaa-máina abimma atakáiye*
one-big-old-man   big   old-man   tree-be-he   insect   he-breaks

S:pro + P:vb + O:d + P:vb + T:O:NP
wemá atáqma aúgemma naráiye, [*min-ábímmá*]
he breaks new he-ate that-insect

Free translation: An old man who lived in the forest was killing insects and eating them raw.

7. CLAUSE STRUCTURE

Clause types may be defined by use of three different types of evidence. Differences in nuclear tagmeme potential and in verb stem class divide clauses into *transitive, intransitive,* and *equational;* differences in external distribution within the sentence and differences in verbal suffix requirements divide them into *final* and *nonfinal;* and differences in external distribution within the clause and/or paragraph and differences in verbal suffix requirements divide them into *subjunctive* and *independent.*

7.1. *General Ordering of Tagmemes*

Since the ordering of tagmemes and the occurrence of peripheral tagmemes are not dependent upon clause type a general statement can be made which will apply to all types.

Nonpredicate tagmemes except the topic tagmeme are not restricted in their order with reference to one another. However, they always occur before the predicate tagmeme. The topic tagmeme occurs either clause initially or clause finally and the predicate tagmeme occurs clause finally except when followed by a topic tagmeme.

There are not usually more than three nonpredicate tagmemes in any one clause. Where multiple tagmeme distinctions are desired for any one action, multiple clause sentences are used rather than using a sequence on several tagmemes in one clause. The following formula reflects the most common ordering of tagmemes with reference to one another with the restriction that there may be no more than three nonpredicate tagmemes.

Cl = (Tp) + (T) + (I) + (L) + (S) + (Acc) + ({O; C}) + (R) + P

Since only the nuclear tagmemes differ in their co-occurrence potential for different clause types the foregoing formula may be considered in two parts:

(1) $Cl_{nu} = (S) + (\{O; C\}) + P$

(2) $Cl_{per} = (Tp) + (T) + (L) + Acc) + (R)$

The clause periphery (Cl_{per}) need not be considered further but the clause nucleus (Cl_{nu}) will have to be restated in terms of clause type. The predicate tagmeme will then have to be examined with reference to further subclassification.

7.2. *Transitive versus Intransitive versus Equational*

The clause nucleus as presented in the preceding section must now be restated in terms of tagmeme potential and manifesting class of the predicate tagmeme. The transitive clause nucleus includes optional subject and object tagmemes and the transitive manifestation of the predicate tagmeme; the intransitive clause nucleus includes only an optional subject tagmeme and the intransitive manifestation of the predicate tagmeme; and the equational clause nucleus includes an optional subject tagmeme and either a complement tagmeme and an optional predicate tagmeme with equational manifestation or simply the equational manifestation of the predicate tagmeme. This may be stated formally as follows:

$$Cl_{nu} = (S) + (\{O; C\}) + P$$
$$Cl_{nu} \rightarrow \{Cl_{nu.tr}; Cl_{nu.intr}; Cl_{nu\text{-}eq}\}$$
$$P \rightarrow \{P_{tr}; P_{intr}; P_{eq}\}$$
$$\{Cl_{nu.tr}; Cl_{nu.intr}; Cl_{nu.eq}\} = (S) + (\{O;C\}) + \{P_{tr}; P_{intr}; P_{eq}\} \rightarrow$$
$$(1)\ Cl_{nu.tr} = (S) + (O) + P_{tr}$$
$$(2)\ Cl_{nu.intr} = (S) + P_{intr}$$
$$(3)\ Cl_{nu.eq} = (S) + \{C + (P_{eq}); P_{eq}\}$$

7.3. *Final versus Nonfinal and Subjunctive versus Dependent*

The interaction of the final-nonfinal and subjunctive-independent oppositions is such that they are best treated together. The differences between the four clause types represented by the intersecting of these components are marked by the form of the predicate tagmeme manifestation and by external distribution.

Final clauses occur sentence finally and the manifestation of the predicate tagmeme must occur with a mood suffix. Nonfinal clauses occur either nonfinally in the sentence or as manifestations of some nonpredicate tagmeme and hence nonfinally within a clause.

Subjunctive final clauses are marked by the predicate manifestation occurring with the beta-person series. Semantically the action of the subjunctive final clause is contingent upon some other action not stated in the context. Distributional restrictions within the paragraph have not been fully studied but there seems to be evidence that these will differ from those of the independent final clause.

$$\text{S.FCl} = \text{P:vb} + \beta + \text{md}$$

Independent final clauses are marked by the predicate manifestation occurring with the alpha-person series.

$$\text{I.FCl} = \text{P:vb} + \alpha + \text{md}$$

Subjunctive nonfinal clauses are those clauses which occur as manifestations of a nonpredicate tagmeme. These have been indicated in the preceding chapter as optional rewrites of the appropriate word level manifestations. They are marked by the occurrence of a noun or nominal suffix with the verb manifestation of their predicate tagmemes, as appropriate for the tagmeme which they are manifesting.

$$\text{S.NFCl} = \text{P:vb} + \text{per} + \text{tg}^{23}$$

Independent nonfinal clauses occur in multiple clause sentences and are marked by the occurrence of relational indicating suffixes or suffix configurations as will be specified in Section 8.

$$\text{I.FCl} = \text{P:vb} + \text{per} + \text{rel}$$

A transitive or intransitive clause may be either independent final or nonfinal or subjunctive final or nonfinal. However, only those equational clauses which have a predicate tagmeme and whose predicate tagmeme is manifested by a verb or verb phrase have the potential for final versus nonfinal and subjunctive versus independent distinctions. Equational clauses which do not have a predicate tagmeme or whose predicate tagmeme is manifested by a nominal word or phrase may not occur nonfinally, and there is no subjunctive versus independent distinction.

7.4. *Clause Types Illustrated by Selective Examples*

Table 55 summarizes the intersecting of these various clause types as distinguished by the distinctive manifestations of their predicate tagmemes.

TABLE 55
CLAUSE DEFINITION

	Transitive P:vb_{tr}	Intransitive P:vb_{intr}	Equational P:vb_{eq}
Final			
Subjunctive	$\text{vb}_{tr} + \beta + \text{md}$	$\text{vb}_{intr} + \beta + \text{md}$	$\text{vb}_{eq} + \beta + \text{md}$
Independent	$\text{vb}_{tr} + \alpha + \text{md}$	$\text{vb}_{intr} + \alpha + \text{md}$	$\text{vb}_{eq} + \alpha + \text{md}$
Nonfinal			
Subjunctive	$\text{vb}_{tr} + \text{per} + \text{tg}$	$\text{vb}_{intr} + \text{per} + \text{tg}$	$\text{vb}_{eq} + \text{per} + \text{tg}$
Independent	$\text{vb}_{tr} + \text{per} + \text{rel}$	$\text{vb}_{intr} + \text{per} + \text{rel}$	$\text{vb} + \text{per} + \text{rel}$

[23] Tagmeme indicating noun or nominal suffix.

Examples will be given of all but the independent nonfinal clauses which will be illustrated in the next chapter under multiple clause sentences.

7.4.1. *Transitive final clauses*

(1) *aónaraune* (P:vb) Independent
   it-I-saw
   'I saw it.'

(2) *tiyáániqtabama tímikaiye* (R:n + P:vb) Independent
   my-work-concerning + me-he-gave
   'He gave it to me because of my work.'

(3) *nóenaq mamé kéyeno* (O:pro + P:vb) Independent
   what + here-get you-come
   'What are you bringing?'

(4) *kemá aáwaqa náiq náiq onááre* (S:pro + O:n + P:VP) Subjunctive
   I + food + eat eat I-want
   'I am going to positively stuff myself with food.'

(5) *wení koínapaqa kemá íma ítaraune* (L:LocP + S:pro + P:VP) Independent
   his going-place + I + not I-heard
   'I don't know where he went.'

(6) *anó-karogaro-namma netuq-wááyúkámá taróq uráiye* (O:NP + S:NP + P:VP) Independent
   big-red-house + plenty-man + work he did
   'A lot of men built the big red house.'

(7) *póma yópáqá ikamuwo* (O:n + L:loc + P:vb) Independent
   pig + garden + you-hit
   'Kill the pig in the garden.'

(8) *imá móragaraqa* (O:n + T:Tem + P:vb) Independent
   bow + one + accom + you-say
   'Sing the song once more.'

(9) *náaraq-taoraqa mi-márámá ámikaaye* (T:TemP + O:NP + P:vb) Independent
   which-time + that-ground + you-they-gave'
   'When did they two give you that land?'

(10) *wení yínataoqa anón-oniqa agayánúnatae* T:TemP + O:NP + P:vb) Independent
   his coming-time + big-feast + we-will-cook
   'At his coming we will cook a big feast.

(11) *púnápó kaatopémá púrénae* (I:n + O:n + P:vb) Subjunctive
   with-knife + potato + he-first-peeled
   'First he peeled the potatoes with a knife.'

(12) *aaragóté aráamma nanáátaae* (Acc:n + O:n + P:vb) Subjunctive
   with-woman + mushroom + we-want-to-eat
   'We want to eat mushrooms with the women.'

7.4.2. *Intransitive final clauses*

(1) *tíwaqnaa uwo* (P:VP) Independent
my-aid you-do
'Help me!'

(2) *aaqá yinénae* (P:VP) Subjunctive
weather it-wants-to-come
'It wants to rain.'

(3) *waíwaakara póiyakara waayúkámá waéwaomiye* (Acc:NP + S:n + P:vb)
with-wild-animals with-domestic-animals + man + he-used-to-sleep
'The people used to sleep with the animals.'

(4) *nóetaba kéyeno* (R:pro + P:vb)
about-what + are-you-coming
'Why are you coming?'

(5) *yaaéna-iraakabaayaama kaagú yááyúqnóbáké kóuraraniye* (S:NP +
L:LocP + P:vb) Independent
green-snake + Kaagu's forest-from + I-think-he-left
'I think the green snake left Kaagu's forest.'

(6) *waagómá môra-wiyoma yauwaré yíniye* (S:n + T:TemP + P:VP)
Independent
man + one-moon + returning he-will-come
'The man will return in one month.'

(7) *ebíbáqá abayaama watáá watáá onétae* (L:loc + T:t + P:VP)
over-there + tomorrow + talk talk + they-want-to-do
'Tomorrow they want to have a discussion over there.'

7.4.3. *Equational final clauses*

(1) *aríkoko wáiye* (S:n + P:vb) Independent
beans there-are
'There are beans.'

(2) *ketí aríkoko wáiye* (S:NP + P:vb) Independent
my beans + there-are
'I have beans.'

(3) *netuq ááráwáámá ketaaí yópáqá máiq uraae* (S:NP + L:NP + P:VP)
Independent
plenty people + our garden + to-be they-did
'A lot of people were in our garden.'

(4) *íbeqa tíwáqnaagoma íma máiye* (T:t + S:n + P:VP) Independent
now + my-help-one + not he-is
'At the present I have no helper.' ('My helper is not here now.')

(5) *eni waíyáárémá íbeqa íráqóne* (S:NP + T:t + P:d) Independent
your bed + now + is-good
'Your bed is now in good condition.'

(6) *turúaani yómmá náakarabiyo* (S:NP + P:p) Independent

Luluai's garden + where-is-it
'Where is Luluai's garden?'
(7) *anómma naammá* (C:d) Independent
big + house
'The house is big.'
naammá anómma (S:n + C:d) Independent
house + big
naammá anóne (S:n + P:d) Independent
house + big
naammá anó kéiye (S:n + P:VP) Independent
house + big it-does
(8) *pógoma* (C:n) Independent
pig-st
'It is a pig.'
(9) *waguráano* (P:vb) Independent
did-you-sleep-st
'Were you asleep?'
(10) *mibáq yópáqá anó kéiye* (L:loc + S:loc + P:VP) Independent
over-there + garden + big is-doing
'Over there the garden is big.'
(11) *púnápó kanáára íye* (I:n + P:VP) Independent
with-a-knife + well it-does
'With a knife is all right.'
(12) *igáráq wemá áá íkegaiye* (Acc:n + S:pro + P:VP) Independent
with-a-bow + he + his-ear does-not-burn
'With a bow he is not afraid.'
(13) *ení pógotaba watáá watáá ánataguraiye* (R:NP + S:NP + P:vb)
    Independent
your pig-concerning + talk talk + it-is-finished
'The discussion about your pig is finished.'
(14) *anón oginénae* (P:VP) Subjunctive
big + he-wants-to-do
'He wants to be big.'

7.4.4. Subjunctive nonfinal clauses

(1) *karí érakakurai kanaama wen amáápaqa yawaíniye* (T:Cl$_{tem}$ + L:loc +
    P:VP)
sickness for-him is-done time + his-homeland + he-will-go-up-and-stay
'When he is well he will go up and stay at his own home.'
(2) *iyákómá ikákainapake iráiye* (L:Cl$_{loc}$ + P:vb)
dog him-he-hit-place-from + he came
'He came from where he killed the dog.'
(3) *yópáq máinakoma nommá tímikaiye* (S:Cl$_{sb}$ + O:n + P:vb)

in-the-garden he-is-person + water + me-he-gave

'The one who is in the garden gave me water.'

(4) *kemá karipé matáinaqa aónaraune* (S:n + O:Cl$_{sb}$ + P:vb)

I + peanut + he-took-person him-I-saw

'I saw him who took the peanusts.'

(5) *kemá kainaatúpaq máanataba íma ítaraune* (S:pro + R:Cl$_{ref}$ + P:VP)

I + Kainantu-at + you-are-there-concerning + not I-heard

'I don't know about your being in Kainantu.'

8. Sentence Structure

A sentence is marked by the occurrence of a mood suffix with a clause, clause segment, or sequence of clauses. A final clause is therefore also a sentence. Since subjunctive nonfinal clauses manifest tagmemes as clause constituents they are not constituents of sentences except through the media of the clauses in which they occur. A sequence of independent nonfinal clauses connected by relational marking suffixes and combinations of suffixes may precede a final clause in a sentence construction.

$$S = (I.NFCl)^n + FCl$$

The number of nonfinal clauses which may occur in any one sentence does not seem to be structurally limited. There may be some higher level limitations such as the paragraph or discourse which are not clear at the present stage of analysis.

Two different categories of sentence types will be discussed. The first includes modal differences and the second relational differences in multiple clause sentences. The latter is of much greater complexity and significance. Differences will be stated in terms of the predicate tagmemes of constituent clause elements.

8.1. *Modal Types*

Differences in modal sentence types correspond to the division of mood suffixes described in Section 3.5. The following eight modal types are defined with reference to the mood suffix or suffixes which occur with the final clause tagmeme identifying them. Further subclassification of types is possible but adds nothing that has not been already dealt with in the description of the mood suffixes. Modal types are:

Indicative = Cl-*e*

Assertative = Cl-{*po: mibo*}

Imperative = Cl-*o$_2$*

Interrogative = Cl-{*o$_1$; abo* + α + *o$_1$; abiyo*}

Designatory = Cl-*miye*

Prohibitive = Cl-*bo*

Causal = Cl-*poa* + ß

Nominal = Cl-{*ma; mo; a; mo* + α + *e*}

The interrogative sentence type must occur if an interrogative pronoun or pronoun phrase occurs manifesting any clause tagmeme. Although the type of mood suffix which may co-occur with any given word or phrase unit is restricted as previously described there are no other restrictions on the type of sentence which may occur when it is manifested by a single clause.

8.2. *Multiple Clause Sentences*

The subordination and coordination of clauses within a sentence is perhaps the most interesting feature of Usarufa syntax. It is certainly the most difficult to learn. Relationships between clauses are indicated by subtle combinations of features. Features which effect relational changes are: choice of person-subject suffix series or combination of series; tense-aspect opposition or agreement; mood suffix selection; verb phrase constructions; and special relational markers. The full range of semantic significance of combinational possibilities is not yet known. A wide range of subtle differences in the relational significance of various clause sequences is evident but at the present degree of competency in the language it is not possible to go into these finer details. This description will deal with the broader constructional types which these various sequences of clauses manifest. The general sentence formula which was given in the preceding section must now be read with both the final and non-final clauses as obligatory: $I.NFCl^n + FCl$.

Three distinct construction types manifest this still quite general formula. Each type is characterized by a particular manifestation of the final and nonfinal predicate tagmemes. The three types are: (1) the future imperative construction; (2) the present aorist construction; (3) the suppositional construction.

8.2.1. *The future imperative construction.* The predicate of the final clause of this sentence construction must be manifested by either a verb in the imperative or by one in the future tense. The form of the verb manifesting the predicate of the nonfinal clause or clauses depends upon whether the action of that clause is conditional or nonconditional and whether the person-subject of the verb is the same or different from the person-subject of the verb manifesting the predicate of the following clause. If the subjects are the same and the action is nonconditional the verb of the first clause will consist of the reduced verb stem and the suffix *ma;* if the action is conditional the form of the first verb will be verb nucleus plus beta person-subject subseries one. If the subjects are different a complex person-subject suffix combination $\alpha_5 + \beta_1$ occurs with the verb nucleus, the alpha suffix indicating the subject of the given nonfinal clause and the beta form anticipating the subject of the predicate of the next clause;[24] if the action is conditional

---

[24] It is important to note that the person-subject agreement or anticipation is between the verb person-subject suffixes. This may or may not be the same as the person of the subject tagmemes of the clauses involved.

an optional conditional suffix (*ma*) may occur following the beta suffix. The formula for the future imperative construction may be stated as follows:

$$\text{I.NFCl}_{\alpha\text{-}5}{}^{(n)} + \text{FCl-P:}\{\text{vb}_{\text{fut}}; \text{vb}_{\text{imp}}\}$$

The relationship between clauses in a future imperative construction is that of events in sequence. This is often best translated by 'and'; however, when an imperative verb occurs in the final clause it may be translated as an infinitive construction.

The matrix in Table 56 gives the structure of the verb forms which occur as manifestations of the predicate tagmemes of each of the constituent clause types.

TABLE 56
FUTURE IMPERATIVE MATRIX

	Independent Nonfinal Clause $\alpha - 5$		Final Clause
	Nonconditional	Conditional	
Different subject	$\overset{\leftarrow \quad \rightarrow}{\text{vb} + \alpha_5 + \beta_1}$	$\overset{\leftarrow \quad \rightarrow}{\text{vb} + \alpha_5 + \beta_1 + (ma)}$	$\text{vb}_{\text{nu}} + no + \text{person} + \text{md}$
Same subject	$\overset{\leftrightarrow}{\text{rvs} + \text{ma}}$	$\overset{\leftrightarrow}{\text{vb} + \beta_1}$	$\text{vb} + \gamma + o_2$

8.2.2. The present aorist construction. The predicate of the final clause of this construction type must be either manifested by a verb with a present continuous or aorist tense-aspect morpheme or if the action is conditional by an abilitative verb phrase. The relationship between clauses may be either causal or temporal depending upon the form of the verb manifesting the nonfinal predicate tagmeme. The structural formula for the construction is:

$$\text{I.NFCl}_{\alpha\text{-}4;}{}^{(n)} + \text{FCl-P:} \left\{ \begin{array}{l} (k\acute{e})_{\text{mx}} + \text{vb}_{\text{nu}} + (ra)_{\text{mx}} + \text{person} + \text{md} \\ \text{VP}_{\text{do-abl}} \end{array} \right\}$$

If there is a causal relationship between the constituent clauses and the subjects are the same or the action is conditional, the form of the verb manifesting the nonfinal predicate tagmeme will be as follows: reduced verb stem plus beta subseries one. If the action is nonconditional and the subjects are different the nonfinal verb form will be: verb nucleus plus the person-subject complex $\alpha_4 + \beta_1$ with the alpha form indicating the subject of the clause with which it occurs and the beta form anticipating the subject to follow.

The actions of temporally related clauses in a present aorist construction are viewed as having taken place at the same time. This simultaneity of occurrence need not be a specific moment in time but covers a period of time during which the events specified took place. If the subject of the nonfinal clause is the same as that of the following clause the verb form will be the same as the same-subject form in the future imperative construction, that is, reduced verb stem plus the suffix *ma*. If the subjects are different the alpha subseries number seven occurs with the verb nucleus indicating the subject of the first clause and that a different but unspecified subject is to follow.

The tense component of the tense-aspect affixes occurring with the final clause may be neutralized by those occurring with the nonfinal clause. The alpha four and alpha seven subseries seem to indicate a narrative past which may or may not refer to actual past events depending upon the tense-aspect affixes with which they may occur. The time significance of the non-final clause is carried over to the final clause.

The structure of the verbs manifesting the predicate tagmemes of the constituent clauses of the present aorist construction is indicated in Table 57.

TABLE 57
PRESENT AORIST MATRIX

	Nonconditional	Conditional
Final Clause	$\left\{ \begin{array}{l} ke + vb_{nu} \\ vb_{nu} + ra \end{array} \right\} + person + md$	$VP_{do\text{-}abl}$
Nonfinal-Causal Different subject	$\overset{\leftarrow \quad \rightarrow}{vb + \alpha_4 + \beta_1}$	
Same subject	$rvs + \beta_1$	
Nonfinal-Temporal Different subject	$vb + \alpha_7$	
Same subject	$\overset{\leftarrow\rightarrow}{rvs + ma}$	

8.2.3. *The suppositional construction.* There are two types of suppositional constructions, contrary-to-fact and subjunctive. In both types the nonfinal clause is marked by the suppositional suffix *raa* and the final clause predicate is manifested by either an abilitative or a future verb phrase construction. The structural formula including the verbal manifestations of the constituent predicates is:

I.NFCl-P:vs + {α₃; ß₂} + *raa* + FCl-P:VP$_{\text{do-abil;fut}}$

The contrary-to-fact suppositional construction indicates that the supposed action or event is known to be contrary to the actual facts of the situation and is marked by the alpha three subseries. The beta two subseries marks the subjunctive suppositional construction which indicates that the supposed action or event could possibly occur.

8.3. *Illustrative Examples of Sentence Types*

The following examples give a sketch of the types of sentence constructions which occur. Translations try to give the English significance of the constructions as simply as possible.

8.3.1. *Modal types*

(1) *oé* (Indicative)
'Yes.'
(2) *ikamónúpo* (Assertative)
'I will certainly hit it.'
(3) *éqááo* (Imperative)
'No!'
(4) *ímiye* (Designatory)
'No. (It is not able to be.)'
(5) *inarúábíyó* (Interrogative)
'Is it a girl?'
(6) *wagíbo* (Prohibitive)
'He shouldn't be asleep!'
(7) *améyuyapoaka* (Causal)
'Because we two will give it to you.'
(8) *ketiwaamá ayaaqtááqa* (Nominal)
'My older brother is tall.'

8.3.2. *Multiple clause sentences*
8.3.2.1. *Future imperative constructions*
(1) *Future, same subject, nonconditional*
    kemá kamááma púqma nanúne
    I + sweet-potato + peel-*ma* + eat-fut-α-1st-indic
    'I will peel the sweet potato and eat it.'

   wemá nommá atíma nániye
    he + water + pour-*ma* + eat-fut-3rd-indic
    'He will pour out the water and drink it.'

(2) *Future, different subject, nonconditional*
timá mínana yíniye
talk-*ma* him-give-α-2nd -ß-3rd come-fut-α-3rd-indic
'You tell him and he will come.'

we kénainaq anáekaq yénúne
he pres. con-eat-α-3rd-ß-1st later come-fut-α-1st-indic
'He is eating, I'll come later.'

anáekaq wemá úkáráápake kumínaka kemaíyúpaq koyúye
later he Ukarampa-from come-down-α-3rd-ß-1st-dual Kemiyu-place go-fut-
   α-1st-dual-indic
'Later he will come from Ukarampa and we two will go to Kemiyu.'

agatáinaq namúne
cook-aorist-α-3rd-ß-1st eat-fut-α-1st-indic
'He cooked it, I will eat it.'

kágayainaq nanúne
pres.con-cook-α-3rd-ß-1st eat-fut-α-1st-indic
'He is cooking it and I will eat it.'

agayáinaq nanúne
cook-α-3rd-ß-1st eat-fut-α-1st-indic
'He will cook it and I will eat it.'

(3) *Future conditional*
áqibo puyéqa puyónúne
if die-ß-1st die-fut-α-1st-indic
'If I die, I die.'

timá ménanama agayániye
talk-*ma* him-give-α-1st-ß-3rd-con cook-fut-α-3rd-indic
'If I tell him (to) he will cook.'

ibiqá yaráinanama íaminiye
cry cry-α-3rd-ß-3rd-con neg-him-give-α-3rd-indic
'If he cries she won't give it to him.'

(4) *Imperative*
agamá naano
cook-*ma* eat-γ-1st-imper
'I must cook and eat.'

timá mínana yíno
talk-*ma* him-give-α-2nd-ß-3rd come-γ-3rd-imper
'Tell him to come!'

akáinama ketí naaôpaq iyo
for-you-put-α-3rd-ß-2nd-con my-house come-γ-2nd-imper
'If you like, come to my house.'

kemá maakáq máunana ááqa ígainc
I here be-α-1st-ß-3rd your-ear neg-burn-γ-3rd-imper
'I am here, you mustn't be afraid.'

8.3.2.2. *Present aorist constructions*

(1) *Present aorist, causal, different subject*

náiyóbaq tikámitaka ibiqá yakáuye
before us-hit-α-3rd-ß-1st dual cry cry-aorist-α-1st dual-indic
'He hit the two us so we cried.'

iraakabayaamá máitana táiyama kákaiye
snake eat-α-3rd-ß-3rd sickness-pres.con-him-put for-α-3rd-indic
'He is sick because he ate the snake.'

ke tááko itaq náunana táiyama tíkaiye
I my-ear-st do-α-3rd-ß-1st eat-α-1st-ß-3rd sickness for-me-put-α-3rd-indic
'I am sick because that is my punishment for having eaten.'

agatáitaq naráune
cook-aorist-α-3rd-ß-1st eat-aorist-α-1st-indic
'He cooked it so I ate it.'

agayáitaq naráune
cook-α-3rd-ß-1st eat-aorist-α-1st-indic
'He cooked it so I just now ate it.'

kágayaitaq naráune
pres.con-cook-α-3rd-ß-1st eat aorist-α-1st indic
'He is cooking it so I will eat it.'

agatáitaq kénaune
cook-aorist-α-3rd-ß-1st pres.con-eat-α-1st-indic
'He cooked it so I am eating it.'

(2) *Present aorist, causal, same subject*

pukuréna timá ítimiye
die-st-aorist-ß-3rd talk-*ma* neg-me-give-α-3rd-indic
'He is dead so he does not talk to me.'

náiyóbaq íma púréq ínanaa únae
before not peel-ß-1st neg-eat-fut-ß-1st do-α-1st abl
'If I had not peeled it I would not be able to eat it.'

(3) *Present aorist, temporal, different subject*

náiyóbaq tikámimma ibiqa íyakauye
before us-hit-α-3rd cry neg-cry-aorist-α-1st-dual-indic
'When he hit us two we did not cry.'

we kumímma e aónane ónae
he come-down-α-3rd you him-see-fut-ß-2nd do-α-2nd abl
'If he comes you will be able to see him then.'

agatáimma kénaune
cook-aorist-α-3rd pres.con-eat-α-1st-indic
'When he cooked it I was eating it.'

agatáimma naráune
cook-aorist-α-3rd eat-aorist-α-1st-indic
'When he cooked it I ate it.'

agayáimma naráune
cook-α-3rd eat-aorist-α-1st-indic
'When he cooks I eat.'

kágayaimma naráune
pres.con-cook-α-3rd eat-aorist-α-1st-indic
'I will eat when he is cooking.'

(4) *Present aorist, temporal, same subject*
ke agamá ke nanáá únae
I cook-*ma* I eat-fut-ß-1st do-α-1st-abl
'If I cook it I will be able to eat it at that time.'

ayáámma káráma ibiqá íyakaiye
his-hand cut-*ma* cry neg-cry-aorist-α-3rd-indic
'When he cut his hand he did not cry.'

8.3.3. *Suppositional constructions*
(1) *Contrary-to-fact suppositional*
aónaunaraa ítanaa únae
it-see-α-1st-supp hear-fut-ß-1st do-α-1st-abl
'If I had seen it (but I didn't) I would know.'

áqibo íma náunaraa táiyama ítikane íne
if not eat-α-1st-supp sickness neg-for-me-put-fut-ß-3rd do-α-3rd-abl
'If I had not eaten it (but I did) I wouldn't be sick.'

áqibo íagayaanaraa ínane íniye
if neg-cook-α-2nd-supp neg-eat-fut-ß-3rd do-fut-α-3rd-indic
'If you don't cook (but you do) he won't eat.'

ketí káari wáikakaa károkapaq koonáá únae
my-car be-α-3rd-supp Goroka go-fut-ß-1st do-α-1st-abl
'If I had a car (but I don't) I could go to Goroka.'

(2) *Subjunctive suppositional*
áqibo íagayeraa ínane íniye
if neg-cook-ß-2nd-supp neg-eat-fut-ß-3rd do-fut-α-3rd-indic
'If you don't cook he won't eat.'

we yénaraa ke aónanaa únae
he come-ß-3rd-supp I him-see-fut-ß-1st do-α-1st abl
'If he comes I will be able to see him.'

áqibo ke wékaraa nanáá únae
if I go-ß-1st-supp eat-fut-ß-1st do-α-1st abl
'If I go I can eat.'

9. Morphophonemics

Morphophonemic rules are divided into five categories: (1) rules which deal with morphophonemic changes effected by person affixes; (2) rules which deal with tone placement and perturbation; (3) rules pertaining to changes effected by the pervasive system of morphophonemic classification which affects morphemes of all classes; (4) general rules which deal with miscellaneous phonemic changes resulting from combinations of specific phonemes either wherever the combination occurs or in specific morphemic environments; and (5) rules for the removal of symbols and signs and for orthographic changes.

The order in which the rules have been given is in general the order in which they should be applied. The order of application between types of rules is usually more important than the order of rules within any one type. In some instances the order of application will not make a significant difference in the results. The order of application in noun constructions is much less important than in verb constructions.

The rules presented here will undoubtedly need to be added to and revised as more data come to hand; however, they seem to be sufficient to account for a significantly high percentage of the material which this grammar will generate.[25] The area most in need of further work is the area of tone placement on verbal forms.

9.1. *Alpha-Beta-Gamma-Delta Rules*

The rules given here are those for changes effected by person affixes. They will be presented under five categories (1) general rules which apply either to more than one person series type or to more than one morphemic environment; (2) alpha rules which apply to specific alpha morphemes and specific morphemic environments; (3) beta rules which apply to specific beta morphemes and specific morphemic environments; (4) gamma rules which apply to specific gamma morphemes and specific morphemic environments; and (5) delta rules which apply to changes effected by delta morphemes.

9.1.1. *General person-subject rules*

(1) x $+$ {α-x $+na;$ ß-x} $+$ *mibo* $\rightarrow$ x $+$ {α-x $+$ *na;* ß-x} $+$ *ibo*

(2) V$\#$ $+$ { ß-x; *ta;* ts; *ro*} $\rightarrow e$ $+$ { ß-x; *ta;* ts; *ro*}

(3) vs-{*e; o*} $\#$ $+$ *no* $+$ α-{2nd; 3rd} $\rightarrow$ vs-*i* $+$ *no* $+$ α-{2nd; 3rd}

(4) x $+$ {*no; ne*} $+$ {α; ß}-*d* $\rightarrow$ x $+$ {*yo; ye*} $+$ {α; ß}-*d*

(5) x-*a*$\#$ $+$ {α; γ}-{$\#c;$ ø} $\rightarrow$ x-*aa* $+$ {α; γ}-{$\#c;$ ø}

(6) x-{*e; o*} $+$ α-$\#u$ $\rightarrow$ x- $+$ α-*u*

(7) x-{*e; o*} $\#$ $+$ {α;γ}-$\#i$ $\rightarrow$ x- $+$ {α;γ}-*i*

---

[25] See Sec. 10 for abbreviations.

9.1.2. *Alpha rules* (α-*rules*)

(1) α-*únata*V + *po* → α-*únatai*V + *po*

(2) α-*únana* + *na* + {*e; ibo*} → α-*únana* + *ta* + {*e; ibo*}

(3) α-*ina*N + *poa* + ß-*na*→α-*i*N + *poa* + ß-*na*

(4) α-*ina*N + *raa* →α-*ika*N + *raa*

(5) ß-*taa*V + *abo* + α-*únata*V + *o* → ß-*taa*V + *abo* + α-*ú*N + *o*

(6) α-sg + *na* + *ibo* → α-sg + *q* + *ibo*

(7) vs-{*e; o*}# + α$_5$-*ena* → vs- + *ina*

(8) vs-*a*# + α$_5$-*ena* → vs- + *ena*

9.1.3. *Beta rules* (ß-*rules*)

(1) {*ne; ye*}$_{fut}$ + ß-1st → {*naa; yaa*} + ß-1st

(2)ß-øQ$_{1sg}$ + *abiyo* → ß-øQ + *iyo*

9.1.4. *Gamma rules* (γ-*rules*)

(1) vs-{*e; o*} ⧧ + γ-øV→vs-{*i;u*} + γ-øV

(2) {vs + *ko;* vs-*oo*#} + γ-øV→{vs + *ka;* vs-*oa*} + γ-øV

9.1.5. *Delta rules* (δ-*rules*)

(1) *ti-δoi*Q1 → *oti*Q1

(2) {*ti; yi*}-δ*o*-vs → {*tim; yim*}-δ*o*-vs

(3) {*ti;yi*}-δ#*v* → {*t; y*}-δ*v*

(4) *a*-δ# {*u; i*}-vs → {*u; i*}-vs

(5) *a*-δ#*ax*→*ax*

(6) {*a; yi*}-δns$_1$-*o*V# → {*a; yi*}-δns$_1$-*o*V + *a*V

(7) {*a; yi*}-δns$_1$-{*u; a; i*}V# → {*a; yi*}-δns$_1$-{*u; a; i*}V + *o*V

9.2. *Morphotonemic Rules*

This section deals with rules of tone placement and perturbation. Nominal stems are classed as either tone type 1 or tone type 2. Verb stems may be either 1, 2, or tone type 3. The rules of tone placement and change for nominal constructions are much simpler than those for verbal constructions and have been checked much more thoroughly. The study of tone placement and change is in beginning stages for verbal constructions and adequate data are not available to make an exhaustive statement of the rules at this time. The rules which are presented here, however, have been checked carefully and represent a statement of tone placement for the most critical forms for determining verb stem classes and subclasses on the morphonemic level. Other verbal constructions seem to be much more uniform in the types of tone patterning which occur, but because it has not been possible to check these as thoroughly as the forms represented here the rules for such constructions have been omitted. The rules for tone placement which are given for verbal constructions represent over three thousand verbal forms.

The morphotonemic rules will be divided into three major categories:

rules for constructions with verb stems of tone types 1 and 2; rules for constructions with verb stems of tone type 3; and rules for constructions with nominal stems and with delta prefixes.

9.2.1. Rules for constructions with verb stems of tone types 1 and 2. In these constructions the final *(v)vcv* or *vv* of the verb stem are the crucial syllables in determining and stating the rules for tone placement. In the citation of verb stems these vowels are either unmarked or marked with the high tone symbol (´). This marking of the citation forms represents a type of subclassification and is not indicative of the innate tone of the verb stem itself. Other marks of significance to the morphotonemic rules are the imperative tone subtypes marked *a* and *b* and the morphophonemic subclassification symbols (V; N; O). Various combinations of these factors plus the tone type of the verb stem and the morphemic construction which occurs affect the tone placement. For any given rule some one or more of these factors may be insignificant in which case the symbol representing that factor will be omitted. For example: vsl—any verb stem of type 1, vs—any verb stem, vsN(R)—any verb stem of morphophonemic class N, vs(R)a—any verb stem of subclass *a*.

The six categories of constructions which will be accounted for here are: (1) alpha present tense third person singular; (2) gamma second person singular imperative; (3) gamma second person dual imperative; (4) alpha future tense forms; (5) alpha aorist forms; and (6) stative forms.

9.2.1.1. Alpha present tense third person singular

$$\{vsl; vs2\} + \alpha\text{-}iV + md$$

$$(1)\begin{cases} vs\{V1; N(R); Q(R)\}\text{-}vcv\,\# \\ vs\{V1; N2R\}\text{-}vc\acute{v}\,\# \end{cases} \rightarrow vs\{V; N(R); Q(R)\}\text{-}\acute{v}c\acute{v}$$

$$(2)\ vsV2\text{-}vcv\,\# + \alpha\text{-}iV + \{e; o\} \rightarrow vsV\text{-}\grave{v}c\grave{v} + iV + \{\acute{e}; \acute{o}\}$$

$$(3)\ vs\{V1; N(R); Q(R)\}\text{-}\acute{v}c\acute{v}\,\# + \alpha\text{-}iV \rightarrow vs\{V; N(R); Q(R)\}\begin{cases} \acute{v}c\acute{v} + iV \\ \acute{v}c + iV\text{-} \end{cases}$$

$$(4)\ \{vsV1\text{-}\acute{v}cv\,\#; vsQ1R\text{-}vc\acute{v}\,\#\} + \alpha\text{-}iV \rightarrow vs\{V; QR\}\begin{cases} \acute{v}c\grave{v} + iV \\ \acute{v}c + iV \end{cases}$$

$$(5)\ vsN2R\text{-}\acute{v}cv\,\# \rightarrow vsNR\text{-}\acute{v}c$$

$$(6)\ \{vsQ2R\text{-}\acute{v}cv\,\#; vsQ2R\text{-}\acute{v}c\acute{v}\,\#\} \rightarrow vsQR\text{-}\acute{v}c\grave{v}$$

9.2.1.2. Gamma second person singular imperative

$$\{vs1; vs2\}\ \{a; b\} + \gamma\text{-}\emptyset V + o$$

$$(1)\ vs(R)a + \gamma\text{-}\emptyset V + o \rightarrow vs(R) + \emptyset V + \acute{o}$$

$$(2)\ vs(R)b + \gamma\text{-}\emptyset V + o \rightarrow v\grave{s}(R) + \emptyset V + \grave{o}$$

$$(3)\ vsQ1R\text{-}vcv\,\# + \gamma\text{-}\emptyset V + o \rightarrow vsQR\text{-}\acute{v}c\grave{v} + \emptyset V + \grave{o}$$

9.2.1.3. Gamma second person dual imperative

$$vs + \gamma\text{-}kaV + o$$

(1) $\left\{\begin{array}{l} vs\text{-}\{vcv;\ vc\acute{v};\ \acute{v}c\acute{v}\}\ \# \\ vsV1\text{-}\acute{v}cv\ \# \end{array}\right\} + \gamma\text{-}kaV \rightarrow vs\text{-}\acute{v}c\acute{v} + \gamma\text{-}k\grave{a}V$

(2) $\{vsN;\ vsQ\}2R\text{-}\acute{v}cv\ \# \rightarrow vs\{N;\ Q\}R\text{-}\acute{v}c\grave{v}$

(3) $vs\text{-}vv\ \# \rightarrow vs\text{-}\acute{v}\grave{v}$

(4) $\{vs\text{-}\acute{e}\,\#\,;\ vs\text{-}\acute{o}\,\#\} + \gamma\text{-}kaV \rightarrow \{vs\text{-}\hat{e};\ vs\text{-}\hat{o}\} + \gamma\text{-}k\grave{a}V$

9.2.1.4. Alpha future tense

$$vs + no + \alpha + md$$

(1) $vs\text{-}v\,\# + no\ \alpha + \rightarrow vs\text{-}\acute{v} + n\acute{o} + \alpha$

9.2.1.5. Alpha aorist

$$vs + ra + \alpha + md$$

(1) $\left\{\begin{array}{l} \{vsQ1R;\ vsN1R\text{-}cvcv\,\#\} \\ vsV1\text{-}\{\acute{v}c\acute{v};\ vc\acute{v}\}\ \# \end{array}\right\} + ra \rightarrow vs\{V;\ Q;\ N\}(R)\text{-}(c)\acute{v}c\acute{v} + ra$

(2) $vsV1\text{-}vcv;\ \acute{v}cv\ \# + ra \rightarrow vsV\text{-}\acute{v}cv + ra$

(3) $\left\{\begin{array}{l} \{vsV2;\ vsQ2R\} \\ \\ vsN2R\text{-}\{\acute{v}cv;\ vc\acute{v}\}\ \# \end{array}\right\} + ra \rightarrow vs\{V;\ Q;\ N\}(R)\text{-}vcv + r\acute{a}$

(4) $vsN2R\text{-}\{\acute{v}c\acute{v};\ vcv\}\ \# + ra \rightarrow vsNR\text{-}\acute{v}c\acute{v} + ra$

(5) $vsN1R\text{-}\{\acute{v}vcv;\ vvcv\}\ \# + ra + vsNR\text{-}\acute{v}vcv + ra$

9.2.1.6. Stative forms

$$vs + koV$$

(1) $vs\{N;\ Q\}(R)\text{-}\{\acute{v}c\acute{v};\ vcv;\ vvcv\}\ \# \rightarrow vs\{N;\ Q\}(R)\text{-}(\acute{v})\acute{v}cv + koV$

(2) $vs\{N;\ Q\}(R)2\text{-}vc\acute{v}\,\# \rightarrow vs\{N;\ Q\}(R)\text{-}vcv + koV2$

(3) $vsV1\text{-}\acute{v}c\acute{v}\,\# \rightarrow vsV\text{-}\acute{v}cv + koV$

9.2.2. *Rules for constructions with verb stems of tone type 3.* The high tone nucleus of verbal constructions with verb stems of type 3 always occurs on the syllables of the verb stem and is usually on the same syllable or syllables in all or most of the various types of constructions. This differs from the heavy influence of morphemic environments characteristic of constructions with verb stems of tone types 1 and 2. Syllable of verb stems of tone type 3 may be marked in one of the following ways: (1) stem unmarked ($\#(c)v$); (2) a medial vowel marked for high tone (-$c\acute{v}$-); (3) an initial vowel marked for high tone ($\#(c)\acute{v}$); (4) a final vowel marked for high tone ($c\acute{v}\#$); (5) the consonant of a penultimate syllable marked with high tone ($\#\acute{v}cvcv\#$); (6) the consonant of a final syllable marked with high tone ($\acute{c}v\#$).

9.2.2.1. Unmarked stems ($\#(c)v$)

(1) $\#(c)v\text{-}vs3b + \gamma\text{-}\emptyset V + o \rightarrow (c)\grave{v}\text{-}v\grave{s} + \emptyset V + \grave{o}$

(2) $\#(c)v\text{-}vs3b + x \rightarrow (c)\acute{v}\text{-}vs + x$

(3) $\#(c)v\text{-}vs3 + x \rightarrow (c)\acute{v}\text{-}vs + x$

9.2.2.2. *Stems with marked medial vowel* (-*cv́*-)
(1) vs-*cv́*-3 + x → vs-*cv́*- + x

9.2.2.3. *Stems with marked initial vowel* (#(*c*)*v́*)
(1) #(*c*) *v́*-vs3 + {ɣ-øV: *no*} → (*c*)*v́*-vs # {øV; *nò*}
(2) #(*c*)*v́*-vs3 + x → (*c*)*v́*-*v́s* + x

9.2.2.4. *Stems with marked final vowel* (*cv́* #)
(1) vs3-*cv*(*c*)*vcv́* + ɣ-*ka*V → vs-*cv́*(*c*)*v́*(*cv́*) + *kà*V
(2) vs3-*cv*(*c*)*vcv́* # + x → vs-*cv́*(*c*)*v̀*(*cv̀*) + x

9.2.2.5. *Stems with marked consonant of penultimate syllable* (#*vćvcv* #)
(1) *vćvcv*3 + *no* → *v̀cv́cv̀* + *nò*
(2) *vćvcv*3 + x → *v̀cv́cv̀* + x

9.2.2.6. *Stems with marked consonant of final syllable* (*cv* #):
(1) (*v*(*c*)*v*)*cvćv*3 + {ɣ-*ka*V; α} → (*v̀*(*c*)*v́*)*cv́cv̀* + {*ka*V; α}
(2) (*v*(*c*)*v*)*cvćv*3 + x → (*v*(*c*)*v́*)*cv̀cv̀* + x
àácv̀cv̀ → *áácv̀cv̀*

9.2.3. *Constructions with nominal stems and/or delta prefixes*
(1) {<x-y>₂; <x + y>; [x + y]₁}
　　　x1 + {y1; y2} → x + y1
　　　x2 + {y1; y2} → x + y2
(2) <x-y>₁
　　　{x1; x2} + y1 → x + y1
　　　{x1; x2} + y2→x + y2
　　　x-*v́*# + y2→x-*v* + y2
(3) {*ti; yi; a*}-δx→{*tí; yí; á*}-δx
　　　{*t; y*} -δ#*v*-x →{*t; y*}-δ*v*-x

9.3. *Morphophoneme Rules* (N, Q, *and* V)
　　All of the morphemes of the language are classified as belonging to one of three morphophonemic classes (N, Q, or V).[26] The criteria for determining the morphophonemic class of any morpheme are types of morphophonemic phenomena which occur contiguously following that morpheme within the same word or descriptive phrase. The rules related to this system of classification will be given in Section 9.3.3. These rules which seem to have diachronic as well as synchronic significance effect allomorphic variants for most morphemes of the language. In specific morphemic environments the morphophonemic class of a given morpheme may be changed or the systemic rules of morphophonemic change neutralized. These environments will be specified in Section 9.3.1. A few morphophonemic changes and/or allomorphic variants seem unrelated to the over-all system of change and are limited to a few morphemic environments. These will be specified in Section 9.3.2.

[26] A few morphemes have not been classified because the evidence from crucial morphophonemic environments is lacking at the present time.

9.3.1. Class changing and neutralizing rules

$$(1) \left\{ \begin{array}{l} \text{vs}\{V; N; Q\} + \{ts_{\text{non-}ra}; \text{per}\} \\ \\ \text{vs}\{N; Q\} + \{ti; yi\}\text{-}\delta ka \end{array} \right\} \rightarrow \text{vs} + \left\{ \begin{array}{l} \{ts_{\text{non-}ra}; \text{per}\} \\ \\ \{ti; yi\}\text{-}\delta ka \end{array} \right\}$$

(2) $\alpha\{V; N; Q\} + ß \rightarrow \alpha + ß$

(3) $x\{V; N; Q\} + b \rightarrow x + b$

(4) $\text{vsQ} + ko \rightarrow \text{vsV} + ko$

(5) $x\{V; N; Q\} + \{kaQ; keV\} \rightarrow xV + \{kaQ; keV\}$ (locatives)

(6) $x\{V; N; Q\} \# \# \rightarrow x$

9.3.2. Extra systemic changes

(1) $\text{vsQ} + ra \rightarrow \text{vs} + ta$

(2) $\text{vsV} + \delta ka \rightarrow \text{vs-}ma + \delta ka$

(3) $\text{vsQ} + a\text{-}\delta ka \rightarrow \text{vs} + ya\text{-}\delta ka$

(4) $\text{vsN} + a\text{-}\delta ka \rightarrow \text{vs} + ra\text{-}\delta ka$

(5) $poa + taaV \rightarrow poa + ta$

(6) $keV2 + ni \rightarrow keV2 + ti$

(7) $ketaaV2 + ti \rightarrow ketaaV2 + i$

(8) $\text{pro.s}_{\text{d; pl; loc-sg}} + ni + na \rightarrow \text{pro.s} + ni + minae$

(9) $xV + rarata \rightarrow x + \{rata; tarata\}$

   $vb + rarata \rightarrow tarata$

(10) $\text{pro}_{\text{int}} + abiyo \rightarrow \text{pro}_{\text{int}}Q + abiyo$

9.3.3. Systemic changes

(1) $xV + \{c; v\} \rightarrow x + \{c; v\}$

(2) $x\{N; Q\} + \{p; t; k\} \rightarrow x + \{qp; qt; qk\}$

(3) $x\{N; Q\} + r \rightarrow x + qk$

(4) $xN + \{w; y\} \rightarrow x + \{qk; qt\}$

(5) $xQ + \{w; y\} \rightarrow x + \{qw; qy\}$

(6) $xN + \{m; n\} \rightarrow x + \{mm/m; nn/n\}$

$$\left\{ \begin{array}{l} \text{per-}xN + \{m; n\} \\ \\ [<\text{nsN}> +<\{m; n\}>]_1 \end{array} \right\} \rightarrow x + \{m; n\}$$

(7) $xQ + \{m; n\} \rightarrow x + \{qm/q; qn\}$

$$\left\{ \begin{array}{l} <\text{nsQ} + m> \\ \\ \text{per-}xQ + m \end{array} \right\} \rightarrow x + q$$

(8) $xN + v \rightarrow x\text{-}n + v$

(9) $xQ + v \rightarrow x\text{-}\{r; q\} + v$

$$\left\{ \begin{array}{l} <\text{nsQ} + v> \\ \\ \text{per-}xQ + \{e; o; a\} \end{array} \right\} \rightarrow x\text{-}r + v$$

$$\left.\begin{cases} [<\text{nsQ}> \ + <v>]_1 \\ \text{per-xQ} \ + i \end{cases}\right\} \to \text{x-}q \ + v$$

9.4. Rules of General Change

(1) vsR-$\{vcv; vv\}$ # + $\{vc; ra\} \to$ vs-v + $\{vc; ra\}$
(2) vs-$\{o; e\}$ # + $\{vc; ra\} \to$ vs-$\{u; i\}$ + $\{vc; ra\}$
(3) vs-ma + yi-$\delta ka \to$ vs-ma + i-δka
(4) a + $ax \to a$ + x
(5) uwu + $o \to u$ + o
(6) u + $o \to uw$ + o
(7) i + $\{e; o\} \to iy$ + $\{e; o\}$
(8) uy + $i \to u$ + i
(9) # #$yì$ + x $\to i$ + x
(10) $kéV_{ts}$ fl vs-#$a \to k$ + a
(11) y + $c \to c$

9.5. Rules of Orthographic Change and Removal of Signs and Symbols

The rules of this section should be the last to be applied.

(1) $\{[<\text{x}> + \{k; p\}]_1; <\text{x} + \{k; p\}>\}; \{k; p\} \to \{g; b\}$
(2) $\{qk; qp\} \to \{k; p\}$
(3) $\dot{v} \to v$
(4) $\{\alpha; \beta; \gamma\}$-x $\to$ x
(5) x-δy $\to$ x-y
(6) x-y $\to$ xy
(7) x + $\emptyset \to$ x
(8) $<\text{x} + \text{y}> \to$ xy
(9) $\{[\text{x} + \text{y}]; [<\text{x}> + <\text{y}>]\} \to$ x y
(10) $ćvcv(cv)^n \to ćvcv́(cv́)^n$

10. ABBREVIATIONS

The following abbreviations appear in this chapter. Some of them are used in the specification of morphophonemic rules, others in general formulas and in the text.

abl = abilitative
Acc = accompaniment tagmeme
accom = accompaniment
act = active
ad = adverbial
ani = animate
asp = aspect
assert = assertative

C = complement tagmeme
c,c = consonant
$ć$ = each succeeding vowel in the word is high
$c̀$ = each succeeding vowel in the word is low
Cl = clause
Cl$_{nu}$ = clause nucleus

Cl_{per} = clause periphery
Cl_{ref} = referent clause
Cl_{tem} = temporal clause
conj = conjunction, conjuctive
cx = complex
d = descriptive, dual
desig = designatory
dir = directional
DscP = descriptive phrase
eq = equational
ex = exclusive
foc = focus
I = instrument tagmeme
IdP = Idiomatic phrase
imper = imperative
impl = impersonal
inani = inanimate
indic = indicative
inst = instrument
inter = interrogative
intr = intransitive
L = location tagmeme
loc = locative, locational
loc_d = directional stems
LocP = locative phrase
loc_p = positional stems
loc_{pn} = place names, personal names
loc.s = locative stem
loc_{sp} = location in space
loc_t = location in time
md = mood
mx = simple
n = noun
nb = number, numeral
NbP = number phrase
neg = negative
nf = noun, nominal formative
nom = nominal
nom.s = nominal stem
NP = noun phrase
n.P = nonpredicate
ns = noun stem

ns_c = common noun stem
ns_d = descriptive stem
ns_{nb} = numeral stem
ns_{nq} = nonquantifiable noun stem
ns_{pn} = personal name
ns_q = quantifiable noun stem
ns_t = temporal noun stem
nu = nucleus
O = object tagmeme
P = predicate tagmeme
p = personal
Pass = passive
per = person affixes
pl = plural
pn = personal names, place names
poss = possessive
$poss_{ab}$ = absolute possessive
$poss_{rel}$ = relative possessive
pres.con = present continuous
pro = pronoun
pro.s = pronoun stem
ProP = pronoun phrase
pro_p = personal pronoun
$pro.s_{obj}$ = object pronoun stem
$pro_{n.obj}$ = nonobject pronoun
$pro.s_{loc}$ = locative pronoun
pro_{loc} = locative pronoun
pro_{int} = interrogative pronoun
R = referent-reason tagmeme, reduced stem types
r = reduplication
ref = referent
rvs = reduced verb stem
rx = reflexive
S = subject tagmeme, sentence
sb = substantive
SbP = substantive phrase
sf.p = substantive suffix potential
sg, sing = singular
st = stative
supp = suppositional
SynP = syntactic phrase
T = time tagmeme

t = temporal
TemP = temporal phrase
Tp = topic tagmeme
tr = transitive
ts = tense-aspect
V = a class of vowels
v, *v* = any vowel
v́ = vowel with high tone
v̀ = vowel with low tone
{*v*; *c*}# = morpheme final
#{*v*; *c*} = morpheme initial
##{*v*; *c*} = word initial
vb = verb
vc = voice
vs = verb stem
VP = verb phrase
x, *x* = any grammatically
    permitted morpheme or
    morpheme sequence

y = any other grammatically
    permitted morpheme or
    morpheme sequence
<x-y> = complex stem
<x + y> = inflection
{x̂; ŷ} = all vowels of x or y are high
{x̌; y̌} = all vowels of x or y are low
1st = first person
2nd = second person
3rd = third person
( ) = optional
/,; = or
→ = rewrite as
[ ] = phonetic, phrase unit
< > = word unit
{ } = alternant choices

XV. *Auyana Texts*

Compiled by HOWARD McKAUGHAN

1. INTRODUCTION

These Auyana texts were recorded on tape in the village of Asempa in
1962. The story teller, or a companion, summarized each text in Neo-
Melanesian. Later the tapes were transcribed with the help of an informant, and then translated using the New-Melanesian as the intermediate
language.

The texts are unanalyzed. Translation is general rather than morpheme
by morpheme. Each stretch of Auyana speech between spaces is to be
equated to the English which has been given in the same order as the
Auyana. That is, when an Auyana word equivalent takes more than one
word in the English, hyphens are used between the English words. The
free translation is a translation, not a paraphrase, though the difficulties
of translation through an intermediate language, especially Neo-Melanesian,
are serious.

Again, as for Awa, the reader-analyst is encouraged to compare the
raw data with the descriptions given. Since most of the descriptive work is
on Usarufa, the texts will be most useful for ascertaining more about the
Auyana relation to Usarufa.

The texts are transcribed with a number of noncontrastive phones. The
intervocalic obstruents are fricative, or flap in the case of the alveolar.
The labial intervocalic phoneme has both voiceless and voiced varieties. It
has been recorded with *f* and sometimes *b,* but is to be pronounced as a
bilabial fricative whether voiced or voiceless. Letters *d* and *r* are used
for the aleveolar phoneme. The six vowels include *i, e, u, o, a,* and *aa.*
The last is the low central vowel and the *a* is the schwa, a mid central

vowel. Prosodic features have not been indicated. Sentence divisions, and even word divisions, are tentative in these texts as they were in Awa.

Again, it is hoped that these texts will prove useful for analysis of the paragraph, and also be useful for students learning to analyze languages.

More stories on origins have been included in this collection. The 'Bat and the Python' story occurs throughout the region as do others of the stories. The compiler believes the texts will prove of content interest as well as linguistic.

2. THE BAT AND THE PYTHON

1. *Mora miyanurai mimbora ontankaq mena.*
   One this-way-did this-one stone-at sat.
2. *Mena numa empaima kuwofimpa iyaakaraampo.*
   Sat headdress down-below Kuwofimpa you-came-up.
3. *Mifa iyaakaraampo ifaqi mbaandantomba maruqa baimakesa inkweto*
   This you-came-up place lot-of-people level-place fix-up singsing did-
   waasarai naaq.
   they it.
4. *Awiyaana manikaiko iyaankaafaya koi kaampan koiqa wiyaakoqa*
   Auyana-two ancestors snake with bat with python-with (python)
   (wiyaa) awiqa miniya kaafaayaanko awiqa wiyaakoiqa efo minda numa
   name this snake name python-with all-right this headdress made-it-two
   uwaamaresaaraiyain ontankaq imaesaraiyai; tinowa epaimemi naaoqarufa
   stone two-sit-down; their-mother at-place near-where garden she-went two-
   kisaufa kumberowa saaraiyai.
   doing-this.
5. *Min ontankaq minuduma mose efai auwaaamifi faimaresarai mesarai*
   This stone this-headdress on-top put feather stuck-in were-there try-out
   tirai maroyana.
   singsing.
6. *Ino aawana aawanaera numa kumiya mosa aawanena sirai maqmai-*
   Mother you-look looking headdress all-right on-top she-look said you-
   nanaano se saraiyai.
   two-try this they-talk.
7. *Mura tinowamba simame saraiyai tirai maroyana.*
   Down their-mother two they-said tried-out dance.
8. *Mindumako imba kwekumu nesaraiyai imba kweku mifo mikaq.*
   This-headdress no all-right fix-it not good this want.
9. *Kainasafimbo iyambo meraindawai aaqa karasuwekai iyafi akaiyana*
   At-fire-place dog is-there ear cut-off fire-in cook-it smell did this-head-
   kasifunta wenawanena mindumaako kumindara anaao suwana.
   dress good look he-said.
10. *Iyanaqa karasuwe saraiyai memi tiyaankaq tasasa pasuwesaraiyai*

Dog's-ear cut they-two there their-hand rub between-two this-headdress
minduma amifaq totuwesarait.
on-top put-it.
11. *Numa mosa faimaresaraiyai.*
    Headdress on-top stick-it-in.
12. *Tirai maroyana mindumako imaimaena marapaqkakasa uwasarain*
    Try-out singsing headdress good ground proper-movement enough you-
eqa umaraifo minkaqmakekai kwaitimaqaanifo kumokayosu suwasarai kwe
made-it this-put-it man's-place-in go-down say-this them go-down.
kumesaraiyai.
13. *Minka timanoi minka wimaresaraiyai oqontu kuwamaimaisarai.*
    This skin this-place two-put-down another-form two-made.
14. *Awanesarai minduma umaisarai umbata maqneremba umaisarai*
    Two-did headdress two-made plenty ornaments two-made go-down.
kunka.
15. *Maresarai kunanoyasa mami ndaantomba empai kuwofimpaq marifan*
    Two-made look this place-man down-there Kuwofimpa place making-
kwetasuwowasa.
singsing.
16. *Uwoi kumbesarai tirai maqmai wenuyasa maandaantombo tumba*
    Two go just-there two-started singsing plenty-men come they all head-
mifa miwiti numa matukesa minkaiqnarai ti numasafesan uwe iye sesan
dress take-off these-two-fellows their headdress oh oh said light put walk-
omba tinkame wenesa.
about.
17. *Aarekowaqi inaamarukowaqi aunkopiriti maitapiritimai wena aneqo*
    Girls young-girls pinch-them go-pinch all same skin-ornaments broke-
aropirasi kotaraqmai tataraqmai.
it broke-them.
18. *Kweuwana uwanena.*
    Do-this look.
19. *Maemoyankakemba in mbiyasesarai siyai: maqawiyana numa siyesiye*
    Were-there these two-talked said: *maqawiyana numa siyesiye aronamiyo*
aronamiyo paasomembo mintosofiyo mantosofiyo mintosofiyowe o e min-
passomembo mintosofiyo mantosofiyo mintosofiyowe o e mintosofiyo man-
tosofiyo mantosofiyo mintosofiyo miyasuyasu maan awiyampake.
tosofiyo mintosofiyo like-this-sang this Auyana.
20. *Kwaasi mbaantuma umentuman umaisa kunkawe.*
    Man this-headdress made-headdress made came-down.
21. *Miyasesa tamai nemowasarai inaamaru mbe sayafaqnamba siyarowa-*
    Same-talk singsing walk-about young-girl all two-came morning two-
sarai kumbai sara.
came-down took-them.

22. *Tinerineo uwamaisamo iyuya tauma piyaqa auwatimaqmai sankweyu-*
Skin-put-on did-this-go on-top shell snail-shell broke-off-give did-went.
wasa.

23. *Aaqaao simamaesareiyai kweyuwana mora wintaabenamo iyuwa*
No two-said he-went one liked-him go-up a-lot go-up.
maenamo iyuwai.

24. *Miwan eqa kaampankon awaininkon ewe sena mosa amuwana iyu-*
This enough bat his-wife yes she-said go-up gave-her went-back.
wekai.

25. *Iyuwerowana awanena mepimi (k)wiyakombo iyuwai awaininko*
Went-back look this snake go-up his girl went-up.
uwoninyai.

26. *Kene enkarese iyampo menda.*
Me like-you I-come this.

27. *Weninaupare aaqa marenanifo umbenai mimbarafa pokai imekai kisau*
Her-place ear think you-me-sit-down this-ground here stay garden
uwandayaufo sena.
make-garden-for-food said.

28. *Mbarena empaimi aawiyan ontanka (k)iiyawanowana ndomba kwe-*
They-go down-below Auyana stone they-went-look water flooded he
fiyuntabena mbae amanoimo mura wimaimo fakariri aqmaromba iyamai-
skin down put take-off put-down come-get put-it-on.
mai anerane.

29. *Weuwana awiman ayama aneraneqa.*
Did-it she-urinate defecated did-it-all-over.

30. *Kweuwana ankembara maaqu waasiko kunkaune kauweq waasiko*
Did-it my-skin no-good man-me go-down good man-me not-like did-it.
raamba nuwamai.

31. *Kumune embe iyondanifo.*
Go-down you just-come-on.

32. *Senambe naipaq tayain anukaq maawayaamba fiyu nafoyaq mafaafena.*
Said ditch base root gripped-with-teeth Fiyu trunk bite-it.

33. *Maafaq ameraamba maufiyena wanena mora uwaaneqa anukaq.*
There tail fastened-on did-it one casuarina rope.

34. *Minkafa kwaao suwana awaininko minkafa mbarena.*
This-one you-go he-said his-wife here she-went.

35. *Naaopaq komerowana; nanowa efo naompaqma iyan aagaayena kwe-*
His-place she-stayed; his-mother all-right house fire she-made warm-self.
kaufuwana.

36. *Minkaq imaena; minkaq imaena naanowan tafenamai iya mosa mai-*
This-place stay; there sit-down his-mother said fire come-up get.
mai.

37. *Aagaisinka renaq kauwono suwana.*
     Made-fire I-warm said.

38. *Iya nkumbaupa min awandampa aanowana aarembo ankaro (m)i-*
     Fire get this room look his-wife put-her this-young-girl what-this.
     namaru maandora.

39. *Sewaq maanda kaweq waasi kowaq ewaq maankumba ewaq weye ono*
     You-talk this good man you-are this you-get this-one you come she-
     suwana.
     said.

40. *Aiqmaqme iyunana.*
     I-sent-away I-came.

41. *Awaao sena kweyiye.*
     No said she-came.

42. *Miyasima suwena waanena nefo minda toqwa uwama kowana.*
     She-said-this talk finish all-right this skirt tie-on stay.

43. *Iyaqoin efo amuqa kaumai(n) minontankaq mena mbaqankarai.*
     Child all-right stomach pregnant this-stone stay bear.

44. *Maqankena waasaqa ufonkwamba iyaankafayamban tumaama mapaq*
     Grasshopper insects snake bird all insects snake bore did.
     ufonkwamba matinkame wewena.

45. *Wenawi moran kwiya mbaqankarai.*
     His-skin one python she-bore.

46. *Maqankowana wanenan efo unaamba imban awiyame mbora iyampoi*
     Gave-birth did all-right net-bag not look one child gave-birth this-this-
     maqankarai iya minininko arumpinkemba maaqmopaq ufonkwambo mau-
     girl belly-in-her all insects this-place walk-about this-person gave-birth.
     woifa kaowenimba weyaamiqa maqankarai.

47. *Maaqankowana samain tarunturena mimpinta miniyampoisomba teu-*
     Bear dry-banana-leaf strip-off-soft-part in-this these-children put-in.
     wamba.

48. *Kowana aarekoni anowa mempakemban iyai.*
     Did-it wife mother down-below came-up.

49. *Mare mare mare mare mare, marena iyena iyoi toqmai ananai suwana.*
     Came-up came came, came came-up come mouth want-look-I she-said.

50. *Qmqm kimboraawaq aawiyasuwenawaq waasi iyampoiyaq maqan-*
     Oh only-one look-good-said man child if-had-given-birth I give-you,
     karainawaq eraq amenauno, ankanawaq oikan anainiyono.
     hand-over face you-look.

51. *Maaqu iyampoisombaniye siyai miyawe suwana aaqaao sena; iyoi*
     No-good children she-said this said no said; come opened my-mother say
     totuwowana kesinowaqiya senan daantaabesa (meq) kofoiwe tafoiwesa
     want-to-suckle (er) go-out come-out fire-in fall-down did burned-up.
     iyafinta seyaafapopoq euwamai keakura.

52. *Ai sena minkanawaq kanawaqa kufasimbai mememi unampimba*
Yipes said these-ashes ashes picked-up got-them bag-in filled-up their-
kwetuwaauwowana nanowan iyai.
mother came.
53. *Maandora ewaq maaniyampoi maaniyan agaaenosu suwana.*
This-what you-do this-child this-fire burned-them she-said.
54. *Uwanena aaqaao etuwaao sunana maenano niyena niyena nifoisuwai*
Said-it no release I-say your-mother came-up opened took-out this fire
sasa maami iya keyakoe.
burned.
55. *Suwana aaroquwamai naaokemba minkakemba (aiq) kaiyaurambani*
Said quickly place this-place (*aiq*) banana cut-it hand-banana cut-it
karamakai feqafu karamena uwanena maandan eqan aafowan itufini aaroqu-
did this enough his-father will-come-hit quickly run your-place go-said.
wamai awaantamba eninaaopa kowosuwana.
56. *Mifeqafu maemaenan kouwana wanena.*
This-ripe-banana took left did-it.
57. *Naopake iyanomba kwemba iyapopoqa euma kowanawanena.*
Place he-came he fall-down stayed were-burned.
58. *Mini yaankafayanko iyaakawena.*
This snake he-came-left.
59 *Maananu ko faika tafaika uwamai kumeme nambe aneka kuwofimpa*
This mountain go-search come-search did-it go-down again go Kuwo-
inkaq kufaituwowana minkaq kumuwana kumbaiwi suwena.
fimpa there ambush-and-stay this she-came-down he went-down swallowed-
her.
60. *Oiqa kunkwegafuwana minka kumuwana minarankamban uwoikum.*
Mouth opened-up this-one came-down this-old-lady unsuspecting.
61. *Oipimba kumbaimenawiq kasuwena niyai.*
Mouth-in went-down swallowed-up came-up.
62. *Marena weyuwana beme eqa kesinomba kuntufuntuwe iyone senan.*
Came went-up he enough my-mother you-killed-her you-come she-said.
63. *Efo ontamba maimai iyafimba kwaakaimarowana maarena minkaq*
Now stone get fire-in heated-it-up he-came this-one he-come-up was-
iyuwana wanenambi ontafaqi maena tone suwana.
there door sit-down food talk.
64. *Mimo tufimba mintomba ninkambai mimbonumba mofamunta marena*
This leaf this-food shake-out this-stone took-it put-it down throw-it
murume tuwowana mifaq aandaampa oiqa ontaraq moikaafuwana.
inside his-mouth down his-throat when-he-came.
65. *Ifaq muratuwowana miniyan kafayako narumpinkaq kwekumena*
This-place down-throw-it this snake belly-in go-down this-fire burned
miniyako kamai kamai kaamai wekumuwana.
burned burned went-down.

66. *Ai sena.*
Yipes he-said.

67. *Ndompinke aafumba nakaime we kumena epai toifinka maime.*
Water-in shoulder rub he go-down place soft-ground sit-down.

68. *Waaekatuwamai kumena empimi werain dompimban efo mimpimba*
Turn-over-and-over go-down down-below stay water-in all-right in-this
kumpuqmai.
go-die.

69. *Isiataraqurai nomparisimo (nontaare) wekofatanaraawefi kumpuwena*
Lying-across-it water-bridge (bridge) jump-over island did this-inside
wanena mimpimba miniyako aafutuwowanan.
this-fire killed-killed-him.

70. *Efo minda aanaoarakankon efo minda owemaan iyampoe sewaq maa*
All-right this his-mother-old now this oh-this child where sorry this
nda tufusiyuwaano simaisuwena kunaraq naaraq aaraq naaraq araqnaaraq
you-killed-mine this-way-talk go-cut cut cut cut cut-up cut.
uwamai.

71. *Maafa sama unamba turena.*
There dry-leaf-banana bag fill-up.

72. *Minunampimba kwetutuwa suwowana awaininkon owema miyaeraq*
This-bag-in fill-up did his-wife oh I-did-this my-husband I-killed-him
kesuwaiqa tufutuwauno sena.
she-said.

73. *Amaafomba taimen asaurai andantokena andantokenan asuuwa maena*
His-heart jerk-out tie-up rope-made rope-made tie-it take she ground
kwena maapa kwemboq aareko kouwana.
she girl go.

74. *Wanenan efo anowa maimaena memi kumupa anainkafamba kunkai*
Did-it now his-mother cook-it this-place down-there behind-place go-
anaikafamba mare mare mare mare mare marena.
down follow went went went went went went.

75. *Aimo aawiyaampa ke manikoma utausenao kuropan efo mifakemba*
Before Auyana it ancestor go(?) left now that-place go other-place(?).
kuwau taumai.

76. *Mifambi anowa mifankouraimbani.*
This-place go-there settle.

77. *Min wiyan araqmaaraq uwamai tutuwa maaena.*
This python cut-it did fill-it-up take.

78. *Kouraimbanifo iyaakeya timaapan efo minda mbaami meraunda kana-*
Go-there Ilakia place all-right this this live *kanaka* skin like-man this-
kaqa auwara waasiko mbemi owanda sambo.
place red rope.

79. *Aasaimo uwamaimo amaafombo mura tutuwamaenamo kunkaimbo.*
Tie-around did-this heart down fill-up-take go-down.

80. *Makaimba mindamaaq kemo undaante faafuta kuwaraq waasiko min-*
    Put-it this I myself black his-skin man this this-one place in-sight put-it
    dambaami afora paaka mbatuwena maeqmaeqa kwesana.
    stay is-there.

81. *Weraisanan efo minda mbarenan efo memo maifakembo simamunaimo*
    It-is-there all-right this put-it all-right long-time here-before I-told-you
    isaandamo aifariqo umaimo sunda.
    you-know at-first I-made talk.

82. *Manikoma kurai aempa mifanko aawiyowena ifako.*
    Ancestor he-go along-here this-place it-is this-place.

83. *Pinisi.*
    Finish.

84. *Uwakuraimbani eqa.*
    Ended so.

1. Once there was a certain person who sat down at a stone. He sat, and his headdress—that place where he sat is down below, the place where you came up from, Kuwofimpa. At this place where you passed, there were a lot of people and they fixed up a level place for a singing, and they danced there. Two Auyana ancestors, a bat together with a snake—the kind of the snake was a python, this snake was a python—these two made up a headdress, and they sat on a stone. Their mother was at a place at a garden near there where the two were fixing their head decorations. 5. There at this stone the two put the headdress on, sticking in a feather, trying it out for a singsing. 'Mama, you look, is it all right, is the headdress all right?' She looked at it upon his head and asked if they tried it; so they talked this way. They called down to their mother and said they had tried it out. They didn't fix it properly; it wasn't as they wanted it. A dog was there at the fire-place, so they cut off his ear. They cooked it in the fire and it had a certain odor. 'You look to see if this headdress is good,' he said. 10. They two cut the dog's ear off, and they rubbed it between their hands, and rubbed it on the top of the headdress. The two stuck it in on top of the headdress and tried it out in a singsing. The headdress was all right. They moved over the ground and it had the proper movement. 'Good, it is fixed up now,' so they put it on.

They went down to the men's place. After she talked to them, they went down. Now here they changed forms and became other [young men]. After they did this, they made the headdress and they made plenty of ornaments, and went down. 15. They two went down, and they were making a singsing down there at Kuwofimpa.

The two went down there, and were just there. They started to dance. Plenty of people came, and they took off their headdresses. These two had on their headdresses and they all said, 'Oh, oh.' They put them on and walked about. All the women and young girls would go about and pinch them as they went back and forth. So they broke the skin ornaments. They kept doing like this. They were there some time, and the two sang: '*Maqawiyana numa siyesiye aronamiyo paasomembo mintosofiyo mantosofiyo mintosofiyowe o e mintosofiyo mantosofiyo mintosofiyo.*' This singing is from this place, Auyana. 20. The one that made the headdress came down. They talked like this, and walked about doing the singsing.

Now of all the young girls, two stayed till morning and the two [fellows] came down, and they wanted them. They put on their skins, and having done this they broke off shells, snail shells, and gave them to them. They did this, and went along. But the two boys said 'Nothing doing,' and went on. One of them liked one a lot and followed him. As for the bat's wife, she agreed, and when he gave it to her, she went back.

25. Now after she went back, the other went with the snake. This other girl went up [saying], 'I like you, so I am coming.' As for her, she thought, "We'll just settle at this place, and we'll make a garden for food.' So they went, and down below at the Auyana stone they went and looked, and the river was flooded, so he put off his [man's] skin, put it down, and came and put [the other] on [he became a python]. When he did that, she urinated, and defecated all over herself.

30. When she did it [he said], 'I'm just like a no good man—I'm not like a real man. I'll go down, and you just come over on me.' He said this and at the ravine, at the base of the tree, he gripped the roots with his teeth, biting into the trunk of the Fiyu tree. With his tail, he fastened onto the one there, and made a rope to the casuarina. 'Now you go along over me,' he said. So his wife went along over it. 35. She stayed then at his place; now his mother made a fire at his house, and he warmed himself. He stayed at this place; he was there, and he said to his mother, 'Go get some wood. Make a fire first, and I'll warm myself,' he said. She went to get the wood, and she saw his wife—the young girl whom he had put there. 'What is it you said? This is a good one. You got this one and came,' she said. 40. 'But I sent her away, and I came.' But she said, 'No,' and she came anyway. The old lady said this, so then the girl put on the full skirt and settled down.

She got pregnant with a child while living at this stone, and gave birth. When she gave birth, there were born to her grasshoppers, insects, snakes, birds, and all kinds of insects. 45. She gave birth to one python—so that is what happened, she gave birth to these things. Now she didn't give birth to just one child, this girl had all sorts of insects in her belly, and having gone about at this place, she gave birth to these things. So she stripped off the soft part of the dry banana leaf after she had given birth, and she put these children in it.

Now the woman, her mother, came up from down below. She came and came and came. She came and at the opening [of the cave where they lived] she said, 'I want to look at them.' 'Nothing doing.' She thought there was only one. 50. 'If I had given birth to only one, and that a good manchild, I would let you look at his face, and hand him over to you' 'The children are not good,' the snake's mother said. After she said this, [the girl's mother] said, 'No'; then, as she came to the opening [cave door], they [the children] said, 'My mother,' and wanted to suckle. They came out all over the place, and they fell into the fire and were burned. 'Yipes,' she said, and she picked up these ashes, got them, and put them in a net bag. Their mother came. 'What is this, what have you done?' 'They got burned in the fire,' she said. But when she said it, [the other] replied, 'No, you let them out, I say.' Her mother, this one, came up here, and opened it, took them out, and they were burned. 55. When she said this, there at that place, she quickly cut a hand of bananas. She cut these ripe bananas. That done, she said, 'His father will come and kill you. Go quickly to your place on the run,' she said. She took these ripe bananas and left.

Now [the father] came home. The child had fallen in and was burned— he found out. So this snake came, and then left. He went searching for her on this mountain, going back and forth, and kept doing that as he came down. Now he went again to Kuwofimpa and there he set up an ambush, and waited. This one, she came down.

60. He went down, and there he opened his mouth and swallowed her up. This one came down, and this old lady, unsuspecting came along, and he swallowed her. Then he came on up. When he came up and arrived, then [his wife] said, 'You have gone and killed my mother, and now you have come.' So she got a stone, and she heated it up in the fire. Now the snake came, and when he came, he was there by the door, and he sat down, and talked of food. Now this leafy vegetable and the food, she took it, and she took the stone in two sticks and put it in the food. She prepared to throw it inside his mouth down his throat when he came and sat down at the door and opened his mouth. 65. So she threw it down his throat, and it went down inside the snake's belly. This fire burned and burned him as it went down. He went down in the water and rubbed his side and sat down in the soft ground. He went down in it and turned over and over and stayed there. He died there in it. Lying across like a bridge, he jumped over and went down and died on that island; so it happened. This fire down inside him killed him.

70. Now this one, the old mother [of the snake] she cried out, 'Oh, oh, you have killed my child, where is he?' and talked this way. Now she went down, and cut him all to pieces. So there she put it on a dry banana leaf in a bag. She filled up this bag and his wife said, 'Oh, this is what I did, I killed my husband.' So she jerked out his heart and tied it up. She made a rope, and having made the rope, she tied it up and took it.

Now the girl left that area. When she did it, then his mother took the bag and followed her, going along behind at that place. She went and went and went. 75. Now our ancestors who were Auyana before left that place and went to another, so these two they went down and then on over there. His mother went there. She cut up this python, filled up the bag and took it. She went there. Now Ilakia is the place. It is at this place they two lived. They are *kanakas*—they have the likeness of men. She tied up the heart round and round, put it in, and took it, and went down. 80. She put it there, and these are black just like I am. At this place not so far, she put it, and it stayed and stayed, and is there. Now it is there—for she put it there. It is where I told you before when I was talking to you before, you remember. The old people went along that level place, that is the place and that is the end of the story.

3. Two Brothers Obtain Wives

1.   Aimosendawesi—aimosendawesi, embominaq—kisau amakopa naun-
    Talk-before—talk-before, this-person—garden mound-up shoots-came-
karurauwana tauwarapimba matapikaiyesi.
up shoot he-go-watch.

2.   Kisaupamba tapikowana uwanena nauwarampi tafikowana numam-
    Garden-to go-watch stay vine go-watch bird-come sit-down shoot this-

bimpi tamauwana fasuwowana minkisaufa komayai.
garden go-stay.

3. *Komauwana arankanko mifaq merowana sena eqaimi numa ke em-*
    Stay old-woman here she-stay talk you-get bird it put him arrow pull-
    bomai kemba auwaiqa metausiyo siyai.
    and-give said.

4. *Meyesuwana efominda kwentuma mbomaena auwaiqa metauqamakai.*
    Said all-right-this take get-it arrow pull-and-give.

5. *Aneka tafikena oqomba fasuwowana mifaq we kuwana wanena kwe*
    Go watch again shoot-it there he go be-there she bird get arrow give-
    numa momaera auwaiqa meamakai.
    him.

6. *Kesi naopa ko yauye su minarankanko we suwanan efo ewe sesarai*
    My place you come said this-old-woman she said all-right yes he-said
    kura.
    went.

7. *Kuwana kwaqanko maime aqankarai.*
    Go bark-cloak she-got covered-him.

8. *Iya isaifo wesena.*
    No not-get-up said.

9. *Aqan kowanan efo mena ifakaqaunkwai kurouwana moran aren*
    She covered all-right there slept-good did one girl's skirt put-on this-
    toqwa uwamai minkeqe isawankarai.
    one stood-up.

10. *Isawankowana awanena minamo waimompinke toqwa uwamai*
    She-standing there this-one sleep-finish skirt got-ready good he-pleased.
    kaweq uwankena.

11. *Iyafasinena anomba areko kufuqan kwe uwamutafena iyawanena*
    Get-up big girl cook-food she give-him get-up this old-woman one-
    min arankankomba araisafena uwankarai.
    given pleased.

12. *Uwankenan efo aiqme nene naopaq waosuwana.*
    Pleased all-right took her place said.

13. *Aiqmena kwe ninaopaq wekuwana awao kaweq uwamai mininimbe*
    Took her his-place went older-brother good look-at this-one look-at.
    awarai.

14. *Meawanena embandabaq konta fakenaq maninimbeq maewaq teno*
    Look-at you-go-get where where this-person get-her go said my-older-
    suwana kesuwao kemundatemba auwaiqa uwamai.
    brother do-what-I-did arrow make.

15. *Kisaufaq uwoiwao we suwana.*
    Garden-place go-do he said.

16. *Auwaiqan umaiena kisaufaq mbata fikena.*
    Arrow made garden-place there watched.

17. *Tumafasuwowana kumuwana minduma baewaq aren toqwa uwasiyo*
    Shot-it fall-down this-bird you-get girl skirt fasten said.
sena.
18. *Iyafakemba suwana, aqa enimpo iyamosendawi aifetiyani.*
    Hard/cross talked, no first-one not-talk-so do-that.
19. *Miyawesuwanan efo minda aneka pasuwowana inkakuwana minduma*
    Talked-this-way all-right this again shot fell-near this-bird took-it
    mowemai are afeqan toqwa uwasi none siyai.
    woman put-on skirt give to-me he-said.
20. *Miyawesuwana embarama uwesempo sena.*
    This-talked your-talk this-way she-said.
21. *Minkusi fakemba suntafena aiqmaena kurai.*
    This crossly talk-like-that took-her went.
22. *We kuwana kwe noqora iyaoiq mamakena we suntafena maquwarasi*
    He went he strong mouth put he talked no-good-girl this him married
    minka kemba kotoqwa uwamakai.
    gave-him.
23. *Embarasempo emo kaika rantaraka kawiqi nimba toqwa uwamusino.*
    You-talk-that-way you talked hard good marry put-on-skirt give-you.
24. *Enaisafe seqawana mbamaqo inimba toqwa; uwa mone sena mbaena*
    Your-talk gave no-good marry put-on-skirt; now I-give said took two
    mamake sarai enawanena afakomba mo awa nowana kaweq inimba
    put-them look-at younger-brother when went looked good marry took he
    maime we kuntafena.
    left.
25. *Kisau nora kunawiq marena oraq uwaaneq wantanamba mindatuwena.*
    Garden big cleared cut-it big casuarina very-big that-one-left.
26. *Uwanena mbinda iyaikunao suwana mbinda kunarai.*
    Left this-one you-clear-branches said this-one cut-it.
27. *Iyafaqafaq we kumu tafena memempaqo kafimo wiyankowano iyun-*
    He-went-up he down came down-below wild-bamboo lean-against went-
    kafi iyotoqwi tuwena.
    up took-away did.
28. *Toqwetuwena efo mememifaq merowana minaimpinkemba kwesuna*
    Take-away all-right on-top he-was-there this-talk I-talk you-angry I-
    agosenda keankisa uwantanaune siyai.
    only-one I-put-garden said.
29. *Miyawesena kweya uwandamaq we uwana.*
    Talk-this-way he made-his-garden he did-it.
30. *Numako tawawanena kofarafa tafarafa wenanomba mamerontafena.*
    Bird saw-him fly go look-at-him was-there.
31. *Iyaiqmai marapaq munankowana seyabaq numako - munankowana.*
    Get-him ground put-him all birds put-him-down.

32. Kumbena awaninkomba kunaiqmai ankaresarai kisaum kweuwande
Go-sit his-wife took put-them-both garden had-food die died.
puqmai sawiyawa.
33. Uwakuraimbani.
That's-all.
34. Iyeyaqmai kumeme kumeme.
Go-up-get come-down come-down.
35. Kumemena nanefo minkaq munankowana minaimpaq merouwase
Come all-right this-fellow come-put this-place down-put now his wi
efo awainimba kufuqa numaisa mifamba maka uwana ndamaq namc
cook-it take-it give-him there do eat eat eat eat eat do do do do do a
namaq namaq we we we we we wena meqefo naupaq kurai.
right place he-went.
36. Naopaq komena awanenan efo awaombako aisanaiqmai tufukai.
Place went settled all-right older-brother cross-at-him fight.
37. Tufutuwena efowena awainini mindawe koime inambaqnaresa if
Fight all-right wife this-one go-take bring-near place-died that's-a
sawiawa uwakuraambani.
38. Eqa pinis.
It-is finished.

1. This is about what has been said long ago. A certain man mounded up
garden. Certain shoots came up and he would go watch the young shoots. H
would go along to the garden and watch the new shoots; a bird would com
and he would shoot it, thus going and staying at this garden. When he woul
be there, an old woman would come there and he said to her, 'You go get th
bird, and you get the arrow and give it to me.' When he said this, then sh
would go and get it, pull out the arrow and come and give it to him. 5. So h
would go and watch again, and shoot [a bird]; and when he would be there, sh
would get the bird but give him the arrow.

'You come along to my place,' that old woman said. When she said it, h
replied, 'OK,' and went. When he went, she got a bark cloak and covered hir
up. 'Now don't get up,' she said. So she covered him, and he went to sleep. H
slept well, and a girl wanting to marry him came in. 10. As she was standin
there, he finished sleeping, and she readied herself; he was very pleased wit
her. He got up, and the girl cooked food for him, and gave it to him; he wa
very pleased with the old woman. He was pleased, so then she told him, 'Yo
take her to your place.'

He took her and after he went, his older brother saw her, and looked at thi
one. He having looked at her asked, 'Where did you go to get this girl?' 'We
my older brother, you just do what I did with my arrow.' 15. 'So you go to th
garden,' he said. He made arrows and went there to the garden and watched o
hunted. So when he shot it, it would fall down. 'You get this bird, and give m
a girl for marrying,' he said. He talked to her crossly, and she said that the firs
one that came didn't talk that way to her. After she talked this way to him, the

this one shot one again, and it fell near her so she took the bird, and he said,
'You give me that girl for marrying,' and when he talked this way, she said,
20. 'You shouldn't talk that way.' He talked crossly and took her and went.
When he went, he had 'made his mouth strong'—was very cross; he talked like
that and she gave him a no good girl for marriage. 'If you had not talked crossly,
I would have given you a good girl to marry. Because of your talk, I gave you a
girl that is no good.'

After she said this, she gave her to him, he took her; the two put them there
and the younger brother looked at her and he [older brother] took her and he
left. 25. He cleared the big garden; having cut it, he left a very big casuarina.
He said [to the younger one] you clear out the branches, and he cut them out.
He went up, and when he got ready to come down, the other who had leaned
a wild bamboo against it [the tree], after he went up, took it away. He took it
away. Now he was left up there—this is what has been said. 'Now I say that
you are angry at me, so I alone will put in a garden and eat,' he [the older brother]
said. He talked this way, and he made his garden and was there. 30. A bird saw
him [the younger brother in the tree], and flew and looked at him, and he was
there. They went and got him, and all the birds put him there on the ground. So
then he went and he took his [brother's] wife, and he settled them there, and he
made a garden and they had food. They all died in the end, and so ends the story.

He went up and got them, and went and went. 35. Now this one came and he
settled them there. Now his [younger brother's] wife cooked the food, gave it to
him there, and he ate and ate. He ate and ate, then he went to his place. He
went and looked at the place, and he was mad at his older brother. He fought
him. He fought him, then went and took his wife [back]. He brought her near this
place, and they died, that's all of it.

4. ORIGIN OF REEDS FOR WRAPPING ARROW TIPS

1. *Maaraumai aafarawai iyaiko maeqmaeq uwai taase aafarawai iyauko*
    This thing brothers two-there did five brothers were.
mauwai.
2. *E mauwai marena kuwana aampaqe sena.*
    Yes they-were there went road said.
3. *Kumba poqai aanon kifa ausamakopa.*
    He-go hole hidden place made-one.
4. *Kwena kuwa tarosamaiena mifaqmi kaukaumakwe kumuwana.*
    He-go fell into-it this-place down-deep he-went-down.
5. *Mora kwaasiko mena.*
    One man was-there.
6. *Aiq kesaanino weko mono su kesaanino weko mono suwana.*
    Oh my-child you came said my-child you came said.
7. *Owe suwanan efo epifaq iya kausuwe sarai.*
    Yes he-said OK here-fire warm they-two this-way.

8. *Teyenakai awainin arankakomba aiqmarena entoniqa koweuwo sena.*
   You-come-we-go old-woman his-wife sent-here you-food go-bring he-
   said.

9. *Iwaimo maya maya unda tainko awanayaiye sima suwe sarai.*
   Possum run run away I-do-it tree we'll-go-find two-talked this-way.

10. *Efo awofaq mowankena kwembarena mefaq imaena samoqa itaisu-*
    OK base went-put-him went-up there-on-top go-sit nut pull-off.
    wena.

11. *Owe maimai waamba mikumiye suwana.*
    Yes there animal go-down said.

12. *Maara mosa awanowana auramba kun tufantuwowana.*
    This-way on-top look his-eye came-down hit-him.

13. *Kuaw puqmae kumawasa efo kuwamaena mowimain.*
    Fell-down died fell-down OK come-get-him go-cook-him.

14. *Efo minda aawaininkonkaq kepai aarankankomba aamafomba taia-*
    OK this his-wife this old-woman [another one] heart pull-out-and-give
    muwana awanena.
    did-it.

15. *Kinda kepaifaq aanda fariqwemarena owe kemba kwaasi tiraqa tufuq-*
    This there vine tie-it-put-it Oh they man offspring killed-him this come
    mai maa tasuwe none sena.
    have-eaten said.

16. *Merowana.*
    Was-there.

17. *Kwem binda mboq tindawe siyaena mbaa tuwaomba miya maum-*
    Him this one come(?) they-said this-one their-older-brother same they-
    bau uwaenan efo moq morawiko kurai.
    waited waited OK again one-of-them went.

18. *Endaarawaq uwawiyo sena moq menkafa kumba me poqaifa ku-*
    You-what happen said again this-place he-go this hole fell-into.
    wafeku.

19. *(Karikaq wesufi fainare e—e—maasenda kweseqa su mpo e—).*
    (Slow eye look er—er—this you-talk I'm talking er—).

20. *Uwana efo menda morawiko kuwafekena mbarena kuwana.*
    Happened OK this another-one fell-in he-went went.

21. *Ae kesifarawao meweteno suwanan owe suwanan efo fukaaqa tufaisu-*
    Oh my-one-kind you-came said yes said OK smoked they-two-ate.
    wesarai.

22. *Tiyenaq iwaimo maya maya unda taifimba ko tufusime ena nowaran-*
    You-come possum run run I-do-it tree go kill-it give-me your-old-
    kamba kwekufuqina tainae (i)kumuwe su.
    mother she-cook-it fix-eat you-go-down said.

23. *Owe simasuwena efo maresarai me awauraq moaankena (men-*
    Yes he-answered OK they-two-went this at-base go-put-him(?) this
    dambe) me samoqa itaisuwowana men auramba kuntufantuwowana.
    nut broke-it-off this eye go-down hit-him.

24. *Menda komaimaenan efo me mokaramai we winena efo aamafomba*
    This-one go-get-him OK this go-cut-him he cook-him-ate OK heart
    taiyamuwana awanena.
    broke-off gave-did.

25. *Minda epibaq we kinarankanko moq mena morawikon aamafombo*
    This this-place she this-old-one again put-it another-one his-heart tie-
    fariqwima konka fariqwimakai.
    it same-with-it fasten-again.

26. *Fariqwimarena oweyaq maa kwaasi tiraqa ekaqa kwenasampo sena*
    Tie-it-put-it Oh-yes this man off-spring just ate-him said did.
    uwana.

27. *Embi kaeqa tufuqna suwena mboq afawa kurai.*
    Enough this-one those-two did-it again this-one he-go.

28. *Afufun kewai marena kuwana moa me poqaifa kuwafe kwena.*
    Third-one he went-along went-down again this hole fell down-in.

29. *(Uq) menda marena kuwanan efo (mi——) eniyambo kogausu-*
    (Uq) there he-went went-down OK (this——) again-fire warm-them-
    wesarai (e——) kesaanimba wetewaq one simasuwesarai.
    selves (enough——) my-child you-have come so-two-talked.

30. *Efo mi tiye itenkaqo iwaimo maya maya unda kotufusi me enano*
    OK this you-come this-place possum run run I-do-it you-kill-give
    arankamba kwe kufuqina tainaawe su.
    this mother old-one she cook come-eat said.

31. *Maarena mboqmi mese samoqa imaisuwena.*
    Went again up-there nut get-throw-it.

32. *Maimai suwana mosa awanowana auramba kuntufantuwo uwana*
    There said up look his-eye hit-it did this-place fall-down.
    mifaqmi kuntuwiq.

33. *Uwakuwana efo minda maesarai mowimai moq mearankamba efo*
    Did-it OK this-one he-got go-cook again this-old-woman OK this-his-
    menamaafomba amuyana.
    heart she-gave-her.

34. *Meimaronkambarowana eqa mbaaran owe sena.*
    This-where-put-first enough this yes said.

35. *Kwenka tifako naarawaq onaunesena.*
    Regarding second what-I-do said.

36. *Paaro unamba tuwasuwena kowanowana embaaramamba we sena.*
    Arrows in-bag fill-up go-look-for what-happened-you he-said.

37. *Menifaq kuwafekwena kowa awanombo owaromba tafiqmae kuwana.*
This-place fell-in go look-for bamboo-tipped-arrow ready-to-shoot he-
went.

38. *Wai namaifaq kokuwana aaqaao ifaqo konafo suwana.*
Man's house he-went no this-place you-no-can-go said.

39. *Naawoaq kemba mifaqo nundawi nune sena.*
Who-is that this-place I-can-walk about said.

40. *Kotafiq mauwana mindaqa sawaaqandowana.*
Go-ready came this-one afraid-of-him.

41. *Owe embeq ki faarumo owimo tosuemiyaamban isa emba ne sinka-*
Yes you this slowly they-did-it came-and-came did this-way you this-
minone sena.
one-want-to-kill-me said.

42. *Kombeinakai iwainko tufuqmai simewaawe su.*
You-me-go possum you-me-kill-give me-you-go said.

43. *Kufuquwamai enanonamina owe simasuwenan; efo mi itai suwowana.*
She-cook-it you-mother-give yes he-answered; OK this went broke-off.

44. *Me mosa awanowana maakumuwana aasekuwana membara muntu-*
This up looked it-came-down jumped-aside this-ground it-went-down-
fuwana.
hit.

45. *(Oweyaq) tufuwinona seqanuna me uwasuwaane sena.*
(Yes) you-want-kill-him I-say this-way you-did said.

46. *Maare kumuwana (kwaaq) mefaimi kwaasin efo seseumai.*
That-way came-down (*kwaaq*) there-up [pointing] man OK shot-and-
shot.

47. *Mimparoimo maekumba tufuqmai kaaweq umarena uwana.*
This-arrow took-left kill-him good put-him did.

48. *Kwe kinarankanko sena waasi tiraaqa awana nesa ka aamafombo*
He this-old-woman said man offspring you-look they-ate this heart
simemba maaqmaaqo unda niye sena.
gave-me all-time I-did this she-said.

49. *Mae muwanan efo minamaafomba kowe maena minayaantamba*
She-took give-him OK this-heart went got this-bone go-get.
kowemaena.

50. *Efo minarankamba tufuqmarena moq mi tufuqmarena.*
OK this-old-woman killed-her again this killed-her.

51. *Efo maafa minda anatatamaena mawimai minanafinta ufereme*
OK this-here this-one bamboo-come-cut come-put-in this-bamboo-in
ufereme.
fill-up fill-up.

52. *Ufeqmarena efai naaompaq moiya akaimarena.*
Filled on-top house he-go fire-made.

53. *Maara kunuwasuwe mowasa kwenefi ai(si)seqeq uwanaawanena.*
    Here come-down was-on-top talk conversed-did happen.
54. *Maanda uyaq seo simasuwena.*
    These who-are talking he-said.
55. *Inamarukomba aiqmarowana kaaq morarasiko iyawanena efi mi-*
    Small-girl sent-her this-one small-girl went-up on-top this-bamboo each
    nanamo kainka kainkaqo kiyawaraqo maqmae maqmae namo.
    partitioned this-fire put and put.
56. *Ufeo faiqyaantambo mayombo maamaromba.*
    It-had filled-up-bone got-it come-put-it.
57. *Iyawanena me kesuwaiq menkesuwaiqa isiyai.*
    She-look this my-husband this-my-husband go-talk.
58. *Minarasiko epi kesinaanon aawaiqa aniye iten kesinaano awaiqa*
    This-girl this my-sister's her-husband he-is this my-sister's her-husband
    (niye) iten kenafo kesinaano efo isenkesuwaiqaniye.
    (is) this my sister's OK that-one-my-husband.
59. *Isimarena uwanena; wembi uwemo simaron.*
    This-way talked; she pointed she-talked.
60. *Aarasi (qa) ifoq kwaasikomba kwembaqme anaano isai maemai.*
    Girl (qa) small man as-to-him older-sister came took-him.
51. *Mauwana.*
    Was-there.
62. *Kaakindaqa kwenki maaqukomba munawowana.*
    For-this-one him this-no-good-one she-left.
63. *Owe siyaena kesafai isimaraunda maa maaemai maaeo sena.*
    Oh she-said mine I-came-marked-out this-one you-came took said.
64. *Efo kwen kinawai komba mbeq simankowana aaqaao sena.*
    OK he this for-her-husband him she-marked no she-said.
65. *Ninkaise we nuwana miya nununuwaenan, efo norawaq onauno sena.*
    Afraid she went did this-did-and-did, OK what I-do he-said.
66. *Epifeq wenompi awaitai ukurenan efo numa faisukena.*
    This-place on-shield feathers tied-it-up OK bird stick-in.
67. *Mindarai maqmae kuwana.*
    This-one made-a-singsing went.
68. *(Me maami sewaqo maami sesumpo.)*
    (Yes this talk this I'm-saying.)
69. *Iyaume iyaume iyaume iyaume.*
    Did did kept doing it.
70. *Iyaumena me metewintana timaapaqo meme taiamifimba epai oka-*
    Did this certain-place that-ground this tree-head-of this Okanorafa
    rorafa timaaqo, meme tonamifaqo we naandambo iyukayemo siyaan (em—
    their-place, this Tomba-tree-head he yellow-reed became they-say (er—
    ee—).
    er—).

71. *Efo maarena aaraiwaqme we kuwana aaqaao sena paarowan kwaqa*
    All-right he-go she-followed he go no she-said arrow shoot-play went he
numai we tuwana unaamba kamoqa kwaatoi mayeqe suwana.
came-now bag net-for-head skirt I'll-get said.

72. *Miyasime iyasime iyasime iyasime sarai.*
    She-talk talked talked talked they two-talk.

73. *Meme okarorafa timaaqo efime wai tonkwaandara taifaq naandaamba*
    This Okanorafa place on-top he-was Tonka-tree tree yellow-reed
iyukwena.
became.

74. *Marapambenda aimpiimban efo aifoq anda koukena usumai usumaina*
    Ground-down-below base-of-tree OK crazy vine she-became twist-up
iyuwana aanawaramba puresi aaqa.
twist-up go-up-on-top neck broke neck.

75. *Inaaq inaama koukena (e—) usumai usumai usumaena iyuwana*
    Oh reed she-became (er—) twist-up twist-up twist-up go-up-on-top
anuwaramba puresi suwowana.
neck-of-vine broke did.

76. *Ikofekaafeq umaena awaofimba kundaa turai mbaniye.*
    Twist-down-falling did base-at-it-go-down go is-there.

77. *Minqa kinda simame su.*
    This-enough that's-all I-told-you said.

78. *Enki pai.*
    It-is finished.

1. There were two brothers in this story, I mean, there were five brothers. Yes, they were there, and he said, 'Its just a road.' He went, but he [an old man] had made a hole and hidden it in that place. He went [the oldest brother], and he fell into it. Now he went straight down it in this place. 5. There was one old man there. 'Oh,' he said, 'my child, you have come. You have come, my child,' he said. The other [brother] replied, 'Yes,' and the two warmed themselves at the fire. 'You come on, and we'll go' [he said].

He sent his wife, and said, 'You go and bring food. Every time I tried to get a possum, he kept running away. We'll go to the tree and find him.' The two talked together this way. 10. So he [the old one] went and put him at the base of the tree, and he went up and sat down in the top. He pulled off a spine covered nut. Then he cried, 'Oh, there, there's an animal going down.' The one down below did this way, looking up, and the nut came down and hit him in the eye and knocked him down. He fell down and he died. After he fell down, then he came and got him and cooked him. Then his wife pulled out this one's heart, and gave it to another old lady. 15. She tied it up with a vine and put it there. 'Oh, they have killed the offspring of a man [a young man]. You have come and eaten him,' she said. And she was there.

Now the brothers said with regard to this one, 'Is he going to come?' But what had happened to this their older brother is the same as we just mentioned. They waited and waited for him.

Then another one of them went. 'What happened to you?' he thought. So this one too went to this place, and he fell into the hole. (Don't stare at me that way, you know the story, I'm telling it OK.) 20. So it happened. Now this other one fell in too. He went down and down. 'Oh, my dear friend,' he said, 'you have come.' 'Yes,' he said. So they smoked, and they ate. 'You come on, there's a possum that keeps getting away when I try to get him, you come on to the tree, and kill it, give it to me, and your old mother will cook it and fix it up good, then you come eat it, and go,' he said. 'Yes,' he agreed, so they two went, and he put him at the base of the tree. So this one again broke off the spiny-nut and it went down and hit his eye and knocked him over. The old man went and got him. Then he went and cut him up, cooked him, and ate him. She broke off his heart and gave it to her. 25. This one, this old lady again put it in this place. She tied up this other one's heart, tying it in the same way, and she tied it and put it there. 'Oh yes,' she said, 'you just ate up this man—that's what you did.'

So—they killed and ate these two. Now this one [holding up the third finger], he also went. The third one went along, and he too fell down in this hole. He went down there, and was in it. And again these two warmed themselves at the fire. 'So, my child, you have come.' Then the two talked together. 30. 'Now you have come. This possum always gets away no matter what I do, so you go kill it, and give it to me. Now this old mother of yours, she will cook it, and you can come eat it,' he said. So he went, and again he went up there, got the spiny-nut and threw it. 'There it goes, there it goes,' he said. He looked up, and it hit him in the eye, and he fell down there. So he got this one, went and cooked him, and again, to this old woman, she gave his heart. This one put it along where she had put the others. She said, 'Yes.'

35. Now regarding the second brother, he thought, 'What will I do?' He filled his bag with arrows and went to look, thinking about what had happened to him. Now he fell into this place. He went looking for them, and he went ready to shoot with his bamboo tipped arrow. He went to the men's house, but the old fellow said, 'No, you can't go to this place.' 'Who is that? Why can't I walk about in this place?' he said. 40. So he came on, ready to fight. The old man was afraid of him. 'Yes,' he thought, 'you're the one. They came along here slowly, that's what they did. They came and came, you must have done it that way. You want to kill me,' he thought.

'Let's go, and let's kill the possum, then you give it to me and go,' he said. 'She will cook it, and your mother will give it to you.' He agreed, and he went up and broke this off. The boy looked up, and it came down, but he jumped aside, and it just went down and hit the ground. 45. 'Ah, you want to kill him; I said do it this way, but you did it that way' [you missed him], the old man said. He came down. 'Look up there,' he said, and he shot and shot the man.

He took these arrows and left. He had killed him, and put him aside. This old woman told him, 'You look, they ate these men, and they gave me their hearts, and all the time, I did this with them,' she said. She took them and gave them to him. He went and got these hearts, and went and got their bones too. 50. And he killed this old lady, and he killed the other one too. Then he came and cut some bamboo and put it in. He filled and filled the bamboo.

Now he went on top of the house, and he made a fire. Then he came down here. Those that were on top [where the hearts were] talked together. 'Who are these talking anyway,' he said. 55. And he sent a small girl to see. This small girl went up and on top she put her torch into each of the rooms. Now each place had the bones in it where he had gone and put them. She went up and looked. 'Ah, this one is to be my husband. This one is mine,' she said.

Now this girl, she thought, 'This is my sister's husband. This one is my sister's husband. This one is my sister's, but that one is my husband.' So she talked along this way. She pointed and said that.

60. Now as to that small one's man, her older sister came and took him. She was there. She left this no good fellow for the little sister. 'Oh,' she said, 'that which belongs to me, I came and designated, and you came and took him,' she said. But as for that one marked out for her husband, she said, 'Nothing doing.' She was afraid, and went, and walked around and around. 'OK, what shall I do?' he [the no good one] said.

65. So he tied onto the shield at this place some cassowary feathers. He stuck in the feathers, and this one made a singsing and went. (Yes, you know this story that I'm telling.) Well, he kept making a singsing, and kept doing it. 70. There at that place, there at the certain ground, in the top of the tree, at Oanorafa, at their place, there in the top of the Tomba tree, he became that yellow reed, they say. All right, he went, and she followed him. He went and she said, 'Don't go,' but he went along shooting his arrows for fun. He came, and she said, 'I'll get my net bag, my net for the head and my skirt—I'll get them first,' she said. She talked and talked this way, and the two talked together. Now he was up on top, and in the Tonka tree, and he changed into the yellow reed.

Now on the ground down below, at the base of the tree is where she was, and she became that crazy vine, and she twisted and twisted, going up to the top, but he broke her neck. She became that other reed. She twisted on up, going up on top, but he broke the neck of the vine. 75. It fell twisting down, and came down to the base of the tree and was there. So that's it, as I told you. And that's all of the story.

[The reed which the man became is used to wrap the tip of arrows, and that which the woman became is used at the base of the tip.]

5. Origin of Reeds for Arrows

1. *Meeq inaamaruma—inaamaruma waikonka meraurai.*
    This-one young girl—young-girl husband did-this.
2. *Taakaaqmakowana paemba umaq umaqan kweu weukwaankoma*
    Marked-her give-gifts for-marriage did did young-man came.
marename.
3. *Marenama minarasinanko kisaan kwewairowana kisaan kwewairowana*
    Came this-young-girl sweet-potato dug-out sweet-potato dug out
aafakon awi awinarai aafakon awi awinumaena minkisaama waironka
younger-brother form became younger brother form changed-to this-sweet-
komena kepai mara tufoufo iyemba nurai.
potato dig-out went-sat this-one ground break-it like-him did.

4. *Mara iye tufoufo we nayemba kisaan aamba maeni mauq mauqa kweu-*
   Ground here break he was-this-way sweet-potato leaf get pile-and pile
wana.
do.

5. *Kwairemo wairemowana eqaifaq aqankowana feqa mofaq komena.*
   Dug-up dug-up this-place sun-out banana base sit.

6. *Akwen aanoqa kepainda naawani aaqnonaq iye suwana.*
   Oh her-brother this-one whose head this said.

7. *Minda enayo tafonaari ndeniye suwana.*
   This your-brother-in-law Tafonari belongs said.

8. *Efo imaisorena mefei naamba man ayafe ndawandewaqiye suwana.*
   All-right understood on-top breast this collar-bone whose-belong said.

9. *Memi enayo tafonaari ndeniye suwana.*
   This your-brother-in-law Tafonari belongs said.

10. *Efo imaimai maanayaambando suwana.*
    OK understand this-hand-whose said.

11. *Min enayo tafonaari ndeniye suwana.*
    This your-brother-in-law Tafonari belongs said.

12. *Maa mora ayaamba ndo suwana.*
    This other arm whose said.

13. *Min enayo tafonaari ndeniye suwana.*
    This brother-in-law Tafonari belongs said.

14. *Maa namuq namba ndowe naanoqa suwana.*
    This stomach big belong-who my-relatives said.

15. *Memi enayo tafonaari ndeniye su suwana.*
    This your-brother-in-law Tafonari belongs say said.

16. *Maa imaisorena maan aisamai ndaawandewaqiyo suwana.*
    This understood this leg who-belong said.

17. *Enenayo tafonaari ndeniye su.*
    Brother-in-law Tafonari belongs said.

18. *Aaqma mora aisamai ndo suwana.*
    This other leg whose said.

19. *Min enayo tafonaari ndeniye su.*
    This brother-in-law Tafonari belongs said.

20. *Akawen aanoqa maan ayanainamban aawandewaqiye suwana.*
    Oh my-older-sister this penis path-belong-who said.

21. *Akwe memindan enayo tafonaari ndeniye suwana.*
    Oh this brother-in-law Tafonari belongs said.

22. *Akwe naanoqa amana wandamban dowe suwana.*
    Oh my-older-sister your private-parts who said.

23. *Akwe memi enayo tafonaari ndema niye su iye suwana.*
    Oh this brother-in-law Tafonari belongs him say his said.

24. *Marena kifaq;*
    Left there;

25. *Kifaq mura pafauwa suwena marena mbeanaawambo memaromba.*
    There down hid went left drum where-put-came.

26. *Komaimai mbe aaraarafamba tumai we wena.*
    Went-got this ridge-on beat he went.

27. *Tafonaariyo tiyarare narare teyarare tafonaariyo tiyarare narare*
    Tafonaariyo tiyarare narare teyarare tafonaariyo tiyarare narare
    tiyarare simaena.
    tiyarare he-sang.

28. *Marena kuwanan afowamba kosimamena sena anofoi kosimaqtimena*
    He-went her-father she-went-talk said father go-talk-all town-mate tell
    aamaarawi simaq timena sena.
    all said.

29. *Imboseqe aimba eqai kembo maku kwaanko mbe kesunafaq tuwewi*
    Isn't talk that-one me put man this my-younger-brother form became.
    umaena.

30. *Kisaan kowewaeraisa wairainka wairaundara komeni.*
    Sweet-potato went-dig-out dig-out break-ground was-there.

31. *Miyamiya we sesa meminda semau semaunana awanena.*
    This-this he talk this tell-him tell-him did.

32. *Menawambo mamaraimba tamaimaena tumaena tisaqa.*
    This-drum put-here came-get beat came.

33. *Maa tune sena.*
    This I-came she-said.

34. *Aqni yaraaqa minka ifiqa.*
    Tears plenty this-place cried.

35. *Tamaena tena suwana.*
    Came-stay came said.

35. *Eqa misenesena afowan antu tuwafaqnarai.*
    All-right this-your-talk her-father bamboo break-it.

37. *Antu tuwafaqnamai naafaauwama tuwena mberowasa.*
    Bamboo break hold-over-fire put was-there.

38. *Entatorupamaresa tukwaenai sesane naumpata inaampakembo mae-*
    Collected-together will-sleep now house women's-inside went-stay.
    mowaine.

39. *Aumbiyamai imauwana awanena.*
    Came-up-top came were-there.

40. *Menomba kuraq maenani mefaqnafimba torenan awaq kesiyaqan*
    This-flame light-it came-up this-room-in light who my-child lie made
    kanaraqan ankarano suwana.
    said.

41. *Manafoima mbenumpo eqaifa maewaawe suwana.*
    This-her-father I-hear this-place you-take-go said.

42. *Eqai kainkaq matorena awareo suwana.*
    This-one room go-light look said.

43. Aqa kemba aawawisawanko mbeqanune suwana.
No me her-brother I-am said.

44. Mboq komaesorena eqai kaqmatorena maana awanao suwana.
Again he-went-get this went-light this look said.

45. Kemba nano kaonune suwana.
I her cousin said.

46. Mbiwiyo kaimbo wemo minkwaasikomo meromba koparafena eqai
This-one room him this-man he-is-here went-there this-place there go-
naume matorena maanawanaao suwana.
light this-you-are said.

47. Kemban afowa mbeqanune suwana.
Me father I-am said.

48. Koparafena uqmai kaqmba matorowana kembaanda aanaafuo mbenune
Went-from-there again room go-light me-this-one her-grandfather I-am
suwana.
said.

49. Kokuraq maena eqainkaq matorena maa nawanaao suwana.
Went-light went this-place he-light this look-like said.

50. Aqa kemba nanawombe nune suwana.
No me her-uncle I-am said.

51. Koweqmaena mbin kwaasikomba aiya mbakaeakaesuwo ayao akae
Came-back this man hair came-burn hair came burn-up.
akaesuwowana.

52. Embi onesena wenomba kounkuqmaena mamarena.
You did-said shield went-made came-put.

53. Aawainko tawaqmaena aayao mapusuqmai maimarena numa kotawaq
Cassowary went-got-out grass pull-out came-braid bird go-get out pull-
maenama pusuqmarena.
out.

54. Efo entoqmaya numaena we kuwana.
All-right decorate self he left.

55. Minininko minkwenomba mosa maimai aneraneq umarena we iyafasi-
This-girl this-shield up took skin put he got-up-left.
nowana.

56. Anoqmenaq watoi mbayeq unaamba mayeq anoqmena wato mayeq
You-stay skirt I'll-get bag I'll-get you-wait skirt I'll-get bag I'll-get she-
unaamba mayeq simaena.
said.

57. We kuwana we aqau sena.
She went he nothing-doing said.

58. (Mbi———) paroimbaisukena parowankwaqan umai uwenena.
(This———) arrow-with-fill arrow-shot-for-fun do do.

59. Tafonaariyo tiyarare narare tiyarare simai uwe we we we we we we wena.
Tafonaariyo tiyarare narare tiyarare simai sang and kept doing it.

60. Mare mare marena mbe taiyamifimban aandaamba kokaruwana.
Went went went this tree-top-in yellow-reed he-went-became.

61. Mbin ininkon ina mbe awaofimba takaruraimban isa.
This girl reed this base-at came-came was.

62. Paroi koumare mininako karamai.
Arrow make this-reed go-cut.

63. Mindamba kuqmai arafi kwimarembi.
This strip-it shaft stick-in.

64. Awaikomba maimai memaraanana.
Man's get this-get-wind-on.

65. Kimparoinkon kosukaimbani oweaei—.
This-arrow straight-good finish—.

1. Now there was a young girl, a young girl belonging to a young man that did this. The parents marked her out for marriage, and he kept giving gifts to his in-laws and came over there. Now when he came, this young girl went to dig out sweet potatoes. When she went out to dig sweet potatoes, he became like her younger brother, he changed to the form of her younger brother and went out where this one was digging out sweet potatoes, sat down there and chipped away at the ground like a child. He was there chipping at the ground and piling up the sweet potato leaves. 5. She was digging and digging them out at this place and when it got hot, they sat at the base of a banana plant. 'Oh,' her brother said to this one, 'whose head is this?' [pointing at her head]. 'This is your brother-in-law, Tafonari's,' she said. All right, he understood this and looked up at her and said. 'Whose is this collar bone up above the breast?' 'This is your brother-in-law Tafonari's,' she said. 10. OK, he understood this and said, 'Whose hand is this?' 'This is your brother-in-law Tafonari's,' she said. 'This other arm, whose is it?' he said. 'This belongs to your brother-in-law, Tafonari,' she said. 'This big stomach, which of my relatives owns it?' he said. 15. 'This belongs to your brother-in-law, Tafonari,' she said. He understood this and said, 'Whom does this leg belong to?' She said. 'It belongs to your brother-in-law, Tafonari.' 'This other leg, whose is it?' he said. 'This belongs to your brother-in-law, Tafonari,' she said. 20. 'Oh, my older sister, whom does this private part belong to?' he said. 'Oh, this belongs to your brother-in-law, Tafonari,' she said. 'Oh, my older sister, who do your private parts belong to?' he said. 'Oh they belong to your brother-in-law, Tafonari,' she said.

25. Then he left there and went down to where he had hidden his drum, where he put it when he came. He got this and then went upon the ridge and beat it as he went along. He sang as he went: *'Tafonariyo tiyarare narare tiyarare tafonariyo tiyarare narare tiyarare.'* He went and went, but she went over and talked to her father, and she talked to all her town mates and told them all that was said. She said, 'That one doesn't talk right, and he took on the form of my younger brother and said those things.' 30. 'He went out to where I was digging and breaking ground for the sweet potato patch, and he talked this way and that way, and I kept telling him the answers. Then he came and got his drum where

he had put it, and he beat it and he came along like that. Then I came here,' she said. She cried a good deal there at that place. 35. She came and was there and said these things.

'That's enough of your talk,' her father said, and her father broke off dry bamboo for the fire. He broke off the bamboo and he put it there over the fire to dry and it was there. Then the men collected together and they went in to sleep. Those others went to the women's house and they went there, and were inside. When they were all there, he came to be there too. 40. With this flame he made a torch and went into one of those rooms and lighting it there he said, 'Who is in there that made those lies to my child?' 'Oh, this is like her father, I am here in this place, you go take him over there,' that one said. Then he went again with his torch to another room and looked in there and asked, 'Are you there?' 'No, I am her brother,' that one said. Again he went and got his torch and went in and said, 'Are you the one?' 45. He said, 'I am her cousin.' So he went over to the opposite door and there was that man there so he went in to that place and lit it up and said, 'Are you the one?' 'No, I am like her father,' that one said. So he went from there again to another room and lit it up and that one said, 'Oh, I am like her grandfather.' So he went with his torch to the next place and lit it and said, 'Are you the one?' 50. 'No, I am her uncle,' that one said. So he came back and then he found him and he burned his hair. He came up and burned and burned him. 'You are the one that did it,' he said.

So that one went and got his shield and came up. He went and got a cassowary from the trap and pulled out grass and came and braided his hair and put a bird [feather] in it. All right, he decorated himself up and then he left.

55. Now this girl when he took up his shield and he put skin on it and left, then she said, 'Oh, you wait, I'll get my skirt and my net bag; you wait so I can get my skirt and my bag,' she said. She went to get them but he said, 'Nothing doing.' He filled up with these arrows and went along shooting arrows for fun and kept doing this. As he went he sang: *'Tafonariyo tiyarare narare tiyarare simai.'* 60. So he went and went and went and then, up in this tree, up in the top, he went and became that yellow reed. This girl came and came up to the base of the tree.

Now you, when you make arrows, you go cut this reed. You strip it and then you stick the shaft into the bamboo. You take the man's reed and then you take this and you wind and wind it on. 65. This is for making good arrows. It's finished.

6. The Origin of Eels

1. *Nuripaqe simema kiqa nona.*
   Nuripa I-tell you first.
2. *(Me—e) tuntamake sarai.*
   (Uh—er) bush-cut-it the-two.
3. *Ke qaqa (em—) tuma tumare saraima.*
   Ke no (er—) cut-and cut two.
4. *Tuma tumare sarai keafarawai.*
   Cut cut two two-brothers.

5. *Keafarawai maa uwin omapi mesarai.*
   Two-brothers this Uwi mountain lived.
6. *Uwin omapi mesarai.*
   Uwi mountain lived-two.
7. *Sifamba aanopaq uraq wimaresarai.*
   Burn-off slowly light the-fire-two.
8. *(S)ifamba uraq wimakesa awaitai ukumai aanopa sebaqsebaq wenom*
   Burn-off light the-fire Muruk-feather twist-it slowly side-by-side shi(
   menda poamba ebai amifaq faimare sarai.
   this Poamba-bird on-top at-its-top stick-in they-two.
9. *Kwetirai mbatuwoyana wetirai matuwoyanan iyamo ukumaimo akain*
   These-two made-a-singsing the-two made-a-singsing fire all-around s
   roya iyako enkunkamaena kunkamaena kunkamaena.
   fires fire burned-and-came burned-and-came burned.
10. *Kunkamaena embi tineqan iko kwembo afako maiqo uamaropaq n*
    Burned-came enough their-skin burn he younger-one hole made-it th(
    faqmi awaitai miyoikaq mura faitumarena kuwafekuwana.
    place feathers tree-opening mouth put-down-close-it went-in.
11. *Awao mbambin iyakon ikamain.*
    Older-brother this fire burn-him.
12. *Ikafuamai kaweq uwakuwana.*
    Burn-him good came-and-burn.
13. *Ai sena kwiyofiq umaena.*
    Yipes said jump-around did.
14. *Epia wintan araawefi toufo toufo araawefin kuwafekwena maandar(*
    Up-over this-there island Toufo Toufo island he-went-on this-he
    kamaimo tokukuqo uwakumba.
    burned-him skinned-off what-is-burned.
15. *Mura fakariri umarena memami kawaindonanda kouwana.*
    Down-go take-off-skin did-it this Kawaina-river went.
16. *(Anaq) afako impinke iyafasinena owe kesuwa ndabaq kourayo ser*
    (?) younger-brother this-hole come-up-from oh my-brother whe(
    go he-said.
17. *Kwaqmae waqmae waamae waqmaena kumuwana minaeran kanar*
    Follow-him follow follow follow go-down this-skin follow follow-hi
    waqmaena kwaqmae waqmae waqmaena.
    follow follow follow.
18. *Kumuana mambarawaifi kuwafekwena.*
    Go-down this-ground-hole go-inside.
19. *Mememi kwoumpi kuwafekurowana kwembo afako marena.*
    This lake-in went-down-inside him brother went.
20. *Memi kwoumpaq kuwaferowana farambai meuwoifa mesukai.*
    This lake went-in pick-him-up along-edge throw-out.

21. Farambai meuwoifa tufantuowana afo menda aqao sena ifaq kuwafe-
   Pick-up on-edge threw-out-hard all-right this no said this-place went-in
rowana (uq) memindan anekaq karambai meuwoifaq mbeq miyan emo emo
(uq) this again pick-up edge this way did did it.
ana.
22. Nenafakomba eqa kwemba ontankaq tufuqmai kawequwana afaara
   Younger-brother enough him stone hit hard-did another-form became
unenan efo mifaq kuwafekuwana.
all-right this go-in-stay.
23. Efo mimbora fimba aufitan kwaiq nankai mimaeq maeq anowi murfaqa.
   All-right at-once here got-blinded eel two-big-ones these stay-here name
Murifa.
24. Murifa mbinda miya nurai yambani minafarawai minafarawai miya
   Murifa all like-this the-two became these-two-brothers these-two-broth-
uwasuwe sarai minkumbae yambani meqnurifaqa.
ers like-this did-this two this-place these-two-because this-Murifa.
25. Minda maniqa.
   These ancestors.

1. Now I want to tell you first about Nuripa. Two people cut the brush there.
The two cut it. The two brothers cleared and cleared the brush. These two lived
at *Uwi.* They burned it off, the two of them, slowly lighting the fire [putting the
flame to it]. When they burned it off, they lit the fire, twisting Muruk feathers
together going along slowly side by side; the two stuck this of the Poamba bird
in the top of the shield. These two made a singsing; the two made it, and they
set fires all around. The fire burned and they came on and on and on.
10. Now their bodies were about to be burned, so the younger brother made
a hole, and he placed the leafy tree [feathers on wood] over the opening, closing
it, and he went down in it. As to the older brother, the fire came and burned
this one. It came and burned, and burned him well. 'Yipes,' he said, and jumped
all around. Now over there there was a beach [by the water], Toufo by name;
and he went on to Toufo island, and here [showing by gesture] he was burned.
15. He skinned off what was burned; he went down [in the water] and took off
his skin, and went into the Kawaina river.
   His younger brother came up out of this hole and said, 'Oh, my brother,
where did you go?' 'And he followed and followed and he went down [saw his
skin] and followed and followed. He went down and went inside this water hole.
He went into this lake, that is, the younger brother went in. 20. But when he
went in, he [his brother] picked him up and threw him out on the edge.
   He picked him up and threw him out on the edge hard. But he [no. 2] said,
'Don't do it,' and went on into this place. But here he got hold again, and in
this way put him and kept doing it. As to his younger brother, enough, he hit
the stone, and he hit it hard [in diving]; he bacame a different thing, and went
into it and stayed there. Here they were blinded, and these two became eels, and
stayed there at Murifa. It is at this place Murifa that the two became like this.

These two brothers, these two brothers, got like this and they stayed there in this place—the place is Murifa. 25. These are the old people.

7. ORIGIN OF NATIVE SALT (LEAF)

1. Na auyana (awiyana) maniko auyampaq mena awiyampaq.
Now Auyana (*Awiyana*) ancestor place-Auyana is Auyana-place.

2. Mefaimi aimompaq emo semba mefai omaq nambo efai awiyana siomaqo
On-top Aimompa they call-it on-top mountain big on-top Auyana our-
waisamo weonda.
mountain is-there all-know.

3. Minomapi mbena min omapi mbena afakomba afakomba waintambo
This-mountain on-he-is this mountain he-is younger-brother brother
indasafena.
shoot-nose do-this.

4. Afakomba wainta indasafena.
Younger-brother shoot-nose do-this.

5. Maampoanafoamaq maampoqnafakemba tawima mayaamba mayaam-
Here-grass-area here-grass-area yam taro taro yam all-food sweet-potato
ba tawima mopakisauma kisaama feqaramba kunkaramai maafaq weyena.
banana-shoot go-down-cut here came.

6. Taima komaitamai komaitamai tanuwaramba komaitamai imboraratan
Tree go-get come-get tops he-go-get one-together tie put-it on-top
asauwa marena efai aimompaq omapimba.
Aimompa on-mountain.

7. Iyawamarena awanenan efo maafambe (afakomba) afakom monka
Did-this did all-right here (brother) brother is-there stick cut-it this
taamban aambusamai minkaq marena ima mbaimai uwoifaq tuwena.
put-it bow get one-side put-it.

8. Imbaimai (auyaq) auyoqawenasena.
Bow-took (*auyaq*) hid-it.

9. Maankaq mema namowawna.
Here you-sit stay.

10. Maankafambo kariq waambo tosomo waambo kariqo we tiname.
This-place small animal come animal small he will-come.

11. (A—)maanka ayaantanden taetore awanena.
(Er—) this with-hand hold-you do-it.

12. Anoan kwambo tiname matamba maisuwe tufuwonafo.
Big animal if-he-comes this-stick you-take don't-kill-him.

13. (E—) tuweana kemo imaendara kemba minkwamba tufuwo su.
(Er—) let-him-go I come-be-here first this-animal kill he-said.

14. Minkwamba tufuwo suwana kwembaafa kwembo wainta indasefena
This-animal kill he-said this-fellow here shoot-the-nose desire shoot-
wainta (niq) indasafena maafaq kunkowana wanenan.
nose (*niq*) want-to-do here go-down did.

15. *Efo wembe afakombowana saawema saawembemi andarafamba min-*
    All-right he younger-brother-is-there wild-cat wild-cat this-vine-along
kaq tuwana.
this he-came.

16. *Memaafau taambo ambusa maromba ofonamba maesuwena misaawe*
    Here stick had-cut had-put-it Ofonamba-tree took-it this-animal hit
tufupa meminanda turatuwowana fifisena tai koturaqwena mberai yaimba
this-vine broke-it spring-apart tree went-and-broke here there happened.
uwakuwana.

17. *Wembaanda (saaqmiqa) kasowana awaaomba (nkake maameraanda).*
    Light (?) sun-come-up older-brother (here you-sit-down).

18. *Omapinke iyawanowana.*
    Mountain-to came-saw.

19. *Kwemba miya urowana awaon kweyena.*
    Him this-way happen older-brother he-came.

20. *Taawimo mewimbo mayaambo tombomaumba mananaefaq foisuwena.*
    Yam taro food he-got this-side threw-it-down.

21. *Maananai foisuwena uwana minkeq iyenan awanaao suwanan.*
    This-side put-it-down did this-one came look said.

22. *Afako mbaara uwasuwena kesuwaao mesaawen tintafeqa (maaq)*
    Brother like-this was my-brother this-wild-cat came (this) this I-killed-
maanda tufundafa.
it.

23. *Mbaanda (taq) mananda turatuwonana fifisena taiko ndenkaqta uwau-*
    This (*taq*) this-vine I-broke-it spring-apart trees to-place happened
wiye suwana.
he-said.

24. *Eqa kanaa none sena.*
    Enough all-right you-are he said.

25. *Kanaa none sena.*
    All-right you-are he-said.

26. *Kwembo waintan indasafena waanafomo warikambo mamumo iya-*
    His shoot-nose did-it animal-skin feathers headdress come-get.
maime.

27. *Ndaasumbo kekoraqo komparoqo uwamaromba.*
    Bracelets upper-leg-ring colored-belt made-put.

28. *Iyamaimai unaampi tuwamaenan awaao menaraaraq iyaemarena efai*
    Came-got bag filled-it older-brother this-ridge went-up-along on-top
araaraq iyaeqmarena efai iyakarantaq ontonemo wesen.
cross-over went-up-along on-top Iyakaranda-at stone call-it.

29. *Ontamba minontamba faisuq maena weyuwana.*
    Stone this-stone lined-them-up put he-went.

30. *(Awaq awaq) afako mifaq faime weyuwana uwo kesuwaoma siyuwe*
    (Uh—er) younger-brother here look-for he-went oh my-brother left-

kwe kone sena.
me he gone said.

31. *Ifiqantamai ifiqantamai kwe yuwana.*
    Cry-he-made cry-make he go.

32. *Iyawamai iyawamai (iyawara).*
    Did-this did-this (did).

33. *Kete kete ayaifakemban eqa (auq) awaaomo weyunkaq menaraaraq*
    There there at-end-of-it enough (*auq*) older-brother gone-on-top this-
    iyaeq marena.
    ridge go-up cross-over.

34. *Iyaeq marena epai waasarin ontampimba waasarin ontamba kufaime*
    Go cross-over on-top Wasari stone-on Wasari stone river go-put room-
    maraumai faqnafaimai.
    put-up.

35. *Kaafaq afakomban ankena.*
    Here put it-is.

36. *Maafaq awaombaena tombomo kufuqo.*
    Here no-one-there food he-cook.

37. *Uwaminda afaqa kinkeq ausamarena.*
    Did-this give-it hole made-it.

38. *Ausamakena awanenan efo meminda (um) efo minkaq mosa waintan*
    Made-it did all-right this-one (um) all-right this-place up shoot-nose
    kwenan.
    did.

39. *Efo waanafoma naasumba kekoraqa komparoqa mandan efo (awaq)*
    All-right animal-skin bracelets upper-leg-ring belt this OK (*awaq*) up
    mosa awena.
    put.

40. *Minka kemba kamemba iyawiyai kumpamba kamemba wiyena maa*
    This place drum tie-on drum-with-handle drum he-went this Wasari
    wasarin dompinkaq we kumena kamemba tuwamaena kwekumena.
    water he go-down drum hit go-down.

41. *Uwoimbaandan donaramba tafiya suqmaena kwe kumuwanan ndona-*
    Went-along sand footprints did-this he go-down sand went-down.
    mai kuwana.

42. *Inaamaru anaamba mepaimi—aroisarakoni naoqa noraqenkoni naoqa.*
    Young-girl plenty this-place—Arokara village Noraqendara place.

43. *Noraqenkoni naoqa aweqara tanomba kweu tanomba kwe kawofimba*
    Noraqendara place edible-leaf mumu made mumu he cook-it he this
    wembe ma kwe kumena.
    he go-down.

44. *Mbema kumbamakena (neoq) waasari ndomba: nawaanawaa nefo*
    This he-sang (*neoq*) Wasari river: *nawaanawaa nefo poq nafopoq*

poq nafopoq kanao kanoa i—; qi tana (suwana).
kanao kanoa i—, qi tana (he said).

45. *Pao suwana memi kamemba tuwamaena kwe kumuwana memin ka-*
    Pao it-said this drum hitting-it he went-down this drum Pao it-said
    memba pao suwana (wiyainkweondae) miyauwamaesa kwasari ndomba:
    (you-laugh) this-way-did Wasari-river singing: *tawanawa nefopoq nafopoq*
    tawanawa nefopoq nafopoq kamao kamao i— (qiq) simamai wekuwana.
    kamao kamao i—, (qiq) this-way-talk go-down.

46. *Mafaq tanomba kwe kauwana kweq (maq) maraumai iyawanomba*
    Here mumu he cooked-it he (*maq*) was-doing come-look this-man-at
    kwembaanda (aq) inamarukon iyawano tanomba kaumakowana inaamaruko
    (*aq*) girl go-look mumu cooked young-girl look things tie-on self.
    iyawanowana umbatan toqwa ikomo.

47. *Marawe unkaq.*
    Like-this did.

48. *Uwanena uwoi mintanomba minka mbeunka nene uwoimbifa kuwaka-*
    Worthless this-mumu this take-away ground worthless go-down-left.
    kurai.

49. *Mifakuwaa kakuwana intanomban aroqnaroq uwamai.*
    This-place went-by mumu quickly did-it.

50. *Mafaq kaumaena memin arasi ananko (minqi—) anainka araiwaq-*
    Here cook-it this girl plenty (?) in-back follow went-down.
    maena kumu.

51. *Maraiwaq maena (meq) kumu uraarafaqa urarafaq mifaq mifaq*
    Followed did (?) down Urarafa Urarafa-place here here (here) this-
    (mifaqu) mifaraq kuminiyenaq iyasuwana.
    place he-is-going they-said.

52. *Mifaq tuwenan anoq uwamai kunuweq.*
    There he-left covertly did-it came-back.

53. *Maename kauronafa emo sentaraq minkaqmi iyamatarai.*
    Come-up Kauronafa you told-me this-place came-cross-over.

54. *Iyamatena mifaq mefaimi tauwarufaq tauwarufaq mifaq mifaq mifaq*
    Crossed-over here on-top Tauwarufa Tauwarufa this-place here here
    wembifaq iyafekuwana efo wembaanda minarasianaanko mbaan kofaiya
    he-here go-up-in all-right this-one these-girls-plenty here go-search come-
    tafaiyaqan uwamaenan.
    search did-this.

55. *Arai awaqmaena kunkwa uwaena.*
    Follow they-went went did.

56. *Iyawanomba kwembaminkaq.*
    She-went-look this-place-at.

57. *(E—) mamifaqa kwemba mamifaq iyametena minkaq araiwaqmaena.*
    (*Er—*) this-place at-it this-place go-over here followed-him.

58. Iyuwanawanena efo minka iyuwana wanena (taq) wemban.
Went-on-top all-right this-place go-up look (*taq*) his.

59. Wemba minka tankoiman uwima uwinku karu kuwana wanena.
Her this-place salty-leaf salt native salt went-down came-up.

60. (E—) kunkaru kuwana wanenan.
(Er—) go-down come-up did.

61. Efo wembe (aq) waikon efo (mineq——) epai mifamemiya i it
All-right him (*aq*) man all-right (this——) on-top this-place-did

warufaqo (emo mami Aamerikamo tamaenda) fimba mimpimba maimb
Tauwarufa (you this-one American you-stay) this-place this-place-in stay

62. Eqa kifinisi.
Enough finished.

1. Now as to the Auyana ancestors, they were at the Auyana place. At Auyana place, on top of the Aimompa mountain they call it, on top of that mountain, he was there on our Auyana mountain that all know. Now it was this mountain that he wanted to shoot the nose [initiate to adulthood] of younger brother. He wanted to initiate his younger brother. 5. So here at grass area down below, at that grassy area, he went and cut yams and taro, t and yams and all kinds of food including sweet potatoes and banana shoots, and he came here.

He got the trees; he went and got the tops of the trees and tied them toget on the mountain of Aimompa. Now when he had done this, he cut a stick his younger brother, and he put it here, but the bow, he got and put to one si He hid the bow. You sit here and stay [said to a listener]. 10. Now along this pla small animals always come. 'A small animal will come, so you hold this w your hand. If a big animal comes, you just hold the stick, it wouldn't be go for you to try to kill it. Let it [the big one] go. I will come and be here first—y just kill this [small one] animal,' he said. 'You can kill this animal,' he said, this one whom he had wanted to initiate, the one he had wanted to initiate, went down here.

15. OK, the younger brother was there, and a big animal, a wild cat came along on this vine. He took the stick he had cut off the Ofonamba tr and he killed this animal; this broke this vine, and the trees sprang apart and t broke everything all over [that the brother had fixed]. When it got light, his old brother (you sit down right here) came to the mountain, and he saw it. T older brother came and saw what had happened. 20. He had gotten yams a what is it—taro and food, and he threw it down on this side. He threw it do here, and this one came and said, 'You look!' His younger brother was like th and he said, 'My older brother, this wild cat came, and I killed it, and I bro this vine, and they sprang apart and the trees went back to their places, a that's what happened,' 'Well, that's OK,' he said. 25. 'That's OK,' he said [t he was really angry].

Now for the initiating ceremony he had fixed the animal skin, feathers, a headdress, and he came and got them. He made the bracelets, upper leg bar and colored rope for the belt, and put them there. He came and got them and filled the net bag, and the older brother went up along the ridge; he got up on top and crossed over and went along, and on top there is the Iyakaranda as they call that stone. He lined the stones up [like a fence] and he went.

30. Now the younger brother went to this place looking for him, and he said, 'Oh, my older brother, you have left me.' He cried and cried, and then he went. He did this and did it. There at that place where it was the end of it [the stone fence] his older brother had gone on top, and crossed over the ridge. He crossed over the top at Wasari stone [name of river source] where he had gone, and he put up a room there. 35. Here he set aside one part for his younger brother. No one was there, and he cooked food for him. When he did this, he would give it to him through a hole in the wall he had made. He made it, and did it this way, so he initiated this one at this place. Then he put up the animal skin, bracelets, upper leg rings, and the special belt; he put these away. 40. He tied up the [skin] drum and with the drum he went along the Wasari river, and as he went, he kept hitting the drum.

He just went along, and some debris in the water from his foot prints went as he went down; the sand went down. Now there were a lot of young girls down there—at Arokara, that is at Noreqendara. At Noreqendara they were making a mumu with edible leaf, and were cooking the mumu, and this one was on his way down. On this—uh—er—that is on the Wasari river he sang: '*Nefopoq nafopoq kanao kanao i—,' qi tana* (he said). 45. As he hit the drum going down, the drum said 'Pao'; 'Pao,' it said (don't laugh) and this is the way he went down the Wasari river, singing: '*Tawanawa nefopoq nafopoq kamao kamao i—';* so he went down saying that.

Now they were cooking the mumu here, and they came to see what he was doing (came to look at him). A girl came to look at this fellow, one that had cooked the mumu, a young girl came to look at him; he had tied on himself a lot of things. He did like this. Now it didn't mean anything to him that they were taking away the ground from the mumu. He just went on by and left this place. He went by the mumu quickly. 50. The girls that had cooked the mumu here followed in back and went on down. They followed him and went down and said, 'He is going here, here to this place, to Urarafa.' He left there, and secretly came back [doubled back]. Now at Wong's place where you told me about—at this place he came up and crossed over. He crossed over there, on top at Tauwarufa—at the place Tauwarufa, here is where he went up and in, so these girls came here and searched all over for this one.

55. They followed him and went and went. She went to look for him at this place. So at this place where he had gone over, she came and followed him. She was on top, and this is the place where she went and looked, where he was. Now this one, the man—she went up where he was at his place, up there at the place belonging to him [to men only probably], and he put her out. At this place she went down and became a salty leaf—she became the native salt. 60. Yes—she became that. OK, as to him, the man, OK there on top at Tauwarufa is where it happened (you came and stopped there—it belongs to foreigners). This is the place where he settled down. The story is finished.

8. ORIGIN OF LANGUAGES

1.   Mendompakemba imbo kwaasimo imbo meronka keakwakaiko.
This-water-down no-man no is-there two-people-married.

2.   Keakwakaiko awaikoma afounamba tuwamai unampimba tutuwana
Two-married her-husband his-penis fill-up net-bag-in fill-up shoulder
ayoiyaq mafaq mosa faferiyuwana.
place up-on put-to-carry.

3.   Awaininko awaamba imba afaqa imba kwerowana.
Wife her-private-parts no vagina no there-is.

4.   Afaqa imba kwerowanan awaamba uwoimbaiq; ai iyaimba uwana.
Vagina no there-is private-parts were-without; road no so-it-was.

5.   Imbo pikoqo imbo foyamba.
No copulate no did.

6.   Ainkwerain dabinaq eraq faano sena.
Path-has if-you-had I have-intercourse said.

7.   Anena uwoi maaminkafamba uwoinaq aawaankabambo umba uwoi
Did just-do this-place do-this private-parts did this penis no success.
afoi mofai nefai.

8.   Kwenaanena awiaraqa tuwamai.
So-this-way semen ejaculate-outside.

9.   Saraiyai maandonandaniya mare mare mare mare saraiyai kofarufa
Two-people this-water-went-up went went went went went-up Kafarufa
niya.
went-up.

10. Kofarufaq iyesaraiyai arifitapa niya.
Kofarufa two-go-up Arifita came-to.

11. Arifitapa imenan efo minkaq naamba mouwamarena anena.
Arifita came-to all-right this house made-one did-it.

12. Arifitapa nefo minka awaiko afoi intoiya moankai ontankaq ontankaq
Arifita all-right this her-husband penis file sharpen-it stone stone-with
moanowana.
filed.

13. Afoi ampaankane kaanaaran kuwamau uwana.
Penis shortened finished short made-it.

14. Awaininkomba munaraanamena maara ke numpoemboq minontanka
His-wife went-and-showed same 1 now-do-you this-stone you-go he-
iyuwo suwanaanena.
said.

15. Awaininko minontankaq minkaq awaamba moanowana moanawana
His-wife this-stone this private-parts filed filed-it did liver file-stone like
anena kwanaru tawai samba moafanku suwowana.
cut-a-gash did-it.

16. *(K)wae ntowai samba moafanku suwowana awanena.*
    Pink stone-file like cut-a-gash did-it thus.
17. *Mimpinkemba awaampinkemba nairakemba maiyaamba karurai.*
    This-place-in vagina-in menstration taro came-up.
18. *Minkakemba fequ karurai.*
    This banana came-up.
19. *Minkakemba motu karurai.*
    This edible-leaf came up.
20. *Uwoi minkakemba karurai.*
    Large-grass this-place came-up.
21. *Mopaq kisauma minkakemba taaqa minkakemba karuwana anena.*
    All garden-things this-place sugar this-place it-came-up so-it-was.
22. *Maanamuqo maampimbo wisenamo maaramo emo amuko komaimena*
    This-belly inside-this got-big like this belly went-down like-before it-
    kanaara tamauwana.
    was.
23. *Kaweqa none siayi.*
    Good you-are he-said.
24. *Kaweqa none senan efo minkaq mesan efo amusa mokaumai.*
    Good you-are he-said all-right this were-there all-right belly pregnant.
25. *Minka niyampoi momakai.*
    This child gave-birth.
26. *Efo awaikon efo awaininkomba famai amuqa kauwankowana minkaq-*
    All-right husband all-right his-wife copulate belly get-pregnant were-
    mena iyampoi mareme mareme mareme mareme.
    there this-child got-more got-more got-more more.
27. *Sawifaqa maqankarai sawifaq iyampoi maqanko.*
    Plenty gave-birth plenty child gave-birth.
28. *Wanaanenan efo taima tawemba ayaiyena naamba marauwamai.*
    Did all-right tree Tawemba cut-down house did-this.
29. *Afaraq mosankena.*
    On-log took-put-up.
30. *Mosankena miniyampoikon ena minkaq imawo suwana.*
    Put-him-up this-child as-to this sat-on said.
31. *Minkaq iya maena aqon tokparesi siyai.*
    This came-up got-on another language talk.
32. *Aqon tokparesi suwana miniyampoikon tafena sena ema omuta none*
    Another talk-place he-said this-child regarding said you Mobuta you-
    siyai.
    are he-said.
33. *Omuta none siyai.*
    Mobuta you-are he-said.
34. *Mora iyampoikomba minafaraq mosa ankouwana aqo tokparesi su-*

Another child this-log up put-him another talk-place said said Awaron
wana sena awaarona none.
you-are.
35. *Awaarona none su.*
   Awarona you-are he-said.
36. *Mora iyampoikomba minafaraq iyamauwana.*
   Another child this-log came-sat-down.
37. *Aqo tok paresi su.*
   Another talk place said.
38. *Suwanan marutafa uwe siyai.*
   Said Marutafa you-are he-said.
39. *Mora iyampoiko minafaraq imaena aqo tok paresi suwana.*
   Another child this-log come-get-on another talk place spoke.
40. *Iyafawe siyai.*
   Iyafa he-said.
41. *Iyafawe suwana mora iyampoi minafaraq mosa ko(u)wana aqo tc*
   Iyafa-belong he-said other child this-log up got-on-top another ta
paresi suwana.
place said.
42. *Iyakiya we siyai.*
   Ilakia-you he said.
43. *Aqon aimba suwana anepaq aimba suwana embi iyakeya none suwan*
   Other language said Anepa language said you Ilakia you-are said.
44. *Mora iyampoi minafaraq mosa ankowana anena tauna aimba siye*
   Other child this-log up-on put-him did Tauna language spoke.
45. *Suwana em tauna none siyai.*
   Said you Tauna you-are he-said.
46. *Mora iyampoi minafaraq mosa mosa ankowana anena kasokana aimb*
   Other child this-log up up put-him did Kasokana language talked di
suwana anena.
47. *En kasokana none siyai.*
   You Kasokana you-are said.
48. *Mora iyampoi minafaraq mosa ankowanan kawaina aimba suwar*
   Other child this-log up put-him-up Kawaina talk spoke Kawaina said-h
kawainawe siyai.
49. *Mora iyampoi minkaq mosa ankowana anena aakaa aimba suwar*
   Another child this up put-on did Aka talk spoke did you Aka you-a
anena e aakaa none siyai.
he-said.
50. *Mora iyampoi minafaraq mosan kowana anena okafa aimba suwar*
   Other child this-log up put-on did Okasa talk he-spoke you Oka
e okafa none siyai.
you-are said.

51. Mora iyampoi minafaraq mosa ankowana anena intona aimba suwana
     One child this-log up put-him did Intona talk spoke you Intona you-are
emba intona none siyai.
said.

52. Mora iyampoi minafaraq mosa ankowana sena kemba arifitapa maanka
     One child this-log up put spoke me Arifitapa this Ofafimba I-am-of said
ofafimba menainune suwana en ofafimba none siyai.
you Ofafimba you-are said.

53. Mora iyampoi minkaq mosan kowana awanena Arora aimba suwana
     Other child this up put-on did Arora talk spoke did you-this-one Arora
anena embaanda arora none siyai.
you-are said.

54. Arora none suwana.
     Arora you-are said.

55. Mora iyampoi minkaq mosan kowana awiyaanan aimba siyai.
     Other child this-log up put Auyana talk said.

56. Sesa awiyaana kembaanta ofoimpimpaqo ofoimpina menai nune siyai.
     Say Auyana me-this-one Ofoimpa-from Ofoimpa can-be I he-said.

57. Awiyaana uwe siyai.
     Auyana you-are said.

58. Uwana efo minkakemba komaimai mepai taundompa niyai.
     Did-this all-right this-one go-get there Fore he-went.

59. Taumpaq weyena anena minda sawifaq aimba simame we yena.
     Fore-of went look this plenty talk they-talked he kept-doing.

60. Sawifaq iyampoi mifamatuq maenan iyai sena.
     Plenty child this-place brought stay said.

61. Kamanompan taunkon amaapa waasima sawifaqa merai.
     Kamano Fore place man plenty are-there.

62. Sawifaqa meraifo sawifaqa meraifo enkakiya sena wanena.
     Plenty are-there-now plenty are-there-now that's-all said did.

63 Kepaika arikitapaq moma karena awanena mokeqai kinkani kankani
    There-at Arikitaipa put-him was-there do there that-place this-place
sena.
he-talked.

64. Awanenamo kepaiki (iya) siyain kanisana nena kakindompa kwaasi
     Was there (?) he-said like-that did not-far-water man few are-there.
kariqa merai.

1. Down at that water where no one lives now, there were two people who were married. Now this couple—the husband put his penis in a net bag and put it over his shoulder in order to carry it. Now his wife as far as her privates were concerned, she had no vagina. She had no vagina; her private parts were just there without anything. There was no pathway. 5. They could not copulate. 'If you had a vagina, I could have intercourse with you,' he said. But at this place all he did

was play around without any success. So they did this way, and he would ejaculate outside. So these two people went up along the river.

They went and went, going up to Kofarufa [pine forest area]. 10. From Kofarufa the two went up and came to Arifita. When they came to Arifita, they built a house. All right, at Arifita, her husband began to file off his penis; he filed it with a stone. He shortened his penis—that's what he did, he made it short. He went and showed it to his wife and said, 'Now just as I have done, you take this stone and go do as I did.' 15. So his wife filed at her privates with this stone. She filed at them. Now the stone for filing was like liver [red], and she cut a gash with it. It was with a pink file-stone that she cut a gash.

So in this place, the place where the menstruation of the vagina was, taro came up. This banana grew, and the edible leaf grew, and 20. large grass grew in this place. All the garden things came up in this place. Sugar came up in this place, and so it was.

Her belly had gotten tight (very big) like this, and now it went down to its original form. 'You are good now,' he said. 'You are good,' he said, and then as they were there, well, she got pregnant. 25. This one gave birth to a boy. Now her husband had intercourse with his wife, and she got pregnant again, and got more children, and got more and more. They got more and more, giving birth to plenty. She gave birth to plenty of children.

Well, then later he cut down a Tawemba tree—he did this at the house; he put one up on a log. 30. He put this child on a log, and this one got up on it and spoke. This one came and got on it, and he talked a different language. When he talked the talk of another place, regarding the child he said, 'You are from Mobuta.' He said, 'You are from Mobuta.' Then he put another child up on the log and he talked another language, so he said, 'You are Awarona' [Fore]. 35. 'You are of Awarona,' he said. So he put another child on a log. He talked another language. He said, 'You are of Marutafa.' Another child came and got up on this log and spoke a different language. 40. 'You are of Iyafa,' he said. 'You belong to Iyafa,' he said, and another child got up on the log. He got up on there, and talked a different way. 'You are of Ilakia,' he said. He spoke another language, and he said, 'You speak the Anepa language, you are of Ilakia.' He put another child up on this log, and he spoke the Tauna talk. 45. 'You are of Tauna,' he said. He put another child up on this log, and he spoke the Kasokana [Fore] talk. 'You are of Kasokana,' he said. He put another child up on this log, and he spoke the Kawaina talk. 'You are of Kawaina,' he said. He put another child up on it, and he talked the Aka talk [Fore]. 'You are of Aka,' he said. 50. So he put up another child on this log, and he spoke the Okasa talk. 'You are of Okasa,' he said. He put another child up on this log, and he spoke the talk of Intona. 'You are of Intona,' he said. He put another child up on this log and he said, 'I am of Arifita, I am Ofafimba,' he said. 'All right, you are of Ofafimba,' he said. He put another child up on it, and he spoke Arora talk. 'You are of Arora,' he said of this one. 'You are of Arora,' he said, 55. and then put up another child on the log, and he spoke the Auyana talk. 'I am Auyana, I am of Ofoimpa, I can be Ofoimpa,' he said. 'You are of Auyana,' he said.

Now all this happened, and he went to get one there at Fore land. He went

to Fore land, and they kept making plenty of languages. 60. They gave birth
to plenty of children and stayed at these various places. Plenty of men are now
there at Kamano and Fore places. Plenty are there now, and that's all, he said.
He put them there at Arikitaipa, and they are in this place and that place [all
over] it is said. It is like that there, but at this water [near] there are only
a few people.

9. SOFT SPOT ON HEAD

1.   Eseq keseq eseq keseq kaimo tombo wenanda aimba emba mi simamenai
You I you I same-time food eat talk you this I-tell-you I-talk origin.
su awouma.

2.   (Ma——) maawiyaampaq maawiyampaq minda tombo nowi kisamo
(Th——) this-place-Auyana this-Auyana this food he-ate sweet-potato
nowi mbafaq mowana.
ate here he-is.

3.   (E—)nowana (me——) mempa imbo tombo nowinbe.
(Er—) is-there (this——) down-below not food ate-it.

4.   Mendonafeumpaq mempime ndonafeumpi benawanena.
This-water-below down-below water-down watch-is-there.

5.   Mimbaena waiqa kaimba efo minda amai tawekwiyena (feqoq).
This-bow-take eel fish all-right this shoot pile-it-up (?).

6.   Nompimba taimawon tokena faimena iyupa minkaq tawanowana ma-
Water-in stick hold-it probe go-up this come-look this taro-is-there.
minka maiyaambankwo.

7.   Mayaamba kowwanaanaq.
Taro is-there.

8.   Maampin ainkwowana.
Here-[head]-hold there-is.

9.   Maapinain kwowana; wanena maana iyaimpa nuwana.
Here-hole there-is; is this-place hole had.

10.   Iwoin mefa mifa mintomba tuwena.
Only here on-top this-food let-it-go.

11.   Uwoi mbaafa kwena (ayamofeq) ayamo kasuwomba ayamo kasu-
Just-do here he-go (hesitation) excrement evacuate excrement come-
womba.
out.

12.   Efowen tamaena wanena.
All-right he-come-take did.

13.   Maiyaraq makena (aqi) iyaraq makowana awanena mindan eqa kokoq
Fire-on go-put-it (?) fire-on go-put-it did this enough hot it-is ate he
uwana nomba kwe mbintonko kaweq anu.
this-food good it-is.

14. We nimbo kisauma uwando kwaasiko kafona.
He not garden make man no-good.

15. Waasiko efo mifaq menan efo moq anekaq kowaiyomba moq maan
Man all-right here is all-right again again go-sleep again this island
araaweraqa maminkakemba mboq mayaune sena.
this-place again I'll-get said.

16. Koqmo (koqo) araawera kaimba kwaiqa faimaena iyumba.
Another (?) island fish eel probe-for he-go-up.

17. Minkakemba taawin imayai taawin imaena awanenan efo (mua) mepaq
This-place yam go-get yam get did all-right here this-fire-on this-hot
meiyaraq makokopan dowana.
he-eat.

18. Miwan asenu.
This was-sweet.

19. Asenuwana wawanena (iyuq).
It-was-sweet did, (?)

20. Minda maa asenone sena mboq kowaiyon kakemba koqon.
This here sweet-you talk again go-sleep then-come-back other.

21. Aaraweraqa maananondompikaq weyena maanondompinkaq weyena
Island this-river-on follow-up this-water follow another island this fish
koqon araweramo minkaq kaimba kwai tafena.
eel will-shoot.

22. Minka ifaumba inkaq feqankwo.
This probe this banana-is-there.

23. Feqankwowana imaena.
Banana-is go-get.

24. Maqme iyaraq makokoq pandowana mindan asenu.
Again fire-on go-heat he-ate this sweet.

25. Asenuwana efo minda ndasuwena.
Sweet all-right this ate.

26. Efo mindan dasuwena moqmoq mepa makokoq pandasuwena wayomba
All-right this ate again-again this-place go-heat ate sleep again again
mboq oqo marena koqon araaweraq iyawanowana minkaq kisaama.
he-go another island-on he-go-up-same this sweet-potato.

27. Kisaambinkaq wowanan efo tamaena efo minkaq makokoq pandowana
Sweet-potato-on be-there OK come-get OK this heat ate-it this sweet.
min asenuwa.

28. Miyan uwandamai uwandamai uwandamai iyawanowana.
Do-this continually eat eat eat.

29. Kwembaanda (kwaq) kwaasiko mbaafa taiya tuwaisuwe numbo.
He-this-one (kwaq) man here-came fire blow-it is-there.

30. Mowana mbaara niwa suwena bena awanowana.
Is-there this-way what he-did go look.

31. *Imba mbaa oiqankwo imba mbaanda kwowana.*
Not this mouth-is not this-one have-one.

32. *Kwowana maampinke tuwowana mampinkembi maampinke tuwowana*
Have these-things would-drop this-one this drop just excrement evacu-
uwoi ayamo komba kwembe mimbutuqa ayantamaena mbanamana.
ate he this-whole excrement-come-get go-eat-and-eat.

33. *Ena kwembi nenan awanomba kwemba miyaweuwanakwena.*
This-way he who was-there-did he this-kept-doing.

34. *Maraume iyaraq imena awanomba kwemba mpinkeq tuwowana mbin-*
Did-this fire-on come watch he this throw-it this-food this-skin this-way
tonko manaum mbaara kuwauwamai manaum kuwamaena kumuwana mbe
go-down this-skin go-take go-down down below excrement evacuate he
empaifan ayamo kasuwomba kwembe muntamuntane.
eat-below-and-eat.

35. *Embaramaa (mefaq) mempakemban imaena baweonda tomba keni*
You-do-this (?) there-below come-is-there do-this food I come-get
maeqa munkwe naune sima suwena.
I-go eat this-way he-talked.

36. *Sima suwenan efo meminkaq mena (anwm—) mena uawanowana*
This-way talk all-right this-one was-there [hesitate—] was-there-do
miyauwana mafa mamifankwau.
who-did-this here he-sleep.

37. *Mamifaq minkwaasikon efo imena kaweuwamai kwawanena.*
Here this-man so he-is good-did this-look.

38. *Kwembo aamunda kwemba aafaq iyaraq akaisuwena awaiyantande*
Him gave him here fire-on cooked-it his-teeth he-ate-so.
untuwenawenena.

39. *Weuwana poin tufuwo su.*
Did-this pig you-kill said.

40. *Poin tufuwo suwana poin tufu.*
Pig kill said pig killed.

41. *Poin tufuwana wanena efo maasawemba maaqamumpin kemba amu-*
Pig killed did all-right grease this-stomach his his-stomach this-fat out
pinke maasawemba mosa maena fima anaroqa (ikakaq) iyaraq marowana
take knife bamboo(?) fire-on put-it dry-it this-thing he-sharpened good
sasaqasuwana kifin awaintamai kawaiq uwamarena.
made-it.

42. *Awaintamai kawaiq uwamarenan efo (meaq) tomba mosa naosuwana*
Sharpen-it good make-it all-right (?) food up you-get-and-eat taro
mayaamba maampinke tuwowana (ma——) morakunuwana.
here-in drop-it (this——) close-go-down.

43. *(Kwe kwe) mifisande maanowi maraumai afekai.*
(He he) this-knife these-lips this-way cut-it.

44. Maanowi maaraumain afetuwena kampuntaramba ayaiyena iyemba
These-lips this-way cut-it kampuntara-tree cut-it this-way his-teeth
awayaamba tamayemba kaweqa nuwamaromba mbe amaimbe nuwamaromba
lined-them-up good did-this-way this chin-bone made-it here cut chin this
maampi afetuwena amaimba maanka mura tamakai.
down put-did.

45. Awaiyaamba efo iyauwamarena.
His-teeth all-right did-this-way.

46. Maandafaitukai efaimifa (nkaq) maanka faituwena.
Here-closed-it-up on-top (?) this-place closed-up.

47. Maanka faituwena awanenan efo maankaq oiqa mura ena maantomban
This-place closed did then this mouth down put-it this-food you-eat.
tao.

48. Maantombandau suwana nomba mankanuwana kaweqa nuwana.
This-food-eat he-said he-ate here-made-it good it-is.

49. Owe kesifarawao kesifarawao ekaq kaweq uramba none one sena.
Yes my-friend my-friend plenty good very you-did you-did he-said.

50. Manafaaqa faiq.
This-hole closed-up.

51. Fauntukaimbani iyaq kikifeqo maqankai iyampoikomba maampimban
Closed-it-up no you-have this-one now-bear-child here-in-this hole is
afaaqa kwaisana maanka mauqmauqa nisa anaandaqi.
this soft make-it you-see.

52. Maambi mbaniqa simemeau (oq) uwanawanena.
Here old-ones I-told-you (?) did-this.

53. Maanda mbura uwamakaisakaimo tomba iyafinkai akaisuwe kaimo
This put-down made-this-way-we food fire-inside cook-it we we-eat.
nauyambani.

54. Eqa ki finisi.
Enough is finish.

1. You and I together eat food. Now I'm going to tell you the origin of this.
At the Auyana place here, he ate this food. He ate sweet potato, and was here.
Yes, but the one there—that is down below—he really didn't eat the food.
Down below on this river, this one would watch. 5. He would take his bow
and he would shoot eel and fish and pile it up. He would hold the stick in the
water and probe around, then go up and look, and here there would be taro.
Taro was there. Now he [that other one] had a hole in here [his head] . There
was a hole here; that's the way it was. 10. There was just a hole here, that is
all, here on the top (of the head), and he would let the food drop in it. He
would just do that, and then he would defecate and out it would come here
[down below]. All right [the other one] he would come and take it. He would
eat this food, and it was good. He did not make a garden. He was just a
no good man.

15. Now this man he was here, and again he went to sleep, and later he said, 'I'll get some more at this bend in the river.' So at another bend in the river, he went up and probed for fish and eel. At this place he would go get yam. He got yam, so here he would heat it on the fire, and eat it. It was sweet. It was sweet, so that is what he did. 20. 'You are sweet,' he said, and then he would go to sleep, planning to come back again the next day. So he would follow the river up to another bend, going along up the river desiring to shoot fish and eel at another bend. He probed there, and then there was a banana there. There was a banana, so he would go get it. He put it on the fire, heated it, and ate it. It was sweet. 25. It was sweet so he ate it, and then he would eat and again and again he would go to a place, heat it, eat, and sleep, and over and over go to another island, doing the same way, and there would be sweet potato. Sweet potato was there, so he came and got it, heated it, and ate it and it was sweet. He would keep on doing this, eating and eating like this.

Now the other one [with the hole in head], this man came and was blowing the fire and was there. 30. When he was there, what he did was go and look at him. He didn't have any mouth; this person didn't have any mouth; this person didn't have any. He would drop these things in [the hole]—this fellow would drop these things, and they would just go through whole, and the other would come and eat them. This is the way he was, the one who was there, and he kept doing it. The other would come and put it on the fire, but he would throw it in and the food, skin and all, would go down this way, and the other would go and take it; it would go down there as excrement does, and the other would eat and eat it.

35. 'You do this down below' [said the poor one]; and came and was there. 'I come and get the food and I eat it.' This is the way he talked. This is the way he talked, this one that was there—he was there, that one who slept there. This man was here so he being there, did this good thing for him. He would give it to him, and he would cook it on the fire and eat it up with his teeth because he could. So he did this, he said, 'You kill a pig.' 40. When he told him to kill a pig, he killed a pig.

When he had killed the pig, then he took the fat of his stomach and taking out the fat of his stomach, he put a bamboo knife on the fire and dried it, then he sharpened it and made it good. He sharpened it up good, then he said, 'You get some food up there and eat it and drop this taro here' [in hole], and he as it went down, he closed it off [at the throat] here.

Then with this knife in this way, he cut his lips [made them]. This way he cut the lips, and with the Kampuntara tree he cut it and in this way he lined up his teeth. He did it good this way, and he made his chin, cutting it here, and he put in his chin. 45. He fixed his teeth up this way. Now he closed it up here on top—here he closed it up. When he closed this place up, then he put it in his mouth, and said, 'You eat this food. Eat this food,' he said, and he ate it, and he had made it good. 'Yes, my friend, my friend, you did it very very well,' he said.

50. So he closed up this hole—it is closed up now. Now when one gives birth to a child, there is this hole, this soft spot; You have seen it, haven't you?

There, I have told you what the old ones did. He put this one there, and made the teeth this way, so now we all cook food on the fire and we eat it. That is the end of this story.

10. THE STONE AXE

1. *Eqi kumba maafaq memaiyaren.*
   This stone-axe here give-it.

2. *Simame mawani aimba awiyaampaq maniko miyanurai.*
   I-talk this talk Auyana ancestor that-one.

3. *Empaima miyamo urain ontamba empewaraifo.*
   Down-below that-one make-it stone is-below.

4. *Min ontanandampaq mena.*
   This stone-from-below it-is.

5. *Mena kanawai iyampoigo kanawai iyampoigo kowiq amai kwewime*
   It-is like-ashes boy like-ashes boy snake find search walk-about.
   inandurai.

6. *Kowiq amai kwimena wewuwana anofowi aamba korowana.*
   Snake find look-for go parents road went.

7. *Aamba korowana kowiq ama kwime nemomba.*
   Road went snake look-for find long-time.

8. *Wewuwanan efo areko efefakemba kunkai.*
   Did-this then girl down-from-up came.

9. *Uwaara timapakemba uwaara timapakemba mare mare mare marena.*
   Foreign area foreign ground came came came came.

10. *Kunanowana uweya mbena kowiqamai kwewiyuwana.*
    Came-down-look just-one person snake look-for.

11. *Afoamo meraindante anoamo meraindante kusuwana kisaufan aamba*
    His-father down-there his-mother down-there thought garden path they-
    kourowana.
    went.

12. *Kourankaqe sena umemba miniyampoi kunaiqmayai.*
    Gone she-said steal this-boy go-take.

13. *Kunaiqme we wena kaema uwamaenamo kumumba.*
    Go-down-get he go small-arrow made-it came-down.

14. *Awaiqo uwamaenamo kumumba munkwamena kaariqi mbunkwamena.*
    Arrow-for-birds made come-down come-give small-bow give.

15. *Kaariqi mbunkwamena sena.*
    Small-bow go-give said.

16. *Numamo auqmaraunda kobasinkwai.*
    Bird saw you-shoot-give-me.

17. *Miyawe suwanan aiqmena kurai.*
    This-way talked took-him went.

18. *Aiqmena nkwe kuwana.*
    Took-him she went.

19. *Eqefo minda naankaraq auqmarano suwańa.*
    All-right this-one where-is you-look said.
20. *Keqai kaandausiya auqmakaune suwana.*
    There ditch-at I-saw she-said.
21. *Minka kuwana.*
    There they-went.
22. *Efo miwamba koyakena ete aaqonka kuwana.*
    Now there went-beyond there another he-went.
23. *Sena naankaraq auqmakano minkeko maena miniyampoigo suwana.*
    He-says where you-see-it there sit-down this-boy said.
24. *Aaqa keqainka auqmakaune minininko sena.*
    No I-see over-there this-mother said.
25. *Miyan kusi mamai aiqme aiqme aiqme aiqme mefaime omapimban*
    This-way came talk took-him took took took on-top mountain go-up
    iyai oraaq omapi imaena.
    big mountain sit-down.
26. *Muranena emba ayatakan kemba kaaroma sema siqmaema kwetene*
    Look-down you long-way me lie you-talk you-took-me you-came he-said.
    sena.
27. *Minkaqimaena ifiqa muratena maankunifiqa muratarai.*
    This-place-sat-down cry come-down for-this-cry go-down.
28. *Maankunifiqa muratena akwe me kesifomo siminkumbo empime*
    For-this-cry come-down oh this my-father my-stone-axe down-there
    maemauntaraqo ontaraqo muratuwaunda imba ndaaumpa aawiyo
    I-sat-down my-door left-it not house hide-it put.
    maraunaq.
29. *Siqmaeq senaraq waaowe sentendafa teraqme kumba tuweraq iyuno*
    You-take-me you-talk you-come go you-said axe I-left I-came said.
    siyai.
30. *Sena maankunko pimba mosa faafeq tuwena minkaqmi.*
    Said this this-thing go-up singsing made for-this.
31. *Ifiqa imbosa wesena isiyena ifiqa mosa tarai.*
    Cry go-up he-talk made-singsing cry go-up did.
32. *Mosa tasuwena uwana iyawena minkaq imaena.*
    Go-up did made-it no-good-go-back this-one came-stay.
33. *Iyarataqa tamai iyuwerai fosena minkakemba koaiqmena.*
    Settled-down for-sure no-good-go-back said this-person took-him.
34. *Kunkai marena tontonasi naaoqa minkaqme naamba munurai.*
    Come-down put-him Tontona place there house made.
35. *Naamba munuwama keanauwanena minke kumbaena.*
    House made finished there stay.
36. *Mbaantafaraq kumuno suwana.*
    Come-where I-come said.

37. *Maanda uwaaratimapa tontonafa kumonesu suwanan efo minkaqmi*
    This-place foreign-place Tontona you-have-come talked now there house
naamba munuwamai.
made.

38. *Uwamarena minkakumbena.*
    Finished-making there-stay.

39. *Kumbena minka kwemba munifoqanurai.*
    Sit-down these him shoot-the-nose.

40. *Miniyampoi munawime minkeqifoqa.*
    This-boy found this-shoot-nose.

41. *Nuwamarowana kesuwaiqa none siyai.*
    Did-it my-husband you said.

42. *Suwana kawequwamai maraumai.*
    Said good-do finished.

43. *Murawanena sena kesino none siyai.*
    Saw-her said my-mother you said.

44. *Karosempo.*
    You-lie.

45. *Kesinome kemba kusiqme awane empaifakemba iyone.*
    My-mother-you me you-got you-saw down-below you-came.

46. *Suwana kemba mimba waai.*
    Said me none man.

47. *Imba mberai isaqawane kesafe emba kunaikaune.*
    Not there-is anyone mine you I-went-get.

48. *Miya sena minkaqmi mosa ifoqa uwamarena.*
    This talk there adult shoot-the-nose did.

49. *Efo minkaqa mesarai kigaum kweuwandesarai minka kaiqa iyampoi*
    All-right this-one two-stay garden made-two this-place two boy give-
maqankarai.
birth.

50. *Maqankesarai mimbararukan imba maesaunesarai.*
    Give-birth this-place no stay-there.

51. *Kuraaoqondamu paresarai kweguyana.*
    They-went another-place two-went.

52. *Aanka kufaiqtuwesa noanta waasi timaaqa awiqa.*
    Road ambushed Nonta man Timaqa name.

53. *Minkaq kuwana noanta waasi kufaituwesan aanka maamora iyampoi*
    This-place went Nonta man ambushed-them road this-one child this
minka kuntufu.
killed-him.

54. *Kuntufuwana awanena kwewena kaweq uwamai imba nafowa me-*
    Killed look-pretend-he go good look no his-father turn-look his-son
kaeqmai aaraakombo tufumba meanarai.

killed turn-look.

55. *Meanomba mifaqwekuwana.*
Turn-look just-left.

56. *Embarena nenkaq kuwana nanowa sena.*
He-went-a-ways little-way he-went his-mother said.

57. *Aaqau eniyampoi tufuwowa awane meuwoimi nonta maekompo mora*
No your-child killed you-look you-carry go cargo-take-go what you-say
sewaq maewaq uwoinkono miyanko sena anowanifiqa.
take-go nothing like-this talk his-mother-cry.

58. *Kontontafena minka komaena kamenafambamakai.*
Cry this-one sit-down drum-give-her.

59. *Kamemba mamora namena marayamba mora kumba mamena.*
Drum one came-gave this-thing one axe come-give.

60. *Maandasamba komaimai aqnomba taqanke minkwaasi minka men-*
This-thing go-get his-head put-at this-man this drum his-head put talk
tamba maqnomba taqankau suwana nkowerenan.
come-back.

61. *Efo noanta tinaq tiyena efo mindambi awiqa.*
All-right Nonta place came all-right this-one name.

62. *Minkafin tiyenan efo minkambini kamenafa tamaimai.*
This-place came all-right this-place drum come-get.

63. *Aqnomba taqankenan efo marauwamai minkumba maqnoamba ta-*
His-head put-it all-right take this-axe at-head put-it.
qankena.

64. *Tamaimai mosa sanaamba maranai sena.*
Come-get go-up top-on put-it said.

65. *Tanoawana minkanarakon efo aasimba minka ekaq fakariri uwamai*
Come-look this-one all-right skin this enough skinned did this-person
minkatai airanoi kwimarena.
skin put.

66. *Nanomba kourowana kanena.*
Body left did.

67. *Efo mamin airamba komaisuwena.*
All-right this skin go-get.

68. *Minairankamban kumba maqnomba mataqankena wanena.*
This-his-skin axe his-head put-it do-it.

69. *Marena we kuwasa.*
Put he go.

70. *Ama timaqa kurai.*
Ama place he-went.

71. *Ama timaqa kuwasan ama kumbaimai minkwaasi kumbaimaimo*
Ama place went Ama come-get this-man come-get good make-it.
kawiqa uwankowana.

72. *Minka komaena araakomba moanowana kwembe aifa kweku aifa*
    Here settle his-son looked him first he-go first he-go said.
weguwana sena.
73. *Aqa ke anowamba me simamena embe tufuwo wemo senda.*
    No he him-his-mother turn talk you killed this said.
74. *Waasi aifa uwoi kwewifo endankwaasiyaq tufuwowaq.*
    Man first go-now what men kill-him.
75. *Senda uwaqiyo siyai.*
    Talk did said.
76. *Miyasuwana uwanena sarai mifaq wewesaraiye.*
    Same-talk did then this-place two-go.
77. *Minkamo tufuyambo amanoimo mowiyainkaqo.*
    This-place two-fought skin left-it.
78. *Maami kumbo aqnomba taqmakaimba epimifankwai.*
    This-one axe head put-it it-is-there.
79. *Epaiq nontawe anaawe wesempi katimaapa waisana.*
    Place Nonta Anawe called place is-there.
80. *Mifaqo mimbiyamo uwamai.*
    This-one became-one-them did.
81. *Mimbifau awiyana maniko koawiyoq kuraimbani.*
    This-place Auyana ancestor hide-it like-that.
82. *Mbaniqa minda eqa finisi sawiqa kowakuraini.*
    Ancestor that all finish no-good go-hide.

1. Give this stone axe here to me. My talk concerns it; it concerns the Auyana ancestors who had it. This stone is from down below.
5. There was a pale young boy, and this boy went there to look for a snake; he walked around looking for one. When he went to look for a snake, his parents went to the garden. They left, and he went to look for the snake for a long time. While he was doing this, a woman came down. She was from Tairora country; she came and came from the Tairora area. 10. She came and saw that there was just one person looking for a snake. 'His father is down there; his mother is down there; his parents have gone,' she said, 'so I will go and steal this boy.'

So she went down to get him. She went, and she made small arrows and went down. She made arrows for birds and came to give them to him. She also made a small bow to give him. 15. She gave him the small bow it is said. She saw a bird—so she said 'You go and shoot it and give it to me.' This is the way she talked to him, and went and got him. She took him and left.

'All right, you look to see where it is,' this one said. 20. 'I saw it there at the ditch,' she said. So they went down there. Now he went on beyond that place. 'Where did you see it?' the boy said, and he sat down there. 'It's not there. I see it over farther,' this woman said. 25. So talking this way, she got him to keep going. They sat down up on top of a big mountain. He looked down, and he said, 'You have brought me a long way, you lied to me; you came and took me away!' He sat down there in that place and he cried. He came down and he cried for this [the axe]. It was for this that he cried having come, and said, 'Oh, my own stone axe, I sat here, and I left it there at my door. It is not hidden in the house. You took me, you just talked and said for me to come, and I left that axe there, and I came up on top,' he said.

30. He said this, and he made up a song about this particular thing [axe]. He cried, and he made up a song about it, and went up crying. He went, making the song, for it wasn't good that he should go back, so they came and were there. They settled down, for she said it wasn't good that he should go back, and took him to keep. She came down, and she made a house, and put him there at Tontona. 35. She made a house, and they stayed there. 'Where am I?' he said. 'You have come to this Tairora [foreign] place, you have come to Tontona.' So she told him, and there made a house. She finished making it, and settled down there.

Then she initiated him (by sticking sharp reeds up the nose). 40. She found this boy, and she initiated him. After initiating him, she said, 'You are my husband, this is good.' When he saw her, he said, 'You are my mother. You lie,' he said. 45. 'You are my mother; you saw me down below, and came and got me.' When he said this, she said, 'But I don't have a husband; there isn't any man for me, so I went and got you.' She talked this way, and initiated him to be an adult there.

Now these two stayed there, and she made a garden, and there she had a child. 50. After she gave birth, they didn't like that place anymore. They didn't want to stay on, so they went off to go to another place. Now a Nonta man ambushed them on the trail—the name of that place is Timaqa. They went, and at this place the Nonta man ambushed them and this one killed the child.

He killed him, and his father had only pretended to watch. 55. His father had not turned to look at his son, and he killed his son. He didn't turn and look, he just left him behind. They went on a ways, and in a little way his mother said, 'Oh no, he killed your child, look, you told me to go on, to take and carry this cargo and you just came along without anything.' She talked like this and his mother was crying. After she cried, this one went and gave her a drum. He came and gave her the drum, and also this thing, the axe, he came and gave her. 60. He went and got it, and he put it at his head. This man put the drum at his head. He said it and came back. Now the name of the place there was Nonta.

He came to that place and he got the drum and put it at his head and he got the axe and put it there at his head. He came and got it and went up on top and put it there, it is said. 65. He came and looked, and he skinned him, and he put his skin there. He left his body. He got his skin. This skin, and the axe, he put them at his head. He did this. He put them there and left. 70. He went to the place Ama. He went to the place Ama; he came down to Ama; this man came, and he fixed it up well. He settled his son there.

She looked and there was her son. 'He went on ahead, he went first,' he said. 'No, but you said they killed him,' his mother said. The man went on ahead; 'What one killed him?' 'They killed him.' 75. 'Now you are just talking,' he said. He talked this way, and he left the skin there, and he put this axe at his head.

It is still there. It is at Nonta. The ground is called Anawe where it is. 80. This one became one of them there. At this place the Auyana ancestors hid those things, as we said. That is all regarding the ancestors. They hid them, it's no good.

11. OLD FOLKS

1.   *(Araq) kwauranko kumba bawanowana.*
     (Er) old-man stone-axe went-sharpen.
2.   *Nonkaq intoi mawanowana awaankamba ifikwena memora waompaq*
     At-water stone-file went-sharpen testicle fell-down one pool went-
     kuwafekuwana.
     inside.
3.   *Muqmi mosa maimarena mora kuwafikuwana mosa maimarena.*
     Again get-up get-put one went-skin-broke up go-put.
4.   *Efo (a—) taaqmunaiqa kewainiqa aanopaq asaaumai kawequ maena*
     OK (uh—) edible-leaf-broke Kewai-leaf-broke gently tie-up good did
     taafo kaumarena.
     got hot-ashes-put.
5.   *Taapon kaumarena mowana (naaq) unaamba kunkweu.*
     Hot ashes-put was-there (?) bag went-start-to-make.
6.   *Kanaamba kunkweuwa suwowana.*
     Unfinished-bag went-started-make continued-on.
7.   *We awaiq wauranko ikepibaq kumbena ifaqa kisaamo araankambo*
     He old-husband this-place went was-there this-place sweet-potato old-
     kaumaraunda kwefasi sinkewe suwana.
     lady I-put-under she-is take-put-by-me said.
8.   *We fasimbakena kepi kewain aiqa maandowana asenuwana.*
     She took-out this Kewai-leaf stem got-tasted sweet.
9.   *Eq miya none sena.*
     Enough this-way you-are said.
10. *Mora mandowana abaara aseseqa unena.*
     Other got-ate very sweet was.
11. *Efo mi tawasumakena fasimbai embi ndamai kaweq uwasuwena.*
     OK this untied-it took-out one ate good did.
12. *We unaamba kweuwana awaiqwauranko minkaqo kisaamo kauma-*
     She bag she-made her-old-husband this-place sweet-potato I-put-under-
     raunda fasisinkarewe suwana.
     neath you-take-out-put said.
13. *Efi indaferaqa fasimban kaune suwana.*
     On-top bed-on I-took-out put said.
14. *Isaafauwaena epi marapaqe suwana.*
     Searched-for down-below ground said.
15. *Sabaununu nuwaena.*

Search look.
16. *Wemba imba kwaisa.*
    It no was-there.
17. *Enkweseni senan efifaq waantamba kwe taufe sunena.*
    Tell-me said on-top stick-for-walking he pulled talking.
18. *Kanaambo emomba kaampakwai tauqmaena.*
    Unfinished-bag made bat-needle pulled-out.
19. *Kimpi anandafi kuwaferena wiya oifinkuwafe kwena.*
    This-place woman's-place went-inside grass opening went.
20. *Mura faimarena kouwana.*
    Down stuck-it-in left.
21. *Efo (minda—) wenayamun awimba awetara tanomba kwe uwana*
    OK (this—) she her-girls Awetara-leaf mumu they made go-down
    kumena kentifo kwe waraisaqanumpo.
    your-father he chasing-me.
22. *Aaroqnaaroq uwamai fasinaaro suwasan.*
    Hurry-hurry do-it take-away said.
23. *Efo mi fasimbai nasuwesaya mainda kouwana wembin kwai kunkusaq*
    OK this opened ate these left him needle came-down punctured.
    kena.
24. *Efo wiofiq weunena.*
    OK jump-about he-did.
25. *Kwembare mare koawanowana wauranko mbaaq taaqa kwewisuwanan*
    They-went go saw-him old-man this sugar-cane tying-up road you-
    aamba araasiyo siyai.
    show-me said.
26. *Aamban araasiyo suwana.*
    Road show-me said.
27. *Menayaafaq iyawanao suwana.*
    Go-look on-top said.
28. *Imba kwaye suwana.*
    Not is-there said.
29. *Menai naraifi kunawanao suwana meawambi koawanawe suwana.*
    There down-below you-go-look said there go-look said.
30. *Imba nuwana kwe fakariri mbin tatayai fakentuwena.*
    Not it-is he came-down this ladder there-left.
31. *Menayaaraqmo wayanai ufaisukowana.*
    This-on-top urinary-tract got-out.
32. *Naanopa—kaekaenoq amarena meminkan ekaneka imau.*
    Gently—Kaekaenoq went this-place here went-in.
33. *Imowana efo minka ferawaato maremarena menka nimaun.*
    Went-in OK this-place Ferawato went-and-went there went-in.
34. *Efo aweqaranta marena menka nimau.*

OK Aweqaranta went there went-inside.

35. *Efo tinowarankanko eka faenturai.*
OK their-mother-old-one enough blocked-it.

36. *Faentumakowana wembi kwaurako kwaqmaeqmaena.*
Blocked-it him old-man chased-and-chased.

37. *Koawanena—kesifarawao maankaniyaq weteo suwana.*
Go-look—my-friend this-place come-here said.

38. *Aaqao imba kwetewe suwana.*
No no they-come said.

39. *Oq maankaqo eqo maa we tene suwana.*
Oh this-place enough here they come said.

40. *Enepai kampuntaramba (naq) ayaye maasimuka tuwesu.*
You-this-one Kampunta-tree (er) you-cut this-my-belly you-hit-said.

41. *Feqa ndaraunana simuqa kwe kurai.*
Banana I-ate my-stomach it too-tight.

42. *Ayaye tuwana taitaiqa nuwanan.*
Cut hit not-strong is.

43. *Efo epiaq arerin ayaye tuwe suwana.*
OK this-one Areri-tree you-cut hit said.

44. *Moqarerin ayayena tufuwana taitaiqa nuwana.*
Again-Areri-tree cut hit not-strong it-was.

45. *Kamemban ayaisuwena tuwana kopiri tapiri simaqa.*
Kamemba cut hit-him went-out come-out did-this.

46. *Simakuwana emba mifaqa mayai (taq) mosa ufeqmakema siyaane*
Did-this him this-place you-get (*taq*) on-top you-fill-yourself you-talk
sena.
said.

47. *Minda minamuqa tufantuwowana kopiri tapiriqa siyai.*
This this-belly hit-did go-out come-out talk.

48. *Mbaniyen enkin ampa mbaniqa enki simameqa sumboqa uwana kon-*
This-way enough short ancestors enough me-talk-you I-said that-way
tai noena noenamba uwakuraimbaniyema.
Kontai-place grass grass happened.

49. *Kindan eqa imbi kisimamo.*
This enough this-it I-told-you.

1. Now there was an old man who went to sharpen his axe. He went to the water to sharpen it with a stone file. A testicle fell out, and it went inside the pool of water. He got it again, and put it there. But the skin broke and the other one fell in. He went and got it and put it down. Then he broke off an edible leaf; he went and got and broke off the Kewai leaf and gently tied them up and put them carefully in the leaves fixing it well and putting them down under the hot ashes.

5. He put them in the hot ashes, and he went and started to work on the unfinished net bag. He went and continued making the bag. The old man went and was at this place, and while he was there, he told the old lady, 'I put that sweet potato under the ashes. Get it out and put it beside me.' She took it out, and she tasted the Kewai leaf, and it was sweet. 'Oh, that is the way you are,' she said to herself. 10. She got the rest and ate it, and it was very sweet.

So she untied it and took it out of the ashes, and she ate the rest and it was good. Then she worked on her net bag, and her husband said, 'I put the sweet potato underneath in that place; you get it and put it by me.' 'I took it out and put it up on the bed,' she replied. He looked for it and she said, 'I put it down below on the ground.' 15. He looked and looked for it. It wasn't there. 'You tell me where it is,' he said, and he pulled out his walking stick from up above while he was talking.

She was working on the unfinished bag, and she pulled out the needle made from the bat. She went down to the woman's place and went in by pushing aside the cane. 20. Down there she stuck the needle in and left. Now she, well, her girls were making a mumu with Aweta leaf, and she went down there and cried, 'Your father is chasing me! Hurry, hurry and open up the mumu,' she said. They opened it, and they ate, then they left together. When he came down, he was punctured by the needle. So he jumped about.

25 . They went, and they saw an old man who was tying up the sugar cane; 'You show me the way,' she said. 'You go look for it up above,' he said. 'It's not there,' she said. 'You go there down below and look,' he said. 'Go look at the place down there,' he said. 30. But it wasn't there so he came on down this ladder and left it there. Now this old man that was up on top exposed his urinary tract. Kaekaenoq went softly into this place [pointing to chest and stomach]. Now after she went in, then Ferawato went into this place—she went in there too. Then Aweqaranta went inside too. 35. Then their old mother blocked it up.

She blocked it up. As to him, the old man chased and chased her. He went to look for her and said, 'My friend, didn't they come to this place?' 'No, they didn't come here,' he said. 'Oh, they came to this place and are here,' he said. 40. 'You take this Kampunta tree limb and cut it, and you hit my belly,' he said. 'I ate bananas, and now my stomach is too tight.' So he cut it and hit him, but it wasn't very strong. So he said, 'You cut the Areri tree and hit me.' So he cut the Areri tree and hit him with it. But it wasn't strong either. 45. Then he cut the Kamemba tree [long thorns on it], and hit him with it. They came out here and all over, that's what happened.

Now as to the old fellow, he said, 'You were at that place, and you filled yourself up there and talked,' he said. He broke this one's belly. And they came out all over, it is said.

That's the way it was with our ancestors—enough. I have told you now—I've said it. That's the way it was there in the grass lands. That's what happened. That's enough, I've told it to you now.

12. FOREST MADE SAFE

1. Awaininkoma awaininkoma toniqa uwamaena kobaraniqa empima

His-wife his-wife bring-food bring bean-sprouts down-below weeds went-
tufake kunumaenamo wekufuquwana.
came cooked.

2. *Kwenawaiko aanopaq wanamaiyare sena kumbaq.*
    Her-husband careful animal-want-hunt said went.

3. *(Maq) kofamaena mana suwena umaq umaq umaq umaq weuwana.*
    (*Maq*) go-shoot came ate-it did did did did did-it.

4. *(Aq) ke aisafiqa maena mamuwana nasuwena kwe kwana mayaqa*
    (Er) this foot get-bring come-give ate he possum find you-go you do-it.
    kondaisama emba kweoni.

5. *Emban kweoni sena umeromerowana (mura aurambo fiqmakaimba*
    You do-this she-said keep-doing-this (down eyes pluck-out I-talk say)
    senaiqa su) endorawaq kowamarewaq wetosoone sena.
    you-do-what you-go-doing you-come said.

6. *Afo (afoq) sawaiye mobaqe kuntoremena.*
    All-right (OK) frog fish went-got.

7. *Memi (aqaq) endoineq wemaiwaq wesene suwana.*
    All-right (*aqaq*) you-what get-what you-talk said.

8. *Auramba aanopaq mura fiqmarenan urifaq maa awanaanda nompi*
    Eyes carefully down take-out-put Nurifa this-place you-saw water
    urifaq mura auramba fiqmarena mifaq kuwafekuwana.
    Nurifa down eyes take-out-put this-place go-inside.

9. *Kwena waaininko marena kunawanomba kwemba fiqmakowana.*
    She his-wife she-go went-down-look he pluck-out-put.

10. *Kumbaena aanafimbamo ufeq wimatuwe mowana.*
    Went-got bamboo went-up put-in is-there.

11. *Nuri nuri nuri su su su.*
    Nuri said said.

12. *Nuri nuri su su su.*
    Nuri nuri said said.

13. *Nuwaenan efo mi menauramba taemokoma onkaefikoma taemikoma*
    Did-this all-right this eye sticks dry-grass young-trees dry-leaf eye-
    taefukoma aurampimba kobeqmain owitakuwana.
    place-in go-inside filled-up.

14. *Toqmaka umaena aanopa ndaaumpa imowana kwembin ara fa-*
    Feel-around did-this carefully house came him mother child live.
    noiyaiko mesa.

15. *Norawaq urewaq one suwana.*
    What you-do she said.

16. *Marena nuriq—imeana.*
    Came *nuri*—is-there.

17. *Inki kanafimba owepamaiyemba.*
    This-place ashes-in curled-up.

18. *Maa qunuwakuwana wanena.*
    This no-good-more he-is.
19. *Efo enamba kusamaenamo wimarena embin auramba maraineq*
    All-right edible-leaf went-got came-up-cooked you eye do-this I-look
    awanaano suwana.
    she-said.
20. *Efo ifau kanamo manaurampimbo kobekuwanamo maemomba.*
    All-right here ashes eye-inside go-in just-there-is.
21. *Maraumai auramba nuwana saqwintu anamo wimaromba menauram-*
    Did-this on-eye did-this mushroom bamboo cooked this-eye-socket
    pimba autuwowana kobekuwana.
    blew-it go-inside.
22. *Ae simasuwena.*
    Yipes cried-out.
23. *Moqmouana moraurampi miyauwasuwowana mena.*
    Again-did-this one-eye-hole did-same-thing is-there.
24. *Efo miyauwasuwe mena norawaq onauno sena umai kawe umarena.*
    All-right did-this is-there what happen-to-me said did good did.
25. *Umipaq taine umika kouwana taine umika kouwana mbarena*
    Forest gift bush he-went gift bush went-he went-go is-there.
    komena.
26. *Wiyakomba amaamban amakai amaamban amena mimbarika*
    Python-to talk gave story gave this-camp we-two-are this-place come
    mbeyaufo minka teo suwana.
    said.
27. *Efo marena minkwiyako aanopaq memora omakaq tamaena fifi*
    OK he-came this-python quietly this-one mountain came *fifi* said.
    suwana.
28. *Taaqa mendan doinkowa siye suwana.*
    Papa this what-noise say said.
29. *Minda uwaintorena taikanenumba torena siye su.*
    This wind-blows scraping-noise noise talking he-said.
30. *Efo marena moq empimika mora taiyaq tatorena fififi suwana.*
    OK come again down-below one tree come-is-there *fififi* said.
31. *Taaqo eqa mbaatenasi ndoinkowaq siye suwana.*
    Papa enough come-something noise-what say said.
32. *Minda taaqo uwaiko kwetorena taiko kanenumba kwetorena niye*
    This father wind blows tree rubbing-together make-noise make said.
    suwana.
33. *Miya simai miya simaiena embo taiyaq tatorena.*
    This-way talk this-way talk close tree came-sat.
34. *Kwemba fifi tasuwana.*
    He *fifi* came-said.

35. *Owe taaqa matenaniye suwana.*
    Oh Papa has-come said.
36. *Aanopaq mifa kenasafawena kumbaimai (wiq) andaampaq mai-*
    Carefully this-place fell-down went-got (*wiq*) inside swallowed.
    wimarena.
37. *Mowana (anowauwana) kwene mbi afowa mbarena ndaaopaq tena*
    Is-there (look) he this his-father go house came his-mother said where
    anowa sena naafaq awewaq teno suwana.
    leave-him you-came said.
38. *Aaqa mifa maefeq afumo neamarena mepaifa miwetenaniye suwana.*
    No this that-banana ripe he-ate there he-come he-said.
39. *Anowa amuqmatuwe maumbauuwaaena uwana.*
    His-mother wait stay-and-stay did.
40. *Kwembai kwembi nampa aayaafaumaena mimaaripi kowawanou-*
    Him this road went-look this-camp went-looked stick (?).
    wana tanaintandena (yamena).
41. *Kotufuqmai minkwiya karanaara karanaara uwamai.*
    Went-hit-it this-python cut cut did.
42. *Uwoifaq tuwena (miq).*
    All-around throw (?).
43. *Ayamunkomba komaena mi minkwiyamo tufuqmaromba.*
    Small-girl go-get-out this this-python go-hit-put.
44. *Komae umaenambe mawima kena poi tatufuwe.*
    Go get-two come-cook for-them pig kill.
45. *Umakena umipaqo winda miya nonafo sena.*
    Did-this bush one-goes this-way not-good said.
46. *Minda tutu simasukai sa miumipa saawifimba kwenaonananiye.*
    This no-good spit-out-she-said this this-bush without-fear you-can-go.
47. *Mi sewaqo isaraundani maniqa.*
    This story I-heard old-folks.
48. *Eqa ekani.*
    Finish ended.

1. His wife—his wife used to bring food; she would go below for native bean sprouts, going below in the weeds, and come and cook them. Her husband said that he wanted just to go carefully hunt possum; so he went. He would shoot it and come and eat it, and he kept doing this. He would get it and bring just the food and come give it to her, and she would eat it. 5. She would say, 'You do this, and you keep doing this,' she said. (I meant to tell that he would pluck out his eyes and put them down.) 'What is it you do? What do you go and do? You keep coming lots of times,' she said.

All right, he went and got frogs and fish. But she said, if you get something, say so. He would carefully take out his eyes, and put them down. At Nurifa (you have seen this place), at this water Nurifa, he would take out his eyes and put them down, and at this place he would go in. Now his wife went down. 10. So she went and got a bamboo and went up and put them in it, and they were there. He kept saying, '*Nuri nuri nuri—*' and kept saying and saying that.

After he did this, then twigs, grass, young sticks, and dry leaves would go inside the eye socket and fill it up. He felt around and did this, and slowly came to the house and was there. The mother and child were there with him. 15. "What are you doing?" she said. He came [saying] '*Nuri—,*' and was there. He came and here in the ashes, he curled up. This fellow wasn't any good anymore.

All right, she went and got some edible leaf and came and cooked it. 'You do this with your eye [looking up], and I will look at you,' she said. 20. All right, what happened was ashes went inside the eye socket, and he was just there [no cure], After she did this, she did it [another thing] to his eye: she took some mushroom and cooked it in bamboo, and blew this into his eye socket. It went in, and he cried out, 'Yipes!'

OK, she did this, and he was there and he said, 'What is happening to me?' Finally she really fixed him. 25. So he went to the forest for the gift for the first born child; he went for the gift, and was there. He told his story to the python telling him his trouble. 'We two [father and child] will be at this camp and you come to this place,' he said. OK, this python came very quietly. He came and this one was there on the mountain. '*Fifi,*' it said.

'Papa, what is that noise?' she [the child] said. 'That is the wind blowing, and the trees making a scraping noise,' he answered. 30. So it came on again and was down there in one of the trees, and it said, '*Fififi.*' 'Papa, enough! something has come! What is it saying?' she asked. Her father said, 'It is the wind blowing and the trees rubbing together and making a noise.' It hissed this way, and having talked this way, came and sat down close to the tree. He came and said, '*Fififi.*' 35. 'Oh, Papa, he has come now,' she said.

Quietly it dropped down at this place, went and got her and swallowed her. She was there, and this one, her father, went and came to the house, and the child's mother said, 'You have come, but where did you leave her?' 'No problem! She has just stopped to eat a ripe banana,' he said; 'She will come.' Her mother waited and waited for her.

40. Finally she went along the road to look for her. She came to the camp and looked. She then went and killed it with a stick, and then cut and cut up the python. She threw the parts all around. She got out the small girl; she went and killed the python and put it around. She got the two and came and cooked; she killed a pig for them. 45. She did this, and said, 'If someone goes to the bush, it isn't good that this happen this way.' She spit it out and said, 'Now you can go about in this forest without fear.' I heard this story from the old people. It is finished.

13. VICTORY OVER SPIRIT

1. Paqa wiyomba kowana mena nafarawaao akwe maankwiyombo kaan-
  This-place moon light is one-kind oh this-moon clear wild-pig I-want-

daraqa afapoi faawaimbaune suwana.
shoot said.

2. *Kwembo afaq waantaun epia naamaifaq tamena.*
    Of-him wild spirit close-by house came.

3. *Ai kesifarawao eqanka sena iseqa oiqan kafuna embe simasuwanesu*
    Oh my-one-kind enough I-talk my-mouth open you go-talk-said said.
    suwana.

4. *Efo kumuwe sesarai.*
    All-right come two-talk.

5. *Imbamaisarai aankafamba kwewesarai paroima (f)omba kwenepi uwo-*
    Bow-got-two road-go two arrow shot he-there outside shoot-finish one-
    ifaq fasuwowana afarawao umaraune suwana.
    kind I-did-good said.

6. *Kwembo afarawao sena aampi famarowana kwena farawao nuwoifaq*
    Him his-one-kind said road shot his one-kind outside shot-it.
    fasuwena.

7. *Kaaro miya simai iyasimaisa kwawanoyana kisaafimba maanan afapoi*
    Lie same talk talk-this-way look garden this wild-pig was-there all-
    mowasan efo minda wenafarawao parafowana.
    right this his-one-kind missed-it.

8. *Kwembo emo naaumpaqo menamo sundaqa aneqa fasuwena kwe mora*
    Him first house-at he-was talked skin he-shoot him one person talk
    naqa sena parafasuwena.
    shot-missed.

9. *Kaaroqa eneqa faune miya semesa tufuqma isarain.*
    Lie skin shot same talked killed would-get.

10. *Efo maama kesarai kwe kaufuwana ayamba saa muwana.*
    All-right this come-put-two he made-a-mumu stomach took-out gave.

11. *Ndompambaena ko afarawao maekouwana wembifaq mu amaara*
    Went-down-to-water go one-kind got-went him-this go-down one-talk
    iwaantaseqa mundasuwena.
    spirit went-ate.

12. *Mi mundasuwena uwana.*
    This go-eat hurry did.

13. *Aroqnaroq umai kaumain efo epaifaq fasimbai kena.*
    Hurry did cooked all-right place-close open-mumu put.

14. *Embe fiqorama kweompo sena.*
    You different-custom you-do said.

15. *Waimbo anafisiemba ndonanafimba fayefayeq uwasuwena amuwana*
    Bone-needle bamboo-small water-bamboo-in punch-holes did gave
    maekourowana.
    took-went.

16. *Kunuwutemba kwe kuwakowana kwenaroq umai kaumai mifa simbai*

Went-fill-it he went-out him-fast made cook this took-out him divided-
kwemba tuwinankenan.
up.

17. *Efo membinda atamimi marewetena naantaikowa kemba suwaaseinono*
All-right him carried took-brought which-tree me can-come-help said
sena simai simai simai ena.
said said said.

18. *Tawanowana ware wandanankon aanopa eniye sena minkaqmena*
Came-looked Ware-tree big-one carefully that's-it said this-place here
maabaq iyuwo siyai iyuwo suwana.
come-up said come-up said.

19. *Ebai kwaare amifa mai suwowana amifaq imenanuwasa.*
On-top Ware head got threw-him top went-up.

20. *Kwembi amara seqa ayaanofiqa intoinanka fintoinankanka ememe saya.*
Him one-talk same-time finger file they-file did-it did it.

21. *Efo maq (qaq) kobaya tabaya umaetuwana kwembin.*
All-right this-one (er) go-look come-look came him.

22. *Ontankwara iyafasindasuwe saya tufintinkomba wareme tuwana*
Stone-of-mumu came-took-away ate gave-out followed came went-up-
kweniyawanomba kwemba.
found him.

23. *Kowankufisa tankufisa umaesa.*
Go-sniffing come-smelling did.

24. *Tuwana imba kurowasa kwembi taemoramaraumai tankufisomba.*
Come no go he tree-base-did came-smelling.

25. *Maaminkaq iyowasa efo aanopa wenaisa fipi kwena(i) safipimba kunun-*
This-fellow gone-up now slow his-toes his his-toes intertwined inter-
kwiso kununkwisoq uwamaesa.
twined did-it.

26. *Amiyaq iyuwana owe kesifarawama eqa maa sinkamo naesa maiyo*
Top went-up oh my-one-kind enough these will-kill me they-come do-
wamaneone suwana.
something said.

27. *Aanoqumain taetoq umai kaweq uwo sena.*
Slowly hold-him-hard did good do said.

28. *Efo minkwaare wandakomba ekaq araapenuwana maeku memena.*
All-right this-Ware big-one enough encircled took-him went-down.

29. *Empina awaifaq mu maantuwena kwe iya fisekuwana awanena.*
This-place steep down throw-him he up-went straightened did-again.

30. *Efo mu kwen arosamupi kwenamupimbe kununkwiso kununkwiso*
All-right down his back his-front intertwined intertwined happened
uwamai kaaqanuwana embe taiwekomba meme kurin awifakaqo nisamo
they-died this small-snake this fence on-edge goes-along you-know sent.

ondawimba aiqmarena.

31. *Kunawanao suwana aifenampaqa ayampaqa oipimba kotusu tatust*
    Go-look said nostrils-in anus mouth went-in came-in enough died di
    wana eqa kaaqaqnumai uwana.

32. *Ekan keqanifo efo kumuwo suwana.*
    Enough he-died OK you-come said.

33. *Efo me mura tuwena.*
    OK this down left.

34. *Uwoi naeiyaimba naopa aano naaompa aumba koukwenan.*
    Nothing no-injuries place slow house sleep went.

35. *Owe kesifarawao esena uqmakuna kemba fiqon tamban onaqa emb*
    Oh my-one-kind you-talk I-go me other custom you-practice you do-
    nune simasuwena.
    he-thought.

36. *Efo mindaumpan ekan aumba taufuasa.*
    All-right this-house enough sleep came.

37. *Amara iyesa aisauwana sena miyayani uwasuweqa mbanteqanuni.*
    One-talks they-came ask-him said I-went did-thus myself-came.

38. *Mesiyai mbani.*
    This-one-talked same.

39. *Noqwamporu owe aei senaq.*
    At-night yes surely tell-it.

1. At this place it was light from the moon, and a certain fellow said, 'O
the moon is clear, I want to go shoot wild pig.' A spirit came close by to th
house. 'Oh, my friend,' he said, 'I want to talk to you.' 'You go ahead,' he sai
'All right, you come on.' This is the way the two talked. 5. The two got the
bows and went along the road.

He [spirit man] shot an arrow, and shot it off to the outside but he said t
his friend, 'I shot it well.' He said this to his friend but he shot it to the side c
the road; his friend shot it outside in the brush. They two went along talkin
this way, but it was a lie. They looked, and a wild pig was in the garden, an
his friend shot and missed it. When he was at the house before, he bragge
that he would shoot its skin [pig]; he said this to one fellow, but he shot an
missed. It was a lie that he shot him; this was the way that they talked abou
how they would kill it and get it.

10. OK, these two came and put it down, and made a mumu, and the othe
fellow took out the stomach and gave it to him. He went down to the rive
his friend got it and also went down; they went down, this one and the spir
went down and ate. When the one went and ate, he [the spirit] did it hurriedl
[swallowed it whole], but he cooked it; he opened the mumu and put it dow
close by. 'You have a different custom that you practice,' he said. 15. The
with a bone needle he punched holes in the bamboo, the water bamboo, and h
gave it to him and he took it and went.

He went to fill it up, but the water ran out of it. The other one [while th spirit was delayed] took out the food from the mumu and quickly divided a portion for him. OK, he carried part of it with him and thought, 'Which tree can help me?' and he kept saying that. So he came and looked and saw the Ware tree—a big one, and he said softly, 'That's the one,' and he was there at that place. It said, 'You climb on up, you climb up here,' it said. The top of the Ware tree picked him and threw him there on top. He went up on top and was there.

20. As to the other one, this fellow meanwhile filed his fingers; they [a group now of spirits] filed and filed their fingers. They went to look for him, and looked all over and so came. They came up to the stone of the mumu and took away all and ate it and came and gave it out to the others, then followed him to search for him. He went sniffing and came along back and forth sniffing him out. Now he had not gone, and he [the spirit] came sniffing for him at the base of this tree.

25. The real fellow had gone up [the tree], and carefully intertwined his toes and intertwined them there. He went up to the top and said, 'Oh, my friend these [spirits] are going to kill me, they are coming, do something.' It carefully held him fast; 'Do it well,' he said.

This big Ware tree encircled and held them, and bent down and picked them up. It threw them down a steep place, then straightened up again. 30. All right, it intertwined down the back and front, and they died. This one, this small snake, that goes along the edge of the fence, you know the one; well, he sent it. 'Go look,' he said, and it went in and out of their noses, anuses, and mouths, and they had died. 'Enough, they are dead, you can come down,' the snake said. So this one came down and left there.

There was nothing wrong with him, so he went slowly to his place to the house for sleeping. 35. 'Oh, my friend, you said let's go, but you have another kind of practice from me, and you do it differently,' he thought. So he came to this house and went to sleep. His neighbors came and asked him about it. He said, 'Oh, I went and did thus and so, and now I alone am come.' He talked this way. But it is at night that it can be told well.

14. MAN ENTERS HEAVEN

1. *Mora amoqnafa umipa areko iyampoi maqankarowasa.*
   One small-bush forest woman child gave-birth-to.
2. *Aiqmaesa taineinesa kwaamba fentaaqa kouwana awanena.*
   They-took get-food-for-feast possum hunt they-go look.
3. *Iyanko aitawisuwena kuwana.*
   Dog put-nose-to trail went.
4. *Afowa araiwaqmaena kuwana.*
   His-father followed go.
5. *Nafakenaq waamba faindaefenaq wiyo sena kuwana maaweraq kurena.*
   Some-place possum he-shot-grab go say go Mawera-tree he-go.
6. *Iyamba aiqmaena kuwana amoquafaq kurena miniyanko taifaq mintai-*
   Dog take go little-bush go this-dog on-top-tree this-tree went-up.

yafan iyuwana.

7. *Afowa mintaiyafa marena iyuwana.*
His-father this-tree go-he went-up.

8. *Wiyomba afaaqa kweropimba iyatusuwena efi wiyompa iyuwana.*
Heaven-in hole heaven-in he-go-up-look on-top heaven went-up.

9. *Kwiyoompaq iyawanowana kwaasiko imbo monka; aareko mimborawe*
Heaven he-go-up-look man no is-there; woman this-one-only just-
weyaa mowana.
one was-there.

10. *Iyuwanaawanena feqa feqa kasiyaamuwana.*
Go-look banana banana break-off-give.

11. *Nasuwena sena enanaafu aamba kouraiye wetenamo aimo wesiname*
Ate-it said your-grandfather road gone when-comes language make-talk
inkaisonafo suwan anena.
don't-be-afraid said did.

12. *Ifakemba minarankanko awaiq wauranko we tuwana ain tasuwana*
This-place this-old-woman her-husband old-man he came talk came-
awanena.
made did.

13. *Maafakembo iyun kwaasiko inkaisuwana mindaifeqo ena naafuwe*
This place he-went-up man was-afraid this-person your-grandfather
sundan efo inkaisonafo suwana.
me-talk so don't-be-afraid she-said.

14. *Minkaq mowana teqa takasi aamuwana.*
This-one-at was banana break-off gave-him.

15. *Nasuwowana, naumpaq mosankena ima paroima awaiqa maimai*
He-ate-it, house go-put bow arrow pronged-arrow got hid-them put
awiyoq marena aupaq marena.
hide put-them.

16. *Mora kariqi eraq wemauna sena aforaq marena.*
One small-one enough I-got-it said in-sight put-it.

17. *Aundoqwaamba aaqa fenowana aunkowana.*
Sleep-night time sundown slept.

18. *Aunkwaowanama piyaima (muritiqa) posaamumba fiyunarampimba*
Slept-was-there Piyaima-tree (?) Posamumba-tree small-Fiyuna-tree-in
kwaamba kwanumemba saawema kwaanonama kwaankoma mena ain
possum squirrel(?) racoon(?) animal animals were language talked.
kwesuwana.

19. *Ainkwesuwana maafakembo iyu kwaasiko mininkuwa maena min*
Made-talk this-place go-up man this-bow go-down-get this he-got did
maisuwena anena akaankaq mofena kwaanumemba mofena.
here shot-him go shoot-him.

20. *Awanena maafandaopa awaaomba putambafarai.*

Look this-place older-brother shot-for-sure.

21. *Araaqa.*
    Died.

22. *Famarowana, owe kembe minda efeq awane faanafo mosundaniye sena.*
    Shot-him; oh me this-one did no-good you-shoot-him me-talk he-said.

23. *Kunawanowanan aqa nuwana.*
    Came-down-look too-bad did.

24. *Poin iya tufuqmai kaumai kwaaq wandan.*
    Pig next-day kill-him cook cloak tie-up-did-it.

25. *Uwamai sawiqiya kwaandan uwamena.*
    No-good what tie-up did-it.

26. *Maantomba maimai awane eninaopa kwekume enawaamba faraam-*
    This-food you-take look your-place go-down your-brother where-shot-
    poifa kunanaao su.
    him go-look said.

27. *Uwana mindafa marena wekumena amaamba amena sena.*
    Did-it this-place he-go went-down story he-gave said.

28. *Enaunandaamba enanokaamba enawaamba enafakomba eninaamaru-*
    Male-cousins father's-sister's-son older-brother younger-brothers sisters
    komba kotaantare awane naoqa tanoniya mufarakeyeane.
    you-call do place mumu-fire go-down-cut-cook.

29. *Maam poima amundambu naao siyai.*
    This pig I-give-you you-eat said.

30. *Maafa marena kunanomba awaomba arowana makwemba kunkaq*
    This-place go-down go-look older-brother shoot-him this mourn put-
    makesa ifiqa kwetowana.
    him cry made-it.

31. *Oenda kesaako isaqa kesuwaamba faraune.*
    Oh my-ear same my-brother shot-I-did.

32. *Ke farauna sena.*
    I shoot-him he-said.

33. *Mimpoima amumba kwaaqwanda uwamaena mumba kena.*
    This-pig he-gave bark-cloak tied go-down put-it.

34. *Anokaomban afakomba kowaante taante kweni inaamaru uwama*
    His-cousins his-younger-brother go-call come-call his young-woman
    karena awanena.
    did did did.

35. *Tawasu suwomba.*
    Rope took-off.

36. *Aqnomba arosaumba ayaantamba auma morawai mipinkemba kuwa-*
    Head back-bone hand body one-time this-one fell-out.
    mai.

37. *We aqonkaq maqmai inkwi amuwana anena.*

He another one-with kind mound-up did.
38.   Efo minda tawasu makarena anena.
       All-right this rope take-off put-it.
39.   Amaara seqa naraimbani eqa sunki.
       His-one-talk one-time they-ate enough finish.

1. Once a woman gave birth to a child at a small bush in the forest. They took him, and in order to get food for the birth feast, they went out to hunt possum. The dog put his nose to the trail and went. His [the dog's] father [owner] went along, following. 5. At a certain place he shot a possum, and said, 'Go get it,' and he went to the Mawera tree. He took the dog and went, and they went to a small bush, and this dog climbed up to the top of this tree.

His owner went and climbed up this tree. There was a hole into heaven there, so he went up and looked and went into heaven—he went up on top into heaven. He went up into heaven and looked, but there was no man there; there was only one old lady—just one was there. 10. He went and looked, and she broke off a banana and gave it to him. He ate it, and she said, 'Your grandfather has gone off. When he comes, he will make talk, but don't be afraid,' she said. So this old woman's husband came to this place and he made some talk. At the place where he had gone up, the man was afraid. 'This person is your grandfather as I told you, don't be afraid,' she said.

So he was by him, and she broke off a banana and gave it to him. 15. He ate it, and he went and put them up in his house, he hid the bow, arrows, and pronged arrows; he put them up and hid them. But one small one, he thought, I'll get and leave in sight. At night after sundown they went to sleep. When they slept, at the Piyaima tree—the Posamuma tree, at the small Fiyuna tree the possum, squirrel, racoon, and another small white-bellied animal—these animals were there and they talked together. When they were talking together, he went up to this place and the man got this bow; he got this one, and he shot him here; he went and shot a small animal. 20. He looked, but at that place he really shot his older brother. He died. When he shot him, he said, 'Oh, I have done this to this one.' 'It is bad that you shot him,' he[the old man] said. He came and looked, and said it was too bad.

The next day he killed a pig and cooked it and tied it up in a bark cloak. 25. What he tied up wasn't good. 'Here, you take this food and go down to your place; go where you shot your brother and see,' he said. He went to go down to this place, and the old man told him this: 'You call your different cousins, older brothers, younger brothers and sisters, and go down and cut it up at the mumu and cook it. I am giving you this pig for you to eat,' he said. He went down to this place, and looked where he shot his older brother, and mourned for him, making a chant. 30.'Oh, this my ear, for I shot my brother, that's what I did. I shot him,' he said. He went down and put this pig which he gave him tied in the bark cloak. 'You call together your cousins and your younger brothers.' so he came and called them and the young women. He took off the rope. 35. Now the head, backbone, hands, and body of this one [the pig] fell out at one time. He mounded it up with other kinds. So he took off the rope and put it there. His relatives all ate it then. That's it—the end.

XVI. Usarufa Text

Compiled by DARLENE BEE

---

1. Two Brothers Get Wives

1. Móra anonuqmagoma anónuqmagoma yaa máina abîmma atákáiye.
One old-man an-old-man tree-at was-he beetle broke-he.

2. Aqaanibo móra waagoma wemá memapaké paképake aimmá ítámena
OK one man he below-from knocking sound hearing-he going-up-going-
uyéqúyéna utáiye.
up-he went-up-he.

3. Áánibo uma máitana aqáániye, tena wemá atáqma áúgêmma naráiye
OK doing was-he-and-he OK saying-I he broke-and raw ate-he that
min ábímmá.
beetle.

4. Aqáániye tena aaqá ékáiye.
OK saying-I atmosphere darkened-it.

5. Abáúmma karáákaq kúmitana keé náakaraq waaénúno téna titana
Sun setting-at going-down-it-and-he I where sleep-will-I saying-he say-
naammá wáipoa waínópo páátémáao tiraiye.
he-and-he house there-is-so-you sleep-will-you-definitely just-say-stay said-he.

6. Ítana ááqiye tena mááyana ítána naammá íma wáipoaqa waínópo
Hearing-he OK saying-I being-they-two-and-he hearing-he house not
páátémáao; ketí yáômma wáiye oqta ítúweka waeyúye; páátémáao tiráiye.
being-it-so-I sleep-will-you-definitely just-say-stay-you; my stick being-it-is
door open-after-we-two sleep-will-we-two; Just-say-stay-you said-he.

7. Mirá téna wemá tiráiye.
Thus saying-he he said-he.

8. Titana máitana awíqmena yópáqá uráaye.
Say-he-and-he being-he-and-he him-carry-he garden-to did-they-two.

390

9. *Uréna yaaqá kobákáténa kamááma kéyubena kábêmma kématena*
Did-he sugar-cane go-picked-he sweet-potato harvested-he greens
kéqokeq yaqtaaqa yókáq wái qtaqtaaqa apáátarimma mamétarata uráaye.
took-he assorted things garden at being-things corn bringing-they-two did-
they-two.

10. *Urétarata móra yáômma komaténa min ánónúqmágómá nokómá*
Did-they-two one garden-stick go-took-he that old-man the-water edge
ááwabaqa móma ítaiye.
going opened-he.

11. *Yáônapo oqtamá ítuwetarata minnóbáq nokómá aúqa pékuraaye.*
Garden-stick-with door opened-after-they-two there-inside the-water
inside disappeared-they-two.

12. *Pékuraitarata mókenaayana aaqá ékaiye.*
Disappeared-they-two going-eating-were-they-two atmosphere darkened-it.

13. *Néta máeq uraaye.*
Eating-they-two staying were-they-two.

14. *Kéneta máena aqaaniye tena aaqá énéna taíwakoma aamá tiráiye.*
Eating-they-two being-it OK saying-I atmosphere darkening-it insects
voice said-it.

15. *Yaatárúgoma, yaatárúgoma aamá titatarátá ítáayuwena mórama wááqa*
The-crickets the-crickets voice saying-it-and-they-two heard-they-two-
mama wírákáraiye.
and-he one bark-cloak taking covered-up-him-he.

16. *Kaayaqá wírakena móra abakéna wagaao titana wemá waguráiye.*
Two cover-up-him-he one pulled-up-he asleep-be-you say-he-and-he
he asleep-was-he.

17. *Taíwakoma aamá tínama ítoreq íitaao aqaaniye téna.*
Insects voice saying-it-if getting-up-you not-listen-you OK saying-he.

18. *Móra wakoma táitawaataakoma pakí tíma íitao.*
One creature lots-of-creatures chirp saying not-listen-you.

19. *Namagó aa tínama íitaao.*
The-bird voice saying-he-if not-listen-you.

20. *Wagurénaraa kemá kaayaq áárámá yaqtoqma ameno; inarúrátá mira*
Asleep-you-if I two women catch you-give-I; unmarried-girl-two thus
téna we timá mílaiye.
saying-he he tall him-gave-he.

21. *Timá mítana aqaaniye tena máiq uráiye.*
Talk giving-he-and-he OK saying-I being was-he.

22. *Uráitana anónuqmagoma we itóuma kéitaitata aabêmma yaráae.*
Was-he-and-he the-old-man he getting-up hearing-he-and they-play
danced-they.

23. *Abê yai marukáq yamáae.*

Play at ground coming-be-they.

24. *Kéyaawana inarúma íráqôn inarurata nopíké utarétarata aabè yaráae.*
Dancing-they-and-she girl good girl-two water-in-from grew-up-they-two play danced-they.

25. *Iqnókóma irotáupapa kukáiye.*
Their-hair their-back-at came-down-it.

26. *Ayaatááq ignomma keitata ignótáugoma kara kááyúkátí iqnótáuraa* Long-their head was-it-they-two their-hair red people's hair-like was-*kéitana.*
it-and-he.

27. *Minnakómá ámîtana ámîtuwena we timá mîkaiye.*
That-one him-giving-and-he him-gave-he he talk gave-he.

28. *Wáápi aqtáuma aména mamé weqeqa yómmá yoqmakááno; titana* Bark-cloak-in wrapping him-give-he bringing going-going garden plant-*yoqmakáune titana.*
have-you; say-he-and-he plant-have-I say-he-and-he.

29. *Yaaq yómmá wáiyo titana yaaq yómmá wáiye titana.*
Sugar-cane garden is-there say-he-and-he sugar-cane garden there-is say-he-and-he.

30. *Kamáá yomma wáiyo titana wáiye titana.*
Sweet-potato garden is-there say-he-and-he there-is say-he-and-he.

31. *Môra yaqtaakoni awíqa úmábûmma uqmakááno titana uqmakáune.*
One thing's its-name Umabumma plant-have-you say-he-and-he plant-have-I.

32. *Titana komatéa aayabiqá kutéa yatóyátó uwo.*
Say-he-and-he go-take-and-you your-backside put-and-then circling do-you.

33. *Kéinatuwa anáekaq yaónaao timá mîkaiye.*
Doing-it-after later come-at-it-look-you talk gave-he.

34. *Mira téna timá mîkaiye.*
Thus say-he talk gave-he.

35. *Aqaanibo timá mîtana we minnakómá anóqmagoma timaminiq tima-* OK talk give-he-and-he he that-one the-old-man telling telling going *miniq weqéna weqéna yópí mómarena úmábûmma yaráqma aayabiqa* going-he garden-in go-put-he Umabumma tearing-and his-backside putting-*kuména min ínarúgórátámá yiqnótáugoratama mititin aqnótáuraa uráiye.*
he those girls-two their-hair-two white woman's-her-hair-like was-it.

36. *Aqaanibo, páákí íráqô táqtáákórata máitarata aamá kéteyana yayimó-* OK, just-so the-good things-two being-they-two voice saying-they-*nawaena wemá amuqá mámakaiye.*
two-and-he come-them-see-did-he he his-pleasure put-for-them-he.

37. *Ááyakoma íráqóne uráiye.*
His-viscera good was-it.

38. *Miráuwatena anurá kóyakena anóama komá ááyaraiye.*
   Thus-doing-he mountain-at go-pulled-he his-mother going her-called-he.
39. *Noqêno, kaayaq áárámá yíwiqme kéune.*
   Mother, two women them-carrying coming-am-I.
40. *Emá naammá kuyubuwo; yaaremá uwo; yuwiqá mama wiyo; kénara*
   You house sweep-you; bed do-you; mat getting make-you; doing-you-if
   awíqme ono mira téna anóama timá titana.
   carrying-doing-I thus saying-he his mother talk say-he-and-she.
41. *Anóama yuwiqá wikéna wanaa popóq uréna áawaqa agaténa kéitana*
   His-mother mat made-she blanket shaking did-she food cooked-she
   minninikaraq awiqmena ko aráiye.
   doing-she-and-he those-brides-with her-carrying-he going arrived-he.
42. *Wemá anóama káonena íráqón amuqá marákaraiye.*
   She his-mother them-seeing-she well her-pleasure put-for-them-she.
43. *Máina ábâko iyáiye.*
   Being-he his-younger-brother came-he.
44. *Ábâko yááyamakena o keti waao móra innimma e timiyo tiráye.*
   His-younger-brother him-called-he Oh my older-brother one bride you
   me-give-you said-he.
45. *Íráqôn innimma awîqme épo; móra innimma e timiyo; ke móra*
   Good bride her-carrying have-you-certainly; one bride you me-give-you;
   mayanúne.
   I one take-will-I.
46. *E keti waamá móra mayaao tiraiye.*
   You my older-brother one take-you said-he.
47. *Kemá emmá íamenaune; emá waayúká íma mamá kaayoné uráane.*
   I you not-you-give-will-I; you people not putting compliment did-you.
48. *Kemá kaayoné eqa kemá páá umá kaunabo emma íamenune téna we*
   I compliment doing-I I just doing burn-I-must-not you not-you-give-
   tiráiye.
   will-I say-he he said-he.
49. *Agaama mamaréna awaón aítauqa wemá aráá aráiye.*
   Scolding put-he his-brother's his-feet he following arrived-he.
50. *Awaón aítauqa aráá ama weqéna weqéna koaónaimma min anónúq-*
   His-brother's his-foot following going going go-him-seeing-he that old-
   mágómá ibîmma máina atákáiye.
   man beetle being-he broke-he.
51. *Weqé weqéna min anónúmágómá ko yaráiye.*
   Going going that old-man go danced-he.
52. *Koaónatuwena komá itana we min ánónúqmágómá tiráiye.*
   Go-him-seeing-after-he going knowing-he he that old-man said-he.
53. *Náakakena yénô; ke táánikoma téna titana.*
   Where-from come-you; my son say-he say-he-and-she.

54. *Ke táániko ke táánikoqa ke náánimma mibáq máin aanibo e páá tiraibo.*
My son my son my son there being OK, you just said-he-definitely.

55. *Emó ketí waam aména yataarama tiráátiyo tiraiye.*
You my brother him-give-you this-thing me-show-you said-he.

56. *Kanaara íye; aráátenupo; páátémáao mira kétima wen áama íma ítáraiye.*
Well is-it; you-show-will-I-certainly; just-say-stay-you thus saying his voice not listened-he.

57. *Miráta tiráiye.*
Thus said-he.

58. *Titana yópáq awíqmena uráiye.*
Say-he-and-he garden-to him-carrying-he did-he.

59. *Min ánónúqmágómá awíqmena kéwímma anónuqmagoma yukea aara*
That old-man him-carrying-he going the-old-man pulling all-right me-
tiráátiyo téna kétimma aáwaqa amítuwe etabai awíramanupo nokáámma
show-you say-he saying-he food you-giving-after later her-carrying-will-I-
páátê iyo téna.
certainly night just-say come say-he.

60. *Awíqma weqéna aáwaqa kómama naaûpake mamé móma ketarata*
Him-carrying going-he food go-getting house-inside-from bringing go-
neqén neqé neqétarata aaqá kéenaimma kéqnaamma auwagaao tiraiye.
put-they-two eating eating eating-they-two atmosphere darkening-it as-before your-body-asleep-be-you said-he.

61. *Kaayaqá paraakéqa mama kéwirakena kaayaqá kábakena.*
Two blankets taking covering-him-he two put-aside-he.

62. *Waayúnóbáqá owana aqáaniye téna wemá yawaguréna anónuqmago*
Pool-inside coming-they-two-he OK say-he he come-asleep-he the-old-
tiraiye.
man said-he.

63. *Yáákaao, yáákaao, yáákaao ke emmá amenúne.*
Easy, easy, easy I you you-give-will-I.

64. *Aúpaqa máiye; kemá aónanune; yáákare kenamáari maméno tima.*
Hidden is-she; I her-see-will-I; slowly I-alone coming-give-I saying-he.

65. *Wemá íma ítáraiye.*
He not listened-he.

66. *Wemá mirá tiráiye.*
He thus said-he.

67. *Koawíqmena emá yáákaao; netuqyáa kaayuka máae.*
Go-him-carrying-he you slowly-do-you; plenty people being-are-they.

68. *Kemá awíqmeqa emmá mámenune.*
I her-carrying-I you coming-give-will-I.

69. *Nonóbáqá naammá wáiye.*
Water-inside house there-is-it.

70. *Waayúka máae; netuqyáá kaayuka máae; awíqmeqa emmá mámenune.*

People there-are; plenty people there-are; her-carrying-I you coming-you-give-will-I.

71. *Yáákaao; yáákaao timá wemá íma ítáraiye.*
Gently; gently saying-he he not listened-he.

72. *Kétaka kááyaq yáqtoqma mátuma weqeo yópí mómareqa yómmá yoq-*
Saying two grabbing come-tying going garden-in going-put garden
makaana yaaqá wáiyo timá.
planted-have-you sugar-cane is-there saying.

73. *Yaaqa wáiyo títakena tiráiye.*
Sugar-cane is-there say-he-for-him-he said-he.

74. *Kamáá yomma wáiyo kamáá yomma waiyo titakena wemá agarenae*
Sweet-potato garden is-there sweet-potato garden is there say-he-for-
tiráiye.
him-he he anger said-he.

75. *Yuwéna abô kégaipo; wemá atáámá ámikaiye.*
Throwing-aside-he his-weariness burning-it-certainly; he wrapping him-gave-he.

76. *Miráte tiráiye.*
Thus-say said-he.

77. *Wemá mómareaq koaónaao timá wemá minnákó ááma íma ítáraiye*
He go-putting go-look-you saying-he he that-one speech not listened-he
anónuqmagon áá.
the-old-man's speech.

78. *We ikaména ikaména weqé weqéna yópím ákaraitana naaégoma aúra-*
He hitting-he hitting-he going going-he garden-in put-them-he-it the-
nobakema ááraranobakema ááyáqnobakema anékema aqnónnóbakema
blood eye-inside-from ear-inside-from intestines-inside-from body-from
koaónawaaena.
head-inside-from go-it-saw-he.

79. *Minnáko abô téna tiráiye.*
That-one my-gosh say-he said-he.

80. *Téqéna awaón naaopaq awíqmena wéna mótiraiye.*
Say-going his-brother's house them-carrying-he going go said-he.

81. *Ketí waaó móra timiyo; timiyo.*
My brother one me-give-you; me-give-you.

82. *Emá kaayoné íyaonabare kaayoné íyaonama maaráitaba yuweqa páá*
You compliment not-seeing-place compliment not-seeing this-concern-
kînnama maré maao; ke íamenune we tiráiye.
ing throw-out just as-before putting remain-you; I not-you-give-will-I he
said-he.

83. *Mirá téna timá mikaiye.*
Thus saying-he talk gave-he.

84. *Timámitana wemá awaaómá yaataabíqá móra kóyokáiye.*

Talk-give-he-and-he he his-older-brother garden-work one go cultivated-he.

85. *Yaataabíqá yómmá ko yoqmaréna yaamá anó tanamma anó tanamma*
Garden-work garden go cultivate-he tree big tree one-big tree-one
komá aayáátáiye.
going chopped-down-he.

86. *Yaauýqnóbáq ánnáma kárataiye.*
Forest-in vine cut-he.

87. *Karéqéna karéqéna karéqéna karéqéna karéqéna marú marabí yuwéna.*
Cutting cutting cutting cutting cutting down ground-on threw-he.

88. *Keti waaô, emá yaamá ko aayáátíkaao téna wemá mátima ámikaiye.*
My brother, you tree go chop-for-me-do-you say-he he come-talk him-gave-he.

89. *Mátima mitana awaaómá kummá kémayena imá kémayena kabáaramma*
Come talk-give-he-and-he his-brother axe taking-he bow taking-he
yubámákéna mi kabáárakaq uténa unááyáátaiye.
ladder getting-he that ladder-on went-up-he go-up-chopped-down-he.

90. *Áánátááyúwéqa wemá kabûmma kó káratuwaitana awaaómá meya*
Finished-after he vine go cut-he-and-he his-brother up-there there stay
mikáq máiq uráiye.
did-he.

91. *Abô; ketí bâko emá yamatíyuwaao; emá ketí bâko yamatíyuwaao.*
Oh, my little-brother you come-put-for-me-do-you; you my little-brother come-put-for-me-do-you.

92. *Kemá nôra itaae; ááq en ánáaqa keti waa kemá mayánúne; mikáq*
I why is-it; your-ear your wife my brother I take-will-I; there being-you
máina pukaao.
dead-be-you.

93. *Mirá kétipike min ínníkárátá iqnó káowarena minínnímmá iqnó káo-*
Thus saying-in-from that bride-with their-hair flowing that bride their-
warena we kóuraiye.
hair flowing-it he went-he.

94. *Kóitana móra numagoma yama aónaraiye.*
Go-he-and-it- one bird coming him-saw-he.

95. *Akáq áánátaiye.*
Finally finished-he.

96. *Itána aónaraiye.*
Understand-he him-saw-he.

97. *Ááqiye, numagómá aónatuwena augeqókoma máqte numagoma tima-*
OK, the-bird him-saw-after-he the-*augeqo*-bird all birds talk gave-he.
mikáiye.

98. *Móra waayuka máiye; ketinógaama awíqmetaa marabítáá kaúne;*
One man there-is; my-cousin him-carrying-we ground-we put-will-I:

máqte numama yero téna.
all birds come-you-all saying-he.

99. *Pááqya numago ti máqte numama iréta maakákémma numagómá*
The-little bird say all birds came-they here-from the-birds him-carrying
awíqme maakáq kákaimma ôq numagoma awíqme maakáq kákaimma
here put-it another bird him-carrying here put-it here thus-back-and-forth
maakáq miráute taute taute tauteta maakaq marauma maraao.
back-and-forth back-and-forth back-and-forth here thus put-you.

100. *Áwîqa aakikígómá awíqmena marabí aáwaqa néqéna yuwéna óniq*
Its-name the-hawk him-carrying-he ground-on food eating-he throw-
kamaama naréna koqá naréna póma naréna yaaqá naré kéitana wemá
away-he earth-oven sweet-potato ate-he bean-root ate-he pig ate-he sugar-
áúgoma táiq umágimma anón naraqa mama kéqnan kéqnan uráiye.
cane ate did-he and-it he his-skin bad was-it big at coming as-before as-
before did-it.

101. *Titana numamá minnakó ááyaraiye.*
Say-he-and-he bird that-one him-called-he.

102. *Ááyateta ye agúmákéta wemá iráábima agamá pubúyâma mákéna*
Him-called-they they gathered-together-they he coals cooking black-
ayammá ayammá (piginibimmá pent) (uturabaibi ayammá) naaé ayamma
paint taking-he paint paint (Pidgin-talk-in paint) (Usarufa-talk-in *ayamma*)
pekaiye.
blood paint painted-he.

103. *Yaayá ayamma pékaiye.*
Green paint painted-he.

103. *Tokón ayamma pékaiye.*
Blue paint painted-he.

105. *Máqte numago ítáta mibaq weawe umágowana wemá minnáko tiráiye.*
All birds knowing-they there waiting doing-ones-they-he he that-one
said-he.

106. *Kemó yewátákórátá uráayakaq wáanibo.*
I those-brothers-two did-they-at be-will-it-certainly.

107. *Kemá páápáq waayukago ôqa íma mirauyuyataba kétena yaatotaamma*
I legendary man-am another not thus-we-two-concerning saying victory-
aakáma anúyaba makáuyaba áárannayaba uqmá weqe wemáwítata mi
plant hiding hill-place wilderness-place planting place he going-he-they that
kááyúkámá únópáq uraae.
people ocean-place were-they.

108. *Únópáq matema merapáq kó etaq uráápota mi kááyúká maranoe.*
Ocean-place taking afar going going-they did-they-so-they that people
put-will-they.

109. *Íyaq maranoa.*
Not put-will-they.

110. Mi máániqá túnama káánatagiye.
That legend say-I finished-it-being-is.

1. Once there was an old man, and this old man was in the forest catching and snapping beetles. Another man hearing the sound of the snapping came up from below. As I have said, he was there and he was snapping the beetles and eating them raw. It got dark. 5. As the sun was setting he said, 'Where will I sleep?' and he [the old man] answered, 'There is a house here so you will sleep there. Be quiet.' As I have said, they two were there and hearing [the answer] he said, 'There is no house so [where will I sleep?]' 'You will definitely sleep here. Shut up. I have a key. We will open the door and we will sleep,' he [the old man] said. Thus saying, he said.

Being there and having spoken, he took him and they two went to the garden. Arriving he picked sugar cane, harvested sweet potatoes, took greens, various things; garden produce, corn, and so forth they brought with them. 10. Having come he took a key, and the old man going to the edge of the water opened [the door]. With the stick they opened the door, and they disappeared inside, inside the water. Having disappeared inside, they went and were eating and it was dark.

They stayed there eating. As I have said, they stayed there eating, and as it was getting dark the insects began to sing. 15. They heard the crickets chirping, and he [the old man] took a bark cloak and covered him [the other man] up. Covering him with two he pulled one up and said, 'Go to sleep,' and he went to sleep. 'If you hear the insects singing, don't get up and listen,' he said. And then he said, 'If you hear any creature, any sort of creature chirp, don't listen. If the birds sing, don't listen.' 20. 'If you are asleep, I will catch two women and give them to you. Unmarried girls [they will be].' As I have said, he told him and he stayed there.

He stayed, and the old man got up hearing them playing. They having come were at the place of playing. They were playing, and a girl, two beautiful girls, grew up from out of the water, and they all were playing. 25. Their hair flowed down their backs. Their hair was long, like white people's hair. That one [the old man] gave them to him, and after he gave them to him, he told him [some things].

He wrapped them up in a bark cloak, and bringing them to him he gave them to him. 'Have you planted a garden?' he asked, and he answered, 'I have planted a garden.' 'Do you have a sugar cane garden?' he asked. 'I have a sugar cane garden,' he answered. 30. 'Do you have a sweet potato garden?' he asked. 'I have,' he answered. 'Have you planted a thing called Umabumma?' he asked. 'I have planted it,' he answered. 'Go get it and put in your backside and circle around. Later after you have finished, come and look at them,' he told him.

Thus saying, he told him. 35. All right, when he had told him, he with the old man continually repeating his instructions went on and on to the garden where he put it down [the package of girls] and breaking the Umabu plant put it in his backside and the hair of the two girls was like a white woman's hair. They were just two wonderful creatures, and when they spoke, he saw them, and he was very pleased. He was wonderfully happy.

Being thus happy, he went pulling them after him to the mountain and called his mother, 'Mother, I am coming bringing two women.' 40. 'Sweep the house, make the bed. Make a mat. If you will do this, I will bring them.' Thus saying he told his mother. His mother made the mat, shook the blankets, and cooked food, so he came with the two brides. His mother seeing them was very very pleased.

While there, his younger brother came. His younger brother called to him, 'Oh, my older brother, give me one of the brides,' he said. 45. 'You have brought beautiful brides. Give me one bride. I will take one. You, my brother, will keep one,' he said. 'I won't give you one. You don't pay compliments and do things to please people. I pay compliments and do things to please, so I shouldn't suffer. I won't give you one.' Thus saying he answered.

He angrily followed his brother's footsteps and came to the place. 50. Following his brother's footsteps he went on and on, and then he saw the old man there snapping beetles. Going on and on the old man went dancing. After he had seen him, he realized he was there, and the old man said, 'Where are you coming from, my son?' saying he asked. 'My son, my son, my son, come off it,' mockingly he said. 55. 'Show me this thing you gave my brother,' he demanded. 'Very well, I will surely show you. Be quiet.' Thus he answered, but he didn't pay attention. Thus he said.

So saying he took him to the garden. The old man taking him he pulled the old man, 'Come on show me!' he said; and he answering, 'First I will give you food, later I will bring her, tonight. So shut up,' he said. 60. He brought him with him and went and brought food from the house, and they ate and ate until it was getting dark, and as before he said, 'Go to sleep.' He brought two blankets and covered him; putting two of them aside he came inside the pool place, and as he said he was [impatiently] lying down, so the old man said, 'Take it easy. Take it easy. Take it easy. I will give them to you. They're hidden. I will see them. Be patient, I alone will come and give to you.' 65. But he didn't listen to him.

He thus spoke [again]. Going to get them he said, 'You take it easy. There are lots of people. I will bring them and come and give them to you. There is a house inside the water.' 70. 'There are people there. Lots of people. I will bring them and give them to you. Take it easy. Take it easy.' He spoke, but he didn't listen.

So saying to him he grabbed two and came wrapping them up, then went to put them in the garden, saying, 'Have you planted a garden and is there sugar cane in it?' 'Is there sugar cane?' mockingly he answered. 'Do you have a sweet potato garden?' 'Do you have a sweet potato garden?' mockingly he answered with anger. 75. Disgustedly he [the old man] became tired of him. He wrapped them up and gave them to him. Thus speaking he said. He went and putting them down said, 'Go carefully watching.' But that one didn't listen to [or obey] his words.

He hitting and dropping them went on and on to the garden, and when he put them down, blood was coming from their eyes, from their ears, from their intestines, from their body, and from their head, and he went and saw it. That one, 'My gosh!' exclaiming he said. 80. So saying he went to his brother's house and carrying them he went and said, 'My brother, give me one of yours. Give me.' 'You have not seen the place of obedience, you have not seen the advantage of giving compliments and pleasure, so concerning this [request] you can just forget it and remain just as you were before. I will not give her to you,' he answered. Thus saying he told him.

After telling him, he and his older brother went to make a garden. 85. While doing the garden work and making the garden, he went and chopped down a very big tree. He cut vine in the forest. Cutting and cutting and cutting and cutting he threw it down on the ground. 'My older brother, you go chop down the tree.' Saying he told him. So he told him, and his older brother taking an axe, taking a bow, and getting a vine ladder, he climbed up the ladder and chopped the top off. 90. When it was finished, he [the younger brother] went and cut the vine, and his older brother remained way up there. 'Oh, my little brother, come and get me. You, my little brother, come and get me.' Why am I doing it? Learn your lesson, your wife, my brother, I will take. You remain there and die.' Thus in his speaking he took the two brides their hair flowing, that bride hair flowing, and he went away.

He went away, and a bird came and saw him [the older brother]. 95. He was really finished [i.e., near death]. He understood what he saw. OK, the bird after seeing him, told all the birds. 'There is a man there. My cousins, we will carry him and put him on the ground. All you birds come,' he said. At the little bird's word, all of the birds came, and from here they carried him and put him there, and another bird carried him and put him there, and back and forth from branch to branch they carried him. 'Put him thus here [they said]. 100. One bird's name was 'the hawk'; he carried him, and on the ground he ate food and throwing aside the dirt, he ate sweet potato from the earth oven, and he ate bean root, and pig, and sugar cane, and he ate and ate, and his body which was withered became big, and it became as it had been before.

So saying he called the birds. He called them, and they gathered together, so he cooked coals and made a black paint (in Pidgin English it is called 'pent'; In Usarufa it is called 'ayamma'), and he took red paint and painted them. He painted them green. He painted them blue. 105. All the birds hearing about it were there waiting, and to those who had helped him he said: 'I, those two brothers have done this and it will remain. I am a legendary man, no one else will do like us two.' Saying, he took the victory plant and planted it on the hillside, in the wilderness out of sight, and he went away, and they, those people [the younger brother and the two women] went over the ocean.

Over the ocean they went afar, and so those people will remember. Or will they not remember? 110. This legend which I am telling is finished.

PART THREE: *Gadsup-Agarabi*

XVII. Introduction

HOWARD McKAUGHAN

Gadsup is spoken near Kainantu by over seven thousand people. The three major branches of this subfamily include the Agarabi, the Oyana, and the Gadsup. The location of the Gadsup relative to the other members of the Eastern Family of the East New Guinea Highland Stock is depicted in Map 2.

The following five chapters cover Gadsup phonology, noun morphology, verb morphology, and syntax, and Agarabi phonology and general notes from textual analysis. The original publishers are noted in the first footnote of each chapter. The Agarabi textual analysis gives an overview of that language. The chapter on phonology by Bee *et al.* presents an important interpretation of nasal vowels not found in the other languages. The interpretation of a five vowel system is the same as for Usarufa, and could be made for the other languages (except Awa). The Gadsup texts which follow the Agarabi textual analysis by Goddard extend the linguistics information on this segment of the study languages.

The phonologies of Gadsup and Agarabi are very close. Where the Frantzes have postulated *b* but not *w* for the former, Goddard has *w*, which has allophones of both stop and fricative varieties for the latter. She does not cite a *b* phoneme. Both speech communities have *y*. In Agarabi the phoneme has alveolar stop and fricative palatal varieties. Both have another alveolar obstruent given as *d* in Gadsup with a flap vibrant [r] as an allophone and *r* in Agarabi without notable variation from the norm. Thus the total consonant inventory is the same in number: *p, t, k, q, b, d, y, m, n* for Gadsup; and *p, t, k, q, w, r, y, m, n* for Agarabi.

The vowel inventories for the two are also the same: *i, a, u, e, aa, o.* The tone systems, however, seem to differ. Goddard indicates two degrees of tone: high marked by the acute accent, and low left unmarked. The Frantzes indicate four for Gadsup: high, low, up-glide, and down-glide.

403

of tone: high marked by the acute accent, and low left unmarked. The Frantzes indicate four for Gadsup: high, low, up-glide, and down-glide. The last two are analyzed only with nouns, since they occur infrequently with the verbs. The two word classes of nouns and verbs are contrasted by opposing tonal characteristics, and unusual phonological feature for a tone language. The Gadsup people use their tone system for a special communicative device in whistle talk. Much can be conveyed since they use the tone and also articulations of the segmental phones in the whistling.

When first published, the articles by the Frantzes on nouns and verbs utilized an orthography with schwa and *a* to indicate the central mid to low vowel and the low front vowel. Here we use *a* for the first, and *aa* for the second to parallel Auyana and Tairora.

Nouns and verbs are characterized by complicated morphologies. Gadsup nouns have five classes instead of the three or two of the other groups. Frantz describes some fifty suffixes occurring with nouns. Not all of these are exclusively used with nouns. The usual number with a base has been found to be two or three at a time, never more than six. The Agarabi texts illustrate only eight suffixes used with nouns (some also with verbs). I suspect that this is not because Agarabi has far fewer than Gadsup, but that the affixes are used to be explicit, specifying what can be indicated by other means. The noun affixes are not at all obligatory, nouns often occurring in texts without affixation.

The verb morphology indicates person (four subject and three benefactor suffixes, and three object prefixes); aspect (five suffixes), and mode (four suffixes). Up to nine suffixes may follow a Gadsup verb, but the only affix that is obligatory to the complex is the subject marker suffix.

Agarabi verbs also permit various affixes. However, there is not enough information to work out correspondences or to identify morpheme for morpheme. Subject markers for Agarabi are similar to those of Gadsup, as are some of the mode markers. However, the aspect system of Gadsup seems to differ markedly from that of Agarabi, which has more of a tense system than aspect or kind of action.

The morphophonemics of the systems are complicated. Individual morphemes are identifiable, but often change almost beyond the point of recognition. The individual morpheme of Gadsup versus the fusions of Tairora are of interest. Perhaps the changes in the morphophonemics will someday move Gadsup toward fusions.

Sentences may contain dependent or independent clauses. As in the other languages, the difference is indicated by a final set of affixes with verbs of independent sentences or clauses, and a nonfinal set of affixes with verbs in the dependent clauses or sentences. Multiclause sentences are more frequent than single clause sentences. Usually independent clauses are preceded by the dependent, there being the possibility of a number of dependent clauses in the sentence.

Gadsup texts follow the Agarabi descriptive materials in the text analysis by Goddard. The texts cited for Gadsup have more 'native reaction' in them than the texts for other languages, since many of them are the work of a Gadsup school teacher. These Gadsup texts will afford the opportunity to compare some items with the Agarabi texts, and also to further the sentence and paragraph analysis of the Gadsup-Agarabi.

XVIII. Gadsup Phoneme and Toneme Units

CHESTER and MARJORIE FRANTZ

1. INTRODUCTION

The segmental phonemes and the phonemic tones of Gadsup will be described in this chapter.[1]

The segmental phonemes each occur with two or more allophones (except the bilabial nasal and glottal stop) which have similar phonetic characteristics and occurrences. The description of the distribution of the phonemes is based upon the four types of syllables observed. The four phonemic tones (two levels, two glides) are described in terms of their contrast and of their distinctive distributional and allophonic characteristics.

The existence of tones was at an early date highlighted to us through the fairly frequent use of 'whistle talk'. In Gadsup whistle talk, not only are the tones conveyed, but also the segmental phonemes of the utterance are articulated.

2. SEGMENTAL PHONEMES

The segmental phonemes of Gadsup consist of nine consonants: *p, t, k, q, b, d, m, n, y;* and six vowels: *i, a, u, e, aa, o.*

[1] This paper was prepared under the auspices of the Summer Institute of Linguistics. The material for it was collected over a period of two years residence at the village of Ommomunta. Much of the detailed checking of this paper was done with the help of two informants, Aupi and Yaduma, both young men of about eighteen years of age. The authors gratefully acknowledge the assistance and encouragement of Howard McKaughan and the editorial help of Alan Pence. The paper first appeared in published form as pp. 1-11 in *Papers in New Guinea Linguistics, No. 5,* Linguistic Circle of Canberra Publication (Series A: Occasional Papers, No. 7) (Australian National University, 1966), and is reissued here by permission.

2.1. Attestation of Phonemes

Consonants consist of two series of stops, a series of nasals, and a continuant. These contrast in identical and analogous environments as indicated in the following examples.

p/t/k/b/m/n/y: pŭnì name of a tree; *tŭnì* 'my face'; *kùmŭ* 'He comes down'; *bûnì* 'I went and they . . .'; *mŭmì* 'pimple'; *númì* 'lice'; *yùnî* 'ashes'.

p/t/b/d/m/n/y: pěnì 'old'; *témì* 'He talks; *bémì* 'He goes'; *děmì* 'He puts'; *ménì* 'shoulder blade'; *némì* 'He eats'; *yémì* 'He comes.'

d/k/m: dúndèqi 'I bore through and then I . . .'; *kùndémì* 'He arrived'; *mùnděmi* 'mushroom'.

k/q: màkè 'now'; *náqé* 'why'.

q/m/n: àmàqî 'meat'; *àmànî* 'barbs'; *àmàmî* 'shadow'.

Vowel phonemes contrast in identical and analogous environments:

i/a/u: àndìmì 'bark'; *àndǎnì* 'scaling skin'; *àndǔnì* 'hollow in tree'.

e/aa/o: ènî 'you' (subject); *àànî* 'road'; *ònî* 'ditch'.

i/e: ìqìdéqú 'I sing/dance'; *èqídèqú* 'I don't want it.'

a/aa: bǎ 'rat'; *bǎa* 'You stay.'

u/o: kúqì 'gourd'; *kòqî* 'bean root'.

2.2. Description

Nonvocoids contrast as to points of articulation: bilabial versus alveolar versus velar versus glottal. They contrast as to type of articulation: stop versus nasal versus continuant, and as to voicing versus nonvoicing. Vowels contrast as to high, mid, and low and as to front, mid, and back tongue positions.

2.2.1. The voiceless stops occur at the bilabial, alveolar, velar, and glottal points of articulation. These stops (except glottal) fluctuate between unaspirated and slightly aspirated. Aspiration tends to be more frequent and pronounced before high vowels. The alveolar stop, articulated with the blade of the tongue, also fluctuates initially to the alveolar affricate [ts]: *tìbáámì* [tsìbáámì] [tʰìbáámì] 'a plate'. A fricative allophone occurs intervocalic for the three stops, respectively: [ɸ] *ápùmî* [áɸùmî] 'his/your shoulder'; [s] *àtìqî* [àsìqî] 'his/your nose'; [x] *àkúmì* [àxúmì] 'his/your muscle'. The fricative allophones will fluctuate to aspirated stops with some speakers. The voiceless glottal stop occurs with one allophone.

The voiced bilabial stop /b/ has two allophones [b] and [ƀ]. The stop occurs following a bilabial nasal, *íyémbémì* [íyémbémì] 'He/it is not here.' The fricative [ƀ] occurs elsewhere: *bémì* [ƀémì] 'He goes'; *ùbìkaǎnò* [ùƀìxaǎnò] 'You fill it up!' With some speakers [ƀ] fluctuates with [b] utterance initial, *báánùdámî* [ƀáánùrámî] [báánùrámî] 'morning'. The fricative allophone [ƀ], when preceding the vowels *aa, a,* and *o,* has less friction, fluctuating to a flat [w] with some speakers: *bónò* [ƀónò] [wónò] 'You go!', *báánì* [ƀáánì] [wáánì] 'a long while'. The voiced alveolar stop /d/ has a flapped allophone [r] occurring intervocalic, *tìdĕmì* [tʰìrɛ̆mì] 'He hits me.'

The nasals occur at bilabial and alveolar points of articulation. The bilabial nasal has one allophone. The alveolar nasal has allophones: [ŋ] occurring preceding velar stop, *únkà̀amî* [úŋkà̀amî] 'snore'; [n] occurring elsewhere: *mànìqì* [mànɪ̀qì] 'legend'; *naduni* [ɑndʋni] 'hole'.

The high, close, front, unrounded frictionized nonsyllabic continuant /y/ varies to an allophone with more prominent friction when preceding high vocoids, and to an affricate [dž] following an alveolar nasal: [ɟ] *kôqyí* [kôqɟí] 'lizard'; [dž] *àqnònyóì* [ɑ̀qnòndžóì] 'his/your hair of head'; [y]*àyăami* [ɑ̀yăamì] 'his/your hand'.[2]

2.2.2. *Vowels.* /i/ the high front unrounded vowel has three allophones: [ɪ] open occurs preceding a nasal or in fluctuation with [i] when following a nasal and preceding glottal stop, *ìndèqú* [ìndèqú] 'I hear', *mànìqì* [mànɪ̀qì] / [mànɪ̀qì] 'legend'; [i] close occurs elsewhere, *dùmìtĕmì* [dʋmìsemì] 'He spits', *ìyònémì* [ìyònɛ́mì] 'It is cold'; [i̥] voiceless, close varies with [i] utterance final, *kàmaămì* [kàmaᴀ̆mi̥] / [kàmaᴀ̆mì] 'sweet potato'.

/a/ the central unrounded vowel has two allophones: [ɑ] low, open, central occurs utterance initial, *àkúmì* [ɑ̀xúmì] 'his/your muscle'; [a] mid, open occurs elsewhere, *ìyămì* [ìyᴀ̆mì] 'a dog', *pàqkă* [pàqkᴀ̆] 'He holds.'

/u/ the high, back, slightly rounded vowel has two allophones: [ʋ] open occurs preceding a nasal, *àmŭnì* [ɑ̀mʋnì] 'top of', *ùndĕmì* [ʋ̀ndɛ̆mì] 'He has arrived (come up)'; [u] close occurs elsewhere, *pùkèqú* [pùxèqú] 'I die.'

/e/ the mid, front, unrounded long vowel has two allophones: [ɛ] open occurs preceding a nasal, *ámènî* [ɑ́mènî] 'tail'; [e] close occurs elsewhere, *táápè* [táápè] 'taro', *èqî* [èqî] 'banana'.

/aa/ is the low, open, front, unrounded long vowel, *áqkaămì* 'bark', *ààpàqî* 'forest area'.

/o/ is the mid, close, back, slightly rounded long vowel, *óyàmî* 'new', *àmŏqì* 'young shoot.'

2.3. *Interphonemic Distribution*

A syllable consists of a single vowel nucleus plus an optional onset and an optional coda: V, VC, CV, CVC. No more than one toneme may occur on any single vowel.

2.3.1. All consonants except glottal stop occur syllable and utterance initial (see Sec. 2.1.). Only nasals and glottal stop occur syllable or utterance final: *mááq* 'house'; *bĕm* 'It is'; *nán* 'rope'; *máάqkìmî* [máάq.kɪ́mî] 'in

---

[2] The high front vocoid [i] / [ɪ] occurs as a syllable nucleus in numerous utterances. As a syllable onset this vocoid occurs with friction [ɟ]. For example: *dìyì* 'He opens', *ìyămì* 'a dog', *yîqî* 'sickness (their)', *ìqî* 'song or dance'.

the house'; *bàmpémì* [b̀àm.pɛ́mì] 'yellow color or plant from which this color is made'; *nándè* [nán.dè] 'how much'.[3] Consonant clusters are only possible across syllable boundaries, namely prenasalization (at same point of articulation) or preglottalization of all consonants except glottal stop: *àmpìmî* 'rotton'; *òmbâdáá* 'You sleep'; *întémì* 'He smiles'; *àndǎnì* 'scaling skin'; *ànkĕmí* [àŋkɛ́mí] 'He thrusts'; *ànnòmì* 'grass, binding at head of arrowshaft'; *ùmmemî* 'a ground beetle'; *áqnònyóì* 'hair of head'; *ààqpèmî* 'his/your underarm'; *àqbemî* 'a boil'; *àqtànî* 'a grass'; *bààqdìnî* 'fly'; *áqkaǎmi* 'bark'; *âqmĕmì* 'He is sick'; *àqnĕmɩ* 'He threw away'; *ààqyámì* 'dead (dried) tree'.

Prenasalized and preglottalized contoids are interpreted as sequences of two phonemes and not as complex units for the following reasons: (A) These contoid clusters occur only medial, never initial or final. (B) All consonants but glottal stop may be preceded by a nasal of the same point of articulation or by glottal stop. (C) The morphophonemic changes which occur when two consonants are juxtaposed by affixation support the thesis that the clusters are sequences of two phonemes (see Chap. XX, Sec. 2).

2.3.2. All vowels occur utterance initial, medial, and final contiguous to any consonant.

Two vowel sequences have been charted in initial, medial, and final positions. In initial position, only the sequences *ai, au, ao, ui, ei, ea, eu, eo, aai, aao,* and *oi* occur. In medial position the following have been observed: /i/, /a/, and /u/ preceded by any vowel; *ae, oaa, io, ao, eo.* In final position clusters are limited by obligatory affixation; thus only /i/ and /o/ preceded by any vowel occur.

The phonetically long vocoids [e], [aa], [o] (of approximately two moras of length) never occur short. It might be possible to interpret them as geminate occurrences of the vowels /i/, /a/, and /u/; however, they are here interpreted as single vowel units for the following reasons:

A. Sequences of the short vowels /i/, /a/, and /u/ contrast in analogous environments with the long vowels /e/, /aa/, and /o/.

ii/e: yáq.kí.ì.nì 'It is a small stick'; *pàq.kè.ní* 'They held and they . . .'; *à.nàà.tí.ì.nì* 'It is a married woman'; *kòq.tè.mí* 'lime gourd's thing'.
aa/a.a: bàan.tà.à.mà 'tall man'; *pên.daǎ.mì* 'strong'; *ò.bá.á.má* 'a long taro'; *à.baǎ.nì* 'flat area'.
uu/o: táá.tù.úq.ì 'axes'; *tíq.tǒq.ì* 'small thing'; *à.pù.úq.ì* 'ripe things'; *ò.pǒq.ì* 'leaf chewed with betel nut'.

B. No more than one toneme occurs on any long or short vowel.

C. Tone perturbation on short and long vowels is parallel in occurrence.

---

[3] The lowered dot (.) is used to indicate the phonemic syllable break. Note that short *a* when lengthened is found in two syllables. Our orthography at first glance gives trouble here, but the syllable structure indicated by tone gives the key. A glide on a single long vowel is marked on the second of two by convention (*aǎ* or *aâ*).

2.4. Frequency

Frequency of phonemes was determined from a study of field notes comprising approximately 5,926 segments and 1,500 grammatical words. The consonants occur with a slightly higher frequency than the vowels. For example, one of the texts contained 513 consonants and 451 vowels.

Each of the nasals occurs more frequently than any one of the stops or the continuant, respectively, the ratio being at least two to one. The velar consonant /k/ and glottal stop /q/ each occur one third more frequently than each of the bilabials / p/ or /b/ or the continuant /y/; and also occur more frequently (almost one-fourth) than either one of the alveolar phonemes /t/ or /d/. The bilabial stops and the continuant, /p/, /b/, and /y/, are the least frequent of the consonants.

The front vowel /i/ is the most frequent, occurring three times more than each of the back vowels /u/ and /o/, and twice as often as each of the two front vowels /e/ and /aa/ and the central vowel /a/.

3. SUPRASEGMENTAL PHONEMES

Four contrastive tones have been noted in Gadsup: / ´/ high, / `/ low, / ˇ/ up-glide, and / ^/ down-glide. We shall first indicate the various contrasts, and then proceed to amplify why it appears advisable to analyze the glides as units and not as sequences of two level tonemes. Finally we will state some of the distributional characteristics of the tones.

3.1. Contrast between the Four Tones

A. Contrast between high and low: *mákùnî* 'earthquake', *màkùnî* 'village'; *béqú* 'I go', *bèqú* 'I stay.'

B. Contrast between high and up-glide: *yápúmì* 'a grasshopper', *kábănì* 'a frog'; *kátŏni* Type of grasshopper, *kŏnămì* 'a fog or cloud bank'.

C. Contrast between high and down-glide: *ódémì* 'a small animal', *ôdémì* 'He is abstaining'; *índè* 'I hear', *aândà* 'trunk of a tree'.

D. Contrast between low and up-glide: *àqněmì* 'He throws away', *ŏqěmì* 'spirit'; *àpù* 'ripe', *àpŭ* 'knot hole in tree'.

E. Contrast between low and down-glide: *ànònî* 'the securing knot for bark skirts', *ànônî* 'obese'; *àànî* 'a path', *aânî* 'the point of . . .'.

F. Contrast between up-glide and down-glide: *ùnaă* 'a bag', *yùnaâ* 'food'; *àkăm* name of a tree, *ààkâm* 'his/your ear'.

3.2. Gliding Tones

As analysis of tone has proceeded, it has been noted that members of the grammatical classes of noun and verb manifest opposing tonal characteristics. Verb stem tones are perturbed only through affixation, whereas noun stem tones may also be perturbed by association with other word bases.[4]

The gliding tonemes are here set up chiefly on the basis of evidence from nouns since glides on verbs are very limited in occurrence. The factors listed below related to the functioning of glides in Gadsup make it appear preferable to interpret them as gliding tonemes.

A. The extent of the pitch difference between the start of the glide and the end point of the glide is less than that between the phonemic high and low tones in a similar environment: *káùyâmî* [káùyãmì] 'a drum', *aâqyûmî* [āāqyũmì] 'that which is set aside or designated for a particular reason'; *òpŏqì* [òpŏqì] 'leaf used with betel nut', *apùúqì* [ɑ̀pùúqì] 'ripened foods'; *indĕnò* [ìndɛ́no] 'You listen!', *indààónò* [ìndààónò] 'You ask!'; *ìtàndáùqî* [isàndáùqì] 'bows', *ànààpûqî* [ɑ̀nààpùqì] 'her/your in-laws or his/your child's wife'; *ànààtî* [ɑ̀nààsî] 'a woman (married)', *àànî* [àànì] 'a path'.

B. Glides occur on all vowels, with only one glide occurring on any single vowel. When the glide occurs on the ultima on a phonetically short vowel preceding a nasal, the particular nasal is lengthened and carries part of the glide tone.[5] However, in the same position preceding a glottal, the vowel takes the whole glide. For example: *àakâmî* 'his/your ear'; *mànĭqì* 'legend'.

C. The starting point of a glide is conditioned by the preceding tone: (a) following a low tone a rising glide begins at low, *ıyămı* [ìyãmì] 'a dog'; (b) following a high tone a rising glide begins at mid, *kábănì* [kábãnì] 'a frog'. In rapid speech, the rising glide is shortened, and may be easily mistaken for a phonetic mid tone; (c) following a low tone a falling glide begins at mid, *àkûqî* [ɑ̀xūqì] 'his/your thigh'; (d) following a high tone a falling glide begins at high, *mêmêmì* [mɛ́mɛ́mì] 'a goat'. The high and low tonemes are not conditioned in this way by preceding tones.

D. When occurring utterance final, an up-glide may fluctuate to a level allotone, the pitch of which is the same as the starting pitch of the glide. For example: a mid to high glide fluctuates to a mid tone, [káyō] / [káyo] 'an ant'. An up-glide or a down-glide preceded by silence begins at low and at mid, respectively, [konamì] 'fog or cloud bank', [òpèmì] 'his/your mouth'.

---

[4] This contrast is apparently a characteristic of the group of languages of which Gadsup is a member. Bee and Glasgow (see Chap. XII, Sec. 3.4) found morphophonemic perturbation of tone on Usarufa nouns and noun phrases to be of a type distinct from that on verbs. McKaughan has in conversation mentioned that Tairora nouns and verbs manifested an obvious contrast after only preliminary analysis. There is also indication of the same sort of dichotomy in other New Guinea Highland languages (see Chap. III on Awa). We do not attempt to predict what may be the conditioning factors of such a contrast.

[5] As implied in Sec. 2.3.1., nasal clusters do occur: *ànómì* 'important man', *ànnŏmì* 'area at small of back'; *ùmŏnì* 'theft', *úmómì* 'day after tomorrow'. Geminate clusters of nasals on nouns do not occur at stem final positions. Length of nasals at such morpheme boundaries is conditioned by the preceding vowel: long following *i, a,* or *u,* and short following *e, aa,* or *o.*

E. The up-glide toneme has a level allotone occurring medially between two high tones which contrasts with the high, down-glide, and low tonemes. *kátònì* (singular) [kásōyúqì] type of grasshopper, *báqdònî* (singular) [b̆áqdòyúqì] 'clothes', *mémêmì* (singular) [mémɛ́núqì] 'goats', *tópádóqì* 'a machete'.

F. To summarize, gliding tones are here interpreted as unit tonemes for the following reasons: glides are of shorter range than sequences from one tone level to another; the starting point of glides is conditioned by the preceding tone in a manner not paralleled by sequences of high and low tones; the up-glide has level allotone; glides occur on all single vowels, and can occur before all consonants including glottal stop.[6]

3.3. Distribution

All tonemes have been observed in utterance initial, medial, and final positions. *ónì* 'stone', *ŏnì* 'face', *ònì* 'ditch', *aânî* 'a point of', *àpù* 'ripe', *àpŭ* 'knot hole in a tree', *àyô* 'his/your hair', *bàqyí* 'tree kangaroo', *kátònî* 'a grasshopper', *báqdònî* 'wearing apparel', *yúpúmì* type of grasshopper, *mémêmì* 'goat'. Sequences of three or more high or low tones have been observed in utterances; however, sequences of no more than three glides occur.

Of the sixteen possible sequences of two contiguous tones, only two have not been observed: up-glide high, and up-glide down-glide. *yápùmì* 'a grasshopper', *báqdónî* 'wearing apparel', *yúpúmì* type of grasshopper, *mémêmì* 'a goat', *màkùnî* 'village', *iyămî* 'dog', *ààyâmî* 'wing', *ŏwĕmì,* 'a spirit', *ônémì* 'He chokes', *aâdaă* 'You call out for him.'

The following summary of the distribution of glides is based on their occurrence on noun stems. They are even more limited in occurrence on affixes and on verbs. Because of the rather severe limitations on the distribution of glides (below), it was not helpful to chart tone sequences on longer than two-syllable words.

Glides occur with one out of every three noun stems (36 percent). Table 58 indicates for each stem group (according to the number of syllables in a stem) the total number of stems analyzed, those stems with glides and their percentage in relation to the total number of stems, and finally the total number of glides observed.

Of the total number of noun stems which have glides, 91 percent of them have glides on the ultima, 9 percent have glides elsewhere (involving 17 stems and 18 glides). Nine stems have more than one glide, one of which does not have a glide on the ultima. Table 59 indicates a breakdown of

---

[6] A possible alternative to this analysis is to consider the glides to be close-knit tone sequences of the high and low tonemes, having special distributional characteristics. This interpretation would seem to present advantages in the description of the level allotones of the up-glide, and in correlating data from nouns with those from verbs. However, it is felt that total complexity is reduced by the analysis presented.

the total glides above, showing the number of glides which occur on each syllable of the stem in relation to the ultima (U); where P is penult, aP is antepenult, and X is the syllable preceding the antepenult.

TABLE 58

OCCURRENCE OF GLIDES WITH NOUN STEMS

Number of Syllables	Total Stems	Stems with Glides	Percentage of Glides	Total Glides
1	42	9	20	9
2	139	49	35	54
3	82	28	34	30
4	18	12	67	13
5	4	4	100	5
Totals	285	102	36	111

TABLE 59

LOCATION OF GLIDES WITHIN NOUN STEMS

X	aP	P	U
3	2	13	93

3.4. *Stress*

Stress is nonphonemic. In analogous environments syllables (A) with *aa, e,* or *o* have more stress than those with *a, i,* or *u;* (B) with high, rising, or falling tones have more stress than those with low; (C) with a phonetic stop onset have more stress than those with nonstop onset. Combinations of these features lead to varying degrees of noncontrastive stress.

XIX. Notes on Agarabi Phonology

DARLENE BEE, LORNA LUFF, and JEAN GODDARD

1. INTRODUCTION

Except for the feature of nasalization which will be discussed in Section 2, the phonology of .ˑgarabi is very much like that of the other languages in the Eastern Family. Allophonic variations differ somewhat from those of its related sister languages but by and large its inventory of phonemes looks very much like that of Gadsup, Usarufa, or any of the other languages in the Eastern Family. The purpose of this paper is to specify the specific nature of the Agarabi phonemes so that a more precise comparison may be made of both phonemic and subphonemic features in the context of the historical development of the languages of this linguistic subgroup.[1]

2. INTERPRETATION

The predominance of open syllables, the strict limitation of types of nonvocalic sequences which may occur, and the limitation of the position of occurrence of nonvocalic sequences combine with features of morphophonemic change to create problems in both the interpretation of nonvocalic sequences and the historical reconstruction of the proto-Eastern phonology. The Nicholsons (1962), Young (1962), Bee and Glasgow

[1] Jean Goddard and Lorna Luff conducted the primary investigation and analysis of Agarabi phonology under the auspices of the Summer Institute of Linguistics. Their report, 'Phonemes of Agarabi' (1962b), is on file in the SIL library at Ukarumpa, Territory of New Guinea. This paper is based on the Goddard-Luff report and has been written by Darlene Bee in consultation with Jean Goddard. It is hoped that this description reflects both the analysis and interpretation which Goddard and Luff have suggested; however, they need not accept responsibility for anything that goes beyond their initial report. This especially applies to the section on the interpretation of nasalization and sequence of nonvocoids.

(see Chaps. XII, XIII), and others have discussed these interpretational problems in relation to specific languages of the Eastern Highlands. These languages include both Eastern and East Central languages so that the phenomenon which underlies the synchronic manifestations is obviously a feature with a good deal of historic depth and significance. The feature of nasalization in Agarabi adds another dimension to the discussion of these nonvocalic sequences and may throw some light on the systems of morphophonemic classification in the languages of the Eastern and East Central Families.

Problems involving the interpretation of vocalic segments include the analysis of central vowels, the phonemic status of pitch, stress, and length, and the interpretation of pitch glides. Each of these will be discussed briefly so that the reader will be able to more easily distinguish the interpretational and systemic differences between Agarabi and the other languages of the Eastern Family.

2.1. *Nasalization*

Before pause Agarabi shows a contrast between oral and nasal vowels. Examples of this contrast follow.

> [ərə] 'dung, rectum', [ərə̨] 'his leg'
> [əme:] 'Give him', [əmę:] 'his throat'
> [əwi] 'poison', [əwį] 'illness'
> [əru] 'bank', [ərų] 'beetle'
> [əro] 'side', [ərǫ] 'fin, tail of bird'

This nasal-oral vocalic contrast is replaced by a sequence of oral vowel plus nasal consonant when affixation occurs and when a word with final nasal vowel occurs nonfinal in a close-knit phrase. The specific nasal consonant which may occur depends upon the shape of the affix or word immediately following the final nasal vowel. Within a word before stops a homorganic nasal consonant occurs; before high and back vowels (*i, u,* and *o*) within a word and before bilabial consonants across word boundaries a bilabial consonant occurs; before either central or low front vowels (*a* and *e*) within a word and elsewhere across word boundaries an alveolar nasal occurs. Examples follow:

[una:] 'string bag'
   plus [iq] verbalizer [una:míq] 'It is a string bag.'
   plus [e] indirect speech [una:né] 'a string bag'
   plus [pi] 'in' [una: mpí] 'in a string bag'
   plus [rą̨q] 'on' [una:ntaq] 'on a string bag'
[oe:] 'new'
   plus [una:] 'string bag' [oé:n uną:] 'new string bag'
   plus [pé:kú] 'leg band' [oé:m pé:kú] 'new leg band'
   plus [tire:] 'corn' [oé:n tire:] 'new corn'

In slow speech vowel nasalization may occasionally replace these nasal consonant at morpheme junctures.

Since there are two nasal consonants and since vowel nasalization is in complementary distribution with them, it would seem most economical to assign nasalization as an allophonic variation of one of these phonemes. However, the economy of this interpretation relates only to the phoneme inventory giving advantage neither synchronically at higher levels of phonological description nor diachronically in comparative and historical reconstruction. An alternative interpretation, considering vowel nasalization as a prosodic or supersegmental feature which may be manifested in specific environments as one or another nasal consonant, simplifies the statement of syllable structure, consonant distribution, and morphophonemic change. This second interpretation also gives a better view of the process of historical development which is involved. The implications of this interpretation with regards to these four areas will be amplified in the following discussion.[2] (Other possible interpretations have been disregarded for purposes of this paper.)

2.1.1. *Syllable structure.* If we regard nasalization as a prosodic feature and sequences of nasal plus consonant as manifestations of that feature, we can describe the syllable in Agarabi as consisting of a vowel nucleus with or without a consonant onset. (The possibility of a glottal coda will be discussed in Section 2.2.) The vowel nucleus may occur with or without the feature of nasalization manifested either as a nasal consonant or as a nasalized vowel.

2.1.2. *Consonant distribution.* The extreme limitation of types, position, and order of nonvocalic sequences suggests that these nonvocalic clusters are not a viable feature of Agarabi phonology. Only nasal consonants and glottal stop precede another consonant; only voiceless stops follow a nasal consonant within the word; and nonvocalic sequences occur only word or phrase medially. Treating nasalization as a prosodic feature not only reduces the number of nonvocalic sequences for which we have to account but it reduces the number of distributional classes with which we have to deal. That is, if we identify vowel nasalization with a nasal consonant we would in addition to the sequences of nasal plus consonant have to set up a distributional class of nasal consonant as distinct from nonnasal consonant.

2.1.3. *Morphophonemic change.* Agarabi morphemes end in either a nasal vowel, an oral vowel, or a glottal stop. These condition the shape of following morphemes. An example of the three classes is given in the following inflectional paradigm.

---

[2] It should be noted that orthographic symbolization does not enter into our discussion. Practical considerations will condition our choice of orthographic representation but need not influence our interpretation of the phonemic status and significance of the phenomenon under consideration.

	'bank'	'beetle'	'root'
stem	[əru]	[ərʉ]	[ərúq]
verbalizer [iq]	[əruíq]	[ərumíq]	[ərúqiq]
'in' [pj́]	[ərupj́]	[ərumpj́]	[ərúqpj́]
'on' [rəq]	[əruráq]	[əruntáq]	[ərúqkáq]
indirect speech [e]	[ərué]	[əruné]	[ərúqe]

The morpheme shape which follows the oral vowel may be regarded as the basic form; the shapes which occur following the nasal vowel and glottal may be described as combinatory features of nasalization and glottal, respectively, without having to postulate allomorphic forms. For example: $V + r \rightarrow Vnt$; $V? + r \rightarrow Vqk$.

2.1.4. *Historical development.* Comparison of cognates of the morphemes with nasal vowels and/or nasal consonant sequences shows that the correspondence is not to nasal consonant phonemes but to the morphophonemic nasal class as described by Bee in Chap. XXXVI.[3] The following cognate set shows the reflexes of the nasal (N) class in parentheses.

* +*yu*N 'seed, seedling'[4]

ʻ*ku(bu)*	Tairora
asu(mú)	Binumarien
ayu(mí)	Gadsup
áy(ú̧)	Agarabi
ayu(mmá)	Usarufa

The analysis of a feature of nasalization for Agarabi as a reflex of a proto-Eastern morphophonemic classification is most attractive. It may, of course, be possible to postulate a feature of nasalization for proto-Eastern with diverse reflexes in the various daughter languages and with Agarabi representing a retention of that feature. In either case it seems wise to distinguish the nasal consonants from the nasal process represented as morphophonemic classification in some of the daughter languages and as nasalization for Agarabi.

Taken by itself no one of the four points discussed is conclusively favorable to one or the other of the suggested interpretations, although each slightly favors the nasalization interpretation. Taken together, however, the over-all economy gained by the nasalization interpretation seems worth the small price of a single additional phonemic feature. This is therefore the interpretation chosen.

[3] Chap. XXXVI (see pp. 741–43, 759–63) gives details of contrast in reflexes of nasal consonants and the (N) class.

[4] The plus sign (+) preceding the reconstruction indicates a postulated inflectional prefix which is lost in some of the daughter languages and retained in others as a fossilized morpheme.

2.2. *Sequences of Glottal plus Consonant*

Having interpreted sequences of nasal plus consonant as manifestations of the nasalization of the vowel nucleus of the preceding syllable, the only nonvocalic clusters which occur are those whose first member is a glottal stop. While there are many distributional and morphophonemic similarities between the nasal plus consonant sequences and the glottal plus consonant sequences there are some significant differences. The combinatory potential of glottal plus consonant is much greater that the combinatory potential of nasal plus consonant, being limited only in that the sequences glottal plus glottal and glottal plus *r* do not occur. The distribution of glottal elsewhere is more restricted than the distribution of nasal consonants in that glottal does not occur contrastively word initially. (It may be of interest to note that the only other phoneme which does not occur word initially is *r*.) On acoustic and articulatory grounds the glottal may be regarded as both non-consonantal and nonvocalic so that our interpretation of the glottal plus consonant sequences need not seriously affect our statement of consonant distribution or syllable structure. Either of two interpretations seems equally valid. The first is to interpret syllable-final glottal as a single instance of a syllable closing nonvocoid, and the other is to interpret the glottal as parallel to the feature of nasalization identifying it with the preceding syllable nucleus. The latter has the advantage of over-all simplicity while the former may strike some as more phonetically plausible. A third interpretation, which would regard sequences of glottal plus consonant as single unit phonemes, is rejected because of the decisive occurrence of glottal word finally *and* because the massive increase in the number of phonemes which would result is without compensating simplicity elsewhere in the system.

2.3. *Vocalic Segments*

Goddard and Luff (1966) suggested a five vowel system consisting of two front, two back, and one central vowel. The central vowel is described as having two variants, one short and high and the other low and long, [ə] and [a:], respectively. [a:] is interpreted as a sequence of [ə] + [ə] which differs qualitatively and quantitatively from the single [ə].[5] A close examination of their evidence shows that an identical situation of contrast seems to exist in the front and back positions. That is, [i] and [u] are high and short while [e:] and [o:] are low and long. Wherever contrast occurs it is both qualitative and quantitative so that the long may be interpreted as a sequence of two short. As long as there is no contrast between a sequence of two like short vowels and a single long vowel this interpretation has everything to recommend it. Such a contrast, though infrequent, can be found for front

---

[5] It should be understood that this interpretation does not disregard the contrast of [ə] and [a:] as in: [kərúq] 'flea', and [ka:rúq] 'nettle'. Recognizing the contrast we interpret it as being the difference between a single phoneme and a sequence of the same phoneme rather than being the difference between two different phonemes.

vowels: [awé:q] 'louse', [awíq] 'his name', [awiíq] 'It is poison' (*awi* poison + -*iq* verbalizer).

It seems reasonable to interpret the back vowels in light of the front vowel contrast and leave the interpretation of central vowels as suggested by Goddard and Luff. The fact that the morphophonemic selection of nasal consonant manifestation of the nasalization feature is different preceding [i] than it is preceding [e:] (*m* and *n,* respectively) and that it is the same preceding both [ə] and [a:] (*n*) suggests that the different treatment of the two pairs of phones is not entirely arbitrary.[6] Vowel length is regarded as an innate characteristic of vowels /e/ and /o/.

Stress is interpreted as a noncontrastive feature of pitch-accent, but more investigation needs to be done to determine the exact relationship of the two with regard to both the rhythm group and the intonational contour.

3. INVENTORY OF PHONEMES

Three classes of phonemes may be defined as consonants, vowels, and neutral. Consonants have three linear and three horizontal distinctions, vowels three linear and two horizontal, and the two neutral phonemes contrast both linearly and horizontally. Table 60 specifies the nature of these distinctions.

TABLE 60

AGARABI PHONEMES

Consonants

	Bilabial	Alveolar	Velar
Oral			
Voiceless	*p*	*t*	*k*
Voiced	*w*	*y*	
Nasals	*m*	*n*	

Vowels

	Front	Central	Back
High	*i*		*u*
Low	*e*	*a*	*o*

Neutral
Glottal
q
Liquid
r

---

[6] The morphophonemic evidence is not in itself conclusive, for [u] and [o] also fall together morphophonemically.

3.1. *Description of Phonemes*

Consonant phonemes divide into two contrastive classes, nasal and oral. Oral consonants further divide into voiceless and voiced. Voiceless oral consonants contrast at bilabial, alveolar, and velar points of articulation. Allophones of voiceless oral consonants occur as follows: aspirated stops, [pʰ], [tʰ], and [kʰ], occur initially and following complex vowel-nasal or vowel-glottal nuclei; fricatives, [ɸ], [s], and [x], occur between oral vowels and may fluctuate with stop allophones. (The alveolar stop and fricative allophones freely fluctuate initially, the bilabial allophones occasionally fluctuate initially, and the velar allophones rarely fluctuate initially, but an unaspirated allophone [k] may occasionally fluctuate with the fricative between oral vowels.) An alveolar affricate allophone [ts] fluctuates occasionally with the aspirated stop initially.

Voiced oral consonants and nasal consonants contrast only at bilabial and alveolar points of articulation. Allophones of voiced oral consonants (*w* and *y*) occur as follows. Voiced stop allophones [b] and [d] occur initially and following complex syllable nuclei. These fluctuate with labialized stop [bʷ], palatalized stop [dʸ] and semivowels [w] and [y]. Between oral vowels, semivowels [w] and [y] occur, which may be accompanied by greater or lesser degrees of friction. A voiced bilabial fracative [ƀ] with or without labialization may fluctuate with [w] between oral vowels. Nasal phonemes /m/ and /n/ occur without allophonic variations. It should be noted, however, that a velar nasal phone [ŋ] occurs before [k] as the homorganic manifestation of the feature of nasalization.

Vowels /i/, /e/, /u/, and /o/ tend to be open rather than close. The central vowel as described in Section 2.3 is the close [ə] when it occurs singlely and the open and long [a:] when it occurs in sequence with itself. Front and back vowels also contrast as to tongue height.

Two neutral phonemes, the liquid, /r/, and glottal, /q/, vary allophonically as follows: The liquid phoneme may be either an alveolar flap [r] or an alveolar trill [ɾ̄]. These seem to fluctuate freely with some speakers using the flap almost exclusively and others using the trill more frequently; still others fluctuate between the two. The glottal stop phoneme may in limited environments occasionally vary to a glottal fricative.

3.2. *Distribution of Phonemes*

Each class of phonemes has a distribution unique to that particular class. Consonant phonemes occur only word or phrase initially and medially as syllable onsets; vowels may occur in all word and phrase positions as the nucleus of the syllable; neutral phonemes occur only word and phrase medially as syllable onsets. The glottal phoneme may occur as part of a complex syllable nucleus word or phrase medially and finally. Nasal consonants may occur medially and finally as manifestations of nasalization and part of a complex syllable nucleus.

Only vowels and voiceless consonants follow a complex nasal-vowel syllable nucleus within the word but all consonants may occur following the nasal-vowel complex across word boundaries. Neutral phonemes do not occur following complex nasal or glottal syllable nuclei.

Up to two vowels may occur as the necleus of a single syllable and two-syllable nuclei may occur in sequence with an intervening nonvocoid. While all vowels may occur word finally, only the long back vowels and the sequence of two central vowels occur finally in verb stems (i.e., /e/, /o/, and /aa/). All onset vowel combinations have been observed in stem morphemes although some combinations are considerably less frequent than others.

4. PROSODIC FEATURES

Nasalization has been discussed at length in Section 2 and will not be further discussed here. However, a second type of prosodic feature occurs contrastively on syllable nuclei. This feature includes two degrees of tone, high and low. These are primarily level tones although a slight pitch glide may be perceived on a single phonetically short vowel when there is a transition from one level of tone to another in succeeding syllables. Otherwise rising and falling glides occur only on phonetically long vowels and are here interpreted as a sequence of low-high or high-low, respectively.[7]

5. CONTRASTIVE SETS

In Table 61 examples are written phonemically. High tone is represented by an acute accent and low tone is unmarked. Nasalization is represented by one or the other of the nasal consonant phonemes depending upon its environment.

---

[7] The interpretation of low-high or high-low tones has been indicated by doubling vowels in such cases and writing a tone (marked or unmarked) over each vowel of the sequence.

TABLE 61
CONTRASTIVE SETS

Vowel Contrasts					
ére 'come'	*érán* 'moss'	*émó* 'wildfowl'	*eyu* 'sand'	*éni* 'your'	
iyeq 'who'	*írá* 'fire'	*írón* 'whitish'	*ínún* 'yesterday'	*ípíq* 'cry'	*ín* 'pandanus'
ote 'divide'	*óná* 'door'	*óro* 'go'	*ópu* 'star'	*oyi* 'rat'	*ón* 'drain'
úte 'cut'	*uraa* 'cane'	*úno* 'weave'		*upi* 'needle'	*ún* 'file'
até 'sweet'	*ara* 'dung'	*aro* 'side'	*ápú* 'knot	*ati* 'knife'	*áán* 'banana'
are 'his rear'	*áná* 'bamboo'	*anon* 'his elder	*ánú* 'mountain'	*awi* 'his urine'	
		áyún 'seed'			

Tone Contrasts			
ánaa 'sharpen'	*anáá* 'leaf'	*áná* 'bamboo'	*anan* 'rope'
	anú 'his tear'	*ánú* 'mountain'	*anu* 'his fat'
	aú 'his skin'	*áú* 'naughtiness'	*au* 'his eye'
óon 'stone'	*oó* 'his mouth'	*ón* 'drain'	*on* 'wild cane'
	oóná 'goods'	*óná* 'door'	*onaa* 'see'

TABLE 61 (Cont.)

Initial Consonant Contrasts

tiwo 'peel'	*yiwo* 'open'				
	yaa 'do'	*paa* 'later'	*waa* 'stay'	*naa* 'eat'	*kaa* 'heat'
			naan 'breast'	*káán* 'two'	*máán* 'law'

Medial Nonvowel Contrasts

ápon 'male'	*aqpoq* 'mud'	*ámpóte* 'break up'
atóo 'soothe'	*aqton* 'tip'	*ántóq* 'nail'
ako 'his chest'		
akun 'cowardly'	*iqkún* 'smoke'	*anku* 'hole'
akááq 'his child'	*aqkaa* 'empty box'	*ánkááróró* 'necklace, beads'
ayó 'his hair'	*aqyo* 'don't'	
awoqo 'find'	*aqwon* 'his navel'	
ámón 'ridge'		
anón 'his elder'	*aqnon* 'his head'	
aro 'side'		
maaqo 'mother, mom'		

XX. Grammatical Categories as Indicated by Gadsup Noun Affixes

CHESTER FRANTZ

1. Introduction

This paper is a preliminary study of Gadsup grammar, treating only those categories indicated by affixes which may occur with nouns.[1] Some of the affixes which may occur with noun bases occasionally occur with other parts of speech.[2] However, we shall investigate the function and the distribution of such affixes when affixed to a noun base, rather than undertake a study of the affixes wherever they occur. We define a noun base as any Gadsup stem which may occur with the nominative suffix (-mi).[3]

In our analysis thus far, we have been able to identify over forty affixes which may occur with noun bases. These affixes do not, however, indicate all grammatical relations between nouns and other parts of the sentence. A Gadsup sentence may contain a number of unaffixed nouns, each with a different grammatical function. Word order in such cases signals the grammatical function involved. The usual word order in Gadsup is subject, object, indirect object, verb: for example, *pumaadaa aakintaa benaano*

[1] The material in this paper was gathered over a period of two years, 1959-61, under the auspices of the Summer Institute of Linguistics. It was prepared under the guidance of Howard McKaughan whose help and encouragement the writer gratefully acknowledges. The article first appeared as pp. 44-63 in *Studies in New Guinea Linguistics*, Oceania Linguistic Monographs No. 6. (Sydney: University of Sydney, 1962). It is reissued here by permission.

[2] For example, the verb 'to go', *bid,* has been observed with the possessive suffix *-iq; benaanoke bid-iq-memi* (like-her-mother go + possessive + verb-ending) 'She walks like her mother.'

[3] Forms enclosed in parentheses indicate the existence of allomorphs. Person names are distinguished from noun bases in that they do not take the nominative suffix (-mi). This paper does not handle person names or pronouns since the distribution of suffixes with them is not completely parallel with that of the nouns.

aamemi (young-man + girl + his-mother + he-give-her) 'The young man gives the girls to his mother.'[4] Within one of the above mentioned slots, there may be a descriptive relationship between two or more juxtaposed noun bases. In such cases, the descriptive relationship is signaled by tone perturbation of the second or "head" word. We shall not, however, attempt here an analysis of noun syntax unless affixes indicate such.

In general, affixes which may occur with noun bases fall into three divisions: (A) internal modifiers, (B) external relators, and (C) utterance indicators. Internal modifiers include those suffixes which modify in some way the base to which they are attached (e.g., plural), and/or which indicate a list relation (see Hjemslev, 1953). These affixes mark no grammatical relationship between the base and other parts of the sentence. External relators include those affixes which mark some relationship between the affixed word base and another word base in the sentence. Utterance indicators include affixes which relate the affixed base to the entire sentence, those which mark the affixed base as an utterance, or those which indicate the type of utterance involved.

2. MORPHOPHONEMICS

Certain basic features of the morphophonemes will be helpful for the reader before turning to the structural categories marked and the distribution of the particular affixes.

Gadsup nouns and affixes fall into five classes. These five classes may be indicated by the final morphophonemes *N, Y, D,* and *K,* with the fifth class characterized by a final vowel. Examples follow:

Class I		Class II		Class III	
iyaN	'dog'	*makuY*	'village'	*poD*	'pig'
noN	'water'	*oY*	'stone'	*naD*	'rope'
kamaaN	'sweet potato'	*bibiY*	'parrot'	*aakaD*	'leg'
-koN	purposive	*-poY*	instrument	*-adaD*	causative
-kiN	'in'			*-aD*	reference

Class IV		Class V	
yaaK	'sugar cane'	*ika*	'fire'
maaK	'house'	*pumaadaa*	'young man'
aanaaK	'wife'	*yaqki*	'stock'
-aakaaK	'small'	*-andaa*	'secured'
-naadoK	'on top'		

---

[4] Except for /q/, the stops have continuant allophones which in general occur between vowels: [ᵽ, s/ts, x/kʰ, ᵬ, r]. Following /n/, an affricate [dž] occurs as an alternant of /y/. Vowels include /i, a, u/ and /e, aa, o/. The latter three are long, and were written /ee/, /aa/, and /oo/, in the earlier publication in some cases. Since that time, the tone analysis has been completed, indicating glides which make long vowels sound longer. In this writing, the /ee/ and /oo/ of the earlier publication has been reduced to /e/ and /o/.

Before vowels, the above morphophonemes are actualized as /n/, /y/, /d/, and either /q/ or /k/. In the case of K, there is partial fluctuation in that some suffixes are preceded by /q/, others by /k/, and others by either.[5] The following illustrate:

Class I: *iyan* + *mindai* > *iyanindai* 'dog's thing'
Class II: *kukuY* + *indai* > *kukuyindai* 'fence's thing'
Class III: *poD* + *indai* > *podindai* 'pig's thing'
Class IV: *maaK* + *indai* > *maakindai* 'house's thing', > *maaqindai* 'house's thing'; *maaK* + *-e* > *maake* 'the house'; *maaK* + *-aaqnaapaqi* > *maaqaaq-naapaqi* 'the base part of the house'
Class V: *baanta* + *-indai* > *baantataindai* 'man's thing'

Gadsup syllables may only be closed by a nasal or /q/. Since there are no consonant clusters within the syllable, the only clusters permitted are those formed at syllable boundaries which must have a nasal or glottal as the first of two. In such instances, the nasal always takes the point of articulation of the following consonant. Geminate clusters of nasals and glottals do not occur when morphemes are juxtaposed. When two consonants are juxtaposed which are not permitted to cluster, the resultant change reflects the position of the first, and the voicing of the second. These changes may be represented as follows where X symbolizes a stop or continuant, a small letter the particular phoneme, and subscript p the point of articulation of the initial consonant of the suffix. No changes occur with Class V words.

A. *Before stops and continuants*

Class I $N + X > n_p X$
Class II $Y + X > y$ (when X is voiced); $> t$ (when X is voiceless)
Class III $D + X > nd$ (when X is voiced); $> nt$ (when X is voiceless)
Class IV $K + X > qX$

Examples follow.

Class I: *iyaN* + *-baankaa* > *iyambankaa* 'dog' (held); *iyaN* + *-kandaa* > *iyankandaa* 'two dogs'; *matiqdeN* + *-yiq* > *matiqdenyiq poni* 'everyone's pig'
Class II: *kukuY* + *bankaa* > *kukuyankaa* 'fence-wood' (held), *kukuY* + *kandaa* > *kukutandaa* 'two fence-woods'
Class III: *poD* + *bankaa* > *pondankaa* 'pig' (held), *poD* + *kandaa* > *pontandaa* 'two pigs'

---

[5] The following suffixes may be preceded by either /k/ or /q/: *-akaD* causative, *-inda* 'thing', *-amaa* 'long', and *-ukaN* reality. Suffixes which are always preceded by /q/ are *-andaa* retention, *-aakaaK* 'small', *-anaa* 'along on', *-anaaK* 'along on top of', *-aamaN* location near, (*-mi*) nominative. The remaining suffixes beginning with a vowel are always preceded by /k/ when affixed to Class IV nouns.

Class IV: *yaaK* + *bankaa* > *yaaqbankaa* 'sugar cane' (held), *yaak* + *kandaa* > *yaakandaa* 'two sugar canes'

B. *Before nasals*

Class I $N + n_p > n_p$
Class II $Y + n_p > n$
Class III $D + n_p > n$
Class IV $K + n_p > qn_p$

Examples follow.

Class I: *iyaN* + *-mu* > *iyamu* 'dog-I', *iyaN* + *-naamaq* > *iyanaamaq* 'with the dog'

Class II: *kukuY* + *-mu* > *kukunu* 'fence-wood-I', *kukuY* + *-naamaq* > *kukunaamaq* 'with the fence-wood'

Class III: *poD* + *-mu* > *ponu* 'pig-I', *poD* + *-naamaq* > *ponaamaq* 'with the pig'

Class IV: *benaanaaK* + *-mu* > *benaanaaqmu* 'his wife-I', benaanaaK + *-naamaq* > *benaanaaqnaamaq* 'with his wife'

The place marker *-paK* does not react to morphophonemic changes, but remains *-paK* after all five classes. Following *-paK,* the following alternants occur: *-ke* > *-te* 'from'; *-kaK* > *-taK* 'on, at'; *-keke* > *-teke* 'like'; and *-kenaa* > *-tenaa* 'belonging or pertaining to'. Other morphophonemic changes will be indicated as the individual morphemes involved are discussed.

3. STRUCTURAL CATEGORIES

3.1. *Internal Modifiers*

Morphemes which modify the word base, but do not show grammatical relations to other word bases, include those marking size, number, quality, retention, place, nominative, and reality.

3.1.1. *Size.* There are four suffixes in Gadsup indicating the size of the word base. These are (*-yakaN*) 'big', *-amaa* 'long', *-aakaaK* 'small', and *-aamuK* 'short' or 'round'. The first of these takes the form *-akaN* following Class I nouns. Suffixes *-aakaaK* 'small' and *-aamuK* 'short' or 'round' occur only with inanimate objects.[6]

kamaan-amaa-yaka-mi (sweet-potato + long + big + nominative) 'the long big sweet potato'

kamaan-akan-amaa-i (sweet-potato + big + long + nominative) 'the big long sweet potato'

kamaan-aakaaq-i (sweet-potato + small + nominative) 'the small sweet potato'

---

[6] Note the following whose morphemic analysis is different, but which seem homophonous with *-aakaaK* and *-aamuK: pod aa-kaaq-i* (pig his + child + nominative) 'the pig's child', *nun aa-muq-i* (bird his + egg + nominative) 'the bird's egg'.

kamaan-aamuq-i (sweet-potato + round-or-short + nominative) 'the short fat sweet potato'

3.1.2. *Number.* Three suffixes denote number in Gadsup: *-uK* plural, *-kandaa* dual, and *-kaamode* trial or 'more than two'. (A) The plural suffix is general, indicating two or more: *aan-uq-i* 'children', *aaqtay-uq-i* 'grasses'. (B) The dual suffix indicates 'two': *baanta-kandaa* 'two men', *pon-tandaa* 'two pigs'. (C) The trial suffix indicates 'three' or 'several': *kukusaamode* 'a few or several fence-woods', *ponkaamode* 'three pigs'.

3.1.3. *Quality or color.* The suffix *-manaa* occurs with a few noun bases to indicate either the quality or the color of the base. Thus *kasiK* 'coals' + *-manaa* > *kasiqmanaa* 'black', *ubo* 'blood' + *-manaa* > *ubomanaa* 'red', *maka* 'ground' + *-manaa* > *makamanaa* 'brown', *paD* 'dirty' + *-manaa* > *pananaa* 'that which is dirty'.

3.1.4. *Retention.* The suffix *-andaa* indicates that the word base so affixed has been secured or retained by a rope or vine: *yunaan-anda duqkemi* 'She has tied up food', *kamaan-andaa-naadoq-paq-i bemi* (sweet-potato + tied-up + on-top + place + nominative it-is) 'The tied-up sweet potato is on top.'

3.1.5. *Place.* The place of the word base is indicated by the suffix *-paK*. This suffix occurs immediately following a few noun bases to indicate the place of the base word:[7] *yunaaN* 'food' + *paqi* 'place' > *yunaampaqi* 'garden', *makuY* 'village' + *paqi* 'place' > *makupaqi* 'village-place', *akunaa* a village name + *paqi* 'place' > *akunaapaqi* 'village of Akuna'. When *-paK* follows locative suffixes, it refers to the place identified by the preceding locative suffix. Since this morpheme is closely related to the locatives in meaning and distribution, further examples are given in Section 3.2.2.6.

3.1.6. *Nominative.* The nominative suffix has two allomorphs: *-mi* with Classes I, II, and III, and *-i* with Classes IV and V: *yunaaN* + *-mi* > *yunaami* 'food', *maaK* + *-i* > *maaqi* 'house', *baanta* + *-i* > *baantai* 'man'.

3.1.7. *Reality.* The genuineness or the superiority of the noun base is shown by the suffix *-ukaN: baqdoy-uk-ukan daano* (clothes +plural +real + you-put-on) 'Put on some real clothes (not flimsy grass ones, but strong bark ones)', *benaano-uka-mi bemi* (his-mother + real +nominative she-is) 'She is his real mother.'

When *-ukaN* occurs following a size morpheme it accentuates that suffix: *yaan-amaa-ukam-po* (stick + long + real + with) 'with the real long stick'. Following the instrument suffix, *-ukaN* denotes veracity: *aayaam-poy-ukam-i* (his-hand + with + real + nominative) 'really or truly with his hand'. *-ukaN* is preceded by the possessive marker *-iK* to indicate that another word base posesses the likeness or reality specified by the base in question: *baanta-iq-uka-mi* 'man + possessive + reality + nominative) 'just like a real man'.

---

[7] *-paK* always follows place names: *ukadampaqi* 'Ukarumpa'.

Another suffix, *-uka*, though similar, has a slightly different meaning. For example: *iyan-uka-i* (dog + real-like + nominative) 'reallike dog' (as in a picture), *benaano-uka-i* (his mother + reallike + nominative) 'his mother (not his real mother, but his father's other wife)'.

3.2. *External Relators*

Certain affixes which may occur with nouns mark grammatical relations between nouns, while others indicate grammatical relations between a noun and a verb.

3.2.1. *Relations between nouns*

3.2.1.1. *Unit relations.* The only *prefixes* which occur with Gadsup nouns indicate what we have called a unit relation. A unit relation is defined as that relationship existing between a part of a whole and the whole itself; that relationship signaling a union of, or unity between, two entities; or that relation indicating some personal affinity. Thus in *ti-yaami* 'my arm', *ti-* makes reference to the whole of which 'arm' is a part. In *aa-biqi* 'his (or your) name', *aa-* indicates the vital union or personal affinity which 'name' bears to the individual referred to by *aa-*.

That which is the whole may be specifically indicated by a noun stem preceding the prefixed noun. In such cases, the noun phrase is closely knit together by the same morphophonemic changes described above between suffixes or stem and suffix. For example: *pod aa-bakuni* (pig his +teeth) 'the tooth of the pig', *ten ti-yaami* (1st-person-pronoun my + arm) 'my arm'. The unit prefix agrees in number and person with the preceding stem (understood or actualized) which indicates the whole. The unit prefixes are as follows: *ti-* first person singular or plural, *aa-* second and third person singular, and *yi-* second and third persons plural.

Certain stems require unit indicator prefixes. These include in general the body parts and kinship terms: *aa-yaami* 'his hand', *aa-naami* 'its handle (the handle of a bag)', *aa-naaqi* 'his wife', *aa-kono* 'his friend'. A few other noun stems optionally take the unit prefix when the unit relationship is required: *iyan aa-nomi* (dog his + water) 'dog-water' (i.e., the liquid formed in a decaying dog), *en aa-bayaani* 'your talk'. Some stems such as *dankumaa* 'corn', and *koi* 'bridge' never take unit prefixes.

The vowel of the unit prefix is subject to certain morphophonemic changes when affixed to a stem which begins with a vowel. These are as follows: /i/ + /o/ > /u/, /i/ + /aa/ > /aa/, /i/ + /o/ > /o/, /i/ + /aa/ or /a/ > /i/, /aa/ + /o/ > /o/, /aa/ + /aa/ or /a/ > /aa/. Examples: *ti-* + *opaqi* > *tupaqi* 'my fingernail', *ti-* + *aaqpemi* > *taaqpemi* 'my armpit', *ti-* + *opemi* > *topemi* 'my mouth', *aa-* + *opaqi* > *opaqi* 'your fingernail'. No morphophonemic changes occur between the vowel of a prefix and the vowel of a preceding Class V noun: *baanta aa-* + *poaqi* > *baanta opaqi* 'the man's fingernail'.

Body parts or kinship terms may occur with the unit prefixes independent of the stem signifying the whole. However, all other nouns occurring with the unit prefixes must be preceded by a noun stem to indicate the whole.

3.2.1.2. *Possession.* We use a cover term 'possessives' for the suffixes (*-iK*), (*-inda*), *-kenaa, -keno* since they all indicate a relationship between the affixed base and some other entity which may vary from a property ownership to simply some vague connection between bases. The suffix *-iK* indicates ownership, *-inda* indicates the ownership of something indefinite, *-kenaa* refers to something which belongs to time or a certain place, and *-keno* refers to a person which belongs to time or a certain place. The suffixes *-iK* and *-inda* have allomorphs *-yiK* and *-yinda,* respectively, which occur with plural bases; *-tiK,* another allomorph of *iK,* occurs with first person pronouns. Examples: (A) *baanta-iq poni* 'the man's pig', *baanta-uq-yiq poni* (man +plural +possessive pig) 'the men's pig', *ten-tiq poni* (1st-person-pronoun +possessive pig) 'my pig', (B) *iyan-inda-i* (dog + -*inda* + nominative) 'the dog's thing' (whether food, foot, etc.), *pod-uq-yinda-i* (pig + plural + -*yinda* + nominative) 'the pigs' ' (foot, thing, etc.), (C) *peyan-enaa-i* 'the old thing', *makutaq-kenaa-i* 'the thing of the village', (D) *maku taqpaq-teno* 'the people of the village'.

3.2.1.3. *Conjunction.* Nouns are joined in a series or list by the suffix *-aa ～ -baa ～ -aate.* Alternate *-baa* occurs with Class V nouns, *-aate* with the last noun of the series, and *-aa* elsewhere. All nouns in the series occur with this suffix: *aaponintaa-baa pod-aa iyan-aate udeno* 'The boy and the pig and the dog went up.'

3.2.1.4. *Accompaniment.* Accompaniment is indicated by the suffix *-naamaK.* The one with whom the affixed noun acts may be indicated by another noun, by the subject pronoun of the verb, by the bound subject in the verb, or understood by context: *yaa-naamaq aaba mademi* (tree + with slide it-took) 'The landslide also took the tree with it'; *aa-naamaq bidade* (child + with I-would-like-to-go) 'I would like to go with the child; *makusaqpaqtenaa-naamaq mademi* (place-thing + with he-took) 'He took (it) with the thing which was at the village.'

Another suffix (*-baK*) indicates that the party referred to by the affixed base also participates in the action expressed by the verb, but does not necessarily carry with it the implication of accompaniment. This suffix has the alternant *-maK* occurring with Class I nouns. Examples follow: *ben aamaaq-baq-i ikankemi* (he his-house +also +nominative it-burned) 'His house also burned down'; *bey-aq-i bidadaa* (he +also +nominative he-would-like-to-go) 'He also would like to go'; *pumaadaa-baq aano-naamaq bidadaa* (young-man + also important-man + with he-would-like-to-go) 'The young man also would like to go with the important man'; *aanoN* + (*-baK*) > *aanamaq* 'the important man also'.

3.2.1.5. *Similarity.* The similarity of one to another is indicated by the suffix *-keke.* This suffix is shortened to *-ke* when confusion does not result from the homonymity with the locative suffix *-ke.* The similarity expressed may be with a preceding noun base, with the subject of the verb, or with as item understood in context. Examples: *aakintaa ben aano-ke bemi* (girl she her-mother + like she-is) 'The girl is like her mother'; *yaampo-teke aademi* (with-stick + like she-hit) 'She was hit (as if) with a stick.'

3.2.2. *Relations between noun and verb.* The following structural relations between noun and verb are marked by suffixes occurring with the noun: purposive, causative, instrument, reference, object of verb 'to hold', and the locative.

3.2.2.1. *Purposive.* The purpose for which the action of the verb is directed is shown by the suffix *-koN: kamaan-kon-ke yemi* (sweet-potato +purposive +like he-comes) 'He comes for sweet potato–like things', *yunaan-kon-aq udenaapi* (food +purposive +question did-he-go-up) 'Did he go up for food?'

3.2.2.2. *Causative.* The suffix *-akaD* indicates that the suffixed noun base is the cause of the action of the verb: *pod aabakud-akan-teke ipiqdemi* (pig his-teeth +because-of +like she-cries) 'She is crying because of something like pig's teeth (as if seeing pig's teeth)', *memay-akan-ipekemi* 'She is afraid because of the snake.'

The suffix *-yikaD* indicates that the cause of the action stems from more than one source: *memay-uq-yikan-iipiqdemi* (snake + plural + because-of + nominative she-is-crying) 'She is crying because of the snakes', *maasiq-den-yikan-i pekemi* (all +because-of +nominative she-is-afraid) 'She is afraid because of all the things.' The affixed noun must agree in number with the plural causative suffix either by being implicit in the stem itself or by affixing a number suffix.

3.2.2.3. *Instrument.* The suffix *-poY* indicates that the action of the verb is accomplished through the instrumentality of the affixed stem: *ika-po yunkaa* (fire +with cook) 'Cook it by fire', *aakintaa yaam-pon-i aadequ* (girls stick +with +nominative hit-I 'I hit the girl with a stick.'

3.2.2.4. *Reference.* The suffix *(-aD)* indicates that the affixed noun is that to which the action of the verb refers. Note the following where this suffix may be translated as 'to' or 'about': *en aapo beniq pod-ani taamidade* (your father his pig +about I-want-to-talk) 'I want to talk to your father about his pig', *beniq pod-ani aatemi* 'He is cross about his pig', *ben aanaak-ani teno* 'You talk to his wife' or 'You talk about his wife.[8] The reference suffix takes the form *-baD* following Class V items: *pumaadaa-bani pekembemi* (young-man +reference she-is-afraid) 'She is afraid of the young man.'

3.2.2.5. *Object of verb 'to hold'.* The suffix *-bankaa* indicates that a particular base is the object of the verb 'to hold'. This suffix is not obligatory

---

[8] The reference suffix *-aD* also has an allomorph *-naD* following all person names.

with this verb, but has not been found with other verbs: *baanta aakintaa-bankaa paqkaante yaandemi* 'The man tried to hold the girl but he fell', *num-bankaa paqkemi* 'He is holding the bird.'

3.2.2.6. *Locative.* A number of suffixes and/or combinations of them indicate various locational relationships between a noun and the verb. The various suffixes observed are as follows: (A) *-kiN* location within; (B) *-kaK* location on, upon, or at; (C) *-aamaN* location near; (D) *-naadoK* location on top of; (E) *-aaqnaa* location next to or at the base of; (F) *-anaa* along on; (G) *-anaaK* along on top of; (H) *-ke* direction from or separation from; (I) *-kaa* direction to. The suffixes *-kiN* 'in' and *-kaK* 'on', 'at' may either indicate the respective locations, or they may designate that the noun base is a place. The internal modifier *-paK* always marks a place. When bases semantically indicate a place, a place marker (one of the three above) is optional, but if not, then a place marker is necessary unless a specific position within that designated by the stem is desired.

Illustrations of the locative suffixes follow:

A. *aana-kim-i daano* (bamboo +in +nominative) 'You put it in the bamboo.'

B. *maku-taq-i bemi* (village +at +nominative) 'He is at the village.'

C. *makuy-aamam-paq yokadade* (village +near +place) 'I want to work near the village place.'

D. *kamaa-naadoq-paq-te maadaano* (sweet-potato +on-top-of +place +from) 'You get it from on top of the sweet potato.'

E. *maaq-aaqnaa-paq ukukemi* (house +at-base-of +place) 'She is standing right next to the house.'

F. *aay-anaa nodaa* (road +along-on) 'I want to walk along on the road.'

G. *oy-anaaq nodaa* (stone +along-on-top-of) 'I want to walk along on top of the stone.'

H. *yunaan-ke-paq-i* (food +apart +place +nominative) 'the place outside from the garden'; *naamun-kin-ke kumemi* (inside +in +from) 'He came down from inside the house.'

I. *maku-taq-paq-taq-kaa nodaa* (village +at +place +on +to) 'I want to go to and walk about on the village.'

J. *pon-taq-paq-i* (pig +at +place +nominative) 'at the pig place'.

3.3. *Utterance Indicators*

Some Gadsup suffixes indicate that the affixed base is a complete and independent utterance. These include the vocative, explicit, predicative, and the person-involvement suffixes. Some other suffixes indicate that the utterance in which the affixed base occurs is a question.

3.3.1. *Vocative.* The suffix *-o* denotes the one being addressed. The resultant form acts as a complete utterance: *baantao* '(You) Man!', *baantauko* *aanaasiuko* 'Men! Women!', *iyaakukanoi* '(You) Very tall one!', *maampan-kino* 'You outside!'

3.3.2. *Explicit*. The suffix (*-e*) marks the noun base as that which is the center of attention, or that which is under specific reference. In response to the question, 'What did you bring today?' one might answer, *kukuye* 'Fence-wood.' This morpheme has the allomorph *-be* occurring with Class V: *ikabe* 'Firewood'.

3.3.3. *Predicatives*. The suffix *-ni* is used to predicate the fact of the base. No verb occurs with this utterance: *iyam-i-ni* (dog +nominative +predica-tive) 'It is a dog.' *pod-indaa-up-i-ni* (pig +thing +plural +nominative + predicative) 'They belong to the pig.' *yunaam-paq-te-pi-ni* (food +place + from +question +predicative) 'Is it from the garden?'

Another predicative suffix, *-no,* is emphatic in character. This morpheme may be used when an individual is not being understood, and a restatement is necessary: *naamunkimino* 'Inside!' *kamaamino* 'It is sweet potato!'

3.3.4. *Person-involvement suffixes*. Three suffixes mark the person-subject involved in an unexpressed verb. These suffixes occur with a noun which, with this suffix, is a complete utterance. The suffixes are *-mu*[9] involving first person, *-mo* involving second person singular or plural, or third person plural, and *-mi* involving third person singular. In response to the question, 'Why have they come?', one might receive the answer, *kamaa-mo-ni* (sweet-potato +3rd-plural +predicative) 'They (have come for) sweet potato.' To the question 'What did you take?', one might receive the answer: *taape-mu* 'I (took) taro.' To the question, 'Whose is this?', one could reply: *baanta-mi* 'It is the man's.'

3.3.5. *Question suffixes*. Suffix *-aa ~ -a ~ -∅* poses a question of identifica-tion: *kamaan-aa* 'Is it sweet potato?' The allomorph *-aa* never occurs in combination with other question suffixes, but marks a complete utterance. The second of the above listed allomorphs occurs with Classes I, II, III, or IV before an interrogative-person suffix, while *-∅* occurs with Class V nouns preceding interrogative-person affixes.[10] Note further examples below.

The suffix (*-aa*) poses a question as to the presence or existence of the affixed base, though the utterance in which such an noun occurs may not be a question. An alternant of this suffix, *-baa* occurs with Class V nouns; this suffix must precede an interrogative-person suffix: *iyan-aa-q-i aabekaano* (dog +existence +interrogative-person +nominative you-bring) 'You bring the dog (when and if it appears).'

The remaining question indicators mark the person or location of an un-

[9] *-mpe,* an alternant of predicative *-ni*, occurs only with *-mu*.
[10] Tone signals the presence of the zero allomorph of (*-a*). If the preceding tone is different, the tone of *-a* is retained as part of a glide on the vowel of the base: *baàntà + -ā + -pì > bàantãpì* (man + interrogative-identification + interrogative-person) 'Is it a man?'

expressed verb. These suffixes include *-pu* first person, *-pe*[11] second person singular, *-po* second person singular, or second and third plural, *-pi* third person singular, and *-ti* location where. An interrogative-person suffix *-q* indicates that the person involved with the affixed base is indicated in the verb. In the first five examples below, the verb 'to take' is assumed by context.

kamaan-a-pu (sweet-potato +interrogative-identification + 1st-person) 'Did I take the sweet potato?'

kamaan-a-pe (sweet-potato +interrogative-identification +2nd-person-singular) 'Did you take the sweet potato?'

kamaan-a-pi (sweet-potato + interrogative-identification + 3rd-person-singular) 'Did he take the sweet potato?'

kamaan-a-po (sweet-potato +interrogative-identification +2nd-person-singular/plural or 3rd-person-plural) 'Did they take the sweet potato?'

kamaan-aa-si   (sweet-potato +interrogative-existence +location-where) 'Where shall the sweet potato be taken?'

kamaan-a-q madekapu (sweet-potato +interrogative-identification +interrogative-person did-I-take) 'Did I take the sweet-potato?'

koqyi + ∅ + *pi koqyipi* (lizard + interrogative-identification + 3rd-person-singular) 'Is it a lizard?'

kamaan-aa-q benaapi (sweet-potato + interrogative-existence + interrogative-person is-there) 'Is there (any) sweet-potato?'

iyan-ad-e-q teepe (dog + reference + explicit + interrogative-person did-you-talk) 'Was it about the dog (just mentioned) that you were talking?'

4. DISTRIBUTION

Gadsup suffixes, though considerable in number, have not been observed affixed to one stem in combinations of more than six. The usual number on one base is two or three. Many of the suffixes occur in more than one order. Numbering such orders results in some seventeen possible positions related to the stem. Since relative orders are not fixed, and since only a few suffixes occur at any one time, it seems best to discuss the distribution of suffixes relative to each other within the categories discussed above, and then in relation to the stem.

In general, suffixes occur with the internal modifiers closest to the base, the external relators next, and the utterance indicators last.

4.1. *Distribution of Internal Modifiers*

Of the internal modifiers, the quality-of-color morpheme directly follows the base, and may only be followed by the nominative suffix. Two size mor-

---

[11] *-pe* may not be followed by any morpheme, whereas *-po* may be followed by the predicatives.

phemes semantically appropriate may occur juxtaposed without restriction as to order: 'big-long', 'long-big', 'big-short', 'short-big', 'long-small', 'small-long', 'short-small', 'small-short'. The internal modifiers usually occur with size morphemes first, then retention, then number, though this order is not fixed. Examples follow:

kamaan-amaa-yaka-mi (sweet-potato +long +big +nominative) 'long big sweet-potato'

upisaa-yakan-amaa-uq-i (bean +big +long +plural +nominative) 'big long beans'

pon-tandaa-yakan-an-i ipiqdemi (pig +two +big +reference +nominative she-cried) 'She cried about the two big pigs.'

pon-dakan-kandaa-ban-i (pig +big +two +reference +nominative) 'with reference to two big pigs'

pumaadaa-amaa-uq-i (young-man +long +plural +nominative) 'tall young men'

maka-manaa-i (ground +quality +nominative) 'brown or ground like'

kamaan-andaa-uq-i (sweet-potato +secured +plural +nominative) 'the tied-up sweet potatoes'

kamaan-amaa-uaa-amaa-i (sweet-potato +long +plural +long +nominative 'the long long sweet potatoes'

The place morpheme occurs either following the base or following one of the locative suffixes: *makupaq* 'village', *makutaqpaq* 'at the village'.

The nominative suffix is mutually exclusive with the person-involvement morphemes and the interrogative morphemes which indicate person or location. The only morphemes which may follow the nominative suffix are the predicative suffixes. Otherwise, if present, the nominative follows all other suffixes.

The distribution of the morpheme indicating reality, *-ukaN,* is the widest of any suffix. This suffix may occur before or following the internal modifiers, but may not interrupt a sequence of size morphemes; before or after the locatives, but again may not interrupt a sequence of locatives; and before or after the possessive suffixes (except that this morpheme does not occur before *-kena*). The reality morpheme may also occur before the other external relators, or after first order of the relators. Examples:

baantu-uk-ukan-amaa-i (man +plural +reality +long +nominative) 'long real-men'

baanta-amaa-uka-mi (man +long +reality +nominative) 'really long man'

makuy-ukam-paq-i (village +reality +place +nominative) 'the real village place'

maku-taq-paq-tenaa-uka-mi (village +at +place +thing +reality +nominative) 'the real thing of the village'

baanta-ukan-iq poni (man +reality +possessive pig) 'the real man's pig' *banta-iq-uka-mi* (man +possessive +reality +nominative) 'the real-like (lifelike) man' (that which possesses the reality of man)

aayaam-poy-uka-mi (his-hand +with +reality +nominative) 'really (truly) with his hand'

aayaan-ukaam-po-ni (his-hand +reality +with +nominative) 'with his real hand'

aayaam-poy-ukan-a-ni tequ (his-hand +with +reality +reference +nominative I-say) 'I am talking about it being really with his hand.'

4.2. *Distribution of Locative Suffixes*

Locative suffixes usually directly follow the base, but may be preceded by an internal modifier. Since these suffixes refer to the location of an action, the place marker *-paK* often occurs with them. Suffixes *-anaa* and *-anaaK* are the only locatives which occur alone, that is, without other locatives or the place marker. Suffixes *-aama*N and *-naako*K must be followed by *-paK,* and *-aaqnaa* must be followed either by *-paK* or *-kaK*. The morpheme *-ke* preceding *-paK* designates 'apart-place', but when following *-paK, -kaK,* or *-kiN,* it designates direction from. The directional morpheme *-kaa* must be preceded by *-paK*. Various locatives and locative combinations: *-kimpaq* locality or area, *-kinkaq* pluralizes stem, *-kaqpaq* 'at place' (e.g., 'He was *at* the place'), *paqtaq* 'around within' (e.g., 'He was walking *around in* the village'), *-kinkimpaq* 'in an area or locality', *-kinkinkaq* 'in the places', *-kimpaqtaq* 'around in the area'. Examples:

yunaan-ke-paq-i 'the place just aside from the garden'
naamun-kin-ke 'from inside'
maku-tim-paq 'village-place' (the area or countryside where the villages are located)
maku-tin-kaq 'the villages'
maku-taq-paq-taq-kaa nodanu 'I want to go to and walk about in the village.'
maku-taq-paq 'at the village-place'
kaandaandaa-naadoq-paq-taq nodanu 'I want to walk about on top of the food-shelf.'
maku-tin-kim-paq nodaa 'I want to walk about in the village country.'
maku-tin-kin-kaq nodaa 'I want to walk about in the villages.'

4.3. *Distribution of Possessives*

The suffix *-iK* may follow the base, a modifier, or the other two possessives. *iK* is the final suffix affixed to the base unless immediately followed by the reality morpheme *-ukaN:*

baanta-uq-yiq poni (man +plural +possessive pig) 'men's pig'
iyaak-iq-ukan-akam-pon-i aademi (long +possessive +reality +big +instrument +nominative he-fought) 'He fought with something like a long big one.'
baanta-inda-iq poni 'man's pig'

peyan-kenaa-iq taasu (old +that-which-is-of +possessive axe) 'the old axe belonging to a man'

Suffix *-inda* may occur after all stems except those referring to time or place. It may follow *-kenaa,* and may be preceded or followed by internal modifiers: *baanta-amaa-inda* (man +long +thing) 'the tall man's (thing)', *makuq-taq-paq-tenaa-inda* village +at +place +thing +belong) 'the village thing belonging to someone'.

Suffix *-kenaa* may be preceded only by the locatives *-kiN, -kaK,* and place marker *-paK,* or by a time base: *maku-taq-keno* (place +at +pertaining-people) 'the people of the village', *nudan-kenaa-ukam-i* (yesterday +pertaining-things +reality +nominative) 'the things of old (really-before)'.

4.4. *Distribution of Other External Relators*

The other external relators may be grouped together. These include reference, similarity, accompaniment, instrument, purposive, causative, object of verb 'to hold', and the series indicator. These suffixes occur in three orders following the suffixes discussed above, with the possibility of the reference morpheme occurring twice: *pod-an-teke-ban-i tequ* (pig +reference +like +reference +nominative I-am-talking) 'Concerning a similar pig—about this I am talking.' Instrument, purposive, causative, and object of verb 'to hold' never follow the others of this group and are mutually exclusive. The similarity morpheme may occur before or after the others, but not more than once. The following illustrate:

yaampo-teke aademi (stick +instrument +similarity he-hits) 'He hit him as if with a stick.'

benaano-ke-ukan-aa benaapo-ke-ukan-aate bemi (his-mother +like +reality +series his-father +like +reality +series he-is) 'He is (looks) very much like his mother and very much like his father.'

pod-ad-ukan-an-i tequ (pig +reference +reality +reference +nominative I-tell) 'I am talking about this matter concerning the pig.'

baanta-naamaq-keke bemi (man +with +like he-is) 'He is staying probably with a man.'

aayaam-poy-aq-i aademi '(his-hand +instrument +also +nominative he-hit) He fought with his hand also.'

pod-akan-teke pekemi (pig +causative +like he-is-afraid) 'He is afraid because of something like a pig.'

pod-ad-teke-temi (pig +reference +like he-talks) 'He is talking about a pig (probably or likely).'

kamaan-kon-aa taape-kon-aase yemi (sweet-potato +purposive +series taro +purposive +series he-comes) 'He came for sweet potato and for taro.'

4.5. *Distribution of Utterance Indicators*

The utterance indicators follow in general the modifiers and external relators. Three orders occur. Order 1: interrogative of identification, interrogative of existence, vocative, explicit; Order 2: interrogative-person, person-involvement; Order 3: predicatives.

The vocative may not be followed by other utterance indicators (only the nominative). The predicatives (regular and emphatic) may be preceded immediately only by the interrogative-person or place markers, by the person-involvement markers, or by the nominative.

XXI. Gadsup Independent Verb Affixes

CHESTER FRANTZ and HOWARD McKAUGHAN

1. INTRODUCTION

We define the independent verb in Gadsup as an inflected base which may occur as the predicate of an independent clause.[1] Independent clauses may be full sentences, and their occurrence does not depend on other clauses in the sentence or discourse. As in other New Guinea Highland languages, the verb is central to the clause since it not only acts as predicate, but also indicates the subject and, optionally, the object and the benefactor of the action.

Gadsup independent verbs contain an obligatory subject marker. Besides optionally indicating an object (some verb stems require such) and a benefactor, the verb may contain affixes to mark various aspect and modelike categories. The affixes are closely knit together phonologically, depending on each other for their different allomorphic variations.

Our aim in this paper is to describe the internal structure of the independent verb. We do not present all possible morphemes since analysis of the Gadsup verb has not yet been completed. Further investigation may lead to modification as well as add to the categories here described. We present this in order that other scholars may compare the languages, especially in the Highlands.

Our method of approach is first to name and describe the various gram-

[1] This paper was first published as pp. 84-99 in *Verb Studies in Five New Guinea Languages,* Summer Institute of Linguistics Publications in Linguistics and Related Fields No. 10, 1964, and is reissued here in this format by permission.

Frantz is responsible for the data and the preliminary analysis. McKaughan is responsible for the theoretical framework and presentation. This paper and others on the Kainantu group of languages form a basis for comparative work to be done later.

439

matical categories indicated in the verb. We then state the distribution of the affixes related to the stem and to each other, giving certain limitations of occurrence and certain required co-occurrences. Finally we turn to the morphophonemic details, describing the stem classes first, and then the affix variants.

2. GRAMMATICAL CATEGORIES INDICATED BY THE AFFIXES

We group the affixes occurring in Gadsup verbs semantically into person morphemes, aspectlike morphemes, and modelike morphemes.

2.1. *Person Morphemes*

Gadsup verbs, as we have noted, must indicate the person performing the action stated by the stem. Besides these subject morphemes, the verb may mark the object or goal of the action, and a person benefited by the action.

2.1.1. *(Su)bject morphemes.* The following suffixes mark person and number subjects: {-u}[2] 'I' or 'we', {-ona} 'you', {-i} 'he', {-o} 'you all' or 'they'. The following illustrate: *kùmèq(ú)* 'I go down', *kùm(ŏnà)mî* 'You go down', *kùmĕm(í)* 'He goes down', *kúm(ò)mî* 'You all/they go down.' The second singular, {-ona}, may contain the singular morpheme -*na,* but since number morphemes do not occur elsewhere, we treat the two as a single unit. The subject of the verb may also be indicated by free pronouns. The free subject pronouns include *tènĭ* 'I', *ènĭ* 'you', *bènĭ* 'he', *màyàuní* 'we' or 'they', *ìkèní* 'you all', and *yènĭ* 'they': *tènĭ kùmèqú* 'I go down', etc.

2.1.2. *(B)enefactor morphemes.* Suffixes -*tink* 'for me/us', -*ank* 'for him/ you', and -*yink* 'for them/you all' indicate both that an action is performed for someone's benefit, and the person to be benefited. Morphemes -*ti, -a,* and -*yi* mark person while -*nk* indicates the benefactive action of the verb. However, -*nk* never occurs without the preceding person morphemes. Hence we treat this sequence as a single unit, calling it the benefactor. The following illustrate: *kùmù(tìnk)ă* 'He goes down for me/us', *kùmù(ànk)ă* 'He goes down for him/you', *kùmù(yìnk)ă* 'He goes down for them/you all'.

2.1.3. *(O)bject morphemes.* Some verbs have an obligatory object prefix whose form is similar to the benefactor person morphemes just described. A very limited number of other verbs may optionally occur with object prefixes. Other stems, although they may sometimes occur in a clause with an object manifested by a noun or pronoun, never occur with object pre-

---

[2] Braces enclosing morphemes, { }, indicate that the morpheme has various alternants. Gadsup phonemes are the following: consonants /p/, /t/, and /k/ which are sometimes slightly aspirated and occur as fricatives intervocalic; /q/; /b/ which is a stop contiguous to a bilabial nasal and a fricative elsewhere; /d/ which occurs as a flap intervocalic; /m/; /n/ which is at velar point of articulation preceding the velar stop; and /y/ which has slight friction in certain environments; vowels /i/, /a/, /u/, /e/, /aa/, and /o/. We have written here high and low tones, and combinations of these for falling and rising varieties: /´/, /`/, /ˇ/, and /ˆ/.

fixes. The object prefixes are *ti-* 'me/us', *a-* 'you/him', and *yi-* 'them/you all'.[3] If a verb stem may occur in a clause with both direct and indirect objects manifested by nouns, then the prefix on the verb indicates an indirect object, not the object. In the sentence *tènǐ ìyàmí bààntá à-mèqú* (I dog man him-gave) 'I gave the dog to the man', prefix *a-* indicates the third singular indirect object, co-occurring with *bààntà* 'man'. In the sentence *tènǐ ìyamí à-dèqú* (I dog him-hit) 'I hit the dog', the prefix *a-* refers to the direct object, 'dog', since an indirect object may not occur with the verb 'to hit'.

The following verbs require the object prefix:[4] *à-mèqú* 'I give to him', *à-tèqú* 'I am angry at him', *à-mànéqú* 'I sneer at him', *à-dèqú* 'I hit him', *á-mòqnéqú* 'I kiss him', *á-yààqéqú* 'I find it.' The verb *on-* 'to look' illustrates a stem which optionally occurs with these prefixes: *à-ònèqú* 'I look at him', but *ònèqú* 'I see.'[5]

Free pronouns may also indicate object, and may co-occur with the prefixes just described: *tèmǐ* 'me', *èmǐ* 'you', *bèmǐ* 'him', *màyàúnì* 'us/them', *ìkèmí* 'you all', and *yèmǐ* 'them': *bèmǐ àdèqú,* or *tènǐ bèmǐ àdèqú,* or *àdèqú* 'I hit him.'

2.2. Aspectlike Morphemes

Aspectlike morphemes with Gadsup verbs indicate kinds of actions usually with time involved. We call the various aspectlike morphemes potential, abilitative, completive, and progressive. The morphemes may all occur together or separately.

2.2.1. *(Po)tential morphemes.* Two morphemes occur indicating actions which are potential, that is, have not taken place at the time a statement is made. One of these, {-idad}, indicates desire: *kùm(ìdád)è* 'I would like to go down'; and the other, {-idan}, indicates certainty as well as immediacy; *kùm(ìdán)ú* 'I am about to go down', or 'I will surely go down.'

2.2.2. *(Ab)ilitative morpheme.* The suffix {-on} indicates an action which has not taken place, but can take place. Future action and ability are connoted by the morpheme: *kúm(òn)téqú* 'I will go down', or 'I can go down', *páqk(ààn)té-qú* 'I will/can hold', *índ(èn)téqú* 'I will/can listen.'

2.2.3. *(St)ative morpheme.* The morpheme {-baq} indicates the state or the existence of an action. In this case the action is viewed as having begun before the statement is made: *kùmè(báq)ú* 'I am on my way down', *màdè-(báq)ú* 'I am doing it', or 'I have been doing it', *pàqkè(báq)ú* 'I have hold of it.'

---

[3] The allomorphs of these morphemes are the same as those described in Chap. XX.

[4] About 14 percent of the verbs analyzed require this prefix. Similar affixes occurring with nouns are described in Chap. XX.

[5] An additional order of prefixes may occur before the object prefix. This order indicates direction. Morphemes include *un-* 'up', *o-* 'along', and *kun-* 'down': *ùn-à-bìkaǎ* 'You bring him from up', *ò-à-bìkaǎ* 'You bring him from over there', *kùnàbìkaǎ* 'You bring him from down.'

2.2.4. *(C)ompletive morpheme.* An action which has been completed is designated by the suffix {-*mok*}: *kùmèq(mók)ú* 'I had come down', *yòkèq-(mók)ú* 'I had worked.'

2.2.5. *(Pr)ogressive morpheme.* An action in progress is designated by the morpheme -*o*: *kùmèk(ó)* 'I am going down', *kùmèn(ó)* 'He is going down', *pàqkèy(ó)* 'They are holding it.'

2.3. *Modelike Morphemes*

Gadsup modelike morphemes include the narrative, interrogative, negative, and augmentative.

2.3.1. *(N)arrative morpheme.* A narrative morpheme, {-*eq*}, indicates that a general statement of fact is in view: *kùm(èq)ú* 'I came down.' If aspectlike morphemes are not present, the time is neutral, conditioned by context: *ád(èm)ì* 'He hits him', but *ád-òn(tém)ì* 'He will/can hit him', *àd(èm)-ón-ì* 'He had hit him.'

With verbs of motion, the narrative morpheme may be replaced by the morpheme {*oq*} indicating that the subject has performed the full cycle of the action designated: *kúm(óq)ú* 'I had gone down (and am now back)', *úd(óq)ú* 'I went up (and am back again).'

2.3.2. *(I)nterrogative morpheme.* A question is marked by the suffix {-*ap*}: *kùmèn(áp)ì* 'Has he come down?', *pàqkèk(áp)é* 'Have you all held it?', *yòkèy(áp)ò* 'Have they worked?'

2.3.3. *(Au)gmentative morphemes.* The suffix {-*no*} (Au₁) marks emphasis: *kúmò(nò)* 'I came down!', *páqkàà(nò)* 'I held it!' An additional morpheme {-*be*} (Au₂) sometimes occurs following (Au₁) marking double emphasis: *kúmònò(bé)* 'I really came down!', *yòkaânò(bé)* 'I really worked!'

2.3.4. *(Neg)ative morpheme.* A negative morpheme is a falling tone occurring simultaneously with the subject morpheme. The abilitative is required preceding the negative morpheme, the two together indicating an avolitional mode, that is, a negative future: *kùmònû* 'It is not good that I go down', or 'I shouldn't go down.'[6]

3. DISTRIBUTION OF THE AFFIXES

Up to nine suffixes may occur following a Gadsup verb stem. The order and morphemes permitted are as follows: + S ± B ± Po ± Ab ± N ± I ± C + Su ± Au₁ ± Au₂, *kùmù-ánk-àdád-òn-ték-áp-ón-ì-nó-bé* 'Had he indeed wanted to go down for him!?' The only morphemes obligatory to this complex are the stem and the subject.

When the stative occurs, it must be preceded by the narrative, but the abilitive and completive in this instance are not permitted: + S ± B ±

---

[6] The negative morpheme may actually be the pattern ` ˆ ˇ since in all observed cases, regardless of the original tone of the preceding stem or affix, the vowel preceding the subject morpheme is low.

Po ± N ± St ± I + Su ± Au₁ ± Au₂, *kùmù-ànk-àdád-é-bàk-áp-ù-nó-bé*
'Did I really want to have gone down for him?'

We have noted that the abilitative is required preceding the negative indicating the avolitional: + S + Ab + Su-Neg, *kùm-òn-û* 'I shouldn't go
down.' When the augmentative follows a subject morpheme without other
suffixes present, the sequence indicates imperative: +S +Su +Au₁, *kúm(ò-nò)*
'I must go down', *kùm(ŏ-nò)* 'You go down!'

When the abilitative morpheme is not followed by the narrative, it must
be followed by the interrogative (with ø alternant). In this case the stative
and completive morphemes are not permitted: +S ± B ± Po ± Ab ± I +I +
Su ± Au₁ ± Au₂, *kúm-òn- ø-ù* 'Will I go?', 'Can I go?'

The completive morpheme may not occur unless the narrative morpheme
is also present: *kùm(èq-mók)ú* 'I had gone down.'

Certain other morpheme sequences are not permitted. Thus when the
stative occurs, the abilitative and the completive morphemes may not occur.
The completive and progressive morphemes are also mutually exclusive.
These and other distributional features will be further illustrated when we
deal with the allomorphic variation of the affixes.

4. Stem Morphophonemics: Related to the Affixes

Gadsup verb stems may be divided into three classes by the suffix alternants which occur with them.[7] For example, the second person singular
subject morpheme has three alternants: *-o~-a~-e*. Verbs which occur
with the first may be grouped as Class I stems, those with the second as
Class II stems, and those with the last as Class III stems (see the matrix in
Table 63). Suffixes which have alternants dividing the verb stems into these
classes include potential morphemes, the abilitative, and certain subject
morphemes.

About 65 percent of the verb stems analyzed occur with a stem-final vowel
preceding the benefactor morphemes. These vowels may be considered
class markers for such stems, since those with final /u/ are in Class I, those
with final /a/ in Class II, and those with final /i/ are in Class III: *kùmù-tìnkaǎ*
'You go down for me', *páqkà-tìnkàà* 'You hold it for me', *ìndì-tìnkàà* 'You
listen for me.' Such stems have alternants without the final vowel preceding
other suffixes: *kùm-èqú* 'I go down, *pàqk-ĕmì* 'He holds it', *ìndènápì* 'Has
he listened?'

A few examples of verb stems not occurring with class markers follow:
Class I, *kud-* 'cook', *puk-* 'die', *up-* 'dig up taro', *kuy-* 'tie', *doy-* 'hold',
dusim- 'put out fire'; Class II, *mak-* 'ration out', *mad-* 'get', *id-* 'marry', *yok-*
'work', *masip-* 'cover up'; Class III, *daot-* 'husk, peel', *diy-* 'open, *kumand-*
'sit'.

---

[7] We have not attempted a description of the allomorphs of stems or affixes which
vary by tone only.

Certain stems having the class marker before the benefactor morphemes occur with final nasal before other morphemes. Since these are limited in number, we list all known stems: *apoqu-* > *àpòqm-éqú* 'I move', *yupuqa-* > *yùpùqm-éqú* 'I caress', *ayapaaqu-* > *áyàpààqm-éqú* 'I carry in my arms', *anaau-* > *ànààm-éqú* 'I leaf through', *yapaau-* > *yápààm-éqú* 'I carry it close to the chest', *anaanaa-* > *ànààm-éqú* 'I put on a handle', *yaqayu-* > *yàqáán-éqú* 'I put on top.'

It is characteristic of Gadsup that the only permitted consonant sequences have initial /n/ or /q/. Hence before morphemes with initial consonants, stem-final consonants undergo the following morphophonemic changes. (A) Voiced stem-final consonants are replaced by /n/: *daud-* > *dáùn-tìnkàà* 'Bend it for me', *dusim-* > *dúsìn-yínkaǎ* 'extinguish it for them', *intuy-* > *ìntûn-yínkaǎ* 'Tie it for them'; (B) voiceless stem-final consonants are replaced by /q/: *mak-* > *màq-tìnkaǎ* 'Ration it out for me', *daot-* > *dàóq-yìnkaǎ* 'Husk it for them', *dup-* > *dùq-tìnkaǎ* 'Chop it for me.'

Stem-final /m/ is replaced by /n/ before *-ank* 'for him': *dusim-* > *dúsìnàn-kaǎ* 'Extinguish it for him.' Stem-final voiceless stops are replaced by /q/ before this morpheme: *mak-* > *màq-ànkaǎ* 'Ration it out for him', *daot-* > *daoq-ankaǎ* 'Husk it for him.'

A few stems with final /y/ drop that phoneme before consonant-initial suffixes rather than having the allomorphs with /n/ or /q/. These include the following: *uqmaay-* 'wrap up', *puntaay-* 'cut down in front of', *yaqkoy-* 'cover', *daqdaay-* 'fold', *uyu-* 'pile up', *kuy-* 'tie', *buy-* 'make a trap', *mantaakuy-* 'press together', *ayaakoy-* 'put food in bag and carry', *koy-* 'dig up', *dubay-* 'break' and *diy-* 'open'. The last two stems listed are Class III; the others are Class I stems. Illustrations: *úqmàa-tìnkaǎ* 'Wrap it up for me', *púntaà-yìnkaǎ* 'Cut it down for them', *yàqkô-tìnkaǎ* 'Cover it for me.'

The benefactor morpheme sequence conditions following morphemes in the same way as do Class II stems. The potential morphemes, abilitative morpheme, and certain subject morphemes have allomorphs with the vowel /a/ or /aa/ following the benefactor: *kùmùànk(àdán)ú* 'I will surely go down for him', *kùmùánk(ààn)téqú* 'I will go down for him', *kùmùánk(àà)* 'I went down for him.'

5. ALLOMORPHIC VARIATION OF AFFIXES

Combinations of suffixes in Gadsup verbs are characterized by a great deal of allomorphic variation. The final form of any inflected verb can best be stated as the product of a succession of selections given on a priority basis. The selectors or conditioners in their order of priority are the subject, stem class or affix *-ank*, and individual suffix morphemes.

5.1. *Allomorphs Conditioned by Subject Morphemes*

The selection of allomorphs of the (Ab)ilitative, (N)arrative, (St)ative,

(I)nterrogative, and (C)ompletive morphemes depends upon the particular subject occurring in the construction. In order to depict this conditioning, and be able to compare the allomorphic variations depending on subject morphemes, we arrange the constructions in a matrix.[8] The axes of the matrix are the particular subject morpheme upon which the selection depends, and the different morphemes selected. See Table 62.

TABLE 62
MATRIX I: ALTERNANTS CONDITIONED BY SUBJECT MORPHEMES

	N	N–C	N–I–C
1st	*kùm(èq)-ú*	*kùm(èq)(mók)-ú*	*kùm(èk)(áp)(ók)-ù*
3rd sing	*kùm(ĕm)-ì*	*kùm(èm)(ón)-ì*	*kùm(èn)(áp)(ón)-ì*
3rd pl	*kùm(ĕn)-ò*	*kùm(èn)(óy)-ò*	*kùm(èy)(áp)(óy)-ò*
2nd sing	*kùm-ŏnà(mî)*	*kúm(ó)-ónà(mî)*	*kùm(è)(p)(ó)-ò*
2nd pl	*kúm-ò(mî)*	*kúm(ók)-ò(mî)*	*kùm(èk)(áp)(ók)-ò*

	Ab–N	N–St	N–St–I
1st	*kúm(òn)(téq)-ú*	*kùm(è)(báq)-ú*	*kùm(è)(bák)(áp)-ù*
3rd sing	*kúm(ìn)(tém)-ì*	*kùm(è)(bám)-ì*	*kùm(è)(bán)(áp)-ì*
3rd pl	*kúm(ìn)(tén)-ò*	*kùm(è)(bán)-ò*	*kùm(è)(báy)(áp)-ò*
2nd sing	*kúm(ìn)-ŏnà(mî)*	*kùm(è)(bàn)-ŏnà(mî)*	*kùm(è)(bá)(p)-é*
2nd pl	*kùm(ìn)-áqkò(mî)*	*kùm(è)(bák)-ò(mî)*	*kùm(è)(bák)(áp)-é*

Particular allomorphs selected are enclosed in parentheses. Symbols on the horizontal axis indicate these morphemes and their linear order. Subject morphemes follow the hyphens.

The following observations come from a study of Table 62. With second person morphemes, unless the interrogative is also present, the narrative morpheme has alternate -*mi* following the person marker. The narrative appears as -*e* preceding the interrogative morpheme if second singular subject is also present (see N–I–C in the matrix). This same allomorph also occurs with both -*e* and -*mi* when stative and second person subject affixes only are present (N-St). Otherwise the narrative morpheme has -*eq* ~ -*ek* with first person, -*em* ~ -*en* with third person singular, and -*en* ~ -*ey* with third plural.[9]

The stative morpheme has the same final consonants in the same distribution noted for the narrative morpheme.

Similarly the completive morpheme has final /k/, /n/, /y/, and ∅ conditioned by the various person subjects (see N-C and N-I-C). This morpheme also has alternants conditioned by the class of the preceding morpheme.

---

[8] We are indebted to K. L. Pike for the term 'matrix'. For matrix theory in linguistics we refer the reader to Pike (1962).

[9] Allomorphs with initial /t/ have the same final consonants: -*teq* ~ -*tek*, -*tem* ~ -*ten*, and -*ten* ~ -*tey*. For the distribution of such see Sec. 5.3.2.

The interrogative has -*ø* alternant when directly following the abilitative with first and second person subjects: *kúmòn(ø)ù* 'Shall I go down?', *kúmìn(ø)ò* 'Will you go down?', *kùmìn(ø)áqkè* 'Will you all go down?' Directly following the abilitative with third singular and third plural subjects, the interrogative has alternants -*an* and -*ay:* *kùmín(án)ì* 'Will he come down?', *kùmìn(áy)è* 'Will they come down?' In other environments the interrogative has alternant -*p* with second person singular subject and -*ap* with all other persons.

The abilitative has alternant -*on* with first person, and -*in* with other persons. This morpheme also has alternants conditioned by the class of the preceding morpheme.

5.2. *Allomorphs Conditioned by Class*

(Su)bject, (Po)tential, and (Ab)ilitative morphemes have alternants conditioned by the class of the stem (or suffix -*ank* which behaves as a Class II stem) if they directly follow such (see Table 63).

Note that in these selections, class conditioning affects only the first vowel of the suffix: /o/ follows Class I, /aa/ follows Class II, and /e/ follows Class III; or /i/ follows Classes I and III, while /a/ follows Class II. The third singular subject, potential morphemes, and the abilitative morpheme if nonfirst persons are involved, all follow the latter distribution (/i/ and /a/), while other morphemes noted in the matrix, and the abilitative with first person subject, follow the former (/o/, /aa/, and /e/).

The second singular morpheme is -*o* ~ -*aa* ~ -*e* if final in the sequence, but -*ona* ~ -*aana* ~ -*ena* when preceding narrative allomorph -*mi*.

The second and third plural subject morpheme has final /q/ when it is the only morpheme following the stem, but has only the vowel elsewhere.[10]

5.3. *Allomorphs Conditioned by Individual Morphemes*

Certain alternants are conditioned by particular morphemes in the immediate environment of the variant selected. The following paragraphs indicate these alternants and their determiners.

5.3.1. The final consonant (or its absence) for alternants of the narrative, completive, and stative morphemes is conditioned first by the particular subject morpheme occurring in the construction (Matrix I), and second by the following morpheme. Thus /k/, /n/, /y/, and *ø* occur with the narrative and stative morphemes preceding the interrogative and progressive, and with the completive morpheme (Matrix I: N-I-C, N-St-I, and N-C). Phonemes /q/, /m/, /n/, /k/ occur with the narrative and stative morphemes preceding other than the interrogative (Matrix I: N, N-C, Ab-N, N-St).

5.3.2. The narrative morpheme has alternants with initial /t/ immediately following the abilitative: *kúmòn(téq)ú* 'I will come down.' As noted, the

10 See Sec. 5.3.4 for a limitation to this general statement.

narrative alternant before the stative morpheme is *-e: kùm(è)báqú* 'I am on my way down.'

5.3.3. The completive morpheme occurs with initial /m/ following /q/, but with initial vowel elsewhere: *kùmèq(mók)ú* 'I had gone down', *kùmèm-(ón)ì* 'He had gone down.'

TABLE 63
MATRIX II: ALTERNANTS CONDITIONED BY CLASS

	1st Su	3rd sing Su
Class I	*kúm(ò)*	*kùm(ì)*
Class II	*páqk(àa)*	*pàqk(ǎ)*
-ank	*kùmùánk(àa)*	*kùmùànk(ǎ)*
Class III	*índ(è)*	*índ(ì)*

	2nd sing Su with N	2nd pl Su with N
Class I	*kùm(ǒnà)mî*	*kúm(ò)mî*
Class II	*pàqk(aǎnà)mî*	*páqk(àà)mî*
-ank	*kùmùànk(aǎnà)mî*	*kùmùánk(àà)mî*
Class III	*ìnd(ěnà)mî*	*índ(è)mî*

	Ab with 1st Su	Ab with non-1st Su
Class I	*kúm(òn)téqú*	*kúm(ìn)témì*
Class II	*pàqk(ààn)téqú*	*páqk(àn)témì*
-ank	*kùmùánk(ààn)téqú*	*kùmùánk(àn)témì*
Class III	*ìnd(èn)téqú*	*índ(ìn)témì*

	2nd/3rd pl Su	2nd sing Su
Class I	*kúm(òq)*	*kùm(ǒ)*
Class II	*páqk(ààq)*	*pàqk(ǎa)*
-ank	*kùmùánk(àaq)*	*kùmùànk(ǎa)*
Class III	*índ(èq)*	*ìnd(ě)*

	Po(certain)	Po(desire)
Class I	*kùm(ìdán)ú*	*kùm(ìdád)é*
Class II	*pàqk(àdán)ú*	*pàqk(àdád)é*
-ank	*kùmùànk(àdán)ú*	*kùmùànk(àdád)é*
Class III	*ìnd(ìdán)ú*	*ìnd(ìdád)è*

C

Class I	*kúm(ó)ónàmî*
Class II	*páqk(á)ónàmî*
-ank	*kùmùánk(á)ónàmî*
Class III	*índ(é)ónàmî*

Allomorphs selected are enclosed in parentheses.

5.3.4. There are certain alternants of the various subject morphemes which have not yet been described. Directly following -*idad,* the first person is -*e;* all other persons are -*aa* following this morpheme: *kùmìdád(é)* 'I wish to go down', *kùmìdád(aa)* 'You/he/you all/they wish to go down.'

Following the progressive morpheme, first and third persons have ∅ alternants. Ambiguity is resolved by the other suffix alternants: *kùmèkó(∅)* 'I am going down', *kùmènó(∅)* 'He is going down', *kùmèyó(∅)* 'They are going down.' Second person forms have not yet been found with the progressive morpheme.

The second person plural has the alternant -*aqko* directly following the abilitative morpheme: *kùmìn(áqkò)mî* 'You all will/can go down.' Usually this morpheme is the same as the third plural: *kùmĕn(ò)* 'They go down', *kúm(ò)mî* 'You all go down.'

Directly following the interrogative morpheme if the stative is also present, the second singular and plural morphemes occur with alternant -*e; kùmè-báp(é)* 'Are you on the way down?', *kùmèbákáp(é)* 'Are you all on the way down?' Note that this combination of suffixes with their particular alternants carries the contrast between singular and plural. If the stative morpheme is not present, the second singular is indicated by -*o* following the interrogative: *kùmèpó(ò)* 'Are you going down?'

5.3.5. The first order augmentative has either -*ne* or -*ni* following the negative: *kùmònû(né)* or *kùmònû(ní)* 'It isn't good that I go down!' Following the alternant -*u* of the first person subject, unless the interrogative is also present, the first augmentative has the alternant -*mpe: kùmìdádèqmó-kú(mpè)* 'I wanted to go down!', *pàqkádánú(mpè)* 'I will certainly hold it!' Following the second or third plural morpheme, if the narrative morpheme is not present, the augmentative occurs as -*ko: kúmò(kò)* 'They/you all go down!', *índè(kò)* 'They/you all listen!' In all other occurrences, the first augmentative has -*no: kúmò(nò)* 'I go down!', *kùmèkápù(nó)* 'Do I go down!?'

5.3.6. The second augmentative morpheme, -*be,* only follows the first augmentative unless the first is not permitted: *kúmònò(bé)* 'I go down for sure!', *kùmùànkàdádòntéqmónkúmpè(bé)* 'I had really wanted to go down for him!', *kùmèkó(bé)* (where -*no* is not permitted) 'I wish to go down!'

6. Addendum: Dependent Medial Verb Affixes

The authors had hoped to complete a study of the Gadsup dependent verb affixes to include in this book. However, this has not been possible. We therefore give an indication of the direction of research for the interest of New Guinea specialists.

As with other New Guinea languages, Gadsup sentences may contain one or more dependent clauses whose occurrence depends on the occurrence of a following clause. Verbs which may occur as the predicate of such clauses are called dependent medial verbs. The dependent medial verb in Gadsup marks in some way two subjects, the first being that of the dependent clause in which the medial verb occurs, and the second being that of the clause to follow. We refer to the second as anticipatory subject markers.

The anticipatory subject markers are -*q* anticipating 'I', 'we' or 'you all'; -*m* anticipating 'he', -*n* anticipating 'they', and the absence of these morphemes (with other identifying allomorphs of other morphemes) anticipating 'you'.

The anticipatory subject markers are -*q* anticipating 'I', 'we' or 'you all'; is the same as the first, or different. If, however, the second subject is the same as the first, the medial verb contains a morpheme -*e* preceding the anticipatory markers, indicating that the second subject is the same. This marker zeros out the first subject markers.

Besides containing markers to indicate both first and second subjects, the dependent medial verb may contain all of the categories described for the independent verb. Thus the medial verb may contain benefactor morphemes, indirect or direct object morphemes, potential morphemes—both certainty and desire—the abilitative, completive, narrative, interrogative, and augmentative morphemes. However the distribution of these morphemes, their limitations of occurrence, and their allomorphic variation constitute a system quite apart from the independent verb.

XXII. Agarabi Narratives and Commentary

JEAN GODDARD

---

1. INTRODUCTION

The narratives presented here have been selected from material gathered in the Agarabi village of Punano in the Kainantu subdistrict of the Eastern Highlands of New Guinea.[1] The materials were recorded during the period from July, 1960, to November, 1965. The choice of subject matter was generally left to the informants and includes folklore, tribal history, customs, everyday events, and village 'news.'

The texts chosen for presentation here represent a cross section of the types given. Sections 2, 3, and 4 relate trips made by a young man to and from his work on an island plantation (two deal with the same trip to show the differences in the two versions of the same story). Sections 5 and 6 describe some of the changes in tribal life due to the coming of Europeans. Sections 7 and 8 relate local events; Section 9 is a related conversation between a woman and her mother. Sections 10 and 11 both deal with the effects of the very prevalent fear of sorcery. Section 12 relates a tribal custom, and Section 13 is a myth common in this part of New Guinea.

1.1. *Orthography*

/p/, /t/, /k/ represent voiceless stops initially and following consonants, and voiceless fricatives [ɸ], [s], [x] between vowels.

/w/ initially and following consonants varies from a voiced bilabial stop [b] to either the labialized stop [bʷ] or the semivowel [w]. Between vowels it is either the semivowel or a voiced bilabial fricative [β].

[1] This paper appeared as pp. 1-25 in *Papers in New Guinea Linguistics, No. 7*, Pacific Linguistics (Series A: Occasional Papers, No. 13) (Australian National University, 1967), and is reissued here, with minor editorial revision, by permission.

/y/ initially and following consonants varies from a voiced alveolar stop [d] to either the palatalised stop [dʸ] or the semivowel [y]. Between vowels it is the semivowel and may occur with or without friction.

/q/ represents a glottal stop; /r/ represents an alveolar flap; /m, n/ are bilabial and alveolar nasals, respectively; /a/ represents [ə]; /aa/ represents [a.]; /e/ represents [ɛ.]; /i/ represents [i]; /o/ represents [o.]; /u/ represents [u].

Periods are used where a sentence terminal is marked by final markers on the verb or where there is repetition of the verb which indicates a dependent sentence. Commas set off parenthetical expressions and afterthoughts as well as series of nouns or clauses.

1.2. *Commentary on Syntax*

In general the grammar description arising out of these texts is centered on the relationships between dependent and independent constructions and on the affixation of nouns and verbs. The following abbreviations will be used in examples which are taken, as much as possible, from the texts to follow.

con = continuative aspect
de = desiderative
dir = directional
ds = subject of dependent verb
emp = emphatic mood
fm = final marker
fu = future tense
ge = gerundive
imp = imperative
int = interrogative
na = narrative aspect
nt = neutral tense
pt = past tense
pf = perfect tense
pr = personal referent
pvs = preview subject marker (indicates subject of succeeding verb)
vbl = verbaliser
1p, 2p, 3p = 1st, 2nd, 3rd person subject suffix
1f, 2f, 3f = 1st, 2nd, 3rd person final suffix

Texts will be referred to by Arabic numerals indicating the section number, with the number of the sentence or major clause in parentheses.

In this section clause structure will be mentioned briefly. Sentences will be dealt with in more detail under two headings: simple sentences and multiclause sentences.

1.2.1. *Clause structure*. In their minimal form Agarabi clauses consist of an obligatory predicate tagmeme; they may be expanded by the occurrence of several optional tagmemes. They divide into two major classes, independent and dependent. Independent clauses are potentially complete sentences; dependent clauses normally occur as part of a larger unit. The major clause types and some of the subtypes will be illustrated in the section on sentences.

There are several optional items which can occur with the predicate in a clause. The normal order, if all occurred, would be: time, location, subject, indirect object/instrument,[2] object/reason/purpose, directional,[3] and predicate. To date there are no examples in which all of these occur. Examples of one to four, always including the predicate, have been noted. There is some freedom of position; for example, the location may follow the subject. Some items have a relatively fixed position, such as the predicate which closes the construction except when there is an afterthought or an item especially emphasized.

1.2.2. *Sentence structure*. Agarabi sentences may also be divided into two classes as independent or dependent. Independent sentences consist of one or more clauses occurring as complete utterances. Dependent sentences may consist of dependent clauses or nonclause constructions as in some responses or exclamations.

1.2.2.1. *Simple sentences*. Simple sentences are those which consist of one clause or short nonclause utterance. Such an utterance may consist of a single word or may be expanded. The following examples illustrate sentences composed of imperative, interrogative, response, and conclusion clause subtypes. The one nonclause sentence which occurs in these texts is illustrated under 'Responses.'

A. *Indicative*

Minimal: *ór-e-m-íq* (go-nt-3p-3f) 'He went.'

Expanded: *aapeiq-páq anaati paqk-e-m-íq* (Afei-at woman hold-nt-3p-3f) 'They caught a woman at Afeipa' 8(1).

B. *Imperative*

Minimal: *óro* 'Go.'

Expanded: *kauqte anam-pín káao* (lime holder-in put) 'Put it in the lime-holder.

C. *Interrogative*

Minimal: *waa-p-o* (stay-int-2f) 'Are you there?'

Expanded: *áá úwít-iyaa-p-o* (road spread-con-int-2f) 'Are you working on the road?'

D. *Response*

---

[2] The slash here indicates that these clause level slots are mutually exclusive.
[3] The directional often occurs as a part of the predicate.

a. *Clause type*

Minimal: *waa-q-u* (stay-lp-lf) 'I am here.'

Expanded: *áá úwít-iyaa-q-ú* (road spread-con-lp-lf) 'I am working on the road.'

b. *Nonclause type*

éeyo 'Yes.'

E. *Conclusion*

Minimal: *ínka-íq*[4] (finish-vbl) 'That is all' 5(9).

Expanded: *mái ááríntá anaati anaatiq-ma i-n aaná-íq* (this girl woman woman-when be-3p story-vbl) 'This is the story of girls and women when they marry' 10(21).

1.2.2.2. *Multiclause sentences.* Multiclause sentences are much more common in narratives than are simple sentences. The most common are composed of one or more dependent clauses followed by an independent clause: *puqkaa-pín káaúq y-e-n war-e-n mó am-iyaa-m-íq* (cigarette-in put do-nt-3p take-nt-3p there give-con-3p-3f) 'Having put it in a cigarette he takes it and gives it to her' 12(5).

It is possible to have only one independent clause in an entire text. For example, Section 2, the short text on the trip to the island, has but one, the last.

A number of minimal clauses (i.e., single verbs) with varying affixes may succeed each other without any intervening words: . . . *karuqya-re-n puríka-n awir-e-n éqy-e-ín múq y-a-n* (throw-out-na-nt-3pvs die-pt. 3ds-3pvs pr-take along-nt-3pvs come up-nt-ge put do-3ds-3pvs) 'She spat it out and died. They took her and, coming, put her . . .' 7(2-3).

In some instances identical clauses are repeated, especially those whose predicates are filled by verbs in the continuative aspect. These indicate a longer duration of time than would be expressed by one. See 2(1): *ór-iyaa-q ór-iyaa-q* (go-con-1pvs go-con-1 pvs) 'I went and went. . . .'

A less common multiverb sentence is the dependent sentence composed only of dependent clauses. Such a sentence anticipates the one which follows. The final clause of the dependent sentence and the initial clause of the succeeding one each occur with the same verb stem but each is affixed differently: *war-e-n mó a-míq-ke-n puqtí-ra-n puqtí-a-ma-* . . . (take-nt-3pvs there pr-give-pt-3pvs puff-na-3ds-3pvs puff-na-3ds-when) 'Having taken it and given it to her, he puffs on it. When she has puffed on it, then . . .' 12(6-7).

A sentence may also occur with included clauses. One quite common occurrence of this is the direct quote. The actual quoted words may form independent clauses which, however, are not sentences in the narrative, but

---

[4] This may be considered a type of equational which also occurs with the verb 'be' following: *ínka-íq e-m-íq* (finish-vbl be-nt-3p-3f) 'That is all.' The analysis of equational sentences is not yet complete.

the objects of the verb *te* 'say'. Thus we have a clause within a clause, with the possibility of more clauses following before the sentence is completed: (A) *ááríntá wa-ram-úno t-e-m-íq* (girl stay-de-1f-emp say-nt-3p-3f) ' "I want to remain single," she said' 8(7). (B) *téqi máráq waá-nte-q-ú-no miqa tí-re-n wé a-paq . . . pon-íq ó e-m-íq* (I here-on stay-fu-1p-1f-emp thus say-na-nt-3pvs his pr-younger-brother pig-vbl dir be-nt-3p-3f) ' "I will stay here," thus he said and the younger brother . . . became a pig' 13(7).

This is, however, not always the case, as the following example illustrates: . . . *a-wiráq-ka-n; ti-pón k-a-q* (pr-take-along-pt-3ds-3pvs pr-body-part burn-3ds-1pvs) '. . . and took her; "I don't want . . ." ' 8(3).

1.2.2.3. *Idioms*. There are several examples of idioms in these texts. The translation is not the literal equivalent of the Agarabi words, but of the underlying meaning. The last example of the previous section is one illustration: . . . *ti-pón k-a-q* . . . (pr-body-part burn-3ds-3pvs) '. . . "I don't want (to do something)". . .' 8(3). *a-ráq óri-kán* (pr-intestines go-pt-3ds-3 pvs) 'She had diarrhoea . . .' 7(1). *íneíne anáá e-n ór-iyaa-m-íq* (thought only was-3pvs go-con-3p-3f) 'They went on having thoughts only of . . .' 5(2). The verb 'go' normally refers to motion, but following the verb 'be' in this case it indicates extensive or repeated action. *pára waá-re-n* . . . (just stay-na-nt-3pvs) 'She was well . . .' 7(1).

The meaning of the foregoing must be derived from context. If it had followed the mention of sickness it would have indicated that the person was still sick. In other contexts the phrase frequently means that the person is just staying around doing nothing, as in Section 5(3).

Another commonly used idiom is illustrated in Section 8. Bampeya is reported to say: . . . *wáántá waráá-nte-q-ú-no* . . . (man get-fu-1p-1f-emp) ' ". . . I will get a (young) man" . . .' 8(3). This saying is equivalent to 'I will get married.' It can be said in jest when there are no immediate plans for marriage or in earnest when it is definite. It is just a statement and does not refer to any particular ceremony.

When reference is made to the actual wedding day, it is called her 'skirt-putting-on-day'. The single girl's divided skirt is exchanged for a married woman's full skirt. The bridegroom is referred to as the "putting-on-man' or the 'putting-on-giving-man', though it is his relatives who actually tie the skirts on the bride and he need not be present.

There is also in this same story what might be termed a 'cultural idiom'. At the beginning we are told that the people of Afeipa took hold of a woman. Actually it is an unmarried girl that is so caught. Prior to this a suitable man has offered for her and her family has agreed to the match. This grabbing of the girl is a kind of public announcement of the impending marriage and she is measured for her skirts which will be made by some of the women. This takes place very close to the day planned for the marriage and usually means that there is now no time for the girl to refuse.

1.3. *Commentary on Morphology*

1.3.1. *Verbal affixes.* There are many verb constructions in these texts. Agarabi verbs not only express action, but, by means of suffixes they indicate the subject and something about the kind and/or time of the action. In addition all verb stems may be affixed to function as either independent or dependent verbs. These functions are determined by distinctive sets of subject suffixes that occur with them and by the possible presence of relational suffixes on dependent forms.

Independent verbs occur as predicate fillers in independent clauses. Dependent verbs occur in the predicates of dependent clauses.

The aspect suffixes illustrated in these texts are *-iyaa* continuative and *-ra* narrative. The tense suffixes are *-e* neutral which replaces the vowel of the preceding morpheme; *-nte* simple future; *-ke* simple past (which alters to *-ka* in dependent forms which have a different subject from the following clause); and *-kaa* perfect. The mood suffixes are *-ram* desiderative; *-nowan* immediate desiderative; |-p|[5] interrogative; *-no* emphatic; and *-po* assertive. Indicative mood is unmarked; the simple imperative mood occurs as the minimal form of the verb.

A. *Continuative.* *ór-(iyaa)-q* 'I (was) going' 2(1) (the context supplies the tense).

B. *Narrative (plus neutral).* *waá-(re)-n* 'She stayed and' 7(1).

C. *Future.* *waraá-(nte)-q-ú-no* 'I will get!' 8(3).

D. *Past.* *n-iyaá-(ke)-n* 'They were eating' 5(3).

E. *Perfect.* *u-(káá)-m-íq* 'He became' 13(1).

F. *Desiderative.* *wa-(ram)-ú-no* 'I want to stay!' 8(7).

G. *Immediate desiderative.* *waraá-(nowan)* 'I want to get now' 8(3).

H. *Interrogative.* *inte-(p)-oó-no* '. . . will you go?' 13(5).

I. *Emphatic.* *ér-e-q-ú-(no)* 'I came!' 8(3).

J. *Assertive.* *ínte-m-i-(pó)* 'It is surely finished!' 4(2).

Independent verbs are always marked for person-subject and, occasionally, for number. The plural affix, however, does not occur at all in these texts—the context is expected to supply this information. Independent verbs occur with final markers following the person-subject suffixes: *ér-e-q-ú* (come-nt-I-fm) 'I came' 3(1). *e-ø-ó-no* (be-nt-you-fm-emp) 'You are!' 9(3). *t-e-m-íq* (say-nt-she-fm) '. . . she said' 9(7).

Dependent verbs are not marked for person-subject in the same way as independent verbs and do not occur with final markers. They always occur with a preview subject marker, the same set of suffixes that occur with independent verbs; but, in this case, they indicate the subject of the following

---

[5] The symbol | | indicates that this suffix stands for all the forms of the suffix, which has several morphophonemic variants.

verb. If both the dependent and succeeding verb have the same subject only the preview subject is marked. However, when the subject of the first clause is different from that of the succeeding clause, there is some indication in the verb of the first clause to show both its subject and that of the following clause: *tí-ka-n wé a-noqé* . . . (say-pt-3ds-3pvs her pr-mother) 'She said (this) and her mother . . .' 7(2). *-ke,* past tense, becomes *-ka* to show that the third person subject of 'say' is a different person from the subject of the next verb. *waá-req e-kén* . . . *tiqpi* 'stay-na-nt be-nt-1ds-3pvs ship-a) 'I waited and . . . the ship . . .' 4(3). *-ké* is the first person subject marker of the first verb with a third person subject of the succeeding verb.

There are several different sets of suffixes to indicate the subject of the first verb. These vary according to the type of temporal or logical relationship between the clauses.

One set of affixes both indicates that the subjects of two verbs are different and also identifies the subject of the verbs, as follows. (This is the neutral tense of *te* 'say'.)

> 1p of dependent verb predicting 2p of next *t-e-ké-ø*
> 1p of dependent verb predicting 3p of next *t-e-ké-n*
> 2p of dependent verb predicting 1p of next *t-e-tí-q*
> 2p of dependent verb predicting 3p of next *t-e-tí-n*
> 3p of dependent verb predicting 1p of next *t-í-q*
> 3p of dependent verb predicting 2p of next *t-í-ø*
> 3p of dependent verb predicting other 3p of next *t-ín*

In the foregoing paradigm, the third person subject of the dependent verb is indicated by the change of vowel of neutral tense suffix, *-e* to í. In the same circumstances, past tense suffix *-ke* is changed to *-ka* as mentioned above.

1.3.2. *Nonverbal affixes.* Agarabi nouns, pronouns, and adjectives may occur unaffixed. When affixed, they may all occur with the same sets of affixes. Those that are illustrated by the accompanying texts include the locatives (of time and space); *-pín* 'in'; {-táq} 'on'; *-naún* 'inside'; *-páq* 'place at'; and {-kéq} 'from'. Others are likeness: {-ten} 'like'; verbalizer: *iq* 'it is', and number: *-kanan* 'two'.

A. *Locatives*

in: *toru waraa-(pín)* 'in the salt water' 2(1). *téqtim-(pín)* 'in our time' 5(4).

on: *táárareq-(táq)* 'on Saturday' 5(4). *mutoq-(káq)* 'on the island' 2(1).

inside: *maaq-(naún)* 'inside the house' 6(4).

place-at: *aapeiq-(páq)* 'at Afeipa' 8(1).

from: *kóróqkaaq-(kéq)* 'from Goroka' 4(8).

B. *Likeness. máqan-(ten)* 'like this' 6(5).

C. *Number. mai-(kánán)* 'these two' 6(3).

D. *Combinations. mínóq-(pím-páq-kéq)* 'from everywhere' 7(4). *mai-(páq-kéq)* 'from this place' 2(2).

1.3.3. *Affixes common to both verbs and nouns.* The only prefixes in Agarabi occur with both nouns and verbs. These are the personal referent prefixes: *ti-* first person singular or plural; and *a-,* nonfirst person singular or plural. The context must supply the distinctions for number and second or third persons. These prefixes occur obligatorily with some nouns and verbs and optionally with others.

When they occur with verbs they function as object, direct or indirect, depending on the meaning of the verb: *(a)-mí-ka-n* 'gave to her' 7(2). *(a)-wir-e-n* 'took her' 7(2). *(ti)-wir-e-n* 'took me' 3(1).

When the personal referents occur with nouns they indicate possession. They are obligatory to all body parts, kinship terms, and a few others such as sickness, fear, yawn, and shadow. They occur optionally with a few others (morphemes in parentheses are optional): *(ti)-naaqu* 'my/our grandfather' 6(1); *(a)-noqé* 'her mother' 7(2); *(a)-wiq* 'her name' 8(1); *(a)-rún* 'her diaphragm' 7(2); (used as an idiom which means 'to be sorry'); *(a)-maaq* 'his house' 7(3).

There is also one suffix which may occur with both nouns and verbs. This is the conditional: *-ma,* 'if/when', which occurs with dependent forms of the verb, with nouns in dependent clauses and with other classes of words as well. Verbal: *puqtí-ra-má e-n* (blow-na-when be-nt-3pvs) 'when she puffs on it . . .' 12(7). Nonverbal: *wé a-yopi-má wa-ín ano* (her pr-brothers-if stay-ge the) 'if her brothers are there . . .' 12(17); *námúró ano-má wákúq y-a-n* (enemy the-when pursue do-3ds-3pvs) 'when an enemy pursued them . . .' 6(3).

2. TRAVEL TO THE ISLAND: A

1. *Óreruqná yáwaaúroq mó manaa táárareq árúreqkún; manteq waaq tun-*
   As-I-was-going at-Rabaul there one week I-spent; Monday I-waited
   teq waaq tarinteq waaq ponteq pá waaq paraanteq áákúráq tíqpi éreín (é)
   Tuesday I-waited Wednesday I-waited Thursday just I-waited Friday morn-
   tiwiraq toru waraapin óriyaaq óriyaaq inuqpáq aìraanipín, mutoqkáq, mo
   ing ship coming (er) took-me over sea I-was-going going in-afternoon on-
   kaaíq yoriyaaq waaq maipaqkeq ínteq érequ.
   island, island, there it-put-me working I-remained from-there when-I was-finished I-came.

   1. As I was going I spent one week there at Rabaul; Monday I waited, Tuesday I waited, Wednesday I waited, Thursday I just waited; and Friday morning the ship coming took me and I was going and going over the sea. In the afternoon it put me there on an island and I remained working; when I was finished, I came from there.

3. TRAVEL TO THE ISLAND: B

1. *Óreruqná yáwaaúroq móráq manaa táárareq árúreqkún; manteq pá*
Ás-I-was-going at-Rabaul I-was-put-down one week where-I-spent;
waaq tunteq pá waaq tarinteq pá waáreq pontea pá waaq ekén paraanteq
Monday just I-waited Tuesday just I-waited Wednesday just I-waited-and
tíqpi ano (é)tiwiren toru waraapin óriyaan óriyaan mutoqkáq móráq
Thursday just I-waited waited on-Friday ship a (er) took-me over sea
yoriyaaq waáreq ínteq érehú.
was-going and-going on-island set-(me)-down working I-stayed I-finished
I-came.

2. *Inkaíq.*
That is all.

1. As I was going I was put down at Rabaul where I spent one week; Monday I just waited, Tuesday I just waited, Wednesday I just waited, and Thursday I just waited, on Friday a ship took me and was going and going over the sea, set [me] down on an island where I stayed working and [when] I finished, I came.

2. That is all.

4. TRAVEL FROM THE ISLAND

1. Intárekún máqtáqe ten.
When-I-finished European spoke.

2. *Ínka éi yei íntemíno; íntemipó.*
Finally your days are-finished; completely-over.

3. *Manteq pá waa, tunteq pá waa, tarinteq yamúq tíqpi ano é awirántemíno.*
Monday just wait, Tuesday just wait, Wednesday Wednesday ship a eh
Tikaq; waáreq ekén. Tarinteq yamúq tíqpi ano ó tiwiraq.
will-take-you. He-said-and; I-waited waited. On-Wednesday Wednesday
ship a oh took-me.

4. *Éreruqná yáwaaúroq méraq waáreq manaa táárareq árúreqkún;*
While-I-was-coming at-Rabaul I-was-set-down I-stayed-and one week
manteq pá waa, tunteq pá waa, tarinteq warutin ano ó tiwiraq.
spent; Monday just waited, Tuesday just waited, Wednesday plane a oh
took-me.

5. *Éreruqná kéwiaani e kúmánén pénitini e wáraq mairaqkeq éreqná*
As-I-came at-Kavieng eh it-landed fuel eh got then as-I-came at-Wewak
wewaake e kúmánen.
eh it-landed.

6. *Mairaqkeq manten éren mantampaq mai warutin ano mé kaaúq yen*
Then it-took-off came at-Madang this plane a this put-down *yen* spoke;
ten;

7. *Téqí yúniq e weraqneq yaaipáq órerúno.*

It-is-dark *yuniq* eh I-return to-Lae return.

8. *Tireqti maraq waatíq wááriti ekén kóróqkaaq ohintin kóróqkaaqkéq*
You-all here stay I-sent-telegram *eken* to-Goroka will-go-up from-*yorun awiranóo. Tíkan kóróqkaaqkéq árawein órún tiwiraq kóróqkaaq* Goroka down get-you. He-said from-Goroka they-came-down *órún* got-us *óqeqú.*
to-Goroka we-went-up.

9. *Ún waaq kaan tááraréq intarekén mairaq kaari ano tiwiren kainantum-* There I-stayed two week completed then car a got-me at-Kainantu *paq moruq yaq érequ.*
put-me-down I came.

10. *Ínkaíq.*
That-is-all.

1. When I finished, the European spoke. 2. 'Finally your days are finished; completely over!' 3. 'Monday just wait, Tuesday just wait, Wednesday a ship will take you!' he said, and I waited. On Wednesday a ship took me. 4. While I was coming, I was set down at Rabaul where I stayed and spent one week; Monday [I] just waited, Tuesday [I] just waited, Wednesday a plane took me. 5. As I came it landed at Kaveing and got fuel; then as I came it landed at Wewak. 6. Then it took off, came and this plane put down at Madang and [the pilot] spoke; 7. 'It is dark, and I am returning to Lae.' 8. 'You all stay here, I have sent a telegram, which will go up to Goroka [so that they will come] down from Goroka and get you,' he said, and they came down from Goroka and got us and we went up to Goroka. 9. I stayed up there and completed two weeks; then a car got me and put me down at Kainantu, and I came. 10. That is all.

5. No Rest-days

1. *Péepaq tinaaqu tiraaqó íqyaa oyaa en tiren awikiyaamíq.*
Long-ago our-grandfathers our-grandmothers not holiday it-is say rest.

2. *Pára yoran íneíne anáá en óriyaamíq.*
Just work have-thoughts only it-is they-went-on.

3. *Óriyaaqín ínáámuníq emá iyámpon káaíkamáen mairaq yunáán táaqen* Going-on child if-there-were child was-born then food they-prepared *niyaáken. Oyaa en tíren pá waamíq.*
ate. Holiday it-is they-said-and just stayed-around.

4. *Taréqaa téqtimpín kamani éren ten, táárarétáq yoqan aaqpiq e taanteq* Now in-our-time government came spoken, on-Saturday work half eh *awikaanóo. Tíkaq, taréqaa téqtimpín maqaa tíkaq téqti tiwikiyááqú.*
on-Sunday rest. Said, now in-our-time thus it-said-and-we resting.

5. *Péepáq tinaaqu tiraaqó mai káyoano, íyaa awikanán íniyaamíq.*
Before our-grandfathers our-grandmothers that group, not rest thinking.

6. *Pára yoran íneíne anáá en óriyaamíq.*
Just work have-thoughts only it-is they-went-on.

7. *Arúwin íneíne anáá en óriyaamíq.*
Fight have-thoughts only it-is they-went-on.
8. *Taréqaa téqtimpín taanteq tiwikeqiyaaqú.*
Now in-our-time on-Sunday we-rest.
9. *Inkaíq.*
That-is-all.

1. Long ago our grandfathers and our grandmothers did not say, 'It is a holiday,' and rest. 2. They just went on having thoughts only of work. 3. Going on, if there were a child, when the child was born then they prepared food and ate. 'It is a holiday,' they said, and just stayed around. 4. Now in our time, the government came and has spoken, 'On Saturday work half [day], on Sunday rest!' it said; now, in our time, it said thus and we are resting. 5. Before our grandfathers and our grandmothers, that group, were not thinking of rest. 6. They just went on having thoughts only of work. 7. They went on having thoughts only of fighting. 8. Now, in our time, on Sunday we rest. 9. That is all.

6. POSSESSIONS

1. *Péepáq tinaaqu tiraaqompín íqyaa oóna waamíq.*
Long-ago our-grandfather our-grandmothers-in no possessions there-were.
2. *Manaa waqyó wán matámen waamíq.*
One bark there-was grease there-was.
3. *Úwé ítana maiqaa yánááq anáá waaqíkan námúró anomá wákúqyan*
Arrows bows that-kind thing only there-were enemy an they-were-pur-
maikánán oóná anáá ámáren. Uqpimpaq káráámpín tíqtoq maaq úwáma-
sued these-two possessions only they-took. Bush-in undergrowth-in little
qáken maipin o wáriyaámiq.
house they-made in-those oh sleeping.
4. *Maqai iyááqín taréqaa kamani éríqkan mínoq pereqti taataq toqpe*
Like-this they-were now government has-come all plates spoons machetes
wítúkaa taaraq taantún mai yánáátíntá aman. Maaqnaún káainwákan mai
knives forks axes this kind-of-thing brought. House-in they-stored-them
ano oónáíq úkan waamíq.
this some possessions become there-are.
5. *Pée-áq íqyaa máqanten oóna waamíq.*
Before no this-kind goods there-were.
6. *Taréqaa kamani érein me tiqtuqaaq káaíkanwákan maipinteq mínoq*
Now government came here stores established in-them all thing taken stored
yánááq aman káainwákan mai ano oónáiq úkan waaíq.
these some possessions become have.
7. *Inkaíq.*
That-is-all.

1. Long ago in our grandparents' time, there were no possessions. 2. There was one bark and there was grease. 3. There were bows and arrows, only that kind of thing; when they were pursued by an enemy they took up these two possessions only. They made a little house in the undergrowth, in the bush and were sleeping in those. 4. They were like this [but] now the government has come and brought all plates, spoons, machetes, knives, forks, and axes, this kind of thing. They stored them in houses and these things have become possessions. 5. Before there were no goods of this kind. 6. Now since the government came and established stores here, it has taken everything and stored in them. These things have become possessions.

7. That is all.

7. SICKNESS

1. *Íqyamúq pára waáren ínúrán arágórikan tíq iyaaqúno tíren.*
Two-days just well at-night had-diarrhoea I sick, she-said.

2. *Tíkan wé anoqé arúnmáqen káákan óreín weweti neqne móo tin érein,*
She-spoke her mother was-sorry at-dawn she-went Bevesi others *moo*
e. Awire yoqtaampaq moruqyetíq waáno, tíkan éreín e awiren arawein yoq-
told come eh. Take-her doctor-at put-her we-may-stay, she-said they-came
taampaq moruqyan waratin amíkan oó ákónááín waratín wíqankaruqyáren
eh took-her going-down doctor-at they-put-her medicine they-gave-her her-
puríkan.
mouth was-tight medicine throw-out she-died.

3. *Awirenéqyeín múqyan wé amaaq wákan weqwaaqtín amaaq kárápan-*
They-brought-her put-her her house she-stayed Bepbati's house was-
taáqín youán karuqyáren maipin e awíqaq kaaekén wákan
partitioned took-down threw-out there eh brought-her I-put-her stay.

4. *Éena námún úwáqyen maipin e awíqan kaaín wákan. Mínóqpímpáqkéq*
Another house they-built this eh brought-her put-her she-stayed. Where
maipin e wán arún yanaaqwaren inúran waamíq.
in-there eh while she-stayed wail there-is-night they-remained.

1. Two days ago she was well, and at night she had diarrhoea; 'I am sick,' said. 2. She spoke and her mother was sorry; at dawn she went and told Bevesi and others to come. 'Take her and put her at the doctor's so we may stay,' she said, and they came and took her; going down they put her at the doctor's; they gave her medicine [but] her mouth was tight and she spat out the medicine and died. 3. They brought her, put her, and she stayed in her house; Bepbati's house was partitioned and they took them down and threw them out and they brought her and I put her there to stay. 4. They built another house, brought her and put her in it and she stayed. While she stayed in there from everywhere they remained the night grieving.

[The girl concerned was about eight years old and died very suddenly. She was brought back from the aid post and put into her uncle's house, which being small, could not hold all the folks who came to mourn. This was a fairly large

number since she was young and her death unexpected. There would not have
been as many for an old woman who was expected to die. The partitions were
removed from the house so more people could get in and then a larger temporary
structure was put up that would accommodate more. She was put there and the
mourning went on for about three days and then she was buried. The mourning
period was longer in the days before European government.]

8. BAMPEYA

1. Aapeiqpaq anaati paqkemíq, mai áárintá awiq waampeyaa.
    At-Afeipa woman they-took-hold, this girl name Bampeya.
2. Paqkaáken anaati óno tíren; yunáán upiyaante óriyaáreqíkaq ááríntá
    They-held-her married-woman you-are said; food to-dig-out they-were-
ano temíq.
going girl the spoke.
3. Peyan wáántá tipónkeín, auyén wáántá waraánteqúno. Tíren me ipaaqen
    Old man I-don't-want, young man I-will-get. She-said-and here left
kaínantumpáq tíqtúaaq woin waaiqpáq e wákááqin. Wé ayopi éreín e awiraq-
in-Kainantu store owner place eh slept. Her brother came eh took-her
kan tipónkaq, téqi mai wáántá waraánowan éreqúno. Tíkan ipaaqen óremíq.
I-don't-want-to, I this man I-want-to-get came. She-said he-gave-up went.
4. Ó wakáaren wáántá káyo ó awirenérein éreqúno. Tíkan ipaaqen óremíq.
    Oh he-spent-night men group oh brought here held-court European spoke.
5. Peyan wáántá ipaaqonóo, auyén wáántá ipaaqonoo, éena wáántá wa-
    Old man forget, young man forget, another man get. He-said yes, she-
raanóo. Tíkan éeyo, tíren óren.
said went.
6. Óreín pára waamíq.
    She-went just she-stayed.
7. Áárintá waramúno temíq.
    Single I-want-to-remain she-said.

1. At Afeipa they took hold of a woman, this girl's name [is] Bampeya.
2. They held her and said, 'You are a married woman!' While they were going
to dig out food, the girl spoke. 3. 'I don't want an old man; I will get a young
man!' she said and left here and slept in Kainantu at the store-man's place. Her
brother came and took her; 'I don't want to, I came because I want to get this
man!' she said, so he gave up and went. 4. He spent the night and brought a
group of men and held court here. The European spoke. 5. 'Forget the old man;
forget the young man; get another man!' he said, and she agreed and went.
6. She went and she just stayed. 7. 'I want to remain single,' she said.
   [In theory a girl is free to choose her husband; but, in practice, she is expected
to marry the one arranged by her family. The man who offered for Bampeya
was approved by her family but was not the one who pleased her. Most girls are

persuaded to accept their family's arrangements, but occasionally the girl rebels and runs away or refuses to associate with the chosen bridegroom. This can cause a lot of trouble for her family, especially if she is to be given in exchange for a bride for her brother, as sometimes happens. This was not so in this case, so she pressed her preference until her family took the matter to the patrol officer who tried to find a middle ground by telling them that she should marry someone else altogether. Actually, she eventually married the man she had chosen.]

9. A SHORT CONVERSATION

1. Purin atiqkááq eompó. Aíne waraanóo. Tekén waremíq.
   Die shortly you-are. Soon take-it. I-said she-took-it.
2. Téhi oén waaqná, tatóreq waraántequno.
   I young still, later I-will-take-it.
3. Éqi purin atiqkááq eóno. Éqi waraanóo. Tequ.
   You die shortly are. You take-it. I-said.

1. 'You are shortly to die! Take it soon,' I said and she took it. 2. 'I am still young, I will take it later.' 3. 'You are shortly to die. You take it!' I said.

[This conversation took place between a young married woman and her elderly mother. Several people were planning to be baptized and the speaker was urging her mother to get baptized, usually spoken of as 'getting water', because she was old and might die soon. The younger woman felt she could wait until later since she was still young. In spite of the implications here, it is not just the older folk who get baptized.]

10. FEAR OF SORCERY

1. Wáántá púmaaraa mínóq áno kaako waren óríwin unáántumpáq anaati
   Men youths all some cargo carrying went at-Unantu women group only
káyo anáá íyúken. Ápáánán péqyen wákan. Téqi ériyaaq taréqaa óneqkún
gathered. Sorcery they-feared they-stayed. I coming now saw that-like-this
maqanten ápáánán péqyen pára waruráq íyúken waamíq.
sorcery they-fear just village-in gathered wait.
2. Ínkaíq.
   That-is-all.

1. All the men and youths went carrying cargo, only the group of women gathered at Unantu. They stayed [together] because they feared sorcery. I was coming now and saw that like this they just wait gathered in the village because they fear sorcery. 2. That is all.

[Fear of sorcery is quite common. In this case all the men had left the village, which is quite unusual; there are ordinarily a few around. The women were afraid that there might be men hiding in the bush at the outskirts of the village waiting to cast spells on them. So they decided to stay together in the village to see if there were any other men lurking about. When it was clear that it was safe, the women would be free to go to the garden.]

11. FALSE ALARM

1. Wáántá púmaaraa kaaqtiráq aapeiqpáq iuqtiyaan waáren mínoq wáántá
   Men youths cards at-Afeipa playing were all men youths just stayed-
púmaaraa pára wákan; wéyáákaq maamaake éqiyaan aíq yánááq áátáqkéq
   there; by-himself Mamake was-coming-up sickness thing on-road up-there
yún waren arawein; téqi áátáqkéq aú wareq érerumpó. É tiwire múq yaq
   took he-went-down; I on-road evil got I-came. Here take-me up-there put-
téqi intááno tíkan
   me I about-to-die he-said.
2. Awiren múq yan wákan ápáán tíreminó tíren ápááq námán árúren
   They-took-him up-there put-him he-stayed spell cast-on-us they-said
onáqkan íqyaa ápáán áremíq.
   sorcery tested if hurt not spell cast-on-him.
3. Pára paaén yánááq ano áremíq.
   Just little thing some hurt-him.
4. Árúran wáken waamíq.
   Hurt-him rest stay.
5. Ínkaíq.
   That-is-all.

1. The men and youths were at Afeipa playing cards, all the men and youths just stayed there; Mamake was coming up by himself when sickness took [him] up there on the road and he went down; 'I got evil on the road as I came! Here, take me put me up there; I am about to die!' he said. 2. They took him, put him up there, and he stayed. 'A spell has been cast on us!' they said and tested the sorcery [but] a spell was not cast on him. 3. It was just a little thing that hurt him. 4. It hurt him and he is lying down. 5. That is all.

[Every sudden, unexpected sickness or accident must be explained. If there is no visible cause for it, sorcery administered by an enemy is the immediate assumption. Most people work and travel in groups for mutual protection; since Mamake was alone, he was vulnerable. Therefore, when he felt sick on his way home his reaction was that someone had cast a spell on him. Every attack of sorcery poses a threat to the whole group so the other men felt themselves also affected by the spell cast on Mamake. They tested to see if it was really sorcery by looking for puncture marks in the man's skin. They believe that sorcery may enter a person's system via nails, bamboo slivers, or something similar which are pushed into the skin.]

12. LOVE POTION

1. Éenapáqma áárintá wááreqín púmaaraa ano ó oqáren.
   From-another-place girl there-is youth some there looks.
2. O onáma awúruq áárintáma wááreqíqkan óweren ó oqáren éremíq.
   There if-he-sees excellent girl she-is he-returns there looks comes.

3. *Éreín atapé me úwáreqiyaamíq.*
Coming love-potion here he-makes.

4. *Atapéiq úáken puqkaapín káaiyaamíq.*
Love-potion having-made cigarette-in he-puts-it.

5. *Puqkaapín káaúqyen waren mó amiyaamíq.*
Cigarette-in having-put-it he-takes-it there gives-it-to-her.

6. *Waren mó-amíqken puqtíran.*
Having-taken-it there give-it-to-her he-puffs-it.

7. *Puqtíramáen mai íráran o wáreqiyaamíq áárintánámáq.*
She-puffs-it then desire-to-marry there he-sleeps girl-with.

8. *Ó wáqkaáren maqyaaq óren.*
There slept several-times he-goes.

9. *Maqyaaq óremáen káánuqmánaaútápi káámikáámitápi ma ó wáren*
Several-times he-has-gone three four-times this there take you I-will-
éqín waráánteqúno mó teq iyaamíq.
marry there he-says it-is.

10. *Mó tíkan ínomá tentin íno en waráánteqúno ten, mó akonaain wááyáá*
There said-this no she-says no you I-will-marry he- says, there this-firm
teq iyaamíq.
talk he-says it-is.

11. *Wááyááríkamái ma en atapé ano araqpímpáq ó peran wéni íneíne*
He-has-said that there love-potion some her-bowels there goes-into
iyaamíq.
his-way she-thinks it-is.

12. *Wéni íneíneíkamá en ó wáren éren iyáán iyáán iyáámá éken éenapáq-*
His-way when-she-thinks then there he-sleeps coming again again it-is
kéq ó waren éreqiyaamíq, éena warupáqkeq.
done from-another-place there he-takes he-comes, another village.

13. *Éena warupáqkéq ó waren me yúqyáren ínkaipó tiyaáken me íreqi-*
From-another village there he-takes here puts-her all-right he-says here
yaamíq.
they-get-married.

14. *Mé ímaken mai íman wáántá ameqiyaamiq.*
Here married then put-on man they-give-her.

15. *Mai iráran iyááqen wáántá wáántá amín mai amáqken yenwaaqiyaamíq.*
This put-on it-is man man they-give-her there he-takes-her they-stay.

16. *Yenwaáken iyámpomá káaen óriyaamá en kókon íyámpomá mó káauq-*
Having-stayed children bearing she-keeps do many children there she-
yen máiráq pon, káákan pon, awiqyan máqen. Aaqtóte tíren árúaqyan
has-borne then pig, big pig, they-get-and take-it. It-is-a-settlement they-say
óriyaamíq.
they-have-killed-it they-go.

17. É weren wé ayopi, wé anoqé nanóo tiran árúaqyan órin wé ayopimá
Eh they-return her brothers, her mother you-eat say kill-it gone her
waaín ano neqiyaamíq.
brothers are-there some they-eat.

18. Ínkaq manaamáen pon, káákan pon, árúran mairaq moaniq tiyaamíq-
Finally if-there-is-one pig, big pig, they-kill then money hand two sticks
kán tirantamíqkán yanka káaeqiyaamíq.
they-put-down.

19. Ínkaq manaamáen tiyaamíqkán tirantan yaamanááqpáq maíqaa káaeq-
At-the-end if-there-is-one hand two five that-much he-puts.
iyaamíq.

20. Maqan túran wareqiyaamíq.
This way they-get.

21. Mái ááríntá anaati anaatiqmáin aanáiq.
This girl women when-they-marry story.

1. If there is a girl from another place the youth looks there. 2. If he sees there that she is an excellent girl he returns looks there and comes. 3. Coming he makes a love potion here. 4. Having made the love potion, he puts it in a cigarette. 5. Having put it in a cigarette he takes it and gives it to her there. 6. Having taken it and given it to her, he puffs on it. 7. When she puffs on it then he sleeps there with the girl, desiring to marry. 8. Having slept there, he goes several times. 9. When he has gone several times and has slept there three or four times he says, 'I will marry you!' 10. Having said this, if she says, 'No!' he says 'No! I will marry you!' this firm talk he says. 11. When he has said that, the love potion goes into her bowels and she thinks his way. 12. When she has thought his way, he sleeps, coming again and again from another place he takes [her] and comes, from another village. 13. He takes [her] from another village and puts her here; 'All right,' he says and they get married. 14. When married, they give her to the bridegroom. 15. This bridegroom, when they give her to the man, he takes her and they stay. 16. Having stayed, if she keeps bearing children, when she has borne many children then they get a pig, a big pig, and [others] take it. They say, 'It is a settlement,' and, after they have killed it, they go. 17. They return and say to her brothers and her mother, 'You may eat.' Having gone to kill it, if her brothers are there, they eat. 18. Finally, if there is one, they kill a pig, a big pig, then they put down money, twenty sticks. 19. At the end, if there is one like this he puts fifteen, that much. 20. They get [it] this way. 21. This is the story of girl and women when they marry.

[When a young man finds a girl who suits his fancy, he goes to her village to begin courting. He shreds some combination of leaves or plants with tobacco and makes it into a cigarette which he then presents to the girl. If she accepts it and smokes it she is agreeing to accept his courtship and the potion is supposed to guarantee that she will also desire him.

When this result has been obtained a marriage is arranged. The girl is given her married woman's skirts in her village and is escorted to her inlaws' home.

Later, when a child is born, the wife or her father-in-law provides a pig or some money to be given to her family. In return her family gets together trade goods or money of equivalent value to give to her.]

13. TWO BROTHERS

1. Péepáq we anoqe wé apoqé puqwíkan wé awaaqé akepo ukáámíq.
Long-ago their mother their father died their elder-brother idle became.

2. Wé apáq waáremíq.
Their younger-brother remained.

3. Waárená wékánán temíq.
They-stayed two spoke.

4. Iyeq tiwiníntenapíno. Tírenan íneíne emíq.
Who will-nurture-us. They-said thought did.

5. Éqi inteq intepoóno tíkan, wé apaq ano temíq.
You wherever go he-said, his younger-brother that spoke.

6. Téqi éena warupáq óroónteqúno. Éqi inteq intepóno tíkan, wé awaaqé
I another place will-go. You where go he-said, his elder-brother spoke.
temíq.

7. Téqi máráq waánteqúno. Míqa tíren wé apaq ano éena wáráráq óren
Here I will-stay. This he-said his younger-brother the another place
poníq ó emíq.
went pig there became.

8. Wé awaaqé ano kotíq emíq.
His elder-brother the bean-tuber became.

9. Úkááreqíkan wé awaaqé ano óreín tipaq interátaq ó waanapíno míqa
Having-become-this his elder-brother the went my-younger-brother
tíren yoten óriyaan ó noqwíkan poníq úwen wé awaaqen úntáremíq.
where there living this he-said search went there when-he-came pig being
his elder-brother bit.

10. Úntáqyen máiráq wákaáren áákúráq yunáán únápemíq.
He-bit-him then slept in-morning food he-dug-out.

11. Pon áremíq.
Pig he-killed.

12. Árúraq yúqyen yanon tááqyen káwé íyóqúren wé awaaqén táaman amín
Having-killed-it put-it earth-oven he-prepared cooking-pot-in roasted
náren meéren wéi warupáq éremíq.
his elder-brother what-was-prepared gave ate returned his home did.

13. Éreín kotíq é emíq.
He-came bean-tuber here is.

1. Long ago their mother and father died and the elder brother became idle. 2. The younger brother remained [as he was]. 3. As they stayed they both spoke. 4. 'Who will nurture us?' they said to themselves. 5. 'Wherever will you

go?' he said and the younger brother spoke. 6. 'I will go to another place. Where will you go?' he said, and his elder brother spoke. 7. 'I will stay here,' this he said and the younger brother went to another place and became a pig. 8. The elder brother became a bean tuber. Having become this the elder brother went; 'Where is my younger brother living?' he said this and went to search; when he got there, being a pig, he [the younger brother] bit his elder brother. 10. He bit him, then slept, and in the morning he dug out food. 11. He killed a pig. 12. Having killed it and put it, he prepared an earth oven, roasted in a cooking pot, and gave what was prepared to his elder brother; he [the elder brother] ate and returned to his home. 13. He came and the bean tuber is here.

[This myth also has a cultural significance. The bean tuber and pig are two important items in the lives of these people, pigs figuring in sacrifices and an annual feast being held when the tuber is harvested. This tale accounts for their origin and a moral is also drawn from it. If you are lazy you will only be a small person and have a small family as the bean tuber is small. If you are industrious you will be important and have a large family as the pig is a large and important animal.]

XXIII. Gadsup Texts

Compiled by HOWARD McKAUGHAN

1. INTRODUCTION

Many of the following texts were written by John Orami, a Gadsup school teacher from the village of Aiyura. John was probably the only Gadsup teacher in the territory at that time (1962). All of the texts dealing with Gadsup customs are both written and translated by John. The compiler checked them, and put them into the orthography generally used in the descriptions. However, if John did not make distinctions, the compiler did not try to do so.

Others of the texts were taped (Sections 2, 8, 12-14), and then John helped in the transcription by dictating from the tapes phrase by phrase. John did not distinguish between the mid and low central vowels, so these are written in his texts with *a*. Texts transcribed from the tapes use *a* and *aa* as in the other languages (except Awa). Prosodic features have not been indicated, but may be possible to add at a future date for those texts on tapes.

Stories 7 and 8 are the same as are 12 and 13. They have been included for comparison of forms. All of the texts should give opportunity to analyze Gadsup further. The texts used by Jean Goddard in her paper are also useful to compare Agarabi and Gadsup. Perhaps some observations on the Gadsup sentence and paragraph will be made by students using these materials.

The format followed for the other languages is retained here. The tentative nature of word and sentence divisions must be kept in mind, although in the texts John wrote, we have a native reaction to these matters.

The content of some of the stories is similar to those from other areas. Some of the customs described are no longer fully practiced by the Gadsup

469

living closer to the subdistrict center of Kainantu. We look to the ethnographers for any organized comments on beliefs and customs. The Gadsup, no less than the other groups, tell of contact with the spirit world and the success of the younger brother in his adventures. If for nothing else, these texts should interest the reader in the oral tradition of the Gadsup.

2. TWO BROTHER STORY

1. Mana maniq kaaruntaabaa banim tsikami mani tsirare.
This story two-brothers were told story tell.

2. Pe kaaruntaabaa baayomi.
Before two-brothers they-lived.

3. Baayomi benapaq uppaq obemi nunoaarure banimi.
They-lived his-younger-brother bush stayed bird-shot is.

4. Manaayokun miniqukimpaq bemi manare banimi obaaekem yeraaem.
An-old-one this-forest stayed she-took-it is come-back he-came.

5. Yebaaikem yaayekankaq oraapitanem.
He-went-back tree-fruit he-watched.

6. Orebanem miniinimano mandem tsemi; maa kebekebe manaam bami
Go-there that-woman used-to-get she-said; here arrow only is bird
naamaaqnaama iyembano.
not-is.

7. Tsirebanemi omanaarem yeraaem.
She-would-say he-would-go come-back.

8. Yebaaekem enaqyaa oraapitánimi.
Went-back again-once-more watch-it.

9. Aaruranimikaaq manaremi maa namaaqnamaa manaa iyembami maa
He-shot-killed she-took-it here bird one not-is here arrow one is she-
kebekebe manaa bano tsiremi.
said.

10. Maa kebekebe manaambami naamaaqnamaa iyembano tsiremi.
Here arrow one-is bird not-is she-said.

11. Aamaamipo tsiremi.
That's-all-right he-said.

12. Paako amanaarem yeraemi.
Arrow go-get come-back.

13. Aapo manaa nurami orapitanimi.
All-right one day he-was-watching.

14. Numi aarumam aaqnuranimi oraaunimi miniaayoku mandemi.
Bird killed throw went-there this-old-one took-it.

15. Aaruekem aaqnuranimi oraaunimi.
He-shot thrown went-there.

16. Mini inimandemi tsemi maaq kebekebemanaam bami maa namaaq-
This woman-there said here arrow-only is here bird only not is she-said.

namaa manaa iye bano tsenimi.

17. *Aamamipo mandaa tsiremi.*
    All-right give-it he-said.
18. *Aamankaakaaq tsenamaq barantepono aayokunininano tsenimi.*
    Straight-right with-me spend-the-night old-woman said.
19. *Eyo tsiremi.*
    Yes he-said.
20. *Aapo banimi aainkaakiqonimi yunaam yunkaaranimi naamandemi.*
    All-right he-stayed evening food she-cooked he-ate.
21. *Aapo manam yubaasikaa kaamunabaa miniuq manam aamenim*
    Then she-took mat bark-of-tree those took give-it-to-him he-made-bed
    ubiqdem baremone.
    he-slept.
22. *Barara ebanimi tsaamemi temi nurampaqmaa yerenaa iqmaa desiyaa*
    Sleep ready-to-go she-told-him said in-the-night it-comes song dance
    iyebaaq ukukaano tsiremi tsaamemoni.
    don't get-up she-said she-told-him.
23. *Aapo tiremi minibaainta baremoni.*
    OK he-said this-man went-to-sleep.
24. *Dukanimi maampaq yereni iqdesemi ukukaran onimi iyebaaq uku-*
    When-he-slept outside arrived singing wake-up did-it don't get-up she-
    kaano tsirem aayokuninimano taamemoni.
    said old-woman said-to-him.
25. *Tsaamenimi eyo tsiremi.*
    She-told-him yes he-said.
26. *Yebaaekem baremone.*
    Go-back sleep.
27. *Dukaakem onimi baanuram aayokunininano yoaabikem nompaq ku-*
    Slept did-it morning old-woman took-him water-place went-down.
    memoni.
28. *Kundaaem neba noyam kaantani aakkeqyarem buamemoni.*
    Went-down Neva stick two cut-down sharpen-it-for-him.
29. *Buamemi tsemi mananoyem mare binte iyebaa kaaruqdaano tsiremi*
    She-sharpen-it she-said this stick take-go don't drop-it she-said she-
    tsaamem.
    told-him.
30. *Tsamemi eyo tsirem; marem bemoni.*
    She-said yes he-said; took go.
31. *Bonimi oraaem yunaankimmaro daapeqdem yaaq kaaotiran aaman-*
    He-went he-arrived in-a-garden stick-in-ground sugar-cane took-off-
    daakaaq uremoni.
    leaves native-ladder went-up.
32. *Undaaemi mini noyam kanda yeredaapeqdem uremi.*

Climb this stick two put-there-stuck-in climbed-on-up.

33. Undaaemi marom kaaotaakem yobaaeqmam impappaq aaunanimi
After-he-climbed-up there take-off leaves turned-down he-looked two-
kaarakintakanda ukukakaayomi yonemoni.
girls were-standing saw-them.

34. Yonaremi aamoyaakendemi umbaaekem kumemoni.
He-saw-and he-was-pleased he-turned came-down.

35. Kumonimi miniqaakintakanda kuqunam yiyaakoreni baami yeyibikem
He-came-down-and those-two-girls lime-gourd-bag sling-from-head
aamoyaakendemi bemoni.
stayed he-took-them pleased he-went.

36. Maakupaq oraaunimi benaabaa aaunaremi tsentipako napaateq mana
Village went-there his-brother saw my-brother where this thing take-it
aaneqne marepono tsentimi.
he-said.

37. Tsentui tsiqebaqi aapakaakeqi mareqyequ tsenimi.
My-body pain find-them bring-them he-said.

38. Manaa tsimeno tsentimi.
One give-me he-said.

39. Iye aamentequmpe temoni benapaqmano.
No I-will-give-you he-said his-younger-brother.

40. Yotibikanaaq mareonapaqbeq maraano tsentimi.
Show-me place-you-get-it take-it he-said.

41. Enaapuyaaq aapaakareq maraano tsiremi benapaaqmano benabaanami
Yourself find-it take-it he-said his-younger-brother his-older-brother
tsemoni.
he-told-him.

42. Tsenimi eyo tsiremi.
He-said-it yes he-said.

43. Dukaakemi baanurami ukukaaemi aakkanaanaa aakkaaram yemoni.
He-slept morning get-up track followed he-came.

44. Yaakem aanon uppaq yeraaem aaunanim aayokuninim banimi.
He-came big forest arrived he-saw old-woman stayed.

45. Yeraaem tsentipaqmaa aameonaa aaneqne make tsimeno.
Arrived my-younger-brother you-gave-him something now you-give-me.

46. Tsentimi eyo uqbinebanakaq aameno tsemi aayokunininano.
She-said yes slowly I-give-you said old-woman.

47. Tsentimi minibaaintamano tsemi makeukam tsimeno tsentipaqma
She-said that-man said just-now give-me my-brother you-gave-him
aameona aneqne.
something.

48. Tentimi aayokunininano tsemi dukaakeq kaakanaaq mareq bono tsen-
He-said the-old-woman said you-sleep tomorrow take go she-said.
timi.

49. *Kaakanaakaraaune make tsimenobare tsentimi.*
   Tomorrow-not now give-it-to-me he-said.
50. *Minibe tsaaqdakaakeq banaakaqi aameno tsemi.*
   That-one after-later-slowly stay give-to-you she-said.
51. *Tsiremi minibaaintabani tsentimi benamaaq baremi.*
   She-said that-man said his-house slept.
52. *Bararanebaami tsiamemi maappaqma yeraena tsiyaai ikkapi aayapi*
   When-he-was-ready-to-sleep she-told-him outside arrived talk song
   tsentiyaai iyebaaq ukkukaano indebaaq ipaq baraano tsiremi tsiaamemoni.
   dancing talk they-say don't-you get-up listen let-sleep she-said she-told-him.
53. *Tsiamenimi eyo tsiremi baremi.*
   Told-him yes he-said went-to-sleep.
54. *Dukem indebanimi nurampaq yereni maampaq aaseni iqdeni omi.*
   He-slept he-heard in-the-night arrived outside talk sing did-it.
55. *Ukkukem karoyaamanaa onimi.*
   He-got-up disturbance they-did.
56. *Aayokuminimano tsemi baani emi tsiaamiqdukequmpe tsentimi.*
   Old-woman said before you I-told-you she said.
57. *Eyo tsirem yebaaikem barem.*
   Yes he-said went-back sleep.
56. *Dukkaakem onimi.*
   Slept he-did.
59. *Baanuram ukkukaaemi tsemi mareyinaq nompaq kumono tsentimi.*
   In-the-morning he-got-up she-said come-we-go water-place go-down
   she-said.
60. *Tsemi nandeq tsimintepono makaqma tsentipaqma aameona aaneqnebe*
   He-said when you-give-me time my-brother you-gave-him thing he-said.
   tsentimi.
61. *Tsaaqdakaaqkeqi aamenteumpe tsiremi.*
   Gently give-it-you she-said.
62. *Yoabikem nompaqi kumemoni.*
   Bring-him water-place went-down.
63. *Kumonimi kumbanimi kaantaan neba noyem aakkeqyarem kutiq aaru-*
   Went-down go-down-and-stay two Neva stick cut-them roughly hit
   remi buamemoni.
   sharpen.
64. *Buamemi tsemi iyebaaq karuqdaano tsaaqdaakaakebaaq mare bono*
   Sharpened she-said don't drop gently take go she-said.
   tsentimi.
65. *Mana noyanuq karaauni.*
   This sticks no-good.
66. *Tsentipaqma aameonaa aaneqne tsemenobare tsentimi.*

My-brother you-gave-him something give-it-to-me he-said.
67. *Mini mare bono mini aamequmpe tsiremi tsaamenimi.*
This take go this I-give she-said she-told-him.
68. *Eyo tsirem marem bemoni.*
Yes he-said took went.
69. *Bonimi maro mini noyankakanda yaaqaandakim daapeqdemi yaaq*
Went did this stick-two under-sugar-cane he-stuck sugar-cane take-off-
kaautiram aamandaakaq uremoni.
leaves ladder climb-up.
70. *Uronimmi umbem kaaotebaanimi.*
Climbed-up stay-up take-off-leaves.
71. *Kaaotembaakemi yobaaeqmaam impaappaa aaonanimi kaan aakinta-*
Take-off-leaves turned down look two girls up-on-nose hole there-is
kanda aasippem boniqnaakaam baanimi yonaaremi.
he-saw.
72. *Tsaaqdaakaakem aayokuqkiqurem tsimiraani tsenaaqi obeqi maandaaiq*
Afterward made-properly-good give-me you-said I-went-bad silly did-
oqnokekunaai maqnukami tsimenamino tsiremi.
foolishness this-kind you-gave-me he-said.
73. *Yeyibikem makupaq bemoni maroremi beyapaq tsiamemi onebaa eyinda*
Took-them village went put-them his-brother told-him see yours beauti-
aayokukiqukam manaa tsimebaa mandaaqukami tsentinda kinke maraano
ful one give-me ugly bad mine and-take he-said.
tsenimi.
74. *Miqnakam mararani obe miqno nokeonamino tsirem benapaqmano*
That-kind want-to-take went do-it something-bad he-said younger-
tsaamemi beyabaami tsentimi.
brother said older-brother said.
75. *Eyo tsirem.*
Yes he-said.
76. *Baakemi uppaqi manaanuram yaasaam benabaa maroraakemi manaa*
Stayed-went forest one-day make-a-clearing his-brother cleared one
baandimana yereqemi yebaakemi.
pine-tree left-it came-back.
77. *Beyapakani yikebaamaro manaaukami yereqeqaaumpo daasinkaano*
His-younger-brother came-and only-one left-behind cut-it-for-me he-
tsirem.
said.
78. *Tsiamimi eyo tsirem benoyo.*
He-replied yes as-he-said-it they-went.
79. *Yeyinaaqmaaqnamaaq benoyo.*
With-wives went-they.
80. *Boyomi obe daayebayomi baakkem.*

Went went cut-down until.

81. *Beyapaq tsiankanem minibaandim yaami uremoni.*
His-brother he-send-him that-pine-tree up climb.

82. *Umbem daayonumpo tsenimi baandimano yenkem inokemone.*
Went-up try-to-cut-branches he-said pine-tree went swell-up.

83. *Inokanimi aamankaq benapaq kumiriq iye emoni.*
When-it-swelled straight his-brother come-down not enough.

84. *Onimi aaqi ubaarankequmpo tsiremi.*
Thus so I-did-it he said.

85. *Beyapaq aanaaqbaq beyenaaqbaq yeyibikem bemoni.*
His-younger-brother his-wife his-wife took-them went-home.

86. *Bonimi tsentibaao naaqeq mandaaiqureq bepono tsiremi.*
He-went my-brother why make-foolishness went he-said.

87. *Minibaandim yaam banim baakkem aarampukonimi aaqnondyobaa*
This-pine-tree up stay until he-was-hungry his-hair grass-skirt fingernail
baqdobaa opakaa miniuqinemone.
he-ate-them.

88. *Naaman kaakiparemi banimi manomani yeonemoni.*
When-eaten all stayed hawk saw-him.

89. *Yionanimi banimi tsiraaqoo naaqiqdukepono tsenimi.*
Saw-him stayed friend what-wrong-with-you he-said.

90. *Miqnimiqnim uremi tsentibaamano tsentinaakaa miniuq yoyibikem*
Thus-and-so did my-brother my-wives all took-them ran-away he-said.
iyaayuiqimpe tsirem.

91. *Manoman tsiamemoni eyo tsiremi.*
Hawk told-him yes he-said.

92. *Manoman bemoni.*
Hawk left.

93. *Bemi aakona nunuq oyibikem yemoni.*
Went friend bird bring he-came.

94. *Yeonanim minibaainta mini baandinkim banimi.*
They-saw that-man that pine-tree stayed.

95. *Aapo tsiremi yeyibikem mareram aakona nunuq tsenini unabike kume-*
All-right he-said bring put friend bird he-told-them bring-him come-
noyo.
down.

96. *Kumoyomi aandakaq mindanaapapaq marokundaayomi tsemi.*
Came-down down down-half-way put-down he-said.

97. *Tseyani aakarukequmpe tsemi.*
Myself found-him he-said.

98. *Aapo beni unabiqman aandakim marokundemoni.*
All-right he brought-him-down bottom put-him-down.

99. *Danimi ondasaayaakem tsaayaakendemi.*

Put-down things-collect collected.

100. Mininunuq yimemoni.

Those-birds he-gave-them.

101. Yimembebanimi ondamaro kakipanimi.

Given-them all-the-things finish.

102. Manomani benaakkanimi yereremoni.

Hawk he-saw left.

103. Yereranimi tsiraaqo etsikaanomi iye aamequmpe tsiremi.

Stayed-behind friend you-who-found-me not give-you he-said.

104. Maa unaankesiqmanaa bano tsenimi.

Here only-old-string-bag is he-said.

105. Mini manda mini aamankaaqi maraantequppe tsenimi.

This you-give this all-right I-can-have-it he-said.

106. Eyo tsiremi unaankasiq mandan aamemone.

Yes he-said old-string-bag take-it gave-it.

107.　Aamenimi yomaarem miyi iyaayemoni.

Gave-it took-it this ran-away.

108. Iyaayonemi aapo tsiremi maro naaumpaq bemi paakobaa yaanaa miniuq

Ran-away all-right he-said put in-house stay arrow stick-to-fight all

ubaremoni.

make.

109. Ubaaremi kempontaami tsiankemone bebaa onaano tsentibaamaa ba-

Made-it certain-bird sent-him go see my-brother where-he-lives he-said.

nanippaake tsenimi.

110. Eyo tsiremi bemoni.

Yes he-said went.

111. Bonimi onanimi kaaippaqi yunaami yokebaayomi.

Went he-saw Kaipa food gardening.

112. Omam yukko opakem yemoni.

Saw rubbish bring came.

113. Yenimi mare yoqabikemoni.

He-came brought-it show-it-to-him.

114. Yoqabikanimi onaremi tsemi obe yonebananaa kopamaaqmaa kitirenaa

Showed-it he-saw-it he-said go watch bean pick-them eat-them finish

naakena kaakiparayaabaaq maretsitsimeno tsenimi.

come-tell-me he-said.

115. Eyo tsiremi bemoni.

Yes he-said went.

116. Obem yonebanini naamankopaamaaqi kaakipaarayomi.

Went watch-them eaten-beans finished-them.

117. Obaaikem yemoni.

He-back he-came.

118. Mare tsiamemi aaqi namani kakipparaano tsenimi.

He-came he-told-him now eaten finished he-said.

119. E tsiremi aapo bemoni.

Yes he-said then he-went.

120. Bonimi obemi yonebanini benabaa namaq beyanaaq namaq yenoyo
He-went he-stayed watched his-brother with his-wives with came garden.
yunaampaq.

121. Yeyomi aakaakaaem kopamaaqi maro iremoni.

He-came quick bean went became.

122. Ipaq aayokukiqukkam kopamaakiq emoni.

There beautiful bean did.

123. Ukkanimi aaqi benaabaanamaq yenoyo beyanaanamaq.

As-it-was then his-brother-with came his-wives.

124. Beyanaq benaba tsiankanimi manaaontim kiqdem kopamaakan aapak-
His-wives his-brother sent-him other-side-of-ditch to-pick bean look-for
kam uremmone.
went-up.

125. Uronimi unonanimi mana mini kopqmaaq aayokukuqukam kopamaaq
Went stayed-saw that this bean very-beautiful bean was-on-stalk saw
intanimi unonem mana mini bani aapakebanaami baanaamino tsiremi.
that this is I-am-looking-for you-are-here she-said.

126. Ye kiqkemoni.

Came pick-it.

127. Kiqkiremi baaqdurem bemi benabaa yeabiqmanaarem beyabaapum
Picked-it put-in-bag went his-brother took-it her-husband went.
benomi.

128. Aamaro aanaraareni kureni.

Then-put cut-bamboo cook-it.

129. Kurirani maro naqeno ikasaareno.

Ready-to-cook go make fire.

130. Saaraan yoqnaa be benabaq mano mini kopamaakinke naaqumanaaq-
Make-fire while his his-brother from that bean he-came-out.
nurem.

131. Pitimanaaqnurem yem.

When-he-exploded came-out.

132. Yem mare isanda daaqyiro bemoni.

Came-out came bow shot he-went.

133. Bonimi naqenoyo maro pako yiro bemoni.

He-went so-on an arrow shot he-went.

134. Bemi baandinaamu aaroninkaaqi mini baandin aampankem maampami
He-went pine-tree head-of this pine-tree grows down Kaipa.
kaaipaq.

135. Aapo sokoma aakeqyaninkaqi mini maampani aanai aampankem.

Then bamboo-arrow cut this down-here bamboo grows.

136. Aapo mini aamuqbaq inima aaruekem nonkim daninkaqi maampami
    Then this pregnant woman killed in-the-water put-over down Kaipa
kaaipaqi mini nomi yuakemi.
this water dammed-it-up.
137. Mini kappaa aainke pakkoma aaroni aainke nomi indaaqemi.
    This little hole arrow shot hole water comes-out.
138. Mini kaaruntaabaaiq mani kaakippemi.
    This two-brother story finish.

1. This is the story of two brothers, a story I am going to tell, told to me. These two brothers lived long ago. As they lived, the younger brother stayed in the bush and killed birds. An old lady used to stay in this forest, and used to take it [the bird] herself while the young fellow would leave and return later. 5. When he would come back, he would watch the fruit on the trees. When he would go there, that woman would get what he shot, and she would say, 'Here is only the arrow, but there is no bird here.' She would say that, and he would go back once again and would watch the tree. He shot it, and she would take it: 'Here, there is no bird, but here is an arrow,' she said. 10. 'Here, take the arrow [here is an arrow], there is no bird,' she said. 'That's all right,' he would say. Then he would go get the arrow and come back.

Now one day he was there watching. He killed a bird, and it was borne along and went where the old one took it. 15. He killed it, and it went along [to where the old lady was]. This woman who was there would say, 'Here is only the arrow, there is no bird here,' she said. 'All right, give it to me,' he answered. The old woman said, 'Are you right to spend the night with me?' He answered, 'Yes.' 20. Now as he stayed, as it was getting toward dark, she cooked food, and he ate it.

Then she got a mat and a blanket and gave those things to him, and he made the bed and went to sleep. When he was about to go to sleep, she spoke to him and said, 'If someone comes in the night with songs and dancing, don't you get up,' she told him. 'OK,' he said, and this man went off to sleep. As he slept, some arrived outside singing, and he started to wake up, but the old woman told him: 'Don't get up,' she said. 25. She told him this, and he said, 'Yes.' He went back to sleep.

After he had slept, in the morning the old woman took him and went down to the creek. When she went down, she cut down two Neva sticks and sharpened them for him. After she sharpened them, she said, 'You take these sticks and go, don't drop them' she said as she told him. 30. When she said this, he answered, 'Yes.' He took them, and went. As he went, he came to a garden, and he stuck them into the ground, and he climbed a ladder to strip off the leaves of the sugar cane. As he climbed up, he stuck the two sticks there in the ground and climbed on up.

After he had climbed up there, he was taking off the leaves, and he turned, and looked down and saw two girls standing there. As he looked, he was very pleased, so he turned and came down. 35. After he came down, the two girls slung their bags on, and he was very pleased, so he took them and went. When he arrived at the village, his older brother saw them. 'My little brother, where did you get these?' he asked. 'I had to work very hard to find them and bring them here,' he said. 'Give me one of them,' his brother said. 'No, I will not give you one,' said his younger brother. 40. 'Show me where you got them, so I can go and get some,' he said. 'Find it and get it yourself,' said the younger brother to his older brother.

The younger brother said this, and the older answered, 'Yes.' He went to sleep and in the morning he got up and followed his track and came along. He came and arrived at the big forest and saw the old woman who was there.

45. When he arrived [he said], 'You gave my younger brother something, now you give it to me.' She said, 'Yes, but take it easy so I can give it to you,' said the old woman. When she said this, that man said, 'Give me right now what you gave my younger brother!' When he said this, the old woman said, 'You sleep, tomorrow you can get it and go,' she said. 'Not tomorrow, but give it to me right now,' he said. 50. 'That is the way it will be, afterward I will give it to you,' she said.

She said it, and she told it to that man, and he slept in her house. When he was ready to go to sleep, she told him that if anyone arrived outside and they talked with talk and dancing, 'Don't you get up,' she said, 'just listen, but go back to sleep,' she told him. After she told him that, he said, 'Yes,' and went to sleep. After he had slept awhile, he heard as they arrived in the night that they were singing and talking outside.

55. He got up as they made the disturbance. The old woman said, 'I told you what to do before,' she said. 'Yes,' he said, and went back to sleep. He slept. In the morning when he got up, she said, 'Let's go on down to the creek,' she said. 60. He said, 'When are you going to give me what you gave my brother?' he said. She said, 'I'll give it to you in a bit.' She took him down to the creek. When they got down there, she cut two Neva sticks and sharpened them roughly. After she sharpened them, she said, 'Don't drop them, take them gently and go,' she said. 65. 'These sticks are not good. You gave my brother something, give that to me,' he said. 'Take this,' she said, 'and go, it is what I am giving you,' she told him. 'Yes,' he said, and took them and left.

When he had gone, he stuck these two sticks in the ground under the sugar cane, and he climbed up a ladder to take off the leaves of the sugar cane. 70. When he had climbed up, he was taking off the leaves. When he was taking off the leaves, he turned and looked down and saw two girls, and up on their noses he saw that there was a hole. 'Afterward you would have given me something well made as you said, but I went and acted foolishly and you have given me this sort,' he said.

He took them and went to the village and showed them and told his brother: 'See, yours are beautiful, give me one of them, and you take an ugly one of mine,' he said. 'That is the sort of thing you wanted to get, so you went and did something foolish,' his younger brother replied to his older brother. 75. 'Yes,' he answered.

One day his older brother went to the forest to cut down everything for making a garden. After he had made a clearing, he left one pine tree and returned.

His younger brother came and there was only one [tree left]. 'Cut out the branches from the tree,' he said. He replied, 'Yes,' and they went out. They went with their wives. 80. When they had gone, they came to where they cut it out. He sent his younger brother to climb up the pine tree. He went up to try to cut out the branches. When he had said this, the pine tree began to swell up. When it had swollen, the younger brother could not get down. 'That's what I did,' he said. 85. He took his younger brother's wife, and his wife, and went home. When he had gone, he said, 'Why has my brother done this foolishness?'

He stayed up that pine tree until he was hungry, and he ate his hair, his clothes, and his fingernails. When he had eaten everything, a hawk saw him. When he had seen him, he said, 'Friend, what is wrong with you?' 90. 'Thus and so my older brother did and he took all my wives and he ran away with them,' he said. The hawk replied, 'Yes.' The hawk left.

He went and got all his bird friends and they came. They saw that man staying up the pine tree. 95. 'All right,' said the hawk, and he told his bird friends to bring him down. As they brought him down half way, the hawk said, 'Put him down now. I myself found him,' he said.

Now the hawk brought him on down to the ground and put him down. When he had put him down on the ground, he collected everything for paying them. 100. He gave it to those birds. When he had given them all the things, he finished. He saw that the hawk was left behind. As he stayed behind, the brother said: 'Friend, I have not given you who found me anything yet. Here is only an old string bag,' he said. 105. 'You give me this, it is all right, I can take it,' he said. 'OK,' he said, and gave him the old string bag.

He gave it to him, and he took it and ran off. When he ran off, he said, 'All right.' He went in a house and made arrows and sticks for fighting. After he had made these things, he sent the Kempontami [bird] and said, 'Go and look for my brother, and see where he lives.' 110. He said, 'all right,' and went. When he had gone, he saw Kaipa where he was making gardens. He saw it, and so he picked up some of the rubbish and brought it. He came and brought it and showed it to him. When he showed it to him and he had seen it, he said, 'Go, and watch, and when they have picked the beans, and have eaten them up, come and tell me,' he said.

115. 'Yes,' he said, and went. When he had gone, he watched them and they ate the beans and finished them. He came back. When he came, he told him, 'Now they have eaten and finished them,' he said. 'Yes,' he said, and then he went. 120. When he had gone, he stayed and watched his brother and his brother's wives, and they came to the garden.

When they came, quickly he changed into a bean. There was a beautiful bean that he had become. As it was a bean, then his brother came with his wives. His brother sent his wives to the other side of the ditch to pick and to go up and look for beans. 125. She went up and she saw that particular bean, and saw that beautiful bean while it was on the stalk and she said, 'This is what I am looking for, you are here,' she said. So she came and picked it.

She picked it and put it in the bag and took it to his brother, going to her husband. Then she went and cut the bamboo to cook it. When she was ready to cook it, she made a fire. 130. When she was making the fire, the younger brother changed over from that bean to himself. When he exploded out of that bean, he came out. He came out and took his bow and shot him.

He went on shooting, and he shot the arrows. When he shot that pine-tree-arrow, the pine tree grew there down at Kaipa. 135. All right, where he shot the bamboo arrow, there is where the bamboo grows. All right, this pregnant woman was killed and where she fell into the water down at Kaipa, the water was dammed up. Now where the arrow shot a little hole, from this hole, the water comes out. This story of the two brothers is finished.

3. SISTER AND BROTHER STORY

1. Nana nuram karuntanaro bayomi.
One day brother-sister lived.

2. Mana nurami yirurem nebanim akaqnamano yekanda yeyibikemi be-
One day killing eat old-man two-of-them bring-them his-place went.
yamapaq bemi.

3. Obayomi mini anonuqmannano benananomi nonana apendum kapo-
When-they-stay this old-one his-older-sister bamboo-for water bottom
daromi amimi mini akintamano nompaq marem kumemi.
make-a-hole give-her this that-girl water take go-down.

4. Kumemi nonyaponimi apendunkinke nomi yankakariq mana ebami
Go water get from-bottom water came-out that did looked did.
onaqkom demi.

5. Yoni pakaremi apendunkim uyaqdemi yapem uremi.
Mud take-it bottom closed get went-up.

6. Non yapiran mini akinta kumbanimi mini ayokunano mini inta arumam
Water get this girl went-down this old-man this boy-child kill-him put
demi manan kandandapaq demoni.
take on-bed put-him.

7. Dukanimi benanano nom kunyaqmanaremi undaemi tsemi mandan
When-slept his-sister water brought-it-up arrived she-said take give-me
danaka mini inta ayapaqurukando tsentimi.
this child cuddle she-said.

8. Ayokuni tsemi eqaa puqamakeq danami nakemi dukano tsentimi.
Old-one said banana ripe gave-him he-eat sleep he-said.

9. Mini akinta mano e tsiremi.
That girl go yes she-said.

10. Apo tsiremi ika tsarakem danimi ayamparimi baremi.
Right she-said-it fire lit did he-felt-tired/weak sleep.

11. Ayamparimi dukami mini akinta mano beyapaq undondemi onanimi
When-tired-and slept that girl go her-brother took-him-up saw died
pukanim onaremi.
saw-it.

12. *Maqnirani tsenoqi kumuna maqnonamino tsiremi.*
    Do-this-sort you-said I-went-down you-did-that she-said.
13. *Apo terem onakaq ika baqdem tsanan upukurem iyayemoni.*
    Right she-said door fire lit burn closed ran-away.
14. *Iyayem bem indentenimi aqnona miniuq kapamemtenimi indemi tsemi*
    Ran went heard head those explode heard she-said so that burnt finish

aqi mini katayemi tsino tsiremi bemoni.
she-said she-left.

1. Once there lived a brother and sister. One day an old cannibal came and took them to his house. When they had stayed there for a while, this old man made holes in the bottom of a bamboo and gave it to his older sister and told her to take it and go down to get water. When she was getting the water, she noticed that it was coming out of the bottom. 5. She took mud and closed off the bottom and went on up.

While this girl was getting the water, the old man killed the boy and put him up on the bed. While the old man was sleeping, his sister brought up the water and when she arrived she said, 'Give me the child so I can cuddle him.' The old man replied, 'I gave him a ripe banana and he ate it, and he is asleep.' The girl said, 'Yes.'

10. All right, after she said that, she made a fire and he felt tired so he went to sleep. When he was asleep, the girl took up her brother and saw that he was dead. 'You wanted to do this sort of thing so you told me to go down, and then you did this,' she said.

Now after she said this, she closed the door, lit a fire, and ran away. When she ran away, she said that she heard his head burst so she said that he was completely burned, and she left.

4. THE STORY ABOUT DONTA

1. *Donta maniq tirare.*
   Donta story I-tell.
2. *Nabantapaqte anasi indandayomi dontapaq umbanimibakemi.*
   Nabanta girl put-skirt-around Donta went-up-and-stayed.
3. *Apo mana narami nabantapaqi poni arureni neni arayomi kumemmoni.*
   Right one day Naganta-from pig killed eat send-word come-down.
4. *Miniq yamuqi oparuqnamaq bepo ubarebayonkim bami.*
   This time Tairora-people-with battle make-war did.
5. *Beni kumbem pon aruremi yunkebanimi.*
   She went-down pig killed she-cook-it-in-mumu.
6. *Benabapu awebanimi dukami.*
   Her-husband sick sleep-on-bed.
7. *Oparuq yemam upukureni yinueno.*
   Tairora-people came stop-from-going-out fight-them.

8. *Aruqumakem aruqumakem benobapum aqebaninkim arumandayom*
They-fought they-fought her-husband sick-in-bed killed he-died.
pukemoni.

9. *Aonayom pukonini masiqdem banta anasi ena makupaq iyayeno.*
Saw dead all-people men women another village ran-away.

10. *Iyayomi mini ininnano panibaumpe tsirem uriyimano unonanimi banta*
They-ran this woman still-there she-said went-up saw men women fire
anasi ika sarebayomi tseni.
make-fire said.

11. *Banta anasi panibeno tsirem urakem undaemoni.*
Men women still-there said come arrived-there.

12. *Mini puka baintaba bana urenaoni.*
That true spirit people went-up.

13. *Yeni banuqi bayomi uremoni.*
Came evil stayed she-went-up.

14. *Beyanduntimi tsemi puka banta baqi urequmpe tsiremi uremoni.*
In-her-mind she-said true men stayed go-up she-said she-went-up.

15. *Unonanimi benabapu kandandapaq dukanimi panidukemino tsemoni.*
When-saw her-husband on-bed sleep still-sleeping she-said.

16. *Poruqma marem marundaninuq marundem karem yimem bemoni.*
Pigs take brought-it-out put-it cut gave-out went.

17. *Beni iye onemoni beyabapuma arurukayom.*
She not see her-husband killed.

18. *Pani bemino mana tsemoni.*
Still alive one she-said.

19. *Pakouq arakendayonuq manani ayoparemi banimi.*
Arrows shot take-it hide stayed.

20. *Apo tiremi benanaqmano pom yimen onaamam bemi okam arapate*
Right said his-wife pig give door went eye one-side saw they-took-it
yonebanini pamanan mankurebayomi yonemoni.
swallow-it-whole show-them.

21. *Apo tiremi yemem bemi asappaq bemi yereyimimam kakipparemi*
All-right said give go road go gave finish saw.
onarem.

22. *Apo aqi mini yererem iyayemoni.*
Right enough that-one leave run-away.

23. *Aqi iyayonim mini banuqmano aqnaqemi abakurenoyo.*
Enough run-away that spirits run-after-to-catch run-after.

24. *Abakuroyomi iyayemi onanini aqi uyakenoyomi.*
Run-away run saw right-away try-stop-her.

25. *Aqi mini yererem iyayemi kumemi.*
Enough that left ran-down came.

26. *Banuqmano uyaqdayomi banana yankakemi.*

Spirits try-to-stop already she-went-away.

27. *Aqi mini ininnano kumakem kundaem benano apo amapaq mampaq*
Enough that woman went-down arrived her-mother her-father home-
nabantapaq.
place down Nabanta.

28. *Marokum beyano apo taamenimi.*
Went-down her-mother her-father told-them.

29. *Yikunan adendeni.*
Sorry did-it.

30. *Pon arurenni akabariq eno.*
Pigs killed make-sacrifice did.

32. *Donta mani kakippemi.*
Donta story finished.

1. I'll tell a story about Donta. A girl was sent from Nabanta to Donta for marriage. One day the people from Nabanta killed pigs and sent word to come down and eat them. This was the time when they were having fights with the Tairora people.

5. She went down there and killed a pig and cooked it in the earthen oven [mumu]. Her husband was very sick in bed. The people from Tairora came and stopped them from going out and started to fight them. They fought and fought and they killed her husband while he was sick in bed, and he died. When they saw that he was dead, all of the men and women ran away to another village.

10. After they ran away, that woman went up and said, 'I think they are still there,' because she thought she saw the men and women as they made fires. 'The men and women are still there,' she said, and she came on and arrived up there. But when she arrived, those people were not really people. She came and found that they were evil spirits. In her mind she said, 'They are real people that are there,' so she went up. 15. When she saw her husband sleeping on the bed, she said, 'He is still sleeping.' So she took and brought out and cut up the pigs and went and gave it out to them. She did not realize that her husband had been killed. 'He is still alive,' she said. He had hidden the arrows with which they had shot him and stayed there.

20. Now after she said these things, his wife gave out the meat, but there at the door she was glancing at them and saw that they took it and swallowed it whole. So when she saw that she had given all of it out, she wanted to escape from them. So this one started to leave, and run away. When she ran, those spirits ran after her to catch her. They ran after her, and as she ran she saw that they were trying to stop her. 25. So she left there and ran down and came. The spirits tried to stop her, but she already had escaped from them.

This woman went down and arrived at the place of her mother and her father at the village of Nabanta. She went down and told her mother and her father about it. They were sorry about what happened. 30. They killed a pig and then made a sacrifice. This story about Donta is finished.

5. THE YAM COMES TO GADSUP FROM MARKHAM

1. *Mana obama makama yenimi.*
   This yam here came.
2. *Mana obama makama yenini.*
   This yam here came.
3. *Mampa dasama abapate uremoni uyapekunama.*
   Down Markham valley came-up mat-under-arm.
4. *Uremi tsemi yabio urina urono ompam yumupina.*
   When-came-up he-said Yabi go-up I-come-too big forest.
5. *Mini tsiremi beyakona yabimi yoabikam makantano dasamapate*
   That he-said his-friend Yabi bring-him both Markham-from they-
   urenoyo.
   came-up.
6. *Ureni makantane iqiq dere uronoyo.*
   They-came-up both song sang came-up.
7. *Mana uroyapaqi umbani mana yabibaka obaba yodeni meno.*
   This they-came-up stayed this Yabi yam they-plant eat-them.
8. *Mana mini obabaka yabiqi iqiq.*
   This these Oba Yabi song.
9. *Yabio marana uronobe; yabio marana uronobe; yabio marana uronobe.*
   Yabi go-along go-up; Yabi go-along go-up; Yabi go-along go-up.
10. *Pompa yamupina marana urono; pompa yamupina marana urono.*
    Big-into forest go-along go-up; big-in forest go-along go-up.
11. *Obao maran urono.*
    Oba go-along go-up.
12. *Marana urono pompa yamupina marana urono.*
    Go-along go-up big-into forest go-along go-up.
13. *Mana mini ukami bami banta anasi oba yokarani mana mini iqiq daremi*
    These that happen stay men women yam want-to-plant this that song
    obo yokeno.
    sing yam plant.
14. *Obama yodama urebami mana mini iqiq demi namariemi.*
    Yam·planted grow this that song sing want-to-weed.
15. *Minureni obai yode neno mana kadsupu makeno.*
    They-did-that yam plant eat these Gadsup people.

1. This is about how the yam came up here. This is how Oba came up here. He came up from down in the Markham valley with his mat under his arm. When he came up, he said, 'Yabi, you go up and I will come up also into that big forest.' 5. This one said that, and he brought his friend Yabi, and they both came up from the Markham. They both came up, and as they came, they sang a song. These came up and stayed here so that they could plant and eat Yabi and Oba.

This is the song about Oba and Yabi. 'Oh, Yabi, let's go up there; oh, Yabi, let's go up; oh, Yabi, let's go up. Let's go on up into the big forest; let's go on up into the big forest. Oba, let's go on up there. Let's go on up into the big jungle; let's go on up there.'

This is what happened, and they stayed; so if men and women want to plant Oba, then they sing this song as they plant it. When they have planted the yam, it grows, and they sing this song also when they want to weed. So these Gadsup people eat and plant the yam.

6. WHY ONLY MEN PLAY MUSICAL INSTRUMENTS

1. *Mana karuntananoyiq maniq.*
   One two-sisters story.
2. *Kakuntanano tonkem apakim bayomi.*
   Two-sisters Tonke-tree hole lived.
3. *Bayonkinke donkamuna ondoba atsebayomi.*
   Live-inside bull-roarer [for music] jews'-harp playing.
4. *Mana pumara indiakondemi yemoni.*
   One young-man heard-about-it came.
5. *Yiraremi yunanuq manam ayopamaremi yemi.*
   Try-to-come food get make-ready came.
6. *Yemi indenini donkamuna ondoba pa atsebami.*
   Came heard bull-roarer jews'-harp still play.
7. *Uranaqompaq yeraem indenimi mindam marorarapate atsentimi in-*
   Kainantu-at arrived he-heard up-there Maronarapa-at playing he-
direm.
heard.
8. *Aqi mini mindam maronara uremi.*
   Now this up-here place went-up.
9. *Undemi indeimmi karuntanano donkamuna ondoba atsebami.*
   Arrived-up he-heard two-sisters bull-roarer jews'-harp they-played.
10. *Beni aqi makuma beyonani apakemi bemoni.*
    He now place stay find went.
11. *Bemi onanimi mindam yaapakim beni donkamuna ondopaq atsebam*
    He look up-there tree-hole he bull-roarer jews'-harp play he-saw-them.
yonemi.
12. *Yonaremi ayani urirani apaka kondemi oqmandemoni.*
    He-saw pass go-up look-for-it can't-find hid-himself.
13. *Oqmantem onebanimi benom akintamano amanda mandandem kume-*
    Hide-himself saw-them her-younger-sister girl ladder took-and-placed-
bami mini baintamano onem.
it climb-down that man saw.
14. *Onebanimi mini akintamano amanda mikaq yereremi yunampaq bemi.*
    Watching that girl ladder that-place put garden went.

15. *Bemi onaremi mini amanda mandandemi aqi mini uremi.*
    Went saw that ladder took-and-put all-right that climb-up.
16. *Undemi onanimi benananomano mana atsem bami onarem.*
    He-climbed saw-her her-elder-sister here play stay saw.
17. *Tsimeno miqya atsana aneqnebe tsemmi.*
    Give-me that playing thing he-said.
18. *Mini akintamano tsemi iye amentequmpe tsemi.*
    That girl said no I-give-you she-said.
19. *Apo tiremi yam mandemi mini akinta arumande.*
    Right he-said stick take that girl kill-her.
20. *Mini bainta mano mini donkamuna ondoba yomarem iyayemoni.*
    That man took that bull-roarer jews'-harp took ran-away.
21. *Benomano yeonaremi akunan akendemi manam masiqemi.*
    Her-younger-sister came-back-and-saw sorry did get bring-her.
22. *Miqnukami bayami make yamuq anonanami anatsimano ondoba don-*
    That-reason why now days you-can-see girls bull-roarer jews'-harp not
kamuna iye atsiya onanonami.
play you-can-see.
23. *Mini banta manobana atsebana onanonami.*
    That men only play you-can-see.
24. *Aqi mini maniq kakippemi.*
    All-right this story finished.

1. This is a story about two sisters. Two sisters lived in a hole in the Tonke tree. They lived inside there and they played the bull roarer and the jews'-harp. A young man heard about it and came there. 5. When he was about to come, he got food and prepared everything and came. He came and he heard that they were still playing those musical instruments. He arrived at Kainantu [formerly called Uranaqompa], and from Maronarapa he heard them playing. So this fellow went up here to that place. When he arrived, he heard the two sisters playing the musical instruments.

10. He stayed near the place and went to find them. He looked and up there in the hole of the tree they were playing the musical instruments, and he saw them. He saw them but when he looked for the path to go up, he couldn't find it, so he hid himself. He hid himself and then saw the younger sister take out and place the ladder and climb down; that man saw it. While he watched, that girl put the ladder in place and then went to the garden.

15. He saw that she went, and he took that ladder and put it up and then that fellow climbed up there. He climbed up and saw the older sister, and he saw her staying there playing it. 'Give me that thing that you are playing' he said. But that girl said, 'I will not give it to you.' All right, and when she said that, he took a club and he killed that girl.

20. That man took the bull roarers and the jews'-harps and ran away. The younger sister came back and saw it, and was very sorry; she got her and buried her.

That is the reason why nowadays you can see that girls do not play the bull roarer and the jews'-harp; you can see that. The men are the only ones that you will see playing them. This is the end of the story.

7. INDIRECT REQUESTS

1. *Mana karauwepaniq maniqi.*
   One Karauwepa story.
2. *Mana nuram karauwepa bemi.*
   One day Karauwepa was.
3. *Banimi benanaqmana am makarani bemoni.*
   Stay his-wife baby born left.
4. *Benanaq yunama iye yunkemoni.*
   His-wife food not cook.
5. *Umpampate bayaranimi kumemi tseni kamanonuqnamaq tsiruon-*
   Upampate-from send-word went-down they-said Kamano-with we-are-
   teumpo isandaba pakoqikaq eurono tsentenini.
   going-to-fight bow arrow you-come-up they-said.
6. *E tsireni.*
   Yes they-said.
7. *Yeni yuruinayo aneqneuq manan ayopenoyo.*
   Come things-for-fighting something take get-ready.
8. *Ayopana aneqnequq bebayomi karauwepa yunami iye nemoni.*
   Ready things went-on Karauwepa food no eat.
9. *Beni bemi beyakandauqkaq maro tsemi isanda bami iqnami iye bako*
   He went his-friends went said bow get string not I-have he-said begged-
   tsiremi inantanomoni.
   them-for-one.
10. *Puka iqnanara tsenaoni mini yunanani tsemoni.*
    Two string not-talk-him that food said.
11. *Yunami iye narukemi tsemoni.*
    Food not eaten he-told-them.
12. *Aqi mini tseremi maro tsenini iqnamuq ameyomi beyoqpemi beni tsemi*
    Right this he-said went told-them string they-gave-him in-his-mind he
    iqnarara sunaka tsimenaino tsemoni.
    said thing I-didn't-ask you-give-me he-said.
13. *Arampukebanimi isandaba miniuq manum ayopemoni.*
    Hungry bows those take get-ready.
14. *Ayoparemi onini uroyomi uremoni.*
    Get-ready did went-up he-went-too.
15. *Aqi mini yirueni benoyo minda indanaq anukim.*
    Right this fight went-on up-here Indana mountain.
16. *Kamanom bainta benamara pako yorapisem yenimi be karauwepa*
    Kamano man same-name arrow put-arrow-point-toward came he

beyaqbaq yorapitsem bemoni.
Karauwepa he-also put-arrow-point-toward went.

17. *Beni benokampen daparonim benokampe daparonim ureni makantano*
     He his-eye shot his-eye shot did both-of-them dead.
pukenoyo.

18. *Piqoyomi yeyan yekandauye boyomi yeyam yekandauye kumenoyo.*
     They-died them carry they-went them carry went-down.

19. *Kumeni marokum masiarukam maniqi bemino.*
     Went-down put-him bury story took-place.

20. *Miqnakami bami yunami iye inantintemi enakaqi manan baekantemi*
     That-is-why happen food not beg another-thing take turn-it-around
pe manikaq miqnukami bami make yamuqi miqneno.
before story that-why happen now these-days do.

21. *Aqi mini kakippemi.*
     Oh this finished.

1. This is a story about Karauwepa. Once there was a man named Karauwepa.
He was there and his wife went to bear a child and left. His wife didn't cook
any food for him. 5. Those from Upampate sent word down there and said,
'We are going to fight with the Kamanos so you come up with your bows and
arrows.' 'Yes,' he said. When they were about to come, they took and got the
things for fighting ready. While they were getting these things ready Karauwepa
did not eat any food. So he went to his friends and said, 'I don't have strings,'
so he was asking for one.

10. He really wasn't asking for a string, he was asking for food. He did not
tell them that he had not eaten food. So when he said this, they gave him strings
for his bow, but in his mind he said, 'I didn't ask for a string, and you gave me
one,' he said. He was hungry, but he took those bows and got them ready. He
got those things ready and as they went up, he went up too.

15. Now this fighting went on up here on Mount Indana. A Kamano man
with the same name put his arrow in his bow and pointed it and came toward
him, and Karauwepa also put his arrow to the bow and pointed it at him and
approached. They both shot into each other's eyes and both were killed. After
they died, they went and carried them, the one up to Kamano and the other
one down here. They went and put him down and buried him; this story actually happened.

20. That is what happened; he did not beg for food he turned it around and
asked for another thing; this story took place long ago, and now they are still
doing this. That is the end of the story.

8. INDIRECT REQUESTS (REPEATED)

1. *Mana karaubepaniq maniq tirare.*
    This Karauwepa story I-will-tell.

2. *Pe karawepa banimi.*
    Before Karauwepa lived.

3. *Benanaq am makaran buonimi.*
   His-wife baby bear went.

4. *Bakeni mampaq upampate baya rayomi kumonimi.*
   They-who-stayed down-here at-Upampate talk sent it-sent-down.

5. *Tseni kamanonuqnamaq tsiruontequmpo isandaba pakoba miniuqkaq*
   They-said Kamano-people-with we-going-to-fight bows arrows those
   mare yeno tseno.
   take come they-said.

6. *Tsireni baya ranim kumemoni.*
   They-said message went/put went-down.

7. *Danim kumonimi aqi mini banta anasi isandaba pakoba yana miniuq*
   Put went-down enough that men women bow arrow club those take
   manam ayopenoyo.
   get-ready.

8. *Manam ayopareni apo bayomi.*
   Take get-ready then they-stay.

9. *Karaubepai yunamaq benanaq iye yunkarukanimi ama karam buonimi*
   Karauwepa food his-wife not cook baby bear went reason-for he-stay.
   tsepo bakemi.

10. *Yunana miniuqbaq iye ami.*
    Food those not there.

11. *Iquankaq manam baeqdemi beyakandaba miniuq bappaq oremi indae-*
    String-for-bow take turn-around/pretend his-friends those to-their-
    moni.
    place went ask.

12. *Isandamana bami iquami iyembaqumpo mare tsimeko.*
    Only-bow stay string I-haven't-got come give-me.

13. *Tsentenini iqnana miniuq ameyomi aqi onamam miqnitsambenone.*
    He-said-to-them string those gave-him enough went-to-door kept-asking.

14. *Tsambemi inantam bebanini puka iqnanani tsino tsireni amenoyo.*
    When-said-that beg he-went-on true string he-talk they-said they-give-
    him.

15. *Amebayomi mini iqnanuq marakem beyiq nanaroq marerem.*
    When-gave-to-him those strings take-them his roof put-them.

16. *Beyoppem tsemi iqnanara tsunaka tsimenano.*
    In-his-mind he-said strings not-talking-about you-gave-me.

17. *Yunanani manam baekeqbanaqi tsimameno tsiremi mareremone.*
    Food take pretend/turn-around you-give-me he-said he-came-put.

18. *Demi apo isandaba miniuq manam ayopamarem mampami aqi urenoyo.*
    Put OK bows those take make-ready down-here enough they-came-up.

19. *Uroyomi apo beyandoqbaq uremoni.*
    When-they-came-up then himself-too came-up.

20. *Undemi aqi mini mindam anokimi indanaq anokimi yirue benoyo.*

Arrived enough those up-here on-mountain Indana on-mountain flight went.

21. *Yirue bebayomi aqi mini mendappate benamara isanda yoremi yenim*
Fight went-on enough this from-up-there namesake bow put-arrow-to-
bemapate yorem bem.
string came one-from-here put-arrow-to-bow went.

22. *Yemi benokampem maro daparonim.*
He-came in-his-eye went shot.

23. *E tsem benokampen daparonim.*
Yes he-said in-his-eye shot.

24. *Ureni makantano pukenoyo.*
They-did both-of-them they-died.

25. *Puqoyoni benakono yekandauye mendam kamanompaq boyoni.*
When-they-died his-friends carry-him one-from-there Kamano-place-to
they-went.

26. *Apo beni yekandauye mampami kumenoyo.*
Then they-went carry-him one-from-down-here they-went-down.

27. *Marokundeni masiqenoyo.*
Went-put-him they-bury-him.

28. *Masiqakam maniqi bani make yamuqi akonoma yunama inantirani*
When-buried story is now days your-friends food beg come not happen.
mare iye naqintemi.

29. *Anteqdem iye inantintemi.*
Straight-away not beg.

30. *Mare enakaqi baeqdemi inantintemi.*
Come another-thing pretend ask.

31. *Pe manikaq miqnukami bami.*
Before story happened it-did.

32. *Aqi mini kakippemi.*
Enough that finished.

1. I will tell you the story about Karauwepa. Karawepa lived long ago. His wife went away to bear a child. Those who stayed down here at Upampa sent a message. 5. When they said it, they said, 'We are going to fight with the Kamano people so you get your bows and arrows and come with them.' When they said this, they sent the message and went down. When they put it, he went down, and the men and women took those bows and arrows and clubs and got them ready. When they had taken them and gotten them ready, they waited. But his wife did not cook any food for Karauwepa, but went off to bear the baby and that's why he stayed behind.

10. There was no food there for him. So he took off the strings from his bow, and went to his friends and pretended to ask for it at their place. 'I only have a bow, I don't have a string for it, so I have come and you give me one.' He said this to them, and those people gave him strings, and then he went out the door

asking them for it. When he went, he asked them but he was not really talking about the strings which they gave him. 15. After they gave it to him, he took the strings and put them up in his roof. In his mind he said, 'I wasn't talking about strings, but you gave them to me. I am trying to ask you for food, and you gave me that,' he said, and he came and put them up there.

After he put them there, he took the bows and got them ready and came on up here. When they came up, then he too came up. 20. When he arrived, then they went on and fought there on the mountain, on Mount Indana. After they fought there, then a person with the same name from up there put his arrow to the string of his bow and came on, and the one from here put his arrow to the string and approached. He came and he shot him in the eye. 'Yes,' he said, and shot him in the eye. They did this, and both of them died.

25. When they died, his friends from over there carried him and went to the Kamano area. And those from down here carried this one and brought him here. They went and put him down and buried him.

So they buried him, and this is the story so that nowadays when your friends beg for food, they come, but they are not really asking for food. They do not ask for it straight. They come and they pretend to ask for something else. This story happened long ago, and it is over. That is the end of it.

9. THE EARLY DAYS

1. *Pena bayouna yunama yoolena nena yurueni ebayonana tsararare.*
   Before lived food plant eat bite do I-want-to-write.

2. *Pena bayouni yirunani tsankoba pakoba miniuqi manan ayopakeno.*
   Before lived fight shield arrow those take-them make-ready.

3. *Ayoparemi apo mini namukonama aruemoni.*
   Make-ready then that enemy fight.

4. *Apo mini yunama yokarani banta rapiman yororami mini anasi ademi*
   Then that food plant men guard around that women do food plant.
   yunami yokakemi.

5. *Manukoma ye onama iye rapitami mare arumandem bakemi.*
   Enemy come see not guard come kill-them went.

6. *Apo mini rapitami yeonemi yebaekem bakemi.*
   Right that guard come-see go-back went.

7. *Apo mini yunam yokarani ana anda apandemi miniponi oni kayakemi.*
   Right that food want-to-plant bamboo trunk split that-with drain cut.

8. *U rapukirani mini ayamponi dapukakemi.*
   Grass pull-out/cut that with-hand pull-out.

9. *Apo bodirani mini moyam bureme miniponi makai bodakemi.*
   Then dig that stick sharpen-it that-with ground dig.

10. *Apo kuku yapamirani kura oya amika miniuqi manam maroremi*
    OK fence split axe stone wedge these take bring split-it.
    apamakeno.

11. *Apandami anasi mano omarakeno.*

When-split women go go-bring.
12. *Tsampi iye omaranteno banta rapitanamana.*
Any not go-take men on-guard.
13. *Pena bayouni minimureni yunami yodeni nakeno.*
Before they-lived that-did food plant they-eat.
14. *Ena anenebani iye indebano penapayouni.*
Other things not think those-lived-before.
15. *Aruin aneneba yunam yodem nam mikanda anenabanana indenoyo.*
Fighting things food plant eat these-two things think-about.

1. I want to write about the people who lived long ago, how they planted and ate food, and fought. The people who lived before got shields and arrows and prepared those things for fighting. They would get those things ready and then fight with the enemy. So if they wanted to plant food, the men would stand on guard and the women would work the ground planting food. 5. If the enemy came and saw that they were not on guard, then they would come and kill them and go away. But if they came and saw that there was a guard, then they would go back again.

Now when they wanted to plant food, they would split the bottom of a bamboo and with that cut out a drain [tube for irrigation]. They would pull out grass; they would pull it out by hand. They would also sharpen a stick for digging and with that dig up the ground. 10. Now for a fence they would split it with a native axe and then take a stone wedge and split. After they split it, the women went and brought what they had split. No one would go and get those things unless men stood on guard. That is what those who lived before did, planting food and eating it. Those who lived long ago did not think about anything else. 15. The two things that they thought about were weapons for fighting and growing food to eat.

10. GETTING FIRE

1. *Mana tsentinapu tsitsimeninan tsirare.*
This my-grandfather told-me he-said.
2. *Ikabana pena bayouna basebayona tirare.*
For-fire before stayed get-fire I-tell.
3. *Mampaq tsanabumpaq tsanabunika kebanimi.*
Down Sanabumpa Sanabu-fire was-burning.
4. *Banta ika basirarapo miqnirara po yereini.*
Men fire wanted-to-get-and want-to-do-that and used-to-come.
5. *Kosokapi bapi tsapurapi minipi manareini mare mini ikakim karuq-*
Grasshopper rat small-animals those-and take-put bring those fire-on
dareni.
throw.
6. *Ye base noyo.*
Come get/take did.
7. *Basebayom banimi apo teremi mana epam akepuno yenoyo.*

Did-get stayed and until that white people came.

8. *Yeyomi mare minikabaq mini sanabum ikabaq ipaq tsoqyaqpaq kakiq-*
   Arrived take that-fire that Sanabu fire went all-together finished.
   pemoni.

9. *Kakipaninni banta anasi mini maniq ubandaninni bemi bakkemi mini*
   When-it-finished men women those story made stayed it-was that another
   qena akepumuno dinani.
   stranger came.

10. *Mini kakipemonini tsenoyo.*
    That finished they-said.

11. *Miqni tseyomi bemini mampami.*
    That they-said stay down-here.

12. *Tsanabumpaqi aqimini tsentinapu tsimeninanni mini ikabani tsequ.*
    Sanabumpa that-is-it my-grandfather told-me that fire I-tell.

1. This is an account that my grandfather told me. I will tell you about the people who lived long ago and how they got fire. Down there at Sanabumpa [just below Ukarumpa], Sanabu was burning. Men, when they wanted to get fire, used to come down there and get it. They would bring there and throw on that fire grasshoppers, rats, and other small animals. They used to come there and get it. They used to keep getting fire there, and they came until the white people arrived. When they arrived, that fire, the fire of that Sanabu, went and it stopped all together. When the fire went out, the men and women of long ago said that it had been going until the foreigners came. 10. That caused the fire to stop they said. They said that; it is down here that they are talking about. What I'm talking about is Sanabumpa, that's what my grandfather told me; I'm telling you about that fire.

11. A LOVE CHARM

1. *Mana mini ampu maneno.*
   This that love-charm song.

2. *Ampu tsararani anukimi masi upeno.*
   Love-charm want-to-burn on-mountain hole dig.

3. *Masi umandemi apo mini upa obemi epariebam yani dukukemi.*
   Hole finished then that forest come-to-white wood they-split.

4. *Dukumam mareiemi mini masiaba kuku ubaremi.*
   When-split bring that hole-around fence build.

5. *Ubandemi apo mini masikam asepeba ikaba miniuq mikim saremi.*
   Finish-building then that hold-in potion firewood these there burn-them.

6. *Sararani mararaenim inini koru omaremi mareremi.*
   When-they-burn they-hope-to-marry woman door-panel they-get they-
   bring.

7. *Apo mini banta akoyumpemi demi asepenama ikamiyokemi.*

Then those men on-back put potion-with make-fire-by-rubbing.

8. *Kamyodemi apo mempa mini masikim ika tsareno.*
When-fire-going then down-there that hole-in fire light.

9. *Tsandeni apo kandada ubandeni mini naropa beni ampui reno.*
When-fire-burns then flat-form make that on-there stay love-charm same.

10. *Banta rapimam yororukami apo mini ampu iqiq rem beno.*
Men guard around then those love-charm song sing stay.

11. *Bami apo mima koruma omarenim akintapi inimmi iyayem yemmi.*
Stay then one-from door-panel took girl-or woman run comes.

12. *Yeraimmi apo mararare tsim bainta maremmi.*
Arrive then suitor say man marry-her.

13. *Manaremi apo mini yerereni beno.*
He-has-married then that they-left go.

14. *Mini ampa reyomkim beni nomi iye neno.*
That love-charm where-sing they-stay water not drink.

15. *Anasi manareni apo mini neno.*
Women married then that drink.

16. *Mika beni apo yayakana akandaumana ne beno.*
There stay then fresh-fruit cucumber eat stay.

17. *Nebakemi manareni apo mini yunam ayokuqi neno.*
When-have-eaten get-married then these food good eat.

18. *Neni apo makupa mini ininapi akintapi abike yeno.*
Eat then village-at those women-or girl-or bring come.

1. This is about the making of a love charm. When people want to burn or cook a potion for a love charm, they dig a hole on the mountain. When the hole has been finished, then they go into the forest and split white wood. After they split it, they bring it here, and they build a fence around the hole. When they have finished building the fence, then they put firewood and the potion into the hole and burn [cook] those there. When they burn it, they hope to get married so they get the door panel from the woman's house and bring it. They put it on the man's back, and then they make a fire by rubbing [sticks together] with the potion. When the fire is lit, then they put it down in that hole and light the fire there. When the fire burns there, then they make a flat platform [bed or table] and they get on there, and they sing the love charm. The men guard around it, and then as they stay there, they sing that love charm.

10. While they stay there, the girl from whom they have taken the door panel, or the woman, comes running. When she arrives, then the suitor says, 'I will marry her.' When they are married, then those go away from there. In the place where they sing that love charm they do not drink water. After the woman is married, then they can drink. 15. While they stay there, they eat only fresh fruit and cucumbers and stay on. When they have eaten that and gotten married, then they eat the ordinary food. They eat it and then they bring the woman or girl and she comes to the village.

12. GIRLS TRAPPED IN A CAVE

1. *Manaa nurami maasiqdem aakintaauq yunaanaa aaneqnebaa yomare*
   One day all girls food something take cave-in came.
   oyapaqkimi yenoyo.

2. *Yebene mare kundeni neni iyararinkaam ebaayom.*
   Came came cook eat played did.

3. *Aami manaa aakintaa baapuiquka miqyapaq bemi onebanimi oni*
   Do one girl ugly out-here stay saw stone come-down saw told-them
   kumentenimi onemi tsiyimemi tsemi mibe.
   she-said look-out.

4. *Mioni kumebano tsentini bono mandaaiqukaanomompo umaaqi tsireni.*
   This-stone come-down they-said you-go you-no-good-one lie they-told-
   her.

5. *Maanda mikimpaq umbeni iyararebaayomi baakem on kumemi uyaake-*
   Up inside went play-continue until stone come-down closed-them.
   moni.

6. *Uyeqdanini baaquiqukan aakintaamano tsemi mini bani tsebanaaqi*
   Closed-them ugly-one girl said that what tell-you you-disregarded up-
   yorureqi mikimpaq baakekomino tsiremi tsiyimiqdem.
   inside you-were-staying she-said told-them.

7. *Iyaayem yenyinoyipo baayoppaq bemoni.*
   She-ran their-parents their-place went.

8. *Bemi yenyinoyipo maro tsiyimemoni.*
   Went their-mother-father came told-them.

9. *Isiyimenini yunaanaa poraa eni yenoyo.*
   When-she-told-them food pig bring they-came.

10. *Mare mini oyabapaq yunkaareni neni indebayomi baakemi manaa*
    Came that near-stone cook eat listen until one by-one die went.
    manaaiquremi pukom bemoni.

11. *Pukom bebanimi baakemi kaantanaanaa maro eqemoni.*
    Die went until two came left.

12. *Eqanimi indaaeseyomi aaqi bendemana yere eqako tsiremi tsiyimemoni.*
    Left asked-them now he-me were left she-said she-told-them.

13. *Tsiyimenini indebaayomi baakem aapo maayaa pukkemoni.*
    She-told-them they-asked until right one died.

14. *Puqonimi maayaa beyaabemi tsiyimeni tsemi.*
    She-died one herself told-them she-said.

15. *Tsemi tseyaam beko tsiremi tsiyimemoni.*
    She-said myself I-remain she-said she-told-them.

16. *Tsiyimenini e tsireni baayom baakem beyaqbaqi pukemoni.*
    She-told-them yes they-said stay until herself-too died.

17. *Puqemi aayaqbaq minibaq iye tsenimi.*
    Die talk that not say.

18. *Aaqi maasiqdem pukeno tsireni baayom baakem.*
    Right all died they-said stay until.
19. *Aampinemi aamonkuqbemi mini oyapaqi diyemoni.*
    Stink smell-went that stone-hole opened.
20. *Diyonini yenyinoyipo undeni beyaraamum aayamppakaq unyuye-*
    Opened their-mother-father went-in his-daughter bones collect-them.
moni.
21. *Unyuyeni maro maasiqenoyo.*
    Collect went bury-them.
22. *Maasiqaareni musaaenoyo.*
    Bury-them made-a-funeral.
23. *Tsikam naniq aaqi mini kaakkippemi.*
    They-say story right that finish.

  1. One day all the girls took some food and went into a cave. They went in and cooked [in bamboo] and ate and they played. As they did this, one girl who was ugly was staying outside and she saw a stone, and saw that it was about to come down, and she told them, 'Watch out! That stone will come down,' she said. They replied, 'You go away, you no good thing, you are lying.' 5. They went inside and continued to play until the stone came down and closed them in.

  When it closed them in, the ugly girl said, 'That is what I told you would happen, and you disregarded what I said and are staying up there inside,' she told them. She ran and went to the place of their mothers and fathers. She went, and came and told their mothers and fathers. When she told them, they brought pigs and food and came. 10. They came and cooked near that stone, and ate, and listened until one by one they died.

  They died until only two were left. When these were left, they asked them and one said, 'Just we two are left,' she told them. She told them this, and they asked until one more died. When that one died, the other told them herself and said, 15. 'I myself only am left,' she said and told them. When she told them this, they said, 'Yes,' and then she herself died too. When she died, then no one said anything.

  'Now all of them are dead,' they said, but they stayed on. Then the smell came up and opened up that cave. 20. When it was opened, their fathers and mothers went inside, collected the bones of their daughters. When they had collected them, they went and buried them. When they had buried them, they made a funeral. This is what they say, and the story is finished.

13. Girls Trapped in Cave (Retold)

  1. *Aakintaauq yeyomi mare on apakim yunaanuq koyaake mare rukeni*
     Girls came go stone hole foods get come put-them cook-it.
yunkebaayomi.
  2. *Yunkebaami manaa baaquiqukam aakintaamano meqyapaq bemi one-*
     Cook one ugly girl there stay saw.
banimi.

3. *Onano kumebanimi tsiyimemi tsemi.*
Stone come-down she-told-them she-said.
4. *Mi oni kumebapo pekeqkaqoko tsentimi.*
That stone will-come-down you-must-be-afraid told-them.
5. *Mini aakintaauq tseni umaaqi tsaanaamipo mare bono.*
That girls said lie what-you-say go go.
6. *Aamankaaq om kumem daaqdaariq iye munkemino.*
Enough stone come-down cover not come-down.
7. *Tsebemi e tsireni banimi enayaaq kumonimi tsentenini.*
They-used-to-say yes she-said stay again come-down she-told-them.
8. *Oni aamankaq iye kumintemino tsireni.*
Stone enough not come-down they-said.
9. *Mikimpaq mini oyanduntimpaq beni yunaanaaminiuq yunkaare neni*
In-that-place that inside-the-cave stop food-those cook eat play.
iyararebayomi.
10. *Iyararebayomi kumentenimi tsiyimentenini tseni.*
Play coming-down told-them they-said.
11. *Oni aamankaaq kumem daaqdaariq iye mukemi tsireni baayom baakemi*
Stone enough come-down cover not do they-said stay until that stone
mini o kumemi daakaaremoni.
down covered.
12. *Daaqdaranini maandaq mikimpaq benioyomi tsiyimemi tsemi.*
Cover up-here inside stay told-them she-said.
13. *Miqnimebani oneqtiyimebanaqi mikimpaqbeqi iyaarareqbaakekomipo*
That-will-happen I-saw-it-and-told-you stay-inside play-continue you-
bekapoko tsiremi bemoni.
stay she-said she-went.
14. *Bemi maro yeyino yipo tsiyimemi tsemi.*
Went came their-mother father told-them she-said.
15. *Yikem yiraamumbaasinaam maaqyami onano kumemi daaqdemino*
Your daughters out-there stone came-down cover-them she-said went
tsirem maro tsiyimemoni.
told-them.
16. *Tsiyimenini yeyino yipo yeni yunaanaa miniporaa aare mare duqkeni*
Told-them their-mother father came food those-pigs kill bring put that
mini aaba aakaabaari oyeukenoyo.
beside sacrifice went-around.
17. *Mare tsaandemi yunkaare neni.*
Came made-fire cook eat.
18. *Aapo ebayom baakemi manaa manaaiqmurem pukembemoni.*
Then do continue one by-one they-died.
19. *Pukembebanimi indaaentenimi aaqi miqnumam mano puqiqi miqnu-*
They-died they-ask-them now how-many go he-die this-many go re-

mam mano beko tsireni baayom baakemi aapo naaqemoni.
main they-said stay continue right what-happen.

20. *Baakem kaantananaa yere eqemoni.*
    Stay two are left.

21. *Kaantananaa yere eqanimi tsemi aaqi maasiqdem puqmam kaakipaaoqi*
    Two left only she-said right all die finish he-me stay she-said.
    bendemanaa beko tsiremi.

22. *Aapo banim baakemi aaqi mini maayaa pukemoni.*
    Right stay continue now that one die.

23. *Pukonini indaaeseyomi.*
    Die asked-him.

24. *Aaqi maayaa puqiqi tseyaam beko tsemi.*
    Then one die myself stay she-said.

25. *Tsentimi aapo e tsireni benaano aapo maampaq maapaq be indebaayom*
    She-said right yes they-said her-mother father outside she stay ask
    baakemi.
    continue.

26. *Aapo maasiqdemi be yandoqbaaqi pukemoni.*
    Right all she herself-too died.

27. *Pukonini indaaetseyomi aayaqbaq iye tenoyo.*
    Die asked-her talk not say.

28. *Aaqi maasiqdemi pukenopo tsireni.*
    Right all died they-said.

29. *Aapo be inde baayomi baakemi aapo naaqemoni.*
    Right she stay listen continue right what-happen.

30. *Aampinnemi mini o aamunkuq aaronimi yemarem uremoni.*
    Stink that stone smell fight-it came went-up.

31. *Uronini aapo undeni naaqenoyo.*
    Went-up right went-in it-happened.

32. *Umam aayampaabaa miniuq beyaraamum aayampaakaq yureni maro*
    Went-in bones those their-daughters bones collect came bury made-
    maasiqaareni musaaoyomi.
    funeral.

33. *Kaakippemi.*
    Finish.

1. Some girls used to come and go inside a cave with food which they collected and put there, and cooked. When they were cooking it, an ugly girl was
there, and she saw something. 'The stone will come down,' she told them, and
said, 'That stone is going to come down, and you must be afraid of it,' she told
them. Those girls said, 'What you say is a lie, go!' 5. 'The stone is not enough
to come down and cover us up,' When they said this she would say, 'Yes,' and
she was there again, and told them it was going to come down. 'The stone will
not come down,' they said.

They would stay inside that place, namely the cave, and cook the food and eat it and play. 10. When they played, she told them that it was coming down but they said, 'The stone won't come down and cover us,' they said, and would stay on until the stone finally came down and covered them up. When it covered them, she told them, 'You stayed there inside,' she said; 'I saw it and told you that is what would happen if you continued to stay inside playing,' she said, and she left.

When she came, she told their mothers and fathers, 15. 'Your daughters are out there and they have been covered up with a stone,' she told them. When she told them their mothers and fathers brought food and killed the pigs and put them near the cave and went around and made sacrifice. They came, made a fire, cooked, and ate.

They continued to do this until one by one they died. When they died they would ask them, 'Now how many are dead?' 'This many remain,' they would say, and it continued like this. 20. Then only two were left. When only two were left, she said, 'All right, all have died but we two remain,' she said. This continued until one of them died. When that one died, they asked her about it. Then that one said, 'I only remain,' she said. 25. When she said this, they said, 'Yes,' and her mother and father stayed outside and continued to ask her if she remained.

All right, now all died, even the last. When she died, they were asking, but nothing was said. So all of them were dead, they now said. Now they stayed on listening, and this is what happened. 30. The smell started, and got into the stone and it went up. When the stone went up, then this is what happened. They went in and collected those bones of their daughters and they came and buried them and made a funeral. It is finished.

14. INVITE YOUR SISTER YOURSELF

1. *Mana make sumeriyaa maniq tiraare.*
   This now Sumeria story I-tell.
2. *Beuntano bayomi benaabaa yunaamaa nentenimi iyaayumaanaarem*
   Mother-and-son stayed her-brother food eat used-to-come came look
   yebanim onaakom onaakom demi.
   look did.
3. *Manaa nuram ipoqbaaqna etseyomi yemoni.*
   One day ceremony-for-nose-piercing they-made they-came.
4. *Yenimi banaabaam aanaaqmano onaarem tsemi.*
   She-came her-brother his-wife saw-her she-said.
5. *Maakepakaa yunaama minipi neseya iyaayumaare yenaabaaino tsiremi*
   Not-now food those eat used-to-come come she-said cross-at-her.
   aasemoni.
6. *Aasenimi aapo onapaq aayokun ininano ika saandem banimi onapaq*
   Cross-at now other-side-of-door old lady fire make stay other-side-door
   okumandemoni.
   sat-down.

7. *Okumantanimi aaqi mini baanta aanaatsi inunaa ikaaiqenoyo.*
   Sat-down right that man woman viand collect-firewood.

8. *Eni benaabaa beyanaaq tsaankemi eyamaasim waaranaana yebena*
   Did her-brother his-wife sent your-sister-in-law go-tell-her come help-
   opaaebanapono tsiremi beyanaaq tsaankemi.
   you he-said his-wife send.

9. *Tsaankemi benanaaq yemi aankapate yebaaekem maro beyabaapum*
   Sent-her his-wife came half-way went-back to her-husband told-him
   tsaamemi maro tsunaami tsipokako tsiremi bako tsiremi beyabaapum
   go I-told-her I-don't-want she-said stay she-said her-husband told.
   tsamemi.

10. *Aaqi aayinkaki onemi rukaakemi baanurami poruq aarobenoyo.*
    Then evening when-got slept in-morning pigs kill.

11. *Aarobebaayomi yebaaekem beyanaaq tsaankemi maro tsinanaa yebem*
    Start-to-kill went-back his-wife sent go tell-her come viand help he-said
    inuniq ebanaapono tsentimi bemoni.
    she-went.

12. *Oraaemi aankapate obaaekem yeremi beyabaapum tsaamemi tsunaami*
    Arrived half-way returned came her-husband she-told-him I-told-her
    tsiponkato tsiko tsiremi mare tsaamemi.
    I-don't-want she-said she-said go told-him.

13. *Tsaamemimi mimipora miniuq aaraakendeni.*
    Told-him those-pigs those killed.

14. *Aaqi mini yunkaabenoi.*
    Now this start-to-cook.

15. *Yunkaboyomi yebaaikem beyenaaq tsiankemi maro tsinam yebem*
    They-cook went-back his-wife sent-her go tell-her come viand soup
    inunaa tsontomaakiq ebanaapono tsentimi.
    do-help he-said.

16. *Benanaaq yemoni.*
    His-wife came.

17. *Yeraaem yebaaikem aankapate bemoni.*
    Arrived went-back half-way went.

18. *Oremi maro tsaamemi tsiponkebako tsiremi bako tsemi maro tsaamemi.*
    Returned to tell-him I-don't-want-to she-said he-stay she-said go
    told-him.

19. *Tsaamimi e tsiremonimi.*
    Told-him yes he-said-to-her.

20. *Aaqi mini pora miniuq onakarabenoyo.*
    Then that pig those start-make-mumu.

21. *Onakara boyomi mini untano onapaq mini aayokinamaq ikasaande*
    Went-make-mumu went that mother-son side-door that old-one-with
    bene okamaq aakom demi.

prepare-fire stay eye used did.

22. *Aaqi mini aayokun tsiaamemi tsentimaasi miqnimiqni aakemidaqi*
    So that old-one she-told-her my-sister-in-law so-and-so has-done this
mana bequmpe baanamaa tsentibaama yerema indaaentina.
I-go you-stay my-brother come ask.

23. *Benanaaqi miqnimiqni tsiraqi mana bequmpe tsirebaaq tsaameno*
    His-wife so-and-so said that I-go she-said tell-him she-said.
tsentimi.

24. *E tsiremi bami.*
    Yes she-said stayed.

25. *Aaqi benabaa daapiqakom demi yemi yenimi mare mini aayokun*
    Then her-brother waited came came came go that old-one asked where
indaaemi napakaq makaq tsentum biyaapono tsentimi.
here my-sister go he-said.

26. *Mini enanaaqi miqnimiqni aakemidami aqi bemino tsiremi benabaami*
    That your-wife so-and-so did right went-away said her-brother told-him.
tsiaamem.

27. *Tsiamemi e siremi aaqi mini beyom aaqnaaemi aabaakuremi.*
    Told-him yes he-said then that his-sister behind ran.

28. *Aabaakurem yemi aanupaq yeraaemi aarentimi yebaaeke eqe bono.*
    Ran-after came hill arrived shouted-at you-go-back no go.

29. *Miqnimiqni aakemidaaqi mana yequmpe yaabaaeke bono tsiremi beya-*
    So-and-so did this I-come go-back go she-said her-brother she-told-him.
baam tsaamemi.

30. *Tsaamimi iyaayem yemoni yere onanimi meqyam ena aanukaaq bonimi.*
    Told-him he-ran came came saw there another hill she-came.

31. *Meqyun untanoo mikake tsenimi.*
    There mother-and-son stay he-said.

32. *Yebaaekem eyanaaq maro aayokukiqure mini pon yunaam yunkaamim*
    Go-back your-wife go properly that pig food cook eat she-said-and
nano tsiremi tsaamemi.
told-him.

33. *Tsaamenimi iyaayem mini aanukaaq yeraaem tsentimi okaan aaimi*
    When-she-said run that hill arrived said same talk told-him.
tsaamemoni.

34. *Tsaamiqdemi aakkaa meqyaq ena aanukaq oraaunimi tenimi okaaniq*
    Told-him all-right there other mountain arrived-there said same she-
tsirem tsaamemi.
said told-him.

35. *Tsaamemi aaqi mini tsumeriyaampaq poq aabasaq oraaemi manam*
    Told-him then that Sumeriyampa hole near arrived took mat stick
yubaa noyana pokim karuqdanimi kumemoni.
in-hole threw-them go-down.

36. *Kumonimi benabaa iyaayem yepakaanumpo tsenimi beontano mempam*
    Went-down her-brother ran try-to-catch he-said mother-son down-there
mini poqaainkim karusaaqemoni.
that inside-hole jumped-down.

37. *Emi aaqyaan konam kumanam danimi uremoni.*
    Did dry fog put-it-up put came.

38. *Uronimi benaabaa ipiqde baninkaake aakanaa aayaanaa aakkeqyamam*
    Came-up- her-brother wept stay ear finger cut-off down-there that hole
mempami mini aaim karuqdemoni.
threw-it.

39. *Karuqdaaremi yebaaikemi bemoni.*
    Threw-it went-back go.

40. *Bonimi oraaunini indaaiseyomi naquqdukepono tsetseyomi.*
    Gone arrived they-asked what-you they-said.

41. *Miqnimureqi kaaqnani sikeqyaake dukeko tsiremi tsiyimemoni.*
    Did-thus-and-so bamboo cut myself he-said he-told-them.

42. *Tsiyimemi tsemi ubikam porukani tsiponkaqumpe.*
    When-he-told-them he-said exchange pigs I-don't-want.

43. *Tsiponkaaqumpe beyanaakani maasiqdem poraa miniuq manam naaum-*
    I-don't-want his-wife all pigs those take in-house put he-said.
paaqmana daano tenimi.

44. *Eyo tsiremi maasiqdem poruq manan naaumpaqmandemoni.*
    Yes she-said all pigs take in-house-put-in.

45. *Danimi aapo manam mini inini ipaq naaumpaq umbeba mana porukaq*
    Put-in right take-it that woman there house go-in-stay that pigs eat
nebaaq baano tsiremi tsaamemoni.
and-stay he-said told-her.

46. *Tsaamenimi eyo tsiremi uremoni.*
    Told-her yes she-said went-in.

47. *Undukanimi nurampaq kunanaanaa kaayaakemdemi mare onakaq*
    Went-inside in-night cane rattan cut-it take door fasten-it hidden-door
aakupandemoni aanaamekaqbaq aakupandemoni.
fasten-it.

48. *Aakupanduremi beyaanaaq tsiaamemi tsemi mini pon yunaanaaq ne-*
    Fasten-it his-wife he-told-her he-said that pig food eat inside stop
baaq naaumpaq baano tsemi.
he-said.

49. *Tsentimi aaqi mini maandaqmikimpaq bemi yunaanaa poraa miniuq*
    He-said then that up-here-inside stayed food pigs those eat she-stayed.
nem bemoni.

50. *Banimi benabaapu mare indaaem tsemi nebunanaaq nepono tsentenimi.*
    She-stayed her-husband go asked he-said what-part you-eat he-said-
to-her.

51. *Aaqi mini tsontomaakaa aaraakaa miniuqi neko tsentenimi.*
    Then that soup insides those I-eat she-told-him.

52. *E tsiremi yebaaikem nokem.*
    Yes he-said went-back walk-around.

53. *Mare indaaentenimi aaqi mini obunaankimi aaraayandeq neko tsentimi.*
    Came asked-her right that skin-outside-part start I-eat she-told-him.

54. *E tsiremi nokem.*
    Yes he-said went-about.

55. *Mare indaaebanimi tsamebanimi baakemi maasiqdem mini poraa*
    Came asked-her she-told-him stay all that pig those eat finish.
    miniuq naman kapippemoni.

56. *Namam kakippanimi mare indaaem tenemi mini maasiqdem poni*
    Eat finish go asked said that all pig eat I-finish said.
    namani kaakippeko tsentim.

57. *E tsirem.*
    Yes he-said.

58. *Yebaaekem bemi obem nokem mare indaaentenimi.*
    Went-back went stay go-about came asked-her.

59. *Aaqi mini koqyunkimi aaraayandeq neko tsentimi.*
    Then that seeds-of-bean start I-eat she-said.

60. *E tsirem.*
    Yes he-said.

61. *Yebaaekem bemoni.*
    Went-back left.

62. *Obem indaaebanim.*
    Stay asked-her.

63. *Obem obaaiqmanarem yerem indaaebanim.*
    Stay came-back arrive ask-her.

64. *Aaqi mini maasiqdem yunaami namani kaakippareqi mini unaankasika*
    Now that all food eat finished that string-bag clothes those things start
    baqdoba miniuq kimi kukandeqi mana neko tsentimi.
    that I-eat she-said.

65. *E tsiremi.*
    Yes he-said.

66. *Yebaaekem nokem obaaekem mare indaaentenimi.*
    Went-back walk-about came-back come asked-her.

67. *Aaqi mana maasiqde aaqneqne naaunkim benim aqneqneuq naakeq*
    Right this all something things in-house some-things I-have-eaten eaten
    namani kaakippareqi mana tsiqnonyoba miniuq kimi kukaandeqi neko
    finish those my-hair those things start I-eat she-said.
    tsentimi.

68. *E tsiremi.*
    Yes he-said.

69. *Yebaaekem bemoni.*
    Went-away left.
70. *Obaakem yemi yeraaemi indaaentenimi.*
    Stayed came arrived asked.
71. *Aaqi mini naamam kaakippaareqi mana paani beko tsentinimi.*
    Right that eaten finished that nothing it-stay told-him.
72. *E tsirem aaqi yebaaekem bemoni.*
    Yes he-said then went-back left.
73. *Onokem mare indaaentenimi aaqi mini tsiaaneqne mareko tsentenimi.*
    Walk-around came asked-her then this sick I-have she-told-him.
74. *E tsiremi.*
    Yes he-said.
75. *Yebaaekem bemoni.*
    Went-away went.
76. *Onokemi yemam indaaentenimi aayaqbaq minibaaq iyen temoni.*
    Went-about came asked-her talk that not say-to-him.
77. *Iye tsenimi.*
    Not she-said.
78. *Aaqi mini pukemino tsiremi onakaqbaq aamaankaqbaq ika indiqdanimi*
    Right this she-died he-said door back-door fire lit burn he-burned-her-up.
    kemi kaataayemoni.
79. *Kataakami bemeno.*
    Burn-up stay.
80. *Aapo benaayopimaa enapate yeraainaai eyanaaqi iyebaaqi tseankaano.*
    All-right his-sister another-place he-came your-wife don't send.
81. *Enapuyaaq oaabiqmam marerebaaq yunaami aayokukiqure aaminanaaq*
    Yourself bring-her come food make-it-properly give eat-it can-go.
    naamandem bino.
82. *Miqnintikemi.*
    That-is-why.
83. *Mana mini maniq kaakippemi.*
    This this story finish.

1. I am going to tell this story about Sumeria [a woman]. There were a mother and her son who used to come whenever her brother would eat some food, and when she came, they would look and look at her. One day he held a ceremony for piercing the nose and pushing the cane down the throat, and she came. When she came, her brother's wife saw her and said, 5. 'Not again! You always run along and come when we eat some food,' she said, and was angry at her. When she was cross at her, she went and sat down on the other side of the door, the place where an old lady was making a fire. After she sat down, then the men and woman got together the viands and the firewood. When they had done this, her brother sent his wife and said, 'Go tell her to come and help you,'

so he sent his wife to her. When he had sent her, his wife just went half way and came back and told her husband, 'I went and told her but she said, 'I don't want to go,' so she stayed back,' she said in telling her husband.

10. When it got evening, they went to sleep and in the morning they were going to start killing the pigs. When they were going to kill them, he went back and sent his wife and said, 'Tell her, "You come and help with the viands,"' and she went. She arrived half way there, and returned and came and told her husband: 'I told her, but she said, "I don't want to go,"' she said as she went and told him. When she told him, they killed those pigs.

Now they started to cook these things. 15. When they had started cooking, he sent his wife to go back and said, 'Go tell her, you come and help prepare the viands and soup.' His wife went. When she went, she went only half way and left. She came back and told him that she said, 'I don't want to,' and stayed; so she went and told him. When she told him, he told her, 'Yes.'

20. Then they went and started to make the mumu of the pigs. When they started to make the mumu, the mother and her son were on the other side of the door with that old one preparing the fire, and she looked and looked [for someone to come after her]. So she told the old one, 'My sister-in-law has done thus-and-so, so I have gone; you stay if my brother comes to ask about me. Tell him that his wife said so-and-so, so I went,' she said to tell him. 'Yes,' said the old one, and stayed behind.

25. When her brother had waited [for some time], he came. When he came, he went and asked the old one, 'Where has my sister gone?' he said. 'Your wife has done thus-and-so, so she left,' she told her brother. When she told him, he said, 'Yes,' and then he ran after his sister. He ran after her and came to a hill and she shouted at him, 'You go back, don't come on. She did so-and-so, so I came, you go on back,' she said and she told her brother.

30. When she told him, he ran and came and saw her and she came up to another hill. 'Stop there, mother and son,' he said. 'Go back; go and prepare properly and eat that pig and food,' she told him. When she said this, she ran and came to a hill and said to him the same thing. After she told him, then she arrived there on another mountain and said to him what she had said and told him before.

35. When she told him she arrived at Sumeriyampa near a hole and took and threw down into it the mat and sticks. When those things went in, her brother ran and tried to catch them and the mother and son jumped down inside the hole. When they did that, a fog came up around there. When it came up, her brother wept and he cut off his ear and his finger and threw them in the hole. When he had thrown them, he left and went back.

40. When he had gone, he arrived and they asked him, 'What is wrong with you?' they said to him. He said, 'I did thus and so, and cut myself with wild bamboo,' he told them.

When he had told them this, he said, 'I don't want to exchange pigs any more. I don't want to do it,' and he told his wife to put all those pigs inside the house. 'Yes,' she said, and she put all those pigs inside the house. 45. When she had put them in, now the woman went and stayed there in the house, and he told her, 'You eat those pigs and stay there,' he told her. When he told her that she said 'Yes,' and went in.

When she had gone inside, that night he cut rattan and locked up the main door and also locked the hidden door. When he had locked them, he said to his wife, 'You stay inside and eat that pig and the food there.' When he said that, then she stayed there inside, and she ate that food and pig, and stayed on.

50. After she had been there a while, he came and asked her and said, 'What part are you eating?' he said to her. Then she told him, 'I am eating a soup of the insides.' 'Yes,' he answered and went back, and went around. He came and asked her again; right, 'I am starting to eat the outside parts,' she told him. 'Yes,' he said, and went about again. 55. He came and asked her again, and she told him that she had finished eating those pigs. When she had finished eating them, he asked her and she said, 'I have finished eating all the pig.' 'Yes,' he said. He went away and stayed, and went about, then came and asked her again. Now she said, 'I am starting to eat the seeds of the beans,' 60. 'Yes,' he replied. He went away. He used to stay away awhile, then ask her again. He would stay away, come back, and when he arrived there, asked her again.

Then when all the food was finished [eaten up] she told him, 'I have started to eat the old string bag and clothes and those things.' 65. 'Yes,' he said, Then he went back, went around, and came back and asked her. Then she answered, 'I have eaten all those things that are in the house, and have finished eating them, and I have started to eat my hair and such things as that,' she said. 'Yes,' he said. He left again. 70. He stayed away, then came, and when he arrived, he asked again. Then she told him, 'I have finished eating, there is nothing left.' 'Yes,' he said, then left again.

He went about, and came and asked of her again. She told him, 'I am sick now.' 'Yes,' he said. 75. He left again. He went around again, and came and asked her, and she did not say anything to him. She did not speak. 'Right, this one has died,' he said, and he lit the door and the secret door with fire, and it was burned up. She remained inside and was burned.

80. Now if you want your sister to come some place, don't send your wife. Bring her yourself, and give food, and do it properly, and she can come and eat it. That is what you should do. Now this story is finished.

15. INITIATION OF THE BOYS

1. *Ipoqbaqna eyonan tsararare.*
Initiation they-do I-will-write.

2. *Ipoqbaqnairani anasi banta yunam koyakemdemi pom aurem uremi*
When-make-initiation women men food collect pig kill do initiate-them.
ipaqbaqnaemi.

3. *Ipaqbaqnairaremi pumara iyen tamemi.*
If-hold-initiation young-men not tell.

4. *Miqnirani miqniqnumpo tsopae ika akano tsiremi baeqdemi akemi.*
When-once-do-something I-do-something you-help fire you-collect he-said pretend collect.

5. *Aonama masiqdem aneqne rereniniquremi.*
    When-he-saw all something get-ready.
6. *Apo mini anombantakaqi tsamemi mini ontequmpo pumaraqukaq*
    Then those big-people tell-them this I-am-going-to-do-something young-
pakano tseni.
people you-catch they-said.
7. *Apo aqi mini pumarauqi pakamam nauni deno.*
    Right now those boys catch house-in put-them.
8. *Apo aqi mini dukeni yunana miniuq mare yimeni neni bayaba miniuq*
    Right then those put/imprison food those bring give eat talk those
tsiyimenieno.
tell-them.
9. *Emi apo mini mankabakumaba miniuq narampa de beno.*
    Do OK those Mankabakumaba those at-night sing stay.
10. *Apo banurami mini nompaq yibike beno.*
    Right morning this water-place bring went.
11. *Nompaq yibike birareni.*
    Water-place bring when-want-go.
12. *Bantauq tsiyinkem bemi maro kappa ayakaq ubiqmam non abakaq*
    Men they-send-them went go small path make water near go-along.
maroremi.
13. *Apo mini karuka yana minuq akeqyarem tsini ayabapaq ayopamam*
    Now this nettles stick those cut that near-road hide-them go-along.
maroremi.
14. *Mini pumara yeyibikeni beno.*
    Those young-men bring-them went.
15. *Yibike tsini ayana kumirani ba bantauq tsiyinkani kum dapiqman*
    When-bring that path go-down before men send-them go-down watch
maro kundami.
go go-down.
16. *Apo mikaqi pumarauqi mikaqi yibike kumeno.*
    All-right that young-men that bring-them go-down.
17. *Yibike kumani apo miqyapate mapate yiro kumeno.*
    Bring go-down all-right one-side other-side hit go-down.
18. *Yiro kumake nonkaq makundani apo mini puka tsireni yirueke non-*
    Hit go-down water-place arrived then that two they-said fight water-in
kimi karuqdeno.
throw.
19. *Nonkim yirumam aqniraneni apo mini onana dakindeni yisippem*
    Water-in hit-them ready-to-throw then that blades-of-grass take-off
aorem nare kumini anareni mini nonkim donan aqneno.
their-nose push-in blood come-down see-it that water-in catch throw-them.
20. *Awnuram kundaini apo mikinke kunubaqdeni mini yopenaimi kuna-*

Throw went-down-there then from-there take-them-out those their-
nami abekeno.
mouth-in come push-down.
21. *Abekeni mini yamuqmana yisiqi kappondeno.*
Push that same-day their nose pierce-hole.
22. *Miqnureni mini yibikeni naumpaq yeno.*
Have-finished that bring-them house-in come.
23. *Miqnurami mipaq dukemi puqmam akakaremi yequkukemi.*
When-done-that there sleep die almost they-get-up.

1. I'm going to write about how they do the initiation. When they make an
initiation, the men and women collect food and kill pigs and then initiate them.
When they hold the initiation, they do not tell the young men about it. 'When I
want to do something, I do this, and you help by collecting firewood,' they say,
and they trick the boys into collecting it. 5. When they see this, they all get
those things ready.

Now those important people talk about it among themselves. They say, 'I'm
going to do something, so you catch those young fellows.' So they catch the
boys and put them in a house. These imprison them and then bring and give
them food and tell them to eat and talk to them. While they do this they sing a
song called Mankabakumaba as they stay there in the night.

10. Now in the morning they take them down to the creek. They bring them
down to that creek when they are ready to go. The men send them along and
they go and make a small path going along near the water. Then they cut nettles
and sticks and hide them near the road where they go along. They then bring
the young men down and go along. 15. When they bring them, they go down
that path, but they send some on down before, and they watch while they go.
All right, now they bring those young boys on down. As they bring them down,
they go along and they hit them from both sides. They hit them as they go
down, and when they arrive at the creek, then they say there is a really big fight,
and they throw them into the water. They hit them in the water, and as they
throw them, then they take the blades [very sharp] of the large grass, and
they push it up their nose and when they see the blood rush out, then they
catch them and throw them into the water. 20. They throw them in and they go
down in it, and then they take them out of there and they come and push it
down into their mouth. They push it in and then that same day they pierce the
hole in their nose [for the pig tusk that hangs from the nose]. When they
have finished all that, they bring them back and come into the house. Then after
that happens, they sleep there and after just missing death, they get up.

16. Funeral

1. *Mana bantama puqona musaeyomi.*
One man death funeral.
2. *Banta puqomi manan dukoni bantaba mini iyen tiyimeno.*
Man die take they-put-him people those not tell-them.

3. *Anoniqukam bainta ukaqmana yuremi yebemi ikom dapikeno.*
   Important people only-ones gather come shell stand-it-up.
4. *Dapeqdama yoanteqimi manam paqbamuremi banta anasi tsamemi.*
   Stand-it-up go-straight take let-it-be-known men women tell-them.
5. *Banta anasi tsaamimi yeni ipiqdeno.*
   Men women tell-them they-come they-cry.
6. *Ipiqdareni manam masiqeno.*
   Cry take bury.
7. *Manam masiqarem apo mini yunana miniuq manan ayopeno.*
   Take bury then that food those take make-ready.
8. *Ayoparem apo mini pora yunana akandemi benaqomi aremi.*
   When-get-ready then that pigs food mumu his-relatives call-upon.
9. *Arami yebami om akandemi nem amemi.*
   When-call-them come stone mumu eat give.
10. *Amimi apo marem bemi.*
    When-they-give-them then take go.
11. *Apo iyema benanontama amimi mini mikaq aruemmi.*
    Then don't relatives give those there fight.
12. *Amimi marem bemmi.*
    Give take go.
13. *Marem bukami apo mini arim bainta apakem.*
    Take went then these kill men find.
14. *Ikom dapekemi moku akaremi uremi arim bainta apakemi.*
    Shell put-it-up native-vegetables mumu did kill man find.
15. *Apakaremi bema etseq maro aremi.*
    When-they-find-it-out he at-sometime go went-kill.
16. *Aruremi moukariem masikaq mare yokemi.*
    Went-kill-him Moukariem grave come plant.

1. This is the funeral for a man who dies. When a man dies, they take and put him aside and do not tell the people about it. The important people are the only ones who gather together, and then they stand up on its edge a certain shell [do magic with it]. They stand it on its edge and when it goes straight, then they let it be known by telling the men and women. 5. After they tell the men and women, they come together and cry. They wail and then they take and bury him. After they take and bury him, then they make ready all the food. When they get it ready, then they cook the pigs and the food, and then they call the relatives together. When they call them together, then they cook it in a stone oven and give it out to eat. 10. After they give it out, those take it and go.

But if they don't give it to the relatives, then there is a big fight there. They give it to them, and they take it and go.

After they take it and go, then those there try to find out what man killed him. They stand up a shell, and they cook a native vegetable and then they find out what man killed him. 15. When they find it out, then at the same time they kill the one who killed him. After they kill him, they plant Moukariem and come there to the grave.

17. GETTING MARRIED

1. *Mana anasi mareyo andaban tsararare.*
   This woman marry custom I-want-to-write.
2. *Pumara anasi maranobani akinta ayopi akinta indaeno.*
   Young-men women to-be-married girl brother girl ask.
3. *Akinta indaentimi mini pumara mararare tsentimi apo mini be ayopiu-*
   Girl ask-her that young-man I-want-to-marry he-said then that he
   nami maro pumaramano ano apomi tsiamemi.
   brothers went young-man mother father tell-them.
4. *Tsiamima pumara ano apoma tsema tsiponkako tsentimi eqiremi.*
   When-they-tell-them boys mother father they-say I-don't-want he-said
   forget-it.
5. *Apo tsema eyo tsentimi amemi.*
   Right they-say yes they-said give-it.
6. *Pumarai iye indaeno.*
   Young-man know they-ask.
7. *Indaerani akintakaqbaq pumara ano aponkaqbaqi indaeno.*
   They-want-ask girl boy mother father ask.
8. *Anasi pumara amirani pumara onama yokema ayampaema abesara-*
   Women boy give boy see work hard lazy not work hard see that married.
   baqma iyeina yokem ayampaebami onemi mini maremi.
9. *Pumara ano apoma onama akintama abesaraebami pumara ano apobaqi*
   Boy mother father see girl lazy boy mother father not get.
   iye maremi.
10. *Onama yokem ayampaimi maremi.*
    They-see work hard get-her.
11. *Apo amiqdukama mararan emi meyaniq narem emi.*
    Then give-her-to-him get-her do to-pay first do.
12. *Miyaniquremi bami manayaqmam ikonapi apappate mana omande*
    Paid stay five moon other-side one get moon go-by put-skirt-around.
    ikonapi yankakaimi iremi.
13. *Iraraemi andina miniuqi manam ayopemi.*
    When-want-to-put-skirt bark those things get-ready.
14. *Apo ayoparemi yunana miniuq mandeni apo mikaqi ireno.*
    Then get-ready food those take-gather then from-there put-skirt-around.
15. *Indami apo mini pumara manom ano apo yemarem bemi.*
    When-skirted then they young-man take mother father come-bring go.
16. *Apo marodukami bami benabapu akakaem iyem yemi.*
    Then went-put-her stay her-husband not-soon not come.
17. *Ipaq bami bakem mana orandepi buimi apo yeraemi ayanaq arurem*

There stay until one year went then arrived celebrate do eat close-to-her
namandemi aqnakaq yemi.
come.

1. I want to write about the custom when women get married. When a young
man wants to marry a woman, the cousins of the girl have to ask the girl. They
ask the girl and if she says, 'I will marry that young man,' then those cousins
[brothers] go and tell the parents of the young man. When they tell them, if the
parents say, 'I don't want it,' then they forget about it.
5. All right, if they say yes, then they indicate that they will get her. They
don't ask the boy. If they want to talk about it, the girl's and boy's parents do
the talking. When a woman is given to a boy, they must see that the boy works
hard and that he is not lazy, but they must see that he works hard if they are to
be married. If the boy's parents see that the girl is lazy, then the boy's parents
do not get her. 10. They see that the one that they want works hard.
So if they want him to get married to her, then they first have to pay. After
the payment has been made for five months or maybe one more month, then
they put the skirt on around the girl [they get married]. When they want to put
the skirt around her, they get those bark things ready. When they get those things
ready, then they get the food together, and then they put the skirt around her.
15. After they get married, then the young man's mother and father come and
bring them and take them there. Then when they go and put her there [in their
house], she stays, but her husband cannot come there very soon. She stays there
up to one year, and then he can come and make a special celebration, and they
will eat and he can go about with her.

PART FOUR: *Tairora-Binumarien-Waffa*

XXIV. Introduction

HOWARD McKAUGHAN

The Tairora-Binumarien-Waffa subfamily of the Eastern Family of the East New Guinea Highland Stock is the last to be described in this monograph. The Binumarien is spoken by 117 people living in three small villages on the northeastern boundary of the Kainantu subdistrict. Waffa is spoken by approximately 940 people living in five villages located at the headwaters of the Waffa River. This area is in the Morobe District south of the Markham River in the Kaiapit subdistrict, and is the only one separated from the rest of the Eastern Family. Tairora is the largest of the three named members of this subfamily and may be divided into a number of dialects. It is spoken by some eight thousand people who live in the mountainous country south of Kainantu in the Kainantu and Okapa subdistricts.

The following chapters describe the phonology of Binumarien and Waffa; give descriptions of the noun systems of Tairora, Binumarien, and Waffa and the verb morphology and syntax of Tairora; discuss sequences of clauses in Tairora; and finally treat the subject morphemes in the Tairora verb complex. Vincents' article on the verb system presented here replaces an earlier study entitled 'Introductory Notes on Tairora Verb Morphology and Syntax' (1962a). Chapter XXVII brings this study up to date, with more data available and a better grasp of the materials than was possible earlier.

The Vincents, in an unpublished manuscript (1962c), list the consonants of Tairora as *p, t, k, q, b, r, h, m,* and *n,* and also prenasalized stops *mp, nt, nk.* Vowels include *i, a, u, e, aa, o.* Word prosodemes of stress are postulated rather than tones as in the other languages, though Stringer and

Hotz describe stress for Waffa too. The relation between stress and tone in these languages is intimate.

Binumarien and Waffa have an alveolar grooved fricative *s* not appearing in Tairora (found in Awa and Auyana). Tairora has a distinctive glottal aspirate *h* which also occurs in Waffa, but not in Binumarien. Both Binumarien and Waffa have five vowels instead of the six of Tairora—less than any of the others of this family. Binumarien and Waffa also have vowel length indicated by gemination of the vowels. This is not the case for Tairora.

The noun structures for Binumarien, Waffa, and Tairora are covered in Chapters XXVII-XXIX. Noun bases for all three may be divided into two classes on the basis of the occurrence of a subject marker suffix. The morphemes in the three languages are cognate: Class I in Tairora takes *-ba,* in Binumarien this class takes *-fa,* and in Waffa it takes *-va.* The class is made up of all personal names and certain listed kinship terms. Class II in each of the three is made up of all other nouns and others of the kinship terms. In addition to the subject marker, Vincent describes some twenty-five noun suffixes for Tairora. As in other languages of the Eastern Family, locatives occupy an important place in the system.

Tairora verbs have suffixed fusions to indicate mode-person-number combinations or tense-person-number portmanteaus. Special sets of these affixes are used with final verbs in independent clauses, and with nonfinal verbs in dependent clauses. Relationships between clauses are outlined in the paper on sequences in Tairora which follows the verb description. The relationships depend on the relative times of the action of the verbs and on the subject of the clause or clauses following, whether they are the same or different.

Harland Kerr discusses possible morpheme cuts to indicate subject pronouns in the Tairora verb complex as seen in the Obura dialect. He concludes that there are morpheme cuts and that basically the morphemes that are so cut are subject person indicators.

The Tairora texts following the descriptive articles were recorded by Alex Vincent. They extend the linguistic material available, permitting further research for interested readers. We look forward to additional material on the Tairora as well as on the Binumarien and Waffa.

XXV. Phonemes of Binumarien

DESMOND and JENNIFER OATRIDGE

1. INTRODUCTION

The segmental and suprasegmental phonemes of Binumarien are presented in this study in terms of their contrast, variation, and distribution.[1]

The Binumarien are a very small group. Within the memory of the older men, they were more numerous, but because of tribal fighting resulting in prolonged residence in the Markham Valley and resultant malaria, their numbers have been greatly reduced. Their neighbors to the west and south are the Gadsup, and to the north the Azera in the Markham Valley. The closely related language of Kambaira is to the southeast. The Binumarien are most closely related to the Tairora though some of the men speak Azera and Gadsup while others speak Gadsup and Tairora as well as their own language. All the men except the very old speak Neo-Melanesian.

[1] This paper was first published as pp. 13-21 in *Papers in New Guinea Linguistics, No. 5,* Linguistic Circle of Canberra Publications (Series A: Occasional Papers, No. 7) (Australian National University, 1967), and is reissued here by permission. The data for this paper were collected by the authors during a stay of two and a half years in the village of Oníkurádarannai while working with the New Guinea Branch of the Summer Institute of Linguistics.

The Administration name for this group of people, Binumarien, was derived from a former village name Pinumaarénai. The people call themselves and the language Afaqina. A large number of informants was used during this time but two middle-aged men, Aaqti and the government-appointed chief, Maraaqaroo, were the principal ones. The tone analysis was done at a linguistic workshop under the direction of Dr. K. L. Pike. The outline for this paper was suggested by the theoretical framework of Pike (1967). Our informants at the workshop were Tata and Kuntaqpi. We wish to record our thanks to members of the institute for help with this analysis.

2. CONTRAST

2.1. Contrast of Segmental Phonemes

p:ᵽ   /putaá/[2] 'rotten', /ᵽukaá/ 'tobacco'; /upeékáa/ 'push into', /aᵽeeka/ 'difficult'

t:r   /raqárárá/ 'will break', /táqárárá/ 'will cross river'; /ᵽaíráka/ type of tree, /ᵽaitáká/ type of frog

t:s   /ᵽatáa/ 'scrape', /ᵽasaá/ type of bird; /túká/ 'root', /suká/ 'sour'

k:q   /ásáúku/ 'your hand', /ásáúqa/ 'old person'; /kukúmá/ type of bird, /ququsá/ 'fence'

i:ee /ᵽiᵽá/ 'He's gone', /ᵽeeᵽa/ 'arrow'; /ᵽainí/ 'dog', /ᵽaééná/ red dye

ii:ee /máríiqa/ 'I have been (there)', /máréeqa/ 'I took it.'

u:oo /múná/ 'smoke', /moóná/ 'the next day'; /uróóna/ 'type of bird', /ooraúná/ type of bird

uu:oo /qtóo/ 'OK!', /qtuú/ type of yam

i:ii /máríno/ 'He stays', /máríino/ 'He has been staying'; /akííqa/ 'head', /ákíqtá/ 'pith (of sugar cane)'

a:aa /mááqá/ 'house', /maqá/ 'ground'; /saaká/ 'sugar', /sáká/ 'fill with water'; /taáká/ type of tree , /táká/ 'frog'

q:ø   (word initially) /qáféqá/ 'I see', /áᵽéká/ 'difficult'; /ó/ 'mouth', /qo/ 'dividing line'; /ququsá/ 'fence', /úqóná/ 'moon'

TABLE 64
CHART OF PHONEMES

	Consonants			
	Bilabial	Alveolar	Velar	Glottal
Stops	p	t	k	q
Fricatives	ᵽ	s		
Nasals	m	n		
Vibrant		r		

	Semivowels	
	w	y

	Vowels		
	Front	Central	Back
High	i		u
Mid	e*		o
Low		a	

* The phonemes /e/ and /o/ never occur singly but only in geminate clusters.

[2] When two /a/ [ˈɑˆ:] phonemes occur contiguously, the vowel quality is changed to [a].

2.2. *Contrast of Tones*

There are two phonemic tone levels, (h)igh and (l)ow. (Only high is marked.)[3]

1-h:h-h /iní murí máríqtánoo/ 'My lemon is here', /iní múrí máríqtánoo/ 'My mole is here.'

h-1:h-h /iní súmpa antáa/ 'Cut my sweet potato', /iní nántá antáa/ 'Cut my forest.'

1-h:1-1 /iní saná suqáa/ 'Cook my taro', /iní paki suqáa/ 'Cook my gum.'

h-1:1-1 /iní sáni máríqtánoo/ 'My stone axe is here', /iní aqti máríqtánoo/ 'My skin is here.'

h-h:1-1 /iní táká suqáa/ 'Cook my frog' /iní paki suqáa/ 'Cook my gum.'

h-1:1-h /iní súmpa máríqtánoo/ 'My sweet potato is here' /iní murí máríqtánoo/ 'My lemon is here.'

3. VARIATION

For the purpose of this chapter a word is defined as the minimal phonological unit which can occur in isolation.

3.1. *Variation of Segmental Phonemes*

3.1.1. Unaspirated stops are /p/, /t/, /k/, and /q/. When occurring intervocalically /p/, /t/, and /k/ are lengthened. [píp·à:nə̀][4] 'insect', [pit·ūt·ū] type of bird, [kuk·ūrə̄] 'beads'.

/p/ and /t/ have voiced variants following nasals at their respective points of articulation. In addition /t/ may vary from an alveolar position to a dental position before /i/ and / e/ in some speakers.

/k/ and /q/ have labialized off glides when they are preceded by /u/ except when followed by /u/: [ukʷə̄sī] 'wood grub', [ə̀ùqʷá:nə̀ì] 'shade'.

3.1.2. Voiceless fricatives are /ɸ/ and /s/: [ə̄pè:k·ə̄] 'hard', [sə̀ínīsə̀] 'small plant'. /s/ has a variant [ts] which occurs word initially. It is used only by some older speakers.

3.1.3. Voiced nasals are /m/ and /n/.[5] A variant of /m/ is [mʷ] which occurs after /u/ except before /u/: [tùmʷə̄nə̄] type of pandanus fruit.

3.1.4. /r/ is the retroflexed alveolar flap [ř]: [řə̀qə̄řə̄řə̄] 'will break'.

---

[3] Low tone /`/ is marked in phonetic representations only.

[4] Throughout this paper, the raising and lowering wedge on the phonetic symbols [ɔˇ] and [əˇ] have been omitted and the symbols written [ɔ] and [ə]. [:] equals two moras of length and [.] equals one and a half moras of length. Phonetic pitch is symbolized [´] high, [⁻] mid, [`] low.

[5] Voiced velar nasal /ŋ/ is a loan phoneme from Azera. It occurs in place and personal names and in a few loan words: /uŋáqa/ place name; /tupúŋa/ 'house post'. Voiced velar stop [g], variant of the phoneme /k/, occurs after /ŋ/ in loan words from Azera: /yaŋkawáná/ place name; /saŋkuma/ 'corn'.

3.1.5. Semivowels are /y/ and /w/. /w/ has a second variant [b] which sometimes fluctuates with [w]: [ɔ̆bá:bɪŋgūsūnɔ̆] type of yam, [kūbɔ̆:nɔ̆nɔ̆] / [kūwɔ̆:nɔ̆nɔ̆] 'small wallaby'.

3.1.6. The high vowel phonemes /i/ and /u/ both have two variants. [ɪ] and [ʋ] occur before nasal initial consonant clusters and [i] and [u] occur in all other positions: [pɪmbʋ́mbúqā:nɔ̆] type of insect, [ít·ít·îê] 'Shut it', [sʋ́mbɔ̆] type of sweet potato, [qùqūsɔ̄] 'fence'.

3.1.7. The mid vowels /e/ and /o/ each have one variant, the phonemic norm: /eetáqtí/ [è:t.ɔ̄qdī] type of rat, / kúkóóqoona/ [kúk.ɔ́:nɔ̆] type of sweet potato.

3.1.8. The variants of the central vowel phoneme /a/ are conditioned as follows: When occurring after /i/ in a VV sequence /a/ has a fronted quality [ə·]: [kɔ̄qdǐə·r̆ŭ] 'worm'. The vowel quality is lowered to low open [a] when two occur together in a geminate cluster, except utterance finally when carrying a high-low tone sequence. In this instance the [ə] quality is retained. The low close variant [ə] also occurs elsewhere.

3.2. *Variation of Tone*

Binumarien has a system of register tones which show only two significant levels. These levels are heard within a simultaneous falling intonation contour which is spread over the utterance concerned. The following examples show how this is applied. Each vowel is one mora of length and carries its own register tone.

3.2.1. In words carrying a series of high tones on all vowels, all tones after the first fall successively lower: /sáárísá/ [sá:r̄isɔ̆] 'cricket'.

3.2.2. A series of word-final high tones following a low tone is phonetically mid: /nammári/ [nɔ̆m:ɔ̄r̄ī] 'water'.

3.2.3. Words carrying a series of low tones on all syllables begin at a low mid level and drop successively lower throughout the word, except when the word occurs utterance finally. The final low tone then rises to form a short rising glide and the vowel on which it occurs is lengthened: /sasoota máráa/ [sɔ̆sɔ̄:t.ɔ̆ mɔ̆r̄ɔ̆ɔ̆] 'Take the wood'; /iní sasoota/ [iní sɔ̄sɔ̆.t.ɔ̆] 'my wood'.

The rising glide has been assigned to low tone because it remains low and the vowel remains short when utterance nonfinal. Its occurrence contrasts with the sequences low-low and low-high, and with high tone in an utterance-final syllable: /sasoota/ type of wood, /sapaa/ 'eel trap'; /karoopaá/ 'water melon', /qumisá/ 'red dye'.

4. DISTRIBUTION

4.1. *Syllables within Word*

4.1.1. *Nuclei.* There are two types of syllables, short and long. The nucleus of short syllables consists of one vowel one mora of length carrying one register tone. The nucleus of a long syllable consists of two contiguous vowels, like or diverse, two moras of length and carries two register tones.[6] Long syllables have been set up because the phonemes /e/ and /o/ never occur singly, but only in geminate clusters.

4.1.2. *General distribution.* The syllable patterns are V and VV optionally preceded by onset of one or two consonants. For description of permitted arrangements in the word, syllables are classed as main, with onset and nucleus, and auxiliary, with no onset.

4.1.2.1. *Main.* There appear to be no limitations of distribution of main syllables either with reference to position in the word or position relative to each other. There may be some minor restrictions on their distribution relative to auxiliary syllables in the word.

4.1.2.2. *Auxiliary.* Word initially only one V syllable or one or two VV syllables occur: /a.qti/ 'skin', /óó.aa.ma.ra/ 'mouth'.[7]

Word medially short auxiliary syllables occur contiguous to long main syllables, and long auxiliary syllables occur contiguous to short main syllables: pee.ú.ná/ type of tree, /pi.oó.sá/ 'wallaby'.

A long auxiliary syllable contiguous to a long main syllable occurs commonly in the speech of young people in words where they omit a glottal stop pronounced by older speakers: /paaqóótáná/ > /paaóótáná/ type of nettle; /kúkóóqoona/ > /kúkóóoona/ type of sweet potato; /tátóóqeesa/ > /tátóóeesa/ type of grub.

Medial sequences of auxiliary syllables have been observed in one word only, /qiú.aa.óó.ná/ 'scrub turkey'.

Auxiliary syllables do not occur in word-final position except in the following example: /róó.i.ráá.i/ 'bamboo cleaning stick'.

4.2. *Phonemes within Syllable and Word*

4.2.1. *Consonants.* All consonants may manifest onset in CV and CVV syllables.

In CCV and CCVV syllables, glottal stop and nasals fill the first consonant position of the onset. Bilabial and alveolar stops, nasals, and semivowel /y/ fill the second. The resulting consonant clusters are as follows: /qp/, /qt/, /qm/, /qn/, /mp/, /nt/, /nn/, /mm/, and /qy/.[8] Of these only /qt/, /qm/, /qn/, and /qy/ have been observed occurring word initially.

4.2.2. *Semivowels.* /y/ and /w/ occur as syllable onsets and are compara-

---

[6] In slow and deliberate speech two clear phonetic syllable pulses are heard particularly on geminate clusters [e.e] [ɔ.ɔ] [a.a].

[7] The boundaries of phonemic syllables are indicated by a dot but are not themselves considered phonemes.

[8] The /qy/ cluster of phonemes is separate from the [qy] conditioned variant of /q/. /qy/ occurs initially in question words and in one word /uqyàa/ 'put'. An alternative analysis of the consonant clusters /qp/, /qt/, /qm/, /qn/, and /qy/ as single phonetically complex phonemes is also possible.

tively rare phonemes occurring most frequently in place and personal names: /aayakaráání/ type of yam, /yankawáná/ place name, /wóówá/ man's name.

4.2.3. *Vowels.* /i/, /a/, and /u/ occur as short syllable nuclei. Long syllable nuclei consist of geminate vowel clusters /ee/, /oo/, /aa/, /ii/, /uu/ and diverse clusters /ua/, /au/, /ai/, /ia/, /ui/, /iu/. The phonemes /e/ and /o/ never occur singly but only in geminate clusters.

The vowel clusters /ui/, /ii/, and /uu/ have not been observed word initially.

All permitted vowel sequences except /iu/ and /uu/ occur in long syllables in medial position. In sequences of main plus auxiliary all vowel combinations have been observed except: /aa/, /ee/, and /oo/ plus /a/; /aa/ and /oo/ plus /u/; /i/ plus /ee/; and /a/ plus /aa/.

/i/, /a/, and /u/ may occur as the vowel of short main syllables in word-final position. All permitted vowel sequences except /ui/, /iu/, and /ii/ may occur as the nuclei of word-final long main syllables.

4.3. *Distribution of Tone*

Tone sequences on words of up to five vowels have been charted. Distributional limitations have been observed only on words of three, four, and five vowels having all long, or short and long syllables.

4.3.1. On three and four vowel words following the first high tone all other tones will be high preceding a final high: /ˊˊˊ/, /ˋˊˊˊ/, /ˊˊˊˊ/. In five vowel words with CVV.CVV.CV syllable pattern, this restriction applies only to the penultimate and final syllables: /ˊˋˊˊˊ/.

4.3.2. Following a high tone on antepenultimate vowel, and preceding low tone on final vowel, a penultimate vowel will carry low tone: /ˊˋˋ/,/ˋˊˋˋ/, /ˊˊˋˋ/,/ˊˊˊˋˋ/, /ˋˊˊˋˋ/.

4.3.3. The tone sequence high-high has not been observed on a final long syllable of a multisyllabic word.

XXVI. Waffa Phonemes

MARY STRINGER and JOYCE HOTZ

1. INTRODUCTION

Waffa has heretofore received very little mention in discussions about New Guinea languages.[1] Preliminary lexicostatistical comparison indicates that Waffa is a member of the Eastern Family as defined by S. A. Wurm (1964; see also Chap. XXXV). It is more closely related to Tairora than to any other language in the family and no doubt is a member of the Tairora subfamily.

The unique feature of a contrast between sonorant and obstruent nasal phonemes distinguishes the Waffa system from the phonemic systems of the other languages in the Eastern Family and perhaps from all other Highland languages.[2] In other features the Waffa phoneme system could be regarded as a typical Eastern Highland system. The following description is presented as a basis for detailed comparison with other Highland systems and as a basis for establishing a practical orthography for Waffa.

[1] This paper, in slightly different format, also appears in *Papers on Seven Languages of Papua–New Guinea* (in press), a publication of the Linguistic Society of New Zealand, and is published here by permission.

The materials upon which this analysis is based were collected under the auspices of the Summer Institute of Linguistics while the authors were residing at the village of Kusing for a total of two years during 1962–66. The authors gratefully acknowledge the help of Eunice Pike and Dorothy James in the analysis of the Waffa phonemic system, and that of Darlene Bee in preparing this paper for publication.

[2] The contrast between an alveolar nasal sonorant and flap is also found in one dialect of the neighboring Tairora language.

2. PHONEMIC INVENTORY

Eighteen consonants, five vowels, and contrastive stress define the Waffa phonemic system. Table 65 shows the intersecting contrastive features which define the segmental phonemes.

TABLE 65

WAFFA PHONEMES

Consonants

	Bilabial	Alveolar	Velar	Glottal
Stops				
Prenasalized	*b*	*d*	*g*	
Nonprenasalized	*p*	*t*	*k*	*q*
Oral Fricatives				
Voiced	*v*			
Voiceless	*f*	*s*		*h*
Nasals				
Sonorant	*m*	*n*	*ng*	
Obstruent	*mm*	*nn*		
Liquids				
Semivowel		*y*		
Vibrant		*r*		

Vowels

	Front	Central	Back
High	*i*		*u*
Low	*e*	*a*	*o*

3. PROBLEMS OF INTERPRETATION

Palatalization, labialization, and prenasalization of consonants; vowel length; and the consonant-vowel status of high vocoids present interpretational problems. The following are the interpretations chosen in the analysis presented in the following sections of this chapter.

3.1. *Palatalization and Labialization of Consonants*

Since vowel sequences are common in Waffa, but consonant sequences do not occur, the palatalization and labialization of consonant phonemes has been interpreted as a sequence of consonant plus high vowel. Two further disadvantages of interpreting them as consonant plus /w/ *or* /y/ are that this would increase the morphophonemic complexity of the verb morphology and it would require the postulation of a /w/ phoneme not otherwise needed in this description of Waffa.[3] For example: [pwǎř ə] /puára/ 'pig', [ndwaːtaino:] /duaátainoo/ 'rotting flesh', [pyέ:no:] /pieénoo/ 'She is weaving', [ndyáuno:] /diáunoo/ 'I am standing'.

3.2. *Prenasalization of Stops*

The prenasalized voiced stops [mb], [nd], and [ŋg] function in single consonantal positions and have been interpreted as single unit phonemes /b/, /d/, and /g/, respectively, since there are no other consonantal clusters. For example: [sɩmbáu] / [sɩmpáu] /síbáu/ 'fly', [ndaːtó:] /daátóo/ 'grandmother', [ɓaíndi] / [ɓaínti] /vaídi/ 'man', [ŋgíːŋgə] / [ŋgíːŋkə] /gíiga/ 'worm'.

3.3. *Vowel Length*

Phonetic vowel length has been interpreted as instances of geminate vowel sequences. For example: /tiínoo/ 'He is coming down', /tínóo/ 'He is saying', /kuáannú/ 'wild cane flowers', /kuáanúu/ 'spit', /nninnúúna/ 'vein', /ninúnna/ 'my sister', /yoópée/ bamboo pipe' /yópee/ 'able'. The distribution of stress justifies the interpretation of geminate sequences as two units rather than one in that either vowel may be stressed, both vowels may be stressed, or both may be unstressed, that is V́V, V́V́, V́V́, or VV. For example: /mmáata/ 'bed', /mmaápu/ 'son', /mmáára/ 'revenge', /mmaimáura/ tree type.

3.4. *Consonant-Vowel Status of High Vocoids*

Syllabic high vocoids are interpreted as /i/ and /u/. Nonsyllabic high front vocoids are interpreted as /y/. Nonsyllabic high back vocoids do not occur apart from labialization. For example: [mɩmí] /mmímmí/ type of worm, [sánéːtu] /sánéétu/ 'lightning', [kɔ́pέyέyɔ] /kópéya/ type of fly, [ɓuéːɓáːɓéː] /vuééváávéé/ 'quickly'.

4. DESCRIPTION AND DISTRIBUTION OF PHONEMES

4.1. *Articulatory Description*

4.1.1. *Consonants* /p/, /t/, and /k/ are voiceless bilabial [p], alveodental [t], and velar [k] unaspirated stops.

/b/, /d/, and /g/ are prenasalized bilabial, alveolar, and velar stops. Voiced allophones [mb], [nd], and [ŋg] occur word initially, and in fluctuation with voiceless allophones [mp], [nt], and [ŋk] word medially. The voiceless

---

[3] In a single instance the analysis adopted here leads to ambiguity. Normally /ii/ represents [iː]. For example, [niːtə] /niíta/ 'with me', [ńíː] /nníí/ 'when you come', [ńiːtaraino:] /nniítarainoo/ 'He is sick.' In just one morpheme for 'you (plural)' does /ii/ represent [yi], that is, palatalization followed by a high front vocoid. For example: [ŋyi] /ngii/ 'your (plural)'. The analysis of palatalization as a vowel has not been abandoned on account of just this one instance of [yi].

allophones tend to occur more frequently in word-final syllables. Examples: [mbú:mə] /búuma/ 'stamens', [yámbá:] / [yámpá:] /yábáa/ 'banana', [ndú:nə] /dúuna/'deafness', [yándá:]/ [yántá:]/yádáa/'elbow',[ŋgi:ŋgə]/[ŋgi:ŋkə]/gíiga/ 'worm'.

/q/ is a voiceless glottal stop [ʔ]. Following pause, word-initial /q/ is manifested as [ʔ] freely varying with zero. There are no words which phonemically commence with a vowel.[4]

/v/ and /f/ are bilabial fricatives, voiced [ƀ] and voiceless [ƥ], respectively.

/s/ is a voiceless alveolar grooved fricative [s].

/h/ is a voiceless glottal fricative [h].

/m/, /n/, and /ng/ are voiced bilabial [m], alveolar [n], and velar [ŋ] nasals.

/mm/ is a nasalized voiced bilabial fricative [m̰].

/nn/ is a voiced alveolar flapped nasal [ň].

/r/ is a voiced alveolar flapped vibrant [ř]. In word-initial position it may occur with a nonphonemic neutral vowel onset.

/y/ is a voiced high front nonsyllabic vocoid. Allophones with friction [ɏ] and without friction [y] occur in free variation. Preceding a high vowel the fricative allophone occurs the more frequently of the two.

4.1.2. *Vowels.* /i/ and /u/ are high front unrounded and back rounded vocoids, respectively. Vocied close, [i] and [u], and open, [ɩ] and [ʋ] variants occur in fluctuation word initially and medially and in stressed syllables word finally. Voiceless variants [I] and [U] occur in fluctuation with [i] and [u] in unstressed final syllables following voiceless stops.

/e/ and /o/ are voiced mid front unrounded and back rounded vocoids, respectively. Open variants [ɛ] and [ɔˆ] occur except in word-final syllables under intonational conditions of high pitch, when the close variants [e] and [o] occur.

/a/ is a voiced low central unrounded vocoid. In vowel clusters an open variant [a] occurs. Elsewhere the phoneme is reflected by a close variant [əˇ].

4.1.3. *Stress.* Contrastive syllable stress may occur on one or more syllables of a word.[5] The following sets demonstrate stress contrasts: /haáya/ 'wing', /háaya/ 'fuzz'; /mmáta/ 'a short way', /mmáta/ 'ground', /mmatáa/ 'spear'; /yeéna/ 'rope', /yéenna/ 'food'; /mmééya/ 'tail'.

4.2. *Distribution.*

Distribution of phonemes will be discussed with reference to the syllable

---

[4] In the orthography used for Waffa literature, word-initial /q/ has been omitted except when it is labialized, since initial /q/ does not contrast with initial vowel.

[5] Some words have no stressed syllables and some have all syllables stressed. These may be identified by frame techniques as used in tone analysis. See Pike and Kindberg (1956) for their application to a language with a stress system very similar to that of Waffa. It should be noted that in the orthography of Waffa literature stress is unmarked.

and the word. For this purpose the syllable and the word will be defined as follows.

A *syllable* is a unit of potential stress having a nucleus of a single vowel and an optional onset consisting of a single consonant or a consonant followed by a nonsyllabic high vowel (see Section 3.1.). The following syllable patterns, therefore, occur: V, CV, and CVV. The V syllable is limited in distribution to word-medial and word-final positions, and two V syllables in sequence have not been observed.

A *word* is a rhythm unit containing one or more syllables. Words containing from one to twelve syllables have been recorded. None, or any, or all of the syllables of a word may be stressed. Phonological word borders have the following phonetic characteristics. Word-initial borders are marked by a consonant and an up-step in pitch. Word-final borders are marked by a vowel, decrescendo, length, and a general down-drift of pitch.

A. All consonants occur in CV and CVV syllables in all positions within words.

B. All vowels occur in V and CV syllables in their positions within words.

C. In CV syllables all combinations of consonant and vowel occur.

D. In CVV syllables not followed by a V syllable, the only vowel sequences which occur are *ua* and *ia,* and this is true for all positions within words.

E. In CVV syllables all consonants are followed by /u/, and all consonants except /q/, /h/, and /y/ are followed by /i/.

F. In the disyllabic grouping CV.V, the vowel sequences *aa, ee, ii, oo, uu, ai,* and *au* occur. In word-final position in vocative forms only, the additional sequences *ao, io,* and *uo* occur.

G. In the disyllabic grouping CVV.V, the vowel sequences *uaa, iaa, uee, iee, uii, iii, uoo, ioo, uai, iai, uau,* and *iau* occur.

5. ILLUSTRATIVE PAIRS OF PHONEMIC CONTRASTS

The following contrastive pairs demonstrate the phonemically separate status of those phonemes which are phonemically most similar.

/p/ and /b/

/yaápa/	'bark cloth'	/sípu/	'door'
/yábáa/	'banana'	/síbáu/	'fly'

/t/ and /d/

/yáata/	ear'	/tínóo/	'He is saying'
/yádáa/	'elbow'	/dínóo/	'He is standing.'

/k/ and /g/

/káaka/	'lime'	/kuátínóo/	'He is talking.'
/káaga/	'dividing mark in garden'	/guátínóo/	'He is splitting wood.'

/f/ and /v/

/faínni/	'dog'	/úufa/	'red'
/vaíni/	'close by'	/óova/	type of yam

/p/ and /f/

/puaáráa/	'single'
/fuáara/	'bearers of house'

/b/ and /v/

/kóobi/	'claws'
/kóova/	'father'

/s/ and /h/

/saívai/	'half'
/haívai/	'He shot.'

/s/ and /t/

/tiínoo/	'He is coming down.'
/siína/	'bow string'

/m/, /n/, and /ng/

/mátee/	'now'
/náammée/	type of tree
/ngámi/	'second son'

/m/ and /mm/

/mmoóka/	'back; leech'	/mmamma/	'skin'
/mókoo/	'live coals'	/kama/	'round taro'

/n/ and /nn/

/nnau/	'house'	/kuáannú/	'a cultivated cane'
/naú/	'yesterday'	/kuáanúu/	'spit'

/r/ and /t/

/mmáráa/	'belong'	/rínóo/	'He is fighting.'
/mmátá/	'ground'	/tínó/	'He is saying.'

/r/ and /nn/

/nnáinoo/	'He is eating.'
/ráinoo/	'He is laughing.'

/i/ and /e/

/tiínoo/	'He is coming down.'
/teénoo/	'we'

/u/ and /o/

/qávú/	'eye'
/qáavo/	'this one'

/a/, /e/, and /o/

/yóonna/	'mud'
/yéenna/	'food'
/yaámma/	'reed skirt'

/i/, /e/, /a/, /o/, and /u/

/nnínóo/	'He is coming.'
/neénoo/	'I'
/naánoo/	'big sister'
/naánna/	'feces'
/nnóonna/	'big'
/nnúuna/	'throat'

XXVII. Notes on Tairora
Noun Morphology

ALEX VINCENT

1. INTRODUCTION

This paper treats the affixes that occur with nouns in Tairora.[1] The analysis presented here is based on spontaneous utterances and stories gathered during two years of field work between 1957 and 1961 under the auspices of the Summer Institute of Linguistics. The writer wishes to acknowledge his debt to Ori, a man of about thirty-five, of the Tairora village of Bantura who has supplied much of the text material and patiently helped in the transcribing of materials from tape.

Tairora phonemes include the following consonants: /p, t, k, q, h, b, r, m, n/ and /mp, nt, nk/. The voiceless bilabial varies between a stop and a fricative; the voiced bilabial is a fricative between vowels and a lenis stop elsewhere. The voiced alveolar tends to be a flapped lateral before the phonemes /u/ and /o/, and a flapped vibrant elsewhere. Prenasalized homorganic stops /mp/, /nt/, and /nk/ are written here as digraphs, though, since they occur initially, they are analyzed as unit phonemes. Other consonants have their usual phonetic values. Vowels include /i/, /a/, /u/, and /e/, /aa/, /o/. The first three are usually short while the last three are long. The phoneme /a/ is mid central and /aa/ is low central. Stress is left unmarked in this paper.

[1] The present draft of this paper was prepared at the University of North Dakota in the summer of 1962 at a linguistic workshop under the direction of Dr. R. S. Pittman of the Summer Institute of Linguistics. The writer gratefully acknowledges the help received from Dr. Pittman and colleagues Bruce Hooley and Forrest Brewer.

2. WORD BASES

Word bases in Tairora can be divided into two main classes, verbs and nouns.[2]

Verb bases occur with portmanteau mood-person-number or tense-person-number suffixes.[3]

Noun bases are those bases which do not occur with mood-person-number of tense-person-number suffixes and which, in addition, have been observed to occur with suffixes marking the following categories: *-ba* subject; *-ra* possession/object; *-tanta* dual subject/dual possession/dual object; *-ka* plural subject/plural possession/plural object; *-o* vocative case; location, *-qi* 'in', *-qaa* 'on', *-ka* 'around', *-kanta* place, *-taari* place, *-nto* 'at', *-ni* 'to', *-na* 'passage', *-runa* 'hollow', *-bau* 'over'; *-hai* direction from; *-nohai* instrument; *-nti* accompaniment; *-hampata* accompaniment; *-ra* reference; *-ra* acquisition; *-kaara* reason; *-bata* connection; shape, *-anta* 'elongated', *-ru* 'small', *-uta* 'bag shaped'.

Pronouns are a subclass of nouns since many of the suffixes that occur with nouns occur also with pronouns. They differ from other nouns in that they are not expandable to the left or right in noun phrases. Pronouns include personal, locational, and interrogative forms. Locational and interrogative pronouns will be listed later. The personal pronouns are listed here for reference so that the examples involving them may be followed more easily. The comma (,) in the following lists is to be read 'or'.

Subject pronouns are:

	Sing	Dual	Pl
1st	*tere, te*	*te(re)-tanta*	*te(re)-nabu*
2nd	*are*	*ne-tanta*	*ne, ne-nabu*
3rd	*bi-ba*	*bi-tanta*	*bi-ka, bi-nabu-ka*

Object or possessive pronouns are:

	Sing	Dual	Pl
1st	*tiri, ti*	*ti(ri)-tanta*	*ti(ri)-nabu*
2nd	*ari, ai*	*ni-tanta*	*ni, ni-nabu*
3rd	*bi-ra*	*bi-tanta*	*bi-ka, bi-nabu-ka*

It will be noted from the pronoun chart that there is no distinction between the third dual subject pronouns and the third dual object/possessive pronouns nor between the third plural subject pronouns and the third plural object/possessive pronouns. The suffix *-tanta* marks dual number

---

[2] Additional analysis may show further classes of word bases, possibly reflexive pronouns, numerals, and adjectives.

[3] For further information on Tairora verb affixes see Chap. XXX.

and -*nabu* marks plural number. *bi-ba ari taba-ira-ma* (person-subject you see-he-has-indicative) 'He has seen you.'[4]

Hyphens are used to indicate Tairora morpheme boundaries. As a single morpheme often needs to be translated by a phrase in English, hyphens are also used to join words of such phrases to indicate that the phrase is a unit. Spaces in the English translation correspond to the spaces in the Tairora examples.

3. NOUN CLASSES

Noun bases are divided into two classes on the basis of their occurrence with -*ba* or -*bano* subject-marker suffixes. The -*ba* class includes the names of people and some kinship terms. *ori-ba bi-ro* (Ori-*ba* go-he) 'Ori went.' *bakaa-ba bi-ro* (elder-brother-*ba* go-he) 'The elder brother went.'

The -*ba* class kinship terms are listed here for reference: *ti qo-ba* 'my father', *ti no-ba* 'my mother', *ti bakaa-ba* 'my elder brother', *ti nakaa-ba* 'my elder sister', *ti nau-ba* 'my uncle (mother's brother)', *ti maabu-ba* 'my aunt (mother's sister)', *ti naaqu-ba* 'my grandfather', *ti taato-ba* 'my grandmother', *ti airaabi-ba* 'my father-in-law', *ti aintaanta-ba* 'my mother-in-law', *ti tonaqo-ba* 'my father-in-law (wife's)', *ti tonano-ba* 'my mother-in-law (wife's)', *ti aitua-ba* 'my brother-in-law', *ti maati-ba* 'my sister-in-law', *ti baraaqo-ba* 'my daughter-in-law', *ti naaqutu-ba* 'my daughter-in-law' (alternate form).

The -*bano* class includes some kinship terms and any noun except a personal name: *qata-bano bi-ro* (younger-brother-*bano* go-he) 'The younger brother went.' *ori-bano hiqiri-ro* (stone-*bano* fall-it) 'The stone fell down.'

The -*bano* class kinship terms are listed here for reference: *ti qata* 'my younger brother', *ti aura* 'my younger sister', *ti baati* 'my husband', *ti naata* 'my wife', *ti maarunti* 'my nephew/niece (brother's children)', *ti maaqu* 'my son', *ti raabura* 'my daughter', *ti nainti* 'my grandson', *ti naunti* 'my nephew/niece (sister's children)' *ti airaamaqu* 'my son-in-law'.

It is of interest to note that the terms for younger brother, younger sister, son, daughter, nephew/niece are -*bano* class nouns whereas the terms for elder brother, elder sister, father, mother, uncle, and aunt are -*ba* class nouns.

---

[4] The following are the reflexive or emphatic pronouns: *tenta* first person (subject, object, possession); *nena* second person singular (subject, object, possession) (also *nina* possession); *nenta* second person plural (subject, object, possession) (also *ninta* possession); *nari, nai* third person (subject, object, possession). In the following examples *tenta* (first person reflexive) is shown occurring in constructions marking subject, object, and possession: *tenta autu-k-unara* (I-myself make-complete-I-have) 'I myself made it' or 'We ourselves made it.' *te tenta tabe-ø* (I myself see-I) 'I see myself.' *tenta naabu-qi bai-ø* (my-own house-in am-I) 'I am in my own house.' *nena* (second person reflexive) is contrasted in the following. *nena autu-ka-anara* (you-yourself make-complete-you-singular-have) 'You yourself made it.' *nena autu-ka-ara* (you-yourself make-complete-you-plural-have) 'You yourselves made it.'

4. NOUN SUFFIXES

Nouns occur with suffixes marking the categories listed in Section 2. In addition they occur with the following suffixes which also occur freely with verbs: *-bau* contrary to fact statement, *-be* reported speech, *-e* interrogation, *-ma* predication/emphasis (*-ma* marks indicative mood when it occurs with verbs).

The suffix orders presented here are only tentative since the analysis is based on a limited amount of data. A maximum of three orders of suffixes has been noted to occur at one time. The *-ba* class nouns have been charted separately from the *-bano* class nouns because suffixes denoting shape occur in different orders in the two classes. Also certain suffixes which occur with the *-bano* class do not occur with the *-ba* class.

The *-ba* class suffix order may be set out in formula form as follows: Base + Order 1 ± Order 2 ± Order 3 ± Order 4.

Order 1: *-ba* subject, *-ra* object/possession, *-tanta* dual subject/dual object/dual possession, *-ka* plural subject/plural object/plural possession, *-o* vocative case. One member of this order must always occur.

Order 2: *-anta* 'elongated', *-ru* 'small', *-uta* 'bag shaped'. The occurrence of a member of this class of suffixes is optional.

Order 3: *-bata* 'and', *-ra* reference, *-nti* accompaniment, *-hampata* accompaniment, *-kaara* reason. The occurrence of a member of this class of suffixes is optional.

Order 4: *-e* interrogation, *-ma* predication/emphasis, *-be* reported speech, *-ai* limitation. The occurrence of a member of this class of suffixes is optional.

The co-occurrence possibilities of suffixes of Order 2 with those of Order 3 is not yet known.

The *-bano* class suffix order may be set out in formula form as follows: Base ± Order 1 ± Order 2 ± Order 3 ± Order 4.

A *-bano* base may occur alone, that is, without suffixes. All suffixes are optional.

Order 1: *-anta* 'elongated', *-ru* 'small', *-uta* 'bag shaped'.

Order 2: *-bano* subject, *-o* vocative case, *-qi* 'in', *-qaa* 'on', *-ka* 'around', *-kanta* place, *-taari* place, *-nto* 'at', *-ni* 'to', *-na* 'passage', *-runa* 'hollow', *-bau* 'over', *-nohai* instrument, *-nti* accompaniment, *-hampata* accompaniment, *-ra* reference, *-ra* acquisition, *-kaara* reason, *-bata* 'and'.

Order 3: *-hai* 'from', *-qai* limitation.

Order 4: *-e* interrogation, *-ma* predication/emphasis, *-be* reported speech.

Unplaced in the above orders is *-bau* contrary to fact statement, which may prove to belong to Order 3, and the number suffixes *-tanta* dual, and *-nabu* plural, which are possibly members of Orders 1 or 2.

Also the possible combinations occurring with the limitation suffix *-qai* are unknown. (These are listed as Order 4 in the *-ba* chart and as Order 3 in the *-bano* chart.)

Note that the second person singular suffix *-ra* or the third person singular suffix *-ro* obligatorily occur following *-nti* accompaniment, *-hai* 'from', and *-nohai* instrument. However, any one of the latter three suffixes together with either of the person suffixes are considered as belonging to the same order. Thus *-nti* accompaniment is considered for the *-ba* class nouns as occupying position 3A and *-ra* second person singular or *-ro* third person singular as occupying position 3B: *ori-ka-nti-ra ani-ra* (Ori-and-with-you come-you) 'You came with Ori.'

For *-bano* class nouns *-nti* accompaniment, and *-nohai* instrument, occupy position 2A and *-ra* or *-ro* occupy position 2B; and *-hai* 'from' occupies position 3A and *-ra* or *-ro* occupy position 3B: *bairi-nti-ra ani-ra* (dog-with-you come-you) 'You came with the dog', *aiqu-nohai-ro ari-ro* (leg-instrument-he hit-he) 'He hit it with his foot' *rai-hai-ro uri-ro* (Lae-from-he come-up-he) 'He came up from Lae.'

Location suffixes have not been listed as occurring with *-ba* class noun bases. However, one example has been noted in text material where the location suffix *-ini* 'at/to' follows *-ra,* which normally marks possession or object: *bi-ra-ini baati qi-ro* (person-object-to husband become-she) 'She became married to him.'

4.1. Subject and Object/Possession Constructions

Subject and object/possession markers occur as first order suffixes with the *-ba* class nouns, and the subject marker *-bano* occurs as a second order suffix with the *-bano* class nouns. Both of these constructions are included in this section so that the construction contrasts involving *-ba* and *-bano* class nouns may be observed.

4.1.1. -ba *class nouns.* The suffix *-ba,* as noted earlier, marks *-ba* class nouns for subject. It also marks singular number. The suffix *-ra* marks a *-ba* class noun for singular object. A subject and an object construction are contrasted below: *bakaa-ba ari-ro* (elder-brother-*ba* hit-he) 'The elder brother hit (him/it)', *bakaa-ra ari-ro* (elder-brother-*ra* hit-he) 'He hit the elder brother.'

When a noun base plus the suffix *-ra* occurs preceding another noun, the suffix *-ra* marks possession. Thus, noun base plus *-ra* preceding a noun is a possessive construction while noun base plus *-ra* preceding a verb is an object construction. The two constructions are contrasted in the following examples: *bakaa-ra naabu tabe-ro* (elder-brother-*ra* house see-he) 'He saw the elder brother's house', *bakaa-ra tabe-ro* (elder-brother-*ra* see-he) 'He saw the elder brother.'

The suffix *-tanta* (*-hanta* with some speakers) marks *-ba* class nouns for dual, and *-ka* marks *-ba* class nouns for plural. There is no distinction between subject, object, or possession forms. Position before noun marks subject or possession. Position after free subject and position before verb marks object. Other free forms and person suffix of verb help avoid ambiguity: *bakaa-tanta aantau aru-ke-tanta* (elder-brother-dual animals hit-completive-dual-subject) 'The two elder brothers killed animals.' *bakaa-ka naabu tabe-ro* (elder-brother-*ka* house see-he) 'He saw the elder brothers' house.' *nahenti-bano bakaa-ka tabe-ro* (woman-subject elder-brother-*ka* see-she) 'The woman saw the elder brothers.'

Thus it will be noted that the behavior of a -*ba* class noun parallels the third person pronoun forms listed earlier. (The pronoun chart also lists an alternative suffix -*nabu-ka*. It may be that further data will show that this alternative form also occurs with other -*ba* class nouns.)

4.1.2. -bano *class nouns.* The -*bano* class nouns are marked optionally for subject by -*bano*. (Some speakers use -*mano* especially after stems containing a nasal consonant.) A longer form -*banora* occurs and may be an emphatic form but further analysis is needed: *qata-bano bi-ro* (younger-brother-*bano* go-he) 'The younger brother went', *nahenti bi-ro* (woman go-she) 'The woman went.'

A -*bano* class noun occurring as object or possessive is unmarked. Position before the noun possessed marks possession and position after the subject and/or other features such as person suffix of the verb help distinguish object: *qata naabu tabe-ro* (younger-brother house see-he) 'He saw the younger brother's house', *are ti qata tabe-ra-e* (you-singular my younger-brother see-you-interrogative) 'Did you see my younger brother?'

A -*bano* class noun is usually unmarked for number. However, -*tanta* dual has been noted to occur and further data may reveal that -*nabu* plural also occurs: *baraata-tanta ani-ø* (girl-dual come-they) 'The two girls came', *baraata-tanta-bano ani-ø* (girl-dual-subject come-they) 'The two girls came.'

The above examples show that -*tanta* dual is not mutually substitutable with -*bano* subject marker. However, -*tanta* does seem to be mutually substitutable with -*ba* subject marker.

4.1.3. *Occurrence of* -ba *class noun markers with* -bano *class nouns.* When the noun is modified by the specifiers *maa* 'this' and *bi* 'that' or when the noun is modified by a clause, the -*bano* class nouns occur with -*ba* class markers: -*ba* subject, -*ra* object/possession, -*ka* plural subject/plural object/plural possession: *bi baraata-ba bare-ro* (that girl-*ba* take-she) 'That girl took it'; note that this contrasts with the -*bano* construction: *baraata-bano bare-ro* (girl-*bano* take-she) 'The girl took it' *maa baraata-ra a-mi-ro* (this girl-*ra* her-give-he) 'He gave it to this girl'; compare -*bano* construction where the object noun is unmarked: *baraata a-mi-ro* (girl her-give-he) 'He gave it to the girl.' *te bi baraata-ka tabe-ø* (I those girl-*ka* see-I) 'I see those girls.' *nahenti-bano bat-o haka-ba bai-ro* (woman-*bano* put-far-past-third-person things-*ba* is-it) 'The things that the woman had put there are there' (literally, 'The woman had put things are there'). *bi-ba nahenti-bano bat-o haka-ra bare-ro* (person-subject (he) woman *-bano* put-far-past-third-person things-*ra* take-he) 'He took the things that the woman had put there.' *te bata-una haka-ra bare-ro* (I put-I-have things-*ra* take-he) 'He took the things that I have put there' ('He took the I have put things').

A few *-bano* class nouns, for example, the names of animals or birds that are personalized in stories, may occur with *-ba* subject, or *-ra* object: *roriqo-ba kara unte-ro* (Parrot-*ba* food cook-he) 'Parrot cooked the food'; compare with the *-bano* construction: *roriqo-bano kara ne-ro* (parrot-*bano* food eat-he) 'The parrot ate the food.' *roriqo-ra tabe-ro* (Parrot-*ra* see-he) 'He saw Parrot'; compare with the following construction where the *-bano* class noun is unmarked: *roriqo tabe-ro* (parrot see-he) 'He saw the parrot.'

Certain clauses when occurring as subject or object of a larger construction may be marked by *-ba* subject, *-ra* object, or *-ka* plural subject/plural object: *qutu b-u-ba-ma bi-ro* (cease go-third-person-far-past-*ba*-emphatic go-he) 'The one who was dead went'; compare: *qutu b-ura* (cease go-third-person-far-past) 'He died.' *qutu b-u-ra tabe-ro* (cease go-far-past-third-person-*ra* see-he) 'He saw the one that was dead (become ceased—deceased).' *baana bai bara-t-o-ka ani-ø* (ghost are take-completive-far-past-third-person-*ka* come-they) 'All the things that were ghosts came.'

A *-bano* noun may occur as subject in apposition with a pronoun. Thus, there are four ways the subject may be indicated: (A) *nahenti bi-ba bi-ro* (woman third-person-subject go-she) 'The woman, she went.' (B) *bi nahenti-ba bi-ro* (that woman-subject go-she) 'That woman went.' (C) *nahenti-bano bi-ro* (woman-subject go-she) 'The woman went.' (D) *nahenti bi-ro* (woman go-she) 'The woman went.'

4.2. *Vocative Case*

The suffix *-o* marks a person addressed and occurs with *-ba* class nouns: *ori-o* (Ori-*o*) 'Ori!' *h-intaanta-o* (my-mother-in-law-*o*) 'My mother-in-law!' *ti bakaa-o* (my elder-brother-*o*) 'My elder brother!'

The vocative marker has been noted to occur with a limited number of *-bano* class nouns: *ti qata-o* (younger-brother-*o*) 'My younger brother!' *ti maaqu-o* (my son-*o*) 'My son!' *ti bainti-o* (my man-*o*) 'My man!' 'My friend!'

A *-ba* class noun may occur in a vocative construction without the vocative suffix: *ori* 'Ori!'. Also a person may tell his own name and the name will occur without a suffix. Thus a person named 'Ori' might answer *ori* 'Ori' when asked his name. These are the only occasions that a *-ba* class noun occurs without what has been termed obligatory first order suffixes.

4.3. Conjunctions

There are two connective suffixes *-bata* 'and' and *-ka* 'and'. *-bata* occurs with both noun classes and *-ka* occurs with the *-ba* class only.

These suffixes indicate that two or more nouns are co-ordinate. They occur suffixed to each noun in the co-ordinate construction.

The following examples illustrate the occurrence of *-bata: ori-ba-bata itai-ba-bata bi-ø* (Ori-subject-*bata* Itai-subject-*bata* go-they) 'Ori and Itai went.' *ori-ra-bata itai-ra-bata tabe -ø* (Ori-object-*bata* Itai-object-*bata* see-I) 'I see Ori and Itai.' *ori-bano-bata katari-bano-bata hiqiri-ø* (stone-subject-*bata* wood-subject-*bata* fell-they) 'Stones and wood fell down.' *ori-bata katari-bata bare-ro* (stone-*bata* wood-*bata* take-he) 'He took stones and wood.'

The following examples illustrate the occurrence of *-ka*. (Note that *-ka* in this construction does not mark the noun base for plural number—see Section 4.1—but marks the fact that more than one phrase head is occurring.) *ori-ka itai-ka bi-ø* (Ori-*ka* Itai-*ka* go-they) 'Ori and Itai went.' *te ori-ka itai-ka tabe-ø* (I Ori-*ka* Itai-*ka* see-I) 'Isee Ori and Itai.' *ori-ka itai-ka naabu tabe-ø* (Ori-*ka* Itai-*ka* house see-I) 'I see Ori and Itai's house.'

The first two examples listed with *-bata* and the first two examples listed with *-ka* are apparently alternative ways of saying the same thing.

In the following example a *-ba-bata* construction cannot be substituted for a *-ka* construction: *te ori-ra no-ka-ma* (I Ori-possessive mother-*ka*-predication) 'I am Ori's mother.'

In the following *-bata* construction note that the *-ba* class nouns occurring with *-bata* 'and' cannot be substituted for *-ka* 'and' constructions: *ori-ba-bata bi-reba* (Ori-subject-*bata* go-he-will) 'Ori will go too.' *kai bainti-bano-bata bai-ro* (no man-subject-*bata* is-he) 'There wasn't a man there.' *bi-ka-bata bi-reka* (person-plural-*bata* go-they-will) 'They will go too.'

In the following expression note that *ori-ka* tells who the person is, other than the speaker, included in the pronoun *te-tanta* 'we two': *te-tanta ori-ka bai* (first-person-dual Ori-*ka* are) 'I and Ori are here' (literally, 'We two and Ori are here').

Often items are simply listed without any connective suffix: *te qamaa kara baara qeta kaaqa ne-ø* (sweet-potato taro yam banana sugar-cane eat-I) 'I eat sweet potatoes, taro, yams, bananas, and sugar cane.'

4.4. Location Pronouns.

Before listing suffixes that indicate location and direction a few comments need to be made about location word bases which can be termed location pronouns. Location pronouns may indicate whether an object is above the speaker, level with the speaker, or below the speaker; whether an object is near or far from the speaker; whether an object is on the other

side of something that is between the speaker and the object. The concept
of distance is relative. What may be considered close at one time may
be considered far at another time when it is being compared with some
place closer.

The following bases refer to objects in a direct line from the speaker.
There are apparently four degrees of nearness in this set. It is clear from
text material, for example, that the form *mia* 'down' is used of objects
that are close and *mua* 'down far' is used of objects that are farther away.
It is not so certain that the forms with reduplicated first syllable are also
marking a similar contrast. However, they are tentatively analyzed as
such here: *mia* 'down', *mimia* 'down more', *mua* 'down far', *mumua*
'down farther', *biti* 'along', *bibiti* 'along more', *butu* 'along far', *bubutu*
'along farther', *bi, biri* 'up', *bibi, bibiri* 'up more', *bu, buru* 'up far',
bubu, buburu 'up farther'.

The following refer to objects (or places) that are on the other side of
something between the object and the speaker. (The object may be a
wall or a mountain.) *beba* 'on the other side of and down—around and
down', *beta* 'on the other side of and level', *bera* 'on the other side of and
up'.

The following also refer to objects that are on the other side of something
between the object and the speaker. This set is used to denote locations
that are relatively nearer to the speaker than those denoted in the preceding paragraph. (Compare *maa* 'here' and *bi* 'there' noted later.) This set
never occurs in close-knit verb phrases, while the preceding set above
does. *maabi* 'on the other side of and down', *maati* 'on the other side of
and level', *maari* 'on the other side of and up'.

Examples of these location pronouns used in larger constructions follow:
te mai-qi baita-ø (I down-in sleep-I) 'I slept down in there.' *naabu
butu-ra-qaa bai-ro* (house along-far-place-on is-it) 'The house is over on
there.' *buku beba-nto bai-ro* (book *beba*-at is-it) 'The book is on the
bottom (of a pile).' *rai beba-ini bai-ro* (Lae *beba*-at is-it) 'Lae is over
down there' (referring to a coastal town). *koroka beta-ini bai-ro* (Goroka
beta-at is-it) 'Goroka is over along there' (referring to a Highland town).
taabu maaqaa maabi-ni bai-ro (Gadsup place *maabi*-at is-it) 'The Gadsup
place is over down there.'

Comparing the three sets listed above it will be noted that often the final
consonant *b* means 'down', *t* means 'level', and *r* means 'up'. This is also
the case with the three direction words which occur only in close-knit
verb phrases: *baabi* 'down', *baati* 'along, level', *baari* 'up'.

The following close-knit verb phrases should be noted as they throw
light on the form of some of the word bases listed: *buabu re-ro* 'He
jumped down' (*re* 'do', *-ro* 'he'). *butu re-ro* 'He jumped along.' *buru re-ro*
'He jumped up.' *beba re-ro* 'He came outside' (literally, 'He came over

and down'; a person usually comes *down* from a house even though the house might be on the ground). *beta re-ro* 'He came over and along.' *bera re-ro* 'He came over and up.' *baabi re-ro* 'He climbs down.' *baati re-ro* 'He climbs over.' *baari re-ro* 'He climbs up.'

Other location pronouns are: *maa* 'here', *bi~mi*[5] 'there', *bai* 'close', *auma* 'close', *niara* 'far'.

Occurring with many location constructions is the suffix *-ra* place. A noun base plus *-ra* is considered a compound word base. Note that a place named after a 'flea' (*taru*) is called *taru-ra* 'flea place'. Most Tairora place names end in *-ra*. Certain location pronouns require *-ra* when they occur with certain location suffixes. In the following examples optional occurrence of *-ra* is contrasted with its obligatory occurrence. In the first example *-ra* is optional; in the second *-ra* is obligatory: *maa-ra-qi* (here-place-in) 'in here', *maa-qi* (here-in) 'in here', *bi-ra-qi* (there-place-in) 'in there'. *bi-qi (there-in) 'in there' does *not* occur.

4.5. *Location Suffixes*

-qi denotes location "in". *naabu-qi bai-Ø* (house-in am-I) 'I am in the house.' *kure-qi bate-ro* (container-in put-he) 'He put it in the container.' *butu-ra-qi bai-ro* along-place-in is-it) 'It is along in there.'

-qaa denotes location 'on'. A further form *-qaata* has been noted with meaning similar to *qaa*. Additional data should clarify the distinction in meaning, if any. *naabu-qaa bai-Ø* (house-on am-I) 'I am on the house.' *kure-qaa bate-ro* (container-on put-he) 'He put it on the container.' *maa-qaa-ma bai-ro* (here-on-emphatic is-it) 'It is on here.'

-ka indicates location 'around'. *kauqu-ka rumpe-ro* (arm-around tie-he) 'He tied it around the arm.' *katari-ka bai-ro* (post-around is-it) 'It is around the post.'

-kanta indicates 'place' or 'area'—especially a flat area. *kainantu-kanta bai-ro* (Kainantu-place is-it) 'It is in the Kainantu area.' *naaho-kanta bi-rera* (garden-place go-I-will) 'I will go to the garden area.' *bata-kanta baita-ana* (ground-place sleep-imperative) 'Sleep on the ground!' *bi-kanta baite-ro* (there-place sleep-he) 'He slept at that place.'

-taari indicates place or area. *mua-taari bi-ro* (down-place go-he) 'He went down there.' *beba-taari bi-ro* (*beba*-place go-he) 'He went down to the coast.'

-nto indicates place 'at'. In data so far this suffix occurs only with location

[5] Allomorph *mi* 'there' occurs in constructions where *bi* 'up' can potentially occur and where allomorph *bi* 'there' does not. Thus ambiguity between the homophonous forms *bi* 'there' and *bi* 'up' is avoided: *bi-ni* 'up-to'; *bi-nto* 'up-at'; *biri-kanta* 'up-place'; *mi-ni* 'there-to'; *mi-nto* 'there-at'; *bi-kanta* 'there-place'. Note further, as illustrated in the above example, that the allomorph of *bi* 'up', as in *biri* occurs where *bi* 'there' can potentially occur.

pronouns: *maa-nto bai-rera* (here-at be-I-will) 'I will stay here.' *mi-nto bai-reba* (there-at be-he-will) 'He will stay there.' *bai-nto bai-ro* (close-at is-it) 'It is near.' *niara-nto bai-ro* (far-at is-it) 'It is far.'

-ni ∼ -ini (allomorph *-ini* occurs after *a* or *aa*) indicates motion toward or position at a place. This suffix has a much wider distribution than *-nto* above: *aakara-ini bi-rera* (Asara-to go-I-will) 'I will go to Asara.' *maa-ini bate-ro* (here-at put-he) 'He put it here.' *mi-ni bu-ana* (there-to go-you-imperative) 'Go there!' *naaho-ni bi-ro* (garden-to go-he) 'He went to the garden.'

-na ∼ -ana (allomorph *-ana* occurs after *i*) is used of passagelike locations. *aato-na oriqete-ro* (ear-passage go-inside-it) 'It went inside the ear passage.' *qenti-ana oqubi-ro* (door-passage sit-he) 'He sat in the doorway.' *mi-na bu-ana* (there-passage go-you-imperative) 'Go along in there!' *maa-na ani-ana* (here-passage come-you-imperative) 'Come along in here!'

Note also: *aiqi-ana* (nose-passage) 'nostril', *raqa-na* (buttock-passage) 'anus'.

-runa is used of hollows such as a river bed, ditch, or drain: *namari-runa oru bi-ro* (water-hollow along go-he) 'He went along the river bed.' *mi-runa bu-ana* (there-hollow go-you-imperative) 'Go along there (in that ditch)!' *aara-runa bi-ro* (road-hollow go-he) 'He went along the road.' *bobara-runa bi-rera* (Bobara-hollow go-I-will) 'I will go to Bobara' (name of low garden area near Suwaira).

-bau indicates location 'over': *tainta-bau raaqu bate-ro* (table-over tip put-he) 'He put (food) over the table.' *iri-bau bi-ro* (bridge-over go-he) 'He went over the bridge.'

Frequently after *-qi* 'in' (but never after *-qaa* 'on') and *-bau* 'over' the suffix *-ra* has been noted to occur. This suffix is tentatively analyzed as the *ra* place noted earlier. Thus a simple word base plus location suffix plus *-ra* is also considered a compound word base: *naabu-qi-ra bai-ro* (house-in-place is-he) 'He is in the house (in the house place).' *ori-bau-ra bate-ro* (stone-over-place put-he) 'He put (dirt) over the stones.' *aahaka-qi-ra-ini bi-ro* (grass-in-place-to go-he) 'He went to the grasslands' (grasslands and forest areas are considered places to go in to). *bi-ra-qi-ra-ini biro* (there-place-in-place-to go-he) 'He went to in there' (to the 'there in' place).

Apart from the occurrence of two location suffixes in the one word noted above, all the location suffixes listed so far occur in mutually substitutable distribution with the exception of *-qi* 'in' which may occur after *-runa* 'hollow'. It is suspected, however, that if *-qi* may occur then at least *-qaa* 'on' may occur also.

-hai ∼ -ihai (allomorph *-ihai* occurs after *a*) indicates direction 'from'.[6]

[6] There are three suffixes that occur followed by *-ra* second person singular or *-ro* third person singular when the subject of the construction is also second person singular or third person singular, respectively. These suffixes are *-hai* direction from, *-nohai* instrument, and *-nti* accompaniment.

This suffix occurs in Order 3 (*-bano* class nouns). The forms follow: *-hai* first person singular and all plural forms; *-hai-ra* second person singular; *-hai-ro* third person singular. *kainantu-hai-ro uri-ro* (Kainantu-from-he come-up-he) 'He came up from Kainantu.' *aupora-ihai ani-ø* (Aupora-from come-I) 'I came from Aupora.' *bi-ra-qaa-hai-ra ani-ra* (there-place-on-from-you come-you) 'You came from on there.' *beba-nto-hai-ro bare-ro* (down-around-at-from-he take-he) 'He took it from the bottom.'

4.6. *Instrument*

nohai (some speakers use *-qohai* or *-qotai* or *-qo*) marks instrument. This suffix occurs in Order 2 with *-bano* nouns. *-nohai* also occurs with the *-ba* class pronoun *bi* which means 'it' or 'that' in *-nohai* constructions. The *-ba* class pronoun form obligatorily occurs with *-ra* which is considered to be the same suffix as the possessive/object *-ra*. *-nohai* occurs following *-ra*. The forms follow: *-nohai* first person singular and all plural forms; *-nohai-ra* second person singular; *-nohai-ro* third person singular.

Examples: *bi-ra-nohai ari-ø* (that-object-with hit-I) 'I hit it with that.' *rori-nohai-ro teqe-ro* (axe-with-he cut-he) 'He cut it with an axe.' *aiqu-nohai-ra utubara-ana* (foot-with-you pick-up-you-imperative) 'Pick it up with your foot!'

4.7. *Accompaniment*

-nti indicates accompaniment of a singular or plural subject with a single person or thing. *-nti* always occurs with *-ka* 'and' in *-ba* class nouns. *-nti* occurs in Order 3 with *-ba* nouns and in Order 2 with *-bano* nouns. The forms follow: (*-ka*)-*nti* first person singular and all plural forms; (*-ka*)-*nti-ra* second person singular; (*-ka*)-*nti-ro* third person singular.

Examples: *nahenti-nti-ro ani-ro* (woman-with-he come-he) 'He came with a woman.' *bainti-bano bairi-nti-ro ani-ro* (man-subject dog-with-he come-he) 'The man came with a dog.' *ta-ka-nti-ra-e ani-ra* (who-and-with-you-interrogative come-you) 'With whom did you come?' *ori-ka-nti ani-ø* (Ori-and-with come-I) 'I came with Ori.' *ai-nti bi-rera* (you-with go-I-will) 'I will go with you.'

-hampata indicates accompaniment by one or more persons or things. This suffix differs from *-nti* in that it does not occur with a person suffix following: *eqara-hampata uri-ø* (white-man-with come-up-I) 'I came up with a white man.'

When *-hampata* occurs with a *-ba* noun, *-ra* object or *-ka* plural must occur between the base and *-hampata*. In this case *-ka* and *-ra* relate *-hampata* to the base: *bi-ra-hampata ni-ø* (that-object-with walk-I) 'I went about with him.' *bi-ka-hampata ni-ø* (those-plural-with walk-I) 'I went about with them.'

4.8. Reference

-ra ~ *-ara* (after *i*) ~ *-ara* (after *u*) indicate reference—person or thing referred to or spoken to. This suffix occurs in Order 3 with *-ba* nouns and in Order 2 with *-bano* nouns. This suffix occurs following *-ra* object, or *-ka* plural with *-ba* nouns: *ori-ra-ra-ma ti-ro* (Ori-object-referent-emphatic say-he) 'He is talking about Ori.' *ori-ara-ma ti-ro* (stone-referent-emphatic say-he) 'He is talking about the stone.' *bi-ka-ra-ma ti-ra* (those-plural-referent-emphatic say-you) 'You were talking about them.' *ti-maaqu-ara bu-an-e ti-ro* (my son-referent go-you-imperative-reported-speech say-he) 'He said "Go away!" to my son.'

4.9. Acquisition

ra ~ *-ara* (after *i*) indicates acquisition. This suffix occurs in Order 2 with *-bano* nouns. When *-ra* occurs with the *-ba* pronoun *bi* 'it', it follows the object marker *-ra* as illustrated below. The suffix *-ra* is tentatively analyzed as being separate from the reference suffix *-ra* above. Note that in the first example listed below allomorph *-ra* occurs after *-u* whereas allomorph *-ara* of the reference suffix occurs after *u* as illustrated by an example above: *aantau-ra bi-rera* (animal-for go-I-will) 'I will go for bush animals.' *naama-ra rate-ro* (milk-for cry-he) 'He (baby) cries for milk.' *iha-ra bi-ø* (fuel-for go-I) 'I went for fuel.' *namari-ara bi-ro* (water-for go-he) 'He went for water.' *bi-ra-ra tubi-ø* (it-object-for come-down-I) 'I came down for that.'

In all the above acquisitional examples a verbal expression may be substituted for the word base plus *-ra: iha bara-rera bi-ø* (fuel get-I-will go-I) 'I went to get fuel.'

Such a verbal expression may not be substituted for word base plus the *ra* reference suffix. This is considered as additional evidence for analyzing the reference suffix and the acquisitional suffix as two different morphemes.

4.10. Reason

-kaara marks the reason ('trouble reason') for a verbal action. This suffix occurs in Order 3 with *-ba* nouns and Order 2 with *-bano* nouns. *-ba* nouns require *-ra* or *-ka* before *-kaara: nana-kaara-e tirori-ro* (what-reason-interrogative dispute-he) 'What is he disputing over?' *nahenti-kaara-ma* (woman-reason-predicative) 'It is because of a woman.' *ori-ra-kaara ari-ro* (Ori-*ra*-reason fight-he) 'He had a fight over Ori' (because of Ori).

4.11. Contrary to Fact Statement

-bau (*-au* with some speakers) marks the preceding noun base as contrary to fact. This suffix occurs with *-bano* nouns and possibly occurs in Order 3 after the base. Further data may show that this suffix occurs with

-ba nouns: *bairi-bau-ma* (dog-*bau*-predicative) 'That isn't a dog!'
The negative *kia* is optional in these constructions: *kia nahenti-bau-ma* (negative woman-*bau*-predicative) 'That isn't a woman!'

4.12. *Predication*

-ma marks a noun as predicate in a construction not containing a verb. It occurs in Order 4 with both *-ba* and *-bano* nouns: *naabu-ma* (house-*ma*) 'It is a house.' *katari-ma* (tree-*ma*) 'It is a tree.' *niara-ini-ma* (far-to-*ma*) 'It is a long way.'

When *-ma* occurs following a noun in a construction containing a verb it emphasizes the noun: *bainti-bano ti huru-ma bare-ro* (man-subject my bow-*ma* take-he) 'The man took my bow.'

When *-ma* occurs with verbs, it marks indicative mood. *-ma* occurs in contrast to *-e* interrogative except where *-ma* occurs emphasizing the verb modifier in an imperative construction. In this type of construction *-e* never occurs: *tota-ma bara-a* (immediately-*ma* take-imperative) 'Take it at once!'

4.13. *Interrogation*

-e marks interrogation, and, like *-ma,* this suffix may occur suffixed to a verb or a noun. When both a noun and a verb occur, *-e* marks emphasis of the verb or noun to which it is suffixed: *naabu-e* (house-interrogative) 'Is it a house?' *ti-huru-e bare-ro* (my bow-interrogative take-he) 'Did he take my bow?' *ti huru báre-ro-e* (my bow take-he-interrogative) 'Did he *take* my bow?'

-e occurs in Order 4 with both *-ba* and *-bano* nouns.

4.14. *Reported Speech*

-be marks reported, shouted, or emphatic speech. It occurs Order 4 with both *-ba* and *-bano* nouns. Compare the following constructions: *naabu-ma* (house-predicative) 'It is a house.' *naabu-be* (house-*be*) 'It is a house!' (shouted or emphasized). *naabu-be ti-ro* (house-*be* say-he) ' "It is a house," he said.'

4.15. *Limitation*

-qai 'only' has tentatively been listed as Order 4 in *-ba* nouns and Order 3 with *-bano* nouns: *uba-qai iri-ro* (sound-only hear-he) 'He heard the sound only.' *katari-qai bare-ro* (wood-only take-he) 'He brought the wood only.' *bi-ba-qai bi-ro* (that-subject-only go-he) 'Only he went.'

-qauta 'only' occurs uniquely with personal pronouns and the inclusive marker *make* (in data so far). The order of this suffix has not been determined: *taaroqa bi-ra-qauta raqa-ke-ro* (nettles that-object-only break-complete-he) 'He broke off nettles only.' *itai-ra ori-ra ai make butu ni ke-ø te-quata taabu magaaini otu ri-ø* (Itai-object Ori-object you inclusive along

walk leave-we we-only Gadsup place-to down walk-we) 'We left Ori, Itai, and you and we went down to the Gadsup place.' *aito-ka nobari-ka make-qauta ani-ø* (Aito-and Nobari- and inclusive-only came-they) 'Only Aito and Nobari came.'

-raa~-araa (after *i*) 'alone' has been noted to occur only with reflexive pronouns:[7] *nari-araa baite-ro* (himself-alone sleep-he) 'He slept alone.' *tenta-raa bi-rera* (myself-alone go-I-will) 'I will go alone.'

4.16. *Shape*

-anta 'elongated', 'tall', *-ru~-uru* (after *a*) 'short', 'small', and *-uta* 'bag shaped' denote the characteristic shape of an object or person. They occur in stories more than in everyday conversation. The elder brother in a story is often the 'tall' elder brother~just as in English stories the hero is handsome. As noted earlier the shape suffixes occur in second order with *-ba* class nouns and in first order with *-bano* nouns: *bakaa-b-anta ani-ro* (elder-brother-subject-long come-he) 'The tall elder brother came.' *kaaker-anta-bano bi-ro* (lizzard-long-subject go-he) 'The long lizzard went.' *taari-anta* (mat-long) 'a long mat'; *turu-ru* (headrest-small) 'a small headrest'; *bainti-ru* (child-small) 'a child' *nahenti-ru* (woman-small) 'a small woman'; *uta-uta* (bag-*uta*) 'a bag'; *abuna-uta* (cape-*uta*) 'a cape'.

4.17. *Suffix Residue*

The following three suffixes, *-haa* 'thing', *-naa* 'person', and *-upiri* 'person or thing' appear to be derivational suffixes, that is, they form compound word bases.

-haa 'thing', 'piece': *soti-haa ti-mi-ana* (shirt-thing me-give-imperative) 'Give me the shirt!' *tutuka-haa-ma* (fence-thing-predication) 'It is a post for a fence.' *qora-haa-ma* (bad-thing-predication) 'That's bad!'

-naa 'person': The resulting compound consisting of word base plus *-naa* is a *-ba* class noun. *bo bata-naa-ba ani-ro* (another ground-person-subject come-he) 'A person from another place came' (i.e., a foreigner) *hoqare-naa-ba-ma* (first-person-subject-predication) 'He is the first'; 'He is the first born.'

When *-naa* follows *-hai* 'from', *-hai* is not followed by either person suffix, *-ra* second person singular or *-ro* third person singular: *aupora-ihai-naa-ba-ma* (Aupora-from-person-subject-predication) 'He is a person from Aupora'; 'It is an Aupora person.'

-naa 'person' contrasts with *-taa* 'enemy person' in the only instance which occurs in the data: *nabu-naa-ba-ma* (clan-person-subject-predication) 'It is a clan member'; 'It is a friendly person.' *nabu-taa-ba-ma* (tribe-enemy-person-subject-predication) 'It is an enemy.'

---

[7] See note 6, above.

-upiri 'person', 'thing': The resulting compound with *-upiri* occurs with suffixes that mark *-bano* nouns. *bainti uara-upiri-bano ihi re-ro* (child little-person-subject song do-he) 'A child, a little one was dancing.'

This suffix also nominalizes a verb expression: *naama na-ira-upiri-bano taaqa ruquti-ro* (milk eat-he-has-person-subject drum hit-he) 'A person who drinks milk was hitting a drum.' (This was said sarcastically of a youth about ten years old.)

-ntauta and *-ntainti* augment the noun base: *nahenti-ntainti bi-ø* (woman-augment go-they) 'A lot of women went.' *uta-ntauta bare-ro* (bag-augment take-he) 'He took a lot of bags.' *bukai-ntauta-ma* (long-augment-predication) 'It is very long.'

5. POSSESSIVE PREFIXES

Possessive prefixes occur with a limited number of noun bases:

	1st sing/pl	2nd/3rd sing	2nd/3rd pl
'name'	*h-utu*	*autu*	*n-utu*
'leg'	*h-iqu*	*aiqu*	*aiqu*
'fear'	*h-aatu*	*aatu*	*n-aatu*
'neck'	*aunta*	*aunta*	*n-unta*

h- is clearly first person, *n-* is clearly plural, and perhaps initial *a* is second and third person singular. (Note that the indirect object pronoun prefixes occurring with verbs are: *h- ∼ ti-* first person; *a-* second and third person singular; *n-* second and third person plural.) The forms for 'fear' occur always as listed above. The other forms occur infrequently—the usual way of indicating possession being preferred, that is, a free possessive pronoun followed by an unprefixed noun: *bi-ka n-aatu qete-ro* (person-plural their-fear fright-he) 'He is frightened because of them.' *h-iqu iha bi-ro* (my-leg fire go-it) 'My leg pains.'

Both free and bound forms may occur together: *ti h-utu* (my my-name) or *h-utu* (my-name) 'my name'. Also to be noted is the difference between the referential term for 'my mother-in-law' which occurs without a prefix and the vocative form which occurs with the prefix: *ti-aintaanta-ba bi-ro* (my mother-in-law-subject go-she) 'My mother-in-law went.' *h-intaanta-o* (my mother-in-law-vocative) 'My mother-in-law!'

6. INTERROGATIVE PRONOUNS

Interrogative pronouns are listed here for reference.

ta ∼ tai 'where'. Allomorph *tai* occurs when there is no suffix present: *tai ni-ra-e* (where walk-you-interrogative) 'Where did you go?' *ta* occurs with any one of the following suffixes: *-ini* 'to'; *-nto* 'at'; *-qi* 'in'; *-qaa* 'on'; *-na* passage; *-ihai* 'from'; *-ra* place. Examples: *ta-ini-e* (where-to-interrogative) 'Where to?' *ta-nto-e* (where-at-interrogative) 'Where at?' *ta-ihai-r-e* (where-from-you-interrogative) 'Where from?' *ta-ra-qi-e* (where-place-in-interrogative) 'In where?' *ta-ra-qaa-e* (where-place-on-interrogative) 'On where?' *ta-ne-e* (where-passage-interrogative) 'Through where?'

ta 'who' (homophonous with *ta* 'where') occurs with any one of the following suffixes: *-ba* subject; *-ra* object; *-tanta* dual; *-ka∼-uka* plural:[8] *ta-ba-be* (who-subject-interrogative) 'Who?'; 'Who is it?'[9] *ta-ra huru-e* (who-object bow-interrogative) 'Whose bow?'; 'Whose bow is it?' *ta-tanta huru-e* (who-dual bow-interr.) 'What two people's bows are they?' *ta-uka huru-e* (who-plural bow-interrogative) 'What people's bows are they?' *ta-ka-nti-ra-e* (who-and-with-you-interrogative) 'Who with (did you come)?'

ta 'who' occurs as an unsuffixed form in the following: *ta-bainti-b-e* (who man-subject-interrogative 'What man?'; 'Who is the man?' *ta-bata-naa-b-e* (who ground-person-subject-interrogative) 'What place are you?'

tabaka and *taire* are two forms for 'when'. *tabaka* is preferred in the North Tairora but is rarely heard in the Central Tairora (Suwaira). The morpheme cuts in these two forms are not clear.

nantiake 'how'. The morpheme cuts here are probably *nanti* 'how', *a* 'do' (uncertain), *ke* 'leave', 'How do I leave it?' *nantinanti-e* 'How many?'

nana 'what' occurs alone or with the following suffixes: *-bano* subject; *-ra* acquisition; *-kaara* reason; *-nohai* instrument; *-nti* accompaniment. *nana* or *nan-e* or *nan-e* 'What?' *nana katari-e* (what tree-interrogative) 'What sort of a tree is that?' *nana-bano-e* (what-subject-interrogative) 'What did it?—What caused it?' *nana-r-e* (what-acquisition-interrogative) 'What for (have you come)?' *nana-kaar-e* (what-reason-interrogative) 'What reason (are they fighting about)?' *nana-nohai-r-e* (what-instrument-you-interrogative) 'What with (did you do it)?' *nana-nti-ra-e* (what accompaniment-you-interrogative) 'What (did you put it) with?'

'Why'. The forms for 'why' conjugate like a medial past tense verb except that there is no clear plural form: *nantimante* occurs with the first person and second and third plural; *nantibare* occurs with the second person singular; *nantibaroe* occurs with third person singular.

The final *-e* is the interrogative suffix. *nantibare kia ani-ra* (why not come-you) 'Why didn't you come?' *nantibaroe kia ani-ro* (why not come-he) 'Why didn't he come?'

---

[8] *-uka* occurs also in *ti bakaa-uka bi-ø* (my elder-brother-plural go-they) 'My elder brother went,' where *bakaa-uka* is an alternative way of saying *bakaa-ka*. Further data might show *-ka* is really two homophonous morphemes, i.e., *-ka* 'and' and *-ka ∼ -uka* plural.

[9] *-be* is considered to be an allomorph of *-e* interrogative in this construction. Another occurrence of *-be* interrogative follows: *tai bu-araba-be* (where go-you-past-interrogative) 'Where did you go?'

XXVIII. The Occurrence and Co-occurrence of Waffa Noun Suffixes

MARY STRINGER and JOYCE HOTZ

1. INTRODUCTION

Noun suffixes in Waffa manifest several types of intricate co-occurrence restrictions such that a description in terms of affix orders and classes gives very little insight into the structure of the system. The method of description presented here focuses on an inventory of noun affixes and a statement of their occurrence and co-occurrence possibilities. It represents a preliminary analysis of text materials collected during two years of field work between 1962 and 1966. The field work was carried out in the village of Kusing under the auspices of the Summer Institute of Linguistics.[1]

The following symbols have been used to aid in the formal description of affix occurrence potential: a plus sign indicates concatenation; parentheses enclose optional items.

2. NOUN CLASSES

Nouns may be divided into two classes on the basis of two sets of suffixes for subject and object markers. Noun stem Class I (ns₁) consists of all proper names and certain kin relationships listed below. The subject marker for this class is -va and the object/possessive marker is -nna. The possessive prefix i- 'your' (singular) will be used with the following examples.

i-koo-va	*i-koo-nna*	'your father'
i-noo-va	*i-noo-nna*	'your mother'
i-vayaa-va	*i-vayaa-nna*	'your elder brother'

[1] This paper, in slightly different format, also appears in *Papers on Seven Languages of Papua–New Guinea* (in press), a publication of the Linguistic Society of New Zealand, and is published here by permission. The authors gratefully acknowledge the help of Darlene Bee in preparing this paper for publication.

i-nnayaa-va	*i-nnayaa-nna*	'your elder sister'
i-nnaugoo-va	*i-nnaugoo-nna*	'your mother's brother'
i-giaayoo-va	*i-giaayoo-nna*	'your mother's sister'
i-nnaaku-va	*i-nnaaku-nna*	'your grandfather'
i-taato-va	*i-taato-nna*	'your grandmother'
i-nniraannioo-va	*i-nniraannioo-nna*	'your father-in-law' (man's)
i-nnummuayaa-va	*i-nnummuayaa-nna*	'your mother-in-law' (man's)
i-nnaaputatioo-va	*i-nnaaputatioo-nna*	'your father-in-law' (woman's)
i-nnaaputuoo-va	*i-nnaaputuoo-nna*	'your mother-in-law' (woman's)
i-nnituoo-va	*i-nnituoo-nna*	'your brother-in-law'
i-mmaugiaa-va	*i-mmaugiaa-nna*	'your sister-in-law'
i-tafaayoo-va	*i-tafaayoo-nna*	'your great grandparents or great grandchildren'

Noun stem Class II (ns$_2$) consists of all other nouns. The subject marker is *-ivo* and the object/possessive marker is *-ivaa*. The kinship terms which occur with this class are listed below.

i-kata-ivo	*i-kata-ivaa*	'your younger brother'
i-nnunna-ivo	*i-nnunna-ivaa*	'your younger sister'
i-vaati-ivo	*i-vaati-ivaa*	'your husband'
i-nnaata-ivo	*i-nnaata-ivaa*	'your wife'
i-nnaaputu-uvo	*i-nnaaputu-uvaa*	'your daughter-in-law'
i-nniraapu-uvo	*i-nniraapu-uvaa*	'your son-in-law'
i-mmaapu-uvo	*i-mmaapu-uvaa*	'your son'
i-raunna-ivo	*i-raunna-ivaa*	'your daughter'
i-nnaudi-ivo	*i-nnaudi-ivaa*	'your sister's children'
i-nneedi-ivo	*i-nneedi-ivaa*	'your grandchild'

3. NOUNS AS SUBJECT AND OBJECT

The distribution of suffixes will be discussed in terms of five formulas in Sections 3, 4, and 5. These formulas will define the occurrence and co-occurrence restrictions of the suffixes. Following are two formulas which show nouns as subject and object.

Suffix restrictions may relate to their occurrence or nonoccurrence or to their status as optional or obligatory. These restrictions depend on both the noun stem class which occurs and on the occurrence of the suffixes.

Following are the readings of the formulas.

In formula 1 noun stems (ns) from both Class I (ns$_1$) and Class II (ns$_2$) can occur alone or with the subject or object suffixes. These suffixes are obligatory when followed by further suffixation. The subject, object, referent, and nonreferent specifier suffixes can be followed by *-nanaa* 'first' or

Formula 1:

$$
ns \quad \pm \quad
\begin{array}{l}
\begin{array}{l} S \\ O \\ Ref \\ Non\text{-}RS \end{array} \quad + \quad (\quad \begin{array}{c} nanaa \\ \\ Md \end{array} \quad) \\[1em]
\hline
\begin{array}{l} S \\ \\ O \end{array} \quad + \quad (\quad ta \quad + \quad \begin{array}{c} (nanaa) \\ \\ (ma) \end{array} \quad) \\[1em]
\hline
S \quad + \quad (noo) \\[0.5em]
\hline
O \quad + \quad (\quad \begin{array}{l} ra_1 \\ ni \\ si + (diri_1) \end{array} \quad) + (nanaa)
\end{array}
$$

Formula 2:

$$ns_2 \quad \pm \quad O \quad + \quad diri_2 \quad + \quad (nanaa)$$

by the mood suffixes. The subject and object suffixes can also be followed by the accompaniment suffix *-ta* plus the optional suffix *-ma* which acts almost like an adverbialiser. The suffix *-nanaa* 'first' can also follow the accompaniment suffix *-ta*. Only subject suffixes can be followed by the indicative suffix *-noo* and only object suffixes can be followed by *-ra$_1$* the reference suffix, or by *-ni* the benefactive suffix, or by *-si* 'to' (of persons) plus the optional suffix *-diri$_1$* 'from'. The suffix *-nanaa* 'first' can also follow these suffixes which follow the object suffixes.

Formula 2 shows affix restriction on noun stem Class II. The noun stem can occur alone or with the object suffixes which are obligatory to the instrument suffix *-diri$_2$* which can also be followed by *-nanaa* 'first'.

Symbols and morphemes are discussed in the order in which they appear when the formulas are read from left to right.

Following are the descriptions of suffixes occurring in the above formulas.

3.1. Subject Marker (S)

3.1.1. Class I

-va singular: *ni-noo-va vi-ra-vai* (my-mother-subject go-far-past-stative) 'My mother went.'

Plural is shown on kinship terms by the formation of the stem. This is described in Section 6 at the end of this paper.

3.1.2. Class II

-ivo singular: *puara-ivo yenna-ivaa nna-i-noo* (pig subject food-object eat-3rd-sing-indicative) 'The pig is eating food.'

-iyauvo plural collective. This suffix is used more specifically when referring

to a group but it is also used as a general plural: *ni yaaki-iyauvo taka-i-vai* (my sugar-cane-pl-collective break-3rd-sing-stative) 'My sugar cane is broken.'

ido plural inclusive. This suffix is used only when referring to an included group: *kiaatanna-ido vi-da kiaa-vai* (girls-plural-inclusive go-pl action-sequence-completive-stative) 'All the girls have gone.'

-iya[2] plural collective with animate *(-iyauvo* can also be used for the animate): *vaidi-iya kua-a-noo* (man-pl-collective go-2nd-and-3rd-pl-indicative) 'The men are going.'

3.2. *Object/Possessive Marker* (O)

3.2.1. *Class I*
-nna singular: *meree-nna ruputua-nee* (Mary-object hit-imperative-singular) 'Hit Mary!' *itai-nna nnau-vai* (man's-name-possessive-house-stative) 'It is Itai's house.'

3.2.2. *Class II*
-ivaa singular: *na suruu-voo vara-u-vai* (I bow-object get-1st-sing-stative) 'I got the bow.' *ni vaidi-ivaa fai-vaa taa-nee* (my man-possessive dog-object look-imperative-singular) 'Look at my man's dog.'

-iyauvaa plural collective: *ni yaaki-iyauvaa taa-nee* (my sugar-cane-pl-collective see-imperative-singular) 'Look at my sugar cane.'

iya plural collective on animate *(-iyauvaa* can also occur on the animate): *vaidi-iya puara-iya hatoka-a-vai* (man-pl-collective pig-object cut-2nd-and-3rd-pl-stative) 'The men cut up the pigs.' *ta vaidi-iya puara-iyauvaa hatoka-a-vai* (we man-pl-poss pig-pl-collective cut-2nd-and-3rd-pl-stative) 'We cut up the men's pigs.'

-idaa plural inclusive: *na sikau-daa vara-u-vai* (I stone-(money)-pl-inclusive get-1st-sing-stative) 'I got all the money.'

3.3. *Referent* (Ref)

-vai singular; *-vai-tana* dual; *-yauvi* plural: This suffix points out the subject or object specifically referred to in a construction. It has been noted that a referent does not occur as the subject of a transitive verb. The singular form does not occur with ns_1.

Examples of ns_1: *i-nayaa-kia-vai-tana kua-a-noo* (your-sister-pl-Ref-dual go-2nd-and-3rd-pl-indicative) 'Your two sisters are going.' *i-nayaa-kia-yauvi kua-a-noo* (your-sister-pl-Ref-pl go-2nd-and-3rd-pl-indicative) 'Your sisters are going.'

Examples of ns_2: *fayai-vai ngiau kua-i-noo* (animal-Ref-sing upwards go-3rd-sing-indicative) 'The animal went up.' *fayai-vai-tana ngiau kua-a-noo*

---

[2] *u* + *i* results in the *i* changing to *u*. *au* + *i* results in the omission of *i*. *noo* causes length on the preceding vowel.

(animal-Ref-sing-dual upwards go-3rd-pl-indicative) 'Two animals went up.' *ni yaaki-iyauvo takai-yauvi oro rai-nara* (my sugar-cane-Subject-pl-collective break-Ref-pl go-up tie-fut-sing) 'I will go up and tie up my sugar cane which broke.'

-da is a plural referent specifier suffix which seems to be used when the number of things referred to is in focus. The number is general and could refer to four or more things: *ngiaammuau-da kua-a-noo* (boy-Ref-pl-specifier go-3rd-pl-indicative) 'The boys are going (a specific number of boys previously in focus).' *na seera-da utua-u-noo* (I stick-Ref-pl-specifier hold-1st-sing-indicative) 'I am holding the pencils.'

3.4. *Nonreferent Specifier* (Non-RS)

-ruta singular; *-ruta-tana* dual; *-rupara* plural. This suffix behaves in the same manner as the referent and the tentative name of Nonreferent specifier has been given to it. It seems to point out a subject or object of special importance which has not been discussed in the course of the conversation. When suffixed to noun stems of Class I, the subject and object markers are obligatory with proper names. Proper names therefore provide an exception to formula 1.

Examples of ns_1: *meree-va-tuta kua-i-noo* (Mary-subject-Non-RS go-3rd-sing-indicative) 'It is Mary going.' *i-nayaa-kia-ruta-tana kua-a-noo* (your-sister-pl-Non-RS-dual go-2nd and 3rd-indicative) 'It is your two sisters going.' *i-nayaa-kia-rupara kua-a-noo* (your-sister-pl-Non-RS-pl go-2nd-and 3rd-pl-indicative) 'It is your sisters going.'

Examples of ns_2: *ikia vo saaba-ruta ni mia-nee* (firewood limiter bundle-Non-RS me give-imperative-sing) 'Give me a bundle of firewood.' *ikia vo saaba-ruta-tana ni mia-nee* (firewood limiter bundle-Non-RS-dual me give-imperative-sing) 'Give me two bundles of firewood.' *ikia vo saaba-rupara ni mia-nee* (firewood limiter bundle-Non-RS me give-imperative-sing) 'Give me bundles of firewood.'

-nanaa 'first': *meree-va-nanaa kua-i-noo* (Mary-subject-first go-3rd-sing-indicative) 'Mary is going first.'

3.5. *Mood* (Md)

-vee indicative; *-nnee* interrogative. These suffixes can also occur on verbal constructions: *meree-va-vee* (Mary-subject-indicative) 'It is Mary.' *vaidi-ivo-vee* (man-subject-indicative) 'It is a man.' *meree-va-nnee* (Mary-subject-interrogative) 'Is it Mary?' *vaidi-ivo-nnee vara gioonna-ivo-nnee* (man-subject-interrogative or woman-subject-interrogative) 'Is it a man or is it a woman?'

-ta accompaniment. The suffix *-ma* can occur following *-ta*. *-ma* shows a close relationship to the following verb and is almost an adverbialiser: *ivo ari-vaati-ivoo-ta-ma kua-a-noo* (she her-husband-subject-accompani-

ment-adverbializer go-3rd-pl-indicative) 'She and her husband are going.'

-noo indicative. The difference between *-vee* indicative and *-noo* indicative is that *-vee* marks the predicate slot and *-noo* marks the subject slot: *apoo-vaa-noo ti-i-vai* (man's-name-subject-indicative say-3rd-sing-stative) 'Apoo spoke.'

-ra$_1$ reference indicates the person or thing referred to, spoken to, or spoken about: *puara-ivaa-ra kua kia-a-noo* (pig-object-about talk say-2nd/3rd-pl-indicative) 'They are talking about a pig.'

-ni benefactive: *nniaammuau-ya-ni iikia-a-noo* (boys-object-benefactive work-2nd/3rd-pl-indicative 'They are doing it for the benefit of the boys.'

-si 'to' occurs in both noun classes with noun stems referring to persons only: *meree-nna-si kua-nee* (Mary-object-to go-imperative-singular) 'Go to Mary.' *gioonna-ivaa-si kua-nee* (woman-object-to go-imperative-singular) 'Go to the woman.'

-diri$_1$ 'from' (direction). The free variant *-di* is also used: *nnau-vaki-di nni-i-vai* (house-in-from come-3rd-sing-stative) 'He (she, it) came from in the house.' *meree-nna-si-diri nni-i-vai* (Mary-object-to-from come-3rd-sing-stative) 'He came from Mary (from where Mary was).'

-diri$_2$ instrument. The free variant *-di* is also used: *na veeva-ivaa-di ruputua-u-vai* (I arrow-object sing-instrument hit-(kill)-1st-sing-stative) 'I killed it with an arrow.'

With the instrument suffix the object suffix can be shown only by the *-a* morpheme. Both forms are used and it has not yet been determined if there is a significant reason for this: *na veeva-a-diri ruputua-u-vai* (I arrow-object-sing-instrument hit-1st-sing-stative) 'I killed it with an arrow.'

4. NOUNS AS LOCATION AND DIRECTION

Following is formula 3 which shows the occurrence and co-occurrence restrictions of noun stems with location and directional suffixes.

Formula 3:

$$ns_2 \pm \begin{Bmatrix} \begin{matrix} ivaki \\ (kieta) \end{matrix} +ki \\ \\ \begin{matrix} nai \\ ivau \end{matrix} + (nni) \\ \\ yaa \\ inataa \\ nni \\ na \end{Bmatrix} + \begin{Bmatrix} (nnai) + nni \\ naa + (nni) \\ ra_2 \end{Bmatrix} + ra_2 \quad \pm \left(\begin{matrix} ngiaa \\ gietaa \end{matrix} \right) +(diri_1) +(nanaa)$$

Formula 3 shows further affix restrictions on noun stem Class II. Of the suffixes appearing in the formula, only *-diri$_1$* 'from' and *-nanaa* 'first' occur in the formulas described previously. The suffix *-ivaki* 'in' or 'at' and the specifier suffixes represented by *-kieta* plus the obligatory suffix *-ki* 'in' or 'to' are obligatory to the optional suffix *-nnai* interrogative plus *-nni* 'by'; or to *-nna* 'through' plus the optional suffix *-nni* 'by'; or to *ra$_2$* 'to.' The suffix *-nai* 'area' plus the optional suffix *-nni* 'by' and *-ivau* 'on' are both obligatory to *-ra$_2$* 'to'. Further suffixes *-yaa* 'on', *-inataa* 'down inside', *-nni* 'by', or *-na* 'inside' can occur following the noun stem.

The above suffixes are optional and can be followed by *-ngiaa* 'along' or by *-giettaa* 'along side'. These are also optional and can be followed by the optional suffix *-diri$_1$* 'from' which in turn can be followed by the optional suffix *-nanaa* 'first.'

-ivaki[3] 'in' or 'at': *tooti-ivaki-di huda ni-mia-nee* (bamboo-in-from cook me-give-imperative) 'From in the bamboo cook it and give it to me.' *na nnoori-ivaki dia-u-noo* (I water-at stand-1st-sing-indicative) 'I am standing at the water.'

Specifiers: *-kieta* singular; *-kieta-tana* dual; *-kiennia* plural. Examples: *nnau-kieta-ki kua-nee* (house-specifier-sing-in go-imperative) 'Go in the house' (referring to a house previously spoken about or referred to). *nnau-kieta-tana-ki kua-tee* (house-specifier-sing-dual-in-go-imperative-pl 'Go to the two houses.' *nnau-kiennia-ki kua-tee* (house-specifier-pl-in go-imperative-pl) 'Go in the houses.'

-ki 'in' or 'to': *nnau-ki hua-nee* (house-in go-imperative) 'Go in the house.' *na nnoori-ki kua-u-noo* (I water-to go-1st-sing-indicative) 'I am going to the water (place).'

-nnai. The area of meaning of this suffix has not been determined: *nnau-vaki-nnai-nni taa-nee* (house-at-?-by look-imperative) 'Look by the house.'

-nni 'by': *nnau-nni taa-nee* (house-by look-imperative) 'Look by the house.'

-naa 'through': *nnau-ki-naa kua-nee* (house-in-through go-imperative) 'Go in through the house.'

-ra$_2$ 'to'. This suffix is used when indicating a long distance: *nnau-ki-ra kua-nee* (house-in-to go-imperative-sing) 'You go to and in the house.'

-nai 'area': *hanikia rura-nai kua-nee* (fence path-area go-imperative) 'Go along the fence path.'

-ivau[4] 'on' or 'around': *yatari-vau rammua-nee* (tree-around tie-imperative) 'Tie it around the tree.' *iri-ivau kua-nee* (log-on go-imperative) 'Go on the log.'

---

[3] The suffixes *-iya*, *-ivaki*, *-ivau*, and *inataa* have the variant forms *-iya*, *-vaki*, *-vau*, and *-nataa*. These may be partially accounted for by morphophonemic rules (not presented here).

[4] See note 3 above.

This locative suffix also occurs suffixed to the referent suffixes. In the singular form the referent suffix is lost and the form appears the same as above. The dual and plural forms retain the *-i* following the noun stem and become *-u* for dual and *-vuna* for plural: *yana-ivau taa-nee* (leaf-(paper)-on look-imperative) 'Look on the book.' *yana-ivai-tana-u taa-nee* (leaf-referent-dual-on look-imperative) 'Look on the two books.' *yana-iyau-vuna taa-nee* (leaf-referent-pl-on look-imperative) 'Look on the two books.'

-yaa 'on'. This suffix indicates a more specific area than *-ivau* 'on': *mmata-yaa varia-nee* (ground-on sit-imperative) 'Sit on the ground.'

-inataa[5] 'down inside': *yava-inataa taa-nee* (clay-pot-down-inside look-imperative-sing) 'Look down inside the clay pot.'

-na 'inside': *na nnoori-na-di vara-u-vai* (I water-inside-from get-1st-sing-stative) 'I got it from in the water.'

-ngiaa 'along'; *-gietaa* 'along side'. The tentative meanings *-ngiaa* 'along around' and *-gietaa* 'along side' have been given to try to distinguish the area of meaning of these two suffixes: *nnau-vaki-nnai-gietaa kua-nee* (house-at-?-along-side go-imperative) 'Go along side the house.' *nnau-vaki-nnai-nni-ngiaa kua-nee* (house-at-?-by-along-around go-imperative) 'Go along around by the house.'

5. OTHER USAGES OF NOUNS

Formulas 4 and 5 show further restrictions of the occurrence and co-occurrence of suffixes with noun stems.

Formula 4:   ns   +   (voc)

Both noun stems of Class I and Class II can be followed by the vocative (voc) suffixes (*-o* singular, *-so* plural) when the noun stem is human. Examples: *Nasitee-o nnia-nee* (man's-name-voc-sing come-up-imperative-sing) 'Nasitee, (you) come!' *vaidi-so rikia-tee* (man-voc-pl hear-imperative-pl) 'Men, listen!'

Formula 5:

$$ns_2 \quad + \quad \left(\begin{array}{c} ra_3 \\ (vai) \quad + \quad (Md) \end{array} \right)$$

Formula 5 shows further affix restrictions on noun stem Class II. The purposive suffix-*ra*$_3$ and the suffixes represented by *-vai* plus the mood suffixes optionally follow the noun stem.

---

[5] See note 3 above.

-*ra*₃ purposive. This suffix indicates the purpose of the action of the verb with reference to the noun with which it occurs: *na ngiaamma-ra kua-u-noo* (I bird-purposive go-1st-sing-indicative) 'I am going for (to acquire) birds.'

-*vai* represents -*vai*₁ and -*vai*₂. -*vai*₁ refers to the stative suffix which occurs with verbal constructions. The person and number are not indicated. This could be considered the predicative when occurring with nouns: *ni fai-vai* (my dog-stative) 'It is my dog.'

-*vai*₂ represents the perfect suffixes. These also occur on verbs and they are marked for person and number. The forms are as follows: first and third singular -*vai;* second singular -*kua;* first, second, and third plural -*ya*. Example: *a vaidi-kua* (you-sing-man-perfect) 'You are (definitely) a man.'

6. KINSHIP TERM STEM FORMATION

Kinship terms in both classes of nouns are prefixed with the possessive pronouns *ni-* first, *i-~ai-* second, *ari-* third singular; *ti-* first, *ngii-* second, *ngiari-* third plural: *ni-napoo-nna nnau-vai* (my-father-possessive house-stative) 'It is my father's house.'

These pronouns are obligatorily prefixed excepting where the person is being addressed: *napoo-o* (father-voc) 'Father!'

There are two terms for father, mother, older brother, older sister, mother's brother, and mother's sister. When the speaker is referring to his father, mother, etc., he uses a different term to that used by anybody else. Thus: *ni-noo-va* (my-mother-subject) 'my mother', *ni-napoo-va* (my-father-subject) 'my father', *ai-kaano* (your-mother-subject) 'your mother', *i-koo-va* (your-father-subject) 'your father'.

Plural is indicated by a change in the stem. Noun stems of Class I have -*kia(iya)* added when the reference is by someone other than the speaker. This seems to mean a special kin relationship: *i-kookiaiya varia-a-noo* (your-father-pl sit-3rd-pl-indicative) 'Your fathers are sitting.'

-*vainna* is added when the speaker is referring to his own kin: *ni-napoo-vainna varia-a-vai* (my-father-pl sit-3rd-pl-stative) 'My fathers sat.'

ns₂ kinship terms have the following plural stem formations: *i-kata-unna-iya* 'your-younger-brother-plural'; *i-vaati-daunna-iya* 'your-husband-plural'; *i-nnaata-daunna-iya* 'your-wife-plural'; *i-needi-tunna-iya* 'your-grandchild-plural'; *i-nnaudi-tunna-iya* 'your-niece/nephew-plural'; *i-nnunna-apu-uya* 'your-younger-sister-plural'; *i-raunna-apu-uya* 'your-daughter-plural'.

In ns₁ the suffix -*ya* occurring on two noun stems connects the two nouns: *meree-ya suaisa-ya kua-a-noo* (Mary-connective Joyce-connective go-3rd-sing-indicative) 'Mary and Joyce are going.' *aheemo-ya air-koo-ya kua-a-noo* (man's-name-connective his-father-connective—go-3rd-pl-indicative) 'Aheemo and his father are going.'

When a kin relationship term from Class II occurs the suffix -*ri* occurs:

munniduu-ya raunna-ri kua-a-noo (man's-name-connective daughter-connective go-3rd-pl-indicative) 'Munniduu and his daughter went.'

XXIX. Binumarien Noun Affixes

DESMOND and JENNIFER OATRIDGE and ALAN HEALEY

1. INTRODUCTION

Binumarien nouns are that class of words which fill the head slot of noun phrases and which do not take person and tense suffixes.[1]

Nouns are divided into two classes on the basis of their different patterns of suffixation. Class I nouns characteristically take *-fa* (singular) and *-sa* (plural) to mark the subject, and *-na* (singular) and *-sa* or *-usa* (plural) to mark nonsubject. Class II nouns, when not preceded by a demonstrative, characteristically take *-fanno* to mark the subject, and *Ø* (singular) and *-uqa* or *-uqaindi* (plural) to mark nonsubject.

Nouns are further subdivided on the basis of prefixation. Nouns of classes IA and IIA take possessive prefixes. In most instances these prefixes are obligatory, but there are a few nouns such as *maaqa* 'house' in Class IIA which have optional possessive prefixes. Nouns of classes IB and IIB do not take possessive prefixes.

Semantically, Class IA consists of some of the kinship terms, Class IB consists of personal names, Class IIA consists of body parts and the remainder ok the kinship terms, and Class IIB consists of all other nouns.

2. SUFFIXATION

Table 66 shows the various suffixes which occur with Class I nouns and Table 67 shows the corresponding system of nonlocative suffixes for Class II

[1] Primary research for this investigation was carried out by Desmond and Jennifer Oatridge. Alan Healey gave assistance in the organization and analysis of the data and is responsible for the material in its present form. Financial assistance was given the Oatridges for Binumarien research from the New Guinea Research Fund of the Summer Institute of Linguistics.

nouns. However, a Class II noun which is preceded by a demonstrative (*mi* 'that', *maa* 'this') takes the suffixes of Table 66 instead. All of the suffix combinations which occur can be ascertained by reading these two charts from left to right without crossing any horizontal lines. It should be noted, however, that *-faqa* 'and' does not co-occur with any of the accompaniment suffixes.

For the interrogative and negative suffixes, the second allomorph listed occurs following the suffixes *-fa, -na, -sa,* and *-faqa,* whereas the first allomorph occurs in all other contexts. In nouns, when certain combinations of vowels occur at a morpheme boundary there is reduction: /aa > a, ii > i, uu > u, ui > u, iaa > aa, aau > au, ae > e/. These reductions deserve a more detailed investigation.

TABLE 66

SUFFIXES WITH CLASS I NOUNS (AND WITH DEMONSTRATIVE PLUS CLASS II NOUNS)

-o vocative

-fa singular *-fa -qara* dual *-sa -qara* dual *-sa* plural	∅ subject			

-na singular
-qara dual
-qanda dual
-usa -namu 'few'
 	
-usa -mara 'few'
 	
usa plural
-sa plural
	∅ object
	-ara (tell) 'about'
	-saara 'because of'
	
	-indi possessive
	    complement
		-kai 'only'
		
		∅
			-faqa 'and'
			
			∅
				-fe ∼ -e
				  interrogative
				-fau ∼ -au
				    negative
				
				∅

-na singular *-sa* (singular)	*-ndiri* accompaniment *-ndiri -qara* accompaniment			
sa plural	*-imbaqa* accompaniment			

TABLE 67

-*o* vocative

∅ singular, plural -*qara* dual -*qanda* dual -*namu* 'few'	-*fanno* subject ∅ subject (when unambiguous)			

∅ singular
-*qara* dual
-*qanda* dual
-*namu* 'few'
 	
-*qmaaka* 'few'
 	
-*uqa* plural
 	
-*uqaindi* plural
 	
-*uqaindi* -*namu*
  plural
	∅ object
	-*saara* 'because of'
	-*ara* (tell) 'about'
	-*indi* possessive
	  complement
	
	-*nno*
	-*nnai*
	-*ko*
	
	-*samu* instrument
	-*samu* -*nno*
	-*samu* -*nnai*
	-*samu* -*ko*
		-*kai* 'only'
		
		∅
			-*faqa* 'and'
			
			∅
				-*fe* ～ -*e*
				  interrogative
				
				-*fau* ～ -*au*
				  negative
				
				∅

∅ singular
 	
-*sa* plural
	-*ndiri* accompaniment
	-*ndiri* -*qara*
	  accompaniment
	-*imbaqa*
	  accompaniment			

TABLE 68
LOCATIVE SUFFIXES WITH CLASS II NOUNS

∅ 'at'	∅ (be) 'at'
mau 'along'	-*saqa* (be) 'at'
-*saa* 'on'	-*ni* ~ -*i* (go) 'to'
amemaana 'under'	-*n(in)dari* ~ -*indari* (come) 'from'
runna 'in' (valley)	-*qari* (come) 'from'
ki 'in' 'into'	-*ndanai* (look) 'toward'
-*ki* -*na* 'inside'	-*indaqa* (look) 'toward'
-*ki* -*aqa* 'among', 'between'	
-*kasaaqa* 'across'	
-*mammaaqa* 'along the side of'	
-*amuaaqa* 'on top of'	
-*amummaqa* 'above'	

Table 68 lists all of the locative suffixes that have been observed on Class II nouns. The majority of the combinations of suffixes in the first column with suffixes in the second column actually occur (but not all). Further inquiry is needed as to whether (A) any two suffixes in the second column co-occur, (B) any of the recurring partials *na, qa, nda, i,* and *ri* are morphemes.

Noun 'suffixes' in many instances seem to belong rather to the noun phrase and may also occur on a nominalized clause. They may also be added to various other complex formations as follows: adjective + -*ikira* 'a person with this quality'; adjective/verb + -*ara* abstract noun; Class II noun and Class I noun + -*na* + -*faqaa* 'a person with this thing'; Class II noun and Class I noun + -*na* + -*siqai* 'a person without this thing'; noun + (-*ara*) + *foqaa* + (-*ira*) 'a person or thing like this thing'; noun + -*anaaqi* 'a person covered with this thing'; noun + locative suffixes + -*aa* 'a person from this location'.

3. PREFIXATION

The possessive prefixes are as follows: *qi*- (before consonants and *i*), *d*- (before vowels other than *i*) 'my, our'; *a*- (before consonants and *i*), ∅ (before vowels other than *i*) 'your (singular)', 'his', 'her'; *ni*- (before consonants), *n*- (before vowels) 'your (plural)', 'their'.

XXX. Tairora Verb Structure

ALEX VINCENT

---

1. INTRODUCTION

1.1. *Background*

This paper is a revision of an earlier paper published in 1962.[1] Additional data gathered since that time have made such a revision necessary. The format of the present paper is similar to the earlier paper and the paradigmatic presentation is largely retained. Some affixes formerly considered fusions of more than one morpheme and left uncut are further divided in this paper.

The verb in Tairora consists of stem plus inflectional affixes.

1.2. *Stems*

1.2.1. *Stem classes.* There are three classes of stems based on the stem-final vowel. These include Class I, stems that end in *i*; *iri* 'hear', *ani* 'come'; Class II, stems that end in *i* or *u*: *bi* or *bu* 'go', *ni* or *nu* 'walk'; and Class III, stems that end in *e* or *a; tabe* or *taba* 'see', *ne* or *na* 'eat'.

The first form of stems with alternants will be referred to as the primary form, and the second will be referred to as the secondary form.[2]

[1] See Alex and Lois Vincent (1962a). The present revision is based on a larger corpus of data gathered over a total of five years field time, roughly half of which time was spent in the Central Tairora (Suwaira) dialect area and a half in the Northern Tairora (Baantura-Aupora) dialect area. The material was gathered under the auspices of the Summer Institute of Linguistics. The writer is indebted to Darlene Bee of SIL and Howard McKaughan, University of Hawaii, for editorial suggestions.

[2] Stems with final *e* rather than *a* have been chosen as primary forms of Class III because this final vowel precedes initial consonants of inflectional suffixes (except liquid *r* in which case the stem-final vowel is sometimes *e* and sometimes *a*). It is also the form when inflectional affixes are absent. *e.g.,* preceding zero third person-number: *nepø* (eat-he) 'He ate.' For similar reasons the primary forms of Class II are those with *i* not *u*.

561

Class I and II stems lose their final vowel before a suffix with initial high vowels: *ti* plus *-urauka* becomes *turauka* 'I said'; *ti* plus *-iba* becomes *tiba* 'He said'; *bi* plus *-urauka* becomes *burauka* 'I went'; *bi* plus *-iba* becomes *biba* 'He went.'

Class III stems occur with final vowel *-a* before a suffix with an initial high vowel: *ne* plus *-urauka* becomes *naurauka* 'I ate'; *ne* plus *-iba* becomes *naiba* 'He ate.'

Other stem changes will be noted as individual morphemes are discussed.

Examples will be given in paradigmatic sets so that stem changes can be observed.

1.2.2. *Stem compounding.* Certain verb complexes may consist of one or more stems (roots), the final stem indicating aspect. Nonfinal stems may occur free. Aspect constructions are analyzed as close knit phrases; further details of this construction are given under Section 3.2.2. This section describes the form of such stems. There are three types of stem compounds.

1.2.2.1. *Nominal plus verb stem.* In certain object-included-in-the-predicate constructions nounlike forms are followed by a verb stem. The nounlike form is referred to as a nominal and is a separate word. Some nominals occur in other constructions clearly as nouns while others occur only in compound stem constructions. The following verb generally has no meaning in isolation. For example, the nominal, *iha* 'firewood' occurs elsewhere as a noun, but the verb, *quare,* occurs only with *iha.* The following examples illustrate: *katari kaara iha quare-ro* (tree branch firewood burn-it)[3] 'He firewooded the tree branch', that is, 'He burned the tree branch.' Compare: *iha bare-ro* (firewood get-he) 'He got firewood.'

In the following example, *antuqa* 'hunger' or 'hunger place' occurs only in a compound stem construction: *h-antuqa h-ari-ro* (hunger-place hit-it) 'It hit his hunger place' or 'He is hungry.'

1.2.2.2. *Nominalized verb stem plus verb stem.* A limited number of verb stems, when occurring as a first member of a compound verb construction, occur with a nominalizing suffix, *-ba* or *-ma.* The secondary form of the verb stem occurs in such constructions. Thus *ti* 'say' becomes *tiba; ri* 'put' becomes *ruba; ne* 'eat' becomes *nama; tabe* 'see' becomes *tabama; ni* 'walk' becomes *nuba.* Two examples follow, the second containing a nominalized verb stem: *uba ti-ro* (talk say-he) 'He said talk' or 'He spoke.' *uba- ti-ba a-mi-ro* (talk say-nominalizer him-give-he) 'He gave him talk' or 'He told him.'

1.2.2.3. *Verb stem plus verb.* Similar to the nominalized verb stem construction, a sequence of verb stems may occur as a single verb either

---

[3] Hyphens between words in the English literal translation indicate bound morpheme breaks in the Tairora which are also indicated with a hyphen. Double hyphens (=) are used when more than one English word is used to translate a single Tairora morpheme.

following the first free stem or following the main verb: *aru-e ke-ro* (hit-interrogative leave-he) 'Did he hit it?' *aru-ke-ro-e* (hit-leave-he-interrogative) 'Did he hit it?'

The secondary form of the verb stem occurs in nonfinal positions.

1.3. *Affixes*

1.3.1. *Prefixes.* Indirect object prefixes occur with a limited number of verbs. Morphemes indicating the indirect object also mark person and number. Person is either first or nonfirst; number is singular or plural only with nonfirst person; *ti-* ∼ *ø-* ∼ *h-* 'me/us'; *a-* ∼ *ø* 'thou/him'; *ni-* ∼ *n-* ∼ *ø-* 'you/them'. As there are only a few verbs concerned all possible forms are listed below.

	1st sing/pl	2nd/3rd sing	2nd/3rd pl
'give'	*ti-mi*	*a-mi*	*ni-mi*
'rebuke'	*ti-ti*	*a-ti*	*ni-hi; ni-ti*
'pain'	*ø-ihabi*	*a-ihabi*	*n-ihabi*
'call'	*h-aare*	*ø-aare*	*n-aare*
'show'	*h-umiqe*	*ø-umiqe*	*n-umiqe*
'hit'	*h-ari*	*ø-ari*	*ø-ari*
'surpass'	*h-aatare*	*ø-aatare*	*ø-aatare*
'seek'	*h-ituti*	*a-ituti*	*n-ihuti; nituti*

Examples: *ti ti-mi-ro* (me me-give-he) 'He gave it to me.' *bika ni-mi-ro* (them them-give-he) 'He gave it to them.' *ti ø-ihabi-ro* (me me-pain-it) 'It pains me' or 'I am sick.'

1.3.2. *Suffixes.* Usually not more than two verbal suffixes follow the verb stem. These may be followed in turn by suffixes (clitics) that occur with other word classes.

The following semantic categories are indicated by verbal suffixes: person, number, mood, and tense or aspect. A further category will be termed focus.

1.3.2.1. *Person-number.* Two number distinctions, singular or plural (free pronouns also mark dual number), and three person distinctions are indicated by the verb. However, these two parameters are fused so that a maximum of four person-number distinctions result: (1) first person singular or plural; (2) second person singular; (3) third person singular; and (4) second and third persons plural.

1.3.2.2. *Tense-aspect.* Three tenses occur: far past, past, and future. Sometimes tense is fused with aspect. For example, the abilitative is future tense plus abilitative aspect.

1.3.2.3. *Mood.* Interrogative and indicative moods are marked by the forms *-e* and *-ma,* respectively. These suffixes also attach to other parts of the clause (e.g., subject or object). When a mood verbal suffix (a fused mood) is present, the free mood suffixes may not occur. The mood verbal suffixes include dubitative, avolitional, contrary to fact, and imperative.

1.3.2.4 *Focus.* There are two focus categories termed subject and non-subject.

2. VERB CONSTRUCTIONS

The structure of verbal affixation is conditioned by distribution in higher level constructions. The following environments condition verb structure: (1) verb in independent sentence-final clauses; (2) verb in dependent non-final clauses; (3) verb in dependent sentence-final clauses; (4) verb in included clauses; and (5) verb in final clause of a quoted sentence.

The structure of the verb will now be described with reference to each of these environments.

2.1. *Verb in Independent Sentence-Final Clauses*

The structure of sentence-final independent verbs can be summarized by the following formula:

$$\text{verb stem} + \begin{cases} \text{mood-per-num} \\ \text{tense-per-num}_1 \\ \text{(aspect)} + \text{per-num} \\ \text{tense-per-num}_2; \text{-}ataa\} + \text{focus} \end{cases} \text{(free mood)}$$

The semicolon is to be read 'or'. Items in parentheses are optional.

All constructions may occur with the interrogative *-e* or the indicative *-ma* free mood markers except the mood-person-number constructions.

2.1.1. *Verb stem plus mood-person-number suffix.* Fused mood constructions include dubitative, avolitional, and imperative.

2.1.1.1. *Dubitative mood.* The dubitative mood indicates uncertainty about a future event. There is no contrast in this mood between second and third person singular forms. Stem changes may be noted from the example of each stem class given, *ti* 'say'; *bu* 'go'; and *ne* 'eat'.

	Class I	Class II	Class III	Dubitative-per-num
1st sing/pl	*ti*	*b*	*na*	-*arera*
2nd/3rd sing	*t*	*b*	*na*	-*irera*
2nd/3rd pl	*t*	*b*	*na*	-*ibera*

Further morpheme cuts may be seen but these cuts are not synchronically productive.

Examples: *hura bu-arera* (tomorrow go-I = dubitative) 'I might go tomorrow.' *biba ba-irera* (he be-he = dubitative 'He might be there.'

2.1.1.2. *Avolitional mood.* The avolitional mood indicates something that the speaker does not wish to happen. There are two sets of these mood-person-number suffixes. No clear difference in meaning has been noted between Set A and Set B except that some forms of Set A may occur with an anticipatory subject marker in a dependent final clause whereas these of Set B do not.

	Class I	Class II	Class III	Avolitional-per-num	
				Set A	Set B
1st sing/pl	*ti*	*bu*	*na*	-arora	-aribaara
2nd sing	*ti*	*bi*	*ne*	-rora	-rabaara
3rd sing	*ti*	*bu*	*na*	-antora	-antaaribaara
2nd/3rd pl	*ti*	*bi*	*ne*	-bora	-baara

Examples: *ruqutubi-rora* (fall-you = should = not) *ruqutubi-rabaara* (fall-you = should = not) Both mean: 'It would not be good if you fell' or 'Be careful not to fall.'

2.1.1.3. *Imperative mood.* Imperative-person-number suffixes indicate second person only, and singular, plural, or indefinite (either singular or plural) number.

	Class I	Class II	Class III	Imperative-per-num
Sing	*ti*	*bu*	*na*	-ana
Plu	*ti*	*bu*	*na*	-ata
Indefinite	*ti*	*bu*	*na*	-a

Examples: *mini bu-ana* (there go-thou = imperative) 'Go there!' *taba-ata* (look-you-plural-imperative) 'You all look!' *iri-a* (hear-indefinite-imperative) 'Listen!'

2.1.2. *Free mood constructions.* Verbal constructions in this section may optionally occur either with -*e* interrogative, or -*ma* indicative mood. There are three constructional types: future- and abilitative-person-number; aspect plus person-number; and tense-person-number, or 'should' plus focus.

2.1.2.1. *Future- and abilitative-person-number constructions.* The future-person-number construction may also indicate desire or intention. Thus *birera* 'I will go' may also mean 'I want to go' or 'I intend to go.' Second and third singular forms are noncontrastive.

	Class I	Class II	Class III	Future-per-num
1st sing/pl	*ti*	*bi*	*na*	-rera
2nd/3rd sing	*ti*	*bi*	*na*	-reba
2nd/3rd pl	*ti*	*bi*	*na*	-reka

(Central Tairora has second singular -*rerara;* third singular -*reraro.*)

Examples: *te bi-rera-ma* (I go-I = future-indicative) 'I will go.' *kaiqa bara-rera* (work get-I = future) 'I want work.' *aaqu ri-reba* (rain do-it = future) 'It will rain.'

The abilitative-person-number construction indicates ability or strong intention for nonpast actions.

	Class I	Class II	Class III	Abilitative-per-num
1st sing/pl	*ti*	*bi*	*na*	*-rara* (*-ainara* in Central Tairora)
2nd sing	*ti*	*bi*	*ne*	*-nara*
3rd sing	*ti*	*bu*	*na*	*-anaro*
2nd/3rd pl	*ti*	*bi*	*ne*	*-bara*

Examples: *qako tabe-nara* (later see-you = can) 'Later you will certainly see it.' *te kia bi-rara* (I not go-I = can) 'I am not able to go.'

2.1.2.2. *Verb stem plus aspect plus person-number constructions.* Two verbal suffixes may follow a verb stem: an optional aspect suffix followed by a person-number suffix. If either no aspect suffix occurs, or if the negative aspect suffix occurs, then the tense implication is past (the implication is prior tense in nonfinal clauses). The person-number suffixes will be referred to as neutral.

The two aspect suffixes are: *-ha* progressive and *-raiti* negative.

2.1.2.2.1. *Progressive aspect.* The progressive suffix *-ha* indicates that an action is in progress. The primary form of the stem occurs before *-ha* (i.e., *i, i,* and *e,* for Class I, II, and III stems, respectively).

Examples: *ani-ha-ro* (come-progressive-he) 'He is coming.' *bai-ha-ra-e* (be-progressive-you-interrogative) 'Are you there?'

2.1.2.2.2. *Negative aspect.* The negative aspect suffix *-raiti* may occur in addition to the use of the negative particle *kia* 'not'. When the negative aspect suffix occurs, the negation of the verbal action is emphasized. The final vowel of the stem is *i, i,* and *a* for Class I, II, and III stems, respectively.

Examples: *kia iri-raiti-ro* (not hear-negative-he) 'He really didn't hear.' *kia taba-raiti-ø* (not see-negative-I) 'I didn't see it.'

2.1.2.2.3. *Neutral-person-number.* First person and second and third plural forms are noncontrastive.

	Class I	Class II	Class III	Neutral-per-num
1st sing/1st/ 2nd/3rd pl	*ti*	*bi*	*ne*	*-ø*
2nd sing	*ti*	*bi*	*ne*	*-ra*
3rd sing	*ti*	*bi*	*ne*	*-ro*

Free subject personal pronouns may be used to avoid ambiguity.

Examples: *te-iri-ø-ma* (I hear-I-indicative) 'I heard it.' *bi-ro-e* (go-he-interrogative) 'Did he go?' *bika bi-ø-ma* (they go-they-indicative) 'They went.'

2.1.2.3. *Focus constructions.* Focus constructions require two suffixes after the stem (i.e., one does not occur without the other). The first order suffix is either a tense-person-number suffix or *-ataa* 'should'. The second order suffix is a focus suffix.

2.1.2.3.1. *Tense-person-number.* The first order tense-person-number suffixes mark past, far past, or future tense. These forms are listed below. The *r* in the first syllable remains *r* when a subject focus suffix follows, but becomes *n* when a nonsubject focus suffix follows:

	Class I	Class II	Class III	Past-per-num
1st sing/pl	*t*	*b*	*na*	*-ura*
2nd sing	*ti*	*bu*	*na*	*-ara*
3rd sing	*t*	*b*	*na*	*-i*
2nd/3rd pl	*ti*	*bu*	*na*	*-a*
				Far past-per-num
1st sing/	*ti*	*bu*	*na*	*-abaura*
2nd sing	*t*	*b*	*n*	*-ura* (*-ora* with Class II stems)
3rd sing,				
2nd/3rd pl	*t*	*b*	*n*	*-u* (*-o* with Class III stems)
				Future-per-num
1st sing/pl	*ti*	*bu*	*na*	*-arira* (or *-aira*)
2nd sing	*ti*	*bi*	*ne*	*-ra*
2nd/3rd pl	*ti*	*bu*	*na*	*-arira* (or *-aira*)
2nd/3rd pl	*ti*	*bi*	*ne*	*-ø*

There is usually a stress contrast between the first and third singular person form: *bu'ainara* 'I will go'; *buai'nara* 'He will go.'

2.1.2.3.2. *'Should' suffix.* With the first order 'should' suffix *-ataa,* the secondary form of the stem-final vowel occurs.

2.1.2.3.3. *Focus suffixes.* There are two sets of second order focus suffixes. To differentiate one set from the other, the first set is termed subject focus because of its correspondence in form to the clause level subject markers. The second set is termed nonsubject focus.[4]

---

[4] The term 'focus' is used for convenience. The same set of markers occur with third person personal pronouns, personal names, certain nouns denoting a 'senior' or 'respectful' type of kin relationship, and relator phrases. In these constructions the markers function syntactically and the subject versus nonsubject distinction is more

The subject focus suffixes are second and third singular -ba; elsewhere -uka or -ka (-ka following high vowels and also following aa in some dialects). The nonsubject focus suffix is -ra. A third suffix could be included in this section, -o ~ -bo assertion, since this suffix cannot occur without the past tense fusions. However, this form also marks reported speech and is described in Section 2.5.1.

The -ra focus suffix with past and far past tense is translated by the perfect and past perfect, respectively: taba-una-ra (see-I = past-focus) 'I have seen it.' taba-abauna-ra (see-I = far = past-focus) 'I had seen it.'

The past and far past suffixes with subject-focus seem to stress tense: tai bu-ara-ba-be (where go-you = past-focus-interrogative) 'Where did you go?' or 'Where have you been?' mini b-ura-uka (there go-I = past-focus) 'I went there' or 'I've been there.' te mini bari-abaura-uka (I there be-I = far = past-focus) 'I used to live there.'

The future-person-number forms have been listed, but examples clearly occurring in the final clause construction are lacking—the future and abilitative forms already described are preferred in future independent clauses. The following examples may be interpreted as a final clause or as an equational clause: te bu-arira-uka (I go-I = future-focus) 'I will go' or 'I am the one who will go.' biba bu-arina-ra (he go-he = will-focus) 'He will go' or 'He is the one who will go.'

The -ataa 'should' plus focus suffix constructions are also difficult to differentiate from equational constructions: te-mini bu-ataa-uka (I there go-should-I = focus) 'I should have gone there' or 'I am the one who should have gone there.'

2.2. Verb in Dependent Nonfinal Clauses

The structure of the verb in nonfinal dependent clauses must be considered in relation to the clause that follows. (The following clause may be a final clause or a nonfinal clause.)

---

clearly seen. (See example of this in Sec. 2.4.) When these forms occur with sentence-final verbs, their function or semantic significance is not clear. The far past and past nonsubject focus -ra constructions occur frequently in text, particularly final in the discourse, and are generally best translated with the past perfect or perfect: mini bari-abauna-ra 'I used to live there,' or 'I had lived there.' taba-una-ra 'I have seen it.' bata-una-ra 'I have it.' The far past and past subject focus constructions occur less frequently, and the past subject forms are often best translatable by English past tense: tai bu-ara-ba-be 'Where did you go?' mini b-ura-uka 'I went there.' However a neutral-person-number construction is used with other verbs, for example, ni 'walk': tai ni-ra-e 'Where did you walk?' mini ni-ø-ma 'I walked there.' The writer suspects that earlier in the history of the language the neutral-person-number forms were restricted to nonfinal clauses, and that now their appearance in final clauses has weakened the usage of the tense-focus constructions. Perhaps too, the abilitative and future fusions (Sec. 2.1.2.1) are fairly recent, and their appearance has caused the future-focus forms to fall into disuse sentence finally.

In many cases (in a two clause construction for example) a change of subject (actor) in the second clause conditions the structure of the verb in the first clause. Two examples illustrate this. In the first example the subjects of the two clauses are the same, that is, first person actor: *te kara ne-Ø bi-rera* (I food eat-I go-I = future) 'I will eat and go.' In the second example the first clause subject is first person and the second clause subject is a different actor, that is, third person: *te kara na-arira-ro bi-reba* (I food eat-I = future-and = he go-he = future) 'I will eat, and he will go.'

Same subject constructions (Sec. 2.2.1) will be described separately from different subject constructions (Sec. 2.2.2).

2.2.1. *Same subject constructions.* In sequences of same subject clauses the verb structure of the nonfinal clause may be identical to the verb structure in the final independent constructions already described. The following constructions may occur: verb stem plus (aspect) plus neutral-person-number; verb stem plus tense-person-number$_2$ plus focus; verb stem plus avolitional or dubitative-person-number; and verb stem plus future-person-number$_1$.

2.2.1.1. *Verb stem plus (aspect) plus neutral-person-number* constructions consist of a verb stem followed by an optional aspect suffix followed by a neutral-person-number suffix as described under Section 2.1.2.2.3. An additional aspect suffix may occur in verbs in nonfinal dependent clauses. This suffix is *-qi* 'simultaneous-sustained', and when this aspect occurs, the verb in the following clause is always a motion verb, for example, *vi* 'go'; *ani* 'come'.

The following action relationships are expressed by these forms.

A. First action in progress while second takes place, signaled by aspect suffix *-ha* progressive in the first clause: *bi-ha-ro tabe-ro* (go-progressive-he see-he) 'While he was going he saw it.' *bi-ha-ro taba-reba* (go-progressive-he see-he = will) 'While he is going he will see it.'

B. Without first action taking place the second action takes place, signaled by negative aspect *-raiti* in the first clause. The free negative *kia* obligatorily occurs: *kia bara-raiti-ro bi-ro* (not take-negative-he go-he) 'He didn't take it and went' or 'He went without taking it' (both actions past). *kia bara-raiti-ro bi-reba* (not take-negative-he go-he = will) 'He will go without taking it' (both actions future).

C. First action occurs simultaneously with the second action, signaled by aspect suffix *-qi* 'simultaneous-sustained'. The verb of the following clause is always a motion verb. The nominalized form of the stem or otherwise the secondary stem forms occur before *-qi: aru-qi-ro tubi-ro* (hit-simultaneous-he come-down-he) 'He hit as he came down' or 'He came down fighting' (both actions are past). *aru-qi-ro tubi-reba* (hit-simultaneous-he come = down-he = will) 'He will come down fighting' (both actions are future). *naabu-qi bari-qi-ro bi-ro* (house-in be-sustained-he go-he) 'He stayed on in the house' (here the action is more 'sustained' than 'simultaneous').

ti-ba-qi-ro bi-ro (say-nominalizer-sustained-he go-he) 'He continued talking' or 'He went along talking.'

D. First action prior to the second action in which the neutral-person-number suffixes occur without first order aspect suffixes, and the first clause action is simply prior to the second clause action: *bare-ro bi-ro* (take-he go-he) 'He took it and he went' (both actions are past). *bare-ro bi-reba* (take-he go-he = will) 'He will take it and go' (both actions are future).

2.2.1.2. *Verb stem plus tense-person-number$_2$ plus focus* constructions consist of the verb stem plus tense-person-number plus focus as described in Section 2.1.2.3. Use of this verb construction in a nonfinal clause indicates that the action relationship is not necessarily sequential or that there is a time gap before the next action takes place: *bate bu-ara-ba taihaira-e bare-re* (today go-you = past-focus where-from-interrogative get-you) 'You (only) went today, so where did you get it from (so soon)?' *enta an-ura-uka hura bi-rera* (yesterday come-I = past-focus tomorrow to-I = will) 'I came yesterday, and I will go tomorrow.'

This latter example could also be analyzed as an equational clause, 'I am the one who came yesterday' plus 'I will go tomorrow.' The resulting meaning would be similar: 'I, the one who came yesterday, will go tomorrow.' *bate bi-ra-ba homa orurante-ra ani-nara* (today go-you = future-focus certain return-you come-you = can) '(If) you go today, you could certainly return today.'

2.2.1.3. *Verb stem plus an avolitional or dubitative mood fusion* constructions consist of a verb stem plus an avolitional mood fusion or a dubitative mood fusion.

The avolitional mood fusions appear in Set A in Section 2.1.1.2. The avolitional first clause indicates the 'undesired reason' for the second clause action. This section should be compared with Section 2.2.2.2. where avolitional different subject constructions are described.

Example: *qutu bu-arora ne-ø-ma* (cease go-I = should = not eat-I-indicative) 'Lest I die, I ate it.'

Dubitative mood (conditional) fusions have been described in Section 2.1.1.1. The dubitative construction in the first clause indicates a condition for the occurrence of the action in the second clause. Only verbs marked for future implications may close conditional constructions. This construction should be compared with the different subject construction in Section 2.2.2.2.

Examples: *bata-irera ti-mi-ana* (put-you = dubitative me-give-you = imperative) 'If you have it, then give it to me.' *ho bari-arera bi-rara* (well be-I = dubitative go-I = can) 'If I am well, I'll be able to go.'

2.2.1.4. *Verb stem plus future-person-number$_1$ (purposive) constructions* contain a verb stem followed by a future fusion suffix described in Section 2.1.2.1. This construction in the first clause marks the purpose for the action of the second clause: *bara-reka ani-ø* (get-they = future come-they) 'They came to get it.' *bira taba-rera bu-ura-uka* (it see-I = future go-I = past-focus) 'I went in order to see it.' *tabe-reba bi-reba* (see-he = future go-he = future) 'He will go in order to see it.'

These constructions should be compared with the different subject construction in Section 2.2.2.3.

2.2.2. *Different subject constructions.* When the following clause subject is different from the preceding nonfinal clause subject, the verb structure is as follows: (1) verb stem plus tense-person-number₃ plus anticipator; (2) verb stem plus avolitional or dubitative plus anticipator fusion; (3) verb stem plus purpose plus anticipator.

2.2.2.1. *Tense-person-number₃ plus anticipator suffix constructions.* The set of tense-person-number suffixes that occur in the nonfinal constructions is similar to the sets listed in Section 2.1.2.3. However, there are important differences, so they are listed in full.

	Class I	Class II	Class III	Past-per-num
1st sing/pl	t	b	na	-ura
2nd sing	ti	bu	na	-ara
3rd sing	t	b	na	-i or -iba
2nd/3rd pl	ti	bu	na	-a or -aba

The third singular suffix has two allomorphs as does the second and third person plural suffix. The first in each case occurs before the anticipatory suffix *-manta* and the second elsewhere.

	Class I	Class II	Class III	Far past-per-num
1st sing/pl	ti	bu	na	-abaura
2nd sing	t	b	n	-ura (-ora with e stems)
3rd sing, 2nd/3rd pl	t	b	n	-u or -uba (-o or -oba with e stems)

The first forms listed in the third singular and second and third person plural precede *-manta* and the second forms occur elsewhere.

	Class I	Class II	Class III	Future-per-num
1st sing/pl	ti	bu	na	-arira
2nd/3rd sing	t	b	na	-ira
2nd/3rd pl	t	b	na	-iba

Anticipatory subject indicators occurring with nonfinal verbs indicate the person and number of the subject to follow.

	Far past, past	Future
1st sing/pl	*-manta*	*-qe*
2nd sing	*-ra*	*-ra*
3rd sing	*-ro*	*-ro*
2nd/3rd pl	*-manta*	*-ø*

-manta anticipates first person and all plural forms in nonfuture constructions. With some speakers, however, *-manta* may be used instead of zero when second and third persons plural future constructions follow.

Examples of nonfinal tense-person-number with anticipatory suffixes follow: *t-i-manta ir-una-ra* (say-he = past-and = I hear-I = did-focus) 'He spoke and I heard.' *are t-ira ani-bara* (you = singular say-future = singular come-they = can) 'When you tell them, they can come.' *t-ira-ra iri-ana* (say-singular future-and you hear-you imperative) 'When he speaks you listen!'

2.2.2.2. Verb stem plus avolitional or dubitative fusions plus anticipator constructions consist of verb stem plus an avolitional or dubitative fusion plus an anticipatory suffix. The avolitional suffixes are Set A, Section 2.1.1.2 and the dubitative suffixes are listed in Section 2.1.1.1.

Anticipatory markers only occur if the following clause subject is second or third singular, and even these markers are absent in the Northern Tairora dialect. Where the following subject is not second or third person singular, there is no anticipatory marker, and the construction is no different from same subject construction described in Section 2.2.1.3.

Avolitional mood plus anticipator construction examples involving different subjects follow: *aru-antora-ro bi-ro* (hit-he = avolitional-and = she go-she) 'Lest he hit her, she went.'

(To avoid confusion between two different third persons, the second third person is translated as 'she' although there is no such gender distinction made in Tairora.) *bika bi-bora te ani-ø* (they go-they = avolitional I come-I) 'Lest they went I came.'

While the above constructions are possible and occur, the preferred way of stating the same thing is by a quote in the first clause. The quoted sentence contains a final avolitional clause: *h-aru-antora-be ti-ro bi-ro* (me-hit-he = avolitional-quote say-she go-she) ' "It is not good that he hits me," she said, and she went.' This example has the same semantic significance as the first example above (see Sec. 2.5.2.2).

Dubitative mood plus anticipator (conditional) construction examples with different subjects follow: *ba-irera-ro bara-anaro* (be-it = dubitative-and = he get-he = can) 'If it is there, he will be able to get it.' *ba-irera-ra biri ti-mi-ana* (be-it = dubitative-and = you bring me-give-you = imperative) 'If it is there, bring it to me.' *an-ibera bi-rara* (come-they = dubitative go-I = can) 'If they come, I can go.'

2.2.2.3. *Verb stem plus purposive plus anticipator construction.* In a sequence of two clauses with different subjects in which the first clause has a 'so that—with the purpose of' type of relationship with the following clause, the verb construction in the first clause is verb stem plus purpose suffix plus -*ra* plus anticipator (with seoond and third singular only).

The purpose suffixes are clearly related to the imperative forms listed in Section 2.1.1.3 and to the forms described in Section 2.3.2. This construction can be compared with the same subject purposive construction in Section 2.2.1.4. Purpose suffixes are:

	Class I	Class II	Class III	Purpose-per-num
1st sing/pl	*ti*	*bu*	*na*	-*ate*
2nd sing	*ti*	*bu*	*na*	-*ane*
3rd sing	*ti*	*bu*	*na*	-*arire*
2nd/3rd pl	*ti*	*bu*	*na*	-*ate*

The first person form is listed here as it was supplied by an informant; however, it is doubtful and an alternative construction using a quoted sentence in the first clause would seem to be the more natural construction. The other forms listed are readily acceptable. In the two following examples a doubtful first person construction is contrasted with a quoted sentence construction: *te ani-ate-ra-ro ti h-aare-ro* (I come-purpose-*ra*-and = he me me-call-he) 'So that I would come, he called me.' *tiri-ara ani-arire ti-ro ti h-aare-ro* (me-ref come-so = I say-he me me-call-he) 'With reference to me, so that he will come, he said, and he called me.'

The suffix -*ra* follows the purpose suffix.

Only second and third person singular anticipatory markers occur in this construction. These markers are -*ra* and -*ro,* respectively (the same markers listed in earlier constructions). They are usually absent in the Northern Tairora dialect. Purposive construction examples: *ne taba-ate-ra autu-ta-una-ra* (you = plural see-purpose-*ra* make-leave-I = past-focus) 'So that you could see it, I made it.' *ti ti-ti-arire-ra-ro tiba a-mi-ro* (me me-rebuke-he = purpose-*ra*- and = she talk him-give-she) 'So that he would fire me, she told him.'

2.3. *Verbs in Dependent Sentence Final Clauses*

There are two dependent final clause constructions. These are termed dependent because they do not occur without a preceding clause. The two constructions are contrary to fact and nonsecond person imperative.

2.3.1. *Contrary to fact.* In the contrary to fact constructions the verb structure is verb stem plus past/far-past-person-number plus contrary to fact.

The tense-person-number morphemes are the past or far past forms listed in Section 2.1.2.3.1.

The contrary to fact suffix is *-itiri* following *ra* and *-tiri* elsewhere.

In the Northern Tairora dialect only the final clause has a contrary to fact verb whereas further south both the final and preceding clause must have contrary to fact (CTF) verbs.

Northern Tairora: *mini bai-ro qutu b-i-tiri* (there be-he cease go-he = past-CTF); Central Tairora: *mini ba-i-tiri qutu b-i-tiri* (there be-he = past-CTF etc.) 'If he had stayed there, he would have died.'

The above examples contrast the same construction where both clauses have the same subject. The following contrasts a different subject construction. Northern Tairora: *ba-i-manta bara-ura-itiri* (be-it = past-and = I get-I = past-CTF); Central Tairora: *ba-i-tiri bara-ura-itiri* (be-it = past-CTF etc.) 'If I were there, I would have gotten it.'

2.3.2. *Nonsecond person imperative.* The purpose-person-number forms (Sec. 2.2.2.3) and the imperative forms (Sec. 2.1.1.3) are clearly related to the nonsecond person imperative forms. In this construction the obligatory preceding clause is always a different subject person from the final clause and is always future tense.

	Class I	Class II	Class III	Nonsecond person imperative
1st sing/pl	ti	bu	na	-ari
3rd sing	ti	bu	na	-arira
3rd pl	ti	bu	na	-ata

Examples: *t-ira-qe iri-ari* (say-(you) = future-and = I hear-so = I) 'Speak so that I can hear' or 'Speak, and I'll listen.' *bata qubi-ka-ira-ro namari bu-arira* (ground dig-leave-(he) = future-and = it water go-so = it) 'He will dig the ground so that the water will go.' *t-ira-Ø t-ira-Ø bu-ata* (say-(you) = future-and = they go-so = they) 'Tell them to go!' or 'You speak to them so that they will go!'

2.4. *The Verb in Included Clauses*

A clause may occur in various nonpredicate positions including subject, object, location, and so on, and in equational predicates. In all such included clauses the affixation of the final verb in the included construction is restricted to those verbs that occur either with the tense-person-number morphemes listed in Section 2.1.2.3.1 or with the morpheme *-ataa* 'should' described in Section 2.1.2.3.2. (An exception is the inalienable possession construction which occurs without either of the above suffixes—this construction will be described at the conclusion of this section.) These suffixes are obligatorily followed by the focus/relator markers except that in these constructions they function as relators.

The focus relators are *-ba* singular subject relator, *-ra* singular oblique relator, and *-uka, -ka* plural subject and oblique relator.

Note that although *-ba* is the subject relator, when the verb in the main clause is intransitive, the oblique relator *-ra* may occur with the subject: *te ø-una-ra bai-ro* (I do-I = past-oblique-relator is-it) *te ø-ura-ba bai-ro* (I do-I = past-subject = relator is-it). Both constructions mean: 'Mine/my thing is there, that is, 'mine' or 'the I-do-have-thing'. The shade of difference between the two constructions would seem to be '*My* thing is there' in contrast to 'My *thing* is there' with emphasis or focus on the possessor or object, respectively.

The *n* forms of the tense-person-number suffixes (Sec. 2.1.2.3.1) occur before the *-ra* relator: *te are taba-ara-uka* (I you see-you = past-I = relator) 'I am the one you saw' or more literally, 'I am the you-saw-one.' *mini bari-ata-uka ani-ø* (there be-should-I = realtor come-I) 'I, who should have stayed there, came.' This construction could also be interpreted as a sequence of two clauses, in which case it would translate, 'I should have stayed there, and (but) I came.'

The last example can also be expressed by *mini bari-ataa-ra ba-i-manta ani-ø* (there be-should-object-relator is-it = past-and = I come-I) 'Where I should have stayed is there, but I came.' Further examples: *enta bata-una-ra bare-ø* (yesterday put-I = past-object = relator get-I) 'I got what I put there yesterday.' *te a-m-una-ra-qohairo auti-ro* (I him-give-I = past-oblique = relator-instrument make-he) 'He made it with what I gave him.'

Inalienable possession constructions do not contain the tense-person-number and *-ataa* 'should' morphemes. Only one verb stem occurs with this affixation: *bata* 'put-have' plus *-a* plus relator. The first order suffix *-a* is lost before the relator *-uka*. Examples: *taaka bukai mare bata-a-ra* (casuarina long leaves has-a-relator) 'A casuarina has long leaves.' *biba abu bata-a-ba* (he eyes has-a-relator) 'He has eyes.' *te tabe bata-ø-uka* (I hat have-a-relator) 'I am a chief.'

The last example may be compared with a tense-person-number construction: *te tabe bata-ura-uka* (I hat have-I = past-focus/relator) 'I have a hat.'

2.5. *The Verb in the Final Clause of a Quoted Sentence*

The verb *ti* 'say' may occur with a quotative object, for example, *ani-an-e ti-ro* (come-you = imperative-quote = marker say-he) 'He said, "Come!"' In this construction *aniane* is the quotative object of the verb *tiro*. The quotative object may contain a sentence or a sentence fragment. This section is primarily concerned with the verb in the final clause of sentences occurring in quotative objects.

Constructions with the verb *ti* are of three types: (1) reported actual speech or thoughts, (2) nonactual reported speech, and (3) *ti* constructions that are not quotes.

2.5.1. *Reported actual speech constructions* involve the reporting of actual speech or actual thoughts. Such speech is often, but not obligatorily, reported in a two clause construction in which the first clause also contains a *ti* verb, for example, *tiharo* 'while he said': *kiapa-ba ti-ha-ro hura ani-rara-be ti-ro* (an = official-subject say-progressive-he tomorrow come-I = can-quote say-he) 'An official said, "I will come tomorrow," he said'; ' "I will come tomorrow," the official said.' The introductory *ti* clause is optional. and the above could be shortened to *hura anirarabe tiro* ' "I can come tomorrow," he said.'

Direct quote constructions are used to express thoughts and intentions, and are often preceded by an expression such as *nai tibakero iriro* 'He said to himself.'

2.5.1.1. *Quotative objects closed by -be.* The quoted sentence within the quotative object is usually concluded by the quote marker *-be* or *e*: *bu-ane ti-ro* (go-imperative say-he) 'He said, "Go!" ' In this example *bu-ana* has become *bu-ane*. Other examples: *bi-rara-be ti-ro* (go-I = can-quote say-he) ' "I can go," he said.' *bi-rera-be ti-ro* (go-I will-quote say-he) ' "I will go," he said.' *taba-una-ra-be ti-ro* (see-I = past-focus-quote say-he) ' "I have seen it," he said.'

2.5.1.2. *Quotative objects closed by the past-quote marker.* The neutral-person-number forms (Sec. 2.1.2.2.3) indicate past tense if no aspect first order suffix is present. These forms may occur in reported speech with the addition of the *-be* quote marker, for example, *bi-ro* 'He went' becomes *bi-ro-be ti-ro* (go-he-quote = marker say-he) ' "He went," he said.' Usually, however, the neutral-person-number suffix is replaced by a past-person-number suffix plus *-o* or *bo* quote marker. These special forms follow.

	Class I	Class II	Class III	Past-per-num	+ quote
1st sing/pl	*t*	*b*	*na*	*-ur*	*-o*
2nd sing	*ti*	*bu*	*na*	*-ar*	*-o*
3rd sing	*t*	*b*	*na*	*-i*	*-bo*
2nd/3rd pl	*ti*	*bi*	*na*	*-a*	*-bo*

In the following examples the neutral-person-tense forms are constrasted with the reported forms: *bi-ro* 'He went' becomes in reported speech *b-i-bo:* *b-i-bo ti-ro* (go-he = past-quote say-he) ' "He went," he said.' *bare-ø* 'I take becomes in reported speech *bara-ur-o: bara-ur-o tiro* (get-I = past-quote say-he) ' "I took it," he said.' *ani-ø* 'They came' becomes in reported speech *ani-a-bo: ani-a-bo tiro* (come-they = past-quote say-he) ' "They came," he said.'

2.5.1.3. *Quotative objects closed by separate past-quote verb construction.* Alternatively the verb stem *i* (which is *ki* in the Barabuna and related dialects) may occur with the past-person-number plus quote marker, as a separate quote marking verb. The quote marking verb closes the quote within the quotative object of the clause. This is distinct from *ti* 'say' the main clause verb. In this construction the neutral-person-number forms are retained with the main verb. Thus the reported form of *bi-ro* 'he went' may be *b-i-bo* (go-he past-quote) or the expanded construction *bi-ro ø-i-bo*. The following examples illustrate the expanded form: *bi-ro ø-i-bo ti-ro* (go-he *i*-he = past-quote say-he) ' "He went," he said.' (Note that Barabuna dialect has *bi-ro k-i-bo*.) *ani-ra i-ar-o ti-ro* (come-you *i*-you = past-quote say-he) ' "You came," he said.'

From the above it can be noted than an expression marked for neutral-person-number such as *biro* 'He went' may be reported three ways: *bi-ro-be ti-ro, b-i-bo ti-ro,* or *bi-ro ø-i-bo ti-ro* ' "He went," he said.' (*ø* stands for the quotative marking verb stem *i* which is lost before the third singular past morpheme *i*.)

A future construction (Sec. 2.1.2.1), when reported, may also occur with the quote marking verb which is marked for past tense as indicated above. The future verb in such constructions always occurs with *-ma* indicative. The structure of the verb in the quotative object is therefore main verb stem plus future-person-number plus *-ma* plus *-i* plus past-person-number plus quote.

Examples: *bi-rera-m(a) ø-ur-o ti-ro* (go-I = future-indicative *i*-I = past-quote say-he) ' "I will go!" he said.'

In Central Tairora the quote marking verb is third person, regardless of the person indicated by the main verb; thus in this dialect the above is *bi-rera-m(a) ø-i-bo ti-ro* (go-I = future-indicative *i*-he = past-quote say-he) ' "I will go!" he said.'

Apart from the reported speech constructions, the quote forms described in this section are also used in calling back and forth and in conversations to emphasize assertions. In such constructions the quote markers serve to indicate an assertive mood: *kia ir-ur-o* (not hear-I = past-quote) 'I didn't hear' (shouted out); *bi-rara-be* (go-I = can-quote) 'I can go!' (assertion); *bi-rera-be* (go-I = future-quote) 'I'm going' (assertion); and *bi-rera-m(a) ø-ur-o* (go-I = future-indicative *i*-I past-quote) 'I'm going!' (assertion).

A reported contrary to fact *-tiri* construction (Sec. 2.3.1) is marked by *-o* quote.

2.5.2. *Nonactual reported speech.* The main formal difference between nonactual reported speech constructions and those of Section 2.5.1 is that the optional preceding introductory 'say' clause of the latter does not occur in these constructions. A further difference is that the quotative object constructions occur in a nonfinal clause only—although in some constructions the quote occurs utterance final. Nonfinal clauses often occur utterance final in certain types of familiar usage—the final clause being 'understood': *taini b-iba-ra-e* (where go-he = past-anticipator-you-interrogative) 'Where did he go?' which is more literally rendered 'Where did he go that you (are there)?' Here it is obvious that there is an understood clause to follow because the utterance-final clause anticipates a second person subject clause. Other formal differences follow.

2.5.2.1. *Mistaken thoughts.* In this construction *-be* marks all quotes except reported neutral-person-number forms. Neutral-person-number forms do not occur; instead the past-quote forms are used. Thus *b-i-bo tima* (go-he past-quote) 'I thought (mistakenly) that he had gone', but not **bi-ro-be ti-ma*. Other examples are *bata-ar-o ti-ø-ma (an-ura-uka)* (put-you = past-quote say-I-indicative (come-I = past-focus)) 'Thinking you had it, (I came).' *hura bi-nara-be ti-ø-ma (irehama ti-ø)* (tomorrow go-you = can-quote say-I-indicative (ask say-I)) '(I asked) thinking that you could go tomorrow.'

2.5.2.2. *Undesired actions.* This quotative construction is an alternative way of expressing the avolitional mood plus anticipator construction in Section 2.2.2.2. In this construction the quoted sentence ends in an avolitional verb (Set A, Sec. 2.1.1.2) plus a *-be* quote marker. A further example is *ti taba-antora-be ti-ro kukeqe-ro* (me see-he = avolitional-quote say-she hide-she) ' "Lest he see me," she said, and she hid.' In the Central (Suwaira) dialect of Tairora the final *-ra* of the avolitional fusion is lost and there is no quote marker. Thus *aru-antora-be ti-ro* becomes *aru-anto ti-ro* ' "Lest he hit him," she said', in that dialect.

2.5.2.3. *Frustrated purpose.* This construction usually, but not always, indicates frustrated purpose. The sentence in the quotative object indicates the frustrated purpose. This quotative construction is referent plus verb stem plus *-arire, -ate* (when referent is plural number): *kaari-ara uba ti-arire t-ura-ro kia uba ti-ro* (car-reference talk say-purpose say-I = past-and = it not talk say-it) ' "With reference to the car, it will talk," I said, but it did not talk', that is, 'I tried to start the car, but it would not start.' Compare this with a purpose construction (Sec. 2.2.2.3): *uba ti-arire-ra-ro kaari autuke-ro* (talk say-it = purpose-ra-and = he car make-he) 'So that the car would talk, he fixed it.'

Other frustrated purpose examples are *ari-ara ani-arire t-iba-ra kia ani-ra* (you-reference come-purpose say-he = past-and = you not come-you) ' "With reference to you, he will come," he said, but you did not come.' *tirinabu-ara ani-ate t-imanta kia bi-ø* (us-reference come-plural-purpose say-he = past-and = we not go-we) ' "With reference to us, they will come," he said, but we didn't go.'

In the three following constructions the quotative clause is always in the first person.

2.5.2.4. *Unrealized intention.* In this construction the quoted sentence ends with a verb marked for abilitative tense (first person). However, the usual *-be* quote does not occur. Instead the final *a* of the abilitative suffix becomes *e*. The following two examples contrast an actual quote with an unrealized intention quote: *te bi-rara-be ti-ro* (I go-I = can-quote say-he) ' "I can go," he said', that is, 'He said that he could go.' *te bi-rar-e ti-ro* (I go-I = can-quote say-he) ' "I can go," he said, but . . .'

Other examples are *mini bi-rar-e t-ura-ro iha b-i-manta bai-ø* (there go-I = can-quote say-I = past-and = it fire go-it = past-and = I stay-I) 'I was going to go there but it burned (I got sick), so I stayed.' *iha quara-rar-e t-iba-ro tebe kia bai-ro* (fire light-I = can-quote say-he = past-and = it matches not be-it) 'He was going to light the fire but there were no matches.'

2.5.2.5. *Unrealized attempt.* In this construction the quoted sentence ends with the reported form of the first person imperative morpheme (Sec. 2.3.2). This suffix is *-ari* which becomes *-are*. It is to be noted that outside of a quote construction this verb occurs in dependent final clauses whereas in this construction a preceding clause is not obligatory. In contrast to unrealized intention, the action of the quotative verb is begun—but then interrupted or frustrated: *tuqantaa bu-are t-u-ra tiri-ara bare-ro* (turn go-I = imperative say-far = past = he-focus forehead-reference get-he) 'He went to turn, and his forehead came up against it.' *bira-qi-hairo uru-are t-uba-ro aruke-ro* (there-in-from come = up-I = imperative say-she = far = past-and = he kill-he) 'She went to come up from in there, and he killed her.'

2.5.2.6. A second unrealized attempt construction has been noted in text material. Very few examples have been recorded. Again there is only a first person form. No quote marker occurs at the end of the quote. The final verb of the quoted sentence is verb stem plus first person-tense-number suffix *-ura: utubara-ura t-uba-ro aqu bi-ro* (grasp-I = past say-he = far = past-and = she fall = in go-she) 'He went to grab her but she fell in (the hole).' *aruka-ura t-iba-ro beba-bano aqi-ana aitare-ro* (hit-I = past say-he = past-and = it arrow-subject just-along go = by-it) 'He tried to hit him, but the arrow missed.'

2.5.3. *ti constructions that are not quotes.* In these constructions both *ti* (which normally means 'say') and the quotative object have purely grammatical function.

2.5.3.1. *Sustained or prolonged action,* consisting of a clause, the final verb of which is verb stem plus tense-person-number plus *-qata*. This construction is then followed by the *ti* verb which agrees in person and number with the clause preceding it: verb stem plus tense-person-number plus *-qata* plus *ti* verb. The main verb is often repeated: *kara n-o-qata* (*n-o-qata,* etc.) *ti-ro* (food eat-he = far = past *-qata* (eat-he = far = past-*qata* etc.) *ti*-he) 'He ate and ate.' *oru b-i-qata ti-ro* (go = along go-he = past-*qata ti*-he) 'He continued going.' *oru bu-arira-qata ti-rera* (go-along go-I = future-*qata ti*-I = will) 'I will go and go' or 'I will continue going.'

This construction may be combined with a 'simultaneous-sustained' construction (Sec. 2.2.1.1.C) to further emphasize the prolonging of the action. Thus the first example above may be expanded *kara n-o-qata ti-ba-qi-ro bi-ro* (food eat-he = far = past-*qata* say-nominalizer-sustain-he go-he) 'He continued on eating and eating.'

2.5.3.2. *Reason* ti *constructions.* This construction consists of clause plus *-ra* plus *ti* verb which is marked for neutral-person-number which agrees with the following clause: *nora kuari ita-iba-ro-ra ti-ro kia ampiqe-ro* (big sun shine-it = past-and = it-*ra ti*-it not grow-it) 'Because the sun was hot, it did not grow.' *kia an-i-manta-ra ti-ø bi-ø* (not come-he = past-and = I-*ra ti*-I go-I) 'Because he didn't come, I went.'

The negative aspect (Sec. 2.1.2.2.2) could be analyzed as a *ti* construction.

3. VERB PHRASE STRUCTURE

Verb phrases are divided into three structural categories. These are characterized by differences in structural configuration and by differences in the auxiliary position. The categories may be summarized by the following structural formulas.

Category 1: {directional; vs^{r-n}} + vb

Category 2: vs + ({*-ma; -e*}) + vb {*bai; te/ke; bi; mi* + *te*}

Category 3: {vb-fut / *-ataa;* (nai + vs)^2} + vb-*i* in which vs = verb stem, raised r-n = reduplicated to nth degree, vb = verb, ( ) = optional, { } enclose alternant possibilities.

The inflectional significance of each category will be discussed below.

3.1. *Category 1*

In this category the initial verb functions as auxiliary to the final verb which is not restricted in either stem selection or structural formation. Two types of constructions are included, directionals and sustained or prolonged action.

3.1.1. *Directional verb phrase constructions* consist of an auxiliary directional preceding the main verb. The directionals include the following forms that are always uninflected: *oru ~ ori* 'go along or up', *buru* 'carry along or up', *biri* 'carry along back', *otu ~ oti* 'go down', *muntu* 'carry down'.

Thus 'Go!' is *bu-ana* (go-imperative); but 'Go and see!' is *oru taba-ana* (go see-imperative).

Other directional phrases involving the direction 'come' have a 'come' verb stem occurring in the auxiliary directional position. These stems are uninflected here but elsewhere may occur inflected. The 'come' stems are *ani* 'come along', *uru* 'come up', and *tubu* 'come down'.

Thus 'Come!' is *ani-ana* (come-imperative); and 'Come and see!' is *ani taba-ana* (come see-imperative).

Examples of directional verb phrases follow: *oru bare-ro* (go = along get-he) 'He went and got it.' *muntu a-mi-ro* (take = down him-give-he) 'He took it down and gave it to him.' *oru bare-ro muntu bate-ro* (go = up get-he carry = down put-he) 'He went up and got it and brought it down and put it (down).'

3.1.2. *The sustained or prolonged action phrase* is an alternative construction to that described in Section 2.5.3.1 (compare also Sec. 2.2.1.1.C). In the auxiliary position before the main verb any number or repeats of the primary form of the main verb stem may occur: *ani ani ani ani ani ani-ro* (come etc. come-he) 'He kept coming.' *kara ne ne ne ne-ro* (food eat etc. eat-he) 'He kept eating food.' *aaqu ri ri ri ri-ro* 'It kept raining.'

The 'go' directional constructions are repeated· in the following way: *otu bi otu bi otu bi-ro* 'He continued going down.' *oru bi oru bi oru bi-ro* 'He continued going along (or up).'

3.2. *Category 2*

The final verb of the phrase in this construction, in contrast to the preceding constructional type, functions as an inflectional auxiliary. The initial verb, which may be regarded as the main verb, is uninflected except for an optional indication of indicative or interrogative mood. The final verb is limited to a specific verb depending upon the inflectional category selected. Four such categories are included: (1) continuous aspect, (2) completive aspect, (3) stative voice, and (4) benefactive voice.

3.2.1. *Continuous aspect* constructions have the inflected verb stem *bai* 'be' as an auxiliary following the main verb: verb stem plus (*-ma; -e*) plus *bai* plus usual inflectional suffixes. The resulting phrase expresses continuous action. Before *bai* the primary form of the verb stem occurs: *aiho bi bai-ro* (air go be-it) 'The air is going (escaping).' *baite-ma bai-ro* (sleep-indicative be-he) 'He is sleeping.' *ne-e bai-ra* (eat-interrogative be-you) 'Are you eating?' *oqubi bai-rera* (sit be-I = will) 'I will continue to sit.'

The following contrasts between continuous phrases and directional verb phrases are to be noted.

Continuous: *u'ri bai-ro* (come = up be-he) 'He is coming up.' *a'ni bai-ro* (come be-he) 'He is coming.' *oru 'bi bai-ro* (go = along go be-he) 'He is going along.'

Directional: *uru 'bai-ro* (come = up be-he) 'He came up and is here.' *ani
'bai-ro* (come be-he) 'He came and is here.' *oru 'bai-ro* (go = along be-he)
'He went along and is there.'

The stress falls on the main verb in both constructional types. The main
verb occurs initially in continuous phrases and finally in directional phrases.

3.2.2. *Completive aspect.* The inflected auxiliary verb stems *ke* or *te*
follow the main verb and the resulting phrase expresses completed action.
The form *ke* may occur independent of a phrase and means 'leave'. The
form *te* is similar in meaning to *ke* but does not occur elsewhere as a main
verb. The nominalized form of verb stems, or otherwise the secondary
forms of verb stems, precede *ke* or *te*. The completive aspect construction
is verb stem plus (*-ma; -e*) plus *ke/te* plus inflectional suffix(es). For
example: *aru-e ke-ro* (hit-interrogative leave-he) 'Did he kill him?' or 'Was
he killed?'

Alternatively the construction may occur as a compound verb: verb stem
plus *-ke/-te* plus inflectional suffix(es) plus (*-ma; -e*). For example: *aru-
ke-ro-e* (hit-leave-he-interrogative) 'Did he kill him?'

In the phrasal construction (first example above) the action of the main
verb is emphasized.

Constructions with *te* and *ke* are often similar in meaning: *kaqa-te-ro* or
kaqa-ke-ro 'He built it.' In clause sequences *ke* may indicate a related action
to follow: *unta-ke-ro ne-ro* 'He cooked (food) and ate it'; while *te* indicates
an unrelated action to follow: *unta-te-ro bi-ro* 'He cooked it and went.'

In some constructions a semantic difference is clearly seen as the following illustrate: *ruba-te* 'put in' (e.g., put in a bag); *ruba-ke* 'put on' (e.g.,
put sand on road); *aqu-te* 'throw over' (e.g., to cover with a blanket);
aqu-ke 'throw it'.

Examples of phrases with *ke* and *te* follow: *quntama-e ke-ro* (bury-
interrogative leave-he) 'Was he buried?' *qenti tinta-ma te-ro* (door close-
indicative *te*-he) 'He closed the door.'

In certain types of action sequences where the verbal action may or may
not be carried on, *bate* 'put' substitutes for *ke* or *te* and indicates that the
action is not carried on, and *bare* 'take' indicates the action is carried on
(or incomplete).

Examples illustrate: *namari kaqa ke-ro* 'He got water.' *namari kaqa
bate-ro bi-ro* 'He got water, put it and went (without water).' *namari kaqa
bare-ro bi-ro* 'He got water and took it and went.' *utaqi ruba te-ro* 'He put
it in the string bag.' *utaqi ruba bate-ro bi-ro* 'He put it in the string bag and
went (without the bag).' *utaqi ruba bare-ro bi-ro* 'He put it in the string
bag and went (with the bag).'

ke type phrases are expandable in the following manner: *ari-ro-ma* (hit-
he-emphasis) 'He hit/killed him.' *aru-ke-ro-ma* (hit-leave-he-emphasis)
'He left him killed.' *aru-ma ke-ro* (hit-emphasis leave-he) 'He left him

killed' (more emphasis on the killed action). *aru taiqa ke-ro* (hit finish leave-he) 'He killed him off.' *aru aqu ke-ro* (hit throw leave-he) 'He killed him! (with vigor).' *aru taiqa aqu ke-ro* (hit finish throw leave-he) 'He killed him off with vigor.' Also note: *nampiqa aqu ke-ro* (swallow throw leave-he) 'He gulped it down.'

3.2.3. *Stative voice*. When *bi* 'go' occurs as an auxiliary following the main verb, the resulting phrase expresses a state of being, that is, that which something has become: *unahi bi-ro* (tear go-it) 'It has become torn' or 'It is torn.' The construction is verb stem plus *(-ma; -e)* plus *bi* plus inflectional suffix(es). The nominalized form of the verb stem or otherwise the secondary form of verb stem precedes *bi*.

Further examples are *baita-ma bi-ro* (sleep-indicative go-he) 'He became asleep' or 'He went to sleep.' *qutu-ma bi-ro* (cease-indicative go-he) 'He became ceased', that is, 'He died.' *abu qimpa bi-ro* (eye extinguish go-it) 'His eyes became extinguished', that is, 'He went blind.'

Because *ke* and *te* constructions are transitive and *bi* stative voice constructions are intransitive, there are important contrasts in the meaning of otherwise identical clauses: *obara-ma bi-ro* (appear-indicative go-he) 'He appeared.' *obara-ma ke-ro* (appear-indicative leave-he) 'He made it appear. *nai bainti bainti taiqa-ma bi-ro* (his = own child child finish-indicative go-she) 'His child became pregnant (with child).' *nai bainti bainti taiqa-ma ke-ro* (his = own child child finish-indicative leave-he) 'He made his own child pregnant', that is, 'He committed incest.'

3.2.4. *Benefactive voice*. This construction consists of a verb stem or the directional forms *muntu* 'carry down', *buru* 'carry along or up', or *biri* 'carry along back' followed by *mi* 'give' plus *-te* plus inflectional suffixes: verb stem or 'carry' directional + *mi* + *-te* + inflectional suffix(es). The nominalized form of the verb stem or otherwise the secondary form of the verb stems precede *mi*.

Examples: *rumpa ti-mi-te-ro* (tie me-give-*te*-he) 'He tied it for me.' *buru a-mi-ta-ane* (carry = along you-give-*te*-you imperative) 'Carry it for me!' *naabu kaqa ni-mi-te-ro* (house build them-give-*te*-he) 'He built a house for them.' Note also: *ire-ro* (ask-he) 'He asked', but *ira a-mi-te-ro* (ask him-give-*te*-he) 'He questioned him.'

The benefactive verb may occur alone: *ho-ma ti-mi-te-ra* (enough-emphasis me-give-*te*-you) 'You have done enough for me.' Only a limited number of verbs may occur in this construction, and the benefactive idea is often expressed by a progressive action construction (Sec. 2.2.1.1): *tiri-ara iri-ha-ro qutu bi-ro* (me-reference hear-progressive-he cease go-he) 'While thinking of me, he died' or 'He died for me.'

3.3. *Category 3*

Two constructions are included in this category. The first indicates either impending action or desiderative mood, and the second indicates reflexive action. The final verb is restricted in stem selection but not in structural formation. The initial verb is restricted in structural formation but not in stem selection.

3.3.1. *Impending action and desiderative mood.* Impending action is indicated by a phrase consisting of two verbs, the first of which is marked with the future forms listed in Section 2.1.2.1, which, however, are often contracted plus the verb *i* 'do' (or the verb *bi* 'go' with some speakers). A 'desire' phrase is the same as above except that the first verb occurs with *-ataa* which in other constructions means 'should'.

Examples: *aaqu ri-re(ba) ø-i-manta bai-ø* (rain come-future do-it = past-and = I be-I) 'It was about to rain, so I stayed.' *bu-ataa ø-ira-ra bu-ana* (go-*ataa* do-future-and = you go-you = imperative) 'It desiring, you go!' or 'If you want to go, go!' Both these constructions are restricted to occurrence in nonfinal clauses.

3.3.2. *Reflexive phrases* consist of *nai* 'himself' plus verb stem plus a repeat of *nai* and verb stem plus *i* 'do' verb: *kia nai ari nai ari i-ata* (not himself hit himself hit do-imperative-plural) 'Don't fight among yourselves.' *nai tiba ami nai tiba ami i-ø-ma* (himself talk give himself talk give do-they-indicative) 'They talked among themselves.'

4. THE VERB IN CLAUSE RELATIONSHIPS

In describing the affixation of the verb it has been necessary to discuss action relationships between clauses. Now follows a summary of the main types of action relationships. Because a same subject clause sequence is often different structurally from a different subject sequence, examples of both are given where pertinent. The first clause usually contains the features that mark the type of relationship with the following clause.

4.1. *Sequential Relationships*

4.1.1. *Simple sequential actions. Same subject* (see Sec. 2.2.1.1.D): vs plus neutral-person-number plus (following clause). Examples: *bare-ro b-u-ra-ma* 'He took it and went' (far past); *bare-ro bi-reba* 'He will take it and go.'

Different subject (see Sec. 2.2.2.1): vs plus tense fusion plus anticipator plus (following clause). Example: *bara-abaura-ro b-u-ra-ma* 'I took it and he went' (far past).

4.1.2. *First action completed.* The distinguishing feature is a completive phrase in the first clause (see Sec. 3.2.2.).

Same subject: ke/te phrase plus neutral-person-number plus (following clause). Example: *qenti bara ke-ro bi-ro* 'He opened the door and went.'

Different subject: ke/te phrase plus tense fusion plus anticipator plus (following clause). Example: *qenti bara ka-i-manta bi-ø* 'He opened the door, and I went.'

4.1.3. *First action continuing. Same subject* (see Sec. 2.2.1.1.A): vs plus *-ha* progressive plus neutral-person-number plus (following clause). Examples: *bi-ha-ro taba-anaro* 'While going he will see it.' *baite-ha-ro tabo-ra* 'While sleeping he saw it' (far past).

Different subject. The distinguishing feature of the different subject construction is a continuous phrase in the first clause (Sec. 3.2.1): *bai* phrase plus tense fusion plus anticipator plus (following clause). Example: *ani ba-i-manta tabe-ø* 'While he was coming I saw him.'

4.1.4. *First action impending.* The distinguishing feature is an impending phrase in the first clause (Sec. 3.3.1).

Same subject: impending phrase plus *-ha* plus neutral-person-number plus (following clause). Example: *bire i-ha-ra bara-ana* 'When you are about to go, take it.'

Different subject: impending phrase plus tense fusion plus anticipator (following clause). Example: *bire ø-ira-ra bara-ana* 'When he is about to go, you take it.'

4.2. *Subjunctive Relationships*

4.2.1. *Conditional relationships.* The distinguishing feature is a dubitative fusion in the first clause (Sec. 2.2.1.3 and 2.2.2.2).

Same subject: vb plus dubitative fusion plus anticipator plus (following future implication clause). Example: *bata-arera a-mi-rara* 'If I have it I can give it to you.'

Different subject: vb plus dubitative fusion plus anticipator plus (following future clause). (The anticipator is absent in Northern Tairora.) Example: *bata-arera-ro bara-anaro* 'If I have it he can take it.

4.2.2 *Purpose relationships. Same subject.* The distinguishing feature is a future fusion in the first clause (Sec. 2.2.1.4): vs plus future fusion plus (following clause). Examples: *bara-rera b-una-ra* 'In order to get it I went.' *bara-rera bi-rera* 'In order to get it I will go.'

Different subject. The distinguishing feature is the related imperative forms in the first clause (Sec. 2.2.2.3): vs plus purposive plus anticipator plus (following clause). (The anticipator is absent in Northern Tairora.) Example: *bara-arire-ra-ro bate-ro* 'So that he could get it, she put it there.'

4.2.3. *Causal relationships.* The distinguishing feature is a reason *ti* construction in the first clause (Sec. 2.5.3.2).[5]

---

[5] The morpheme *-bera* may replace the anticipatory first person form *-manta*. A causal relationship is indicated in such constructions: *b-i-bera bai-ø* 'Because he went, I stayed.'

Same subject and different subject: nonfinal clause plus *-ra* plus *ti* plus neutral-person-number plus (following clause). Examples: *bate-ro-ra ti-ro bi-ro* 'As he had it he went.' *bata-iba-ro-ra ti-ro bi-ro* 'As he had it she went.'

4.2.4. *Avolitional relationships.* The distinguishing feature is an avolitional fusion either closing the first clause or occurring in the quotative object of the first clause. See Sections 2.2.1.3, 2.2.2.2, and 2.5.2.2.

Same subject: vs plus avolitional fusion plus (following clause). Example: *taba-arora bai-ø* 'Lest I see it I stayed.'

Different subject: vs plus avolitional fusion plus anticipator plus (following clause). (Anticipator absent in Northern Tairora.) Example: *taba-arora-ro bi-ro* 'Lest I see him, he went.'

Avolitional quotative construction: avolitional quotative object plus *ti*-person-number plus (following clause). The first example equals *same subject* above, and the second example equals *different subject: taba-arora-be ti-ø bai-ø* ' "Lest I see it," I said, "I stayed." ' *tiri-ara taba-antora-be ti-ro bi-ro* ' "Concerning me, lest he see it," he said, "he went." '

4.2.5. *Contrary to fact relationships.* Two clauses have an interdependence in contrary to fact constructions. The contrary to fact feature is indicated in the second clause in Northern Tairora and on both clauses in Central Tairora (Sec. 2.3.1).

Same subject: Northern Tairora: (neutral-person-number clause) plus (vs plus far past/past fusion plus *-tiri*).

Central Tairora: (vs plus far past/past fusion plus *-tiri*) . . .

Examples: *bairo taba-i-tiri* and *ba-i-tiri taba-i-tiri* 'If he had stayed, he would have seen it.'

Different subject: Northern Tairora: (vs plus tense fusion plus anticipator) plus (vs plus far past/past fusion plus *-tiri*).

Central Tairora: (vs plus far past/past fusion plus *-tiri*) . . .

Examples: *ba-i-manta taba-ura-itiri* and *ba-i-tiri taba-ura-itiri* 'If he had stayed, I would have seen him.'

Note that future contrary to fact relations are indicated by the clitic *-baube* (sometimes *-bau* or *qau*) in the first clause followed by a future of abilitative clause. Same and different subject constructions are identical if a neutral-person-number verb is in the first clause: (vs plus neutral-person-number) plus *-baube* plus (future/abilitative).

Examples: *bate-ø-baube a-mi-rara* 'If I had it, I would give it to you.' *bate-ø-baube bara-anaro* 'If I had it, he could take it.'

When the first clause verb is future tense, then same and different constructions contrast.

Same subject: (vs plus future fusion) plus *-baube* plus (future/abilitative clause). Example: *bi-rera-baube bita-rara* 'If I were going, I would take him.'

Different subject: (vs plus future fusion plus anticipator) *-baube* plus (future/abilitative clause). Example: *bu-arira-ro-bau-be bu-anaro* 'If I were going he could go.'

4.2.6. *Nonsecond person imperative relationships.* Two clauses have an interdependence in the nonsecond person imperative construction, and the distinguishing feature is a nonsecond person imperative fusion occurring in the final clause. The first clause is obligatorily a different subject (Sec. 2.3.2): (vs plus future fusion plus anticipator) plus (vs plus nonsecond person fusion)

Examples: *t-ira-qe iri-ari* 'Speak and I'll listen!' (Note that the second person is being addressed, but the final first person clause indicates the imperative relationship.) *t-ira-ro iri-arira* 'Speak so he can hear!' *biba tim-ira-qe bara-ari* 'He will give it to me so that I can get it.'

4.3. *The Verb in Narratives*

The suffix *-ntau* (*-ta* in Central Tairora) narrative past occurs sentence finally, but not discourse finally, in narratives where the tense is far past. Its use appears to be stylistic—it being possible to substitute a neutral-person-number form or a far-past-person-number form in such sentence-final positions. The primary form of Class I and II stems and the secondary form of Class II stems occur with *-ntau.*

Examples: *ti-ntau* 'I (or any person) said.' *bi-ntau* 'I (or any person) went.' *na-ntau* 'I (or any person) ate.'

XXXI. Sequences of Clauses in Tairora

HOWARD McKAUGHAN

---

1. INTRODUCTION

One of the characteristics of the languages of the Eastern Highlands of New Guinea is the distinction between utterance-medial and utterance-final forms of the verb (Wurm, 1962a). Since the verb usually contains in its internal structure the obligatory clause level elements (subject and predicate), and because of the formal differences between the nonfinal and final verbs, it is possible to describe the various types of clauses in sequence by reference to the characteristics of the verb in each clause.[1]

Tairora exhibits various relationships between clauses in sequence within a single sentence. Alex Vincent describes the Tairora verb morphology, and deals with some of the possible sequences of clauses in sentences in Chapter XXX. In depecting the verb morphology, Vincent resorts to verb paradigms. These seem to me to be useful in this case even as I found verb paradigms useful in describing the Maranao verb structure (McKaughan, 1958).

The use of paradigms to describe language material is not new. Hockett (1954) mentions this approach as the oldest model of grammatical description. He describes the IA (Item and Arrangement) and the IP (Item and Process) models, but indicates that the older, which he terms WP (Word and Paradigm) model, needs elucidation. Robins (1959) and Matthews (1965) have given some formality to such a model and Pike has suggested

---

[1] Field work was done under the auspices of the Micro-Evolution Studies, University of Washington, supported by NSF grants G-17283 and G-22676. This paper was first published in *Oceanic Linguistics* 5, No. 1 (1966):1-12, and is reissued here by permission. (See Chap. XXXV for a discussion of the language family to which Tairora belongs.)

588

similar possibilities in various articles dealing with what he terms matrix theory (Pike, 1962b, 1963a, 1963b). Paralleling Hockett's IA and IP designations, I suggest IM (Item and Matrix) for an expansion of the third model. WP would be restricted to the morphology with the matrix a broader reference to the syntax as well. It may be that this model, and even the other two, should be thought of, not as systems of approach for the description of grammar. But as techniques within a larger framework of studying the structuring of language. This larger framework, it seems to me, probably includes both the analysis of language and its description.

Here I would like to underline my contention for many years to classes of beginning linguists. I insist that discovery procedures and/or analytical techniques should be kept separate from descriptive models. How one analyzes a language, what techniques he uses to discover elements, whether he mixes levels, uses his own intuition or that of his informant, whether he utilizes distribution features, process factors, classifying regularities, or grammatical functions—no matter what his field method may be, the linguist usually does not and probably should not use the same approach to describe his results. Description follows, or at least should follow, analysis.

My suggestion here is that a matrix is a valuable tool for analysis, but that this tool must be used with all the cautions a field worker uses when dealing with an informant. The matrix display provides a way of discovering new forms and combinations whether the matrix is a verb paradigm or a chart of the contrastive features of phrases or clauses.

In this paper I use paradigmatic sets of material and matrices to display the kinds of clauses found in Tairora when juxtaposed within a single sentence. In this sense I have used matrices as a descriptive device. The device is not conceived of as a descriptive model, but is only a device within a larger framework. While in New Guinea, I used the technique with an informant as a discovery procedure. I came away satisfied that I had added information to what Alex and Lois Vincent had written, helped define the kinds of clauses in Tairora, and had pointed up the particular contrasting features of these clauses.

As a discovery procedure, the technique has certain dangers which lie along the lines of 'discovering' too much. It may be that informants cooperate a bit too well. Analogy and logic may give forms not often used. Since my acquaintance with Tairora was all too brief, I sent my conclusions to the Vincents for checking. The Vincents have spent years with the Tairora and thus were able to use the language in checking the data. They used the same informant I had used, but came up with a few comments—one of them to the effect that 'the informant was surely agreeable the day he worked with you!'

In my use of the IM approach for field work, I set up all the combinations of clauses in sequence derived from the Vincents' study. I generated paradigmatic sets varying the subjects for all persons in first and second clauses, and also all combinations of the tenses from one clause to the next. Many of the forms generated had not come to light in text material or in other elicited data.[2] I then checked the sentences thus generated with an informant for his acceptance, using various safeguards typical in such investigation. I have thus supplemented the material presented by Vincent in the preceding chapter and organized it here.

A brief statement of the Vincents' treatment of the Tairora clause is in order. The clause is defined as a construction which contains one main verb, a main verb in turn defined as one marked for person and number (see Vincents' earlier article, 1962a). The following are the Vincents' designations of clauses in sequence: (A) actions in series, (B) first action completed before the next takes place, (C) first action continues while the second takes place, (D) simultaneous actions, (E) first action impending as second action takes place, (F) conditional relationships, (G) contrary to fact relationships, which may be divided into past, negative and future types, and (H) causal relationships. I shall refer to these sequences respectively as series, sequential, inclusive, simultaneous, impending, conditional, contrary to fact, and causal.

The clauses in the sequence differ from each other depending first on whether the subject is the same for both clauses, or is different, and second on the kind of sequence involved. If different subjects are involved in the sequence, a morpheme is included in the verb of the first clause to anticipate the subject to come. The verb in such clauses also contains a contrastive set of tense-aspect/person/number portmanteaus. This set of portmanteaus also occurs even if the subjects are the same if the nonfinal clause is dependent for its occurrence on another clause in the environment. Another set of tense-aspect/person/number affixes occurs with verbs which are in the final clause of the sequence. The portmanteaus making up these sets are described by Vincent in the preceding chapter.

A syntax paradigm or matrix displays the various possibilities with as little vocabulary change as possible. Just as a word paradigm uses one base with several affixes, so the clause sequence paradigm may be illustrated best by using only the necessary bases for each kind of sequence. The bases *ne~na* 'eat' and *bi~bu* 'go' will suffice for illustrating all the sequences to be described here. Other auxiliaries such as *ke* or *te* completed action and *bai* 'to be' are required in certain constructions, and therefore will appear in the paradigmatic illustrations. We now turn to such paradigms for the sequences of clauses in Tairora.

---

[2] See Shand (1964), Reid (1964), Lusted, Whittle, and Reid (1964) for the application of matrices to Philippine languages.

2. CLAUSES IN SERIES

2.1. *Same Subject*

A series of actions all of which have the same subject is indicated by the juxtaposition of clauses containing verbs which have final or closing tense-aspect-subject morphemes, or mode-subject morphemes. Where possible the third person singular forms are used to show the various possible combination of tense-aspects, or modes in the series. A hyphen within a form set off by spaces marks a morpheme boundary—the phonemic sequence following the hyphen being the tense-aspect-subject marker, or the mode-subject marker. Verb paradigms for the various person subjects are cited by Vincent in Section 2 of Chapter XXX.

ne-ro bi-ro 'He ate and went.' (neutral + neutral)
ne-ro bi-reba 'He ate and will go.' (neut + future)
ne-ro bu-anaro 'He ate and can go.' (neut + abilitative)
ne-ro b-iba 'He ate and went.' (neut + past)
ne-ro b-ura 'He ate and left (a long time ago).' (neut + far past)
ne-ro b-ira 'He ate and has gone.' (neut + perfect)
ne-ro bu-ariraba 'He ate and leaves.' (neut + customary)
na-reba bi-ro 'He will eat and go.' (fut + neut)
*na-anaro bi-ro 'He can eat and go.' (abil + neut)
na-iba bi-ro 'He ate (recently) and went.' (past + neut)
*n-ora bi-ro 'He ate (a long time ago) and went.' (far past + neut)
na-ira bi-ro 'He has eaten and gone.' (perfect + neut)
na-ariraba bi-ro 'He eats and goes.' (customary + neut)
ne-ra bu-ana 'You eat and then you must go.' (neut + imperative)
*na-ana bi-ra 'You must eat and go.' (imperative + neut)
ne-ro bu-antora 'He ate and should not go.' (neut + avolitional)
*na-antora bi-ro 'He should not eat and go.' (avolit + neut)
ne-ro b-irera 'He ate and probably shouldn't go.' (neut + dubitative)
*na-irera bi-ro 'He probably shouldn't eat and go.' (dub + neut)

Any combination of the above verbs representing sequences of clauses in a series with the same subject was accepted by my informant as valid. For example, *na-reba bi-reba* 'He will eat and will go' or 'He will go to eat' (fut + fut); *na-reba bu-anaro* 'He will eat and can go' or 'He can go to eat' (fut + abil). In a sequence of clauses of same subjects the last verb is sufficient to indicate past or far past. If the action is quite recent, then the last verb may be neutral.

Starred forms are those Vincent questioned. Upon further work with the same informant, they concluded that the forms at first accepted by him as valid were actually not used. It would seem that the matrix approach has elicited a wider range of forms than other eliciting techniques did. Why? Are there really two underlying grammars, perhaps one an active range of acceptable grammatical patterns, and the other a passive range? If two such grammars exist, which one should we be trying to describe? Further careful work, it seems to me, is needed to reach a conclusion as to the place such forms have in our grammatical descriptions.

Series of actions which have the same subject, then, require verbs containing what we may call a final set of tense-aspect-subject markers or mode-subject markers. If we symbolize this set by 'f' and the verb stem as 'S', we may represent the series as (S + f) + (S + f).

2.2. Different Subjects

If a series of actions with different subjects is to be indicated, then the nonfinal clause must contain a verb with a contrastive set of tense-aspect-subject markers, and an anticipatory subject marker to indicate the subject to come. Only three tense-aspects occur with these nonfinal forms. The final clause usually contains a form having the same tense as that of the nonfinal verb. We will cite the third person neutral final form to represent all such possibilities. In the following examples, and throughout the paper unless otherwise noted, the first 'he' in translation refers to a different subject from that of the second. The series paradigm, then, where subjects are different, is as follows (the tense-aspect-subject of the first verb appears after the first hyphen, and the anticipatory subject marker after the second hyphen):

na-iba-ro bi-ro 'He ate and he left.' (past nonfinal + neut final)

n-oba-ro b-ura 'He ate (a long time ago) and he went.' (far past nonfinal + far past final)

na-ira-ro bi-reba 'He will eat, and he will go.' (fut nonfinal + fut final)

Clause sequences which are in series with different subjects may be represented by the following where 'nf' indicates a nonfinal set of tense-aspect-subject markers and 'as' indicates an anticipatory subject marker: (S + nf + as) + (S + f).

3. CLAUSES IN SEQUENTIAL RELATION

3.1. Same Subject

A sequence of clauses in which the action of the first is finished before the second takes place is indicated, when the subjects are the same, by a verb stem followed by one of the verbal auxiliaries *ke* or *te*, which in turn occur with the final set of tense-aspect markers in he first clause. The verb in the last clause occurs with a final set of tense-aspect markers. Any combination of the various possibilities seems permissible. The entire range may be illustrated as follows: *ne ke-ro bi-ro* 'He finished eating and then went.'

The syntactic formula for the sequential relation with clauses having the same subject is (S + *ke/te* + f) + (S + f) where the italics indicate the Taiora auxiliary verbs.

3.2. *Different Subjects*

The sequential relation, when different subjects are involved, is indicated by nonfinal forms of the tense-aspect morphemes and the anticipatory subject markers occurring with *ke* or *te,* which follows a main verb stem in the first clause, and a verb stem plus final tense-aspect markers in the second clause. It should be remembered that only three tenses are possible with nonfinal forms. All combinations of these three in the first clause followed by the full range of final portmanteaus in the second may occur.[3] The sequence may be depicted by the following: *nama*[4] *ka-iba-ro bi-ro* 'After he finished eating he went'; or by formula as (S + *ke/te* + nf + as) + (S + f).

4. Clauses Having the Inclusive Relation

4.1. *Same Subject*

A sequence of clauses in which the first action continues while the second takes place, if the same subject is retained throughout, is indicated by the juxtaposition of clauses containing verbs with the final set of tense-aspect markers on both verbs, with the addition of the progressive suffix *-ha* after the stem of the first verb: *ne-ha-ro bi-ro* 'He went while eating.' The only tense-aspect permitted in the first clause is the neutral, with no limitations in the second clause. This sequence may be represented also by (S + *-ha* + neut f) + (S + f).

4.2. *Different Subjects*

The inclusion relation between clauses which have different subjects is indicated by using a verb stem followed by the auxiliary *bai* which must occur with a nonfinal set of tense-aspect markers followed by the anticipatory subject markers: *ne ba-iba-ro bi-ro* 'While he was eating, he went.' The formula representing this sequence is (S + *bai* + nf + as) + (S + f).

5. Clauses Having Simultaneous Actions

Clauses with simultaneous actions and the same subject are marked by the suffix *-qi* (*q* indicating glottal stop) and the final tense-aspects after the

---

[3] I suspect now that my informant's reaction needs to be tested further. Had I written out all the possibilities and sent them to Vincent, I rather imagine he would have found objections.

[4] *nama* is an allomorph of *na* 'eat' (see A. and L. Vincent, 1962a:26). The form *nama* usually occurs in this construction though *ne* is also possible.

verb base in the first clause, and the regular final verb in the second clause: *nama-qi-ro bi-ro* 'He was eating and going (at the same time).' In these cases, only the neutral tense may occur with the first verb: (S + -*qi* + neut f) + (S + f).

When different subjects are involved, the form is the same as that for different subjects in inclusive relations (Sec. 4.2): (S + *bai* + nf + as) + (S + f).

6. Clauses with Impending Relations

To mark the first action as impending when the second takes place, the first clause contains a verb with a future final form followed by the auxiliary *i,* which in turn occurs with -*ha* and the neutral final forms when subjects are the same, but with nonfinal forms and the anticipatory subject markers when different subjects are involved. Same subject: *na-reba i-ha-ro bi-ro* 'He went when about to eat'; different subjects: *na-reba iba-ro bi-ro* 'When he was about to eat, he went.' The formulaic sequences are as follows: same subject: (S + fut f + *i* 'do' + -*ha* + neut f) + (S + f); different subjects: (S + fut f + *i* 'do' + fut nf + as) + (S + f).

7. Clauses in Conditional Sequences

Same and different subjects do not contrast in conditional relations. A verb with the dubitative-mode-person suffix occurs in the first clause, while the second contains a regular verb with final endings: *na-irera bi-reba* 'If he eats, he'll go (same or different subjects).' This sequence may be represented by the syntactic formula (S + dubitative) + (S + f).

8. Clauses Having Contrary to Fact Relations

Sequences indicating contrary to fact relations occur with past, negative, and future implications.

8.1. *Past*

Only the person may be altered in sequences with the same subject, the contrary to fact morphemes occurring in the second clause: *ne-ro b-itiri* (the past nonfinal form has a zero allomorph with -*itiri*) 'If he had eaten, he (same subject) would have gone'; (S + f) + (S + past nf + -*itiri*). Note that nonfinal forms are used in the second clause in this kind of sequence. If different subjects are involved in the clauses, the first clause has a regular nonfinal verb, while the second has the conditional affix complex: (S + nf + as) + (S + past nf + -*itiri*); *na-iba-ro b-itiri* 'If he had eaten, he would have gone.' The person and tense-aspect may be altered in the first clause of such sequences with different subjects, but only the person may be altered in the second clause.[5]

8.2. *Negative*

In negative contrary to fact sequences, the first clause does not take place, so the second cannot. The morpheme *-bau* occurs following the tense-aspect markers in the first clause. Neutral final forms are used in the first clause when the same subject occurs throughout the sequence, and future nonfinal forms occur in the first clause if different subjects are involved. The second clause may contain either the future or the abilitative, but not other tense-aspects. The negative contrary to fact sequence of clauses may be represented as follows: *ne-ro-bau bi-reba* 'If he had eaten, he (same subject) would have gone' or *ne-ro-bau bu-anaro* 'If he had eaten, he (same subject) could have gone.' The syntactic formula is (S + neut f + *-bau*) (S + fut or abil f). For different subjects, where the first verb must also contain the anticipatory subject: *na-ira-ro bau bi-reba* 'If he had eaten, he would have gone' and *na-ira-ro bau bu-anaro* 'If he had eaten, he could have gone.' The formula: (S + fut nf + as + *-bau*) + (S + fut or abil f).

8.3. *Future*

The contrary to fact sequence with future implications may be illustrated by the following: *na-reba i-ha-ro-bau bi-reba* 'If he were about to eat, he (same subject) would go' or *na-reba i-ha-ro-bau bu-anaro* 'If he were about to eat he could go'; (S + fut f + *i* + *-ha* + neut f + *bau*) + (S + fut or abil f) for same subject, and the following for different subjects: *na-reba i-ra-ro-bau bi-reba* 'If he were about to eat, he would go' or *na-reba i-ra-ro-bau bu-anaro* 'If he were about to eat, he could go'; (S + fut f + *i* + fut nf + as + *-bau*) + (S + fut or abil f).

9. CLAUSES HAVING THE CAUSAL RELATION

Clause sequences in which the first gives the reason for the second have only been observed with different subjects. Nonfinal forms are used with the verb in the first clause with the suffix *-bera* following them. The sequence is illustrated as follows: *na-i-bera bi* 'Because he ate, I left' (S + nf + *-bera*) + (S + f). Only first person forms have been noted following *-bera*.

Thus far we have been describing clauses as they occur in sequence in the sentence. In order to summarize, we arrange the contrastive features of the

---

[5] In Suwaira, a different dialect of Tairora, the contrary to fact forms are retained in both clauses for both same and different subject sequences: *na-itiri b-itiri* 'If he has eaten, he (same or different subjects) would have gone' (S + past nf + *-itiri*) + (S + past nf + *-itiri*).

clauses described above by the matrices (with formulas) used to elicit the forms from the informant. The contrastive features include the distribution of the various clauses with relation to each other, or in the sentence, and certain internal formal features.

Clauses occur either nonfinal with respect to other clauses, or final (i.e., last in the sequence of two or more). In addition to these features of distribution there are formal contrastive features which may be grouped under the terms independent and dependent. Independent nonfinal clauses contain verbs with final tense-aspect sets of suffixes, plus some other morpheme such as *ke* (or *te*) completed action, *-ha* the progressive, *-qi* used with simultaneous actions, *-bau* used in negative or future contrary to fact sequences, and *i* 'do'. Independent final clauses contain a verb with final tense-aspect sets without these additional morphemes. The dependent nonfinal clauses contain a verb with nonfinal tense-aspect sets of suffixes plus an anticipatory subject marker. Dependent final clauses contain a verb with nonfinal tense-aspect sets, but no anticipatory subject marker. These facts may be arranged in the matrix in Table 69, the kernel matrix for Tairora clauses found in sequence.

The clause sequences may easily be fitted into the matrix. Dependent final or nonfinal clauses may only occur if there are other clauses in the environment. Independent final clauses may occur as complete sentences. I suspect that the independent nonfinal clauses may also occur as complete sentences, but this needs testing.

By arranging our facts in this matrix, we reduce the clauses to four major types, and group them by formal characteristics. The application of the matrix to the clause types brings order to what may otherwise seem to be an unordered listing of clause types. The matrix also brings into focus the relationships between the various clauses, that is, both contrasting features and similarities.

TABLE 69
Tairora Clause Sequences

	Independent	Dependent
Final	S + f	S + nf + *-itiri*
	Independent final clause	Dependent final clause
Nonfinal	S + f + other morpheme or dubitative	S + nf + as
	Independent nonfinal clause	Dependent nonfinal clause

I should indicate, however, that other matrices are possible. For example, one could work with transitive-intransitive verbs. Very good matrices—good in that the cells can be filled nicely—are possible, but do not result in reaching something basic to Tairora structure. In other words, contrasting features displayed in matrices do not necessarily reveal basic structure.

We note further that certain limitations are difficult if not impossible to indicate in such matrices. This matrix does point out the over-all relationships, but the details necessary to a more comprehensive description are not apparent. For example, there are certain limitations in tense relationships (only the neutral tense occurs in the independent nonfinal clause when an inclusive relation is indicated), and also with particular persons (only the first person has been permitted following *-bera* in causal relations). I have indicated a few, but probably not all, of these limitations in my discussion of the paradigm cited.

Analysis for such sequences, it seems to me, is fairly complete. That is, we know what the basic facts are, how the system works, and can put all the forms we locate into their proper cells. However, we are not prepared to generate all and only the possible acceptable clause sequences in Tairora. I conclude that an IM approach helps to order the facts, helps to discover units, helps to align contrastive features, and helps to summarize relationships between constructions (patterns). It seems to me that the tool is therefore important in analytical and discovery procedures. I am not, however, convinced that it is quite as useful in description, at least as an over-all model for presenting a grammar powerful enough to generate even theoretically all and only the possible sequences.

Although not attempted in this paper, a set of rules from which one could generate the data could be set up to describe these sequences. The independent final clause seems to be basic. From this clause one can derive the independent nonfinal clauses, then, by transformations, generate also the dependent nonfinal and final clauses. The restrictions are numerous, but with sufficient patience and perhaps more data, they could be indicated in such a set of ordered rules. I leave this for a later date or possibly for others.[6]

---

[6] The contrary to fact final clause, since it is dependent upon the occurrence of a preceding clause, is the only instance given in this paper of nonfinal portmanteaus in a final clause. Vincent indicates that other dependent final forms have been discovered, but I do not have the data.

XXXII. Subject Morphemes in the Tairora Verb Complex: Obura Dialect

HARLAND B. KERR

1. INTRODUCTION

This chapter is particularly concerned with the structure of sentence-final verbs of the Obura dialect of Tairora.[1] According to Vincent (see Chap. XXX) and McKaughan (see Chap. XXXV), Tairora verbs contain complexes of morphemes best described as fusions,[2] where Gadsup in the same family contains sequences of identifiable morphemes, greatly altered by the environment. Regularity in the sixteen verbal paradigms of Tairora is apparently obscured by this postulated fusion. The structure of the Obura verb paradigms, however, would suggest that there is greater regularity than at first suspected. Elementary internal reconstruction of the subject morphemes in the various Obura paradigms and a limited amount of data from two other dialects[3] point to a regular system, and brings to light certain

---

[1] Obura is a dialect of, at most, some few hundred people in the southeast division of Tairora. The data were collected from the medical orderly, Kuaampa, at Obura by Alex Vincent, who is responsible for the identification and naming of the paradigms. Vincent is planning to carry out research on the paradigms of all Tairora dialects. This paper was written during tenure of a postdoctoral fellowship at the Institute of Advanced Projects of the East-West Center, University of Hawaii, during the latter half of 1966. It was revised in 1968 in consultation with Alex Vincent.

[2] 'Most other suffixes are portmanteau to indicate (1) mood-person-number, or (2) tense-person-number' (A. and L. Vincent 1962a:6). 'Sometimes in Awa . . . and always in Tairora . . . the subject morphemes are so fused with the tense or mode indicators as to be indivisible' (Chap. XXXV, Sec. 4.2.2.1).

[3] These two dialects are Northern Tairora, and Suwaira. Most of Vincent's published materials are based on the former dialect. Suwaira lies between Northern Tairora and Obura, and is referred to as the Central dialect.

simple interacting features of the system which result in superficial irregularity.

The underlying regularity was first indicated by a study of two Obura verbs *ti-* 'to say' and *bu-* 'to go'. The affixes taken by these verbs are typical of Obura verbs in general. They differ, however, from other verbs since the root initial consonant of each is replaced by a glottal stop when followed by certain subject affixes. When the distribution of the glottal stop initial form of each root was plotted against the five subject categories distinguished by the subject affixes of the sixteen paradigms, four patterns were discovered. In certain paradigms the verb root retains its regular consonant with each of the five subject categories. With other paradigms the glottal stop initial form of each root occurs with first person subjects, and the regular form of each root with second and third person subjects. The four patterns are indicated in Table 70 which lists the distribution of the alternating root initial consonants of the verb *bu-* 'to go'. These four patterns represent four sets of paradigms. Paradigms of the same set share distinctive affixial features which bring to light the underlying regularity of the Obura verb system.

TABLE 70
STEM CONSONANT ALTERATION PATTERNS

Stem Consonant Pattern	Subject				
	1st sing	1st pl	2nd sing	3rd sing	2nd/3rd pl
1	*b-*	*b-*	*b-*	*b-*	*b-*
2	*b-*	*b-*	*q-*	*b-*	*q-*
3	*q-*	*q-*	*b-*	*b-*	*b-*
4	*q-*	*q-*	*b-*	*q-*	*b-*

2. THE FOUR PATTERNS OF PARADIGMS

The four sets of paradigms divide into two formally distinct groups, one group consisting of the pattern 1 only, the other group consisting of the other three patterns 2, 3, and 4. The verb of each group consists of three fairly well defined sectors, an initial root sector and two affixial sectors. In pattern 1 the affixes of the first affixial sector register distinctions of tense, and the affixes of the second affixial sector register distinctions of subject. In the paradigms of patterns 2, 3, and 4 the affixes of the initial sector register distinctions of subject, and together with the affixes of the final sector identify the paradigm as a perfect or a stative paradigm, or one which is neither perfect nor stative, and determine additionally tense distinctions.

2.1. *The Paradigms of Pattern 1*

Three paradigms named by Vincent neutral or near past, progressive,

TABLE 71
THE PARADIGMS OF PATTERN 1

Neutral or Near Past	*ti-* 'to say'	*bu-* 'to go'	*na-* 'to eat'
1st sing	tina	bina	nena
1st pl	tita	bita	neta
2nd sing	tira	bira	nera
3rd sing	tiro	biro	nero
2nd/3rd pl	tita	bita	neta
Progressive			
1st sing	tiqa	biqa	neqa
1st pl	tiqa	biqa	neqa
2nd sing	tiqara	biqara	neqara
3rd sing	tiqaro	biqaro	neqaro
2nd/3rd pl	tiqata	biqata	neqata
Future			
1st sing	tirera	birera	narera
1st pl	tirera	birera	narera
2nd sing	tirera	birera	narera
3rd sing	tirero	birero	narero
2nd/3rd pl	tirerata	birerata	narerata

and future, respectively, fall together under pattern 1.[4] They are listed in Table 71 which includes along with paradigms of the verbs *ti-* 'to say' and *bu-* 'to go' the equivalent paradigms of the verb *na* 'to eat'. The paradigms of the verb *na-* 'to eat' have been added to facilitate the reconstruction of an original, but no longer viable suffix-initial vowel in the paradigms of pattern 1, and the identification of a currently viable morphemic vowel in suffix-initial position (which has been absorbed into the root sector) in the paradigms of patterns 2, 3, and 4.

An original suffix-initial vowel *i* can be reconstructed for the paradigms of pattern 1. It has merged with the regular root vowel *i* of the verb *ti-* 'to say' and replaced the regular root vowel *u* of the verb *bu* 'to go'. With the verb *na-* 'to eat' it has merged with the root vowel to produce the vowel *e* in the near past paradigm and the progressive paradigm, but it has not merged with the root vowel but appears to have been lost in the future paradigm of this verb. This reconstructed vowel is not currently functional in the

---

[4] According to Vincent (see Chap. XXX) Northern Tairora (and presumably also the other dialects) have three tense categories, far past, past, and future. This conclusion is based on a strictly synchronic analysis of his data. It would seem, however, that the three tenses of pattern 1 paradigms agree with the three tense categories found in a large number of Highland New Guinea languages, past, present, and future. The corresponding paradigms in Tairora as named by Vincent are neutral or near past, progressive and future. In Chapter XXX Vincent identifies both progressive and near past or neutral as aspects rather than tenses.

paradigms of pattern 1. It is difficult to determine what its earlier function may have been, but it is at least a distinctive feature of the three paradigms which fall together under this pattern.

Apart from the reconstructed initial vowel *i* (which has been incorporated in the root sector and is no longer functional) there are two orders of suffix. These two orders and their members are indicated in Table 72 which gives a morphemic breakdown of the suffixes of pattern 1 paradigms. The forms of the first order identify the tense of the paradigm. Neutral or near past tense-aspect is represented by a zero form *(ø)*, and progressive tense-aspect by the suffix -*qa*.[5] Future tense-aspect is represented by a complex form -*rera*. The second segment of this form, *ra*, has been lost with second person singular and third person singular subjects in Obura, but it is retained with these subjects in the neighboring dialect of Suwaira.[6]

TABLE 72

THE SUBJECT AND TENSE SUFFIXES OF PATTERN 1 PARADIGMS

bu- 'to go'

Subject	Stem	Neutral or near past		Progressive		Future	
		1	2	1	2	1	2
1st sing	*bi-*	ø	-*na*	-*qa*	ø	-*re*	-*ra*	ø
1st pl	*bi-*	ø	-*ta*	-*qa*	ø	-*re*	-*ra*	ø
2nd sing	*bi-*	ø	-*ra*	-*qa*	-*ra*	-*re*	(-*ra*)	-*ra*
3rd sing	*bi-*	ø	-*ro*	-*qa*	-*ro*	-*re*	(-*ra*)	-*ro*
2nd/3rd pl	*bi-*	ø	-*ta*	-*qa*	-*ta*	-*re*	-*ra*	-*ta*

The form -*ra* included in parentheses is missing in the Obura dialect but present in the same paradigm of the adjacent dialect of Suwaira.

The forms of the second order identify the subject of the verb. The semantic dimensions of the bound subject pronoun system are person and number. A given bound subject pronoun identifies either the person of the subject or the number of the subject, but not both person and number. When the subject is plural it is identified by the bound subject pronoun -*ta* which identifies the number of the subject only. When the subject is singular, the person of the subject is identified by the bound subject pronouns -*na*, -*ra*, and -*ro* specific for first, second, and third persons, respectively. These

[5] The Vincents in their paper on Tairora verb morphology (1962a) define neutral as follows: 'The neutral tense indicates that the time viewed is indefinite or unimportant. Usually the action is viewed as being present, or at least just having taken place.' The progressive suffix indicates that an action is in progress.

[6] In the Suwaira dialect the second person singular and the third person singular suffixes of the future paradigm are -*rerara* and -*reraro*, respectively.

forms automatically connote singularity, but this is only an incidental function of the three person forms -na, -ra, and -ro.

A first person singular subject is reflected in the verb of the neutral (near past) paradigm only. In the other two paradigms it is a zero element. The zeroing tendency of first person singular is also apparent in the unusual paradigmatic structure of all the paradigms of pattern 4. It is particularly apparent in the paradigms of the dialects north of Obura (Northern Tairora and Central Tairora). In these dialects there is no contrast between first person singular and first person plural. A single form identifies both. This form proves to be a form which relates to the first person plural bound subject pronoun of Obura. Evidently in all the paradigms of these dialects first person singular has dropped from the paradigm and first person plural has been retained for both.

2.2. The Paradigms of Patterns 2, 3, and 4

The paradigms of patterns 2, 3, and 4 or the verbs ti- 'to say', bu- 'to go', and na- 'to eat' are listed in Tables 73-79. The unanalyzed paradigms are listed in Tables 73, 76, and 78. These tables have been included to show the morphophonemic processes involving the vowel of the root and the immediately following suffix vowel. Tables 74, 77, and 79 list the suffixes of the various paradigms without the root. Two orders of suffix are recognized in each paradigm. The forms manifesting them are sometimes possibly complex. The suffixes of the first order basically identify the subject of the verb. As a result of morphophonemic interaction the initial vowel of the first order suffix is sometimes incorporated in the verb root sector, or so merges with the vowel of the verb root that no clear morphemic boundary can be established between root and suffix. The form of the first order suffix listed in Tables 74, 77, and 79 (and other tables) is either the actual form of the suffix (when there is a clear morphemic boundary) or a reconstruction (when root and suffix sectors have merged).

The complexity and apparent irregularity of the verbal paradigms of Tairora come in large measure from the forms of the first suffix sector. For this reason particular attention is devoted to an analysis of these forms, which are listed in Table 75. The bulk of this paper is an attempt to bring to light a common and highly viable system of relationship between these forms within each paradigm. Many of the forms are complex forms, but their function is basically the same in all paradigms. They identify the person of the subject.

The suffixes of the first order have a significant secondary function. They also characterize the paradigm of which they are a part, and in consequence connote the distinctive tense-aspect of that paradigm. The term tense-aspect cannot be defined simply for paradigms of patterns 2, 3, and 4. But the tense-aspect of these paradigms may be roughly equated with tense of pat-

TABLE 73
THE PARADIGMS OF PATTERN 2

	ti- 'to say'	*bu-* 'to go'	*na-* 'to eat'
Past perfect			
1st sing	*tura*	*bura*	*naura*
1st pl	*tunara*	*bunara*	*naunara*
2nd sing	*qianara*	*quanara*	*naanara*
3rd sing	*tira*	*bira*	*naira*
2nd/3rd pl	*qiara*	*quara*	*naara*
Past stative			
1st sing	*tuba*	*buba*	*nauba*
1st pl	*turahua*	*burahua*	*naurahua*
2nd sing	*qiaraba*	*quaraba*	*naaraba*
3rd sing	*tiba*	*biba*	*naiba*
2nd/3rd pl	*qiahua*	*quahua*	*naahua*
Reported near past			
1st sing	*tuqo*	*buqo*	*nauqo*
1st pl	*turo*	*buro*	*nauro*
2nd sing	*qiaro*	*quaro*	*naaro*
3rd sing	*tiho*	*biho*	*naiho*
2nd/3rd pl	*qiabo*	*quabo*	*naabo*
Progressive perfect			
1st sing	*tusira*	*busira*	*nausira*
1st pl	*tunasira*	*bunasira*	*naunasira*
2nd sing	*qianasira*	*quanasira*	*naanasira*
3rd sing	*tisira*	*bisira*	*naisira*
2nd/3rd pl	*qiasira*	*quasira*	*naasira*
Contrary to fact (past)			
1st sing	*tutiri*	*butiri*	*nautiri*
1st pl	*turatiri*	*buratiri*	*nauratiri*
2nd sing	*qiaratiri*	*quaratiri*	*naaratiri*
3rd sing	*titiri*	*bitiri*	*naitiri*
2nd/3rd pl	*qiatiri*	*quatiri*	*naatiri*

tern 1 paradigms. However, where in pattern 1 tense was simply indicated by a first order form (or absence of a first order form), there is no form (or absence of a form) specific for the tense-aspect of any of the paradigms of patterns 2, 3, and 4.

In stative paradigms the tense-aspect of the paradigm is inferred from the dinstinctive association of first order and second order suffixes which basically identify the person and number, respectively, of the subject, and only secondarily connote the tense-aspect of the paradigm. It might perhaps be inferred from this, as Vincent first and later McKaughan did in preliminary studies of Tairora, that the forms are actually portmanteau forms which represent the fusion of subject and tense-aspect forms. It is contrary, however, to the structure of the first order forms to treat them as portmanteau forms. The second order forms of stative paradigms -ba and -hua are even more obviously simple monolexemic forms which identify the number of the subject, singular and plural, respectively.[7] It may also be relevant to note that Wurm (1964b) has stated that the verbal affixes of languages of the East New Guinea Highland Stock are generally not portmanteau forms.

In perfect paradigms the second order suffix -ra characteristically identifies the paradigm as a perfect paradigm. It is part of a complex form -sira in the progressive perfect paradigm of pattern 2 (Table 74). The distinction between past perfect (pattern 2, Tables 74 and 75), far past perfect (pattern 3, Tables 77 and 75), and perfect (pattern 4, Tables 79 and 75) is indicated by the person-marking forms of the first order.

Those paradigms which are neither stative nor perfect are reported near past and contrary to fact (pattern 2, Table 74, dubitative (pattern 3, Table 77), abilitative and avolitional (pattern 4, Table 79). The suffixes of the second order in the abilitative paradigm basically identify the subject of the verb.[8] When the subject is singular it is identified by the same person marking forms as those already identified in Paradigm I: -na first person, -ra second person, and -ro third person. When the subject is plural the suffix is -ra. The second order suffix of the avolitional paradigm is -ra. This is homophonous with the second order suffix of perfect paradigms, but is not equated with this suffix. It may, however, equate with the second order suffix -ra of the dubitative paradigm, and both may in turn equate with the final segment -ra of the complex future tense suffix -rera of pattern 1 (Table 72). Grounds for this will be discussed later. The contrary to fact paradigm is identified by the second order suffix -tiri which is unique to this paradigm, and has no subject connotation. The reported near past paradigm of the same pattern (pattern 2, Table 74) is identified by the verb-final vowel -o. It is separated from the form of the first order by glottal stop (q) or h when that form is a vowel (u and i, respectively). When it follows the reconstructed form -r(a) the reconstructed sequence -r(a)-o reduces to -ro (hyphens within a form indicate morpheme breaks).

---

[7] These forms are matched by -ba and -uka, respectively, in the corresponding paradigms of Northern Tairora. The latter form (along with Obura -hua) probably relates to the third person plural number suffix -nabuka of the free personal pronoun system of Northern Tairora. The suffix -ba is the singular number suffix with the third person free personal pronoun, and like -nabuka is limited to third person pronouns.

[8] The abilitative paradigm is the only paradigm in patterns 2, 3, or 4 in which the sector 2 suffixes specify the person of the subject.

3. THE FIRST ORDER SUBJECT PRONOMINAL SUFFIXES OF PARADIGMS OF PATTERNS 2, 3, AND 4

The first order subject pronominal suffixes of the paradigms of patterns 2, 3, and 4 are listed in Table 75. Many of these forms are complex forms. All of them consist of an initial vowel referred to as the V segment, and many of them have a final segment referred to as the CV segment. The first person forms of far past perfect and far past stative paradigms (pattern 3, Table 75) include an intermediate segment -*ba*.[9] In the reported near past paradigm the vowel *o* of the second order has been included in the representation of the first order forms which would otherwise be atypically consonant final.

TABLE 74

THE FIRST AND SECOND ORDER SUFFIXES OF PATTERN 2 PARADIGMS

bu- 'to go'

Subject	Stem	Past perfect		Past stative		Reported near past	
		1	2	1	2	1	2
		V	CV	V	CV	V	CV
1st sing	*b*-	*u*	*ra*	*u*	*ba*	*u*	*qo*
1st pl	*b*-	*u* *na*	*ra*	*u* *ra*	*hua*	*u* *r*(a)	*o*
2nd sing	*qu*-	*a* *na*	*ra*	*a* *ra*	*ba*	*a* *r*(a)	*o*
3rd sing	*b*-	*i*	*ra*	*i*	*ba*	*i*	*ho*
2nd/3rd pl	*qu*-	*a*	*ra*	*a*	*hua*	*a* *b*(a)	*o*

Subject	Stem	Progressive perfect		Contrary to fact	
		1	2	1	2
		V	CV	V	CV
1st sing	*b*-	*u*	*sira*	*u*	*tiri*
1st pl	*b*-	*u* *na*	*sira*	*u* *ra*	*tiri*
2nd sing	*qu*-	*a* *na*	*sira*	*a* *ra*	*tiri*
3rd sing	*b*-	*i*	*sira*	*i*	*tiri*
2nd/3rd pl	*qu*-	*a*	*sira*	*a*	*tiri*

A reconstructed suffix vowel is enclosed in parentheses.

The first order forms listed in Table 75 are referred to as bound subject pronouns, or bound subject forms. This section and the following sections are devoted to an analysis of these bound subject pronouns, and will be basically concerned with the relationship obtaining between these forms in

---

[9] This suffix is probably a retention of a proto suffix associated with a far past tense proto paradigm. It is a feature of the first person singular, dual, and plural suffixes of the far past paradigm in Awa, and in Awa as in Tairora is restricted to first person.

each paradigm. This relationship is substantially the same in all paradigms, and probably reflects a feature of a proto language which is at least as old as that from which the East-Central and Eastern Families of languages have developed. While the basic system of relationship is essentially the same in all the paradigms, and seems to have been retained virtually unchanged from the proto language, it does not rigorously determine the segmental shape of the bound subject pronouns. The superficial diversity of forms manifesting a given subject (e.g., first person singular) tends to obscure the elementary and deep-seated relationship which exists between the forms. Despite such diversification the elementary rules governing the fundamental structure of the forms remains unchanged.

4. THE BOUND SUBJECT PRONOUNS OF PATTERN 2 PARADIGMS

4.1. *The Initial V Segment*

The initial V segment is an obligatory component of all bound subject pronouns. In pattern 2 (as in pattern 3 and 4 paradigms) it characteristically identifies the person of the subject, but does not specify the number of the subject (Table 75). This is consistent with the function of the bound subject pronouns of the paradigms of pattern 1 which identify the person of the subject when the subject is singular and the number of the subject when the subject is plural, but basically do not denote both person and number.

In recognizing the person-marking function of the V segment it is essential to recognize the recessive role of third person in Obura paradigms. This is particularly obvious in plural situations, when third person is consistently identified by the bound subject pronoun which identifies second person plural. This according to Wurm (1964b) is a feature of the bound subject pronoun system of verbs in all languages of the East New Guinea Highland Stock. In pattern 2 paradigms, however, third person achieves formal identity when singular. A third person singular subject is consistently identified by the vowel -*i*. But when a plurality of third persons is involved third person loses its specific personal identity and is subsumed under the vowel -*a* which identifies second person.

The person-marking vowels of the V segment are: -*u* first person, -*a* second person, and -*i* third person. On the basis of evidence presented in a later section these three person-marking vowels are probably a retention from a proto language at least as old as that from which the Eastern and East-Central Families have developed.[10]

The following morphophonemic processes operate when the V segment vowel and the vowel of the verb root are juxtaposed. The two high vowels *i* and *u* behave alike and differ from the mid (central) vowel *a*. When a sequence of two high vowels (*ii, uu, iu,* or *ui*) occurs, the first high vowel

TABLE 75
THE BOUND SUBJECT PRONOUNS OF PATTERNS 2, 3, AND 4

Pattern 2

Subject	Progressive perfect V CV	Past perfect V CV	Past stative V CV	Reported near past V CV	Contrary to fact V CV
1st sing	*u*	*u*	*u*	*u*	*u*
1st pl	*u na*	*u na*	*u ra*	*u r(o)*	*u ra*
2nd sing	*a na*	*a na*	*a ra*	*a r(o)*	*a ra*
3rd sing	*i*	*i*	*i*	*i*	*i*
2nd/3rd pl	*a*	*a*	*a*	*a b(o)*	*a*

Pattern 3

Subject	Far past perfect V CV	Far past stative V CV	Dubitative V CV
1st sing	*a ba*	*a ba*	*a ngye*
1st pl	*a ba na*	*a ba ra*	*a re*
2nd sing	*u na*	*u ra*	*i re*
3rd sing	*u*	*u*	*i re*
2nd/3rd pl	*u*	*u*	*i be*

Pattern 4

Subject	Perfect V CV	Stative V CV	Abilitative V CV	Avolitional V CV
1st sing	*a i* / *a-ni*	*a ri*	*a ni*	*a ndyo*
1st pl	*a na*	*a ra*	*a na*	*a ro*
2nd sing	*i na*	*i ra*	*i na*	*i ro*
3rd sing	*a i* / *a-ni*	*a ri*	*a na*	*a ndyo*
2nd/3rd pl	*i*	*i*	*i ba*	*i bo*

is dropped. When a sequence of a high vowel and the mid vowel occurs *(ua, ia, ai,* or *au)*, there is no reduction and both vowels are retained unchanged. When a sequence of two mid central vowels occurs, the two mid central vowels are replaced by a single low central vowel orthographically represented as *aa*. It should also be noted that when in the paradigms of pattern 2 the roots *ti-* 'to say' and *bu-* 'to go' are followed by the mid central vowel *a*, the regular consonant of these two roots is replaced by glottal stop (*q*). This replacement also occurs when these two roots are followed by the vowel *a* in paradigms of patterns 3 and 4.

---

[10] The vowels *-u, -a,* and *-i* have the same person-marking function in cognate paradigms of Awa of the same family, and in Bena-bena (see Young 1964:52) of the contiguous East-Central Family. The same is true of other languages of the two families.

4.2. *The Final CV Segment*

Except for the reported near past paradigm of pattern 2 the CV segment is restricted to first person plural and second person singular. Within each paradigm the CV segment of the second person singular bound pronoun is the same as the CV segment of the first person plural bound pronoun. The two occurrences could be treated as homophonous accidents. But it is more satisfactory to identify them as the same form. This, however, seems to pose a major problem of definition of function. In one instance it is a feature of a second person pronoun, in the other feature of first person pronoun. In one instance it is a feature of a singular pronoun, in the other a feature of a plural pronoun.

Pike (1963b) has reacted to the somewhat unique problem posed by the cognate feature in Fore of the contiguous East-Central language family. He is primarily concerned with the unique pattern which shows up when the various bound pronoun forms are plotted on a matrix chart, and notes that among two different bound personal pronoun systems of Fore the pattern remains the same though the forms involved in each pronoun system are different. He could have made a similar observation about each of the languages of the Eastern Family. He accounts for this pattern as a field phenomenon, and in describing the minimal formal units of each pronoun system in Fore postulates a relatively complex portmanteau role for them. The solution, however, proposed by Pike seems more complex than the facts demand.

The CV segment is interpreted as a monolexemic form, rather than a portmanteau form. It is assumed that it either specifies the person of the subject or the number of the subject, but not both the person and number of the subject. Its function in the bound subject pronoun system of the paradigms of patterns 2, 3, and 4 is best accounted for by assuming that it specifies the person of the subject. In order to understand this it is important to realize that the term first person plural is a misnomer in the bound subject pronoun system of Tairora. First person plural is not a first person pluralized, but it is a combination of specific persons that do not lose their specific identity in plural situations.[11]

The CV segment of the second person singular and first person plural bound subject pronouns of pattern 2 paradigms is interpreted as a person form, second person. This would imply that the second person singular pronoun is a combination of two forms, a V segment and a CV segment, each of which independently denotes second person. This is possibly unusual. However, it may be useful to note the formal make-up of the free

---

[11] A similar situation obtains in Usarufa personal pronoun systems in which it is possible to focus one or other of the persons involved in such a plural situation.

numeral 2 in Tairora and two languages closely related to it, Binumarien and Waffa.

Numeral 2 in Tairora is *taara-quanda,* in Binumarien *qaara-qanda* and in Waffa *taara-bai-tanna.* The first and last segment of each word may function independently as a marker of duality either in the free personal pronoun system, or as part of the free numeral 3 (formed by combination of numeral 2 plus numeral 1) or part of the free numeral 4 (formed by reduplication of a form specifying free numeral 2 or duality).

It is concluded that second person singular in the bound subject pronoun system of the paradigms of pattern 2 is a combination of two segments V and CV. They combine together to specify second person singular, but may function independently in other pronouns, and in such independent function continue to specify second person. Again it is necessary to state that the term second person singular is a misnomer. The subject specified by this pronoun is better designated second person. When the subject is singular, number is irrelevant and the bound subject pronoun refers only to the person of the subject. Such singular bound subject pronouns might be better referred to as person (rather than personal) pronouns.

The first person plural bound subject pronoun is now interpreted as a simple combination of a first person form (the V segment *u*) and a second person form (the CV segment). The bound first person plural subject pronoun *una* of the two perfect paradigms, *ura* of the past stative and contrary to fact paradigms, and *ur(o)* of the reported near past paradigm is not a portmanteau form signaling both the person and number of the subject. It is a combination of two person forms, second person and first person, which automatically connotes plurality. Number, then, is incedental to person, and first person plural like the singular bound subject pronoun is best referred to as a person rather than a personal pronoun.

It will be noted that in pattern 2 (and also pattern 3 and 4) the CV segment of the second person (singular) bound subject pronoun is *-na* in all perfect paradigms and *-ra* in all stative paradigms. This difference may prove to be only a morphophonemic difference. It is treated as such by Vincent (see Chap. XXX). Bee (personal communication) is of the same opinion. The form of the CV segment in paradigms which are neither perfect nor stative may equally prove to be the product of morphophonemic interaction with following suffixes.

5. THE CV SEGMENT OF SECOND-THIRD PERSON PLURAL BOUND SUBJECT PRONOUNS

In the paradigms of pattern 2 (Tables 74 and 75) the CV segment is restricted to the second person singular and first person plural bound subject pronouns with one exception. The second-third person plural bound subject pronoun of the reported near past paradigm also has a CV segment. This particular CV segment can only be interpreted adequately in the context of the bound subject pronouns of all the paradigms of patterns 2, 3, and 4 (Table 75).

In each of the paradigms of patterns 2, 3, and 4 the second-third person plural bound subject pronoun is represented by the V segment only, or by the V segment plus a CV segment in which the consonant is always *b*. The paradigms in which the bound second-third person plural pronoun is represented by a form of the type V + *b*V are reported near past (pattern 2), dubitative (pattern 3), and avolitional and abilitative (pattern 4). None of the perfect or stative paradigms includes a second-third person plural pronoun of the V + *b*V type. It should also be noted that the V + *b*V form manifesting second-third person plural in these paradigms is the same as the second person singular form of the same paradigm except for the consonant. Assuming that these formal features point to some underlying identity of the four paradigms just cited it may be relevant to note that each in some way correlates with future tense.

Abilitative tense-aspect, Vincent says, indicates ability or strong intention for nonpast actions' (Chap. XXX, Sec. 2.1.2.2). Frantz and McKaughan (Chap. XXI, Sec. 2.2.2) describe the comparable tense-aspect in Gadsup of the same family as 'an action which has not taken place but can take place. Future action and ability are connoted. . . .' Avolitional tense-aspect refers to an action 'that the speaker does not wish to happen' (Chap. XXX, Sec. 2.1.1.2).

Vincent's description of the reported speech constructions shows a clear connection between reported speech and future tense. In Northern Tairora a reported speech suffix *-be* indicates that speech is being reported, but is also used to indicate the intentions or thoughts of the subject as in such a sentence as *bi-rera-be ti-ø* (go-future-reported say-I) 'I thought I would go.'[12] Bee's definition of future tense-aspect in Usarufa of the same family may further elucidate a possible connection between the future paradigm and the reported paradigm. She describes future tense-aspect in Usarufa as 'a tense-aspect indicating an action which has not yet taken place or an action which the speaker either has not observed or is not certain as to the reliability of its occurrence' (Chap. XIV, Sec. 3.3.1).

The future implications of the contrary to fact paradigm are evident in the following example from Northern Tairora: *maaqaini baitiri qutuma bitiri* 'If he had stayed at his place, he would have died.'

The future implications of dubitative are clear from Vincent's definition in which he says it is used to indicate uncertainty about a future event

---

[12] The equivalent expressions in Obura are not available in the data at hand.

(Chap. XXX, Sec. 2.1.1.1). The connection is further reinforced by his description of a conditional construction (Chap. XXX, Sec. 2.2.1.3). In Northern Tairora *ba-i-rera* means 'He might be there.' *ba-i-rera ami-ena* means 'If he is there, give it to him', literally, 'He might be there, give it to him.'

Formal grounds for equating reported near past, dubitative, avolitional, and abilitative paradigms with the future paradigm of pattern 1 are indicated in the future paradigm of Northern Tairora cited below.

Future	*ti-* 'to say'	*bu-* 'to go'	*na-* 'to eat'
1st sing/pl	*ti-rera*	*bi-rera*	*na-rera*
2nd/3rd sing	*ti-reba*	*bi-reba*	*na-reba*
2nd/3rd pl	*ti-reka*	*bi-reka*	*na-reka*

This paradigm is to be equated with the Obura future paradigm of Tables 71 and 72, and no other paradigm. This is indicated by the fact that the stem vowel of the verbs 'to say' and 'to go' is *i*, while the stem vowel of the verb 'to eat' is *a*. As pointed out previously this is an irregularity unique to the future paradigm among the Obura paradigms, and reflects a reconstructable but no longer viable suffixial vowel *-i* which has been absorbed into the stem sector with the first two verbs, but has been lost with the verb 'to eat'. It is therefore interesting to note that in this Northern Tairora future paradigm the second-third person singular bound subject pronoun consists of an initial segment *-re* (which probably equates with the initial segment of the Obura future tense suffix *-refa*) and a final segment *-ba*.

The medial future paradigm of Northern Tairora confirms still more clearly the distinctive association of the suffix *-ba* with future tense. In this paradigm listed below the suffix *-ba* is an obligatory feature of the bound second-third person plural pronouns. The same suffix also appears in the bound subject pronouns of the medial past, and medial far past paradigms. But with these paradigms the *-ba* is optional.

Future medial		Past medial	
1st sing/pl	*na-ari-ra*	1st sing/pl	*na-ura-*
2nd/3rd sing	*na-i-ra*	2nd sing	*na-ara-*
2nd/3rd pl	*na-i-ba*	3rd sing	*na-i-/na-i-ba*
		2nd/3rd pl	*na-a-/na-a-ba*

Far past medial	
1st sing/pl	*na-abaura-*
2nd sing	*n-ora-*
3rd sing, 2nd/3rd pl	*n-o-/n-o-ba*

It would seem from the above medial paradigms that -ba is associated with third person rather than second person, since in no instance is it a feature of a bound second person singular pronoun. It is a feature of each of the bound second-third person plural pronouns, in which the identity of second and third person have been neutralized. But since second person singular is not associated with -ba it is reasonable to assume that with second-third person plural pronouns -ba is a third person rather than a second person feature. In the free personal pronoun system of Tairora -ba is a common final suffix of the third person singular pronoun (either optional or obligatory in most dialects). It specifies singular number, and does not occur with the first person or second person singular pronouns. It is assumed then that -ba is probably derived from the singular suffix associated with third person singular free personal pronouns. Where it is a feature of bound subject pronouns its vowel probably harmonizes with the regular vowel of the other suffixes which substitute for it. In verbal paradigms it has come to associate with thrid person (in particular third person plural) in paradigms which have a future connotation.

There are probably then formal as well as semantic grounds for equating the reported near past, dubitative, avolitional, and abilitative paradigms with future tense of pattern 1. The contrary to fact paradigm of pattern 2 though it lacks the second-third plural marker -bV should also be identified as a futurelike paradigm.

If the foregoing is a valid equation, it may be reasonable to suggest that perfect paradigms and stative paradigms of patterns 2, 3, and 4 equate with near past tense, and progressive (i.e., present) tense, respectively, of pattern 1. The perfect tense is used by Vincent to translate near past with the -ra suffix (see Chap. XXX, Sec. 2.1.2.3).[13]

6. THE BOUND SUBJECT PRONOUNS OF PATTERN 3

There are three pattern 3 paradigms, far past perfect, far past stative, and

[13] Vincent defines the perfective suffix as a nonsubject focus suffix and the stative suffixes as subject focus suffixes because of their correspondence in form to the clause level subject markers (see Chap. XXX, Sec. 2.1.2.3.3). The paradigms referred to as perfect and stative paradigms in the present paper are, however, definitely sentence-final paradigms, not nominalized clauses or sentences. Vincent points out that the -ra nonsubject focus suffix with past and far past is translated by the perfect and past perfect, respectively. The past and far past suffixes with subject-focus seem to stress tense. In his paper it would seem that the suffix referred to as the perfect suffix -ra and the stative suffixes -ba and -uka/-ka (equivalent of Obura -hua) also occur with future-person-number forms. Such a combination is not listed among the Obura paradigms under study. It is significant that Vincent comments that the future-person-number forms have been listed, but examples clearly occurring in a final clause construction are lacking—the future and abilitative forms already described are preferred in future independent clauses. The future examples he actually cites may be interpreted either as final clauses or equational clauses. There is obviously some co-occurrence restriction between future tense and Vincent's focus (perfect and stative) affixes.

dubitative (Tables 76 and 77). The bound subject pronouns of the first suffix order have been extracted from these paradigms and listed in Table 75.

TABLE 76

THE PARADIGMS OF PATTERN 3

	ti- 'to say'	*bu-* 'to go'	*na-* 'to eat'
Far past perfect			
1st sing	*qiabara*	*quabara*	*naabara*
1st pl	*qiabanara*	*quabanara*	*naabanara*
2nd sing	*tunara*	*bunara*	*nonara*
3rd sing	*tura*	*bura*	*nora*
2nd/3rd pl	*tura*	*bura*	*nora*
Far past stative			
1st sing	*qiababa*	*quababa*	*naababa*
1st pl	*qiabarahua*	*quabarahua*	*naabarahua*
2nd sing	*turaba*	*buraba*	*noraba*
3rd sing	*tuba*	*buba*	*noba*
2nd/3rd pl	*tuhua*	*buhua*	*nohua*
Dubitative			
1st sing	*qiangyera*	*quangyera*	*naangyera*
1st pl	*qiarera*	*quarera*	*naarera*
2nd sing	*tirera*	*birera*	*nairera*
3rd sing	*tirera*	*birera*	*nairera*
2nd/3rd pl	*tibera*	*bibera*	*naibera*

As in the paradigms of pattern 2 the initial V segment identifies the person of the subject. First person is identified by *-a* in each paradigm. Second person is identified by *-u* in the perfect and stative paradigms, and by *-i* in the dubitative paradigm. Third person is recessive in both singular and plural situations and is subsumed under the vowel identifying second person.

When the V segment and the vowel root are juxtaposed the morphophonemic processes are the same as those noted for the paradigms of pattern 2 except when the root vowel *a* of the verb *na-* is followed by the high vowel *u*. The sequence *au* becomes *o*.

The segment *ba* is associated with the first person V segment in the far past perfect and far past stative paradigms. Since it is restricted to these two paradigms it automatically connotes far past tense.[14] In the same two paradigms the CV segment is restricted to the second person singular and first person plural pronouns. It is *-na* in the perfect paradigm and *-ra* in the stative paradigm as in the corresponding paradigms of pattern 2. In these two paradigms of pattern 3 it evidently specifies second person as in pattern 2.

The dubitative paradigm has for its CV segment *-re*. It is a feature of

---

[14] See footnote 9.

the second person singular pronoun -*ire,* and is the final segment also of the first person plural pronoun -*are.* Its occurrence as part of the pronoun (*ire*) representing third person singular is attributed to the recessive nature of third person in the dubitative paradigm. Third person singular is represented by the form which basically specifies second person singular, just as third person plural is represented by the form which basically specifies second person plural.

The second-third person plural pronoun is -*ibe.* It identifies the dubitative paradigm as one of those paradigms which equate with the future paradigm of pattern 1, and is the same as the second person singular pronoun -*ire* except for the consonant.

Certain parallels between the dubitative paradigm of pattern 3 and the future paradigm of pattern 1 may be relevant in attempting to account for the CV segment -*re* tentatively identified as a second person form in the dubitative paradigm. There are grounds for suspecting that it may originally have been the first segment of the complex future tense suffix -*refa* of the future paradigm (see Tables 72 and 77). The complex form -*rera* may once have been a functional future tense suffix in the dubitative paradigm. However, in both the future and dubitative paradigms the complex form is in the process of degeneration. In the future paradigm the second segment -*ra* has been dropped when the subject is second person singular, or third person singular. In the dubitative paradigm the initial segment -*re* has been replaced by -*ngye* and -*be* with first person plural and second-third person plural subjects, respectively.

The behavior of the V segment vowel *i* of the dubitative paradigm is further grounds for equating the dubitative and future paradigms. This vowel has replaced the regular root vowel of the verbs *ti-* 'to say' and *bu-* 'to go' yet it has not merged with the root vowel of the verb *na-* 'to eat'. On the other hand the corresponding vowel *u* of the far past perfect and far past stative paradigms has merged with the root vowel of *na-* to produce a single vowel *o* (see Tables 76 and 77). This nonmerging characteristic of the

TABLE 77

The First and Second Order Suffixes of Pattern 3 Paradigms

bu- 'to go'

Subject	Stem	Far past perfect			Far past stative			Dubitative		
		1		2	1		2	1		2
		V	CV		V	CV		V	CV	
1st sing	*qu-*	*a*	*ba*	*ra*	*a*	*ba*	*ba*	*a*	*ngye*	*ra*
1st pl	*qu-*	*a*	*ba* *na*	*ra*	*a*	*ba* *ra*	*hua*	*a*	*re*	*ra*
2nd sing	*b-*	*u*	*na*	*ra*	*u*	*ra*	*ba*	*i*	*re*	*ra*
3rd sing	*b-*	*u*		*ra*	*u*		*ba*	*i*	*re*	*ra*
2nd/3rd pl	*b-*	*u*		*ra*	*u*		*hua*	*i*	*be*	*ra*

vowel *i* when juxtaposed to the root *na-* has its parallel in the future paradigm (see Sec. 2.1).

Although the preceding evidence is not conclusive it is consistent with the assumption that both the future paradigms and the dubitative paradigms once shared a common future tense suffix *-rera*. This complex suffix is evidently in the process of degeneration in both paradigms.[15] In the dubitative paradigm the final segment *-ra* has been retained as the sector 2 suffix. The initial segment *-re* has been equated with the second person CV segment. It is now a viable segment of sector 1.

TABLE 78
THE PARADIGMS OF PATTERN 4

	ti- 'to say'	*bu-* 'to go'	*na-* 'to eat'
Perfect			
1st sing	*qiaira / qianira*	*quanira*	*naanira*
1st pl	*qianara*	*quanara*	*naanara*
2nd sing	*tinara*	*binara*	*nenara*
3rd sing	*qiaira / qianira*	*quanira*	*naanira*
2nd/3rd pl	*tira*	*bira*	*nera*
Stative			
1st sing	*qiariba*	*quariba*	*naariba*
1st pl	*qiarahua*	*quarahua*	*naarahua*
2nd sing	*tiraba*	*biraba*	*nerabe*
3rd sing	*qiariba*	*quariba*	*naariba*
2nd/3rd pl	*tihua*	*bihua*	*nehua*
Abilitative			
1st sing	*qianina*	*quanina*	*naanina*
1st pl	*qianara*	*quanara*	*naanara*
2nd sing	*tinara*	*binara*	*nenara*
3rd sing	*qianaro*	*quanaro*	*naanaro*
2nd/3rd pl	*tibara*	*bibara*	*nebara*
Avolitional			
1st sing	*qiandyora*	*quandyora*	*naandyora*
1st pl	*qiarora*	*quarora*	*naarora*
2nd sing	*tirora*	*birora*	*nerora*
3rd sing	*qiandyora*	*quandyora*	*naandyora*
2nd/3rd pl	*tibora*	*bibora*	*bibora*

---

[15] The Suwaira future paradigm is probably the most regular paradigm. The Obura and especially the Northern Tairora future paradigms lack the symmetry of the Suwaira paradigm, which may well be the most transparent reflection of the earlier form of this paradigm.

7. THE BOUND SUBJECT PRONOUNS OF PATTERN 4 PARADIGMS

There are four pattern 4 paradigms, perfect, stative, abilitative, and avolitional (Tables 78 and 79). The bound subject pronouns of sector 1 have been extracted and listed in Table 75.

TABLE 79
THE FIRST AND SECOND ORDER SUFFIXES OF PATTERN 4 PARADIGMS

bu- 'to go'

Subject	Stem	Perfect		Stative		Abilitative		Avolitional	
		1	2	1	2	1	2	1	2
		V	CV	V	CV	V	CV	V	CV
1st sing	*qu-*	*a (n)i*	*ra*	*a ri*	*ba*	*a ni*	*na*	*a ndyo*	*ra*
1st pl	*qu-*	*a na*	*ra*	*a ra*	*hua*	*a na*	*ra*	*a ro*	*ra*
2nd sing	*b-*	*i na*	*ra*	*i ra*	*ba*	*i na*	*ra*	*i ro*	*ra*
3rd sing	*qu-*	*a (n)i*	*ra*	*a ri*	*ba*	*a na*	*ro*	*a ndyo*	*ra*
2nd/3rd pl	*b-*	*i*	*ra*	*i*	*hua*	*i ba*	*ra*	*i bo*	*ra*

7.1. *The V and CV Segments of First Person and Second Person Pronouns*

The initial V segment of the bound subject pronouns identifies the person of the subject as in the paradigms of patterns 2 and 3. *a* identifies first person (as in pattern 2) and *-i* identifies second person. Third person is recessive in both singular and plural situations. When singular it is subsumed under the second person vowel *-i*. When plural it is subsumed under the first person vowel *a*.[16]

---

[16] The recessiveness of third person is a feature of most pronominal systems of the languages for which data have been collected from the East New Guinea Highlands Stock. In the free personal pronoun systems of languages of the contiguous East-Central Family the zeroing tendency of third person (from which derives its recessive behavior) is manifested by the absence of a pronoun-initial consonant present in first and second person nonsingular pronouns. The pronoun-initial consonant with nonsingular first and second person pronouns, however, cannot be assigned full morphemic status. The singular third person pronoun similarly lacks a pronoun-initial consonant carried by the first person and second person singular pronouns. In the case of the last two singular pronouns, however, the pronoun-initial consonant can be given full morphemic status. Hence third person in the third person singular pronoun of these East-Central languages is a regular zero morpheme.

In languages of other families third person is also a zero form in third person singular pronouns. But these languages seem to reject the formal vacuum and replace the expected zero form with another form. The replacing form can usually be traced to a form functioning elsewhere in the same pronominal system, commonly a dual number form (if the language recognizes this number category).

The free personal pronoun system of the Eastern Family contrasts very clearly with that of the contiguous East-Central Family, and most other languages of the other families. This is most evident in the singular pronouns. Outside of the Eastern Family the first person singular free personal pronoun is usually *n-* initial. In the Eastern Family the second person singular free personal pronoun is virtually always consonant-initial. In the East-Central Family it is always *k-* initial. In the Eastern Family this

The CV segment poses a more complex problem than the V segment, but its function is essentially the same as it is in the paradigms of patterns 2 and 3. This is most obvious in the perfect and stative paradigms (Tables 75 and 79). In these two paradigms the second person CV segment is manifested by -*na* and -*ra* respectively as in the corresponding paradigms of patterns 2 and 3. In the avolitional and abilitative paradigms the equivalent CV segment is -*na* and -*ro,* respectively, and is a feature of both the second person singular and first person plural pronouns.

Without exception the first person plural pronoun combines the first person V segment and the second person CV segment of each paradigm as in the paradigms of pattern 2. The unexplained complexities of the bound subject pronouns of the paradigms of pattern 4 are (A) the CV segment which is part of the first person singular pronoun of each paradigm, and which is manifested by a different form in each paradigm and (B) the segmental homophony of the first person singular and third person singular pronouns in the perfect, stative, and avolitional paradigms, and the segmental homophony of the first person plural and third person singular pronoun of the abilitative paradigm.[17]

These complexities may ultimately resolve themselves into a single problem. This is suggested by data from the Northern and Central (Suwaira) dialects. In these two dialects there is no formal opposition of first person singular and first person plural pronouns in any paradigm. A single pronoun specifies both first person singular and first person plural. This is illustrated by the far past paradigms of Northern Tairora, which equate with the corresponding pattern 3 paradigms of Obura (Table 77).

pronoun is vowel-initial, and with a number of exceptions (4) this vowel is *a-,* possibly equating with the affix vowel *a* of bound possessive pronoun and bound indirect object pronoun sets in the Eastern Family wich functions as a second-third person singular pronoun. In other families (particularly obviously in the contiguous East-Central Family) the third person singular free personal pronoun has a zero third person. In the Eastern Family by marked contrast it seems possible to reconstruct a third person form (for third person singular free personal pronouns). This form can, however, only be expressed submorphemically as a feature of bilabialization.

As an incidental feature the structure of the singular free personal pronouns of the Eastern Family clearly demarcates all the languages of this family from all the languages of the contiguous East-Central Family, and in a less precise way from the languages of the other families of the same stock.

[17] The third person singular forms do, however, differ in a suprasegmental feature. According to Vincent's orthographic representation of what is probably ultimately to be interpreted as a tone difference the first person member of the pair is marked for stress on or following the root. The third person singular member of the pair is marked on the penultimate syllable of the suffix sequence. It is almost certain, however, that the third person singular and first person forms were not only segmentally homophonous, but identical earlier in the history of the language. The suprasegmental difference is a later development.

	Far past perfect	Far past stative
1st sing/pl	*-a-ba-u-na*	*-a-ba-u-ra*
2nd sing	*-u-na*	*´u-ra*
3rd sing, 2nd/3rd pl	*-u*	*-u*

The Suwaira abilitative paradigm, which equates with the Obura abilitative paradigm of Table 78, also illustrates.

	Abilitative
1st sing/pl	*-a-i-na-ra*
2nd sing	*-i-na-ra*
3rd sing	*-a-na-ro*
2nd/3rd pl	*-i-ba-ra*

The form of the first person plural pronoun in each of the far past paradigms of Northern Tairora can be derived by combining the first person form *-aba* and both the V and CV segment of the segment of the second person singular pronoun of Obura. It is obvious from this that these were originally first person plural forms in Northern Tairora, which have come to identify both singular and plural first person. Similarly the first person singular and plural pronoun *-a-i-na* of the abilitative paradigm can be derived by combining the first person V segment *-a* with both the V and CV segments of the second person singular Obura pronoun *-i-na*. This is further confirmation of the assumption that first person plural is formed by a combination of first person and second person forms.

In accounting for the present first person singular pronoun of each pattern 4 paradigm in Obura the following assumptions are made in the light of the preceding data from Northern Tairora and Central (Suwaira) Tairora.

A. The current first person singular pronouns were probably originally first person plural pronouns formed by combination of the first person V segment and both the V and CV segments of the second person singular pronoun.

B. The number contrast (singular versus plural) was neutralized by loss of the first person singular form. The first person plural form with the shape -V-V-CV was retained for both singular and plural first person.

C. During this time the second person singular pronoun (with the form V-CV) was retained unchanged in each paradigm.

D. Subsequently the contrast has been restored by the development of a new first person plural pronoun formed on the regular model by combination of the V segment of the first person pronoun and the CV segment only of the second person singular pronoun, at least in the perfect, stative, and abilitative paradigms.

E. The pronoun with the form -V-V-CV (which just previously had specified both first person singular and first person plural) was now restricted to first person singular. Since this pronoun no longer specified first person plural it had no further need to reflect the systematic formal relationship of first person plural and second person singular, and may thereby have been free to change its shape.

We assume then from the above that earlier in the history of the pattern 4 paradigms of Obura the following first person plural forms probably existed: perfect and abilitative *-a-i-na* and stative *-a-i-ra*. The former pronoun is currently attested in the abilitative paradigm of Suwaira, whose first person singular and plural pronoun is *-a-i-na* (followed by the suffix *-ra*). Subsequently these forms came to be first person singular pronouns and changed shape. The former became *-ani* alternating in the perfect paradigm with *-ai*. The latter became *-ari*.

The postulated shift of *-a-i-na* to *-ani* and *-a-i-ra* to *-ari* has its parallel in a Tairora kinship term which reflects a proto kinship term of the Eastern Family (see Chap. XXXVII). The reconstructed form is *-nau-i-nta* used by a mother's brother for ego and his or her siglings. This proto term has become *naunti* in Tairora. Similarly the reconstructed term for husband *-waa-i-ta* in the proto language underlying the Eastern Family has become *baati* in Tairora.

Attempts to internally reconstruct such a cycle of events are not, however, the concern of this paper. The basic aim of the paper has been to note the systematic formal relationship which obtains between second person singular and first person plural pronouns in all the paradigms of patterns 2, 3, and 4. Attempts to account for the segmental homophony of the first person singular and the third person singular pronouns of paradigm 4 paradigms are, however, more consistent with this aim.

7.2. *The Segmental Homophony of Third Person Singular and First Person Pronouns in Pattern 4 Paradigms*

With the exception of the abilitative paradigm first person singular and third person singular are segmentally homophonous. In the abilitative paradigm third person singular is segmentally homophonous with the plural first person pronoun. This is consistent with the suggestion that these homophonous forms were all originally plural first person forms in the paradigms in which they occur.

The homophony of the third person singular and first person singular pronouns could be generally accounted for by assuming that third person in these paradigms is again a recessive person, and that this recessiveness manifests itself by the lack of a specific third person form. However, since the paradigmatic system seems to reject this formal vacuum, another form has been substituted for the zero, and this form has been drawn from within the existing system. The question remains to be asked why in pattern 4 paradigms a first person pronoun, and more specifically a currently or originally plural first person pronoun, has filled the zero vacuum.

The answer to this may perhaps be found to parallel the suggested explanation of the appearance of a basically first person plural pronoun in first person singular function (see Sec. 7.1). It is obvious, when comparison is made with other dialects, that first person pronouns of these dialects which function as both singular and plural pronouns equate with the current first person plural pronoun in the cognate Obura paradigm. This can only be explained by assuming that originally there was a contrast between first person singular and first person plural in all dialects, but this has broken down. It has broken down following the loss of the first person singular pronoun form from each of the paradigms. It is logical, following the loss of the first person singular pronoun, that first person plural should substitute for it. But this does not follow from the fact that first person plural is a first person singular pronoun pluralized. It follows rather from the fact that first person plural is a person pronoun combining first person and second person. First person plural and first person singular have first person in common. By virtue of this semantic overlap first person plural has come to substitute for the lost first person singular.

We may perhaps extrapolate from this and ask why first person plural should (if it is a person pronoun) combine first person and second person rather than first person and third person. The former equates with a first person plural pronoun of the inclusive subtype. The latter is equally a first person plural pronoun, but of the exclusive subtype. The answer to this might well be that if third person has no formal identity of its own, a first person plural pronoun would be expected to be compounded from a first person and a second person form. However, if by any chance third person were to have a formal identity of its own, this argument could not stand. It would be expected in this case that first person plural could be as well represented by a first person plus third person combination as a first person plus second person combination.

It has been pointed out (see footnote 16) that in fact third person in the free personal pronoun system of all the Eastern languages does have a formal identity of its own, even if the proto feature which this reflects can only be stated submorphemically as a feature of bilabialization. It is also apparent that in paradigms of pattern 2 the third person does have a formal identity of its own, and it is marked by the vowel i in these paradigms. This is almost certainly a reflection of the proto language, since third person (when singular) is similarly marked by the suffix $-i$ in the cognate paradigms of Awa, Gadsup, and presumably other languages of the Eastern Family, as well as Bena-bena, Gahuku, and probably other languages of the contiguous East-Central Family.

We note also that in the simple tense paradigms of pattern 1 the person-marking forms of the second suffix sector are *-na* first person, *-ra* second person, and *-ro* third person. Also in Northern Tairora the anticipatory subject forms which occur on the medial verb inflected with far past and past tense to indicate the subject of the following verb are *-ra* second person singular, *-ro* third person singular, and *-manta* first person singular, and plural first, second, and third persons. It is evident that these subject forms follow the pattern of pattern 1 paradigms of Obura, for which with the exception of the neutral (near past) paradigm the forms are *-ra* second person, *-ro* third person, and *-ta* plural (for all persons). If this plural suffix *-ta* were additionally to mark first person singular (which is represented as zero in the progressive and future paradigms of pattern 1 in Obura) the parallel would be complete.

We assume from the foregoing that in the total grammatical system the suffix *-ro* is to be interpreted as a third person suffix even though in the avolitional paradigm of pattern 4 it occurs atypically as a second person form. Even this exception, however, may point to the true function of the form *-ro*.

7.3. *The Segmental Homophony of Third Person Singular and First Person Singular Pronouns in the Avolitional Paradigm*

We now propose that in the paradigms of pattern 4 the paradigmatic system may in part be accounted for by assuming that in these paradigms the usual dominance of second person over third is reversed. We note in particular the avolitional paradigm, and the current form which marks both first person singular and third person singular, *-andyo*. It is suggested that this rather irregular sequence of phones can be reconstructed as **-aniro*. The initial vowel *a-* is quite regular for pattern 4 paradigms. The following segment *-ni* is almost demanded by the corresponding form (either *-ni* or *-ri*) in each of the other paradigms of pattern 4. This leaves only the final segment *-ro*. We assume that this segment is best equated with the form which functions most commonly as a third person form in other sectors of the language. We now assume that **-aniro* is not a regular first person singular form, nor a regular third person singular form, but that it was originally a first person plural form like all the other irregular first person forms of pattern 4. To account for all these facts we must postulate a first person plural pronoun which combined a first person form **ani* (still a viable first person singular form in pattern 4 paradigms) and a third person form **-ro* (still a viable third person singular form in pattern 1 paradigms and also in medial paradigms).

From this by a further extension we may assume that the process which resulted later in the loss of the former first person singular form from the avolitional paradigm was simultaneously accompanied by a loss of the third person singular form from the same paradigm. The zeroing tendency of first person (singular) is quite apparent in the pattern 1 paradigms of Obura, and even more so in all the paradigms of the Northern and Central dialects. This certainly has set the stage for the appearance of a first person plural form in place of a first person singular form. But it has already been noted that third person (both singular and plural) has an even more pronounced zeroing tendency in the Eastern languages, and still more of a zeroing tendency in the languages of related families (see especially footnote 16). The structural pressure of the zeroing tendency of third person in other paradigms may well account for the loss of a third person singular form from the avolitional paradigm. Again, however, the zero vacuum has been rejected and a form has been substituted in place of the zero. Since first person plural would seem to have been a combination of first person plus third person it overlapped semantically with the third person (singular) pronoun. By virtue of this overlap it substituted for the lost third person singular form.

It remains then to account for the form -ro with the second person singular pronoun of the avolitional paradigm. It has already been pointed out that the systematic parallel between second person singular and first person plural is one of the most consistent systematic patterns in the paradigmatic system. With two exceptions the first person plural pronoun combines the V segment vowel of the first person singular pronoun with the CV segment of the second person singular pronoun. The two exceptions do not break the pattern. They combine the first person singular V segment and a following segment -ba (limited to first person and to the far past paradigms of pattern 3 and almost certainly a retention from the proto system underlying the Eastern Family) together with the CV segment of the second person singular pronoun. Against this pressure it would hardly be surprising if the originally second person singular pronoun of the avolitional paradigm matched by a first person plural *-aniro did not come into step be replacing its former CV segment (probably *-ra) with the originally third person form -ro.

This explanation may seem unnecessarily involved. However, it does seem to harmonize with the facts, and some such explanation most ultimately be forthcoming to explain the irregularity of the first person singular form -andyo and its segmental homophony with the third person singular form. Those familiar with the inflectional structure of languages of the Eastern Family must be struck by the remarkable grammatical diversity of structure, despite the fact that any language of the family in no case shares less than fifty-eight cognates (by the Swadesh hundred-word list) with its most different sister language. The grammatical diversity cannot be accounted for simply by sound change. It is obvious that there has been a considerable measure of analogic change to account for such diversity.

If this is a correct reconstruction of the history of the form -andyo, it may equally explain the parallel between the form of the first person singular and third person singular pronoun in the perfect and stative paradigms of pattern 4. The third person singular pronoun of the abilitative paradigm, as already noted, however, is the same as the first person plural pronoun in sector 1. This paradigm additionally differs from the other three pattern 4 paradigms in the appearance of subject person-marking forms in sector 2. It is possible that the current first person singular form *-a-ni-na* of this paradigm stems from an originally first person plural pronoun combining in this instance a first person form *-a-ni* and the second person CV *-na*. The final segment *-na* may by analogy with the paradigms of pattern 1 (which originally possibly all had *-na for their first person singular pronoun) have been equated with the first person singular form *-na*. With this as a base for analogy the other sector 2 subject forms of the pattern 1 paradigms have filled out the paradigm to give *-ina-ra* (second singular) and *-ana-ro* (third singular) either replacing an existing set of forms in this position, or simply taking up a position not previously occupied by a suffix. The suffix *-ra* with the plural abilitative pronouns might well equate with the plural suffix *-ta* of pattern 1 paradigms.

It remains to be determined why the third person singular pronoun of the abilitative paradigm is not segmentally homophonous with the first person singular form *-ani* but instead is homophonous with the first person plural pronoun. The first person singular pronoun was almost certainly an original first person plural pronoun, like the other first person singular pronouns of pattern 4 paradigms. But the terminal suffix *-na* which follows the form *-ani* now clearly marks this as a first person pronoun. This may well have precluded it from substituting for the third person singular as well as the first person singular pronoun following the process of zeroing of these persons. By contrast in the avolitional paradigm the internally reconstructed original first person plural pronoun *-ani-ro had for its terminal suffix the form *-ro clearly identifying it as a third person form (or compound). This would have predisposed it to substitute for both first person singular and third person singular following a period of person zeroing.

7.4. *Suprasegmental Differences between First Person Singular and Third Person Singular Pronouns*

Although the third person singular pronouns of the perfect, stative, and avolitional paradigms are segmentally homophonous with the first person singular pronouns they all differ suprasegmentally. This difference is registered orthographically by Vincent as stress, though the difference is actually one of tone. As a general rule stress falls on the penultimate suffix sector syllable with third person singular, and on some other syllable with first person singular.

It is almost certain that these segmentally homophonous forms were in fact originally identical forms, and that the suprasegmental differences are a recent development. If this were not so it would be hard to account for the segmental homophony of the forms within a given paradigm, but the diversity of the forms between paradigms.

8. CONCLUSIONS

Whatever the validity of the postulated reconstructions and explanations of the earlier sections it is fairly clear that there is a systematic relationship between the first person plural pronoun on the one hand and the first person singular and second singular pronouns on the other in each of the paradigms under study. This systematic relationship is accounted for by assuming that first person plural is a person pronoun which combines a first person pronoun and a second person pronoun form. Plurality with first person is an incidental feature deriving from a combination of persons.

This explanation would account for the characteristic occurrence of a feature associated with the second person singular cell of a personal pronoun matrix in the first person plural cell of the same matrix. Considerable diversity of forms from one matrix to another is allowed for within the confines of this systematic restriction. In light of this, the field explanation suggested for this phenomenon as it is manifested in Fore of the contiguous East-Central Family seems more complex than the facts demand.

This systematic feature of personal pronoun systems is not restricted to Tairora, but is a feature of all the languages of the Eastern Family. It is equally a feature of the languages of the East-Central Family along with Fore, and is found in the personal pronoun systems of languages in other families of the stock. It is evidently a feature which traces back to a very remote proto system, but is still currently viable in Tairora, and presumably also in many other Highland New Guinea languages. The system is extremely simple, but allows for almost unlimited diversification when it is overlaid by a process of neutralization of number contrasts and later rejuvenation of the contrast with first person pronouns, and further overlaid by the zeroing potential of third person in particular, and first person in lesser measure. Significantly second person exhibits no zeroing tendency, though it may perhaps sometimes be outranked by third person in certain sectors of the pronominal system.

XXXIII. Tairora Texts

Compiled by ALEX VINCENT

1. INTRODUCTION, *by Howard McKaughan*

These Tairora texts, told by a villager from Bantura, were collected in 1962. Vincent transcribed and translated a number of them without the aid of the informant. Question marks enclosed in parentheses in the literal translation indicate that the meaning of the Tairora word (also in parentheses) was obscure at that point.

Vincent's transcription did not mark sentence breaks. These have been added by the editor and may not be correct. The editor has also modified Vincent's free translation, and has placed hyphens between English words when more than one word translates a single Tairora word. The order in the literal translation is the same as the Tairora word order, word by word, but not morpheme by morpheme. Not all morphemes in the Tairora word are translated, nor is the order within the sequence of English words connected by hyphens of necessity the same as the morphemes in the Tairora word. The editor has also modified Vincent's orthography so that it approximates that used in the descriptive chapters.

There are six vowels in Tairora: *i, e, u, o, a,* and *aa*. As in Auyana and Gadsup, the last is a low central vowel, and *a* is the schwa, a mid central vowel. Consonants include voiceless stops *p, t, k,* and *q;* continuants *b* (a bilabial fricative), *r* (an alveolar flap), and *h* (a glottal aspirate—lacking in the other languages); and nasals *m* and *n* (the velar nasal being an allophone of *n*). The Vincents (1962c) also postulate prenasalized stops *mp, nt, nk* as single phonemes which they say occur initially and medially in words but never finally (the latter being true of all consonants).

Tairora lacks the semivowels found in the other languages. The bilabial semivowel is an allophone of *b,* found after back vowels but not with all speakers. This phoneme, though usually fricative, may be a lenis stop initially. It is always a stop following the nasal if one prefers to analyze the homorganic nasal and stop as a sequence rather than a unit phoneme. The *y* of the other languages, not found in Tairora, appears sometimes as *k*. After high front vowels the glottal aspirate may fluctuate with allophone [s]. Note that this sound does not appear as a phoneme in Tairora as it does in Awa and Auyana. The alveolar voiced phoneme *r* has the stop varient [d] after *i* and with some speakers a flapped lateral in initial position preceding central and back vowels.

Vincent postulates word stress instead of the tone postulated for most of the other languages. Note that Oatridge (see Chap. XXV) proposes tone for Binumarien, and that Stringer and Hotz (see Chap. XXVI) describe stress for Waffa (the former is more closely related to Tairora than the latter). Vincent has transcribed the texts indicating stress with an apostrophe (') before the syllable in question. The relation between tone and stress in Tairora needs explication. I prefer to leave open the question as to which it is. Comparative study of word prosody is needed, and may help make a conclusion.

As has been indicated for the other languages, the text materials presented here are valuable for further analysis of Tairora, for practice in applying descriptions given and for testing them, for study of levels above the sentence, and finally, for the folklore contained therein. The similarities between Tairora stories and those of the other languages are obvious. Again, we leave the analysis and ordered comment about customs and beliefs to the ethnographers.

2. PYTHON STORY

1. *Kuna'kaata ti'rerama; 'buri, kuna 'buriqa.*
   Python I-will-say; story, phython story.
2. *Bainti nahentiba'norama oru kuna bara'te.*
   Man woman went-along python took.
3. *'Bairo ku'na barate 'baaubaroma kunabano bira 'bata ni'baairo.*
   He-was python took he-was-and-he python him took walk-he-was.
4. *'Nini'roma baainti bara 'amiro baainti bara a'mubaroma biba baainti*
   He-walked man took he-gave man took he-gave-him-and-he she
taaiqa'mabiro.
child she-became-pregnant.
5. *Baainti taaiqamabiro ba'riroma ba'tero bata.*
   Child she-became-pregnant she-waited she-bore bore.
6. *Kuna ba'taqu ko'naiquana kubeqa ba'taqu ko'naiqana 'korina ba'taqu*
   Python put bore-things lizard put bore-things reptile put bore-things
konaiqana ('kaakera) ba'taqu konaiqana 'kuburora ba'taqu ko'naigana.
(?) put bore-things reptile put bore-things.

7. *Me'maru ba'taqu ko'naiqana 'hampi haka bata'kero bata'kero bira*
   Snake put bore-things crooked things she-bore she-put her things
   'aautaha (huhuqaa) (ra'tutukero) (huhuqaa) (ra'tutukero).
   (?) (?) (?) (?).

8. *U'taqira ru'bakero.*
   Bag-in she-put-in.

9. *Ba'tobaro u'taqira ru'bakeroma hiri'tero 'baairo.*
   She-put bag-in she-put-in she-hung-up she-was.

10. *'Baaubaroma bira 'noba erantonai 'baauanihairoma 'bibiroma nai*
    She-was-and-she her mother Erandora she-was-from she-went her
    raa'buraba'nora uaro'raqira 'biro.
    daughter place-where-was went.

11. *Biro oru'robaroma aae tiro ti'noba bi'haire aniaro*
    She-went she-arrived oh she-said my-mother there-from you-come.

12. *Tu-tubaro o te bi'haima aai 'tabererama ani'ro tiro.*
    She-said-and-she oh I there-from you I-will-see I-come she-said.

13. *Tuba-roma oru baaitoba'roma u'ta kiama nai 'nora bata umi'qaro.*
    She-said-and-she went-along she-slept-and-she bag not her mother
    too she-showed.

14. *Aqira'kero ho bira (aauta) no rum'pakero hirito'nainima 'baairo.*
    She-forgot-it well her (?) mouth she-tied-up hung-up-place it-was.

15. *Bu-rubaroma bira noba aara bi'rebe (aa—) bira raa'burabano aara*
    She-go her mother road to-go (er—) her daughter road to-go.
    bi're.

16. *Bi'haroma nai 'nora ti'bamiroma koqe'makera baaintika raqiki'ene*
    While-she-went her mother she-told good-leave children-over watch
    tiro.
    she-said.

17. *Raqiki'harama raqiki'harama kiama kuban'tuke 'tabaane tiro.*
    While-you-watch while-you-watch not untie look she-said.

18 *'Aqi kanta baai'hara biraq'aima bira aaitutu'ane tiro.*
    Just place while-there them-only her watch she-said.

19. *Tuba'roma baai'haro baai'haro aaitutuma 'tabokieroma.*
    She-said-and-she while-there while-there watched she-wondered.

20. *Bira raa'bura aaraini 'bubaro 'nana haka nana baainti bata'kero*
    Her daughter road-to she-want-and-she what things what child she-
    ru'bateroe kia kuban'tuke 'tabaane ti'roibo.
    bore she-put-inside not untie look she-said.

21. *Kaai te kuban'tuke 'tabaare tiro.*
    Wait I untie I-will-look she-said.

22. *Tibakero oru u'ta biqu muntubi.*
    After-she-said went-along bag took-off brought-down.

23. *'Kero uta (ba—) no rumpa'tora; kubantu'kobaro no rumpan'tora*
She-went net-bag (er—) mouth she-had-tied; she-untied-and-it-mouth
kubantu'kobaro ku'beqabano korirabanora uri'tariro nari'era nari'era i'ha
she-had-tied she-untied-and-it lizard reptile came-up-out each-one each-one
ra'taqu.
fire fell-in.

24. *Rabaaqa'bubaro han'tarabata oru baauqitero.*
Became-seized ashes went-along she-gathered-up.

25. *Ani baauqitero baati (h)uaaqira ruba'tobaro.*
Came she-gathered down bag she-put-inside.

26. *Ru'batero aqi bira 'nora 'muntukabano 'nona tin'tabubaro aae ti'roma*
She-put-inside just her mother's heart mouth it-became-closed oh
tiraaburabano 'nena baainti 'koquera 'batakera bataa'ro tima te kuban-
she-said my-daughter your child good you-bore you-put I-said I-untied-it
'tukema 'uraroma iha taqu tubi baai'bo tiro.
I-did-and-it fire fell came-down they-did she-said.

27. *'Tibakeroma hantarabata baati rubake'roma no rum'pake ba'taro.*
She-said ashes down she-put-inside mouth tied she-put.

28. *Batobaro bira raa'burabanora kaaiqaqira naa'hoqira 'biunahi 'tabo-*
She-put-and-she her daughter work-in garden-in she-went-from
baro 'biunaihai 'tabobaro biba to'nabubanora hiipaama'tobaro hiipaama-
she-saw-and-it she-went-from she-saw-and-it it cloud it-settled-and it-
tero rape'bubaro.
settled it-became-dispersed.

29. *Aae tinoba nantia baainti kaibaroe beta to'nabu utu'tero rapebi'bo*
Oh my-mother how children she-left-and-it over-there cloud it-
tiro.
settled it-became-dispersed she-said.

30. *Noqu'nabu an'tukero.*
Vegetables-some she-cut.

31. *'Barero 'kaaqa ra'qake barero kaaqa raq'akero teqe teq'e.*
She-took sugar-cane she-broke-off she-took sugar-cane she-broke-
off cut cut.

32. *Kero ru'babarero qeta aqu'tabura tu'ikero ruba'barero kante kante.*
She-did she-put-inside-and-brought banana ripe twisted-off put-
inside-and-brought ran ran.

33. *Kan'tero orure.*
She-ran she-came.

34. *'Tabobaro orure'roma maa'qaaini orure'roma nai 'nora ire'roma*
She-saw she-came to-place she-came her mother she-asked what-
nantiararoe baainti (aa—) nantiararoe.
did-you children (er—) what-did-you.

35. Tonabu ututero rapebi taba anu'ro.
Cloud settled dispersed saw I-came.

36. Ti'tubaro a'qaau tima te 'baaiha aaitutuma tabaauraikiema nana
She-said-and-she oh-no I-said I while-here I-watched I-considered
baainti tiraaburabano batakeroe ruba'taibo.
what child my-daughter she-bore she-put-inside.

37. Ti'bakema 'kaaiqe oqike 'tabaare ti.
I-said wait I-take-out I-will-see I-said.

38. Kaiqe oqike tabaare ti.
Wait-and-I I-take-out I-will-see I-said.

39. Tibake biqu muntu bikema no rumpa'taanara kubantu.
After-I-said took-off brought-down I-did mouth you-had-tied-up
untied.

40. 'Naaqunta 'kaauraroma uritariha taquqi.
String I-did-and-it they-came-up fell-in.

41. Tibibanta baauqita baati rubate.
They-went-and-I I-gathered-up down I-put-inside.

42. Maan'tarabata ru'bateuro.
This-happened-and I-put-inside.

43. 'Tubaro ho ho ti'ro.
She-said-and-she oh oh she-said.

44. Baainti baaintiaaube tiro.
Children not-children she-said.

45. Aakaau baaintima mintiakeriaro tiro.
Wild children the-same-you-did she-said.

46. 'Ora haka baainti'mibo tiro.
Bad things children she-said.

47. Maara qetataaiqahaanta rubabare'rama kaaqa (etatanta) (taina)
These bananas you-put-in-and-take sugar-cane (?) (?) you-put-in-and-
rubabare'rama kiama an'tabira tuqan'tabira i'ene ti'ro.
take not you-turn-around you-turn-around do she-said.

48. Ho 'binanainima kantarantara.
Well the-place-where-I run.

49. Ho miniqai ho bi bi bi bi.
Well there-only well go go go go.

50. Birama oru 'tabairaroma naabu baainto baai'rarama biti 'taberama
You-go go-along you-will-see-and-it house close it-will-be-and-you
tinaabu bitiqai 'baaibo 'tirama oru biraaqaa baai'harama no'raqaa baai-
over you-look my-house over it-is you-say go-along there-on while-on-there
'harama 'kaaqa bata qeta bata naane tiro.
hill-on while-on-there sugar-cane and banana and eat she-said.

51. Tu'bamubaro ho bira tun'teqiro bi bi bi.
She-told-her-and-she well her she-was-told went went went.

52. *'Bibiro oru tabobaro naabubano ho tin'taama.*
    She-went went-along she-saw-and-it house well it-was-closed.
53. *Baaubaro oru no'raqaa baai'haro.*
    It-was-and-she went-along hill-on while-she-was.
54. *(Oba) ('taqa) baai'haroma kaaqa bata qeta bata 'nebaaubaro kunabano*
    (?) (?) while-she-was sugar-cane and banana and she-was-eating-and-
aai.
he python came.
55. *Taba'meqero nantia kaararo to'nabu utute tabe.*
    Saw-and how it-was-left-and-it cloud it-settled saw.
56. *Anu'to tu'baro aq'au bira 'noba tinoba baa kuban'tukero nana baainti*
    I-came he-said-and-she oh-no her mother mother question she-untied-
batakeroe.
it what child she-bore.
57. *Tiraaburabano ruba'teroibo kai kuban'tuke tabaare.*
    My-daughter she-put-inside wait I-untie I-will-see.
58. *Ti'bakero biqu man'tubike.*
    She-said took-off brought-down-and-left.
59. *Kubantukaibaro iha taqu tirobibo tiro.*
    She-untied-it-and-it fire fell they she-said.
60. *Bibaro baauqitakeroma rubate'roma baa'ka biroibo tiro.*
    It-went-and-she she-gathered she-put-inside earlier she-went she-said.
61. *'Tubaro 'iriro kan'tero.*
    She-said-and-he he-heard he-ran.
62. *Ani bona ra'taquke.*
    Came another-passage circled-around.
63. *'Tabobaro bita'robaro kan'tero oru bona ra'taquke.*
    He-saw-and-she she-had-gone-by he-ran went-along another-passage
circled around.
64. *'Tabobaro bita'robaro kantero bona oru ra'taquke.*
    He-saw-and-she she-had-gone-by he-ran another-passage went-along
circled-around.
65. *'Tabobaro bita'robaro o kunabano minti 'aqiro bu'qata buqata tiro.*
    He-saw-and-she she-had-gone-by er python the-same as-he-did went
went he-said.
66. *Oru bona ra'taquke 'tabobaro kia bita'robaro e maini ti naanti'eraini*
    Went-along another-passage circled-around he-saw-and-she not she-
ani bariaro tiro.
had-gone-by oh here my the-place-behind came you-are he-said.
67. *Orurante bi'hairo.*
    He-came-back there-from.

68. *Anaiharo 'tabobaro biba no'raqaa baaiharo 'kaaqa bata 'qeta bata 'ne.*
While-coming he-saw-and-she she hill-on while-there sugar-cane and banana and ate.

69. *Baaubaro aqi betara hairoma (maqira) aniro.*
She-was-and-he just over-there from (?) he-came.

70. *(Aqira) (aqira) (biaqira) nam'piqa'maqukero.*
(?) (?) (?) he-swallowed-her.

71. *Nampiq'amaqukero bi bi biro eqa aniran'tero 'nabuqi oru baaita.*
He-swallowed-her went went he-went again he-went-back house-in went-along sleep.

72. *Naabuqi oru 'aampe 'aampeqamabi 'roma.*
House-in went-along coil he-coiled-himself.

73. *Kahe kahe'mabiroma baaitate 'baairo.*
Coil he-coiled-himself he-slept he-was.

74. *'Baaubaroma bira raaburabano burubi aauha tabe'roma 'ehai barakero bira rai'hakeroma 'baaiti noquqi keroma 'noquara bata nonku'karo.*
He-was-and-she her daughter went-along belly she-saw bamboo she-took it she-split-off-sliver down vegetable-greens she-put greens and she-put-in.

75. *Nonkutero un'te baairo.*
She-put-in cook she-was.

76. *Un'tebaaubaroma biba noqu biba i'tabiro.*
She-cooked-and-it it greens it it-became-cooked.

77. *Bi'raqaahairo bira (hurubiroqaqi) kuna arara ta'taqu'kobaro.*
There-on-from it (?) python guts cut-open.

78. *Aqi bira 'noba biriqihai naare 'abutanta bata ani'roibo.*
Just her mother there-in-from blood middle and she-came.

79. *Anire nai raabura ai.*
She-came her daughter came.

80. *Taatoaqu'kobaro tenta minti'rerabe tenta nora mintiakaau'narabe tiro.*
She-cut-open myself I-will-do-that my mother I-had-done-that she-said.

81. *Ti'bakero bi'raqai tu'biniro nai nokantiro naabuqai (u)tutu'makero.*
Said-that only she-came-down her mother-with house-only they-burned.

82. *Tuta'kobaroma bi'raqira kuna aauha taqu'tububaro.*
They-burned-and-he there-in python belly it-became-burned.

83. *Nai baainti titaqu'tubaro.*
His children became-burned.

84. *Nai raaburaqai bara bi'takero orurabara'kero eranto'naini bu'ramibo.*
Her daughter-only took she-took she-came-to Erandora she-went.

85. *Minti ti'bakero ina'raiqa 'tiamanta tenta buri iru'naiqanama.*
She-same they-said a-little they-said-and-I myself story heard.

1. I'll tell about the python; the python story. Men and women used to marry pythons. The one she took [married] was a python and the python walked like a man. He walked and she married the man and he gave it to her; she married him and he gave it to her and she became pregnant.

5. She became pregnant and gave birth. She gave birth to python things, lizards, reptiles, and snakes, and all sorts of things. She gave birth to snakes and these terrible things and when she gave birth she [?]. She then put them in a net bag. She put them in a net bag and hung it up and she was there. 10. She was there and her mother who was from Erandora went and came to where her daughter lived. She [her daughter] said, 'Oh, Mother! you have come here from there!' She said this and then she [her mother] said, 'Oh, I have come from there to see you!' She said this and she went along and she slept, but she [her daughter] did not show the net bag to her own mother. She avoided it, and she left it [the net bag] hung up with the mouth tied.

15. She went and her mother was going to go along the road. When she went, she told her mother, 'Look after the children well. While you are looking after them, don't untie it [the net bag] to look in it. Just be there and watch them from a distance!'

After she [the daughter] said that, she [the mother] was there watching and she wondered about it. 20. Her daughter had gone off along the road and she said to herself, 'What kind of children did she give birth to that she said don't untie and have a look? Wait, I'll untie it [the bag] and look.' After she said that, she went and took the bag off and put it down. She went and untied the mouth of that bag that she [her daughter] had tied up; she untied the mouth that had been tied up, and the lizards and reptiles came up [out of the bag] and each one fell into the fire. They were seized by it [killed], and she gathered them up with the ashes. 25. She gathered them up and put them back in the bag. When she put them in the bag, she [the mother] closed the mouth of it and she said, 'Oh! my daughter, I thought you had given birth to a good child, and I untied it [the bag] and they fell down into the fire, that's what happened.' After she said that, she put the ashes back in [the bag] and tied the mouth [of the bag] and put it back.

After she had done that her daughter, from where she had gone to work in the garden, saw that the cloud which had settled [over her house] had dispersed. 'What did my mother do to the children that the cloud which had settled has dispersed?' she said. 30. She then cut vegetable leaves. She took them and broke off and took sugar cane and cut it up. She did this and put it in [her net bag] and she twisted off some bananas that were ripe and put them in [her bag] and went [home] running. She ran and came there. When she saw it, she came and she arrived at her place and asked her mother, 'What did you do to the children?' 35. 'I saw that the cloud which was settled became dispersed, and I came!'

After she said this, her mother said ' "Oh no," I said as I was here watching, and I wondered and I thought, "What sort of child did my daughter bear and put inside [the net bag]? Wait, I will take it out and see! Wait I will take it out and see." And after I said this, I took it [the bag] off and put it down and untied the mouth which you had tied.' 40. 'I did this to the string, and they came out and fell into the fire. They went in, and I gathered them up and put them back in [the bag]. These things happened, and I put them inside the bag.'

After she said this, she [daughter] said, 'Oh, no. The children are not children.' 45. 'You did this and they are wild children,' she said. 'These are bad sorts of children,' she said. 'You put these bananas and sugar cane inside [your net bag] and don't turn around, don't come back at all,' she said. 'You run to your place. You just run and go there, and keep on going.' 50. 'Keep going till you see that a house is near and then look over and say, "Over there is my house!" and then go up and wait up on the hill and eat the sugar cane and bananas,' she said.

After she told her that she [her mother] did as instructed and kept going and going. She went till she saw it, and the house was there. It was there and she went up and waited on the hill. She was there and she ate the sugar cane and bananas, and the python came. 55. He saw how something had happened to the settled clouds. 'I came,' he said, and she [the daughter] said, 'Oh, no, my mother said, "What sort of child did my daughter bear?" and then she untied it. "Wait, I will untie and look!" and then she untied it. "Wait, I will untie and look!" she said. When she said this, she took it [the bag] off and put it down. Then she untied it and they fell into the fire and they were burned,' she said. 60. 'She went and gathered them up and put them back in and she's already gone!' she said.

When she said this, he understood it and ran. He came and circled around one place. He saw that she had gone by; then he ran and circled around another place. 65. He saw that she had already gone by, and he saw that she had gone by so he circled around again and ran up to another place; the python continued doing this, going and going. He circled around another place and saw that she had not gone by and he said, 'Eh! you have come here and are behind me.' He came back from there. While he was coming, he saw that she was up on the hill eating sugar cane and bananas. She was there, and he just went over there from where he was and came up on her. 70. Then he grabbed her and he swallowed her.

After he swallowed her, he went back again to the house and slept. He went back and coiled himself up at the house; he coiled up and slept. While he was there, the daughter came along and saw his [distended] stomach, and she took some bamboo [type used for cutting] and split off a sliver and put it down into the greens. 75. She put it in there, and she cooked them. She cooked them, and they were cooked. She took them from there and threw them to him and it cut open the python's stomach. Her mother came out from in there; she came out with the blood. She came out to her daughter. 80. She cut it open and said, 'I will do that, and I have done that for my mother.'

After she said that, she came down with her mother, and they burned the house. They burned it and the python also became burned. His children were burned too. She took her daughter and went down to Erandora. 85. That is what they told it to me, and I have heard the story that way.

3. POPIRE AND PAPIRE

1.   Popi'reka paapi'rekama.
Popire-and Papire-and.

2.   Kabe'roraqi baai'haroma.
Kaberora-in they-lived.

3.   Popi'reka paapi'reka; 'baaubaroma 'butura o'reqarainima i'ha quara-
Popire-and Papire-and; they-were-and-he over-along there Oreqara-
amite'haroma.
at fire lit-and-gave-for-them.

4.   On'tera bariqo'mano tuba'roma 'eqara ara'rera 'eqara ara'rera.
Ontera (? actor) he-invited-and-he feathers to-stick-in feathers to-
stick-in.

5.   'Baaubaroma bitanta 'arake ba'rema ara'kema.
They-were-and-he the-two they-stuck-in they-took they-stuck-in.

6.   'Baaintintiera hanta bata'tema bara'ke nimi'tema.
Children-for two they-put-for they-took they-gave-them.

7.   Nari'eraahanta ara'kehanta e'baara 'batate.
For-themselves-two they-stuck-in-two secret they-put.

8.   'Kantaba narierahanta arake bata'tema.
Arm-band for-themselves-two they-wove they-put.

9.   Bika 'baaintintiera ara'ke 'nimite.
Their children-for they-wove they-put-for-them.

10.   Kaahu'naa 'baaintintiera ku'take 'nimite narieraahanta 'kutake 'batate.
Wrist-band children-for knitted gave-for-them for-themselves-two
knitted put.

11.   Baaqa 'baaintitiera aautu 'nimite 'naitantara 'baaqa 'autuka 'batate.
Front-skirt children-for made gave-for-them themselves-two front-skirt
made put.

12.   'Ekaa 'haka barake 'baaintintiera 'baahehe haka barake 'nimite.
All things took children-for decoration things took they-gave-for-them.

13.   'Naihanta bara'ke 'batate.
Themselves took put.

14.   Bata'tehanta 'baaintihakara ne popi'reka paapi'reka (i'hainihanta)
Put-two to-the-children you Popire-and Papire-and (?-two) (?-two)
(be-rabihanta) 'baaihatanta kia koqemabaai oraiqaa'mabuka.
are-two not good-are bad-become.

15.   Baaintinti 'aarana bumanta'ma ba'rema buba'roma ho bika 'tubitare
Children road-passage they-went-and-they they-took they-went-and-he
bumanta'ma bi'tanta aqira'ke.
well they went-down-by they-went-and-they the-two forgotten.

16.   Hanta baai baaiha nihu'tu.
Two were while-there watched-them.

17. *Baaumanta bira baaintinti bara i'ha um'piqi.*
They-were-and-they their children took fire as-it-lighted.

18. *Bibibibinabu buru butu'raqaa no'raanana bata'tema (oka) 'baahehema*
Went-went-plural brought-along there-on entrance they-put (?) decor-
ba'rehanta(nabu) naabuqi ori'qete ha'raaraqi.
ated did-two house-in went-inside dance-circle-in.

19. *Ori'qetema buru ihi u'tintaau.*
Went-inside brought dance they-circled.

20. *I'hi buru u'tukema ihi'rantaau.*
Dance brought circled they-danced.

21. *'Re baauba'roma 'bitanta ho bara 'baahehemake 'naihanta ba'rehan-*
They-did-and-they the-two well took decorated themselves-two took-
tananta muntubitare (maantana).
two they-went-by (?).

22. *Otu i'ha qumpubumanta butu 'tabema 'butuqai 'bobatanaa i'ha qumpi.*
Down fire lit-and-went-and-they along they-saw along-only another-
person fire light.

23. *'Tubibo tu'boma a'qau kia 'baainti bata bariera'mibo.*
He-comes-down they-said-and-they oh-no not man too they-were.

24. *Ekaa'qaima 'anuro.*
All-only we-came.

25. *Baaka'qora hantama popi'reka paapi'reka mini 'kaaunarahanta ba-*
Old-men two Popire-and Papire-and there we-left-two they-are.
ri'ebo.

26. *'Bira'maara 'ekaama 'ara ba'rema 'anuro.*
That-place all stuck-in took we-came.

27. *Tubo a'qau 'butuqa 'oba qumpi ani'ribo tubo a'qau tiro.*
They-said-and-they oh-no over-there torch lit they-come they-said-
and-they oh-no they-said.

28. *Kia ekaa'ma 'anuro tiro.*
Not all we-came they-said.

29. *'Ekaa anu naramibo.*
All we-have-come.

30. *Bira bakaqorahanta biraqaa kaau'naramibo tiro.*
Their old-men-two there-on I-have-left they-said.

31. *Mintituba'kema buru utu'kero 're baau'raqi bi'tanta oru 'bima oru*
After-they-said-that brought circled danced it-was-in the-two went-
no'raarana oru u'tehantama.
along went went-along entrance went-along circled-two.

32. *Popi'rebama hini no'raarana oru.*
Popire one-side entrance went-along.

33. *Buroboma hini no'raarama paapi'reba oru'rehanta.*
He-went-and-he one-side entrance Papire they-came-two.

34. *Maa bi'raqihanta buru ihi'rantau.*
That there-in-two brought danced.

35. *Ihi 're baaubaroma na'hentimanora (e) bi'tantaka ba'raata 'baainti-*
Sing did they-were-and-they woman (er) the-two-around girl people
bano'nora u'tutorarama ti.
they-encircled I-say.

36. *Utu'tohantama bi'tanta aqini uqai'taane 'tima.*
Encircled-two the-two to-side get-out-of-way they-said.

37. *Aqini uqai'taane (ma) baaka'qora (ma) tema biri ihi 're baruro.*
To-side get-out-of-way (uh) old-men (uh) we-are brought sing do
we-are.

38. *'Kia baainti'aauma biri ihi 're baruro tiro.*
Not men brought sing do we-are he-said.

39. *Baaka'qorama biri ihi 're uro tiro.*
Old-men brought sing do we he-said.

40. *Mintitibakehantama i'hi ra'baqi bibi'bima.*
After-the-two-said-that sing as-they-did went-went-went.

41. *'Aatitare bumanta bitanta aatita're bumanta'hantama ho tubi'reka*
To-dawn it-went-and-they the-two to-dawn it-went-and-they enough
umanta biba na'henti a'nintau.
go-down they-did-and-they they women they-came.

42. *Ba'raata 'baainti bitanta biraini tanta a'nubo.*
Girl persons the-two to-them follow they-came.

43. *A'qau tiro.*
Oh-no he-said.

44. *Kia tema baainti'aauma baka'qoramuro tiro.*
Not we man old-men-we-are he-said.

45. *Minti ti'bakehanta bika a'nintau a'nubaroma bi'tanta tan'taqi ani.*
The-same they-said-two they came they-came-and-they those-two
follow came.

46. *A'nima bi nai maa'qaini biri 'kantaau biri.*
Came went their-own place-to brought they-did-leave brought.

47. *'Koboma bi'tanta tihama a'qau tehanta baaintiaaube baaka'qorama*
They-left-and-they the-two they-said oh-no we-two men old-men two
hantama a'ni.
came.

48. *Hanta bomano ani kaankaara utu'mabubo.*
Two one came bat he-became.

49. *Bomano ku'na utamabiro.*
One python he-became.

50. *Minti'abuma bi nahentika ani 'tabema.*
That-they-did those women came they-saw.

51. *Anirante aqira'kema 'bintaau.*

They-went-back forgot they-went.

52. *Nena baaintimanoe buru 'raaraau tu'rarama 'baaqu hakamanora*
You men brought danced I-said-and-you terrible things you-are they-
iriaro tiro.
said.

53. *Tiba 'kehanta aqira'ke aniran'tehanta bika'bintaau.*
They-said-two forgot they-went-back-two they-went.

54. *'Bubantama bika mintima i'hitintaau.*
They-went-and-they they the-same they-sang.

55. *Mi'tanta kia baainti'aau tetanta a'nuro.*
The-two not men we-two we-came.

56. *Ua'haka a'nuro ihi minti tibakehanta.*
Bad-things we-came song same they-said-two.

57. *Mitanta 'tintaau.*
Those-two they-said.

58. *Popi're i paapiro taao rurue popi'rei paapi're taao rurue popire i paapire i taao rurue popire paapire taao rurue oe eqe oe eqe oe iae oe eqe oe eqe oe eqe ue iae oe eqe.*

59. *Bitanta mintibakehanta ihi tintaau.*
The-two the-same-said song they-did-sing.

60. *Ho 'bi'qenama.*
Well the-end.

1. There were two, Popire and Papire. They lived in Kaberora. Popire and Papire; they were there and those at Oreqara made a fire for them. The Ontera people invited them so they made feather headdresses. 5. They were there and the two of them were making feather headdresses. They made some for their children and put them to one side. They made some for themselves and secretly put them to one side. They wove arm bands for themselves and put them to one side. They made some for their children too. 10. They knitted wrist bands for their children and knitted some for themselves, and put them down. They made skirts for their children and they made skirts for themselves and put them to one side. They took all things; they made all decorating things for their children. They took these for themselves and put them down. The two put them down for the children and Popire and Papire had some for themselves.

Popire and Papire were no good, old, bad. 15. The children went along the road [to dance], and they took [their things] and went; they went off [to dance] and the two [old men] were left behind forgotten. They were there and watched them. They stayed behind, their children lit fires [torches]. They went along and came to the entrance, and they decorated themselves and went inside the dance house and circled around. After they circled around they danced. 20. They danced circling around. While they were dancing, the two decorated themselves and went, lit fires [torches], and started down.

And they [the people at the dance] looked over and saw that someone had lit a torch. 'Over there more are coming down,' they said, but they [the children of Popire and Papire] said, 'Oh no, there are no more people! All of us have come!' 25. 'Only two old men, Popire and Papire, that we left behind are there! All from that place have brought their things and we came.' They said this, but they [others] replied, 'Oh no, over there they are coming with torches,' but they said, 'No! It is not so, we have all come. We all have come!' 30. 'We only left behind two old men!' they said.

After they said that, the two came to the place and circled, and they went to the entrance and the two circled. Popire went to one entrance. He went there, and Papire went to the other entrance. The two came there and in there they danced. 35. They sang and were there, and the women and girls gathered around the two of them, I say. They encircled the two and the two said, 'Get out of the way! Get out of the way, er, we are old men and we brought [ourselves] and are singing. We aren't men who have come to sing!' they said. 'We are old men singing!' they said. 40. After they said that, they continued singing and kept doing it.

At dawn the two went to go and when the two went to go, the women came. The girls came following the two. 'Oh no!' they said. 'We are not men— we are old men!' they said. 45. They said this, and they went along, but they came and they [girls] followed them. They came and brought them to their place. They left, and the two said, 'Oh no! we two are not men! We are two old men!' but they came.

Then one of them turned into a bat. The other one turned into a python. 50. After they did that those women came and saw them. They returned and gave up on them and left. 'We thought you were men who came and danced but you are terrible things!' they said. They said that, and they gave up, and as the two left, they went back. They went and they sang that. 55. 'We two are not men, we came. We bad things came,' and the two sang that song. These two sang: *'Popi're i papire taao rurue popi'rei papi're taao rurue popire i papire i taao rurue popire papire taao rurue oe eqe oe eqe oe iae oe eqe oe eqe oe eqe ue iae oe eqe.'* The two said these things and sang that song. 60. Well, that's the end.

4. TWO BROTHERS

1. Aairi'naaka koqa'kuka ba'kaaka ti'erira 'iria.
Airina-and Koqaku-and information I-will-say-and you-listen.

2. Aairi'naaba koqa'kuka baa'raqu an'take.
Airina Koqaku-and traps cut.

3. Barero koqakuba 'araro.
He-took Koqaku he-put-in.

4. Ekaa baainti bakuntema 'araqiro 'araqiro baa'raqu 'araqiro.
All men the-place-of he-put-in he-put-in traps he-put-in.

5. Ni ni ni ni ni ni ni ni ni.
He-went went.

6. *'Niroma qata biri tibamiha'roma qata . . .*
   Went younger-brother took-along he-told-him younger-brother . . .
7. *Kaaibu kaku'pububoma baa'raqu 'arero.*
   Nuts they-fell-off-and-he traps he-put-in.
8. *Bihai anire 'tabobaro kaaibu kaku'pububoma qata baramiroma*
   There-from came-to he-saw-and-it nuts they-fell-and-he younger-
   'maarama kakupuke'hara ba'taane tiro.
   brother he-took-and-gave-him these you-take-them-off you-put he-said.
9. *'Tubaro bibaa kaku'pukero.*
   He-said-that-and-he he he-took-them-off.
10. *Bate'haro bate'haroma nai 'boqa anta qutu 'namakero.*
    While-he-put while-he-put he some part cracked-between-teeth he-ate.
11. *Boqa qutu 'nobo hia'kiubo 'tabero ekaa hini anta bakura.*
    Some cracked he-ate-and-it it-was-tasty-and-he he-saw all side part it-
    was-there.
12. *Qutu namaqu'karo qutu namaquke'roma kero.*
    Cracked he-ate-up cracked he-ate-up he-left.
13. *Hini anta baku'raqai bato'boma 'niro ba'kaaba bi'haairo ani bara*
    Side part that-was-there-only he-put-and-he he-went-about elder-
    aaiqa'roqa arama kero.
    brother there-from came took the-same-place put-in he-left.
14. *Haam'pakiharo 'tabobo hini kia ba'kubaro hiniqai ba'kubaro aairi-*
    He-put-together he-saw-and-it side not it-was-there-and-it side-only
    'naarara ti'haro.
    it-was-there-and-he to-Airina he-said.
15. *Taaini ekaa kaaibu unara na'maqukaa'ro.*
    Where-to all nuts I-do-have you-have-eaten-up.
16. *Ti'tubaro aqau ti.*
    He-said-and-he oh-no said.
17. *'Naauro hia'kima na'manakeuro tiro.*
    I-ate it-was-tasty I-ate-them-up he-said.
18. *Minti tibakobo biraqaa kaa'bumiqakero ruqutu'kero.*
    That he-said-and-he there-on fighting-stick-he-struck he-hit-him.
19. *Raauq'iro maa'bini 'onkaiqirama baabi aqu'karo.*
    He-picked-him-up down-there steep-place down threw-him.
20. *Ruqutu'kero ba'tero bara baabi 'onkaiqira baabi aquko'boma biba*
    He-hit-him he-put-him took down steep-place down he-threw-him-
    otu bi'raqira baai'haroma.
    and-he he went-down there-in he-was-there.
21. *'Baaubaroma taa'roqa aquru'babiro hi'qiriro.*
    He-was-there-and-it nettle it-had-become-dried it-fell.
22. *Ubaai 'utiro aquru'babiro biraqaa hiqiri muntukaqaa 'aarakobo bi-*
    Wind it-blew it-had-become-dried there-on fell heart-on stung-him-

'hairo korumpu'mabiro.

and-he there-from he-became-startled.

23. *Himpiro biba oru ta'roqa raqa'kero.*

He-got-up he went-along nettle he-broke-it-off.

24. *Min'tana ra'raau munti bi kero.*

That-thing pull brought down went he-left.

25. *Bara aarakero aara'kobo baatamano koqe 'ubaro bi'raqi hai himpi*

Took stung-himself stung-himself his-body good it-did-and-he there-

uri'tarero.

in-from got-up he-went-up-past.

26. *Oru 'qentana baai'haro ba'kaarara taarienta'bata tururubata abu-*

Went-up at-door while-he-was-there to-older-brother mat-long-too

'nautabata naabu kaa'raiqabata bara beba timi'ene ti'ro.

headrest-small-too cloak-too house post-too take down-over give-me he

said.

27. *'Kierianta bata tuba'roma ha'ntaqanabu bata tuba'roma bara beba*

Rafter-long too he-said-and-he *kunai*-some-too he-said-and-he took

amiro.

down-over he-gave-him.

28. *Bara beba a'mubaro bare'rama baaintimano baaibo 'bibitira baaibo*

Took down-over he-gave-him-and-he you-take man he-is over-here

ti'baqira otu 'birama kia baaintibano bata baaina kanta 'nenaraakanta otu

he-is you-speak go-down you-go not man too he-is place you-alone-place

bari'ene tiro.

go-down you-stay he-said.

29. *Minti tibakero atitaa'kobo otu.*

That after-he-said he-ordered-him-off-and-he went-down.

30. *Biharo otu biharo otu biharo otu.*

While-he-went went while-he-went went went went.

31. *Biharo baaintibano ba'kura aaitutu'aqiro biharo babi biribi.*

Went man he-was watched go pass-by went.

32. *Otu bi otu bi otu.*

Went-down went went-down went went-down.

33. *'Tabobo kia baaintibenobata otu bakukanta otu.*

He-saw-and-he not man-too went-down he-was-place went-down.

34. *Qen'tubo kia baainti otu bakukanta otu.*

It-became-dark not man went-down he-was-place went-down.

35. *Bikanta baaitero otu baai'haroma ho buqa'nohairoma buaq'nohairoma*

That-place he-slept went-down while-he-was-there enough hand-with

aabe.

hand-with mark.

36. *Bate'haroma te maaqaa baai'tema hura maaqaa hai be'bare.*

While-he-put I here I-sleep tomorrow here-at from I-will-arise.

37. *Naabu ka'qararabe ti.*
House I-can-build said.
38. *Ka'qake maaqaama 'baairarabe tiro.*
I-have-built here-at I-can-stay he-said.
39. *Maakantama kaiqa bara utu 'nararabe tiro.*
At-this-place work take plant I-can-eat he-said.
40. *Tibakero baai'tabiro.*
After-he-said he-went-asleep.
41. *Qentaqiro.*
it-was-dark.
42. *Baaitaba'rora naabu 'kaaraka buru aaiqu aru' barero.*
He-slept house post-over brought leg he-hit-it.
43. *Himpiro 'tabobaro naabubano nai qumina kaqa'bubo baai'tero araraa*
He-got-up he-saw-and-it house itself nothing it-became-built-and-he
to'aqi be'bare.
he-slept next-day in-the-morning came-outside.
44. *'Tabobaro karakaaqa manora kia aqi nai 'ekaa hakabanora aqu-*
He-saw-and-it food thing-there not just itself all things ripened-it-was.
'kobun'tobura.
45. *Bakubaro ekaa haka nai qumina ba'kubaro otu 'tabero bebare tabero.*
It-was-there-and-he all things itself nothing they-were-there-and-he
went-down he-saw came-outside he-saw.
46. *Te ho maakarakaaqa neha maaqaa 'baairarabe tiro.*
I enough this-food while-I-eat at-here I-can-stay he-said.
47. *Quaramano baairibano kokoraamano nai nana hakamano ekaa haka*
Pig dog fowl itself what thing all thing all thing itself nothing that-
ekaa hakamano nai qumina bikanta ba'kurarama ti.
place it-was-there I say.
48. *Te maakarakaaqara na'hama quara aantaaura neha 'baairaramuro tiro.*
I this-food while-eating pigs animals while-eating I-can-stay he-said.
49. *Biraqaa bii'haro nariera 'kaiqa barero.*
There-on while-there he-alone work he-took.
50. *Roriqai barero oru katari tuqi baaubo tuqi baaubo ba'raata 'taaraqanta*
Axe-only he-took went-along tree chop he-was-and-they chop he-was-
ba'raata taaraqanta o'tirante ha'buka ra'baqi naamairuna u'rintaau.
and-they girls two girls two went-back-up fish they-trapped water-along
they-came-up.
51. *Ra'baqi u'ri.*
As-they-trapped came-up.
52. *Uru 'tabobo biba teqoba hankamano otu ba'heqi tu'tububo u'taqira*
Came-up they-saw-and-it he he-had-cut chip went-down trap-in it-
oru bara burubi ke.
went-down-and-they in-the-net went-along took brought left.

53. *'Tabero bara birauru totabarero urihatanta aaitutu'aqi uri.*
They-saw-it took thing holding-took while-coming-up-the-two they-watched came-up.

54. *Ha'buku ra'baqi uri uri uru.*
Fish as-they-trapped came-up came-up came-up.

55. *'Tabobo biba ka'tari an'te baaumanta aairi'naaba ante uru.*
They-saw-and-he he tree cut he-was-and-they Airina cut came-up.

56. *Bira 'okara baaintaau katari 'okara.*
Its trunk they-waited tree trunk.

57. *Biba bini ante baaumanta bitanta okaraqi oru baaubo anta kobo tubi.*
He up-top cut he-was-and-they they-two trunk went-along they-waited-and-he cut he-completed-it-and-it came-down.

58. *Katari biba nta'qubiro.*
Tree it it-became-jammed.

59. *Anta kobo tubi katari biba nta'qubiro.*
Cut he-completed-and-it came-down tree it it-became-jammed.

60. *Minti'aqi bubo te katari antake baauro batete otu.*
It-did-that it-went-and-he I tree cut I-did-it-and-you quickly go-down.

61. *Buarabama otu nena ntaqu.*
You-went go-down you-yourself jam.

62. *Ntaqubibaririaro tiro.*
You-become-jammed he-said.

63. *Tibakero tubu.*
After-he-said-that came-down.

64. *Bentaqiro bentaqiro ben'tero kero.*
As-he-pushed as-he-pushed he-pushed he-completed-it.

65. *Tubu 'tabobo maa bitanta biraqi bakubo nehanta tana hai uruabo ti.*
Came-down he-saw-and-they those they-two there-at-they-were-and-he you-two where from you-came-up said.

66. *Tubo te hanta o'tirante namairuna urure habuka rabaraba uru(re).*
He-said-that-and-they said two came-back-up water-along came-up-to fish trapping came-up.

67. *Tabauro katari maa teqaara hanka otu.*
We-saw-and-it tree this you-cut piece went-down.

68. *'Bumanta 'tabema maa biqana totabarema aare baria'naraqaa ururo;*
It-went-and-I I-saw-it this thing holding-took you you-are we-came-
tubo tere tentaraa maaqaa maa katari ante baaurama uriabo.
up; they-said-and-he I I-alone here-on this tree cut I-was-and-you you-came-up.

69. *'Biqebe tiro.*
Let's-go he-said.

70. *Bikaqai(bara) nti'tabarero kara'kaaqa oru an'tuke 'numanta baraburu*
They-only-took he-took-them food went-along cut he-gave-them-and-

unta ne'haro.
they took-brought cooked ate.
71. *Numanta ne.*
     He-gave-them-and-they ate.
72. *Baaite nehanta hura bua'te ti.*
     Sleep you-two tomorrow you-go said.
73. *Tumanta bika baaite.*
     He-said-and-they they slept.
74. *Aqau kia te birarabe na'kaaba baainti ami'taabamibo.*
     Oh-no not I I-can-go elder-sister man she-is-given-to-him.
75. *Tere ehaara baauraaukabe aaurabano tubo aaurara maa biba baainti*
     I single I-came young-sister she-said-and-she about-the-young-sister
     amitaabemibo te na'kaaba ti'haro te ehaara baauraaukamuro.
     this she man she-is-given-to-him I elder-sister she-said I single I-came.
76. *Ho minti tiba tabokiehanta.*
     Enough same say the-two-saw.
77. *No biraini baati qintaau.*
     Enough to-him husband they-became.
78. *Baati 'qaabihanta baki'hama.*
     Husband the-two-became they-were-there.
79. *Ba'kubaro karakaaqa hanta utu na'maqi bi.*
     They-were-and-he food two plant they-ate went.
80. *Baaubaroma bira ba'kaabanta koqa'kuba kia naahobata ba'kubo biba*
     They-were-and-he his older-brother Koqaku not garden-and it-was-
     u'tuba umu'tiqa ara'bubaro.
     and-it he he-had-planted weedy-grass it-had-become.
81. *Uriku'mabubaro kara naainara tabobo kia bakubo buhaarimano*
     It-became-overgrown food that-which-is-eaten he-saw-and-it no it-
     buhaarimano bakubo matimano baatamano bata kia bakubo 'buhaarian-
     was-there-and-it bone bone it-was-there-and-it flesh body too not it-was-
     tamano (bakubaro) bari.
     and-it bone-long (it-was-there-and-he) was-there.
82. *Tabokiero kaairaqe qata bira naantiera bua're tiro.*
     He-saw-it you-wait-and-I young-brother him after I-will-go he-said.
83. *Bira naantiera otu.*
     Him after go-down.
84. *Biha tabaare.*
     While-going I'll-see.
85. *Ti'bake otu bibaaubo bira bakaabanta otu bihato otu biharo otu.*
     After-he-said-that went-down he-was-going his elder-brother went-
     down went went went went.
86. *Baainti nihutu'aqiro otirante baainti bakura.*
     Men as-he-watched-them came-back-up men they-were.

87. *Nihutu'aqiro otu bi otu bi otu bi otu bi.*
He-watched-them went-down went went went went . . .

88. *Qata bano bira ba'tuka otu 'robaro ho biranaatahanta ani tabe ani*
Younger brother his village went-down he-came-to-and-he enough
tabe.
his-wife-two came saw came saw.

89. *Buru qatra ti'bamima maa (aai) ba'kaaba maarira tubu.*
Took-along younger-brother-to they-told-him that (er) your-brother
up-there come-down.

90. *Baairibo titubaro nehanta kara'kaaqa an'tu barema buru naabuqi*
He-is-there they-said-and-he you-two food cut take bring house-in
'untaate.
you-cook.

91. *Naabuqi unte'hama quara aaraai 'tintira 'hoquka ekaa haka i'erinara*
House-in while-cooking pig tusk head-band rattan-waist-band all
baahehe haka ierinara bara biri timi'ete.
things I-have decorating things I-have take bring give-me.

92. *Tumantama bitanta ani eo tibake ani kara'kaaqa qanti.*
He-said-and-they they-two came yes after-they-said came food cut.

93. *Bare naabuqi bate ani bare buru a'mubaro ne naabuqi baaihama*
Took house-in put came took brought they-gave-him-and-he you
quara 'aaraate ti.
house-in while-there pig call said.

94. *Te oru maanto uba tieri i'rima' nehanta quara 'aaraate tubaro qen-*
I go-along at-here noise I-will-say hear you-two pig call he-said-and-
tana bakubo baahehema barero maanto uriha hmmmm ti'tumanta bitanta
they doorway they-were-and-he decorate took at-here coming-up hmmm
naataauhanta tiha maaai ti.
he-said-and-they they-two wives-two said here said.

95. *Tubarobetanta hmmmm tibaai minti ti'baqiro a'nuqata a'nuqata aai.*
They-said-and-he hmmm he-was-saying same he-said coming coming
came.

96. *Ba'kaaranta aai.*
Elder-brother came.

97. *Aaiqi'nohairo raaqitabarera hini rahi'taqukoraa'ma ti.*
Nose-with caught-and-took side threw-heavily I-say.

98. *Bi'hairo aai hini raaqitabarero buru rahi'taqukora babi.*
He-came-from-there came side caught-up-and-took brought threw-
heavily brought.

99. *Ruqutukero biribi ruqutukero babi babi ruqutukero biribi ruqutukero*
He-hit-him brought-back he-hit-him brought brought he-hit-him
ba'kaara oraaiqakoramaama ti.
brought-back he-hit-him about-the-elder-brother he-left-him-badly I-say.

100. Konkoma bubuqaa ma̧a'qiri tuqarabu'raraama ti.
Dust particles tongue it-rubbed I-say.

101. Tuqara'bubaro aqau tiro.
It-became-rubbed-and-he oh-no he-said.

102. Qatara aaiquara manomahari baairibo.
To-younger-brother your-pig hitting-me it-is.

103. Bara'kaane ti'tubaro bira naatatanta maaiqai ti'bake ti.
Take-it-away he-said-and-they his wives-two come they-said say.

104. Baaubo biraqira ruqu'tuke biraqaa bata'tero.
They-were-and-he there-in hit-him there-on he-put-him.

105. Anirantero aaiquma aautu'taro anirantero buru(maa) biha'kara
He-went-back legs he-made he-went-back brought (er) those-things
aqirakero.
he-threw-away.

106. Buru aqirakero orurantero bihairo a'niro 'aaitare naabuqi oru.
Brought he-threw-away he-came-back there-from he-came passed-by
house-in went.

107. Baai'haroma 'naatatanta otu ba'kaaranta bite uru'ate tiro.
While-he-was-there wives-two go-down elder-brother take come-up
he-said.

108. Koqakura otu bi'taate.
Koqaku go-down get-him.

109. 'Tumanta tubuhanta bi'tabare buru naabuqi ke.
He-said-and-they the-two-went-down got-him brought house-in left.

110. Namaai aarake baata tuntu'aquke kara'kaaqa raa'quke bate a'mubaro
Water heated body bathed food tipped-out put they-gave-and-he food
kara'kaaqa 'nero.
he-ate.

111. Baai'tomanta ara'raa qentaqira baai'tabubaro taari buqi ami'tobaro
He-slept-and-they next-day in-the-night he-went-to-sleep-and-he mat
baai'tabubaro bu'kera a'taara taaraqanta bini biri.
spread-out he-gave-it-and-he he-went-asleep-and-he cassowary bamboo-
container two above brought.

112. Hiritero a'taaini nto'matero.
He-hung-up the-bottom he-pierced.

113. A'taaini nto'matero tero.
The-bottom he-pierced he-did.

114. Biabi bakaara muntukaqaa batatobo hi'qiri.
Down elder-brother heart-over he-put-and-it it-dripped.

115. Hi'qiriharo bukera bahaberamano.
It-was-dripping cassowary fat.

116. Qa'tara nana haka manoari 'baaibo ti.
To-younger-brother what thing hit it-is said.

117. Nana haka mano tiqaa hiqiri hiqiri baaibo.
What thing me-on drip drip it-is.

118. Ti'tubaro buana batakanta baai'taane ti.
He-said-and-he go ground-place sleep said.

119. Minti 'baaimanta baaitau'naraqimibo tubo baaitero.
The-same it-was-and-I I-have-slept he-said-and-he slept.

120. Qa'tara bara'kaane tiro.
To-younger-brother take-it-away he-said.

121. 'Nanahaaumano hiqiri hiqiri baaibo tubaro buana bata kanta baai-
What-thing drip drip it-is he-said-and-he go ground place sleep.
'taane.

122. Minti baaimanta baaite baunaraqibe ti.
The-same it-was-and I-slept I-have said.

123. Minti ti'baqiro bibiro burubaro aati'tabubo aati'tabubo bira ba'kaa-
The-same as-he-said he-went brought it-dawned-and-he it-dawned-
rantabano noruquare tiro.
and-he his older-brother I-will-enlarge he-said.

124. Bibi'ti kanta baku'raraama ti.
Out-here place it-was I-say.

125. Bira baatamanora eqa mare aamura kakanairiaqra boqaara 'ibaau-
His body banana leaf new it-flattened-out like it-was I-say.
raraama ti.

126. Bira baata 'kaahairo minti'qakero.
His body all-over it-was-left-like-that.

127. Baaitobo araraa orihi'ramiro kara'kaaqa oru qantu quara aantaau
He-slept-and-he next-day he-made-a-stone-fire food went-along cut
arukero.
pigs animals he-killed.

128. Kara'kaaqa orihautu'kero a'mubaro ba'tera baai'tera hura bu'ane.
Food he-cooked-in-stone-oven he-gave-it-and-he you-put you-sleep
tomorrow go.

129. Tubo baai'tobaro qen'taqira biraqai tuqan'taakero.
He-said-and-he he-slept-and-he night-in him-only he-turned-over.

130. Tuqan'taakero bita 'uriro nai maaqaaini kero.
He-turned-him-over took he-came-up his place-to he-left.

131. Kero ekaa haka tuqantaa tanta tantama kobo bira ba'kaaba ba'kura-
He-left all things turned-over over over he-left-and-he his elder-
qaata ekaa kara'kaaqamanora tuqan'taa aqukobo uru baairo.
brother he-was-at all food turned-over he-threw-and-he came-up he-was.

132. Araraa ba'kaabanta baaitero be'barero tabobaro kia bira maaqaa
Next-day elder-brother he-slept he-came-outside he-saw-and-it not his
ba'kubo aau tenta maaqaama ururo tenta qatanti muani baau'raauka.

place it-was-and-he oh my-own place I-came-up-to my-own younger-brother-with down-to I-was.

133. (Maa) nantiake maaini uru'ro ti.

(Er) how here-to I-came said.

134. Tibakero baaitero.

After-he-said-that he-slept.

135. Bebarero tabobo ekaa kara'kaaqamanora orau'tiro bakuraraama ti.

He-came-outside he-saw-and-it all food plentifully it-was-there I-say.

136. Ho te maa neha baairarabe.

Enough I this eating I-can-stay.

137. Tibakero tibakero baai'haro neharo.

After-he-said-that after-said-that he-was-there he-ate.

138. Bi kara'kaaqara qatara ti'haro batema uru'ane tiro.

That food-about to-younger-brother he-said today come-up he-said.

139. Hurama uruane te o'rihaqukute aai kara'kaaqa qantuke unta amitare-

Tomorrow come-up I I-will-make-a-stone-oven your food cut cook

muro.

I-will-give-you.

140. Tubaro minti'ene tiro.

He-said-and-he the-same he-said.

141. Tibakero baaitero.

After-he-said-that he-slept.

142. Araraa to'aqira qata bano bebarero uriro uri uri uri uri.

Next-day in-the-morning younger-brother he-came-outside he-came-up came-up came came came came.

143. Uriro 'bibitiraqaa ba'kubaro ba'taqi biqetero.

He-came-up over-there it-was-and-he in-ground he-went-inside.

144. Ba'taqi biqetero bi kara'kaaqa amito'raqira mpaqike.

In-ground he-went-inside went food he-had-given-him-in took-away.

145. Barero a'niro ururante biro.

He-took he-came he-went-back-down he-went.

146. Naai maaqaa bare bubo qatara kara'kaaqa amitaau'narabe ti'tubo

His place took he-went-and-he to-his-younger-brother food I-have-

te naai baaka bare tu'bimuro.

given-you he-said-and-he I itself earlier took I-came-down.

147. Ho ti'bake biraqaahai bare biro.

Enough he-said-that there-from took he-went.

148. Ho biqena'ma ti.

Enough the-end I-say.

1. You listen to what I have to say about Airina and Koqaku. Airina and Koqaku cut traps [cut small sticks to use for traps]. He brought them, and Koqaku put them in. [He stuck them in the ground—the trap was made by

bending over a stick with a noose attached.] He went about all the places
where people were, putting in traps as he went. 5. He went went went went.

He went and told his younger brother ... The nuts [pandanus nuts] had
fallen off and he put traps there. He came to that place, and saw that the nuts
had fallen off, and so he took them and gave them to his younger brother and
said, 'Take these [nuts] off, and put them down!' [The nuts are in a big cluster
on a stem.] He said that and he [younger brother] took them off. 10. While
he put them down, he cracked some between his teeth and ate them. He
cracked some and ate them, and he saw that they were tasty so he ate all of
part of what was there. He cracked and ate them, and left. He only put out
part of what was there, and the elder brother came back from walking about,
and he took them [the nuts] to put them back in the same place and he left.

While he was putting them together [he put the nuts back into the original
sockets on the stem], he saw that some were not there and only some were
there and he spoke to Airina. 15. 'Where are all the nuts that are mine? You
have eaten them!' He said that and he [the younger brother] said, 'Too bad. I
ate them, they were tasty and I ate them up!' he said. After he said that, he
[the older brother] struck him with a fighting stick and hit him. He picked him
up and threw him down over the cliff. 20. He hit him and put him down and
took him and threw him down into a steep place, and he [younger brother]
went down in there.

He was there and a nettle [leaf] that had become dried fell. The wind blew
it, and it fell there on his heart and stung him, and from there he became
startled. He got up and he went along and broke off nettles. He pulled them
down and left. 25. He took them and stung himself with them, and his body
became all right, and he got up from in there and went up.

He went and while at the doorway, said to his older brother, 'Take, bring
down and give me a mat and a headrest and a cloak and a house post.' He
said, 'A rafter too, and some *kunai* [grass for thatch] too!' and he [elder
brother] took and brought them down to him. He took them and gave them to
him and he said, 'Take these things; men are here and men are there, but as
you are talking you go on where no men are; you go and stay at a place where
you are alone.'

After he said that, he ordered him off, and he [younger brother] went
down down down, and kept going. 30. As he went down, he watched and left
behind the places where people lived. He went down, down; on and on. He saw
that it was a place where people did not go; he went down there. It became
dark; it was a place where people did not go.

35. At that place he slept, and while he was there, he marked out with his
hand a place. 'I will sleep here, and tomorrow I will get up. I will build a
house,' he said. 'When I have built a house, I will be able to stay here,' he said.
'At this place I will be able to work, plant, and eat,' he said. 40. After he
said that, he went to sleep. It was dark. While he slept, he brought his leg over
a house post and hit it with his leg. He got up and saw that the house had
become built of itself, and he slept, and the next day in the morning he came
outside. He saw that food just of itself had come and it was all ready ripened.
45. All things just of themselves were there; he came outside and he saw it.

'While I eat this food I can stay here!' he said. He got up and saw that the house had become built of itself, and he slept, and the next day in the morning he came outside. He saw that food just of itself had come and it was all ready ripened. 45. All things just of themselves were there; he came outside and he saw it.

'While I eat this food I can stay here!' he said. Pigs, dogs, fowls, what; all sorts of things just of themselves were there, I say! 'While I am eating this food, while I am eating these pigs and animals, I can stay here,' he said.

While he was there he began to work. 50. He took an axe and went along and while he was chopping a tree, while he chopped the tree, two girls came up along the river trapping fish as they came. As they trapped they came up. They came up, and they saw that a chip [from the tree] which he had cut had gone down into the trap, into the net, and they took it out and brought it and left there. They looked at it and brought it with them as they came up, looking at it as they came. As they trapped fish they came on up, and kept coming. 55. They saw that he, Airina, was cutting a tree; he was cutting a tree and they came on. They waited at the base of the tree. He was on top cutting [the tree], and the two came to the base of the tree and waited, and he cut it [a branch] and it came down. The branch got jammed. He cut it through, and it came down and jammed, and it continued to do this. 60. It did this and he said [to the tree], 'I cut you and you quickly go down. You go down, and get yourself jammed! You always get jammed.' After he said that, he came down. He pushed it and freed the branches.

65. He came down and saw that the two [girls] were there and he said, 'Where have you two come up from?' After he said that, they said, 'We two have come back up along the river trapping fish, we came up. We saw that this piece of wood that you cut had gone down. It came along and we saw it and bringing it with us, we came up to where you are'; after they said that, he said, 'I am alone here and I was cutting this tree when you came up. Let's go!' he said.

70. He took them and cut food and gave it to them, and they brought it and cooked it and ate. He gave it to them, and they ate it. 'You two sleep and tomorrow go!' he said. After he said that, they slept. 'Oh no! I'm not going; my elder sister is given to a man.' 75. 'I am single,' the younger sister said, and then the older sister said about the younger sister, 'She is given to a man, I am the older sister, I am single!' The two continued talking like that and they wanted him. So the two married him. They were there married to him.

They were there and the two planted and ate food and went along. 80. They were doing that and the older brother, Koqaku, did not have a garden [garden produce] and that which he had planted was overgrown with weedy grass. It became overgrown, and he looked for something to eat, and it wasn't there; bones, just bones were there but flesh and body were not there, [just] bones were there and he was there. He saw it and said, 'Wait! I will follow after my younger brother!' So he went down after him. 'I am going and I will see him.'

85. After he said that, he went down; his elder brother went down, down and kept going on down. He passed the places where men were, and there were men along the way. He watched them he went down down down. His younger

brother went down to his village, and he came there, and then his two wives
came and saw him [elder brother]. They went and told [took talk to] the
younger brother, 'Your elder brother has come.' 90. 'He is up there!' they said;
and 'You two cut food and take it to the house, and cook it,' he said. 'While
you are cooking in the house, bring me my pig tusk, cassowary headband,
rattan waistband, all things, all things that I use for decorating myself and give
them to me!' He said this, and they said 'Yes!' and after they said it, they went
and cut the food. He took it and put it in the house and came and they gave
him [the things] and, he said, 'You give the pig call while you are there. I will
go along and when you hear the noise I make, you two give the pig call!' and
they stayed in the doorway, and he decorated himself and came up saying,
'Hmmmm,' and his two wives called him [he turned into a pig] saying, 'Here!'
95. They said it and he came saying, 'Hmmmm,' and as he said that he came,
came, and kept coming.

He came up to his elder brother. With his nose he caught him up and took
and threw him heavily to the side, I say! He came back and caught him up
and brought him and threw him heavily to the side. He took him and hit him;
he brought him back and hit him; he took him and hit him; he left his older
brother in a bad way, I say! 100. His tongue became rubbed with dust, I say!
After it got in the dust, he [elder brother] said, 'Oh no!' Then, to his younger
brother, 'Your pig is hitting me! Take it away!' he said, but the two wives only
called 'Come!' They were there and he hit him in there and put him on there.

105. Then he went back, he ran quickly, and went back and put aside his
things. He threw them aside, then he came back and went by into the house.
While there he said to his two wives, 'Go down and bring up my elder brother!
Go down and get Koqaku!' He said this, and the two went down and got him
and brought him into the house and went out. 110. They heated water and
bathed his body and put out food and gave it to him and he ate the food.

He slept, and the next day—er—that night, after he went to sleep, he
spread out a mat for him and he went to sleep again, and he [younger brother]
hung up two bamboo containers of cassowary oil. He hung them up, and he
pierced the bottoms. He pierced the bottoms. He put them down over his
older brother's heart, and it dripped. 115. It was dripping there, that cassowary
oil. He said to his younger brother, 'What is hitting me? What is dripping and
dripping on me?' He said this and he told him, 'Go away with you, sleep on
the ground. It always does that when I sleep!' so he [the elder brother] slept
again. 120. Then he said to his younger brother, 'Take it away. What is dripping
and dripping?' and he [his younger brother] said, 'Go away with you! Sleep on
the ground! It always does that when I sleep!'

They continued like this till it became dawn and his elder brother said, 'I
will enlarge,' and it [his body] was out here, I say! 125. His body was like a
new [curled up] banana leaf, the way it unfolded [enlarged], I say! His body
[as a result of the cassowary oil dripping on him, his body had gotten flat]
was left like that. He slept and the next day he [younger brother] made a stone
oven, and he went and cut food and killed pigs and animals. He cooked the
food in a stone oven and gave it to him, and said, 'Put [take] it to one side
and sleep and tomorrow go!' He said that and he [elder brother] slept and he

[the younger brother] turned him. 130. He turned him over, and he took him [while he slept] and came up with him to his own [the older brother's] place and left him there. He left and he turned over all things and left them there and his elder brother was there and he turned over all food and threw it there and came up and was there. [The younger brother 'turned over' food from his place so that it came up at his elder brother's place.] The elder brother slept and the next day he came outside and he saw that it was not his [younger brother's] place, and he said, 'Oh! I've come up to my own place—I was down there with my younger brother. How have I come up here?' he said.

After he said that he slept. 135. He came outside and saw that all kinds of food were there, I say! 'Well, I can stay here now that I have this food to eat!' He said this, and he stayed there and ate. He said to his younger brother about the food, 'Come up today,' he said. 'Come up tomorrow and I will make a stone oven and cook your food and give it to you.' 140. He said this, and he replied, 'You do that!' After he said that, he slept. The next day in the morning the younger brother came outside and came up, and up. He came up and over there where it was he went inside the ground. He went inside the ground; he went into the place where the food was he had given him [into the stone oven]. 145. He took away the food and took it back down to his own place. He took it and went and he [the elder brother] said to his younger brother, 'I have given [prepared] food for you!' and he [the younger brother] said, 'I took it earlier and I came back down!' He said that, and he took the food from there and went off with it. Enough, that's the end!

5. ESCAPE FROM SPIRITS

1. *Baainti'naaqua 'taaraqanta bo'haahanta 'nibaukama.*
   Youth two one-two wait.
2. *'Nibaukama baainti'naaqua bomano aai'habubaro.*
   Wait youth one he-sickened-and-he.
3. *Aai'habubo bo'mano 'kiama bira 'bateta oru 'tabero.*
   He-sickened-and-he one not him continually went he-saw.
4. *Aqirakeroma 'baairo aqirake ba'kuboma biba nari'era aai'habubo*
   He-forgot-him he-was forgot he-was-and-he he he-alone he-sickened
   'bariro 'qutubiro.
   he-was he-died.
5. *'Qutubi'roma 'bariro e'robaroma aqi ba'kurara ti'haroma ani'ene*
   He-died he-was afternoon-and-he just he-was he-said come he-said
   ti'roma 'tibaaintio tiro.
   my-friend he-said.
6. *Tora'kahanta na'ntaqi aan'taaura hanta bua're tiro.*
   Moonlight-two bush-in animals-for two we-go he-said.
7. *Tuba'roma 'biqehanta buare tibakero keba 'bata huru 'bata ba'reh*
   He-said-and-he come-two we-go he-said arrow and bow and took-two.
   'antama.

8. *Toraka bi'hahanta haampaaqu'maqi bi.*
    Moonlight went-two as-they-shot they-went.
9. *Baanama'noma arana 'arutoboma aqiba'kubama aha'kaqi 'aquke.*
    Spirit road-along he-shot-and-he alive-one in-grass shot.
10. *Baanamano 'naiquqana nkaqubare'roma aqibakubura aha'kaqihairoma*
    Spirit his pulled-out-and-took alive-one from-in-grass went-along
    oru bi'qana 'nkaqu 'amiro.
    those pulled-out gave-him.
11. *Ho minti'aqihanta 'bima otu 'taboboma quarama'noma ho'haaqira*
    Enough two-did-that they-went went-down they-saw-and-it pig fence-
    ni'baairo.
    in walk-it.
12. *Ho'haaqira ni'baaubaroma otu hanta bara rata'qukema quara'hanta*
    Fence-in it-was-walking-and-they went-down two took cornered pig-
    a'rintau.
    two they-killed.
13. *Aru'ketantama ba'tema.*
    Two-killed-it put-it.
14. *'Naaqunta ra'pe bare katari te'qakehanta bare 'rumpe.*
    Vine broke-off took pole two-cut took tied.
15. *Katari bara'kehanta 'rumpe 'quara ru'mpeha 'taboboma biba 'baa-*
    Pole two-took tied pig tying he-saw-and-he he spirit blood ahead
    nama'nora naare 'naane hi'qirube 'aaiqiana'hairo mpui'nero.
    it-fell-and-he nose-passage-from licked-and-ate.
16. *Mpuinoba'roma 'tabero.*
    He-licked-and-ate-it-and-he he-saw.
17. *O'o tiro 'baanamanorama titibi'tabarerama tubi'riaro baaintimano-*
    Oh he-said you-brought-me you-came-down said man-not he-said.
    aaube tiro.
18. *Ti'bake hanta bara rumpa bare otu muntu'hanta ba'tehanta.*
    He-said two took tied brought went-down brought-down-two put-two.
19. *'Ori bara 'aqukuke i'ha tu'take hanta quara 'toqe.*
    Stone took piled-up firewood lighted two pig cut.
20. *Quara to'qake hanta ba'tema.*
    Pig cut two put.
21. *Bira 'atitema namari oru ni'hara ka'qaane tiro.*
    Him told water go-along while-walking get he-said.
22. *'Baanara tu'boma baainti qorainti'mano tuba'roma 'baana qorain-*
    Spirit he-said-and-he man male he-said-and-he spirit male he water
    timano biba na'mari kaqa'reba 'biro.
    to-get he-went.
23. *Namai oru kaqareba bu'boma biba babi na'mai taqu aqireka'roma.*
    Water went-along to-get he-went-and-he he brought water bamboo

he-threw-away.

24. *'Baana baai bara'reba buba'roma biba batete kero.*
Spirit people get he-went-and-he he put left.

25. *Ori 'ira'kero baaka mpaqi aqukeroma 'hini antaiqakero nai bate-*
Stones he-made-an-oven early took-and opened one-part he-divided
'roma bira amite'roma.
himself he-put him he-gave-for-him.

26. *Bira baainti qoraintibano qi'eta ('kaamakero) 'bare'roma.*
Him man male head (?) he-took.

27. *Taai'raqi baari'rero.*
Pandanus-tree-in he-climbed.

28. *Taai'raqi baarire'romaburu taaira'qaata bata'tero orurantero tubiro.*
Pandanus-in he-climbed pandanus-upon he-put he-came-back he-
came-down.

29. *Ori kan'kaarumake 'barero.*
Stones gathered-up he-took.

30. *Ka'tai te'qake ba'rero.*
Wood cut he-took.

31. *Bi'raqai 'barero buru 'taairakanta ba'te hanta quara oru bi'raqaa*
That-only he-took brought pandanus-place put two pig went-up there-
baai'haro ne'haro baairo.
on he-was he-ate he-was.

32. *Ne'haro.*
He-ate.

33. *Ba'kuboma maa 'baana qoraintimano baana baai'baraka barero aniha*
He-was-and-he this spirit male spirit they-that-were he-took while-
'tabobo.
coming he-looked.

34. *Biba maa ori mpaqi'aquke.*
He this stones took-away.

35. *Bato'raqi quaraqai nai ami'toba.*
He-had-put-in pig-only himself he-gave.

36. *Ba'kubo ani bi'raqai barakero na'makero.*
It-was-and-he came it-only he-took he-ate.

37. *'Aaiquara taa'rararo.*
Legs-for he-trailed.

38. *Taa'rararoma niha 'tabobo 'kiaqai ba'kubo.*
He-trailed while-walking he-saw-and-he not-only he-was-and-he.

39. *'Bateni ku'raankantakero buru 'tabobo 'taaira mare 'kanta ba'kubo.*
Then he-looked-up brought he-looked-and-he pandanus leaves place
he-was.

40. *'Taaira mare 'kanta ba'kubo 'tabero.*
Pandanus leaves place he-was-and-he he-looked.

41. Aai te na'rera quara aru'taaunara taainie ba'rera buru ne baria'ro tiro.
Oh I I-will-eat pig I-have-killed where-to you-took brought eat you-are he-said.

42. Minti ti'bakero bi'raqi ne maaini baaiqe tenta 'naane baarire 'quara
Same after-he-said there-in you here wait-and-I myself first I-will-
oru bara baabi kaariraro naa'te.
climb pig go-up take bring take-and-you you-eat.

43. Ti'bakero oru 'biro oru 'taaira baau oru 'biro.
After-he-said went-up he-went went-up pandanus over went-up he-went.

44. Ori tan'tabubo raauntu'kora (buahaa'raauru) biraqai ruqutu.
He-came near he-swung-at-him (?) him-only hit.

45. 'Aqukora mi'aqira bebe tiro.
He-threw down-there-in watch-out he-said.

46. Bira 'be tiro.
Him go he-said.

47. Bira baainti ruqutu 'aqukora otu 'biribo tiro.
Him man hit he-threw go-down he-went he-said.

48. Tubaro baana baainti biti hairo mia hairo kaabu bira aa'bata ruqutu.
After-he-said ghost man there from down from club him motionless hit.

49. 'Aqukero aa'bata taiqama aqu'karo bira bara ba'tero.
He-threw motionless finish he-threw he-threw him took he-put.

50. Bomanora kaai te baari ruqu'tukaa're tiro.
Another wait I up I-will-hit he-said.

51. Mintitibakero oru biro oru 'tabobo orikatu mpaqi ba'rora.
Same-he-said went-up he-went went-up he-saw-and-he stone took-away he-took.

52. Baana bira 'paamaqira ('katu) ruqutukorara 'mati ruqutu.
Spirit him forcefully (?) he-hit-him I-say hit.

53. 'Aqukora be be be tiro (bihana) baaintima ruquturo.
He-threw watch watch watch-out he-said (?) man I-hit-him.

54. Ruqutukauro otu bi'ribo tiro.
Hit-him went-down he-went he-said.

55. Biti hairo biri hairo raauqi kaabu 'baantaara bira aa'bata ruqutu.
Over from up from as-he-swung club spear him motionless hit.

56. Aqukorara mati (e) bobano kaai te oru bua're tiro.
He-threw I-say (er) another wait I go-up I-will-go he-said.

57. Biba oritanta'bubo kaabu utubarora minti'aqi aqukorara mati.
He came-close-to club picked-up-he as-he-did-it he-threw I-say.

58. Ho 'minti'aqiro 'minti'aqiro 'minti'aqiro ruqu'tu ruqu'tu ruqu'tiro.
Enough as-he-did-it as-he-did-it as-he-did-it hit hit he-hit.

59. *'Behi aautukorara 'mati.*
    End made-he-left I-say.
60. *'Behi aautukero 'aatitare bubaro.*
    End he-made-left light it-became.
61. *Biba aqi bika nun'takaranahairo tu'bitarero.*
    He just their necks-over-from he-went-down-past.
62. *Ho bi'roma uri u'riro uru.*
    Well he-went came-up he-came-up came-up.
63. *'Taboboma naa bi'ka iqira'te.*
    He-saw-and-he that they cry.
64. *Baaubo baainti bira tarae biti'raqa qutubira bate 'tibariabo tubo.*
    They-were-and-he man him who over-in-there he-has-died today
    you-are-talking he-said.
65. *Ho mintima bi'rama 'qutubibo tubo.*
    Well the-same it-is-he he-is-dead he-said.
66. *Ho biba ti tibi'tabareroma nibaaimanta 'ninima maa taai'raqi baarire*
    Well he me he-took-me we-went-and-I went-and-went that pandanus-
    quara hanta aruke bara muntu un'take hanta bira hini raai'ramite tenta
    in I-climbed pig we-two killed took brought-down cooked two him part I-
    hini raai'rake bare buru taai'raqaa baarire.
    divided myself part I-divided took brought-up pandanus-on I-climbed.
67. *'Baana ne.*
    Spirit ate.
68. *Baaubaroma 'baana baaibarataika ti aruke na'reka iamanta ruqutu*
    I-was-and-they spirit they-that-were me kill they-will-eat they-did-
    ruqutu ruquti.
    and-I hit hit hit.
69. *'Behi 'aautukema te maa tubu'ro tiro.*
    End I-made I here I-came he-said.
70. *Minti 'tubaro ho tiro.*
    The-same he-said-and-he well he-said.
71. *Ho biba aai biribo tiro.*
    Well he you he-went he-said.
72. *Beba huru 'kaabuqai 'baqa rubakero barero aa'batai'qaabunaini buru*
    Arrow bow club-only cloak got he-took the-place-of-motionless-one
    'aauha baau aru'qiro burara'mati.
    brought belly over as-he-hit he-went-I-say.
73. *Arubo bira noba qoba maa bira ('kaaratuba) biraqihairo nora'iqoka.*
    He-hit-and-they his mother father that his (?) there-from big-fight.
74. *Ba'roraramta min'tikerou'rama.*
    They-took-I-say that-they-did.
75. *Ho biqena'mati.*
    Enough the-end-I-say.

1. Two youths went around always together. One of the youths became sick. When he got sick, the other one didn't come to see him. He forgot about him; he forgot about him and he sickened more and died. 5. He died and in the afternoon he was there and said to the one who was alive, 'Come! my friend. Let us go in the bush in the moonlight to hunt animals.' He said this and he [the other] said, 'Let's go!' [come], and they took bows and arrows and the two went. They went along in the moonlight shooting as they went.

The spirit shot along the road while the alive one shot into the grass. 10. The spirit pulled out and took his own [arrows] from the grass and also pulled out the others and gave them to the alive one. Well, the two continued like that, and they went down and saw that a pig was walking inside a fence. It was walking inside the fence, and the two went down and cornered it, and the two killed the pig. The two killed the pig and put it down. They broke off vine, and the two cut a pole and brought it and tied it up. 15. While the two took the pole and tied up the pig, he saw that the spirit licked up the blood that had come out from its nose. He licked it up and he watched him. 'Oh,' he said, 'You are a spirit that has brought me and come down! You are not a man!' he said. After he said that the two took and tied it [the pig] and they brought it down and put it there. They piled up stones [to heat] and prepared the firewood, and cut up the pig.

20. The two cut up the pig and put it down. He then told him, 'While you are walking about get some water!' He said that to the spirit, the man said that and the spirit went to get water. He went to get water and he brought it; but he threw away the bamboo for water. That spirit left and went off to get the other spirits. 25. He [alive one] fixed the stone oven and opened it before the usual time and divided it [the pig] and put some for himself and he put down some for him. The man left the head and took the rest. He climbed up a pandanus tree. When he climbed up the pandanus tree, he put it [the pig] up there then he brought them up in the pandanus and while he was up there, he ate the pig. He ate it.

While he was up there, the spirit got the other spirits and came and looked for him. He had opened the oven. 35. He had put it there, and only the part of the pig he had given him was there. He [spirit] came and ate it. Then he trailed the footprints. He trailed him but saw that he wasn't there. Then he looked up and saw that he [man] was in the pandanus. 40. He was up in the pandanus and he saw him. 'Oh, the pig that I killed to eat, where have you taken it to eat?' he said. After he said that, he said [to the other spirit], 'You wait here, and I myself will climb up and get the pig and bring it so you all can eat!' After he said that, he went up the pandanus. But when he came close he [alive one] swung and knocked him down. 45. He threw him down and said, 'Watch out! He has gone down!' he said. He knocked him over and 'He has fallen,' he said. When he said that, he knocked him down senseless. He knocked him down, and he fell senseless and he put him aside. 50. Another said, 'Wait, I'll go up and hit him.' He said that, and he went up and saw that he [alive one] had taken and brought up stones. He hit the spirit forcefully and knocked him down, I say! As he fell, he said, 'Watch out! I hit him; I hit him and he went down!'

55. This way and that way he swung the club and knocked them senseless. They fell and another said, 'Wait, I'll go up!' But when he came close, he [alive one] knocked him down with the club. He continued like that, hitting, hitting, hitting. He made an end of them all! I say! 60. He made an end of them, and at dawn he came down. He came down over their necks and left. He came on up. He saw that they [villagers] were waiting. So he said, 'Who died?' and they said, 65. 'It is he who died.' He told them, 'He took me and while walking I climbed up a pandanus, we two killed a pig and brought it. We killed a pig and brought it. We killed it, and I divided part for him and part for my own, and went up a pandanus. The spirit ate—er—I was eating when the spirit with the other spirits came to kill and eat me, and I hit them and hit them and made an end of them. After I made an end of them, I came down here.'

70. He told them all about it. They said, 'Oh, he took you and went!' They got arrows, bows, and clubs ready and took them to where the one who was motionless was, and he shot him, I say! They shot him, and his mother and father had a big feast because of it, I say! That's what they did. 75. Well, that's all, I say!

6. THE STORY OF BOY, MOTHER, AND HER DOG HUSBAND

1. *'Maaquma'noma bira 'norara tiharoma quara aru 'timiraqe un'take*
   Son his mother-to he-said pig kill you-give-me-and-I cook I-will-eat.
   'naare.

2. *Quarara haantuqahari'ribo tu.*
   Pig-for I-am-hungry said.

3. *Tuba'roma e'o.*
   He-said-and-she all-right.

4. *Tibakeroma i'haquaraane tubo iha aquke biri.*
   After-she-said-that fire-make she-said-and-he firewood carried brought.

5. *Ba'tobo ori mpaqi'ene tubo ori mpaqike biri ba'tobo.*
   He-put-and-she stones take-away she-said-and-he stones took-away brought he-put.

6. *Batobaroma biba quara aruke un'taane tubo orihaquku'tero quara un'tero.*
   He-put-and-she she pig kill cook she-said-and-he he-made-a-stone-oven pig he-cooked.

7. *Quara aru'kero.*
   Pig he-killed.

8. *Aruke'roma quara bonku unte'haroma to'qakero batero.*
   He-killed pig one he-cooked he-cut-up he-put.

9. *'Norara ara'rauta kanteba'rera buru tutu'ane tiro.*
   Mother-to intestines run-take-you bring rub he said.

10. *Tubo ara'rauta tutukero barero biri ba'tero.*
    He-said-and-she intestines she-rubbed she-took brought she-put.

11. Ba'teubaroma biba tutuke biri bate ubaroma biba minti'ma tiro.
Put-she-did-and-she she rubbed-them brought put she-did-and-she she
this he-said.

12. Are kai te maa hu'nkaauru unte nebo.
You wait I this piece-little cook eat.

13. Tubaroma a'qua ti'roma are biritaanarama.
She-said-and-he oh-no he-said you you-have-adopted-it.

14. Te naremuro ti.
I I-will-eat said.

15. Tubaroma biba biri ba'teroma ba'te.
He-said-and-she she brought she-put-it put.

16. Ubaroma are biritaa'nara te naremuro.
She-did-and-he you you-have-adopted-it I I-will eat.

17. Tubaro kia ami'rarabe tubo tuba'roma e'o.
He-said not I-can-give-you he-said-and-she said all-right.

18. Ti'bakero bira na'mai 'taqu ba'ramiro kante namai aatitaakero.
After-she-said-that him water bamboo she-took-and-gave-him run
water she-sent-him.

19. Namai aati'taaqi biharoma oru namai ka'qaane tubo oru bi.
Water sending while-going go-along water get she-said-and-he went-
along went.

20. 'Baaubo namai bebanto ubati'baqi.
He-was-and-it water underneath as-it-made-noise.

21. Bibaaubo ho biba aqiqai bibaaubo biba baaka a'ntaaura bira 'noba
It-was-going-and-he enough he just-only he-was-going-and-she she
'kero.
prematurely level his mother she-left.

22. Antaauruaqukero baaka ira aqu'kero 'tabobo i'tabubo baaka mpaqi
She-leveled-it-out prematurely put-on the-food she-saw-and-it it-
aqu'kero.
became prematurely took-away she-threw.

23. 'Maaqu qi'etabata kaauqubataqaqai amitero naiqai bara rubake bare
Son head-and forelegs-and-only she-gave-for-him she-herself-only
biro.
took put-in-bag took went.

24. Bare'bubaro bira 'maaqumano biraqiraini qumina nu'ba tabero.
She-took-and-went-and-he her son along-in-there in-vain searched he-
saw.

25. Nuba namariera aitutu'qaqiro a'niro biro anirante.
Searched water-for he-hunted-for he-came he-went he-came-back.

26. Aqirakero biro oru.
He-forgot-about-it he-went went-along.

27. *'Tabobo (maa) biba namakero 'bi.*
He-saw-and-she (er) she she-ate went.

28. *Buubo biraqaahairo oru biraqi qi'eta urubata kaauqurubata amitora.*
She-went-and-he there-on-from went-along there-in head-little-and forelegs-little-and she-had-given-for-him.

29. *Biraqaau hantaqai nero.*
Them-only two-only he-ate.

30. *Oriqai ututuqaautumake ba'tero kero.*
Stones-only he-picked-up he-put he-left.

31. *Baai'tero.*
He slept.

32. *Araraa to'aqi be'barero 'unti ri'baaubo 'unti ri'baaubo ri'baaubo*
Next-day morning he-came-outside grass-arrow he-was-doing grass-
ri'baaubo ri ri ri ke.
arrow he-was-doing doing doing do do do left.

33. *'Boru 'borumake bata'tero.*
One he-left-one he-put-them.

34. *Qen'taabubaro ani baai'tero.*
It-became-dark-and-he came he-slept.

35. *Ara'raa to'aqi bebarero qunti aqi 'baaubo 'birante nai raq'aauta*
Next-day morning-in he-came-outside grass-arrow throwing he-way-
kaaqaqai tabaauru'kaaqai.
and-it it-came-around his G-string hit testicles-hit.

36. *Qunti aqi 'baaubo aqi 'baaubo aqi 'baaubo aqi 'baaubo aqi 'baaubo*
Grass-arrow throw he-did throw he-was throw he-was throw he-was
aqi 'baaubo aqi 'baaubo aqi 'baaubo aqi 'baaubo aqi 'baaubo.
throw he-was throw he-was throw he-was throw he-was throw he-was.

37. *Ekaama qunti bubo bo'haiqa aqu'kobo bibrio nai nora naama*
All grass-arrow it-went-and-he one he-threw-and-it it-went his mother
qi'etaqaata buru.
breast nipple brought.

38. *Rahiti'kobo rahiti'kobaro min'tanaka bi bi bi bi 'biro.*
It-struck-and-he it-struck-and-he over-that-way went went went went he went.

39. *Bira maaqumano bibi'biro oru 'tabobo biba (maa) bira'qaata 'baaubo*
Her son he-went-went went-along he-saw-and-it she (er) there-on she-
oru kaaiqa tokaini baai'tero.
was-and-he went-along garden outside-edge he-slept.

40. *Kaaiqa 'tokaini oru baaita'tero.*
Garden outside-edge went-along slept.

41. *Ba'kubo bira noba niro.*
He-was-and-she his mother she-walked.

42. *Bi'hairo tubu'robaro 'rero himpubaro.*
There-from she-came-down came-to he-got-up.

43. *'Kaauruqai batatora kahairo utu'barare tiro.*
Digging-stick-only she-had-put from I-will-pick-it-up she-said.

44. *Buhi'tika tabobo biba biraqira ba'kubaro biraqai barakero.*
She-spread-it-apart she-saw-and-he he there-in he-was-and-she him-
only she-took.

45. *Bira noba bira 'maaqu kaa'bumiqakero.*
His mother her son she-hit-him-with-a-stick.

46. *Ruqutukero tuqutukero 'tabero.*
She-hit-him she-hit-him she-saw.

47. *Ba'tobo biraqihai bira qi'eriba ani bi'taberero.*
She-put-him-and-she there-in-from her co-wife came she-took-him.

48. *Bira qi'eriba ani bitabarero ani ba'tabarero 'biro.*
Her co-wife came she-took-him came she-took-him she-went.

49. *'Biroma buru baairi naabuqirama kero.*
She-went brought dog house-in she-left.

50. *Baairi qorainti oru barero bara'tero.*
Dog male went-along she-took she-took-completely.

51. *Bira 'noba bira noba baairi qorainti oru baatiqibiro.*
His mother his mother dog male went-along she-husbanded-him.

52. *Baai'haroma ani ba'tabarereme buru 'kobaroma baairi ha'mpata ba-*
She-was came she-took-him brought she-left-him-and-he dog with he-
'kubo tanto baaintimano baaibo tubo a'qau kia baaintimano baaibo.
was-and-he where man he-is he-said-and-he oh-no not man he-is.

53. *Baairi qorainti baatiqunarabe ti.*
Dog male I-have-married said.

54. *Ti'bakero baairi qorainti baatiqaata baki'haroma kara un'take batcha-*
After-she-said-that dog male married-to she-was-there food cooked
'roma baairi' erama boqa batero.
she-put dog-for some she-put.

55. *Baaintiera boqa ba'tobo biba baaintimanoqai ani.*
Child-for some she-put-and-he he child came.

56. *Baairi amitora qamaara bata nama'kero.*
Dog she-had-put-for-him sweet-potato and he-ate-up.

57. *'Nebaaubaroma biba minti'ma tiro.*
He-was-eating-and-she she this she-said.

58. *Nahenti biba aqau baairi amitaau'narabe tubo buana baaqu baairian-*
Woman she oh-no dog I-have-given-for-him she-said-and-he go damn
tabe tiro.
dog-long he-said.

59. *Baaqu baairianta kia (araara) kaaiqa bata ba'raintana qumina ni*

Damn dog-long not (?) work and he-does nothing walk he-is he-said.
baaintanabe tiro.

60. *Qumina ni baaintana kia ami'tarara.*
Nothing walk he-is not I-can-give.

61. *Te kaaiqa ba'raarirauka narerabe tiro.*
I work I-have-done I-will-eat he-said.

62. *Minti tibake'haroma biba qa'maa 'ne 'baairo.*
Same while-he-said he sweet-potato ate he-was.

63. *Nebaaubo iri'tabokiero.*
He-was-eating-and-he he-heard-and-pondered.

64. *Baaqu baairianta ami'reraube.*
Damn dog-long I-cannot-give.

65. *Tubo baairibano iri'qiro biro buru ekaa 'baairaqira baairi taintimano-*
He-said-and-he dog as-he-hear one-went brought all men's-house-in
qai bakuraqira buru.
dog many was-in-there brought.

66. *Baairi ti'bamiharo maa baainti bi'habe ti'haroma 'tirierabuarama maa*
Dog he-told-them this child that-is he-said concerning-us those damn
baaqu 'baairibe kia koqe baairibano baaube qora baairimanobe tu.
dogs not good dog no-good bad dog he-said.

67. *Tinabuma minti tiribo tubo kerama.*
About-us that he-said he-said-and-they leave-it.

68. *Baairaro qen'tirare en'taqirama bi'tabare uru'ane ti.*
You-wait-and-it it-is-dark-and-you in-the-night take-bring come-up
said.

69. *Baaiti bi'rau bi'tabare uruane ti.*
Child him-only take-bring come-up said.

70. *Tibakero baairibano ekaa buru i'ha 'quara ba'kubo baainti birau*
After-they-said dog all brought fire lit they-were-and-he child him-
bitabarero aatitaakero buane ti.
only took-brought ordered-him go said.

71. *'Baairaqira baairaqi bu'ane tubo biba uriro uru.*
Men's-house-into men's-house-in go he-said-and-he he came-up came.

72. *'Tabobo baairibano 'naaquraqaa abutana 'naaquraqaa oqubuare tubo*
He-saw-and-they dog center-pole-on middle center-pole-on I-will-sit-
baairibano beraqihairo raauraau tubaro otu unu 'barero.
down he-said-and-they dog up-there-from *raurau* they-said went-down jaws
took.

73. *Mumua hiniqihairo raauraau tubaro uru unu 'barero.*
Down-there-from other-side *raurau* they-said came-up in-jaws took.

74. *Baainti arukero arukero arukero arukero arukero arukero.*
Child killed killed killed killed killed killed.

75. *Ekaa na'maqukero.*
    All they-ate-up.
76. *Arukero na'maqukeroma kakahiru'qaima ua'raauru bi'raumanoqai*
    Killed ate-up finger-little-only a-piece it-only house post-at it-became-
    naabu kaaraini kuke'qabiro.
    hidden.
77. *Naabu kaaraini kukeqai ba'kubaroma bira noba baai'tero.*
    House post-at hidden it-was-and-she his mother she-slept.
78. *Araraa to'aqirama baairi biba otu bura.*
    Next-day morning-in dog he down he-had gone.
79. *O'tureroma ti'haroma qamaara otu bubo baaintibano hanto tubibarabe*
    She-came-to she-said sweet-potato went-down they-went-and-she child
    tuboma a'qau tiro.
    where he-went-to-and-you she-said-and-he oh-no he-said.
80. *Kiama te baaintibano bata baaka maini tu'bibabe.*
    Not I child and earlier here he-came-down.
81. *Tubo aqau kia baaintibano tu'biribo.*
    He-said-and-she oh-no not child he-came-down.
82. *Tubaroma biba 'iriro.*
    He-said-and-she she she-heard.
83. *Aqirake baki'haroma i'habibe tibakeroma bira noba i'habimuro ti.*
    She-forgot-about-it she-was-there I-pain she-said his mother I-pain
    said.
84. *Are buane.*
    You go.
85. *Baairiarabe kaai'qarabe ti'tubaro baairibano kaaiqara bubaro biba*
    To-the-dog for-work she-said-and-he dog for-garden he-went-and-she
    ori'qetero.
    she went-inside.
86. *'Baairaqira tabobaro oba umpike 'tabobaro naaremano ba'kubaro*
    Men's-house-in she-saw-and-it torch lit she-saw-and-it blood it-was-
    naare bakubaro rantero.
    and-she blood it-was-and-she she-searched.
87. *Biraqihairo baati kakahiru'qaima barero.*
    There-in-from along finger-little-only she-took.
88. *Kakahiruqai bare'roma muntu bata'tero batatero muntu.*
    Finger-little-only she-took brought-down she-put she-put brought-
    down.
89. *'Nai qi'erira ti'bamiro mintimaa baainti aru'ke.*
    Her co-wife she-told this child killed.
90. *Maa baairi ekaama na'makeiama.*
    Those dogs all they-ate.

91. *Maa bira kakahirube titubaro homa tiera iruro ti.*
    This his finger-little she-said-and-she enough you-spoke I-heard said.
92. *Batatero ani ba'kubaro e'robaro baairi baaintimano 'niniro naabuqira*
    She-put-it came she-was-there-and-it it-was-afternoon-and-he dog
ekaa oriqetabiro.
man went-about house-in all they-went-inside.
93. *'Baairaqi tu'naaraqai toqakero tuburu'bakero.*
    Men's-house-in rattan-only cut split-into-strips.
94. *Kaiotu qentiqai tin'takero.*
    Went-down door-only she-closed.
95. *Tin'takero baairi baaintibano baai'tabubo tu'naara 'utubarero.*
    She-closed dog man he-went-asleep-and-she rattan she-picked-up.
96. *Qenti ribiraabimakeroma aqu'kero.*
    Door she-roped-up throw.
97. *Bata'tero i'ha qenta'naiqana tu'taka.*
    She-put-it fire in-the-doorway she-dropped.
98. *'Tabobaro naabu tu tu tu tu tu tutakobo baairi biba biraqi kaau kaau*
    She-saw-and-it house around around around around around she-
ti'haroma.
dropped-and-they dog he there-in howl howl they-said.
99. *'(Qu'tibaaubaro) i'hamanora ta'toaqu'kobo ekaa behi aautu'bura.*
    (?) fire it-burned-up-them-and-they all they were-destroyed.
100. *Bira noba oru rabarakero bu'rama.*
    His mother went she-went-down she-went.
101. *Ho bi'rama.*
    Enough that's-it.

1. A son said to his mother, 'Kill and give me a pig so that I can cook and eat it. I am hungry for a pig,' he said. He said this and she said, 'All right!' Then she said, 'You make a fire!' and he brought firewood. 5. He put it down and she said, 'Bring some stones!' and he got stones and brought them and put them there. He put them down, and she said, 'Kill a pig and cook it!' and then he made a stone oven [pit in ground with fire to heat stones, covered with earth for oven effect] and cooked a pig. He killed a pig. He killed it and he prepared a pig and cut it up and he put it there.

He said to his mother, 'Run and take these intestines and clean them.' 10. He said this, and she cleaned the intestines and brought them back and put them down. She put them there, and she cleaned them and brought them back and put them down and said this, 'You wait! I'll cook this little piece and eat it!' She said this, but he said, 'Oh, no! You are the owner of the pig! I'll eat it!' he said. [The owner cannot eat his own pig as he is the parent of the pig.] 15. He said that and she brought it and put it down. She did this, and he said, 'You are the owner of the pig; I will eat it. I can't give you any!' he said, and then she said, 'That's all right.'

After she said that, she gave him a bamboo for water and sent him running for water. [Water is poured into the oven through a bamboo to make steam, giving the effect of a pressure cooker.] She sent him for water and said, 'Go and get water!' and he went for it. When he was there, the water went under the ground, making a noise as it went. It was going under, and he just kept going, and she quickly leveled out [the stones] and his mother left. She leveled it out, put in the food early, and saw that the food had become cooked; she took it away [the dirt] and threw it to one side. She gave her son the head and forelegs only [of the pig] and she put the rest in her net bag and left.

[Meanwhile] her son searched in vain along there for water. 25. He searched and hunted and went here and there and then he came back. He gave up and went and went back. He saw that she had eaten [the pig] and gone. She went, and he came from there and she had given him the head and forelegs [bits of them]. He ate only those two parts. 30. Then he tried eating stones, but he put them down and left. He slept.

The next day in the morning he came outside and he made a lot of arrows out of grass and kept doing that for a long time. He would make one, leave it, and put them down. It became dark and he came and slept. 35. The next day in the morning he came outside and he threw [shot] the grass arrows and they [did not go straight] came around and hit him in his privates. He continued throwing grass arrows, throwing and throwing and just continually doing that for a long long time. He threw all the grass arrows and one that he threw went along and struck his mother on the nipple of her breast. It struck her, struck her, and he followed the way that it [the grass arrow] had gone, going and going along.

Her son went and went and went, and saw that she was there; she was there and he went along and slept on the outside edge of the garden. 40. He went and slept on the outside edge. He was there and his mother came along, she came, and he got up. She said, 'I will pick it up,' namely the digging stick from where she had left it. She parted the grass and saw that he was there so she took him.

45. His mother hit her son with the stick. She hit him and hit him where she saw him.

She put him aside and then her co-wife came and took him. Her co-wife came and took him and went. She went and brought him to the dogs' house and left him there. 50. She [his mother] had gone and married a male dog. His mother, his mother had married a male dog. She came and took him and brought him and left him with the dogs and he was there, and he said, 'Where is your man [husband]?' and she said, 'Oh, no! There aren't any men. I married a male dog,' she said.

After she said that and was married to a dog, she was there, and she cooked food and put it out; she put out some for the dog. 55. She put some for her child, and her child came. He ate that sweet potato which she had put out for the dog. While he was eating it she said this. 'Oh, no!' the woman said, 'I have given this for him,' and he said, 'Go away, it is a damn fool dog!' he said. 'He doesn't do any damn work; he does nothing!' he said. 60. 'He does nothing, so I'm not giving him any; I work, so I will eat,' he said. After he said that he ate the sweet potato and was there.

While he ate [the dog] heard and thought about it. 'I'm not giving any to that fool dog,' is what the dog heard and this one went and told all the dogs in the men's [dogs'] house. The dog said to them, 'That child that is here said that we were damn fool dogs; not good dogs, but that we are bad dogs is what he said about us.'

After he said that they said, 'Wait until it is dark and then bring him up here with you. Just bring the child and come up here,' they said. 70. After they said it, the dogs were at the fire and he [the other dog] brought the child, and he ordered him to go in. 'Go in to the men's house,' he said, and he [the boy] came up. He saw that the dogs were at the house center pole, and he said, 'I will sit down there,' and all the dogs from up there growled and took him in their jaws. The dogs from down on the other side growled and took him in their jaws. They killed him, killed, killed, killed him! 75. They ate him all up. They killed and ate him, and a piece of his finger only became hiddedn by the wall posts.

It became hidden and his mother was asleep. The next day in the morning the dogs came down. She came and she said, when they came for sweet potato, 'Where has my child gone down to?' But he [dog] said, 'Oh, no. The child didn't come down here earlier.' He said, 'Oh, no, the child hasn't come down.' He said this, and she didn't ask further, but she told the dog, 'I am sick,' his mother said, 'I am sick. You go!' 85. She said it to the dog so he went to the garden and she went inside. She looked in the men's house; she lit a torch [of wild cane] and saw that there was blood there; she searched about. From along in there she picked up the piece of finger. She took it and brought it down and put it down. She told her co-wife this. 'They have killed the child.' 90. 'Those dogs have eaten him all up. This is a piece of his finger!' she said and she [co-wife] heard what she said.

She put it down and waited and in the afternoon her dog husband came and all [the dogs] went inside. In the men's house, she cut rattan and split it into strips. She went down and closed the door. 95. She closed it and the dogs had gone asleep, and she picked up the rattan. She roped up the door.

Then she dropped fire in the doorway. She dropped it all around the house and the dogs cried out howling from inside. The fire burnt them up and destroyed them all. 100. Then his mother went, she went on down. That's it!

7. ERENDORA WOMAN

1.   *Nahenti.*
      Woman.
2.   *'Bonkuma'nora minta'haka batoba'roma eka 'haka 'eka 'haka 'eka*
      One those-things she-put-and-he all things all things all things all
'haka eka haka bara'keroma bate'roma.
things she-took-away she-put.
3.   *Kaiq'ara 'biro.*
      To-work she-went.

4.　*Kaiqara buba'roma bi'raqira ba'kuba'roma to'nabu'mano utu'taro.*
　　To-work she-went-and-it in-there they-were-and-it cloud it-settled.

5.　*'Naabu bira ututoba'roma baainti 'bonkuma'nora butu aaitu'tikeroma.*
　　House it it-settled-and-he man one along he-watched.

6.　*'Nanahaka ba'tairaqi'e.*
　　What-things have-been-put-it.

7.　*Butu'raqaa mi'ntiro 'baaibo.*
　　Along-there it-is-like-that it-is.

8.　*'Kairaqe te bi oru 'tabaare tiro.*
　　You-wait-and-I I go go-along I'll-see he-said.

9.　*Ti'bakeroma 'biro oru 'tabobaro na'hentiba'nora 'eka haka 'naabuqi*
　　He-said-that he-went go-along he-saw-and-she woman all things in-
　　bi'raqi ba'toboma 'eka haka minta 'haka 'okaaube (i) oq'okabe 'taqube
　　house in-there she-put-and-he all things those things whiskers (uh) jews'-
　　aanu'maarabe eka 'haka bata'tora.
　　harps bamboo flutes all things she-had-put.

10.　*Biraqi ba'tora biba oriqe'tero.*
　　There-in she-had-put he he-went-inside.

11.　*Eka 'hakama 'barero.*
　　All things he-took.

12.　*A'niro eka 'haka bare'roma 'biri.*
　　He-came all things he-took-and brought.

13.　*Ani'baauboma na'henti biba 'tabobo kia bi'raqi to'nabu rupe'mabubaro*
　　He-was-coming-and-she woman she she-saw-it not there-in cloud it-
　　'tabobo kia bi'raqi bata to'nabu ru'pebubo.
　　became-dispersed-and-she she-saw-and-it not in-there and cloud disperse.

14.　*Ai te batauna'hakarama 'bareroma 'bibibo tiro.*
　　Oh I I-have-put-things he-took he-went she-said.

15.　*A'niro a'ni tabobo kia ba'kubaro 'naabu bi'raqi uqaa'taakero.*
　　She-came came she-saw-and-it not it-was-there-and-she house there-in
　　she-moved.

16.　*Ran'tobo kia ba'kubo bi'raqi 'hairoma taa'raramaqi taa'rara'maqi*
　　She-searched-and-it not it-was-there-and-she there-in from she-trailed
　　taa'rara'maqi a'niro ani
　　she-trailed she-trailed she-came came.

17.　*Taboboma ho 'barero ani raabara'kero.*
　　She-saw-and-he enough he-took came he-came-down.

18.　*A'nubo bira 'aaiqu an'taka ani ani ani.*
　　He-came-and-she his tracks searched-for came came came.

19.　*A'niro ho 'tabobo eran'tona no'rantaqaata baari'rero.*
　　She-came enough she-saw-and-he Erendora upon-the- peak he-climbed.

20.　*Baarirero minta'naqaa ba'kubaro na'henti biba 'aahaaqiro kan'tero.*
　　He-climbed there-on he-was-and-she woman she panting she-ran.

21. Eran'tonaini aai'haini oru 'bubo biba bi'raqaa hairoma otura'bara
To Erendora steep went-up she-went-and-he he there-on from came-
ori bi'raqi tu'tubiro.
down-to rock there-in he-went-down.

22. Ori bi'raqi tu'tubiroma.
Rock there-in he-went-down.

23. Hini 'biniro aanu'maara buaqa'kobo biba mini oru 'kaauru utuba'rero.
One-side he-went-to flute he-blew-and-she she there went-along dig-
ging-stick she-picked-up.

24. Ori mpehim'paahima tabobo biba 'kiaqai orimano 'irubo eqa biba
Rock struck she-saw-and-it it not-only stone it-heard-and-he again he
beta 'boraka oru'rero.
along another-place he-came-to.

25. Bi'raka buru aanu'maara u'nequ'nera uba tubaro biba bi'raka oru-
At-there brought flute Unequne noise he-said-and-she she there-at
'rero.
she-came-to.

26. 'Buru umi'na kanta mpehim'paahi ori 'tabobo ori'mano kempu'kai-
Brought empty place struck rock she-saw-and-it rock it-was-strong-
qubaro aqira'kero
and-she forgot-about-it.

27. Ori'rantero biri hini anirero.
Came-back brought other-side came-to.

28. 'Bubo biba aanu'maara bu'aqakobo biba eqa mini 'kaauru utuba'rero.
She-went-and-he he flute he-blew-and-she she again there digging-
stick she-picked-up.

29. Mpehim'paahubo 'kiaqai oribano 'irubo 'aqirakero.
She-struck-and-it not-only rock it-heard-and-she forgot-about-it.

30. Eqa aniran'tero beta hini 'orurobo ho minti'baaubo min'kuna ba'riro.
Again she-came-back along other-side came-to-and-they enough were-
doing-that-and at-there were.

31. Enta'mabubo 'aqirakero.
It-became-dark-and-she forgot-about-it.

32. Popoha'mabubo oru'rantero 'aaitarero nai 'maaqaa bu'rama.
She-became-tired she-came-back she-passed-by her place she-went.

33. Ho biqenama ti.
Enough that's-the-end I-say.

1. There was a certain woman. This one took all sorts of things and put them aside; she took and put many many things in there. She went to work. She went to work and the things were in there [in the house] and a cloud settled there. 5. It settled on the house and a man saw it. 'What has been put in there? Over there it is like that. Wait! I'll go and see,' he said.

When he had said that, he went and saw that the woman had put all things in there in the house; she had put in all those things, whiskers, jews-harps, bamboo, flutes, all those things. 10. She had put everything in there, and he went inside. He took everything. He came, and he took and brought everything away. While he was coming, the woman concluded that it was not in there; the cloud had dispersed, and she realized the things were gone because the cloud dispersed. 'Oh,' she sighed, 'somebody has taken the things I put and has gone.'

15. She came and came, and saw that the things weren't in the house, and she moved things aside. She searched, but they were not there, so from there she trailed him and trailed and trailed him and saw and he came. She saw him, and he had gone down with the things. She followed him and saw that his tracks had gone down, so she came and came. She came and then saw that he had climbed up on the peak of Mount Erendora.

20. He had climbed up and was up there and the woman ran panting. She went up the steep side to Erendora, and as she went he went down into a rock; he went down inside there, right down in there. He went from side to side in the rock blowing on a flute, and she picked up a digging stick. She tried to pry away the rock but she saw that it didn't move, and he went to another place [in the rock]. 25. There he brought it and Unequne made a noise on the flute, and the woman came over to that place.

He brought it and at that empty place she pried at the rock, but she saw that the rock was firm. So she gave up there. She came back to the other side. She went there, and he blew on the flute, and she again picked up the digging stick. She pried but the rock didn't move (hear) and she gave up. 30. Again she came back to the other side, and she continued like this and they were there. It became dark and she gave up. She became tired and came back and passed by and went to her own place. That's the end of what I have to say.

8. THE AXE IN THE WATER

1. *Baainti 'bonkuma'noma i'haqai rubari'baaiba.*
   Man one firewood one-who-splits.

2. *I'haqai rubari'baaibama 'taauni 'kanta 'taauni kanta baai'haroma.*
   Firewood one-who-splits town place town place he-lived.

3. *I'haqai rubari'baaibama na'mai 'aanta'raini otu.*
   Firewood one-who-splits river bank-to went-down.

4. *Baai'haroma i'ha rubari 'baairo.*
   He-was-there firewood split he-was.

5. *I'ha rubari'haroma 'rori 'muntu tuta'kobo na'maiqira tu'tubiro.*
   Firewood while-he-was-splitting axe brought-down he-dropped-and-it water-into it-went-down.

6. *Na'mai tu'tubibo mpo ti'ro kia 'monu ba'ta monu bata bakimantama*
   Water it-went-down-and-he oh he-said not money and money and it-
   i'naara 'monu nohaai barataau'nara.
   is-there-and-I little money with I-have-taken.

7. *Rorira na'maiqira tu'takero.*
Axe water-into he-dropped-it.
8. *'Nantiakeaau 'bararabe ti'ro.*
How I-can-get he-said.
9. *I'qiratero.*
He-cried.
10. *I'qiratebaau'boma na'henti bi'raqihairo na'maiqiba'ku na'henti bauru-*
He-was-crying-and-she woman there-in-from water-in-was woman
'reroma.
she-came-up.
11. *'Nanare are i'qirate baria'ro tu'boma 'rori 'maaqi tu'takaauro na-*
What-for you cry you-are she-said-and-he axe there-in I-dropped-and-
'maiqi tu'tubimanta i'qirate ba'ruro.
it water-in it-fell-and-I cry I-am.
12. *Kia 'monu nora 'monu batau'raaukabe inaara 'monu nohai rori paaimi-*
Not money big money I-put little money with axe buy-I-have he-said.
'qaataaunarabe ti'ro.
13. *Tuba'roma bi'ba ti'haroma 'are 'baaiqe 'te oti'qete na'maiqihai bara*
He-said-and-she she she-said you wait-and-I I I-go-down-in water-
buru ami'are ti'ro.
in-from get bring I-will-give-you she-said.
14. *Ti'bakero oti'qete'roma koru baku'monura (aa) 'rorira koru baku'ra.*
After-she-said-that she-went-down-in gold it-was-money (er) axe gold
it-was.
15. *'Rorira bara 'buru ami.*
Axe took brought gave.
16. *Umiq'oboma a'qau ti'ro.*
She-showed-him-and-he oh-no he-said.
17. *Ti 'rori 'aaini 'aqu ba'taarabe ti'ro.*
My axe iron handle it-has he-said.
18. *'Aaini'be ti'ro.*
It-is-iron he-said.
19. *'Aaini 'roribe ti'ro.*
Iron axe-it-is he-said.
20. *Aaini rori'mibo ti'tubo eqa o'turabara tu'tubiro otu kukuqe'tabiro.*
Iron axe-it-is he-said-and-she again down-came-to she-went-down down
she-became-hidden.
21. *Monu baku 'rorira bara buru 'amubo a'qau ti'ro.*
Silver it-was axe took brought-she gave-him-and-he oh-no he-said.
22. *Terenara 'rori otu ran'take buru timi'ene.*
My axe down you-search bring give-me.
23. *'Aaini ba'kiramibo 'aaini 'aqu ba'taara.*
Iron it-is iron handle it-has.

24. *'Aaini 'roribe ti'tubaro biba eqaa 'monu ba'kura 'rori 'bara 'buru*
   Iron axe he-said-and-she she again silver it-was axe took brought
a'mubo bara buru a'mubo ti'haroma minti'matiro o tent(a)ina 'aqu ba-
she-gave-him-and-he took brought she-gave-him-and-he he-said this-he-
'taararama 'aaini ba'taara 'rorierama 'turo.
said oh mine handle it-has iron it-has axe-about I-said.

25. *Tubo oturabara e'qa bi'raqira kukuqe'tabiro otu 'aaini ba'kura 'rorira*
   He-said-and-she down-came-to again there-in she-became-hidden
'bara uru'robo e bi'rama ti 'rorimibo ti'ro.
down iron it-was axe took she-came-up-and-he yes it-is my axe he-said.

26. *Ti'bakeroma rori bi'ra ami'roma kori ba'kura.*
   After-he-said-that axe it she-gave-him gold it-was.

27. *'Rorira ba'tero monu ba'kura rorira ba'te 'kero.*
   Axe she-put silver it-was axe she-put left.

28. *'Amiro are u'qaama tiria'ro tiro.*
   She-gave-him you true you-spoke she-said.

29. *Are u'qaama rori'era a'ro.*
   You true axe-about you-spoke.

30. *Tiba'keroma bira monu 'amiro monue 'rori u'qaama tiera'bera 'amuro*
   After-she-said him silver she-gave-him silver axe true because-you-
tiro.
spoke-I I-gave-you she-said.

31. *Tiba'kero a'mubo 'bareroma oru 'biro buru nai 'naabuqi ba'tero.*
   After-she-said she-gave-him he-took went-along he-went brought his-
own house-in he-put.

32. *Buru bato'boma bira ta'taaqa bira baainti 'bonkumano naabu kaa-*
   Brought he-put-and-he his next-to his man one house he-had-built he-
'qoba bira ori'qete 'taboboma bira rori ba'toba 'tabema.
came-inside he-saw-and-it his axe it-had-put-and-he he-saw.

33. *'Taaihaira maa monu 'aqu ba'kira bata 'kori ba'kirama rorira bata*
   Where-from these silver handle it-has and gold it-is axe and where-
'taaihaira barara'be ti'ro.
from you-get he-said.

34. *Tuba'roma bi'ba ti'haroma o na'maiqi otu iha rubaribaauraro 'rori*
   He-said-and-he he he-said oh water-in went-down wood I-was-split-
otura na'maiqira tutubimanta iqira'te.
ting-and-it axe down-to water-into it-fell-down-and-I I-cry.

35. *Baaura na'maiqi hairo na'henti'mano bara baairi timi'ramibo tiro.*
   I-was-and-she water-in from woman took up she-gave-me he-said.

36. *Bara buru 'timirabe.*
   Took brought-up she-gave-me.

37. *Tubo ikai tentara bata otu minti'ake ba'raare tiro.*
   He-said-and-he wait I-alone too go-down the-same I-will-get he-said.

38. *Tiba'kero nai 'roriha ba'rero muntu.*
    After-he-said his axe he-took brought-down.
39. *Iha rubariare tiro.*
    Wood I-will-split he-said.
40. *Muntu na'maiqira aqu'kero.*
    Brought-down water-into he-threw.
41. *Na'maiqi aqu'kaibo nahentimano bi'hairo uru'rero 'nanare iqirate*
    Water-in he-threw and-she woman there-from came-up-to what-for
    baria'ro tiro.
    crying you-are she-said.
42. *Tuboma 'rori maaqi muntu 'aqukemuro.*
    She-said-and-he axe there-in brought-down I-threw.
43. *Tu'boma otu biba 'kori bakura rorira bara buru 'amubo.*
    He-said-and-she down she gold it-was axe took brought-up she-gave-
    him.
44. *E bi'rama ti'rori'mibo tiro.*
    Yes it-is my-axe he-said.
45. *Tiba'kero butura utubarobaro biba ti'haro aq unahaa'ma tiria'ro tiro.*
    After-he-said over-there she-took-and-she she she-said ah lie you-say
    she-said.
46. *Kia aai 'roriaaube tiro.*
    Not your axe-not she-said.
47. *Aqira'kera bu'ane tiro.*
    You-forget-it go she-said.
48. *Kia bate ba'renarabe tiro.*
    Not today you-can-take she-said.
49. *Minitiba'kobo aqira'kero ururabarakero uru'rama.*
    After-she-said-that-he he-forgot-about-it he-came-back-up he-came-up.
50. *Ho bi'qenama.*
    Enough the-end.

1. There was a man who was splitting firewood. The one who split firewood lived in a town, there in a town. Now the one who split firewood went down to the bank of a river. He was there splitting wood.

5. While he was splitting wood he dropped his axe and it feel down into the water. As it went into it, he said, 'Oh! I haven't got any money and the money is there and with my little money I bought my axe.' He dropped the axe into the water. 'How can I possibly get it back?' he said. He cried.

10. He was there crying and a woman who lived in there, a woman who lived in the water came up. 'What are you crying for?' she said, and he said, 'I dropped my axe and it fell into the water so I am crying. I haven't money—a lot of money, and with my little money I bought my axe,' he said.

After he said that, she said, 'You wait and I'll go down into the water and get it and bring it and give it to you.' After she said that, she went down in [the water] and brought a gold, silver—er axe—a gold axe. 15. She brought the axe and gave it to him. She showed it to him, and he said, 'Oh no! My axe is iron with a handle. It's iron,' he said. 'It is an iron axe,' he said. 20. 'It is an iron axe,' he said, so she again went down [into the water] and became hidden. Then she took a silver axe and brought it up and gave it to him, but he said, 'Oh, it's not the one. You go down and find my axe and bring it up and give it to me. It is an iron axe; it has an iron handle. It is an iron axe,' he said and she again brought a silver one, she took a silver one and gave it to him, she took it to him and he said, 'Oh, mine has a handle; I'm talking about an iron axe.'

25. After he said that, she again went down out of sight into there [the water] and she came back up with an iron axe, and he said, 'Yes, that's it, that's my axe.' After he said that, she gave him the axe and she put down the gold one. She put down the silver one, too, and left. She gave them to him. 'You spoke truthfully,' she said, 'You spoke truthfully about the axes.' 30. After she said that she gave him the silver one—the silver axe—'Because you spoke truthfully, I gave them to you,' she said.

After she said that, she gave them to him and he took them and brought them and put them in his house. He brought them and put them there, and the man who had built a house next to him [his neighbor] came inside and saw that the axes were there. 'Where did you get the silver axe and the gold axe, where did you get them from?' he said. After he said that, he [the wood chopper] said, 'Oh, I was splitting wood down by the river and my axe fell into the water so I was crying.' 35. 'I was doing that, and a woman from in the river took them up and gave them to me,' he said. 'She took them and brought them and gave them to me.'

After he said that, he [the neighbor] said, 'Wait! I'll go alone and do that and get them,' he said. After he said that, he took his axe down. 'I will split wood,' he said. 40. He took it [axe] down and threw it into the water. After he threw it into the water, the woman from there came up and said, 'What are you crying for?' He said, 'I brought my axe down and threw it in there [water].' After he said that, she went down and took a gold axe and gave it to him. 'Yes, that's it; that's my axe,' he said. 45. After he said that, he took it but she said. 'Forget it and go!' she said. 'You can't have it,' she said. After she said that, he gave up on it and went back. 50. That's the end.

9. KONKO AND MANABO

1.   *'Konkoka, 'konkoka manaa'boka.*
    Konko-and, Konko-and Manabo-and.

2.   *'Konkobama bariharo 'butura konkoraini bariha 'tabaabaauboma*
    Konko he-was along-there at-Konkora he-was he-was-looking-and-
manaa'bobama (maa) 'taruraini biraqaa iha quarate'haro.
he Manabo (er) at-Tarura there-on fire he-lit.

3.   *I'ha quaratero taru'ara 'oba qumpike'haro oba qumpikeharo tabeba-*
    Fire he-lit for-fleas torch he-kept-alight torch he-kept-alight he-was-

'rubaro 'konkoba 'bariha buabu aaituti'baauboma manaa'boba i'ha qumpike-
looking-for-and-he Konko while-there over-there he-was-watching-and-he
'haro taru ari'barubaro aaitutuma tabe aaitutuma taba aaitutumake.
Manabo fire he-kept-alight flea he-was-hitting-and-he he-watched saw he-
watched saw he-watched.

4.   *'Nanahakarabe iha qumpibarubo tiro.*
     What-things fire he-is-lighting he-said.

5.   *Konkoba bariha 'aaitutuma tabero 'aaitutuma 'tabero.*
     Konko while-there watching he-saw watching he-saw.

6.   *Manaa'boba manaa'boba i'ha qua'rebaaubo i'ha qua'rebaaubo aaitutu-*
     Manabo Manabo fire he-was-lighting-and-he fire he-was-lighting-and-
'ma 'tabero.
he watching he-saw.

7.   *'Nanahaie oba qumpi bari'bo tiro.*
     What-things torch lighting he-is he-said.

8.   *Oba qumpike'haro 'tabebaaubo biba tarubanora baatan'taka ora*
     Torch he-kept-alight he-was-looking-and-he it flea body-long-around
aautibaaubo.
bad it-was-making.

9.   *'Kaakiantaka abuan'taka ibaaubo aaitutuma.*
     Hair-long-around eye-long-around it-was-and-he watching.

10. *'Tabero.*
     He-saw.

11. *Konkoba tu'biro muntu.*
     Konko he-came-down brought-down.

12. *Biraqaata Konkoba buru'raqaata bari'haro*
     There-upon Konko-actor up-there-upon he-was-there.

13. *Bari'haro kaau aau'tukero.*
     He-was-there trade-items he-prepared.

14. *Kaau 'aautukero barero tu'biro.*
     Trade-items he-prepared he-took he-came-down.

15. *Muntu biraqaa bata'tobo quara rabaa'kukero.*
     Brought-down there-on he-put-and-he pig carried-in-arms.

16. *Biti a'mubaro biba Konkoba aaiqiqai tua'herate baaubaro baairi*
     Along he-gave-and-he he Konko nose-only up-high he-was-and-he
rabukukero biti a'mubaro aaiqiqai tua'herate 'baaubaro ori'qetero.
dog carried-in-arms along he-gave-and-he nose-only up-high he-was-and-
he he-went-inside.

17. *Kaau pu'kaari barero muntu.*
     Cowrie-shells he-took brought down.

18. *A'mubaro aaiqiqai tuaherate baaubo minti'ma tabe.*
     He-gave-and-he nose-only up-high he-was-and-he the-same saw.

19. *Minti'ma tabo'kiero.*
The-same he-wondered.

20. *Taru ra'baaqabu'kero.*
Flea he-seized.

21. *Taru ra'baaqabukero.*
Flea he-seized.

22. *Bia'bi biraqaa bata'tero.*
Downward there-on he-did-put.

23. *'Konkoba maara bi'rarama 'tuburo.*
Konko that it-for I-came-down.

24. *Tubaro oba 'qumpikero.*
He-said-and-he torch he-lit.

25. *U'quaatamakero 'konko'maqi'raini bata u'qaatamake.*
He-moved-it-aside in-the-dust ground moved-aside.

26. *'Aribarubaro 'aribarubaro taruara oba qumpiqibi biharo ari ari ari.*
He-was-hitting he-was-hitting for-fleas torch as-he-lit he-went hit hit
hit.

27. *A'rikero taqu mpiqabubo barero.*
He-left-hit bamboo it-became-full he-took.

28. *Konkoraau'tainibe tiro.*
The-place-is-Konko he-said.

29. *Butura bo'raauba barira.*
Over-there Borau he-is.

30. *Bo'raauba barira.*
Borau he-is.

31. *Bi'taari bira'qaarama kon'korautainibe tiro.*
Over-there-place there-upon the-place-is-Konko he-said.

32. *Manaaboba maarira'qaata bariro.*
Manabo over-up-there he-was.

33. *Bari'haro biba oba qumpi.*
While-he-was-there he torch lit.

34. *'Baaubaro aaitu'tikero*
He-was-and-he he-watched.

35. *Biba tu'biro muntu 'amubo quara rabuku.*
He he-came-down brought-down he-gave-him-and-he pig carried.

36. *'Amubo aaiqiqai tuaherate baaubo baairi rabuke.*
He-gave-him-and-he nose-only up-high he-was-and-he dog carried.

37. *'Amubo aaiqi tuahe baaubo na'henti a'mubaro aaiqi tua'herake 'baau-*
He-gave-him-and-he nose up-high he-was-and-he woman he-gave-
baro taru rabaaqubu.
and-he nose up-high he-was-and-he flea seized.

38. *A'mubo te bi'rara tubu'raukamuro.*
He-gave-and-he I it-for I-came-down.

39. *Tibakero mi'ntubo taru rabaaqabira.*
    After-he-said he-did-that-and-he flea he-seized.
40. *Rabaaqa'bikero 'taquqira un'tamubo bara buru kero.*
    He-made-seized bamboo-in put-in-and-gave-and-he took brought he-left.
41. *Buru 'kerama 'taari buqikerama koqe'make bata'te'rama bi'raqaama*
    Brought you-leave mat you-spread-out good-leave you-put it-upon
    taru qa'hia'raane tiro.
    flea you-tip-out he-said.
42. *Minti tubaro eo.*
    Same he-said-and-he OK.
43. *Ti'bakero barero oru 'biro buru.*
    After-he-said he-took went-along he-went brought.
44. *Biraqaata kero.*
    There-upon he-left.
45. *Taari buqike ba'tero taru 'qahia'kobo tarubano baatan'taka abuan-*
    Mat spread-out he-put flea he-tipped-out-and-it flea body-long-around
    'taka hairo kaakiruka hairo tiro.
    eye-long-around from hair-little-around from he-said.
46. *Ikai taruba'noma hari baaibo tiro.*
    Oh flea me-bit it-is he-said.
47. *'Be 'taba bi'rarama koqa autuanarami'ribo.*
    Now see it-for trade-goods you-have-made.
48. *A're bata bira qumpihara 'tabaane tiro.*
    You too it while-lighting you-look he-said.
49. *Minti ti'raama.*
    That he-did-say.
50. *Boraauba burura konkoraau'taini bari.*
    Borau up-along at-Konkora is.
51. *Bariboma (maare) manaabora biraqaata mintiakerora.*
    He-was-and-he (?) Manabo there-upon he-had-done-that.
52. *Manaaboka Konkoka.*
    Manabo-and Konko-and.

1. There were these two, Konko and Manabo. Konko lived along over there at Konkora, and he kept watching, and Manabo there at Tarura [Tarura = the flea place] kept lighting fires. He lit a fire, keeping a torch alight for fleas, he kept a torch alight as he was looking for fleas and Konko watched from across there and there was Manabo keeping a fire alight, killing fleas, and he watched and watched and watched. 'What is he looking for with the fire?' he said. 5. Konko continued to look, watching and watching from over there.

Manabo had a fire alight and he watched him. 'What is he looking for with the torch?' he said. He [Manabo] kept the torch alight and saw that the fleas were all over his body making it bad. They were in his hair and his eyes and he [Konko] watched. 10. Konko came on down. Konko was then there. When he got there, he prepared items to trade. He prepared the items for trade and took them and came down. 15. He brought them down and put them there, carrying a pig in his arms. He offered it to him for trade, but Konko only held up his nose, then he [Manabo] carried a dog along and offered it to him but he [Konko] only held up his nose; then he [Manabo] went inside. He got cowrie shells and brought them down. He offered them to him but he only help up his nose; he did the same thing. He did that, and he wondered about it. 20. He seized a flea. He seized a flea. He put it down on the ground. Konko said, 'That's what I've come down for.' After he said that, he [Manabo] lit a torch. 25. He moved things aside, he moved the dust about. He hit and hit them, lit a torch for the fleas, and kept hitting, and hitting. He kept hitting them until he filled up a bamboo and he [Konko] took it. 'The place where it happened is Konkora,' he said.

It was over where Borau lives. 30. Borau lives over there. Yes, Borau lives there. 'That place near there that is what is called Konkora,' he said. Manabo lived over there. While he was over there, he lit a torch. He [Konko] watched him. 35. Then he came down and brought it [trade goods] and offered it to him and he [Konko] held up his nose, so he carried a dog to him. He offered it to him, but he [Konko] held up his nose, and then he offered him a woman, but he held up his nose, and then he seized a flea. He offered it to him, and he [Konko] said, 'That's what I came down for!' After he said that he [Manabo] seized fleas. 40. He seized fleas and put them in a bamboo and he [Konko] took them and left.

He [Manabo] said, 'Take these and spread out a mat carefully and on it tip out the fleas!' After he said that, he [Konko] said, 'Okay!' After he said that, he took them and brought them up there [to his place]. He left there. 45. He then spread out a mat and tipped out the fleas, and the fleas went all over his body, his eyes, and his hair. 'Aeee," he said, 'Oh! the fleas are biting me!' he said. 'Now see! That's what you gave trade goods for! You, too, can light it. [a torch] and look for them!' he [Manabo] said. That's what he said. 50. Borau lives up there at Konkora. He was there when Manabo did that. Manabo and Konko!

10. THE GIRL AND THE BANANAS

1.   Ba'raata 'baaintima; ba'raata baaintima bumi'qaate aqa ru'baaqama-
     Girl child; girl child gathered-together no gathered-together gathered-
tero rubaaqamatoba'roma 'kaaiqa ba're baairo.
together-and-she work did they-did.

2.   'Kaaiqa ba're baauboma baainti bonku'mano baainti bonkuma'nora . . .
     Work did they-were-and-she person one person one . . .

3.   Ba'raata baainti 'ekaa ru'baaqamatero kaaiqa ba're baauboma bare-
     Girl person all gathered-together work did they-were-and-she while-

'*haroma ba'raata bonkuma'nora burubi 'taboboma baainti ba'kaabata*
she-worked girl one went-along she-saw-and-he man elder-brother younger-
qataba'nobata qatamano bura nan'taqira naabu ka'qake'roma naabu ka-
brother younger-brother up-there bush-in house he-built house he-built.
'*qake'roma.*

4. *Na'ntaqi naabu ka'qakero koboma 'baairo 'baaubaroma biba baaiha*
   Bush-in house he built he-did he-was he-was-and-she she while-there
'*tabobo tonabu'banora 'naabu utu'tora naabu utu'toboma.*
she-saw-and-it cloud house it-had-settled house it-had-settled-and-she.

5. *Buraqi nanahaka batate'roe nanahaka batate'roe buraqi kaiba'roe*
   Over-there-in what-thing he-did-put what-thing he-did-put over-there-
to'nabu ututaibo.
in it-was-put cloud it-settled.

6. *Kai te oru bi oru tabaare tiro.*
   Wait I go-along go go-along I-will-see she-said.

7. *Ba'raata baainti ne maaqa 'baaiha kaaiqa ba're baaiqebe tiro.*
   Girl person you-all at-here wait work did you-are-and-I she-said.

8. *Tibakeroma bi ba'raata oru biro oru 'taboboma baaintimano bi'raqi*
   She-said that girl went-along she-went went-along she-saw-and-he
ba'kiro.
man there-in he-was.

9. *Ba'kubaroma qentana oru o'qubi baai'haroma 'qentana oru baai-*
   He-was-and-she doorway went-along sat while-she-was doorway went-
'*haroma bebarairaqe qieta tutua're tiro.*
along while-she-was you-come-outside-and-I hair I-will-twist she-said.

10. *Qi'eta tutuare tuboma biba tiharo a'qau ba'kaarara kia bebara aira*
    Hair I-will-twist she-said-and-he he he-said oh-no elder-brother not
i'ene.
outside come you-do.

11. *Naabuqi bari'ene minti tiba'tero bi'berama kia te bata be'bararabe*
    House-in stay the-same he-said-for-me he-went-and-I not I too I-can-
te naabu'qima baai'rerabe tiro.
go-outside I house-in I-will-stay he-said.

12. *Tuba'roma a'qau tiro beba'rairaqe qi'eta tu'tirerama 'turo tiro.*
    He-said-and-she oh-no she-said you-come-outside-and-I hair I-will-
twist I-said she-said.

13. *Tuboma a'qau tiro kiama te otu birarabe tiro.*
    She-said-and-he oh-no he-said not I go-down I-can-go he-said.

14. *Kia te bata otu birarabe te maaqima 'baairabe tiro.*
    Not I too go-down I-can-go I here-in I-can-stay he-said.

15. *Tubaro kiaqai i'rubaro ba'raata biba ori'qetero.*
    He-said-and-she not-only he-didn't-heed-and-she girl she she-went-
inside.

16. Ori'qetero bu'kera 'baqa bira 'utuba'rora aa'qi aaun'takara rabaaqa-
    She-went-inside cassowary thigh-bone it she-had-picked-up just neck-
bumun'tu (bike'roma) homa babi ka(kero) ariro.
pipe seized-brought-down (?) well down left she-hit.

17. Baabi'kero bira 'qaima aunta'kara 'behi 'aqukaro qutu'ma biraqi
    Down-she-left him only neck-pipe end she-threw ceased there-in he-
biro qutu.
went ceased.

18. Bubo ba'raata biba tubitarero 'aiquma aautotero.
    He-went-and-she girl she she-went-down-by legs she-made.

19. Tu'bitarai bu'boma bira ba'kaaba niharo tabobo.
    She-went-down-by she-went-and-he his elder-brother while-he-walked
he-saw-and-it.

20. To'nabumano ekaa ruqe'mabubo kia'buqai to'nabu ba'kubaro (eee)
    Cloud all it-became-dispersed-and-it not-only cloud it-was-and-he
nanahakamano nantie tiqata i'bo tiro.
(eh) what-thing how my-younger-brother it-did he-said.

21. Te qata kaau'naraqi to'nabu burura ruqemabi'ribo tiro.
    I younger-brother I-have-left-in cloud over-up-there it-became-dis-
persed he-said.

22. Ka'ntero oru 'tabobaro i'haqira aaunta teqa'kobo i'haqira tu'tububo.
    He-ran went-up he-saw-and-he fire-in neck she-cut-and-he fire-in he-
fell-and-it.

23. 'Untabubo unta hira'maqiro uriro uru 'tabobo bi'raqi bira'qata bira-
    It-smelled-and-he smell as-he sniffed he-came-up came-up he-saw-
qai mpaqi'kero bata'tero.
and-he there-in his-younger-brother there-in he-took-away he-did-put.

24. Mpaqike bata'tero aae tiro ti'qata nanti aautua'bo tiro.
    Took-away he-did-put oh he-said my-younger-brother how he-made
he-said.

25. Oru'rantero aaiqu taa'raramaqiro tu'biro tubu.
    He-returned-down legs as-he-trailed he-came-down came-down.

26. 'Tabobo ba'raata baainti kaaiqa ba'roraqaata ba'kubo 'tabero.
    He-saw-and-they girl person work she-had-done-at she-was-and-he
he-saw.

27. Aare maa ba'raatabama tiriqata ari'riaro tiro.
    You this girl my-younger-brother you-killed he-said.

28. Minti ti'bakero qata qu'bikero ba'taqi 'quntero.
    The-same after-he-said younger-brother he-dug ground-in he-buried.

29. Quntaa'tero qeta an'ta buru a'nta buru a'nta buru ma'kero qeta
    He-buried-him banana cut brought cut brought cut brought he-finished
qunta'maqi uru uru u'riro.
banana as-he-buried came-up came-up he-came-up.

30. *Baainti be'banto qun'taatero.*
Man underneath he-buried.
31. *'Quntaatero qeta 'aahiera quntaaqiro ura uru.*
He-buried banana rim as-he-buried came-up came-up.
32. *U'riro bubu qeta mpiqa'kero mpi'qake'roma.*
He-came-up brought banana he-filled-up he-filled-up.
33. *Bata qubi'kero rahi'ramateroma ba'raata 'baaintiara oru 'baaitaate*
Ground he-dug he-pressed-down girl persons-to go-along you-all-
tiro.
sleep he-said.
34. *Oru 'baaima oruran'tema ani qeta 'maaqihai mpaqi'ke naa'te tiro.*
Go-along stay you-return-down come banana here-in-from take-
away you-all-eat he-said.
35. *'Tuba'roma ba'raata baaintimano bi'aniro 'kaaiqa ba're 'amitero oru*
He-said-and-they girl persons went-and-came work did gave-for-him
'baaubaroma qeta aqu'tabiro.
went-up they-were-and-it banana they-became-ripe.
36. *Aqutabuboma bi'hairo aa'robaroma 'aniro.*
They-became-ripe-and-he there-from he-sang-out-and-they they-came.
37. *'Ekaa ba'raata baaintiara qeta mpaqi'ene 'tubaro biraqi'hairo mpa-*
All girl persons-to banana take-away he-said-and-they there-in-from
'qiro.
as-took-out.
38. *Mpa'qiro mpa'qiro qeta otubi otubi otubi'roma.*
As-took-out as-took-out banana down-went down-went down-to-went.
39. *Biba'raatara biba baainti 'arukora biba'raatara aare 'qeta mpaqi'ene*
This-girl-to she man she-had-killed that-girl-to you banana take-out
tiro.
he-said.
40. *'Tubaro 'baabi 'qeta mpaqiqiro uru'are tu'ra.*
He-said-and-she down banana as-she-took-out I-will-come-up she-said.
41. *Baainti bata mpaqi buru'bi kero qmm tiro.*
Man too as-took-out brought-up she-left ugh she-said.
42. *Tuqaan'taa buare tubaro.*
I-will-turn-around I-will-go she-said.
43. *Bi'raqira bu'kera 'baqa 'bata biba'raatara 'behima aqu'karo.*
There-in cassowary thigh-bone too that-girl-concerning end he-threw.
44. *Aaunta 'karara bi'raqira 'bira 'bata ba'raata bata baainti bata 'qeta*
Neck pipe there-in him too girl too man too banana too down there-
bata baabi biraqira aqu'karo.
in he-threw.
45. *'Kero rahi'raakorarama.*
He-left he-has-pressed-down.

46. Ho bi'qenamati.
   Well the-end-I-say.

1. There were some girls; some girls gathered together and they worked [did garden work]. They were working and one of them—one of them—one of them . . . All the girls gathered together and were working when one of the girls went along and saw that two brothers had gone and built a house up in the bush. They built the house in the bush and lived there and she saw that a cloud had settled on the place! 5. It had settled on the place and she said, 'What has been put in there that caused the cloud to settle. Wait! I'll go along and look!' She said to the girls, 'You stay here and work and I'll [go and see].'

After she said that, that girl went and saw that there was a man in there. He was in there and she went and sat in the doorway and while she was there she said, 'Come outside and I will twist your hair!' 10. But after she said that he said, 'Oh no! My elder brother said, "Don't go outside! Stay in the house," and because he said that I cannot go outside. I will stay in the house!' After he said that she said, 'Oh no! Come outside and I will twist your hair.' But he said, 'Oh no! I cannot go down; I cannot go. I can stay in here!' 15. He didn't heed her so the girl went inside; the girl went inside and with the thigh bone of a cassowary that she had brought she stabbed him in the throat and killed him. She made an end to him.

He died in there and the girl went by and ran away [made legs]. She went by and his elder brother while walking saw that the cloud had all dispersed. 20. There was no cloud: 'What has happened to my younger brother,' he said. 'The cloud has dispersed from the place where I left my younger brother,' he said and ran up and saw; she had cut his throat and he had fallen into the fire. It smelled [from burning] and he [elder brother] sniffing the smell came up and saw that his younger brother was there and he took him [out of the fire] and put him down; he put him down and said, 'Oh, what has happened to my younger brother?' 25. Then he returned down trailing [the girl's tracks] as he came.

He came down and saw that the girl was at the place where they had done work and he saw her and he said [to himself], 'You are the girl who killed my younger brother.' After he said that he dug [a hole] and buried his younger brother in the ground. After he buried him he cut bananas and brought them and he filled up the hole with the bananas. 30. He buried the body underneath the bananas. He filled up the hole with bananas and dug ground and pressed it down.

Then he said to the girls, 'Go and sleep and stay there and then come down and come and take out bananas from in there and eat them!' 35. After he said that the girls went and did their work and the bananas ripened and he came and called them and he said to all the girls, 'Take out bananas!' and they came and took them out and the bananas went down and down, and then he said to the girl who had killed the man, 'You take out bananas,' and 40. she said, 'I will take a banana and come up.' [She went to take a banana] but she pulled out the body too! 'Ugh!' she said, 'I will turn around,' she said [she went to

turn around] but he [older brother] slew her with a cassowary bone and he cut her neck! Then he threw him, the girl, and the bananas down in there and
45. filled in the earth. Well, that is the end—I say!

11. How a Woman Committed Suicide

1. *Bainti'mano nai 'naata ruqutu'kero.*
   Man his wife he-hit.
2. *Ba'taibaro 'toma'kero bi'aautuba'rero quara naaqun'taqai 'barero 'buru*
   He-put-her-and-she she-depressed went pig rope-only she-took car-
   ka'tariqira baari'rero kan'tarutero.
   ried tree-in she-climbed she-tied-it.
3. *Kan'taru'tero bi'raqira 'aaunta beta'kero.*
   She-tied-it there-in neck she-put-through.
4. *'Taaqiku'mabubo bira 'baatimano beta'kero tu'tubiro.*
   She-became-choked-and-he her husband she-put-it-through she-went-
   down.
5. *Tu'tubo bira 'baati'mano qumi'na bi'rara.*
   She-went-down-and-he her husband nothing for-her.
6. *Ranta tabo'kiero oru 'tabobo ka'tariqira ba'kubaro oru qantu'kero.*
   He-searched wondering went-along he-saw-and-she tree-in she-was-
   'barero biri.
   and-he went he-cut he-took brought.
7. *'Kobaro baai'tobaro ara'raara 'quntero.*
   He-left-and-she she-slept-and-he next-day he-buried-her.
8. *'Quntaa'kero baai'tero ti'baniharo naai 'nabunaa'kara 'hurama kara-*
   He-buried-her he-slept he-told-them her clan-to tomorrow food cut
   'kaaqa qan'tuke ba'tema 'hurama nai 'naatara 'qumpaaraiqi'rebe ti'ro.
   put tomorrow his-own wife-for will-feast-for-dead he-said.
9. *Minti'tubaro bira 'nabunaaka i'rubaro 'oru i'ha aqukero.*
   He-said-and-he her clan they-heard-he went-along firewood carried.
10. *Biri ba'tero 'kara antu'kero biri.*
    Brought he-put food he-cut brought.
11. *Ba'tero ba'tero ara'raara to'aqira be'barero quara aru'kero.*
    He-put he-put next-day morning-in he-came-outside pig he-killed-it.
12. *Bira ba'taakero 'ori aquku'kero tuta'kero aan'taaurumakero.*
    It left-it-with stones piled-up he-set-alight he-leveled-out.
13. *Orihira'tero.*
    He-put-food-in.
14. *Bata raba'tero namai qihiqa'tero.*
    Ground put-on water he-poured-in.
15. *Ti'baniharo bi'ra 'baain'tintibaraa bi'ra 'naauba 'naaquba baai'raba*
    He-told-them her brothers-and-sisters her uncle grandfather he-was

ba'tema 'maaqaa a'niraqema quara 'aantaau 'ona ami'ere tiro.
today here-on you-come-and-I pig animals possessions I-will-give-you he-said.

16. *'Tubaro 'ani 'baaubaro o'riha mpaqi'kero.*
    He-said-and-they came they-were-and-he stone-oven he-opened-it.

17. *'Quara 'aantaau kara'kaaqa 'baatamakero.*
    Pig animals food he-divided-out.

18. *Ba'tero bira'qaata 'onana aautu'kero.*
    He-put there-on possessions he-made.

19. *A'mubaro 'barero bu'rama.*
    He-gave-them-and-they they-took they-went.

20. *Ho bi'qenama ti.*
    Enough the-end I-say.

1. A man beat his wife. He left her and she was depressed and went and took a pig rope and climbed a tree and tied it to the tree. She tied it and put her head in there [the noose]; she put her neck [head] through it. She became choked, and because of her husband, she put it through and dropped down.

5. After she dropped, her husband searched in vain for her. He searched wondering and then went along, and saw that she was in the tree, and he went along and cut her down and took her. He left her and she slept [stayed unburied], and the next day he buried her.

After he buried her, he slept and then he told her relatives that tomorrow he would cut food and put it and the next day he would make the payment feast. After he had said that, her relatives heard it and he went and brought firewood.

10. He cut food and brought it. The next morning he came outside and killed the pig and put it with the food. He left it, and he piled up the stones and heated them and spread them out. He put in the food. He covered it with dirt and then poured in water [to make steam]. 15. Then he said to her brothers, sisters [includes cousins], her maternal uncles, and grandfathers, 'Come today, and I will give you pigs, animals, and goods.' After he said that, they came and were there, and he opened the stone oven. He divided out the pigs, animals, and food. He put it there and he made up the possessions. He gave it to them and they took it and went. 20. That's the end of what I have to say!

12. THE PARROT LOSES ONE TOE

1. *Ro'riqobama na'mairuna 'oru biro.*
   Parrot water-along went-along he-went.

2. *Ro'riqoba oru biro 'ekarori raa'qu namaqiro.*
   Parrot went-along he-went pebbles took-away he-ate.

3. *Raqu na'maqiro oru bi'roma be'raini oru 'buboma karaapaaanta'mano*
   Took-away he-ate went-along he-went up-and-around went-up he-

bu'hairo bi'abi tabamakeroma bububu tubo kan'teroma 'tubiro.
went-and-he crow-long over-from downward he-saw go-along come-down
he-ran he-came-down.

4. *Tu'biroma tubu 'taberoma 'tibaainto bi'haire urua'ro tubo tema maai-*
He-came-down came-down he-saw my-friend there-from you-came-
'haima maaruna uriha 'ekarori raaqu na'maqi.
up he-said-and-he I here-from this-along while-coming-up pebbles took-
away I-ate.

5. *U'rima maqaa ururo.*
I-came-up here-on I-came-up.

6. *Tubo bi'raqaahairoma minti'ma tiro.*
He-said-and-he there-on-from the-same he-said.

7. *Karaapaaantamano 'tibaaintio 'aniqe hanta bua're tiro.*
Crow-long my-friend you-come-and-we two we-will-go he-said.

8. *Bitabare buru kaarira baai'taane.*
I-take-you bring I-will-leave-you-and-you you-sleep.

9. *Tu'boma a'qau tenta ururante maini tenta 'maaqaa birebe.*
He-said-and-he oh-no myself I-return-down to-here my-own place-on
I-will-go.

10. *'Tubaro ro'riqoba 'tubaro roriqoba tiharo aqau kara'paarara a'niqe*
He-said-and-he parrot he-said-and-he parrot he-said oh-no crow-to
tenta 'maaqaa otu 'buare.
you-come-and-we my-own place-on go-down we-will-go.

11. *Tubo a'qaau nia'raini aai maaqaa 'baaibo ti maaqaa 'baaintoma*
He-said-and-he oh-no a-long-way your place-on it-is my place-on
'baaibo tiro.
close it-is he-said.

12. *Minti 'tubo ho 'biqe hanta aai maaqaa oru baai'taare tibakero.*
The-same he-said-and-he OK you-go-and-we two your place-on go-
along we-will-sleep he-said.

13. *Bi'tabarero oru 'biroma buru.*
He-took-him went-along he-went brought.

14. *Kara'paaba ro'riqora bi'tabarero oru biro buru nai 'maaqaaini nai*
Crow parrot he-took-him went-along he-went brought his-own place-
maaqaini bi'tabarero.
on-to his-own place-on-to he-took him.

15. *Buare tira burubi aqira oriqirama 'karo.*
I-will he-has-said brought-along just rock-in he-left-him.

16. *Ori'qira maaqira 'baairaqema qa'maaqai 'barehama muntu maini*
Rock-in place-in you-wait-and-I sweet-potato-only while-getting bring-
ami'ere tiro.
down to-here I-will-give-you he-said.

17. *Tuboma biba ro'riqoba minti'ma tiro*
　　He-said-and-he he parrot the-same he-said.

18. *Ti'roma naabu'qira maa'qaaini tibi'tabarera bi'reba(ra) bo'qaara ti-*
　　He-said house-in place-on-to me-you-take you-will-go like me-you-
　　tiba'tabarera u'rirama buru'bi.
　　took you-came-up brought-up.

19. *Aqira o'riqira keriaro.*
　　Just rock-in you-left-me.

20. *Kaa'raauma tenta 'maaqaa buro tiro.*
　　You-left-me-and-I my-own place I-go he-said.

21. *Minti 'tubo biba ti'haroma a'qau maaqi 'baairaqe 'ninihama 'bateta*
　　The-same he-said-and-he he he-said oh-no here-in you-wait-and-I
　　qa'maa ba'rema muntu ami'are tiro.
　　walk-walk today sweet-potato I-take I-bring-down I-will-give-you he-said.

22. *Minti'akero burubi ori'qira ke'roma maa'qaaini biro.*
　　After-he-did-that went-along rock-in he-left place-to he-went.

23. *Karaa'paaba karapaaantamanora maaqaini oru baai'haroma qa'maa*
　　Crow crow-long place-to went-along while-he-was-there sweet-potato
　　un'take.
　　cooked.

24. *Ba'toboma ne'haroma bara beba ru'babarero u'taqira rubabarero.*
　　He-put-and-he he-ate took came-outside he-put-in-and-took bag-in
　　he-put-in-and-took

25. *Tu'biroma muntu 'tibaaintio tiro.*
　　He-came-down brought-down my-friend he-said.

26. *Qa'maa tubu ba'raane tiro.*
　　Sweet-potato come-down get he-said.

27. *Tubaroma tubu ba'raro.*
　　He-said-and-he came-down he-took-it.

28. *Bebarero bare'roqai tuburantero.*
　　He-came-outside he-took-it he-returned-back.

29. *Biraqi oriqoba baaiha ne'haro 'baaubaroma oru baai'tero.*
　　There-in parrot while-there while-eating he-was-there-and-he went-
　　along he-slept.

30. *Araraa to'aqi qa'maa 'barero.*
　　Next-day morning-in sweet-potato he-took.

31. *Bare'roma kan'tero tubu'rero.*
　　He-took he-ran he-came-down-to.

32. *'Tibaaintio qa'maa tubu ba'raane tubo bibaqai tubu qa'maa barero.*
　　My-friend sweet-potato come-down get he-said-and-he he-only come-
　　down sweet-potato he-took.

33. *Bare'roqai oriqi oriqetero 'ne.*
　　He-took-only rock-in he-went-inside eat.

34. *Baaubaro biba tuburantero maa'qaini biro.*
    He-was-and-he he he-returned-back place-to he-went.
35. *Ho minti'aqi bi bi bi bi.*
    Well as-he-did-that went went went went.
36. *Biubaroma bira 'naatamano hampe'qiroma.*
    He-did-and-she his wife became-curious.
37. *Ham'peqamakeroma bi'raqira tiqi'eta i'hamabi'ribo ti'roma.*
    She-became-curious there-in my-head it-pains-me she-said.
38. *'Baatiera u'ta 'barera bu'ane qa'maarabe tiro.*
    To-husband bag take go for-sweet-potato she-said.
39. *'Te tiqienta iha naabuqi baaitate baai'rarabe tiro.*
    I my-head pains house-in asleep I-will-stay she-said.
40. *Tubo u'qaama tiriaro.*
    She-said-and-he truth you-speak.
41. *Tibakero bareroma biro.*
    After-he-said he-took he-went.
42. *Buba'roma biba bira 'naatabanora tu'biroma aaiqú taarara'maqi tu'biro*
    He-went-and-she she his wife she-came-down legs as-she-trailed she-
    tubu 'tabobo biba ori'qira ba'kubo tibaaintio qa'maa beba ba'raane titubo
    came-down came-down she-saw-and-he he rock-in he-was-and-she my-
    qa'maa beba ba'raane.
    friend sweet-potato come-outside get she-said-and-he sweet-potato come-
    outside get.
43. *Ti'tubo biba utuba'robo.*
    She-said-and-he he picked-it-up.
44. *A'qaau tiro.*
    Oh-no he-said.
45. *'Tibaintiba bo'qake tiba'kero burubi kamuro kia bate bebararabe tiro.*
    My-friend very he-said brought-up I-left not today I-can-come-out-
    side he-said.
46. *Te maaqima 'baarirarabe tiro.*
    I here-in I-can-be he-said.
47. *Minti 'tubaroma biba tuburante.*
    The-same he-said-and-she she returned-back.
48. *Oriqira buboma biba haanama tabokie'roma.*
    Rock-in he-went-and-she she what-do she-considered.
49. *Nai na'hentibano pa'haara ra'peiro.*
    His woman skirt she-tore.
50. *Pa'haara ra'pepaamake bata'teroma tuburanteroma oru 'biroma oru*
    Skirt tore she-put she-returned-up went-up she-went went-up house-
    naabuqi ba'kuboma biba karapaaba bi'hai anubaroma bira naatamano
    in she-was-and-he he crow there-from he-came-and-she his wife the-same

mintima tiro.
she-said.

51. Aqaau tiro.
Oh-no she-said.

52. Nanahaaba bitabare burubi kaarababe.
Who took brought you-did-leave.

53. Baai'hara ba'kiraqe otu buraroe ti pa'haara ra'pepaamake.
You-stay you-stay-and-I go-down I-went-and-he my skirt tore.

54. Ba'taimanta u'ruro tiro.
He-put-and-I I-came-up she-said.

55. Ba'taimanta u'roro tubo biba mintima tiro.
He-put-and-I I-came-up she-said-and-he he the-same he-said.

56. Taba ai tibamibarabe tiro.
Who you he-told-you-and-you he-said.

57. Te bira baainti e'baara bitaba buru'bi kemu'ro tiro.
I him man secretly took brought-along I-left he-said.

58. Minti ti'bakero bo biba tuburan'tero kan'teroma 'roriqai tubu bare-
That he-said go he he-returned-up he-ran axe-only came-down he-
'roma.
took.

59. 'Kari kari tubu bare'roma tubire'haroma 'tibaaintio qa'maa beba
Stone-axe stone-axe came-down he-took he-came-down my-friend
ba'raane ti 'tubo 'beba qa'maa ba'raare tiro.
sweet-potato outside get he-said he-said-and-he outside sweet-potato I-
will-get he-said.

60. 'Kaauqu tu'tuboma qataa bara te'qaqukaro.
Arm he-stretched-out-and-he joint took he-cut-off.

61. Teqa'kobo biba tuburantero oriqi oriqete'haroma tibaaintio qumina
He-cut-off-and-he he he-returned-up rock-in while-he-went-inside my-
(raaiqaake'rama) hari'riaro.
friend nothing (?) you-hit-me.

62. Ai 'naatamanora nai 'tubu maa bira ba'haaqaihairo qa'maa ba'raane
Your wife herself came-down er there outside-from sweet-potato get
'timanta beba kaauqu tu'turaroma ti utuba'raimanta te maaini (ukinkirima-
she-said-and-I outside arm I-stretched-out-and-she me she-took-and-I I
'kema) naabuqi uri'qeteuro.
here-to (?) house-in I-came-inside.

63. Oriqi uriqe'tauraroma bira ai 'naatamanora naima pa'haara rape-
Rock-in I-came-up-inside-and-she her your wife herself skirt she-tore.
'rikero.

64. Unaha ti'bakaibama.
Lie she-has-said.

65. *Ti muntu 'buqa teqakeria'ro tiro.*
Me brought-down finger you-cut-off he-said.

66. *Minti tubo ae u'qaama tiriaro.*
That he-said-and-he oh true you-speak.

67. *Nai are utu'barora tima buru.*
Herself you I-took I-said brought.

68. *Nai rape'rike buru ti'bakaima te buqa te'qamakeuro tiro.*
Herself tore brought she-told-me-and-I I finger I-cut-off he-said.

69. *Minti 'tibake oturante naata irare.*
That he-said went-back wife to-ask.

70. *Bibubaroma biba biraqaahairoma ihi (antaqi) tibakeroma minti'mihi*
He-went-and-he he there-on-from song (?) he-said that-song he-said.
tiro.

71. *Rorio roroie ompura rorie rorio rorioe aarabaa rorioe rorio rorioe a*
rorio rorioe ompu'raa rorioe rorio rorio'e aarabaa rorioe rorio oiaae baai'aa
oioe oio oioe baaiaa oioe oio oioe.

72. *Minti tibakero otu'raakero 'roriqoba nai 'maaqa bu'rama.*
This he-said he-went-down parrot his-own place he-did-go.

73. *Ho biqena'ma ti.*
Well the-end I-say!

1. A parrot went along the river. A parrot went along eating pebbles as he went. He went up and around and up and around eating as he went, and a crow looked down and saw him and he ran and came down. He came down and saw him and said, 'My friend, you have come up from there!' and he [parrot] said, 'I have come up along here and while I came up I ate pebbles.' 5. 'In coming up, I arrived here.' After he said that, he said the same thing. Crow said, 'My friend! Come and we will go. I will take you and bring you and leave you and you sleep!' But he [parrot] said, 'Oh, no! I will return down to my own place!' 10. He said this and he said it to the parrot, but the parrot said to the crow, 'Oh, no! Come and we will go to my own place!' But he [crow] said, 'Oh, no! Your place is a long way away! My place is close!' After he said that, he [parrot] said, 'OK, let's go and we will go and sleep at your place.' He took him and went.

The crow took the parrot and went and took him to his own place. 15. He said, 'I will take you there,' but he brought him and left him in a rock. 'You stay in this rock, and I will bring you sweet potato and give it to you,' he said. He said this and the parrot said this. He said, 'You said you would take me to your place and you took me and brought me and left me just in a rock. You just left me at this rock.' 20. 'You left me and I am going to my place,' he said. After he said that he [crow] said, 'Oh no! You stay in here and after I have walked about, I will get sweet potato and bring it down and give it to you!'

After he said that, he left him in the rock and went to his place. The crow went to his place, and while he was there he cooked sweet potato. He put it there and ate, and then put some in a bag and came down. 25. He came down and brought it and said, 'My friend! Come down and get sweet potato!' He said this and took it to him. He came outside and took it, and he returned. While in the rock he ate and he [crow] went [home] and slept.

30. The next day in the morning he brought sweet potato. He took it and ran and came down. 'My friend! Come down and get sweet potato!' he said, and he came down and got the sweet potato. He went inside the rock and ate it. He was there and he [crow] returned up and went to his place. 35. He continued doing this. As he did this, his wife became curious. She got curious, and she said, 'My head pains me, and I will stay here and sleep!' 40. She said this, and he said, 'You speak the truth!' After he said it, he took it [bag] and went.

When he had gone, his wife came down; she came following his tracks and came down and saw that he [parrot] was in the rock; so she said, 'My friend, come outside and get sweet potato; come outside and get sweet potato.' She said this and he started to pick it up. 'Oh, no!' he said, 'my friend that brought me said strongly that I am left here, and I cannot come out today. I must stay here,' he said. After he said that, she went back. He went into the rock and she considered what to do.

Then his wife tore her skirt. 50. She tore her skirt and returned back and was there in her house, and the crow came back and his wife said this. 'Oh, no!' she said. 'Whom did you bring up and leave? You stayed away and while you stayed, I went down and he tore my skirt. Then he did that, and I came up. He did it and I came up,' she said. 55. 'He did it, and I came up,' she said, and he said this: 'Who told you [about him]? I brought that man secretly up here and left him!' he said.

After he said that, he returned up and ran and got an axe and came down. He came down and got a stone axe, a stone axe, and said, 'My friend, come outside and get sweet potato!' and he said, 'I will go outside and get sweet potato!' 60. He stretched out his hand and he took and cut off the joint [finger]. He cut it off and he [parrot] went back inside and said, 'My friend, you hit me for nothing. Your wife herself came down and from outside said, 'Come and get sweet potato! and when she said that, I stretched out my arm and she grabbed me, but I came back in this house, in this rock. I came back inside the cave, and your wife herself tore her skirt. She told you a lie.' 65. 'You came down and cut off my finger!' he said.

After he said that he [crow] said, 'Oh, you speak the truth, for she said, "I will take you!" and then went and tore her skirt herself and told me and I cut off your hand [finger]!' After he said that, he went to ask his wife. 70. After he went, then he [parrot] sang this song: *'Rorio rorioe ompura rorie rorio rorioe aarabaa rorioe rorio rorioe rorio rorioe ompu'raa rorioe rorio rorio'e aarabaa rorioe rorio oiaae baai'aa oioe oio oioe baaiaa oioe oio oioe.'* After he sang that he, the parrot, went down to his place! Well, that's the end, I say!

PART FIVE: *Linguistic Relationships*

XXXIV. Introduction

HOWARD McKAUGHAN

The final part of this study of the languages of the Eastern Family of New Guinea first presents a discussion of the divergence of the four major languages, Awa, Auyana, Gadsup, and Tairora; and then in two further articles delineates some comparative and historical characteristics. The first two treatments have been published elsewhere with the only modification here being in orthographic representations consistent with the descriptive articles. The divergence paper is based largely on statistics from the phonologies and lexicons of the languages. Some preliminary steps in reconstruction are suggested, and some observations made on grammatical similarities and differences.

In chapter XXXVI Bee has pushed the comparative work forward by presenting some sixty reconstructed stems for the family. She outlines the reflexes found in the reconstructions, and in addition describes the phonemes of each language (using Tairora, Gadsup, Agarabi, Usarufa, Auyana, and Awa) as they relate to their own systems. She then compares the phonemes as parallel points of related systems viewed as wholes, and gives the allophonic and distinctive feature structure of each phoneme.

In the last chapter Harland Kerr discusses the Proto Kainantu kinship system giving us a treatment of the nuclear kin terms. He adds nine reconstructions to the nine kin terms Bee included in her paper, refining a few points in Bee's reconstructions.

In one instance Kerr suggests a morpheme *-Wa where Bee has reconstructed the vowel class. Data from Avia, Kumpora, other dialects of Auyana and the Usarufa, and an indication of the use of -ka, -wa, and -kawa in Ilakia-Awa support Bee's reconstruction rather than Kerr's. Kerr has suggested a possible meaning of 'seniority' for the suffix he reconstructs. This could be the case for the morphophonemic class that Bee reconstructs instead of the morpheme. It may be that the morphophonemic classes in these languages at one time had lexical content. If so, seniority-juniority may have been involved. Kerr's suggestions along this line for the kinship system as his parameter are quite in order, but they may be questioned with a wider perspective in view. My conclusion is that the semantic value of the morphophonemic classes must, at least at this point, remain indefinite.

One important part of the kinship system found in the Guawa (Gadsup-Auyana-Awa) has not been touched upon yet: the ego generation kin categories. Kerr concludes, most likely, that cross-cousin terms are not part of the earlier Tagauwa (the three of Gauwa plus Tairora), but further investigation is needed. If terms are reconstructed for the three subfamilies in Gauwa, we should look for a trace of these in the Tairora subfamily. At this point it looks as though the cross-cousin part of the system of Gauwa was not a part of the proto system.

Though the earlier statistical study had to be based on data that have since been refined, the resulting conclusions are still valid. This is encouraging since Wurm's early groupings based on even rougher data than mine are also confirmed. The usefullness in this area of lexicostatistical work for classificatory purposes is thus more firmly established.

On the basis of both the statistical evidence and the comparative-historical studies, we conclude that Tairora, Binumarien, and Waffa split off from the proto language first. The other three, Awa, Auyana, and Gadsup, moved together in time until the Awa split off from that subgroup. Auyana, Kawaina, and Usarufa remained with the Gadsup, Agarabi, and Oyana the longest, though probably the final split of the subfamilies was not as long after the Awa split as was the time between this split and the Tairora break-off point.

Within the Eastern Family we now need to look at the languages in each subfamily. The impressions are that Waffa split first from the Tairora-Binumarien, that Usarufa split first from the Auyana-Kawaina, and that the Agarabi is the most different of the Gadsup subfamily. Further investigation of the Southern Tairora is needed to complete the over-all picture. Details are coming to light as we press the comparative-historical study.

Bee's suggestion that we consider the Eastern Family as made up of four subfamilies is a good one. I have, in my paper on divergence (Chap. XXXV), suggested four languages with dialects for each. The Usarufa, Agarabi, Waffa, and Binumarien, with Auyana, Gadsup, Tairora, and Awa should in all probability be considered languages belonging to the four subfamilies. The subfamilies in turn, I suggest, may be referred to either by hyphenated terms naming each language in the subfamily, or by the names Awa, Auyana, Gadsup, and Tairora. The naming of languages, or the calling certain speech communities by names that infer languages, is largely a matter of historical accident. Since we have no firm criteria to reverse this accident in the cases of Agarbi, Usarufa, Waffa, and Binumarien, I accept these as names for 'languages'. Kosena, however, loses as a language name since it is so closely identified in form and structure to the Central Auyana through its identity with Arora.

Awa is now known by the one name, and its dialects need not be given the status of languages, though their differences may be as great as, for example, Auyana and Kawaina. Certainly Southern Tairora may be as divergent from Northern Tairora as is Agarabi from Gadsup. But so little is known of the Southern Tairora that the general name will no doubt be brought down for the whole area. At this point I should indicate that linguistic information for the Southern Tairora is the one large gap in our study of the Eastern Family. We look to the Summer Institute of Linguistics to help in this matter.

Names should not influence our notion of relationship, and though I am quite willing to accept at this time the names we have mentioned as referring to languages, I point out that this is because of the weight of history and convenience rather than because of the linguistic distance between the groups established by the naming process.

Thus the Awa, Auyana, Gadsup, and Tairora subfamilies are composed of the following languages: (A) Awa; (B) Auyana, Usarufa, and possibly Kawaina; (C) Gadsup, Agarabi, and possibly Oyana; and (D) Tairora, Binumarien, and Waffa.

In summary the basic relationships of these languages to each other are now quite clear. The systematic comparative-historical work by Bee and Kerr confirm and refine the conclusions reached through my earlier study on divergence.

XXXV. A Study of Divergence in Four New Guinea Languages

HOWARD McKAUGHAN

1. INTRODUCTION

The first step in a study of language diversification is to determine which languages in a given area are genetically related, and which are not.[1] S. A. Wurm of the Australian National University has provided a basic, though tentative, classification for the languages of the Highlands areas of New Guinea. In this classification, Wurm links five language families to a single East New Guinea Highlands Phylum (1961a, c; 1962a, b, c). Such a classification is helpful in a study of the prehistory of the area since, if it is valid, it indicates the probability of a common source, or related sources, for the languages now in the Highlands.

This paper helps to substantiate Wurm's work by carefully examining the divergence in a single family of languages located in the Eastern Highlands, Kainantu subdistrict. Though I recognize only four major languages in the family, there are a number of dialects in each language (Wurm and Laycock 1961). The family is small, having some 30,000 speakers with 11,200 to 15,000 per language and constituting about 4 per cent of the total number included in the East New Guinea Highlands Phylum (Wurm 1961c). Wurm refers to the group as the Gadsup-Auyana-Awa-Tairora family.

The best way to study linguistic divergence is through what is called the comparative method (Hockett 1958:485 ff.; Greenberg 1957). This is the

[1] Field work was carried out in 1961–62, and further research done at the University of Washington 1962–63. The writer is indebted to Professor James Watson for his stimulation and help, and also to members of the Summer Institute of Linguistics, New Guinea Branch, for their cooperation in the field. This paper was originally published in *American Anthropologist*, 66:98–121, and is reissued here by permission.

oldest of our linguistic tools and the most reliable. Unfortunately, its full application requires a great deal of data and time. Hence, statistical methods are being worked out as a quicker way to get results even though these may not be as conclusive as those arrived at through the comparative method (Cowan 1959).

In making his classification, Wurm has primarily used glottochronology (Swadesh 1950; 1952; 1955a, b; 1959; 1962), the best known of the statistical measures, or what for our purposes we shall regard as lexicostatistics (see Hymes 1960a:41-44 and 1960b for bibliography). I have also applied this method to data from the four study languages including a number of dialects of each. My results support Wurm's conclusions in so far as these pertain to language relationships.

A second statistical measure of language divergence employed here is less well known. In its essential features, it was introduced by Grimes and Agard in a study of linguistic divergence in Romance languages (1959). Grimes refers to the method as a measurement of degrees of difference (1962:287); we refer to it here as *phonostatistics* since it is a statistical expression of the relative phonological difference between pairs of related languages. In practice this method lends support to the lexicostatistical conclusions, and also gives a basis for further comment on language relationships.

A final section of the paper gives a survey of the structural characteristics of the study languages, and includes results obtained from a preliminary application of the comparative method. These structural studies confirm the conclusions drawn from the statistical studies and help to validate them as measures of language divergence.

2. LEXICOSTATISTICAL STUDY

Both of the statistical studies herein are based upon three separate vocabulary lists. List I is basically the latest Swadesh 100-word list (1955a:133-37); List II has 100 additional items, many especially related to the Eastern Highlands languages; List III has some 345 entries collected from a central village in each of the four languages.[2]

The lexicostatistical results obtained by comparing items in List I are given in Table 80. In this table, as well as in Tables 81-83, numbers below the diagonal indicate the percentage of shared probable cognates for any two dialects. Numbers above the diagonal indicate the glottochronological time depth in years separating any two from a common origin. Table 81 gives the results of comparing items in List II, and Table 82 the results obtained from a study of List III.

---

[2] See Sec. 7 for Lists I, II, and III with entries for the central dialects of the four languages.

TABLE 80

LEXICOSTATISTICAL PERCENTAGES AND ABSOLUTE TIME DEPTHS
(Based on List I)

	Awa			Auyana			Gadsup			Tairora		
	Mo	Il	Ta	As	Ko	Ka	Oy	Ak	To	Ab	Bat	Bai
Mo		286	341	690	756	750	1046	1053	1108	1124	1094	1400
Il	88.4		177	657	698	720	1046	998	1046	1150	1195	1438
Ta	86.3	92.6		560	631	622	933	958	1007	1083	1108	1350
	(89.1)		(268)	(676)			(1022)			(1215)		
As	74.2	75.2	78.3		48	193	776	900	843	1094	1150	1357
Ko	71.9	73.9	76.0	97.9		145	751	950	984	1150	1170	1373
Ka	72.4	73.2	76.3	91.9	93.9		809	972	1007	1170	1290	1401
	(74.6)			(94.6)		(129)	(888)			(1239)		
Oy	63.5	63.5	66.7	71.4	72.2	70.4		357	385	1150	1170	1373
Ak	63.3	63.9	66.0	67.7	66.3	65.6	85.7		48	1094	1177	1357
To	61.8	63.5	64.6	69.4	65.3	64.6	84.7	97.9		1170	1272	1410
	(64.1)			(68.1)			(89.4)		(263)	(1248)		
Ab	61.4	60.8	62.5	62.2	60.8	60.2	60.8	61.2	60.2		48	304
Bat	61.2	59.6	61.8	60.8	60.2	57.1	60.2	60.0	57.6	97.8		300
Bai	54.6	53.6	55.7	55.5	55.1	54.5	55.1	55.5	54.1	87.7	87.9	
	(59.0)			(58.5)			(58.3)			(91.2)		(217)

2.1. Mechanical Observations

Village names representing the various dialects are given along the top and side of the tables by abbreviations using the first two or three letters of each name. Dialects are arranged by rank, in so far as is possible, with those showing the greater affinity closer to the diagonal. The reader must make certain adjustments when the figures do not follow in the exact sequence suggested. Language groups are indicated in the larger squares. Numbers in parentheses within the squares are the mean percentages or average time depths between all dialects of one language and those of the intersecting language.

2.2. Support for a Core Vocabulary

An outstanding observation to be made from the lexicostatistical study is that List I shows much higher cognate relationships than Lists II and III. Each of the latter shows a decreasing over-all percentage of cognates. This

TABLE 81

LEXICOSTATISTICAL PERCENTAGES AND ABSOLUTE TIME DEPTHS
(Based on List II)

	Awa			Auyana			Gadsup			Tairora		
	Mo	Il	Ta	As	Ko	Ka	Oy	Ak	To	Ab	Bat	Bai
Mo		571	859	2120	2135	1980	2335	2390	2390	2335	2390	2390
Il	78.0		790	1940	1940	1980	2210	2150	2150	2010	1945	2170
Ta	68.9	71.0		1525	1480	1480	1810	1980	1980	2135	2200	2250
	(72.6)		(740)	(1770)			(2155)			(2203)		
As	39.8	43.1	51.6		75	150	1395	1480	1480	2135	2260	2440
Ko	39.6	43.1	52.7	96.9		125	1330	1600	1600	2330	2395	2460
Ka	42.4	42.4	52.7	93.7	94.7		1410	1650	1650	2320	2390	2390
	(45.3)			(95.1)	(116)		(1511)			(2347)		
Oy	36.3	38.3	45.6	54.6	56.1	54.2		360	360	2180	2240	2370
Ak	35.9	39.4	42.4	52.6	50.0	48.9	85.6		0	2110	2055	2240
To	35.9	39.4	42.4	52.6	50.0	48.9	85.6	100.0		2110	2055	2240
	(39.5)			(52.0)			(90.4)	(240)		(2178)		
Ab	36.3	41.9	39.6	39.6	36.4	36.5	38.9	40.0	40.0		23	555
Bat	35.5	43.0	38.5	37.5	35.5	35.5	37.9	41.0	41.0	99.0		520
Bai	35.9	39.0	37.8	34.7	34.4	35.9	35.8	37.9	37.9	78.7	79.8	
	(38.6)			(36.2)			(38.9)			(85.8)	(366)	

indicates clearly that certain vocabulary items have a higher retention rate than do others, and supports the contention that there is a *core* vocabulary which changes less over time than do other vocabulary items (Swadesh 1950:157).

2.3. *Language and Dialect Relationships*

Notwithstanding the difference between the lists, we observe that each list indicates quite similar groupings. Highest percentages of cognates show that (Mo)buta, (Il)akia and (Ta)una are dialects of one language—*Awa;* that (As)empa, (Ko)sena and (Ka)waina group as another—*Auyana;* that (Oy)ana, (Ak)una and (To)mpena group as a third—*Gadsup;* and that (Ab)iqera, (Bat)ainabura, and (Bai)ra group as the fourth—*Tairora.*

All lists indicate that Tairora is the most divergent language of the four, and that Auyana stands about equidistant from the Awa and Gadsup. The Awa, Auyana, and Gadsup shared a common history after the Tairora

TABLE 82

LEXICOSTATISTICAL PERCENTAGES AND
ABSOLUTE TIME DEPTHS
(Based on List III)

	Awa		Auyana	Gadsup	Tairora
	Il		As	Ak	Ab
Il			2480	3200	2900
As	34			2510	3100
Ak	25		33		2900
Ab	28		26	28	

TABLE 83

LEXICOSTATISTICAL FIGURES FROM S. A. WURM

	Awa	Auyana	Oyana	Gadsup	Tairora
Awa		1800	. . .	. . .	. . .
Auyana	46		1450	1800	2550
Oyana	. . .	53		850	2500
Gadsup	. . .	46	69		2450
Tairora	. . .	33	34	35	

split-off, but the divergence between Awa and Gadsup at the poles of this subgroup indicates that this common history was not long.

The present geographical location of the Auyana between the Awa and Gadsup is in line with these facts. Auyana shares a common border with Oyana of the Gadsup, and Tauna of the Awa also shares a border with Auyana; but no Gadsup dialect shares a common border with an Awa dialect (see Map. 3).[3]

2.4. *Comparison with S. A. Wurm's Studies*

Table 83 gives the lexicostatistical figures gleaned from various soures by S. A. Wurm.[4] It will be noted that Wurm's figures lie usually between my

[3] The writer is indebted to D. R. Lycan for his assistance in the project, for the programing of the statistical data, and for mapping of the divergences.

[4] Sources for these figures are Wurm (1960:134; 1961a:20) and correspondence from Professor Wurm. Some of the percentage figures cited in the table were derived from time depth figures given by Wurm. I have cited only the single figure, an average from the range given by Wurm.

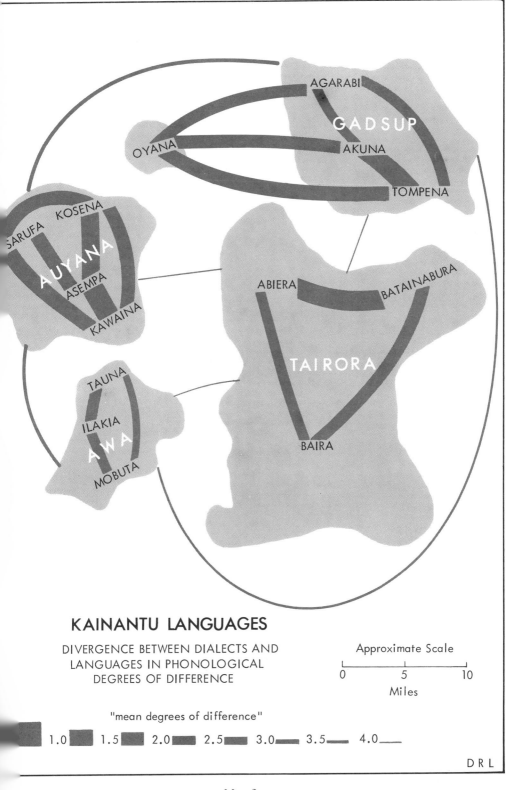

KAINANTU LANGUAGES

DIVERGENCE BETWEEN DIALECTS AND
LANGUAGES IN PHONOLOGICAL
DEGREES OF DIFFERENCE

Approximate Scale

0   5   10
Miles

"mean degrees of difference"

1.0   1.5   2.0   2.5   3.0   3.5   4.0

DRL

Map 3

Lists II and III. However, the general facts are the same, that is, Tairora is the most divergent of the four languages; Oyana and Gadsup belong together; Awa and Gadsup stand equidistant on both sides of Auyana (though in 1961a:20 Wurm places Auyana closer to Gadsup than to Awa).

Wurm's figures average 950 years more in time depth than do mine from List I. But Wurm based his calculations upon the larger Swadesh 215 list with some modifications (1960:125 and 1961a:16). Hence the variance in our figures is largely due to the difference in vocabularies used.

However, it must also be stated that any two investigators will come out with different answers even if they should use the same word lists, simply because the method calls for personal judgment as to what is cognate and what is not. In this we find the greatest weakness of the method for dating purposes, for a difference of 5 or 6 per cent makes a difference of two hundred years or more, depending on where in the scale that 5 per cent difference lies.

Even so, two different investigators (Wurm and myself) with different languages, have come out with results of a classificatory nature which are so similar that they can be said to be the same, even though percentage figures vary considerably.

3. PHONOSTATISTICAL STUDY

The second measure of linguistic relationship is the phonostatistical study—so named because it is a study of the differences that exist in the sounds of related languages.

3.1. *Approach*

As noted in the introduction, the basic approach to a phonostatistical study was suggested in an article by Grimes and Agard (1959). Based on K. L. Pike's comments regarding the ranking of sounds (1943:1288ff.; 1967:329-31), and E. V. Pike's criteria of rank (1954:26-29), each sound in the study languages is coded in such a way that the difference between any two sounds can be calculated numerically.

Phonological change usually proceeds by minimal steps along one phonetic dimension at a time (Austin 1957). A basic assumption is, then, that the longer two items have diverged, the greater will be the phonetic difference between them. For example, *cuatro* 'four' from Spanish is phonetically more like Latin *quattuor* than it is like *vier* of German, or *four* of English (cf. *fidwor* of Gothic). Yet all four of these words are genetically related. The first two show a greater affinity to each other than they do to either of the last two. On the other hand, *vier* and *four* are closer to each other than these are to the Latin or Spanish. In other words, *vier* and *four* show a span of common history which is divergent from the common history seen in *cuatro* and *quattuor*.

In order to measure the divergence involved in such instances, we set up a scale by assigning numbers to the minimal distinctions necessary to deal with the phonologies of the study languages. Four dimensions are sufficient for measuring the Kainantu languages: (A) point of articulation, (B) degree of constriction of the air stream, (C) velic action, and (D) laryngeal action. By assigning numerical values to these four dimensions and summing the values for all four, we can compare the phonetic difference between any two sounds. This comparison will give us the 'degrees' of difference between the items under consideration.

However, it is important to emphasize again that we do not compare just any two words. The first requirement is that the words to be compared be related. As indicated above, Grimes has insisted that only material be used which has been proven cognate by a rigid application of the comparative method. I have departed from this rigidity because I feel the method is usable at a stage in our investigation far ahead of the time when comparative results can be available. Further, I find that very often two lexemes bear resemblances for which we cannot give an early account by the comparative method. These either remain hidden to us for lack of evidence available, or because of intrusions that cannot be traced. Hence I am suggesting that the phonostatistical measure be applied to languages which are assumed to be genetically related by the lexicostatistical measure, and that all items which have been considered as probably cognate in such a study be compared phonologically.

Without a doubt, certain sounds will be compared in this process which may not have had a common source. Even a gross phonetic comparison of words that look enough alike to be (wrongly) considered cognate, however, will tell us something about phonological difference if not divergence. It is my conviction that the possibly invalid comparisons will not distort the results sufficiently to obscure information.

My working hypothesis has been that if the phonostatistical results compare favorably with the lexicostatistical findings, and if the conclusions of each can also be supported by structural studies, then we can be assured of the validity of the statistical measures as tools for the study of language relationships. Results do assure the validity of the statistical tools in a satisfying way.

3.2. *Methodology*

Table 84 gives the code used in this study. Each column represents a dimension as described above. We proceed by comparing any two words which have been considered cognate in the lexicostatistical study. For example, we may compare the words meaning 'ear' in Akuna and Asempa: *akɔ* and *aqɔ*. Analytically, the coded value of the first word is 6601 3102 6501; of the second 6601 4199 6501. The number 9 indicates that a par-

TABLE 84

CODIFICATION

p	1102	*t*	2102	*k*	3102	*q*	4199
p̶	1202	*s*	2202	*kw*	3202	*h*	4299
b	1101	*d*	2101	*g*	3101		
b̶	1201	*r*	2201	*g̶*	3201		
w	1301	*y*	2301				
m	1111	*n*	2111				

i	5401			*u*	7401
e	5501	*ə*	6501	*o*	7501
eh	5601	*a*	6601	*ah*	7601

Loss of consonant 9499   Loss of vowel 9299

Note: *eh* is a low front vowel; *ah* is a low back slightly rounded vowel.

ticular dimension is nonsignificant (summing 9 with any other number thus gives 0). The only difference between these words, then, is 1.

In the Tairora village of Abiqera, the word for 'ear' is *ato*. This word has been considered cognate with the two just mentioned (even though at present I have not found a systematic correspondence between the final vowels). The phonostatistical comparison with Asempa would be as follows:

$$
\begin{array}{llll}
6601 & 4199 & 6501 & \textit{(akə)} \\
\underline{6601} & \underline{2102} & \underline{7501} & \textit{(ato)} \\
0000 & 2000 & 1000 & \text{total } 3
\end{array}
$$

The words in Asempa and Abiqera differ by three degrees. We conclude in this case that Asempa and Akuna are more closely related than are Asempa and Abiqera, that is, as far as this word is concerned, Abiqera has had a separate development longer than have Asempa and Akuna.

All probable cognates for which there are data in the previously mentioned lists are compared in this way. When a word is not considered cognate, or when it has not been elicited, no comparison is made. The total degrees of difference for all probable cognates must be summed. A mean difference is than calculated, taking into consideration only the number of words which have been compared in any two languages. These degrees of difference represent the average amount of phonological difference per word in the various pairs of dialects. The mean degrees of difference may then be arranged in a matrix where every pair of the dialects studied is located.

3.3. *Results Tabulated*

The material for this phase of the study was programmed in Fortran for the IBM 709 by Richard Lycan, University of Washington. Tables 85, 86,

TABLE 85

PHONOSTATISTICAL MEAN DEGREES OF DIFFERENCE
(Based on List I)

	Awa			Auyana			Gadsup			Tairora		
	Mo	Il	Ta	Ka	As	Ko	Oy	To	Ak	Ab	Bat	Bai
Mo												
Il	1.73											
Ta	2.20	1.00										
		(1.64)										
Ka	2.72	2.71	2.69									
As	2.74	2.66	2.47	0.58								
Ko	2.83	2.73	2.69	1.02	0.52							
		(2.69)			(0.71)							
Oy	3.07	3.05	3.16	2.54	2.29	2.29						
To	3.09	2.85	2.98	2.72	2.41	2.69	1.75					
Ak	3.18	2.90	3.02	2.77	2.47	2.74	1.83	0.06				
		(3.03)			(2.55)			(1.21)				
Ab	4.18	4.11	4.07	3.67	3.47	3.45	3.39	3.44	3.39			
Bat	3.98	4.13	4.10	3.58	3.40	3.27	3.43	3.56	3.51	0.27		
Bai	3.73	3.80	3.83	3.94	3.66	3.54	3.62	3.42	3.37	1.70	1.70	
		(3.99)			(3.55)			(3.46)			(1.22)	

and 87 indicate the mean degrees of difference found in a study of Lists I, II, and III, respectively. Matrices are arranged in so far as is possible with the smallest numbers toward the diagonal. These pairs show the least phonetic divergence, and therefore the greatest affinity. An average figure appears in parentheses for each language group.

3.4. *Observations Corroborating Lexicostatistical Studies*

Phonostatistical tables compare favorably with those given for lexicostatistical studies. The smallest differences are between dialects of the same language, grouping Mobuta, Ilakia, and Tauna as *Awa;* Asempa, Kosena, and Kawaina as *Auyana;* Oyana, Akuna, and Tompena as *Gadsup;* and Abiqera, Batainabura, and Baira as *Tairora.*

In each of the phonostatistical tables we also note that Auyana occupies a position between Awa and Gadsup. Table 85 shows Auyana a bit closer to Gadsup while Table 86 shows Auyana a bit closer to Awa. Note that this is just the reverse of the lexicostatistical results for Lists I and II—

TABLE 86

PHONOSTATISTICAL MEAN DEGREES OF DIFFERENCE
(Based on List II)

	Awa			Auyana			Gadsup			Tairora		
	Mo	Il	Ta	Ka	As	Ko	Oy	Ak	To	Ab	Bat	Bai
Mo												
Il	1.93											
Ta	2.04	1.00										
		(1.65)										
Ka	2.48	2.40	2.88									
As	2.60	2.52	2.83	0.24								
Ko	2.52	3.00	3.17	0.70	1.00							
		(2.71)			(0.65)							
Oy	3.72	3.88	3.71	2.97	3.00	2.92						
Ak	3.55	3.78	3.91	3.00	2.92	3.05	1.49					
To	3.69	3.94	4.00	3.09	3.03	3.21	1.64	0.20				
		(3.80)			(3.02)			(1.11)				
Ab	3.77	3.87	3.62	3.60	3.48	3.88	3.06	2.85	2.94			
Bat	3.96	4.03	3.59	3.67	3.61	4.03	2.97	2.85	2.94	0.43		
Bai	4.72	5.14	4.82	4.53	4.44	4.59	3.52	3.61	3.61	1.70	1.73	
		(4.17)			(3.98)			(3.15)			(1.29)	

indicating that the margin of difference is so small (as Table 87 for List III portrays), that we conclude that Auyana is about equidistant between Gadsup and Awa. On the other hand, Gadsup and Awa show greater divergence from each other than does either of these from Auyana, again paralleling the lexicostatistical results.

The average difference for all dialects of Tairora indicates that this languages is the most divergent of the four. Differences between Awa and Gadsup seem to be as great as between Tairora and the others. According to the results in Table 86 Gadsup and Tairora are even a little close than Gadsup and Awa, a fact which we will comment on later (Sec. 3.5.3).

In summary, Gadsup, Auyana, and Awa form a subgroup with some parallel development—Gadsup and Awa the most divergent within it, but Tairora and Awa distinctly more divergent than Gadsup and Awa. Tairora seems to have had a longer and more independent development than any of the others. The phonostatistical measure for these data thus supports the lexicostatistical index.

TABLE 87

PHONOSTATISTICAL MEAN DEGREES OF DIFFERENCE
(Based on List III)

	Ilakia	Asempa	Akuna	Abiqera
Ilakia				
Asempa	2.51			
Akuna	3.48	2.53		
Abiqera	4.06	3.58	3.21	

3.5. Extended Observations

3.5.1. *Comparative results between lists.* It is worthy of note that Lists I, II, and III show relatively little difference in phonostatistical mean degrees of difference. There are differences, but these are individual, and cannot be characterized by an over-all pattern from list to list. Our lexicostatistical studies indicate a real difference between lists, pointing up the factor of a core vocabulary. Since in the phonostatistical studies we are considering only probable cognates, variation between lists should come only from differences in judgment as to what is cognate and what is not. I would venture to suggest that if assured cognates only were considered instead of cognates determined by inspection, the results in each list would be the same. I have therefore combined Lists I and II and indicated the mean degrees of difference for that combination in Table 88. In general, our further observations will be made from this combined matrix.

3.5.2. *Relations between dialects within language groups.* Mobuta, Oyana, and Baira are the most divergent of the dialects in Awa, Gadsup, and Tairora, respectively. Both the phonostatistical and the lexicostatistical figures agree. Dialects in the Auyana are closer to each other, no one of them clearly more divergent than the others. In the Awa, Mobuta and Tauna are the most widely divergent pair. Ilakia and Tauna group a little closer than do Ilakia and Mobuta. These phonostatistical results reflect the spatial relation of these dialects.

Spatial dimensions are also paralleled by linguistic relationships in the following instances. Akuna and Tompena are linguistically and geographically quite close. The linguistic relationship between Oyana and the other Gadsup dialects, on the other hand, indicates a greater separation in both time and space.

In contrast, Kosena is quite far geographically (as distances go in this language family) from Asempa, yet more closely related to Asempa than

TABLE 88

Phonostatistical Mean Degrees of Difference
(Based on Lists I and II Combined)

	Awa			Auyana			Gadsup			Tairora		
	Mo	Il	Ta	Ka	As	Ko	Oy	Ak	To	Ab	Bat	Bai
Mo												
Il	1.83											
Ta	2.12	1.00										
		(1.65)										
Ka	2.60	2.55	2.78									
As	2.67	2.59	2.65	0.41								
Ko	2.67	2.86	2.93	0.86	0.76							
		(2.70)			(0.64)							
Oy	3.39	3.46	3.43	2.75	2.65	2.60						
Ak	3.36	3.34	3.46	2.88	2.69	2.89	1.66					
To	3.39	3.39	3.49	2.90	2.72	2.95	1.69	0.13				
		(3.41)			(2.78)			(1.16)				
Ab	3.97	3.99	3.84	3.63	3.47	3.66	3.22	3.14	3.16			
Bat	3.97	4.08	3.84	3.62	3.50	3.65	3.20	3.20	3.22	0.35		
Bai	4.22	4.47	4.32	4.23	4.05	4.06	3.57	3.51	3.49	1.70	1.71	
		(4.08)			(3.76)			(3.30)			(1.25)	

Oyana is to Akuna. This linguistic closeness is paralleled by the remembered history of the removal of Kosena from the village of Arora, situated very close to Asempa (and of the same dialect as Kosena). Given time, and independence from the other Auyana dialects, we would expect Kosena to become the most divergent of the group which includes Kawaina and Asempa—a possibility that does not seem as probable now as it would have been before the coming of the Europeans.

Later in this paper (Sec. 3.6) we will observe the relationships between Usarufa, a fourth Auyana dialect, and those mentioned here. Usarufa is the most divergent of the Auyana dialects, an indication that Usarufa has been separated from other Auyana dialects for the longest period of time, and that it has also been geographically independent of the others.

Abiqera and Batainabura of the Tairora are very closely linked linguistically. In this case, these villages are farther apart geographically than Akuna and Tompena. There are also a number of villages in the areas of Abiqera and Batainabura which have little linguistic divergence from each other. In fact, there are more villages speaking what we may term a 'Tairora Valley' dialect of Tairora than there are villages speaking any one dialect of any of the other languages. In conjunction with this, we note that there is little geographically to hinder communication in the Tairora Valley area. As we will note later in this chapter (Sec. 3.5.3), the Tairora separates Oyana from the other Gadsup dialects. We conclude that the Tairora pushed into the area rather than that the Gadsup dialects moved away from each other across the Tairora. These facts are noted here to give the further suggestion that the Tairora Valley people seem to have pushed into the valley area at about the same time, and while coming into the area must have had a good deal of contact with each other. Linguistic relationships thus seem to portray an interaction in the Tairora Valley area which is not paralleled by interaction in other languages, at least over as wide an area.

3.5.3. *Relations of various dialects across language boundaries.* Some evidence from the phonostatistical tables seems to indicate that certain dialects of different languages have had longer contact and show less divergence than do others. For example, the phonostatistical figures indicate less divergence between Gadsup and Tairora than they do between Tairora and the other languages. This may mean that Gadsup has shared a boundary with Tairora longer than with the other languages. This striking Tairora-Gadsup relationship leads me to suggest that phonostatistical figures may reflect geographical relations across language boundaries, as well as between dialects of the same language. Note that Oyana evidences closer relations to the Auyana than do the other Gadsup dialects. This no doubt reflects a long-standing border relation between Oyana and the Auyana dialects, especially Kosena and Asempa.

As indicated in Section 3.5.2, the Tairora villages now separating Oyana from the other Gadsup dialects seem to represent an intrusion. The Gadsup dialects have shared a common border with Tairora for approximately the same period of time, as seen by the fact that each has about the same phonostatistical relationship to the Tairora. The Oyana relationship to Auyana indicates stability of location for these peoples, but the difference between Oyana and Akuna-Tompena indicates a separation of both time and space.

No Awa dialect seems to be especially close to any of the Auyana dialects. Lists I and II yield varying results on this question. We can only conclude that there has been no particular long-standing influence between, for example, Tauna and Kawaina, the present closest neighbors across this language boundary. The same seems to be true of the Awa-Tairora boundary, although I do not have material from an Awa village that borders a Tairora village. The rugged terrain of the Awa territory suggests a possible isolation of the Awa from both Auyana and Tairora (as well as Gadsup), and even from village to village within the Awa. It would be of interest to know whether at present the Awa show a greater tendency toward either independence or fission plus isolation in their cultural traits, than do the Tairora of the Valley area. These, at any rate, may be the extremes within the area under study.

3.6. *Observations Related to Two Additional Dialects*

Material from two other dialects, Agarabi and Usarufa (Chap. XII; Bee 1961a, b), has been available for much of List I. Phonostatistical results indicate that Agarabi groups with Gadsup, and Usarufa with Auyana (as Wurm concluded in his studies, 1960, 1961a). Agarabi is the most divergent of the Gadsup dialects, though it does show slightly closer relations to Oyana than to the Akuna-Tompena area. This is of interest since Oyana does not at present share a common border with Agarabi, as do Akuna and Tompena. Agarabi also has a slightly higher divergence from the Tairora dialects than do others of the Gadsup dialects. This indicates that the Agarabi have been spatially farther from the Tairora than have the Oyana, Akuna, and Tompena.

Usarufa is the most divergent dialect of the Auyana, indicating a longer separate development for Usarufa from the more central Auyana dialects. On the other hand, Usarufa shows more affinity to the Gadsup, especially Oyana, than do the other dialects of Auyana. The closeness of Usarufa and Oyana linguistically may be in error, since the figures are based on less material than that used for the other languages and dialects. However, it is quite likely that Usarufa and Oyana once shared a common border. The Usarufa people claim that they were once a much larger group, occupying a much larger area than they do now. (Kosena is said to be on Usarufa ground.) Thus Usarufa may have come at one time between the other Auyana dialects and the Gadsup. Phonologically the Usarufa and Oyana constitute links between the Auyana and Gadsup languages.

Tables 89 and 90 give the lexicostatistical and phonostatistical figures for Agarabi and Usarufa as related to the other study dialects.[5]

4. STRUCTURAL STUDIES

The results obtained by lexicostatistical and phonostatistical studies are further supported by a study of the structural characteristics of the languages in their present form, and also by those facts which I have been able to glean from the application of the comparative method. Though Capell (1962a) suggested structure statistics as another measure of linguistic relationship, the specific techniques for such a study have not been worked out. The structural comparisons that follow, however, though not

TABLE 89

LEXICOSTATISTICAL PERCENTAGES

(Based on List I)

	Awa			Auyana				Gadsup				Tairora		
	Mo	Il	Ta	As	Ko	Ka	Us	Oy	Ag	Ak	To	Ab	Bat	Bai
Us	66.7	67.0	69.2	82.8	82.6	81.9		67.4	68.9	64.9	62.4	56.5	56.4	51.6
Ag	61.8	62.7	64.5	70.1	67.5	64.9	68.9	89.6		83.1	80.3	61.0	59.7	55.8

TABLE 90

PHONOSTATISTICAL MEAN DEGREES OF DIFFERENCE

(Based on List I)

	Awa			Auyana				Gadsup				Tairora		
	Mo	Il	Ta	As	Ko	Ka	Us	Oy	Ag	Ak	To	Ab	Bat	Bai
Us	2.60	2.80	2.66	1.27	1.22	1.67		1.41	2.14	2.07	2.04	3.33	3.34	3.57
Ag	3.20	3.07	3.07	2.61	2.40	2.64	2.14	1.67		1.82	1.81	3.43	3.63	3.95

formally statistical in nature, do confirm our conclusions drawn from the lexical and phonological comparisons.

4.1. *Phonological Structures*

4.1.1. *Present status.* Each of the four languages in view has at present a series of voiceless stops including /p/, /t/, /k/, and glottal /q/; a voiced series consisting of /b/ and /d/; and the nasals /m/ and /n/. Auyana and Awa have both the bilabial and alveolar semivowels /w/ and /y/, whereas Gadsup has only /y/ phonemic of the two; Tairora lacks both of these in its phonemic system. Auyana and Awa have an alveolar sibilant phonemic, /s/, but Gadsup and Tairora do not have this sound as a phoneme. Awa has the voiced velar /g/ phonemic, but this sound is subphonemic in Auyana, grouping with /k/. Tairora has a glottal aspirate /h/ not found in the other languages.

Auyana, Gadsup, and Tairora exhibit six vowels in their systems: /i/,

---

[5] Data for the Agarabi are from the field notes of Professor J. B. Watson, and for the Usarufa from Miss Darlene Bee of the Summer Institute of Linguistics. The data for the Agarabi are from the village of Ayamoentenu.

/ə/, /u/; and /e/, /a/, /o/. Awa has a seven vowel system with front vowels /i, /e/ and /eh/; back vowels /u/, /o/ and /ah/; and central vowel /a/ (allophones [a] and [ə]).

Each system is thus distinguished from the other: Awa from Auyana, and from the others, by one additional vowel; Gadsup from Auyana and Awa by the absence of the bilabial semivowel and the sibilant phonemes; and Tairora from the others by the absence of semivowels and sibilants as well as the presence of a unique glottal aspirate. This is basically the relationship already noted: Tairora the most divergent; Awa, Auyana, and Gadsup a subgroup with Gadsup the most divergent of that subgroup.

Though a number of the phonemes in these languages are the same, they are often composed of different allophones. Thus the bilabial sounds group differently in Gadsup and Auyana, and even differently in specific Auyana dialects. In Gadsup there are three bilabial phonemes: /p/, /b/ and /m/. The first includes the allophones [p] and [b], the second allophones [b], [b], and [w], and the third the single allophone [m]. The Asempa dialect of Auyana has four bilabial phonemes: /p/, /b/, /w/ and /m/. The first has a single representation as do /w/ and /m/, but the second has allophones [p], [b], and [b]. But the Kawaina dialect of Auyana has five: /p/, /f/, /b/, /w/, and /m/. A contrast has developed in the Kawaina between voiceless and voiced obstruents.

The contrast between [p] and [b] making /f/ and /b/ both phonemes in Kawaina was introduced in the following way. The proto phoneme */m/ has various reflexes in the Auyana dialects. Initially, and preceding bilabials, it is /m/ in all dialects: andampa 'mouth', maiya- 'taro.' Following /u/ it is /m/ in Asempa, but /w/ in Kawaina: aumə and auwə 'egg.' Following /i/ it is /m/ in Asempa, but /y/ in Kawaina: taimə and taiyə 'tree'. Intervocalically it is /m/ in Asempa, but /b/ in Kawaina: numamə and nduwabə 'bird'. Because this phoneme becomes /b/ intervocalically in Kawaina, a contrast is introduced between [p] and [b] not found in Asempa. These two sounds fluctuate noncontrastively in Asempa, but note the contrast in the following words from Kawaina: uwipəqə 'forest', ufəqə 'grass land', and abəmə 'bark'. Cognates in Asempa are umipəpə 'forest', ubəqə (upəqə or ubəqə) 'grass land', and amambə 'bark'.

In noting these reflexes of */m/ we have also observed that not all semivowels in present Auyana dialects trace back to an original */w/ or */y/. Such complications may be multiplied in a detailed study of the changes which have taken place, and in reconstructing earlier stages of the languages. For this study we can only indicate briefly what the results of a comparative study are to date.

4.1.2. *Earlier stages.* Comparative studies within each of the four languages tentatively yield the following phonological systems.

	Consonants	Vowels
A. Pre-Awa	*p t k q*	*i u*
	f s	*e ə o*
	b d g	*eh a ah*
	w y	
	m n	
B. Pre-Auyana	*p t k q*	*i ə u*
	f s x k^w	*e a o*
	b d	
	w y	
	m n	
C. Pre-Gadsup	*p t k q*	*i ə u*
	f s	*e a o*
	b d	
	w y	
	m n	
D. Pre-Tairora	*p t k q h*	*i ə u*
	b d	*e a o*
	m n	

These reconstructed systems display again the same grouping of languages we have noted throughout our study. The only major difference between these systems and the present day systems is the voiceless fricative series in the Awa-Auyana-Gadsup subgroup, not found in the Tairora. Auyana exhibits the fullest of the series and seems to fall between Gadsup and Awa.

Though the Tairora does not have a fricative series phonemic, such phones do occur in the various dialects, and the early phonemes in the voiceless series thus represent sets of correspondences with such in them. For example, the Tairora Valley dialect exhibits a reflex /k/, while quite consistently the southern dialect exhibits a reflex /s/, both from */k/ *kauqu: sauqu* 'hand'; *bukera: busera* 'cassowary.'

4.1.3. *Earliest stage.* Some of the sound correspondences of these languages show further their relationship to each other. The following examples are arranged to indicate the proto phonemes and their reflexes. Reflexes are enclosed in parentheses. The letter 'I' after the proto phoneme indicates initial sounds, 'M' indicates medial.

	Awa	Auyana	Gadsup	Tairora	
*p	*(p)uk-*	*(p)uk-*	*(p)uk-*	*(q)ut-*	'die'
	(p)oedahq	*(p)oimə*	*(p)oni*	*(q)uəda*	'pig'
*b	*(m)ada-*	*(m)ada*	*(m)aka*	*(b)ata*	'ground'
	(m)ina	*(m)ində*	*(m)ini*	*(b)ihə*	'that'

		Awa	Auyana	Gadsup	Tairora	
*w		(w)eh	(w)aiyə	(b)antə	(b)ainti	'man'
		(w)ahte	(w)atoi-	(b)aqdo-	(b)aqa	'clothing'
*m		(m)ahna	(m)andə	(m)ənə	(m)ahə	'this'
		(m)adotah	(m)ədombəq	(m)ənoməni	(m)ədomədi	'owl'
*t	I	(t)ahyahte	(s)iyankai	(t)iyankəni	. . .	'ten'
		. . .	-(s)i	(t)equ	(t)i	'say'
		. . .	. . .	(t)eni	(t)ede	'I'
	M	ma(t)awe	mə(s)awembə	bə(t)apemi	bə(h)abera	'fat'
		a(t)i-	ki(s)i	i(t)i	i(h)i	'sneeze'
*d	I	(n)agaq	-(nd)əbə	(n)əni	(n)aədə	'vine'
		(n)o	(nd)ombə	(n)omi .	(n)amədi	'water'
	M	mo(d)a	mo(d)ə	mə(n)ə	. . .	'one'
		a(d)u	ə(d)uq	. . .	-tə(d)ə	'thigh'
		ma(d)otah	mə(d)ombəq	mə(n)oməni	mə(d)omədi	'owl'
*y	I	(t)eh	(t)aimə	(y)ani	(k)atadi	'tree'
		(t)ahq	(t)aqə	(y)aqi	(k)aqə	'sugar cane'
	M	i(y)a	i(y)əmə	i(y)əmi	bai(d)i	'dog'
		a(y)ah	a(y)a-	a(y)a	. . .	'hand'
*n	I	(n)u	(n)umbə	(n)umi	(n)umə	'bird'
		(n)ah	(n)ambə	(n)ami	(n)amə	'breast'
	M	o(n)i-	o(n)təmbə	o(n)i	o(d)i	'stone'
		a(n)o	a(n)u	a(n)o	a(d)u	'neck'
*k		(t)auya	(k)amoyə	(k̇)auyə	(t)aqə	'drum'
		(t)o(t)oriq	(k)o(k)oq-	(k)o(k)oq	(t)o(t)oqəi	'warm'
*g		ma(d)a	ma(d)a	ma(k)a	ba(t)a	'ground'
		-(d)a(d)a	-(d)a(d)ao	-(k)a(k)ə	-(t)a(t)odə	'grandmother'
		po(d)iah	pa(d)oimə	pa(k)oni	. . .	'arrow'
*h		namu(q)	. . .	nəmi(q)i	nəbu(h)i	'grass'
		koko(q)	ko(q)ə	ko(q)i	ko(h)o	'bean'[6]
		. . .	. . .	i(q)i	i(h)i	'sing'
*q		ah(q)	a(q)ə	a(q)i	a(q)u	'rain'
		anu(q)	anu(q)ə	aku(q)i	tu(q)ə	'root'
*i		(i)taq	(i)sao	(i)ndə	(i)di-	'hear'
		(i)bitehq	(i)biqi	(i)piqi	(i)qira-	'cry'
*e		na(e)	na(e)mə	nar(e)	nar(e)	'blood'
		aw(e)	am(e)-	am(e)-	b(e)-	'tail'
*u		n(u)	n(u)mbə	n(u)mi	n(u)mə	'bird'
		(u)bo	(u)pu	(u)po-	(u)bi-	'dig'

[6] This set is the only one I have with initial /k/ throughout. I am somewhat dubious as to its validity.

	Awa	Auyana	Gadsup	Tairora	
*o	(o)ni-	(o)ontəmbə	(o)ni	(o)ri	'stone'
	n(o)na-	(o)ya-	(o)ni	(o)də	'ditch'[7]
*a	(ah)mapi	(a)mbə	(a)ni	(a)rə	'path'
	(ah)ka-	(a)qə	(a)kə	(a)to	'ear'
*ə	(a)yu	(ə)rambə	(ə)yumi	(ə)uru	'seed'[8]
*ai	t(eh)	t(ai)mə	y(a)ni	kat(ai)re(Bat)	'tree'
*ai	. . .	aw(ai)-	ab(a)kuni	ab(ai)	'tooth'
	w(eh)	w(ai)yə	b(a)ntə	b(ai)nti	'man'
*au	(au)peq	(au)pəq	(o)pəqi	m(au)təq-	'hidden'
	. . .	t(au)	y(o)i	k(au)hi	'hair'

Most of the vowel phonemes, and the reflexes of */m/, initial */n/, and */q/ show the genetic relationship of the four languages. The reflexes of */p/, */b/, initial */y/, and */h/ show Tairora split from the other three languages. If we refer to the earliest stage of this family as Tagauwa, then we can say that Tagauwa split into Tairora and a proto language from which we have the Awa, Auyana, and Gadsup. This pre–Awa-Auyana-Gadsup group may be referred to as Gauwa.

Table 91 depicts the history of the initial consonants showing the split of Tairora and Gauwa from the earliest stage Tagauwa. The Gauwa in turn split into the three languages: Awa, Auyana, and Gadsup. The reader can trace the various splits for each initial consonant by comparing phonemes across the table.

These data indicate that Awa and Auyana are slightly closer to each other than are Auyana and Gadsup. However, certain of the medial consonants (reflexes of */k/, and the vowels */ə/ and */a/), as well as structural evidence to follow, show Auyana and Gadsup to be related about as closely as are Awa and Auyana.

4.2. *Grammatical Structures*

A survey of some of the grammatical features of the languages under discussion will add support to our study. Each language is characterized by a fairly complicated noun and verb morphology. Various affixes attached

---

[7] Words for 'stone' and 'ditch' in Gadsup differ in tone: óní and òní, respectively. I have not indicated tone in this chapter since it needs more study in some of the languages.

[8] The distinction between the central mid vowel [ə] and the central low vowel [a] proved to be a problem in recording data. Awa evidence unites the two into one phoneme but has /ah/. Gadsup has a short and long variety of the low central quality [a], the short variety uniting with [ə] to make up the phenome /ə/, and the long variety forming a single variety of /a/. This fact was discovered by Chester Frantz after the writer had left New Guinea. Some similar allophonic distribution may be true for the other languages. My data now need revising with this in view.

TABLE 91

INITIAL CONSONANT HISTORY

Tairora		Tagauwa		Gauwa		Gadsup	Auyana	Awa
q	<	$*p$	>	$*p$	>	p	p	p
b	<	$*b$	>	$*m$	>	m	m	m
b	<	$*w$	>	$*w$	>	b	w	w
m	<	$*m$	>	$*m$	>	m	m	m
t	<	$*t$	>	$*t$	>	t	s	t
d	<	$*d$	>	$*d$	>	n	nd	n
k	<	$*y$	>	$*y$	>	y	t	t
n	<	$*n$	>	$*n$	>	n	n	n
t	<	$*k$	>	$*k$	>	k	t	t
t	<	$*g$	>	$*g$	>	k	d	d
h	<	$*h$	>	$*q$	>	q	q	q
q	<	$*q$	>	$*q$	>	q	q	q

to word bases indicate semantic categories and grammatical relations. Thus noun affixes may indicate size or shape, number, location; and show such relations as similarity, conjunction, possession, accompaniment, and so forth. Nouns may also contain morphemes to indicate that the word base is called (vocative), predicated (predicative), or questioned in one way or another (interrogative).

The verb complex may indicate persons involved in the action as subject, object, or benefactive; the tense or aspect of the action; and also the mode of the action. Verbs are either independent (see especially Chap. VI) or dependent (Chap. VII) with some difference in the morphemes permitted in the complex to distinguish them. Dependent verbs occur in clauses which predict other clauses. Such verbs contain a morpheme anticipating the subject of the action predicted. They may also contain morphemes to show intraclausal relations as to time or kind of action.

Both noun and verb complexes in these languages are also character-ized by a great deal of morphophonemics. Tairora verbs on the one hand contain complexes of morphemes best described as fusions. Gadsup verbs, on the other hand, contain sequences of identifiable morphemes whose shapes are greatly altered by environment. Note the following:

Tairora fusions indicating person subject and tense-aspect (see Chap. XXX):

na-arera 'I/we might eat.'	na-rera 'I/we will eat.'
na-irera 'You/he might eat.'	na-reba 'You/he will eat.'
na-ibera 'You/they might eat.'	na-reka 'You/they will eat.'

Gadsup variants of the narrative morpheme indicated by parentheses, preceded or followed by subject morphemes (see Chap. XXI):

kum-(eq)-u 'I go down.' *kum-onə(mi)* 'You (pl) go down.'
kum-o(mi) 'You (sing) go down.' *kum(en)-o* 'They go down.'
kum(em)i 'He goes down.'

The modification of morphemes in their phonological and morphemic environments is part of the study of linguistic change and is used by comparativists for the internal reconstruction of a language. Much remains to be done in the Kainantu languages that I have not attempted in this paper. Here I can only point out some of the structural comparisons depicting the linguistic relationship existing between these languages.

4.2.1. *Noun structure*

4.2.1.1. *Morphophonemics.* Awa (see Chap. IV), Auyana (Chap. XI), and Gadsup (Chap. XX) have noun classes based upon the final phoneme of the noun base. The first two have three classes: Class I with final /q/, Class II with a final nasal, and Class III with a final vowel. Gadsup has these three, where the first may end with either final glottal or /k/, and two additional classes for nouns whose bases end with /y/ or /d/. Tairora noun bases all end with vowels and thus do not fall into these classes (see Chap. XXVII).

The following examples illustrate:

Class	Awa	Auyana	Gadsup	Tairora	
I	*tahq*	*taq-*	*yak-*	*kaqə*	'sugar cane'
II	*iyan*	*iyən-*	*iyən-*	*bairi*	'dog'
III	*ida* (Mo)	*idə*	*ikə*	*ihə*	'fire'
IV	*poedahq*	*poi-*	*pod-*	*quəda*	'pig'
V	*wita*	*kuri*	*kukuy-*	*tutuka*	'fence'

These facts show a Tairora split from the other languages, and a close relationship between Awa and Auyana as well as Gadsup and Auyana.

4.2.1.2. *Affixes.* Noun affixes in the four languages are usually suffixes. Suffixes indicating size and number usually occur closest to the noun base followed by grammatical relation markers, and finally there are markers to indicate that the complex is a complete utterance, independent of other utterances. All four languages have the suffix *-o* for the vocative. The predicative morphemes (translated 'It is a ———') are for Awa *-mire ~ -re ~ -e;* for Auyana *-we ~ -ye ~ -e;* for Gadsup *-ni* or *-e* (explicit); and for Tairora *-ma* or *-be.* Interrogative morphemes are varied. Awa has a number indicating various shades of doubt or question: *-po, -pomo, -rabiramo,* and so forth. Auyana has *-waqi ~ -yaqi ~ -aqi.* Gadsup has a group which also indicates person involvement: *-pu, -pe* ~ *-po, -pi* (first, second, and third person interrogative, respectively). Tairora has *-e*.

The only prefixes occurring with nouns are those indicating person. Certain nouns are characterized in all four languages as obligatorily containing a person possessor. These same, or very similar morphemes, occur with the verbs to indicate the indirect or direct object of the action, or the benefactor of the action. The person morphemes follow:

	1st sing/pl	2nd/3rd sing	2nd/3rd pl
Awa	*ni-* ~ *nu-*	*a-*	*si-*
Auyana	*s-* ~ *si-* ~ *su-*	*a-* ~ *o-*	*t-* ~ *ti-* ~ *tu-*
Gadsup	*ti-*	*a-*	*yi-*
Tairora	*h-(ti-* in verbs)	*a-*	*n-*

The following suffixes illustrate further some of the interrelations between the four languages.

	Awa	Auyana	Gadsup	Tairora
'in'	*-piq*	*-pin*	*-kin*	*-qi*
'on, at'	*-taq*	*-daq* ~ *-kaq*	*-kak*	*-qa* ~ *-qata*
conjunction	*-kakaq,* *-seq,* *-reh*	*-wadaq*	*-a* ~ *-ba* ~ *-ate*	*-ka* ~ *-bata*
place	*-peq*	*-pqə*	*-pək*	*-da*
'from'	*-ten*	*-ken*	*-ke*	*-hai*
similarity	*-tahnsan*	*-dan* ~ *-kan*	*-keke* ~ *-ke*	. . .
plural	*-do* ~ *-so* ~ *-madin* etc.	*-ton* ~ *-yon*	*-uk*	*-ka* ~ *-uka*
dual	*-tade* ~ *-te* ~ *-natade*	. . .	*-kəndə* ~ *-təndə*	*-təntə*
reference	*-sabe*	*-tabe* ~ *-yabe*	. . .	. . .
classifier	. . .	*-ma* ~ *-a*	*-mi* ~ *-i*	. . .

4.2.2. *Verb structure*

4.2.2.1. *Subject morphemes.* The only morphemes which are obligatory to the verb complex (besides the base) in all four languages are the subject indicators. Subject morphemes usually mark first person (singular or plural), second singular, third singular, and second or third plural. Sometimes in Awa (see Chap. VI), and always in Tairora (Chap. XXX), the subject morphemes are so fused with the tense or mode indicators as to be indivisible. Though individual morphemes cannot be identified for the person subjects in Tairora, the fusions often have characteristic vowels which seem to be vestiges of the person markers. Morphemes indicating the persons follow; the characteristic vowels for Tairora are also noted. Parentheses indicate possible alternants.

	Awa	Auyana	Gadsup	Tairora
1st sing/pl	*-ga ∼ -q*	*-u*	*-u(m)*	/u/
2nd sing	*-na(q)*	*-a*	*-ona*	/a/
3rd sing	*-da ∼ -q*	*-i*	*-i*	/i/
1st pl	*-na(q)*	. . .	. . .	. . .
2nd/3rd pl	*-waq ∼ -q*	*-a ∼ -o*	*-o*	

4.2.2.2. *Benefactive morpheme.* There is a benefactive morpheme in Awa, Auyana, and Gadsup, but not in Tairora. This morpheme with the different person markers preceding it is cited here for comparative reference.

	Awa	Auyana	Gadsup
1st sing/pl	*-nin(t)*	*-si(nka)*	*-ti(nk)*
2nd sing/pl	*-a(t)*	*-a(nka)*	*-a(nk)*
3rd sing/pl	*-ri(t)*	*-ti(nka)*	*-yi(nk)*

4.2.2.3. *General structure.* The following is an indication of other structural categories that may occur in the verb complex. These are not formulas for descriptive purposes, but generalizations for comparison.

Awa

$$+ \text{ Stem } \pm \text{ aspect } + \left\{ \begin{array}{l} \text{tense-subject} \\ \\ \text{tense-subject-mode} \end{array} \right\} \pm \text{ mode}$$

Auyana

$$+ \text{ Stem } \pm \text{ -ma } + \left\{ \begin{array}{l} \text{completive 1} \\ \\ \text{completive 2} \end{array} \right\} \pm \text{ stative } \pm \text{ tense } + \text{ subject}$$

$\pm$ mode

Gadsup
$+$ Stem $\pm$ potential $\pm$ abilitative $\pm$ narrative $\pm$ interrogative $\pm$ completive
$+$ subject $\pm$ augmentative 1 $\pm$ augmentative 2

Tairora
$+$ Stem $+$ tense-subject $\pm$ mode or $+$ stem $\pm$ mode-subject

Tairora does not mark the aspects found in the other languages in the verb complex. If an object, direct or indirect, occurs, person morphemes to indicate this usually follow the stem in Awa, and precede the verb stem in

Gadsup, Auyana, and Tairora. Certain verbs in each of the languages require an indirect object person marker in the verb.[9]

5. GENERAL IMPLICATIONS

This paper supports Wurm's general classification of Highlands languages in New Guinea by a careful examination of the divergence resulting in four major languages and a number of dialects in the Kainantu subdistrict. More broadly, the study implies that quite good results of a classificatory nature can be obtained from a very small percentage of the total lexical inventory. This is because certain lexical items are relatively stable (Swadesh 1950:157). This paper further attests to a core vocabulary of such items. The core vocabulary includes the highest probable percentage of comparable lexical items in pairs of languages, and therefore makes it feasible to postulate linguistic relationships from a very limited amount of data.

The material here also supports Grimes's contention (1962) that phonostatistics is a more refined index of linguistic relationship than lexicostatistics. This is because almost all of the comparable phonological elements occur in a limited corpus. However, the phonostatistical measure decreases in value as the linguistic separation between languages increases. Under such conditions, lexicostatistics retains its value, but as distance increases, I would suggest more reliance upon structural studies. This leads me to express a hope that, following Ellegard (1959), Kroeber (1960), Capell (1962a) and others, a formal technique of structure statistics will be developed.

This paper also points out the variance in absolute glottochronological time depths calculated by different investigators and from different vocabularies. If lexical studies are to be used for dating purposes (see Chretien 1962, Gudschinsky 1956, Longacre 1960), great care must be exercised in the choice of lexical elements representing the core vocabulary. The figures given in Table 80 seem to me to be too shallow to allow for the amount of divergence between Tairora and the other languages. It may be that the more we refine the core vocabulary, the greater should be the retention rate used in the calculations.

6. SPECIFIC CONCLUSIONS AND IMPLICATIONS

We have seen that Awa, Auyana, Gadsup, and Tairora are members of a single language family. Tairora split from the proto form of these languages early, while the other three shared a longer common history.

---

[9] It may be that in these languages, nouns and verbs which require person prefixes (or the verb suffix for Awa) to indicate possession or indirect object have a higher retention rate than other lexical items. The word lists contain a fairly high percentage of nouns of this kind.

The Awa-Auyana-Gadsup subgroup shows a type of radial fission whereby Awa and Auyana are related to each other to about the same degree as are Gadsup and Auyana, while Gadsup and Awa show much longer separation from each other.

Moreover, the spatial order of these three members of the Gauwa subfamily matches the genetic order. Thus the farther apart the languages are geographically, the farther apart they are linguistically. In fact the farther apart two dialects are spatially in any one of the Kainantu languages, generally speaking, the more distant they are linguistically. All members of the larger family are contiguous to each other, moreover, with no outliers beyond the family bounds which have migrated earlier than remembered history; nor is any alien language located within the family bounds.

I find no evidence in the Kainantu family to suggest a major exception to this pattern of divergence. Only local movements within the family are at present evident, such as the Tairora Valley intrusion between two Gadsup dialects and Binumarien (a Tairora dialect needing more study) enclaved in the Gadsup area. In other words, I conclude that the Gauwa subgroup of the Kainantu Family either moved into the present area without disrupting its present spatiolinguistic pattern, or that this subgroup evolved largely or wholly *in situ.* If the latter is the case—and it seems to me the more likely possibility, then these people have been in the Highlands area —indeed, in this part of the Highlands—at the very least for 1,000 years, based upon glottochronological figures which seem quite conservative. I leave to others the implications of this possibility in relation to such questions as population expansion in the Highlands and the introduction of the sweet potato.

Wurm's map of the East New Guinea Highlands Phylum (1961c) indicates that each of the language families in the Stock is in a block which shows no alien intrusions. Generally speaking the languages closest to each other are more closely related, and the most aberrant members are located on the edges of each family. Duna, the farthest west of the Phylum, is the most aberrant family of the Stock. These facts seem to follow a spatiolinguistic relationship parallel to that found in my study of the single Kainantu Family. No alien language outside the Stock seems to be located within the bounds of the Stock, nor do we know of members of the Stock located outside of its bounds. We may then ask the question: did these languages also evolve *in situ,* or did they move into the area somehow preserving their present spatiolinguistic patterns? If they evolved *in situ,* then they have been in the Highlands area for a long time indeed.

A study of the spatiolinguistic relations of the language families in the Highlands Stock, along with suggestions by Dyen (1956) regarding his language distribution and migration theory, might help us locate the homeland of the progenitors of the Stock, at least within the Highlands. If other languages have been in the area, we can only assume that they have either been absorbed, or pushed to the outer edges of the area now occupied by languages belonging to the Stock.

One final point: Wurm has listed eight languages in the Kainantu family (1960:126; 1961c). Throughout this paper I have referred to Oyana, Agarabi, and Usarufa as dialects rather than languages, leaving only four major languages in the family. I have been influenced in this decision by the relationships which the Oyana and Agarabi have to Gadsup, and the Usarufa to Auyana—relationships as close as that of Mobuta to other Awa dialects or Baira to other Tairora dialects. I group the languages into the following dialect areas: Oyana, Agarabi, and Akuna-Tompena areas for *Gadsup;* Usarufa, Central Auyana, and Kawaina areas for *Auyana;* Northern and Southern areas for *Awa;* and at least the Tairora Valley and Southern areas for *Tairora.* Binumarien may be a third dialect of Tairora and there may be another dialect between the Tairora Valley and the Southern area, namely the Suwaira dialect. The Tairora dialects need further study as to their number.

7. APPENDIX

Three lists have been used for the statistical studies. These lists are reproduced here with certain modifications. In the original study Lists I and II were made up of forms from one central and one peripheral village making a total of eight forms for the study languages. I have cited in this appendix only one form from each language. The form cited is usually from a central village of the given language: Ilakia for Awa, Asempa for Auyana, Akuna for Gadsup, and Batainabura for Tairora.

List I is basically the 100 items from the Swadesh list (1955a:133-37). The following from that list are not included: feather (made up of hair + bird), hear (included in know), drink (included in eat), and lie, person, swim, round, horn (not appropriate for the Eastern Highlands of New Guinea). I have therefore substituted the following: arrow, bamboo, bow, father, grass, house, mother, and sugar cane.

List II contains 100 additional items often related to the cultures of the Eastern Highlands peoples. Twenty-five of these are from the longer 215-list of Swadesh (1950). List III contains some 345 entries selected from materials elicited from each of the four languages.

The orthography used here is consistent with that used in the descriptive studies of this volume. However, the forms are not written phonemically in all cases. Since entries are not always from the same dialect, the reader should not attempt a phonemic analysis from these lists. It should also be remembered that the lists were collected before much of the descriptive analysis was done. The lists could and should be refined, recognizing morphemes within entries and some either incorrect or at least doubtful renderings. However, these are the lists used for the statistical studies and are excellent examples of what the analyst uses for his early study.

The lists are arranged with English entries numbered followed by the entries from the four languages. If an entry was not elicited, its place is marked by ellipses.

7.1. *List I*

	Awa	Auyana	Gadsup	Tairora
1. 'all'	*moke*	*amapaqa*	*masiqdemi*	*ekaa*
2. 'arrow'	*poriah*	*paroima*	*pakoni*	*beba*
3. 'ashes'	*tanah*	*kanama*	*yuni*	*hantama*
4. 'bamboo'	*ana*	*anama*	*ana*	*taqu*
5. 'bark'	*ahweh*	*aamaamaba*	*aqkaami/ yagwami*	*aabahi*
6. 'belly'	*amuq*	*amuqa*	*amuqi*	*auha*
7. 'big'	*aanotah*	*anomba*	*inoqna*	*nora*
8. 'bird'	*nuwo*	*numama*	*numi*	*antau*
9. 'bite'	*ungiye*	*unkara*	*unkano*	*kaqaka*
10. 'black'	*pabutsa*	*aubutamba*	*kasiqi*	*bankora*
11. 'blood'	*nehe*	*naema*	*naarei*	*naare*
12. 'bone'	*ayahnta*	*ayaantamba*	*ayampai*	*buhaarima*
13. 'bow'	*iq*	*ima*	*isandai*	*huru*
14. 'breast'	*nah*	*naamba*	*naami*	*naama*
15. 'burn'	*tehre/otorehq*	*kwegai*	*ikankemi*	*itero*
16. 'claw'	*ayahnobeq*	*aisabuqa*	*opaqi*	*kakahi*
17. 'cloud'	*irabuya*	*ainamba*	*konama/ayoni*	*tonabu*
18. 'cold'	*titiriq*	*taugwiqa*	*ironemi*	*antero*
19. 'come'	*tiye*	*tiyo*	*yeno*	*aniena*
20. 'die'	*pukire*	*pukai*	*pukono*	*qutubiro*
21. 'dog'	*iya*	*iyamba*	*iyami*	*bairi*
22. 'dry'	*totoragoye*	*kasaqnagwi*	*kasaguke/ oyama*	*ahaara*
23. 'ear'	*ahre*	*aqa*	*aakami*	*aato*
24. 'eat/ drink'	*nahno*	*nare*	*naano*	*naana*
25. 'egg'	*au*	*auma*	*amuqi*	*auru*
26. 'eye'	*aura*	*auramba*	*okami*	*abu*
27. 'fat (grease)'	*mayehwe*	*masawemba*	*basapemi*	*bahabera*
28. 'father'	*(a)bowa*	*(a)bowama*	*(ena)poi*	*(ti)qora*
29. 'feather'	*ayo*	*ayauma*	*ayoi*	*kauhi*
30. 'fire'	*ira/eku*	*irama/iyaba*	*ikai*	*iha*

	Awa	Auyana	Gadsup	Tairora
31. 'fish'	nontah/ koeyaq	noyaaqa/ kuma	noyana/ kauya	. . ./ haabuka
32. 'fly'	(k)ogo	kwasimba	baaqdini	baubaari
33. 'foot (sole)'	aitaru	aisamima	akarakumi	aiqutubu
34. 'full'	orahpeh	ogwitarai	ubikemi	mpiqero
35. 'give'	awiq	ami	ameno	amina
36. 'go/walk'	pokaiq	koro	bono	buana
37. 'good'	kaweq	kawiqa	abokuqi	koqeba
38. 'grass (kunai)'	namuq	owaima	owana/ namiqi	naabuhi
39. 'green'	ʹaukaka	sokomba	yanamanai	bukana
40. 'ground'	marako	marama	maka	bata
41. 'hair'	(a)yahra	-tauma (aayara = Ka-waina)	-nyoi	kauhi
42. 'hand'	ayahnobeh	ayaamba	aayaami	kauqu
43. 'head'	ayaqno	aqnomba	aaqnomi	qieta
44. 'hear/ know'	iro	enisa	indequ	iri
45. 'heart'	awahbo	amaaboomba	amukuni	muntuka
46. 'hot'	totoqi	kokoqa	kokoqmemi	totoqa
47. 'house'	nah	naamba	maqi	naabu
48. 'I'	ne	kema	teni	tere
49. 'kill'	subio	tufuo	areqi	ququbiro (are 'hit')
50. 'knee'	arau	arauma	akona/ akoraumi	tori
51. 'leaf'	ahnah	anama	anai	mare/itu
52. 'liver'	aru	aruma	anonomi	tubu
53. 'long'	tahtahi	ayaataqa	iyaaqi	bukai
54. 'louse'	nu	numba	numi	numa
55. 'man'	weh	kwaima	banta	bainti
56. 'many'	ahnde	nesuqa/ suwifaqa	amuqna	airi
57. 'meat'	awehq	amaqa	amaqi	mati
58. 'moon'	iyo	(k)wiyomba	ikona	tora
59. 'mother'	(a)nowa	(a)nowama	(ana)noi	(ti)nora
60. 'moun-tain'	taweh/omaq	omaaqa	anui	batamuatu
61. 'mouth'	aweh	andampaq	abani	no
62. 'name'	awiq	awiqa	abiqi	autu

	Awa	Auyana	Gadsup	Tairora
63. 'neck'	*anuo*	*anuwaramba/ awaima*	*anokami*	*aru*
64. 'new'	*o/nauna*	*aunama*	*onana/oyami*	*araaka*
65. 'night'	*inokahpeq*	*noqwamba*	*ayupumi/ nurambaqi*	*entaqira*
66. 'nose'	*abiah*	*aiqa*	*asiqi*	*aiqi*
67. 'one'	*mora*	*morama*	*manaa*	*bohaiqa*
68. 'path'	*ah*	*aambi*	*aani/aami*	*aara*
69. 'rain'	*ibo/ahq*	*aaqa*	*aqi*	*aaqu*
70. 'red (blood)'	*ehtah/nehe*	*karogarom- ba/naema*	*korami/ naarei*	*. . ./ naare*
71. 'root'	*anuq*	*anuqa*	*anuqi*	*tuqa*
72. 'sand'	*arahwe*	*araiya/amai*	*epayauni*	*nuqama*
73. 'say, I'	*iraruwo*	*siyo*	*sequ*	*tiena*
74. 'see'	*tagaho*	*awanao*	*onaano*	*tabaana*
75. 'seed'	*ahyu*	*auma/aramba*	*ayumi*	*auru*
76. 'sit down'	*maratuo*	*maraqmai*	*kumandeno*	*oqubuana*
77. 'skin'	*au*	*awarasima*	*anda*	*paha*
78. 'sleep'	*tugehq*	*aunkwai*	*barano*	*baitaana*
79. 'small'	*ma/pehgariq*	*kitoqa*	*tsitoq*	*inara*
80. 'smoke'	*amuniq/ aune*	*umumba*	*iqkuni/ inumuni*	*mura*
81. 'stand up'	*irigaho*	*usasina*	*ukukaano*	*himpuaana*
82. 'star'	*oq/wehyoq*	*oqa*	*bayo*	*opu/bahoqura*
83. 'stone'	*oniki*	*ontamba*	*oni*	*ori*
84. 'sugar cane'	*tahq*	*taaqa*	*yaaqi*	*kaaqa*
85. 'sun'	*popoqnah/iyo*	*aabauma*	*ikona*	*kuari*
86. 'tail'	*ehwe/awe*	*ameraamba*	*ameni*	*beka*
87. 'that'	*mina*	*mindama*	*mini*	*biha*
88. 'this'	*mahna*	*maanda*	*mana*	*maana*
89. 'thou'	*are*	*ema*	*eni*	*aare*
90. 'tongue'	*anehbi*	*amaabi*	*anapini*	*maaqiri*
91. 'tooth'	*aweh* ('mouth')	*awaiyaamba*	*abakuni*	*aabai*
92. 'tree'	*ta/awahnga*	*taima*	*yaani*	*katari*
93. 'two'	*tahtare*	*kaiqa*	*kaantani*	*taaraqanta*
94. 'water'	*no*	*nomba*	*nomi*	*namari*
95. 'we (excl.)'	*ite*	*kesama*	*yikenama*	*tenabu*
96. 'what'	*aneq*	*noneqi*	*nepi*	*nana*
97. 'who'	*entebo*	*nawaqi*	*yepe*	*tababe*
98. 'white'	*tehyahntah*	*waiemba*	*epani*	*eqara*

	Awa	Auyana	Gadsup	Tairora
99. 'woman'	ahre	arema	anaatsi	naenti
100. 'yellow'	pehyaq	sebomba	miqyunawa-nemi	tatabauqa

7.2 List II

	Awa	Auyana	Gadsup	Tairora
1. 'adze'	poka	kakumi	karaqa	haipi
2. 'after-noon'	tunsoreriq	eninkaqa	ayinkaqi	erairika
3. 'armpit'	ayahbepeq	aabemba	aaqpemi	aakama
4. 'arrow-shaft'	. . .	arama	akai	bebaqu
5. 'axe (stone)'	konaro/poka	koraroba	kuntaqi	kaarima
6. 'back bone'	abobiah	arosamba	akoyumi	taubaqabu-haari
7. 'bad'	ahbabaq	sawiqa	tampiqmemi	oraha
8. 'banana'	potera	teqa	eqi	etaa
9. 'bark cloak'	wah	(k)waaqa	kamuna	abuna
10. 'bark skirt'	wahte	aimba	andini	pahara
11. 'beads'	. . .	akaroro	ankaroro	haankaaroro
12. 'bean'	arikokoq	koqa	koqi	kohe
13. 'bean (native)'	abehpero	pisa	naba	eqi
14. 'betel nut'	pareya	iyumba	iyui	ihu
15. 'bow string'	tapuri	kaafima	iqnaami	hinta
16. 'boy'	animai	iyampoi	anintai	baintima
17. 'branch'	ayahnowe	am(a)ima	ayaamani	kaara
18. 'brother (older)'	(a)wahwa	(a)waoma	(ena)bai	(ti)bakaara
19. 'brother (younger)'	(a)baka	(a)bakoama	(ena)paqi	(ti)gata
20. 'casso-wary'	kuwaira	augwaima	buyemi	bukera
21. 'casso-wary headdress'	kuwiara	augwaima	titinami	titira

	Awa	Auyana	Gadsup	Tairora
22. 'casuar- ina (hard)'	*arah*	*karaimba*	*aka*	*taaka*
23. 'casuar- ina (red)'	*nahrempah*	*nebaamba*	*naremi*	*naarempa*
24. 'charcoal'	*tarasa*	*(ira)bimba*	*(ika)kuni*	*qarampaa*
25. 'cheek'	*aqmo*	*oqmauma*	*aqpaani*	*aurubu*
26. 'chin'	*awai/awehi*	*amaimba*	*anaanaani*	*maatiri*
27. 'cough'	*ingokoq*	*(a)untamba*	*umisequ*	*quntutiro*
28. 'digging stick'	*yera*	*taumba*	*yaumi*	*kauru*
29. 'eel'	*kuri*	*kwaaiqa*	*baari*	*baanti*
30. 'elbow'	*ayayo*	*ayaanaumba*	*ayaaqomi*	*kaantaa*
31. 'face'	*auranabiyah*	*oiqa*	*oni*	*biri*
32. 'fall down'	*inahnsubire*	*kuntimba*	*yandono*	*ruqutubiro*
33. 'fence'	*wita*	*kurima*	*kukuni*	*ubika*
34. 'finger nail'	*ayahnobeq*	*ayaanofiqa*	*opaqi*	*kakahi*
35. 'five'	*mobesah*	*ebaqaasi*	*manaayaaq- | mani*	*kauquru*
36. 'to fly'	*puwambuwa*	*ararabena kore*	*akemi*	*atabarero*
37. 'forehead'	*ayai*	*auweyaamba*	*apemi*	*tiri*
38. 'forest'	*taikahpeq*	*umipaqa*	*uqpaqi*	*nanta*
39. 'four'	*tapotahpa*	*eyimba*	*eribami*	*taraqanta*
40. 'frog'	*iyo*	*awaima*	*kabani*	*eqaboka*
41. 'garden'	*so*	*kisau*	*anayopaqi*	*naaho*
42. 'girl'	*ahrari*	*arasi*	*akintai*	*baraata*
43. 'grand- father'	*(a)nahboweh*	*(a)naapuko*	*(ena)napu*	*naaqura*
44. 'grand- mother'	*(a)rahraweh*	*(a)raarao*	*(ena)kaaka*	*taatora*
45. 'grass- land'	*uwo*	*ufaqa*	*upaqi*	*qukau*
46. 'habarika . . . (reed on arrow)'		*nandamba*	*sabarimi*	*habarika*
47. 'hawk'	*kuqnu*	*murombaqa*	*manomani*	*maromari*
48. 'he'	*wega*	*kwema*	*beni*	*biba*
49. 'heavy'	*umehiq*	*umbaintai*	*umaniremi*	*maramentero*
50. 'husband'	*(a)wehka*	*(a)waiko*	*(ena)wapui*	*baati*
51. 'leg'	*ai*	*aisamima*	*akani*	*aiqu*

		Awa	Auyana	Gadsup	Tairora
52.	'lime'	kiriyeqna	kanama	kotte	auhe
53.	'lime gourd'	tanunsu/ kurinara	kwemoqa	kuqi	timona
54.	'lips'	omuq/aruo	oyawima	abarana	mauru
55.	'morning'	ahbiai(peq)	aabeama	baanudami	toaqi
56.	'navel'	aunta	amobiq	aqbankumi	mauntaba
57.	'nephew'	ahninka	anaabego	nonta	naunti
58.	'net bag'	unah	unaamba	unaami	uta
59.	'no'	aqao	aqau	ao/iye	aqau
60.	'old'	naho	airamba	peyami	naaruara
61.	'old man'	wehura/ore	anonuqmaima	ayokuni	bainti tarura
62.	'old woman'	oreni	araankamba	ayokurinini	naenti konta
63.	'oposum (kapul)'	mengamehnga	waamba	tapurai/wami	antauma
64.	'owl'	memonta	memontaamba	memoni	memora
65.	'pine'	mahni	kobima	bandimi	toqukera
66.	'pit pit shoots'	ahmuru/ahyu	uwoima	uwaanu	ubaara
67.	'python'	agania	kwiyame	kandam	kuna
68.	'rat'	umoq	(k)waima	bai	tubura
69.	'rib'	awai	arausamba	akoyami	antera
70.	'reed skirt'	wahte	awiwatoima	baqdoni	kiera
71.	'run'	pehirahnuo	isaisi	iyayono	kantaana
72.	'shield'	tehnge	kweuqa	yaani	kainke
73.	'short'	wahto	akima	baakaqi	eqo
74.	'shoulder'	ako	ayoima	apumi	kururu
75.	'sister (older)'	(a)nane	(a)nanoa	(ena)nanoi	nakauba
76.	'sister (younger)'	anunka	aunko	aumi	aura
77.	'snake'	waya	osimba	memani	memaru
78.	'sore'	namo	namomba	namomi	numuara
79.	'spit'	witehni	awiraima	tikaanoi	taara
80.	'stick'	tegara	taamba	yaami	kairiqa
81.	'strong pit pit (small bamboo)'	kori	kiyama	omi	kunkara
82.	'sweet potato'	topah	kisaama	kaamaami	qama
83.	'take'	meaho	mayaqo	marequ	baraana

	Awa	Auyana	Gadsup	Tairora
84. 'taro'	*ango*	*maiyamba*	*yami*	*kara*
85. 'ten'	*tahyahte*	*siyankai*	*tiyankani*	*kauquruntanta*
86. 'thigh'	*aru*	*aruqa*	*akuqi*	*aru*
87. 'three'	*tahmoro*	*kamboma*	*kamore*	*taraqanta-*
				bohaiqa
88. 'throat'	*aoto/ehwehi*	*amosamba*	*ameni*	*aunta*
89. 'thumb'	*ayanaobona*	*ayanabomba*	*apomi*	*enara*
90. 'trunk'	*(a)wai*	*(a)boima*	*(a)ndai*	*okara*
91. 'twenty	*naigunya-*	*mora kwai*	*mana bainta*	*kauqurutan-*
(one	*yahngu/*			*taaiquru*
man)'	*aiguyahngu*			
92. 'vine'	*nahgaq*	*andama*	*nani*	*naqunta*
93. 'wallaby'	*nabanta*	*kawima*	*kabenami*	*tabenara*
94. 'wet'	*tantanagiq*	*tasiasi*	*noniqmemi*	*puta*
95. 'wife'	*(a)nahnkawa*	*(a)waninko*	*(ena)naqi*	*naata*
96. 'wind'	*toiriq*	*undama/*	*tisobaani*	*ubai*
		taukwiqa		
97. 'wing'	*weto*	*aiyoima*	*aayami*	*aroka*
98. 'yam'	*ahwehq*	*taawima*	*obai*	*oba*
99. 'yes'	*kowe*	*owe*	*eyo*	*eo*
100. 'youth'	*mahbi*	*ifoaqa*	*pumara*	*bainti nankua*

7.3. *List III*

	Awa	Auyana	Gadsup	Tairora
1. 'afraid'	*ahre*	*inkaisi*	*pekemi*	*qeta*
2. 'alike'	*monserah*	*mirama*	*miquo*	*mintiena*
3. 'alive'	*ogamieh*	*merai*	*paanibemi*	*aqibairo*
4. 'ances-	*manika*	*maniko*	*maniqi*	*bariqa*
tors/spirit				
beings'				
5. 'ancient'	*naho*	*naoqa*	*peyukami*	*naaru*
6. 'angry'	*taunsahiq*	*awaqa*	*aseno*	*titiro*
7. 'ankle'	*aitaura*	*aisaumba*	. . .	*auroka*
8. 'ant'	*tawehngi*	*kasiqa*	*kayoi*	*tompiqara*
9. 'anus'	*arahngai*	*ayafu*	*araimi*	*rahana*
10. 'arm'	*ayah*	*ayaamba*	*ayaami*	*kauma*
11. 'ask'	*kaseuno*	*aisao*	*indaiyono*	*inaana*
12. 'awake'	*totumiyano*	*aubare*	*auremi*	*himpuana*
13. 'baby'	*-nahni*	*umaramba*	*akaqinta*	*naati*
14. 'bachelor'	*itaq mahbi*	*awagwaasi*	*atsetsaami*	*ehaara*
15. 'bald'	*ayahqno*	*aqnon tuwaig-*	*ayakoka*	*hintara*
	bausa	*wiemba*		*muqubira*

	Awa	Auyana	Gadsup	Tairora
16. 'ball'	topoq	kwaarima	poqyami	potara
17. 'band (for arm)'	kera	kwairamba	yaankami	kaantaba
18. 'band (woven)'	ahbahra	uwaima	iyoqi	kota
19. 'band (wrapped)'	taqnu	aibaqa	annomi	aunaaru
20. 'bandi- coot'	abinahwa	airaqa	akemi	qiroka
21. 'bank'	ahkorapeq	aipaqa	aaqpaqi	butuhini-
22. 'barb'	sehikara	karamaka	amani	aubi
23. 'bat'	tahpah	kaampaamba	panemi	kaakaara
24. 'bear, to'	maqmereiq	marankarai	makaano	batatero
25. 'bed'	mahriq	asipa	kandandai	tainta
26. 'behind (in back)'	anehe	naaemba	aqnaimpaqi	naantierai
27. 'belch'	kahq	narunaaruq	tsimandemi	antarahabu- kaibo
28. 'below'	awanahpeq	amendampaqa	makakaqi- bemi	bebanto
29. 'bend down'	tehiberiahre	kibaiqa	makamono	. . .
30. 'blind'	aurabireh	kabika	okampun- tinkami	qimpamabiro
31. 'blink'	mututu	awanantaqa	mukumuk	impankero
32. 'blow (w/mouth)'	tubiyaho	tubaya	puqtemi	buaqa
33. 'blue'	mangora	sokomba	sokmi	qihiqama
34. 'body'	anonka	auma	oi	batama
35. 'boil'	ake	karebuqa	abemi	meiqa
36. 'braid'	ti	wekusai	undequ	buntake
37. 'brain'	(a)biqno	(a)wimba	(ti)sinkuni	qiqiparama
38. 'break'	andero	ankaigwi	ukaraano	raqake
39. 'breathe'	aiyanaiya	aama	aumi	aanaimati
40. 'bridge'	tahre	tarema	koi	irima
41. 'bring'	mewesuwo	mayo	mareyi	baraania
42. 'bury'	uqmarahao	utai	dabaqo	untaana
43. 'butter- fly/moth'	pahparah	parebaremba	pepemi	pepenaaro
44. 'buttocks'	(a)wahowaya	(a)yema	(ti)rema	raqa
45. 'buy'	paiqmaro	meyomba	meyaniqo	onautua
46. 'calf (of leg)'	ehweh	amaima	amaaqi	aibaqo

	Awa	Auyana	Gadsup	Tairora
47. 'call out'	ahrabuno	kweaye	aaraano	aaraana
48. 'carry in arms'	tehwiyah	. . .	ayapaqono	kaqate
49. 'carry on head'	mewe	aqmainantie	ayaapono	aqumabarero
50. 'carry on shoulder'	oraraqmiyaho	aukwataq- mena	apunateno	tabukubare
51. 'chest'	(a)wi	(a)intama	(a)mimini	mimira
52. 'chew'	tautauq	unkaqna	unkunemi	uniro
53. 'chief'	turuwa	turuama	tabemunoi	tabebetaara
54. 'child'	ani	iyampoi	aami	bainti
55. 'choke'	tirahq	tiraqa	onemi	raqotubiro
56. 'chop'	ehpiwo	asai	duqkukono	tuquwa
57. 'circle'	kenahngenah	kokutauko	yeuku	utututu
58. 'clay'	tehmarako	kariqa	apumaka	entoka
59. 'climb'	kokiqnah	taiyaga	indokaano	barintero
60. 'close (shut)'	kakarinarah	kaataamara	orabaqono	aqutero
61. 'clothing (skirt)'	wahte	watoima	baqdoyami	baratara
62. 'collar- bone'	ayah beqara	. . .	. . .	kuabekera
63. 'comb'	kom	paasama	kaaqiyi	aahi
64. 'cook'	tiro	kaufu	yunkaano	qunte
65. 'copulate'	tiotioq	amuqnante	ayokami	iki
66. 'count'	tantaho	torausu	yaandaano	kaarantiro
67. 'crawl'	kamengame	ambaena kwewi	mankaqman- kaqmemi	rariribiro
68. 'crazy'	ahbabatinani	aifoqa	ananimemi	uberakuqiro
69. 'croco- dile'	karahrabah	. . .	ebari	ebaari
70. 'crooked'	tabirahbiya	taisarei	koeqikemi	rararero
71. 'cross'	tauntaiq	aisamba	koneno	atiro
72. 'cry'	ibitehq	ibiqante	ipiqi-	iqiratero
73. 'curve'	pugenta	taunkaimba	apurintimi	taurini
74. 'cut'	karoro	kare	aqkaano	teqero
75. 'dance'	abahq	araimara	tikoni makequ	ihintero
76. 'dark'	tungikiriye	tunkura	ayupumikemi	konkiraiqiro
77. 'daughter'	ayahunka	ayamuko	damummi	airaabura
78. 'day'	wekah	sankarai	kakaqi	enta
79. 'deaf'	ahkambu	aqankaukai	aqikonkemi	aato titamabiro
80. 'decorate'	. . .	toqwainkweye	kabayapira	bahehemama- tero

	Awa	Auyana	Gadsup	Tairora
81. 'deep'	iye wahto (not short)	ayaataqa	bontemi	baruqba
82. 'defecate'	tetarehre	aiyema kewqena	arankaano	rahate
83. 'dew'	tari	kawimba	ipundai	berabumama-tero
84. 'different'	iye montante	kaqomba	iye miqnukemi	boma
85. 'dig'	ubo-	ufuo	upono	ubiena
86. 'dirty'	nawera	pirikai	pani	kaimaamama
87. 'dissolve'	puwaqnagoye	kaqnagwi	ubantemi	tabiteroma
88. 'ditch'	nonawehq	oyaami	oni	ora
89. 'doze'	kotehqme-miyehq	augafaqa	muqnaromequ	tauntero
90. 'drag'	abari aiyaq	tabisi	yirepiqta	rarauruana
91. 'dream'	aonahiq	kaimba	tunkaqidukequ	tairamatabe
92. 'drop/fall'	meyagoye	kuntimbu	papasemi	tutakero
93. 'drum'	kamoya	komoyamba	kauyami	taaqa
94. 'duck'	pahto	kubima	nukumi	nontubu
95. 'earth-quake'	mari	marima	makuni	batura
96. 'edge'	ayehrapeq	awibaqa	akoyamami	biti
97. 'enough'	aire	aqani	amankaqi	homa
98. 'excre-ment'	teq	ayamba	arai	raha
99. 'eye-brow'	auwanahnto	auwanantau-ma	okanayoi	abu naabu
100. 'far'	iyewahto	nempaqa	iyakaqi	niaraini
101. 'fast'	pehirah	isaasi	akaikai	kantero
102. 'fasten'	tahuruno	kararu	dammequ	kantaru
103. 'feverish (hot)'	otorehq	aubimbakem-ba	koqnaami	ihitero
104. 'few'	tahmoro	kabiqa	kamore	taraiqa
105. 'file'	ensa	itooma	umi	ubi
106. 'fill'	orabehranao	ema kubero	ubikaano	ibiqana
107. 'fin'	owe	aiyoima	aokyunoqi	bebekau
108. 'finished'	parabagoiq	anaisawi	kakipemi	taiqero
109. 'first'	ebeq	aibaqa	aqnaim	abuni
110. 'flat area'	arubi	aruma	abaani	uqitakanta
111. 'flea'	tahnu	nuumba	kadu	taru
112. 'float'	ara	mayaqmaena	nonadupaqi	namai tubikanta bairo

	Awa	Auyana	Gadsup	Tairora
113. 'flute'	*pureresah*	. . .	. . .	*burera*
114. 'fold'	*kahwengah*	*taisamarai*	*punkandeno*	*rairakero*
115. 'food'	*tautauq*	*tomka*	*nami*	*karakaaqa*
116. 'forget'	*ibitagoiq*	*awinkawi*	*abinkaano*	*teurumake*
117. 'fruit'	*ara*	*aramba*	*akami*	*taba*
118. 'get'	*meniyo*	*mayao*	*maraano*	*barabu*
119. 'get (as in marry)'	*paoiq*	*aarembere*	*anasimarequ*	*amitaaba*
120. 'ginger'	*ki*	*kwimba*	*bimi*	*haaka*
121. 'grab'	*totorao*	*tabimea*	*orabe*	*rabaqabute*
122. 'grass-hopper'	*paqnori*	*pintaaqa*	*kasoni*	*kaintaqa*
123. 'grate'	*kaniq*	*kawakai*	*aneano*	*taintimanti*
124. 'grave'	*mairia marako*	*taaritaima*	*baamasiqi*	*baiti matipa*
125. 'grow'	*kirehq*	*iyeni*	*ampamintemi*	*ampiqaanaro-rama*
126. 'grunt'	*kiunkiuniq*	*ankambam-barei*	*aamagono*	*kekematiro*
127. 'hand, strong'	*pubeq*	*-mbapaqa*	*bempapaqi*	*kauquta*
128. 'hand, weak'	*ayahnepeq*	*ayanepaga*	*ayanopaq*	*kaataini*
129. 'handle'	*aq*	*asamba*	*akai*	*aqoma*
130. 'hang up'	*irarao*	*inkaqnumara*	*apodono*	*hiritaana*
131. 'hard'	*yoqeh*	*eseki*	*eraani*	*kepuka*
132. 'hat'	*kanoq*	*kaamoga*	*kabe*	*tobaqa*
133. 'hatch'	*kuwaqmara-rehre*	*tuwaqmakai*	*dibakaka-pakemi*	*noramanora*
134. 'hidden'	*aupeqmarao*	*aupaqa*	*oqpaqi*	*mautaqakero*
135. 'hoarse'	*owatautareta*	*amoimbasi*	*ayapikaya*	*auntakara*
136. 'hold'	*tahtoro*	*tatora*	*andorono*	*tote*
137. 'hole'	*abahrabahq*	*abaqa*	*masiqi*	*maiga*
138. 'house, men's'	*wehnenah*	. . .	*baaqnamaqi*	*baira*
139. 'how many'	*erauwe*	*norameq*	*naqde*	*natinanti*
140. 'hungry'	*arupibiq*	*ainkwankai*	*tanidebagu*	*naataamiru*
141. 'hurry'	*suansua*	*kabigabi*	*eraro*	*batetsiena*
142. 'intestine'	*ayeh*	*ayaqa*	*araqi*	*arara*
143. 'itch'	*niweweiq*	*kakamakama*	*amikebami*	*kuku*
144. 'jews-harp'	*ponto*	. . .	. . .	*oqoka*
145. 'join'	*tukiarao*	*augwiyu*	*oqbikaano*	*hampakiro*

	Awa	Auyana	Gadsup	Tairora
146. 'joint'	o	aumba	omi	aata
147. 'juice'	tehno	anomba	anui	nora
148. 'jump'	kiwo	tokabaraq	karusaqono	butunte
149. 'kanga- roo, tree'	ayahba	kwaamba	kabenami	tabenara
150. 'kick'	turuturuq	tufuo	kabiankaano	raputakero
151. 'kidney'	puruyuyah	awaamoyamba	anaqnaami	. . .
152. 'kiss'	mkoqnankoq- na	amoqnao	amoqnaano	moqana
153. 'knock'	pakibaki	tuwatuwaqa	kukukequ	rutuatuamire
154. 'lake/ pond'	kawau	kayumba	abarumi	baruba
155. 'lame'	kutikutiq	kararema	denkaqmemi	rentuqama- qiro
156. 'lap lap (men's cloth skirt)'	ambanta	ampantama	oqpaqta	tabata
157. 'lazy'	guweraro	kabonama	kusiqmemi	popohero
158. 'lean against'	tekiqmemi- yaho	komusu	munkukeqi	muntubi
159. 'let go'	tapik(u)wao	ibetuwa	uqkikaano	tutakaana
160. 'leave it'	. . .	. . .	eqa	eqaana
161. 'lie'	pehepehe	kampaqa	umaqi	unama
162. 'light (fire)'	ira bario	iya nagao	taremi	iha quraana
163. 'lightning'	okekwehq	apayauma	apayu	qaquaka
164. 'line up'	perairah	aisotara	diribayono	abuqabuqi
165. 'look'	tagaho	awano	onaao	tabe
166. 'lose'	taqnobagiq	ibetuwa	dompirono	aqakimake
167. 'lungs'	tentarurahru	. . .	anaqnami	eqarauntai
168. 'make it'	piaho	onam	ubaraano	kaqaana
169. 'medicine woman'	. . .	pukaarinimba	uqwatsa	uhiakaa
170. 'midday'	waikah	waiwai	bayankomi	ikaraqa
171. 'middle'	akahnabubu	abumpimba	abanakaqi	tabarana
172. 'moan'	mukaqmukaq	esega	nunkikisin- temi	keketiro
173. 'molar'	ehronkai	awairunkwai	anayakuni	baantubora
174. 'mos- quito'	akaruq	kaama	kamemenka	aaquqa
175. 'mound up (dirt)'	. . .	kisaramba	amurono	baurukaana

	Awa	Auyana	Gadsup	Tairora
176. 'mud'	*toseh*	*toima*	*yoni*	*hora*
177. 'mumu (oven)'	*purikahruno*	*pasina*	*oyokaano*	*orihampaqia*
178. 'mush-room'	*arah*	*araamba*	*kuqina*	*narubu*
179. 'narrow'	*tobuya*	. . .	*kaqkaqmu-kemi*	*ampara*
180. 'near'	*wahto*	*ewaaqa*	*aqdekaqi*	*bainto*
181. 'needle'	*wei*	*waima*	*ubai*	*uqa*
182. 'nest'	*ana*	*anaamba*	*anaami*	*antau*
183. 'nostrils'	. . .	*aibemba*	*asipaimi*	*aiqiena*
184. 'not'	*ire*	*imani*	*iye*	*kia*
185. 'nothing'	*iregeq*	*uwoi*	*paani*	*umina*
186. 'open'	*tio*	*awaumara*	*diyeno*	*qantarauna*
187. 'other'	*mo*	*oqomba*	*ena*	*boma*
188. 'outside'	*mahpeq*	*maqarubaqa*	*maapaq*	*bahaqaini*
189. 'over there'	*tebeq*	*mekui*	*mipaqi*	*mini*
190. 'pain'	*niriq*	*aiqa*	*tiqmemi*	*aihabiro*
191. 'paint (native)'	*peni*	*moqa*	*kabaani*	*buika*
192. 'palm (hand)'	*ahyanaru*	*ayanarumba*	*akumi*	*kaqutubu*
193. 'pan-danus'	*kanabah*	*inama*	*imi*	*akaara*
194. 'peel'	*puwiraho*	*asima*	*abanteno*	*abahike*
195. 'penis'	*pegara*	*apoiko*	*ape*	*aake*
196. 'person'	*morani*	*kwaasima*	*akaami*	*boru*
197. 'pile up'	*moaqmoaq*	*abobo maiaa-taraamba*	*daurono*	*taurintau-rimbataana*
198. 'pillow'	*kunuba*	*kunimima*	*kunu*	*turu*
199. 'pinch'	*paririone*	*piriti*	*puntiqdami*	*antata*
200. 'pitpit'(1)	*ubah*	*uwoima*	*oboyaami*	*oba*
201. 'pitpit'(2)	*one*	*omba*	*omi*	*ohaqera*
202. 'pitpit'(3)	*wiahno*	*kwiyama*	*uwaanu*	*kunkara*
203. 'place'	*mahpeq*	*naopaqa*	*apaqi*	*maaqa*
204. 'place (suffix)'	*-peq*	*-paq*	*-paqi*	*-ra*
205. 'plant'	*mahndu*	*aramba*	*yunandumi*	*kubu*
206. 'to plant'	*uqmareq*	*uqmare*	*amunude*	*utuana*
207. 'plate'	*kunuba*	*tabiqa*	*tsibaami*	*taanu*
208. 'play'	*neqnehq*	*aabema*	*iyararono*	*ruhe*

		Awa	Auyana	Gadsup	Tairora
209.	'point'	aweh	aima	ani	biara
210.	'poison'	. . .	uwaa	ubampini	uhiaka
211.	'pregnant'	mukarinimimiehq	amukwaqa	konkequ	taiaqbiro
212.	'press'	prahpah	taabasena	ubisonaano	tataurua
213.	'pry'	tiyuwo	kantoma	dapequ	aqiatukero
214.	'pull'	abariwe	tabisi	dapono	rarauruana
215.	'push'	paguntane	abusu	abekono	ahuqira
216.	'put'	maraho	marao	daano	bataana
217.	'put on skirt (marry)'	kiwo	. . .	irequ	irero
218.	'quarrel'	ahwahiq	aisamba kwesei	yirumbayaani	tiroriena
219.	'quick'	siansia	kabigabi	eraru	butete
220.	'rainbow'	ora	oisamba	apondami	ontanta
221.	'raw'	tegarabiehq	augwayambakwai	oyami	araaka
222.	'return'	wehuraq	kowerao	obaikeqiyeqi	orurante
223.	'ripe'	putagoiq	abuma	apui	abuabu
224.	'roll'	pabebabeq	(k)warereqa	bayabayaqemi	kobiri kabiri biro
225.	'roof'	abogah	naanamima	obani	naabuqieta
226.	'rotten'	kambarekiq	ankuqa	ampimi	ampontuqabiro
227.	'rough'	. . .	nagai	aka	akakembeni ahabairo
228.	'round'	aiteh	monumba	amuqi	potariboara
229.	'rub'	tobari	agoyaama	yotsiqtsiq naano	raqutuana
230.	'run'	pehirahnuo	isasio	iyayono	kantaana
231.	'salt'	oyaq	uwi	uni	oroqu
232.	'scream'	ayahtiye	(k)wa(k)wa ga(k)weti	baqiremitsi	oioitiro
233.	'sew'	unah kogahnie	aru	anduqkono	haqiriena
234.	'shadow'	awahngaqnah	amamba	amami	maraqura
235.	'shake'	piribari	toratoraqa	uqmimindono	rirariena
236.	'share'	taraqme	timatai	makequ	karamiena
237.	'sharp'	awehrakahq	. . .	mandayamuq	baihero
238.	'sharpen'	intoya	ontoaaqa	baqtayeno	upiaraana
239.	'shelf'	tahbe	taarema	kandanda	tainta
240.	'shield'	tehge	kweuqa	yaani	kainke

	Awa	Auyana	Gadsup	Tairora
241. 'shoot (of plant)' (1)	*ahmura*	*aruma*	*amoqi*	*noqa*
242. 'shoot (of plant)' (2)	*ahyu*	*aruma*	*aanka*	*aimaratero*
243. 'shoot (to)'	*pahno*	*farai*	*daqarequ*	*ampaquana*
244. 'show'	*tiagawo*	*arasinka*	*yoakequ*	*humiqaana*
245. 'shrub area'	*uqmataupeq*	*umipaqa*	*upaq*	*ukauqi*
246. 'shut up'	*ahyamiano*	*aisera*	*ayamambaano*	*ebarabariena*
247. 'sick'	*awahre*	*aiqa*	*aqebami*	*orobara*
248. 'side'	*aro*	*awibaqa*	*abapaqi*	*aubahini*
249. 'singsing'	*abahq*	*ima*	*iqi*	*ihintaana*
250. 'sky'(1)	. . .	*arupiqa*	*inaru*	*naarubu*
251. 'sky' (2)	*iyopeq*	*kwiyompaqa*	. . .	. . .
252. 'sleepy'	*tugahgaiq*	*(k)we(g)wai*	*tunidebaqu*	*abutauntero*
253. 'slice'	*tehraho*	*aresi*	*ompequ*	*toqaana*
254. 'slipped'	*nahnsubiq*	*yebeqan*	*bandini*	*baurinta-baruqu*
255. 'slow'	*pehwehtie*	*wempake*	*naniebu*	*akomakera*
256. 'smash'	*ehmpegoiq*	. . .	*inkamequ*	*rukabubiro*
257. 'smell (a)'	*sunsuniq*	. . .	*abokuqunda*	*umtamabiro*
258. 'smell (to)'	*akiaki*	*kwiyumba*	*amunkuqi*	*uhiraana*
259. 'smile'	*wireh wirehiq*	*wiyaima*	*inteno*	*naraihiana*
260. 'smooth'	*niq*	*aukwarima*	*bandiruka-memi*	*muquhiutu-taire*
261. 'sneeze'	*atiantiq*	*kisiqasi*	*asindeno*	*ahiramantiro*
262. 'snore'	*kahragahra*	*unkararoqa*	*unkaami*	*karankai*
263. 'soft'	*tehboboi*	*amomantai*	*uqdenemi*	*nuqerero*
264. 'some/ few'	*tahmoro*	*sebakaqa*	*yekamore*	*taraiqia*
265. 'son'	*ahninga*	*aaninko*	*kaqi*	*maaqu*
266. 'sore'	*namo*	*namomba*	*namomi*	*numuara*
267. 'sorry'	*niruntantanie*	*arumba kweye*	*aimpo*	*mbo*
268. 'spider'	*kontah*	*upaqnaamba*	*baqnoi*	*ontautara*
269. 'spirit'	*awa*	*kwantagwasi*	*bami*	*tabaru*
270. 'split'	*pehbehnuo*	*pasao*	*dupamequ*	*rubarikaana*
271. 'spread'	*abayaro*	*abini*	*apequ*	*auruma*
272. 'spear (to)'	*tehtehbiyao*	. . .	*aukaano*	*ranteramake*

	Awa	Auyana	Gadsup	Tairora
273. 'squash'	poruporuq	kusima	dusi	kuhi/toru
274. 'stab'	tehtehbiyaho	airare	ankakequ	tantiqakue
275. 'stare'	tagaho	auranten kararai	uono	kukeqakaro
276. 'startle'	kurinah	kantumba	anduqdono	raakumabiro
277. 'steal'	ebo	umemba	umorono	mura barero
278. 'steep'	totupeq	. . .	aiyepaqi	aihaini
279. 'stink'	kunguniq	ankuqa	amunkuq-	untama-
280. 'straight'	agigi	arupima	antekemi	abuqabu
281. 'straighten'	aeroairaho	arupinurai	akunkaano	abuqabuma
282. 'stretch'	tabiriq	sapiqa	tampiqnaano	raqikikaana
283. 'string'	nagai	andama	amuqnani	naqunta
284. 'string (to; as beads)'	tunugiwo	tokwi	ananequ	taqima kaana
285. 'strong'	toqweq	usisiandei	erarukai	kempuka
286. 'suck'	mitiqmitiq	kwegwampie-nei	umpiqpiqsequ	mbarikaana
287. 'sunlight'	tahraq	aabauma	aqkarani	kuariabu
288. 'sunrise'	kiampogoiq	abanusei	akarani	kuari buru-hunkubiro
289. 'sunset'	tupekoiq	kuafeqwi	aqikumpekemi	buruhunkubiro
290. 'swallow'	narunsao	nawikai	nabiqtequ	nampiqakaana
291. 'sweat'	tungio/munsinsi	umuqnamba	koqnaami	toqabu
292. 'swell'	torehq/muwi	kwentorai	pamequ	noqakero
293. 'tadpole'	ahmbaruqnah	. . .	birabiaeq	kampaqo
294. 'tatoo'	. . .	aufai nagai-makai	apunisantemi	ararubatairo tabaari
295. 'tear (to)'	tubaugoiq	tapeqwi	daqkakemi	anahiena
296. 'tear (from eye)'	aqno	aqnuma	obanomi	auquru
297. 'temple (of body)'	ahta	awamuqa	(ti)qwani	buakaara
298. 'thick'	abae	amokoqa	amakoqi	nora
299. 'thin'	tobuya	amantaima	aqyamana	ampara
300. 'think'	iwiauq	imayaan	indidequ	irikaana
301. 'thirsty'	tahbebeye	nawaqwankai	tiyebaqu	namainata-miro
302. 'thorn'	tahwe	awima	amuqi	auqu
303. 'throw'	tupegwaho	metua	aqnequ	aquana

	Awa	Auyana	Gadsup	Tairora
304. 'thunder'	*puruburuq*	*wiyonaima*	*inarua-*	*narura-*
305. 'tickle'	*karikariq*	*karobiqa*	*aparoriqono*	*kamparoriena*
306. 'tie'	*pantenuo*	*kararu*	*intuyono*	*rumpaana*
307. 'testicles'	*awahnta*	*awainkamba*	*aramuqi*	*taba*
308. 'tired'	*aiyanaiya*	*awesarini*	*taumiqdeu*	*abu tauntero*
309. 'tomor-row'	*ahbiyah*	*apaya*	*kakana*	*hura*
310. 'touch'	*biehre*	*taetora*	*ayokaono*	*taana*
311. 'trap'	*andayanka*	*koboqa*	*aanai*	*kuhe*
312. 'trash'	*katu*	*kankamba*	*onapaqi*	*orakarakaqa*
313. 'top'	*webeq*	*sanampaqa*	*amuni*	*turu*
314. 'truth'	*puri*	*araiqa*	*pukante-qunku*	*uqa*
315. 'trunk'	*awai*	*aboi*	*andai*	*abarana*
316. 'turn'	*teheraho*	*waera*	*baiekaano*	*tuqantara*
317. 'twist'	*ibiyuwo*	*ufama*	*indindu*	*uquramiro*
318. 'uncle'	*abowa*	*anaugoma*	*aqo*	*naura*
319. 'untie'	*pukeraho*	*intutue*	*uqtupono*	*antukaana*
320. 'urine'	*wi*	*awima*	*yibi*	*biera*
321. 'vagina'	*awah*	*afaqa*	*api*	*kohu*
322. 'vein'	*onu*	*anumba*	*anunani*	*aururu*
323. 'visible'	*aboraq*	*imbananpaqa*	*apoqtaqi*	*oqaamabairo*
324. 'vomit'	*mugiq*	*mima*	*biseno*	*burubihikaana*
325. 'waist'	*aunta*	*amuqanda*	*annomi*	*teqo*
326. 'wait'	*pehitare*	*etukenaq*	*eukaano*	*bariena*
327. 'wall'	*tibi*	*kaataima*	*akumi*	*poroba*
328. 'want'	*nitehq*	*wankai*	*tsimuqikemi*	*bira hantuqa hariro*
329. 'war'	*webeh*	*uwaama*	*yiruni*	*raqiro*
330. 'wart'	*mumureh*	. . .	*mumunaami*	*buri*
331. 'wash'	*peroperoq/ pabepabeq*	*pera*	*nonokequ*	*biqaana*
332. 'watch'	*pehitare*	*taparai*	*dapiseno*	*aituqibariena*
333. 'water-fall'	*kokuba kokuba*	*nomba kwegumi*	*iyai*	*namai tubiro*
334. 'weak'	*tabirahbiq*	*amoima*	*maamami*	*quqeraira*
335. 'weave'	*kireq*	*kusai*	*undaano*	*araana*
336. 'web'	*abanah*	*upaqnaamba*	*akaanoi*	*omamaru nabu*
337. 'well'	*kaheriye*	*eqankai*	*asopaano*	*koqeba bairo*
338. 'whisper'	*muniq muniq*	*simusimuqa*	*tiqpuqnaaono*	*atoqima tiba/ ami bairo*
339. 'whistle'	. . .	*uposinai*	*uboteno*	. . .

	Awa	Auyana	Gadsup	Tairora
340. 'why'	anentabe	noraqinaq	naqe	nantimatae
341. 'winded'	tahgarahgaq	ayaqayaqa	aundaano	anamanoma- raqutukero
342. 'wipe'	to bari kwaho	kankamba	dauyono	qunkakaana
343. 'word'	ehweh	aima	bayaani	uba
344. 'worm'	topehya	kuqarema	ini	ahequ
345. 'wrap'	pantenuwo	asaumakai	ukono	apuqakaana
346. 'yawn'	awainta	amaimbati	tinanikaatsequ	anai tiro

XXXVI. Comparative and Historical Problems in East New Guinea Highland Languages

DARLENE BEE

1. INTRODUCTION

The linguistic terrain of New Guinea is covered with virgin forests of untouched problems of synchronic and diachronic analysis, description, and comparison. Almost any area chosen will reward its investigator with opportunities for pioneer work in one area of linguistic research or another. The Eastern Highlands of the Territory of New Guinea are no exception. Although some areas of research in the Eastern Highlands are rapidly becoming familiar ground there are many areas which have hardly been touched. One such area is that of historical reconstruction and comparative analysis. McKaughan has taken a step in that direction in his study of 'Divergence in Four New Guinea Languages' (see Chap. XXXV) where he suggests a reconstructed phonemic system for the Eastern Family. The purpose of this present paper is to take a few more steps into the frontier of comparative and historical research in New Guinea.[1] For this study the seven languages of the Eastern Family will be used and levels below and beyond the phoneme will be investigated. An attempt will be made to reconstruct some actual linguistic forms and problems awaiting solution will be pointed out. Material for this study has been drawn from the author's personal field

[1] This paper was prepared for a seminar in Problems in Comparative and Historical Analysis held at the University of Hawaii, Fall 1964, and conducted by Professor George Grace. The author is indebted to Professor Grace for his encouragement and suggestions. A grant from the East-West Center made possible the author's study at the University of Hawaii and sincere appreciation is expressed to the center. The paper first appeared pp. 1-37 in *Papers in New Guinea Linguistics, No. 4,* Linguistic Circle of Canberra Publications (Series A: Occasional Papers, No. 6) (Australian National University, 1965), and is reissued in this form by permission.

notes, from published and unpublished papers of colleagues from the New Guinea Branch of the Summer Institute of Linguistics, and from extensive word lists collected by Howard McKaughan.

Tairora, Binumarien, Gadsup, Agarabi, Usarufa, Auyana, and Awa will form the basis of the discussion presented here. Wurm's classification and subclassification of these speech communities rather than McKaughan's have been adopted. The basic difference between the two classifications is one of status rather than grouping. Wurm classifies the seven speech communities together as the Eastern Family with four subfamilies: Gadsup, Auyana, Awa, and Tairora which are respectively composed of the following languages: Gadsup and Agarabi, Auyana and Usarufa; Awa; and Tairora and Binumarien. McKaughan does not recognize the subfamily division but classifies Wurm's subfamily groups of languages each of which have several dialects. Agarabi and Usarufa are regarded by McKaughan as merely the most divergent dialects of Gadsup and Auyana, respectively. His conclusions are based on statistical evidence which although extensive is subject to interpretational differences of opinion. The general groupings of the two classifications are however in agreement. The status ranking of the speech groups whether language versus dialect or family versus subfamily is at the present stage of analysis relatively unimportant. In any case statistical information is only one type of information needed for the assignment of status labels.[2]

Not only is the comparative and historical analysis of New Guinea Highland languages in its infancy but these languages have characteristics which make such analysis particularly difficult. The present discussion is primarily concerned with the Eastern Family but many of the points which will be made are true throughout the Highland area. With reference to the Eastern Family at least four factors need to be given careful consideration: (A) the polymorphemic shape of linguistic forms, (B) extensive and complex morphophonemic systems, (C) interpretation and distribution of contoid clusters, and (D) borrowing. The extent and nature of the influences of these four factors cannot be specified until the comparative studies anticipated here have been completed. However, it is important that one should be prepared for confusions on several levels as the result of these factors so that if possible one might avoid traveling too far up blind alleys created by combinations of them. The brief general description of the nature of the problems which arise even at an early stage of analysis is intended as a warning, not an answer.

In the beginning stages of the search for sets of sound correspondences one hopes to find a nucleus of monomorphemic forms upon which to base

---

[2] McKaughan in including both lexico- and phonostatistic information makes the evidence from statistics more convincing but other considerations, such as degrees of intelligibility and grammatical comparison, are also important.

initial hypotheses. Such a nucleus is almost impossible to find in Highland languages. Polymorphemic forms are the rule rather than the exception. In Usarufa, for example, monomorphemic words do not occur in isolation so that at least two morphemes must be taken into account. Some categories of words which are especially fruitful in their yield of cognates, for example, kinship terms and body parts, are in most of the languages of the Eastern Family always polymorphemic. Heavy verbal inflection in all of the languages not only makes it difficult to establish equivalent sets of forms but almost excludes this class of words from the search for monomorphemic forms. One may, however, still be rewarded with a form in a given language which synchronically seems to be monomorphemic. But such rewards are hard come by and often prove to be polymorphemic on the diachronic level. Therefore the necessity of familiarity with the morphemic structure of each language can hardly be overstressed. The accuracy of the reconstructions which are postulated will be increased in proportion to one's familiarity with the morphemic structures involved. The author's familiarity with the structure of Usarufa has proven of great value and one could wish for a similar competency in each of the other languages.

The Highland languages are characterized by systems of morphophonemic change which tend to mask the true nature of historical change and which make the recognition of cognates difficult. A thorough study of the morphophonemics of each language should be undertaken as part of the comparative and historical analysis of each family of languages. Materials for such a study are not yet available for the Eastern Family but information on the morphophonemics of some of the languages has been gleaned from various papers and has proven very helpful (see Chaps. IV, XI, XX; R. and R. Nicholson 1962). Although no information of a direct nature has been available for Tairora, Binumarien, or Agarabi, comparative studies show that there is evidence of some similar active or fossilized morphophonemic processes to that which has been recorded for the other languages of the family. Morphophonemic information from Fore of the East Central Family seems to indicate that a remarkably similar system of change is operative there. It looks as though it may be possible to reconstruct a protomorphophonemic system and that this will provide insight into the development of the phonemic and morphemic systems of Highland languages. A summary of the information in hand about the various morphophonemic systems follows.

All of the languages for which morphophonemic information is available have a system of morphophonemic classification which includes all or most of the morphemes of the language and other cosystems of morphophonemic change which are restricted to particular morphemes or morpheme classes. The former seems to be an inherited system while the latter seem to be developments within individual languages. Although there are differ-

ences in the extent of the circumstances for application of the more pervasive type, depending upon the particular language, the similarities are
striking. The general principle of the system is that the phonemic shape of
a given morpheme is determined by the morphophonemic class of the
morpheme which precedes it. Usarufa, Awa, and Auyana as well as Fore
have three such morphophonemic classes and Gadsup has five. Cognate
morphemes within the Eastern Family belong to corresponding morphophonemic classes.[3] The regularity of this class correspondence is very significant
and may provide evidence for determining whether two forms are cognate
or not. It also may give some clues as to the analysis of polymorphemic
forms. The specific nature of the changes which occur may be seen in Table
92. The information from Fore has been included for comparison even
though it does not directly pertain to this present study. Morpheme-initial
phonemes which appear along the horizontal axis are changed when preceded by morphemes belonging to the morphophonemic classes indicated
along the vertical axis as specified by the cells formed by the intersection of
the two axes. A blank cell indicates that the information concerning that
particular sequence is lacking. Ellipses indicate that the language in question
does not have that particular phoneme. In some cases as indicated by
phonetic brackets allophones are given. The chart is to be read as follows:
following a morpheme of class N (second row division) the phoneme /p/
becomes /mp/ in Gadsup and Auyana; /qp/ in Usarufa; /p/ in Awa and /p:/
in Fore. It should be stressed that these are synchronic changes active within
each language but which are diachronically corresponding. Tairora and
Binumarien have regular correspondences to some of these sequences but
evidence thus far seems to indicate that these may be fossilized forms and
not synchronically productive. Nevertheless it is important to recognize these
correspondences. The sequence N + /m/ regularly corresponds in Tairora
to /b/ and in Binumarien to /m/.[4] The sequences V/N/Q + vowel (v) correspond as follows:

$$
\begin{array}{llll}
 & \text{Tairora-Binumarien} & & \\
V & + v & r + v & r + v \\
N & + v & r + v & n + v \\
Q & + v & q + v & k + v \\
\end{array}
$$

---

[3] Whether or not this class correspondence extends outside of the Eastern Family
needs to be investigated. Also to be investigated is the correspondence in terms of
cognate morphemes of the five Gadsup classes to the three classes of the other
languages. This should reveal whether Gadsup has developed two additional classes
or if an originally more complex system has been reduced to three in all the other
languages.

[4] The Tairora and Binumarien reflexes of N which are given in Section 3 may
be explainable in terms of other complex sequences but it is not immediately obvious
what the nature of these might be.

It is important to realize the implications of these morphophonemic processes. Each polymorphemic form whether a compound of more than one stem or a stem plus inflectional affixes will reflect both morphophonemic and historical change. The specification of the relationship between the two is a task that the comparative linguist in New Guinea can hardly avoid.

TABLE 92

PHONEME CHANGES RESULTING FROM MORPHEME COMBINATIONS

Class		*p*	*t*	*k*	*b/w*	*d/r*	*y*	*m*	*n*	Vowel (v)
V	Ga *p*	*p*	*t*	*k*	*b*	*d*	*y*	*m/n*	*n*	V + v
	Us	[b]	*t*	[g]	*w*/[g]	*r*	*y*	*m*	*n*	V + v
	Au	*p̑*	*s*	*g*	*gw*	*k*	*y/t*	*m*	*n*	*w/y* + v
	Aw	[b]	[r]	[g]	...	...	*y*	*w*	*n*	V + v
	Fo	*b*	[r]	*g*	*w*	...	*y*	*m*	*n*	(V + v)/V
N	Ga	*mp*	*nt*	*nk*	*mb*	*nd*	*ny*	*m*	*n*	*n* + v
	Us	*qp*	*qt*	*qk*	*qk*	*qk*	*qt*	*m:*	*n:*	*n* + v
	Au	*mp*	*nt*	*nk*	*nkw*	*nk*	*nt*	*mb*	*nd*	*n* + v
	Aw	*p*	*t*	*nk*	...	...	*ns*	*m*	*n*	*n* + v
	Fo	*p:*	*t:*	*k:*	*nkw*	...	*nt*	*mp*	*nt*	*nk* + v
Q	Ga	*qp*	*qt*	*qk*	*qb*	*qd*	*qy*	*qm*	*qn*	*k/q* + v
	Us	*qp*	*qt*	*qk*	*qw/qk*	*qk*	*qy*	*qm/q*	*qn*	*r* + v
	Au	*p*	*t*	*k*	*kw*	*k*	*t*	*qm*	*qn*	*r* + v
	Aw	*p*	*t*	*k*	...	...	*s*	*qm*	*qn*	[r] + v
	Fo	*p:*	*t:*	*k:*	*qw*	...	*qy*	*qm*	*qn*	*q* + v
Y	Ga	*t*	*t*	*t*	*y*	*y*	*y*	*n*	*n*	*y* + v
D	Ga	*nt*	*nt*	*nt*	*nd*	*nd*	*nd*	*n*	*n*	*d* + v

In the phonemicization of the languages of the Eastern Family prenasalization, preglottalization, and consonant length have been interpreted either as clusters of consonant phonemes or as single complex unit phonemes depending on the language and the analyst.[5] For comparative work, however, it is important to consider these sequences as units corresponding as units to other units. These need not be single phoneme units but may, if desired, be considered higher level units and treated on the phoneme level as clusters.

[5] The Vincents for Tairora adopt a unit solution; the Lovings for Awa, Marks for Auyana, Luff and Goddard for Agarabi, and Frantz for Gadsup have chosen a cluster; and Bee (in Chap. XIII) suggests that both solutions are equally possible for Usarufa.

The result of further historical study may furnish clues as to which synchronic interpretation is more likely but it need not necessarily dictate the choice of interpretation for any given language.

Complex sequences as indicated above occur only between vowels in all of the languages of the Eastern Family except Tairora. They also are often clearly the result of morphophonemic processes (see Table 92). However, this restriction in the distribution and occurrence of sequences of contoids is parallel to the complementary distribution of allophones of single phonemes in some languages and to restrictions on noncomplex phonemes in others. Rather than being a determinant for choice of interpretation these restrictions tend to emphasize the necessity of keeping initial and noninitial correspondence sets separate.

The seven languages considered here are spoken by populations living in an area approximately one hundred miles long and fifty miles wide. Such geographic proximity promotes multilingualism and linguistic borrowing. The evidences of the former are legion and although less easy to recognize the latter has surely played a significant role in the development of Highland languages. In languages without a written tradition borrowing is not only difficult to recognize but often almost impossible to prove. The regularity of the incorporating processes of the language in question is hard to distinguish from the processes of historic change. However, it is important to be alert to the evidences and influences of linguistic borrowings when the conditions for such borrowing are so manifestly present.[6]

The reconstructions which follow are based on an examination and analysis of one hundred and eighty cognate sets of forms. The Summer Institute of Linguistics survey list (Bee and Pence 1962) was used as a starting point but lists of more than one thousand forms were examined for each of the languages except Binumarien and Agarabi where only the SIL list was available. The least complicated and most transparent sets of cognates have been chosen for presentation here. To keep the influences of the various factors described above to a minimum, complex sequences of contoids have been avoided as much as possible and the least morphemically complex forms have been chosen. Only two verbal forms have been included. Except for the indication of morphophonemic class (N, V, or Q) which has been reconstructed in the cases where there is fairly clear evidence to do so, no attempt has been made to reconstruct anything more than stem morphemes. Where morphophonemic class has been reconstructed the reflexes in the various languages are morphemes (active or fossilized) not phonemes as such.

---

[6] The recent borrowings from Neo-Melanesian demonstrate correspondence regularity. It may prove interesting to compare these borrowings from Neo-Melanesian with inherited cognate sets to see if there is a parallel in phoneme and morphophonemic correspondences.

These reconstructions are only tentative and are intended to serve as stepping stones to more precise analyses. Vowel reflexes and reflexes of complex contoid sequences in particular need more detailed study and may alter some of the present reconstructions. The comments following each reconstruction usually indicate specific problem areas.

No attempt has been made to standardize the orthographies for the different languages. The orthography used for each language is that used by the linguist who prepared the lexical list from which the forms have been taken. In some cases these lists were made after preliminary phonemic analysis and are only partly phonemic. The following summary of orthographic devices which have been used may prove helpful:

/:/	Binumarien length	/ˆ/	falling tone
/./	Gadsup and Auyana length	/q/	glottal stop
/'/	stress	/ə/	Tairora mid central vowel
/´/	high tone	/eh/	Awa front low vowel
/`/	low tone	/ah/	Awa back low vowel

In addition from individual languages are the following representations of phonemes:

Gadsup

/t/s/	for the /t/ phoneme	/a/	for the /ə/ phoneme
/w/b/	for the /w/b/ phoneme	/a./	for the /a phoneme
/r/d/	for the /r/d/ phoneme		

Usarufa

/p-/-b-/	for the /p/ phoneme	/-k-/	for the /qk/ complex
/k-/-g-/	for the /k/ phoneme	/mm/	for the /m:/ complex
/-p-/	for the /qp/ complex	/nn/	for the /n:/ complex

Awa		Agarabi	
/p-/-b-/	the /p/ phoneme	/h/	for the /h/q/ phoneme
/t-/-r-/	the /t/ phoneme	/h/	for the /ə/ phoneme
/k-/-g-/	the /k/ phoneme	/aa/	for the /a/ phoneme

In the reconstructions hyphens (-) indicate morpheme boundaries and a plus preceding a reconstructed form indicates that the prefix which is postulated has become fossilized in those languages which retain an overt reflex of it.

2. RECONSTRUCTIONS

1. 'armpit'	*ɔpɔ-N	Ta.	´akɔ
		Ga.	àppè.mí
		Us.	áábèmma
		Au.	á.'bémbà
		Aw.	ahbé

Comment: The reflexes of *N should be noted. Gadsup, Usarufa, Auyana, and Awa regularly show *mi, mma, mba* and loss, respectively. The loss in Tairora while not uncommon is but one of several reflexes of *N.

2. 'arrow'	*paro-V/kwe-	Ta.	'bebɔ
		Bi.	pè:pà
		Ga.	pàkò.nì
		Ag.	úwé
		Us.	paromá
		Au.	pà'ròimá
		Aw.	póriah

Comment: Since each language has a number of specialized terms for arrow types it is difficult to be sure that equivalent terms have been chosen. Gadsup, Usarufa, Auyana, and Awa seem likely to be cognate terms although the Awa vowel reflexes are unusual. The Tairora, Binumarien, and Agarabi terms are likely cognate and seem to reflect some kind of reduplication.

3. 'bag'	*una-N	Ta.	u'tɔ
		Bi.	uqa
		Ga.	ù'ná.mì
		Ag.	unaan
		Us.	unáámma
		Au.	ù'ná.m'bá

Comment: The Tairora and Binumarien forms though probably cognate are irregular. Although Tairora /t/ and Binumarien /q/ regularly correspond they are not the usual reflexes of */n/. It is possible that Tairora *tɔ* and Binumarien *qa* are reflexes of *N but these would normally be reflexes of *Q.

4. 'banana'	*qe-Q	Ta.	'qetɔ
		Bi.	è:qa
		Ga.	è.qì
		Ag.	áán
		Us.	eqá
		Au.	te'qá
		Aw.	peraré

Comment: This is the only example of initial */q/ therefore it is a rather uncertain reconstruction. However the set of correspondences does not match any other initial consonant.

| 5. 'bean' | *ko-para-N | Ta. | 'kohe |
| | | Bi. | o:ɸa:ɸana |

Ga.	*ko.qí*
Ag.	*mataah*
Us.	*koqá/kobárámmá*
Au.	*kòqá*
Aw.	*tobárá*

Comment: The Binumarien, Awa, and Usarufa forms seem to indicate a polymorphemic stem complex. The Usarufa forms mean the root of the native bean and the bean itself respectively. Whether such a distinction is made in the other languages is not clear. This is a case of */k/ being reflected in Tairora as /k/ rather than /t/ and may indicate a later borrowing.

6. 'belly'   *-*mu*-Q

Ta.	*'auhe*
Bi.	*amuaqa*
Ga.	*ámùqi*
Ag.	*amúh*
Us.	*'ámûqa*
Au.	*'ámùqà*
Aw.	*ahmibiuq*

Comment: The initial vowel may be attributed to a third person possessive prefix. This set of nasal correspondences is unique.

7. 'blood'   *nade-V

Ta.	*'nare*
Bi.	*píqdìká*
Ga.	*nà'rei/korà'mi*
Ag.	*nááre*
Us.	*naaemá*
Au.	*nàè'má*
Aw.	*kóraq/onu*

Comment: Loss of medial */d/ in Usarufa and Auyana is unique. The Awa forms do not appear to be cognate to the forms from the other languages except the alternate Gadsup form. The Binumarien form seems unrelated.

8. 'breast'   *nɔ-N

Ta.	*'namǝ*
Bi.	*ná:m:á*
Ga.	*ná.mí*
Ag.	*naan*
Us.	*náámma*
Au.	*'ná.mbà*
Aw.	*nah*

Comment: Tairora reflex of *N unusual.

9. 'brother (older)' *-kwɔ-   Ta.   bɔkarɔ
                                     Bi.   apasa:pa
                                     Ga.   tènti wai
                                     Ag.   awahe
                                     Us.   awaaóma
                                     Au.   àwà'ómá
                                     Aw.   awahwá

Comment: All of the languages reflect polymorphemic forms but the stems bɔ, pa-, -wa-, -waa-, -wa- and -wah-, respectively, are obviously cognate. Regular.

10. 'brother (younger)' *pa-Q   Ta.   'qɔtɔ
                                     Bi.
                                     Ga.   'páqi
                                     Us.   ábáqà
                                     Au.   ábá'komà
                                     Aw.   ábákawa

Comment: Polymorphemic forms but stems reflect regular correspondences.

11. 'cloud'   *kona-N   Ta.   to'nɔbu/uro'murɔ
                                     Bi.   o:námú
                                     Ga.   ko'nami/àyòni
                                     Ag.   áyón
                                     Us.   konnámmá/kunnomimá
                                     Au.   ài'námbá
                                     Aw.   saboná/irabúyá

Comment: Tairora bu, Binumarien mu, Gadsup mi, and Usarufa mma are regular correspondences of *N. Initial */k/ is /t/, loss, /k/, and /k/ in these languages, respectively.

12. 'come'   *ye-   Ta.   'aniro
                                     Ga.   yé.nò
                                     Us.   (y)iyo
                                     Au.   tiyó
                                     Aw.   sire

Comment: The Tairora form is probably not cognate to the others. (y) in the Usarufa form indicates that it is lost in this particular form of the verb and retained in others. The difference in the vowels reflects morphophonemic change.

13. 'daughter'   *-dɔmu-N   Ta.   ra'burɔ
                                     Ga.   dàmúmmì

Us.	*ayáámûmma*
Au.	*a'yámùko*
Aw.	*ayahungáwa*

Comment: This is the only example of this set of correspondences for the reconstruction of */d/*. Also the loss of */-m-/* in Awa is unique. The initial vowels in Usarufa, Auyana, and Awa are third person possessive prefixes. As in most kin terms the final syllables of the various forms represent formatives of one kind or another.

14. 'dog'	**iya-N*	Ta.	*'bairi*
		Bi.	*paini*
		Ga.	*ìyámì*
		Ag.	*iyan*
		Us.	*iyámmá*
		Au.	*i'yámbá*
		Aw.	*iya*

Comment: The Tairora and Binumarien forms are obviously cognates as opposed to the forms from the other languages. However, since dogs are late introductions into these cultures, the history of these forms is likely to be other than direct inheritance.

15. 'ear'	**ɔ-Q-ra-N*	Ta.	*a'to*
		Bi.	*ááqô:*
		Ga.	*à.kàmì*
		Ag.	*aahtarén*
		Us.	*áárarammalááqa*
		Au.	*'á.qà*
		Aw.	*ahre*

Comment: A polymorphemic form has been reconstructed here to account for seeming irregularities in correspondences. The two terms in Usarufa provided the clue to this explanation. The first of the two terms refers to the external ear and means literally 'ear-fruit'. The second of the two terms refers to the inner ear, the understanding or mind.

16. 'ground'	**bara-V*	Ta.	*'batə*
		Bi.	*maqa*
		Ga.	*màkà*
		Ag.	*wárá*
		Us.	*maramá*
		Au.	*màrà'má*
		Aw.	*marakó*

Comment: This set of reflexes for */r/* needs still to be justified.

17. 'grease (fat)'   *watawe-N   Ta.   'bɔhɔberɔ/ka'ntebu
                                        Bi.   paqkame:na
                                        Ga.   bàsàpémi/ano.ni
                                        Ag.   anu
                                        Us.   matewémma/ainómma
                                        Au.   masawémbe
                                        Aw.   maiyawe
Comment: This is one of the few good sets of correspondences for */t/.

18. 'father'   *po-V   Ta.   'qo
                                        Bi.   akoɸa
                                        Ga.   apo
                                        Ag.   apohé
                                        Us.   aboámá
                                        Au.   abo'wámá
                                        Aw.   abowá
Comment: As with other kin terms the forms except the Tairora are
polymorphemic.

19. 'fence'   *kuru-V   Ta.   tu'tukɔ/tu'bik
                                        Ga.   kukuni
                                        Us.   kurumá
                                        Au.   kurimá/kusa'má
                                        Aw.   wíra
Comment: The two terms in both Tairora and Auyana seem to indicate
that these are polymorphemic but the correspondences are still quite good.

20. 'fire'   *ida-V   Ta.   i'hɔ
                                        Bi.   iqda
                                        Ga.   ikai
                                        Ag.   írá
                                        Us.   iramá
                                        Au.   ira'má
                                        Aw.   ira
Comment: Reflexes of V in Gadsup, Usarufa, and Auyana are i, ma,
and ma respectively. Elsewhere there is loss.

21. 'flying fox'   *kɔmpɔ-N   Ta.   'kankarɔ
                                        Bi.   ka:ka:na
                                        Us.   kaapaammá
                                        Au.   ka.mpa.mba
                                        Aw.   tahpah
Comment: This is one of the few clusters postulated for the proto form
and needs more confirmation.

22. 'fruit'   * +*ra*-N   Ta.   *təbə*
    Ga.   *akami*
    Us.   *arammá*
    Au.   *arambá*
    Aw.   *ara/sera*

Comment: The initial vowel on all of the forms but Tairora may be fossilized third person prefixes which are now restricted to body parts and kin terms. Tairora forms regularly lose these prefixes.

23. 'ginger'   *kwi-N   Ga.   *bími*
    Us.   *wímma*
    Au.   *kwímba*
    Aw.   *ki*

Comment: This is the only occurrence of /k/ in Awa as a reflex of */kw/.

24. 'grandfather'   *-*nɔpu*-V   Ta.   *'naqurə*
    Us.   *anáábúómá*
    Aw.   *anahbuwá*

Comment: Stem correspondences are regular.

25. 'grandmother'   *-*rərao*-V   Ta.   *ta'torə*
    Ga.   *-kaka*
    Us.   *aráráómá*
    Au.   *-rarao*
    Aw.   *àrahrawá*

Comment: The Awa -*wa* is a separate morpheme and probably not a reflex of */o/.

26. 'hand'   *-*yɔ-u*-   Ta.   *'kauqu*
    Bi.   *asáúku*
    Ga.   *aya.mi*
    Ag.   *ayaan*
    Us.   *ayáámma*
    Au.   *áyáamba*
    Aw.   *ayahn*

Comment: The Tairora and Binumarien forms seem to indicate that there has been a change from an N class to a Q class. This may be accounted for by the presence of /u/ in these forms which has no corresponding reflex in the other languages and may be representative of some proto morpheme.

27. 'he'   *kwe/bi-   Ta.   'bibɔ
                                    Bi.   mipa
                                    Ga.   bèni
                                    Ag.   wehi
                                    Us.   wemá
                                    Au.   kwe'má
                                    Aw.   wega

Comment: Tairora and Binumarien forms go back to *bi while the other languages have forms going back to *kwe. Other pronoun forms seem to indicate that both forms may have been inherited. Evidence from other related language families will prove valuable here.

28. 'head'   *-qno-N/pia-   Ta.   qi'etɔ
                                    Bi.   akiaqa
                                    Ga.   aqnomi
                                    Ag.   ahon
                                    Us.   aqnómma
                                    Au.   aqnómbá
                                    Aw.   ayeqnó

Comment: The Awa form seems to suggest a polymorphemic shape other than the usual for body and may explain the Tairora and Binumarien forms which do not seem to be cognate with the Gadsup, Agarabi, Usarufa, or Auyana.

29. 'house'   *nɔ-N/mɔ-Q   Ta.   'nabu
                                    Bi.   maaqa
                                    Ga.   máqi
                                    Ag.   maah
                                    Us.   naammá
                                    Au.   na.m'bá
                                    Aw.   nah

Comment: That two different stems are represented here is suggested by Tairora maqa 'home place'; Usarufa mááqa 'home or place'; and Gadsup i'na.mi 'sleeping house for men and women'.

30. 'husband'   *-kwɔ-   Ta.   'bati
                                    Ga.   wapui
                                    Us.   awaiqá
                                    Au.   awai'ko
                                    Aw.   weh

Comment: There may be some significance to the /i/ in all of the forms but Awa, but what it is is not clear from present evidence.

31. 'knee' *-rau-N Ta. *'tori*
              Bi. *aqo:ri*
              Ga. *àkò.ní/àkūqì*
              Ag. *árón*
              Us. *araayummá*
              Au. *àràum'ba*
              Aw. *arau*

Comment: The class correspondence is imperfect and may indicate some morphemic process not accounted for by this reconstruction.

32. 'liver' *-ru-N Ta. *'tubu*
              Bi. *an:a:ma*
              Ga. *ákúqì*
              Ag. *amaapón*
              Us. *árumma*
              Aw. *aru*

Comment: The Binumarien and Agarabi forms seem not to be cognate with the other forms. The Gadsup reflex of *N is not the normal one and needs to be further investigated.

33. 'louse' *nu-N Ta. *nu'mɔ*
              Bi. *árú*
              Ga. *númì*
              Ag. *nun*
              Us. *nûmma*
              Au. *nùm'bá*
              Aw. *nu*

Comment: The Binumarien form is probably not cognate. The Tairora reflex of *N is the same as in the form for breast.

34. 'man' *kwe-(t)-V Ta. *bainti*
              Bi. *ɸaiqi*
              Ga. *bàntà*
              Ag. *wáántá*
              Us. *waamá*
              Au. *kwài'má*
              Aw. *weh*

Comment: A form in Usarufa *wáátigoma* 'man or person' seems to suggest that there may be a need to reconstruct some sort of */t/ phoneme, here indicated in parentheses. It may have been a complex sequence. This set of correspondences should be compared with those for 'husband'. The difference between bound and free in some of the languages should be noted.

35. 'meat'   * +*ma-(t)*-Q   Ta.   *məti*
                                       Bi.   *amaqi*
                                       Ga.   *àmàqi*
                                       Ag.   *ámáti*
                                       Us.   *amaqá*
                                       Au.   *àmàqá*

Comment: The initial /a/ of all the forms except the Tairora may represent a fossilized possessive prefix. It is not clear whether the final syllable of each form represents reflexes of *Q or whether /t/ should be reconstructed.

36. 'mother'   *-*no*-V   Ta.   *'no*
                                       Bi.   *anopa*
                                       Ga.   *ènà noi*
                                       Ag.   *anohé*
                                       Us.   *anóama*
                                       Au.   *a'nówama*
                                       Aw.   *anówa*

Comment: See the comment for 'father'.

37. 'name'   *-*wi*-Q   Ta.   *'autu*
                                       Bi.   *auqu*
                                       Ga.   *àbìqì*
                                       Ag.   *awih*
                                       Us.   *awîqa*
                                       Au.   *á'wíqa*
                                       Aw.   *awiq*

Comment: It is not clear whether the Tairora and Binumarien forms are cognate with the other forms or not but it seems rather doubtful.

38. 'nose'   *-*hi*-Q   Ta.   *'aiqi*
                                       Bi.   *aiki*
                                       Ga.   *àsìqi*
                                       Ag.   *átíh*
                                       Us.   *aiqá*
                                       Au.   *aiqá*
                                       Aw.   *abiyah*

Comment: This is the only example of this set of correspondences reflecting */h/ and needs confirmation.

39. 'one'   *boda*   Ta.   *bo'haiqa*
                                       Bi.   *mò:qdá:*
                                       Ga.   *màna*

Ag.	*manaa*
Us.	*môrama*
Au.	*mò'rámà*
Aw.	*morá*

Comment: The Gadsup and Agarabi forms are probably not cognate with the forms from the other languages.

40. 'penis'   *-poi-*

Ta.	*'ake*
Ga.	*àpè*
Us.	*abema*
Au.	*apoiko*
Aw.	*pegara*

Comment: This set of correspondences should be compared with the set for 'armpit'. The retension in Tairora of the reflexes of the initial *a* prefix is unusual.

41. 'pig'   **poe*-V

Ta.	*'quərə*
Bi.	*kúára*
Ga.	*póni*
Ag.	*pon*
Us.	*pomá*
Au.	*póima*
Aw.	*poérahq*

Comment: The Awa form may be polymorphemic although it is also possible that the *-rahq* is a reflex of *V.

42. 'rain'   **ɔ*-Q

Ta.	*'aqu*
Bi.	*àːkù*
Ga.	*àqi*
Ag.	*ááh*
Us.	*aaqá*
Au.	*à.qá*
Aw.	*ibo*

Comment: Compare with 'ear'.

43. 'road (path)'   **ɔ*-N

Ta.	*'arə*
Bi.	*àːnà*
Ga.	*à.ni*
Ag.	*páríparih*
Us.	*aammá*
Au.	*aambá*
Aw.	*ah*

Comment: Compare the reflexes of N here and the reflexes of Q in the set of correspondences for 'rain'.

44. 'root'   * +*ru*-Q/+*nu*-Q   Ta.   *'tuqə*
                                            Bi.   *atùkà*
                                            Ga.   *ákùgí/ánùqì*
                                            Ag.   *arúh*
                                            Us.   *ánûqa*
                                            Au.   *á'núqà*
                                            Aw.   *ánúq*

Comment: Compare with 'liver'. Gadsup has forms reflecting both of the reconstructed forms while Tairora, Binumarien, and Agarabi reflect only *-*ru*-Q and Usarufa, Auyana, and Awa reflect only *-*nu*-Q.

45. 'say'   **te-*   Ta.   *'tiro*
                                            Bi.   *qiqdano*
                                            Ga.   *sequ*
                                            Ag.   *temíh*
                                            Us.   *tiyo*
                                            Au.   *siyo*
                                            Aw.   *irarúwo*

Comment: All forms are polymorphemic but the stems in all but Awa are clearly cognate. Compare these forms with the forms for 'come'.

46. 'seed (planting)'* +*yu*-N   Ta.   *'kubu* 'seedling'
                                            Bi.   *àsùmú*
                                            Ga.   *àyùmi*
                                            Ag.   *áyún*
                                            Us.   *ayummá*
                                            Au.   *àràmba/aumá*
                                            Aw.   *ahyu*

Comment: Neither of the Auyana forms are cognate with the others. Tairora reflects the regular loss of initial vowel of possessive prefix. Although retained in the other languages it is not now productive with this stem.

47. 'shoulder'   **-pu-N*   Ta.   *'ubu/kururu*
                                            Bi.   *akumu*
                                            Ga.   *ápùmi*
                                            Ag.   *apun*
                                            Us.   *ábûmma*
                                            Au.   *àyóimá*
                                            Aw.   *ako*

Comment: An initial /g/ would be expected for the Tairora form. The Auyana and Awa forms seem to be cognate neither with one another nor with the forms from the other languages.

48. 'smoke' *(u)mu*-N Ta. *'murə*
                                         Bi. *muna*
                                         Ga. *íkkùni*
                                         Ag. *íhkún*
                                         Us. *úmúmma*
                                         Au. *ú'múmba*
                                         Aw. *aúne*

Comment: There is not enough evidence to determine whether the Tairora and Binumarien forms reflect a loss of initial */u/, or whether the Usarufa and Auyana forms reflect an addition. The Gadsup and Agarabi forms may be compounds with the words for 'fire'. The Awa form is probably not cognate.

49. 'sugar cane' *yɔ*-Q Ta. *'kaqə*
                                         Bi. *sààká*
                                         Ga. *yà.qí*
                                         Ag. *yááh*
                                         Us. *yaaqá*
                                         Au. *tà.qá*
                                         Aw. *sahq*

Comment: Perfectly regular.

50. 'tail' *+be*- Ta. *'bekə/rə'tirə*
                                         Bi. *aratira*
                                         Ga. *ámèni/amendimi*
                                       Ag. *amé*
                                         Us. *améráamma*
                                       Au. *à'méra.mba*
                                       Aw. *ehwegárá*

Comment: Most of the forms in this set appear to be more complex than the form reconstructed. However, there is insufficient evidence for the reconstruction of a more complex form and some type of compounding may be in evidence.

51. 'taro' *ya*-N Ta. *'kərə*
                                         Bi. *sàná*
                                       Ga. *yàmi*
                                       Ag. *umánti*
                                       Us. *yammá*
                                     Au. *mai'yámbà*
                                   Aw. *ango*

Comment: Compare with 'sugar cane'. The Auyana form looks as though it might be a compound cognate with both the Agarabi form and the forms reflected in Tairora, Binumarien, Gadsup, and Usarufa of *ya*-N.

52. 'ten'   *tiyənkə-   Ta.
                                        Bi.   qisaukuara
                                        Ga.   tìyánkani
                                        Ag.   tiyaamikán
                                        Us.   tiyáákae
                                        Au.   sì'ánkai
                                        Aw.   neangú

Comment: These are polymorphemic forms meaning roughly 'my two hands'.

53. 'that'   *bi-   Ta.   bihə
                                        Bi.   muquna
                                        Ga.   mini
                                        Ag.   ma
                                        Us.   minnáma
                                        Au.   mi.ndámà
                                        Aw.   miná

Comment: The Binumarien and Agarabi forms are probably not cognate with the others.

54. 'thigh'   *-ru-Q   Ta.   'abundərə
                                        Ga.   àkùqì
                                        Us.   árûqa
                                        Au.   árúqa
                                        Aw.   arù

Comment: Compare with 'liver' and 'root'. The Tairora if cognate with the other forms is an unusual correspondence.

55. 'this'   *ma-   Ta.   'mana
                                        Bi.   maana
                                        Ga.   màna
                                        Ag.   mi
                                        Us.   maannáma
                                        Au.   mà.ndáma
                                        Aw.   mahna

Comment: Compare with 'that'. The Agarabi forms seem to be reversed.

56. 'tongue' *-mɔpi-V   Ta.   maq'iri
                                        Bi.   ámá:kírí
                                        Ga.   ànàpini
                                        Ag.   amaapín
                                        Us.   amáábîma
                                        Au.   àmá.bí
                                        Aw.   anehbi

Comment: The /n/ reflex of */m/ in both Gadsup and Awa is unusual.

57. 'tree' **yə-V* Ta. *kə'təri*
Bi. *sàqárí*
Ga. *yà.ni*
Ag. *yáá*
Us. *yaamá*
Au. *tài'má*
Aw. *wangá/teh*

Comment: Compare with 'sugar cane' and 'taro'. The Tairora and Binumarien forms may indicate that a more complex form should be reconstructed.

58. 'water' **no-N* Ta. *nə'məri/nə'məi*
Bi. *namari*
Ga. *nò.mi*
Ag. *nón*
Us. *nommá*
Au. *nòmbá*
Aw. *nò/waní*

Comment: The Awa form *waní* may tie in with the Tairora and Binumarien forms.

59. 'wife' **-nɔ-Q* Ta. *'natə*
Ga. *tenti nàqi*
Us. *ánáaqa*
Au. *àwài'nínkó*
Aw. *anahkawa*

Comment: Compare with 'breast' and 'house'.

60. 'wind' **uwə-V (ukwə)* Ta. *u'bai*
Bi. *úpáí*
Ga. *tìsòbá.nì*
Ag. *uwaa*
Us. *uwááma*
Au. *ùndámà*
Aw. *soiriq*

Comment: Both of the suggested reconstructions seem to be equally possible. The Auyana form which would be expected to provide the deciding evidence is an unusual correspondence.

3. REFLEXES

The reflexes of each of the phonemes reconstructed in the preceding section are given below. The most common reflex for a given language is listed first followed by other reflexes either regular or unique. If a given reflex occurs only once or twice it is followed by a number in parentheses which indicates the number of the form in Section 2 which contains the correspondence set in which that particular reflex occurs. A number in parentheses immediately following the reconstructed phonemes indicates that there is only one occurrence of that particular phoneme. If no number appears after a given reflex it indicates that the reflex is fairly common and examples may be found by checking the index of reconstructed phonemes in Section 4. A diagonal line between two symbols indicates two orthographic representations of the same phoneme. Initial-only reflexes are marked by a hyphen following the symbol; a symbol between two hyphens indicates a reflex limited to medial position; and reflexes which are not limited as to position of occurrence are unmarked.

*/p/   Ta. /q/; /-k-/ (1, 40); loss (47)
        Bi. /k/; /-p-/ (5)
        Ga. /p/; /-pp-/ (1)
        Ag. /p/
        Us., Aw. /p-/-b-/
        Au. /p-/-b-/; /-p̶/ (40)
*/t/   Ta. /t-/; /-h-/ (17); /-nt-/ (34); /-t-/ (35)
        Bi. /q-/; /-qd-/ (17)
        Ga. /t/s/; /-q-/ (35); /-nt-/ (34)
        Ag. /t/; /-nt-/ (34); /-t-/ (35)
        Us. /t/
        Au. /s/
        Aw. /-y-/ (17)
*/k/   Ta. /t-/ (11, 19); /k-/ (5, 21)
        Bi. loss (5, 11); /k-/ (21)
        Ga., Us., Au. /k/
        Aw. /t/
*/r/   Ta. /t/; /-b-/ (54)
        Bi. /q/; /-t-/ (44); /-p-/ (5)
        Ga. /k/
        Ag. /r/; /-ht-/ (15)
        Us., Au., Aw. /r/
*/d/   Ta. /-h-/; /r/ (7, 13)
        Bi. /-qd-/
        Ga. /d-/ (13); /-k-/ (20); /-r-/ (7)
        Ag. /r/
        Us., Au., Aw. /r/; /-y-/ (13); loss (7)
*/b/   Ta. /b/
        Bi., Ga., Us., Au. /m/
        Ag. /w-/ (16); /-m-/ (50)
        Aw. /m-/; /-w-/ (50)

*/w/ Ta. /b/
Bi. /p-/ (17); /-p-/ (60); /-m-/ (17)
Ga. /b-/ (17); /-b-/ (37; /-p-/ (17)
Ag. /-w-/ (37, 60)
Us., Au., Aw. /m-/ (18); /-w-/ (37, 60, 17)

*/kw/ Ta. /b/
Bi. /p/ (2, 60); /ƥ/ (9, 34)
Ga. /b/w/
Ag., Us. /w/
Au. /kw-/; /-w-/
Aw. /w/; /k-/ (23)

*/m/ Ta. /m-/; /-b-/ (13); loss (6)
Bi., Ag., Us., Au. /m/
Ga. /m/; /-n-/ (56)
Aw. /m-/ (55); /-mb-/ (6); /-n-/ (56); loss (13)

*/n/ Ta., Bi., Ga., Ag., Au., Aw. /n/
Us. /n/; /-nn-/ (11)

*/y/ Ta. /k/
Bi. /s/
Ga., Ag., Us. /y/
Au. /t-/; /-y-/
Aw. /s-/; /-y-/; /t-/ (57)

*/q/ (4) Ta. /q/
Bi., Ga., Us. loss
Au. /t/
Aw. /p/

*/h/ (38) Ta., Bi., Us., Au. loss
Ga. /s/
Ag. /t/
Aw. /b/

*/mp/ (21) Ta. /nk/
Bi. /k/
Us., Aw. /k/
Au. /mp/

*/nk/ (52) Bi., Ag., Us. /k/
Ag., Au. /nk/

*/qn/ (28) Ga., Us., Au., Aw. /qn/
Ag. /hn/

*/ɔ/ Ta. /a/; /ə/ (9)
Bi. /a:/aa/; /a/ (9)
Ga. /a/; /a./; /ai/ (9)
Ag. /aa/; /a/ (9)

Au. /a./aa/; /a/ (9, 25); /ai/ (59)
Aw. /ah/
*/a/   Ta. /ə/; /a/; /ai/ (39)
Bi. /a/; /ai/ (5, 39)
Ga. /a/; /a./ (3); /ai/ (20)
Ag. /a/; /aa/ (3, 7)
Us. /a/; /aa/ (3, 7)
Au. /a/
Aw. /a/; /a./ (3); /o/ (2)
*/ə/   Ta. /ai/ (34, 60); /a/ (30); /ə/ (57)
Bi. /ai/ (34, 60); /aa/ (29); /a/ (57); /ua/ (52)
Ag. /aa/; /a/ (52)
Ga. /a/; /a./ (52)
Us. /aa/; /ai/ (30); /ae/ (52)
Au. /ai/
Aw. /eh/
*/e/   Ta., Us., Au., Aw. /e/; /i/ (12, 45)
Bi. /e:/; /i/ (12, 45)
Ba. /e/; /e./ (2, 4, 12); /ei/ (7)
Aw. /e/
*/i/   Ta., Bi., Ga., Ag., Us., Au., Aw. /i/
*/u/   Ta., Bi. /u/
Ga., Ag., Us., Aw. /u/; loss (26)
Au. /u/; /i/ (19); loss (26)
*/o/   Ta., Ga., Ag., Us. /o/
Bi. /o/; loss (18, 36)
Au. /o/; /oi/ (2)
Aw. /o/; /ia/ (2)
*/ao/   (25) Ta. /o/
Ga., Aw. /a/
Us., Au. /ao/
*/au/   (31) Ta., Bi., Ga., Ag. /o/
Us. /aayu/
Aw. /au/
*/oi/   (40) Ta., Ga., Us., Aw. /e/
Au. /oi/
*/oe/   (41) Ta., Bi. /ua/
Ga., Ag., Us. /o/
Au. /oi/
Aw. /oe/
*/ia/   (28) Ta. /ie/
Bi. /ia/

*N   Ta. /bu/; /rə/; /mə/ (8, 33); /bə/ (22)[7]
       Bi. /mu/; /na/; /m:a/ (8, 33)
       Ga. /mi/; /mmi/ (13); /ni/ (31, 43, 48); /qi/ (31, 32)
       Ag. /n/
       Us. /mma/
       Au. /mba/
       Aw. loss
*V   Ta. loss; /rə/; /ri/ (56, 57); /kə/ (19)
       Bi. loss; /rq/; /ri/ (56, 57)
       Ga. /ni/; loss; /i/ (7, 20)
       Ag. loss; /n/ (41, 56)
       Us. /ma/
       Au. / ma/; loss (56)
       Aw. loss
*Q   Ta. /t/ + vowel; /q/ + vowel
       Bi. /q/ + vowel; /k/ + vowel
       Ga. /qi/
       Ag. /h/; /ti/ (35)
       Us., Au. /qa/
       Aw. /q/; loss (54)

4. INDEX OF RECONSTRUCTED PHONEMES

The following list gives the forms in Section 2 in which each phoneme occurs.

*/a/   2, 3, 5, 7, 10, 11, 14, 15, 16, 17, 20, 22, 35, 39
*/ao/   25
*/au/   31
*/ɔ/   1, 8, 9, 13, 15, 21, 24, 25, 26, 29, 42, 43, 49, 52, 56, 59
*/b/   16, 27, 39, 50, 53
*/d/   7, 13, 20, 39
*/e/   1, 2, 4, 7, 12, 17, 27, 45, 50
*/ə/   29, 30, 34, 52, 57, 60
*/h/   38
*/i/   14, 20, 23, 27, 37, 38, 52, 53, 56
*/ia/   28
*/k/   5, 11, 19, 21
*/kw/   2, 9, 23, 27, 30, 34, 60
*/nk/   52
*/m/   6, 13, 29, 35, 48, 55, 56
*/n/   3, 7, 8, 11, 24, 29, 33, 36, 44, 58, 59

[7] The Tairora and Binumarien reflexes of *N in numbers 3, 5, 15, and 31 are not clear.

*N	1, 3, 5, 8, 11, 13, 14, 15, 17, 21, 22, 23, 28, 29, 31, 32, 33, 43, 46, 47, 48, 51, 58
*/qn/	28
*/o/	2, 5, 11, 18, 28, 36, 39, 58
*/oe/	41
*/oi/	40
*/p/	1, 2, 5, 10, 18, 24, 28, 40, 41, 47, 56
*/mp/	21
*/q/	4
*Q	4, 6, 10, 15, 29, 35, 37, 38, 42, 44, 49, 54, 59,
*/r/	2, 5, 15, 16, 19, 22, 25, 31, 32, 44, 54
*/t/	17, (34), (35), 45, 52
*/u/	3, 6, 13, 19, 24, 26, 32, 33, 44, 46, 47, 48, 54, 60
*V	2, 7, 16, 18, 19, 20, 24, 25, 34, 36, 41, 56, 57, 60
*/w/	17, 37, 60
*/y/	12, 14, 26, 49, 51, 52, 57

5. SYSTEMIZATION OF PHONEMES FOR THE EASTERN FAMILY

In the preceding sections phonemes were viewed as separate from their respective systems and were compared as historically corresponding. This section will attempt to present the phonemes of each language as they relate to their particular systems and to compare them as parallel points of related systems viewed as wholes. The allophonic and distinctive feature structure of each phoneme will be presented.

The information concerning phonemic contrasts and allophonic variation is drawn directly from the analyses of colleagues who have been studying the various languages for periods ranging up to five years.[8] Some analyses are more tentative than others but have been accepted as the best at present available. A phonemic statement was not available at the time of this study so no systemization of the phonemes of Binumarien will be presented.

On the basis of the available phonemicizations a distinctive feature analysis has been made of each system. To facilitate this analysis a slight change has been made in the phonemicization of [ŋ] in Gadsup, Auyana and Awa. On the basis of shared features [ŋ] in each of these languages has been assigned to /m/ rather than /n/ since no change need be made in the complementary distribution statement except the /m/ to /n/ substitution. Also to simplify the distinctive features analysis the complex contoid sequences have throughout been omitted from consideration. They are in effect treated as clusters of phonemes, but this is not intended as an endorsement of that particular interpretation.

In order to compare the relevant features of each system more readily

[8] See Bee (Chap. XIII), C. and M. Frantz (Chap. XVIII), Goddard and Luff (1962b), R. Loving (Chap. III), Marks (1964a), and A. and L. Vincent (1962c).

they have been arranged in table form (see Table 93). The four categories indicated are: consonants, vowels, complex contoid sequences, and distinctive features. Phonemic differences of note are the following: the lack of a /y/ phoneme in Tairora; the labiovelar and fricative series in Auyana; the

TABLE 93

RELEVANT FEATURES

	Consonants				Vowels			Complex Sequences			Features
Tairora	*p*	*t*	*k*	*q*	*i*	*u*		*mp*	*nt*	*nk*	Consonantal,
	b	*r*			*e*	*o*					Vocalic, Compact,
	m	*n*				*a*					Grave, Nasal,
											Tense, Strident
Gadsup	*p*	*t*	*k*	*q*	*i*		*u*	*mp*	*nt*	*nk*	Consonantal,
	b/w	*d/r*			*e*	*ə*	*o*	*qp*	*qt*	*qk*	Vocalic, Com-
	m	*n*				*a*		*mb*	*nd*		pact, Grave,
		y						*qm*	*qn*		Nasal, Tense
									qy		
Agarabi	*p*	*t*	*k*	*h/q*	*i*		*u*	*qp*	*qt*	*qk*	Consonantal,
	b/w	*d/r*	*g*		*e*	*ə*	*o*	*qb*	*qd*		Vocalic, Com-
	m	*n*				*a*		*qm*	*qn*		pact, Grave,
		y	*r̃*								Nasal, Tense
Usarufa	*p*	*t*	*k*	*q*	*i*		*u*	*qp*	*qt*	*qk*	Consonantal,
	m	*n*			*w*	*a*	*o*	*qw*	*qy*		Vocalic, Com-
	w	*y*						*qm*	*qn*		pact, Grave,
		r						*m:*	*n:*		Nasal, Sharp-
											Flat
Auyana	*p*	*t*	*k*	*kw*	*q*	*i*	*u*	*mp*	*nt*	*nk*	Consonantal,
	b	*d*	*g*	*gw*		*e*	*ə*	*o*	*mb*	*nd*	Vocalic, Com-
	p	*s*					*a*	*qm*	*qn*		pact, Grave,
	m	*n*									Nasal, Tense,
	w	*y*									Sharp-Flat,
		r									Discontinuous
Awa	*p*	*t*	*k*	*q*	*i*		*u*	*mp*	*nt*	*nk*	Consonantal,
	m	*n*			*e*	*ə*	*o*	*qp*	*qt*	*qk*	Vocalic, Compact,
	w	*y*			*eh*	*a*	*ah*	*qm*	*qn*		Grave, Nasal,
		s						*nw*	*ns*	*dw*	Strident, Discon-
											tinuous

/r/ versus /d/r/ contrast in Agarabi; the lack of /d/r/ phoneme in Awa and its seven vowel system; and the Usarufa five vowel system. Difference of distinctive features are: Auyana and Tairora, strident-mellow; Usarufa and Auyana, sharp/flat-plain; Auyana and Awa, continuous-discontinuous; and Tairora, Gadsup, Agarabi, and Auyana, tense-lax.[9]

Finally the differences between the allophones, distinctive features and historical sources of the phonemes of each language will be considered. Distinctive features are coded as follows. *A:* Consonantal; *B:* Vocalic; *C:* Compact; *D:* Grave; *E:* Nasal; *F:* Tense; *G:* Sharp-flat; *H:* Strident; *I:* Discontinuous. *Subscripts 1:* plus; *2:* minus; *3:* irrelevant.

Coded in parentheses immediately following the phoneme symbol are the features which are the same for that particular phoneme in all the languages. Those features which occur only in some but not all of the languages are listed by code in parentheses following the language or languages where they are distinctive. Following the distinctive features are the allophones of the given phoneme in each of the languages. Lastly the protophonemes are cited which are reflected by the phoneme in question. Where no indication is given as to the historical source of a given phoneme there is no evidence yet available as to the nature of that source. Since a statement of the Binumarien phonemes is not available there can be only an indication as to the source of a given phone. Because the specifications of the vowel phonemes do not vary as greatly as the consonants only the latter have been included.

/p/ $(A_1B_2C_2D_1E_2)$

Ta.	(F_2H_2) [p], [p^h], [ø]	
Bi.		*/kw/; */w/; */b/; */-p-/
Ga.	(F_2) [p], [ø]	*/p/; */-w-/
Ag.	(F_2) [p^h], [ø]	*/p/
Us.	(G_2) [p], [p^h], [b], [ß]	*/p/
Au.	$(F_2G_3I_1)$ [p]	*/p/
Aw.	(H_3I_3) [p], [b], [ß]	*/p/; */q/; */h/

/t/ $(A_1C_2D_2E_2)$

Ta.	$(B_2F_2H_2)$ [t]	*/t/; * /k-/; */r-/; *Q
Bi.		*/-r-/
Ga.	(B_2F_2) [t], [ts], [s]	*/t/; */h/
Ag.	(B_2F_1) [t^h], [s]	*/t/; */h/; *Q
Us.	(B_2G_2) [ṭ], [t], [s]	*/t/
Au.	$(B_2F_2G_2I_1)$ [t]	*/y-/; */q/
Aw.	$(B_3H_2I_1)$ [t], [d], [r]	*/k/; */y-/

---

[9] A unit interpretation of long nasals would introduce the tense-lax opposition in Usarufa.

/r-d/ (A_1E_2)
      Ta. $(B_3C_2D_2F_1H_2)$ [ľ], [ř], [d]   */d/; *V; *N
      Bi.   *V
      Ga. $(B_3C_2D_2F_1)$ [d], [ř]   */d/
      Ag. $(B_3C_2D_2F_3)$ [ľ], [ř], [t], [ty] */d/; */r/
      Us. $(B_1C_3D_3G_3)$ [ľ], [ř]   */d/; */r/; *Q
      Au. $(B_1C_3D_3F_3G_3I_3)$ [ľ], [ř] */d/; */r/; *Q
/b-w/ $(A_1B_2C_2D_1E_2)$
      Ta. (F_1H_2) [b], [β], [w]   */b/; */kw/; */w/; */-r-/; *N; */-m-/
      Ga. (F_1) [b], [β], [w]   */kw/; */w/
      Ag. (F_1) [p], [β], [w], [w̟] */kw/; */-w-/; */b-/
      Us. (G_3) [w]   */kw/; */-w-/; */b/
      Au. $(F_1G_3I_1)$ [w]   */-w-/; */b/
      Aw. (H_2I_2) [w]   */kw/; */-b-/
/k/ $(A_1B_2C_1D_1E_3)$
      Ta. (F_2H_2) [k], [k]   */y/; */-p-/; */k-/; *V
      Bi.   */p/; */k-/; *V; *Q
      Ga. (F_2) [k], [x]   */k/; */r/; */-d-/
      Ag. (F_2) [k], [x]
      Us. (G_2) [k], [kʰ], [g], [g] */k/; */kw/
      Au. $(F_2G_2I_1)$ [k]   */k/
      Aw. (H_2I_3) [k], [g], ⌊g⌋ */kw-/
/y/ $(A_1B_2D_2E_2)$
      Ga. (C_1F_1) [y], [y̟], [dž]   */y/
      Ag. (C_1F_3) [y], [y̟]   */y/
      Us. (C_3G_1) [y], [y̟]   */-d-/; */y/
      Aw. $(C_1F_1G_3I_2)$ [y]   */-y-/; */-d-/
      Aw. $(C_3H_3I_2)$ [y], [z]   */y/; */-d-/; */-t-/
/m/ $(A_1B_2C_3D_1E_1)$
      Ta. (F_3H_3) [m]   */m-/; *N
      Bi.   */m/; */b/; */-w-/; *N
      Ga. (F_3) [m], [ŋ]   */m/; */b/; *N
      Ag. (F_3) [m]   */m/; */-b-/
      Us. (G_3) [m])   */m/; */b/; */w-/
      Au. $(F_3G_3I_3)$ [m], [ŋ] */m/; */b/; */w-/
      Aw. (H_3I_3) [m], [ŋ]   */m/; */-b-/; */w-/
/n/ $(A_1B_2C_3D_2E_1)$
      Ta. (F_3H_3) */n/
      Bi.   */n/; *N
      Ga. (F_3) [n]   */n/; */-m-/; *N *V
      Ag. (F_3) [n]   */n/; *N; *V

	Us.	(G_3) [n]	*/n/; *N
	Au.	$(F_3G_3I_3)$ [n]	*/n/; *N
	Aw.	(H_3I_3) [n]	*/n/; */-m-/
/q/	$(A_2B_2C_3D_3E_3)$		
	Ta.	(F_3H_2) [ʔ]	*/p/; */q/; *Q
	Bi.		*/t/; */n/; */r/; *Q
	Ga.	(F_3) [ʔ]	*/h/; */q/; *Q
	Us.	(G_3) [ʔ]	*Q
	Au.	$(F_3G_3I_3)$ [ʔ]	*/h/; */q/; *Q
	Aw.	(H_3I_3) [ʔ]	*/h/; */q/; *Q
/h/	$(B_2C_3D_3E_3F_3)$		
	Ta.	(A_3H_1) [h], [s]	*/t/; */d/; */h/; */y/
	Ag.	(A_2) [h], [ʔ]	*Q
/s/	$(A_1B_2C_2E_2)$		
	Bi.		*/y/
	Au.	$(D_2F_2G_3I_2)$ [s]	*/t/
	Aw.	$(D_1H_1I_1)$ [ts], [dz]	*/y-/
/kw/	Au	$(A_1B_2C_1D_1E_2F_2G_1I_1)$ [kw]	*/kw/
/ƥ/	Bi.		*/-p-/; */kw/
	Aw.	$(A_1B_2C_2D_1E_2F_2G_2I_2)$ [Ø]	*/p/
	Au.	/gw/ $(A_1B_2C_1D_1E_2F_1G_2I_1)$ [gw]	
	Au.	/g/ $(A_1B_2C_1D_1E_2F_1G_2I_2)$ [g]	
	Au.	/b/ $(A_1B_2C_2D_1E_2F_1G_2I_1)$ [b]	
	Au.	/d/ $(A_1B_2C_2D_2E_2F_1G_2I_1)$ [d]	
	Ag.	/g/ $(A_1B_2C_1D_1E_2F_1)$ [g]	
	Ag.	/r̄/ $(A_1B_2C_2D_2E_3F_1)$ [r̄]	

XXXVII. The Proto Kainantu Kinship System of the East New Guinea Highlands

HARLAND B. KERR

1. INTRODUCTION

This paper attempts to reconstruct proto kinship terms of the proto language from which have developed the four major language divisions of the Eastern Family of the East New Guinea Highlands Stock.[1] The four divisions have been named Tairora-Binumarien, Auyana-Usarufa, Gadsup-Agarabi, and Awa.

Lexicostatistical studies with the Swadesh 100-word list set Tairora apart from Auyana, Gadsup, and Awa. It differs more or less equally from each of these three languages (58-59 percent shared cognates), which in turn exhibit a greater percentage of shared cognates (64-75 percent) *inter se*. The percentage of shared cognates is, however, considerably diminished in the nonbasic vocabulary. In a list of 345 entries collected from a central village in each language division, Auyana and Awa (which shared 75 percent cognates in the 100-word list) shared only 34 percent cognates (see Chap. XXXV).

---

[1] This paper was commenced in 1964 during field service with the Summer Institute of Linguistics in New Guinea. It was carried further during a period as a postdoctoral fellow at the Institute of Advanced Projects of the East-West Center, University of Hawaii, in the latter half of 1966. At this time the author was collaborating with members of the Micro-evolution Studies Project working from the University of Washington. Particular thanks are due to Howard McKaughan through whom the author was introduced to the Micro-evolution Project and to James B. Watson for his subsequent interest, encouragement, and advice. Thanks are also due to Darlene Bee, whose prior comparative studies in the Eastern Family have laid the foundation for this paper. The term 'proto Kainantu' for the title of this paper has been adopted at Watson's suggestion. The area under study is coextensive with what has previously been defined by Wurm (1964a,b) as the Eastern Family of the East New Guinea Highland Stock.

McKaughan (Chap. XXXV) has suggested the name Tagauwa for the proto language of the Eastern Family. Lexicostatistical and preliminary comparative studies point to a preliminary separation of Tagauwa into two groups, one giving rise to the present Tairora-Binumarien division, the other (named by McKaughan 'Gauwa') giving rise to Auyana-Usarufa, Gadsup-Agarabi, and Awa. To qualify as a proto Tagauwa term a given term must currently be attested in the Tairora-Binumarien group (which is referred to as the Taibi group), and in at least one language division of the Gauwa group.[2]

The postulated proto kinship terminology and the conclusions drawn from certain systematic features of this terminology must be tentative at this stage of comparative studies. McKaughan (Chap. XXXV) and Bee (Chap. XXXVI) have both done preliminary studies, but little is yet known about the details of allophonic variations of postulated proto phonemes. This stems in large measure from the complexity of the problems facing the comparativist in this family. According to Bee it is almost impossible to find a nucleus of monomorphemic forms on which to establish comparative studies in Highland languages (see Chap. XXXVI, Sec. 1). Various systems of morphophonemic change in Highland languages tend to mask the true nature of historical change and make the recognition of cognates difficult.

Despite such limitations there is a growing nucleus of workable comparative data. The kinship terms of the Eastern Family seem to be a particularly fertile source of cognate words. There seems to have been remarkably little change in the root sector of these terms, and reconstructions of the proto root of a particular term is comparatively straightforward. There is, however, considerably less agreement between the four language divisions with respect to affixes.

A distinction was made in the proto kinship system between two categories of kin, roughly defined as senior and junior kinship categories, respectively. This dichotomy is attested in each of the four language divisions. It is reasonably certain that the senior category was identified in the proto system by a first order suffix, which is still reflected in the daughter languages, by currently viable forms. The evidence for this proto suffix is most convincing among those terms which are applied to Go and G +1 consanguineal kin. It is rather uncertain whether the proto system included a suffix specific for the junior category of kin. But whether the proto system had such a suffix or not three of the four language divisions have a form characteristically associated with this category. It is improbable that these forms, *-bano* in

---

[2] The term Taibi has been chosen for this group according to the system adopted by McKaughan in previously naming the proto language underlying the Eastern Family of languages, Tagauwa, and the proto language underlying the Gadsup-Agarabi, Auyana-Usarufa, and Awa divisions, Gauwa.

Tairora, *-ko* in Auyana and Usarufa, and *-kawa* in Awa stem from a common proto form.

Bee in her reconstruction of proto roots for the Eastern Family (Chap. XXXVI) has postulated three morphophonemic classes of roots. This is an extension of her studies of Usarufa in which she assigns all forms, root or affixial, to one of these three classes, identified by a postscript -N, -V, and -Q, respectively (Chap. XIV, Sec. 1.2). In Usarufa the senior kin group is characteristically associated the the -V morphophonemic class, and the junior kin group with either the -N or -Q morphophonemic classes.

According to Bee (Chap. XIV) Usarufa noun stems may occur with a nominal suffix *-ma,* which Bee calls a mood affix (Chap. XIV, Sec. 4). The juxtaposition of the nominal suffix *-ma* and a noun stem is followed by morphophonemic interaction the outcome of which is determined by the postulated morphophonemic class of the nominal stem or the preceding suffix to which *-ma* attaches. In some combinations *-ma* remains *-ma* (following a vowel class V form). In other situations (following a glottal class Q form) it becomes *-qa,* while in others (following a nasal N class form) it becomes *-mma.* The nominal suffix therefore reflects the morphophonemic class of the form to which it attaches. A similar situation obtains in Auyana and Awa for both of which three noun classes have been postulated on the basis of a reconstructed or current stem-final phone: glottal, nasal, and vowel. There are five allied classes in Gadsup.

The evidence justifying recognition of two kin categories, senior and junior, in the proto language is presented in the first section. The kinship terms themselves are presented and discussed in three following sections, the first dealing with consanguineal kin of the Go, G +1, and G +2 generations, the second with affinal kin of the G-1, Go, and G +1 generations and the third with consanguineal kin of the G-1 and G-2 generations. In a concluding section attention is drawn to those kinship terms, already reconstructed, which appear to share a common proto root.

Data from two dialects of Auyana (Kosena and Asempa) are cited in this paper. Unless otherwise stated the term Auyana implies the Kosena dialect of Auyana. The term Tairora implies the Northern Tairora dialect area unless otherwise stipulated. The bulk of the data dealt with in this paper have been obtained from published materials of or personally supplied information from members of the Summer Institute of Linguistics, and in consequence is mainly representative of areas in which members of the institute are working. A considerable body of additional data has been collected by members of the Micro-Evolution Studies Project. Much of it agrees with data collected by members of the SIL. Where there are differences (due in large measure to differences of dialect studied) the differences have not been such as to invalidate the proto reconstructions postulated in this paper.

No attempt has been made to reconstruct tone or stress, although it is certain that Auyana, Usarufa, Gadsup, Agarabi, and Awa are tone languages. Vincent recognizes stress but not tone in Tairora. Where relevant, footnotes will note pertinent tone or stress information. While it will be essential to take note on tone and/or stress in the future refinements of comparative studies in the Eastern Family, failure to take note of such features does not seem to have seriously affected attempts to reconstruct the segmental form of the proto kinship terms in this paper.

Readers of this paper will face inevitable orthographic problems in relating the orthography of this paper with the orthography adopted in the various papers from which information has been drawn. The orthographies in previous papers have not been rigorously phonemic, for instance a word medial *k* in Usarufa is phonetically a complex sequence *qk*. Orthographic agreement between languages has been difficult, if not impossible, to achieve. As far as possible the orthography adopted in this paper has been chosen to harmonize as much as possible with published information, and to highlight relevant phonetic details for reconstruction. Readers should consult Bee's comparative paper (Chap. XXXVI, Sec. 5) for a concise charted summary of the vowels, consonants, and complex phoneme sequences of the languages of the Eastern Family.

2. THE AGE AND GENERATION STATUS SUFFIXES

According to Vincent (Chap. XXVII, Sec. 3) 'noun bases are divided into two classes on the basis of their occurrence with *-ba* or *-bano* subject-marker suffixes. The *-ba* class includes the names of people and some kinship terms. . . . The *-bano* class includes some kinship terms and any noun except a personal name.'[3]

The kinship terms which take the suffix *-ba* are listed below.

Consanguineal
G +2: grandfather, grandmother
G +1: father, mother, mother's brother, *(father's sister)
Go: older brother, older sister

Affinal
G +1: father-in-law and mother-in-law of both male and female ego
Go: brother-in-law, sister-in-law
G-1: daughter-in-law, son-in-law

The kinship terms which take the suffix *-bano* follow:

Consanguineal
Go: younger brother, younger sister

---

[3] It was apparent to Vincent in making this comment that the suffixes *-ba* and *-bano* indicated a systematic classification of the kinship terms.

G-1: daughter, son, nephew and niece (terms used by mother's brother and father's sister for ego's sibling group)

G-2: grandchild

Affinal

Go: husband, wife

The suffix *-ba* is used with all consanguineal kin of a higher generation than ego, and consanguineal kin of ego's sibling group who are older than ego. The suffix *-bano* is used with consanguineal kin of a lower generation than ego, and siblings younger than ego. Among terms for affinal kin *-ba* is used with terms specifying affinals of a higher generation than ego, and Go affinals other than ego's spouse. The suffix *-bano* is used with affinal kin of a younger generation than ego, and with the spouse terms, husband and wife. The dichotomy registered by these two suffixes distinguishes a group of kin on the one hand who may be roughly defined as senior kin, and a group of kin on the other hand who may be roughly defined as junior kin.

The senior-junior dichotomy of kinship terms seems to have been a feature of the proto language. Within the Gauwa group corresponding affixes register a similar dichotomy of kinship terms in the Auyana-Usarufa and the Awa language divisions.[4] The Gadsup-Agarabi language division does not register this dichotomy, since this division commonly fails to retain proto affixes which languages of the other divisions retain.

In Auyana the junior kinship terms carry a first order suffix *-ko*. Senior kinship terms include a first order suffix *-wa*. This suffix remains *-wa* following roots which are *o* final as in 'father' (*bo-wa-ma*) and 'mother (*no-wa-ma*). It becomes *-o* following roots which are *a* and *aa* final as in *raara-o-ma* 'maternal grandmother' and *waa-o-ma* 'older brother'. The same suffixes are present in Usarufa, but one minor difference (probably orthographic) must be allowed for. Bee represents the senior suffix *-wa* by *-a* in such terms as *bo-a-ma* (*bo-wa-ma*) 'father'.[5]

In Awa kin of the junior category have for their first order suffix a possibly complex form *-kawa*. Kin of the senior category have the first order suffix *-wa*.

The suffixes marking kin of the senior category are then: Tairora *-ba,* Binumarien *-fa,* Auyana *-wa* (fluctuating to *-o*), Usarufa *-a* (probably

---

[4] The classifying suffixes of the Gauwa languages mentioned in this section are associated with the second-third person singular prefix *a-*. This prefix is a reflex of a proto prefix reconstructed as **a*, and is dealt with in Section 4.1.2. When it is replaced by a first person prefix (singular or plural) in these languages the classificatory suffixes are dropped (note Chap. IV, Sec. 2.1.7).

[5] The seniority suffix *-al-o* is an optional feature of those Usarufa terms in which it occurs according to Bee (personal communication). Its absence implies a measure of informality in referring to the senior kin.

Where a term, either of a daughter language or the proto language, consists of more than one morphemic unit these units are separated from each other by a hyphen.

originally *-wa* if not currently so, also fluctuating to *-o*), and Awa *-wa*. This suffix is reconstructed as **-Wa*. The vowel has evidently been retained virtually unchanged in each of the three language divisions which retain the suffix. The proto phone **W* is reflected by Tairora *b* (which varies from a voiced fricative *ɓ* to *w*), Binumarien *f,* and Auyana and Awa *w*. the same correspondence set is a feature of the root-initial consonant of the proto term for husband, and older brother.

The suffixes marking the kin of the junior category are Tairora *-bano,* Binumarien *-fano,* Auyana and Usarufa *-ko,* and Awa *-kawa*. It is improbable that these forms reflect a common proto suffix, though they do strongly reinforce the assumption that the proto language registered a dichotomy of senior and junior kin.

The suffixes cited above have other functions in addition to reflecting the seniority status of a particular term. Tairora *-ba* is a subject-marking suffix which additionally connotes singular number. Binumarien *-fa* has much the same function. The suffix *-ko* has been defined as a stative suffix in Usarufa by Bee (see Chap. XIV) and has a similar function in Auyana.[6] In Awa the seniority-juniority suffixes are dropped when the possessive pronominal prefix (which is an obligatory feature of kinship terms) is first person (singular or plural). Since second person plural is identified by the same form as first person plural the seniority suffixes are dropped when this prefix has second person plural for referent. A similar situation obtains in Usarufa and Auyana.

The languages do not agree exactly in the kin classified as senior and junior, but the agreement is sufficiently close to justify the assumption that the classification is a retention from proto Tagauwa. Each of the languages agrees in classifying the following as senior kin: *consanguineal G + 1* father, mother; *Go* older brother, older sister; *affinal* brother-in-law. Each of the languages also agrees in classifying the following as junior kin: *consanguineal Go* younger brother, younger sister; *G-1* son, daughter; *affinal* husband, wife, daughter-in-law and her parents-in-law. With the exception of Gadsup and Agarabi (whose terms lack any suffix) the languages also agree in identifying grandfather and grandmother as senior kin.

It is perhaps surprising that husband and wife, and the parents-in-law of a female ego, should be categorized as junior kin. It will be pointed out in a later section however that the roots of these terms are homophonous (and possibly identical) with the roots of other terms. With these roots the

---

[6] Since this paper was written Bee has made the following comments about the distribution of *ko* and its function. In Usarufa and Auyana the suffix *-ko* may occur with most stem morphemes. It does not occur with pronouns, personal names, or kinterms of the category referred to as 'senior'. In the case of the category called 'junior' the *-ko* suffix usually occurs with the stem but neither it nor the senior category marking device is obligatory. The *-ko* suffix functions as a stative marker with verbs and as a personalizer or activator of nonverbs.

seniority-juniority suffixes may have a derivational function rather than a classificatory function.

The term for father's sister is reconstructed with the seniority suffix *-Wa*. In Auyana, however, the term carries the juniority suffix *-ko,* while in Usarufa two terms are applied to father's sister, one *maamu-o-ma* carrying the seniority suffix *-o,* the other *maamu-ko-ma* carrying the juniority suffix *-ko.* This apparent inconsistency is resolved by noting that the root reconstructed as **maaMu* (as also probably the root of the term for mother's brother **nau*) is a reciprocating term root. It is assumed that in the proto language these two roots attached the seniority suffix to specify father's sister, and either dropped this suffix or replaced it with a juniority suffix to specify female ego's brother's children. In certain of the daughter languages this contrast has not been retained. One of the terms has been dropped and the other retained to signal both the junior and senior reciprocating kin groups.

3. Consanguineal Kinship Terms

3.1. *Kin of the Go and G +1 Generations*

The kinship terms applied by ego in each of the four language divisions of the Eastern Family to his own siblings and to his parents and their siblings are listed in Tables 94 and 95. The tentatively reconstructed proto term is listed at the bottom of each column citing the terms used by each language for a given category of kin. That part or those parts of terms in the daughter languages which do not seem to reflect the proto term are placed in parentheses. As already indicated a term to be recognized as a feature of proto Tagauwa (i.e., the language from which the four language divisions derived) must be attested in Tairora-Binumarien and at least one of the three language divisions of the Gauwa group. Those forms in the kinship terms which reflect a feature evidently stemming from proto Taibi or proto Gauwa but not attested as a proto Tagauwa feature are underlined. Thus the Tairora term *ba-*KAA*-ba* 'older brother' consists of three forms, an initial root *ba* and a final seniority suffix *-ba* both of which reflect a proto Tagauwa form, and a first order suffix -KAA which reflects a proto Taibi form.

The reconstructed kinship terms of Tables 94 and 95 are listed together in a single table, Table 96. This table has two major dimensions, the dimension of sibling relationship with two major categories, parallel sex siblings and cross sex siblings; and the dimension of generation with two major categories, ego's generation and parental generation. Each category of the dimension of sibling relationship is subcategorized for age. There are two age subcategories, older and younger. Within the parental generation a distinction is registered between male and female parental generation.

Table 96 assumes a male ego, but female ego uses the same term as male

TABLE 94

G + 1 CONSANGINEAL KINSHIP TERMS

	Father	Mother	Father's Sister	Mother's Brother
Tairora	*qo-ba*	*no-ba*	*maabu-ba*	*nau-ba*
Binumarien	*ko-fa*	*no-fa*	*maamu-fa*	*nau-fa*
Auyana	*bo-wa-(ma)*	*no-wa-(ma)*	**maamu-(ko-ma)**	*naao-o-(ma)*
Usarufa	*bo-a-(ma)*	*no-a-(ma)*	*maamu-o-(ma)/*	*nau-(ma)*
			maamu-(ko-ma)	
Gadsup	*po*	*no*	*maamu*	*(aqo)*
Agarabi	*po-(qe)*	*no-(qe)*	*maamu*	*(kaako-qe)*
Awa	*po-wa*	*no-wa*	*waau-wa*	*(po-wa)*
Tagauwa	*-Po-Wa*	*-no-Wa*	*-maaṀu-Wa*	*-nau-Wa*

TABLE 95

GO CONSANGUINEAL KINSHIP TERMS

	Older Brother	Younger Brother	Older Sister	Younger Sister
Tairora	*ba-*KAA*-ba*	*qa-ta-(bano)*	*na-*KAA*-ba*	*u-ra-(bano)*
Binumarien	*fa-*SAA*-fa*	*ka-qa*	*na-*SAA*-fa*	A*u-na*
Auyana	*waa-o-(ma)*	*ba-(ko-ma)*	*naa-*NO*-wa-(ma)*	*u-n-(ko-ma)*
Usarufa	*waa-o-(ma)*	*ba-q-(ko-ma)*	*naa-*NO*-a(ma)*	*u-q-(ko-ma)*
		ba-qa		*u-m-(ma)*
Gadsup	*waa*	*pa-qi*	*naa-no*	*o-mi*
Agarabi	*waa-(qe)*	*pa-q*	*naa-*NO*-(qe)*	*u-n*
Awa	*waa-wa*	*pa-q-(kawa)*	*naa-no-wa*	*o-(nanaa-wa)*
Tagauwa	*-Waa-Wa*	*-Pa-*QV	*-naa-Wa*	*(a)u-*NV

ego for each of the kin groups listed. In referring to the kin represented in Table 96 it will be useful to adopt the expression 'sibling group'. Ego's sibling group consists of ego and his siblings, his father's sibling group consists of father and his siblings, and mother's sibling group consists of mother and her siblings. Each cell in Table 96 is named by the basic kin person specified by the relevant kinship term. Thus the cell which includes father and father's brother, both named by the same proto term *Po, is named the father cell, and the term will be referred to as the father term. The basic kin of the cells of the top row together with the left hand side column listing the kin of ego's sibling group constitutes the biological family of which ego is a member. The kin of the two cells making up the bottom right-hand corner of Table 96 represent the first degree of remove from the biological family.

TABLE 96

Sibling Relationship	Generation		
	Ego's	Parental	
		Father's	Mother's
Parallel Sex	OB *-Waa-Wa	F, FB *-Po-Wa	M, MSr *-no-Wa
	YB *-Pa-QV		
Cross Sex	OSr *-naa-Wa	FSr *-maaMu-Wa	MB *-nau-Wa
	YSr *-u-NV		

3.1.1. *Proto roots of G +1 consanguineal kinship terms.* Reconstruction of the majority of the roots listed in Table 96 is relatively straightforward. The reconstructed term for father is *Po*. The initial consonant is well attested by the same correspondence set in other kinship terms (grandfather, daughter-in-law, and younger brother) and the terms for tongue and pig (items 56 and 41, respectively, in Chap. XXXVI). The vowel of *Po* is convincingly attested by the vowel *o* in each daughter language. The proto term *no* 'mother' is attested by the form *no* in each daughter language. The identity of form in each language might be construed as evidence of wholesale borrowing from a common source, but this seems improbable.

The proto term *maaMu* 'father's sister' is reasonably well attested. The vowels of the cognate word in each language are identical and have presumably been retained virtually unchanged from proto Tagauwa. The initial consonant *m* is reflected by *m* in each language except Awa where it is reflected by *w*. The same correspondence set is a feature of word-initial consonant of the proto term for sister-in-law (*maaTi*). The medial consonant *M* is reflected by Tairora *b*, Binumarien *m,* and by *m* in each Gauwa language except Awa in which it is lost. The same correspondence set is a feature of the medial consonant of the proto term for daughter (*DaaMu-NV*).

When the distributional characteristics of the various correspondence sets are better known, *M* will probably be equated with *m*. The cognate term for father's sister *momo* and *maamu* in Kamano and Fore, respectively, of the contiguous East-Central Family strengthens this assumption.

The root *nau* of the term for mother's brother is attested in languages of both the Taibi and Gauwa groups. It is reflected by *nau* in Tairora and Binumarien, and by *nau* and *naao* in Usarufa and Auyana, respectively. It

is not retained in the term for mother's brother in Agarabi, and is replaced
by the father term in Awa. However, in Agarabi (and also in Gadsup) a
reflex of *nau functions as the root of a term (no-i-nta-q and no-nta,
respectively) used by mother's brother for ego's sibling group. *Nau was
probably a reciprocating root in proto Tagauwa, held in common by the
terms used for ego for mother's brother and by mother's brother for ego's
sibling group.

The Gadsup term for mother's brother is aqo. This may be related to
terms used when addressing mother's brother in other languages of the
family. The Tairora term of address is aqo, and the Usarufa term (a probable cognate) is kaakoqa.

3.1.2. *Proto roots of the Go consanguineal kinship terms.* Among the
terms applied to kin of ego's sibling group reconstruction of the root consonant is straightforward. *P of the younger brother root *Pa is well
attested by the same correspondence set in the root of the term for father,
grandfather, and daughter-in-law and such nonkinship terms as pig and
tongue (see Chap. XXXVI, items 41 and 56). *W, the root-initial consonant of the older brother root *Waa, is attested by the same correspondence set in the seniority suffix *-Wa, and in the root of the term for husband, *Waa. The root-initial consonant *n of the older sister root *naa is
reflected by n in each of the daughter languages.

The proto vowel of the younger brother root *Pa is reflected by a in
each of the daughter languages, and has presumably been retained unchanged
from the proto language. The vowel of the proto roots for the older sibling
terms poses some minor problem of reconstruction. The vowel a of the root
of these terms in Tairora and Binumarien of the Taibi group has probably
been retained virtually unchanged from proto Taibi. The corresponding
vowel aa of these roots in all the languages of the Gauwa group has probably been retained unchanged from proto Gauwa. It is assumed that the
vowel aa of the Gauwa roots has been retained unchanged from proto
Tagauwa and that the vowel a of the Taibi roots reflects the conditioning
of the vowel aa of the suffixlike element -kaa of Tairora and -saa of Binumarien, which is unique to the Taibi terms.

Tairora, Binumarien, Gadsup, Agarabi, and Auyana have a six vowel
system, which consists of three pairs i and e, u and o, a and aa. The first
member of each pair is phonetically short, the second member phonetically
long. In this paper the vowel represented as a by Bee in Chapter XXXVI
is represented orthographically as aa to highlight the fact that it is phonetically long in contrast to the vowel represented as a. The shift of the proto
Tagauwa root reconstructed as *naa- 'older sister' and *Waa- 'older brother'
to na- and ba-/fa-, respectively, in Tairora and Binumarien has involved
the replacement of the phonetically long vowel aa by its phonetically short
counterpart a.

This conclusion is supported by the fact that the reconstructed roots of older sister and older brother are probably identical with the reconstructed roots of wife and husband, respectively. In the case of the terms for husband and wife, the Taibi languages, Tairora and Binumarien, have retained the phonetically long root vowel *aa* of the proto Tagauwa terms (see Table 100).

The stem of the proto term for younger sister is reconstructed as a single vowel *u-*. In Binumarien of the Taibi group, however, this root vowel has fossilized with the prefixial second-third person singular possessive pronoun *a-*, which is still a viable prefix in the other languages, and with other kinship terms in Binumarien. The root vowel *o-* of the Gadsup term *omi* must similarly reflect the influence of this prefix. The proto term for younger sister is therefore reconstructed as *(a)-u*. The initial *(a)* is to be interpreted as a possessive prefix which is reflected unchanged in the daughter languages, except that in Binumarien it has fossilized with the root vowel of the term for younger sister.

While the Awa stem vowel *o-* of the term for younger sister is equated with the proto root it may later be necessary to treat the Awa term as an innovation unique to Awa. The possible cognate term in Usarufa (*Unanaama*) applied to a particular subgroup of parallel cousins (male ego's mother's sister's children, or female ego's father's brother's children) is said by Bee to derive from a root *ðuV* which means skin.

TABLE 97

G + 2 Consanguineal Kinship Terms

	Grandfather	Grandmother	Paternal Grandparent
Tairora	*naaqa-ba*	*taato-ba*	. . .
Binumarien	*naaku-fa*	*taato-fa*	. . .
Auyana	*naabu-o-(ma)*	*raara-o-(ma)*	*(ai-saabu)*
Usarufa	*naabu-o-(ma)*	*raare-o-(ma)*	. . .
Gadsup	*naapu*	*kaaka*	. . .
Agarabi	*naaqu*	*raa(qo)*	. . .
Awa	*naapu-wa*	*taata-wa*	. . .
Tagauwa	*-naaPu-Wa*	*-taata-Wa*	. . .

3.1.3. *Proto suffixes of the reconstructed terms for ego's younger siblings.* The proto term for younger brother consists of a root (*Pa-*) and a following suffix. The suffix is reflected by Tairora *-ta*, Binumarien *-qa*, Usarufa (and probably also Auyana) *-qa*, Gadsup *-qi*, and Agarabi *-q*. This set of cognate affixes is a feature of several proto terms reconstructed by Bee (see Chap. XXXVI) as Q class. In Usarufa the suffix *-qa* is the form taken by the nominal suffix (-ma) following a stem of the glottal (Q) class. This suffix is currently viable in Usarufa. However the cognate segment in the terms of Tairora and Binumarien are probably fossilized with the root.

In Usarufa and Auyana the suffix -ko is optionally interpolated between the root and the nominal suffix. As previously noted this suffix identifies the term of which it is a part as a junior kin term. When interpolated it reflects the glottal (Q) class status of the root. This is indicated by the preglottalization of the initial consonant (-q-ko) in Usarufa, and by the absence of voicing or prenasalization of the initial consonant of this suffix in Auyana.[7] The Auyana and Usarufa terms for younger brother are therefore doubly marked for juniority.

The possibly complex form -kawa of Awa similarly identifies the term for younger brother as a junior category term. As in Auyana-Usarufa the feature of preglottalization of the initial k establishes the root as a Q class root, and confirms the junior status of this term.

The term for younger sister also consists of a root plus a suffix. In Usarufa (and presumably also in Auyana) this suffix is the form taken by the nominal suffix following an N class stem, that is, -mma. This establishes the junior status of the root. This is confirmed by the optional occurrence of the juniority suffix -ko. When this suffix attaches to the root in Auyana the N class status of the root is confirmed by the prenasalization of the suffix initial consonant: u-n-(ko-ma). Since the prenasalization reflects the N class status of the root, it appears together with the root in Table 95. In Usarufa, however, a nasal stem followed by a suffix which is consonant initial (other than nasal consonant initial) is reflected by a feature of preglottalization. Thus instead of the expected term u-n-(ko-ma) in Usarufa the term is u-q-(ko-ma). (The only complex sequences in Usarufa are preglottalized seqences, unlike Auyana which has only prenasalized complex sequences.)

The cognate segments of Usarufa -mma (of the term u-mma) in Tairora and Binumarien are -ra and -na, respectively. These segments are no longer viable affixes, but are fossilized with the preceding root. This processing of fossilization has evidently also involved the impersonal possessive prefix a-.

3.1.4. *The proto suffix of the reconstructed terms for ego's older siblings.* The older sibling terms are reconstructed with the suffix *-Wa. This suffix has been retained by the older sibling terms in Tairora and Binumarien of the Taibi group, and Auyana-Usarufa and Awa of the Gauwa group. It is predictably absent from the terms of the Gadsup-Agarabi language division. However, in Agarabi the older sibling terms have for their word final suffix -qe, a suffix shared by only three other terms, father, mother, and the irregular term (kaaka-qe) used reciprocally between mother's brother and ego's

---

[7] Bee in Chap. XXXVI has represented the preglottalized -qk as k. It should be further noted that the expected prenasalized complex sequence -nk is also manifested as -qk in Usarufa, which has no prenasalized complex sequences as does Auyana.

sibling group. (*kaakoqe* is not a reflex of the proto term **nau*.) Among those terms which reflect proto terms *-qe* would seem to be specific for senior kin of the biological family.

In addition to a reflex of the seniority suffix **-Wa* the older sibling terms of the Taibi languages carry a first order suffix which is limited to these two older sibling terms. This suffix is *-kaa* in Tairora (e.g., *ba-kaa-ba* 'older brother') and *-saa* in Binumarien (*fa-saa-fa* 'older brother'). It evidently stems from proto Taibi, but is not a feature of the older sibling terms in the Gauwa languages.

The older sibling terms in the Gauwa languages lack a suffix with the specific function of the Taibi suffix just mentioned. But the term for older sister includes a first order suffix *-no*. This suffix evidently stems from proto Gauwa and has been retained unchanged in all the Gauwa languages. It has no matching form in the Taibi group. The form *-no* may relate to the root *no* 'mother', and suggests that older sister is in some way equated with mother. In Fore, of the contiguous East-Central Family, there are two terms for older sister. One term *na-mana-ne* is used for both older and younger sisters. The term specific for older sister is *na-nona-nto-we*. This term means little mother and breaks down into the following components, *na-* (my), *nona* (the root), *-nto* (diminutive), *-we* (nominal suffix held in common with free personal pronouns).

3.2. *Kin of the G +2 Generation*

3.2.1. *The proto roots of the G +2 consanguineal kinship terms.* Except in Auyana only two terms are applied to kin of the G +2 generation. These two terms are the grandfather and grandmother term, respectively. The root of the former reconstructs as **naaPu* and the root of that latter as **taata*.

The grandfather root reconstructed as **naaPu* is well attested by reflexes in each of the four language divisions. The initial consonant and the vowels of this root are identical in each language and have probably been retained virtually unchanged from proto Tagauwa. The medial consonant **P* is one of the best attested sound correspondences of the Eastern Family.

The initial syllable of the grandmother root **taata* poses no problem. The vowel *aa* has probably been retained unchanged from proto Tagauwa. The initial consonant **t* was probably an alveolar consonant in the proto language as it is now in each of the daughter languages except Gadsup where it is reflected by *k*. The same set of correspondences is a feature of the terms for male ego's in-laws of the Go generation which reflect the proto term **i.tua*. Correspondence of Tairora *t,* Binumarien *q,* Gadsup *k,* and Awa *t* is also a feature of the terms for ear and knee (Bee, Chap. XXXVI, items 15 and 31, respectively, represents this set as **r*).

The second syllable of the grandmother root is reconstructed with the same initial proto phone *t as the first syllable. The vowel of the second syllable is reconstructed as *a*, but is reflected by *o* in the Taibi group of languages. In each of the languages of the Gauwa group except Agarabi the proto vowel *a* of the second syllable is reflected by *a*, and has presumably been retained virtually unchanged in those languages from the proto language.

The term for grandmother in Binumarien has probably been borrowed from Tairora. The term for grandmother in Agarabi *raaqo* is also probably not a simple reflex of the proto term, and may be an analogically changed reflex. The initial syllable of *raaqo* probably reflects the initial syllable of the proto root *taata*, just as the initial syllable of the Agarabi grandfather term *naaqo* also probably reflects the initial syllable of the proto root *naaPu*. But the final syllable -*qo* of both Agarabi grandparental terms (*naaqo* and *raaqo*) is probably a common innovation unique to Agarabi. This final syllable is also a feature of the term for a female's grandson *naaqo*, and may be related to the final syllable -*qu* of the term *neequ* used by a male ego for his grandson.

Bee has reconstructed the grandmother root with a final vowel *o* following the vowel *a* of the second syllable. This vowel is presumably reconstructed by Bee to account for the vowel *o* of the second syllable of the Tairora-Binumarien root *taato*, and the vowel *o* of the Usarufa and Auyana term *raaraoma*. In this paper it has seemed better to equate the vowel *o* of the grandmother term in Usarufa and Auyana with the seniority suffix -*wa* of such Auyana terms as *bo-wa-ma* 'father', *no-wa-ma* 'mother', *iro-wa-ma* 'brother-in-law'.

The reconstruction of the Tagauwa grandmother root as *taata* implies that the second syllable had a central vowel, although only the Gauwa languages agree in having a mid central vowel *a* in this syllable. The Tairora term (probably borrowed by Binumarien) has for its root *taata* with a back vowel in the second syllable. The root of the grandparent term (used for both males and females) in Bena-bena and Kamano of the contiguous East-Central Family tends to support the reconstruction of central vowel in the second syllable. The Bena-bena and Kamano root is *taata*. This East-Central root also tends to justify the representation of the consonant of the Tagauwa grandmother root *taata*.

Auyana is inique among Eastern languages in having three terms for consanguineal kin of the G +2 generation. The material grandparental roots are regular, and simple reflexes of the proto grandparental roots *naaPu* and *taata* ('grandfather' and 'grandmother', respectively). A third term unique to Auyana (and possibly restricted to the Kosena dialect) is used for paternal grandparents of either sex.

3.2.2. *The proto suffix of the G +2 consanguineal kinship terms.* The first order suffix of the grandparental terms is the seniority suffix *-Wa*. It is reflected by Tairora *-ba,* Binumarien *-fa,* Awa *-wa,* and by a form which fluctuates phonologically from *-wa* to *-o* in Auyana and *-a* to *-o* in Usarufa. The basic form of this suffix in the Auyana-Usarufa language division is probably *-wa.*

The seniority suffix is not a feature of the grandparental terms of Gadsup and Agarabi. This language division is characterized by its failure to retain proto affixes retained by other languages of the Eastern Family.

4. AFFINAL KINSHIP TERMS

4.1. *Reciprocating Terms Used between Affinal Kin of the Go and the G +1 Generations*

Much of the superficial complexity of the terminological system relevant to affinal kin is resolved by noting the common use of reciprocal terms between a parent-in-law and a child-in-law. This is highlighted in Table 98 which lists on the left-hand side terms used reciprocally between male ego and one or both of his parents-in-law, and on the right-hand side the terms used reciprocally between female ego and one or both of her parents-in-law.

4.1.1. *Female ego reciprocating term.* The relative diversity of terms in the male ego section contrasts with the relative uniformity in terms of the female ego section. The term for daughter-in-law is clearly a cognate term in each language. The root reconstructs as **naaPu,* and the suffix equates simply with the proto suffix **-QV.*

The reciprocal use of this proto term between a daughter-in-law and both her parents-in-law is attested in languages of both the Taibi and the Gauwa group. In Binumarien the reflex of **naaPu*-QV (*naakk-qu*) is used reciprocally between a daughter-in-law and both parents-in-law. In Gadsup and Agarabi of the Gauwa group the reflex terms *naapu-qi* and *naapu-q,* respectively, are also used reciprocally between a daughter-in-law and both parents-in-law.

The same proto term **naaPu*-QV is reflected by the Tairora term for daughter-in-law and the term used by her for her father-in-law. The term for her father-in-law is not, however, a direct reflex of the proto term. The suffixial element has shifted to prefixial position in this term. It appears that the Tairora daughter-in-law reflex of **naaPu*-QV (*naaqu-tu*) first became **tu-naaqu* and subsequently *to-naqo.* Tairora and Binumarien have six vowels, three phonetically short, *i, a,* and *u,* matched by three phonetically long vowels, *e, aa,* and *o,* respectively. The shift of **tu-naaqu* to *to-naqo* has involved the replacement of *u* by its long equivalent, and *aa* by its short equivalent.

The Tairora term for mother-in-law of the female ego (*to-nano*) may also be an indirect reflex of the proto term **naaPu*-QV. Given *to-naqo* as the father-in-law term it is conceivable that the final element of this term (*qo*) has been equated with the root of the term for father (also *qo*) (see

TABLE 98

RECIPROCAL IN-LAW TERMS

	Son-in-Law	Male Ego's Parents-in-Law		Daughter-in-Law	Female Ego's Parents-in-Law	
Tairora	*a-i-raa*-MAQU	*a-i-raa*-MAKU	(F/M-in)	*naaqu-tu*	*to-naqo*	(F-in)
Binumarien	*a-i-raa*-MAKU	*a-i-saa-m-(ba)*	(F/M-in)	*naaku-qu*	*naaku-qu*	(F/M-in)
Auyana	*a-i-saa-m-(ba)*	*a-i-taa-m-(ma)*	(F/M-in)	*naabu-qa*	*naabu-qa*	(M-in)
Usarufa	*a-i-taa-m-(ma)*	*(nda-qi)*	(F/M-in)	*naabu-qa*	*naabu-qa*	(F/M)-in)
Gadsup	*(nda-qi)*	*(a-naa-n)*	(F/M-in)	*naapu-qi*	*naapu-qi*	(F/M-in)
Agarabi	*a-(naa-n)*	*a-taa-na-(wa)*	(F/M-in)	*naapu-q*	*naapu-q*	(F/M-in)
Awa	*a-taa-n-(kawa)*	*(M-in)*				
Tagauwa	**-(a)-i-Raa*-N	**-(a)-i-Raa*-N		**-naaPu*-QV	**-naaPu*-QV	

Table 94). The term for mother-in-law has possibly then been derived from *to-naqo* by replacing the final element *qo* with *no* which functions as the root of the term for mother.

The proto term **naaPu-QV* is reflected by Auyana and Usarufa *naabu-qa* used for a daughter-in-law by both parents-in-law, and by her for her mother-in-law.

Awa is the only language division which no longer attests the reciprocal usage of the proto term **naaPu-QV*, but the reflex *naapu-q* is still retained for daughter-in-law.

Table 99 is the source table for the parent-in-law terms cited in Table 98. It lists all the terms used by male and female ego for their parents-in-law. A number of the terms used by female ego for her parents-in-law clearly do not reflect the reciprocal proto term **naaPu-QV*. Among them are the following: *watena* 'father-in-law' and *ataana* 'mother-in-law' in Awa; *warendo* 'father-in-law' and *araara* 'mother-in-law' in the Asempa dialect of Auyana) *warenda* 'father-in-law' in the Kosena dialect of Auyana. Such terms used by female ego for her parents-in-law might suggest that in the proto system female ego used two different terms for her parents-in-law rather than a single reciprocal term **naaPu-QV*. The evidence for two proto terms is, however, slender, and is not supported by any other evidence than the existence of the above terms. The following evidence seems to rule out the possibility. (A) The only term used for daughter-in-law in all languages of the family clearly reflect the proto term **naaPu-QV*. The other proto term (if it ever existed) might be reflected by *watena, ataana,* and *araara* but could not have been used reciprocally unless by some remarkable process of convergence no language has retained it for daughter-in-law. (B) Even if there were a proto term used nonreciprocally for one or other parent-in-law it is improbable that each of the above four terms reflects it. (C) *ataana* of Awa is better accounted for as a reflex of a proto term used reciprocally between a male ego and his parents-in-law.

4.1.2. *The male ego reciprocating term.* It is difficult, and may perhaps with the available data be impossible, to reconstruct a term or terms used between a son-in-law and his parents-in-law. It is, however, reasonably certain that a term was used reciprocally between these two kin groups in the proto language. In the Kosena dialect of Auyana the term *ai-saa-m-ba* is used reciprocally between a son-in-law and both parents-in-law. *ai-taa-m-ma* has the same function in Usarufa. In the Gadsup-Agarabi language division *nda* (Gadsup) and *anaan* (Agarabi) are used reciprocally in the same way. In the Awa division the term for son-in-law (*a-taa-n-kawa*) differs from the term for his mother-in-law (*a-taa-n-wa*) in the terminal suffix. The former carries the juniority suffix *-kawa* and the latter the seniority suffix *-wa*.

In Binumarien of the Taibi group *ai-raa-maku* is used reciprocally be-

TABLE 99

G + 1 AFFINAL KINSHIP TERMS

| | Male Ego's | | Female Ego's | |
	Father-in-Law	Mother-in-Law	Father-in-Law	Mother-in-Law
Tairora	*a-i-raa(bi-ba)*	*a-i-(ntaanta-ba)*	*to-naqo-(ba)*	*to-na-(no-ba)*
Batainabura	*a-i-raa(bi)*	*a-i-(ntaanta)*	*a-i-raa(bi)*	*(a-i-ntaanta)*
Binumarien	*a-i-raa-(maku)*	*a-i-raa-(maku)*	*naaku-qu*	*naaku-qu*
Auyana				
Kosena	*a-i-saa-m-(ba)*	*a-i-saa-m-(ba)*	*(warenda)*	*naabu-qa*
Asempa	*warendo*	*(a-raara)*	*(warendo)*	*(a-raara)*
Usarufa	*a-i-taa-m-(ma)*	*a-i-taa-m-(ma)*	*naabu-qa*	*naabu-qa*
Gadsup	*(nda-qi)*	*(nda-qi)*	*naapu-qi*	*naapu-qi*
Agarabi	*(a-naa-n)*	*(a-naa-n)*	*naapu-q*	*naapu-q*
Awa	*(watena-wa)*	*a-taa(na-wa)*	*(watena-wa)*	*(a-taana-wa)*
Tagauwa	**-(a)-i-Raa*	**-(a)-i-Raa*	**-̄naaPu*-QV	**-naaPu*-QV

tween a son-in-law and both parents-in-law. A cognate *ai-raa-maqu* specifies son-in-law in Tairora. It is assumed that each term derived from a proto Taibi term used reciprocally between a son-in-law and his parents-in-law.

It is assumed then that in proto Tagauwa a son-in-law and his parents-in-law referred to each other by a common reciprocal term. This term has not been retained in the Gadsup-Agarabi division, but at least remnants of it have been retained in the other three divisions. The remnant retained is reconstructed as **(a)-i-Raa*-N. The N class affiliation of the presumed stem **Raa-* is deduced from the terminal segments *-m-ba* and *-m-ma* of the Auyana (Kosena) and Usarufa terms, respectively, and may perhaps also be reflected by the segment *-na* of the Awa term for male ego's mother-in-law and the segment *-n* of the term for son-in-law. The segment *-n* of the latter term is clearly not an integral feature of the preceding root since it is dropped when the term takes one of the regular possessive prefixes (*wa̱ 'you'*, *wena* 'his', or *iqteti* 'our/your'). Compare Awa *ataankawa* (Table 99) with *atenataa*.

The initial segment of the proto remnant **(a)-i-Raa*-N consists of a possessive prefix **a-* and a prefix **i-* which may specify the maleness of ego in affinal linkage. The same prefixial sequence is a feature of the term used between a male ego and his brothers-in-law. The first order suffix *-i* is also a feature of the reconstructed term for husband.

The initial prefix **a-* is enclosed in parentheses to identify it as a possessive pronominal prefix for which other possessive prefixes could be substituted in the proto language. It is fairly certain that this particular prefix **a-*

has been retained unchanged in each of the daughter languages. It is a viable prefix in the languages of the Gauwa group, but in the terms for younger sister, son-in-law, and brother-in-law is fossilized or semifossilized in the languages of the Taibi group. Note the Tairora term *ti aura* 'my younger sister' in which the prefix *a-* is retained though the possessive pronoun is first person singular. Note also *ti airaabi-ba* 'my father-in-law', *ti aintaanta-ba* 'my mother-in-law', and *ti aitua-ba* 'my brother-in-law', all terms used by male ego in Tairora. The prefix **a-* is similarly fossilized in the cognate Binumarien terms.

The possessive pronoun set to which *a-* belongs also functions as an affix set with verbs. It is pertinent to note that it is an indirect object prefix set with certain Tairora verbs, and an optional indirect object suffix set with certain verbs in Awa. In Gadsup the same set functions as an object set prefixed to the verb stem. It is safe to assume that the affix set in the proto language functioned both as a possessive prefix set and a verbal affix set. The fact that it appears in verbs in one daughter language in prefix position and in another in suffix position lends some weight to the suggestion that the Tairora terms used by a female ego for her parents-in-law have involved a shift of a proto suffix to prefix position (see Sec. 4.1.1).

The stem segment of the proto term has been reconstructed as **Raa-*. The vowel of this segment has been retained unchanged in the daughter languages which retain it. The initial consonant **R* is reflected by Tairora and Binumarien *r*, Usarufa *t*, Auyana *s*, and Awa *t*. This sound correspondence set is so far limited to this cognate word set among the sixty sets identified by Bee in her comparative chapter, and the few additional sets identified in this chapter. Correspondence of Auyana *s* and Usararufa *t* is, however, a feature of several cognate word pairs in this language division.

The stem **Raa-* has been identified as an N (nasal) class stem, although grounds for this identification are restricted to languages of the Gauwa group. Since the Gadsup term *nda-qi* carries a suffix characterizing the stem to which it attaches as a Q (glottal) class stem it is unlikely that this term reflects the proto term. The Agarabi term *a-naa-n* carries a terminal *-n* which is probably a suffix identifying the preceding stem as an N or V class stem. It is pos.̤. ꞏ that this term also reflec . ꞏ ριᴏ.ꞏ ꞇrm, and that proto **R* is reflected by Agarabi *n*.

The terms of the Taibi group no longer retain evidence of the class of the stem. In place of the expected suffixial elements these terms in Table 98 carry a suffix unique to the Taibi group and presumably stemming from proto Taibi. These forms *-maqu* of Tairora and *-maku* of Binumarien may have derived from the term for son, *maaqu* in Tairora and *maaku* in Binumarien. These terms in turn have probably been derived from the proto daughter-in-law root **naaPu* reflected by Tairora *naaqu* and Binumarien *naaku,* by a shift in point of articulation of the root initial nasal consonant from alveolar (for the female term) to bilabial (for the male term).

The proto term *(a)-i-Raa-N is probably not reflected by the possibly cognate terms for father-in-law *warendo* of Auyana (Asempa dialect), *warenda* of Auyana (Kosena dialect), and *watena-wa* of Awa. These terms are not used reciprocally, nor is there any evidence that they stemmed from an earlier reciprocal term. In Asempa and Awa these terms are used for the father-in-law of both a male and female ego. Another term is used for mother-in-law of both male and female ego. Similarly in the Batainabura dialect of Tairora one term *airaabi* is used for father-in-law of both male and female ego, and another term *aintaanta* is used for mother-in-law of male and female ego. Either there has been convergence in three of the language divisions or else this system has an alternate system in proto Tagauwa used along with the reciprocal terms reconstructed as *(a)-i-Raa-N and *naaPu-QV, respectively. It is improbable that the Tairora term *airaabi* and the Auyana and Awa terms *warendo* and *watena,* respectively, are cognates. It is assumed then that these terms do not reflect an alternate system in the proto language.

4.2. *Kinship Terms Used between Affinal Kin of the Go Generation*

4.2.1. *Brother-in-law and sister-in-law.* The available data permits the following conclusions. (A) Apart from the two terms for spouse only two other terms of proto origin would seem to be used between affinal Go kin. (B) One of these two terms is reconstructed tentatively as *maaTi-Wa. The only term used between sisters-in-law in each language is a reflex of this term. (C) The second term is reconstructed tentatively as *i-tua-Wa. The only term used between brothers-in-law in each language is a reflex of this term.

The consistent use of only the one term between sisters-in-law and the consistent use of only the one term between brothers-in-law in each language probably points to the basic function of these two reconstructed terms in the proto language. *maaTi-Wa was probably used between female in-laws of the Go generations, that is, by female ego for her brother's wife, or husband's sister. *i-tua-Wa was probably used between male in-laws of the Go generation, that is, between a male ego and his sister's husband, or wife's brother.

In the daughter languages (and possibly also in the proto language) the function of the two terms reconstructed as *maaTi-Wa and *i-tua-Wa is extended beyond the basic reciprocal usage. In the Taibi group *maatiba* (Tairora) and *maaqifa* (Binumarien) is used by a male ego for his brother's wife. In this extended use the specified kin is a female as in the basic use. A reflex of the proto term *i-tua-Wa identifies a female ego's brother-in-law (husband's brother or sister's husband) in Tairora, Binumarien, and Gadsup.

TABLE 100

GO AFFINAL KINSHIP TERMS

	Ego's Sister-in-Law	Ego's Brother-in-Law	Ego's Sister-in-law	Ego's Brother-in-Law	Wife	Husband
Tairora	*maati-ba* BW/HSr	ᴀɪ-*tua-ba* HB/SrH	*maati-ba* BW	*a-i-tua-ba* SrH/WB	*naa-ta*	*baa-ti*
Binumarien	*maaqi-fa*	ᴀɪ-*qua-fa*	*maaqi-fa* BW	*a-i-qua-fa*	*naa-qa*	*faa-qi*
Auyana	*mai-(ko-ma)* BW/HSr	*(waaya-o-ma)* HB/SrH	*(waaya-o-ma)* BW	*i-ro-wa-(ma)* SrH/WB	*(wani-n-ko-ma)*	*wa-i-q-(ko-ma)*
Usarufa	*maai-(yo-ma)*	*(waaya-o-ma)* HB/SrH	*(waaya-o-ma)* BW	*i-ro-a-(ma)*	*naa-q-(ko-ma)* *naa-qa*	*wa-i-q-(ko-ma)* *wa-i-qa*
Gadsup	*maati* BW/HSr	*ko* HB/SrH	*ko* BW	*ko* SrH	*naa-qi*	*waa-(pu)*
Agarabi	*maati*			*i-ro* SrH	*naa-q*	*waa-(pu)*
Awa	*wəi-(a)wa*			*e-to-wa* SrH/WB	*naa-q-(kawa)*	*w-e-q-(kawa)*
Tagauwa	*-maaTi-Wa*			*-(a)-i-tua-Wa*	*-naa-QV*	*-Waa-i-QV*

Again in this extended use the specified kin is a male as in the basic usage. However, this extension of the usage of the terms is not consistent in all the languages for which information is available. In Gadsup the male reciprocal term *ko* (a reflex of *-tua*) has been extended to male ego's sister-in-law as well as to female ego's brother-in-law. In Auyana *waaya-o-ma* (which probably derives from the proto term *maaTi-Wa* possibly indirectly by borrowing from Awa) is used for female ego's brother-in-law and male ego's sister-in-law.

The male affinal term of the Go generation is reconstructed as *i-tua-Wa* but should perhaps be reconstructed as *ai-tua-Wa*. The initial vowel *a* of the latter reconstruction is now a fossilized feature of the reflex terms in the Taibi language group. It is still viable in languages of the Auyana-Usarufa and Gadsup-Agarabi divisions, where it seems to function as an impersonal prefix (roughly translated as 'someone's') which is dropped when the term attaches the regular personal prefixes. Within Awa of the Gauwa group, however, this form *a* is fossilized and has combined with the following prefix-like form *i-* to product the single vowel *e*. To indicate this situation the reconstruction *i-tua-Wa* is extended to *(a)i-tua-Wa*.

The Tairora term of the Taibi group is the most transparent reflection of the term reconstructed as *(a)i-tua-Wa*. The two vowels *ua* of the root have merged to produce a single vowel *o* in each of the languages of the Gauwa division. This merging must therefore stem from proto Gauwa.

As already noted the initial element *a* is probably a possessive prefix. The following prefixlike element *i-* may signal affinal maleness of ego in affinal linkage. It is a prefixial feature of the tentatively reconstructed reciprocal term used between a male ego and his parents-in-law *(a)-i-Raa* as well as the term under study, which is used between male ego and his brothers-in-law. It may perhaps be equatable with the suffix *-i* of the proto term for husband reconstructed tentatively as *Waa-i-*QV. It has previously been noted that in the Tairora terms for female ego's father-in-law and mother-in-law (*to-naqo-ba* and *to-nano-ba*, respectively) the prefixial segment *to-* probably reflects the proto suffix reconstructed as *-*QV. If this is a correct interpretation (at least in Tairora) there has been metathesis of an affix from a suffixial to a prefixial position.

The root-initial consonant *t* of *(a)-i-tua-Wa* is reflected by Tairora *t*, Binumarien *q*, Usarufa and Auyana *r*, Gadsup *k*, Agarabi *r*, and Awa *t*. The same correspondence set is a feature of the term for grandmother, and also the terms for ground and knee (Chap. XXXVI, items 16 and 31). The proto suffix *-Wa* which identifies the term as a senior kin term, is reflected by Tairora *-ba*, Binumarien *-fa*, Auyana *-wa*, Usarufa *-a*, and Awa *-wa*.

Among the various reflexes of the reciprocal sister-in-law term reconstructed as *-maaTi-Wa*, the Awa reflex seems to have undergone the most pronounced change. The root initial *m* is reflected by *w* and the medial consonant *T by the absence of any consonant. The same changes are involved in the derivation of Awa *waau* from the proto root *maaMu* of the term for father's sister. The initial root vowel *aa is reflected by Awa ɔ, a change possibly conditioned by the now contiguous vowel *i*. The interpolation of the vowel *a* between the reflex root *wɔi* and the seniority suffix -*wa* cannot be explained yet, but hardly invalidates the recognition of the Awa term as a reflex. The Awa reflex has possibly been borrowed by Usarufa and Auyana, which designate male ego's sister-in-law by *waaya-ma* and *waaya-o-ma,* respectively.

In the languages other than Awa the two root vowels of *maaTi-Wa* have been retained unchanged (or virtually unchanged), and the root-initial consonant is reflected by *m.* The medial consonant *T is reflected by Tairora *t* and Binumarien *q.* This is a regular correspondence within the Taibi group. But the reflexes of this medial consonant in the Gauwa languages are not consistent with those expected for the proto consonant represented as *t in this chapter. When the distributional characteristics of the various proto phones are better known, however, it is likely that proto *T and proto *t will be equated as the same proto phoneme. Meantime the proto phone *T of *maaTi represents a unique correspondence set. The proto sister-in-law term also carries the seniority suffix *-Wa.

4.2.2. *Husband and wife.* The proto terms for husband and wife are reconstructed as *Waa-i-QV and *naa-QV, respectively. The root of the former is the same as that reconstructed for older brother, and the root of the latter is the same as that reconstructed for older sister. The distinction between husband and older brother, and between wife and older sister is signaled by the affixes. Both the affinal terms would seem to have Q class roots, a feature reflected by the following suffix reconstructed as *-QV for both. The suffix associated with the term for wife is the same as the corresponding suffix of the term for younger brother in each language, previously reconstructed as *-QV. The suffix associated with the term for husband is also reconstructed as *-QV although the evidence for this is not quite so convincing. The difference in the vowels reflecting this suffix when it occurs with the husband root *-Waa may, however, reflect the presence of the reconstructed first order suffix *-i of the proto husband term. It has been suggested in earlier sections that this proto suffix *-i may equate with a proto prefix *i- in the proto terms for male ego's brother-in-law and in the reciprocal term used between male ego and his parents-in-law. It was further suggested that it specified the maleness of an affinally linked ego.

The evidence for a first order proto suffix *-i is most obvious in the Usarufa terms *wa-i-q-ko-ma* (and its alternate form without the juniority suffix -*ko, wa-i-qa*) and Auyana *wa-i-q-ko-ma.* The shift of the proto vowel of the root (*aa) to *a* in these two languages may reflect the influence of the contiguous vowel *i*. In Awa the root vowel *eh* almost certainly reflects the influence of this vowel, but in light of the Awa term for female ego's sister-in-law, *wehi-awa* (which reflects proto *maaTi-Wa), it is assumed that the suffix vowel *-i* has been dropped from the Awa term *weh-q-kawa* rather than merged with the root vowel.

In Tairora (*baa-ti*) and Binumarien (*faa-qi*) the suffix vowel reconstructed as **-i* would now seem to be reflected by the vowel of the word final suffix reconstructed as *-QV. It is possible that in this language group the proto term *Waa-i-QV first became *Waa-Q*i* before shifting to *baati* and *faaqi* in Tairora and Binumarien, respectively, either by a process of vowel harmony with subsequent loss of the first order suffix **-i,* or by a single step process in which this suffix replaced by the vowel of the final suffix *-QV. A similar process has been involved in the history of the Tairora term for male ego's sister's children (*nau-nti*) which reflects **nau-i-nta.*

Whatever the history of the final suffix *-QV of the proto term for husband, the form of the reflexes of this suffix in the daughter languages shows that the root is a Q class root. It follows from this that the term for husband (like that for wife) is a junior kin term. This is further confirmed by the optional suffix *-ko* which occurs with these terms in Auyana and Usarufa, and the suffix *-kawa* which occurs with the Awa terms.

5. G-1 AND G-2 CONSANGUINEAL KINSHIP TERMS

5.1. *Son and Daughter*

It is simple to reconstruct terms for son in the Taibi group and for the Gauwa group, but since the reconstructed terms for these two divisions have virtually nothing in common and are almost certainly not cognates, it is not possible to postulate a final proto term for proto Tagauwa. The proto Taibi term is reconstructed as *maaPu and the proto Gauwa term as *a-ni-N.

It is highly probable that the proto Taibi term is an innovation unique to this division, and that it has been derived from the root of the proto term for daughter-in-law, *naaPu-QV, by shifting the point of articulation of the root-initial consonant from alveolar to bilabial. This is indicated in Table 101, which includes the term for daughter-in-law in each language along with the terms for son and daughter. The term for son-in-law has also been included in this table. The final segment of the term for son-in-law in Tairora and Binumarien (as already noted) is unique to these two languages, both segments *-maqu* and *-maku,* respectively, are cognates. It is possible that these two segments derive from the proto daughter-in-law root *naaPu via the derived term for son *maaPu just postulated for proto Taibi.

Since the Tairora and Binumarien terms for son are probably a reflection of a derived innovation peculiar to the Taibi group it is improbable that they reflect a proto Tagauwa term for son. This makes it more prob-

TABLE 101

G − 1 Kɪɴsʜɪᴘ Tᴇʀᴍs

	Son	Daughter-in-Law	Daughter	Son-in-Law
Tairora	MAAQU	*naaqu-tu*	*raabu-ra-(bano)*	*a-i-raa-(maqo)*
Binuma-rien	MAAKU	*naaku-qu*	*raamu-na*	*a-i-raa-(maku)*
Auyana	*a*-NI-N-*(ko-ma)*	. . .	*yaamu-n-(ko-ma)*	. . .
Usarufa	*a*-NI-Q-*(ko-ma)*	. . .	*yaamu-q-(ko-ma)*	. . .
			yaamu-m-(ma)	. . .
Gadsup	NI-N*(i)*	. . .	*raamu-mi*	. . .
Agarabi	*(a)*-NI-N	. . .	*raau-n*	. . .
Awa	*(a)*-NI-N	. . .	*yaau-n-(kawa)*	. . .
Tagauwa	. . .	*-naaPu*-QV	*-DaaMu*-NV	*-(a)-i-Raa*-N

able, though it cannot prove, that the proto Gauwa term *a-ni-N reflects the proto Tagauwa term for son. The proto Gauwa term is analyzed as an initial prefix *a- probably equating with the proto possessive prefix postulated for other proto terms, and a root *ni. The feature of prenasalization of the following suffix -n-ko in the Auyana term *aninkoma,* the final nasal consonant -n of the Agarabi and Awa terms *anin,* and the final suffixlike segment -ni of the Gadsup term *nini* strongly support the assumption that the root *ni is a nasal (N) class root. From this it may be inferred that the term is a junior kin term. This is confirmed by the optional occurrence of the juniority suffix -ko with the Auyana and Usarufa terms.[8]

The term for daughter in each language reflects a proto Tagauwa term reconstructed as *DaaMu-NV.[9] As noted by Bee (Chapter XXXVI) the sound correspondence set reflecting the root-initial proto phone is unique to this term. It is reflected by Tairora and Binumarien *r* in the Taibi group, and in the Gauwa group by *y* in the Auyana-Usarufa and the Awa divisions and *r* in the Gadsup-Agarabi division. The root medial proto phone *M* is equated with the root medial proto phone of the reconstructed root *maaMu 'father's sister', although the Agarabi term *raaun* on this assumption should

---

[8] The feature of preglottalization of the suffix-initial consonant in the Usarufa term *aniqkoma* does not invalidate this conclusion. As noted previously Usarufa lacks the prenasalized complex sequences of Auyana and has in their place cognate preglottalized sequences. Auyana lacks preglottalized complex sequences.

[9] The reconstruction *DaaMu-NV is the same as Bee's reconstructed term *-damu-N. The upper case *D* has been adopted in this paper to indicate that this symbol cannot be taken as an approximation of the phonetic norm of the reconstructed phone. The upper case *M* has been adopted to distinguish it from the root-initial proto phone of the term for father's sister *-maaMu.

be *raamun*. The Awa root reflex of **DaaMu* has lost the medial consonant and replaced the initial consonant by a semivowel (in this case *y*). A similar double sound shift affecting the initial and medial consonant of the root is a feature of the Awa root reflexes in *wehiawa* (reflecting **maaTi-Wa*) and *waauwa* (reflecting **maaMu-Wa*).

The evidence clearly establishes that the root reconstructed as **DaaMu* is a nasal (N) class root, and the first order suffix reconstructed as *-NV has the same reflexes as that reconstructed for the term for younger sister **(a)u-NV*. The term is therefore a junior kin term, and this is confirmed by the optional occurrence of the suffix *-ko* with the Auyana and Usarufa terms, and the optional occurrence of the suffix *-kawa* with the Awa term.

5.2. *Nephew and Niece*

No distinction is made between nephew and niece. The sex of the senior kin referring to his nephews and nieces determines the root of the terms used between them. As already indicated this root has been reconstructed as **maaMu* for a female ego (father's sister) and as **nau* for a male ego (mother's brother).

The evidence is fairly convincing that when kin of the two generations referred to each other, a seniority suffix previously reconstructed as *-Wa* indicated superordination. In the case of the term used by ego's sibling group for father's sister the seniority suffix *-Wa* is reflected by Tairora and Binumarien *-ba* and *-fa,* respectively. It may also be inferred from the Usarufa term *maamu-o-ma*.[10] This Usarufa term, however, is also used by father's sister for ego's sibling group. The appearance of the seniority suffix *-o* in a term applied to junior kin does not undermine the interpretation of this affix as a seniority marking suffix. It points rather to a breakdown in the proto system which presumably added the seniority suffix to the proto root only when the term applied to the senior kin, and either dropped it or replaced it when the senior kin addressed or referred to the junior kin. This breakdown has occurred in all the languages of the Gauwa group, and presumably stems from proto Gauwa.

This breakdown is evident in the Auyana term for father's sister (*maamu-go-ma*). The suffix *go* is the form taken by the suffix *-ko* following a stem of the V class. The suffix *-ko* is a juniority suffix. A V class stem is a senior class stem.

The breakdown is further evident in the Agarabi term *maamun*. The final *n* identifies the stem to which it attaches as an N class stem, and this in turn identifies the stem as a junior class stem. *maamun* is, however, used by father's sister for the junior kin category (ego's sibling group), as well as by ego's sibling group for father's sister.

---

[10] According to Bee, 'father's sister' may be referred to in Usarufa by the term of address *maamúqo*.

TABLE 102

RECIPROCAL TERMS FOR G — 1

	Father's Sister	Female Ego's Brother's Children	Mother's Brother	Male Ego's Sister's Children
Tairora	*maabu-ba*	*maabu-(nti-bano)*	*nau-ba*	*nau-nti*
Binu-marien	*maamu-fa*	*maamu-(qi-mara)*	*nau-fa*	*nau-qi-(mara)*
Auyana	*maamu-(go-ma)*	*(naabe-i-go-ma)*	*naao-(go-ma)*	*(naabe-i-go-ma)*
Usarufa	*maamu-o-(ma)*	*maamu-(o-ma)*	*nai-(ma)*	*nau-(ma)*
	maamu-(ko-ma)	*maamu-(ko-ma)*	. . .	. . .
Gadsup	*maamu*	. . .	*(aaqo)*	*no-nta*
Agarabi	*maamu-(n)*	*maamu-(n)*	*(kaako)*	*(kaako)*
				no-i-nta-q
Awa	*waau*	. . .	*(po)*	. . .
Tagau-wa	*-maaMu-Wa*	*-maaMu*	*-nau-Wa*	*-nau-i-nta*

It is uncertain whether, when a female ego (father's sister) referred to her nephews-nieces, the term carried a juniority suffix in proto Tagauwa, even though it is reasonably certain that a distinction was made between the subordinate and superordinate terms sharing the root *maaMu. Only the term used by father's sister for nephew-niece in Tairora (*maabu-nti-bano*) suggests this. But no suffix cognate to the Tairora *-nti* is found in the corresponding term of any Gauwa language. The Binumarien term *maamu-qi-mara* in Table 102 is probably a descriptive term and should not be equated with the Tairora term.

The evidence is more convincing that the term used by mother's brother for his nephews-nieces attached a juniority suffix to the proto root *nau. This suffix is probably reflected by Tairora *-nti* in the Taibi group, and by Gadsup *-nta* and Agarabi *-inta* in the Gauwa group. Assuming that the suffixes in both language groups are cognates, the proto term used by mother's brother for ego's sibling group is reconstructed as *nau-i-nta. The suffix *-i* may well equate with the suffix *-i* of the proto term for husband reconstructed as *Waa-i-ta, and with the proto prefix *i-* of the term used between male ego and his parents-in-law, *(a)-i-Raa, and the term used between male ego and his brothers-in-law, *(a)-i-tua. It was suggested that the affix *i* of these last three terms specifies the maleness of ego affinally linked. The term reconstructed as *nau-i-nta involves a male ego (mother's brother). It may also be that the relationship between mother's brother and his nephews-nieces is rated as essentially affinal.

Assuming that the term *nau-i-nta is a correct reconstruction, the shift from this proto term to the Taibi term *naunti* (Tairora) has involved a replacement of the final suffix vowel by the intitial suffix vowel *-i*. A similar shift has been postulated to account for the Tairora and Binumarien reflexes (*baa-ti* and *faa-qi*, respectively) of the proto term for husband **Waa-i-ta*. The final suffix *-nta* may perhaps consist of two segments, an initial *n* representing a feature of prenasalization conditioned by the morphophonemic class of the stem *nau*, and the suffix proper *-ta*. By this analysis the stem **nau* would be determined to be a nasal (N) class root. This would be consistent with the fact that the root **nau* in this context is the stem of a junior category term.

Several of the terms of Table 102 are not reflexes of the reconstructed terms. An alternate term used by male ego (mother's brother) for his sister's children *kaako* is used reciprocally between these two kin groups. This term may, however, be a reflex of a proto term of address, at least a proto Gauwa term. In Usarufa an obvious cognate *kaako-qa* may be used as a term of reference for mother's brother, but is generally a term of address.[11]

The Auyana term *naabe-i-go-ma* is used by a female ego (father's sister) for her nephews-nieces, and also by a male ego (mother's brother) for his nephews-nieces. The origin of this term is uncertain. The root *naabe* bears some resemblance to the root of the grandfather term *naabu-o-ma*. Both roots are V class roots. This is inferred for the latter from the seniority suffix *-o* and for the former by the suffix *-go*, which is the form the juniority suffix takes following a V class stem. The suffix *-i* of the term *naabe-i-go-ma* tends to suggest that it is basically a term used by a male ego (mother's brother) rather than a female ego (father's sister).

5.3. *Grandchildren*

Usarufa is the only language which uses a reciprocal term between grandparents and grandchildren. It is improbable then that this is a retention from the proto language. In Usarufa a term which is a reflex of the proto term for grandfather (*naabu-o-ma*) is used reciprocally between a grandfather and his grandchildren. A term which is a reflex of the proto term for grandmother (*raara-o-ma*) is used reciprocally between a grandmother and her grandchildren. As with the terms for nephew-niece just dealt with, the sex of the senior kin determines the root used in the reciprocal term.

Apart from Usarufa, Agarabi is the only language which uses the same term for a grandparent as a grandchild. This term *naaqo*, however, is not used reciprocally, but is used by any grandchild for its grandfather, and by a grandmother for her grandson.

The root of the proto term for grandchild is reconstructed as **naa-*.

---

[11] Bee indicates that 'mother's brother' may be referred to Usarufa as either *kaakóqa* or *noganéqa* as well as the usual term of reference *anaumá*. These are generally, however, used as terms of address.

It has been retained virtually unchanged in the Gauwa languages. In the Taibi group it is followed by a possible prefix -*i*. The shift of the proto vowel *aa* to its phonetically shorter equivalent *a* in the Taibi languages is attributed to the following *i*. (Note a similar vowel shift in the Auyana and Usarufa term for husband, *wa-i-ko-ma,* which reflects the proto term **Waa-i-ta.)*

It is uncertain whether the suffixlike element -*i* following the root of the Taibi terms is a retention from proto Tagauwa. There is no evidence for such a suffix among the cognate terms of the Gauwa languages.

It is equally uncertain whether the grandchild term was classified as a junior or senior kin term in the proto language, though it is only reasonable to assume it was a junior term. The Awa term *naa-wa* with its final suffix -*wa* is classified as a senior kin term. The nasal segment *n* of the suffix -*nti* in the Tairora term suggests that the root is classified in this language as an N class root, and the term as a junior kin term. This apparent contradiction may perhaps reflect the fact that in the proto system the terms used between grandparents and grandchildren shared a common root, to which attached seniority or juniority affixes. The evidence does not strongly favor this. However, it is perhaps significant that the Auyana term for grandfather (*naabu-go-ma*) exhibits internal contradiction. The suffix -*go* is a juniority suffix. But the initial *g* of this form can only be explained by assuming that the root is a V class root. A V class root in the kinship system is characteristically a senior kin term root.

Until more is known about the terms for grandchild in the Eastern Family only a root **naa-* will be reconstructed.

6. Form and Function in the Kinship System of the Eastern Family

It has been noted earlier that the terms for older brother and husband, and older sister and wife shared the same root in the proto language.[12] The distinction between older brother and husband and between older sister and wife was determined by the proto suffix. If, however, the roots constructed as **Waa* and **naa,* respectively, were inherently V class or Q class, and the suffix to which they attached in the proto system was simply a nominal suffix (with no class marking function) it is difficult to account for this situation. Certain roots apparently have potential for belonging to two classes. If we postulate morphophonemic classes, it is more or less implicit that the class is an inherent feature of the stem, and that this inherent feature stems from the form of the stem. It is evident, however, that the term morphophonemic class must have semantic overtones. This would seem to be borne out by the fact that among the kinship terms V class roots are the

---

[12] It is highly probable that these roots are also related to the roots of the terms for man and woman, respectively.

roots of terms which specify senior kin, while N and Q class roots are the roots of terms which specify junior kin.

The classificatory system is evidently not a pure one since the same root may function in a term which is classed as senior, and also in a term which is classed as junior. A root is evidently able to change class (at least within the kinship system). It may be that the affix which attached to the proto root was classificatorally neutral in the proto system and merely reflected the class of the root by the product of its morphophonemic reaction with the root. It is, however, possible that as the classificatory system shifted from a pure classificatory system, the various forms of the suffix (conditioned by morphophonemic interaction) achieved independent status, and prior to fossilization with the root may have had a derivational function. It is also possible that after a suffix became fossilized the now complex root later attached the currently viable nonderivational nominal suffix.

It is certain that the root of the grandfather term reconstructed as *naaPu-Wa and the root of the daughter-in-law term reconstructed as *naaPu-QV were segmentally homophonous in the proto language. It is possible that they were in fact identical, and that the difference in the terms was signaled by a difference in the classification of the root. In the case of the grandfather term the root was classified as a V class root and attached the seniority suffix *-Wa. In the case of the daughter-in-law term the root was classified as a Q (glottal) class stem and attached a suffix (*-QV) reflecting this fact. This then would account for the reason why the daughter-in-law term was used without change when the daughter-in-law referred to her senior affinal kin (mother-in-law and father-in-law). There was no option for the seniority suffix to replace the *-QV suffix, since the seniority suffix had already been pre-empted for the grandfather term.

It would seem that with the passage of time the difference between the grandfather term and the daughter-in-law term has ceased to be a definable viable difference, and the roots have at least in Usarufa and Tairora ceased to be recognized as the same. In Usarufa they differ in tone and in Tairora they differ in stress placement.[13]

It may be of interest to note the consonantal and vocalic parallels between the roots of the ego axis and the roots of the parallel sex axis of the chart under Table 96. Grounds for this are perhaps implicit in the semantic overtones of the morphophonemic classificatory system. (The term parallel sex axis is used to indicate the fact that the term for father also applies to father's brothers, and the term for mother also applies to mother's sisters.)

If we exclude the term for younger sister we note that the vowels of the

---

[13] The Usarufa terms for daughter-in-law and grandfather with the first person possessive prefix keti- are ketináábuqa and ketináábúmá, respectively. The difference between the roots in Tairora are registered orthographically as stress differences (though the language is actually tonal) as follows 'naaqu 'grandfather' and naa'qu 'daughter-in-law'.

terms in the ego axis are central vowels **aa* and **a*. The roots of the parent terms have the same vowel, the back vowel **o*. We note also that the root of the term for older sister is **n* initial as is the root of the term for mother. Similarly the root-initial consonant of the term for younger brother (**P*) is identical with the root-initial consonant of the term for father.

In the kin chart of Table 96 only the roots of the terms which apply to members outside the biological family are bisyllabic, and the vowels of the two syllables are *a* and *u* in both.

The root of the term for younger sister is formally unusual if there is any significance to the above observations. It is the only root which is not consonant initial, and it carries a back vowel *u*, which is found only in the terms of the two kin (father's sister and mother's brother) outside the biological family. It may be relevant to note an interesting feature of the same kinship sector in two languages of the contiguous East-Central Family. In Bena-bena and in Fore as in the languages of the Eastern Family both the sex and age of ego's siblings are relevant in defining the terms he applies to them. However, a possible four-way contrast is reduced to three by the collapse of two of the terms. In both languages the term for younger sister and younger brother is the same. In each language the term for older sister is distinct from the term for older brother or younger brother. This term is, however, not unique. In Bena-bena it is the same term as the term for father's sister. In Fore the root of the term for older sister is the same as the root of the term for mother's sister. In effect then, older sister while formally distinct from older brother and younger brother has no formal identity of her own but takes for her term or the root of her term a form used for the sister of her father or the sister of her mother. This might perhaps be interpreted as pointing to a zero role for older sister in the structure of her biological family. Characteristically in the Eastern and East-Central families she marries outside the group to which her biological family belongs. The zero role of younger sister is perhaps implicit in the fact that she has no term of her own, but is named by the term for younger brother. While this has no direct relevance to the formal system suggested for the terms of Table 96 it does at least point to the slight possibility that there is some correlation between the form and the function of certain kinship terms. It might, however, be significant in the light of this that the vowel of the term for younger sister in the Eastern Family is the back vowel *u*, and that this vowel also appears in the terms applied to mother's brother and father's sister.

It is obvious that the above observations and statements are highly hypothetical, and that future research may discredit them. They are presented here only because it is becoming increasingly clear that the morphophonemic classificatory system which comes to light in studies by Bee and in this paper point to some unusual correlation of formal and semantic features in at least the terms of the kinship system of the Eastern Family.

REFERENCES CITED

NOTE: *Unpublished items are in the files of the Summer Institute of Linguistics, New Guinea Branch, Ukarumpa, E.H.D., unless otherwise noted. Starred items appear in this volume.*

Austin, William M.
1957   'Criteria for Phonetic Similarity,' *Language* 33:539-44.

Bee, Darlene
nd.   Extensive field notes and lexical material. Unpublished.
1961a   'A Comparative Study of Usarufa and Kosena.' Unpublished.
1961b   'Usarufa Personal Pronouns and Pronominal Prefixes.' Workshop papers, Summer Institute of Linguistics, New Guinea Branch. Mimeographed.
1964   'Toward Cross Cultural Comparison of Kinship Terminology.' Unpublished.
*1965a   'Comparative and Historical problems in East New Guinea Highland Languages,' pp. 1-37 in *Papers in New Guinea Linguistics, No. 4*, Linguistic Circle of Canberra Publications, (Series A: Occasional Papers, No. 6) Canberra: Australian National University.
*1965b   'Usarufa: A Descriptive Grammar.' Ph.D. Dissertation, Indiana University.
*1965c   'Usarufa Distinctive Features and Phonemes,' pp. 39-68 in *Papers in New Guinea Linguistics, No. 4*, Linguistic Circle of Canberra Publications (Series A: Occasional Papers No. 6) Canberra: Australian National University.
1966   'Binumarien Grammar Essentials for Translation.' (Data from Desmond and Jennifer Oatridge.) Unpublished.

Bee, Darlene, and Kathleen Barker Glasgow
  *1962   'Usarufa Tone and Segmental Phonemes,' pp. 111-27 in *Studies in New Guinea Linguistics*. Oceania Linguistic Monographs No. 6. Sydney: University of Sydney.

Bee, Darlene, and Alan Pence
  1962   'Toward Standardization of a Survey Word List for Papua and New Guinea.' Unpublished.

Capell, A.
  1949   'Two tonal languages of New Guinea,' *Bulletin of the School of Oriental and African Studies* 13:184-99.

  1949/50 'Distribution of Languages in the Central Highlands, New Guinea,' *Oceania* 19:104-29, 234-53, 298-315.

  1962a   'The Techniques of Structure Statistics,' *Oceania* 33:1-11.

  1962b   *A Linguistic Survey of the Southwestern Pacific*. South Pacific Commission Technical Paper No. 136. Nouméa, New Caledonia.

Chretien, C. Douglas
  1962   'The Mathematical Models of Glottochronology,' *Language* 38: 11-37.

Cowan, H. K. J.
  1959   'A note on statistical methods in comparative linguistics,' *Lingua* 8:233-46.

Crawford, John Chapman
  1963   *Totontepec Mixe Phonotagmemics*. Summer Institute of Linguistics Publications in Linguistics and Related Feilds No. 8.

Dyen, Isidore
  1956   'Language Distribution and Migration Theory,' *Language* 32: 611-26.

Ellegard, Alvar
  1959   'Statistical Measurement of Linguistic Relationship,' *Language* 35:131-56.

Elson, Benjamin, and Velma B. Pickett
  1962   'Beginning Morphology and Syntax.' Summer Institute of Linguistics, Santa Ana, California.

Franklin, Karl and Joyce
  1962   'Kewa I: Phonological Asymmetry,' *Anthropological Linguistics* 4:29-37.

Frantz, Chester
  *1962   'Grammatical Categories as Indicated by Gadsup Noun Affixes,' pp. 44-63 in *Studies in New Guinea Linguistics*. Oceania Linguistic Monographs No. 6. Sydney: University of Sydney.

Frantz, Chester, and Howard McKaughan
   *1964   'Gadsup Independent Verb Affixes,' pp. 84-99 in *Verb Studies in Five New Guinea Languages.* Summer Institute of Linguistics Publications in Linguistics and Related Fields No. 10.

Frantz, Chester and Marjorie
   n.d.   'Gadsup Lexical List.' Unpublished.
   *1966   'Gadsup Phoneme and Toneme Units,' pp. 1-11 in *Papers in New Guinea Linguistics, No. 5.* Linguistic Circle of Canberra Publications (Series A: Occasional Papers, No. 7). Canberra: Australian National University.

Goddard, Jean
   *1967   'Agarabi narratives and commentary,' pp. 1-25 in *Papers in New Guinea Linguistics, No. 7,* Pacific Linguistics (Series A: Occasional Papers, No. 13). Canberra: Australian National University.

Goddard, Jean, and Lorna Luff
   n.d.   'Agarabi lexical list.' Unpublished.
   1962a   'The final verbs of Agarabi.' Unpublished.
   1962b   'Phonemes of Agarabi.' Unpublished.

Greenberg, Joseph H.
   1957   *Genetic Relationship among Languages, and the Problem of Linguistic Subgroupings.* Essays in Linguistics. Chicago: University of Chicago Press.

Grimes, Joseph E.
   1962   'Measures of Linguistic Divergence,' pp. 27-34 in Preprints of Papers for the IXth International Congress of Linguists, Cambridge, Mass.
   1964   *Huichol Syntax.* The Hague: Mouton & Co.

Grimes, Joseph E., and Frederick B. Agard
   1959   'Linguistic Divergence in Romance,' *Language* 35:598-604.

Gudschinsky, Sarah C.
   1956   'The ABC's of Lexicostatistics (Glottochronology),' *Word* 12: 175-210.

Healey, Alan
   1962   'Linguistic Aspects of Telefomin Kinship Terminology,' *Anthropological Linguistics* 4:14-28.

Hjemslev, Louis
   1953   *A Prolegomena to a Theory of Language.* International Journal of American Linguistics, Memoir 7.

Hockett, Charles F.
    1954   'Two Models of Grammatical Description,' *Word* 10:210-31.
    1958   '*A Course in Modern Linguistics*. New York: Macmillan.

Hymes, D. H.
    1960a   'Lexicostatistics So Far,' *Current Anthropology* 1:3-44.
    1960b   'More on Lexicostatistics,' *Current Anthropology* 1:338-45.

Kroeber, A. L.
    1960   'Statistics, Indo-European, and Taxonomy,' *Language* 36:1-21.

Littlewood, R. A.
    1972   *Physical Anthropology of the Eastern Highlands of New Guinea*.
               Anthropological Studies in the Eastern Highlands of New Guinea,
               Vol. I. Seattle and London: University of Washington Press.

Longacre, Robert
    1960   'Review of *Mapas de clasificación de Mexico y las Américas*, by
               Morris Swadesh,' *Language* 36:397-410.
    1964   'Prolegomena to Lexical Structures,' *Linguistics, an International
               Review* 5:5-24.

Loving, Aretta, and Howard McKaughan
    *1964   'Awa Verbs, Part II: The Internal Structure of Dependent Verbs,'
               pp. 1-30 in *Verb Studies in Five New Guinea Languages*. Sum-
               mer Institute of Linguistics Publications in Linguistics and Re-
               lated Fields No. 10.

Loving, Richard E.
    *1966   'Awa Phonemes, Tonemes, and Tonally Differentiated Allo-
               morphs,' pp. 23-32 in *Papers in New Guinea Linguistics No. 5*,
               Linguistic Circle of Canberra Publications (Series A: Occasional
               Papers, No. 7). Canberra: Australian National University.

Loving, Richard and Aretta
    n.d.   'Awa Lexical List.' Unpublished.
    1961   'Phonemes of Awa.' Unpublished.
    *1962   'A Preliminary Survey of Awa Noun Suffixes,' pp. 28-43 in *Stu-
               dies in New Guinea Linguistics*. Oceania Linguistic Monographs
               No. 6. Sydney: University of Sydney.

Loving, Richard, and Howard McKaughan
    *1964   'Awa Verbs, Part I: The Internal Structure of Independent Verbs,'
               pp. 31-44 in *Verb Studies in Five New Guinea Languages*. Sum-
               mer Institute of Linguistics Publications in Linguistics and Re-
               lated Fields No. 10.

Lusted, Ruth, Claudia Whittle, and Lawrence A. Reid
    1964   'The Use of Matrix Technique in an Analysis of Atta Personal
               Pronouns,' *Oceanic Linguistics* 3:138-60.

McKaughan, Howard

    n.d.   Auyana, Awa, Gadsup, Tairora lexical lists. Microevolution Studies Project files, University of Washington.

    1958   *Inflection and Syntax of Maranao Verbs*. Publications of the Institute of National Language. Manila: Bureau of Printing.

    *1964   'A Study of Divergence in Four New Guinea Languages,' *American Anthropologist* 66:98-121.

    *1966   'Sequences of Clauses in Tairora,' *Oceanic Linguistics* 5: 1–12.

Marks, Doreen

    n.d.   'Kosena lexical list.' Unpublished.

    1961   'Auyana Nouns.' Unpublished.

    1964a   'Auyana Phoneme Paper.' Unpublished.

    1964b   'Auyana Final Verbs.' Unpublished.

Matthews, P. H.

    1965   'The Inflectional Component of a Word-and-Paradigm Grammar,' *Journal of Linguistics* 1:139-71.

Nelson, H.

    n.d.   'Preliminary report on proto-Kainantu kinship.' Microevolution Studies Project files, University of Washington.

Nicholson, Ruth and Ray

    1962   'Fore Phonemes and Their Interpretation,' pp. 128-48 in *Studies in New Guinea Linguistics*. Oceania Linguistic Monographs No. 6. Sydney: University of Sydney.

Oatridge, Desmond and Jennifer

    n.d.   'Binumarien Lexical List.' Unpublished.

    1965   'Sentence Final Verbs in Binumarien.' Unpublished.

    *1967   'Phonemes of Binumarien,' pp. 13-21 in *Papers in New Guinea Linguistics No. 5*, Linguistic Circle of Canberra Publications, (Series A: Occasional Papers, No. 7). Canberra: Australian National University.

Pike, Eunice V.

    1954   'Phonetic Rank and Subordination in Consonant Patterning and Historical Change,' *Miscellania Phonetica* 2:25-41.

Pike, Kenneth L.

    1943   *Phonetics*. Ann Arbor: University of Michigan Press.

    1962a   'Practical Phonetics of Rhythm Waves,' *Phonetica* 8:9-30.

    1962b   'Dimensions of Grammatical Constructions,' *Language* 38:221-44.

    1963a   'A Syntactic Paradigm,' *Language* 39:216-30.

    1963b   'Theoretical Implications of Matrix Permutation in Fore (New Guinea),' *Anthropological Linguistics* 5:1-23.

    1967   *Language in Relation to a Unified theory of the Structure of Human Behavior*. 2nd rev. ed., The Hague: Mouton & Co..

Pike, Kenneth L., and Willard Kindberg
    1956   'A Problem in Multiple Stresses,' *Word* 12:415-28.

Pike, Kenneth L., and Graham Scott
    1963   'Pitch Accent and Non-accented Phrases in Fore (New Guinea).'
            Zeitschrift für Phonetik, Sprachwissenschaft und Kommunika-
            tionsforschung, pp. 179-89.

Pittman, Richard S.
    1954   'The Priority of Valence over Phonological Attachment and Rela-
            tive Order in Description: A Grammar of Tetelcingo (Morelos)
            Nahuatl,' *Language* 30:6-8.
    1959   'On Defining Morphology and Syntax,' *International Journal of*
            American Linguistics 25:199-201.

Reid, Lawrence A.
    1964   'A Matrix Analysis of Bontoc Case Marking Particles,' *Oceanic*
            Linguistics 3:116-37.

Robins, R. H.
    1959   'In Defense of WP,' *Transactions of the Philological Society,*
            pp. 116-44.

Shand, Jean
    1964   'A Matrix of Introducer Tagmemes,' *Oceanic Linguistics* 3:110-15.

Stringer, Mary, and Joyce Hotz
   *1971   'The Occurrence and Co-occurrence of Waffa Noun Suffixes,'
            Seven Languages of Papua-New Guinea. Linguistic Society of
            New Zealand. In press.
   *1971   'Waffa Phonemes,' *Seven Languages of Papua-New Guinea.*
            Linguistic Society of New Zealand. In press.

Summer Institute of Linguistics, New Guinea Branch (SIL)
    1961   Workshop papers. Ukarumpa, Territory of Papua and New
            Guinea. Unpublished.

Swadesh, Morris
    1950   'Salish International Relationships,' *International Journal of*
            American Linguistics 16:157-67.
    1952   'Lexicostatistic Dating of Prehistoric Ethnic Contacts,' *Proceed-*
            ings of the American Philosophical Society 96:452-63.
    1955a   'Towards Greater Accuracy in Lexicostatistic Dating,' *Interna-*
            tional Journal of American Linguistics 21:121-37.
    1955b   'Towards a Satisfactory Genetic Classification of Amerindian
            Languages,' *Anais do XXXI Congresso Internacional de Amer-*
            icanistas, Sao Paulo, pp. 1001-12.
    1955c   'Amerindian Non-cultural Vocabularies.' Rev. ed. Mimeographed.

1959 'Linguistics as an Instrument of Prehistory,' *Southwestern Journal of Anthropology* 15:21-35.

1962 'Linguistic Relations across Bering Strait,' *American Anthropologist* 64:1262-91.

Vincent, Alex R. and Lois
   n.d. 'Tairora Lexical List.' Unpublished.
   *1962a 'Introductory Notes on Tairora Verb Morphology and Syntax,' pp. 4-27 in *Studies in New Guinea Linguistics*. Oceania Linguistic Monographs No. 6. Sydney: University of Sydney.
   1962b 'Tairora Dictionary.' Unpublished.
   1962c 'Tairora Phonemic Statement.' Unpublished.

Watson, J. B.
   1963 "A Micro-evolution Study in New Guinea," *Journal of the Polynesian Society* 72 (No. 3): 188-92.

Wurm, S. A.
   1960 'The Changing Linguistic Picture of New Guinea,' *Oceania* 31:121-36.

   1961a 'The Linguistic Situation in the Highlands Districts of Papua and New Guinea,' *Australian Territories* 1, 2:14-23.

   1961b 'Research Report, New Guinea Languages,' *Current Anthropology*, pp. 114-16.

   1961c Languages of the Eastern, Western and Southern Highlands, Territory of Papua and New Guinea. Map. Canberra: Australian National University.

   1962a 'The Languages of the Eastern, Western and Southern Highlands, Territory of Papua and New Guinea, in A. Capell, ed., *A linguistic survey of the South-Western Pacific*. South Pacific Commission Technical Paper No. 136. Noumea, New Caledonia.

   1962b 'Comment on A. Capell, *Oceanic Linguistics Today*,' *Current Anthropology* 3:421-22.

   1962c 'Oceanic Linguistics,' *Oceanic Linguistics* 1:1-11.

   1962d 'The Present State of New Guinea (non-Melanesian or Papuan) and Australian Historical and Comparative Linguistics.' Paper read at the 9th International Congress of Linguistics, Cambridge, Mass.

   1964a 'Australian New Guinea Highland Languages and the Distribution of their Typological Features,' *American Anthropologist* 66:77-97.

   1964b *Phonological Diversification in Australian New Guinea Highland Languages*. Linguistic Circle of Canberra Publications (Series B: Monographs, No. 2) Canberra: Australian National University.

Wurm, S. A. and D. C. Laycock
   1961 'The Question of Language and Dialect in New Guinea,' *Oceania* 32:128-43.

Young, Robert A.
    1964   'The Primary Verb in Bena-Bena,' pp. 45-83 in *Verb Studies in Five New Guinea Languages*. Summer Institute of Linguistics Publications in Linguistics and Related Fields No. 10.

Young, Rosemary
    1962   'Phonemes of Kanite, Kamano, Benabena and Gahuku,' pp. 70-110 in *Studies in New Guinea Linguistics*. Oceania Linguistic Monographs No. 6. Sydney: University of Sydney.

Index

Language names are abbreviated and placed in parentheses after corresponding page references for the user's convenience: Agarabi (Ag), Auyana (Au), Awa (Aw), Binumarien (Bi), Gadsup (Ga), Tairora (Ta), Usarufa (Us), Waffa (Wa). These designations appear after the last page number of a series rather than with each page listed. Citations from Part V on Linguistic Relationships are not followed by language designations since they are usually general references to the family.

Abilitative: aspect, 441, 449(Ga), 566, 604n, 610, 618(Ta); mode, 262, 272(Us); phrases, 295(Us)

Accompaniment: noun suffix, 186(Au), 299(Us), 430, 437(Ga), 541(Ta), 551-52(Wa), 558(Bi)

Acquisition: noun suffix, 542(Ta)

Adjectives, 456(Ag)

Adverbs: illustrated, 293(Us)

Affinal kinship terms, 237(Us), 783-92

Affixes: combinations of, 457(Ag); with dependent medial verbs, 448-49(Ga); summarized for nouns, 20(Aw), 185-87(Au), 424-25, 427-32(Ga), 456-57 (Ag), 531, 533-45(Ta), 558-60(Bi), 715-16; summarized for verbs, 38-39, 57(Aw), 187-89(Au), 252-53, 261-63 (Us), 439-42(Ga), 455-56(Ag), 563-64 (Ta), 714, 716-18. *See also* Noun affixes

Agamusi: Awa village, 7

Agarabi, 226, 403, 414, 450, 708-9, 741, 769

Aiyura: Gadsup village, 469

Allophones, 766-68. *See also* Phonemes

Amoraba: Awa village, 8, 9

Anticipatory clause markers, 61-62(Aw)

Anticipatory subject, 57-59(Aw), 259(Us), 449(Ga), 455-56(Ag), 571-72(Ta)

Aorist tense, 252, 309-10, 312-14(Us)

Arora: Auyana village, 179

Asempa: Auyana central village, 179, 324

Aspect: abilitative, 441, 449(Ga), 566,

604n, 610, 618(Ta); benefactive, 47-48 (Aw), 717; completive, 47(Aw), 442, 447, 449(Ga), 582(Ta); constructions, 562(Ta); continuative, 48(Aw), 455 (Ag); continuous, 581(Ta); habituative, 48(Aw); inceptive, 49(Aw); narrative, 455(Ag); negative, 566, 569 (Ta); potential, 441, 449(Ga); progressive, 442, 448(Ga), 566, 600(Ta); progressive-perfect, 603, 604, 605(Ta); punctiliar, 48(Aw); repetitive, 49 (Aw); stative, 441, 447, 448(Ga); summarized, 47-50(Aw), 187-88(Au), 441-42(Ga), 455(Ag), 565-66, 569, 581-83(Ta)

Assertive mode, 261, 271(Us), 455(Ag)

Augmentative: mode, 54(Aw), 442, 448, 449(Ga); noun suffix, 186(Au), 545 (Ta)

Auxiliary verb, 84(Aw), 294(Us), 580, 581, 582(Ta)

Auyana, 3, 8, 179, 181, 205, 225, 226, 742, 769

Avolitional: compounds, 60(Aw); mode, 51(Aw), 564-65, 570, 572, 578(Ta); relations, 586(Ta)

Awa, 3, 226, 607n, 620, 742, 769

Axis-relator phrases, 68, 76-78(Aw)

Azera: language neighboring Binumarien, 517

Aziana River, 9

Bantura: Tairora village, 530, 625